Edwin Booth

EDWIN BOOTH
A Biography and Performance History

Arthur W. Bloom

McFarland & Company, Inc., Publishers
Jefferson, North Carolina

The present work is a reprint of the illustrated case bound edition of Edwin Booth: A Biography and Performance History, *first published in 2013 by McFarland.*

All photographs are courtesy of the Hampden-Booth Library at the Players Educational Foundation.

LIBRARY OF CONGRESS CATALOGUING-IN-PUBLICATION DATA

Bloom, Arthur W., 1939–
Edwin Booth : a biography and performance history / Arthur W. Bloom.
 p.   cm.
Includes bibliographical references and index.

ISBN 978-1-4766-8126-9
paperback : acid free paper ∞

1. Booth, Edwin, 1833–1893. 2. Actors—United States—Biography.
3. Booth, Edwin, 1833–1893—Criticism and interpretation. I. Title.
PN2287.B488B58 2020   792.02'8092—dc23   [B]   2013018025

BRITISH LIBRARY CATALOGUING DATA ARE AVAILABLE

© 2013 Arthur W. Bloom. All rights reserved

No part of this book may be reproduced or transmitted in any form or by any means, electronic or mechanical, including photocopying or recording, or by any information storage and retrieval system, without permission in writing from the publisher.

Front cover: Edwin Booth in costume as
Hamlet, 1870 (Library of Congress)

Printed in the United States of America

*McFarland & Company, Inc., Publishers
Box 611, Jefferson, North Carolina 28640
www.mcfarlandpub.com*

For David Birney and Lawrence McCauley,
Keepers of the Flame

and my grandchildren,
Rachel Stephanie Jacobson
and
Rebecca Emily Jacobson

Acknowledgments

The author is indebted to Raymond Wemmlinger of the Hampden-Booth Theatre Library at the Players Educational Foundation; to Louise Taper and the late Barry Taper for their gracious hospitality in admitting to me to their Booth collection; to the Huntington Library for its support of my research in the Los Angeles area; to Norma and Harvey Beit, David Birney, Jessica Bloom, Sarah and Gregory Jacobson, Julius Novick, Phyllis Spaeth, and Phyllis and William Warfel for their assistance in travel to collections; to Michael Gaunt, Michael A. Morrison and Julius Novick and, above all, to Rena F. Bloom for their editorial assistance; to Gregory Jacobson and Mike Schumer for their technical assistance, to Jean Seaman for allowing me to see Boothden; to Frank Zool for his copy of Booth's letter dated February 26, 1872; to Geraldine Duclow of the Theatre Collection of the Free Library of Philadelphia; to Robert Cohen for the use of his Booth material and to Johanna Forte for her assistance in examining the Booth costumes at The Players.

Table of Contents

Acknowledgments vi

Introduction 1

Part I: Biography

One. 1833–1849: "Born to the stage" 5

Two. 1849–1852: "A long legged stripling … awkward as a young duck" 11

Three. 1852–1856: "Full of promise … and Bowery rant" 17

Four. Professional and Family Life, 1856–1860 29

Five. 1857–1860: Booth, Mary Devlin and Adam Badeau 36

Six. America and England, 1860–1862: "At a larger circumference" 50

Seven. 1862–1863: "Tell Molly I'm coming" 61

Eight. 1863–1865: "If it goes a year, keep it up!" 68

Nine. Edwin and John Wilkes Booth: "Life's too short to spend in grieving" 74

Ten. 1865–1867: "Something to keep us above the surf" 89

Eleven. Mary McVicker: "The best actress we've had for a century" 93

Twelve. Booth's Theatre, 1867–1869: "A temple to art" 98

Thirteen. Booth's Theatre, 1869–1871: "The currency of good intentions is not bankable money" 103

Fourteen. Booth's Theatre, 1871–1883: "So much for high-old-art" 106

Fifteen. Family Life, 1870–1880: "My house has been a hospital" 112

Sixteen. England, 1880–1881: "The verdict of foreigners" 119

SEVENTEEN. 1881–1882: The Death of Mary McVicker   124

EIGHTEEN. Europe, 1882–1883: "The most important engagement of my life"   128

NINETEEN. 1883–1886: Touring and Family Life   135

TWENTY. The 1886-1887 Season: "It is time to harvest all I can"   142

TWENTY-ONE. 1887–1888: Booth and Barrett   149

TWENTY-TWO. "The Booth and Barrett Social Company"   156

TWENTY-THREE. 1888–1889: The Second Booth and Barrett Tour   161

TWENTY-FOUR. 1889–1890: Touring with Modjeska   166

TWENTY-FIVE. 1890–1893: Illness, Last Tour and Death   170

PART II: PERFORMANCE HISTORY   177

Notes   297

Bibliography   344

Index   347

Introduction

This is a biography and full performance history of Edwin Booth, the foremost tragic actor of the nineteenth-century American theatre. It stems from a desire to exhume and understand the past, focuses on primary sources and avoids, whenever possible, statements unverifiable by valid documents. It assumes that the past is knowable through a rigorous examination of its artifacts—letters, promptbooks, financial records, broadsides, playbills, newspaper advertisements, reviews, extant costumes and books and magazine articles from the period.

The artifacts with which the biographer works, however, not only provide factual information but also allow for multiple interpretations. Confronted, for example, with the slavish subservience in Mary Devlin's letters to Edwin, the reader may see her as a victim of Booth's prejudices; as a person bent on reforming her own life and that of her husband; as a martyr to the ideals of womanhood held by nineteenth-century men; as a champion of romantic realism in the American theatre; as a clever young woman artfully manipulating the person on whom she is financially and socially dependent; as a practical woman who wisely knows the price to be paid for the privilege of not having to earn a living; as a woman in love; or as any combination of the above. In like manner, the relationship between Booth and Adam Badeau might be seen as platonic, homosexual, self-serving, symbiotic and/or educational. What is the significance of Mary calling herself Edwin's "daughter" or Booth calling Horace Howard Furness, the editor of the Shakespeare Variorum, "sweetheart?"

It is impossible to answer such questions with absolute certitude. Consequently what follows is one scholar's "version" of Edwin Booth, and certainly not the versions that his friend William Winter or his sister Asia Booth Clarke wrote. No Booth biographer can have the last word about so complex a life, and I am aware of at least two other Booth biographies currently under way, which is not surprising. Booth's life was so filled with ups and downs, so theatrical, so replete with adventure, sadness, success and disaster that it reads like a novel, as do most of the biographies already written about him. His earliest twentieth-century biographer, Richard Lockridge, called Booth's life "a melodrama of abashing theatricalism."[1]

He has been seen as a pillar of nobility, an icon of the American theatre, virtually a god. This is the view of William Winter, whose *Life and Art of Edwin Booth* (1893) was an expanded version of a text published in 1872, when Booth was still alive. To Winter, who "honored and loved him," Booth was "intellectual and spiritual," the cause of "all good things upon the American stage."[2]

Other nineteenth-century biographers waxed equally lyrical. In *The Elder and the Younger Booth* (1882), Booth's sister Asia echoed Winter's adulation, writing that "as a citizen and as a man, Edwin Booth has been always devoted, upright, true; the kindest and most tender of sons to an erratic father and to a widowed mother, in every other relation, as brother, husband, father, friend, worthy of affection and of all praise." In 1886 Booth's future co-star Lawrence Barrett wrote that "Eulogy and praise stand mute in the presence of such merits," having just eulogized and praised Booth for nine pages. When Booth's daughter Edwina published an edited collection of her father's letters in 1894, she declared that her intention was to "reveal" his "depth of soul, a firmness of purpose, a high resolve to battle against life's struggles."[3]

Adulation continued in the twentieth century. For Eleanor Ruggles, in her 1953 best-seller *Prince of Players*, Booth was "an actor whose greatness would tower over the talents of today." For L. Terry Oggel, in his excellent 1992 bio-bibliography, Booth was "intuitive and sensitive, tolerant and patient ... astonishingly self-effacing and scornful of pretentiousness." Their visions of Booth are not without validity. He was publicly modest, often had high artistic aspirations and was financially generous to friends and family, but he was also childish about money, prejudiced (in typical nineteenth-century fashion) against African Americans and Jews, snobbish and, above all, ambivalent about being an actor, the latter a particularly strange and unpleasant trait in a theatrical leader. The noble Edwin Booth legend does not represent the total story of a man engaged in the competitive commercial world of nineteenth-century American theatre.[4]

Booth has also been seen as a tragic figure whose personal life mirrored the Shakespearean characters he played, particularly Hamlet. His was certainly a sad life. His father drank; he himself drank to excess as a young man; he was addicted to tobacco; his first wife died young; his brother assassinated the president; his scenery, costumes and props were lost in a fire at the Winter Garden Theatre; the theatre he founded went bankrupt; he was physically injured in a carriage accident; his second wife died after a lengthy physical and mental illness; his beloved daughter married a man he detested; and out of necessity, he continued to perform after having suffered a stroke. In his darker, more melodramatic moments, he asserted that "Life is a horrible imposition, at the best; therefore I can not mourn for those that die, but rather grieve for those who are born to such penalties. The moment we begin to breath we begin to decay, & as Lear says: 'we cry that we are come unto this stye of fools.'"[5]

If Booth was Hamlet-like in his moodiness and prone to milk his tragic persona, his letters also reveal a playfulness and a sharp wit far closer to the Hamlet of Act II than the nineteenth century's ideal of an introspective, supersensitive, self-absorbed romantic prince. In his early twenties Booth would have been far more suitable playing the roguish Prince Hal in *Henry IV, Part I*. He rode horses; he loved beer, rich food, cigars and pipes. He was attracted by and attractive to women well into his fifties, when he was still checking out the ankles of ladies hitching up their dresses as they boarded a streetcar. A year before he died, he told William Winter that "I was always of a boyish spirit and if my physical health were good, I should still be very boyish. But there was always an air of melancholy about me that made me seem much more serious than I ever really was."[6]

Booth himself saw his life as governed by a wheel of fortune, although he never understood that he was one of the forces driving that wheel. In good times he came to expect that bad times were coming. Life was filled with both "buffets and rewards," he admitted. "What an up & down my life has been!" "What a strange fate mine has been! Up to the highest notch in my profession, down to the depths in my domestic affairs! My sad tale would make a most incredible story — if I cd write it."[7]

He tried to write it but finally concluded: "In my most serious moods, I become careless & flippant & grow disgusted with all I write. Heigho! I shall never be an Hauthor [sic] (God be thanked!)." He was, however, well aware that biographers were lying in wait. The Booths were the nineteenth-century equivalent of the Kennedys; even minor family members were news. Edwin hated the publicity, but he prepared the way for posthumous biographies by saving his voluminous correspondence. More than 2,000 letters to, from and about Booth exist, and new ones surface fairly often. At some point more letters probably existed, but Booth moved his belongings a great deal, and, as the nineteenth-century aphorism went, "three removes are as good as a fire." That large numbers of people treasured letters from him is not surprising — he was a celebrity — but the number of extant letters *to* him testifies to the fact that he kept thousands of them for "many years"; "Why?" he asked himself? "God only knows! Too lazy to destroy them, I suppose." It was more than laziness, because in later life Booth began to re-read and annotate some of his letters, implying a recognition and perhaps a desire or need that such letters become grist for biographic mills. He may have been trying to make some sense of his life.[8]

If all the information available about Booth were lined up end to end, it would prove bewildering and boring, although it is tempting to a biographer to show off his scholarly skills by recording endless details. My family claims I have a tendency to write: "On Thursday, June 3, 1891, Edwin Booth went to the dentist." It is, rather, the task of any biographer to create *a story* if not *the story*.

My version of Booth's story is inextricably enmeshed in the workings of the nineteenth-century American theatre. Consequently this is a book about travel, about nasty hotel rooms and bad food, about jolting rides on railroads, about box office receipts and managers, about drafty dressing rooms and cheering audiences, about money made and lost. It's about the organizational change that occurred after the Civil War and how it affected the traveling star.

It is also a personal story, and in that aspect, mine is admittedly not the noble Booth. I have chosen to emphasize the human and often the negative aspects of his life while simultaneously attempting to encompass his complexity. I admit it's the dirt that is the fun, and there are moments when I feel I have come not to praise Booth but to bury him. Certainly the adulation he has received needs an antidote. His was a life of paradoxes: he was noble, but he could be vicious; he was fun-loving as a young man but grew increasingly self-absorbed to the point of posturing. He was melancholy but also witty. His life was a turbulent mixture of ups and downs, but his popularity ensured that he was always financially able to recover. He saw himself as the victim of a deprived childhood, but he was not born poor, and he died rich. He was monetarily successful but a childish businessman. He was obsessive about his health but spent forty-two years of his sixty-year life earning a living in the strenuous rough-and-tumble world of nineteenth-century American theatre. He disliked most of the managers and actors with whom he worked, but consistently aligned himself with individuals whose work or honesty he deplored. He was a great professional actor beset by internal demons that molded his acting and his life. While he never consciously made the transition to modern psychological realism as an actor, there were triggers within him and forces without that produced his performances onstage and off. The external melodrama of his life was matched by the internal drama of its hero.

I have taken him "all in all." Consequently this is a book about his personal life, about his acting and about the nineteenth-century theatre which he produced and which produced him. Linked together, these elements form my version of the life and art of Edwin Booth.

Part I: Biography

CHAPTER ONE

1833–1849: "Born to the stage"

Edwin Thomas Booth was born on November 13, 1833, on a farm near Bel Air, Maryland, twenty-five miles from Baltimore. His twelve-year-old brother, Junius Brutus Jr., known as June, rode through a spectacular display of the Leonid meteor shower to fetch the doctor. The falling celestial debris, interpreted by some religious groups as a harbinger of the end of time, came to also be seen as a sign that Edwin Booth would be the savior of the American theatre. Booth, always cynical about such adulation, later referred to it as "a grand 'Star' performance."[1] The Booths sent June for the doctor, because he was the eldest male family member at home. The theatrical season was in full swing, and on the night of Edwin's birth, his father, the British-born American star Junius Brutus Booth, was playing Richard III at New York's Bowery Theatre.

Mary Ann Booth, who had already borne seven children, sent for a doctor, rather than the traditional midwife, in case Edwin's birth proved to be difficult. He was born with a caul, a membrane across his face, widely regarded as the sign of a charmed life. Booth later contended that the disasters which befell him were the result of the loss of the caul, a convenient way of explaining misfortunes, even those for which he bore a primary responsibility.[2]

The Leonid shower and the caul provided Booth with entertaining stories later in life but were less significant than the fact that Edwin, like all the children of Junius Brutus and Mary Ann, was illegitimate. According to his younger sister Asia, who took great pains to legitimize her family, their father had married their mother in England on January 18, 1821, when he was twenty-four and she was eighteen. To have done so, however, would have been bigamous, because in 1821 Junius Brutus Booth was already married to a Belgian woman named Mary Christine Adelaide Delannoy, by whom he had two children. They had met in July 1814, when he was eighteen and Adelaide twenty-two. They were married on May 8, 1815, when she was four months pregnant. Their first child, Amelia, died in infancy; their second, Richard, born on January 21, 1819, survived to manhood. Junius Brutus met Edwin's mother, Mary Ann Holmes, around October 1820; they ran off together three months later, and, in May 1821, left for America. Mary Ann was two months pregnant when they sailed, and Edwin's oldest brother, Junius Jr., was born in America on December 22, 1821. Edwin's sister Asia contended that "if ever there was perfect love, it was between my father and mother." Her mother, however, had her doubts. In 1881 she wrote to her grand-daughter: "I am not a great advocate for marriages," and she had good reason.[3]

In 1843, when Edwin was ten, Richard, son of Adelaide and Junius, came to America, toured with his father and settled in Baltimore. Three years later, Adelaide arrived and lived in Baltimore from November 1846 until her death in 1858. By December 17, 1846, she had become aware of the location of the Baltimore house that Booth had purchased for himself, and "the Holmes," as Adelaide referred to Mary Ann. She filed for divorce on February 27, 1851, and her petition was granted on April 18. Junius Brutus Booth married Mary Ann Holmes less than a month later, on May 10, 1851, the day of their son John's thirteenth birthday. Edwin was seventeen at the time. It is likely that at some point in his adolescence he became aware of his parents' marital status and consequently of his own illegitimacy.[4]

Adelaide died when Edwin was twenty-four, and her tombstone in Baltimore's old Roman Catholic cemetery identified her as the "Wife of Junius Brutus Booth." Following the announcement of Adelaide's death in *The New York Evening Post*, Edwin, who was playing at Baltimore's Holliday Street Theatre at the time, wrote to its editor: "I see by your issue of yesterday a notice of the death of 'Mrs. Mary Booth, at one time married to J.B. Booth, and mother of EB, tragedian.' Oblige me by contradicting that statement. My father was married but once, and then to my mother, who, thank God, still lives." The newspaper was confused about Booth's relationship to the deceased, but in all likelihood Edwin knew who she was. Asia Booth Clarke wrote in her father's biography: "By a boyish misalliance, contracted in Brussels in the year 1814, there was one son, who, if alive, is still a resident of London, and of whom we possess no further knowledge." Edwin later wrote to his daughter Edwina: "Y^r Aunt Asia's memoir of father tells of his first foolish marriage at about 18 to an adventuress of nearly 50 — she saw the woman once (in her girlhood in Balt^o) I never did."[5] By deprecating their father's first marriage, both he and Asia were attempting to legitimize their mother and themselves.

Whether or not the elder Booths ever discussed their marital status with their children, Edwin grew up in a family with a secret that may have been one source of his sense of unworthiness. Throughout his mature life he strove for respectability, courting social acceptance by people outside the theatre through his professional aspirations and personal demeanor. Booth's sense of illegitimacy exacerbated the shame that came with being an actor in the nineteenth century.

Between 1821 and 1850, Junius Brutus and Mary Ann had eleven children. In late November or early December, 1828, one of their children died in Boston. Edwin apparently never knew the child existed.[6] In February 1833, three other children, Elizabeth, Mary Ann and Frederick, died in a cholera epidemic. Their deaths must have been horrible. Cholera, spread through contaminated water or food, led to death from diarrhea and vomiting, possibly within hours. At least one of the children died on February 4, and Junius Brutus Booth returned home for the burial. Edwin was born in November 1833, nine months after these deaths. Edwin's conception may have resulted from his parents' need for comfort or simply from the fact that Junius Brutus was home.

Junius was thirty-seven when Edwin was born; Mary Ann was thirty-one. They named him Edwin Thomas for the early nineteenth-century American tragedian Edwin Forrest and the comic actor Thomas Flynn, who had been Junius's traveling companion. He was brought up in a family with five siblings. His oldest brother, Junius Brutus, Jr., was almost twelve years his senior; his oldest sister Rosalie Ann, born on July 5, 1823, was ten years older than Edwin; his sister Asia Sydney (sometimes Asia Frigga), born on November 20, 1835, was two years younger; and his younger brothers John Wilkes and Joseph Adrian born on May 10, 1838, and February 8, 1840, respectively, were four and seven years his junior. During a family visit to England in 1836 another older brother, Henry Byron, died of smallpox (Edwin, three at the time, was saved through inoculation).

Mary Ann Holmes Booth, Edwin's mother. In 1881 she wrote to her grand-daughter: "I am not a great advocate for marriages," and she had good reason.

A year after Edwin's birth, Junius Jr. began acting professionally, and by 1839 he was working regularly and consequently no longer at home most of the year; Rosalie, a recluse who suffered from tuberculosis, was devoted to Mary Ann and remained at home all of her life, treated like a child. Asia described her as having been "from childhood, more or less an invalid." Edwin, brought up by his mother and by a black woman he referred to as his "Mammy," became, *de facto*, the oldest male member of the family when his father and his older brother were not at home, and they were often not at home.[7]

Like any touring star, Junius Brutus Booth spent most of the year away from his family, traveling from city to city, performing his great roles— Richard III, Sir Giles Overreach in *A New Way to Collect Old Debts*, Sir Edward Mortimer in *The Iron Chest*, King Lear, Hamlet, Iago, Pescara in *The Apostate*, Othello and Shylock. These were the family stock-in-trade, and all would be handed down to Edwin like family property.

Although the Booths were dependent on the theatre for a living and occasionally performed together, they never formed a family company. Only two of the surviving Booth children, Edwin and John, made the theatre a life-long profession, and John's life was not long. June eventually ran a hotel, and Edwin's youngest brother, Joseph, left the theatre to become a doctor. Neither sister ever performed, a fact that is significant, because for a theatrical family in the antebellum period to keep its daughters off the stage required wealth and a desire for the respectability traditionally denied actors.

From birth until he was almost seven, Edwin lived on the Bel Air farm his father had bought in 1822. It was a crowded place, housing Junius Brutus, Mary Ann, their children, Junius' sister Jane Mitchell, her husband, their seven children and various hired servants and rented slaves. By June 1840 Junius Brutus had moved the family to Baltimore, and, five years later, on September 20, 1845, he purchased a three-story house at 62 North Exeter Street. The Booths became an urban family.

In 1845, when Edwin was twelve, a neighbor boy named John Sleeper took his part in a street fight. John's father was dead, and he eventually took his mother's name, Clarke, as a surname. He and Edwin became friends and later brothers-in-law and professional partners. Clarke remembered him as "a slim delicate lad, sensitive, gentle even shy" but not particularly "moody or studious." He was counteracting the mature image of Booth as Hamlet-like.[8]

One of Booth's fondest childhood memories was receiving lessons in the neighborhood of "Old Town" from a woman named Susan Hyde. Booth remembered "Miss Susan" as "a little old school marm ... with glasses & cork-screw curls" and wrote: "She taught me all I know — A.B.C., the sum total of my erudition.... I'm her boy still." When she died in 1888, he recalled: "She was <u>woman</u> all through; in the true sense of that word: gentle in manner, soft in heart and low in her estimation of her worth: excellent things in woman! She gave me my first school-whipping and I've loved her ever since. The marks of this discipline, it seems, cut to the heart. God bless her! She is gone, but the welts of her rattan still tingle, but pleasantly in my memory." While being caned by a teacher in the nineteenth century was normal, Booth's enjoyment of it may be significant.[9]

"Miss Susan" was the most educated woman he had ever met, but he loved her, because she was "gentle in manner ... and low in her estimation of her worth" and yet could beat him when he misbehaved. He would want a woman who was both subservient and yet dominant when she needed to be so. His first wife was the former; his second the latter; and out of the continual "beatings" that accrued to him, in later life, he formed his persona — someone who could take a beating and recover from it. His later business dealings were so naïve that they make him look as if he wanted a beating.

Despite the efforts of Miss Susan, Edwin came to see himself as uneducated, "travelling since childhood almost without a home." His father, Junius Brutus, could speak and write

French, some Italian and possibly Hebrew and prided himself on his knowledge of the Bible, the Talmud and the Koran. Edwin complained: "I never was at school more than a week or so at a time. I grew up in ignorance, allowed by an indulgent mother who knew nothing more than that she loved her child and a father who, although a good man, seemed to care very little what course I took."[10]

Booth was particularly aware of his deficiency in languages. He spoke and wrote French poorly, and self-consciously mangled what he knew as if to display what he did not, using "Genesee squaw" for "Je ne sais quoi," signing letters "Bonne Swore!" or "Adoo! Adjew!" In 1876 he joked with his daughter, Edwina, that he would have earned honors at Eton had it not been for the "unfortunate accident that I never went to school there except in dreams. How often, oh! how often have I imagined the delights of a collegiate education! What a world of never-ending interest lies open to the master of languages."[11]

Booth also complained of his lack of writing ability. He was besieged by correspondence he could not bring himself to answer. As late as 1885 he complained to his friend, the critic Laurence Hutton: "I scramble through a page and on revision find it 'full of omissions,' ... misspelt words set in a sort of hybrid grammar of my own construction which would puzzle the devil himself to comprehend."[12] Before the educated men and women whose attention he craved and sometimes bought, Edwin's emphasis on his illiteracy was somewhat deliberate. The pose charmed people who admired him as America's foremost tragic actor.

John Sleeper Clarke remembered that when a boy, Edwin "was a capital horseman and played the violin, also the banjo; and when Negro minstrelsy came into vogue, in imitation of the original 'Ethiopian Serenadors,' he used to masquerade at social gatherings with blackened face as 'Dandy Jim of Caroline.'" In his adulthood Booth reveled in recounting his youthful minstrel performances while simultaneously despising minstrelsy as a competitive but inferior form of entertainment. Booth engaged in the nineteenth-century sport of denigrating black people by performing an exaggerated version of their perceived nature while reminding a private audience that he had risen far above such theatrical shenanigans of his boyhood.[13]

His amateur theatrical performances were well remembered by boyhood friends, some of whom became professional actors. These performances took place in found spaces—improvised theatres variously recollected—"an old stable loft on South Street," a "woodshed ... with mother's old quilt for curtains, and two or three 'dips' for a light," a cellar in Calvert Street, where "the Negro janitor who had charge of the building agreed to keep our doings from the people overhead, if we allowed him to be doorkeeper and take half the proceeds." Booth also performed at school. In an interview with *The Cleveland Herald*, Clarke corroborated the fact that he and Edwin had performed "The Quarrel of Brutus and Cassius" as well as "selections from different tragedies, at our school exhibitions."[14]

The elder Booth was ambivalent about his son becoming an actor. As an adult Edwin contended that his father had urged him to be a carpenter. Yet from 1847, when Edwin was fourteen, until September 1852, he served as his father's dresser and companion on tour, despite the fact that his mother felt that he "should remain at school." His biographer William Winter referred to him as "the chosen ... guardian of that wild, strange genius, possessing a greater influence over him than was exercised by any other person." Winter saw this as Booth's apprenticeship—the passing of the theatrical torch. Edwin was far more ambivalent. He admitted that he learned acting techniques from his father, but he also believed that he was not Junius Brutus's favorite child: "My presence seemed necessary to him when at work, although at other times he almost ignored me, perhaps because his other children were more vivacious and amused him more."[15]

During his lifetime Junius Brutus Booth was regarded both as a drunkard and as eccentric to the point of insanity. As a mature man Edwin continued to wrestle with his father's reputation—both on and off stage. The official explanation he created in a brief biography of Junius

Brutus was that his father was filled with a Hamlet-like humor. He contended that "Great minds to Madness closely are allied. *Hamlet*'s mind, at the very edge of frenzy, seeks its relief in ribaldry." He claimed that like Hamlet, Junius Brutus was so immersed in his roles that he resorted to jokes to keep him from insanity.[16]

Junius Brutus' behavior, however, was hardly Hamlet's feigned "antic disposition." If it had been pretended, there would have been no need for the actor Thomas Flynn or Richard Booth or Junius Jr. or Edwin to accompany him. He missed performances; he was obsessive; he was violent — when a child died, Mary Ann was afraid to go home. From a modern standpoint, Junius Brutus was also an alcoholic. Edwin did not see it that way. He conceived of a drunkard as someone who consumed a great deal of alcohol, whereas, as he remembered, the "fineness" of his father's "organization was so acute that a bottle of porter (his favorite beverage when fatigued) or a single glass of brandy-and-water, would produce the same effect" as copious amounts of liquor.

Given the fact that he traveled with his father, Edwin could not help but be aware of the elder Booth's real and reputed mental condition. Junius Brutus Booth's "eccentricity" was stock-in-trade newspaper filler throughout the nineteenth century. Even his daughter Asia, always at pains to protect the dignity of her family, published anecdotes of his disappearance before a performance as Shylock, of his attempt to hold a funeral for his favorite horse, and of his absences from home for hours at a time. Her memories make it clear that Junius Brutus's alcoholism and/or periodic insanity necessitated a chaperone, someone to get him to the theatre and keep him out of the saloon.[17]

In February 1834 Booth was accompanied by an "attendant and companion" named John. Both Mary Ann and June were traveling with him in the fall of 1834, and all of the children were with them that year in New York. Thomas Flynn, for whom Edwin was named, was doing the job in March 1838; Richard Booth, Junius's son by Adelaide Delannoy, accompanied his father in 1843; and June, who performed with him in 1841, 1845 and 1847, was presumably available at those times to guard against his father's eccentricities. Mary Ann performed with him in Baltimore on October 22, 23, 25 and 26, 1847.[18]

Edwin Booth as a young teenager with his father Junius Brutus Booth Senior. "My presence seemed necessary to him when at work, although at other times he almost ignored me, perhaps because his other children were more vivacious and amused him more."

Edwin probably became his father's companion in 1847, when he was fourteen, because he was the only person left at home to do the job. June was already working as a touring star. Rosalie and Asia were inappropriate, because they were women. Joseph and John were too young. That left Edwin. An image of the young Edwin was later provided by an actor named Henry Sedley who, as a boy, was sent to deliver to a message to Junius Brutus:

> Mr. Booth met me kindly; ... but there seemed ... in his manner ... a depression, which indicated mental suffering.... He was habitually taciturn.... Edwin was like him. I have been with the two for what seemed an hour when neither spoke a word. Mr. Booth ... complained a little that Edwin would not study. It was his wish, he said, to give him a classical education, but the boy would have none of it. So he took him travelling with himself, that he might be of some use, he added, and be kept out of mischief. Edwin presently came in — a slight, dark, shy-looking lad of fourteen. The father introduced us, calling his son "Ted," and said something about our being so unlike, one being so brown, the other so fair. Mr. Booth then insisted upon having refreshments. He took brandy and water, ... Edwin a "port-wine sangaree," and I lemonade. EB's face looked mature for his years.... His manner ... reflected the gravity ... of his father's. Both ... left on my boyish mind the impression that they were either brooding over some sorrow or anticipating one.[19]

Sedley was writing in 1893, five months after Edwin's death. Like John Sleeper Clarke, he was reacting to Booth's mature image, but, unlike Clarke, he contended that the qualities that characterized Booth's adulthood were evident as a boy. Not all of these qualities were positive. At the age of fourteen, Edwin was already drinking, in this case a "port-wine sangaree," a drink composed of Madeira, water, sugar and nutmeg.[20]

He was also started on tobacco at an early age. After he had had his first serious stroke in 1889, Booth claimed that he had been "weaned on tobacco," and his daughter wrote: "Father has related how, when a small boy, his father unconsciously initiated him in the habit of smoking, by allowing my father to light his cigar then return it to his father, proud of his manly achievement." Edwina contended that gradually her father became addicted.[21]

Sedley contended that although Junius Brutus doubted his son's talent or fitness for the profession, as a teen-age boy, Edwin continually spoke about becoming an actor. He began taking fencing lessons from his brother Junius and received a foil point in his right eye. Fortunately the point was "buttoned," but the eye "blackened, ... became suffused with blood and for days was in a state of dangerous inflammation. The white ... was ... like crimson velvet."[22]

As an adult, Edwin publicly recalled his father with admiration for his abilities as an actor and with nostalgia for his eccentricities. Privately he lamented the senior Booth's failure to educate him and admitted that the eccentricities were part of a strain of madness he saw running through the family. He came to agree with June that "all Booths are more or less eccentric — There is a 'General Booth, of the Salvation Army' I've heard of; crazy as a loon, I suspect."[23] It was, however, his apprenticeship with his father that led him eventually to regard his choice of a profession as inevitable, despite parental opposition. In January 1864, he told George J. Mason, a writer for the *Spirit of the Times*:

> I was born to the stage.... I was familiar with its traditions ... pleasures and ... hardships, from my earliest boyhood. I was relieved from ... the pains and disappointments of those who are "stage-struck." But my familiarity with the business, while it saved me from the mistakes which novices make, deprived me of the buoyancy and hopefulness ... experienced by those who approach the profession from the outside, strangers to its hardships, and filled only with an enthusiastic idea of its possible successes.[24]

From his boyhood on, Booth was aware that a life in the theatre necessitated arduous travel, the discomfort of hotel rooms and food and the work of performing six or seven times a week, but there is no evidence that he ever seriously considered another profession.

Chapter Two

1849–1852: "A long legged stripling ... awkward as a young duck"

Edwin Booth made his professional debut on September 10, 1849, in Boston. He was not quite sixteen years old. According to the story recalled by his sister Asia, the young man was standing in the wings half an hour before his father was to go on as Richard III. The play's prompter, also cast as the messenger Tressel that evening, was annoyed at having multiple tasks and convinced Edwin to take his place as Tressel on stage. Edwin got into costume and sought out his father, who looked him over and said:

"Who was Tressel?"
"A messenger from the field of Tewksbury."
"What was his mission?"
"To bear the news of the defeat of the king's party."
"How did he make the journey?"
"On horseback."
"Where are your spurs?"

Edwin apparently had not thought of the spurs. His father said: "Here, take mine," and the young man removed the spurs from his father's boots and put them on his own.[1]

The date of Booth's debut is accurate and was reported as early as 1857, when he made a triumphant return to Boston, but the story also has elements of theatrical contrivance. The hero accompanies his famous father to Boston; the father discourages his theatrical ambitions; *Richard III* — his father's greatest hit — is the play. The theatre's prompter chooses not to appear and persuades the young man to take his place — a variant on "the star gets sick, and the understudy goes on." Edmond tells his father only at the last moment, because he knows his father will disapprove. The boy performs for the first time, and in Shakespeare, the playwright with whom he will become identified, although it is ironic that his Shakespearean debut occurs in a role added to *Richard III* by the eighteenth-century playwright Colley Cibber. And Booth, who becomes famous later for his attention to costume detail, actually forgets an important part of his wardrobe.

Although the date of Booth's debut is accurate, the impromptu substitution story is fabricated. The prompter in question was Jacob Wonderley Thoman, who had a major role in the afterpiece *Slasher and Crasher* but was not listed in the September 10 broadside, although he had already played Tressel to Booth's Richard on August 20. That he might have given up a minor role is credible, but a broadside had to be up more than a half-hour before the performance, and Edwin had been already listed on the broadside as Tressel. Moreover, advertisements of his appearance had been placed in three Boston newspapers. The last-minute aspect of the story is untrue.[2]

A more likely scenario presupposes a guiding principle of nineteenth-century American theatre — the pursuit of financial gain through novelty. Nineteenth-century audiences went to the theatre with a frequency difficult to imagine in the modern period. They patronized theatres, plays and stars the way modern audiences tune in to their favorite television programs, but, compared to today, the available audience population was infinitesimally smaller. Consequently nineteenth-century theatre attractions quickly exhausted their audiences, and so, to attract patrons, theatre managers needed novelty. Women performing male roles, female children performing opposite each other in adult male and female roles, female children performing adult male roles opposite adult actresses, fathers performing with sons, mothers with daughters, sisters and brothers with each other, amateurs performing leads, sometimes anonymously, sometimes not — all were common conventions of the period used to draw customers into the theatre. The theatrical debut of a major star's son was but another such ploy to lure patrons into the theatre.

While Tressel was Edwin's first professional appearance, it was, at best, a halting beginning to his career. A performance that marked the beginning of a serious career in the nineteenth-century theatre was normally repeated on a regular basis for financial gain, the actor in question establishing himself in a role. Edwin's Tressel did not fit this pattern. It was not repeated until a year later, and it was no triumph. Henry Sedley later remembered: "Edwin's performance, while entirely inoffensive, was ... colorless.... He was almost inaudible and seemed to have but slender appreciation of the overwhelming purport of his message to the king.... Good judges of acting did not assuredly augur future greatness from it."[3]

For the son of a theatrical family, Booth's debut came late — when he was sixteen years old, and had been touring with his father for two to three years. In comparison his brother June began performing at thirteen. Edwin may have spent his time on tour taking care of Junius Brutus. Given the elder Booth's deteriorating physical and mental condition, making sure he got to the theatre, went on stage, and returned to the hotel may have been a full-time job. But it did provide a form of apprenticeship. Edwin watched his father act. He later claimed that Junius Brutus forbade him to leave the dressing room, expecting him to concentrate on school work, but that he listened through a keyhole and learned dramatic interpretations by ear. Nineteenth-century dressing rooms were usually in the basement, so this assertion is probably false. His friend E. C. Stedman wrote that Edwin had told him that he "would sit in the wings for hours, listening to the play, and having all its parts indelibly impressed on his memory."[4] Given his later difficulties with memorization, it is doubtful that the texts were "indelibly impressed on his memory," although it is likely that he spent time watching his father from the wings.

Edwin grew up in a period in which interpretation was everything. Audiences knew the plays intimately and had seen them performed by dozens of actors. Junius Brutus Booth was famous for his interpretations, and Edwin inherited, in the sense of claimed, these interpretations. For most of his early career, he was compared to his father; it was natural for any nineteenth-century audience to do so. And while Edwin would come to reject the robust romantic style in which his father performed, this very rejection represented an artistic decision that could only have been made by observing that style and trying it out early in his career. When the late nineteenth-century actor Otis Skinner asked Booth to compare himself with Junius Brutus, Edwin was to say: "I think I am a little quieter."[5]

He did not perform Tressel during the rest of the season, or at least he was not advertised for the role. Instead he began to work on a line of more important roles — namely that of male juveniles. On September 27, 1849, he played Cassio in *Othello* at the Providence Museum. Tressel can be any age, but Cassio must be a handsome young man for Othello's jealousy to make sense. On September 29 he performed Wilford to his father's Sir Edward in *The Iron Chest*. Wilford is the virtuous secretary of the evil Sir Edward Mortimer. It was this role Booth repeated soon after in Norfolk, Pittsburgh, Charleston and Philadelphia. All of these were benefit nights for his father. Benefits were performances at which the honoree received all the box office receipts after expenses had been paid.[6]

In antebellum America, a stock actor (one contracted to a particular company in a particular city to play a particular type of character for one season) might perform six nights a week from late summer through May or June. Edwin's performances were seven in a season in which Junius Brutus Booth worked from August 20, 1849, until June 1, 1850, as a touring star playing a variety of theatres. There was little sense that he was beginning a career. It is even possible that Edwin was not with his father all the time. For instance, something went wrong with Junius Brutus in Richmond in 1849. He was scheduled to appear as Richard III on April 1, but "a crowded audience were disappointed, as he could nowhere be found at the time of the performance." Apparently he had gone to a nearby plantation to visit friends and neglected to notify his family. Edwin wrote to John Sefton, stage-manager of the Richmond Theatre, asking about his father's whereabouts. Sefton responded, and Edwin was sent to retrieve his father. Junius Brutus had to borrow $50 to get them back to Baltimore. It seems likely that Edwin was serving only as an intermittent guardian.[7]

He was certainly at home in the summer, when American theatres were traditionally closed. On August 2, 1850, he and John Sleeper Clarke produced a "Grand Dramatic Festival" in the courthouse in Bel Air. Booth was almost seventeen and Clarke a year younger. The "festival" was a series of speeches and scenes, including Hamlet's "To Be or Not to Be" (Booth), the dagger scene from *Macbeth* (Booth), the Cassius/Brutus argument from Act IV of *Julius Caesar* (Booth as Brutus; Clarke as Cassius) and portions of *Richard III* (Booth), *The Merchant of Venice* (Clarke), Kotzebue's *The Stranger* (Clarke), Otway's *Venice Preserved* (Clarke as Jaffier) and *Richelieu* (Booth as Richelieu), plus a second half with "Yankee Stories" and Clarke's "peculiar illustrations of a young man's first appearance as an actor."[8]

The lack of activity that characterized Edwin's first season as an actor also marked his second year — 1850–1851. He did, however, add several roles to his repertoire — Hemeya, the noble Moorish antagonist to Pescara, the evil Spanish governor in Richard Sheil's *The Apostate*; Laertes in *Hamlet*; and Titus, the rebellious son whom Lucius Junius Brutus must put to death in John Howard Payne's *Brutus*— all within a juvenile line of business. Edwin remembered a notable incident during a performance as Titus:

> In the last scene when all was hush as death and while *Brutus* (my father) was holding his son *Titus* (me) in close embrace at their final parting, a senseless fellow in front made some rude remark which disturbed both audience and actors. Raising his head from off my breast, my father, without lapsing from the stern Roman character of judge, with a lightning glance toward the fellow said — "Beware I am the headsman!" ... All in front and on the stage seemed paralyzed until the thunder of applause that followed broke the spell.[9]

Edwin's first New York appearance occurred on September 27, 1850, at the National Theatre on Chatham Street. The National was a second-rate working people's theatre in a rough neighborhood. The fact that Junius Brutus Booth was playing there indicates a decline in his career.[10] The *Spirit of the Times* commented: "It is said that for faithful attendance during an engagement, he cannot be relied upon and for that reason is not sought by our first-class theatre men."[11]

At the National Edwin played Wilford to his father's Sir Edward Mortimer and Hemeya to his father's Pescara. In the company were Joseph Jefferson (later to become the foremost comic actor of the nineteenth-century American stage) and his first wife Margaret Lockyear Jefferson, who both played opposite Edwin in his first New York performance. Jefferson remembered him as "a handsome youth ... a lithe and graceful figure, buoyant in spirits, and with the loveliest eyes I ever looked upon. We were friends from the first." Their friendship lasted for the rest of Booth's life.

On November 9, 1850, Edwin performed Hemeya to his father's Pescara at the Adelphi Theatre in Washington, and won his first review: "Mr. Edwin Booth ... played the part of *Hemeya* in very creditable manner, giving the audience ample evidence that the mantle of the father will fall upon the son." In January 1851 Booth received a letter from thirty-four young men in St. Louis, asking him to accept a complimentary benefit and saying "you have already mounted an eminence that places the glittering prize of triumph in full view." The invitation was polite hyperbole, and there is no indication that such a benefit, in which an actor's friends traditionally attempted to sell out the house, ever took place. On the back of the invitation, the seventeen-year-old Booth kept daily accounts of the money he was spending for items such as bread, butter, milk, raisins, soap and candy.[12]

On April 5, 1851, back at New York's National Theatre, Edwin may have substituted for his father, playing his first lead — Richard III. The elder Booth rehearsed in the afternoon but suddenly announced that he was ill. When Edwin remonstrated with him, his father said: "Play it yourself." Edwin contended that the theatre's manager told him: "there is not time to change the bill; we must close the house — unless *you* will act the part." The carriage was at the hotel door with a trunk of costumes strapped to it. Edwin's friend and biographer the critic William Winter believed that Junius Brutus faked illness in order to give his son a chance and that Edwin was still memorizing lines as he got into his father's costume, a set of clothes too large to fit his slender frame. "No announcement was made of a change in the cast," and the audience who came expecting "Mr. Booth ... in his last appearance ... lapsed into silence" when they discovered the substitution. Later in life Edwin came to believe that his father sneaked into the theatre that night to watch him perform.[13]

Junius Brutus Booth was certainly scheduled to play Richard III on April 5. There is no newspaper review of Edwin's substitution, but the chances of a local critic venturing down to the National on that particular night were scant. Like Edwin's debut, his first Richard III occasioned no notice. The performance supposedly occurred on the elder Booth's benefit night, but, in actuality, the benefit was for "the juvenile prodigy Master Murray," and the elder Booth may have decided to become ill because he did not want to perform. That Edwin was thrust into the role of Richard with the speed implied is unlikely.

Nineteenth-century actors were expected to be "up in all the legitimate parts" and ready to go on in four hours time. Edwin, however, was neither his father's understudy nor a nineteenth-century stock actor, and lead tragedy was not his line. If he could do Richard III at a moment's notice, the implication is that he had been studying the part, watching his father perform and learning the lines or picking enough of them up to stumble through a performance. To his future manager, Benjamin Baker, who claimed to have seen this performance, Edwin looked like "a long legged stripling ... awkward as a young duck." Yet despite Baker's perception of his lankiness, Edwin was successful. He was "called out" at the end of the play and led forward by his Richmond, the veteran actor John R. Scott. Scott expressed the young man's gratitude to the public, introducing him as "the worthy scion of a noble stock" and adding, under his breath, "I'll wager they don't know what that means."[14]

Edwin's New York performance of Richard III was a turning point in his work as an actor. He later remembered:

> Thenceforth he [Junius Brutus Booth] made no great objection to my acting occasionally with him, although he never gave me instruction, professional advice or encouragement in any form. He had doubtless resolved to make me work my way unaided; and though his seeming indifference was painful then, it compelled me to exercise my callow wits; it made me *think*!"[15]

By the time the Booths opened in Richmond, Virginia, on April 21, 1851, Edwin's career had expanded. At the age of eighteen he began performing every night, playing Richmond to his father's Richard III, as well as four other roles in six days. In Washington in May he did Edgar in *King Lear*, Gratiano in *The Merchant of Venice*, Macduff in *Macbeth* and Young Norval in John Home's *Douglas*. He was playing "seconds," as the theatrical term had it, to his father. By the end of the 1850–51 season he was performing at least ten roles. It was a far cry from the forty roles any stock company actor played in his line of business, but Edwin was in a strange position. He was not a stock company actor coming up through the ranks, and he was not a touring star. He was an added attraction, a minor moon orbiting around his father. It may also have been difficult to cast him, because he was taking over the roles for which a given theatrical management had normally contracted its juvenile man.[16]

The Booths concluded the 1850–1851 theatrical season with four performances at the National Hall in Washington D.C. In *King Lear*, the *Daily National Intelligencer* noted that "Mr. Booth was well supported by Mr. Edwin Booth." Both Booths, however, had a problem. The *American Telegraph*'s critic wrote: "In *Macbeth* young Booth played well; but the elder Booth was drunk. We mean it literally — he was drunk and staggered some; interpolating sections of *The Merchant of Venice*" into *Macbeth*.[17] The next night was worse.

> The curtain rose at a late hour, and Mr. Booth, senior, was the most drunken Sir Edward Mortimer that ever looked into an iron chest or an empty tumbler; and Mr. Booth, junior showed very good powers of imitation in this particular.... An effort was made to play the tragedy of "Douglas" but young Norval [Edwin Booth] had made such progress in the road of dissipation, as to excite the sympathy of all beholders for his melancholy mother. Seeing how things were tending Mr. Taylor [another member of the company] had quietly put on his hat and gloves, picked up his cane and walked off.... Most of the ladies in front and many of the gentlemen, retired very early also.[18]

On May 28, 1851, Edwin appeared as Richmond in *Richard III* at the Holliday Street Theatre in Baltimore. It was his first advertised performance without his father. His whereabouts between the end of this season and February 11, 1852, when he played Antoine Bellard at the Front Street Theatre in Baltimore and on the next day Titus to his father's Lucius Junius Brutus, are a mystery. He performed without his father as Lykon in *Ingomar* for Jean Davenport's benefit on March 6, 1852. This was followed by only two more appearances— Wilford in Charleston on April 26 and Edgar in Baltimore on June 2. The Baltimore appearances prove that he was there in February; the occasional appearances in April and June imply that he was touring with his father. Where did he spend most of the 1851–1852 theatrical season?[19]

One possibility is that he was engaged to play utility roles at $6 a week. The Baltimore *American Commercial Advertiser* does not list Edwin in any cast, but a program for March 13, 1852, shows him playing Herman in Schiller's *The Robbers* and Lord Rivers in *Day After the Wedding* at the Holliday Street Theatre in Baltimore. Consequently Edwin may have spent most of 1851–1852 playing in stock.[20]

Another explanation for Edwin's scant appearances was that his father's professional clout in the East may have weakened to the point that he could not get a decent engagement or insist that local managers take on his son. Junius Brutus' performances during 1851–1852 ran counter to the pattern typical of an actor of his stature. If well booked and popular, a touring star opened in a city on Monday, played every evening that week, took a benefit on Friday and gave a final appearance on Saturday night. On Sunday the star traveled to a new town to open the following day. Stars seldom visited a city more than once a year, because the popularity of their repertoire declined the more it was exposed. Yet between August 11, 1851, and June 3, 1852, Junius Brutus Booth played four times in New York, five times in Baltimore and twice in Philadelphia. And several of these engagements lasted only three days or less. The odd schedule probably means that in the eyes of theatre managers, Booth could not be trusted. Moreover the predominance of performances in Baltimore implies that he was at home much of the time, and for a nineteenth-century touring star to be at home during the season meant that he could not get an engagement or that he was ill, or both. Edwin was dependent on his father's employment, and his father was only sporadically employed. Facing this lack of work, Edwin and his father decided to move west; their motivation was money.

Chapter Three

1852–1856: "Full of promise ... and Bowery rant"

In July 1852 Edwin Booth accompanied his father to San Francisco. According to William Winter, the idea for the tour originated with the family's oldest son, Junius Jr., who "had visited California." June, however, had done far more than "visit." Like his father, he had escaped westward with a second wife. As early as 1841 when he was twenty, June was married to Clementina (Mary) DeBar, described by a contemporary as "a most versatile actress, but far from prepossessing of feature." She was thirteen years older than June. On February 6, 1851, the twenty-nine-year-old June and a seventeen-year-old actress named Harriet Mace were arrested after a performance for being "entirely too familiar." The arrest was at the instance of Clementina, who charged that "since the 6th of February at Brookline," Massachusetts, June, as a married man, had been "guilty of adultery" and Harriet, "being unmarried," was guilty "of fornication. They were carried to Brookline, Mr. Booth giving $400 bail and Miss Mace $50" and were remanded "to appear at Dedham on the 4th Monday in April for trial." No evidence about the disposition of Clementina's suit or June and Harriet's trial has yet been discovered but the love triangle may have been settled amiably. June and Clementina divorced, and she remained on good terms with the Booth family; in later years she visited Asia, and her daughter (June's stepdaughter) Blanche DeBar performed with Edwin when he was a star.[1]

June and Harriet, called Hattie, made their debut at San Francisco's Jenny Lind Theatre on October 4, 1851. Although June was not a talented actor (one reviewer wrote that his husky voice and twitching arms, legs and body detracted from his verbal interpretations), his California performances were described as "the best ever seen on the Pacific coast," and his stay was financially successful. On March 18, 1852, according to *The San Francisco Daily Herald*, he "announced his intention of leaving immediately for the Atlantic States, with the view of inducing his father to come to California." He and Hattie made their last San Francisco appearance on March 19 and returned east.[2]

The hope of profits in the west was a motivating factor for actors throughout the nineteenth century. The Booth family would not have undertaken a California trip without the expectation of financial gain. The 5,245-mile journey from New York to San Francisco was expensive; typically the first-class one-way cabin fare for the entire journey was $315 per person.[3]

The journey was also arduous. Junius Brutus, Edwin, June and Hattie left New York on June 21, 1852, on the steamship *Illinois*. The steamer made the thousand-mile journey to Aspinwall on the Atlantic side of Panama in eleven days. The Booths paid two dollars each to be transferred onto small boats called yawls to get on shore. Travelers at the time found Aspinwall "covered with eight to ten inches of water." Frame "slab hotels, boarding houses and bordellos" stood on stilts connected by "flimsy wooden footwalks" amidst "the stench of the slops in the lagoon-like interior of the island."[4]

They stayed overnight at one of Aspinwall's three hotels for three dollars a head and then, for five dollars each, took the six A.M. train west for the fifty-five-mile journey across the isthmus. They rode across three thousand yards of swampland and through a "barrier of mangrove," where Edwin saw monkeys cavorting in 150-foot-tall trees. From the end of the line, a mile east of Barbacoas, they traveled to Gorgona on a river no more than one hundred yards wide, using a bungo, a flat-bottomed hollowed-out boat of guayacan logs. It was rainy season, and the Booths traveled at night because it usually rained in the daytime, making the current too swift. They were paddled or poled up the river by what travelers described as three or four sweating "half-naked natives" who often had to enter "the water to propel the boat past a sunken tree or sandbar."[5]

They slept overnight at Gorgona, a collection of cane huts with palm tree roofs and two or three American frame buildings perched high on a cliff overlooking the Chagres River. From Gorgona, they took a boat to Cruces and traveled the remaining twenty-three miles across the isthmus to Panama City on mules. The road, seven feet wide with rough curbstones on each side, descended into ravines ten to thirty feet deep and only three feet wide at the bottom. As the wood grew deeper and darker and the tough clay soil became saturated with rain, the road became a gulley so narrow that two people could not pass each other. Mud, four or five feet deep, came up to the mules's bellies.[6]

After twenty-four hours on muleback the Booths reached the grassy plains near Panama City and entered the town of crumbling walls, red-tiled roofs, old churches, and cathedral towers coated with pearl oyster shells. Its roadways were narrow and filthy, and, according to a contemporary traveler, "licentiousness" walked "the streets unblushingly and ... every ... man, woman and child — smoke[d] cigars and [drank] wine and liquor." Women carried "their babies astraddle of their hip"; children were "always naked," and drinking water was available only for cash.[7]

The Panama City harbor was so silt-filled that steamers had to remain two miles from shore. Consequently, for fifty cents, passengers and their baggage were carried on the backs of natives to canoes. Then for two dollars each they were rowed out to their ship — the steamer *California*. The Booth party left Panama on July 11.[8]

The trip up the west coast took seventeen days. The *California* arrived in San Francisco at 6 P.M. on July 28, 1852. It had taken the Booths thirty-seven days to reach California from New York. The theatre's company as well as groups of ordinary citizens greeted them, and, according to a member of the company named J. J. McCloskey, Edwin was so handsome that he quickly became "the most observed man in San Francisco."[9]

The Booths began to rehearse the day after arriving. According to McCloskey, Edwin, who could not wait to try the allurements of San Francisco, complained: "Oh, come on! Let's cut all this and go out and see the town!" As the rehearsal lengthened, he began to slur his words, and his father snapped: "That won't do! Come, come, come!" The young man drawled his line: "The weary sun has made a golden set." "For God's sake!" broke in the elder Booth, "where does the sun set? Well, show it then! Point to it! Nod your head! Do something!" McCloskey, writing after Booth's death, remembered a dashing but professionally irresponsible young man.[10]

Two days after they had arrived, Junius Brutus Senior opened at the Jenny Lind Theatre as Sir Edward Mortimer in *The Iron Chest*. A thousand people crowded the house. Although his voice was not as "vigorous as in former days," critics saw him as "a splendid ruin, aged and crumbling, but majestic and magnificent even in its decay." Edwin was described as a "judicious actor" who had "inherited a large share of the genius of his father."[11]

Ferdinand Ewer, the editor and theatre critic for San Francisco's *Placer Times and Transcript*, was immediately struck by him and later wrote: "He played under some embarrassment but still with ... naturalness and good judgment." Seven years older than Booth and a Harvard graduate, Ewer was one of the first public figures to recognize Edwin's ability. He was the type of man whom Edwin always cultivated — an educated, respectable member of society who was also a fan.[12]

Despite Ewer's enthusiasm, the Booths' thirteen San Francisco performances were not financially successful. A local correspondent for the *Spirit of the Times* wrote of the elder Booth in *Richard III*: "Richard, I am sorry to say, was not himself.... His voice could not be heard half way across the theatre, although his action and by-play were worthy of his palmiest days."[13]

The Booths made the 150-mile ten-hour journey to Sacramento, where they opened at the American Theatre on August 19. Edwin performed every evening and, on September 2, had his first benefit, playing Jaffier, the noble conspirator in Thomas Otway's *Venice Preserved*. When his father saw him in the black velvet tunic traditional in the role, he said: "You look like Hamlet; why did you not act Hamlet for your benefit?" Edwin replied: "If I ever have another, I will." Apparently his father's expectation was that Edwin, at the age of nineteen, was ready to perform a role the size of Hamlet.[14]

In later life Booth remembered Sacramento as a financial failure and wrote to a friend, the author Thomas Bailey Aldrich: "The town was always a wretched one for theatricals; my father acted to empty benches here in the 'golden days,' when the streets and gambling-houses were crowded." In actuality the Booths played Sacramento for three weeks, the length of time that Edwin, as a mature star, performed in a city as large as Chicago. They would not have stayed nor would the management have kept them, had they not been making money. The weather in Sacramento was unmercifully hot, reaching a hundred and one, and ticket prices were high. Both elements might have kept audiences away, but reviews were glowing. Edwin was cited as sustaining his part "with great credit," and his benefit was artistically successful. The *Union* wrote: "The young tragedian achieved a gratifying triumph ... and for his excellent personation of the character was presented with a beautiful scarf by one of the fair auditors present." Edwin was nineteen, and his physical beauty was appealing to female audience members. This appeal would persist for the rest of his life.[15]

The Sacramento run closed on September 6, 1852, and Junius Brutus went on to an engagement alone at the Adelphi Theatre in San Francisco beginning September 27. The result was disastrous. A correspondent for *The Weekly Placer Herald* wrote: "There has been a great rush to the theatre to see Booth; but his old admirers come away — sadly disappointed. Last night he was reported to have been so drunk as to have fallen twice on the stage." On October 1 the elder Booth sailed back to San Juan del Sud, Panama, leaving his sons in California. Junius Junior had established a career in San Francisco, and Edwin had decided to remain, probably out of a sense of adventure.[16]

After what the *New York Times* described as "a very flattering and successful engagement" at the St. Charles Theatre in New Orleans, Junius Brutus Booth embarked on the Mississippi steamboat *J.S. Chenowith* for Cincinnati. He caught a cold on the ship during a rainstorm, which, in a century without antibiotics, turned into what was called "consumption of the bowels." He became speechless and died on board on November 30, 1852, at the age of fifty-seven. On December 9, his body arrived in Baltimore, and he was buried the next day in Green Mount cemetery.[17]

News of his death reached San Francisco via the steamship *Cortes* on the evening of January 5, 1853. June, who was in town, learned of his father's death that night and went on performing the following evening. Word of the elder Booth's death was published in Sacramento on January 12.[18]

Immediately after his father's departure from California in October 1852, Edwin had joined a troupe headed by Dan Wilmarth Waller and his wife Emma, touring the Northern mining towns of Marysville, Shirt-Tail Bend (sometimes called Shirt-Tail Canyon), Nevada City, Red Dog, Rough and Ready, Grass Valley, Poverty Flat and Downieville.[19] This was a period in his life that spawned adventures in which he reveled but never wanted to repeat. Later, in 1886, he wrote to Lawrence Barrett from Derrickville, Pennsylvania, where he was performing before oil miners who reminded him of the gold rush prospectors he had known in 1852:

> I expected to weary the [o]ilers & to be invited, perhaps, to "git"—as the miners of California did in ye days of lang syne, when I galloped through the woes of [Sir Edward] Mortimer & the Stranger—in Hangtown [Placerville] & Jackass Gulch near Shirt-tail Bend, in the Northern mining camps. Ah! Those merry days of Youth! Will they never come again? No, thank God! unless you beguile me into other "show towns" beyond the pale of Civilization's luminous wings & things; "Tombstone," mayhap, or "Hell-&-fetch it." Don't![20]

The Waller troupe traveled on horseback, and Edwin acquired considerable riding experience and skill. In 1875 Waller remembered: "he is as fine a whip as lives, and a splendid rider besides. In the early days of California he and I rode side by side every day. I thought him then the most daring rider I ever met. He would take the trunk of one of those big fallen trees out there even though there was a road around it, and a big rock or a high banked stream were nothing either to him or his horse."[21]

From October 16, 1852 through January 1, 1853, the Waller troupe performed a wide repertoire in Nevada City and Grass Valley, California.[22] Reviewing *The Merchant of Venice,* the Nevada City critic noted of Edwin's Gratiano: "Anyone seeing him would perceive how much a piece may be acted when no word is spoken." It was the earliest evidence of the introspective style for which Booth became famous. Audiences perceived of him as involved in the action even when he was silent.

The rains began in early November and by mid-month it was snowing hard. By the end of November the snow was ten feet deep in Downieville, and settlers made snow tunnels to the "stores in the vain hope that some crackers or a bit of flour ... might be found to eat." On December 31, 1852, the Waller company left Nevada City for Grass Valley, where they were hemmed in by a snowstorm. Edwin

Edwin Booth as an older teenager. Booth mainly remembered California for the fun in what he called "the nursery of my professional babyhood," the time when he was "full of promise ... and Bowery rant."

learned of his father's death during January 1853 either through a letter or, more likely, a copy of a San Francisco newspaper which had published a death notice. Determined to escape his snow-bound community, Booth joined a group of men and, according to Winter, walked for two days and one night, through snow that was two to three feet deep, to the river port of Marysville, fifty to sixty miles away. This story may be exaggerated, but somewhere between January 5, 1853, when word of Junius Brutus Booth's death first reached San Francisco, and January 15, when Booth was advertised as having been "engaged" at the San Francisco Theatre, he walked through the snow, crossed the Yuba River by ferry, took a steamer or stage coach to Sacramento, went by boat to San Francisco and began to perform.[23]

June was running the small San Francisco Theatre and playing to "tolerable houses." He immediately advertised "Mr. Edwin Booth" as Fred Jerome in *The American Fireman*, which opened on February 2. Years later Booth would regale his acting company by performing the play's most memorable line: "A San Francisco Fire Boy is the noblest work of God."[24]

According to Winter, Booth went from leading tragedian to utility actor at the San Francisco Theatre, three times—"a lesson for crushed tragedians." A "leading tragedian" performed the major male roles in a play; a utility actor performed walk-ons. Winter, however, was exaggerating Edwin's humble beginnings and his struggle to achieve greatness. While his opportunities to appear in tragic roles were limited to ten performances at the San Francisco Theatre between February 2 and October 23, 1853, Booth seldom played utility roles; he specialized in juvenile parts important enough to be mentioned in the limited space of newspaper advertisements. Moreover specializing in comedy was not a punishment; it was what every nineteenth-century stock company actor did, at least part of the time. Twenty years later Booth saw it as a valuable experience. "When I was learning to act tragedy, I had frequently to perform comic parts, in order to acquire a certain ease of manner that my serious parts might not appear too stilted."[25]

The San Francisco critic Ferdinand Ewer extolled Booth's "severe accuracy and chasteness" but noted that "Mr. Booth devotes too little time to study." Edwin typically went on the stage without having studied or memorized his parts carefully. On March 24, Ewer wrote: "Mr. E. Booth will, with a little care and study, make an eminent actor, and at no distant day." Edwin needed to learn his roles, but then "a little care and study" was what the entire company needed. According to San Francisco newspapers, new pieces were "produced with such rapidity that a proper time for studying the parts" was not possible. Often lines had "to be completed by the ready wit of the actor or botched altogether."[26]

On April 21, after three months of comic acting, Edwin played Richard III in a benefit performance for the company's scene painter, who probably hoped that the novelty of young Booth in his father's greatest role would be profitable. The critical results were mixed.[27] Ferdinand Ewer wrote: "During the first three acts it was evident that Mr. Booth was not doing himself justice. His performance was not even.... As the piece developed, however, Mr. Booth warmed up, and it was reserved for the fourth and fifth acts for him to achieve a triumph."[28] What Ewer saw became characteristic of Booth's Richard III and other parts. He would save himself for the strenuous closing acts of the play. His next venture into Shakespeare came on April 25, when he performed his first Hamlet. At this point Ewer heralded Booth as the equal of the leading American tragedian Edwin Forrest.

> Never in the history of the drama did such a spectacle present itself. A young man, nineteen years old, appeared in Hamlet, for the first time, and played it in a style of excellence which puts to the blush any attempt in the same character we have seen in California. We do not mean to say that Mr. Edwin Booth's Hamlet has the polish of that of his father, so far as reading and grace of gesticulation are concerned.... Nor is Mr. Edwin Booth's Hamlet without its faults. He has not had sufficient experience.... There was a slight awkwardness ... in some of his movements.... Nor was he entirely

letter perfect; but how immeasurably little does so slight an error seem before the greatness of that general conception to which he has vaulted.[29]

While Booth regularly became friendly with people like Ewer, men who criticized his work positively and whose level of erudition he considered superior to his own, he also made friends with those with whom he could have fun. During his time in San Francisco, he encountered David C. Anderson, a character actor in the line of old men, who became Edwin's comrade for life and was eventually known as "Uncle Dave, the friend of Edwin Booth." Anderson was twenty years his senior and became both a pal and a surrogate father. In later life Edwin wrote voluminously to Anderson in a style far less formal than the style he reserved for his other correspondents, and Anderson, into old age, called him "Ned," the boyhood name Booth discarded as he became famous.

This was the bohemian period of Booth's life. He was a great favorite with the ladies and acquired a group of riotous male friends. Booth, Anderson and the journalist/songwriter Stephen C. Massett lived in a section known as the Mission. At first they camped in a tent among the sandhills. Eventually they purchased several lots and built a little two-room shanty out of dry-goods boxes and tree boughs. They called it the Rancho and styled themselves "comedians and rancheros" in the city's directories. They kept horses, did their own cooking and washing, invited members of the company to dinner, wrote out elaborate menus in the mode of fashionable New York restaurants and then served fat bacon and coffee followed by corncob pipes. In later life Booth delighted in reminding Anderson of "our old 'ranch,'" of the buckwheat cakes they had once shared and of their mutual delight in kidneys and an after-dinner pipe. "Dost remember how in the hoary days of yore, we used to set our special days for a regular square meal of kidneys? Ah, the merry days of youth! What a sin you could not stay!"[30]

The actor and playwright Henry Sedley, who had known Edwin as a boy, became his companion through the 600–700 miles of his western wanderings in what Sedley called "stages and saddle." After Booth's death he wrote:

> There was scarcely any domestic life in California in those days. For a young man of Edwin's situation, apart from the theatre, the hotel, the bar-room, and the gambling-room were almost the sole resorts available, and to keep fairly clear of evil habits, which Edwin in the main did, was correspondingly praiseworthy. At this time Edwin picked up a little Spanish.... In mining towns, salons, the haunts of the Monte and the Faro dealer and always from the lips of the dusky senoritas, who turned the roulette wheels; this speech was common, and a few words or sentences of it were often in Edwin's mouth.[31]

Every morning at ten Booth and his actor-housemates, dressed outlandishly and riding mules and horses, came down Mission Road to the theatre. Sedley remembered Edwin "habitually wore long boots—what people there called 'top-boots,' they being really 'Hessians'—a plain suit of dark stuff, an overcoat hanging on the shoulders—the arms not being thrust through the sleeves, so looking like the outer jacket of a Hussar—and a slouch felt hat."[32]

As part of his bohemianism Booth was often drunk when performing. Later nineteenth-century writers saw this as an inheritance from his father and praised his eventual ability to overcome "the thirst in the blood" that lay "like a lurking tiger waiting for its opportunity."[33] Writing to his wife-to-be Mary Devlin, Edwin confessed that while his vices did not include "murder, robbing and such petty offenses" but did include drinking and fornication:

> Before I was eighteen, I was a drunkard, at twenty a libertine. I knew no better. I was allowed to roam, at large and at an early age, in a wild and almost barbarous country where boys become old men in vice very speedily.... Sin was in me, and it consumed me while it was shut up so close; so I let it out, and it seemed to rage and burn more fiercely than ever.[34]

The confession Booth made about being a "libertine" implies that he had committed what he considered sexual "sin." In 1874 he wrote to David C. Anderson recollecting "the old time 'when youth beat high, and'— I've forgotten the rest of the quotation, but perhaps 'tis best unsaid, now you're a married man, in fact we're both married men — and ought not to recollect any of our halcyon 'dido,' [mischief] ought we? Let's be good!" While California during the Gold Rush lacked women of virtue, whores were available, and someone taught Booth where his "cojones" were. By the time he was nineteen Edwin had formed both an addiction to alcohol and an ambivalence about his relationship to women that would haunt him for the rest of his life.[35]

Over the next year and a half in June's San Francisco theatre Booth performed opposite a series of important American actors — James Murdoch, Matilda Heron and Laura Keene, but most frequently with Catherine Sinclair. Sinclair's ability as an actress was bolstered by the notoriety of her scandalous public divorce from the stage star Edwin Forrest, a notoriety on which she capitalized by billing herself as "Mrs. Catherine F. Sinclair, formerly Mrs. Edwin Forrest."

Edwin became Sinclair's leading man in the domestic melodramas that were her specialty. He was not completely successful. *The Daily Alta California*'s critic wrote: "Claude Melnotte was a very irregular and defective performance in the hands of Mr. Booth." Ewer agreed, writing: "We would drop a word of caution touching a mannerism, which it would be well for him not to fall into. We allude to a certain prolongation of words in pronunciation, which gives them a drawling sound." The mannerism became characteristic of Booth's performances for the rest of his life.[36]

After Sinclair's engagement, June closed the theatre for repairs. The renovated San Francisco reopened on June 11, 1853, with a company of twenty that included Booth. It was in this new company that Edwin played Romeo for the first time, on June 27, 1853. Ewer thought it "one of the best pieces of acting we have ever seen." On August 2, Booth got his second opportunity to play Iago — the first time before a metropolitan audience, albeit unfortunately opposite an Othello played by a local amateur. His Petruchio earned him his first review in a New York City newspaper from a San Francisco correspondent for *The Spirit of the Times*, and he went on to his first performances of Sir Giles Overreach on September 6 and Shylock on September 8 (his benefit).[37]

Two days after the benefit, June's venture at the San Francisco Theatre closed. After some painting and repairing it reopened under Catherine Sinclair's management on September 19, 1853, with a performance of *The School for Scandal* featuring Sinclair as Lady Teazle and Edwin as Charles Surface. Ewer wrote: "Mr. Booth adds to his artistic allurements the utmost degree of good taste in costume, and the bearing and personal appearance of a perfect gentleman. His light comedy is the best we have ever had in California." His work, however, was still marked by his failure to memorize lines.[38]

While workmen were excavating a completely new home for the company, Sinclair and Booth toured to Sacramento, opening there on October 23. After a week, however, the tragedian James E. Murdoch joined Sinclair in Sacramento Theatre and took over Booth's roles. With a bigger name to support her, Sinclair no longer needed Booth, and his name disappeared from the theatre's newspaper advertisements. When the new San Francisco Theatre, soon to be rechristened the Metropolitan, opened on December 24, 1853, Edwin was a member of the company, again supporting Sinclair and touring stars like Murdoch. When they were not present, he got a chance to shine. On December 25, he performed Richard III, and the critic of the *Daily Alta California*'s critic wrote: "Mr. Booth needs only time, study and care to make him a really good actor." The call for more study plagued him through performances of the title role in *Pizarro* and Sir Thomas Clifford in *The Hunchback*. When he played Richard III on January 17, 1854, the reviewer for *The Golden Era* slammed the production without even mentioning Booth by name: "Many ... were not altogether satisfied as to whose Richard it was, whether Shakespeare's or whether it was 'got up' expressly for that occasion by some aspiring 'supe.'... An indiscriminate slaughtering took place in which all hands were murdered outright.... To speak plainly ... the tragedy was extremely farcical."[39]

On April 6, the English-born American star Laura Keene opened at the Metropolitan in San Francisco, and Booth became her leading man. She was greeted, according to a local critic, on opening night by a cheer "so boisterous and prolonged" that it frightened her. Her performances, however, were not financially successful, and she closed after three nights. The *Daily Alta California* ascribed her lack of success to illness after a long sea journey. Ewer, however, placed the blame on Booth. "Miss Keene has not performed in San Francisco as well as she is capable of performing. Her pieces came onto the stage without sufficient preparation. Some of the important actors around her were not perfect in their parts. We regret to say that this remark applies with too much truth to Mr. Edwin Booth." If Ewer, who was a fan of Booth's work, said this, Edwin's failure to master his part must have been extreme.[40]

In early July an exodus of San Francisco actors bound for Australia began. It may have been caused by a financial depression that hit the city beginning in 1854. Edwin's departure may have been the result of the reviews he was getting and the fact that his last benefit on June 6 was poorly attended. By July 25, along with David Anderson, he had booked passage on the "bark *M. A. Jones*" and left for Australia on August 1.[41]

Laura Keene went with them. She had taken over the management of San Francisco's Union Theatre and had been scheduled to perform on July 31 but failed to show up for the performance. She had sailed that afternoon for Australia with Booth and Anderson.[42]

Did Booth and Keene leave together with the intent of performing in Australia? Did the idea of performing together occur during the trip? Either way the Australian tour was so unsuccessful that it was hardly worth the seventy-two-day journey from San Francisco. The *M. A. Jones* arrived in Sydney on October 11, and Anderson, Keene and Booth opened a two-week run at the Victoria Theatre on October 23. The critic for *The Empire* praised Booth's Claude Melnotte, the Stranger and Hamlet, but wrote that Edwin "appeared to be suffering from influenza, or some vocal ailment, which rendered him at times inaudible."[43]

Booth, Anderson and Keene left Sydney on November 8 on the S.S. *Yarra* and arrived in Melbourne on November 13, in time for Edwin to celebrate his twenty-first birthday by getting drunk. The Melbourne *Argus* was not impressed by Booth's "national peculiarities of intonation" but said that he possessed "naturally a good voice" and "excellent stage face and figure." Booth, Anderson and Keene left on the propeller steamer the *City of Norfolk* on December 1, 1854. The entire Australian adventure had lasted forty-nine days.[44]

Booth arrived in Honolulu after a sixty-three-day journey from Melbourne and Georgetown via Tahiti. In Hawaii he and Laura Keene supposedly had a disagreement which led to her leaving the company and continuing to San Francisco, while he stayed on, began his managerial career and give thirty-nine performances at the Royal Hawaiian Theatre in February and March 1855.[45]

How true is the claim of the Booth/Keene disagreement? The *City of Norfolk* arrived on February 17 and left on February 24. Plus marks next to the names of individuals on the passenger list indicate the names of people who disembarked at Honolulu. No mark appears next to Keene's name. Keene arrived with the company but probably never left the boat. Whatever led her to decline disembarking in Honolulu had occurred before the ship arrived. To the group coming from Australia, Booth added "the best dramatic talent on the islands," winding up with six men and one woman in the company and scheduled the troupe to open on February 24, the day Keene left Hawaii.[46] Obviously something happened between the two actors, but what it is and when it occurred is not clear.

It is odd that Booth waited one week after arrival to begin performing. This was against nineteenth-century theatre practice. Something stopped this company from opening as soon as they got there. Twenty-seven years later, in 1882, the San Francisco correspondent of the *New York Dramatic Mirror* contended that he had visited the Hawaiian theatre in 1855 and saw "a very interesting little quarrel ... going on between the people on the stage about the business of the piece." He visited New York in 1859, "dropped into Laura Keene's theatre, and there recognized the lady as one of the participants of the rehearsal dissension." If the San Francisco correspondent saw Keene rehearsing, she may have intended to perform and then changed her mind, producing the subsequent delay. Keene was the company's star. Losing her may have necessitated a change in the kind of plays the company performed and in their casting.[47] If the San Francisco correspondent is accurate, then the lack of a mark next to Keene's name on the ship's passenger list is inaccurate.

With Keene gone Booth was left with one woman, not enough for any nineteenth-century company. Consequently a male actor named Rowe undertook female parts. In later life Booth remembered Rowe playing Lady Anne and described him as:

> a stumpy fellow with bandy legs, cross eyes and with all his front teeth gone. He chewed tobacco furiously, and he spoke with a strong German accent. His only knowledge of the stage proved to have been from once working as a "grip" behind the scenes of some theatre in "the States."... I thought I should burst with mortification, for her bandy-legged waddle, her cross-eyed leer, her toothless mouth and her German accent were something indescribable. And while she stood mourning at her dead husband's bier, her ladyship had broken her solemn pledge and was actually chewing tobacco.... We shortened the play a good deal.... The two English armies were of course made up of Native Sandwich Islanders, and to see the followers of Richard and of Richmond fighting the battle of Bosworth Field in burnt cork was something.... But there was a curious sequel to the performance. After the play, while I was dressing, King Kamehameha was ushered into my room.... He patted me familiarly on the back: — "Mr. Booth, I saw your father play Richard in New York twenty years ago."[48]

Booth's and his sister Asia's account of Kamehameha IV's attending a performance has the king sitting backstage, because he is in mourning for his predecessor and lending Booth his chair to use as a throne during the show. Edwin gets to sit in a royal seat. Royal regard was an issue much on the mind of both Booth and his sister when Asia was writing *The Elder and the Younger Booth* in 1881–1882. Booth, then in England, had been snubbed by the royal family. How likely were his father's and Edwin's earlier encounters with Hawaiian royalty?

At the age of fifteen, only five years earlier than the reported encounter with Edwin, Alexander Liholiho (later Kamehameha IV) visited the United States and kept a diary of the trip. At no point does he mention going to the theatre, although he writes about attending the opera and other places of amusement. He left Boston for Washington on May 25, 1850. On the way, he stopped briefly at Baltimore and had dinner at the American Hotel. At the time Junius Brutus Booth was performing in the city, but Liholiho did not stay long enough to see him act. The elder Booth had played Richard III the night before, and it is possible that the Hawaiian prince heard about the performance or even met the actor at dinner. No matter what he told Edwin, he never saw Junius Brutus perform. The statement that he saw the elder Booth perform "twenty years" before 1855 is impossible. Alexander Liholiho would have been an infant.[49]

The new king was influenced by English tradition. Consequently, when Kamehameha's predecessor, Kauikieauoli, Kamehameha III, died on December 15, 1854, the Hawaiian court went into mourning for three months, although the mourning seems to have been more nominal than real. Kamehameha IV appeared in church, gave an official reception at the palace and accepted an invitation to dinner from the American diplomatic mission. There would have been no reason for him to hide backstage during Booth's performances on March 22 or 24, 1855, when Edwin played Richard III. The three months of mourning were over. Moreover, on

March 29, 1855, the day after Booth left for San Francisco, Kamehameha IV attended a theatrical performance. The story of the king sitting backstage is a fabrication.[50]

Twenty-three years after his Hawaiian sojourn, Booth wrote to William Winter: "Many years ago, at the Samoan group of islands— S.[outh] P.[acific] I was told that the male natives were <u>circumcised</u>. My curiosity, however, was confined to— well to other things. By-the-by, now do they circumcise females?" In 1881 Booth wrote to his friend, the novelist, poet and essayist Edmund Clarence Stedman: "In my youth I spent some happy months at several islands in the South Pacific & my fancy often floats me thither; I lived on fruits, pig & pöe-pöe." Edwin's mature recollections of his South Pacific sojourn were of sex and food.[51]

Booth left Honolulu, accompanied by David Anderson, on the clipper schooner *Lady Jane* on March 28 and arrived in San Francisco thirteen days later. When he reopened, at the Metropolitan Theatre on May 2, playing Benedick, he got top billing over Mrs. Catherine Sinclair, but he had not done the role for more than five months, and the results were inadequate. Ferdinand Ewer again felt that Edwin needed "devoted study."[52]

Even when Booth was undisciplined, however, he could be effective. When he played Armand Duval to Jean Davenport's Camille on May 28, he discarded her rehearsal instructions, upstaged her during the death scene and brought the house to its feet with applause.[53] Edwin had found a new way to act Duval's reaction to Camille's death. The critic for *The Wide West* wrote:

> The rendition ... of Armand by Mr. Booth was sufficiently an improvement to make up for all shortcomings. The last scene was given with no diminuation of the effect hitherto attendant on it. We were pleased to observe that in assuring himself that his beloved was really no more, Armand contented himself with simply showing the difficulty of unclasping his hand from hers and did not repeat the lifting of her body from the couch by her arm and let it fall heavily back.[54]

Booth was absent from San Francisco from June 15 to July 10, while he was part of the B. [Ben] F. Moulton troupe performing in small California mining towns. A fellow actor, Frank Mayo, remembered that Edwin "rode on the band wagon, and Ben Moulton, the manager, beat the big drum. Moulton didn't know a note of music, but he was a powerful drummer. We had a cornet and a clarionet. I think the man that played Baradas in Richelieu was the driver of the team. Booth sat by his side." The Moultons were a financially strapped company unable to pay their hotel or advertising bills. It is even possible that Moulton deserted the company in Downieville. They were the most unprofessional company with which Booth worked in California.[55]

On August 4, a company of twelve actors from San Francisco's American Theatre opened in Sacramento "with the addition of Edwin Booth." Business was consistently poor, although the repertoire of the company was very ambitious, including Booth's only attempts at Demetrius in *A Midsummer Night's Dream*, Malvolio in *Twelfth Night* and Antipholius of Ephesus in *A Comedy of Errors*, as well as performances as Richard III, Macbeth and Hamlet. When Adelaide and Joey Gougenheim, one of the many sister acts that played romantic comedy in the period, came to star on September 6, Booth joined them as their leading man for a tour to Marysville and the American Theatre in San Francisco where they opened on October 8.[56]

On November 27, he continued in the same line of business at "the old Sacramento Theatre ... under the management of Mrs. C. N. Sinclair." This tour spawned Edwin's first hit, the first part he repeated over a substantial period of time — *The Marble Heart* by Charles Sedley. Sedley suggested that Booth play the light comedy role of Volage, but J. J. McCloskey persuaded Edwin that Raphael, the tortured artist in love with Marco, a cold beautiful woman, was a better part. In 1906 McCloskey provided an anecdote about opening night:

> Salaries were behind three weeks. Our boarding house lady ... informed us at breakfast ... that unless the "ghost" walked shortly, we would be compelled to subsist on bread and water. We had received

... a number of new plays, among them being *The Marble Heart*. We ... read it and saw a big success awaiting us.... The play was put in rehearsal.... While dozing one afternoon, [Booth] overheard our prompter tell the landlady that things looked bright, that the papers were working up the new play and that the only fear we had was for "Ted." He said, "I don't think he can rise to the heights of such melodramatic acting as Raphael requires." ... The rehearsals were nearly ended, and still Booth would attend and gave no evidence that he had even read the part, for he stumbled over the words, then laid the book down and asked someone to read his lines. His head, he said, was in such a condition that he was unable to see a word. Consternation was seen in the faces of ... all; here was our only hope ... to get our back salary, to eat our Christmas dinner and to put money in our pockets, and the one we most depended on was destroying our hopes. Some said that it would be better to call the play off ... but he promised that he would be all right on the night of the performance. After the last rehearsal, ... I inquired how he felt, and with a wink of his eye ... he said, "Keep your eye on me on me tonight," and I did.... The audience rose at him, and he was forced to return and bow his thanks.... We ate our Christmas dinner with gold in our pockets.[57]

The Marble Heart opened on December 10, 1855. Booth was hardly the immediate success that McCloskey described. The critic for the *Sacramento Daily Union* wrote: "Mr. Booth was deficient in the text, and moreover acted the part of the sculptor too tamely, although in the scene of the parting with Marco, he was exceedingly effective." By the third night, however, Booth knew the role. The play was an enormous success and ran for eighteen nights. It was such a hit that even bad weather did not prevent women from coming to the theatre.[58]

Benjamin A. Baker, then manager of the Metropolitan Theatre, brought the company back to San Francisco, and Booth, Sinclair and Sedley opened *The Marble Heart* there on January 14, 1856. Like David Anderson, Baker became a father figure to whom Booth turned after his father's death. Born in 1818, he was thirty-eight when Booth met him; Edwin was twenty-three. Baker, "an old stager," who had worked as a prompter and "walking gentleman" at Mitchell's Olympic in New York, had written Frank Chanfrau's hit *A Glance at New York*. He had managed the Howard Athenaeum in 1850 and National Theatre in Washington in 1851 and was one of the first people to see Booth's potential.[59]

In the winter of 1856, Booth, Sedley and Sinclair traveled to Oroville for three performances. Charles Sedley remembered: "a desperate fight took place in the auditory of a mining-town theatre when Edwin was on the stage.... Revolvers were freely used, and several shots were fired in the direction of the foot-lights. We afterwards found bullet holes in the proscenium."[60] What sounds like a fable was somewhat true. The Oroville newspaper reported:

> Concerning the row in the Theatre on Sunday night last, in which three persons were shot, we wish to say as little as possible .... One of the heroes of the shooting match has been discharged and the other held to bail in the sum of $2,000 for his appearance after a three days ... investigation into the circumstances ... of the quarrel.[61]

On April 26 Benjamin A. Baker reopened the Sacramento Theatre with Booth and Elizabeth Thoman (the divorced wife of the stage manager who had given Booth his chance to play Tressel) as its stars. It was a major turning point in Edwin's career. Between April 26 and May 3, he performed Richard III, his first Othello, Bertram, his first Lucius Junius Brutus in *Brutus* and Sir Giles Overreach. His comic roles were abandoned, and for the first time, he was tasted life as a serious tragic actor. When he returned to San Francisco to perform at the Union Theatre run by June, he was doing Hamlet, Claude Melnotte, Brutus, Othello, Richard III, Sir Edward Mortimer, Macbeth, Shylock, Pescara, Sir Giles Overreach, Romeo and Richelieu. It was essentially his entire adult repertoire.[62]

Baker opened the Sacramento Theatre again on June 5 with *The Apostate*. Booth gave only three performances, the last one a benefit for Baker, who was returning East to pave the way for Edwin. Subsequently Booth began to tour to Jackson, Georgetown, Placerville, Auburn and Nevada. William Winter contends that Booth was known as the "Fiery Star," because a fire broke out in each town the company played as soon as they had left. But given the rapid manner in which they were built, gold-mining towns were prone to fire, whether Booth was there or not. A fire that destroyed three quarters of a mile of property in Placerville broke out on July 6, 1856, the day after Booth closed. On July 19, two days after his benefit there, Nevada City burned, destroying "every church, hotel, livery stable, printing office and business house."[63]

On August 19, 1856, Booth began his final engagement in Sacramento. He had a Grand Complimentary Farewell Testimonial on August 23, at which he performed Richelieu, and yet another Grand Complimentary and Farewell Benefit on September 1, as Iago. Charles Pope later remembered giving up a night so Edwin could have a benefit to raise the money he needed to return east and even volunteered to appear.[64]

> This I was most happy to do, although I had never met Edwin. On the evening of the day on which this matter had been so pleasantly arranged, I heard a knock at my dressing room door. I was in the act of changing my dress for the last act of Ingomar. A slender graceful form slipped into the room. A pair of luminous eyes shone out from a beautiful Oriental face, illumined by as sweet a smile as ever came from a finely chiseled mouth. A hand was extended, which met with a firm and cordial grip. Only the brief simple words, "thank you" came from his lips, and he disappeared.[65]

What Pope was remembering is that he volunteered his services for Booth's last benefit, playing Othello to his Iago. He remembered not only Booth's eyes—the feature that struck virtually everyone who met him for the rest of his life—but also the "Oriental quality of his face." In the period, "Oriental" connoted Middle Eastern or Semitic. Booth looked Jewish to his contemporaries, and in the nineteenth century, looking Jewish was exotic. To those around him he was dark and mysterious.[66]

Ben Baker had convinced Edwin to return East. He later said: "He was wasting his time out there, and I knew he would never amount of anything, being so convivial." On September 3, Booth was given a farewell benefit at the Metropolitan Theatre in San Francisco, performing his first King Lear. On September 5, he left for Panama on a steamer called the *Golden Age* and reached Panama City on September 18. The steamer anchored two miles from shore, and Booth and his luggage were carried in a small boat toward land. When the boats reached shallow water, passengers were transported to land on the backs of "negro" porters just as they had been four years earlier, but there the similarity ended. There was now a railroad terminal "situated along the beach." For twenty-five dollars Booth traveled across the isthmus in five hours. It was a far more elegant ride than it had been four years before. He took the steamer *Illinois* to New York. It was the same boat on which he had left the East four years earlier. Whereas going to Panama had taken thirty-seven days in 1852, returning took only twenty-four. He also returned financially solvent, contending later that he had left California with "a draft for $500 in my pouch."[67]

Booth did not return to California until 1876, and he remained of two minds about his Western experience. On October 29, 1872, he wrote: "I sigh for the Sierra and pine for Lone Gulch and Shirt-Tail Bend, to say nothing of Cock-Tail Canyon, and the rough-and-tumble patrons of wild California." Five years later, however, he wrote to David C. Anderson: "I can't feel the least affection for Frisco.... I doubt if I shall ever again go there." The experience had been mixed, but in time, Booth mainly remembered the fun in what he called "the nursery of my professional babyhood," the time when he was "full of promise ... and Bowery rant."[68]

Chapter Four

Professional and Family Life, 1856–1860

Ben Baker arrived in New York from California in August 1856 to set up Edwin's first eastern starring tour — a tour that began in Baltimore, ranged as far west as New Orleans and Mobile and included thirteen cities in nine months. According to the legend he later promulgated, Baker initially had difficulty finding work for his protégée. He told Booth that Laura Keene wanted to engage Edwin for a hundred dollars a week but that he had turned her down, telling Booth: "If we're going to be run over, let it be by a coach and four, not a dirty coal cart." Given the fact that Keene had left Booth's company in Hawaii, Baker probably fabricated her offer. He approached Caleb [E. A.] Marshall, manager of the Broadway Theatre, a natural venue for Booth, because it was the only New York theatre consistently producing serious drama. Unfortunately Marshall wanted a three-hundred-dollar per night guarantee that would have obligated Baker and Booth to make up the difference if box office receipts fell below that figure. Again Baker said he turned down the offer and told Marshall: "You don't know this young man. You refuse my demands now, but six months hence, you'll come to me for him." Both men were right. Six months later, Edwin had become a star, but a provincial star; it would take several years to establish his reputation in New York.[1]

Subsequently Baker persuaded the mid–Atlantic theatre manager John T. Ford to hire Edwin for an engagement at the Front Street Theatre in Baltimore, and Booth made his eastern reappearance there on October 15, 1856. He began with Hamlet, the role with which he would ultimately be most associated. Booking Edwin into Baltimore was a theatrically wise move. Although it was a second-rate American theatre town, the fact that it was Booth's home would guarantee audiences and prepare him for the big time.[2]

His strategy worked. From Baltimore on Booth became what later theatre-goers would call a "matinee idol," the darling of female theatre-goers. George Kunkel, Ford's partner, wrote that Booth's Baltimore engagement was "a fine success.... Our houses at present are the most fashionable we have had in this theatre; three evenings this week we have had ladies in the second Tier, and last evening Booth's benefit the Parquette was crowded with ladies.... It seemed to me there were two ladies for every gentleman in the house."[3]

When he returned from California Booth was immediately treated as a serious actor of the first magnitude and remained so for the rest of his life. The *Richmond Daily Dispatch* critic had seen Booth's father as Lear and approached the son's performance with doubts, but "halfway through the first scene ... we were convinced ...the genius of the elder Booth still lived.... Here is a young man, only twenty-two, who assays [*Lear*] with all its difficulties, and in his *second* performance ... wins ... complete success."

Booth was actually twenty-three, but playing Lear at twenty-three is still an amazing achievement, particularly because it necessitated disguising the physical beauty that had become Edwin's trademark. He possessed what newspapers described as "a fine, classical, intellectual and handsome face and a graceful, well-proportioned figure" and had inherited his father's vocal quality, line readings ("emphasis"), enunciation and "easy and natural" manner.[4]

Not everyone was convinced. His Sir Giles Overreach reminded a New Orleans critic "of the great impersonation of his father," but he felt that "the son has yet a great deal to do before he attains the eminence ... enjoyed by the elder Booth" and that Edwin slurred over "great opportunities of fine acting," and spent his time making "points."[5]

Making "points," or producing startling momentary dramatic effects at critical points in the text that elicited show-stopping applause, was what every mid-nineteenth-century actor did. Audiences were expected to applaud these moments the way modern opera buffs are expected to shout "bravo!" Nineteenth-century actors believed that if audiences did not stop the show with applause, something had gone wrong. When Booth performed Richelieu at the Winter Garden Theatre in 1867, the audience, anticipating his famous "Curse of Rome" speech, actually applauded before the "point" rather than after. They knew it was coming. In objecting to Booth's "making points," the New Orleans critic was ahead of his time, foreshadowing the coming of realism with its emphasis on an actor's immersion in his role.[6]

As a rising star, Booth faced both professional and personal problems. He conserved his energy, and his performances consisted of uninteresting opening acts followed by emotionally spectacular climaxes. The critic for the *Boston Evening Transcript* described the points Booth scored during his fifth-act dream sequence and death in *Richard III*:

> He plunges madly forward and falls on his knees—his teeth chatter against each other—his eyes glare and seem bursting from their sockets—his voice gushes forth at intervals or is lost in hurried and impotent attempts at expression.... [In the Death scene] he stumbles and falls on his side, and in this position holds Richmond at bay; he then, by superhuman energy, regains his position, and after receiving his mortal wound, lifts himself to more than his natural height, and falls at [Richmond's] feet.[7]

While Booth dazzled audiences with physical pyrotechnics, the voice for which he would become famous gave him trouble. A New Orleans critic wrote in 1859: "Mr. Booth was in bad voice last night. His utterance was husky, and his reading was rapid and indistinct in many parts." He spent his life obsessed with his vocal and other symptoms. While this may seem hypochondriacal to a modern reader, it indicates a reasonable level of caution for a nineteenth-century actor, a person whose livelihood depended on physical, particularly vocal, stamina. The constant changes of temperature in trains and hotels, as well as the large size and variable acoustics of American theatres, mitigated

Edwin Booth in his early twenties. Note the curly hair much admired by female audience members. "What eyes he has! The most brilliant and expressive I ever saw.... Nearly all the women are in raptures about him, and I heard many expressions such as 'Well now, ain't he pretty?' 'Oh, there he is again, I don't care for anything when he is not there'—from the surrounding ladies. He annoyed ... me by having one pertinacious lock of hair hanging over his forehead, through the play, which we were always wanting him to put back, but he wouldn't."

against good health. It was harder to be healthy than today, and minor problems, like colds, were major ones. An actor's throat had to be kept warm, and Edwin was warned that "close shaving and open collars will not do around here."[8]

Booth's future wife Mary Devlin and his friend Adam Badeau attributed these vocal problems to smoking. Badeau wrote: "You must stop smoking: I heard yesterday that the opera singers consider it ruinous to the voice. I really fear you injure your voice by such extreme smoking." Booth, however, did not stop smoking; an addiction to tobacco plagued his life and may have eventually contributed to the strokes that killed him.[9]

Booth's second problem as a young star was his manager Ben Baker, the first of two men in this period to develop a fanatical attachment to him. Baker provided local newspapers with "puffs" about the young actor, billing him as "The Prince of the American Stage" and "The Wonder of the Age."[10] These claims unwittingly set Booth up as a target, and New York critics, in particular, took aim and fired: "Booth has an agent who does him more harm than good.... His success would have been ... more decided, if he were not ... injured by ... puffery.... When he ... summarily cuts—'cuts' is the word—all connection with pandering parasites, we shall behold a great actor."[11]

Sitting in his dressing room in Louisville after a performance as Sir Giles Overreach, Booth described touring with Baker in an 1858 letter to the rising comic star Joseph Jefferson, whom he had first met in 1850. He wrote as he was waiting for Baker to knock at the door, the signal for him to go on in a one-act farce that would end the evening's performance. He described the hideous train ride that he and Baker had taken from Baltimore to Louisville on April 22.[12] The journey took all day, and there were no stops for food along the way. Booth felt ill; he disliked touring with Baker and the engagement had not begun prosperously.

> We left Baltimore on Friday last (I say we — meaning my royal self — Ben goes for nothing — save in rail-cars and steam boats), arrived here — after a delightful gut-shaking — last evening, right side up with care — neuralgia and sore throat abroad — good times for work (in a pig's) Opened tonight with "Sir Giles" to a slim house — my share amounting to somewhere between ought and eighty-ought — "who steals my purse steals—" [Booth was implying that his purse was "trash"]. I hope to do a smashing business here, and if tonight is any criterion, I undoubtedly will, but where the smash be, I leave you to imagine.... [Henry E.] Willard will probably have Laura [Keene]'s place next season, for a star theatre. — why don't you try it on? — I think it would be a good hit — put the sharing terms down to the lowest match, and play the stars — t'would s knock the others — for stars are sick of acting in N.Y. for *nix* — I speak feelingly, and "am zealous in the cause."[13]

Booth was tired of touring and wanted Jefferson to operate a theatre in New York in which Edwin could star and receive a percentage of the net profits. He was so anxious that he was willing "to put the sharing terms down to the lowest match"—that is, he was willing to share profits after all expenses had been paid and on a fifty-fifty basis.

Booth's annoyance with Baker was growing. It extended to his bad breath and snoring, qualities Edwin could not help noticing if, as Baker contended, they shared the same room. They began touring together in 1855. In March 1858 Booth wrote to Junius. "I think I shall drop Baker shortly — don't know though, he's a useful pup." While Baker annoyed Booth, he also provided services the young star needed. He negotiated Edwin's contracts. He sewed his costumes and served as his dresser. He gave up his own clothing and boots for Edwin to wear on stage. He cooked his food. He ran lines with him. He negotiated publicity with local newspapers. He packed the props and costumes with which they toured.[14] By July 1858, however, Booth was convinced that Baker was financially dishonest and expressed his exasperation in a parody of biblical verse, probably written either to June or to David Anderson. Only a fragment of the letter has survived; it reveals Booth's malicious wit, his verbal cleverness, his dependence on Baker financially and personally, the casualness with which he could discuss various bodily functions and his problems with alcohol. The fragment begins with the imaginary Baker (the prophet) addressing "Ted" [Booth's youthful nickname] who is recovering from a drunk:

> 14 "Arise, and come with me, as thy prophet—thou worthless one—have I not made thee what thou art? Did I not take thee from the dirt in 'Oro' [Oroville] and make thee great?—and wilt thou now be thus ungrateful—dog?"
>
> 15 In this wise did Benjamin, the prophet, say unto Ted—the sobered one; for albeit drunkenness was manifest in the legs, in the chest, the ankles, the toe-nails—yea even the Kok [Cock] and Kuu-jonas [*cojones*, Spanish for testicles], yet verily, the headpiece was right:
>
> 16 And therefore Ted, the wise one, said "Nay I will not go unto the Temple [theatre] with thee—give me Koktail and bid the Temple come hither unto me so it want me."
>
> 17 And it came to pass, when Ted had made this sage remark, his knees gave way and he did fall—Selah!
>
> 18 Many were the words and cross that passed between great Ted and Benjamin his prophet.
>
> 19 Sickness came upon the house, and Ted did puke, yea he did puke even unto the danger of his boot heels; but health came back and smiled—though Ted made oath he never would again. & cetera!
>
> 20 Many days, and many nights did Ted revolve within himself—yea even unto sickness, the abuse he had received from the dog he had fed.
>
> 21 And it came to pass that in the month of July, which is this present one, they came upon the town where Buffaloes had been—therefore was it called so.
>
> 22 Nightly did Ted hold forth the nightly crowds in the Temple of this place, [word indecipherable] were the dinners the prophet cooked.
>
> 23 Now woe unto him who buildeth castles in the air, and teareth down his Booth: Each month hath a 4th—so hath July: Yea, was it not on this day the Yenkees puked up the Briton's pill? So ... will I puke up this dough and discharge myself of my Baker.
>
> 24 And it came to pass that on the 4th of July, when all hearts were exceeding glad with wine and 'chootin'-crackers,' Benjamin the Guttermouth, did say cringingly—like unto a sneaking cur—"Oh master—lord of Tragedy—greater than all—who wear the sock and buskin—behold me thy prophet, thy slave, thy worshipper, here at thy foot willing to tender up my ledgers of thy season past,"
>
> 25 Now Ted—the cunning one—had carefully perused these ledgers, and did know, yea—even unto a tittle, the extent of his servant's crime—therefore he said unto him—"Nay—I will not doubt thee—I'm sure thy books are right—put them up—I have full confidence in thee—but sit thee down in quietude, and hearken unto my voice—I have much to say to thee."[15]

What Booth said is lost, but he believed that Baker was swindling him, and whatever Baker "did hearken" to on the fourth, by July 23, 1857, Booth was soon looking around for his replacement. It was the first of various situations in which Edwin felt betrayed by friends, particularly in a financial sense. He did, however, need "some one to help me in dressing, packing" and subsequently hired twenty-one year-old Henry Flohr, who remained with him from 1858 to 1859 through the 1877-1878 season.[16]

He needed far more than a dresser; he needed to acquire professional discipline. The call for "study" resounds through his early reviews, with critics urging "patient study and practice" or "prudence and study or "a little more practice and study." He still approached roles without sufficient memorization or the amount of textual research for which he later became famous. Even during his triumphant 1857 adult debut in Boston, the critic for the *Boston Evening Transcript* thought that in Hamlet's soliloquies, Booth took "unpardonable liberties ... with the text."[17]

Critics were also concerned that he had inherited "the infirmities of his distinguished progenitor," and, as Booth's biblical satire of Baker indicates, they were right. Edwin drank heavily. In a world in which tea and coffee were more expensive than distilled liquor, Booth, in his own words, "thought little & drank a heap." The Cincinnati *Enquirer* critic hoped that "our young friend Edwin Booth is not about to deviate from the path of ... regular habits, and follow in the footsteps of his illustrious predecessor."[18] Booth had already deviated. Deviation was a polite description for the drunkenness that had occurred on stage the previous evening as documented in the *Enquirer*:

> When Mr. Booth appeared upon the stage last night, it was evident that he was in no condition to play his part. The audience greeted him with hisses, and though he made several attempts to read the words of the play and the actors and actresses endeavored, by a boisterous manner, to rouse him, he failed to recover himself, and the curtain was dropped on the first scene of the first act. The stage manager informed the audience that in consequence of Mr. Booth's "indisposition," Richelieu would not be performed and that those who wished would have their entrance fee refunded.[19]

Despite these problems, Booth's tours, which he referred to as "campaigns," were increasingly successful outside New York. In March 1857 after Richelieu's "curse of Rome" speech in New Orleans, he was "called out, and coming before the curtain, was literally pelted with bouquets from all parts of the house." When he opened a month later in Boston, Booth later remembered that "it was intensely cold & a snowy, sleety night nearly froze the scanty audience." The literati of the city, however, gathered to welcome the actor they regarded as heir to the throne. His first entrance was met with two minutes of applause, and he was called before the curtain both at the end of the fourth act and at the end of the play. Booth left the stage to "deafening and long continued applause." According to William Winter, the Boston run convinced Edwin that he was going to have a career as an actor. He later wrote to his brother June: "In this city [Boston] theatricals are better supported and appreciated than in any other, the profession is looked upon with better grace — actors are respected. I speak from experience — the theatre is nightly visited by men of standing — families of the first class &c., and the profession is considered one of the first walks of art — as it should be — and its exponents are respected accordingly."[20]

New York, however, was another story. Booth's reputation had come to the notice of William Stuart, and it was through Stuart that Booth got his first break in New York. On May 4, 1857, he made his New York debut as a star at Burton's New Theatre. Hundreds of spectators came to witness the "son of Booth" open in *Richard III*, but the reviews were mixed and hurt subsequent attendance. As he had in Boston Booth gave an unequal performance. The reviewer for *The New York Herald* wrote: "Portions of the fourth act [of *Richelieu*] were given with so much fire and effect as to call down repeated rounds of applause from a very critical house. Mr. Booth, before he can attain the position to which he aims, will have to learn to strengthen and elaborate the parts of his performance which are now weak. The public expects more than one or two flashes of lightning illuminating a level plain."[21]

Booth's New York engagement was extended until May 30, but he was still disheartened by his mixed critical reception. After New York he opened at the Walnut Street Theatre in Philadelphia and then "dropped the sock and buskin for the present and [took] up the shovel and the hoe," returning to the Bel Air farm, supposedly to till the ground until the following season.[22]

While Booth may not have been pleased with his New York reception, Burton had apparently been financially satisfied, because he hired the young star to open his 1857–1858 season in New York. Lawrence Barrett, who was a stock actor at Burton's playing seconds to Booth, later remembered that by this time Edwin had begun behaving like a manager, giving orders to subordinate members of the company about how and where they should stand, essentially directing the productions in which he appeared. By 1858 he was sketching out pictures of the scenery for *Richelieu*. By October 1859 he was furnishing prompt books, property lists, scene lists and scenic maquettes (small-scale models), all of which indicate a managerial urge he attempted to satisfy over the next fifteen years.[23]

Booth's New York reviews were not positive.[24] The critic for the *New-York Daily Tribune* wrote:

> This young actor will have a career before him if he will adopt a good school, and lay aside the traditional deformities of the English tragic want of school. First he should give up the tide of gutterly intoned words, which is a time-dishonored specialty of that harsh, noisy, ruffianly old mode of acting. Next he should learn to look the person to whom he is speaking full in the face, and not with his countenance and body to the audience act at them, occasionally glancing sideways at the person addressed.[25]

Outside New York, however, the 1857–58 tour to fifteen cities in eleven months was successful, but the contrast between Booth's success as a provincial star and his mediocre critical reception in New York continued. A second New York engagement during the 1857–1858 season did not draw well, and, according to *The New York Clipper*, when he reopened at Burton's on April 5, 1858, for the third time in one season, he was met by "a slim but appreciative audience."[26]

No matter what newspaper critics thought, public opinion of Booth's acting had turned to idolatry. On April 12, 1858, he participated in a benefit at Wallack's Theatre, honoring and raising money for Henry C. Jarrett, who had just been publicly fired from his position as acting manager (director) at Burton's Theatre. Outside it was pouring rain; when it was announced that even standing room tickets were sold out, hundreds went away disappointed, and some spectators paid money to simply look at the stage and then leave. Producing what a New York critic called "groans, whistles and thumpings," the men in the upper balcony were "packed like herrings." The audience may have been sympathetic toward Jarrett, but they had come to see Booth.[27]

At the end of the 1857–1858 season, Booth returned home to Baltimore to rest for the summer. He was worth approximately five thousand dollars and had enough money to erect a monument of New England granite over his father's grave.[28]

Edwin had established himself as a touring star, but he disliked the life and wanted a permanent home. Mary Ann had rented out the Bel Air farm, and she, Rosalie, John and Joseph moved to Baltimore in the fall of 1855, but Edwin hated the city and dreamed of bringing the family together in Boston. He also wanted to shed the burdens of taking care of his family. To Edwin the natural solution lay with his older brother Junius. As a young man Edwin had been fond of June, writing him letters in the late 1850s that were playful in tone and sexually frank. He had been an affectionate uncle to June and Harriet's daughter Mary when she was a child ("I suppose Mary is a great big girl now, and has forgotten all about her pet; tell her I love her dearly, and long see her very much"). Now he wanted June to leave California and come east.[29] On October 31, 1858, he wrote to his brother:

> You are dea[r]ly beloved by me and all the family — Poor mother is ever wishing for your return; oh how happy it would make her were you with her, and comfortably situated. By the bye I have serious notions of buying a house here [Boston], and moving Mother and all in to live, Mother says <u>yes</u> — and I am sure everything would be much more pleasant than in that den of corruption and oblivion Baltimore, Then, as Boston is a favorite city of yours — we could all be together in one house as it should be — what say you give me your ideas on the subject, and say "<u>yes</u>," & (I hope) "I will come." I think you could do well — there is such a scarcity of good actors now — especially in N.Y. & Boston — believe you could live comfortably and make money I think.... How delightful it would then be to have us all together in a family knot — Yourself in a comfortable and respected position — the head of the family — as you should be — Given <u>my</u> back isn't strong enough yet to bear the weight — besides I must 'keep moving' — there's no home for me — until I have <u>lost my pretties</u> and have ceased to draw.[30]

When Booth wrote this letter in 1858, he was "hot." His good looks ("pretties") were pulling in ("drawing") audiences. At the age of twenty-five he was a traveling star with little time for family life. Yet he knew that someone had to take care of Mary Ann who, at fifty-five, was already known as "poor mother," the epithet Booth used for her for the next thirty-three years. The term implied some sense of enfeeblement, an inability to take care of herself, a dependence on others and ultimately a dependence on him. It was the viewpoint he came to hold about most of the Booths.[31]

Mary Ann was enfeebled by age, Rose by a combination of mental and physical problems and Joseph always remained in Edwin's eyes a disaster. He was twelve when Edwin left for California and sixteen when he returned. When Joe was eighteen, Edwin described him as a "great big lubberly boy — does nothing but smoke his brains out, as I used to — can't get any employment in Baltimore ... and he has no idea of the stage." Given the fact that Joseph had no ability as an actor but was part of a theatrical family, he naturally became part of a backstage operation, namely assistant treasurer at the Holliday Street where Edwin began his 1858–1859 season.[32]

The 1858–1859 season was Booth's first on the road without Ben Baker. From Louisville in December 1858 he wrote to June: "I have done very well this season thus far, and much more comfortably than with Baker — you can't imagine what relief it is to be rid of him."[33] The season was financially rewarding. On February 6, 1859, Booth wrote to his friend the artist Walter Brackett from New Orleans: "I have banked over $700 more in six months than I did in all last season — so much for agents." Booth's health, however, both physically and mentally was tenuous: "I feel as blue as an indigo boy. My health is about as fluctuating as a game of bluff.... but tonight I have a thundering headache — caused by cold. My business here [New Orleans] is good — very good if it only holds out."[34]

Edwin Booth in his mid-twenties. "I must 'keep moving'— there's no home for me — until I have lost my pretties and have ceased to draw."

Reviews of Booth during the 1859–1860 season were, as usual, mixed. Even in its review of Booth's success in the Jarrett benefit, the *Spirit of the Times* cautioned that Booth's genius required "a master-hand to control it." He was a "rough diamond ... rapidly becoming polished." He had already met the two people who would work on the polishing.[35]

Chapter Five

1857–1860: Booth, Mary Devlin and Adam Badeau

During his first year as a touring star Booth met two people with whom his personal and professional life would be entwined over the next six years. The first was Mary Devlin, a sixteen-year-old actress who became his first wife; the second was a twenty-five-year-old drama critic and homosexual named Adam Badeau. They would, at least in Badeau's view, become rivals for Booth's affections. Mary won hands down, but both people played a role in developing Booth's artistic aspirations and curbing his alcoholism.

Edwin was heterosexual, but, as a young man, his experience with women consisted of sex with prostitutes and offers from female spectators, and he came to avoid any physical or emotional contact. His friend the businessman William Bispham wrote: "I never knew a man who had such an aversion to being caressed as he had. He shrunk instinctively from any physical manifestation of personal affection." Adam Badeau wrote of Booth's youthful success: "Hundreds of women flung themselves at him in those days: they sent him notes in verse and prose, flowers, presents of jewels, shawls, feathers to wear on the stage; they asked for appointments; they invited him to their houses; they offered to go to his; but he cared nothing for any of them."[1]

Booth was hardly a virgin. All of the men in the Booth family — Edwin, his father and his brothers June, John and Joseph — were sexually active. In 1879 when a dry goods clerk named Mark Gray attempted to kill Booth, rumors circulated that Gray was actually Booth's illegitimate child. Ben Baker, then house-bound in New York with rheumatism, countered the rumor with: "I never in my life knew a young fellow who cared less for the company of women.... The girls couldn't make love to him worth a cent, and he shed most letters like a duck sheds water. The women were ... going wild over him; yet he shunned female society and used to laugh at their ardency." Booth's comment was that "Ben Baker's report ... was kindly intended, but not altogether 'so.'" Indeed, during their travels together, Booth wrote to his brother June about Baker: "He's a good soul — thinks almost as much of me as you do, but somehow or other, I can't find the same affection for him — no matter he'll go his length for me 'specialy when a cunt is weeping on my account."[2]

With his "Oriental" good-looks, Edwin was an exotic, physically attractive man, and if indeed he "shed" letters from female admirers "like a duck sheds water," it was because he had received so many of them. Female fans became rapturous in the mere anticipation of seeing him. In November 1858, Louisa May Alcott, then twenty-six, wrote to her sister Anna: "Miss K asked me to go to see Booth for the last time on Saturday. Upon that ravishing thought, I brooded all the week very merrily, and I danced, sang, and clashed my cymbals daily."[3] Ms.

Five. 1857–1860: Booth, Mary Devlin and Adam Badeau

Alcott was not the only woman clashing her cymbals. Offers piled up. Some were from obviously young women:

> I saw you last winter in Hamlet, and since that time you have never been absent from my thoughts. I have been to see you many times this winter — and now notwithstanding strong opposition declare my love. It is true I have seen nothing of the world (having just left school) but I know you are my congenial spirit. I am an orphan and have no one to interfere with me — and need a strong kind heart and arm to lean upon. Of course I would insist on your leaving the stage having enough to support us both in luxury.[4]

Some were from more mature women: "I think as well as you do, that it is unwomanly and unbecoming in a woman telling her love, but, surely you would forgive me if you [knew] how long I have worshipped you in my heart of hearts.— I have been to see you personate Hamlet this evening. What a Hamlet! What a man: It is now three o'clock and I am still thinking of you." When Adam Badeau's estate was sold at auction on December 16, 1901, it included a letter to Booth from "E.T.," asking for "but one glance of your eye." While little is known of the provenance of these letters, Booth obviously did not destroy them upon receipt. The fact that Badeau possessed one may even indicate that he passed them around.[5]

Like actors today Edwin was an object of his audiences's fantasies, and female admirers filled the seats at his performances. At his 1857 benefit in New Orleans, "Mr. Booth was beckoned to a private box at the side of the stage, where one of the ladies gracefully placed on his head a wreath of evergreens, with his name inscribed upon it. From a private box on the other side was thrown to him another beautiful wreath, with the following inscription — "From the Ladies of New Orleans to the Young Roscius."[6] At his second Boston benefit in 1857 the actress Matilda Heron

> became so enthusiastic that she rose from her seat and applauded lustily, and stripped from her hand a white kid glove, which she flung at the feet of our young tragedian, who picked it up and gracefully bowed.... After the performance Mr. Booth called at the Hotel of Miss Heron and gallantly offered ... the glove that she had thrown, but she requested him to keep it, and whenever he chanced to look upon it, imagine that it contained a hand with a heart in every finger, that would always beat with enthusiasm at his success![7]

Edwin Booth c. 1856. Note the "Oriental" [Semitic] good looks. "A pair of luminous eyes shone out from a beautiful Oriental face, illumined by as sweet a smile as ever came from a finely chiseled mouth."

The incident wound up in the newspapers. Who knew what was said in Heron's hotel except the two people involved? One of them or their representatives or both informed the newspaper. Heron was about to follow Booth as the lead attraction at the Boston Theatre. She was an established star; he was a rising one. The romantic overtones of the incident were mixed with the participants' understanding that the public image of their private lives sold tickets.

Adam Badeau believed that Booth "never injured a pure woman in his life," "injured" being a euphemism for sexual intercourse, but Edwin was well acquainted with women who would allow him to "injure" them, although they could hardly be described as pure. Nineteenth-century men were not expected to abstain from premarital sex; indeed they were expected to prepare for monogamy by sowing wild oats. Edwin admitted to being a libertine by the age of twenty, but the women he knew, in the sexual sense, were likely to be the prostitutes he encountered or the native women of Samoa. He was almost twenty-five before he had intercourse with someone he considered "virtuous."[8]

The woman in question was probably Josephine Orton, known as Josie. She and Booth appeared together at a benefit for the American Dramatic Fund in New York on August 2, 1858.

Josie Orton. "Can't brag on her acting so much as what we do in secret."

Five. 1857–1860: Booth, Mary Devlin and Adam Badeau

On October 31, 1858, six days after he had opened at the Boston Theatre where Josie was a member of the company, Edwin, wrote to his brother June about a singing chambermaid. "There is a little sweetheart of mine crazy to go to Cal.... I talked her out of it, and my p—k into her, told her that I would ascertain from you all about it &c, she is singing chambermaid, I won't mention her name—I think you know her—can't brag on her acting so much as what we do in secret." By December 12, a month after he had left Boston, Booth really had something to brag about—what he called "the premonitory symptoms of a glorious *clap*, produced I think by a strain only, for the woman is virtuous &c hope soon to be rid of that trouble—it's the first ever."[9]

Born in Brooklyn in 1843, Josie Orton had "received a splendid education, especially in music," and, in 1858, was working her way up the theatrical ladder, having started in minor roles at Barnum's American Museum in New York. She was fifteen years old when she had an affair with Booth; he was twenty-five. While Edwin's sense of propriety prevented him from mentioning her name, just as it prevented him from spelling out words like "prick" and "damn," Orton is the most likely candidate for the "singing chambermaid" because of her musical background and the roles she played.[10]

She may not, however, have been responsible for his venereal disease; in fact he may have been responsible for hers. By October 7, before he played Boston, Booth, already experiencing the symptoms of his "glorious clap," confided as much to Badeau who responded: "So you are unwell.... is it that horrid apprehension realized?" It is, of course, possible that the affair with Orton began in August, when they first appeared together.[11]

By twenty-five Edwin was already sexually aware enough to recognize the signs of syphilis—probably a skin irritation on his genitals, itching, joint pains and fever. In his letter to June, twelve years his senior, Booth admits he is bragging, because getting venereal disease was, for him a sign of manhood and because the woman was "virtuous." Given the fact that Booth had gotten his "p—k into her," her virtue might seem questionable, but for Booth the fact that she was not a professional whore was delightful. In fact it was her virtue that assured him that he had but "a strain." Booth had made it with a woman who was not a prostitute; that she may have given him syphilis or that he may have given it to her was inconsequential. Twenty-one years later Booth's friend the artist Jervis McEntee told him "I thought for young men no influence was more restraining and ennobling that companionship with women. He agreed with me and repeated that he had been deprived of it in early life."[12] His early sexual experiences with women had left him with a jaundiced and somewhat self-pitying view of his place in the world. Even before he met Josie Orton, whores had turned Booth off women, and Ben Baker's dishonesty had turned him off men. He was looking for a lady. He wrote in 1858:

> A certain sadness has pervaded my whole nature even from child-hood; ... there was a time I dreamed myself completely happy but it was short-lived, for a too early contact with the world, and a knowledge of the wickedness spilt all my milk, and I have been a hater—ever since. I scarcely let a day pass without repeating the grace of old 'Appemantus' [from Shakespeare's *Timon of Athens*]—
>
> > "Immortal Gods! I crave no help—
> > I pray for no man but myself:
> > Grant I may never grow so fond
> > To trust man on his oath or hand.
> > Or a dog that seems a sleeping
> > Or a wanton for her weeping.
> > Or a keeper with my freedom,
> > Or my friends, if I should need 'em"
>
> There, so much for friends and wantons—both of which had a hand in souring my disposition at too early an age.[13]

As he wrote the above, Booth's ability to form serious relationships with either sex was being tested by the woman who became the great love of his life—Mary Elizabeth Devlin. Edwin's friend Joseph Jefferson created the sentimental and somewhat inaccurate legend of the Booth-Devlin courtship at a memorial after Edwin's death. According to Jefferson, in September 1855, when he began his second season as stage manager at the Baltimore Museum, the company's over-all manager Henry Jarrett:

> brought a ... girl who had been given to his care and placed her in mine—a beautiful child, but fifteen years of age. Her family, a most estimable one, had met with some reverse, and she had decided to go upon the stage to relieve them from the burden of her support and ... to contribute to the comfort of her father.... She lived in my family as the companion of my wife for three years and during that time became one of the leading actresses of the stage.[14]

Fifteen-year-old Mary Devlin, called Mollie and sometimes Molly, became Edwin Booth's first wife, the object of his life-long love, the mother of his only surviving child and the person with whom he chose to be buried. She was not, however, quite the innocent novice portrayed by Jefferson in 1894, with Booth recently and Devlin long dead. Born on May 19, 1840, in Sand Lake, New York, one of three daughters of a "poor but honest tailor," Mary Devlin moved to Troy, New York, in 1848 with her family and appeared there on the stage on May 4, 1852, when she was not quite twelve. She studied at the Mechanics' Institute in New York and with a music teacher named Mrs. Seguin, whose family opera company toured America. She performed as a dancer at the Troy Museum in 1854, at the age of fourteen, and by May 17, 1855, when she was fifteen, she was playing breeches roles for her benefit at the Howard Athenaeum in Boston. She first appeared in New York on June 28, 1855, and performed with Jefferson at John Drew's National Theatre in Philadelphia beginning May 16, 1856. Thus she had been on the stage for six years prior to meeting Booth, had played Boston, New York and Philadelphia and had shown off her legs in breeches roles for her benefit.[15]

Jefferson employed Devlin as a stock company actress at the Richmond Theatre during the 1856–1857 season. On November 23 Booth arrived in Richmond. He opened the next day in *Richard III* and on November 25, 1856, he played Romeo to Devlin's Juliet. Again Jefferson created a legend. "One morning I said to her: 'To-morrow you are to rehearse Juliet to the Romeo of our new and rising young tragedian.' ... I knew at the conclusion of that rehearsal that Edwin Booth and Mary Devlin would soon be man and wife." Mary was sixteen years old; Edwin was twenty-three.[16]

Jefferson's story implies that he had a hand in promoting the romance, but Joe was actually in Washington in late November when Booth and Devlin first performed together. Either Booth or Ford's partner George Kunkel or Henry Jarrett selected Devlin to play Juliet, because Edwin needed a leading lady. Any pretty young girl would have done. Devlin's name was not even mentioned in advertisements for the November 25, 1856, performance. The casting problem that plagued Booth's entire career provided an introduction to both of his wives. He needed an actress for leading female roles.

Booth later claimed that, upon meeting Mary, he immediately wrote to his mother. "From the day I met her, I felt the influence of her kindred spirit—purer—holier than mine, but still a kindred one." At the time, however, Edwin, like any touring player, moved on, and Mollie stayed behind with the company to which she was contracted. By the fall of 1857, the Jeffersons had moved to New York, leaving her in Baltimore. At the age of seventeen Mary was on her own.[17]

Booth was accustomed to adoration—from women and from men. As a young man, his physical beauty immediately struck everyone who met him. Five months after he met Mary, Edwin found an admirer in Adam Badeau, who introduced himself by letter on May 17, 1857.

Born in New York City on December 29, 1831, Badeau was a stout, red-faced social butterfly. According to the writer Henry Adams, his habits were "regularly irregular" [meaning that he drank], but he was "very intelligent, a good newspaper-man." On June 15, 1857, Badeau, who wrote for the *New-York Sunday Times* under the *nom de plume* "The Vagabond," wrote to Booth who had just appeared at Burton's Theatre and received mixed reviews. Badeau enclosed an essay on tragedy which, he claimed, contained a "direct reference" to Edwin's performances.[18]

He compared Booth's acting favorably to that of the French actress Rachel as well as to the actors Edwin Forrest, James William Wallack and Matilda Heron, thus establishing, at the beginning of their relationship, that he saw Edwin's acting in both male and female terms. Badeau offered to share his knowledge of the acting of David Garrick, Edmund Kean and Sarah Siddons as well as the dramatic criticism of William Hazlitt, and to help Booth use this knowledge to improve his own performances.[19] Badeau wrote that Booth, like Kean, was criticized for "the unconcern of his conceptions" and "the fitfulness of his performances." In a letter dated June 15, 1857, he offered to help Booth:

> I have read every scrap that I could find in print about you....You cannot, you must not misunderstand me nor my motives. You have no warmer friend in New York than I am.... [Al]though I have a connection and influence with the press, I am independent of it as a means of support. I shall be most happy on your return, to exhibit my earnestness by serving you in any way in my power, by introductions, by public notices. Meanwhile, if you come to New York..., you must not fail to call on me; if I am in town, it would be a positive unkindness to leave me unvisited. I beg you also to write to me and assure me that you do not misconstrue my conduct, ... that you appreciate the sincerity and ardour [*sic*] of the regard entertained for you by... Your most cordial friend and admirer, Adam Badeau.[20]

Although the two men had never met, the length and passion of the letter demonstrate the depth of Badeau's emotional and intellectual involvement. Badeau's obsession with Booth, the tantalizing offer of patronage, the subservient begging for attention and above all the fear that he might be misconstrued or unappreciated by someone he did not know, all point to a level of hero worship that Badeau knew he had to sublimate and that Booth would eventually find disturbing.

Booth sent Badeau presents and even gave him money. His appreciation is not surprising. He had just finished his first season as a touring star, and he had been heavily criticized for a lack of "study." Given Edwin's sense of educational inferiority, he was flattered by the attention of a seemingly literate individual who thought him a god. The two men rehearsed together, making decisions on line readings and interpretation; Badeau attended performances, seated sometimes in a private box provided by Booth, and took notes. For both the young actor and the young critic, it must have been a heady experience.[21]

Badeau presented himself as a man of learning, something Edwin always aspired to be. Badeau introduced him to the avant-garde artistic currents of the day. Booth needed the tutoring. Adam admired Edwin as a herald of emerging Romanticism on the stage—comparable to Frederick Church's paintings of untamed nature, Charlotte Bronte's moors, Turner's seascapes or the "noble savage" of the American West. While Badeau admitted that the quality of Booth's acting was inconsistent, Edwin's emotionalism on stage, what Badeau called "one touch of real feeling" overwhelmed his audiences four or five times every night.[22]

Over the next few years Edwin visited Badeau in his home on the Hudson and at the Long Island estate of Badeau's patron Richard Busteed, an attorney who served as counsel to the corporation of the City of New York. Badeau lectured Booth on smoking and sexual profligacy. They developed a voluminous correspondence, Booth writing fifty letters to Badeau in 1858 alone. Badeau, in turn, furnished Booth with an entree into a society of literate New Yorkers and Bostonians—many of whom became Booth's friends and correspondents, including the abolitionist Julia Ward Howe and the poet William Cullen Bryant. It was a step toward respectability that nineteenth-century actors, and particularly Edwin Booth, craved.

Edwin saved Badeau's initial letter for the rest of his life. Forty-six years after they met, Badeau recalled that "from that time dated a peculiar intimacy." The nature of that intimacy was intellectual, personal, professional and, on Badeau's part, romantic/sexual. The term "peculiar intimacy" conjures up latent or not-so-latent homosexuality in the twenty-first century, but it is more likely that Badeau was boasting of his influence on the most important actor in nineteenth-century America rather than disclosing personal secrets. How aware Badeau, Booth and eventually Devlin were of Adam's homosexuality is impossible to know. Nineteenth-century men, prior to the work of Freud, had such a disbelief in or ignorance of homosexuality that they were able to use actions and language that a modern reader finds redolent with sexual connotations.

Victorians were aware of homosexuality and lesbianism but lacked the language and willingness to discuss it. They indulged in innuendo and produced correspondence charged with what has been described as homo-social relationships. The Baltimore *Sun* quoting the *New York Mirror*'s characterization of the actress Charlotte Cushman, who was famous for playing Romeo, as "*Macready in petticoats*," commented "Nuf ced." The same newspaper reported that Charlotte's sister, "MISS SUSAN CUSHMAN being asked ... if it were not true she was to be married, said that she did not intend to marry unless she could find a person of really masculine mind. 'Then,' said her interlocutor, 'why don't you marry your sister Charlotte'?" Readers were left to figure out the implication by themselves. *The New-York Times* reported that Cushman and her friends Emma Stebbins and Harriet Hosmer were "were wont to call themselves ... three jolly bachelors."[23]

As Jonathan Ned Katz points out, "the sexual was cordoned off from comradeship. 'Love' was not usually thought then to harbor eros.... A 'lover' was the object of romantic pursuit, not a partner in sex." During the nineteenth century, overt physical affection between members of the same sex was common. "Love" and "lover" were frequently employed without any sexual subtext. When his friend Richard Cary was killed during the Civil War, Booth wrote a condolence letter to Richard's sister and signed himself "ever your friend and servant and your brother's lover." In 1878 Ferdinand Ewer, by then a New York minister, wrote to Booth: "I am woman enough to have a very gentle & true love for you." In 1883 Booth referred to his daughter's fiancé as her "lover." On June 17, 1888, he referred to his friend the critic Horace Howard Furness as "beloved" and "sweetheart." None of this was meant sexually.[24]

Booth was resolutely heterosexual. He shared the Victorian assumption that in men "virility and ... worthiness [were] roughly synonymous." He was appalled when, in 1883, male members of the German acting troupe with whom he was performing, demonstrated their admiration by kissing him. It is reasonable to assume, however, that he became aware of homosexuality if not during the rough life he had led as a youth taking care of his father, then during his years in the "homo-social" world of the California mining camps. Badeau was a closeted homosexual in a period in which exposure would have meant social disgrace. His infatuation with Edwin degenerated into hero-worship that is difficult to disassociate from sexual connotations. Badeau referred to Booth as "a god," "my prince," "the man I love best in the world." He referred to his correspondence to Edwin as "love letters." When Booth failed to write, Badeau became testy: "As to your delay in writing, at first I was hurt, then indignant, and now am quite indifferent. Be silent as long as you choose. I can live."[25]

In addition to seeing Edwin in New York, Badeau longed to be on the road with him, but in this respect Mary Devlin had the upper hand. On February 23, 1858, Booth returned to Richmond for a two-week engagement and performed with Devlin. This time when he left, she accompanied him to Baltimore, where they acted together until March 20, Mary playing Lady

Anne to his Richard III, Cordelia to his Lear, Juliet to his Romeo, Julie de Mortimar to his Richelieu, Katherine to his Petruchio, Florinda to his Pescara and, in a breeches role, Wilford to his Sir Edward Mortimer.[26]

The fact that Mary and Edwin were traveling together makes it tempting to hypothesize a serious relationship, but this does not necessarily prove that they were romantically linked. Booth was always on the lookout for leading ladies who could perform his repertoire. Later in that spring of 1858, Mrs. Hudson Kirby supported him at the Boston Theatre and then went with him to Burton's New Theatre in New York as a leading lady. After Baltimore Booth went on touring alone, leaving Devlin to perform at Baltimore's Holliday Street Theatre. Word about Booth and Devlin, however, was getting around. In late March 1858 Edwin wrote to June: "Don't believe any reports of my marriage if you hear it — I've heard it myself, and doubt not but it has reached you ere this."[27]

On April 26, Devlin joined Charlotte Cushman on Cushman's farewell tour of Baltimore, Boston and New York.[28] Charlotte's niece by marriage, Emma Crow Cushman, who saw Mary play Juliet to Charlotte's Romeo in St. Louis in 1858, described her as

> a very young girl whose simplicity and inexperience lent themselves specially to this character, for which Miss Cushman had herself taken great pains to drill her.... She wore her own beautiful hair in ringlets down her back and everyone must have felt a thrill when in the balcony scene.... Romeo returned again for a last embrace and finally pressed one of these ringlets to his lips.[29]

The Washington, Baltimore and Richmond manager John Ford disagreed about Mary's appeal. He decided not to retain her as a member of the 1858–1859 Richmond company, telling his stage manager that although she was "a sweet dear girl," she was also "played out." Mary's youth limited her to roles like Juliet; she was not a leading lady and certainly not a star. She was a stock company actress, and after her tour with Cushman she was without a job. Had she been seriously involved with Booth, this was a moment she could have retired into matrimony. Instead she made plans to join the Boston Theatre company in the fall of 1858.[30] On June 2 Booth wrote to his Boston friend, the nature and portrait painter Walter Brackett:

> I hope the Bostonians will treat my little friend Miss Devlin well; she's a good little girl and very talented.... Now Walter, if I had a wife ... such as you have, I think I'd be a happy fellow, and tell all the word to go to hell, but there is no prospect of my ever attaining such blessings — it's all very well to say "oh she'll come along by and by" — but my dear boy, she has been along — and passed on me too — just as I had a full hand — my game's blocked; I'll live and die an old maid.[31]

The letter implies that Mary has turned him down or passed him by. She was, however, writing to him, and within two weeks after Booth swore to die as an old maid, Brackett suggested the possibility of marriage. Booth responded: "I had a letter from Miss Devlin today; I am glad that you admire in her the same charming qualities which first attracted me; she is indeed a dear, sweet girl, innocent as a babe, and I would give the world to see her high in her profession, and happy withal; but Walter, marrying wouldn't achieve the latter — no, on the contrary, 'twould be to render her most wretched; I love her as a sister — nothing more." The shame Booth felt about the life he had led was a psychological barrier to forming permanent relationships. Mary was a sweet and innocent babe; Edwin saw himself as damaged goods.[32]

The Booth/Devlin relationship reached the newspapers in early July 1858, when the *Spirit of the Times* reported that "Mr. Edwin Booth will shortly lead to the altar the talented actress and very estimable girl, Miss Mary Devlin." Later that month, Booth wrote to Brackett: "Miss D. Is up in the country — at Paradise Valley (the angel) Monroe County Pennsylvania — should you write to her — don't congratulate her on her wedding — 'taint so." Booth was still resisting the now-public possibility that he and Devlin were to marry, and for her part, Mary was continuing with her career.[33]

She first performed as a member of the Boston Theatre company on September 15, 1858. Josephine Orton was employed in the same company, and the two women often appeared together on stage. Thus Mary was around when Edwin was putting his "p—k" into Josie."[34] Devlin was generally relegated to comic afterpieces. When Booth appeared there as a touring star, however, she played Margaret to his Sir Giles Overreach and Lady Helen to his Sir Edward Mortimer and appeared with him and Orton in a comic afterpiece called *Only a Half-Penny* for his benefit on October 29. It was unusual both for Mary to appear in serious plays and for Booth to appear in farce. It is tempting to think that their romance may have been the cause, but in the case of the benefit, Booth's decision to perform may simply have been financial. The farce was new, and, like any nineteenth-century actor, he wanted a "bumper." Mary remained with the company to which she was contracted. Booth moved on to fulfill his contractual obligations, but by January 1859 he was referring to her as "dear Molly" and that year visited her at the home of her sister Kate Devlin Magonigle and Kate's husband John Henry Magonigle. John Henry, known as Harry, would become Booth's life-time friend, business associate and eventual caretaker."[35]

As his relationship with Mary developed, so did the complexity of Booth's friendship with Badeau. On February 6, 1859, he wrote to Walter Brackett from New Orleans: "[Badeau] is not here—thank God—nor is he likely to be—he's a good fellow, but one of those whom I admire at a distance." Badeau, however, kept track of Booth, even from a "distance." After Edwin gave a lackluster performance and subsequently attended a champagne party at the Charleston Hotel, Badeau badgered him by letter to remain sober and keep himself "clean" (free of venereal disease) and about the necessity of careful preparation for his performances.[36]

There is no sign that Edwin felt embarrassed by Adam's attention. He did, however, begin to tease Badeau with the excessiveness of these emotions, accusing him of having "Booth fever." For his part, Adam was disturbed by what he felt for Edwin. He was repressing something and knew that "there are some feelings [in] ... nature that get rampant when long deprived of their natural vent. I am, however, very calm." This thought, however, led him to: "So the fellows have gone mad about you in Charleston, not the women; ... that's what you get for being 'so handsome!' Wouldn't you be in demand in Turkey?" Both Adam and Edwin knew that the stereotypical Turkish sexual specialty was pederasty, and Badeau no sooner joked about this than he coyly teased Edwin:

> I don't know what to make of you of late, you are so amiable (Don't relapse to prove you are still yourself.) You spoke of seeing me next summer absolutely without my suggesting it; the first time in our acquaintance that such a thing occurred; and when I ask you to pay me a visit, you accept without any wry mouths, and in the very next letter. Am I really to suppose that you are getting fond of Ad?[37]

By June 1859, however, the person of whom Booth was getting fond was Mary Devlin. In her first extant letter to Edwin, Mary wrote: "I have made my arrangements for next season (I hope they will be the last)." She was contemplating leaving the stage after the 1859–1860 season. Since she had no means of supporting herself except acting, her talk of retiring suggested she planned to marry. By early June 1859 she was writing coyly to Edwin: "Are you well yet, and are you a good boy?—and do you ever think of me?... God bless you, that is my nightly prayer."[38]

The preceding April Badeau had written: "Be a good boy and don't forget your manners (so often broken) to Ad."[39] The question is, did they mean the same thing? The phrase "are you a good boy?" implies that, in some manner, Mary had become aware that Edwin was not always or had not always been "a good boy." Badeau certainly knew he had not. Mary's reference is most likely to "drink," the same problem that Badeau had raised two months before. Both people were concerned with Booth's alcoholism; Adam as a man, could address it directly; Mary, as a woman, was constrained to be circumspect. The phrase "Are you well yet," however, implies physical illness, and while Mary may be referring to his throat problems, she could also be alluding to venereal disease.

That summer Devlin worked at Niblo's Gardens in New York, and Booth visited Badeau in Jamaica, Long Island. Back in New York Edwin fell off the wagon and went on a "spree." Mary "nursed" him, and by mid–July they were engaged. She addressed him as "My darling Edwin" and told him: "I begin to realize, fully, the indescribable joy, and intense happiness, you ... have bestowed upon me — ah I shall so study to deserve it — by giving my whole thoughts, and heart and <u>soul</u> into your loved keeping."[40]

Mary's belief that she had given her "whole thoughts, and heart and soul" into Edwin's "loved keeping" was not sentimentality. He had taken complete control of her life and insisted that she leave the stage and spend a year in seclusion to purify herself from the taint of having been an actress. Booth took her to Philadelphia and introduced her to his

Mary Devlin Booth. "Are you a good boy, and do you ever think of me?"

mother, to his sister Rose and to his brother Joseph (his sister Asia refused to meet her) and then began to "purify" her by setting her up in a house in Hoboken. Mary immediately wrote to her sister to "come on," to join her so she would have a proper chaperone. As C. Dallett Hemphill points out the common belief in the period was that "being in public posed dangers to women," who needed "protection in the form of an escort."[41]

Since Mary no longer had any means of support, Edwin paid the bills. She wrote to Ben DeBar, canceling her theatrical engagement with him and sent a copy to Edwin; she wrote to Richard Smith Spofford, Jr., a Boston lawyer with whom she had been romantically involved, and kept a copy of the letter for Booth to prove she had done the right thing. She not only stopped working in the theatre; she promised to stop going to the theatre and confessed to him when she broke her promise. She apologized for her fondness for a woman who once apparently swore in Edwin's presence. She apologized for even thinking of "things which you have forbidden me to think of." Her subjugation to him was immediate and total.[42]

For his part Booth congratulated himself that he had done the right thing—for himself. On July 26, 1859, he wrote to mutual friends of his and Mary's. He began with an admission of guilt. In his own eyes Edwin was tainted by the society he had kept, the "wild oats" he had sown "at a very early age": He admitted having "sought the society of those whose influence ... would ... bring misery and shame." He "tossed and tumbled in ... bed at night, ... thinking of all the girls" he knew and finally decided "Mary is the girl for me — there's no use in trying to give her up, and if she will leave the stage I'll make her M^{rs}. B."

To the modern reader Booth's statement seems as hypocritical as that of the young girl, fresh from school, who threw herself at him but added: "of course I would insist on your leaving the stage." Brought up in a family tainted by illegitimacy and in which women did not work, embarrassed by his father's drinking and lunacy and living in the tough world of rural American theatricals, Booth felt simultaneously superior to theatre people and inferior to the people he met in the outside world. In order to validate himself, he insisted that Mary become an educated lady

> Mary has all the qualities of heart — and of mind, though undeveloped — which I most need to make life cheerful to me. The few years she has passed on the stage have not been detrimental to her in the least, and if she will, as I am sure she must, in the year I have set apart, give up all thoughts of the profession as far as she is concerned, and by study improve her mind, she will make me a happy individual.... Doubtless you will think it strange that I have denied the fact so long; my only excuse ... is the prejudice I have against actresses, and had I ever observed the slightest indication of coarseness or vulgarity so common among persons in the profession, I would never have taken this step; I never could have loved her.[43]

In a letter to his friend the artist Walter Brackett written on September 12, 1859, Booth claimed that he had hesitated only on Devlin's account. He was unworthy of her — a "cold unloving man" with a "withered heart." She was "a fragile flower" growing in "a rude unweeded soil," — the theatre. Booth contended to Brackett that he had avoided Mary to avoid "the wretched life hers would be if linked with mine; I could only give her a calm, undemonstrative heart, of which she would soon weary, and sigh for something more in keeping with her own ardent nature." He assured Brackett how difficult his decision to marry Mary had been.

> I had almost vowed I would never marry — had resolved never to marry an actress; that was the only striking flaw in the whole catalogue of the long list of good on Mary's part. After a deal of tossing and troubling of brains and bedclothes, for it cost me many sleepless nights, I came to the conclusion that the knowledge she had gained of the trials and vicissitudes of an actor's life, would be an advantage; and as she had never mingled with members of the profession, she had always kept her reputation clear.

Suddenly Mary's years with the Jefferson family, the breeches roles, the tour with Charlotte Cushman were swept away. Mary had never "mingled." Booth implied that she had no off-stage relations with actors, forgetting or ignoring the fact that she had actually lived with the Jeffersons.

> I ran my eye along the brilliant line of wealth and beauty (from which I might have chosen as worthless a heart as my own perhaps), but saw only the humble actress with the angel's soul; I put aside all the choice and rare exotics, plucked a simple daisy, and taking it from the scorching, unpitying glare of public eye — I planted it in the deepest, and most sacred recess of my gloomy soul; she'll not find her new sphere so bright and cheerful, but I hope and pray a far more comfortable one. Of course all this will give rise to a deal of talk — perhaps a deal of scandal.[44]

The scandal that Edwin alluded to was the fact that, in actuality, he had reduced Mary from the status of a person who earned her own living to that of a kept woman. When she died, her obituary in *The New York Herald* said that Booth had placed her in a Canadian convent to complete her education. He had actually set her up in a private home in Hoboken. It was, however, a move done, in both their eyes, for her own good. There is no evidence that Mary Devlin ever objected to Edwin's viewpoint. She was in love with him; he had "bestowed" himself upon her as a gift, and she studied to be deserving. Edwin Booth loved Mollie Devlin, but he did not, however, see her as an equal nor, in fact did she. By the summer of their engagement, she referred to herself as "your ... little daughter," and he, in turn, referred to her as a "girl." Mary would become: "a dependent, undeveloped," or, at least, less-developed "daughter to her husband" a viewpoint she held of him until death. She constantly referred to herself as his "baby."[45]

Five. 1857–1860: Booth, Mary Devlin and Adam Badeau

The idea that Mary had to become educated and give up the stage, the "rude unweeded soil" in which she was stuck, came, to Edwin, in part, from his family. Edwin's sister Asia shared his prejudices. She believed "actors, morally and socially deceive us" and consequently loathed Mary Devlin. Mary was Irish. Asia and her younger brothers John and Joseph were believers in the anti-immigrant Know-Nothing party, keeping two small party flags draped over their door in Bel Air. Asia could accept Edwin's alcoholism, because it was "an inherited disease," but not his intention to marry a poor Irish actress— a "deep designing artful actress." Speaking of Mary, she wrote: "I'd like to write a letter on her face with this pen."[46]

Actors who married actresses in the period often found a touring partner for life and founded theatrical dynasties. Mr. and Mrs. W. J. Florence, Mr. and Mrs. James W. Wallack, Mr. and Mrs. John Drew and Mr. and Mrs. Edmon S. Connor all toured together. Booth was having none of it. By making Mary give up the stage, he was acting like a respectable gentleman, not like an actor. He wanted Mary to improve her mind. Mary consented to "forget if possible as I shall that the Stage ever claimed me as its votary." Moreover she would not ask questions. "You need never tell me, Edwin what your motive is for having me seclude myself this one year.... It is for me and _me_ alone, that your bounty gives so much ... and all the improvement you desire in me, is because you known 'twould make me happier."[47]

Mary, however, knew that no matter how much she subordinated herself to Booth, he was not perfection. She knew that his "past life" had "taught" him "a sad, but ... useful lesson." She knew about the lessons he had learned, because, as he told Elizabeth Stoddard: "she wept when I laid my blackened heart bare to her." When she asked Edwin to advise his brother Joe "to avoid the passions of the world, which inevitably bring sorrow upon men," she may have been warning Edwin as well. She was there to make sure that Edwin remained "a good boy" which implies that she knew what she was dealing with.[48]

If Mary needed to be purified, so apparently did Edwin, who took Mary's trial year to cure himself of venereal disease. They each practiced a kind of self-denigration that prompted them to affirm each other's worth. Mary imagined him as a broken toy whose shattered pieces would be cared for by a child, an image that implies both a disparagement of herself as a child poor enough to cherish a "broken" toy and of Edwin as being damaged. Mary also reminded him that his "goodness" lay beneath a "seemingly cold exterior."[49] They both knew that he was not a romantically demonstrative man.

During the summer of 1859, as the intensity of Booth's relationship to Mary increased, so too did his friendship with Adam Badeau. The two men went to Baltimore together and then traveled twenty-five miles by carriage to spend a night together in the Bel Air farmhouse that Junius Brutus had built as a retirement home. Booth's mother, sister and brother Joseph had moved to Baltimore, and alone in the house, Edwin and Adam rummaged through the elder Booth's books, letters, journals, playbills and costumes. They "pored over" an edition of the Koran, "getting authority for all sorts of wickedness." They put two sofas together, found an old mattress and covered themselves with Junius's costumes. Badeau dozed off as Edwin was telling him stories. Adam later wrote: "some of his fair admirers would not have slept, so long as he talked, and would doubtless envy me my snooze on his arm. But 'twas dark, and I couldn't see his eyes."[50] It was, for Badeau, the most erotic moment of their relationship.

Booth selected Badeau to serve as a guardian of Mary Devlin during her term of purification. If Booth entrusted his fiancée to another man, the implication is that he trusted them both; Mary was safe in her innocence; Adam was safe, because, as Mary said: "he is not like other men." During the 1859–1860 season, Badeau periodically visited Devlin in Hoboken and then reported to Booth.

Mollie was ambivalent about Adam. She reassured him of Booth's friendship and praised him lavishly to Edwin. At the same time, she regarded Badeau as "very weak in many respects," a slave to "the goddess Fashion," and eventually "an intolerable bore," desirous of playing Boswell to Booth's Johnson. On December 28, 1859, she wrote to Edwin: "I sometimes feel as though he were a love-sick school girl, I am consoling.... He says he will bid you Adieu, on your wedding day, that he does not expect your attention after that — I consoled, as well as I could, the 'neglected child.'"[51]

By mid–August 1859 Mary's lessons had begun. She acquired a French teacher and a guitar teacher and visited the Dusseldorf gallery, a center for German visual art, to elevate her artistic taste. In an attempt to cleanse herself of the taint of having been an actress, she also became a puritan. She gave up reading Victor Hugo, because her French tutor insisted that her "mind was too youthful and too ardent to read this author without being intoxicated." She turned vehemently against the theatre or at least against the historic and domestic melodramas that competed with Booth's artistic intentions and which, in Mary's view, "taught immorality from the stage ... in its most dangerous and seductive form." In her desire to purify herself, in both her own as well as in Edwin's eyes, Mary even criticized the company she met at Jefferson's house and descended into snobbism with her recently bought French sophistication: "How very glad I am — that I have always held at a proper distance 'peoples du Theatre'— when I was 'of them'!"[52]

Booth shared her misgivings and hinted to Mary that he might give up the stage. In 1860 she wrote to him: "I have too high an appreciation of the divine spark God has gifted you with, and which you entrust to my care, ever to cause you to seek another sphere than your natural one."[53] If Mary was assuring Edwin that she would never cause him to leave the stage, the issue must have been raised. Mary's reply, however, may reveal an underlying practicality veneered by a moral pose. Both she and Edwin must have known that their financial future depended on Booth's continued success as an actor. Was he pretending to consider leaving the stage so as to justify his insistence that she do so or did they both share a distaste for the profession in which Edwin would spend the rest of his life? Was their disdain for the stage a game in which they complemented each other's high moral tone?

Mary clearly understood what her duty was as his future wife. "My future ambition, will be to see you, great and good, and if, devotion of mind, and intellect [and] affection — can accomplish it, you shall be everything that the world has predicted." She was to become a "True Woman," a nineteenth-century term that suggested purity, piety, domesticity and submissiveness. Victorian women were not the equal of their husbands; equality of the sexes was, in fact, seen as "unnatural." While the 1860 Married Women's Property Act gave wives in the state of New York "the right to their own property and earnings," the issue was moot in the case of Booth and Devlin. She had no property, and even before their marriage, Edwin insisted that she stop earning money.[54]

In April 1860 Adam Badeau wrote: "I'm delighted that you are to be free from disease. Keep so, for Heaven's sake.... pray, stay a god!"[55] Booth was cured of venereal disease and could proceed toward marriage. On April 5, 1860, Adam wrote to "My Prince." He had been obsessively waiting for a letter, getting enraged by Booth's failure to write and his own need to do so. Aware of the hopelessness of his position, he told Booth that he wanted to stop what appears, to a modern reader, to be obsessive behavior:

> Ned I think we two may as well give over making each other unhappy. I've tired of it; besides I think I generally get the worst; I suffer ten times worse than I can make you feel, so if you please we'll be good natured the next time. But I vow you always give me good cause for my naughtiness. And all my exacting, jealous, ridiculous behavior proves just one thing. What it is you may guess.

"What it is you may guess" is a tantalizing hint about what was going on in Badeau's mind. He was experiencing a love that not only dared not speak its name but for which he did not have a name. As Edwin and Mary's marriage approached, the thought of their having children was repulsive to Adam.

> You write quite as if you were in earnest about Italy. We must think of one thing: suppose you are to have children!! In a year from now, I suppose there will be some squalling ugly little creature to interfere with the Coliseum and Venice. Hang it. Don't you call it after me. I won't be godfather, I warn you.

Badeau wrestled with his knowledge of Booth's sexuality, teasing Edwin that he loved others, while simultaneously admitting how obsessed he became with Booth when he saw him.[56] Booth, tired of Badeau's infatuation, responded forbidding Badeau to address him as "Prince" and accusing Badeau of being jealous of Mary. For his part, Badeau realized that his feelings about Mary were complicated. He recognized the "true woman" in her, the help-mate she would be to Edwin, but he knew that she held a place in Edwin's heart that he coveted for himself, and it drove him to rage:

> I'm frightfully jealous, not of Mary, but about her. She, good girl, would not hurt even one particle, I know; I'm almost fond of her, myself; I'm sure I'm grateful to her; she does every thing she can for me; and when I have the blues & feel very low spirited, she cheers me delightfully (I think she's capital for that as you'll find out some day.) ... But I have seen for some time evidence enough not only of her growing importance but of my own eclipse. I wish to God I'd never seen you. It's a frightful thing to live out of one's self; to be buried alive in somebody else. To depend on that body for your own happiness..... Damn you, God bless you.[57]

Edwin and Mollie were married in New York on July 7, 1860, with Booth's brother John Wilkes and Adam Badeau serving as witnesses. The marriage took place in the study of the Rev. Samuel Osgood at No. 154 (later No. 118) West 11th Street. It was a small private ceremony, because Booth feared that a large formal public wedding would injure his popularity with female fans. Friends of the Booths received "wedding cards" announcing the event, but the Magonigles were the only guests. According to Badeau, after the wedding, "Wilkes threw his arms about Edwin's neck and kissed him."[58]

The couple spent their wedding night in a hotel in Albany and honeymooned in a cottage on the Canadian side of Niagara Falls. Adam Badeau later claimed that after a week, Booth invited him to join them and that he spent two weeks there with Edwin and Mary. Edwin and Mary spent most of the summer at Niagara and by late August, Booth's mother and youngest brother Joe had joined them. On August 21, Asia Booth Clarke, as usual, expressed her distaste for Mary: "Mother and Joe are at Niagara with Ned and Miss Devlin or whatever they call her — Why don't she go under the Falls or try to swim in the whirlpool I wonder."[59]

Mary and Edwin settled at the Fifth Avenue Hotel. There they met Lillian Woodman who would marry Booth's friend Thomas Bailey Aldrich. In her memoirs published sixty years later, Lillian recalled the Booths as happy in their companionship, constantly refusing invitations to social events.

> After ... dinner, there would be the chat round the fire, the Prince lying on the black bearskin rug, face downward, supported by his elbows, going over the play for the evening, Mrs. Booth giving him his cues; then the rapid drive to the theatre, arriving long before the audience came in order that Mr. Booth might have time for his make-up. He always went with us to the box — always came there for us at the end of the play.[60]

Asia Booth Clarke had a quite different view of the Booths's social life: "Did Ned hold receptions at this hotel? — I hear of such swarms of visitors. Adam is entirely given up — He wanders forlorn and broken-hearted."[61]

Chapter Six

America and England, 1860–1862: "At a larger circumference"

However complex the relationships were among Booth, Mary Devlin and Adam Badeau, Mary and Adam had a positive effect on Edwin. They discouraged Edwin's drinking and encouraged his artistic ambitions. Reclaiming men from vice was a typical female responsibility in the nineteenth century; in Booth's case it was a duty that Adam also took upon himself. He wrote: "You feel, you say, like an artist; and ask if it's owing to Water, Mollie, or Adam? Lest you should make a mistake, you'd better cling to all three; especially the first, who can't speak for himself, however he seems to have spoken plainly enough. For God's sake, don't desert so true a friend."

Mary wrote to Elizabeth Stoddard: "Edwin — well you know the demon that persues [sic] — a noble ungoverned spirit like his. He is so gentle, so yealding [sic], so abstemious now: & I advise with him & he promises that the victory shall be his." The victory was hard-won and never complete. Booth's bad habits continued through the early years of his marriage. Fifty-eight years later, Lillian Aldrich remembered his drinking at parties after performances in 1862 and telling her: "Since daylight I have not slept. No one can imagine the call of that desire. When it engulfs me, I could sell my soul, my hope of salvation, for just one glass."[1]

In the long run, however, tobacco, which was socially acceptable, proved a more formidable opponent than alcohol. Even Mary, who did not like the smell of tobacco and wanted to limit her husband to two pipes a day, pictured Edwin sitting in an armchair, with his "great meerchaum." She undertook the traditional Victorian role of "influencing" or, as she put it, "advising" him. While there is no evidence that she ever opposed him, she did guide him, and Booth's domestic helplessness after her death implies her authority in household matters. She was, however, unsuccessful in curbing the smoking habits that contributed to the strokes that eventually killed him.[2]

Both Mollie and Adam also encouraged Edwin's plan to go to Europe, an idea that emerged as early as December 1859 when he wrote to his brother June: "I must begin to look towards England." For his part Booth did not care where he went as long as he got out of the theatrical cultural wasteland of America:

> I'm "orph," but whether for Italy, France, or "Merrie England" depends upon — away, away from — here at all events. Art degenerates below the standard even of a trade in America. My taste is becoming vitiated; my love of it is dying out; and I need a recuperation.... I can go on traveling through this country for, perhaps five, years longer, and make a great deal of money; but money is not what I want — nor position either, unless I can feel within, the consciousness of deserving it. Fortune has

placed me in (for my years) a high, and many think, an enviable position, but I feel the ground tremble beneath my feet, and I'm perfectly well aware that unless I am at a larger circumference than the rim of the "almighty dollar" (which one can't help in America), I'll go down "eye deep" in the quicksand of popular favor.[3]

In late May 1860, a month before his marriage, Edwin believed his plans were set and wrote to Lawrence Barrett: "I am to open on the 3d of Sept^r ... [in Boston], and after that go to Europe." Mary Devlin, initially apprehensive about the trip, had come to count on it. Booth and Badeau discussed the possibility of Adam joining Mary and Edwin as a "companion du voyage," because Badeau spoke both Italian and French, but, as Edwin told his friend, the Boston businessman Richard Cary: "The only trouble will be, I shall have a wife to look after." For his part Adam thought that Edwin would be creating an intolerable *ménage a trois*. "A pretty fool I'd feel like tagging around Europe in your train, waiting for the crumbs that fell from the rich woman's table. When you could spare a moment of a thought now and then, glad to get it! Damnation, damnation, damnation. Hell."[4]

Booth postponed the European trip for a year and performed in the fall of 1860 in Boston, Baltimore and Philadelphia. For most of that time, he was ill, suffering "dreadfully with neuralgia in [his] neck & shoulders," an illness he was often able to overcome by immersing himself in his stage roles. "Except when actually engaged in my professional duties (and sometimes even then)," he wrote, "I have been in continual pain."[5]

Booth later claimed that "while at Antietam dead men lay rotting on the blasted fields ... the theatres were crammed to their flag-draped roofs." If this was true, Booth was not there to witness it. He was in England in the fall of 1862 when Antietam took place, and he certainly had not seen uniformly crammed theatres in 1860–1861. In Baltimore, where Booth was engaged for four weeks, his performances had to be terminated after eighteen nights. He commiserated with the theatre's manager, John T. Ford: "I sincerely ... wish you safely out of Balt^o— that's saying as much as man can say—your own Mother couldn't wish you anything better than that—eh?"[6]

Booth had more success at Philadelphia's Arch Street Theatre, with *The Fool's Revenge* being a "bully hit," but work in melodrama, he thought, endangered the status conferred by his Shakespearean roles, placing him on the same level as Edwin Forrest and Charlotte Cushman, whose reputations were based on melodramatic characters (the title roles in *Metamora* and *The Gladiator*; Meg Merriles in *Guy Mannering*). He wrote to Lawrence Barrett: "I'm rather afraid ... — lest I should get a sort of *Metamoric* or *Meg Merrilic* reputation instead of '*Shakes.*'" Edwin was also aware that his "pretties" would not last. "Tomorrow is my benefit—birth-day, I mean, I'm 27! D-m-it! I must never get past that—I'll soon lose me 'Young American'—I must go back to the 25's!"[7]

In an attempt to establish himself as a serious actor, Booth began a seven-year relationship with the Winter Garden Theatre in New York. The theatre's manager, "fat and fluffy" William Stuart, would be instrumental in developing Booth's career. The two men had worked together during a benefit at Wallack's in 1858.[8] Edwin later wrote that after the benefit, Stuart:

> approached me in a most cordial manner with reference to a "repeat," & (if I remember rightly) an engagement at that house.... Having heard queer things of "W.S.," I "fought shy" of the gentleman. Previous to this, however, on the strength of my popularity (in spite of my irregularities at that time), and the fame I was acquiring in the West & South, S. offered me (by telegram) a position to support Miss H[eron] as "Armand," which I pooh-pooh'd & respectfully declined.[9]

Booth did not want to be a supporting actor in New York City; he had decided to be a star, and the Winter Garden gave him that chance. Opened in the fall of 1859 by the triumvirate of Stuart, the playwright Dion Boucicault and Boucicault's actress wife Agnes Robertson, the Winter Garden was in trouble by January 1860 and needed a box office attraction. The Boucicaults and Stuart parted ways over Boucicault's controversial play *The Octoroon,* and in June 1860 *The Spirit of the Times* reported: "The houses have not been for some time past very good, and it behooves the manager to do something better ere longer or he will 'go to the well.' There are many things at this theatre needing a radical change."

That fall, Stuart hired Hart James Jackson (also known as A. W. Jackson and "Black Jackson") as his theatre manager and Booth as his star. Edwin joined the Winter Garden because it afforded him both monetary as well as artistic rewards. He was newly married, and his family was not doing well financially. He was already supporting his mother and Rosalie and Joe, and in January 1860 was forwarding money to California to help get June out of debt.[10]

Edwin and Mary set up housekeeping at 104 East 14th Street, and Booth wrote to Lawrence Barrett: "I've taken up housekeeping at last, and have put all my pictures, books and articles of vertu here with me (my articles of 'virtue' also—of course)." On November 26, 1860, he opened at the Winter Garden. From the beginning, his relationship with Jackson and Stuart was tense. He wanted them to hire competent supporting actors like Lawrence Barrett; they wanted Booth to pay the actors' salaries. He found he had "a hard hill to hoe."[11] The venture proved to be another example of Booth's propensity for aligning himself with unscrupulous managers whom he grew to despise.

Booth wanted to be a Shakespearean actor. His quiet, introspective Winter Garden Hamlet pleased some critics and displeased others. *Frank Leslie's Illustrated Newspaper* reported: "His is a Hamlet to please schoolgirls and very young men; it is lachrymose, sentimental, gloomy."[12] His opening coincided with performances in the same role by Edwin Forrest, returning to the stage after four years of retirement. Forrest had opened with Hamlet at Niblo's Gardens on September 19, 1860, and was still performing a round of characters when Booth began at the Winter Garden. The critic for *The New-York Times* compared Booth and Forrest as representatives of "the intellectual and physical schools" and wrote of Booth's opening night performance: "Mr. BOOTH played ... as if ... he had so much dread of the loud-voiced Forrest school that he went to the other extreme of whispers. In portions of the closet scene, a few paces from the stage, he was nearly inaudible.... He has little muscular force, but with several faults, he has decided and discriminating intellectual talent." The critic for the *New-York Daily Tribune* agreed that Booth was a "quiet" actor 'but felt this was his greatest strength, because "with Mr. Booth quiet is not lack of intensity. He is the first Hamlet for many a day who, in the closet scene, does not consider it necessary to rave and rant at the Queen like a drunken pot-boy.... He is the first Prince of Denmark for many a year who had dared ... to conduct himself like a gentleman and not a blackguard."[13]

However favored by critics, Booth's engagement in Shakespearean roles did not do well financially. Both audiences and critics however, responded positively when he switched to the melodramatic *Richelieu* on November 30. After the curse of Rome speech, the audience "shouted, stamped their feet, waved handkerchiefs, and continued their demonstration for several minutes." The production ran for two weeks, and Jackson suspended the theatre's free list (complimentary tickets available to stockholders).[14] One reason the play was so popular was that to contemporary audiences, *Richelieu* contained echoes of the impending Civil War:

> The inclination of the great mass of Northerners was for peace and a resort of diplomacy to calm the excited South, and significant lines of the aged Cardinal Richelieu to his page: "Take [or Put] away the sword—States can be saved without it" evoked thunders of applause. At a later date, when all efforts at adjustment had failed and the Northern spirit was roused to arms, the same applause was awarded to a still more striking phrase: "First employ all methods to conciliate; failing those—all means to crush!"[15]

As usual, Booth was disappointed that audiences preferred him in a melodramatic role. He wrote to his friend Richard Cary: "*Richelieu* has made *the* mark. There are constant inquiries at the box-office for it; just my luck .... I can't go south, sure. Hurry up and make your fortune that we may have a decent theatre. The company is most atrocious here; they ruin all I attempt. Be sure *my mark is made* here, I'll draw like a blister, and with the best people too." There is, however, no evidence that Cary had either the money or the skill to run a theatre. It was up to Booth.[16]

He might have been pulling in audiences ("draw like a blister"), but Booth disliked the Winter Garden experience. Jackson was interested in making money. He hired twenty-five year-old Amy Elliot Dinsmore, "a young lady said to be of great theatrical promise and the [adopted] daughter of a celebrated oculist," as Booth's Juliet, presumably thinking her social prominence would fill seats. Unfortunately Dinsmore's voice "was for many whole scenes nearly inaudible in the remoter parts of the house." Edwin did not want to work with such amateurs; he wanted more control over the theatre in which he performed.[17]

The critic for *Frank Leslie's Illustrated Newspaper* wrote: "Whether the name on the programme be Pescara, Hamlet, Richard or Richelieu, we see only Edwin Booth, a young man with a pleasant voice, good eye and somewhat pallid countenance, and black hair standing much in need of the attention of the hairdresser."[18] Females in the audience, however, seemed mostly interested in his physical beauty. Mrs. Sam Cowell, whose husband was a music hall entertainer, wrote in her diary:

What eyes he has! The most brilliant and expressive I ever saw.... Nearly all the women are in raptures about him, and I heard many expressions such as "Well now, ain't he pretty?" "Oh, there he is again, I don't care for anything when he is not there"—from the surrounding ladies. He annoyed ... me by having one pertinacious lock of hair hanging over his forehead, through the play, which we were always wanting him to put back, "but he wouldn't." He was very light and buoyant in Petruchio, only a little too boyish; jumping about the stage, and playing all manner of school-boy antics, but now and then ranting a speech in very tragic style.[19]

Booth was increasingly disgruntled with his career. Although convinced that New York theatre was "a gonner for actors," he also hated "barnstorming" and wrote to Barrett: "I *must* pursue the path fate has marked out for me—but 'tis ... a thankless one. I'd rather there was no such thing as *storming*—I'd rather stay in one place & have a home, but, of course, I'd like to stand *A. 1.* in my trade."[20]

Booth went off to Philadelphia to play Macbeth with the "*Col.*" The "colonel" was Charlotte Cushman. Booth's epithet for her implies his recognition of her masculine, martial qualities, particularly as Lady Macbeth, a role she played with a helmet resembling a beard, a style inherited from Edwin Forrest's Macbeth costume. After the first night of *Macbeth* business fell off, and the management lost one thousand dollars. Booth reported that Cushman was "down on" him "as an actor; [she] says I don't know anything at all about 'Hamlet,'" and he found her sexual ambivalence amusing. He told friends that when they played *Macbeth*, he wanted to tell her: "Why don't you kill him. You're bigger than I am."[21]

Back at the Winter Garden, Booth's audiences began to dwindle, and critics were still divided in their opinions. On February 11 Booth began work as Shylock. Opening night had a poor house, perhaps because of competition from the American premiere of Verdi's *Un Ballo in Maschera,* but despite several nights of bad weather, his version of what was called the "sordid Jew" and "the mean cuss of a Jew" caught on with both critics and audiences, and business was good by the end of the week.[22] The critic for *The Evening Post* wrote:

Shylock is the character ... best suited to Mr. Booth's Asiatic intensity which seems to belong to his nature. As he is seen first approaching from across the bridge in his oriental garb .... he looked the Jew to the life.... If Mr. Booth has Hebrew blood in his being, his assumption must be classed as a work of art.... He realized the very height of Hebrew intensity when he gives his final dogged and deliberate No! to the final appeal for mercy.... Nothing could be finer.... than the unmingled irony and dignity of his bow in acknowledgement of the mock magnanimity of the Court and his final exit.[23]

When Booth began to alternate Iago and Othello with J. W. Wallack, Jr., it was his Iago that garnered the most praise. The critic for *The Daily Tribune* wrote:

Perhaps the strongest feature of Mr. Booth's Iago is his *plausibleness*— he is no vulgar melodramatic villain;. full of scowlings and writhings, so transparent in his malice that Othello could not fail to see motives; he does not go up and down, ranting his devlish designs at the top of his voice in bellowing tones that would have frighted the whole Isle of Cyprus.... He is a gentleman in dress and bearing... During the great scenes at the third act ... the whole colloquy is conducted on his part in a voice that is never raised above the ordinary key of a conversational tone.... In the fifth act, in the last scene, after he has delivered his final speech, he rivets the eyes of the whole house on himself, during the progress of the whole scene, *without speaking a word*.[24]

By the end of the 1860–1861 season all forms of entertainment were experiencing the war's impact everywhere.

Theatres, concert saloons, and all other places continue to feel the blighting influence of the war, and those who cater for amusements are all in a fog.... Managers stand aloof in dread of the approaching conflict and dare not advance without the utmost caution. [Entertainers] of "high and low degree" are turning their attention to the land of gold [California] or to European soil. Some have already left for Europe, and others are departing to follow.... Most places of amusement now open, here and elsewhere, are running on half salaries, and even this will not last much longer. It is not so much owing to the scarcity of money as to the interest taken in the war and in the operations of our volunteers. Parties who start out to visit a theatre or music hall, in many instances [stop] at a military rendezvous, or remain in the street to witness the parade or departure of some regiment bound to the seat of war.[25]

As his box office at the Winter Garden declined, Booth's relationship with its management disintegrated. On July 1, 1861, he wrote to Barrett, who continued to ask for work: "I am bound to the hog Jew for 4 weeks in the fall & he knows I wanted you but rather than pay he'd let me act without a company." "Hog Jew" was one of Booth's favorite disparagements and the earliest example of the casual anti–Semitism that characterized his life and the world around him. He used "Jew" as an all-purpose slur, often directed at people, not necessarily Jewish, who he felt were cheating him financially.[26]

Although contracted to Jackson for a four-week run in the fall of 1861, Booth was not planning to return to the Winter Garden. He was hoping for an engagement in England. By June 1861 Mary Devlin Booth, three months pregnant, was facing the "dread packing of trunks." The Booths went off to Umbagog Lake in Bethel, Maine, where Edwin, joined by his friend the artist Walter Brackett, spent his summer fishing for trout. By early August he had completed negotiations with J.B. Buckstone of the Haymarket Theatre in London. He either did not bother to find out anything about the company he was joining, or his views of the profession were so jaundiced that he simply did not care. It would prove to be yet one more example of Booth's ineptitude as an artist/businessman.[27]

Edwin and Mary, by then five months pregnant, left for Europe on August 7, 1861, on the *Arabia*. After an eleven-day crossing, they arrived in Liverpool, stayed a day and went on to London. By August 30 they were renting rooms at 15 Bedford Place, a four-story brown brick house off Great Russell Street between Russell and Bloomsbury Square, a block and a half from the British Museum. The fashionable neighborhood was populated by physicians, surgeons, solicitors and architects. The Booths arrived too early for the theatrical season, which began in October. Mary wrote to Richard Cary's sister Emma that Edwin was "very nervous and anxious; if he should fail, the disappointment would almost crush him."[28]

Edwin Booth as Iago. "Perhaps the strongest feature of Mr. Booth's Iago is his *plausibleness*—he is no vulgar melodramatic villain; full of scowlings and writhings, so transparent in his malice that Othello could not fail to see motives; he does not go up and down, ranting his devlish [sic] designs at the top of his voice in bellowing tones that would have frighted the whole Isle of Cyprus.... He is a gentleman in dress and bearing."

Booth's anxiety was warranted. He opened as Shylock on September 30, 1861, at the Haymarket Theatre. According to William Winter, "the public received him kindly, but actors and critics were cold." They were expecting a successor to Edmund Kean, an actor of the old romantic school who would tear a passion to tatters like Junius Brutus Senior. They found a studied and controlled actor. "Mr. Edwin Booth ... scarcely corresponded to the ... prediction that he would prove to be an actor of the fiery impulsive school. Those who ... expected that old-fashioned rant ... must have been grievously disappointed at ... his ... steady and well considered performance."[29]

Booth's Shylock was a characterization by a twenty-eight-year-old actor of an elderly man, performed, oddly enough at this point, without a beard. Like his early versions of Richelieu, his Shylock was inconsistent. According to one critic, "the trembling, stooping, staggering decrepitude ... gave way every now and then to muscular tightness and manly vigour."[30]

Some critics responded positively to the "extreme levity" with which Booth's Shylock treated "the terms of the bond" with Bassanio and Antonio, his scene with Tubal and to the "spasmodic sobs ... clinging hands, tottering footsteps" with which Booth dramatized Shylock's "baffled hopes and ruined prospects" during his final exit. Most critics, however, were unmoved by the performance, and Buckstone's Haymarket company, accustomed to playing comedy, was not up to requirements of what was considered a Shakespearean tragedy. The production as a whole looked under-rehearsed.[31]

> Scenes were shifted before the stage was clear; Jessica kept her lover waiting at the window an unconscionably long time; the curtain rose on scattered groups of scene-shifters and carpenters; there was a gross waste of time between the acts; and worse than all, the stock players of the establishment were anything but equal to, or well up in, the parts assigned them. The prompter is no doubt a useful official, but he should not be too frequently appealed to. Better management on the stage, it must also be said, would prevent a scene from being shifted, while yet the actors were in front of it, uttering the words set down for them.[32]

Mary Devlin Booth attended the *Merchant* opening in the sixth month of her pregnancy, an unusual occurrence in the Victorian period when pregnant women typically remained at home. The next day she complained to Emma F. Cary:

> Several of the morning journals—fortunately of but little account ... came out, in the most unkind censure of Shylock at the Haymarket—the part Mr. Booth chose for his first appearance not daring, after so long a rest to task his strength with any character, requiring more physical power. The Times—the journal of most consequence, did him some justice but still its praise was luke-warm.... This tone of criticism certainly could not fail to chill, and depress, one so sensitively organized as my dear husband—but he knew there was against him, pre-existing prejudice.... The enthusiasm of the audience was unbounded.[33]

On October 6, Booth wrote to Lorimer Graham, a wealthy American whom he had known in New York and who traveled on the same ship to England: "My debut is considered by many a successful one, but I am far from being pleased—or even satisfied with it."[34]

Booth's London engagement was characterized by a series of miscalculations. Charlotte Cushman had warned him against opening with *The Merchant of Venice*, and Mary thought that "'Shylock' was perhaps the worst part he could have chosen." Mary also blamed his lack of success, in part, on his unwillingness to bribe critics, an issue that would surface later in his relationship to William Winter: "Of course," she wrote to Emma Crow Cushman, "the press might have been secured, but I am happy to say Mr. Booth has too much dignity of character to beg praise." Edwin may also have fallen victim to the strong anti-Northern sentiment prevalent in England during the early years of the Civil War. Mary wrote: "'Tis much to be regretted that he came here just at the time he did. The prejudice strong against the 'Yankee'—& the public surfeited with Shakespeare."[35]

Booth went on to play Iago, Sir Giles Overreach, Richard III and Richelieu. His reviews continued to be mediocre. As Shylock, Iago and Sir Giles Overreach, London critics found him tame, "a good though not a great actor... wanting ... fire and intensity," "careful and conscientious," "creditable and respectable." His Richard III, on the other hand, was laughed off the stage by the opening night audience. Buckstone had hired armor from Astley's Theatre. It took two weeks for the property men to clean it up, but they forgot to oil it. One actor's raised arm and sword got stuck in the air; another walked around with a stiff leg and a third had his visor slip down and catch his ear and had to play with his head tilted to one side.[36]

Booth's next role — Richelieu — was heralded as "a step in the right direction." *Bell's Life in London* told its readers: "He simulates age exceedingly well, and expresses with sufficient effect the vanity, humanity, and merits of the Cardinal as well as his subtle wiliness and far-reaching policy." There were, however, reservations: "He does not give the requisite prominence to the humour with which the part abounds. Too much effort, also, is apparent at times in the enunciation of words and phrases.... We would caution him on some American accents which offend English ears. 'Commend' for instance is accented on the second syllable; and 'gallant' (the adjective) on the first."[37] The critic for *The Literary Gazette* pointed out serious inconsistencies in the performance, problems that he would never completely solve, in part because they are built into the text.

> Throughout the play *Richelieu* is represented as physically infirm, nay, all but moribund: through physical exhaustion he drops, and all but dies upon the stage, and from this state he rises to rant and stagger and rave in a voice that would do credit to a Thames waterman.... His hand, one moment powerless at his side, is the next wagged about to an extent that threatens permanent dislocation; and his head which at one time he can scarce raise from his pillow the next turns, nods and oscillates upon his shoulders.[38]

On October 13, 1861, Booth wrote to the American painter Thomas Hicks: "Are you one of those who deemed my advent here would set the Thames on fire? ... At all events I can assure you that the Thames is as wet as ever.... I have not heard from Badeau since I left home — is he still alive?"[39]

Badeau was very much alive. Both he and Booth's Boston friend Richard Cary had joined the Union troops, Cary as a soldier, and Badeau initially as a correspondent for his newspaper and later as an aide to generals Quincy A. Gillmore and Thomas W. Sherman in combat. By June 30, 1861, he had served under General William Tecumseh Sherman. On November 3 Booth wrote to Walter Brackett: "What do you think — I had a letter — an indignant one —from Badeau the other day!!!! He's gone on an expedition to fight the rebels: if he gets sea-sick, and vomits over the side of the frigate, he'll lose his glasses, sure as a gun! Then he might shoot Cary instead of our enemy."[40] Adam's relationship with Edwin was changing. Badeau had found "real and exquisite happiness" in his "profound and tender and anxious love" for a young soldier named James Harrison Wilson.[41] Badeau's nickname for him was "Left Arm." The relationship was revealingly described in a letter Adam wrote to Edwin on December 4, 1862, from the headquarters of the first division of the Department of the Gulf in Carrollton, Louisiana, where he was a captain and aide-de-camp, complaining about the terseness of Booth's last letter:

> The Left Arm [Wilson — penciled in] writes me fifty pages at a time; ... and what's more, Sir, letters just as crammed with affection, just as demonstrative as any you ever received from a man. I don't think I'll ever show them to you, but I'd like you to realize that such profusion and tender and anxious love as you have been the object of is not unparalleled. Perhaps you will consider my soldier friend "unmanly." On the very morning of the terrible 17th of September [the battle of Antietam] he added such words as these: "7 A.M. Heavy firing has already begun. I go at once to the front. God bless you, my true heart." All day long, through the thicket of the fight, he says he thought of me and wished that I was by his side. Do you understand Ned, that 'tis out of my confidence that I tell you this; not out of maliciousness. I can't tell more than one or two in the world of it. You are one of these. I am proud to excite such an affection in such a noble nature. I don't have any of the anxious excited feeling you used to know of, but this new affection gives me real and exquisite happiness. I tell you of it ... as you used to tell me of Mollie. But I wonder how — No, I won't say anything. I shouldn't. Tell Mollie all; she is my friend, true and tender; I love her, Sir. What d'ye think of that? Or am I distant and out of mind? Am I thought of as a comparative stranger, and have you outgrown (both of you) all the past? I am changed, but the past has left an impress on me

Edwin Booth as Richelieu. "Throughout the play *Richelieu* is represented as physically infirm, nay, all but moribund: through physical exhaustion he drops, and all but dies upon the stage, and from this state he rises to rant and stagger and rave in a voice that would do credit to a Thames waterman."

forever. I shall always be a different man from what I would have been had I never known you. I shall always feel in some sort more intimate with you than with any one else. Tis queer that now, tis I who give the confidences, and demand the sympathy. By the way, Left Arm went to the play and saw Booth as Richard.... My Ned, for all I write as I do about my Left Arm, I haven't felt as kindly towards you, old fellow since I left the North as I do just now. I can't root out — all traces of what was once so firmly knit around my heart strings. Can you? ... I've got a Left Arm, and 'tis nearest the heart, but it never will supply the place of the Right One — and sometimes even yet I feel out for what once was — and when I find it gone I am sad.[42]

On April 12, 1862, Booth wrote to Badeau who, in Edwin's view, had become a man: "I am delighted in the change in you. I knew the war would do you good, and a little rough usage on the battle field — with a few soldiery oaths will complete the glorious work. But joking aside I am gratified to know that you have devoted yourself to labor ... and have give up the 'fopperies' of life." Edwin promised: "In regard to our letters—I will, as soon as possible, collect all of yours ... and return them." Badeau had apparently expressed concern about the letters he and Booth had exchanged. He was embarking upon a military career, and he needed to cover his tracks.[43]

Booth, like Badeau, had found other friends, such as Lorimer Graham and his wife, who had been part of the bohemian/intellectual/artistic set of New York. Mary was entering her last trimester, and Booth and Graham began touring the sights of London together—what Booth described as "this large wilderness of London ... through every nook & corner —church-yards— high-ways & by-ways— in search of the 'mighty dead' and their haunts while living; every place of interest about London set down in the guide-books." Unlike Graham, however, Booth was not wealthy. He later told him: "Would to Heaven your beautiful idea of our living could be carried out; but living in Byronic palaces don't spread one's bread — although it might cost as much as 'twould to live here [in America] in a dark and dingy brown-stone." Booth had to work, and performing before an English audience during the American Civil War was not easy. The plays Booth did were English, and London audiences had been nurturing traditions about them for years. On November 3, 1861, he wrote to Walter Brackett: "The prejudice against the 'd-d Yankees' is so strong just now that the Bull won't 'cotton' to 'em at any price.... I have at least succeeded in waking up the dull ... Britishers to a sense of something beyond the Macready-worship which has ever surrounded the play of Richelieu. I shall take a turn through the provinces."[44]

After London, Booth performed in Manchester, where the fledgling Henry Irving played Laertes to his Hamlet, Cassio to his Othello and Bassanio to his Shylock. Booth told Walter Brackett that after Manchester he would "rest awhile — out of town — I'm going to take 'a cot in the valley I love' in the 'syllabubs' of the town." The "cot," a small house with a garden that Booth rented until May 1862, was 5 Stamford Villas in Fulham, between Walham Green and Stamford Bridge. Stamford Villas was a terrace of twenty-three attached houses with gardens backing onto the grounds of the London Athletic Club. Fulham was much too far away for a nightly carriage commute to the theatre district, and Booth had decided to suspend his work in England. He was physically exhausted and suffering from "a terribly swelled face & toothache."[45]

His retirement may also have been due to the impending birth of his child. Edwin hoped for a boy. He was thinking about it even before he married Mary; in fact he was expecting it from the moment she got pregnant. But Booth's only surviving child, a girl named Edwina Marie Frances for her father, was born on December 9, 1861, in Fulham. Like most nineteenth-century women, Mary gave birth at home. The Booths were not expecting the child until two weeks later, but at 11 P.M. on December 8, Mary woke Edwin to say she was in labor. Booth described the birth in a letter to Thomas Hicks:

At One A.M. I was sent "adrift" in my night gown & slippers to find a doctor (the servant being dispatched for the one we had previously engaged); at two A.M. I was several miles out of my vicinity and up to my knees in mud — the night being stormy & I a stranger. Three A.M. found me by my wife's side with a strange M. D. (that I had found in the mud!! on Fulham Green) on 'tother side of the bed. Fortunately, however, our own D<u>r</u> arrived, and dismissed the queer looking stranger I had picked up — at half past three A.M. Four A.M. found me on the verge of agony, and five A.M. found me <u>father</u>! And you will be pleased to hear my friend, a happy one.[46]

Edwina was born at 4:30 A.M. Edwin later claimed that he had draped the American flag over Mary's bed so that his child would be born, as he put it, under the "stars and stripes"; however, he never made any such claim until after his brother had assassinated Lincoln, and Edwin had become "vitally patriotic." Following the birth, Booth wrote to Lorimer Graham: "<u>I am a father</u>! Oh! Graham you know not the <u>phelinks</u> of <u>phather</u> — <u>phancy</u> mine!!" After he informed his immediate family, Asia Booth Clarke wrote to her friend Jean Anderson: "They are going to call the child Edwina. Did you ever hear of anything to beat that? Joe [Booth's youngest brother] always changes everything, so he calls the name Ed<u>w</u>ina, like wine you know."[47]

Five weeks after Edwina's birth, Mary wrote to Emma C. Cushman that the delivery had been easy but that she could only nurse out of her left breast, the right breast and arm being too painful. Her sister-in-law Asia referred to this as a "broken breast." Mary hired a nurse to look after the baby, who, by mid–February, had to be put on a bottle. Her childbearing experience gave Mary a level of authority that does not appear in either her previous letters or the notebooks she kept. Edwin, stiff with rheumatism, was afraid to handle the baby; Mary began giving out advice to pregnant friends. Motherhood, however, did not make her an independent woman. After a dull social visit, she wrote to Edwin: "I made up my mind ... never to go anywhere again without my darling husband."[48]

Although Edwin was no longer acting, the Booths decided to stay in Europe. As of January 1862, Mary hoped they would spend the following winter on the continent where it would be warmer. By the spring, however, Booth had decided to return to Boston for the fall 1862 season. As he told Richard Cary, he was coming home "a poorer but wiser man than when I left there," and the fact that he asked Cary not to mention his return to anyone implies that he was trying to avoid questions about the success of his visit.[49]

Edwin visited Paris alone from March 3 through 9, staying at the Hotel des Arts at 7 Cité Bergère in Montmartre, but found no theatre there interested in engaging him. He returned to England, planning to take Mary and Edwina to Paris on March 20 and to remain there until the fall season in New York began. Unfortunately pain in his knee and a poison ivy rash that covered him "head to foot" postponed the trip until May 1.[50]

The Booths stayed in Paris for two months. They went to see the great French actor Frederic Lemaitre in *Don Cesar de Bazan*; they toured the Louvre, the Père Lachaise cemetery. the Luxembourg Gardens, the Bois de Boulogne and the Champs Elysées. Booth took the time to study costumes at the Louvre, particularly those needed for *Richelieu*, and, under Mary's guidance, contracted for a new set of Cardinal robes.[51]

They left for London on July 26 and went from there to Liverpool, where they embarked on what Edwin described as "that horrible mighty monster the G<u>t</u> Eastern." Built between 1854 and 1859, the *Great Eastern*, with her combination of six masts, a paddle wheel and screw propulsion, was reputed to be "the largest and most comfortably appointed ship in the world." To Booth, however, she was "dirty beyond description, and the food &c, &c, is little less than frightful." Edwin disliked the stateroom they had booked in Paris and complained to the English purser that he wanted a "room with more light." The purser was unhelpful, but Mary made arrangements to exchange rooms with a fellow traveler.[52]

Edwin, Mary, Edwina and Edwina's French nurse arrived in New York on September 1, 1862. He contemplated returning to England in the summer of 1863 and the fall of 1864, but the 1861–1862 trip had been, at best, a lukewarm financial and artistic success, and Booth did not return to England until 1880. In later life his memories of his initial experiences there were not positive. In 1877 he wrote to William Winter: "Nine months of pea-soupic atmosphere and coal-sootie inhalation failed to warm my bowels towards John Bull."[53]

Chapter Seven

1862–1863: "Tell Molly I'm coming"

The Booths left Europe in a hurry, because Edwin thought his work at the Winter Garden would begin on September 1, but his engagement was postponed until the 29th. Edwin and Mary entered into the lively social life of its literary bohemia. James Lorimer Graham, a wealthy American they had met in Europe, arranged an introduction to Richard Henry Stoddard and his wife Elizabeth Drew Barstow Stoddard. Stoddard was a literary reviewer for *The World*; Elizabeth was a short story writer, novelist and poet, later described as "an angular individualist" with a "sharp ... tongue" who "frequently made enemies by its injudicious use."[1]

The Stoddards were poor, living in a rooming house on Tenth Street and Fourth Avenue, but they were the center of an artistic salon. Through them the Booths met the writers Thomas Bailey Aldrich, Edmund Clarence Stedman and Bayard Taylor, the sculptor Launt Thompson, the painters Sanford Robinson Gifford, Eastman Johnson and Jervis McEntee and McEntee's brother-in-law the architect Calvert Vaux. Booth found a drinking companion in Stoddard, and both he and Mary were attracted to the intellectual/social milieu in which Richard and Elizabeth moved.

Although his social life was "brimming o'er," Edwin's plans to elevate the art of American theatre with the help of his friend the Boston businessman Richard F. Cary were crushed when Cary died, shot through the head at the battle of Cedar Mountain, Virginia, on August 9, 1862. Edwin fell back on his own resources. This meant the Winter Garden and touring.[2]

He reopened there on September 29, under Jackson's management, and played through November 17, 1862. Performing against the combination of Edwin Forrest and James Hackett at Niblo's Gardens, Booth attracted "poor but honest" audiences. His New York press was generally negative, and given his long-standing popularity in Boston, it is not surprising that he left New York and took a lease as manager of the Boston Academy from November 24 through December 20. The issues that plagued all of his managerial efforts beset him there — how to balance the financial burdens of a manager while furthering the careers of his friends and developing productions that lived up to his standards. Consequently Booth turned the day-to-day operations of the Boston Academy over to William Stuart, one of his Winter Garden managers. It was not a wise move. Good actors were expensive, and Stuart, who was working for Booth, was obligated to make money for his employer. Even if they had wanted to invest the money in a superior company, it was mid-season. Actors of any stature already had contractual engagements. Stuart was forced to use actors on "furlough" from Laura Keene's New York company, which never performed the kind of repertoire Booth played, and their lack of preparation showed.[3]

Despite these reservations, however, the Boston venture was a financial success. On November 30, 1862, Booth wrote: "Thus far my speculation has been very successful — and if it continues throughout the three [actually four] weeks (for which time I have taken the theatre) I shall realize at least $4,000.... The war does not seem to affect business — certainly not mine — in the least.... This is my first attempt at management and it has given me a thirst for it."[4] Of course, in actuality, Booth had been sharing his managerial duties with Stuart. He was not undertaking the full responsibilities of running a theatre.

Mary accompanied Edwin to Boston, but she was not well. The Booths hoped to have another child, a boy they intended to name Alva, but Mary had developed gynecological problems. In December she called in Dr. Erasmus Miller, and, as she wrote, with "fear," "dread" and "loathing," underwent a gynecological examination. To be near her doctor during treatment, she retreated to a furnished cottage in Dorchester, Massachusetts, while Booth was obliged to go to Brooklyn to fulfill an engagement.[5]

Booth returned to Dorchester on January 4, 1863, and wrote to Stoddard: "I found Mollie and baby ill — I was scared last night — poor Mollie was in great suffering & the doctor had to be summoned. She is better today; baby ditto." On January 19 Mary wrote to Elizabeth: "Dr. Miller ... says I am very much better & will be perfectly cured even before the time he thought." She could, however, no longer sit up for long periods of time.[6]

In late January she rallied. On the 21st she and Edwin went to the theatre in Boston to see John Wilkes Booth perform Pescara in *The Apostate*, and the next day Edwin wrote to Richard Stoddard: "Mollie is getting on well." This same day, however, Mary wrote to Emma Cushman: "Dr. Miller is very skillful, & his family very kind & attentive to me. 'The rest is silence.' ... I am not very well."[7]

Shortly before February 9 Edwin returned to work at the Winter Garden in New York, leaving Mary in Dorchester. In his biography, William Winter, always careful to preserve Booth's reputation, wrote that Mary's health was "impaired" but that she was not seriously ill. Establishing this part of Booth's legend was important to Winter and also to Booth. He later claimed in a letter to Adam Badeau: "I left her in bloom of health and hope, joyful and loving, throwing kisses to me as I parted from her."[8] That Mary was in "the bloom of health" is doubtful. Edwin would eventually be beset by guilt at having left her.

Mary urged Booth's friends to "take care of him" — by which she meant "keep him from drinking," and Thomas Bailey Aldrich and Launt Thompson began to chaperone him. They could hardly have been effective. Edwin's drinking showed in his acting. Elizabeth Stoddard wrote to Mary: "Sick or well, you must come. Mr. Booth has lost all restraint and hold on himself. Last night there was the grave question of ringing down the curtain before the performance was half over. Lose no time. Come." Mary, however, was too ill. She wrote; "I cannot come. I cannot stand. I think sometimes that only a great calamity can save my dear husband."[9]

The calamity came. On February 11, 1863, Mary went to see John Wilkes perform again, this time in the dual leads in *The Corsican Brothers*. Her letter to Edwin about the performance the next day was her last extant piece of writing. Lillian Aldrich, writing in 1920, recounts that John Wilkes Booth told her "that two days before he [Edwin] left [Boston], Mrs. Booth had suggested that, as she would be alone again, she should go to [Boston] and ask a friend to return with her. There had been a snowstorm, a delay in the horse-car, and standing on the snow she had waited for it and taken cold. On her return to the house she said to the maid: 'Take me upstairs and put me to bed. I feel as if I should never be warm again.'" If Lillian Aldrich was reporting John correctly, he was probably avoiding the fact that Mary went to Boston to see him act.[10]

By February 18 Dr. Miller had called in another physician, John Ware, president of the Massachusetts Medical Society. His daughter Frances kept a diary and recorded what she heard of Mary's last days. On February 18 Frances she wrote: "that poor, dear, little Mrs. Booth was dangerously ill of inflammation of the bowels."[11]

Booth was receiving mixed messages. On February 18 Orlando Tompkins, manager of the Boston Theatre, telegraphed him saying that "Dr. Miller has just written me saying Mary continues comfortable & don't think your return necessary."[12] On the morning of the next day, February 19, Miller wrote:

> I am happy to say that Mrs. B. has passed a comfortable night — The pain in the bowels & nausea has left her, & she suffers only from debility & wind, occasionally, in the stomach. She would of course be perfectly delighted could you be with her, but says, under the circumstances, she would prefer you should fulfill your engagement, inasmuch as were you here you could do nothing to relieve her physically.[13]

A telegram from Tompkins on February 19 says: "Mary is better," but another telegram that same day reads: "Mary is comfortable. No worse. Dr. Miller thinks you had better come on tomorrow morning [Friday, February 20], leave early A M and get here about four (4) o'clk remain until Sunday night." Mary was in no pain but "completely prostrated." Tompkins asked Dr. Ware "to sign a certificate, saying it was absolutely necessary for Mr. Booth to come on from New York," and they expected him on Friday. Booth, however, did not start for Boston until 8 A.M. on Saturday, February 21, and he was too late.[14] Mary died that morning at 8:30 A.M. She was twenty-three years old. Frances Ware wrote in her diary:

> Mr. Tompkins came this morning before breakfast, for Father to go out and see Mrs. Booth, who is dying, and they are afraid she will not live till her husband come. They did not telegraph till yesterday morning, and he has not come yet. Father went, but she died before he got there, peacefully and without pain. She just ceased breathing. The doctor told him that Edwin Booth had been going on very badly in New York, appearing on the stage, intoxicated, and when he first went, he wrote regularly to her, every day, and then almost ceased. She probably knew the cause and that worried her in addition to her illness.... Mr. Brackett is going to meet him at the Depot and go out with him.... I kept hearing the words of his last telegram, "Tell Molly I'm coming," when poor fellow, she was lying still and dead in the faraway house.[15]

Although her gynecological problems may have weakened her, Mary died as the result of an illness that settled in her stomach and intestines. On March 11, 1863, Booth wrote to Elizabeth Stoddard: "I lost my father in just the same manner. With the same disease he died."[16] The fact that Edwin failed to reach Mary in time weighed heavily on him and led to the perpetuation of a family legend. Booth's daughter told her son, Edwin Booth Grossman (Ted):

> The facts as related by my dear father are merely these. On his return from a yachting trip to Old Point Comfort with Lorimer Graham, he resumed his engagement at Winter Garden Theatre — opening in "Hamlet," having left my young mother with me (a baby of fifteen months) & the nurse in his rented house in Dorchester — Mass. During this interval my mother fell ill with a severe cold — & doctor wired my father that he saw no cause for immediate alarm. After 3 days — the [cold] grew worse — & the doctor wired my father to come at once. This telegram which arrived during the performance was withheld by the manager of the Winter Garden theatre — until after the performance that night — too late for my father to reach my mother's bedside before she died; after he left — for Boston — at once. He never forgave Stuart — the manager for this![17]

Thus, in the official Booth family version, the villain conveniently became William Stuart, but in the extensive correspondence he wrote after Mary's death, Booth never mentioned Stuart; the two men continued to work together for another four years and, at the time, Edwin's objections to the Winter Garden were focused far more on "Black Jackson," Stuart's fellow manager at the Winter Garden. The legend was designed to cover up the fact that Edwin did not start for Boston when the Boston manager Tompkins suggested. He started a day later. Dr. Miller and Tompkins' communications had been positive, and Edwin may not have been neglectful.

The situation, however, left him with guilt and the need for a scapegoat. The "manager" villain, who originally may have been Jackson, was a convenience.

According to Frances Ware, Booth's "grief was demonstrative and theatrical. He rushed into the house quite frantic, and they brought his baby which he embraced so violently and distractedly that he frightened the little thing, who began to cry."[18] Mary lay on her bed "almost covered with flowers" for three days and was interred at Mount Auburn Cemetery on February 24, 1863. Only the immediate family and a few friends were invited. Booth's mother, who had arrived the day before from Philadelphia, his brother John Wilkes, his brother-in-law John S. Clarke, the Boston comedian William Warren, Julia Ward Howe and one of her daughters and the poet Thomas William Parsons and his wife Anna attended.

It was too cold to go to the grave. An Episcopal minister read the funeral service in the cemetery's chapel over an open coffin. Mrs. Parsons told Frances Ware that Booth "waited till everybody had gone, ... and after a while stooped and put one of the rose buds into her hand and patted it gently and tenderly as one would to a child, then kissed her forehead and cheeks and then went away." Having treated his wife as a child in death as he did in life, Booth returned to Dorchester with his mother.[19]

It was too cold to break ground, and the coffin was kept in a vault or "receiving tomb" until summer, when Booth had to go through a second burial approximately a week before what would have been his third wedding anniversary. The occasion brought out a melodramatic gesture reminiscent of the fifth act of *Hamlet*. Booth described it in a letter to Adam Badeau:

> I got back from Boston two or three days ago whither I had gone... to place my darling in the ground; my own grave is dug beside her — I jumped into it, and wondered how long it would be (and inwardly prayed it might be soon) before I should be laid there.... Tomorrow is the glorious 4th — do you remember 3 years ago about this time? Next Tuesday I shall look at my bridal bed in vain for that which lay there once, so full of trembling Heaven.[20]

Mary's death had a profound effect on Edwin's personal life, and, for a short while, on his professional life as well. He withdrew from acting and initially refused to see anyone. He blamed himself and particularly his drinking for hastening Mary's death. He certainly had been drinking. On March 3, 1863, Asia Booth Clarke, vindictive even after Mary's death, wrote: "It is better for her that she died so early — for her wonderful influence had wonderfully ebbed away of late and Ned was at his old wild ways again."[21] The Reverend Samuel Osgood, who had married the Booths, urged Edwin to start working again, but on March 7, 1863, Booth responded: "I can only regard my profession as the means of providing for the poor little babe she has left with me; the beauty of my art is gone — it is hateful to me — it has become a trade."[22]

Leaving the theatre temporarily was not hard to do, given the time frame involved; Mary died in February, and the theatrical season ended in May. Booth's mourning put him out of work for three months. At the same time, withdrawing from the Winter Garden early had a financial penalty. Booth forfeited salary when he broke his contract. He had played only eleven performances before Mary died, and left Stuart and Jackson with a hole in their schedule and a contract for the following season that he was reluctant to honor. Their reaction was to withhold salary. At this point Booth's animosity focused on Jackson so intensely that it brought out the casual anti–Semitism that often surfaced when he was angry. On July 1 he wrote to Lawrence Barrett who was once again asking for work:

> Jackson & I have not exchanged a word either by letter or verbally since the sad night of my departure in February. I am bound to the hog Jew for 4 weeks in the fall & he knows I wanted you but rather than pay he'd let me act without a company — as you know. When he speaks, and not 'till then, I will do all I can to forward your wishes; I shall not approach him until he breaks the ice — he has treated me very badly, and if such a beast can feel shame — I fancy he experiences that sensation at present.... I have no idea when I begin nor has Jackson — for I may throw him yet.[23]

Seven. 1862–1863: "Tell Molly I'm coming"

Going into seclusion deprived Booth of the income from three to four months of touring, and no matter how keenly he felt Mary's loss, he had to make a living in the theatre. Late that summer he wrote: "My hill-work begins next month — I must now commence a train of thinking that may lead me back into the old ruts of my hateful life — at present I dread the plunge into it." The rut that Booth dreaded included drinking. He was not happy about returning to the stage, but he knew nothing else.[24] Six months after Mary's death, Booth resumed his career.

Facing life as a single parent, he needed a house and someone to take care of his daughter while he was working, particularly when he was touring outside New York. This meant providing a home for his mother, his sister Rosalie and his brother Joseph, all of whom were entrusted with Edwina's care. By May 18, 1863, he had taken a six-month lease on a furnished residence in New York at 107 East 17th Street. Buying a house, however, proved difficult. "I've tried a thousand times to get a house. I suppose I'll have to wait til my grave is dug.... The only security I can give in the house business is to pay in advance. D—n the house! D—n me! D—n the world! D—n, d—n, d—n!" Finally, on June 11, Booth purchased a house at 28 East 19th Street. On June 15 he wrote to Adam Badeau saying that he planned to move there in the fall.[25]

The relationship between Badeau and Booth continued to change. Adam wrote to Booth from New Orleans, offering his condolences about Mary and, to some degree, apologizing for his past conduct. "You know that I loved her too; from the first hour when you took to me visit your promised bride, all through the year of engagement when you trusted her so much to my care; on your honeymoon and afterwards crazy and foolish though I was."[26]

Badeau was reinventing himself in the Union army, abandoning his pose as an effete man of letters and becoming a soldier and a man of affairs. "Left Arm" Wilson recommended him to Ulysses S. Grant, then Commander of the Army of the Tennessee, and on May 19, 1863, Grant requested that Capt. Badeau report to him for duty. A week later, before Badeau could do so, Union Maj. Gen. Nathaniel P. Banks's army moved against the Confederate stronghold at Port Hudson on the Mississippi River. In the battle that followed, Badeau was hit by a bullet that shattered the bones of the instep of his left foot. He was evacuated to New Orleans.[27]

The news reached New York on June 6, and Booth read in a morning newspaper that Badeau's foot could be saved. Fearing that this was not true, he wrote immediately saying "I pray God you may not be taken away." Badeau lay in an army hospital until July 1863, when he was brought back to New York.[28] When Badeau asked to recuperate in Booth's rented home on 17th Street, Edwin replied: "My house is at your service & you know it. You will find it upside down as we are preparing to move into our new one on 19th St, but as you say you can put up with anything nowadays & can get about. Go there as soon as you can — Mother is there, and John will be on hand for a little while yet."[29] In 1893, shortly after Booth's death, Badeau claimed:

> I lay in hospital for many weeks, and he wrote me constantly. In July I was taken to New York and arrived just before the [draft] riots of that year. I was carried to Booth's house. He and his brother Wilkes bore me to Edwin's bed, which he gave up for me.... I remained at his house until it was possible to remove me to the country; both he and his brother dressed my wounds, and tended me with the greatest care. I saw much of him during the months of my convalescence.[30]

When Adam arrived in New York he did not initially stay at Edwin's home. He moved to Booth's house sometime after September 14, by which time Edwin was in Albany. The likelihood of Badeau being carried to bed by the Booth brothers is remote, although he referred to Edwin's nursing his wounds in a letter after Lincoln's assassination. Even after Booth's death Edwin was still Adam's romantic hero, carrying him to bed.[31]

Both Badeau and Booth bore emotional scars. Badeau's was the knowledge of human feelings he could not name and could discuss only in secret. When he told Booth about his feelings for "Left Arm" Wilson ("Do you understand Ned, that 'tis out of my confidence that I tell you this; ... I can't tell more than one or two in the world of it.") he probably came as close as he could to saying what he felt. He may not have known what to call his feelings; he may not have been sure of what they were, but he knew they were not something he could discuss in public.

Booth's scar was a sense of guilt about Mary Devlin, and following her death, he had no difficulty in discussing it; he wallowed publicly in his guilt, emphasizing how cold he had been to her: "Mary's love was too deep, too holy for such a selfish, beastly being as I.... I was ever cold, indifferent, and even have made her weep most bitterly when like a statue, I received her deep devotion."[32] Booth even realized that there was a link between the way he treated Adam Badeau and the way he had treated Mollie. He told Badeau: "You know too well what that coldness is—what you do not know is how hateful it renders myself unto myself.... She is gone and I am awakening to the appalling truth that I am a demon!"

What was Edwin Booth guilty about? What had he done to Mary Devlin to make her weep? Charlotte Cushman wrote to her niece Emma Crow Cushman: "Edwin Booth is not a gentlemen and to my mind has not more gentlemanly instincts, which would make him hesitate to hurt a woman or give her pain, than Mr. Edwin Forrest." She classified Booth among men "who would ... descend into being 'Masters' merely for the sake of ... showing their power over a weak woman." Cushman did not like men and probably did not know a lot about Booth's personal life, but Edwin himself provides a clue to his guilt in a letter written on May 21, 1863, to Lorimer Graham: "I, spoiled and fondled by the world from childhood, could not appreciate her devotion."[33]

The problem in the marriage between Mary Devlin and Edwin Booth was that an inexperienced woman in the lower ranks of her profession married an experienced man at the top of his—a man constantly admired, a man accustomed to being a sexual object, an icon worshipped by both men and women. Consequently when she worshipped him, it was nothing new; he was indifferent to her adoration; he loved her but not with the intensity with which she loved him. When she died, he felt guilty; the feeling of his own unworthiness which he had experienced prior to their marriage reasserted itself. He wanted reassurances that she was in heaven; he wanted her forgiveness.

Booth turned to spiritualism. A month after Mary's funeral, he wrote to Adam Badeau:

> I'll tell you what happened to me two nights before Mary left me. I was in New York, in bed; it was about two in the morning. I was awake; I felt a strange puff of air strike my right cheek twice.... I turned in bed, when I felt the same on the left cheek.... I distinctly heard these words, "Come to me, darling; I am almost frozen." When I was in the cars on my way thither, little dreaming that she was so seriously ill, I saw, every time I looked from the car window, Mary dead, with a white cloth tied around her head and chin.... I, who have ever laughed at such things, now feel mystified, and half believe that such things may be. Surely they can do no harm; for if Mary should come to me, I feel that my soul would become purified.[34]

Edwin began visiting mediums almost immediately after Mary's death. In the summer of 1863, he wrote to Badeau: "I have longed for a letter from Miss Edmonds on the subject [spiritualism], but have rec'd none."[35] "Miss Edmonds" was Laura Edmonds, a wealthy young woman and a spiritualist who had known Richard Cary, Mary Devlin and Edwin prior to Richard's and Mary's death. She had been an ardent fan even before Booth sought her professional help and described Booth's effect on her in the gushing language that Louisa Mae Alcott used. She was another of Edwin's bubbling tea kettles. She went to see *Hamlet* nine times and invited Booth to her home for "a good dose of raps [the manner in which Edmonds's spirits signaled their presence]."[36]

Booth turned to Edmonds and spiritualism looking for comfort from his guilt about Mary Devlin; Edmonds's letters, however, betray a deep concern for him, possibly an obsession, possibly love. Booth was having the same effect on her that he had on female members of his audience. She had begun to visit him privately at his home, and she wrote: "How much I've missed that face I won't say.... I shall hope soon to see you as long as it does not seem to you out of place — my going to you — and as it is a matter of anxiety to me I'll waive all ceremony."[37]

Booth liked Edmonds; Asia thought their relationship might go further, but Booth became skeptical about spiritualism and resumed his interest in other women. On September 13, 1864, a year-and-a half after Mary died, he wrote to Adam Badeau: "Miss Mason ... was in a stage box tonight ... and on Saturday was in front — she *is* pretty." By September 25, 1864, he was involved with a young Philadelphia woman named Blanche Hanel, and by April 1865, little more than two years after Mary's death, they were engaged.[38]

Chapter Eight

1863–1865: "If it goes a year, keep it up!"

Edwin Booth prepared for his later managerial career by operating theatres in Boston, Philadelphia and New York. Doing so was part of his mission to reform the American stage — a mission he had discussed with Mary Devlin and Richard Cary. To fulfill it Booth focused on the Boston Theatre, the Walnut Street in Philadelphia and particularly the Winter Garden in New York.

When he returned from England in 1862, he began work as an actor at the Winter Garden under the management of its leasee William Stuart and its manager "Black Jackson" and continued to perform there intermittently until March 23, 1867. He loathed Jackson and merely tolerated Stuart as a business necessity, but he lacked the managerial experience to run theatres by himself. Moreover, since he performed in all three venues he needed someone else to run day-by-day operations in each place. Booth remembered that in the fall of 1863:

> [John Sleeper] Clarke and I became "enthused" with the idea of establishing ourselves in the Metropolis as permanent stars in a theatre of our own. Our object was solely to elevate the tone of our art, without even ½ an eye to the dollar, for we well knew there was not "millions in it"; no, we would take our chances at making money outside of New York & be satisfied with the glory of the good work we would accomplish there. C[larke] & I talked excitedly with each other & to Stuart of our grand air-castle, at which the old foxy adventurer smacked his lips & encouraged us.... until at last he was "one of us."

Booth was writing after the New York theatre, of which he was the sole owner and manager, had failed, and his assertion that his "object was solely to elevate the tone of our art without even ½ an eye to the dollar" was prompted by the financial failure of that undertaking. In Booth's version Stuart had talked his way into the partnership of the Winter Garden, making Booth and Clarke believe he was "a sort of fixture in the lease ... and that he had such influence with the La Farge boys [the owners of the building] it would be an easy task to get rid of the 'd-d old Jew,' as the Irish-Israelite [Stuart] himself styled Jackson." Stuart called Jackson a "Jew"; Booth called Stuart an Irish Jew. Their mutual anti–Semitism reflects financial mistrust all around.[1]

On September 1, 1863, Stuart, Clarke and Booth signed an agreement to lease the Winter Garden theatre from September 1, 1864, until February 1, 1866. Each man had a one-third interest in the theatre. Stuart as manager, got an extra $70 a week and one benefit a year to devote himself full-time to the Winter Garden, and Clarke and Booth each got half of the nightly net profits, but only after the plays in which they appeared had paid back their production costs.[2]

When Booth reopened as Hamlet at the Winter Garden on September 21, 1863, he was still an employed actor under the management of Stuart and Jackson. The overall production was slipshod. The critic for *The New York Herald* wondered "Why should Ophelia be forced to wear crinoline when our fashionables are all leaving it off?" Booth received excellent reviews for his own interpretation. *The New York Clipper* noted that he "never mouths nor rants, nor makes faces, nor tears a passion to tatters."[3]

While Booth was performing in New York, the Walnut Theatre in Philadelphia was offered for sale, and by November 18, 1863, he and Clarke had decided to buy it, making him not only the future leasee of the Winter Garden but also part owner of the Walnut. Booth later remembered: "my popularity and reputation were such that I did not hesitate a moment to enter into what was then a mighty undertaking, $100,000 worth of theatre, feeling perfectly secure I alone could do it, & with Clarke's aid ... I 'went in' without fear."[4]

By November 1863 Booth, performing with a "disgusting" company in Boston, was "so racked with pains & aches & d-d bad temper, ... so lame" he could "scarcely walk," and "in such a bad humor from the pain" that he could "scarcely talk." He was determined not to return to the Winter Garden as an employed actor as long as Jackson was part of its management. He opened instead at Niblo's Gardens in New York on March 28, 1864, in Tom Taylor's *The Fool's Revenge*, a version of Hugo's *Le Roi s'Amuse*, now best known for its operatic version, *Rigoletto*.[5] The production was crude. The actor playing the Duke knew neither the text nor his cues. Rose Eytinge, who played Bertuccio's daughter Fiordilisa, recalled in 1905:

> In dressing *Fiordilisa* ... I designed a costume composed of satin and rare silver embroidery and diaphanous draperies.... I might more readily have been taken for the daughter ... of the reigning duke than for the child of the court fool. Being dressed (and truth to tell, feeling very well satisfied with my appearance), I went to the greenroom. Thither came Mr. Booth. When he saw me, he fell back aghast. I inquired the cause of his amazement. He told me I was far too richly dressed for the daughter of a man of his rank, and he explained to me that my dress should have been unobtrusive and of cheap material. I was overwhelmed with shame,—in fact was on the verge of tears,—when the dear, gracious fellow took me by both hands and turned me round about, and, with an amused glint in his eye, said: "Well! By jingo, the result of our blunder is so fine I think we'll have to let it stand."[6]

The problem that Eytinge's costume presented would not be solved until actors no longer had to provide their own stage clothing. *The Fool's Revenge*, however, proved to be a financial success, and although he had already performed it in Boston, Baltimore and Philadelphia, the New York run made the role of Bertuccio one of Booth's melodramatic staples.[7]

Back at the Winter Garden, Jackson suddenly retired into private life due to an unspecified "terrible domestic bereavement." His departure was the source of general theatrical glee. The *New-York Daily Tribune* referred to his managerial stint as "the worst management that ever crushed down the drama to the lowest depths of degradation." On April 4, 1864, five months before their contract actually began, Booth, Stuart and Clarke took over the management of the theatre.[8]

Booth wrote to Lawrence Barrett on May 25 that he and Clarke had agreed that Stuart was to have "all the management in his own hands" and that they would "not interfere in any way."[9] This freed Booth for another project—a performance of *Julius Caesar* in which he would play Brutus with his brothers John Wilkes and Junius Brutus Jr. as Antony and Cassius. What Booth thought would take "a week or two" actually took six months. During the summer of 1864 his brothers June and John went off to western Pennsylvania to look after their oil well investments, and the proposed production of *Julius Caesar* was postponed.[10]

At the same time that they were fitting up the Winter Garden, Booth and Clarke were attempting to turn the Walnut Street, which Booth considered "dirty & dingy," into "the prettiest theatre in America." In August 1864 he wrote to Launt Thompson: "We are fitting up our concern here, as well as the Winter Garden; we did hope to pay off $45,000 on our mortgage next October, but I fear our plans with S[tuart] and H[amlet] will keep us back.[11] His financial concerns proved unnecessary. He and Clarke were so successful that during their first year at the Walnut, they were able to raise $50,000 of their $80,000 mortgage and actually paid off the entire debt in three years.[12]

Booth's primary focus, however, was on the Winter Garden and particularly on the scenery, costumes and props for a production of *Hamlet*. He had essentially taken over all the theatre's managerial tasks, relegating Stuart to public relations with the press. On August 26, 1864, he wrote to Emma F. Cary (Richard Cary's widow): "I have been kept as busy as though I had been acting all this while, for it is my wish to 'bring out' several of the Shakespearean plays in a superior style, and the whole arrangements of the affairs is in my hands; I've been in the scene room & wardrobe night & day lately. Everything looks fair & prosperous for the coming season at the 'Winter Garden,' & when I begin (Oct 3rd) it is the wish of all concerned that I be 'kept at it' until next April — when I shall act in Boston."[13]

Booth, Stuart and Clarke formally opened their Winter Garden management on August 18, 1864. Their advertisement proclaimed the theatre "A CONSERVATORY OF ART devoted to the production of TRAGEDY AND COMEDY in the most perfect form and especially to the culture of an American Drama." It promised that Booth would appear that season in "one or more original parts expressly written for him," but in actuality the theatre initially featured John Sleeper Clarke in a round of comic characters.[14]

While Clarke was performing at the Winter Garden, Booth opened his own 1864–1865 season at the Walnut in Philadelphia on September 5. He wrote to Launt Thompson on September 16: "You have no idea how I suffer after playing (the hardest work in the world). I am ill, and fagged out from the effects of last night's bellowing as Richard. But it pays! I have cleared over two thousand dollars in these two weeks."[15]

Booth closed at the Walnut on October 1, and went on to his "regular work" at the Winter Garden, where he was having *Hamlet* "done up." He was planning a major revival in the historically accurate style of the English producer Charles Kean and was directing the production personally.[16] The production was postponed, however, partly because John Sleeper Clarke was doing good business at the Winter Garden and partly because of Edwin's health. Booth wrote to Emma Cary deprecating the coming production of *Julius Caesar* by comparing it to the work of the acrobatic Hanlon Brothers:

> I have been quite ill ... nor am I yet in a condition for work; but I must soon get at it for a long winter campaign. On Friday the 25th, *without fail*, the long-talked-of benefit "to Shakespeare" will take place at the Winter Garden, with the "Brothers Booth"—à la Hanlon—as the mainsprings, and beginning on the following night *Hamlet*, in a new dress ... will fret his brief hour every night until further notice.... For the last four weeks I've suffered terribly with headaches, and while I write, I feel ... "they have not buried me deep enough."... Every little noise seems to split my pate across.[17]

After playing 101 nights in an assortment of plays, Clarke closed at the Winter Garden on November 24, 1864, and the next day, Edwin and his brothers finally appeared together in *Julius Caesar* at the Winter Garden in a benefit for the erection of a statue to Shakespeare in Central Park. Their mother watched from a box. Ticket prices were high. The dress circle and parquette were $1.50, the family circle was a dollar, and orchestra chairs were five dollars each. Edwin wrote that "Tickets for the W. S. are going like hot cakes & wd. Have done so at $2 head."[18]

The benefit brought in $3,000. The occasion, however, was marred by a panic in the streets due to a possible attempt that night to set fires to three Broadway theatres, including the Winter Garden.[19] *The New York Clipper* described the chaos:

> When the curtain rose on the second act, a fire was discovered in one of the front rooms of the Lafarge Hotel, just over the entrance to the theatre. Almost in an instant, the firemen were on hand,

and several of them with hose in hand came rushing pell mell into the vestibule of the theatre, crying fire.... Women screamed and ran terrified from the dress circle.... We saw several magnificent dresses completely stripped from ladies, also bonnets and furs lying under the feet.... The police arrived and by main force compelled the audience to remain quiet.[20]

Following the Shakespearean benefit Booth opened as Hamlet and performed the role for a hundred nights, from November 28, 1864, until March 22, 1865, an unprecedented four-month run in the days when theatres used a revolving repertory. The reviews and public response were exceptionally positive. Booth's introspective Hamlet was already well known. What was particularly new and striking were elements of the scenery and staging. According to *The New-York Daily Tribune* the production used moveable 'tormentors,' or hinged wings at the front of the stage which, after the rising of the curtain, were pushed forward so as to enclose the scene. "Hitherto 'tormentors' had been painted in harmony with the decorations of the auditorium

Edwin Booth as Hamlet. "If Booth was Hamlet-like in his moodiness and prone to milk his tragic persona, his letters reveal a playfulness and a sharp wit far closer to the Hamlet of Act II than the nineteenth-century's ideal of an introspective, supersensitive, self-absorbed romantic prince."

and never changed from one end of the year to the other, so that the ridiculous spectacle [was] night after night ... presented of ladies and gentlemen entering a wood, a hut, an open landscape or what not through gilded ... doors. In *Hamlet*, at the Winter Garden, these wings [were] ... shifted with each change of scene." The effect was that of a modern box set.[21]

Edwin Booth as Hamlet (Act V costume). "I have been to see you personate Hamlet this evening. What a Hamlet! What a man: It is now three o'clock and I am still thinking of you."

The changing tormentors were part of fourteen sets used to illustrate the play in the pictorially realistic manner of Charles Kean. When Hamlet asks Polonius, "Do you see yonder cloud," traditionally actors had advanced to the footlights and placed the cloud in the galleries. Booth played the scene looking out a broad open window. Act III, scene i ("To be or not to be" followed by the "Nunnery" scene) was handsomely set is an audience chamber. Lucia Gilbert Calhoun recalled the staging four years later:

> A stately double staircase leads to a gallery, from which small doors open on the corridors without. In a deep embayed window Ophelia kneels— Hamlet is thus freed from the inconvenience of walking over her train without seeing her, which was part of the old order of things. From a low arched door beneath the stairway glides the Prince, his head bent, his hands clasped before him, his step slow and uncertain. He steadies himself by the balustrade, moves on again mechanically, is stopped by a chair, sinks into it — still silent, still utterly absorbed. In another moment ... "To be or not to be," is uttered in a voice almost inaudible.[22]

By December 10 the play was being advertised as "Booth's Hamlet," and *The New York Clipper* was reporting that "the house has been crowded nightly and even standing room has been known to bring a high figure." The ads on Christmas Eve read: "Come and Bring the Children." On December 31, *The New York Leader* advised its readers: "Not to have seen "Hamlet" at the Winter Garden is not to have seen the tragedy acted." In December 1864 the Winter Garden took in $19,633; only Niblo's Garden, which was playing the Irish and Yankee comedians Mr. and Mrs. Barney Williams, took in more. By January 11, 1865, *Richelieu* was ready, but *Hamlet* was too financially successful to withdraw. In February Stuart began to schedule Saturday matinees, still a novelty in Civil War–era America.[23]

The long run took its toll. Nineteenth-century actors were unaccustomed to long runs in one play. On January 14, 1865, the critic for *The New York Leader* pointed out that "the minor actors might be freshened up a little. Mrs. Wallack [Gertrude] seemed very tired the other evening, and the company imitated her ennui. Eventually even Booth became bored with the role and described its success as "terrible."[24]

Booth was pushed toward the hundredth performance by William Stuart. In a note written in 1874 to the manuscript of Winter's *Life and Art of Edwin Booth*, Booth remembered:

> The one-hundred night run was certainly due to Stuart, I was heartily sick and wearied of the monotonous work, and several times during it suggested a change of bill, for I felt that the incessant repetition was seriously affecting my acting as at that time I was unused to such a thing. But Stuart, wild with his wonderful success, would exclaim, "No, not at all my dear boy! Keep it up, keep it up! If it goes a year, keep it up!" And so we kept it up.[25]

Several months before *Hamlet* opened in New York, Booth had made plans to perform in Boston. After the New York run, he went to Philadelphia where the three-year-old Edwina was staying with his sister Asia and took her with him for what he thought would be a three-week season. He opened at the Boston Theatre on March 27 to a house with "every seat ... filled" and "all available standing-room ... occupied."[26] His hundred nights of Hamlet had made Edwin a national icon.

He would soon need the prestige. On Good Friday, April 14, 1865, Booth played a farewell benefit in Boston as Sir Edward Mortimer and Don Caesar de Bazan.[27] He was scheduled to play a farewell matinee as Hamlet the following day, but by then his brother had killed the president of the United States.

Chapter Nine

Edwin and John Wilkes Booth: "Life's too short to spend in grieving"

The Booths were always a disjointed, if not a dysfunctional, family, mainly because three of them — Junius Brutus Senior, Edwin and John — were stars. In the eighteenth century, before any significant number of American cities could support a resident company, actor families maintained cohesion by traveling and performing together. As American cities grew populous enough to support resident stock companies, some actors were able to play in one city at least for a season. Performers such as William Warren at the Boston Museum or Mrs. John Drew at Philadelphia's Arch Street Theatre even became prominent citizens of the towns in which they entertained. The comic actor and theatre manager John Blake Rice, for instance, was elected mayor of Chicago in 1865. After the Civil War, when touring "combination" companies (touring groups of actors performing one or more plays) replaced resident stock companies, actors had the benefit of each other's company for at least a thirty-six-week season. If they went out year after year, they could, as in the case of Joseph Jefferson, recreate the antebellum family troupes they remembered.

The Booths fell somewhere in between. Although Edwin traveled with his father as a boy, he never belonged to a family company. Female members of the family did not appear on stage. June occasionally performed with his father in 1839, 1845 and 1846; Junius Brutus Senior toured with June and Edwin for nine weeks in California; June employed his younger brother Edwin sporadically between 1852 and 1856; and Joe spent a season touring with Edwin in 1859–1860, much the way Edwin had toured with his father in 1849. John appeared with Edwin only three times, and all three of the Booth brothers, June, Edwin and John, performed together for one night only.

In the nineteenth-century theatre, the family that played together stayed together. The Booths were often apart because they were neither a stock nor a traveling company. They were individual stars, and they traveled alone, accompanied occasionally by a valet, manager or family member, or, in the case of Junius Brutus Senior, a necessary chaperone.

Mary Ann, Rosalie and Joe lived together for forty-five years in what Edwin described as "the Booth lunatic asylum," but Edwin and John saw each other only intermittently. Consequently when Edwin turned out to have a brother who was a presidential assassin, he could easily deny having known him well. On July 28, 1881, sixteen years after the assassination, Booth wrote to the autograph collector Nahum Capen, who had requested information about John:

> I can give you very little information regarding my brother John. I seldom saw him since his early boyhood in Baltimore. He was a rattle-pated fellow, filled with Quixotic notions. While at the farm

in Maryland, he would charge on horseback through the woods, "spouting" heroic speeches with a lance in his hand, a relic of the Mexican war, given to father by some soldier who had served under Taylor. We regarded him as a good-hearted, harmless, though wild-brained boy and used to laugh at his patriotic froth whenever secession was discussed. That he was insane on that one point, no one who knew him well can doubt. When I told him that I had voted for Lincoln's reelection, he expressed deep regret, and declared his belief that Lincoln would be made king of America; and this, I believe, drove him beyond the limits of reason. I asked him once why he did not join the Confederate army. To which he replied: "I promised mother I would keep out of the quarrel, if possible, and I am sorry that I said so." Knowing my sentiments, he avoided me, rarely visiting my house, except to see his mother, when political topics were not touched upon, at least in my presence. He was of a gentle, loving disposition, very boyish and full of fun—his mother's darling,— and his deed and death crushed her spirit. He possessed rare dramatic talent and would have made a brilliant mark in the theatrical world. This is positively all that I know about him, having left him a mere school-boy when I went with my father to California in 1852. On my return in '56, we were separated by professional engagements, which kept him mostly in the South, while I was employed in the Eastern and Northern states.... All his theatrical friends speak of him as a poor, crazy boy, and such his family think him.[1]

Booth's letter exemplifies the legend he created about his relationship to his brother and is, with its appeal to his father's and his own patriotic associations, patently self-serving. Some of it is true, but its basic disclaimer is false. John and Edwin spent their childhood together, shared the same professional life, were in touch by mail and, as adults, lived together for months at a time. Edwin knew nothing about the plot against Abraham Lincoln, but he certainly knew John.[2]

Booth was five years old when John was born in 1838, and assuming that he began traveling with his father in 1847, the two boys spent nine years of their childhood together. John was fourteen when Edwin left for California; they were then separated for four years, and, by the time he returned, John was already touring. Their professional paths, however, crossed. In Baltimore, on August 27 and in Richmond on October 1 and 9, 1858, and April 22 and 27, 1859, John played "seconds" to his brother—Richmond to Edwin's Richard III and Horatio to his Hamlet. On May 2, 1859, they were on far more equal footing, with Edwin playing Iago to his brother's Othello at John's Richmond benefit.[3]

Their fraternal bond also reasserted itself when Edwin returned from California. Edwin spent the summer of 1857 on the Bel Air farm and the summer of 1858 at the family home in Baltimore, and it is possible that John spent time with him. John's letters to Edwin were caring: "How are you getting along. I had hoped to hear from you before this.... God bless you, write soon. And believe me I am ever your affectionate brother." John may have visited Edwin during the latter's Boston engagement in May 1861. On January 29, 1863, when Edwin and Mary were living in Dorchester, and John was performing in Boston, Mary Ann Booth wrote to Edwin: "I have had several letters from Wilkes and he tells me he has seen you often." John was one of the two witnesses at Edwin's wedding and one of the mourners at Mary Devlin Booth's funeral. At the time of the funeral, June was still in California; Asia disapproved of Mary, and Joe had run away. John was the brother who came to celebrate and grieve.[4]

The two brothers played the same roles—Claude Melnotte, Richard III, Shylock, Raphael, Petruchio, Hamlet, Pescara, Macbeth, The Stranger, Romeo, Charles de Moor in *The Robbers*, Iago and Othello, all part of the stock in trade they had inherited from their father. They also faced the same problems. Both were negligent about the memorization of lines. Edwin wrote to June on December 12, 1858: "John is getting along well in Richmond Va. the folks know him there and like him—He'll make a good actor, but he says he's not comfortable—he don't like the study." Both were criticized for unclear enunciation, and both were physically slight men attempting heroic roles. As the *Indianapolis Gazette* of January 7, 1863, said of John: "his physique, perhaps would not serve as a model for a fighting gladiator." Yet both were often praised for onstage beauty and athleticism and were popular with female members of the audience because of their physical attractiveness. After having seen John in *The Corsican Brothers*, Mary Devlin wrote to Edwin: "The combat was strictly 'gladitorial'—the muscles of his arms—for his sleeves were rolled up—eclipsing everything else besides. 'Look at his arm'—every one exclaimed—& highly delighted the audience seemed at this exhibition." Over-billed by managers anxious to promote them as their father's artistic heirs, both made a great deal of money as actors, and both hated the travel necessitated by being a star. Edwin wrote to Lawrence Barrett: "Storming about the county is sad work—a home is better; my brother John—successful as he was—is sick of it & is determined to go into the stock & there make a stand."[5]

John was ambivalent about his professional relationship to Edwin. In part he traded on Edwin's success, just as both men traded on their father's reputation. Writing to Edwin about his 1858 stock experience in Richmond, John objected to the fact that "everyone knows me already. I have heard my name—Booth—called for one or two nights, and on account of the *likeness* the papers deigned to mention me."[6] Edwin, on the other hand, admired John's work on stage. Even after the assassination, when he denied knowing his brother, he lauded him as a potentially great actor. On January 21, 1863, he and Mary went to the theatre in Boston to see John perform, and the next day, Edwin, forgetting their 1858 and 1859 performances together, wrote:

John Wilkes Booth. "I saw last night—for the first time—my brother act; he played Pescara—a bloody villain of the deepest red you know, an ***admiral*** of the red ... and he presented him—not underdone but rare enough for the most fastidious 'beef-eater.'"

I saw last night—for the first time—my brother act; he played Pescara—a bloody villain of the deepest red you know, an *admiral* of the red ... and he presented him—not underdone but rare enough for the most fastidious "beef-eater." ... I am happy to state that he is full of the true grit—he has stuff enough in him to make good suits for a dozen such player-folk as we are cursed with; and when time and study round his rough edges, he'll bid them all "stand apart," "like a bully boy, with a glass eye"; I am delighted with him & feel the name of Booth to be more of a hydra than snakes and things ever was.[7]

That Edwin and John's political differences caused a deep rift is doubtful. Secession was an issue on which they disagreed and avoided discussing. Edwin was not a political animal. He voted for Lincoln in 1860, when he was twenty-seven years old, but it was the first time he ever voted, and there is no evidence that he ever voted again. He was vehemently opposed to the South, writing to Adam Badeau: "Send me Jeff Davis' head & I'll play for your benefit." He had, however, no intention of enlisting and counted on his "rheumatic shinbones" to "save" him from the draft. When Booth was depressed after Mary's death, Adam Badeau, hoping perhaps that they

Nine. Edwin and John Wilkes Booth: "Life's too short to spend in grieving"

could be together, urged him to enter the army as an officer. Edwin's reaction was: "Poor fellow! He amuses me." Moreover, John's allegiance to the confederacy was not strange to the Booths, who were, as Edwin admitted, "Southern-born." Maryland was in Union territory, but it was a border state below the Mason-Dixon line and filled with southern sympathizers.[8]

Edwin also had no interest in emancipation; there is no reason to think that he favored slavery, but his attitude toward people of color was, at best, ambivalent. He gave money toward the "elevation of ... down-trodden people (the Negro)," and he showed paternalistic concern for the African Americans in his employ, particularly a "yellow gal" named Betty Smith.[9] Mrs. Charles Calvert, a member of Booth's company in 1881–1882, recalled that Betty Smith

> whilst at Philadelphia, suffered from a "raging tooth," and Booth, knowing it would be difficult to extract, placed a $10 bill in her hand and told her to go to one of the first-class dentists. She returned at the end of four hours. She had been to five of the most skilful men, who all declined to help her on account of her race. One of them said, in a kindly tone, "I am really very sorry for you, but you see, if by any chance it was known that my instruments had touched a coloured woman, I should lose the whole of my practice." Booth added, "And this is Philadelphia, Mrs. Calvert. The City of Brotherly Love. The City that during the war was amongst the loudest to proclaim the equality of the couloured race!"[10]

Writing in 1911, Mrs. Calvert remembered Booth inveighing against hypocrisy, but Booth's generosity probably had a practical side. With her "raging tooth" cured, Betty was presumably a better employee. Moreover, his own letters betray a racial prejudice that went back to his childhood and was so deeply imbedded in him as a nineteenth-century man that he had no sense of it.

> I asked my sister, Rose, the other day—at L[ong] Branch, if father ever owned a slave.... She said "No—father bought a woman servant, because he could not hire an obedient one, but as she threatened to beat Mother's brains out with a fence-rail, he gave her free papers three days after purchase & sent her away." Then he afterwards 'leased' for ten years a black girl named Hagar who asked him at the end of 3 to set her free from lease, wh. he did—on the promise to return to her owner, Judge Bond of Harford Co. Of course, she didn't go back & father had to pay for her. A rabid Republican or Democrat rather, my father could not hold slaves.[11]

Edwin was proud that his father never owned slaves but only rented them. What he found distressing was that the slaves were disobedient or violent or simply ran away. The black people Edwin knew as a boy were servants; they probably were the only black people he ever knew, and when they did not serve appropriately, the word that sprang to his lips was "nigger." "It is 12½ o'clock and d–nigger has forgot my supper—I'm hungry as the devil too." When an African American waiter welcomed him back to a hotel and asked about his daughter, Booth, forced to be polite in public, seethed in private: "The buck dark head waiter here welcomed me with a hearty shake of the hand & kind inquiries after [Edwina]. Fraternal fiend."[12]

Booth could be generous toward individual black people, but he tended to see African Americans as minstrel show caricatures, "darks" who "howled with fun."[13] He played and sang minstrel songs as a boy and loved Negro-dialect jokes:

> A darkey praying for God to "he'p dis de nigger—don't sen' yer son, come right down yerself—for dis 'ant no chiles' play!" ... A busted balloon fell & scattered a cotton-field of darks, who thought God had come down among them. One old rheumatic couldn't get away & thought he'd make the best of the situation, so, slouching up to the balloonist, he remarked: "Good mornin' Massa Jesus! How's yo Pa?"[14]

In 1876, touring the South for the first time in seventeen years, he found "reception grand! Balmy Summer weather here" but lamented that there was "Little money, I fear, but much nigger." He described Savannah on February 12, 1876, as having "streets lined with beautiful trees (and ugly darkies)," and he found a cotton press "very interesting — not, however, to the little niggers who sometimes get mixed in the cotton (being of the same color, you know, it's difficult to distinguish <u>wool</u> from cotton) & get their little selves 'squished' out flat & thin as wafers; then they ain't little niggers any more."[15]

The possibility that Booth actually saw black children mangled by machinery is unlikely. His second wife was on the tour, and had she seen such a thing, she would have collapsed both emotionally and physically. Moreover he was writing to his fifteen-year old daughter whom he also regaled with stories of the uneducated information about Mammoth Cave provided by their guide — "a bright young colored chap." The story about "little niggers" getting "'squished' out flat" was Booth's version of an amusing story to tell a teenager.[16] In his attitude toward black people as well as in his casual anti–Semitism, Booth was simply a nineteenth-century man.

The differences between Edwin and his brother John were not about slavery but about secession and even more about personal behavior. The Booths were actors; they were expected to perform. After the assassination, June wrote of John: "Knowing his sympathy for the South, I was very much afraid he might go over the lines and I begged of him not to be so foolish. I told him to follow his profession."[17] The family's disapproval of John was not about what he believed but about what he did. He stopped acting.

According to his sister Asia, John was "crazy or enthusiastic about going for a [soldier]. I think he will get off. It has been his dearest ambition, perhaps it is his true vocation." Asia was right. On November 11, 1859, John joined the Richmond Greys, the Virginia militia, to guard the captured John Brown. He marched to Charleston on November 19 and actually watched as the old abolitionist was hanged on December 2, 1859. Edwin disapproved of John's enlistment, and Mary wrote to him: "Your news regarding the mad step, John has taken — I confess did not surprise me — if you remember, I told you I thought he would seize the opportunity. 'Tis a great pity he has not more sense — but time will teach him — although I fear the discipline is hardly severe enough to sicken him immediately with a 'soldier's life.'" On December 28, 1859, she continued to "grieve for John's trouble — foolish boy what can he be thinking of — talk to him Edwin seriously, ere he destroys his youth."[18] Apparently Edwin was not only in contact with John but also, in Mary's mind, had some influence over him.

While the two brothers differed in their political views, Mary and Edwin remained cordial toward John throughout the Civil War. On February 28, 1862, while in London, Mary wrote Edwin: "I must write a congratulatory letter to John — and in it say what <u>I think</u> of his kindness etc." Given Mary's perpetual deference to Edwin, the emphasis on <u>I think</u> may have served to separate her feelings from his, although it is doubtful that Mary would ever have written to anyone of whom Edwin disapproved. The "kindness" referred to was financial. While in England the Booths ran short of money, and Edwin wrote to June, still in California, asking him to repay a two-thousand-dollar loan. June, however, had invested Edwin's loan unwisely in a mining speculation, and it was John who "sent the money ... needed."[19]

When they returned from England, Edwin took Mary to see his brother perform. In the spring of 1863, after Mary's death, with the Civil War raging, John wrote to his business partner Joseph H. Simonds: "When did you see Ned. Love to him and Mother."[20] After Mary's death, Edwin even considered living with John: "Mary being in heaven, I am thrown back to my filial duty to provide a home for my mother who has not had one since my father died. Once settled there may be some comfort for her in having her children about her, for it will be a home for John and mother and my other brothers, should they return."[21]

When Edwin was looking for a house, he assumed "my brother will help me out in such an undertaking, and I ought to have something to leave behind when I go, besides my combat swords and soldier clothes." He was well aware that June was not in good financial shape, and Joe was a bohemian wastrel. The family member he could count on financially was John. John was also one of numerous family members and friends who stayed at the house that Edwin rented at 107 East 17th Street and later at the one he purchased at 28 East 19th Street. Just before he was to open in *Hamlet*, Booth wrote to Adam Badeau: "J. Wilkes is ...on the sofa at this junction in tother room, as I've spent all my money for a dining room carpet." Edwin may not have had a bed for him, but John still had a place in his home.[22]

Edwin had no compunction about telling Badeau, a wounded Union officer, that John would be occupying the house while Badeau recovered there. In 1893, shortly after Booth's death, Badeau claimed:

> I remained at his house until it was possible to remove me to the country; both he [Edwin] and his brother dressed my wounds, and tended me with the greatest care. I saw much of him during the months of my convalescence, and early in 1865, when I was again taken to New York after an attack of camp fever; Wilkes Booth was once more at his brother's house. He was excessively handsome, even physically finer than Edwin, but less intellectual in his manliness.... Under Edwin's roof I thought him very captivating.[23]

Whether or not John actually dressed Adam's wounds, Adam's reminiscence indicates that Edwin and his brother were living together at least on an intermittent basis. When Badeau recuperated and returned to the front, Edwin, still in mourning for Mary, wrote him:

> [John Sleeper] Clarke came the day or the day after your departure and has been telling stories & talking business all day & night; John Booth also has disturbed my equanimity by his "love ditties," some of which you heard, and hair-breadth 'scapes in dark passages with "the most beautiful creations in the world, upon my sacred honor" &c. &c. &c. All very charming to hot-blooded youth, but ...disgusting to one in my condition.[24]

While the Booths were aware of John's pro–Southern sympathies, he was not the bad boy of the family. That distinction went to Joe. Joe, the untalented Booth who wound up in the box office, consistently got his family's attention by misbehavior. He had been studying medicine in New York, but in March 1862 enlisted in the navy and disappeared. On April 8, 1862, Booth wrote to Badeau from Paris: "I have [learned] the painful news of my brother Joe's sudden & mysterious departure from his home — leaving a few lines to inform his mother that he had enlisted; he was the pet of the whole family, and particularly mine — it pains me very much! We can find no trace of him." That he was Edwin's pet is doubtful; Edwin supported him and had found him jobs in the theatre, but his other letters disparaged Joe, and in later life the relationship between the two brothers was so bad that Edwin consistently referred to Joe as a lunatic.[25]

Joe visited England and subsequently shipped out for Australia. On October 20, 1862, Junius, still in California, wrote to Edwin:

> Joe seems an enigma, but I think I can guess him. I would not say so to Mother but I am afraid he is not sound in mind. His insane manner of enlisting & subsequent conduct in Engl[d] & his departure for Aus[a]— seem to point that way, mind I do not say positive insanity but a crack that way, which Father in his highest moments had to [sic] which I fear runs more or less thro' the male portion of our family myself included.... Asia seems to think that you are angry with Joe, but I could not detect any thing of the kind in your letter — I am sorry that you and Asia are not on more loving terms — but I fear Asia has a little of the family taint — which I hope time may cure — & John who was to be my constant correspondent, wrote one letter & there stopped.[26]

The spring and summer of 1864 was the first time since 1856 that most of the Booths were together. Joe was still gone, but June and his daughter Marion (later called Marie) left California on April 23, 1864, and arrived in New York on May 16, finding "Edwin at home, just finished at the Winter Garden." Between April and August, various members of the family, including John, congregated in New York, Boston and New London, where they visited William Stuart's seaside house. John wrote letters from the 19th Street address between June 9 and July 24, 1864.[27]

In a statement written after the assassination and designed to emphasize the difference of political views between John and the rest of the Booth family, June asserted that Edwin and John Sleeper Clarke "would not argue with" John "for they considered him a monomaniac on the subject & not worth arguing with.... About this time the latter part of August, he had a severe family quarrel on politics after that politics was never allowed in the house — I and Edwin went to Phila on the 1st of Sept [1864] & John Booth went to Canada so said to play an eng^t [engagement]."[28]

June's chronology was misleading. The quarrel took place between August 2 and 7, 1864, when Clarke, John Wilkes and Edwin left for Philadelphia. No matter how severe the argument, Edwin and John and John Sleeper traveled together and began living at Clarke's Philadelphia home with their mother and Edwina. In Philadelphia John was ill for three weeks with erysipelas in his right elbow. Edwin wrote: "Dear mother is happy with her children about her, thank God! but she still has an absent one, the youngest boy — strange, wild and very moving; he causes us all some degree of anxiety."[29]

On November 28 Edwin began what would be his historic one hundred nights of *Hamlet*. The same day the three brothers "stood for characters in JC to be painted." Edwin stayed in New York. Junius went to Boston, to appear at the Howard Athenaeum, and John, his "neck bad with boils" went to Washington.[30]

Perhaps more than their political division, the issue of money caused dissension between Edwin and John. Edwin had come to think of his mother, Rose, Joseph and John as dependent on him financially, and the idea rankled John, who, after all, had sent Edwin and Mary Devlin money when they were in England. On January 17, 1865, he wrote to June from Washington D. C. where he was about to play Romeo[31]:

> Dear brother you must not think me childish when I say that the *old* feeling roused by our loving brother has not yet died out. I assume *he thinks* I *live upon him.* And it's only for dear Mother that I have gone there at all when in New York and as I cannot live in that city without living at home. And for this reason I would be home all the time, I thought it best not to be in the city at all. And as I like *this place next,* and my business at present calls me here, I thought I would here make my stand.[32]

The "business" referred to may have been something other than acting, although John continued to work in the theatre. June contended in his statement that in early February 1865 he "went to Washington & was informed that" John had played one night in borrowed dress." When he "questioned him about not wearing his own," John "said he had left his wardrobe in Canada":

> He confessed that after the quarrel alluded to in August [1864] that he went to Canada & shipped his wardrobe to the South to play there for the future — that he had disposed of most of his property in gifts, for he did not mean to take anything he had made in the North but to go there & act.... but that the vessel had been sunk by a gunboat and his wardrobe was lost — so he had now given up the idea of going south.... as he had no wardrobe he could not act.... I was thankful that his wardrobe was lost & hoped that he had given up all thoughts of going south. — he assured me he had.

The next day June "left for Philadelphia and did not see John again until about Feb. 11 [1865] when he stopped in Phila. for one day — & left for NY" where he saw him ... on the 14th [February 14, 1865] as [June] passed through the city on [his] way to Boston." Thus John had the opportunity to see Edwin play *Hamlet,* although it is not certain that he took that opportunity. If the two brothers saw each other at this time, it was likely their last encounter.[33]

John "took his stand" on the evening of Good Friday, April 14, 1865. The news reached Edwin in Boston that his brother had assassinated Abraham Lincoln during a performance of *Our American Cousin* at Ford's Theatre in Washington. According to Lillian Aldrich, Booth learned of the assassination through a black servant who entered his bedroom early the next morning and said: "Oh Massa Edwin ... you never could guess what has happened! Somethin' dreadful! The President has been shot. And oh Massa Edwin, I am afraid Massa John has done it." The story is apocryphal. Aldrich was not in Boston at the time, and the servant's lines have a minstrel-show quality. Moreover there is no evidence that Booth ever traveled at the time with a black servant, and it is unlikely that a waiter in the hotel would refer to him as "Massa."[34] John Thompson, a stenographer, claimed in 1877, that on the night of the assassination, Booth was attending

> a sort of little supper .... at the Parker House, Boston in room 70.... We were having a good time, and I suppose it was half-past twelve when Ned Booth rose with a glass of champagne in his hands to give a toast. He was just raising the glass to speak, when the door opened, and a boy came in with a telegram he handed Booth. He took it, and saying, "Excuse me a moment," he put down the glass and opened the envelope. As he read his face turned white, and uttering, "My God!" he sank down with his head on the table, and wept. The telegram fell on the floor and was picked up and read aloud. It said that John Wilkes Booth had shot Abraham Lincoln at Ford's Theatre that night.[35]

Despite its melodramatic tone, Thompson's version is a possibility. The assassination occurred at approximately 10:15 P.M. There would have been time for a telegram to reach Booth at a post-show supper. News reached others in Boston before the next morning. By 7 A.M., Henry C. Jarrett, manager of the Boston Theatre, had written Booth of his intention to "close the Boston Theatre until further notice" and asked him "Please signify to me your cooperation in this matter." In return Booth published a letter thanking Jarrett for "relieving" him of "his engagements." During the afternoon a detective searched Booth's trunks and correspondence and published a letter in the Boston *Evening Transcript* exonerating Edwin of any "knowledge that such an act was contemplated." Booth retired from the stage for six months and wrote an abject public apology. He never performed in Washington again.[36]

The assassination had a short-lived but devastating effect on the American theatre. *The New York Clipper* reported: "Everything has been deranged by the atrocious crime, engagements broken, time curtailed, entertainments postponed, speculations ruined, hopes deferred and aspiration nipped in the bud." Members of the theatrical profession met in New York and Baltimore on April 17 and in Washington and Philadelphia on April 21 and drafted a letter of condolence. With two exceptions, New York theatres remained closed until after the funeral on April 19.[37]

In New York, Launt Thompson visited Booth's mother in New York to find Rose "all alone— waiting for some definite information." Mary Ann had gone to Philadelphia to be with her five-month-pregnant daughter Asia. On April 16, Judge John B. Murray, upon consultation with Louis L. Delafield, a prominent New York lawyer, wrote to Edwin: "We have decided that it is best for you to remain for the present in Boston and in a few days when you are composed and your mind more tranquil, you may feel it to be better to come to your own home in New York." Murray's letter arrived too late. Booth had already left that day for New York.[38]

Friends and strangers came to Booth's defense. On April 17, 1865, the Boston *Transcript* published a letter from the Rev. George H. Hepworth stating that Booth had cast the only vote of his life "last November for Mr. Lincoln." On April 18, 1865, a similar letter from Judge J. W. Edmonds, Laura Edmonds' father, testified to Edwin's "unwavering loyalty" and praised his "keen sympathy with the cause of emancipation" and his "high regard for the lamented Lincoln." On April 21 Henry C. Jarrett did the same, and Emma Cary published excerpts from his letters to her brother Richard in the *Boston Evening Transcript*. Her brother-in-law Louis John Rudolphe Agassiz, the Swiss-born naturalist who served as professor of zoology and geology at the Lawrence Scientific School in Cambridge, Massachusetts, and was past president of the American Scientific Association, publicly endorsed Booth. Launt Thompson organized a group to write a condolence letter expressing their friendship to him. It was signed by Jervis McEntee, McEntee's brother-in-law, the landscape architect Calvert Vaux, Thomas Bailey Aldrich, Thompson and nine others. People hesitant to have their names linked with the assassination sent Booth anonymous letters signed "Justice," or "One of your party" or simply signed with their initials. Looking at a landscape entitled "The Coming Storm," owned by Booth and exhibited that month at the National Academy of Design, Herman Melville wrote: "All feeling hearts must feel for him." There were, however, also letters suggesting that Booth change his name and that Secretary Stanton take him into military custody.[39]

On April 29, *The New York Clipper* reminded its readers of Edwin and June's loyalty and promulgated a story of Booth saving the life of Lincoln's son Robert:

> The Union cause has had no stronger nor more generous supporter than Mr. Edwin Booth.... Not a month since Mr.... Booth was proceeding to Washington. At Trenton there was a general scramble to reach the cars which had started, leaving many behind in the refreshment saloon. Mr. Booth was proceeded by a gentleman whose foot slipped as he was stepping upon the platform, and who would have fallen at once beneath the wheels had not Mr. Edwin Booth's arm sustained him. The gentleman remarked that he had had a narrow escape of his life, and was thankful to his preserver. It was Robert Lincoln.... In some way the incident came to the knowledge of Lieut. Gen. Grant who at once wrote a civil letter to Mr. Edwin Booth and said that if he could serve him at any time he would be glad to do so. Mr. Booth replied, playfully, that when he (Grant) was in Richmond he would like to play for him there.[40]

Booth needed friends, even long-lost ones, and searched them out. On June 13, 1865, David C. Anderson wrote from San Francisco. He had not heard from Edwin in five years, but his response helped to cement their friendship for the rest of Anderson's life.

> After a silence of nearly five years to hear from you, and in such melancholy times makes my old heart ache.... The world does not condemn you or yours for the crime of another; on the contrary, they deeply sympathize with you in your affliction. There is not a day passes but I meet sundry friends of yours and June's, who seem to take a lively interest in your future.—They say "you must not think of abandoning your profession, you belong to the people, the American people—and they will not allow you to seclude yourself from them."[41]

On April 16 Booth wrote to Adam Badeau, by then a lieutenant colonel serving as Ulysses S. Grant's military secretary, and presumably in a position to provide meaningful support. (Edwina called him "Laftan"; Joseph Booth described him as Grant's "segar-holder"). It may have been a dreadfully embarrassing task. Booth began by saying "it has been so long a time since I last wrote you." He admitted to Badeau that he had found John "loveable" and that all the family had found "a source of joy in his boyish and fighting nature."

> Poor mother. I go to New York today expecting to find her either dead or dying.... Abraham Lincoln was my president for in pure admiration of his noble career and Christian principle I owe what I never did before, I <u>voted</u> and for <u>him</u>. I was two days ago one of the happiest men alive. Grant's magnificent work accomplished, the devils defeated and sweet Peace turning her radiant face upon our country. Now what am I? Oh, how little did I dream my when on Friday, I was, as Sir Edward Mortimer, exclaiming, "where is my honor now? Mountains of shame are piled upon me" that I was not acting but uttering the fearful truth. I have a great deal to tell you of myself and the beautiful plans I had for the future, all blasted now but must wait until my mind is more settled. I am half crazy now.[42]

Badeau replied on April 19. His letter, intended to comfort Edwin, was cagey. He was an army officer and secretary to the most prominent general in the Union army, and he had also known and possibly lived with a presidential assassin. He had to make it clear to whoever might see the letter that he had no knowledge of John's political affiliations.

> I have not written to you before because I was trying to hope that it was not true. Need I tell you now how I feel for you to whom this terrible blow is more terrible than to any man in this nation. I

cannot understand it. Your brother never in any hearing spoke a word that seemed like sympathy with the rebellion. Try dear Ned and bear up under this overwhelming calamity. I need not tell you that I feel for you still the same regard as ever. Try and be a man; and you have a consolation in the thoughts of another world where your comforter awaits you, and where sufferings and calamities will all be past — Once more dear Ned, my heart bleeds for you.[43]

That John had "never in any hearing spoke a word that seemed like sympathy with the rebellion" is doubtful, although he may have been as careful around Badeau as Badeau was now being with Edwin. The letter is sympathetic enough, although the irony of Badeau telling Booth to "be a man" may not have been lost on either party. The relationship between the two men was coming, if not to an end, to a hiatus. Badeau was making a career for himself in the military, and it is possible that being infatuated with the brother of a presidential assassin was an embarrassment to him. By October 23, 1866, in a letter to Booth, Adam, who still owed Booth money, no longer had expectations about Edwin's affection. On February 12, 1869, Booth wrote: "though Ad & I are not so intimate as we were — I have not in my heart one unkind impulse. Events have changed & separated us — but I daresay we will all meet at the other end after the journey's done."[44]

Edwin was surrounded by supporters, but other members of the Booth family, not to mention anyone even tangentially connected with the assassination, were far less fortunate. The investigating court, under H. L. Burnett, its judge advocate, cast its net wide. Between April 14 and May 9 fifty-nine people were arrested, many simply for "expressing satisfaction at the murder of the president." Actors' costumes, underwear, dressing cases, prompt books and property books were confiscated. Laura Keene, who was performing before Lincoln the night he was killed, was detained in Harrisburg, Pennsylvania. The wardrobe manager of Ford's Theatre was arrested, as were Junius' step-daughter Blanche DeBar and her uncle Ben.[45]

At the time of the assassination June was performing at Pike's Opera House in Cincinnati. His diary reads: "played eng[agement] up to date, this morn news came of the death of the President & John's deed last night in Washington The excitement was so great that I remained in the Hotel till the night of Monday the 17th." June "left for home" at 10 P.M. on the 17th and arrived in Philadelphia at noon on the 19th. He informed the U.S. Marshall of his presence and on the 23rd, recorded in his diary: "read a false ac^t [account] of the letter I wrote to John from Cin^{ti} on the 12th. On April 25, on the basis of this "newspaper report," he was arrested at Asia's home, "placed in a close carriage, ... driven to the Baltimore depot and taken on the first train to Washington" where he was jailed in the Carroll Prison.[46]

John Ford, owner of the theatre in which Lincoln was shot, was arrested on April 18, as were his two brothers, one of them, H. Clay Ford, having accidentally left a knife in the presidential box while arranging it for the evening. John Ford's mail was censored, and he was not allowed to see his wife and children.[47] He later wrote a description of the conditions under which the prisoners lived:

> I was consigned to a barred and locked garret room in the Carroll Prison in Wash$\underline{n}$. The room contained a bag of straw and some dark blankets and their usual accompaniments. No chair, table or convenience whatever save a slop bucket and a stone pitcher. When I wrote — I did so on the floor & when I wanted to sit down the straw was the only accommodation.[48]

On April 19, Booth's brother-in-law, John Sleeper Clarke, brought to Marshall Millward of Philadelphia a sealed envelope that John Booth had addressed to himself and left with Clarke in November 1864. It contained United States bonds, oil stocks and a letter denouncing Lincoln and indicating his intention of kidnapping the president. Burnett ordered his arrest on April 26, and the next day Clarke was arrested and confined in the same prison as June and the Fords. Ford recorded that Clarke was "brought in, kept like a malefactor in a small room & on prison fare, forbid to speak to any one or see a paper." The Clarke home on 18th and Summer Streets in Philadelphia was searched from top to bottom. Although he was later released, Clarke never forgot his arrest, and the fact that he was hauled into jail while Edwin was not touched rankled for years. When Edwin was shot at in 1879 Clarke complained that "the ... Booths ... get all the notoriety without <u>suffering!!</u> for it ... Look at <u>me</u> I was dragged to jail by the neck—literally <u>dragged</u> to prison—and Edwin goes scot-free gets all the fame—sympathy—who thinks of what <u>I</u> endured."[49]

John Wilkes Booth was killed at Garrett's farm near Port Royal on the Rappahannock River on April 26, 1865, twelve days after the assassination. According to Lillian Bailey Aldrich, his mother had been called to Philadelphia because her pregnant daughter Asia was "seriously ill." Accompanied by Thomas Bailey Aldrich, Mary Ann started for the ferry boat that would take her to Jersey City, where she was to catch the train for Philadelphia.[50] On April 27, 1865, Booth, in New York, wrote to Mrs. John B. Murray:

> At last the terrible end is know [sic]—fearful as it is it is notwithstanding a blessed relief. Poor Mother was telegraphed for & started in the 11.½ train—learning the news of her boy's fate on the ferry boat. Junius' arrest on suspicion does not trouble me more than the alarm & the added disgrace (if there can be more than what is already heaped upon us) to our poor house.[51]

In early May the situation of Edwin's incarcerated family improved. On May 5, Clarke was put with June and they were "allowed to go into the yard." On May 5 June "wrote a statement of all I knew regarding John to Sec. E. Stanton. Sent out & got my meals from Ms. Whitney till the 1st of June." Suddenly, however, Joe resurfaced. Arriving on a steamer from California, he was arrested six miles "down the river," interrogated on May 12, and released, on bail, on May 14.[52] On May 11, 1865, Booth wrote to John B. Murray in scrawled pencil:

> My troubles will never cease. I have just learned that another of my brothers—Joseph—on his arrival this day has been arrested & is at 3⁰⁰ Mulberry S^t—the Hdq^{rs} of the police—I believe. I had no idea he was in this part of the world, and telegraphed yesterday to ascertain his whereabouts—thinking he was still in California somewhere. My first impulse was to go to you—then to Genl [John Adams] Dix—then to him, but have concluded to be quiet—for my turn may come sooner than I anticipate. When will this trouble leave me? I am at my wit's end & can think of nothing but the sea of misery that seems to be swallowing up everything connected with me. Pray pardon my pencil scratches—I could not use the pen so firmly—I am so anxious & disturbed.[53]

John Sleeper Clarke was released on May 26, but, although Burnett recommended June's release on June 2, he remained imprisoned until June 23.[54] On May 30, Booth visited him:

> I spent the day (yesterday) in Washington, and the greater part of it with my brother Junius—I dined with him—in his 'quarters' I was called for the defense—to prove that J. Wilkes had such power over the minds of others as would easily sway those with whom he associated, &c. &c; the idea is to set up a plea of insanity for [the accused members of the assassination plot] Herald [David E. Herald] or Paine [Payne was an alias for Lewis Thornton Powell]—or some of them. I told [William E.] Doster [the counsel for the accused] all I knew of John, and he concluded it w^d be as well not to call me. The Washington 'Star' had a description of me—stating I was there as a witness—I daresay the press all over the country will be filled with my 'arrest' and all sorts of awful things. I then left the court (after taking a good look at the criminals) and drove to C[arroll] Prison & stayed with June until 5 o'clk. I had all sorts of good words & Junius ... sh^d be speedily released &c.[55]

In contrast to his brothers June and Joseph, John Sleeper Clarke and the Ford brothers, Edwin was not arrested.[56] He was at one of the highest points in his career. The hundredth performance of Hamlet had occurred only three weeks before the assassination; he was a national icon, and at least his brother-in-law felt that the assassination had elicited sympathy for Edwin that helped his career.

Personally, however, he may not have been so lucky. At least a month before the assassination, Booth had become engaged to a woman named Blanche Hanel, whom he had met through his interest in spiritualism after Mary Devlin's death. Blanche came from a wealthy land-owning family in Philadelphia. Asia regarded her as a "fashionable flirt" but a "stickler for decorum." Word that Edwin was engaged had reached Elizabeth Stoddard, who did not know the lady's identity and wrote to her brother Wilson on March 16:

> Your news of Edwin's marriage is about as astounding as the rest. Is it Laura Edmonds or Maty Woodman? ... He will undoubtedly go to the devil sooner or later. All the elements that make up life are in his composition, except one — that of courage.... Think of Edwin's marrying again. I pity the woman, unless she has a dramatic genius superior to his and then she can overpower him. I shall be most curious to learn who the person is. His family will have to retire again.[57]

In light of the assassination, Edwin wrote a letter of relinquishment to Blanche in early May, but she apparently did not accept his offer to call off their engagement. On May 3, 1865, the Boston hostess Mrs. James T. Fields recorded in her diary that it was "all right between" Booth "and the lady he was about to marry.... Have seen a lady who knows the person to whom Booth is engaged — said that her letter telling him she was true passed his letter of relinquishment on its way to Philadelphia." On May 6, 1865, Booth wrote to Emma F. Cary: "All I do [know] of [Philadelphia] is that there is one great heart, firm and faster bound to me than ever. Sent in answer to dear Mary's prayers, I faithfully believe it; She will do what Mary struggled, suffered and died in doing."[58]

By May 21 Booth was in Philadelphia, staying with Asia. He may have chosen Philadelphia to be near Blanche. There were rumors that the engagement was off, but on May 22, 1865, Asia wrote to Jean Anderson: "The reports of Blanche and Edwin are without truth. Their marriage was not to have been till September and I don't think it will be postponed as that is a long way off yet. Edwin is here with me." On May 23, Booth wrote to John B. Murray: "I am where it is good for me to be, and where that which is gloomy cometh not. My blessed lady is most beautiful! My lady full of grace and goodness and great happiness at my increasing happiness for the future."[59]

Blanche's father, however, eventually objected to the engagement. Jervis McEntee wrote in his diary:

> Booth ... told me all about his engagement to Miss Harel [sic] of Philadelphia. When Wilkes shot the President, her father desired the engagement broken, but Booth immediately wrote her releasing her. She did not give him up, however, at once but when he next met her, she received him coldly and talked of her first duty being to her father &c and so it ended, luckily as he thinks for both.[60]

McEntee was writing fifteen years after the event. The break-up was not quite as sudden as he set it down, but by November 24, 1865, Blanche had broken her engagement, and Edwin, resigned to the fact, wrote to Emma F. Cary:

> My affairs are quite unsettled — I don't know yet when I shall act — or what I shall do next. As to the *unfortunate matter* — it *is* at an end. I have faith in Providence. All is well. (The lady is a dutiful daughter & must not be blamed for obeying and clinging to her father).... Mother is very much broken, I think, poor soul! ... She seems to have still a lingering hope in her heart that all this will prove to be a dream.[61]

While Booth's letter to Emma Cary appears definite, on February 15, 1866, Asia Booth Clarke wrote to Jean Anderson Sherwood:

> About Blanche Hanel, she was at the Continental but Edwin was in New York all of the time and never saw her. She called to bid me goodbye before leaving, and I suppose they [Blanche and her father] will not remain long abroad — when perhaps if nothing worse occurs, their marriage will take place. She is a great stickler for decorum, as all fashionable flirts are, before the world so has

every way endeavored to avoid the false rumor of a secret marriage, when her very care has led people to surmise that the event took place.⁶²

In the long run, Booth felt that he was lucky to be rid of Blanche. In later life, she dyed her hair and acquired what he called a "fast" reputation. On October 9, 1887, he wrote to Edwina:

> When I discovered her real nature I was thankful to be free from her. She had some good traits & was a favorite with her fine friends, but I discovered in her (after I became engaged to her) qualities that suggested the probability of what has resulted; I hope I shall not meet the lady. Spiritualism led me into that danger from which you and I were rescued by a terrible calamity; your uncle John affording her an excuse to break off our connection.⁶³

As a family, the Booths, of course, were permanently marked and scarred by the assassination. A number of women claiming to be John's widow descended on the family for financial support. Edwin warned his mother "about the sharpies who wish to get money" and insisted that "she hold no communication with weeping imposters." Rosalie, however, supported one such family, giving them ten thousand dollars over twenty years.⁶⁴

Everything possibly connected with John Wilkes Booth became news. Stories abounded about the wardrobe trunk that went down with the ship in Montreal, was salvaged and came into the possession of the actor and theatre manager McKee Rankin, who, in turn, sold it to Barton Hill, acting on Edwin's behalf. Booth himself believed that another trunk belonging to John was stored at the National Hotel in Washington "under the seal of the war department." After Booth's death, the actor Otis Skinner perpetuated a legend that Booth had burned his brother's belongings at three A.M. on a snowy night in late winter of 1873, but it is most likely that John's belongings were destroyed in an 1867 fire at the Winter Garden. There is also a possibility that the trunk salvaged in Montreal was burned at the Winter Garden and that another trunk retrieved from the National Hotel in Washington was the one Booth destroyed.⁶⁵

Misinformation about the disposition of John's body also accumulated. Booth requested his brother's body on April 29, 1865, but the request was denied. On May 20, *Frank Leslie's Illustrated Newspaper* published a full-page drawing purporting to show the body being dumped into the Potomac. In actuality, John's body was initially buried ten feet below the brick or flagstone flooring of the prison's No. 1 wareroom — a portion of the prison between the warden's dwelling and the prison proper. Eventually, in October, 1867, when the old penitentiary was being demolished, the wooden box containing the body was reburied with the corpses of the other conspirators a few feet from the north wall, upon orders of General Grant, then acting secretary of war. In the opinion of Baltimore's *The Sun*, "it seems to be now well settled that none of the remains are to be given up to their friends."

Edwin, however, continued his attempts to obtain John's body. In July 1867 he wrote to Edwin M. Stanton, the secretary of war, but received no reply. Then on September 11, he wrote to Grant.⁶⁶ Grant did nothing, and on February 10, 1869, Booth wrote to President Andrew Johnson:

> May I not now ask your kind consideration of my poor Mother's request in relation to her son's remains. The bearer of this (Mr. John [C.] Weaver) is sexton of Christ Church, Baltimore, who will observe the strictest secrecy in this matter — and you may rest assured that none of my family desire its publicity. Unable to visit Washington, I have deputed Mr. Weaver — in whom I have the fullest confidence and I beg that you will not delay in ordering the body to be given to his care. He will retain it (placing it in his vault) until such time as we can remove other members of our family to the Baltimore Cemetery and thus prevent any special notice of it. Your Excellency would greatly lessen the crushing weight of grief that is hurrying my Mother to the grave by giving immediate orders for the safe delivery of the remains of John Wilkes Booth to Mr. Weaver, and gain the lasting gratitude of Yr. Obt. Servt.⁶⁷

Johnson was about to leave office. He hated Grant to the point of refusing to attend his successor's inauguration. Grant, in turn, refused to ride in the same carriage as Johnson. Booth had already failed with Grant, and he may have felt that Johnson, with little to lose, was worth a try. Weaver gave the letter to Andrew Johnson personally on February 12. On February 15, 1869, Johnson ordered Major General G. D. Ramsey, Commander of the Washington Arsenal, to disinter John's body. At 4 P.M. that day, Weaver, accompanied by Marr & Harvey, D. C. undertakers, drove into the arsenal. It took forty-five minutes to dig around the box which was then pulled up by box hooks. The top was removed, and John's body was found wrapped in two or three grey government blankets. The body was "a mass of blackened bones. Upon one foot was an old army shoe, and upon the other a boot cut open upon the top." John Ford, who accompanied Weaver, wired Edwin "Successful and in our possession here." The body was taken to Marr & Harvey's funeral home on E Street in Washington, put in a larger pine box and then taken to Weaver's funeral home at 22 Fayette Street in Baltimore, where it was placed in "a splendid metallic coffin." The entire procedure took less than a day.[68]

Conflicting accounts exist about what happened to the body at Weaver's. *The New York Times* reported that during the afternoon of February 16, hundreds of people visited the Baltimore funeral parlor and "some were allowed to see the remains." In order to get souvenirs, they tore the blankets in which the bones were wrapped to shreds. The Baltimore *Sun*, on the other hand, told its readers that the body was kept in "strictest privacy."

On February 17, Joseph Booth and his mother arrived from New York, and he "and a few others" identified the remains of his brother. The body was interred on February 18 in a vault in the Green Mount Cemetery in Baltimore. According to the Baltimore *Sun*: "There was no one present on the occasion but Mr. Weaver and his assistants." The Booths had decided to have John's corpse buried with the remains of Junius Brutus Booth Senior and the three dead Booth children.[69] Mrs. Elijah B. Rogers, the Booth's Bel Air neighbor, wrote:

> Mrs. Booth wrote me to go to Mr. Weavers and give him the directions on the farm to get the Children. And I did so and they were put in A Casket. Altogether John was placed in A elegant Casket alone and taken and put in Mr. Weavers vault for A few days til they all could be bureyed to gether in the lott. I got A piece of John's harre for the family. It was not so black and Shiney as it was long ago. He was burryd in the Penetiniary yard in Washington they did not intend to let but few knew where he was, A great many people surmised many things, that he was dead, and some sayed that his heart was in the Pattent office in Washington, all not Correct, poor fellow.[70]

On June 17, 1869, the remains of Junius Brutus Booth, along with the monument that Edwin had placed over his father's body, were removed from the Baltimore cemetery and reinterred in Green Mount Cemetery. On June 26, John's body was taken from Weaver's vault and carried by six "old friends of the deceased acting as pallbearers" to be buried in an unmarked grave at the foot of his father's monument. At 1 o'clock Frederick James, an assistant at Christ Church and assistant minister at St. Luke's Hospital, New York, robed in gown and surplice, read the funeral service of the Episcopal church over the graves. At the conclusion, John's body was lowered in the grave, and the remains of the other children, Frederick, Elizabeth and Mary Anne, contained in one box, with silver plate, were laid on top of his coffin. Mary Ann Booth was present, dressed in deep mourning, and accompanied by Junius, Edwin and Rosalie. After the grave had been filled, several ladies placed bouquets on the mound.[71]

Asia was not present because by the time John was buried, the Clarkes had left America. Asia contended that at the time of the assassination, Clarke had asked her for a divorce. If so, their marriage survived the trauma, and the couple went on to have more children. Clarke sailed for England in early September 1867 and made his stage debut there on October 16 at the St. James Theatre. Asia followed in March 1868, bringing the children and thinking initially that she would "be away for two or three years." Although she detested England, she never returned or saw her mother, June, Rose or Joe again.[72]

The newspapers were relentless, and Edwin called the writers "heartless curs" and "penny-a-liners"; wherever he turned, there were people reminding him of what his brother had done.[73] On March 1, 1876, undertaking his first southern tour since the Civil War, he wrote to Natt Levin, a friend in Charleston:

> Two nights more & my engagement ... will be ended. It has been unusually agreeable in all respects but one — The "bloody shirt" has been fluttered in my face by the press in nearly every place to such an extent that I doubt very much if I shall visit the South again in a hurry. In the North I am not daily reminded of the disgrace & misery that can never be forgotten by me or any of my family, but here they seem to delight in the hyena process of resuscitating the buried carcass of our grief.[74]

The reminders of the assassination were endless. In 1877 R. B. Garrett, on whose father's land John had died, wrote to Edwin, offering him a lock of John's hair and assuring him that "my mother and sisters did everything in their power to make your brother comfortable in his last hours even when they did not know who he was, and had they known it would have made no change in them." As late as 1887 Booth received a letter asking for a loan of $100 from a woman who claimed "it was a Cousin of mine that put your Brother across the river to the Virginia shore, & a friend who set his leg."[75]

Despite the "most extravagant inducements," Booth consistently refused to act in Washington after the assassination. In 1885 he wrote to Lawrence Barrett, who was arranging his 1886–1887 tour:

> Nothing could induce me to act in Washington. I have not only refused large terms, but declined an invitation signed by all the "crowned heads" from President Arthur down. It comprised a series of letters elegantly bound, gilt-edged etc. This may be mere sentiment in me, but 'tis a strong one & will hold 'till my "silver cord is broken." I cannot will not go there.[76]

Forgoing Washington enhanced his image of suffering nobility. It also helped his Baltimore box office, since whenever he performed there, special trains were regularly scheduled from Washington. In the long run, close associates of Booth knew that "Such a calamity would have ruined any other actor — but it has done him good." At the time Edwin simply went on; as he wrote to Jervis McEntee: "Ah well! Life's too short to spend in grieving."[77]

Chapter Ten

1865–1867: "Something to keep us above the surf"

The Booth family returned to the stage during the 1865–1866 season. John Sleeper Clarke opened at the Winter Garden in New York City on September 4, 1865, but subsequently sold three weeks of his New York engagement and spent November resting in Philadelphia. He may have wanted to be with his family, because on August 20 Asia had given birth to twins, Creston and Lillian. Initially June was indolent. On December 3 he wrote in his diary: "have passed most of my time the last 3 months in reading—& idling my time—am undecided as to my future—see no likelihood of acting yet."[1]

Faced with temporary unemployment after Lincoln's assassination, Edwin and Clarke concentrated on the continuing renovations to the Walnut Street Theatre. The Walnut improvements, his management at the Winter Garden and commuting between Philadelphia and New York enabled Edwin to take his mind off his brother John. On September 24, 1865, he wrote: "I have been vastly busy—thank the Lord, who sends in our deepest troubles something to keep us up above the surf.[2]

In addition to refurbishing the Walnut, Booth was preparing for his return to the stage in New York. He collaborated with a Winter Garden actor named Henry Hinton on an edition of "acting versions" of the plays in which he performed. There would have been no reason to begin such an edition if he had not intended on returning to the stage, because the books sold best in conjunction with his engagements. The question was not whether Booth was coming back but when. By early August 1865 there were rumors that he would resume acting. Moreover, if running two venues was not enough, by the end of December 1865 he and Clarke began negotiating for a lease on the Boston Theatre. They obtained the lease in January 1866 for $16,000 a year and became the theatre's managers for the 1866–1867 season.[3] Edwin was throwing himself into work, and that meant spending and owing money. There was only one way for Booth to guarantee an income. He went back to acting.

He reappeared as Hamlet at the Winter Garden on January 3, 1866. As early as November 1865 *The New York Clipper* predicted that he would receive "such a reception ... as has seldom if ever been witnessed on the American stage."[4] As Booth's comeback approached, however, he encountered vicious criticism from the New York *Herald*'s editor, James Gordon Bennett:

> The public must be surprised to learn that a Booth is to appear on the New York stage the coming week. We know not which is most worthy of condemnation, the heartless cupidity of the foreign manager [Stuart was Irish], who has no sympathy with the feelings of the American people or the shocking bad taste of the actor himself in appearing. Will he appear as the assassin of Caesar? That

would be, perhaps, the most suitable character and the most sensational one to answer the manager's purpose.... The blood of our martyred President is not yet dry, and the very name of the assassin is appalling to the public mind, still a Booth is advertised to appear before a New York audience.[5]

The newspaper's diatribe actually helped Booth. The opening night reception was enormous, and *The New York World* told its readers: "The extraordinary warmth of this magnificent demonstration was, in part, due to the fact that the public sense of decency has been recently outraged by a most brutal attack upon Booth's fair name in the *Herald*.[6] *The New York Clipper* reported:

Long before the doors were open, Broadway was so blocked up with ladies and gentlemen that the casual passer-by ... was obliged to cross the street. The street in front of the theatre was ... crowded with private carriages.... Owing to the great crowd, a large police force was sent for, and after a little while, a line was formed to the box office, and the doors opened.... In less than fifteen minutes, with the exception of seats that had been previously secured, there was not a seat to be had in the house, and scarcely a spot to stand on. At twenty minutes to eight, the curtain rose on the scene of the platform before the palace of Elsinore. Very little interest was felt by the immense concourse of people in this scene, but when the scene changed to the audience room in the palace, and Edwin Booth was discovered seated, ... the audience rose to their feet, the ladies waving their handkerchiefs, the gentlemen their hats, and cheer upon cheer was sent up.... For four minutes the audience stood cheering and waving their handkerchiefs and head coverings. Mr. Booth was so overcome that his head drooped, but recovering himself, he walked to the footlights when the applause commenced again and with renewed vigor. At last silence reigned and the play proceeded.... At the close of the second act, three groans were asked for the *Herald* and they were given from every part of the house. The curtain descended at exactly twelve o'clock, but the audience remained seated, calling for Booth; he appeared, and bowing his acknowledgements, walked across the stage, and retired.... As the audience rose to leave the theatre, three groans were proposed for James Gordon Bennett, and the crowd gave them with a will.[7]

On March 27, 1866, Booth ended his engagement at the Winter Garden, and on April 23 he opened at the Walnut Street.[8] While performing there, his mind was already on Boston. On April 22, he wrote to Emma Cary: "I am very busy. I have taken the Boston Theatre — I could get it for only one year & the terms of the lease are such as to render it hazardous to attempt anything like what I did at Winter Garden.... The theatre is too large and I see my mistake too late." Booth did not anticipate that the Boston venture would be successful. He may also have been hard pressed for money. Consequently he and Clarke accepted three other investors in the lease.[9]

As they were only two of five partners in the lease, Booth and Clarke together only received one quarter of the profits. Booth wrote to his friend the judge John B. Murray: "Had I been smart I could have made $30,000 as a manager of this theater alone exclusive of my share as an actor — but, just like me, I see these chances after they have skipped & gone; as it is I shall make about $8000 at most." Booth's dreadful business sense had come to the fore once more as it had in his relations with Ben Baker and continued to be with William Stuart.[10]

Edwin was still hoping to produce *Othello* in New York that season and *Romeo and Juliet* the following fall, although he was worried because "Stuart is rather dilatory & needs 'pushing up.'" Clarke was supposed to "attend to all the business affairs" of the Walnut Street, just as Stuart was to attend to the business affairs of the Winter Garden, but both theatres were most profitable when Booth appeared in them, and when he was around, he inevitably wanted to be involved in managerial decisions.

Booth opened in a production of *The Merchant of Venice* at the Winter Garden on November 24, 1866. During his time there, he began rehearsing privately with a German actor named Bogusmil Dawison, who played Othello in German to Booth's English-speaking Iago.

We have been rehearsing it together for our own edification, in his room at the hotel.... Dawison and I think of acting Othello some night in New York. He is a <u>great</u> actor, and it is delightful to meet a true Shakespearian, although of a foreign type, and to feel the <u>link</u> vibrating between us— can you imagine anything so <u>jolly</u>? By Jove! I never experienced anything more pleasant.[11]

Their plan was to perform the third act of *Othello* for a benefit, but as they worked on it, Booth saw a more daring possibility—a full polyglot production. The *Othello* that opened on December 29, 1866, was performed in both German and English much the way Booth would also do an English-speaking Macbeth to Fanny Janauschek's German-speaking Lady Macbeth in Boston on November 3, 1868, and the way he would tour Germany and Austria seventeen years later. Mme. Methua-Scheller performed alternatively in German and in English, depending on whether she was talking to Dawison or Booth. "In all her scenes with Dawison ... she spoke in German, and in the same scene, while conversing with Emelia, she would instantly change to English." The critic for *The Albion* noted wrote: "So far as the 'confusion of tongues' was concerned the experiment proved a success, the three principal actors displaying a keen scent for 'cues.' ... We only noticed only one or two instances in which an actor proceeded with his part, before his predecessor had given the word"; however, so little attention was paid to the *mise-en-scène* that "modern drawing room furniture" was used in the fourth act.[12]

On January 29, 1867, Booth's newly-mounted four-act version of *The Merchant of Venice* opened at the Winter Garden with Booth playing Shylock to Methua-Scheller's English-speaking Portia. In comparison to the Winter Garden's revivals of *Hamlet* and *Richelieu*, *The Merchant of Venice* was a failure. By March 9, *The New York Clipper* was reporting: "Business was not very good with the 'Merchant of Venice' last week. There is a satisfaction in knowing that Mr. Booth will not play it 'one hundred nights' but will withdraw it shortly for the production of *Othello* which is in preparation."[13]

The Winter Garden *Othello* never occurred. On March 23, 1867, a fire broke out in the theatre. It began in the northwestern end of the theatre, under the stage and was discovered shortly after 8:30 A.M. by the assistant property master. He immediately called the head carpenter, and together they found flames in the area of the dressing rooms, raised the alarm and attempted to pump water on the growing fire. Stuart, who was reading a newspaper in his bedroom at the rear of the theatre, opened his door and discovered "that the entire light traceries of the stage were enveloped in flames. He was forced to flee in his nightshirt, pants and overcoat, leaving his watch and a wallet containing $96 behind." By 9 A.M., the entire interior of the building was on fire. At 9:15, the roof of the theatre collapsed, carrying a portion of the north wall. A few moments later the back wall fell outward, crushing a barbershop located behind the building.

The Winter Garden theatre was a $300,000 loss. Booth and Stuart's scenery for *Hamlet*, *Richelieu*, *The Merchant of Venice* and a forthcoming production of *Othello*, valued at $30,000, was destroyed. Much of Booth's wardrobe, props, costumes (worth $30,000–$40,000), manuscripts and theatrical portraits were incinerated, including heirlooms from his father and probably from his brother John. He estimated his personal losses at $60,000. Neither Booth nor Stuart was protected by insurance, the cost of insurance for a theatrical enterprise being prohibitively expensive.[14]

Just prior to the disaster John Sleeper Clarke had sold his interest in the theatre to Booth for $10,000; Booth was the loser. Stuart became the guest of his fellow manager Henry Jarrett at the Metropolitan Hotel and was given the proceeds of a benefit performance of *The Black Crook* at Niblo's Garden. On April 4 Booth appeared as Hamlet in a benefit for the artists and employees of the theatre at the Academy of Music and then went to Boston to work. An amusing notice from Boston speculated that "As Mr. Booth lost all his wardrobe by the Winter Garden fire, he will appear in his shirt sleeves."[15]

The uneasiness that had always existed between Stuart and Booth became a feud that lasted for nineteen years. Stuart contended that he had been instrumental in furthering Booth's career, particularly by pushing him to complete the hundred nights of Hamlet in 1864–1865. Booth contended that "further than furnishing rubbish for the press in the way of puffs, and 'boshy' advertisements—[Stuart was] totally incompetent to hold any position in a theatre, unless it be as a sort of 'entertaining partner' to keep the critics merry." Yet it is clear that it was Stuart who paid the bills in the theatre, because on September 6, 1867, Booth gave Stuart $1,234.27 "being his share of outstanding bills and in liquidation of same."[16] Stuart was obviously doing more that just entertaining the press, but not in Booth's mind. On June 13, 1867, Booth wrote to John B. Murray:

> Nor do I consider the Winter Garden loss a calamity—for, although it cost me some little $—more or less, it has released me from Stuart. [Joseph] Jefferson truly said—"if you had lost a dozen theatres, & as many wardrobes, it would be a cheap release from him." I was a mad fool—an idiot ever to associate with S.[tuart], & I have now cut free forever from him.[17]

The animosity never ended. By 1874 Booth was contending that Stuart had "tried to throw me overboard when he thought John's madness had set the seal upon my destiny," an unlikely possibility, since Booth's popularity with the public was always assured and provided Stuart with a way to make money. When Booth received poor reviews in Philadelphia, he wrote: "The papers have abused me ... influenced by a bad man with whom I was previously associated in the 'Winter Garden' management—himself a 'literary Bohemian' and a most plausible villain." Stricken with heart disease, Stuart died destitute on December 27, 1886, in the Harlem Hospital where he was lodging as a pensioner. Booth's comment was: "So Stewart [*sic*] is gone at last! I wonder that he held out so long."[18]

By the end of 1867 Booth was through managing the Boston Theatre. On June 23, 1870, Booth leased the Walnut in Philadelphia to Clarke for nine thousand dollars. After the fire the heirs of the LaFarge estate, who owned the Winter Garden property, decided not to rebuild. By March 29, 1868, the Winter Garden's ruins were replaced by a dry-goods store. It would not be the last theatre so fated.[19]

Chapter Eleven

Mary McVicker: "The best actress we've had for a century"

Little more than two months after the Winter Garden fire, Booth played an engagement at McVicker's Theatre in Chicago. He had not been there since June 1858, when James McVicker's stepdaughter, then nine years old, danced for him at dinner.[1] When he met her again in the spring of 1867, she was eighteen; he was thirty-four. They fell in love, and two years later Mary Frances McVicker became Booth's second wife.

She had been a theatrical child. Born Mary Runnion on September 17, 1848, she was the stepdaughter of James Hubert McVicker (1832–1885) and the child of his wife Harriet G. Myers Weaver Runnion McVicker (1821–1904). In 1859 her stepfather put his Mary on the stage as Little Eva in *Uncle Tom's Cabin*.[2]

She was eight years younger than Mary Devlin. Both of them were actresses, but unlike Devlin, who performed in stock companies that stayed in one place for a season, McVicker was a touring child star who moved each week from one city to another. According to Joseph Jefferson, Devlin's parents were so poor that she was forced to go on the stage; McVicker came from a theatrically successful family. While her stepfather never had the financial resources that Booth commanded, he was a prosperous businessman. Unlike Mary Devlin, who either hated the theatre or pretended to hate it in order to purify herself for Edwin's sake, Mary McVicker had grown up in the theatre and liked being part of it. While not young enough to be his children, both of Booth's wives were young enough for him to dominate.[3] Dominating Mary Devlin had been easy; she craved it. Dominating Mary McVicker was more difficult. Unlike Devlin, who was pretty, physically weak and docile, Mary McVicker was witty, sharp-tongued, domineering, physically strong, an astute businesswoman, an alcoholic and eventually, perhaps always, mentally ill.

As a child she performed, like Booth or any nineteenth-century actor, every day of the week, took a weekly Friday benefit and had specialty pieces in which she delighted audiences with her imitations of Italian opera singers and the French tragedienne Rachel. During the 1859–60 season at the age of eleven, she began working as a touring star with a repertoire of ten tailor-made plays. In September 1860 she appeared at the Chicago Theatre in "a portion of Hamlet." By the spring of 1864, however, Mary, then thirteen, had left the stage to be educated in a seminary.[4]

According to the *Chicago Tribune* she began acting again "at Booth's request" when he played McVicker's Theatre in 1867, performing Juliet to his Romeo on June 7. It was the role in which he had first performed with Mary Devlin. Her initial appearance may have been a novelty designed to augment the box office, but Edwin was impressed with Mary's acting. Two days after they first performed together, he wrote to Launt Thompson: "Miss Mary McVicker has made a great success as 'Juliet' here with me. She deserves all the encouragement she can get, and I believe will be the best actress we've had for a century in this country."[5]

By mid–July 1867 he had offered McVicker a place as a leading lady. Since she was not an experienced actress in mature roles and he had never toured extensively with anyone, the offer could only have been made for one or both of two reasons. Mary worked cheap, and Edwin was in love. They began performing together in the fall of 1867. Mary played Ophelia, Juliet, Pauline in *The Lady of Lyons*, Tarquina in *Brutus*, Margaret Overreach in *A New Way to Pay Old Debts*, Julie in *Richelieu*, Florinda in *The Apostate*, Desdemona, Emilia, Lady Macbeth, Beatrice, Lady Anne in *Richard III* and Katherine in Garrick's truncated version of *The Taming of the Shrew*.[6] Traveling with Edwin's brother-in-law J. Henry Magonigle as Booth's newly appointed manager, and with Mary's mother, presumably as a chaperone, Booth and McVicker opened in Baltimore on September 9, 1867, and toured through May 2, 1868.[7]

In December Joseph Booth wrote to his brother: "Hoping your health continues good and Mary's also, give my love to her." On February 23, 1868, Asia Booth Clarke wrote: "I suppose Edwin will eventually be married to Mary McVicker a strange union, but he has only himself to please and no one cares to oppose him." By May 18, Booth and McVicker were planning to marry and spent the summer living together in Long Branch, New Jersey.[8] It was there that Mary McVicker first met the six-year-old Edwina Booth.

Booth's responsibility for raising Edwina had weighed heavily on him. The necessity of touring meant separation, but even in his Winter Garden days, when he was spending months on end in New York, he had little time available for his child. When Edwina was two years old, he wrote: "I see little of my 'bird' [Edwina] except at meals, for I am seldom in the house at other times. She is dreadfully opposed to my acting every night." When Booth told her that he had to earn their daily bread, she replied "I don't want any bread."[9]

When Edwina was seven, her father came to a difficult decision. He believed that her grandmother was spoiling her, indulging her the way she had indulged Edwin; moreover Edwina was learning what he considered bad habits from the family's servants. Edwin decided to put her in school. He chose the Ursuline Convent Academy a Catholic institution run by nuns in Morrisania, a section of what is now the Bronx.[10]

The Booths were to have a long flirtation with Catholicism. As early as 1852 Asia was quoting a favorite nun in a letter to her Baltimore friend Jean Anderson. In 1855 she was attending a Roman Catholic church, and by August 1864 she had converted. In addition, Mollie Booth (Junius Jr.'s daughter) and three of Asia's children were all Catholics. Edwina herself would eventually convert to Catholicism.[11]

Booth's decision to place his daughter in boarding school coincided with the growth of his relationship to Mary McVicker. Edwin, Edwina and Mary, whom he called "Marinee" lived together at Long Branch during the summer of 1868, and that September Edwin placed his daughter in school. He wrote to her on September 5:

> Poor little Mama went back to Long Branch yesterday crying for you & me, and yet full of hope that we would both return to her — very good children; she will call to see you when she next comes to the city — Remember all the good advice & teaching Dear <u>Marinee</u> gave you — (I call her <u>Marinee</u>, but remember she will soon be your <u>Mamma</u>, and you must call her by that title — for she loves you, darling, better than anyone on earth, except your Papa.[12]

Whereas Edwin had referred to Mary Devlin as his child, he referred to Mary McVicker as if she were his mother. Mary was assuming dominance in the Booth household. Booth saw Mary as her stepdaughter's role model and guide. During the summer it had been her job to discipline

Edwin Booth and Edwina Booth, c. 1864. Note the coarsening of Booth's features, probably due to alcoholism. "I see little of my 'bird' [Edwina] except at meals, for I am seldom in the house at other times. She is dreadfully opposed to my acting every night." When Booth told her that he had to earn their daily bread, she replied "I don't want any bread."

Mary McVicker Booth, Edwin Booth, Edwina Booth, c. 1870s. "You will, I know, do all you can to be a truthful, good, obedient little daughter. Remembering what <u>Marinee</u> (or <u>Mamma</u>, as you will call her) did for you during the Summer and to be like her in all things."

Edwina and report on her behavior to Edwin just as he expected the nuns and mother superior to provide Edwina with "some serious occupation for her little 'rattle-pate — something to keep her steady and out of mischief" and to write to him about her progress. When she was only six and a half, Booth was concerned about her "improvement and development into a good and true woman," including her tendency to dress "too <u>gaily</u>, ... one of the faults" he thought she "would soon dislike as much as she had come to dislike candy." He wanted her to be a lady

> as your darling mamma (now in Heaven) was and as little Marinee (Your Mamma that will be — I hope) is.... Remembering all the while, my darling, that the angels in Heaven have always their eyes on you, and know all your thoughts, and when little children deceive and tell fibs it makes them very sad, and the naughty ones are sure to be found out and punished. So you will, I know, do all you can to be a truthful, good, obedient little daughter. Remembering what <u>Marinee</u> (or <u>Mamma</u>, as you will call her) did for you during the Summer and to be like her in all things Thus you can make your papa very happy & the good sisters too will be so proud of you & so happy to write me word of my little daughter — for they will tell me everything just as <u>Marinee</u> did at Long Branch; & you know how very sad it makes me to hear of Edwina's ill-behaviour.[13]

In February 1869 Booth and McVicker moved to New York and continued to live together. Mary remained his leading lady on stage and a force to be reckoned with off-stage. When in 1869 Dr. R. Ogden Doremus called to ask Booth to do a reading of Byron's *Manfred* Mary was in Edwin's dressing room and exclaimed: "Please don't ask Edwin to read *Manfred*. He is already so overtaxed by the labors of the theatre, — superintending the costumes ... and the working of the complicated scenes, etc., that he cannot get the sleep he needs."[14]

Women did not appear in dressing rooms, particularly in the dressing room of a man to whom they were not married, much less discuss his sleeping habits. Mary and Edwin were, by this time, behaving as man and wife to the outside world. On June 7, 1869, they were married in Long Branch at the home of her stepfather. The wedding was private, as had been Booth's wedding to Mary Devlin. Given the fact that they had been living together for at least a year, it had to be private. One month after they were married Edwin took Mary for a vacation at the State Insane Asylum in Utica. Its director A. O. Kellogg had become friendly with Edwin, who admired the psychological profile of Hamlet that Kellogg had published. Kellogg invited the Booths to visit for a rest. From there they toured to Hector, saw the Finger Lakes of central New York and spent the rest of the summer at Long Branch.[15]

Not only was the wedding private, the marriage had been kept a secret even from Booth's friends. On June 22, 1869, Booth wrote to John E. Russell: "Forgive me, my dear boy, for neglecting you — I certainly thought I had told you ... that I w<u>d</u> marry <u>Mary</u> — you <u>knew</u> it, at all events.... Be assured I have not made a mistake & all is well & happy with me now."[16] On August 22, he wrote to Tom and Lillian Aldrich

> I never told a human being of my engagement or approaching marriage save those who <u>asked</u> me of it. Had you done so — I sh<u>d</u> have said <u>so</u>, but you didn't & so I concluded not to obtrude my affairs upon you. Several (after ascertaining the facts) began to advise, &, as I once told you, but two people in the world know anything about such matters — I resolved to "confess nothing nor deny nothing." You'll both like the little girl — I know. Edwina & she are very good & love each other dearly — in fact I was half jealous of each by turns.[17]

This letter makes it clear that Booth had not introduced Mary even to the Aldriches, and his reference to friends giving him advice implies that such advice may not have been positive. Some of Booth's friends perceived problems from the beginning. Laura Edmonds was glad to hear about Mary McVicker, but once McVicker and Booth were married, Mary made a point of destroying Edwin's relationship with Laura. After Mary's death, Laura wrote to Edwin:

> When Mrs. B. called upon me; she gave utterance to words that showed me, that from no fault of yours or others, your friends would drop off. She said <u>she meant to have</u> it so, & she was going to cut off Edwina too [from Booth]. Then <u>I</u> spoke <u>my</u> part & told her, she <u>couldn't</u> do <u>that</u>, & that to pursue her plan would bring down misery all round — & most upon herself. That you had noble friends & needed them, they would be help, not a hindrance to her happiness. Of course, she had no desire to cultivate <u>me</u>, after that.[18]

The seeds of discontent in Booth's second marriage were apparent early on, but before they ripened into public humiliation about his private life, Edwin faced both the highest and the lowest points of his professional career — the erection and failure of Booth's Theatre.

Chapter Twelve

Booth's Theatre, 1867–1869: "A temple to art"

Booth's work at the Winter Garden, the Walnut and the Boston theatres was prologue to the great event of his artistic life, an event envisioned as early as 1860, when he wrote to Richard F. Cary: "Hurry up and make your fortune, that we may have a decent theatre." Booth imagined that "a decent theatre" would raise his profession and himself to a level of respectability that would allow him to overcome the fact that his birth was illegitimate, his father alcoholic and insane and his brother a presidential assassin. Five years after Cary's death in 1862, Booth thought his previous managerial work had prepared him to run what he described as his own "shop," and his admirers saw him as the hope of the American theatre.[1] A tourist, looking for intellectual entertainment, wrote to him:

> Having nothing to do evenings we looked New York through in the theatrical line, — and with all our respect to that metropolis — must say — we got enough of it. Our prayer for you is hasten up the Temple and save the city from the doom of Sodom! Legs! Legs! Legs! Everywhere & not a brain. I ... think you will be a bold one if you put Hamlet "on" again. To gain a chance for business I even suggest that you put Ophelia into silken tights.[2]

The destruction of the Winter Garden theatre freed Booth to build the "Temple," but in order to do so, he needed money. "It's a 'big job,'" he wrote, "and I may sink under it." Immediate aid, however, was not forthcoming. Booth found his mistake when he approached the enthusiastic art lovers he knew as well as his admiring friends. Instead of abandoning the project, however, he gave way to what he called a "sort of desperate feeling of determination to proceed unaided." Having "$80,000 on hand to pay down," he asked his brother-in-law Harry Magonigle to "hunt up sites."[3] Magonigle would eventually manage the theatre, some of Booth's tours and become Edwin's caretaker in old age.

By June 2, 1867, Booth had purchased four adjacent plots of land on 23rd Street and Sixth Avenue. He paid $254,500, taking out what became the first of many mortgages. In fact Booth may not have put all $80,000 down on the land, since by the following fall he had also hired people to design and construct scenery, costumes and properties and had employed James Renwick, the architect of St. Patrick's cathedral, to design what he described to Lawrence Barrett as a "temple to Art."[4]

Booth thought his theatre could be completed in three months. He appears to have had no sense of what was involved in constructing a large building, particularly in the middle of Manhattan. Excavations began on June 15, 1867. Several houses on the land were torn down, and a stone ledge underneath the surface was blasted away. Booth began touring in the fall, and the job of supervising construction fell to his brother Joseph and his business partner Richard Robertson, whom William Winter later described as "a commonplace tradesman."⁵

According to the agreement between them, Robertson was to invest between $75,000 and $150,000 of the $500,000 needed for construction. Booth was to provide the rest so that, with the $254,000 already spent on land, Edwin's total investment in the land and buildings amounted to between $600,000 and $675,000. Robertson was to receive three-sevenths and Booth four sevenths of the profits. For an outlay of 15 percent to 30 percent of the construction cost, Robertson was to receive 42 percent of the net profits. In Edwin's opinion, moreover, "Robertson ... never invested a cent of solid money in Booth's Theatre." What he did was borrow whatever money he provided and repay his debts, in part, out of his share of the profits.⁶

The Booth Theatre designed by James Renwick was an elaborately decorated building of light-colored New Hampshire granite. It measured 108 feet in height and 98 feet in depth and stretched 184 feet along 23rd Street (the front of the theatre) and 79 feet along Sixth Avenue (the section devoted to studios). The stage envisioned was 55 feet wide and 75 feet deep; the 1,783-seat horseshoe auditorium was "heated and ventilated by hot air pipes that ran beneath the floors." Scenery could sink into a 32-foot pit beneath the stage or rise above the 50-foot proscenium opening into a 75-foor fly loft. Supporting such a theatre required touring. Booth was not even present to lay its cornerstone. The comic actor James Hackett performed the ceremony on April 8, because Edwin was acting in Philadelphia, raising money for construction he could not watch.⁷

By the end of February 1868 Booth was having to face up to his first big mistake — his choice of repertoire. In a letter to Edwina, age seven, he included instructions to Joseph: "Tell Uncle Joe to tell [Charles W.] Witham [Booth's scene designer] that after all I may be obliged to begin with *Romeo & Juliet* instead of *The Winter's Tale*." That Booth had actually contemplated opening his theatre with *The Winter's Tale* demonstrates his commercial naiveté. While the play was not unknown in the nineteenth century (the doubling of Hermione and Perdita occasionally provided a star female role), it was never a popular hit like *Hamlet*, *Richard III* or *The Merchant of Venice*. Booth's instincts were artistic, not managerial. He wanted to branch out beyond the normal Shakespearean repertoire. It was a fatal financial error, because nineteenth-century audiences wanted to see what they already knew. In addition Booth was inspired by the historical realism of the English actor-manager Charles Kean, noted for his lavish Shakespearean spectacles. Booth's taste would produce spectacles that matched the grandeur of his theatre's interiors but which contributed to his financial ruin.⁸

The theatre Booth envisioned would fulfill one of his life-long dreams—elevating theatre to the level of sculpture and painting. He would attain respectability through association with "real" artists not just theatre artists, an idea that characterized his friendships, his relationships with his wives and daughter and later his vision of The Players. By October 25, 1867, with one mortgage already on the theatre, he hoped to satisfy his desire for artistic respectability and simultaneously defray expenses by renting out stores and studios on the theatre's Sixth Avenue side. By April 1869 he had all of the studios filled with artists and doctors, and he and Mary had decided to move to a suite of the theatre rooms. What he was building was an art center in which he found a home.⁹

Edwin had hoped to open his theatre in December 1868 and began hiring actors in June. In actuality it would be eight months before he needed them. When he realized that the theatre would be incomplete in December, he could only offer contracts beginning February 1869 and lasting through the following spring, and stock company actors were accustomed to nine-month engagements. This limited the quality of his casting. Minor actors, however, were readily available and worked cheap, and these were the people he employed. To "play seconds" opposite him, he chose Edwin Adams, who had drinking problems but who promised that "the advice given me in your character of 'Dutch uncle' will be strictly heeded — for I assure you I can 'keep my elbow as straight as any mans.'" Unfortunately Anna LaCoste, who was to play leading juvenile tragedienne roles (Ophelia, Juliet) died, and Booth substituted Mary McVicker, assuring Richard Robertson that "Mary ... is well & very happy — She is acting better than ever.... Mary's got all all the stuff — except the beauty."[10]

The fact that Booth needed to assure Richardson of Mary's health and happiness implies that she was experiencing neither state. Booth's statement about her lack of beauty may simply have been a reference to her lack of height or perhaps her lack of a full-bodied and consequently healthy shape. Certainly her reviews suggest that she was charming to look at on the stage. Mary's main drawback was that she was an ingénue, and using her meant that Booth also had to engage Fanny Morant as his leading heavy tragedienne. He also hired Emma Waller, with whom he had performed in California in the 1850s, as well as her husband, D.W. Waller, who became the theatre's stage manager and prompter. Booth's brother-in-law, J. Henry Magonigle, was appointed his business manager, and Joseph remained as treasurer. He described them as "as good a company as it is possible to obtain in the country," but only Adams had a substantial reputation.[11]

These personnel choices were sentimental — the paying of debts to old friends, the provision of jobs to family members, the selection of the woman who to become his wife. The company's lack of prestige, however, may also have reflected Booth's reluctance to perform with actors whose abilities might rival his own. "As a friend later admitted, 'Mr. Booth never had a good supporting company. He chose them particularly for their inferiority in order that he might shine by comparison.... He was really quite a child in the world we live in.'"[12]

His childishness was reflected in his relationship to his business partner Richard Robertson. Robertson was a slick businessman, but he knew nothing about running a theatre. Although touring, Edwin was still making decisions about whether tickets should be raffled to prevent speculation, how to handle out-of-town orders, whether policemen should be employed to ward off scalpers, whether to increase the salary of the house scene painters, how to program the following year's repertoire, whether or not to rent scenery, what stars to hire, how the costume designer could save money by shopping at secondhand clothes stores, what was wrong with the rigging system etc. He was out of town, performing seven shows a week and trying to manage all the details of his theatre long-distance.[13]

Robertson had invested time and money (albeit probably not his own) in the building and supervised its construction and felt he should serve as more just an investor in its profits. In early January 1869, a month before the theatre opened, he cajoled Booth into deeding him three-sevenths of the building and land, in addition to his three-sevenths profit share.[14] But this action neither increased Robinson's investment nor reduced Booth's indebtedness.

Booth's Theatre opened on February 3, 1869, with *Romeo and Juliet*. The interior was opulent. The audience area was ventilated by an overhead fan. According to descriptions in local newspapers "boxes ... were fitted with gas lights ... simultaneously ignited in full view of the audience." Chairs were upholstered and separated by iron arm-rests, and the orchestra pit was sunk beneath the stage so that "the musicians were nearly out of sight of those seated in the parquette." The theatre's only drawback was its lack of lobby space, which made it difficult for women dressed in the period's wide dresses to move. It rained on opening night, and the lobby became congested. Audience members were admitted in single file, causing "a bustle at the door," torn dresses, "a wreck of bonnets and a crush of toes."[15]

The orchestra played the national anthem, and Booth, dressed in evening clothes, appeared before the curtain and made a short speech. He thanked Robertson for his help in erecting the building and told the audience that he was about to play Romeo when the Winter Garden burned, and thought it fitting to take up his career in New York where he had left it. The gigantic chandelier was extinguished, and the curtain rose to reveal a sixty-foot high square of Gothic architecture including a forty-foot-tall Romanesque church. On stage right and left hinged flats produced the effect of a box set, surrounding the acting area with scenery. "With a certain amount of creaking the scenery, automated by ... hydraulic rams powered by huge steam engines, flew up or down from the fly-loft and rose or sank through the stage floor in full view of the audience." Booth wrote to William Winter: "the rising & sinking scenes often had a good effect & were applauded — especially when the two movements occurred simultaneously.[16]

The scenery was praised in the press, but McVicker and Booth were savaged. Mary, "clothed in a white satin skirt looped with pearls and cut pompadour, trimmed with silver bullion fringe," was described in *The World* as having "an immature face ... too small to be expressive, and too attenuated to be pleasing, ... an exceedingly fragile body ... and a voice deficient in quality and power." The *Daily Star* noted that Booth "made Romeo look like a sheep, cavort like a monkey, and chatter like a parrot." The *Spirit of the Times* said that he "hopped about like a clog-dancer or a sonambulic-velocipedist, who fancied himself astride a bicycle." The critic for *The New York Leader* wrote that Booth "makes Romeo at times to whine like a simpering, whimpering school-girl; at others to prance like an organ-grinder's monkey and at others to move about like a half idiot."[17]

Booth chafed at what he considered not only critical hostility but also critical indifference, particularly that of his friend the *Tribune* critic William Winter: "Winter has done all he could — having pledged to do as little as he possibly could.... Winter's conduct has really hurt me — I have always felt an affection for him."[18] There was, however, a reason why William Winter was avoiding Booth. Edwin had tried to bribe him. On February 7, 1869, four days after the theatre opened and bad reviews began appearing, Booth had offered to lend Winter enough money to join The Century Club.

> You know ... that I am a member of the "Century." ... I ascertained that you were desirous of joining the Club ... but that you were obliged to decline on account of pecuniary considerations. Now, bearing a grateful memory of your past services, I venture even at the risk of wounding your delicacy to offer you assistance. Knowing you to be a thorough gentleman, and possessing a keen sense of dignity myself — I would not suggest this if I had any object in view other than that of aiding a deserving fellow being....I think you are entitled to at least the thanks of the better paid fellow.... If I have offended you, my dear boy, don't retain any ill feeling toward me beyond the moment.... I often do foolish, hasty things — without duly considering the result.... I enclose a check which you may light your segar with in disgust.... I have nothing to gain by this.... but I candidly admit, if I should need your aid in order to carry out the intention I have regarding the drama, I will not hesitate to ask it.... As for the future — I shall never ask or expect more than you can in justice do.[19]

At the end of the letter Winter scribbled in pencil: "I did not accept the gift."[20] It is no wonder that he kept his distance. His suspicions were well founded as shown by a letter Booth wrote a week later to John E. Russell: "Took your hint & (keep it 'twixt us — mum) gave Wm W.... $100, and used the pretext of Century, as you suggested. He received it, and with several letters of gratitude &c, &c, has quietly dropped me altogether. So much for so much! Don't ever breathe a word of this, but keep it sacred & destroy this evidence of the fact."[21]

Booth's attempt to bribe Winter was actually subtle in the period. In 1868 *The New York Clipper* denounced the regular employment of critics by theatre managers:

> A manager, investing heavily in a speculation, ... considers the subornation of professional critics a portion of his duties. He devotes a portion of his capital to secure a certain space in journals.... Employing the services of a competent writer, sometimes drawn from an influential daily, ... frequently maintained as a stipendiary to his own establishment, the manager crowds the newspaper columns with adulatory comments ... prepared at his suggestion.[22]

That Booth had resorted to bribery implies that he was terrified. *Romeo* had the potential for being financially successful, but the potential was not being realized. By prevailing New York prices, tickets were expensive — $1.50 in the parquette circle, one dollar in the balcony and second circle and fifty cents in the gallery. The completed building seated 576 on the main floor and 1,277 more in its three balconies, giving it a box office potential of approximately $2,183.00 per performance. The problem, however, was that "the upkeep of the company cost the management $2,330 weekly." More than a third of this was paid to actors, whose salaries ranged from $100 a week (Fanny Morant) down to six dollars. In addition mortgages on the property and short-term loans made to support the productions had to be met. Booth lost money even if the house was full.[23]

On April 12, 1869, Booth opened in *Othello*, playing the title role, with Mary McVicker as Desdemona and Edwin Adams as Iago. Again the elaborate realistic scenery was praised, but Booth had decided on a role that was not within his range. Both he and McVicker were pilloried in the press. The reviewer for *The New York Albion* wrote: "Nature has denied [Booth] that physical prowess that we naturally associate with deeds of valour." *The Citizen* praised Booth's Othello for its "delicacy" but wrote that Mary McVicker "dresses nicely, looks nicely, sings quite nicely, and doesn't act at all." The reviewer for the *Daily Star* wrote that "Mr. Booth's cork was evidently on a strike and worked only on occasion, for, instead of giving us a sight of a first-class darkey, he made up as a streaky quadroon — sort of Vanilla Ice with Chocolate mixed" and also noted that "Miss McVicker dressed beautifully, knew her lines perfectly — and that's about all."[24]

Two years after his work was so admired that his career survived his association with a presidential assassin, Booth had become an object of critical venom. He had set himself firmly on the pinnacle of American theatrical culture, and he was despised for the self-glorification that his theatre's grandeur suggested. By its grandeur the theatre raised expectations that neither he nor the company he employed could meet. Its size and spectacular scenery may have actually worked against the intimate style of acting that Booth had developed, and its cost made efficient operation financially impossible. Booth's reputation, which had led him to think that he could become the American equivalent of Charles Kean, was destroying his chance to have "a decent theatre." The temple was becoming a tomb.

Chapter Thirteen

Booth's Theatre, 1869–1871: "The currency of good intentions is not bankable money"

When the spring 1869 season closed, Booth's Theatre reverted to being a traditional stock company, and Edwin hired Blanche DeBar, identified in newspapers as his "niece" but really his stepniece (the daughter of Junius' first wife), as his leading lady.[1] She was unfortunately tarred with the brush, and *The New York Leader* was unrelenting:

> This lady has many of [Booth's] characteristics. Like him, what she lacks in ability she makes up in egotism. She has evidently mistaken her vocation.... Her voice lacks sympathy, and allied to an ungraceful appearance excites anything but admiration.... Mr. Booth alone is responsible for the engagement and retention of such sticks. We say to him that the currency of good intentions is not bankable money.[2]

By the end of June business was poor, and Booth needed to make money by touring in the fall.

Beginning the next season, on August 2, 1869, Joseph Jefferson, who had not appeared in New York in three years, packed the house for forty-nine performances of *Rip Van Winkle*. Booth's was hanging out its "standing room only" sign nightly, but Jefferson was also getting a certainty (a fixed salary) of $500 a week plus fifty percent of the gross receipts at every matinee. Edwin was forced to sell his house on 19th Street. He rented rooms for his mother, his sister Rose and his brother Joseph, and he and Mary moved from their large space in the theatre into what he described as a "lesser suite of rooms" in the building.[3]

While Jefferson was flourishing in New York, Booth opened his 1869–1870 season with engagements in Philadelphia and Boston followed by an Eastern seaboard tour with a company from June's theatre, the Boston Museum. Accompanied by Mary, he was back on the road, plagued by horrid food, an ear infection, "a dreary cold," and a company that was poor to middling.[4] He was performing in the kind of productions that his own theatre was meant to reform.

He was scheduled to reopen in New York as Hamlet on December 2, but the opening was postponed until December 13 "in consequence of illness." The illness was Mary McVicker's. Booth's second wife apparently intended to continue her career after marriage, a decision in which he may have concurred based not only on her wishes but also on his need to economize. Mary, however, was so sick she could not leave the house, and Booth substituted Blanche DeBar as Ophelia. He either had no time to find another ingénue, or he simply chose to ignore the wretched notices she had received the previous summer.[5] Reviews were mixed. The critic for the *New-York Daily Tribune* described Witham's twelve elaborate sets as "magnificent" and praised the performances. *The New York Albion*'s critic, however, wrote: "The company contains many sad sticks who should be abated as stage nuisances."[6]

It was Booth's intention to run *Hamlet* for one hundred performances, closing on May 1, but it lasted only until March 19, 1870. The abbreviated run may be due to the competition provided by Charles Fechter's *Hamlet*. It may also, however, have reflected Booth's exhaustion, his fear that the public would tire of Hamlet and his need to make money. "I take off Hamlet chiefly because I do not wish to surfeit the dear pub with it — as it is my standby. It must be done a little each season, and partly because I am not ambitious to act solely for the sake of acting, and — although the receipts are large, the expenses are correspondingly so — and if a change will increase the $ why — let us change."[7]

It was a bad managerial decision. Booth began playing Sir Giles Overreach, Claude Melnotte and Macbeth. The results were artistically mediocre.[8] The critic for *The New York Clipper*, writing in dialect under the penname "Our Jim," a semiliterate person visiting the theatre, gave his opinion of *The Lady of Lyons*: "E. Booth maid luv as if his hart wassent in it, as if it wus goin to be a funeril instead of a weddin.... As a luvver he issent a grate sucksess.... The lions runs 3 nites, and was atended by the elites uv sossiety, menny of whom was females and yung gurls of a prekoshis an susseptibbil age."[9]

The Lady of Lyons was followed by *Macbeth*, which was, like Romeo, never one of Booth's most successful roles. The critic for *The New York Times* wrote: "Mr. Booth has habitually a scholar-like stoop of the shoulders, an unsteadying bowing of the legs, a stealthy rather than an open and unconstrained gesture.... His Macbeth smacks too much of the closet and too little of the field.... In general his appearance is too much that of Hamlet in military clothes." Booth was too tired to bother. On April 2, 1870, he wrote to John E. Russell: "I am at *Macbeth* — it serves as a mere rehearsal for a future elaboration — for after *Hamlet* I am used up & too weary both in head & hinges to do anything with so huge a part. I am surprised how badly I act it."[10]

By May 1870 the financial realities of Booth's Theatre were becoming apparent. Profits from the theatre's season beginning February 1869 were $102,000, but during 1869–1870, the box office took in only $85,000; and would drop to $70,000 during 1870–71. Plans to produce *The Winter's Tale* were set aside, and Booth announced that his next major revival would be *Richelieu*, always one of his most popular plays.[11]

Jefferson had agreed to a four-month run in the fall of 1870, opening the second full season on August 15 and again freeing Edwin to earn money by touring. As Booth wrote to William Winter: "My only (or rather my chief) object is to get away that I may let my ground lie fallow & gather i the West the harvest waiting there for me."[12] The money Booth made on the road was turned over to Robertson, who used it to pay off the short-term loans with which he kept the theatre afloat. These loans were made, in large part, by Oliver Ames, a Massachusetts political figure, and his father, Oakes Ames, an American capitalist and United States representative from Massachusetts.[13] They would eventually play an important role in the theatre's failure.

By October 11, 1870, Robertson needed Booth to stop making money on the road and start performing *Richelieu* immediately after Jefferson closed in order to bolster Booth's Theatre's sagging box office. Edwin had no choice. There was no time to get another star, because actors of any significance had already signed contracts to appear elsewhere. Mary was ill, and Edwin was sick of traveling. He wrote to his friend, the businessman William Bispham: "When that pile of granite is paid for, I'll retire and act only once in a while by way of recreation."[14]

Richelieu opened on January 9, 1871. The costumes were new, and although the scenery was taken from *Romeo and Juliet*, the critic for the *Evening Post* called it "the most magnificently mounted play ever seen in this city." The critic for the *New York Evening Express* thought that Booth was particularly brilliant in bringing out the humor in the role although the supporting cast was "by no means what might be desired." Despite the fact that the theatre finally had a hit, Booth decided to terminate the run five weeks after he opened. He wrote to John E. Russell on February 12, 1871: "I shall withdraw Richelieu in its full success—to bring it on at the close of my eng^t, however. Shall do Benedick for the first time in New York & what a howl there'll be against my idiocy & unfunny attempts at Comedy—hey!"[15] He was courting failure by abandoning one of his strongest roles to perform one of his weakest.

Booth was marking time until his next great Shakespearean production—in this case, the first in which he did not appear. On April 25, 1871, Lawrence Barrett opened in a lavish revival of *The Winter's Tale*. It was a seldom produced Shakespearean play that had not been seen in New York for twenty years and one that Booth had been considering when he first conceived the idea for his theatre. The production was noted for its eight realistic sets. Local critics were impressed by the "real and painted figures so blended as to present to the spectators the effect of thousands of human beings group in multitudinous masses." In like manner the stage business was meticulously delineated. "The crowd of soldiers and people who fill up the scenes and enact the incessant by-play ... never stand staring stupidly at the audience.... They are given specific duties to perform, and instructed how to perform them."[16]

Despite the care with which the play had been mounted, however, it opened to a box office of $927 and averaged only between $400 and $600 per night. Despite adverse criticism, *Much Ado*, with Booth, had cleared a profit of $2,400; *Winter's Tale*, without him, lost $10,000. By June 17, 1871, Booth was resting at Long Branch, New Jersey, in a home that he and Mary had purchased on 18 or 19 acres of property.[17] Meanwhile, the theatre was reduced to having the comic soubrette Lotta Crabtree. She was not an appropriate choice. *Frank Leslie's Illustrated Newspaper* reported:

> The distressing report that Lotta opens at Booth's, is fully confirmed. The pestilence-fly, the harbinger of cholera, has also appeared in New York. We trust that Miss Crabtree, whose sphere is—well anywhere rather than Booth's, may not be the precursor of the plague of clogs, banjos, winks, kicks, and female cigars, raging in the theatrical hemisphere and now possible at this once classic theatre.[18]

Lotta's appearance was distressing because Booth's Theatre was a monument to Edwin's determination to elevate the American stage. He had set a standard for the kind of work he produced, and both critics and public expected him to live up to his ideals. Lotta Crabtree was not the kind of attraction audiences expected to see there. Her run at the theatre failed financially, losing $200 a week, and Booth's economic prospects for the 1871–1872 season were not good.[19]

Chapter Fourteen

Booth's Theatre, 1871–1883: "So much for high-old-art"

By March 4, 1871, Booth had begun negotiating for the kind of serious performers his theatre's reputation demanded. Negotiating with stars, however, meant holding time for them in the theatre's schedule. Moreover since they would appear only in their specialty pieces, using the theatre's company as support, their performances postponed Booth's own productions, notably a planned revival of *Julius Caesar*.

Booth offered a contract to the American actress Charlotte Cushman, who was interested in making her first appearance in New York since 1863. On May 18, 1871, she wrote: "I think I will consent to the engagement." The operative words were "I think I will." Cushman told Booth that she was still suffering from a "local difficulty, which <u>may</u> have to be removed." In actuality she was ill with cancer and undergoing a water treatment.[1]

Cushman was a shrewd businessperson. She requested a "certainty" rather than a share of the profits; she set no amount but asked Booth to suggest what he could afford and what she would be worth to him. It put him in the position of making an offer she could either accept or reject. While theoretically Booth, as a manager hiring an actor, was in the driver's seat, Cushman, by delaying her decision, made him dependent on her decision rather than she on his.

By July 1 he had sent an offer. Cushman found it unacceptable, but she did not reject it; instead she countered, implying that she would definitely accept an engagement but just not on the terms Booth had offered. She wanted the money her male counterparts were paid.[2] She also wanted to open "with the privilege" (the possibility of extending a successful engagement as long as it brought in money). Booth, however, needed a definite commitment.

By July 23 he was begging: "Give me some <u>positive</u> reply concerning the proposed engagement. You can appreciate my anxiety & will excuse it— when I tell you that Mr Forrest and others are 'hanging by the eye-lids' for some definite offer from me." In actuality there is no evidence that Booth was negotiating with Forrest, who had resolutely declined to act either with him or at his theatre.[3]

On July 27 Cushman wrote that her doctor had agreed to her acting, but she reopened negotiations. Booth was now willing to pay her the same amount for a matinee as for an evening performance. She eventually accepted the certainty Booth offered, but even with contracts signed, Booth was still worried: "Now comes Cushman at a big certainty with her. Opera season soon to begin & she'll carry me up Salt River sure.... My only hope to pay expenses on the year will be in the revival of *Hamlet* & *Julius Caesar*."[4]

Despite his financial concerns, Booth made an important decision by midsummer 1871.

Robertson, always concerned with the bottom line, was pushing Booth to produce popular entertainment like the hit musical *The Black Crook*. Booth, in turn, wanted to run the theatre on his own. On October 2, 1871, he bought Robertson out. The Booths sold their house and land in Long Branch for $60,000 in return for Robertson's share of the theatre building, its trappings and its box office receipts.[5]

It was a terrible choice. Booth was now the sole owner of the property but had bought back a percentage of the land and building he had deeded to Robertson in January 1869. He actually purchased back something he had given away. The mortgages on the building and the loans made to support past seasons were still extant, and Edwin was accountable for them.[6]

Booth finally presented *Julius Caesar* on December 25, 1871. The production, a year in preparation, employed three hundred persons, including a supporting cast of twenty-five and twenty-four extras.[7] It played eighty-five performances over twelve weeks, the longest run of any of the Booth's Theatre revivals.

Before *Caesar* closed, Booth had played all three leading roles, opening as Brutus and beginning Cassius on March 4 and Marc Antony on March 11. Critics thought that his Cassius had the "devilish cunning" of his Iago, and his Antony, the "slight and youthful appearance and refined manner ... in good keeping with our conception of that 'curled darling' of Cleopatra." Booth, however, was unhappy with his reception: "All the papers abuse my Brutus, Cassius, and Antony — so I suppose I'm a fraud, but as long as I draw and have debts to pay, I shall not retire." By early March's Booth's "draw" was dwindling; the play was not making money; Booth had touring commitments, and the production closed on March 16.[8]

On April 22, 1872, Booth presented what would become his final revival — *Richard III*. Most of the scenery was new, and the reviews were positive. Despite this, the production played only two and a half weeks. Edwin wanted to get out of New York and particularly out of his theatre. His financial affairs were in desperate shape. He decided to remain out of New York "one season & if possible two," taking a company on a tour of thirty or forty weeks, avoiding "large towns & cities." He would go into small-town America to make money.[9]

In the fall of 1872 he toured the eastern seaboard with productions of *Hamlet* and *Richelieu*, supported by twenty-one actors, many of them members of the New York company. A Springfield, Massachusetts, critic wrote: "To expect that the support would be what Booth deserves and the play demands, is, of course, more than a provincial city could reasonably hope for, and it was therefore nothing surprising to see the other parts, in general, only respectably filled."[10]

Booth was well aware of the second-rate nature of the productions, but the freedom from his New York enterprise exhilarated him. He wrote to Thomas Bailey Aldrich:

> I am off scouring the provinces for the stray ducats that lie around loose. So far my trip has been very pleasant in every way — with here & there a weak town, but the old-fashioned fun I have in extemporizing stages and scenes compensates me for the "sparcity" of shekels. It reminds me very much of my early California tramps; I have my own company — no rehearsals and the travel is done by short stages of not more than 2 hours [at] the longest. — I do wish you were here [Portsmouth, New Hampshire] tonight — to see me bury Ophelia "above-board"; there is but a six x six square hold, into which my large-legged-Laertes [F. C. Bangs] could not leap — and so I've "faked" (as we mummers style a make-shift) a grave above the stage; Ophelia's coffin, mind you, is packed with Yorick's skull & bones, swords, spears & c, while we travel[11]

The "ducats" that Booth earned poured into New York, but no matter how financially successful the tour, it produced an inadequate amount of money to allow him to continue to run his New York theatre. Halfway through the 1872–1873 season, approximately four years after he opened the theatre, his control over it came to an end. In all he had produced eight Shakespearean plays in spectacular style plus contemporary and standard works, most of them star vehicles like Joseph Jefferson's *Rip Van Winkle.* On January 30, 1873, Booth leased the theatre to his brother June for five years at $73,000 per year. He still owned the building, but he was giving up producing plays in it. Foregoing artistic control over the theatre, however, did not absolve him from debt. By this time the building, which he still owned, had $350,000 in mortgages against it. He hoped that the rent June paid on the lease would allow him to liquidate his debts "instead of paying them off to keep the company together & producing plays." He had failed artistically; he was trying to keep his head above water financially. He and Mary rented their rooms in the theatre and sold their furniture.[12]

The 1873–1874 season at Booth's Theatre started out well, with Joseph Jefferson playing a starring engagement as Rip Van Winkle. On September 17, however, as Joseph Booth wrote in his daily notations on the theatre's box office record: "This morning a panic began in Wall St and some of the best Banks and Firms suspended, it looks like a financial chaos—a Black Friday once again." In the financial crisis, rents and home sales declined. Meat, poultry and butter prices fell. Retail clothing establishments sprang up in all parts of the New York City with placards announcing "No person allowed to go out without some clothing, either at our or your price." Booth's Theatre began to make less each week it was open.[13]

Booth owed $45,000 in loans he had personally made and $70,000 in loans made by Robertson in addition to the theatre's mortgages. Bankers were unwilling to extend Booth's mortgages. On October 15, Edwin wrote to Tom Aldrich: "I have no definite news from New York yet; all is suspense—in a few days the worst will be known."[14]

June was having trouble paying his operating expenses, much less paying rent to his brother. This meant that Edwin was not getting money from the theatre toward the mortgage payments. The financial panic of 1873 reduced attendance, increased the demand for rapid payment by creditors and made additional money impossible to borrow. In deep financial trouble Edwin turned to his father-in-law for advice. McVicker advised selling the theatre, paying off his debts and beginning again. If that did not work, he advised bankruptcy. Booth wrote: "My crisis is deferred daily—I s'pose the smash will come soon."[15]

The "smash" came three days later, on November 12, 1873, when upon the advice of his lawyer T. J. Barnett, Booth "conveyed all his interest in the real and personal estate to a lawyer named Clarke Bell ... for the benefit of his creditors." Barnett had so advised Edwin because Bell knew Booth's principal creditors Oakes A. and Oliver Ames. The advice was questionable; Booth was turning his financial affairs over to someone who was not necessarily a disinterested party; he was a business acquaintance of the people to whom Booth owed money. By the next day, his fortieth birthday, Edwin was out of the theatrical management business but still seriously in debt. Conveying his affairs into the hands of Bell did not free him from the financial responsibilities for the debts and mortgages he had contracted. He wrote to William Winter: "I believed myself to be worth at least what I have put into that concern—all I have earned since '63— some $500,000 & lo! I awake from the dream without a penny & a debt of some $100,000 hanging over me." Booth finally took his father-in-law's advice (by then seconded by Barnett) and declared bankruptcy on February 2, 1874.[16] He retreated into a sense of wronged nobility, writing to William Bispham:

> This is by no means the heaviest blow my life has felt, and I shall recover from it very shortly, if my creditors have any feeling whatever. My disappointment is great, to be sure, but I have the consciousness of having *tried* to do what I deemed my duty.... With a continuance of the health and popularity the good Lord has thus far blessed me with, I will pay every "sou." ... Of course I see some years of hard work before me—all for a "dead horse" too. Not a very cheering prospect; but I'll worry it thro', and thank God with all my soul when I cry "quits" with my neighbor.[17]

Although he did not have enough money to pay off his mortgages, Booth was not at a loss for cash. He wrote to John E. Russell: "the Law permits me to keep what I earn, & I shall thus have a hoard enough to indulge my soul and a big 'loaf' all (or for the greater part of) next year." In all, Booth's income at the time was "said to be $75,000 a year."[18] His expectation was that he could free himself of debt through the income of a year's touring.

On April 7, 1874, Junius Brutus Booth Jr. also went bankrupt and assigned his lease of the theatre to the commercial producers Henry C. Jarrett and Henry D. [Harry] Palmer, whose theatrical expertise was what Edwin called "the leg drama ... the gorgeousness of nudity & nastiness." Clarke Bell began the process of turning the theatre over to Jarrett and Palmer for the next three years. Booth's Theatre went up for sale on November 5, 1874. Oliver Ames, who was one of Booth's creditors, paid $109,000 in excess of the mortgages or the equivalent of $385,000.[19]

With the theatre's loss, Booth searched for people to blame and found them all around him. His actors were ill-equipped to play the legitimate drama:

> Could I have possibly got about me a company of sufficient strength to do it [the legitimate drama] justice ... there could have been very little loss from the business. As it is actors are a set of mere vain, self, brainless idiots—seeking only their own personal glorification which consists in paper-puffery and large types on the play-bill.[20]

He blamed the critics, one of whom turned out to be married to the woman Booth had had an affair with fourteen years before. A nasty article in the *Boston Globe*, in 1874, was, in Booth's opinion, "doubtless written by a little jew-fiddler, the thing of Josie Orton of the Boston Museum — he was the dramatic 'critic' of that paper when I acted there."[21] He blamed his brother June, whose management, in Edwin's opinion, "has at one fell swoop destroyed all the prestige that the Other B. had established." He blamed Clarke Bell, who according to the court official assigned to the bankruptcy, had run the theatre after Booth assigned it to him and made money, which he never disclosed. He blamed his lawyer, T. J. Barnett. Most of all Booth blamed Richard A. Robertson. On March 2, 1875, he wrote to John E. Russell: "I am 'gyved' foot-bound, tongue-tied and legally, dead, you know.... Remember this R. A. R. can and will make use of every little straw to break my back with—he is desperately mad!" In Booth's view, "I fell among thieves, and came out plucked of every feather."[22] The theatre continued to operate; Booth sued Jarrett and Palmer over their continued use of his name and lost.

The bankruptcy had an impact on the whole Booth family. Joe, no longer working at the theatre, began living with his mother in Long Branch, spending his time walking to the post office, building fences, hunting, fishing and gardening. On November 29, 1874, Booth wrote to Edwina at school telling her she would have to spend the Christmas holidays there, because he and Mary had to go to Chicago where Edwin was scheduled to perform.[23] Booth's personal property was seized and appraised for sale, including his library, wardrobe, props and paintings by Jervis McEntee and Sanford Gifford.

Booth dismissed Barnett as his attorney and employed a Chicago lawyer named Comilins Van Schanck, recommended by McVicker. Van Schanck forced Clarke Bell to surrender all of Booth's notes and by May 2, 1875, had arranged with Ames and the bank "to take 20 cents" on the dollar.

Relinquishing control of his theatre in January 1874 meant that Booth spent the rest of his career touring. During those subsequent seventeen years, the organization of the American stage changed from "stock" companies that performed a variety of plays in one location, with scenery, costumes and properties drawn from their store rooms, to "combination" companies that went out on the road from a theatrical metropolis, generally New York, with one play, employing actors particularly suited to their roles and using scenery, costumes and props selected for that play. Within these two extremes, however, there were a variety of theatrical organizations:

(1) Stock companies that performed in one place and did not employ touring stars. These were already rare by the time Booth started his career.

(2) Stock companies that used touring stars. Booth used stock companies exclusively prior to 1867 and continued to perform with them part of the time until 1880. Booth referred to this type of company as "the stock."

(3) Stock companies that toured without stars. For instance, in February 1858, A. McFarland, manager of the Detroit Theatre, brought the entire John Ellsler and Felix A. Vincent company from Cleveland to Detroit for a series of performances.[24] As a star, Booth never performed with such a troupe.

(4) Combination companies supporting a star but formed out of previously existing stock companies. These companies toured in a variety of plays, sometimes with or without scenery, becoming in effect a traveling stock company/combination. They generally had a fairly limited range geographically and lasted only a month or two. If they traveled without scenery, their sets were supplied by the theatres in which they performed. Booth performed intermittently with such companies from 1867 until 1877.[25]

(5) Independently formed touring companies that carried scenery and enough actors for the leading parts, filling in minor roles with members of the stock companies they encountered in cities along the way.[26] Booth never worked with this kind of company, although the plays he performed required supernumeraries who were picked up from place to place, often from the ranks of college students.

(6) Independently formed combination companies carrying a full complement of actors and touring in a variety of plays with or without their own scenery. Booth used this type of combination company intermittently from 1867 until the spring of 1880, during the 1881–1882 season and exclusively from 1883 until the end of his career in June 1891. The elaborate scenery he transported around the country was reserved for longer runs; when playing only one or two performances, Booth's company reverted to the stock scenery owned by the theatre. In the case of *Hamlet*, for instance, it always used such scenery.

(7) Independently formed combination companies that toured in one play with scenery and costumes. Booth never performed in such a company; this final stage developed late in his career. The theatrical roster for 1891–1892 showed that 128 out of 227 dramatic companies were doing only one play — 56 percent, so 44 percent were still doing more than one.[27]

In the years that followed the bankruptcy Booth's Theatre continued to operate, but Edwin appeared at Daly's Fifth Avenue Theatre in late 1875 and at the Lyceum Theatre in New York in November 1876 through January 1877. Finally, on January 6, 1878, he returned for a six-week stay at Booth's. Playing there with his own company, he wrote to William Winter: "Will it not be odd if my engagement at Booth's sh$^{\underline{d}}$ close that house? I think it will." By that time he was financially in the clear as a result of touring. He wrote to David C. Anderson: "Just think — two years ago I hadn't a dollar & owed some $30,000, and now I am talking about taking my ease!" There were periodic rumors that Booth would regain control of the theatre, but Edwin had had his bellyful of management. When he heard that his brother-in-law John Sleeper Clarke had "bought another theatre," his response was Malvolio's "Mad! My masters, mad!"[28]

In time Booth came to understand his responsibility for the theatre's failure. The box office simply could not support the elaborate productions in the style of Charles Kean. On January 20, 1881, he wrote to Lawrence Barrett:

> When I see the ruin that has been wrought by "revivals" I am grateful for my huge losses at Winter Garden & Booth's. Had I gone on "mounting" the drama, it would have thrown me & true art also into the mire — just where it lies here, hidden under the rubbish of theatre gew-gaws. If you ever manage a theatre again — do as I shall do, if ever I control another — do all you can to subdue the painter & costumer & spend the money, thrown away on them, for good plays & actors.[29]

He also came to understand that his lack of financial and managerial expertise made the project's demise inevitable: "I look back now at my folly with self-contempt; to think what I might have done — had I first banked my dollars and built the theatre later."[30]

On December 22, 1881, the building and land were sold for $550,000, less than half its original cost. Booth again believed he might close the theatre with a two-week engagement beginning April 17, 1882, but it was his future co-star Madame Modjeska who gave the last performance there, on April 30, 1883. The theatre closed as it opened, with a performance of *Romeo and Juliet*. Its new owners announced that it would be turned into a "drygoods shop." By October 13, 1883, the Sixth Avenue front of what was formerly Booth's Theatre had entirely disappeared. As early as 1877, when he heard that there was a possibility of the theatre becoming a department store, Booth wrote: "Yes, the old shop is to be a shop indeed; a dry-goods mart — I believe. So much for high-old-art! Sic transit etc."[31]

Chapter Fifteen

Family Life, 1870–1880: "My house has been a hospital"

The poet, novelist, lecturer and journalist Elizabeth Oakes Smith wrote in 1851:

> It is often said, "A woman's world is in her affections, her empire is home." This is only in part true, and true only to a part of the sex. There is a large class to whom the affections hold a very subordinate part — women who find it irksome to sustain the relations of wife and mother, and who would never have assumed them, but because public opinion has made it desirable.[1]

Mary McVicker was one of these women. Despite having appeared with Edwin Booth for two seasons, she gave up her stage career when she married him, perhaps unwillingly, possibly due to ill health, probably because both Edwin and the world around her expected it. She did not, however, give up the theatre. Over the next decade she was an active participant in the management of his career and dominated his personal life. The 1870s also saw a serious decline in her mental and physical health, which took its toll on their marriage.

Edwin and Mary were married in June 1869, and by late October she was pregnant. The baby was almost a month late. The doctors in attendance convinced the Booths that Mary had miscalculated. They all thought it was a joke, but the result was disaster. Mary was a physically small woman, and the baby was so large (10-½ pounds) that the attending doctors were forced to use forceps, which slipped twice and damaged the child's head. Edwin assisted at the birth, which came at 11:30 P.M. on July 3, 1870.

Initially the baby, named Edgar, seemed, according to Booth, "well and strong," but by 4 A.M. he had died. The task of telling Mary fell to Booth. She was given chloroform for five days, and while she was still under its influence, Edwin buried Edgar in a grave near Mary Devlin's in Mount Auburn Cemetery. Her physicians expected Mary McVicker to die, but Booth decided that the sea air would benefit her and brought her to Long Branch, where she improved.[2]

Two months later Booth opened at McVicker's Theatre in Chicago, and Mary was with him. On September 29 he wrote to the actress Jean Davenport Lander: "Thank Heaven her health is stronger although hotel living is not conducive to good digestion, yet the change of scene & air, and occupation (taking care of me) have all combined to keep her comfortable & as happy as possible under the circumstances."[3]

Mary was back to her occupation, taking care of Edwin. She became a combination dresser and business representative, fully engaged in every aspect of Edwin's work and life. She let her opinions on scheduling be known. She had a hand in casting his supporting company. She packed his wardrobe into large trunks. She helped him dress and prepared the wigs he wore. When an engagement ended, she settled the accounts, making sure that Edwin got what he had earned. She bossed servants around. She bossed Booth's tour managers around as if they were servants. She was always there, as Edwin put it, "keeping me up when I am overworked and depressed by the many annoyances of my profession."[4]

Mary insisted on doing the work, and Edwin became dependent on her. On January 1, 1876, he wrote to Edwina: "poor little Mama is busily breaking her back over the trunks—you know we poor men are not permitted to do any labor of that kind." The Booths had servants; yet when he and Mary attended funeral services he wrote: "I must 'hurry up'; my wife is waiting to brush me up before starting on our melancholy visit." Mary supervised him every time he left the house.[5]

Between March and June 1871 Edwin bought a home on 19-½ acres of property in Long Branch. Most of the property was purchased in Mary's name. There was no financial reason at the time for doing so. Edwin was not facing bankruptcy in 1871; he was simply pleasing his wife. Life at Long Branch, however, was hardly idyllic. Mary was ill, subject to what Booth described as "fits and flops," and Edwina saw what was happening to her stepmother.[6]

On October 1, 1871, the Booths were ready to close the house and move to New York for the 1871–1872 tour. Edwin expected to leave the "colored persons" to clean the house, but Mary, always in need of control, was unwilling to trust them. Booth wrote: "The Branch is deserted— my servants there are cleaning house & dear Mary is up to her eyes in dust & yellow soap— cleaning the rooms." Mary was a wealthy woman, a person who owned land, a house and horses. Yet there she was "up to her eyes in dust & yellow soap," apparently unable to believe that the house would be cleaned if she did not do it herself. The house needed to be cleaned, because on October 2, 1871, the Booths sold it and its land to Richard Robertson to buy Robertson's share of Booth's Theatre.[7]

Edwin immediately began thinking of buying another house. On August 13, 1872, he and Mary purchased a house in Cos Cob, Connecticut, on approximately eight acres of land at Studwells Point, on the west bank of the Mianus River. Named Cedar Cliff, it had been built by Charles M. Barras, author of *The Black Crook*, the great musical hit of the period. Booth was amused that he was now doing business with a man who represented exactly the kind of theatre he despised: "Barras & Shakespeare, Booth & Ballet, legs & legitimate. It's a delightful spot— a fairy spot—with every kind of pleasure close at hand, boating, bathing, fishing & driving at your very doorstep."[8] It was to be his happiest home, but he purchased it at the very moment that he was going bankrupt.

A week before the Booths purchased Cedar Cliff, Booth's lawyer T. J. Barnett accompanied Edwin and Mary to see the property and subsequently wrote to Booth about the experience. Using a military metaphor, he painted a picture of Mary as a senior officer drilling her troops.

> Since—Knowing (Instinctively)—the Major General to be exceedingly stormy in bad weather (as she is mild & beneficent under pleasant skies)—I was in hourly expectation of drum-head Court Martial, & bloody execution. However, thank Heaven the Gen. Is content.... salute her! I often think of Farmer Booth, in his Slouch Hat, Scotch suit, Jersey carriage ... so patriarchical in his ways & so plagued—like Socrates—with a fierce wife![9]

The Booths spent the summers of 1872 through 1875 at Cedar Cliff.[10] By January 29, 1873, Mary was pregnant again. Edwina, who was back in school, wanted a brother, and her father wrote:

> What put that little brother in your head? Who told you? Was it in the papers? No darling, the good God has not seen fit to bring our baby-boy back to us—but I pray that He will, for your sake—as well as ours. Perhaps, if we are good & try to do our duty towards our fellow creatures, He will let your little brother come from Heaven soon.—It often happens tho' that when we set our hearts on having one particular thing, God sends something else—to try us & to chasten us. And it may be ... that seeing us all so anxious for a little brother, He may see fit to send a sister instead; this w^d be as

great disappointment to us all, but He knows best & if it should be so—if He ever sends us either—we must be patient & bless God all the same."[11]

Being pregnant did not stop Mary from working. By early February she was, in Edwin's words, "up to her eyes in trunks" preparing for Booth's tour to Detroit and Chicago, where Booth described his mother-in-law in terms that were less than flattering: "If M<u>rs</u> M<u>c</u>Vicker gets any fatter you'll never see her any more, for she'll explode & disappear in infinitessimal [sic] fragments! Why she's fatter than Mama!!!!"[12]

Mary's pregnancy was showing, and by early March, the baby was kicking. On March 2, 1873, Booth wrote to Edwina: "Pip (the dog), is yelping tonight to you—and so is your little brother."[13] Unfortunately Mary miscarried. This time, there was not enough to bury. On June 13, 1873, Booth wrote to Edwina: "Mama was completely broken down & had to go to bed (& there she remained for two days & nights.) ... I am hurrying now to get Mama back to Cos Cob—away from the hot city."[14]

The summer of 1875 was peaceful until August 16. Booth and his friend the psychiatrist A. O. Kellogg were driving the four miles from Cos Cob to Stamford when a portion of the harness gave way, and both men were thrown from the wagon. Kellogg hit the ground and was stunned. Booth was thrown against a telegraph pole and slid down it on his belly into a patch of poison ivy. Kellogg ran for help, and a local resident cradled Booth in her arms, bathed his head with water and gave him brandy. Booth had bruised his stomach and broken five ribs and a bone in his elbow. The first newspaper accounts contended that the accident might prove "fatal."[15]

A wagon with a mattress and pillows was used to transport him to Cedar Cliff. He was conscious but in great pain. Mary immediately became incapacitated. Edwina, then thirteen, had a bed put together for her father in the library so that he would not have to walk stairs and called two doctors from Stamford. His pain from what he eventually called his "break-rib" ride was so intense that chloroform was administered in small doses.[16]

Booth's mother, his two brothers, Harry Magonigle and his in-laws, the McVickers, arrived. Meanwhile, Mary had recovered enough to realize that there was money at stake. Booth had contracts to appear for both Augustin Daly and John Ford, and Mary wired both theatre managers about the accident. Having taken care of business, she proceeded to "faint several times during the night" and remained "prostrated and under medical care," leaving Edwina in charge.[17]

By September 4 Booth had strength enough "to sit bolt upright & totter a la Lear about the room." He wrote to Edwina who was back at school: "Your dilapidated dad walked alone upstairs last night & slept in his own bed, the first time in 3 weeks! More than that, the mutilated old gent actually took a bath."[18] On September 12 he wrote again:

> Little Mamma takes good care of the "child," but my baby—the "larbard fin" [left arm]—is a great nuisance ... —it is very heavy. I do nothing but nurse my baby while Mamma is hard at work—cleaning house, & getting things in readiness for our closing up. I am getting stronger every day, & walk about the farm without assistance.[19]

Mary was "hard at work" because the fall 1875 tour was approaching, and Booth had contractual obligations. Moreover, he was still paying off debts from the bankruptcy of the theatre. On October 5, he wrote to his friend the journalist John E. Russell: "I have little to say of myself—being in every sense, 'dead broke'; my bank, my bones and my engagement are so badly fractured that there is little chance for ... repair." He felt himself "pirouetting on the ragged edge" of his "last greenback," because he was "in limbo" with his "lim(oh!)."[20]

Despite Edwin's illness and probably because of his financial situation, he and Mary were in New York by October 24, 1875, and he began work the next day, performing Hamlet with his arm in a sling. He soldiered on, going from New York to Philadelphia, and in January 1876, he and Mary began to tour the South with John T. Ford. As Ford described them: "Edwin was conscientious, gentle and kindly familiar with all the company, Mrs Booth was at times anxious and nervous but very considerate — always so upon reflection."[21]

By April 1876 Booth's arm was well, but Mary was sick again, and Edwin was beginning to believe that she needed a fresh-air long-term care. He wrote: "My wife is not well — I wish I could go at once to Colorado & keep her there for the next six months; physic does her no good, & only the natural influences of air [and] water can set her up." Edwin was beginning to face the fact that Mary had consumption.[22]

The Booths sold the Cos Cob house on April 26, 1876. Booth wondered: "if we'll ever have a home again! Not until I've got a solid 'corner stone' at all events." Edwin, Mary and Edwina spent June 1876 living with his banker E. C. Benedict in Greenwich, Connecticut, and made plans to travel west in the fall. Again, despite her declining health, Mary spent August packing their trunks.[23]

The Booths took Edwina out of school and decided that she would travel with them, accompanied by a governess, because, as Booth wrote: "She now needs her mother's care & Mary needs her society also." At fifteen Edwina may have been finished with schooling, but it also may be that Edwin felt he needed another family member with him. By August 6 they were in Chicago, and on August 18 Booth, Mary, whom Edwin described as "as school-teacher & general superintendent of the Booth establishment," Edwina, her governess and the McVickers set off for California by rail. The tour was successful, and the "delightful climate had a wonderful effect on Mary & Edwina," though Edwin thought that Mary, although doing "full justice to her wittles & pillow," was "too much of a worker, bodily & mentally, to grow fat."[24]

The way back east was tougher. On November 19, 1876, Booth wrote to the San Francisco theatre manager and actor John McCullough: "Mary had little sleep & broke up after we reached Chicago; she is still on the sick list." As her health declined, Edwin announced that he would not be performing in New York next season and that "his present intention" was "not to be very active for some time to come." Whatever his intentions he had to make money. By September 10, 1877, he opened in Chicago.[25]

In the spring of 1878 the Booths continued to tour. They traveled slowly, breaking up their journeys with overnight stays. Edwin contended that this was to "to avoid night travel on my wife's account," but, given his complaints about traveling, it probably had as much to do with his own comfort.[26] He was rehearsing, performing, traveling, "playing nurse" to Mary and suffering from "dyspepsia."

The season ended on May 4, and the Booths went back to New York. From May 1878 on Mary's health declined rapidly. Booth wrote to Jervis McEntee: "Her trouble is excessive nervousness."[27] The reference to "excessive nervousness" is Booth's first hint of the psychological problems that would dominate Mary McVicker's life.

On Shakespeare's birthday, April 23, 1879, Booth performed *Richard II* at McVicker's Theatre in Chicago. At 10:30 P.M., Booth was beginning the third scene of Act V. "The bell rung, the lights had been turned down and the curtain rose to plaintive music upon ... the dungeon of Pomfret Castle.... Booth began the famous soliloquy: 'I have been studying how I may compare this prison where I live unto the world.'" He got to "For no thought is contented." At that point, a twenty-three-year-old dry goods clerk named Mark Gray, seated about fifteen feet from Booth, stood up and fired a pistol at him. A man in the gallery yelled: "Cheese it! Cheese it!" Booth, thinking that a pistol belonging to a member of the audience had misfired, looked up. Gray fired a second shot which made a hole in the flat about three feet from where Booth was sitting. The audience began to scream. Booth walked calmly to the front of the stage and silently pointed at the would-be assassin. Men rushed at Gray; the spectator next to him pinioned his arms; and finally the "officer of the theatre" disarmed him. Gray allowed himself to be led from the auditorium without resistance.

Mary was in Edwin's dressing room when a company member rushed in shouting: "The people in front are shooting your husband." She fainted. After Gray's removal Edwin came to the front of the stage, and the audience cried out: "Three cheers for Booth," waving their hats and their handkerchiefs. He told them he needed to leave briefly to comfort his wife, exited and having assured Mary, returned to continue the scene and finish the play.

By the time Gray was taken outside, a mob had gathered, shouting: "Hang him! Kill him! Lynch him!" As he was led away Gray commented: "I don't see how I happened to miss him! I am sorry I that I didn't take some lessons on pistol practice before I tried this thing." Another ludicrously comic touch was provided by Mary's stepbrother Horace McVicker, who claimed that the assassin had been found carrying a copy of *Richard II* and had fired out of exasperation for Booth's departures from the text.

Following the performance, Edwin and Mary went by carriage to the Grand Pacific Hotel. Booth immediately admitted a reporter. Inevitably the question was asked: "Do you think that his deceased brother J. Wilkes had any showing in the motive?" Booth's dresser Henry Flohr answered: "Several years ago Mr. Booth received a number of anonymous letters ... saying that he had made lots of money out of that affair [the assassination], and unless he divided with certain parties he would be shot."

The comedian William H. Crane, playing in Chicago at the same time, took the viewpoint that there was no such thing as bad publicity.

> Mr. Crane was of the opinion that it was a material benefit to Mr. Booth, seeing it had turned out so harmlessly.... Mr. Crane ... was at the theatre (McVicker's) just one moment before 8, and he was surprised to see such a poor house for the leading exponent of Shakespeare, and he thought Booth was in hard luck; but now his fortune is made for the next three years.[28]

Crane was partially correct. *The Louisville Commercial* noted: "Many will go now, not to see *Hamlet* make eyes at his mother but to see some frenzied-looking drummer fire at Booth from one of the proscenium boxes." On July 27, 1879, Booth wrote: "It is sad to know that little-souled things endeavor to throw doubt on this terrible fact, by calling it an advertising trick." On May 10, a twelve-man jury judged Mark Gray insane and remanded him to the insane asylum at Elgin.[29]

By the time of the assassination attempt, Edwin had developed a "deep black spot" on his tongue "as large as a silver dollar." In June 1879 he put himself under the care of Dr. Ghislahi Durant who diagnosed it as "nigrities, or langue noire."—a "black to yellowish brown discoloration of the dorsum of the tongue due to staining by exogenous material such as the components of tobacco." There were several relapses, but ultimately the tongue resumed its normal color and appearance.[30]

Edwin and Mary spent that summer at Saratoga. They took rooms at the Grand Union Hotel, "not in the hotel proper, but in a cottage" and planned to stay until fall. Laurence Hutton remembered:

> the mother and I chanced to find the Booths at the Grand Union Hotel in Saratoga and at their request we occupied two vacant rooms in a little suite engaged by them, in one of the most retired cottages in the Grand Union grounds. We were together a month or two, dining at the same table and spending most of our waking hours as one family.... Mrs. Booth, always a nervous invalid, began to show signs of the mental lack of balance which finally sapped her life.... During her frequent attacks at Saratoga and later, when the two families met in New York and in London, sometimes she was very trying, but I never knew of [Booth] to show a sign or utter a word of impatience. He bore meekly with everything she said and did, made excuses for her [and] concealed her irritability and irresponsibility; he held her in his arms, as if she were a baby, for hours and nights together without a murmur.[31]

Mary's cough became perpetual throughout the fall and winter of 1879–1880. When she visited Jervis McEntee's studio on January 21, 1880, she "looked very ill and was almost out of breath when she reached" his room. She was a fighter, however, and refused to see a doctor; the disease worsened.[32]

Despite his wife's deteriorating physical condition, by February 14, 1880, Booth had decided to take his family to England. It was a strange decision. By this time anyone around Mary must have sensed the possibility that she had pulmonary tuberculosis. At the time the common remedy was travel to climates considered suitable for recovery. The popular belief was that the damp foggy climate of a city like London was bad for consumptives. It would eventually become a point of contention between him and his in-laws.[33]

Edwin had convinced himself that what he wanted to do — perform in London — would be good for his family's health. In actuality, it mattered little where he took Mary; Robert Koch would not report his finding of the tuberculosis bacilli until March 24, 1882, and what Mary needed to definitively cure tuberculosis — streptomycin — would not be invented until 1943.[34] It is, nevertheless, odd that Booth, who must have been privy to the consensus about consumption, chose to take his wife to a place generally viewed as deadly.

As her physical health deteriorated, Mary's mental health changed. She lost the singing/speaking voice of which she was so proud, and she began to feel alienated from Edwina. Edwina wrote to her father:

> I don't know what is the cause of this change in Mamma's conduct — she is quite reserved towards me ever since before dinner, though nothing occurred that I know of to cause it, unless it is that she feels badly.... She says she feels she has lost her voice and is trying to resign herself to the one thing she regrets so bitterly. I tried to cheer her up about it, but she wouldn't be cheered ... Poor Mamma I know how hard it is for her to lose her only accomplishment but I will pray earnestly for its return for it was a pleasure to us all.[35]

Mary had never been the Victorian ideal of woman or motherhood, and at this point, instead of devoting herself to Edwin's needs, Edwin was forced to devote himself to hers. Being ill increased her domination over the Booth household. As Mary grew physically and mentally worse, Edwina began to assume her mother's place in her father's life.[36] Edwin began to see in her the Mary he had lost as a young man, and Edwina was pleased by the comparison.

Booth was strangely myopic about his wife's illness. On March 5, he wrote to William Winter: "I've had a very sick wife all this winter, and I hope the change — from New York to Boston [where Booth was going to fulfill an engagement] will help her, but the east winds are to be feared."[37] He may have feared the east winds which made Mary Devlin deathly ill, but it never occurred to him to leave Mary McVicker behind. She probably would not have allowed it.

On April 23, 1880, Booth wrote to William Winter, "My wife's health is no better. She absolutely lives on cream, ... eats nothing & is little more than a skeleton. Her mother has just arrived, quite ill too, and that worries her a great deal."[38] The fact that Mary's mother had joined the Booths in New York was upsetting not only because she was ill but also because the relations between Edwin and his in-laws, particularly his mother-in-law, had deteriorated. Mary and her mother had begun spreading malicious gossip about Edwin. On June 29, 1880, he wrote to William Winter: "It was my intention to write a history of my miserable association with the McVicker family. You could not credit, Will, the vile & wicked things I've been told by husbands of women to whom my crazy wife & her wicked mother have 'confided' their sorrows."[39]

All the Booths were ill during May and June 1880. Jervis McEntee thought Mary looked "very badly" and had "an ominous cough." Edwina suffered from what her father called "a diptheritic attack." On May 17, 1880, he wrote: "My house has been a hospital — wife & daughter both sick.[40]

On May 14, 1880, while Booth was visiting Jervis McEntee's studio, a letter arrived from Lawrence Barrett "proposing to give [him] a dinner before he [went] abroad."[41] Booth was, as always, reluctant to be displayed publicly offstage, and McEntee proposed a small breakfast at the Century Club for "25 to 30 prominent people"; however, on May 22, 1880, Laurence Hutton invited Booth to a full-blown "breakfast" in his honor at Delmonico's at noon on June 15.

Edwin had never been honored at a "breakfast" and worried about his speech; Jervis McEntee worried about the possibility of Booth getting drunk. In actuality, he drank enough during the breakfast that the following day, he could not remember how he got home.[42] Booth had good reason to get drunk. As he wrote to William Winter: "A series of troubles" had "been seething for some time before the feed." The night before the breakfast, Mary left Edwin and went to live in a New York hotel with her parents. Three days later she had not returned, and Booth had to admit: "The chances are that my wife will not go to Europe — but remain awhile with her parents in the West."[43]

On June 21 McEntee visited the Booths and found that Mary was back and talking about the European trip. On June 22, 1880, Booth and William Bispham took her down to see the *Gallia*, the ship on which the Booths had booked passage. Booth wrote to Thomas Bailey Aldrich: "Mary ... has at last decided to go 'if it kills her.'"[44] Writing from the *Gallia* on the way to Europe, Booth revealed that he may have had other reasons for wanting to take Mary abroad:

> The damage that Mary & her vile-tongued mother ... have done me — is more than you suppose. I've been busy the past few months listening to & refuting horrible stories about myself.... If it were not for my domestic misfortune, all would be jolly. I anticipate little enjoyment ... in my "pleasure trip" through Europe.[45]

Booth was right. The trip through Europe would prove no pleasure.

Chapter Sixteen

England, 1880–1881: "The verdict of foreigners"

In order to be acknowledged as a major tragedian or comedian, an American actor — Edwin Forrest, Charlotte Cushman, Joseph Jefferson, Lawrence Barrett — had to gain the respect of European, particularly English, audiences and critics. As *The New York Mirror* of December 4, 1880, wrote, in the view of nineteenth-century American actors, "the verdict of foreigners" was "the verdict of posterity."[1]

In mid–March 1879 rumors reached Booth that the English tragedian Henry Irving was considering an American tour. Booth began thinking about the possibility of performing at Irving's Lyceum Theatre in London while the English actor played the United States.[2] He wrote to Irving proposing "that I shall go to your theatre during your ... visit to this country, to perform under your management." It must have been a difficult letter to write. Irving had been a stock actor in 1861 when Booth was already a star. Now Irving had a theatre to offer and Booth had none.

Booth got no answer. Irving may not have been planning an American tour that year, since he did not actually come to America until 1883. He may have been reluctant to support a rival or to incur the financial risk. Despite the fact that he had no prospects in England, in the fall of 1879 Edwin began planning a London trip and hoped to have an engagement there by midwinter.[3]

The Booth family sailed on June 30, 1880, and had what Edwin called "a canal-like voyage." After nine days the ship docked at Queenstown, Ireland, and Edwin, Mary, Edwina and "Black Betty" Smith went off to Cork and the lakes of Killarney. Booth was unimpressed by Ireland, but he was relaxed and playful. With a pipe of Irish wood in his mouth, he wrote to David C. Anderson, in a vaudeville Irish dialect:

> Arrah Galoo! Hoo-roo! Mabokalush faleen sackdalergerwhack, me bye. I'm on the sod wid a dudeen o' the rale auld bog-wood in me jaw, acushla! ... Did you ever come here? Don't! ... I won't again, mavourneen. Saving the antiquities & the foul weather, we can bate [beat] 'em in Yankeedom. Lakes & hills & all the beautiful scenery & sights they boast of are 'way behind us, so they are.[4]

Before he landed in Ireland Booth had received a telegram from Walter Gooch, manager of London's Princess's Theatre, famous for Charles Kean's spectacular Shakespearean revivals. By 1880 the theatre had fallen on hard times, and Gooch was looking for a stellar attraction to renew its former glory. Booth had his brother-in-law John S. Clarke negotiate a contract.[5]

After an extensive tour of England and a trip to Oberammergau, Munich and Paris the Booths returned to London, and Mary was placed under the care of a specialist in diseases of the throat and loss of voice. Booth wrote that the doctor spoke "encouragingly of her case," but that she had "a terrible cough" and was "very hoarse."[6] That he had been willing to drag Mary through the round of tourist attractions indicates that he was either unaware of the seriousness of her condition, in complete denial or simply did not give a damn about her.

He opened at Princess's on November 6, 1880. Nothing went well. Reviews were mixed, with a number of critics aligning Booth with "the old and stilted school," a style that had been supplanted by the psychological realism of Henry Irving. Mary remained a "very weak invalid & ... under treatment." She spoke in whispers most of the time. Booth wrote to Jervis McEntee that Irving had "not *yet* recognized [Booth's] existence" and had announced the reopening of his own Lyceum Theatre production of *Hamlet*, which made Edwin anticipate "another press onslaught." Above all, Booth described Princess's, as managed by Gooch, as "unpopular with the first-class element, for years a sort of 'Bowery'—given up" to melodrama and a sort of "'Cheap John' management with a wretched company and poorly furnished stage—compared with Irving's superior settings." He felt himself surrounded by "stupid actors & worse carpenters & scene-painters, who did everything contrary to [his] orders."[7]

Booth's detestation of Gooch and Princess's was fueled by the fact that his engagement ended "just as the London season proper" began, and he feared that he would "not have a fair lick at the nobs." Getting a "lick at the nobs" was part of the vindication that Booth sought. At the same time he was not going to go to them; he wanted them to come to him. Socializing was never easy for Booth. He was exhausted after performances, and he was taciturn around people he did not know. In a December 1880 interview the journalist Joseph Hatton pointed out that "It is Booth's habit after acting to go home; and it is not his practice to lunch at clubs or pay complimentary visits.... He rarely takes wine, and he lives the life ... of a recluse."[8]

Unfortunately, as Hatton pointed out, "success on the stage without the aid of a small exchange of amenities" was "rare." Booth agreed: "A success here means social slavery." He needed to socialize in order to fill seats in the theatre, but his social decisions reflect the snobbism of a man who simultaneously felt inferior and superior to the people he courted. He had numerous invitations but accepted only "Sunday dinners from the choicest ladies." He was made an honorary member of various clubs but visited none. What he was holding out for was attention from members of the royal family. He made fun of royalty behind their backs, but he was insulted when they ignored him.[9]

> Have had the Queen's right-hand man, Lady [Jane] Ely, Dowager Marchioness & c &c, not only in the box, but behind the scenes. She is trying to coax her Majesty to have me read at Windsor. The Duke of Connaught [Prince Arthur, son of Queen Victoria] came last night but the other Yankee shows— the midgets & minstrels— occupy the leisure moments of Herr Wales & his party — perhaps he'll come next week & see [*The Fool's Revenge*].[10]

Booth thought Victoria and her son, the Prince of Wales, too "stuck up" to patronize him and eventually referred to the portly Edward as "the Royal Whale."[11]

On October 7, 1880, Booth was proposed as an honorary member of the Garrick Club by the English producer Squire Bancroft and seconded by Henry Irving. Given the fact that Irving had previously ignored Booth, this may have been the first step towards a rapprochement. On November 15 Booth finally heard from Irving directly: "It would be a delight ... to meet you again & to renew a brief acquaintanceship." Irving went so far as to visit Booth at his hotel suite rather than making Booth come to him. Irving alluded to Booth's "letter of 18 months ago but did not apologize ... for not answering it." Booth found Irving "boorish" with his way of looking sideways at his guest and mumbling between "compressed lips," but, hearing him described as "a good fellow," Edwin returned the call the next day. By the end of January, they had had several meetings, and Booth was finding him "pleasant."[12]

Booth played at Princess's Theatre for eight weeks and wound up with a weekly average of just under 49 pounds, although Gooch took in 572 pounds per week. The reason for this disparity is that Gooch gave Booth 50 percent of the net, not the gross, receipts. On January 1, 1881, John Sleeper Clarke renegotiated his brother-in-law's contract, and Booth's engagement was extended until March 12. Booth was dissatisfied with the terms, and his dissatisfaction was expressed in anti–Semitism. Gooch became my "cheap–John" or "my cheap–John Jew" manager.[13] He contended that Gooch had underpaid him, surrounded him with cheap sets, costumes and actors, and was cutting short his engagement in order to make money by returning to the melodrama and spectacle for which his theatre was famous.

Othello opened at Princess's on January 17, 1881, with Booth alternating Iago and Othello. As in America critics were almost unanimous in their condemnation of his Othello. His Iago, on the other hand, was declared a "masterpiece," "brilliant," "artistic," "intelligent" and "scholarly."[14]

Unfortunately *Othello*'s financial success was affected by a snowstorm that newspapers called "the worst in 50 years." The shops and streets were deserted, and many of the theatres closed. The icy atmosphere of the theatre, especially behind the scenes, so affected Booth that he often rubbed his hands to keep them warm while on stage. He felt he had received "the faintest of faint praise from the few critics who ventured out."[15]

As the snow fell, Mary's health deteriorated, and her behavior became increasingly eccentric. Sometime during the run of *The Fool's Revenge*, the English actress Madge Robertson Kendal, her husband, W. H. Grimston Kendal (manager of the St. James Theatre), Sir John Hare (Kendal's partner) and his wife went to see Booth perform. At the end of the play Booth "sent round" to ask them to come and see him. What they found was Mary in an agitated state. According to Ms. Kendal:

> We were received on stage by Mrs. Booth, while the men went to his dressing room. Not having met us, Mrs. Booth, as she advanced to shake hands, asked, "Which is Mrs. Kendal and which is Mrs. Hare?" Mrs. Hare drew herself up to her full height and replied, "I have never been on the stage." As she shook hands with me, Mrs. Booth said: "Well, Mrs. Kendal, my step-daughter went to see you play and ... said she had cried for two whole acts." I was on the point of blushing at the compliment when she added: "But, there, oh Lord! She's *easily* moved." She went on to tell us that she was Mr. Booth's second wife and that the girl was "only her step-daughter." She talked more quickly than anyone I had ever met.[16]

Mary still went out to dinner parties. At one given by the artist Sir John Everett Millais, Madge Kendal reintroduced her husband to Mary, warning him that "Mrs. Booth goes on and on and on, like Niagara Falls." Mary, however, who was unable to speak by that time, "took out a notebook and wrote on a page, "I have laryngitis. I can't speak. I ought not to be here." She continued to write notes all during dinner to Henry Irving, who finally turned to Mrs. Kendal and said: "What does this lady mean? I can't pass the whole of my dinner writing notes to her."[17] Edwin had to face a diagnosis of his wife's fatal condition "Mary has had no respite from pain since we've been here, coughing night & day, eats nothing & loses flesh rapidly. She has some disease in the wind-pipe & the doctor has had fears of consumption of the throat."[18]

Asia, who had moved to England after the Civil War, visited Mary and wrote to her brother: "She told me long ago that Edwina often shook and pinched her when she was asleep — worked her roughly and made awful faces ... to frighten her — and dared her to tell her father — saying he would never believe her.— It was so ludicrous but I only said 'What a shame Mary, and you have been so good to her.'" Mary seemed to know she was dying. Asia wrote: "After I had kissed her — she said —'Oh Asia — my life is going from me Asia — my life is going from me!'"[19]

During the second week of February Booth lunched with Irving "and related the history of [his] foolish engagement with [his] present manager, then asked if [Irving] could spare a few Matinees at his theatre during the 'Season,' &c." That evening Irving called on Booth and proposed that they play Othello and Iago three times a week, alternating the roles. Booth accepted and thought that Irving had "acted very kindly."[20]

By March 19 just as his professional life was improving, Booth became convinced that Mary was dying. Her physician called in Dr. William Jenner, whose reputation was based on his skill with typhoid fever and tuberculosis. Both doctors advised Booth that Mary's left lung was infected and recommended deceiving her about her condition "in order not to hasten the end and to make the ... few months remaining to her ... as pleasant as possible." Booth wrote to Jervis McEntee: "She has so often said that she does not want to know it until a week at most before she dies that we all think it best to keep her ignorant of the fact—so long as she is able to be about." She ate nothing; her memory was gone, and she was unable to write. Apparently Booth did not notify the McVickers, because it was the doctors who finally wrote to Mary's parents about her condition. For his part Booth began to worry that her death would restrict his professional life: "In the fall I have engagements made for several provincial cities. If the doctors' predictions are verified, my engagement with Irving will be upset—for the world would consider me heartless, I presume, to follow my vocation before some months have elapsed."[21]

Edwin also recognized that Mary had been the dominant force in his family's domestic affairs. He wrote to McEntee: "If you knew how helpless both Edwina & I are you'd be amazed! All these years that Mary has controlled my domestic affairs; she has not permitted the slightest interference on Edwina's part & my indolent nature has yielded everything." His behavior toward Mary was akin to his behavior toward the business managers with whom he had worked. He simply handed them control and did the same with her. At the same time Booth still regarded her as his child.

> For twelve years (nearly) I have nursed her like sick baby, but despite the care of this, and the evil that has been wrought by her semi-lunatic brain of late years, I felt for her that strange affection that the mother feels for the "black-sheep" of her family.... I think of the oral slavery that both Edwina & I endure—for the sake of quiet and regard death as our liberator, as well as a relief to the poor soul who suffers so.

Despite her doctors' insistence on bed rest, Mary continued to go out, much to Edwin's embarrassment. He found himself performing "with the constant dread ... that she will be doing some outrageous thing." In March 1881 she began raving. Edwin hired nurses to watch her night and day. He wrote to Harry Magonigle: "She is too far gone ... to understand a word that is said to her." He was advised to place her in an asylum but could not bring himself to do so. His mother-in-law, whom Booth characterized as "a vile-tongued virago & slanderer," arrived on April 4. He was forced to endure "Mistress McWicked," walking around with "a hell-cat's glare in her pale green eyes."[22]

On April 12, three weeks before opening, Booth and Irving began rehearsals alone before bringing in Ellen Terry, who played Desdemona, and the rest of the company.[23] When the entire troupe assembled, Booth was amazed at Irving's artistic control:

> Mr. Irving is despotic on the stage. At rehearsal, his will is ... law, whether it concerns the entry of a Messenger with a letter or the reading of a letter by Miss Terry.... He sits among his players watching every movement, listening to every word, constantly stopping anyone—Miss Terry as well as the messenger—who does not do exactly right. He rises, explains the fault and that part of the scene is immediately repeated.... Over and over again the line is recited or a bit of action done, until all is perfect.[24]

Booth and Irving opened on May 2, 1881. It was an odd production. Initially Irving played Iago to an Othello whose height was far less than his. Due to the difference in their height, Booth's Othello was "a slight lithe Oriental," who appeared "reluctant to lay very savage hands on ... Irving." He was never the noble Moor. The real problem was, as the critic Dutton Cook wrote, "We have here two simply masterly Iagos, two insufficient Othellos." The two men alternated in the two roles for twenty-two performances.[25]

By May 16 Booth had made the decision to sail to New York, along with Mary, her parents, Edwina and a doctor and nurse but to leave his theatrical wardrobe in England, where he intended to return with Edwina on August 17 in order to complete a provincial tour. On May 22, 1881, he wrote to William Winter: "My engagement ... with Irving ... is very great in all respects—only my domestic misery prevents it from being the happiest theatrical experience I've ever had."[26]

Booth's engagement with Irving ended on June 15. On June 6, 1881, he had written to David C. Anderson:

> My engagement ... has been ... agreeable and *ponderously* successful; it could run several weeks, if not months longer. I have made a solid mark here, but as Fate will have it, I must leave in the midst of my success, to be forgotten ... in a few months. But it does not make me miserable; my life has been so full of ups & downs that I calmly accept any rise or fall.... The past two years have been fraught with sorrow for me and for Edwina. Poor Mary was never right—her brain was too great for her fragile body, and both are now wearing out. The end is near.[27]

Chapter Seventeen

1881–1882: The Death of Mary McVicker

On June 18 the Booths and the McVickers sailed from Liverpool to New York. Edwin's plan was to take Mary to New York, spend about a month and a half in America, leave her with her parents and return to England with the nineteen-year-old Edwina. They landed on June 29, and went to apartments in the Windsor Hotel. The McVickers attempted to stop Edwin from paying Mary's bills, and during the first week in August Mary stopped seeing him. He compared her to Rip Van Winkle's shrewish wife Gretchen: "M̲r̲s̲ B., like Gretchen, drove me from her room a month ago last Saturday & I've not seen her since.... The D̲r̲ found her in pain tother day & feared it was the result of stimulant, the mother, I'm afraid, gives her too much."[1]

It is possible that Mary's mental condition may have been exacerbated by alcoholism. Mary's mother provided her with liquor. After Mary's death Booth wrote that "she was doubtless kept under alchoholic [sic] influence ... from the day her mother took her from me. The mother first inculcated that bad habit in the poor girl & often said, in excuse for Mary's conduct, 'It is Mary's life—she can't live without it.'"[2]

By September 15, 1881, Booth and Edwina needed to leave, Edwin to visit his mother in Long Branch and then his banker E. C. Benedict in Greenwich, Edwina to see Jervis McEntee's niece Julia Vaux at Rondout, near Poughkeepsie. As Booth wrote, "our house is now so distressful that 'tis better she should be away from it as much as possible."[3]

Father and daughter were preparing for a life without Mary; they needed a home. As he had at Long Branch and Cos Cob, Booth turned his attention to the possibility of a rural retreat. In July he went to Newport, Rhode Island, "to look after a lot of ground" outside the town's fashionable area that he had "bought some few years" before but had never seen. Upon his return he wrote to Jervis McEntee: "I should like to live there—if I ever live anywhere permanently this side the 'Summer-land.'"[4]

Edwina's immediate future would be centered on a childhood friend named Downing Vaux. Like Edwina, Downing was the child of a famous father—Calvert Vaux, an Englishman who had emigrated to America in 1850 and joined the firm of the noted American landscape architect Andrew Jackson Downing, for whom his son was named. In 1856 he moved to New York and became a partner of William Law Olmstead. Between 1857 and 1877 they designed and built Central Park.[5]

Booth knew him through Vaux's brother-in-law, the painter Jervis McEntee. Booth met both men in 1861, at one of the bohemian soirees of Richard and Elizabeth Stoddard. Jervis and his wife Gertrude had no children, a gap partially filled by their nephew Downing, whom McEntee described as "a great comfort."[6]

In 1881 Downing was a 24-year-old architect working in his father's firm. Downing and Edwina had known each other since childhood. He sent letters to her while she was in Europe and exhibited interest in those she sent to his sister Julia. Almost immediately upon her return to America, Downing and his mother called at the Windsor Hotel, and arrangements were made for Edwina to go to the McEntee/Vaux homes in Rondout, New York, near Poughkeepsie.[7]

Edwina spent time that summer in Rondout, visiting with Julia and Downing. He was a good-looking, athletic young man. On July 25, 1881, Booth wrote to Jervis McEntee: "Edwina had a jolly time at Rondout, ... and since Saturday has been with Julia.... They went to see a regatta in w^h Downing took part & I've no doubt she will be full of his prowess, &c." Edwina was of marriageable age, and Downing Vaux was the young man to whom her affections were turning.[8]

Jervis McEntee invited the Booths, father and daughter, to spend a weekend in Rondout. They arrived on September 24, and during the next three days, Edwin sat up late with Jervis "talking over his troubles." On September 26, McEntee recorded: "Booth talked frankly with me yesterday concerning [Downing] and Edwina. They seem fond of each other, and ... Booth told me he was more than satisfied with Downing and thinks only of Edwina's happiness." The next day McEntee "had a confidential talk with Downing and made him very happy." Three days later McEntee wrote: "A letter came from Downing telling me that ... Edwina had accepted him as her lover in their parlor at the Windsor Hotel. Her father was present and was pleased."[9]

The engagement was announced formally on October 22. Victorian engagements normally lasted four to eight months; it was September; Booth was going on tour and taking Edwina with him. They would be back by May. A June wedding would have been normal.[10]

Booth needed to work, to support himself, to build the home he was contemplating, to pay the bills of his estranged wife and now to provide for the daughter he loved, who was engaged to a man without substantial financial means. By 1881 resident stock companies were gone; Booth needed a combination company (a group of actors who toured together in one or more plays) but had neither the time nor the inclination to form one. Consequently he engaged himself to Henry E. Abbey for a thirty-week season to begin at Booth's Theatre on October 3, 1881, go out on the road and end about May 1, 1882.[11]

On November 13, 1881, Mary died at 4 P.M. at the house her parents had rented at 13 West 53rd Street. She was thirty-three years old. The official cause of death was pulmonary and laryngeal phthisis or consumption of the lungs and throat. A telegram was sent to Edwin at the St. George Hotel in Philadelphia at 7:50. It was his forty-eighth birthday. He cancelled the rest of his Philadelphia engagement, and traveled with Edwina to New York the next day.[12]

Edwin and Edwina spent the day and evening at the 53rd Street house. Draped in white satin and looking "extremely natural," Mary lay in an open rosewood coffin, surrounded by flowers. At nine P.M. that evening, her body left New York's Grand Central depot, accompanied by Edwin, Edwina, the McVicker family, Laurence Hutton and William Winter and arrived in Chicago on the morning of November 18. A funeral service was held at 2 P.M. Mary had "Standing Room Only" for her Chicago farewell. "Every seat in the church" except for "the few in front ... reserved for the mourners was occupied, and the aisles and space about the entrance were crowded with ladies and gentlemen standing up."[13]

During the service James McVicker "shook with heavy sobs." In contrast Booth seemed "calm," his face "immobile." He sat apparently unmoved, watching the preacher or the coffin or the floor in front of him. Now and then he wiped his eyes with a handkerchief, although the reporter for *The Chicago Daily Tribune* pointed out that "so far as could be seen his eyes were dry." When people filed past the open coffin, he turned in his seat and leaned with his elbow on the back of it. Since he was seated "at the end of the seat and directly adjoining the aisle" down which the mourners passed after viewing the remains, people naturally turned and looked at him. He kept his back toward them until all had gone by. After the service Mary's body was interred in Rose Hill Cemetery in Chicago." The tombstone cites her as "Mary McVicker Wife of Edwin Booth 1842–1881." His name is larger than hers.[14]

By the time she died, Edwin's vision of Mary had become one of condescending pity and loathing. She was "a devil." Even when he described her death in later life, he was far from forgiving. "Have you watched a kitten purring itself to sleep? It did not hurt her to part from loved ones for — she had not loved any one but herself." He received a condolence letter saying: "none who loved her could wish her back again."[15] It was unintentionally ironic but could have summed up Booth's own feelings.

Two days after Mary was buried, Edwin, accompanied by Edwina, rejoined the Abbey company in Baltimore, before embarking on a New England whistle-stop tour.[16] After Baltimore the company's baggage was checked for Waterbury but unfortunately placed in a car taken to Bridgeport. Booth and company arrived in Waterbury on the 4:14 P.M. train on November 28, the day they were scheduled to play, but no baggage came with them. Finally, by 7 P.M., the lost property was traced to a car standing on a side track in Bridgeport. It was obviously too late for the Waterbury performance. The local newspaper described the result — an accidental modern-dress production.

> When the curtain was finally rung up at about 8:30, it disclosed ... the entire company attired in street costume. Booth stepped forward to the footlights explained the situation and said that they would go ahead and give the three principal acts of Hamlet, doing the best they could without suitable wardrobe and properties. or the audience could have their money refunded. The announcement was received with some applause.... Only about 60 or 70 people left the hall and probably the first performance of "Hamlet" in this country by actors in street and traveling apparel took place. It gave the effect of a superior rehearsal by daylight.... In the first scene the two gentlemen in bobtail coats, Bernardo and Marcellus, appeared very much as other young gentlemen do without occupation, and the Ghost, another substantial fellow citizen, seemed to happen in to see what they were about — the whole scene being, in effect, decidedly unconventional and highly entertaining. The King [looked like the] ... president of the United States of Denmark, while his Gertrude was apparently ready for "the road."[17]

By the end of December, Booth was exhausted and wrote to Laurence Hutton: "O if I could but cancel the rest of my time with Abbey! I am wearied until death." Of course he could not stop. He was under contract.[18] Travel, however, became a bit easier in January when Abbey provided Booth and Edwina a special private train called the Jerome Miller, complete with personal chef, for their tour through New England, Pennsylvania, Louisville, Memphis, Galveston, New Orleans, the South and Midwest.

His accommodations were luxurious, but Booth still complained. "I have been so jolted & bumped over the rails that I ache from head to heels & have not had strength to write a letter.... Everything is dirty here. For many nights I have not slept more than two hours per night.... No amount of ducats could induce me to repeat this trip, luxurious as it seems to have our own car & modern conveniences; the jolting is terrible & the constant dread of being dashed to pieces is a foretaste of hell & blazes."[19]

Booth's "dread" of train travel was well justified. Underneath the "Jerome Miller" was a heating apparatus "supplied with coal by two self-feeders on either side." In early January 1882 the train lurched while Booth was giving himself a sponge bath, and his ankle was burned by the hot-air pipe that ran along the floor. He had just been inoculated and the vaccine virus in his blood infected the burn, or so he believed. His arm had to be cauterized and plastered from the vaccinations. Moreover, his jaw was swollen, probably from an infected tooth.[20]

As the tour wound through upstate New York, toward its final two weeks at Booth's Theatre, Edwina left her father to visit Downing's family at Rondout, and Booth wrote:

Being alone, I gave up my car at Buffalo & it started home [Worcester, Massachusetts], but after it has passed this point it jumped the track and was badly damaged — no one hurt — the colored porter telegraphed to this effect. Had we been aboard, the shock w^d have been serious to both [Booth and Edwina]. It's a wonder that it kept the rail so long, for we went over some wretched roads & at a fearful speed sometimes. Thank God tomorrow will end my country work & that I shall soon be out of harness.[21]

Back in New York, almost "out of harness," Booth was plagued by "insulting letters" from James McVicker. He consistently refused to appear at McVicker's Theatre in Chicago but enjoyed the fact that his father-in-law wanted him there ("The whizzing of Time brings round its revenge"). He referred to them as "the McVinegars" and "the McWickeds." Rumors persisted about future marriages to Mattie Woodman, Lillian Woodman Aldrich's sister, and to Ida Vernon, an actress in Booth's company, but Booth wrote to William Winter on December 6, 1883: "Marry again? — Wheh! — No sir! Though I had a taste of its bliss in my early venture I had a hell of it for nearly thirteen years in my second marriage and that has scared me from such risks." As he put it in minstrel show dialect, "Ah ben deah honey!"[22]

Chapter Eighteen

Europe, 1882–1883: "The most important engagement of my life"

Before Booth left Europe, his manager, Wynn Miller, was already arranging a London season for the summer of 1882, and a week after Mary's funeral, *The New York Mirror* announced that Edwin would return to England. He had written to Irving, asking to perform again at the Lyceum, but Irving had no room in his schedule. Consequently Booth turned to the Adelphi Theatre on the Strand, and on May 6 received confirmation of a six-week engagement. He wrote to Miller instructing him to "get a powerful company, excellent scenery, dresses, &c, and every adjunct that can be obtained to silence fault-finders so far as the 'mise-en-scène' is concerned."[1]

The return engagement was to include performances in Germany, a tour that Booth had contemplated when he went to England in 1880. He wrote: "My heart is set on Germany.... There the fame is to be acquired. [My] sole ambition [is] to obtain the German endorsement. England has done for me all that she is likely to do."[2]

Although Edwina had been engaged a suitable amount of time, her wedding was postponed until October 1883, so that she could accompany her father back to Europe. Downing, absorbed in business affairs, made and then broke plans to travel with them. Instead, his sister Julia Vaux was selected as Edwina's traveling companion, both young women to be served by the Booths' maid, "Brown Betty" Smith.[3]

As they were about to leave again for Europe, Edwina fell ill, and Booth immediately postponed his trip. The initial diagnosis was neuralgia, but by May 19 it had changed to what Booth called "Pleurisy with threatened Pneumonia." From London Miller cabled that Booth was financially liable as of the 26th, but Edwin replied: "My daughter hangs twixt life & death & no considra [sic] in the world could induce me to risk a 'jot,' though all the theatres ... could offer were at stake.... One lung was half full of water (Pleuro-pneumonia)."[4]

He was not concerned artistically. London was not the focus of the tour, and Booth wrote to Miller:

> [Robert] Pateman [Booth's leading comic actor] can rehearse the play [*Richelieu*] & see that the scenes & props are correct — if anything sh^d be wrong it makes little difference to me, for I can jump in at the last moment & accommodate myself to my surroundings. In one rehearsal I can correct any ... error that may occur.... I shall be in London Sat: 24th, or perhaps the night of 23rd — a quick Sunday night rehearsal may be needed, but I doubt it; one on Monday morning will suffice.... My Richelieu dress ... might be got out, hung up to get the wrinkles out, & my wig dressed.[5]

Edwina and her father left for England on the 14th, taking a doctor, who remained with them until July 3, by which time she had recovered.[6] Their ship landed at Queenstown, Ireland, on the evening of June 24. Edwin left his daughter, Julia Vaux and Betty Smith in Liverpool and hurried to London where he rehearsed *Richelieu* at the Adelphi until 4 P.M. on June 26, 1882, and opened that evening for a six-week engagement. Booth wrote to Anderson from the Hotel Brunswick: "Reception *great*, business—*English*— papers kind — weather too good for theatres— audiences fashionable and very enthusiastic every night — if they don't count many. After I close here, we shall take a trip to Switzerland & get back for rehearsals 1st week in Sept. then start for the [provincial English] tour 'till Xmas after which for Germany." When Booth wrote that "Business" was "English," he meant mediocre.[7]

A contract arrived from Berlin, but Booth didn't like it and decided to wait a few days before signing. The weeks turned into months. On September 24 he wrote to William Winter: "the German tour is not yet complete — I have signed only for Berlin, Jan. 16th, and four other palaces Hamburg, Bohn [sic], & I think Hanover is one of the other two, there are twelve cities to be bored." As usual Booth knew little of his business affairs. In actuality, there were only eight.[8]

Business in London continued, what Booth called "bad & fashionable," and he expected that he would "lose a little" not only on this Adelphi venture but also on his tours of the provinces or Germany. He visited Oxford, attended a midnight supper given in his honor by Henry Irving at the Lyceum Theatre (where he got very drunk), and he and Edwina and Julia planned a visit to the Netherlands, Germany, Switzerland and Paris before he returned to London in early September to rehearse for his provincial tour.[9]

On August 8 the Booth party left for a whirlwind month of sightseeing. In the first four days Edwin, Edwina, Julia, Betty and their Dutch guide covered Brussels, Antwerp and Rotterdam. Dutch beer began to bring out the youthful "Ted" in the almost-fifty-year-old Booth, who saluted David C. Anderson with an irreverent version of Rip Van Winkle's famous toast:[10]

> Here we are in Dutchland on the Maas. Clean, sober & polite are the people & many of them speak English perfectly. No *Darks* since we left London & Betty is stared at wherever we go. Cigars are excellent & cheaper than at home — haven't yet tried their pipes, but their beer is bully! I'm full of it now! ... I shall try to send a greeting to you from Bingen as we go up the Rhine. This tour is Edwina's & I go as she directs, but I notice that I pay all the bills! Have you ever been here? 'Tis unlike all other places (just a smack of Venice perhaps) and I could spend a month here in full enjoyment of it: —'specially the beer! The beer is bully! I like the Dutch. The women are pretty, the men affable & *the beer is bully!* Here's your goat-o-hel! .... if we had *six* instead of *one* month [I] would be happy; the nightmare of my Provincial towns in England still haunts me! If I had a decent pen I'd write more nonsense, but the only one I have doth beat the Dutch & they're hard to beat, 'specially on their beer — their beer is Bully (with a big B this time) and don't you forget it! Here's your Goot-hel, unt ur family's Yaw![11]

From Rotterdam the Booths took a boat up the Rhine to Heidelberg, where they spent three days. Booth, having caught what he described as "a severe cold in damp Dutchland" and lonely for male companionship, stayed up until midnight, smoking and medicating himself with alcohol. The Booth party stayed at the Grand Hotel Victoria in Interlaken, Switzerland, with a view of the Jungfrau, and then went on to Lucerne, Geneva, Paris and back to London, where, beginning September 5, Edwin went into a week's rehearsal — an exceptionally long period in the nineteenth century.[12]

In mid–September 1882 Booth undertook a tour of Britain, visiting Sheffield, York, Scarborough, Harrowgate, Newcastle-Upon-Tyne, Dundee, Aberdeen, Glasgow, Edinburgh, Hull, Leeds, Dublin, Manchester, Liverpool and Birmingham. He always opened with *Richelieu*, followed, during a week's run, by *Hamlet, The Fool's Revenge, Othello*, a repetition of *Richelieu* and on Saturday evening a double bill of *Merchant of Venice* and *Katherine and Petruchio*. He typically received between 55 and 65 percent of the box office.[13]

Artistically and financially, the results were not always positive. Booth encountered many of the same problems he faced in America. Competition from alternate events like the St. Leger horserace in Doncaster hurt his houses in nearby Sheffield. "Inclement weather" produced poor houses in Manchester, a place Booth referred to as "the watering pot of England." Backstage crews were sometimes incompetent.[14] The company that supported Booth had its share of "dogans," Booth's term for inept actors. On October 3 during the final scene of *Hamlet* at Dundee, one of them accidentally stabbed Booth in the right arm. The wound plagued Edwin for more than a month. On October 22 he wrote to Winter:

> Your last ... reached me the day after I had been slightly stabbed by a 'dogan' who stood in defense of the King, in the final scene of Hamlet, and owing to my own treatment of the wound, I have suffered the torments of erysipelas (in both arms) ever since—even now the itching is intolerable, & I am bandaged o'both sides with ointment & lint.... With both arms swollen & itching all the while, I have not ceased acting.... Had to fence left-handed, which arm you know is so badly mashed that I can barely use it, and the exertion caused that member to swell, so the next night I had both fins in limbo.[15]

Off-stage the tour was often pleasant. Booth and Edwina and Julia had "delightful times" at York and Harrowsgate and found Scarborough "a heavenly place when the sun shines" where they could have "a stroll about the quaint place & on the beach" and enjoy the air, which he thought "better than that of Newport." Financially, however, it was disappointing. On September 27, 1882, Booth wrote a facetious letter from Newcastle: "My tour has been very agreeable so far—except in the way of dollars, I barely pay expenses, but I am gaining practice & experience, w^h I need so much."[16]

On the morning of October 12, 1881, while Booth was playing Glasgow, Calvert Vaux found his son Downing, Edwina's fiancé, unconscious in his gas-filled room. Downing "had left his gas burning and it had evidently blown out and the door blown closed." A doctor was called, and oxygen administered. By 3:30 the next afternoon Downing was "still unconscious."[17]

Booth heard of the accident when he reached Leeds on October 30. McEntee and the Vauxes told him that Downing was out of danger, and Booth immediately cabled that Downing should join them in England "to get a good long rest from business." It proved to be impossible. On November 1, 1882, Jervis McEntee wrote in his diary: "Downing gets on very slowly and on Monday sat up half an hour. Booth cabled to him to join them, but poor fellow, he is helpless."[18]

Downing, "somewhat improved," though still "dull and silent," decided to join the Booths anyway and sailed for Europe on the *Servia* on December 13. The English provincial tour ended, and by the 18th Booth was at Morley's Hotel on Trafalgar Square in London. Downing arrived in London on December 22 and spent Christmas with the Booths. Edwin wrote that he was "very weak," but his "presence ... relieved Edwina," and Booth believed that he would "steadily improve." On December 27 the Booth party started for Berlin "by easy stages." They anticipated arriving on January 1 so that Booth could begin rehearsals. Booth expected to "*open & shut, too, perhaps*" on January 15 and wrote to David Anderson: "It may be a startling fizzle!" He had given up the idea of a touring company of any kind in Germany and faced instead "a fresh company in every city I visit. A terrible task it will be!"[19]

He arrived in Berlin as planned on January 1, 1883, ready to begin rehearsals for *Richelieu* at the Victoria Theatre on January 3. On the 2nd, however, his German representative and stage manager of the tour, Emanuel Lederer, informed him that the manager of the Victoria Theater had canceled his contract, supposedly on the basis that the "prompt books for the German Co. were not sufficiently clear." In actuality, the manager had opened a spectacular entitled *Frau Venus* on Christmas Day and refused to interrupt the run. "At the eleventh hour [a female] star at the Residenz (a smaller house) was taken ill," and a theatrical agent arranged for Booth to "jump in hap-hazard." Edwin was not completely satisfied. He wrote to his friend the critic

Laurence Hutton: "the Victoria is too large & cheerless, the Residenz too small for tragedy, but snug & cozy — better for me artistically, but holds few pfennigs. The papers are full of my praises & if I do not lose my way among the gutterals, may make a 'hit.'" Rehearsals began in early January, with Booth using an interpreter to provide him with cues. He came to believe that he could understand their German when he was acting, because he was actually reciting the English text in his mind.[20]

Booth opened on January 11 in *Hamlet*, "without scenery at all appropriate & costumes of the queerest description." To his delight he found the company, which was both local and German, "really excellent — good in every particular."[21]

The United States minister to Germany and the German crown prince, later Emperor Frederich Wilhelm, were present at the opening. "At the end of each prominent scene," Booth "was called before the curtain three to five times," and at the end of the play, he was recalled twenty-four times. The crown princess came twice during the run; the crown prince four times. The latter declared that for the first time, he had seen a "real prince" on stage. Booth's dream had come true. Royalty, at least German royalty, was paying attention.[22]

Berlin society was "won over," and Booth, who normally lived "in strict retirement," began to accept invitations. A reception at the court of Emperor William I had been arranged by the crown prince but did not take place in consequence of the death of Prince Karl, brother of the elderly emperor. Booth, however, "received ... the portraits of the Crown Prince and Crown Princess shortly before his departure from Berlin." He wrote to Laurence Hutton: "This is a superb city & in summer must be delightful. The air is cold & crisp — just as we have it at home at our best ... Am mighty glad to get out of the fogs of London and away from the bad cooking & sameness of provender; here we have excellent food in great variety, & properly prepared: we 'gorge' after our long English fast."[23]

Downing, however, continued to worry him. "My girl is happier in having Downing here, ... but the poor fellow's condition causes her anxiety — physically he is all right, but the shock to his brain has dimmed his memory & renders him almost helpless at times, but a few weeks rest & care will 'bring him round,' I hope."[24] By January 29, however, when Booth was performing King Lear in Berlin, there was little hope left.

> Poor Downing's condition is very distressing. I had the highest authority (Dr. Leyden) on brain & nerve diseases to see him three times, & he says it will be a *long* time, with careful treatment, before he fully recovers; he should not have come, but we all thought it the best for both Edwina & him. He has improved in minor matters very much, but all his ambition is gone, & he is apathetic, Edwina to him is no more than his sister — he sometimes forgets (or seems to) that she is here or of any interest to him. Julia long ago lost her love for Europe... Edwina having Downing only in the body present, his spirit being absent, as it were, is wretched of course. The result is they go home next Sunday from Bremen in the Donau.... I shall be anxious to hear of their safe arrival. The separation will, I hope & believe, create a re-action in Downing's condition & restore Edwina's natural feeling towards him, as it is there seems to be a cloud between them.[25]

From Berlin, Booth went to on to Hamburg, where he opened on February 15, 1882. After his first performance, as reported in *The New York Herald*, "the [male] actors fell upon his shoulders and in continental fashion kissed him on both cheeks, while the women wept and sobbed as they shook hands with him. He did not relish the kissing. In vain he cried out 'Mind the paint!' And at last in a sort of comic desperation, he exclaimed 'If kissing be the correct thing, please stand aside, gentlemen, and let the ladies advance.'"[26] On February 18, 1883, he wrote to David Anderson:

> My success is if possible increased here. The people (and I'm told the Press) seem wild over me. The stage-director ... your very counter-part (I call him "Uncle Dave" — he played Polonius with me, too) — who was pupil to Ludwig Devrient (Germany's greatest tragedian) hugs me, kisses my hand

& calls me "*Meister.*" The manager, who saw & well remembers *Talma* does *the* same & both declare me their equal. Much for two old fogies to admit. The actors & actresses weep & kiss *galore* also & the audience last night formed a passage from the lobby to my carriage till I was in & off, *yet* I was nearly an hour in the theatre after the play [*Lear*].So far as the men-kissers go, I feel with old *Pericles* "I never liked these *buggers*" but I see no particular objection to the ladies— there are so many fair & callow ones that it compensates for the *Queens* & *heavies*. Having a surfeit of public applause, for it seems as though I had it— through Father, being with him so long— the most is but as little to me, but this personal enthusiasm from actors— old & young, is a new experience & stimulates me strangely. I feel more like acting than I've felt for years & wish I could keep it up here in Germany for six months at least, but *alas* my time is limited, & the old man waxeth weary— in his *joints.* You've heard ere this about the silver wreath & the Press Testimonial in Berlin: had to make *my usual* speech. Think of acting five acts of Tragedy without a *hand*! Merely a very subdued "Bravo" now & then— but when the drop falls *call* after call & *bravos* by the bushel make it up. I daresay applause (if I ever get it) in the midst of a scene will confuse me hereafter.[27]

After the performance of *King Lear* on February 22, Booth took eight curtain calls, and when the curtain finally fell, "a whole bevy of pretty young girls— actresses & otherwise— rushed up with open arms" and in Edwina's words, "actually embraced and kissed papa as he stood on the stage still in Lear's robes!!" Then the director of the theatre, all the members of the company, some in costume and some in evening dress, presented Booth with a silver laurel branch on a silk cushion. He thanked the company, although only those nearest could catch his words, because the audience had not left their seats and continued to applaud. Finally the curtain was raised again, and Booth made a short speech. As he and Edwina left the theatre, "its doors were surrounded by well-dressed ladies and gentlemen ... many of them giving 'three cheers'" and "lifting their hats as they did so." The next morning, "a chorus of male voices serenaded" Booth from the corridor outside his room at the Hotel de L'Europe.[28]

The Booths traveled from Hamburg to Bremen on February 23, and Edwin immediately went into rehearsals for *Hamlet*, *King Lear* and *Othello*. Although his polyglot performances were described by Bremen critics as a "Mischmasch" of languages, his season there ended with the same tributes he had received in Berlin and Hamburg. By now, directors in various German cities were soliciting an engagement, but Booth intended a holiday of several weeks in Italy and then a month at leisure in London before sailing to America in late June. He regarded his German tour as "the most important engagement of my life," but was "tired and full of aches." By March 17 he realized that he would not have the time to visit Italy after his Vienna engagement, and would have only two weeks in London before he sailed home.

He closed in Leipzig on the 21st, went with Edwina to Dresden and Prague "to see the sights," while Wynn Miller left with Booth's "traps" [luggage], his interpreter and his valet for Vienna on the 23rd.[29] Booth wrote to Winter from Dresden:

> I can hardly realize that my dream of twenty years ago is so near its end. In a week or so I shall terminate at Vienna the series of engagements towards wh. I have looked with hope, fear and despair— for I hardly believed I should ever accomplish them, or if— not so successfully. My health is excellent, a little fatigued & occasionally a cough depresses me, but on the whole all was never better.... 'Tis time to sit down & begin to be old.[30]

Booth opened as Hamlet at the Stadt Theater in Vienna on March 31, 1883. He was scheduled to close on April 8 but was held over until April 17. Initially the audience was unresponsive, because most of them could not understand English. Booth's supporting cast were, of course, acting in German, and one of the comic newspapers, reviewing Booth's Lear, illustrated the problem: "Two stout ladies are attentively watching Lear, who is tearing his hair. One of them asks in an audible whisper, 'What is the old man crying about, do you know?' 'Oh no wonder he is desperate, he can't understand a word his own flesh and blood says to him,' answers the other."[31]

Viennese critics were initially annoyed by the amount of movement Booth brought to his roles, but eventually spectators warmed to Booth's performances and called him out after every act. During *Hamlet*, applause stopped the show after the Nunnery scene, an unusual event in a culture in which it was generally reserved until the end of the play. Booth, however, thought he "was dull & heavy as the spritely Dane" and that in terms of Othello, Viennese audiences wanted a "howler" like Salvini who would "yank Desdemona about the floor like a clothes bag." When he gave his last performance in Vienna—an evening for the benefit of the Concordia Club, an association of Viennese authors and journalists—wreaths were handed to him from the audience.[32] After returning to his hotel, Booth had to send his carriage back to the theatre to collect the floral tributes left there, some of them hoops of roses and camellias the size of carriage wheels. Despite his reservations about Viennese audiences and weather ("a horrible place for throat & lung diseases"), Booth spoke of his Vienna engagement as "the summer of his life." Sending Wynn Miller ahead to London with his "traps," and "sojer-clothes" (costumes), Booth left Vienna on April 19, 1883, and arrived in Paris on April 25.[33]

He did not look forward to his Parisian experience. "Paris has no charm for me now—twenty years ago it had; I must agonize through a fortnight there & dine & Opera most of the time, I suppose." Sarah Bernhardt had just completed her run. There was nothing in the theatres Booth wanted to see, and as he wrote to David Anderson: "I'm sick of theatres just now." Edwina dragged her father shopping, and Booth stayed home at night "from sheer fatigue." He was tired; he had given up the chance to see Italy or do further sightseeing in England in order to rest before leaving for America; he even turned down an invitation to have supper on May 7 with Henry Irving, the Prince of Wales and James Russell Lowell. He planned to sail to America on the *Gallia* on June 9.[34]

The Booths had been receiving what Edwin described as "very encouraging news" about Downing after his return to America in February. Although "his recovery was slow" and he was clearly "far from well," he had expressed "anxiety about his profession," which Booth saw as "the best evidence of his restoration yet given." In her father's eyes Edwina was "by turns hopeful & depressed as his letters vary," but a letter she had written while touring Germany set off a disastrous reaction.[35]

On May 7, Downing left his home at 15th and Irving Place and went to breakfast with his family. During breakfast, a letter from Edwina arrived. After reading it, he picked up his "satchel and spring overcoat" and left, presumably for his father's business. He never arrived at the office. Around noon Calvert Vaux sent a messenger to find out why his son was detained and later went around to Downing's rooms to find him, but he was not there. Alarmed, the Vaux family began to check with local hospitals. Downing's mother, his uncle Jervis McEntee and Julia Vaux arrived around 9 P.M. from Rondout, and Julia suggested that Calvert visit Downing's rooms again. A servant reported seeing Downing around 7 P.M. and hearing him pouring out water as if he were washing himself, but he was gone by the time Calvert got there, leaving his satchel with an empty unfired revolver as well as his gold watch and chain and other articles of jewelry. The family notified the police but were advised to wait a day before sending out "a general alarm." McEntee spent all night in the front parlor of the house in which Downing had his room, while Calvert Vaux stayed outside in the street, watching the house. The next day McEntee and Downing's sister combed the city parks, and Downing's brother Bowyer searched for him in the Bowery and Staten Island. McEntee continued to spend the night in Downing's room.[36]

On May 8, Calvert Vaux went to the police, fearing, in the words of Jervis McEntee: "that his son's mind has become unsettled and that he was either wandering aimlessly about the City or had committed suicide. A general alarm describing the missing man was sent ... to all the police stations in the city." The news of Downing's disappearance made the New York newspapers on May 9, and McEntee telegraphed Booth at the American Exchange, London: "Downing disappeared seventh. No tidings. Jervis." That night Downing returned to his room at 11 P.M. He had been wandering about in the country. After speaking to Downing on the 10th, McEntee wrote to Booth advising "him and Edwina not to ... consider any plans for the future." Booth wrote to McEntee: "I dread now to think of the consequences of this affair. How will it end? Will his brain be ever restored? Who can tell! ... What is to be the future of these two—on whom we all set such hope!!"[37]

To David Anderson Booth poured out his heart. "What a curse is on the Booths & for what? We must go back beyond my records that I have found for the cause of all the horrors that are heaped on us! God help us!" The Booths sailed for home on June 9, and in time Booth came to see the 1882–1883 European tour as a mixed blessing. He continued to flirt with the idea of returning to Germany as late as 1887, but, in actuality, he would never again leave America.[38]

Chapter Nineteen

Touring and Family Life, 1883–1886

During the 1880s Booth experienced the death of his oldest friend, his mother, his wife, two sisters and his eldest brother, and he became increasingly dependent on his daughter and aware of his need to find a home for her and for himself. Edwina sought to take Mary McVicker's place, but in the 1880s even she would desert him for a husband, and Booth would be alone.

When he and Edwina returned from Europe in June 1883, Booth was vague about his personal plans: "I want first to get a roosting place ... and then to spend as much of the summer as I can at Newport."[1] He also faced the problem presented by Downing Vaux, whom he saw as mentally incompetent.

Edwina and her father vacationed with the McEntees and Vauxes for three weeks. During her visit to Rondout, Edwina decided to break her engagement. On July 16, 1883, Booth wrote to Jervis McEntee: "I could see that she ... wanted to speak of something that troubled her.... At last, ... she relieved her heart by a relation of ... the terrible trial she had endured the past few weeks—all of which she has written to Downing.... Bad as this misfortune seems for both of them, how much worse, ... would be their fate were they married! ... I must beg of you Jervy to ... make him realize how incapable he is ... to assume the responsibility of marriage."[2] Downing received the letter just before dinner the next day. McEntee urged him to accept Edwina's decision. Booth, in turn, sought to occupy Edwina's mind and time with their new house in Newport, Rhode Island, soon to be christened Boothden.[3]

The Newport home represented a considerable upswing in social prestige from Long Branch and Cos Cob. Newport was one of America's most fashionable summer resorts, and since the Booths toured most of the year, they were "home" primarily in the summer. In January 1879 Edwin had spent $3,658 for 3.658 acres on a stretch of land known as "Paradise," three miles east of downtown. Eventually he owned almost ten acres. The house was finished by August 1, 1883.[4]

In September 1883 as Edwina was recovering from her break with Downing, Booth's oldest brother Junius died. Edwin had never thought much of him as an actor. When Mary Anderson told him that his brother had said: "I would rather plough all day than act half the night," Edwin replied: "Quite right, too; Junius would have ploughed better than he ever acted." By 1872 after a life spent acting and managing theatres in Boston and New York, June and his third wife, an Australian-born actress named Marian Agnes Lane Rookes Perry, had settled in a cottage in Manchester-by-the-Sea, Massachusetts, and by 1878 they had built a hotel on the site called the Masconomo House, where they entertained their guests with "readings." June continued to act intermittently, but by February 1879 he was plagued by arthritis; his wife Agnes was often out of work, and Edwin was forced to support them with "loans." When June was not able to meet the notes, Edwin simply cancelled them.[5]

On September 12, 1883, June, who had been ill for several weeks with bladder and heart problems, was seized with a "paralytic shock." His wife Agnes was summoned from Philadelphia where she was performing. Joseph Booth came from Long Branch and Edwin from Newport. The brothers spent September 16 together, and at 11:10 P.M. that night, June died. He was buried in Manchester's Rosedale cemetery.[6]

By the time of June's death, Edwin had decided that he needed not only a summer home in Newport but also a permanent winter residence. He had found one by September 25 on Chestnut Street in Boston, the fifth house he had purchased since the 1860s.[7] He wrote to Jervis McEntee on September 27, 1883:

> My resolve to buy in Boston was not a sudden one, or rather I sh<u>d</u> say 'twas the result of a long cherished wish to make that city my home. Edwina's mother died & is buried there: she [Mary Devlin] & I had determined to settle there, when circumstances would permit me to settle anywhere, & as I am now on the "home stretch" and do not mean to travel much—never, I hope beyond Baltimore, I made up my mind to "fix" myself at once provided I could get a house to suit me.... Next spring I hope to move my worldly goods & <u>deeds</u> to "Yankeeland" & "set up my everlasting rest" at the "Hub."[8]

By late August he had decided on a brief tour to Boston, New York, Philadelphia, Baltimore and Brooklyn, using the theatrical firm of Brooks and Dixon as managers.[9] Booth gave them the right to choose the theatres in which he performed, the supporting company and the costumes and scenery they used. His producers were interested in making money. Consequently the company, composed of what *The New York Mirror* called "professional pigmies" traveled without scenery, dependent on the stock settings of theatres in which they performed what Booth described as their "slaughterous work."[10] Playing in New York, he wrote to Winter:

> You can form no idea of the miserable condition of the Star theatre! Filthy dirty & so crowded with rubbish that I am in dread every night lest some accident may occur. It is impossible to get anything decent in the way of scenery or <u>props</u> & I will not be able to produce all the plays in consequence.... Such a hole I've not been in for many years—I mean in this country. The rats carry off everything that is lying about loose & raise merry 'h-11 & Tommy' in my dressing room. I think the old rattle trap ought to have been condemned years ago—it never could have been safe.[11]

Downing was back at work in New York by the time Booth played the Star. He appeared at the apartment Edwin had rented, and Booth, who was out at the time, became furious. McEntee "urged him to keep away from them," but Downing insisted on his rights. Booth wrote Downing "a firm but kindly letter" and received what he described as a "a disrespectful silly &, in a certain sense, threatening ... half-lunatic epistle" in return. On December 30, 1883, he wrote to McEntee: "I have been told that he carries a pistol & ... he will in some sudden freak do something desperate."[12]

At the end of the 1883–1884 season Edwin and Edwina returned to Boothden, where he remained, until at least October 12. On July 27, 1884, he wrote to Jervis McEntee: "The place is very beautiful, but ah, the cost of it! This place & the Boston house have been a fearful pull on me, & my expenses have increased infernally, while my income has decreased correspondingly." The European tours and the abbreviated 1883–1884 tour had been unprofitable. He had also made a bad $20,000 stock investment.[13] To make money, Booth needed to tour.

For the 1884–1885 season he turned to R. M. Field and the Boston Museum company, hoping to find better support than he had endured during the previous season. The Field company had only four rehearsals before opening. Although Booth "felt no interest whatever in the weary work," he "gave three honest hours to it; from 10 A.M. 'till three at least & perhaps longer," writing to Laurence Hutton, "at 52 this is not funny."[14]

By Thanksgiving he and Edwina were back in Boston and felt "at home and cozy."[15] At

Christmas 1884 he wrote to Launt Thompson: "Edwina has had her time well occupied with younger friends— unmarried girls."[16] Edwina's time, however, had been "occupied" with more than those. On November 24, 1884, she wrote to a young man named Ignatius Rupert Grossman to invite him to visit her home accompanied by a female friend, presumably included for propriety. In the note Edwina promised "that you shall continue to have all your bachelor freedom, and no restraint, but to come and go as you please. This invitation you must know is a joint one from my father as well as from myself." Ignatius was unable to come, but the two met at the opera, and on November 29, Edwina wrote to him expressing her regret that he could not visit and saying: "I had hoped to become better acquainted with you over a cup of tea than a box at the opera would permit." In December he sent her a birthday gift of "toothsome sweetmeats."[17]

The son of two Hungarian immigrants, Ignatius was nine years older than Edwina and had lived with the family of Celia Thaxter, a minor New England writer. By February 17, 1885, Booth was aware of him as one of Edwina's beaus and wrote to her: "I'll talk of 'Ignat' ... & tother fellows when I have more time — my love to them."[18] He was writing to her because Edwina no longer accompanied her father on tour but stayed at home to pursue her social life.

Booth opened at the Fifth Avenue Theatre in New York on December 10 with five thousand dollars worth of tickets already sold, played there for six weeks and immediately undertook a two-week tour of eleven New England towns, Boston and Philadelphia. On April 13, 1885, he wrote to Winter from Philadelphia: "This is my last week, thank God! And when my Ristori week is ended & the all-important event of my life is passed, I shall hope for a long unbroken season of rest."[19] The "Ristori week" was two performances of *Macbeth* at the Academy of Music in New York with the Italian tragedienne Adelaide Ristori. The results were artistically slapdash although financially profitable. The producer Daniel Frohman recalled:

> The house was crowded. Over three thousand people witnessed the performance. Many of the ultra-fashionable ... paid as high as five dollars each for seats.... The management used stock sets that had been knocking around the city for years. Supers had been mustered at the last minute at one dollar each.... And to cap the climax a small cat walked across the stage and yawned in open defiance.[20]

The "all-important event" that Booth referred to was his daughter's wedding. Edwina and Ignatius were engaged by April 12, 1885, and Ignatius began making arrangements for a private railroad car to carry him and Edwina to New York, where they would embark on a European honeymoon, presumably financed by the bride's father. Ignatius had no money, and from the beginning, Booth was wary of his future son-in-law. He introduced him to his banker, E. C. Benedict, and provided him with letters of credit but made sure that only Edwina could sign the checks.[21]

Booth made no effort to hide his discomfort from either his friends or Edwina, but the date and place were set — the parlor at 29 Chestnut Street at noon on May 16. Booth and Edwina began "discussing flowers and other marriage matters." His uneasiness, however, continued. He could find nothing wrong with the man who had come "in the dark to steal my treasure" but the fear he experienced bespoke a neurotic need to keep "all I have"— namely his daughter. Edwina received "all sorts of golden opinions" of Ignatius, but Booth approached the wedding as "an ordeal that 'dazes' me to think on.... 'Till after the event I can give no thought to myself— what I shall do, where go during her absence abroad."[22]

On May 16, 1885, Edwina Booth married Ignatius Rupert Grossman. At the wedding Booth is said to have turned to the Boston comedian William Warren and said: "Let us escape from here, and have a smoke together upstairs in my den." Booth accompanied the bride and groom to New York and saw them until May 20 — the day before they sailed for their European honeymoon.[23]

Three days after they left Booth, still in New York, wrote to his now-married daughter: "Since I left you Wednesday I have been in a dize — everyone endeavoring to prevent me from loneliness... Until I know that you are safe beyond the ice-bergs & other sea-dangers I cannot be quite at rest."[24] On August 14, 1885, he wrote to William Winter: "I have felt my girl's absence very keenly & have not had a very cheerful summer."[25] The omission of Ignatius' name from Booth's letters was indicative of his feelings about the man who had taken his daughter away. It was Edwina's company he needed. Ignatius did not exist. Booth often wrote about his daughter as if she were traveling alone. When he mentioned her husband, only his last name was used. Booth had called Edwina's first fiancé Downing; he referred to her husband as "Grossman." He would call him worse things as time went on.

By the time she returned from her honeymoon, Edwina was pregnant. To Booth, she looked "pale & thin," but she assured him that she felt well, had a good appetite and was getting lots of sleep. He had to conclude: "She is happy & that's all I can ask for. Grossman seems devoted & very tender & I hope for the best from what I see of them."[26]

A month after Edwina returned from her honeymoon her grandmother, Mary Ann Holmes Booth, died. Booth had been Mary Ann's primary support since he was twenty-five. By 1858 he was already referring to her as "poor mother," an epithet he used for the next twenty-five years. Mary Ann actually lived until eighty, and her letters, even in old age, reveal a person filled with gossip and an interest in the economic aspects of the theatre.

After leaving the farm in Bel Air, Mary Ann spent most of life in hotel rooms and apartments, supported by Edwin and living with Rosalie and Joseph.[27] As her age increased, Edwin became increasingly dependent on David C. Anderson and his wife Marie as her caretakers. David visited Mary Ann daily, cheering her up with an "hour or two of jollity." In late January 1884 she fell in her apartment, fractured her hip and never fully recovered. On July 27, 1884, Booth wrote to Anderson: "I think poor mother seems to get no better, & I fear her fate is fixed — never to walk again, & poor, dear Rose! How patient & long-suffering her life has been! Their case is pitiable & I wish I could relieve it."[28]

It was Anderson, however, and not Mary Ann who died first, cared for, in his last illness, by Joseph Booth. Edwin attended the funeral supporting Marie Anderson, Dave's widow, on his arm. He continued to support her for the rest of her life, and after Mary Ann's passing she became a care-giver for his sister Rose.[29]

Mary Ann Holmes Booth died at 3 A.M. on October 22, 1885. The cause of death was officially diagnosed as "Pneumonia Aetieronia Embolism and Heart Failure." Ten days before she had caught a cold, and only two days before pneumonia had set in.[30] Booth wrote to Edwina:

> Poor grandma passed away at three this morning. I did not arrive until seven. How strange that it should be my lot always in such cases to arrive too late! ... Joe is of little use, poor Rose — of none at all. She fell into a stupor about 7:30 last night and died so at three.... 'Tis for poor Rose I feel most anxious — she has just sighed, barely loud enough for me to hear, "I wish I was gone too"; poor, poor soul! I must arrange something now for her.... For some nights past she [Mary Ann] insisted that Rose should sleep in the same bed with her — she felt too nervous to be alone, & Rose was asleep beside her, when the nurse woke her & informed her of Mother's death. I am waiting for the doctor and the embalmers — I can't endure the idea of placing the body on ice.[31]

On October 24, 1885, the funeral party arrived in Baltimore on the 12:45 train. After the graveside service the Booths did not wait to see the grave filled in but left immediately for dinner at a local hotel and then caught the five P.M. train back to New York. Although two of June's children attended their grandmother's funeral, Edwina and her husband did not, presumably because she was pregnant. After the funeral Booth wrote to Lawrence Barrett: "She looked about forty & very beautiful — as I remember her in my boyhood."[32]

Two weeks later Booth was back touring under Fields' management, with the Boston Museum company for a fourteen-week season during 1885–1886. He was feeling "an aged party" and during the summer, decided to forego Hamlet in the future, a promise he found impossible to fulfill. The season began late again — in Baltimore on November 9 — and then moved to New York, Brooklyn, Boston and Philadelphia. The schedule was grueling. In November 1885 Booth performed fourteen characters in a two-week run at Baltimore and eight characters in a week-long run in Brooklyn.[33]

In Boston Booth stayed at his new Boston residence, 29 Chestnut Street, but relations with his daughter and son-in-law were deteriorating. On December 4, 1885, McEntee wrote in his diary: "I asked him if Edwina and her husband lived with him, and he said they did but that they had their separate suite of apartments, and ... kept a good deal to themselves and seemed too absorbed in and very fond of each other." What seems natural for a newly married couple was for Booth a sign of avoidance. Booth loved his daughter and was emotionally dependent on her; in turn, she loved him and was financially dependent on him, but it would soon become clear that they could not live together.[34]

He opened his New York engagement with *Hamlet* on February 1, 1886, supported by the Boston Museum company.[35] He went on to give twenty-eight performances in ten different characters; however, weariness and possibly the onset of neurological problems that would eventually take his life surfaced during the New York run. On February 27, 1886, he wrote to Edwina:

> I had a most curious experience with Brutus (Julius Caesar) with w^h I closed my engagement. Having so recently acted it (seven times) and with such success I gave myself no concern about it, but when I found myself on the stage, I could not recall more than a few lines of my speech throughout the play. I made a "mess" of it & yet I was in excellent condition otherwise. It mortified me extremely for I calculated on that part to give a satisfactory close to my engagement — the matinee & last night's performances of the part were better but I had had a scare & it "took the <u>act</u> out of me."[36]

Booth stopped touring on March 13 to spend time in Boston with his pregnant daughter. He was frightened. His first wife had suffered from gynecological problems that developed shortly after childbirth. His second wife had delivered a ten-pound still-born boy and had miscarried a second child. Booth's first grandchild Mildred, possibly named for Mollie Devlin, was born on March 24, 1886. According to Booth, the delivery was difficult. Edwina remained in bed for almost a month, and Booth wrote to Lawrence Barrett that she was "so feeble that neither Grossman nor I have been permitted to see her. Poor girl! My anxiety is dreadful but the doctors assure me all is well with her. God bless the child!"[37]

Before Mildred was born, Booth had contracted for a brief spring tour with the Italian tragedian Tomasso Salvini. Artistically it proved unsatisfactory, and in terms of Booth's reputation, it would be a disaster. By spring 1886 Booth and Salvini were rehearsing, and Booth wrote to Laurence Hutton: "Just from rehearsal — the greatest mess you ever saw! Shakespeare a la Macaroni!"[38]

On April 26, 1886, Booth and Salvini opened as Iago and Othello in what Booth still described as "a terrible mess of Shakespeare & Macaroni" at the Academy of Music in New York City.[39] Three days later, Jervis McEntee recorded in his diary:

> The moment Booth came in, we all noticed something was wrong. We could not hear a word, and his voice sounded thick, and as the noise of people coming in late subsided, it was apparent Booth was hampered by some disadvantage. Of course we suspected what was the matter, and we were all full of anxiety. He had to be prompted several times; his utterance was thick and spiritless, and he repeated his phrases. In the scene between him and Othello where he insinuates Desdemona's infidelity and where the Moor in his phrensy [*sic*] throttles him and flings him on the floor. he ...

staggered backward towards the front of the stage and fell backward at full length upon the footlights breaking the guard rod in his fall. Some one from the audience sprang [up] and assisted him to rise, when he went on with his part. But the strain ... was terrible. I went over to Mrs [Richard Henry] Stoddard's box on the opposite side of the house to see if she noticed anything wrong. She only said she heard people in the next box say when he fell, "he is drunk."[40]

Booth's friends rushed to his aid in print. Salvini's manager said that he had been with Mr. Booth nearly all of Wednesday and felt sure the tragedian had not been drinking. Mr. Perry, treasurer at the Star Theatre, and William Bispham both said that Booth "was worn out by hard work and long rehearsals." Booth himself showed up looking "bright" at the eleven o'clock rehearsal next day, saying that he had been affected by an attack of vertigo. "Similar attacks have troubled me often before; yesterday it was caused, I think, by a bilious attack." Salvini commented: "He have trouble in ze head.... It was ze nervousness, you see, nodding but ze rush of blood to ze — what you call? — brain." In the long run Booth blamed Salvini, saying "the fat boy pushed me."[41] Alcohol may have contributed to the attack, but it also may have been a harbinger of the stroke that would fell Booth two seasons later. He admitted to Edwina that he had also lost his balance in Philadelphia and Boston.

In July 1886 Booth wrote to Lawrence Barrett: "Edwina is getting on nicely now — she has a trained nurse to regulate her diet &c, and no doubt she will steadily improve." Edwina had also taken the first step to detach herself, Ignatius and the baby from her father by renting a summer home at Narragansett Pier. She told Booth that she did not want to summer in Newport. He was free to visit Narragansett, but it would not be his home.[42]

Tomasso Salvini. "On April 26, 1886, Booth and Salvini opened as Iago and Othello in what Booth described as 'a terrible mess of Shakespeare & Macaroni.'"

In Edwin's eyes, Ignatius was systematically getting "rid of Edwina's old 'stand-bys' — friends as well as servants," including Betty Smith who, in Edwin's words, did "not wish to go 'Grossman.'" Booth claimed that he was "letting Edwina and her family have my houses, furniture & horses at their expense, helping them in taxes, gas &c." The truth was that Booth no longer wanted either the Newport or the Boston house without Edwina. His dislike of Ignatius was growing. From all appearances Ignatius was a loving husband and father, but he was financially dependent on his father-in-law, and that rankled Booth, On July 17, 1886, he wrote to Winter:

> I must sell this house [29 Chestnut Street] & get rid of 'Boothden' as soon as possible in order to support my son-(of a b–h) in-law, who does nothing but spend money, smile, & live on his wife's father. A jolly old home is mine — would you not rather have your child in heaven? — I would. Particularly if I knew that her husband was in <u>Hell</u> where he belongs.[43]

Edwina became pregnant again in June, but she did not tell her father until mid–September, when Booth replied to her letter: "I pray to God that you may be mistaken, premature old age and harrowing cares at the best are the consequences of frequent maternity to a young woman." He despised his son-in-law and began to refer to him as "Ignausea," but he wrote to William Winter on September 19, 1886: "Edwina ... is evidently very happy & perhaps the strange companionship is for the best. A woman's love is incomprehensible. I shall sell the Boston house & return to New York. I shall never again attempt to settle down outside a graveyard."[44]

Chapter Twenty

The 1886–1887 Season: "It is time to harvest all I can"

As early as October 9, 1884, Booth knew that he would be again "obliged to 'tour' this country — even to California." As he wrote to Jervis McEntee: "the years are crowding fast & thick upon me; it is time to harvest all I can before my sun-set." For what he thought of as his farewell, however, Booth needed someone to take care of the business and logistical details that were part of any tour. Before the 1886–1887 season, he began what would become a five-year collaboration with the actor Lawrence Barrett, who offered to arrange Booth's tour, to hire actors and support staff and negotiate bookings, travel, hotels and publicity in return for a percentage of the profits. On July 1, 1885, Booth placed himself under contract to Barrett for thirty weeks between September 13, 1886, and May 9, 1887, each week to include six nights and one matinee. He received 80 percent of the net profits, which left 20 percent for Barrett.[1] Barrett was touring on his own and could not manage Booth in the sense of accompanying him; Arthur Branscomb Chase, who had worked as Barrett's tour manager since July 1885, was the natural man to take charge of the company's day-to-day operations. The correspondence among the three of them provides the most thorough picture so far available about the day-to-day operations of a late nineteenth-century tour.

Competition to book the combination was fierce. *The New York Mirror* told its readers:

> The out-of-town managers are all anxious to secure Booth. One manager has offered the entire receipts of a night of Booth in any play. Another, who is known to be both successful and shrewd, says: "I want to round up my managerial laurels with Booth. It is my ambition to secure the tragedian for just one night and then lay down the sceptre of local management."[2]

Chase negotiated ticket prices with the theatre managers along the way. Theatre seats ranged from two dollars and fifty cents down to twenty-five cents. In Far West cities such as Los Angeles and San Francisco, the high price could go up to three dollars, and a box could go for as much as ten to thirty dollars. Chase was also in charge of complimentary tickets, which he used to butter up railroad officials who, in turn, gave the combination better rates. Members of the company, on the other hand, got no comps at all. Chase and his associates also served as ticket takers to make sure that no one slipped into the theatre without paying.

The company consisted of fifteen male actors, six female actors, a child who traveled with her mother, a manager (Chase), four advance men, a super-property man, a treasurer and Booth's valet Frank Lodge, who also doubled as the leader of the singing quartet used in *The Merchant of Venice* and the carrier of the prompt books and photographs that boys sold in front of the theatres. Harry Magonigle joined Booth as his valet in Chicago. "Stage staff" and a "wardrobe mistress for the supers" were hired en route. Following the practice of nineteenth-century American theatre, almost no roles were doubled. There were, for instance, twenty-two actors in *Macbeth*, and only Kate Molony and Walter Thomas played more than one part. Molony performed Fleance, Thomas played Donalbain, and both played apparitions in Act V.[3]

Rehearsals began on September 6, 1886, seven days before the Buffalo opening. The actors assembled at 11 A.M. at the New York Academy of Music, where Barrett was appearing nightly. The supporting company, scenery and costumes were drawn from Barrett's company, but despite Barrett's presence at the opening rehearsal, Booth took control. In one morning the troupe rehearsed two plays; the next day they did three in four hours. They rehearsed for four days to become "letter perfect" in *Hamlet*, *Richelieu*, *Macbeth* and *Othello*.[4] The company was able to mount these four plays in two weeks because its members had performed their roles before. They were all aware of the traditional business, and some of them had even done the same parts with Booth.

On their last Saturday in New York company members were given trunk labels marked "Theatre" and "Edwin Booth Company Hotel," the former for the costumes, shoes, wigs and make-up, the latter for their personal belongings. The company left by the Erie Railroad at 7 P.M. on Saturday September 11 and arrived in Buffalo at 7 A.M. the next day. Booth, however, avoided night travel and consequently did not arrive until 7 P.M. Sunday. Cast members unpacked and hung up only those costumes needed for the three-day Buffalo run.[5]

On September 13, they opened with *Richelieu*. Evening performances began at eight. Booth entered the theatre through the stage door shortly before seven. The call-boy called "half-hour," "quarter hour," "overture" and then "Act First." Members of the cast, normally in make-up and costume ten minutes before curtain, went upstairs from their basement dressing rooms and took their places as the overture ended and the curtain music began. The first scene of *Richelieu* was played in front of a drop. The curtain fell and then rose again for Booth's star entrance. He was greeted with a round of applause. The scene was played; the curtain fell again, and Booth signaled the actors on stage to "hold the picture" for a curtain call. It was the only one he took with other actors.[6]

From then on, as distance permitted, Booth played seven performances a week, including a Saturday matinee. He did not perform on Good Friday, on Sundays or on Wednesday matinees, although additional matinees were added on Thanksgiving, Christmas, New Year's Day and Washington's birthday. The schedule was flexible, particularly in terms of smaller American cities. For instance, Booth was scheduled to play Lancaster, Pennsylvania, on New Year's Eve, but when a better offer came along, Chase simply suggested to Barrett that they change Lancaster to the previous night.[7]

Longer runs always began with Richelieu. Booth found the part physically easy; the Cardinal is an elderly man, and the play required no heroic physical action. It was always followed by *Hamlet*. *Richelieu* established Booth's presence in town; *Hamlet* brought in the money. *Merchant of Venice* and *Katharine and Petruchio* were always performed together, and it is typical that if Booth played Hamlet at a matinee, he did one of his easier roles—Iago, for instance—in the evening. There was, however, no attempt to plan out the entire season at the outset. With the Buffalo opening looming, Chase was still lining up venues. Two months into the tour, he actually added a two-week extension.[8]

On tour the company depended on the local management for scenery, special effects and extras, and the results were poor. A reviewer for the *Detroit Tribune* wrote: "The stage thunder, the constant bungling shifting of scenes, the weak-kneed supers supposed to represent the stalwart soldiers all operated to destroy the illusion"; however, no one came to see the scenery or the extras.[9]

After three days and four performances in Detroit, the company left to play a week in five

Michigan cities. One of the advance men had arranged for the troupe to take a boat from Kalamazoo across Lake Michigan and then a train to Milwaukee, where they were to open the next evening. Facing heavy rain and strong winds, Chase cancelled the boat trip and engaged a special sleeper that left at 1 A.M. and took the troupe around the southern tip of the lake in what Booth described as "a fearful storm." They stopped in Chicago, where he had breakfast, and proceeded north to Milwaukee. During the trip, a Hungarian Gypsy band serenaded the star in his private car. Chase made ten members of the company pay two dollars each for the extra train, but he charged the extra sixteen dollars for Booth's private car to the company account.[10]

Chase was concerned that Booth stayed in his "delightful room at Milwaukee's palatial West Hotel from morning until night" enjoying the food of its "excellent chef." He tried to get Booth "to drive or walk" and told him "he was fighting against nature to confine himself indoors so much." Booth replied that "he had been fighting that way for thirty years, & it had become second nature with him." When the company moved on to Minneapolis, Booth agreed to take a party of six of the company's actresses to Minnehaha Falls.[11]

The trip proved disastrous. Booth developed a bad cold, and although he wrote to Edwina that it did not interfere with his acting or voice, it made him "very stupid & dull, — tired all over."[12] His throat was hoarse; his nose was inflamed; "a hard week's work" had "greatly tired" him and he was not eating well, but there was no possibility of resting. Every seat had been sold for the entire Chicago engagement.

After performances in St. Louis and Cleveland, the company traveled by "special sleeper" to New York. No one was optimistic about the financial success of Booth's upcoming season at the Star Theatre. Chase estimated that the expenses would "run over $5,000 which would leave but small profit compared to what he could get elsewhere." Booth, who felt that New Yorkers had had "a surfeit" of his acting, attempted to cut his engagement from four weeks to two.[13]

Tickets went on sale on October 28. Unfortunately the Statue of Liberty was unveiled that day, which, combined with rainy weather, resulted in an advance sale of only $1,014.00. Booth opened at the Star on November 1. It was the night before the presidential election in which Rutherford B. Hayes defeated Samuel J. Tilden by one electoral vote, and Booth competed with fireworks, meetings and parades. As predicted, the box office in New York fell far short of what it had been elsewhere.[14]

Booth's health got worse during his second week in New York. On November 7, he complained to Barrett: "I have had a week of gripes (today quite ill) — either from a cold or the poison of cured [canned] vegetables, against which there should be a law condemning the seller to be canned and the carrier to be damned or doomed to feed on no other food.... My supper is come.... 'tis gruel & milk; my only commerce now: — almost all I eat or drink gripes me with a hand of iron."[15]

By November 7, 1886, Booth was experiencing bowel pain. He performed in "great pain," on November 8. The stage was cold, and the only heat in his dressing room was provided by a gas stove. The next day it was difficult for him to sit upright, and he lay flat on his back. Alarmed by the possibility of "inflammation of the bowels," the disease he believed had killed both his father and Mary Devlin, Booth cancelled his next six appearances.[16]

He stayed in his room for ten days, treated by Dr. St. Clair Smith, who remained his physician for the rest of his life. He had a dressing room built for him backstage at the Star Theatre and wrote to Edwina: "I live on rice, tea & toast & bread & milk.... I find that solid food causes pain in its passage through the intestine."[17]

When Booth resumed playing the following Monday, he did so under reduced prices and with a repertoire that omitted *Macbeth* and *Richard III*, plays that he and Chase felt were too demanding. Chase feared that his star's "illness has dampened the engagement greatly — as the public have stopped buying & will not resume until they are convinced he is himself again."

Chase promised to "work" the Saturday and Sunday papers thoroughly to increase the box office, but it was of little avail.[18]

The company opened in Boston on December 6, and there, as usual, Booth's popularity held. His health, however, remained poor. The day after opening, he wrote to Barrett: "I've had an almost incessant headache for several weeks & even now I am in pain. What the deuce causes it I know not; the D^r has pill-ed me powdered me, but still I ache." Despite the pain Booth continued to perform. On December 16, 1886, he wrote to Barrett: "I have done some pretty bad work, notably with Lear, last night, whose wits were really wild with a hellish 'pain upon my forehead here'; yet the critics approve!"[19]

After Boston, Booth played one-night stands in Massachusetts, New York, Delaware and Pennsylvania from December 20 through January 1, 1887. He traveled with only a parlor car and not a sleeping car, staying in hotels in each city, either walking to and from the theatre each night or taking a carriage.[20] On January 2, 1887 he wrote to William Winter from the Everett House in New York:

> Edwina was ill-abed when I left her, but she is better & has been down stairs of late; she is on the way [pregnant] again! The heavy-hipped Hungarian hog, who, "like a full-acorned boar cries 'ugh!' and mounts" will soon kill the poor fragile girl, or beget a breed of puny weaklings—following too fast to permit the mother to gain strength to nourish them. My anxiety for her is constant & very great.[21]

On January 4, Booth wrote to Lawrence Barrett: "I have now a difficult & somewhat painful letter to write Edwina, touching our ~~separation~~ change of house-hold relations—at her own suggestion cued (to coin a word) by the Rabbi of her tribe—or rather of the tribe she has joined."[22] Booth was formalizing their separation by selling both his Boston and his Newport homes. From his viewpoint that separation had been instigated by Ignatius.

The tour continued in Philadelphia and Baltimore. An effort was made to get Booth to play Washington or, at least, to recite portions of his plays there in costume and make-up. Given his resolution after Lincoln's assassination, Booth refused both offers, writing to Barrett: He "The enclosed was sent by the tempter who promised a special car full of pretty girls to carry me to Washington if I'd go. Now, isn't it dernedable that I can't accept such sweetmeats? I could no more read or recite with my toggery & war-paint than I could swim the Hellespont." As usual, special trains were run from Washington to Baltimore to carry spectators for each performance.[23]

After Baltimore Booth played Pittsburgh, Cincinnati, Louisville, Memphis and New Orleans. Chase told him that the trip from Louisville to Memphis would be overnight after the Wednesday night performance and that he would not arrive in Memphis until 4:30 P.M. the next day, leaving two and a half hours before he had to be at the theatre. "Booth ... heaved a sigh" and said: "Mr. Chase I have never traveled like this before." Chase replied: "Mr. Booth you never was so active as now"; Booth just gave him "a look."[24]

Although theatrical business in New Orleans had been very bad that season, Chase believed that unless "the River floods and they are up to danger line," nothing could "stop the Booth boom now." The reality, however, was different. It rained hard for two days. and "the bottom ... dropped out of N. O." In addition Booth had arrived during Mardi Gras, and as he wrote to Edwina: "All the city will be in the streets—of course the theatres will be empty." He loathed the St. Charles Hotel: "simply beastly—in every respect; I have not had a morsel of palatable food here." In all he thought "New Orleans ... very dull & dirty; —I shall be glad when I get away, and to California.[25]

For Booth's cross-country comfort, Barrett had rented a sixty-six-foot private car called the "David Garrick," which cost $3,000 for the entire journey without meals. Chase saved on money by having what Booth called "several of the 'lead' animals of my team" join him in his "private" car. The chosen actors helped to "part pay" for the cost of train carriage. Barrett sent books to "comfort" Booth "through the Texas tour," and the company left for Galveston at 7:20 P.M. on February 20, arriving and opening the next day.[26]

Magonigle became the car's steward, serving breakfast at eleven, dinner at three and supper after midnight to Booth, Chase and sometimes the young women of the company. The rest of the troupe, alerted by a gong when the train pulled in to a town, scrambled to eat their meals in station restaurants during twenty-minute stops. On Sunday, when the company did not perform, supper for Booth was milk, crackers, cheese and Apollinaris (imported table water). No alcohol was allowed, including beer and wine. Booth treated the company to a "pic-nic" on the beach in Galveston. After Galveston, the company moved to one-night stands in Houston, Dallas, Austin and San Antonio.[27]

The company started for California from San Antonio at 7:30 A.M. on February 27 and arrived at 6 P.M. on March 1. Booth found the "three days passage through the desert, from San Antonio ... very wearisome," and described his trip "through a vast desert of sand ... fatiguing, hot & dusty." He thought that the "Indians" whom he referred to as "Mexican greasers ... a dirty but picturesque lot." He was, however, enchanted by a mirage which "lasted for several miles," "a lovely stretch of water, in which were reflected the snow-hills near by, and other objects close at hand."[28]

Booth arrived in Los Angeles exhausted and found that Barrett's advance men had not done their job. Los Angeles was "overcrowded," and Chase had difficulty finding lodgings for the company. The "ladies of the company" wound up in a boarding house, where Chase slept on a cot. Harry Magonigle and other members of the company slept in the David Garrick. Only Booth retired with "a hot soak & a sleeping draught" in a hotel where the food was "as nicely cooked & served as at Delmonico's" and awoke "fresh" the next morning. Performances at the Grand Opera House in Los Angeles sold out and produced what Chase called "the largest profit so far the season," with 1,000 people being turned away at each performance.[29]

At 1 A.M. after the March 5 evening performance, the company left what Booth called "this land of fruit and flowers" on a special train and arrived in San Francisco at 8:30 P.M. the next night. There Booth gave up the "David Garrick," because he would be spending five weeks in the Palace Hotel. Booth, Chase, and three of the company's ladies went to the Palace Hotel, while the rest stayed at the Baldwin, which was part of the theatre in which they played. Booth found his hotel rooms "decorated with camellias ... & vines of maiden hair," an arrangement of violets that spelled out "Welcome Edwin Booth" and a huge star of roses.[30]

On March 7, 1887, Booth opened in *Hamlet*. The performance began with Act I, scene ii — the first scene at court. Before the curtain went up, Booth stood in the middle of the stage to make sure that the extras were placed correctly. His stage manager stood by to give the curtain signal. Booth sat in his chair left center near the footlights. He was about to approve the curtain signal by nodding his head when he spied Elizabeth Saunders, the California actress with whom he had performed in the 1850s, standing in the first wing. The curtain music was playing, but suddenly Booth got up and went over to embrace Saunders, while the orchestra played the curtain music three times over; the stage managed fumed, and the audience waited. Finally the curtain went up, and the audience that "filled the boxes, orchestra and dress-circle, crowded the galleries and swarmed the side aisles" gave Booth a five-minute ovation. Booth bowed to them from his chair. According to Kitty Molony: "Men stamped.... Fair women clapped their hands 'til their gloves burst; the air was white with waving handkerchiefs.... Old men ... arose to their feet, tossed their silk hats in the air." They kept applauding — he smiled at them — more applause — he stood up and sat down — more applause; he stood up again, bowed again and sat down — more applause; he stood up, bowed and waited — more applause and finally he walked down to the footlights and stood there crying. When the curtain fell on Act V, women in ball dresses climbed onto their seats, screaming for Booth.[31]

Booth had hoped to spend a week at Yosemite, but "the season" was not "favorable," and after three days rest in Monterey, with the cast on full salary, he opened at San Jose and went on to Stockton and Sacramento, all of which paid the company ninety percent of the gross.

On April 9, 1887, when Booth was playing Sacramento, Edwina gave birth to a nine-pound boy whom she and Ignatius named Edwin Booth Grossman. Ignatius sent a six-word telegram and followed it up with one of 107 words. Booth's reaction was: "A beggar on horseback is a rough rider when the animal aint his'n. I'm glad to know that everything so far is well at any price, but my anxiety will not cease 'till Edwina is safely out of the woods."[32]

On April 10 the company started for Salt Lake City where, as Booth wrote, "all my wives await me." They breakfasted at Reno on April 11, had dinner at Humboldt and supper at Elko, Nevada, and breakfast on April 12 in Ogden, Utah.[33] On April 16 Booth wrote to Barrett:

> Salt Lake has gone well, not greatly; the Morms are rather depressed at present, & I'm told they are selling real estate & hoarding ducats; ... I shall send several trunks from Omaha & a lot of wardrobe &c, can be also sent East—as but little will be required thenceforth.—The weather has been delightful all the week & the hotel well fooded; an excellent cook;—ours, of the D[avid] G[arrick] is otherwise. He has been presenting the ladies & others of the corps, with bouquets this week & a charge is made against me for his gallant acts.... [Carl] Ahrendt [who played Polonius and Kent] has lost a bottle of brandy from the car & one of the Cº a flask of whisky; both tipples incite to gallantry & "nig will be nig" when dars rum aroun'. I may wrong the noble dark, but it looks s'pecious, ain't it, honey?[34]

From Salt Lake City, the company went to Cheyenne, Denver and Omaha. At this point Booth and Barrett were facing a new railroad law which made carrying a lot of luggage very expensive. Booth hoped it would "have the effect of ridding the country of the show-rubbish and be the means of reviving the old stock-system." As a result Booth began to divest himself of his theatrical wardrobe, carrying only what he would need for the next month.[35]

It would be a rough month. Barrett had originally planned four weeks of one-night stands, but Chase thought it "would be a little too hard at the close of the long season for Mr. Booth," The regular season was due to end with a week split between Omaha and Kansas City, but Barrett scheduled an extension until May 14 — 2 weeks spent in twelve different cities.[36]

Booth continued moving east. Gradually the repertory dwindled to Hamlet and Richelieu. The last two weeks were a series of one-night stands in theatres in which Booth got ninety to ninety-nine percent of the profit or certainties of $2,000. Managers simply wanted to have Booth play in their theatre. They wanted *Hamlet* but Booth often decided on *Richelieu*. It was the easier role.[37]

The company reached Indianapolis. There a young man named Malcolm Dale Owen wrote to his family about a scheme he employed for getting good seats at a Booth performance:

> Almost immediately after our arrival ... about 3:30 P.M., we went to the box office; we found we could get fine seats, from scalpers at about $6.00 each, but we decided that as we were only millionaires, not billionaires, we would not purchase those. We next asked what the price of standing room down stairs would be. "$2.00 was the answer; that was more like it, but we afterwards found that standing room in [the] dress circle was only $1.00, so concluded to take those tickets. There were six of us in our party.... We ... set out for the Opera House. The play was given in English's Opera House, because it is the largest there. We reached our destination at quarter of seven, giving us fifteen minutes before the doors opened, but we knew that it was "first come, first served" so did not object in the least to being early. On account of some delay of ushers, we were not admitted till 7.15 and from that time until eight, we had to guard the two aisles nearest the center. [Four of the young men] took possession of aisle to right of center, [two of the young men] the one left. By being "awfully" nice to the usher, he let us go down the aisle a very few moments after the curtain

arose. I was the first to make the brake [sic].... The occupants of the seats adjacent looked daggers at us, but we smiled serenely & proceeded to the very front of the dress circle, where we took seats that were equally as good for a view of the stage as the seven dollar seats by our sides, but the upholstery of our seats was not luxurious to say the least, in fact they were so hard that [one of the young men] is sore yet. You understand that we were sitting on the steps of the aisle, — they were covered with some kind of carpet. It was quite a lark & we could see perfectly.... Booth soon made us forget all else, even the hard seats.[38]

On May 7, Booth performed in Columbus, Ohio, and then took an overnight train to New York to begin work on a benefit at the Star Theatre in New York for the elderly actor C. W. Couldock, who was celebrating his fiftieth year on the stage. The benefit had been in the works since early December 1886, at which point Booth had asked Barrett to perform with him. Given the noteworthiness of the occasion, they rehearsed twice on Sunday and on Monday morning for the matinee performance. Then Booth traveled to Harrisburg, Pennsylvania, for a Monday evening performance, returned to New York, and the benefit went on during a matinee on Tuesday, May 10. Booth opened the afternoon with the third act of *Hamlet*, and John T. Malone, who played Claudius, was able to double as Brutus opposite Lawrence Barrett in the quarrel scene from *Julius Caesar*. The benefit netted $4,200 for Couldock — what Booth normally earned in two performances.[39]

Following the benefit Booth did four one-night stands in New England. The rest of the company traveled on with the "David Garrick." The tour ended in Worcester, Massachusetts, where the "David Garrick" was put into storage. The company returned to New York, and Booth made his way alone back to Boston. When his train left, the entire company saw him off at the station. "The ladies shed tears.... At parting he gave his property man and the several other minor employees $100 each."[40] They may have adored him, but Booth had not been impressed with them. Only four of the actors in the 1886–1887 company were retained the following year. Barrett was planning a far more sophisticated troupe, and Booth was planning a new home.

Chapter Twenty-One

1887–1888: Booth and Barrett

Despite Booth's persistent grumblings, the Booth-Barrett combination created for the 1887–1888 season lasted until Barrett's death in 1891. In her autobiography Clara Morris reports that Booth, having been complimented on his "good work" under Barrett's management, replied:

> Good work, eh? Well, why should I not do good work, after all Barrett has done for me. Why I never knew what c-o-m-f-o-r-t spelled before. I arrive — someone says: "Here's your room, Mr. Booth." I go in and smoke. At night, someone says: "Here's your dressing room, sir," and I go in and dress, and smoke, and then act. That's all, absolutely all, that I have to do, except to put out my hand and take my surprisingly big share of the receipts now and then. Good work, eh? Well, I'll give him the best that's in me, he deserves it.[1]

Two weeks into the 1886–1887 season, when it was already clear that managers were willing to pay exorbitant amounts for Booth alone, he received a letter from Barrett proposing that they tour together the following year. He protested vehemently and immediately accepted.

> "Thou torturest me, Tubal!" ... My dear boy — I have barely set my foot upon the road which I thought to travel for the last time, when you appall me (one or two p's?) by your proposition to prolong the agony another weary year! ... Why, I haven't yet begun to devote you to the infernal gods for what you've done to me this season.[2]

Arthur Branscomb Chase, the company's road manager, immediately saw the artistic and financial possibilities of a "combination" and even suggested the possibility of a $3 ticket.[3] On September 27, 1886, he wrote to Barrett: "I estimate 150 nights with yourself & Mr. Booth combined at $3,000 gross (which I consider low) would amount to

	$450,000
Less local managers 10%	$ 45,000
-----	$405,000
Expenses of Co. etc.	$ 55,000
Net Profits	$350, 000
To Mr. Barrett 40%	$140,000"[4]

Chase's math suggested that Booth might make as much as $210,000 for the season. In actuality his share of the profits turned out to be $249,896.47.

Barrett signed and forwarded the contract on October 1, 1886. It placed Booth under Barrett's management for "not less than twenty five consecutive weeks, beginning on or about the second Monday of October 1887, Booth to receive sixty percent of the net profit and Barrett forty percent. Booth signed it on October 15, and Chase was jubilant, anticipating "a wonderful tour."[5]

Barrett brought a level of managerial skills to the enterprise that Booth desperately needed. By October 10, 1886, a full year before their tour actually began, the two stars were discussing actors and staff for the following season. Chase advised Barrett: "You will find the whole profession ... only too eager to get with you" and later contended that Barrett had had "over 2,000 applicants" for places in the company. Barrett approved of rehiring Chase immediately, and, with Booth, began to decide which of the "little folk" to retain. Barrett's preference for a leading lady was a young actress named Mina Gale, but Booth thought that Gale's ears stood out too much and complained that she would have "to go sidewise" to make entrances and exits "to avoid being caught between the wings." By December 26, 1886, the major actors for the following season, including Miss Gale, had been selected and most of the people traveling with Booth during the 1886–1887 season had already been dropped from consideration without their knowing it. During 1887–1888 the thirty-seven company members would give 255 performances in a journey of over 16,000 miles.[6]

Offers were already pouring in, and Chase was a ruthless negotiator. The manager of the Columbus Theatre offered ten thousand dollars for a week, and Chase told Barrett: "I shall answer him 'not enough.'" The manager of a theatre in Kansas City offered the same amount for three nights and a matinee; again Chase replied: "it's not enough" and got $18,000 or $4,500 per performance. Where he was forced to take certainties [a set fee], Chase got at least $2,000–$3,000 a night. In general, however, both he and Barrett preferred a percentage of the house, so sure were they of the season's potential. Chase arranged for a 90 percent/10 percent split in Los Angeles. Chicago, New Orleans, San Francisco and St. Louis all agreed to 85 percent.[7]

The new federal interstate railroad law, however, required "full fares" rather than cut rates for theatre companies with "no excess baggage allowed." Knowing that this would cut into Barrett and Booth's profits, Chase advised Barrett: "Don't you think it would be unnecessary to carry scenery & props for productions. I find in the large cities the theatres get up the plays very nicely — And ... you might wait until a year later & announce a limited Booth-Barrett tour of the large cities only ... grand productions if you thought it advisable." Booth agreed and wrote to Barrett: "It would be best for us to carry only two or three drops — & stone arches ... & the stenciled inexpensive material for hangings.... I think we can have all important scenes painted for us in the principal theatres. — even if we pay for them 'twould be cheaper than carrying them with us — the wear & tear would be terrible, & render them shabby after the first transportation."[8]

For the theatrical profession as a whole, the existence of the upcoming Booth-Barrett company presented some problems. Other attractions were loathe to schedule shows opposite the combination, and the cost of attending a Booth-Barrett production resulted in decreased attendance before and after their appearance. After the tour an actor in the company named Milton Nobles told the readers of *The New York Mirror*:

> This is an era of "trusts" and "combines," and the Booth-Barrett tour was a mammoth "trust," and the local managers and more humble attractions have been the victims.... Throughout the country — particularly, the one and two-night stands — they simply killed the business for six or eight weeks in the midst of the season. The coming of this great "combine" was known months in advance. It was an event that no theatre-goer could think of missing. The theatre ... is supported by the industrial classes. The clerk, book-keeper, artist, artisan and small tradesman, with incomes ranging from nine hundred to two or three thousand a year, are the main support of the drama. They allow themselves a certain amount of money during the season for amusements. To see the Booth-Barrett "combine" cost them just five times what it would cost to see Louis James, Annie Pixley, Fred. Warde, Maggie Mitchell or Milton Nobles. This is for the matter of tickets alone. So great an event demands unusual preparation in the matter of toilets, gloves, carriages etc. for wife or sweetheart. All of these extra expenses must be met by rigid economy before the coming, and the total abstinence after the departure of the great "combine." ... Booth and Barrett played to a three-

Edwin Booth and Lawrence Barrett in San Francisco, March 1888. "This is an era of 'trusts' and 'combines,' and the Booth-Barrett tour was a mammoth 'trust,' and the local managers and more humble attractions have been the victims.... Throughout the country — particularly, the one and two-night stands — they simply killed the business for six or eight weeks in the midst of the season."

thousand dollar house, and the local manager got three hundred dollars. Three or four attractions preceding this engagement had, on former visits, played to houses ranging from four to eight hundred dollars. Owing to the great expectations aroused by the coming of the "combine," their business this season was less than half what would, under ordinary circumstances, they have played to. The rule applies with still greater force to the month following the great event.... Several managers in the South told me that their season had been ruined by the Booth-Barrett tour and that the organization could never play these cities again excepting upon the same terms and at the same prices as other first-class attractions.[9]

By June 20 Chase was already figuring out the complicated railroad schedule that would take the company south. It is easy to imagine Booth's eyes glazing over when he read:

Leave Baltimore 9.50 A.M. arrive Richmond 2.49 P.M. Leave Richmond 10.49 A.M. Arrive Norfolk 2.30 P.M. Leave Norfolk 11.45 P.M. Special to Wilden 89 miles Can probably arrange to have regular train that is due at Wilden 10.00 A.M. hold until 2 A.M. for your arrival which train arrives at Charleston 3.30 PM. Leave Charles[ton] 6.10 A.M. Arrive Savannah 10.15 A.M. Leave Savannah at 10 A.M. [the next day] Arrive Macon 4.50 P.M.[10]

By August Chase was working with Barrett to determine repertoire. As initially planned, Booth was to perform Brutus in *Julius Caesar*, Macbeth, Shylock, King Lear and Hamlet. Barrett would do Cassius, Macduff, Bassanio, Edgar and the ghost in *Hamlet* as well as one of his specialty plays—*The King's Pleasure*. They would alternate Othello and Iago. The exact schedule, however, had to be determined city by city. Chase believed that *Julius Caesar* was "the 'piece de resistance' that the public would be most anxious to see."[11]

Ticket prices for 1887–1888 were advanced over anything Booth had ever known—from $2.50 to $5.00 with boxes going for $15 to $40. Ticket prices were so high that even when attendance was down, profits were up. It was anticipated that by the end of the Chicago run the Booth-Barrett combination would take in $70,000 and that they would clear $200,000 for the entire season.[12]

Barrett assumed full control of both the artistic and financial aspects of the tour and continued to do so for the rest of the season, which improved both the casting and the staging of the productions.[13] *The Omaha Republican* reported late in the season:

Mr. Barrett superintends rehearsals personally, as a tutor conducts his class. He devises stage business, the exits, the entrances, the crossings of the stage, the movement of this man when he says this, the attitude of that woman when she says that, the doing of the mob, the action of the servants, in short everything. He learns every part. When the same play continues throughout a week, it is of course not rehearsed, unless for some special reason, after the opening night of the week. But when the piece to be presented on a certain night has not been given for some time, or if it has not been given in this particular theatre, there is a rehearsal in the day time. Everybody in the company attends all rehearsals. Mr. Booth himself is always there, goes through his business and gives his cues."[14]

The Omaha reporter was only partially correct. Barrett led his actors through the play like Henry Irving had done when Booth performed with him in London, but Edwin had no need to rehearse his own roles and was not present for the company's rehearsals.

The 1887–1888 tour was similar to that of the preceding year. The company opened in Buffalo and toured westward as far as Kansas City, then made its way back east to Philadelphia, Boston and New York. It then turned southeast and eventually traveled to New Orleans, its jumping-off spot for Texas and California. Moving east, it toured through major western cities such as Denver and Omaha, then retraced its steps to the Midwest and ended in Brooklyn. In all, between September 12, 1887, and May 19, 1888, it covered seventy-one cities.

Booth traveled, as he had the previous year, in a Worcester Excursion Car. Although called the "Junius Brutus Booth," it was actually a refurbished version of the "David Garrick" used the preceding season and contained a parlor or reception room, a dining room, library, smoking room, kitchen, bath and sleeping compartments for both him and Barrett. Although they left the "Junius Brutus Booth" for long-term hotel stays, Booth and Barrett used it exclusively during one-night stands. The rest of the company traveled with seventy pieces of luggage on the second section of a train "made up of an engine, a baggage car, one coach and a sleeper."[15]

By the tour's second city—Detroit—Booth had realized that its big hit would be *Julius Caesar* and wrote: "I'm glad of it—for Brutus is a very easy part of me.... I've regarded it more of a rest than even 'loafing' with my pipe." The early stops were also made easier by the fact that when Booth did his four-act version of *The Merchant of Venice*, Barrett performed *The King's Pleasure* as an afterpiece, relieving Edwin of the burden of playing *Katherine and Petruchio*. By the time they opened in Chicago, however, this practice was abandoned, and the company began performing the longer, five-act version of *Merchant*. At that point, Barrett also began playing Laertes instead of the Ghost in *Hamlet*, because, as Booth wrote: "The two pieces [*Merchant* and *Hamlet*] do not seem to draw—the public want us both in one play & as the Ghost [Barrett] has so little to do, they hold back for *Othello* & *Caesar* where both hold the stage throughout the play." Barrett's work increased, while Booth hoped to confine himself primarily to Shylock, Brutus and Iago which he called "the three easiest of my characters." He was not able to do so. While 106 of his appearances during the season were as Brutus and 57 as Iago, he still gave 35 performances as Hamlet and only 25 as Shylock.[16]

By the time they reached Chicago, Booth had decided to spend the rest of his career under Barrett's management. The two men walked each day, and Booth wrote to his daughter:

> Barrett is very earnest and devoted, and works like a horse over the rehearsals; showing good taste and thorough knowledge of stage-management & is sincerely proud of his work as second to me. Time & experience have robbed his youthful vanity and he is satisfied to be "mine ancient".... I think I will, hereafter, so long as I continue to act, play short engagements with Barrett—he can fill his regular seasons with new productions, when I am idle—& so I may glide gently & gradually into the shade, instead of making an abrupt "flop" of my last act. He is an excellent stage manager & not only executes his own ideas but carves out whatever I suggest—but which for many years I have lacked energy to put into practice.[17]

The Chicago engagement closed on October 22, and the company left the next day for Kansas City, Missouri. Booth was anxious about opening the Warder Opera House, a theatre whose walls were not yet plastered and whose roof, as far as he knew, was "but partly finished," but tickets were selling rapidly at large prices and as he wrote to Thomas Bailey Aldrich: "So we do it on the per-airies." His concerns were well founded. He arrived on October 24 to find "that the theatre was yet unprepared" but was assured that "all would be right for the night's performance." The hotel was also newly finished, and Booth and Barrett were given large handsome, cold apartments, with every convenience, few of which worked. The hot water was cold; the cold water was mud; the fireplace was very small and the heaters had no steam. As they were about to leave for their dressing rooms, Chase arrived with the news that the theatre would not be ready in time, and the two actors consented to give a Wednesday matinee in lieu of Monday night's performance.[18] On Tuesday night, they opened in *Othello*. Edwin Milton Royle, who had a walk-on role, described the experience:

> When we first looked upon the New Warder Grand Theater [*sic*], it boasted of four walls without a roof, window or door. At seven o'clock on the night we were to play there, it was still a forest of scantling and scaffolding. An army of workmen was busy, and by nine o'clock chairs—undertaker's chairs—were appropriately put in, and the doors, or places for doors were thrown open to the public.... The people in the "boxes" looked out from under carriage robes and blankets.... We had one set which did for all the scenes in "Othello." For the Senate, we had one Doge, two Senators and one Doge's chair, all of which we carried. A magnetic young man by the name of Augustus Thomas was

energizing as a local stage-manager.... The second night we played "Julius Caesar." ... I had on, besides my underclothes and my toga, three woolen shirts, three pairs of tights, and a thick wig.... The hit of the entire week, however, was made not by Booth or by Barrett but by the drunken porter in "Macbeth" when he said: "This place is too cold for hell."[19]

From Kansas City the company went to St. Louis. By this time Barrett was not feeling well. During the preceding summer, Barrett had begun showing the beginning stages of the glandular disease that would plague him for the rest of his life. By St. Louis, he was increasingly ill with what Booth called "gout in his throat" and was traveling with an Armenian masseur to ease the pain. By Pittsburgh, his "health [was] better, but his neck [looked] large in consequence of the swelled glands." He refused to tell his family, and Booth cautioned Edwina not to mention it. By late February both men were considering going to Hot Springs, Arkansas, for three weeks in May. A doctor had recommended a cure for Barrett's "glandular affection" but the trip was cancelled when another physician vetoed the hot springs and recommended "mountain air, and absolute repose."[20]

At the end of the season, the company traveled east to New York City, where, on May 21, Booth participated in a testimonial performance of *Hamlet* at the Metropolitan Opera House for the actor Lester Wallack, who was ill, although he hated the recipient and loathed the event. He wrote to Barrett: "I hardly see how I can refuse— for <u>W.</u> is recognized in his sphere as a leader & <u>professionally</u> merits our support; personally—?" He wrote to Edwina: "It will be a hard day's work for me, to honor a most unworthy man, for whom no one has a personal respect, but whose name is high up, on the list of heroes of the Past."[21]

In addition to an all-star cast in the speaking roles including Barrett as the Ghost, the Polish actress Helena Modjeska as Ophelia and Joseph Jefferson and his comic co-star W. J. Florence as the gravediggers, the thirty-five supernumerary roles went to minor nineteenth-century actors. "Scene shifters took particular delight in running flats into a bunch of stars

Lawrence Barrett and Edwin Booth, 1880s. Note the pipe in Booth's mouth. "Why should I not do good work, after all Barrett has done for me. Why I never knew what c-o-m-f-o-r-t spelled before."

to the detriment of costumes and the agony of corns.... The 'grips' treated the stars just as they would any twenty-five cents a night 'super.' It was a rare chance to settle old scores." Jefferson, who did not appear until Act V, spent most of the performance in his street clothes. To make his entrance Booth had to walk through the crowd "with both his hands stretched out, as though he was getting ready to swim" in order to part the waves of actors between him and the stage. The local critic reported: "the distinguished body of auxiliaries's exit after the play scene evoked so much applause that several of ... Booth's lines were lost in the uproar." Over 3,500 people attended, and the performance sold out at $19,500. Wallack was barely able to stand up and walk on stage to say thanks. His wife received $21,600 from the performance, supposedly as an annuity but she had to use some of it during her husband's last illness and to pay for his funeral.[22]

The season had ended in Brooklyn and the company had dispersed before the Wallack benefit. Barrett returned to his farm in Cohasset. Booth went to Baltimore for the funeral of his sister Asia, who had recently died in England.[23]

There was no doubt that the combination would continue. As a reporter in Youngstown, Ohio, had written: "Booth and Barrett say they will remain together until one of them dies." On June 8, 1888, Booth wrote from Boston where he had recently given up his home on Chestnut Street: "The ... tour ended gladly & now all but I — are taking their ease for the Summer; I am homeless & hang up at hotels ... with my pipe & reflections—which there are many & not over cheerful. No matter: the play will soon be ended."[24]

Chapter Twenty-Two

"The Booth and Barrett Social Company"

On June 6, 1887, when Booth dedicated the Actors' Fund memorial in Evergreen Cemetery in Brooklyn New York, he told the assembled crowd:

> Time has not grown so old since the most prominent ones of our profession, though admired ... by the public, ... were socially viewed askance, and regarded as merely players.... Vagabondage ... is ... the cruel condition of our calling — the actor can hardly have a permanent abode.... Homeless ... he has been or he may ever be in the pursuit of his vocation, which rends all but a fortunate few nomadic.[1]

Booth's decision to erect a monument to the advancement of the theatre was motivated by the homelessness he had known both as both a boy and a man. The Booth/Grossman household had broken up in May 1887, and Edwin wrote "I have relinquished house-keeping for all time — letting Edwina and her family have my ... furniture & horses at their expense, helping them in taxes, gas &c.... I am well, but there's a void, of course, that — well, we each of us all has made that void, I suppose, and we must take our share of its ache." Booth was once again a man without a home.[2]

His real home, of course, was the theatre, but he thought it was a slum. As a young man he had internalized society's views of actors as "socially viewed askance." He would not marry Mary Devlin until she was purified of theatrical taint. He wanted Booth's Theatre to be a temple that would elevate an art form. In 1876–1877, a time when Booth needed money, the manager of the Bowery Theatre had offered him all the receipts of the house if he would play a two-month engagement there to establish the theatre as a first-class "star" house. Booth declined. The Bowery, known for its blood and thunder melodramas, was beneath him. The desire for a home was part of this desire for respectability. He wanted someplace permanent, a place he could come home to, a place he could use to store his memorabilia. The solution to his housing problem was The Players, a club he would come to refer to as "my abiding place in New York for all future time that may be mine."[3]

During the 1886–1887 season, when he was touring the west in the "David Garrick," he had Harry Magonigle bring several actors from their Pullman into his private "Smoking Room" and proposed to them his plan for a gentlemen's club for actors. In the summer of 1887 he joined a group of friends — Thomas Bailey Aldrich, Lawrence Barrett, Laurence Hutton, William Bispham and Booth's banker, E. C. Benedict — to cruise off North America on Benedict's steam yacht *Oneida*. What had started as an excursion of a "few days" eventually became first a three-week, then a month-long "stag party" that Booth expected would be "bully."[4]

Thomas Aldrich later claimed that it was his happy fortune to suggest the name of the club during the cruise, a claim that Booth supported. Since Aldrich and Hutton had left the cruise by July 31, The Players was conceived, at least in name, sometime between July 21 and 31. The following October, however, Booth was still vague about his plans and wrote to William Bispham: "I ought to make an effort, before I quit, to establish some abiding-place for my profession, where the 'legitimate' may find a home. Something may yet be accomplished."[5] At that point he was contemplating both a gentleman's club for actors and a home for indigent members of the profession.

The organization's formal inception occurred on January 6, 1888, when seventeen men including Booth, Barrett, the producer A. M. Palmer, Joseph Jefferson, General William Tecumseh Sherman (a theatre enthusiast), Samuel Clemens (Mark Twain), Thomas Bailey Aldrich, Judge Joseph F. Daly, John Drew "and other men prominent in literary and dramatic circles met at lunch at Delmonico's to found 'the Players' Club,' somewhat after the pattern of the Garrick Club in London."[6] Its objectives were:

> To provide for social intercourse among the members of the dramatic profession, artists and the patrons of art.
> For the formation of a dramatic library and a house for dramatic records.
> To collect historical data of the stage in general and of the American stage in particular.

Articles of incorporation were promptly drawn up by a committee chaired by A. M. Palmer. Booth was touring, and the practical details of establishing the club were turned over to his friend William Bispham, who had business experience working for William H. Wallace & Company, Iron and Steel manufacturers. By January 18, 1888, Bispham was corresponding with the famed architect Stanford White, who was already ordering furniture for the building. He made it clear to White that Booth had sole control over whatever went into the building and assured him that if anything not specified in the contract were purchased, Booth would pay for it."[7]

The board of directors of the incipient club responded to Booth's role in the club's founding by electing him president. On April 19, 1888, he wrote to Edwina: "I am not glad of my election, for the office sh<u>d</u> be in the hands of a strong, <u>positive</u> man, and my nature is not of that quality. Besides, I am too easily bored & confused by business & discussions. Once fairly started, I will resign in favor of a <u>practical</u> party, but 'tis best that my name be used as the first President of such an institution." Booth remained The Players' president until his death, but in actuality, it was impossible for either him or Joseph Jefferson as vice-president to run the club, because both men were usually touring. The day-to-day duties fell to William Bispham.[8]

By early May Bispham had found a future home for The Players at No. 16 Gramercy Park South. Laid out in 1831, Gramercy Park was the neighborhood where the old "Knickerbocker" families lived. Number 16, on the south side of the park was a townhouse, dating from before 1846, built in Gothic Revival style with a full brownstone front. It had been the residence of the late Congressman Clarkson N. Potter. His widow, Virginia Mitchell Potter, donated the house and land on May 28, 1888, selling it to Booth for one dollar, but her name disappeared completely from the history of the club. Edwin took credit for purchasing the building and land, which he then donated to the club. Booth's out-of-pocket expenses were for the building's redesign and refurbishment by Stanford White. It was a substantial donation but not quite as substantial as it became in legend.[9]

White replaced the high stoop and cast iron verandas of the original house with a new wide basement entrance with a two-story colonnade. There was a porch, a "loggia" in the Italian Renaissance style, decorated with two huge projecting wrought-iron lanterns, like those on the façade of Florence's Palazzo Stozzi. The basement level contained a reception room, a billiard room, a wine room, a coat room and the offices of the club. From there, guests took a broad oaken staircase to a Great Hall containing a massive fireplace flanked by two firedog andirons and a marble mantel carved with the masks of comedy and tragedy. At the rear of the house, facing a small garden, White placed a grill room, with a long members' table suggestive of an ancient English tavern. The room was decorated with shelves, lined with pewter and glass, old blue Delft platters, and Toby jugs. On the second floor was a Reading Room furnished with deep chairs and tables piled high with books and periodicals and racks of newspapers, a conscious evocation of a London gentlemen's club. There were also two huge fire-proof Yale-lock safes that reached almost to the ceiling. These were to be used to store the precious theatrical objects owned by the club in case of fire. Upstairs were the founder's private rooms and other bedrooms. All this combined to project the atmosphere of a house long inhabited by a patrician family. It was the home that Booth had never had.[10]

On June 4, 1888, Booth and Barrett met with White and found his plans perfect, although the cost was double what Booth originally intended. Nevertheless, he "gave the word 'Go'" and wrote to Laurence Hutton: "Work will start at once. He even suggested mottos to be placed on the walls: "What think you of this as a motto for the 'grill'—Lets 'mouth it as many of our Players do'? & for the Toilet—: 'Nature her custom holds, let Shame say what it will'? Would not appropriate mottoes for each room be a novel feature?" Remodeling the building eventually went $20,000 over estimate. Booth wrote to Lawrence Barrett: "The changes, furnishings &c &c, will cost me $70,000 at least; the architect says $65,000. Whew!" Booth's distress over the cost must, however, be weighed against the fact that during the 1886–1887 season he made $211,000 and during the 1887–1888 season $249,000. He could afford the gift.[11]

The creation of The Players allowed Booth to divest himself of the books and pictures he had carted from one home to another and which, by the 1880s, were stored in a warehouse. In addition to his gifts, books, portraits, death masks, sculptured busts, and bronze bas-reliefs poured in. By December 4, 1889, The Players had received so many "pictures" that Booth wrote that it "puzzles us where to hang them."[12]

While the club's collection of historical theatrical memorabilia was very successful, its membership list was far more problematic. Booth's remedy to what he considered the justifiable low esteem in which actors were held was a club in which actors would be elevated through their contact with eminent members of the non-theatrical world. He believed that only those actors who met his standard of decency could be so elevated. His vision of The Players was elitist and betrayed a personal disdain for his fellow professionals who he felt lacked "ambition and self-respect" and who wasted "the better part of their nature in happy-go-lucky, Bohemian habits, ... a set of mere vain, selfish brainless idiots—seeking only their own personal gratification which consists in paper-puffery and large type on the play-bill."[13]

He was able to blackball people he felt unsuited for The Players. Initially among these was the noted comedian William J. Florence, who ironically later became a member of the club's Board of Directors. Initially Booth had been against Florence's membership, but in May 1888 he had "a chat with Florence" and later wrote to Barrett: "He is full of the true faith—was serious & talked well; not a sign of levity but sincere & correct in all he said. He hoped he could join us & I had to tell him his name was up; he was delighted & says he has books &c, &c, to donate. I guess he's O.K.—I only feared that he was too convivial, even for us." Florence was noted for being "convivial," and Booth associated conviviality with the bohemianism he deplored.[14]

The club's vice-president, Joseph Jefferson, was highly diplomatic and circumspect on the issue, writing to Booth that he was "such a hayseed that he [feared] that he would not be able to name many, if any, actors worthy of membership." Jefferson did not want to get involved, fearing that if the standards set for lack of conviviality were too high, no one would "scape whipping." Booth got the message and on July 12, 1888, wrote to Barrett:

We must be careful to not let personal feelings influence us in our selection. After all — there may be many of us "a little off" and the worthy President himself might wince a wee bit if put to Inquisition; and how would our "Vice" stand the question on <u>vices</u>? But, 'tis not what we <u>was</u>, but what we <u>is</u>, and <u>will be</u> must be our motto.... We will look up, not down; forward not backward.[15]

By December the work was done, and Booth deeded the building to The Players on December 31, 1888, for one dollar, the same amount Mrs. Potter had charged. The New Year's Eve deeding ceremony marks the official opening of The Players. As described in the local press, at 11:45 P.M. members marched up the marble steps to the reception room while "a menial with a scrubbing brush" kept the steps "like the reputations of them that walk over them 'unspotted from the world.'" As the clock tolled midnight Booth and The Players drank from a loving cup presented by William Warren to Joseph Jefferson and by Jefferson to the club. Barrett placed a wreath on Booth's head that Edwina had sent along with a card that read: "Hamlet, King, Father," and Edmon S. Connor, the oldest living American actor present, stepped from the crowd and kissed Booth's hands. After that the festivities began with dinner in the grill room whose walls, seen under White's chandelier (adapted for both gas and electricity), were decorated with "the great antlers of a monster elk" presented to the club by Barrett and a "bristling boar's head with protruding tusks," reflective of the masculine taste of its membership. Booth and Barrett did not get to bed until 5 A.M., and both woke up feeling "wretched" the next day.[16]

Booth spent the first day of 1889 packing his belongings at his hotel to move to The Players. He was setting up a home for himself in which he could lead the social improvement of actors. The deed specifies that Booth "together with his friends and servants shall during his natural life have the free and uninterrupted use and occupancy of the third floor."[17]

For the first year of the club's existence, Booth was not alone. He maintained only two rooms on the third floor, leasing others to Barrett. By June 1890, however, the precariousness of Barrett's health forced him to give up his rooms. Booth appropriated one of them for his own uses.[18] A clipping from the period describes his suite as

> elegant as pretty woman's boudoir.... There is a plain table for cards, perhaps, on it, the pipes, a half dozen or more of good usable ones, beside which is the canister of tobacco, the match-box, the ashtray, the comfortable chair.... A crazy-quilt made of elegant materials and exquisite colors has his monogram in letters of gold in the center of it. A pillow sham of Irish point lace and the handsome canopy of the finely wrought brass bedstead, together with the quilt, suggest an ideal couch of luxuriant ease. A delicately painted picture of his first wife hangs to the right of his bed. On his chiffonier is a picture of his beloved daughter and ... grandchildren, also one of his newest grandson, photographed by himself.... On a lounge in his parlor is an artistic slumber-pillow made of chamois-skin, delicately tinted with pink.... Over the lounge is a mirth-provoking sketch of Irving and Booth drawn by a clever caricaturist.... An oil painting of his daughter hangs in a conspicuous place over the mantel.[19]

It is ironic that what Booth had actually created for himself was more a nineteenth-century luxury hotel suite than a Victorian home. It was the kind of space in which he had spent most of his adult life.

There were doubts about the club's success and its tone from its inception. Booth expected it. On January 6, 1889, he wrote to Edwina: "Some of the disappointed papers & cheap actors are pitching into the club as a glorification of Edwin Booth and his daughter, &c. But they can't get in. I will have made enemies of all the theatrical critics, since none will be admitted & no dramatic papers permitted on our tables; so you must expect to see your daddy much abused hereafter." "The location," wrote one journalist, "seems hardly suitable for a club, being retired and rather dull, and in a few years, it will probably be considered decidedly down town." *The New York Dramatic Mirror* berated the one-hundred-dollar initiation fee and the forty-dollar-a-year membership cost as well as the control exercised by a board of directors elected for life.

A *Times* correspondent wrote that the club was "entirely too aristocratic an affair. Actors, as a rule do not care to go there, for they meet so very few people in whom they are interested." From the point of view of *The Mirror*, it really was a private club, "about as hospitable and inviting as a deserted palace, guarded by mutes. There ought to be a sign over the door written in this way: 'The Booth and Barrett Social Company.'"[20]

Chapter Twenty-Three

1888–1889: The Second Booth and Barrett Tour

Booth and Barrett signed a contract for the 1888–1889 season on October 20, 1887. It called for thirty consecutive weeks beginning September 15, 1888, but, from the beginning, it was doubtful that they could fulfill that long an obligation. Barrett's health was problematic. By the summer of 1888 he was seriously ill. He rented out his home in Cohasset and leased a house in Southboro, Massachusetts, where, as Booth wrote to Edwina, he hoped to get "strong and rugged by using a sulphur treatment at Richfield (Sulphur) Springs."[1]

Although he did not look well, by September Barrett was preparing not only for their joint 1888–1889 tour but also for future combinations with other stars. The immediate plan was to travel less, avoid one-night stands and concentrate on eastern cities, playing four-week engagements in Boston, Philadelphia and Chicago. Despite the plans, the 1888–1889 tour was longer than that of the preceding year.[2]

By December 1887 the season was booked through January 1889, and Booth and Barrett were already casting. Programs show seven new members, only two of whom had previously performed with Booth. In all the combination had eighteen male actors and four female actors. They were, in keeping with Booth's wishes, all chosen as much for their proper personal demeanor as they were for their talent and suitability.[3]

The major difference between the 1888–1889 tour and that of the preceding year was the presence of elaborate scenery and costumes as well as vocal and instrumental music in *Othello*, *Julius Caesar* and *The Merchant of Venice*. In their first three stops—Kansas City, Minneapolis and St. Paul—Booth and Barrett still employed the stock scenery provided by local theatres, but in Chicago they picked up the sets designed for them by Ernest Albert, the scenic artist of the Chicago Opera company and used them for the rest of the tour. With the new sets for *Julius Caesar*, *Othello* and *The Merchant of Venice*, after Chicago Booth and Barrett traveled with five carloads of supposedly historically correct scenery, costumes and properties. Ironically, despite the scenic elaboration, the best patronized show of the Chicago run was *Hamlet* with the old scenery.[4]

Meanwhile, Barth and Barrett were having plenty of amusement over the applications they received "from society people to serve as supernumeraries in their productions." *The Daily Chicago Tribune* reported:

> There seems to be an earnest ambition among a number of young ladies and gentlemen ... to take part in the performances, apparently for the simple object of being able to say that they have acted with Booth and Barrett.... During the last two weeks a number of well-known Chicago people have

appeared as the Roman army and Vatican population..... The "super" who has caused the most sensation is a young Chicago millionaire, who drives to the stage door every night in his private turnout and joins the noble army of supernumeraries, receiving 50 cents for his labors during the evening. When the play is over, this young fellow re-enters his carriage, waiting at the stage door, and drives to his club."[5]

What Booth called "dreadfully depressing weather" injured business in Chicago, Cincinnati and St. Louis. Consequently Booth and Barrett began an informal public relations campaign. Both men, being great walkers, spent their leisure hours on the street. Local newspapers reported that they "attracted general attention and were instantly recognized" wherever they went, Barrett in "a high white hat of prehistoric antiquity" and Booth in an "equally novel" outfit with a dark hat.[6]

Having canceled their Memphis and Nashville engagements on account of a yellow fever scare, the Booth and Barrett company closed in St. Louis on October 27 and traveled that night to New York in a special train comprising five baggage cars, two Pullman sleeping cars, a dining car and two passenger coaches. The two stars stayed overnight at the Hoffman House and then went to Boston to see their families.[7]

The company opened in New York on November 12, alternating *Othello* and *The Merchant of Venice*, using the Chicago scenery. The productions boasted over one hundred auxiliaries, a double quintet of selected singers, and a group of supernumeraries composed of what a New York critic described as "fresh young girls and bright faced youths from Dion Boucicault's Madison Square dramatic school."[8]

The student supernumeraries received nine dollars a week, three times what an ordinary supernumerary was paid. On one occasion, when a student was required for a part in a school play, a reporter for *The New York World* took his place. His resulting report is revelatory about the nature of this lowest rung in the theatrical hierarchy. Wandering around bewildered backstage, the reporter was directed to climb two flights of winding stairs, and found a dressing room where two other "supes" were making up. They immediately told him to "peel off as quick as he could" and handed him a pair of tights, with one blue and one white leg, a velvet doublet that buttoned up the side, a brown silk coat and a pair of brown kid shoes with pointed toes and French heels. One of the young lords applied the make-up:

> First came a covering of cocoa butter, which made the face very greasy and which ... was used to prevent cosmetics from injuring the skin. Then a generous application of fresh paint was applied and rubbed ... on all parts of the face and neck. After this had been ... smoothed down, two big dashes of red paint were put on each side of the eyes and a third daub almost covered his chin. [These were rubbed] gently until the reporter was left with a pretty pair of pink cheeks. The chin was also slightly colored in the same manner. Two little daubs of carmine were then placed on the reporter's lips.... The young lord then blackened the eyebrows and eyelashes. "I see that you have been getting your hair cut," said the young lord "so I'll let you wear my wig. You can get one tomorrow and my hair will be all right for one night." At this moment a voice was heard at the foot of the stairs. "All up for the first act! The young lords quickly grabbed their swords, and, thrusting one to the reporter, told him to stick it in his belt and follow them.... The reporter [asked] "what he was to do when he went on the stage." "Follow me and do just as I do," was the reply.... Stand near me but above all ... don't drop your sword when you take it out.... Don't stumble against any of the scenery and keep your face towards the audience as much as possible. Keep away from Booth and Barrett, and don't knock against anyone.... As they entered the stage, Othello [played by Barrett] turned towards them. "Salute," whispered the lord, quickly, at the same time raising his finger to his cap.... "Draw your sword halfway out." ... In a second, the lords were told by Othello to "keep up your bright swords for the dew will rust them." ... "Draw out your sword and hold it in front of you to protect Othello" ... "Now we will walk out and salute just as the curtain goes down."

A local critic reported that the "supernumeraries ... had ... been drilled according to 'Meiningen methods.'" The reference was to the painstakingly rehearsed staging typical of the Meiningen

Company, the court theatre of the German state of Saxe-Meiningen, led by Georg II, Duke of Saxe-Meiningen. The description of a rehearsal given by the reporter, however, indicates illustrative and coarse group responses as evidenced in the duel between Cassio and Montano, fought, at rehearsal, without swords.[9] Barrett, who played Othello, is directing.

> "Now, then, you see, Montano is wounded," cried Mr. Barrett. "Sympathy on the part of the women." The girls ... all tried to look doleful and murmured to one another while pointing to Montano. "Now I say, 'I love thee Cassio, but nevermore be officer of mine.'" Consternation on the part of the women. Up went the hands and they tried to depict consternation.... "The next point comes when I say, 'Sir, for your hurts myself will be your surgeon. Lead him off.'" You see he is weak, he staggers. Sorrow on the part of the women. They were all very much overcome, and a few of the most industrious wrung their gloved hands. "Very good. That is all to-day. Be here to-night at 7."

The company closed in New York on January 5, 1889, and went on to Pittsburgh, Baltimore and Boston. While in Baltimore, Booth and Barrett and various company members attended the burial of Booth's invalid sister Rosalie who had died in New York on January 15, 1889, at the age of sixty-six. Booth buried her on January 17th between the matinee and evening performances.[10]

In Boston a local critic wrote of Booth's Brutus: "If there was aught to wish were otherwise, it was an exhibition of weariness or listlessness which may have come from over-exertion or indisposition, and which was also the cause, probably, of Mr. Booth's occasional tripping in his speech." The "listlessness," "the tripping in his speech" and the headaches were all forebodings. In Philadelphia, Booth's health continued to deteriorate. He did not feel well, and he did not know why. "I am positively fagged out, but not by work, which has been comparatively light the past two seasons. It think it is the result of some liver derangement, and yet — with the exception of this chronic fatigue — my health seems better than ever it was."[11]

On April 3, 1889, in Rochester, according to the local newspaper, "every seat in the auditorium was filled" and "a large number" of people "were standing in the lobby and aisles. At exactly fifteen minutes past eight the curtain went up for the first act" of *Othello*. Unfortunately the dialogue could not be heard because of the noise made by latecomers. Some people thought that the theatre had poor acoustics, but "those familiar with the theatre and with Mr. Booth's voice and manner on the stage knew at once that the actor was ill, especially as he raised his hand to his head several times." The company got through the first act, and as the second act was being prepared, Booth, backstage, felt an increase in the "oppressive heaviness that he had experienced for several days." He said nothing, and the first scene of act II, Othello's appearance before the Venetian signiory was given. The curtain fell, and before the second scene could begin, Booth succumbed to his physical weakness. He became dizzy; he could not see and he became unsteady. A local physician named C. R. Sumner was called and reached the actor's room just as the curtain was rung up for the second scene. "Barrett and the other members of the company were forced to enter upon the stage in ignorance of what might be the result of the doctor's examination.... At the close of the scene Mr. Barrett hastened to [Booth's] dressing-room, ... where he was informed by Dr. Sumner that the symptoms were those of paralysis."[12] Before the third act, Barrett came out and told the audience:

> My colleague has shown symptoms of breaking down for three or four days past, and his condition tonight is so serious that it is impossible for him to act. We had hoped that he would rally from this attack and that he would be able to play his part to-night, but one of your physicians Dr. Sumner says that it would be perilous for him to attempt it. Mr. Booth has sustained a partial stroke of paralysis, and we fear that this is the beginning of the end.... The world has probably heard for the last time the greatest actor who speaks the English language. We shall, of course, cancel all engagements, and I hope we shall be able to remove Mr. Booth to his home.... The management will make such arrangements as may seem best, for refunding the money.[13]

Booth felt somewhat better before he left the theatre and was able to enter his carriage at the stage entrance without the assistance of Barrett or Dr. Sumner, both of whom accompanied him to the Powers Hotel. He walked to his room without being supported and slept through the night with Sumner at his side.[14]

The company was scheduled for Buffalo the last half of the week. A company member was dispatched to the railroad station to obtain tickets for Booth and Barrett on the Central Flyer, leaving for New York at 10:30 A.M. the next day. The next morning Booth got up at 8:30 A.M. and had breakfast in his room at nine. Dr. Sumner called and found his patient's condition much improved. Shortly after ten o'clock, Booth and Barrett were driven to the New York Central depot, preceded by members of their company. The two men sat secluded in the ticket office while members of the combination gathered in groups outside and talked in hushed tones. A reporter gained admission to the ticket booth and asked Booth how he was feeling. Booth looked at him in rather a surprised way and replied: "I am pretty well thank you." Just then Barrett, who wished to prevent anyone from talking to Booth, touched the arm of the reporter and said: "What is it?" The newspaper man replied that he was asking after Mr. Booth's health. Barrett replied: "He is very well this morning. He will be all right after a few days' rest. He is going to his home in New York to-day and I hope after ten days or so that he will be able to resume his engagements." The reporter later wrote, "Booth did not look remarkably bad, neither did he act in any unusual manner. He was very pale and his face had a yellowish tint that was not altogether pleasant. He was attired in an heavy ulster and a heavy scarf encircled his neck. Over his shoulder was thrown a small satchel. Mr. Barrett was attired in a similar manner and carried a fancy cane and an umbrella." Booth walked to the door, through it to the train house and into a seat in the drawing-room car, which took him to New York. Following his departure, however, Dr. Sumner told another reporter that Booth had "sustained a slight stroke of paralysis which prevented his power of speech. The paralysis affected his entire left side.... I think that within a few years, Mr. Booth will suffer a final attack, which may rob America of its greatest actor." Arthur B. Chase said: "I have no doubt that the immediate cause of Mr. Booth's attack was excessive cigar smoking. He smokes about twenty strong imported cigars a day and frequently uses a pipe. I told Mr. Booth this morning that I thought this was the cause. He smiled and said: 'I could not give up my cigar.'"[15]

Barrett did not accompany Booth to New York, deciding to stick to the original schedule, and he and the rest of the company left for Buffalo by train. Accompanied by his valet, Frank Lodge, Booth arrived back home in New York at 7:30 that evening. A local reporter described him as leaving the train wearing "a derby hat and a long overcoat," and walking down the platform at a moderate pace and without any assistance, carrying "a light satchel slung over his shoulder while a wooden toothpick rested between his lips." "His figure was erect and his step firm. Mr. Booth's physician Dr. St. Clair Smith, Booth and Barrett's New York agent Jerome H. Eddy and the reporters of the morning papers were there to greet him. He told the reporters: "I have had no paralysis; my illness was loss of voice, caused, I think, by excessive smoking. When he was spoken to about Mr. Barrett's speech, he smiled and said: 'Barrett had got frightened, lost his head and let his feelings run away with him.'" By April 6 Booth was resting at The Players and claiming that the attack had been brought on by tobacco.[16]

The company continued without Booth to Buffalo and Toledo with Lawrence Barrett starring alone. Their share went down to seventy-five percent, but Booth still got his cut despite the fact that he was not acting. He rejoined them in Cleveland, opening there on April 15 with nearly all seats sold for four performances. Between the acts, he told a reporter that he had never felt better in his life. "I am a boy again," he said. "No more paralysis for me. I have given up smoking altogether. It was a pretty hard struggle, but I have conquered and feel infinitely better. I am confident tobacco was the sole cause of my trouble, and that it was merely temporary."

Twenty-Three. 1888–1889: The Second Booth and Barrett Tour

Booth's abstinence from tobacco, however, was far from total: On April 15, 1889, he wrote to Edwina from Cleveland: "I smoked but five from breakfast to bed time, instead of my usual twenty or so! I think that is a pretty good reduction for one who was weaned on tobacco." By May 11, he admitted; "I <u>some days forget</u> how many smokes I've had, but rarely go beyond six per diem."[17]

In Indianapolis, Booth and Barrett had picked up their new private railroad car "Haselmere," built for them by the Pullman Palace Car Company. It contained private sleeping apartments, a drawing room, a parlor, a library, a dining room, a kitchen and a bath and had hot and cold water, electric lights and the services of a waiter, cook and porter. In time, however, Booth and Barrett discovered that the car's plumbing did not produce hot water.[18]

The tour moved westward with the company spending the following week in Iowa and Nebraska. The health of both stars began to deteriorate again. When Booth rejoined the company in Cleveland, he found Barrett looking "badly — his neck is a fearful sight!" and determined to visit a spa in Germany early in July. Booth attempted to reassure Edwina about his own physical condition, but he also complained about being bilious, lazy, tired, sleepy and having vision problems. His daily naps began coming earlier. He was taking five different kinds of medicine and having difficulty remembering when to take each dosage.[19] On May 7, 1889, Booth wrote to Thomas Bailey and Lillian Woodman Aldrich from Utah providing an assessment of his physical condition:

> Your dear ... letter ... found me very much better but still quite weak. It was a startling little episode & Barrett was excusable for his scare; I was scared myself, tho' less so I fancy than those about me. Three days prior to the collapse I had partially lost the full strength of my right arm, & about one year ago I had a similar attack (loss of coherent speech) w^h lasted about an half an hour; this time I turned green, had a chill & was unable to articulate or use the proper words to express myself, with loss of memory of the text of my part altho' clear enough otherwise — this lasted about 2 hours — About the 9th day after (at my rooms — in N.Y.) my left eye lost its lustre & was nearly closed while my right one was distended & was quite painful; my vision was double.[20]

Booth and Barrett arrived in San Francisco on May 10, 1889, by special train accompanied by thirty company members. The local newspaper reported that neither of the tragedians appeared to be in very good health, and that Booth looked particularly delicate.[21] The day after they arrived, Booth wrote to Edwina that they had canceled their trip to Monterey, and by May 13, Barrett had already cancelled their dates in Los Angeles, Portland, Butte and Helena and was working to cancel the fourth week of their engagement in San Francisco. The San Francisco manager John Maguire initially wanted a high fee to change attractions but eventually made arrangements with Helena Modjeska to fill their engagements, employing a number of actors from the company. Booth wrote to Edwina that Barrett felt "weary" and was "anxious to get to Germany as soon as possible."[22]

On June 2, Booth and Barrett started for New York with sixteen of their company members while others joined the actress Modjeska to tour the northwest. The trip took six days including a delay in Chicago, which allowed Booth "the opportunity to wash, shave, get a decent meal at the hotel, and to write letters." Barrett sailed for Europe on June 19th; Booth went to visit Edwina's family in Narragansett. They both needed a rest. The second Booth-Barrett tour had grossed $414,121.00, but both men were ill and knew, as businessmen, that the public needed a new combination.[23]

Chapter Twenty-Four

1889–1890: Touring with Modjeska

Booth and Barrett had experienced the monetary and artistic success of working in a star "combination." What they needed, however, was a new star. The person they chose was Helena Modjeska.

Modjeska was born Helena Opid (or Opido) in Krakow, Poland, on October 12, 1840. She married her guardian, Modrzejewski, and thus her name, a feminized version of his, became Modrzejewska and was eventually shortened to Modjeska. After her husband's death Modjeska married a young Polish patriot and journalist named Karol Brozenta Chlapowski. They settled in Warsaw, where she worked as an actress. In 1876 they emigrated to California, where they attempted to set up a utopian Polish community. She learned English and made her American stage debut at San Francisco's California theatre in 1877.[1]

Booth met Modjeska and her husband in March 1878 at the home of the Boston publisher Robert Montgomery Field, and found "the Count [as Chlapowski styled himself] & his charming Modjeska ... very pleasant folks." He renewed their acquaintance while in England, often attending Modjeska's Sunday drawing-room salons. He eventually found their pretensions to being Polish nobility silly and referred to the "he Modjeska" as "The Count Slapslowski or Dasslowski or Slasslowski."[2]

On December 9, 1888, Booth wrote: "It may be that I'll have Modjeska next season; As Lady Macbeth she will be a good card, & in all my other plays, she will be considered better than any other that I can get." By February 1889 he had decided to tour with Modjeska, now 48, while Barrett acted separately in a new play. By March 23 Barrett placed her under contract, as a salaried employee for "thirty weeks of performances" to extend over a thirty-two week period.[3]

According to the initial plan Modjeska and Booth were to open in October at the Broadway Theatre, giving *Macbeth* "the finest production" it had ever had in New York. Booth received a contract for twenty-five weeks. In practice, the tour lasted 30 weeks.[4]

Modjeska was not interested in being a "leading lady" like Minna Gale, who had toured for the last two seasons with Booth and Barrett. Leading ladies were simply members of the company. Modjeska was a star and insisted on equal billing with Booth. By February 1889 Barrett, who was still acting as the tour's producer, was hiring actors; the line of "leading man" (the second most important male actor in the company) went to the rising star Otis Skinner. The company consisted of at least twenty-seven actors including a quintet of vocalists plus supernumeraries.[5]

With the exception of a Fourth of July trip to his banker E. C. Benedict in Greenwich, Booth spent the summer of 1889 alternating between The Players and Edwina's summer home at Narragansett Pier. The schedule implies that he was probably getting on better with his daughter and her husband. Modjeska spent her summer working, having thirty-five new costumes made from designs she found in the Astor Library.[6]

Neither Barrett nor Booth were in good health. Booth wrote to Laurence Hutton: "Barrett went direct to Germany; his disease is serious & I fear the dear fellow will have great difficulty to be rid of his disfigurement." European spas did not help. On September 23, 1889, having seen his partner, Booth wrote: "I have serious doubts of Barrett's continuance; his face looks worse than ever and is fearfully sensitive." His own health was delicate. He was perpetually tired and slept until noon all summer.[7]

Rehearsals began at the Broadway Theatre in New York on September 16. Modjeska was to play Julie to Booth's Richelieu, Lady Macbeth to his Macbeth, Ophelia to his Hamlet, Portia to his Shylock, Fiordelisa to his Bertuccio and Beatrice to his Benedick. In addition she was scheduled to appear in two of her specialties—Friedrich Schiller's *Mary Stuart* and *Donna Diana*, a one-act comedy by Westland Marston which she performed, as part of a double bill, whenever Booth played *Don Caesar* or *The Fool's Revenge*.[8]

Booth, Modjeska and Barrett rehearsed in New York for four days. Edwin felt that rehearsals went well but that "the gentle Pole's accent is very heavy and the text bothers her very much."[9] In Pittsburgh Booth had less than one day to re-rehearse with Modjeska prior to their opening on September 30 in a six-act version of *The Merchant of Venice*. By this point Booth found his "foreign lady ... difficult to understand." On October 3 he wrote: "M$\underline{s}$ Ophelia was a superb piece of acting, but she is indistinct & speaks too low; her dresses charming." Whatever Modjeska's drawbacks, her combination with Booth "did a very large business" in Pittsburgh, and the local correspondent for *The New York Mirror* predicted that that they would do "the largest business of any theatrical organization on the road this season."[10]

By Cleveland Booth was thoroughly disappointed with Modjeska and fed up with her husband:

> I doubt if you will like Modjeska; she is so hampered by her accent: her art (which is excellent) is cramped and "dislocated," as it were, by the difficulty she has with our language. 'Twas my mistake in engaging her—I had forgotten her accent. She is a very pleasant lady—but is nervous & hysterical at times, while her dirty little Count fusses about like a poodle. He goes to Cal: next week to look after their ranch—I hope he'll stay there during our season.[11]

Modjeska's vocal problems were caught late in the tour in an interview by a reporter from *The Toledo Blade* who reproduced not only her syntax but also her rather frank appraisal of her own abilities.

> When I have a new part to take, first I must see myself in it. If I can see myself in it, then I know I can do that. You see how it is ... it is not that I must only have a part I like—a part I can put myself in. NO, no it is not that, but I must see myself in the part from top to toe. If I do not—even to hear the tones of my voice—then I know I cannot do well to that part.... Lady Macbeth I cannot see myself in that.... I could do it. I would study. I could do—With study. But it would be all skill, study—and it would not be the same.... With my voice—it would be hard to make my voice to be the voice of Lady Macbeth. I cannot hear in my voice those hard tones. I could study. Yes, I can study hard; and with care and study—but, after all, she is so sharp, like a knife ... and I am so round, like a spoon.... So you see it would be like a fat Camille.... Yes I like to act all the time. I cannot help it. But it is tiring. Not at the time, after.... Ophelia is easy. Simple. There is not much to act. You just have a little 'hysterics' and so on, and that is not hard.[12]

On October 14 Booth and Modjeska opened *Richelieu* at New York's Broadway Theatre.[13] During the run at the Broadway, *The New York Herald* insinuated that Modjeska was taking legal measures to dissolve her contract with Barrett and that "the chief reason ... was that ... Booth's conduct towards her had been ungentlemanly," the implication being that he had annoyed her with his personal attentions.[14] A *Dramatic Mirror* representative, interviewing Modjeska, found her "much disturbed by the *Herald*'s publication," claiming "Not only is there not this awful disagreement between Mr. Booth and myself, but there has not even been a cross word or an ugly look between us."[15] Booth blamed the scandal on reporters who had been barred from membership in The Players and wrote to Edwina: "I never heard a breath of reproach against Modjeska and I presume I sh^{d} consider myself lucky in 'scaping such scandals so long. The idea of two grandparents being so scandalized has a ludicrous aspect, and, as a man, the report will not seriously affect my reputation, but to drag a lady's name through their filth is a very serious affair."[16] In time, however, Booth came to suspect that Modjeska had planted the story for publicity. After she suffered a sprain later in the season, he wrote to Edwina: "How 'the whirligig of Time brings its revenges'—and the Polish attempt to scandalize me has its reward, too."[17]

After a Christmas vacation, Booth and Modjeska resumed touring for a month in New England followed by a week in Brooklyn. At the last evening performance in Brooklyn, Modjeska sprained her ankle during *Macbeth*, and "limped heroically through the play" but was unable to continue when the company went on to Philadelphia and Baltimore. At this point Barrett was too ill to tour, and Minna Gale, "temporarily disengaged" due to his illness, stepped into her roles.[18]

Booth was annoyed at Modjeska's disability, although it did not significantly affect business which he pronounced "great ... in spite of Lent." In truth he did not miss her and felt that "Gale gave more than satisfaction to the audience." Moreover, without Modjeska, the company's salaries went from $2,890 to $1,575. Her husband, whom Booth now referred to as "the Count de Cigarette Boyenta," promised her early return, but when Modjeska's doctor told him that she would be unable to act until March 8 in Chicago, Booth wrote to Edwina: "I hope she won't hurry." Booth himself was now in reasonable health. On February 16 he wrote to William Bispham: "'tis remarkable how the old nag draws in his decadence! Perhaps 'tis his last 'spurt' on the home strech!"[19]

Modjeska began to perform again on March 3 in Baltimore, but the two had little contact off stage. Booth stayed at the Mount Vernon Hotel. Modjeska and her husband occupied the Langtry suite of rooms at the St. James. According to a local newspaper, she "was compelled to remain quietly at her hotel," because her ankle "was still weak and encased in a steel splint." They usually arrived at the Holliday St. Theatre about 7:15 or 7:30, coming in closed carriages, went to their respective dressing rooms and did not see each other until the play began.[20]

By the time they reached Chicago, Modjeska was dancing "around as though she had not been ill" and Booth was afraid she would "slip her old bones again." On April 3 Booth, who was seven years older than his 48-year-old co-star, wrote to Edwina: "'H. W.' & 'H. W.'—(Holy Week & Hellish Weather) have hurt the business considerably, but last night a boom began & the prospect is now fair.... The M^{dme} begins to limp a little & has sent for a doctor today. The old girl is too kittenish with her antique bones, & I've no doubt but that she'll feel the sprain the rest of her life."[21]

From April 17 until the tour's end on May 10, Booth and Modjeska played seventeen different cities and three matinee/evening performances. He was determined that in the future, he would endure "God willing, no more 'barn-storming' & no more double days' work." The trek through small Midwestern towns found the company in theatres reminiscent of Booth's days in California.[22] Otis Skinner recalled a dreadful theatre in Vincennes, Indiana, where the *Hamlet* scenery would not fit on the stage. Booth came off after the first act "sputtering with mirth":

"Did you see it? Did you see it?"
I certainly had.

"I nearly said it!" he exclaimed.

What he had seen — what we all saw — was a long reflecting board shielding the gas footlights from the audience; on its white surface, painted in huge black letters, was this admonition:

DO NOT SPIT IN THE TROUGH

"I was fascinated by it," he said, "What if I should say, 'To be, or not to be — do not spit in the trough — that is the question. Whether it is nobler in the mind to suffer the slings and arrows of outrageous fortune or to take arms against a sea of troubles and by spitting in the trough — end them.'"[23]

By the time he reached Dayton, Ohio, Booth was exhausted. On May 5, 1890, he wrote to Edwina: "I've had ... a horrible attack of dyspepsia the past week.... I have a sty on my eye — aches in various parts of my skeleton & have the horrors generally.... I will try your dentist this summer, for my teeth are going rapidly, & I must be doctored at once. This is my last week, thank God." The season ended on May 10. Barrett was so ill that he had had to abandon his tour in midstream, have an operation and travel to Europe in hopes of finding cures at a spa. Owen Fawcett, Booth's lead comedian, declined an engagement for the following year and wrote in his diary: "Not at all sorry that the season is coming to a close — the last few weeks have been more than disagreeable." Otis Skinner later wrote that during the tour he had seen Booth's "physical powers sapping and his performances routine and perfunctory." The end was in sight.[24]

Chapter Twenty-Five

1890–1893: Illness, Last Tour and Death

By the summer of 1890 Booth, approaching the end of his career, felt that he was also approaching the end of his life. He had already suffered one stroke, and his legs were weak. By June 10, 1890, he "rarely" left The Players, going out only for a "mechanical massage" treatment known as the "Swedish cure," which as he wrote was "about all the exercise" he could "endure." He described his condition as "premature antiquity." He missed Edwina and, as he wrote to William Winter, "(strange as it seems) I miss her mother, as I go nearer to her, more than I ever did." He had apparently learned to endure Ignatius Grossman, because the endless vindictiveness against him expressed in previous letters ceased. Eventually his letters to everyone except Edwina ceased.[1]

He spent part of June and July 1890 at the Jefferson compound at Buzzards Bay, Massachusetts, where the air and the company always improved his health. In late August and early September, however, while visiting the Grossmans at Narragansett Pier, he was "laid flat" by what he described as "uric acid in the blood." He collapsed at the knees, and his "head spun like a 'buzz' saw whenever [he] sat upright." He could "barely stand alone & creep unaided," but he still assured his partner Lawrence Barrett: "I shall soon be on my pins again."[2]

Given the state of his health, Booth knew that he could not maintain a schedule of seven or eight performances a week. He was determined that there would be "no more such work.... The nervous strain begins to 'tell' on me seriously, & I shall hereafter hold a tighter rein on my young ambitions." In November 1889 he wrote what he described as "a long positive letter to Barrett refusing to act Matinees & less than one week anywhere & not more than 15 weeks the next season."[3]

On November 3, 1890, Booth and Barrett began their last tour at Albaugh's Theatre in Baltimore. They were originally booked for the Boston Theatre, but their contract was cancelled because of the successful run of the theatre's current hit. They were paid $1,500 in compensation and opened at Boston's Park Theatre instead. The company that two years previously had cleaned up all the money available in a particular venue now took second place to the latest novelty.[4] Booth wrote from the Thorndike Hotel in Boston: "I am getting gradually stronger on my pins & clearer in my wits, tho' my tongue slips frequently & my knees totter occasionally, I thought I had St. Vitus' dance at daybreak this morning, when I rose to shut the window."[5]

After Boston Booth's seven-week fall season ended with one week in Providence. There, according to the local newspaper, during *Julius Caesar*, he "seemed unable to concentrate his thoughts upon the task at hand and frequently appeared to be unfamiliar with the text. He hesitated, corrected himself, then went on as if awakened to the situation [and] seemed insecure in moving abut the stage." It had, in all, been a seven-week season. The company went on, with Barrett as its star. Booth did not rejoin them until they opened at the Broadway Theatre for a four-week season beginning March 2, 1891.[6]

He continued to be weak. The day before opening in New York, his grandson, almost four years old, knocked him flat, managing a narrow escape when his grandfather fell on him. According to a local newspaper, off-stage he looked "pale and ill" and "walked slowly and painfully, leaning heavily on a cane." He no longer performed on Saturday evenings and played only Shylock and Brutus the first week and Hamlet and Iago the second. On March 7, he wrote to Edwina: "I have felt better every day; but as the play progresses, I seem to lose power; my tongue keeps clear tho' it slips a word or two, now & then; but my legs get tangled and are weary after a few moments' standing.... I feel remarkably well — most of the time, but am constantly tired; I could sleep, all day as well as all night; even now, while I write, I can scarcely keep my eyes open.[7]

On March 18, 1891, Barrett arrived at the Broadway Theatre to play De Mauprat in *Richelieu*. Booth was told he was ill.

> I immediately went to him.... He was seated in a chair against the wall and had not yet taken off his hat or overcoat. The coat-collar was turned up, so as almost to hide his face, and he had been crying. He became calm at once. I urged him to go home, but he insisted on playing, and he managed to get as far as the end of the third act; but when he bent over me, after I was on the Cardinal's bed, he whispered, "I cannot go on."[8]

Lawrence Hanley finished the play as Mauprat, and Barrett was taken to the Windsor Hotel with a high fever, a severe cold and threatened pneumonia, although his case was reported to the public only as an attack of influenza. Barrett's wife arrived from Boston, and he was attended by two doctors, who recommended that he stay in bed for at least ten days. Booth visited his partner on March 19, but Barrett "was in a burning fever.... It pained him to talk, and he asked [Booth] to keep away for fear his breath might be infectious."[9]

Barrett died on Friday, March 20, 1891, at 9:45 P.M. Booth learned of his death from Theodore Bromley the following day at 12:30 P.M. He got up, played a matinee and then called on Mrs. Barrett at the Windsor Hotel to express his sympathy and stayed for an hour. Both Barrett and his wife were Catholics, but the Catholic church forbade its services to a Mason. Consequently the funeral service was conducted in the hotel parlor on Monday, March 23, 1891, at 10 A.M.[10]

That night the Broadway Theatre was closed, but the night after the funeral, the company resumed work, performing *Hamlet*. Booth wrote to Edwina: "I, of course, am free." Barrett's death voided their contract, but Booth decided that "for the sake of the company, I shall fulfill my time to pay their salaries, this week here; and next week — in Brooklyn, as they were engaged by Barrett for my eng.ᵗ After which they will be out of employment the balance of the season." Booth finished his New York run with a matinee of *Hamlet* on March 26, 1891.[11]

After New York he immediately moved to the Academy of Music in Brooklyn for what would be his last engagement. There he ended his career with six performances, Barrett's estate still receiving his share of the profits. On April 4, 1891, Edwin Booth gave his last performance — a matinee of *Hamlet*— at the Brooklyn Academy of Music. It was a role he knew he should have given up years ago, but the public demanded it. By 1 P.M. people began to pour through Montague Street to the Academy in crowds and the rush did not diminish until after the curtain had risen. The line in front of the ticket seller's window reached through the door out upon the porch of the Academy. As reported by *The New York Times*:

> The big auditorium was crowded by more than 3,000 persons. The money taken in at the box office amounted to $2,664.50.... Every available foot of standing room was occupied. The steps in the

orchestra circle, balcony and upper gallery were used as seats in violation of the law, by people who refused for the time to recognize authority. The reason for the unusual crowd was the settled public belief, in spite of all reasonably authoritative contradictions, that in yesterday afternoon's representation of the play most closely associated with his fame, Mr. Booth would unostentatiously say farewell to the stage. The orchestra had been driven upon the stage [behind the scenery] and seventy-five chairs were placed inside the orchestra rail. People were sitting on the steps of the aisle in the dress circle and gallery. Mr. Booth wore the black wig he first used in *Hamlet* a year or so ago. His movements on the stage were easy and graceful, but his lack of physical strength was plainly apparent. Excepting those lucky people who had choice seats in front, nobody heard all he said. His voice was husky, and there was scarcely a trace of his old fire in his speech and action in the play scene, in the frenzy at its close, or in the famous "Is it the king?" of the Queen's closet. None of these episodes awakened applause. There were bursts of polite enthusiasm, though, after "To be or not to be," the repulse of *Ophelia*, and the rebuke to the courtiers. The famous actor was followed through it all, however, with loving interest. After the close of the last act there was a great demonstration. The curtain was raised twice for Mr. Booth [to] bow his acknowledgements. Then he was summoned before the curtain twice and called upon for a speech. In a low and tremulous voice that could not be heard except in the front row of seats, he spoke as follows: "Ladies and Gentlemen: I hardly know what to say to you. I have said all I can say. I thank you for your kindness, and I hope this will not be the last time I shall appear before you. I intend to rest next year and care for my health but hope to appear again in the near future. Next season I shall pay some attention to my health, and I think I shall return to you strengthened. I again thank you and hope it will not be for the last time. Au revoir, not adieu."[12]

There was quite a crowd on the stage when Booth emerged from his dressing room. He found his supporting cast standing in a double line to greet him. All shook hands with him and Booth was obliged to kiss some of the ladies good-by. Two policemen were waiting to escort him to his carriage. Outside on Montague Street, there was a great crowd. The stoops of the house opposite and the windows of the Brooklyn Library were all occupied. According to a local newspaper, when Booth came in sight, 2,000 voices united in a mighty cheer. He bowed his acknowledgment gravely. His carriage was waiting in front of the main entrance of the Academy, half a block away. The policemen led him through the throng, and the cheering continued. With some difficulty he reached the carriage, bowed once more to the admiring crowd, and was driven over the bridge to Gramercy Park.[13]

Booth was repulsed by the attention and wrote to Edwina: "The manager quietly encouraged the sensation reports that 'twas my 'farewell,' and the reports slobbered their sweet gush, full of spite, all over me." Even before this performance, however, he had decided "to cancel all my engagements for next season." He remained at The Players, sending down orders for food on small cards: "Broiled Bacon Omelette with parsley — Hominy — coffee, Indian Cakes Syrup, Toasted Roll."[14]

In May Booth went to Stockbridge with Edwina and her family and by the end of June he was at Buzzards Bay with the Jeffersons. By August he had joined Ignatius and Edwina and his grandchildren at Narragansett. He wrote to William Bispham: "My general condition is improved immensely, but indigestion still affects me. My legs and head are steady — no cane for six weeks past, few headaches, and unusual vigor.... I really do not smoke so much since I left home; the desire is subsiding, I am confident." By the fall he was back in New York, complaining "Your melancholy friend Ye Hemorhoidal [sic] Hamlet unlike his Papa's Ghost, doesn't walk often by our watch now-a-times.... I've had a good summer and am in much better health — but I still sit still & read the advertisements, as formerly — do not go out much."[15]

During the winter of 1891–1892 his health continued "about the same," and he wrote to William Bispham: "I go as far as the grill-room during the day, and several nights a week, I tea or dine with my daughter.... My lassitude is such that I'm no equal to giving you a decent letter. Mentally and physically I am about 'played out,' but I am in so much better *trim* that I feel

Twenty-Five. 1890–1893: Illness, Last Tour and Death

encouraged to hope for steadier pins and a clearer head in the near future." As he wrote to William Winter: "I have reached the full length of my tether & can say no more than to wish you well — in health and all other things that make life worth living."[16]

He spent the summer with his daughter in Narragansett. On October 2, 1892, Booth and the Grossmans went to a hotel called Laurel House in Lakewood, New Jersey, where he was seen in a dark, almost black, frock coat and waistcoat with a black cravat and white shirt, "making his way feebly through the corridors with the assistance of a heavy oaken cane." He refused to have a physician or even an attendant with him. He normally got up now about nine or nine-thirty in the morning, spent a half an hour getting himself ready and then had breakfast either in his room or in the hotel dining room. On October 5 he suffered an attack of vertigo, fell in his room and hit his head. His son-in-law Ignatius Grossman was quoted as saying: "I suppose ... that were he to get well, he would want to go back to the theatre, but he never speaks of it, or, I believe, thinks of it." Yet Booth still tottered to the smoking room to light a cigar, and when Edwina appeared in the doorway, like a gentleman, he struggled to his feet and with weak unsteady steps advanced to meet her. Every day he walked around the hotel's verandah for exercise, played with his grandchildren and took rides with Ignatius and Edwina. Occasionally he was able to walk down to the lake. He was finally either reconciled to his son-in-law or in no condition to prevent his presence.[17]

On November 13, 1892, Booth spent his fifty-ninth birthday in his room at The Players. Seventy-five club members sent up a written greeting and he received letters of congratulations and flowers. He spent the day reading and smoking. A reporter for the *New York Herald* wrote:

> Those who saw him said his brain seemed stronger than when he came back from Lakewood, but that he was very weak in the lower limbs. I saw him at 5:45 o'clock in the evening, when Mr. McGonigle supported him from the private elevator to a carriage.... He seemed scarcely able, even with a strong arm locked in his, to drag himself along, and he sank into the carriage with a weary sigh as if he had come a long journey. He asked to be excused from talking.... He was driven around to No. 12 West Eighteenth street, where his daughter Edwina (Mrs. I. R. Grossman) lives, and took dinner there ... with her and her husband.[18]

In the days that followed Booth could be seen walking around Gramercy Park or Union Square. Adam Badeau wrote:

> I called just as he was about to try to walk, and he asked me to go with him. He had to be assisted to the door, and when he reached the street, I proffered him my arm. He took it and leaned heavily. He stumbled as he walked, and it took us half an hour to move around the block of buildings in which the club-house stands. Then he was tired, and wanted to go in, and I knew that my friend would not recover.[19]

By December 21, 1892, Booth's mind was going. He no longer could form coherent sentences. He wrote to Edwina:

> 'Tis almost impossible to write now — its so dim with my ideas & I I can spells, Harry should speak of matter I was so uncertain of. I had not decided & I am all uncertain. For 3 days I have had no repose & must suffer tomorrow of course. Dr Smith I must not go to the South at all, & I think it a bad trip for all of us, but I'll take it at risk, but I can write only more not even speech. Let it write yr a day or so. Will so you tomorrow & try the election also. [Edwina appended a note: "Dear Mr Bispham: This note is so incoherent that I am somewhat alarmed lest Papa have another attack of Paralysis — Will you kindly read it, I wonder if he has his doctor with him."][20]

On New Year's Eve 1892, Booth made his last appearance before the members of The Players. He had written out a short speech in an illegible hand, and when it was suggested to him that a copy be made he replied: "I am afraid it's of no use. My eyes are always very moist when I see them all, and I do not think I could see to read it, even if it were copied." The evening was presided over by the producer A. M. Palmer, and the honored guest was President-elect Grover

Cleveland. On the stroke of twelve Booth drank from the loving cup which was then passed to the other Players.[21]

On February 11, 1893, William Winter visited Booth for the last time. By February 19 Magonigle was staying overnight with him and William Bispham and Ignatius Grossman's brother-in-law Charles Carryl were watching him through the day. Electricity was applied almost daily to his back, first four and later two times a day, and his theatre-going was confined to matinees. He seldom went out or even downstairs. On April 3, 1893, he saw Alexander Salvini play Don Caesar de Bazan at the Manhattan Opera House. It was the last time he went to the theatre.[22] On April 17, he wrote to Edwina from The Players:

> I rose very late this morning, and brought with me an all-night and permanent headache, which still sways me after a long nap on the sofa — till just now; I hope to get rid of it and be with you for a while this evening.... If I should not get out, don't worry; I am quite well — except my stupid headache, that will perhaps keep me in the house. Nothing worse.[23]

It was Booth's last letter. That evening, he visited his daughter's home for dinner. On April 18, 1893, he suffered another attack of vertigo, and a small stroke during the night. The next morning at 10:30, Magonigle found him "lying in bed speechless and seemingly unconscious." Booth's doctor St. Clair Smith pronounced it a case of vertigo probably brought on by excessive smoking. It was a fiction that could not last.[24]

On April 21 his doctor admitted publicly that Booth had had an "aphasia ... of a paralytic character" but not a "cerebral aphasia." Booth was speaking, albeit articulating with difficulty. Edwina spent a few minutes in the morning with him, and Ignatius remained at his bedside all day long. Ladies' Day (the one day women were admitted to the club) scheduled for April 24 (in celebration of Shakespeare's birthday), was indefinitely postponed. Smith visited the actor three times during the day and that evening made the following public statement: "Mr. Booth was attacked yesterday morning by partial aphasia and some paralysis of his right arm and right side of his face in all probability due to a slight hemorrhage in the brain."[25]

By April 27 Booth "was dull and listless ... and failed to recognize even the attendants ... at his bedside." On June 3 his condition deteriorated; he was attacked by "an exhausting fit" of vomiting, which brought him near suffocation. He continued, however, to take nourishment until June 5, when he lapsed into unconsciousness. He appeared to be gasping for air; consequently the "the three windows in his room were opened at the top and bottom and the curtains drawn aside." During the afternoon of June 5, Joseph Jefferson, his son, Charles Burke Jefferson, and William Bispham called on Booth. Jefferson stood at his bedside for fifteen minutes, but Booth did not recognize him. Edwina, Harry Magonigle, Ignatius and his sister and her husband, Mr. and Mrs. Charles P. Carryl, sat up all night with the dying man, along with a trained nurse and physician. "At 1:10 A.M. "all of the electric lights of the clubhouse and street were suddenly extinguished, probably by a freak of the electric current. Two minutes later [they] shone again." Booth died 5 minutes later at 1:15 A.M. on June 7, 1893. The *New York Times* reported that he passed away in his daughter's arms. At 1:17 Dr. Smith appeared at a window of the clubhouse and gave a signal with his handkerchief to the crowd waiting below.[26]

Funeral services were held on June 8 in the Little Church Around the Corner. Booth's body was placed in a massive plain oak casket trimmed with brass and taken to the church with no flowers on it except a laurel wreath from Edwina. Two carriages carrying the pallbearers preceded the hearse; a carriage with the chief mourners followed it, and virtually the entire membership of The Players followed on foot.[27]

The procession entered the church to Chopin's Funeral March. In addition to the chief mourners, people from all phases of Booth's life were present — Mrs. Benjamin A. Baker (the widow of his first manager), his later managers Henry E. Abbey and Arthur B. Chase, Alexander

Salvini (Tomasso's son), J. J. McCloskey (his fellow actor from Gold Rush California), Dr. St. Clair Smith, H.C Jarrett (who took over the Booth Theatre), Stanford White (the architect of The Players), Adam Badeau and Edmund Clarence Stedman (one of the many literary people Booth cultivated as a friend). The service lasted only fifteen minutes.

The casket was then taken to Boston, where the mourners proceeded by carriage to Mount Auburn Cemetery. Four to five hundred people crowded around as the short Episcopal service was said. As the coffin was to be lowered into the grave, Edwina prostrated herself upon it, weeping and crying, "My father, oh, my father." She placed a bunch of violets on her mother's grave, and Ignatius led her away. The spectators pressed around the open grave to get floral mementoes.[28]

Fifteen years later, having decided to move to Europe, Edwina had the Booth material in her possession auctioned. There was little interest. An admirer of Booth's turned away, choking back tears, saying: "It reminds me of the Roman soldiers shaking dice for the clothes in the story of the Crucifixion."[29] Booth would have found the statement lachrymose. The items on sale were not holy relics. They were the tools of his working trade. He had no illusions about the theatre. As he wrote to the father of an aspiring actor:

> It is a life of wearisome drudgery; and requires years of toil and bitter disappointments to achieve a position worth having.... Had nature fitted me for any other calling, I should never have chosen the stage; were I able to employ my thoughts & labor in any other field I would gladly turn my back on the theatre forever. An art whose professors and followers should be of the very highest culture, is the mere make-shift of every speculator & boor that can hire a theatre or get hold of some sensational rubbish to gull the public. I am not very much in love with my calling as it now is (and, I fear, will ever be).[30]

He romanticized the life of a common laborer: "O father, father, why didn't I take your advice & learn a trade@ (my sign) 'E Thomas Booth — Cabinet maker & job-carpenter, Bel Air, Me^{d}.'" The truth was that he did learn a trade, one that served him well for the rest of his life. He was an actor, and when in 1890 he wrote to Edwina that his father had wanted him to be a cabinet-maker, he added: "But Nature cast me for the part she found me best fitted for & I have had to play it, and must play it, till the curtain falls. But you must not think me sad about it. No; I am used to it & am contented."[31]

Part II: Performance History

The following chronology of Edwin Booth's known performances includes the date of the engagement; the theatre and its location; the character performed and the play in which the character appears, unless Booth performed the title role. When the location is self-evident through the name of the venue, the city and state (or country) may be omitted; and the theatre is given upon the initial date only in the case of consecutive appearances at the same theatre. Nineteenth-century theatres were often called "opera houses" or "museums" to make them seem more respectable. While some were used for multiple purposes, including concerts, exhibitions or revivals, they either housed, or essentially were, traditional theatres. Some of the plays in which Booth performed are probably lost to history, and many early performances were impromptu presentations cobbled together by the company and compiled from a number of works. Scripts, characters and play names were not standardized, and newspapers varied in what they called a particular play. In some cases, as stated in the entry, the role or play performed is unknown.

1849–1850

9/10/49; Boston Museum; Tressel, *Richard III*
Edwin's debut as Tressel came at the beginning of Junius Brutus' 1849–1850 season, and on the first Monday of the third week of his Boston run. He had already acted Richard III three times during this engagement, and his son's appearance in a fourth performance may have been designed to bolster the house on a traditionally slow night. Edwin later remembered that after the show, the elder Booth "coddled" him in their hotel, feeding him gruel and dressing him in his own worsted nightcap so he would not catch cold. At the time, the young Edwin thought it an ironic comment a brief performance.

9/27/49; Providence Museum; Cassio, *Othello*
9/29/49; Wilford, *The Iron Chest*
11/17/49; Avon Theatre, Norfolk, Virginia; Wilford, *The Iron Chest*
2/16/50; Charleston Theatre, South Carolina; Benefit of Junius Brutus Booth; Wilford, *The Iron Chest*
5/22/50; Connor's Arch Street Theatre, Philadelphia; Wilford, *The Iron Chest*

1850–1851

9/27/50; National Theatre, New York; Wilford, *The Iron Chest*
10/1/50; Tressel, *Richard III*
10/4/50; Hemeya, *The Apostate*
11/2/50; Holliday Street Theatre, Baltimore; Titus, *Brutus*
11/8/50; Adelphi Theatre, Washington, D.C.; Hemeya, *The Apostate*
12/10/50; Brooklyn Museum; Wilford, *The Iron Chest*, advertised as Millord, *The Iron Chest*
12/21/50; Providence Museum; Titus, *Brutus*
1/8/51; Lowell Museum; Hemeya, *The Apostate*
1/14, 16/51; Titus 2x, *Brutus*
2/24/51; Adelphi Theatre, Washington, D.C.; Richmond, *Richard III*
2/26/51; Hemeya, *The Apostate*
2/27/51; Cassio, *Othello*
2/28/51; Laertes, *Hamlet*
4/5/51; National Theatre, New York; Richard III, first known performance
4/21/51; Richmond, Virginia; Hemeya, *The Apostate*
4/22/51; Richmond, *Richard III*
4/23/51; Cassio, *Othello*
4/25/51; Wilford, *The Iron Chest*
4/26/51; Titus, *Brutus*
4/28/51; Richmond, *Richard III*
5/5–6/51; National Hall, Washington, D.C.; Edgar, *King Lear*
5/7/51; Richmond, *Richard III*
5/14/51; Gratiano, *The Merchant of Venice*
5/16/51; Macduff, *Macbeth*; Gratiano, *The Merchant of Venice*
5/17/51; Wilford, *The Iron Chest*; Young Norval, *Douglas*

Booth told Francis Wilson that he found a costume for Young Norval by borrowing "the dress the leading lady wore as Helen M'Gregor in *Rob Roy*," shortening the skirt, wearing it as a kilt and wearing the back of the costume's top across his chest.

5/29/51; Holliday Street Theatre, Baltimore; Richmond, *Richard III*

1851–1852

8/2/51; Court House, Belair, Maryland; Richard III selections; Macbeth dagger scene, *Macbeth*; Hamlet "To be or not to be," *Hamlet*; Richelieu selections, *Richelieu*; Brutus quarrel scene, *Julius Caesar*
8/8/51; Same roles as 8/2/51; *The Apostate*, role unknown
2/11/52; Antoine Bellard, *The Carpenter of Rouen*
2/12/52; Holliday Street Theatre, Baltimore; Titus, *Brutus*
3/6/52; Benefit of Jean Davenport; Lykon, *Ingomar*
3/8/52; Gaspar, *The Lady of Lyons*
3/13/52; Herman, *The Robbers*; Lord Rivers, *The Day After the Wedding*
3/26/52; Charleston Theatre; Wilford, *The Iron Chest*, billed as Millford, *The Iron Chest*
6/3/52; Holliday Street Theatre, Baltimore; Edgar, *King Lear*

1852–1853

7/30/52; Jenny Lind Theatre, San Francisco; Wilford, *The Iron Chest*
7/31/52; Allworth, *A New Way to Pay Old Debts*
8/1/52; Laertes, *Hamlet*
8/2/52; Virolet, *The Mountaineers*
8/3/52; Cassio, *Othello*
8/4, 6/52; Gratiano 2x, *The Merchant of Venice*
8/7/52; Hemeya, *The Apostate*
8/8/52; Calverton Hall, *The State Secrets*
8/9/52; Francis, *The Stranger*
8/11/52; Titus, *Brutus*
8/12/52; Edgar, *King Lear*
8/13/52; Wilford, *The Iron Chest*
8/14/52; Cassio, *Othello*
8/15/52; Malcolm, *Macbeth*
8/19/52; American Theatre, Sacramento; Wilford, *The Iron Chest*
8/20/52; Allworth, *A New Way to Pay Old Debts*
8/21/52; Gratiano, *The Merchant of Venice*
8/23/52; Laertes, *Hamlet*
8/24/52; Hemeya, *The Apostate*
8/25/52; Edgar, *King Lear*
8/26/52; Titus, *Brutus*
8/27/52; Richmond, *Richard III*
8/28/52; Virolet, *The Mountaineers*
8/30/52; Richmond, *Richard III*
8/3152; Calverton Hall, *The State Secrets*
9/2/52; Booth's benefit, Jaffier, *Venice Preserved*; Calverton Hall, *The State Secrets*
9/3/52; Titus, *Brutus*
9/6/52; Richmond, *Richard III*
10/16/52; Dramatic Hall, Nevada, California; Role unknown in *The Stranger*; Stuckley, *The Gamester*
10/20/52; Laertes, *Hamlet*
10/26/52; Gratiano, *The Merchant of Venice*
10/29/52; Role unknown in *Richard III*
11/10/52; Laertes, *Hamlet*
11/15/52; Role unknown
11/18–12/3/52; Grass Valley; Roles unknown
c. 11/26/52; Laertes, *Hamlet*
12/3/52; Laertes, *Hamlet*
12/11/52; Dramatic Hall, Nevada; DeMauprat, *Richelieu*; Roles unknown in *Jack Cade*; Role unknown in *Gisippus*; Role unknown in *Romeo and Juliet*; Role unknown in *Evadne*; Role unknown in *Brutus*
12/22/52; Role unknown in *Othello*
12/24/52; Role unknown in *Gisippus*
12/26/52; Iago, Third Act only, *Othello*
12/26/52; Macduff, Third Act Only, *Macbeth*
Booth began playing Iago in an evening of scenes that included the third act of *Othello* with the Waller company in Nevada City on Dec. 26, 1852, and did his first full performance in San Francisco on Aug. 2, 1853. He performed it approximately three times a year until the 1857-1858 season, when it became an increasingly important part of his repertoire.
12/31/52; Icilius in *Virginius or The Roman Father*
1/1/53; Complimentary Benefit for Waller Troupe; Icilius, *Virginius or The Roman Father*
2/2/53; San Francisco Theatre; Fred Jerome, *The American Fireman*
2/3–4/53; Fred Jerome 2x, *The American Fireman*
2/5/53; Henry Meadows, *Rosina Meadows*
2/6/53; Fred Jerome, *The American Fireman*
2/10/53; Phillippe, *The Child of the Regiment* or *The Trumpeter's Daughter*
2/12/53; Title role, *Charles II*
2/14/53; Cassio, *Othello*
2/18/53; Henry Hamilton, *Maidens Beware!*
2/19/53; Lord Sparkles, *Love in Livery*
2/21/53; Frank Heartall, *The Soldier's Daughter*
2/22/53; Harry Stanly, *Paul Pry*
2/23/53; Charles Franklin, *Sweethearts and Wives*; Lord Sparkles, *Love in Livery*
2/25/53; Sir Charles Rivers, *The Trumpeter's Wedding*
2/27/53; Charles Rivers, *The Trumpeter's Wedding*
2/28/53; Role unknown, *The Miller's Maid*
3/2/53; Dick Dowlas, *The Heir at Law*
3/4/53; Frank Heartall, *The Soldier's Daughter*
3/7, 9/53; Dick Dowlas 2x, *The Heir at Law*
3/11/53; Young Marlowe, *She Stoops to Conquer*
3/14/53; Young Marlowe, *She Stoops to Conquer*
3/16, 18/53; Henry Stanly 2x
3/21–24/53; Role unknown, *The Invisible Prince* 4x; Mr. Bromley, *A Lesson to Merchants* a/k/a *Simpson & Co.*
3/25/53; Mr. Bromley, *A Lesson to Merchants* a/k/a *Simpson & Co.*
3/26/53; Sir Charles Rivers, *The Trumpeter's Wedding*; Role unknown, *The Invisible Prince*

3/27/53; Role unknown, *The Invisible Prince*
3/28–29/53; St. Val 2x, *A Lesson for Ladies*; Role unknown, *The Invisible Prince* 2x
3/30/3; St. Val, *A Lesson for Ladies*
3/31/53; Mr. Bromley, *A Lesson to Merchants* a/k/a *Simpson & Co.*; Role unknown, *The Fair One with the Golden Locks*
4/1/53; Charles Unit, *My Sister Kate*
4/2/53; Young Marlowe, *She Stoops to Conquer*
4/3/53; Dick Dowlas, *The Heir at Law*; Role unknown, *The Fair One with the Golden Locks*
4/4/53; Dick Dowlas, *The Heir at Law*
4/5/53; Sir Charles Rivers, *The Trumpeter's Wedding*
4/6/53; Col. Mannering, *Guy Mannering*; St. Val, *A Lesson for Ladies*
4/7/53; St. Val, *A Lesson for Ladies*
4/8–9/53; Walker 2x, *Leap Year*; Mr. Bromley 2x, *A Lesson to Merchants* a/k/a *Simpson & Co.*
4/10/53; Walker, *Leap Year*
4/11–12/53; George 2x, *The Green Bushes*
4/13–14/53; Furlbond 2x, *The Yellow Dwarf*; Walker 2x, *Leap Year*
4/15–17/53; Furlbond 3x, *The Yellow Dwarf*; Sir William Wisby 3x, *The Roebuck*
4/18/53; St. Val, *A Lesson for Ladies*; Roland, *All for Love or The Lost Pleiad*
4/19/53; George, *The Green Bushes*
4/20/53; Furlbond, *The Yellow Dwarf*; Sir William Wisby, *The Roebuck*
4/21/53; *Richard III*
4/22/53; Furlbond, *The Yellow Dwarf*; Walker, *Leap Year*
4/23/53; Capt. Absolute, *The Rivals*
4/24//53; George, *The Green Bushes*
4/25/53; Booth's benefit, *Hamlet*, first known performance
4/26–27/53; Captain Absolute 2x, *The Rivals*
4/28–29/53; Dombey 2x, *Dombey and Son*
4/30/53; Dombey, *Dombey and Son*; Sir William Wisby, *The Roebuck*
5/1/53; Captain Absolute, *The Rivals*
5/2/53; *Richard III*
5/3/53; Henry Hamilton, *Maidens Beware!*
5/4/53; Dick Dowlas, *The Heir at Law*
5/5–6/53; Lydon 2x, *The Last Days of Pompeii*; Mr. Bromly, *A Lesson to Merchants* a/k/a *Simpson & Co.*, 2x
5/7–8/53; Lydon 2x, *The Last Days of Pompeii*
5/9/53; Paul Lafont, *Love's Sacrifice*
Of Booth's performance in Lovell's melodrama *Love's Sacrifice*, the Sacramento critic wrote: "Mr. Booth, as the deceitful, artful and subtle Lafont, acquitted himself with great satisfaction to the audience. With a true conception of the part, with attractive person, and clear and sonorous voice, he depicted the character to the life. Mr. Booth ... possesses all of the elements of a distinguished actor, and with due study, united to greater experience, will doubtless hereafter rank among the foremost of his profession."

5/10/53; Claude Melnotte, *The Lady of Lyons*, first known performance
5/11/53; Francis, *The Stranger*
5/12/53; Paul Lafont, *Love's Sacrifice*
5/13/53; Francis, *The Stranger*
5/14/53; Charles Surface, *The School for Scandal*
5/15/53; Walker, *Leap Year*
5/16/53; Charles Surface, *The School for Scandal*
5/17/53; Claude Melnotte, *The Lady of Lyons*
5/20/53; Benedick, *Much Ado About Nothing*, first known performance
5/21/53; Benedick, *Much Ado About Nothing*; Petruchio, *Katherine and Petruchio*, first known performance
5/22/53; Charles Surface, *The School for Scandal*
5/23/53; Benedick, *Much Ado About Nothing*; Petruchio, *Katherine and Petruchio*
5/25/53; Dazzle, *London Assurance*; Petruchio, *Katherine and Petruchio*
5/29/53; Claude Melnotte, *The Lady of Lyons*
6/11/53; Duke Aranza, *The Honeymoon*
6/12/53; Captain Absolute, *The Rivals*
6/13/53; George, *The Green Bushes*
6/14/53; *Hamlet*
6/15/53; Walker, *Leap Year*
6/16/53; Sir Valentine May, *St. Cupid; or Dorothy's Fortune*
6/17/53; Sir Valentine May, *St. Cupid; or Dorothy's Fortune*
6/19/53; Young Marlowe, *She Stoops to Conquer*
6/20/53; Mr. Bromley, *A Lesson to Merchants* a/k/a *Simpson & Co.*
6/21/53; Sir Alfred Highflyer, *A Roland for an Oliver*
6/22/53; Captain Absolute, *The Rivals*
6/23/53; Harry Stanly, *Paul Pry*
6/24/53; Richmond/Tressel, *Richard III*
6/25/53; Dick Dowlas, *The Heir at Law*
6/26/53; Mr. Bromley, *A Lesson to Merchants* a/k/a *Simpson & Co.*
6/27/53; Romeo, *Romeo and Juliet*, first known performance
6/28/53; Frank Heartall, *The Soldier's Daughter*
6/29/53; Sir Alfred Highflyer, *A Roland for an Oliver*
7/1–2/53; St. Cyr 2x, *Lucille*
7/4/53; Lord Sparkles, *Love in Livery*
7/6/53; Romeo
7/7, 8, 10/53; Charles Oakley 3x, *The Jealous Wife*
7/11/53; Duke Aranza, *The Honeymoon*
7/13/53; Harry Stanly, *Paul Pry*; Petruchio, *Katherine and Petruchio*
7/14/53; Charles Oakley, *The Jealous Wife*
7/15/53; Claude Melnotte, *The Lady of Lyons*
7/17/53; St. Cyr, *Lucille*; Petruchio, *Katherine and Petruchio*
7/18/53; Jabber, *Breach of Promise*; Michael Magnus *The Angel of Attic*

7/19/53; Michael Magnus
7/20/53; Jabber, *Breach of Promise*
7/22/53; Henry Hamilton, *Maidens Beware!*
7/23/53; Jabber, *Breach of Promise*
7/24/53; Michael Magnus
7/25/53; Don Manuel, *Where There's a Will There's a Way* a/k/a *The Queen's Husband*; Jabber, *Breach of Promise*
7/26/53; Don Manuel, *Where There's a Will There's a Way* a/k/a *The Queen's Husband*
7/27/53; Jabber, *Breach of Promise*
7/28/53; Don Manuel, *Where There's a Will There's a Way* a/k/a *The Queen's Husband*
7/29/53; Mr. Bromley, *A Lesson to Merchants* a/k/a *Simpson & Co.*
7/30/53; Captain Absolute, *The Rivals*; Jabber, *Breach of Promise*
7/31/53; Don Manuel, *Where There's a Will There's a Way* a/k/a *The Queen's Husband*
8/1/53; Petruchio, *Katherine and Petruchio*
8/2/53; Iago, first known full performance, *Othello*
8/5/53; Dazzle, *London Assurance*
8/8/53; Frank Heartall, *The Soldier's Daughter*
8/10/53; Givemesum, play title unknown; Don Manuel, *Where There's a Will There's a Way* a/k/a *The Queen's Husband*
8/11/53; Givemesum, play title unknown; Young Marlowe, *She Stoops to Conquer*
8/12–13/53; Givemesum 2x, play title unknown; Col. Terrier 2x, *The Barrack Room*
8/14/53; Col. Terrier, *The Barrack Room*
8/15–16/53; Benedick 2x, *Much Ado About Nothing*; Givemesum 2x, play title unknown
8/17, 19/53; Gratiano 2x, *The Merchant of Venice*
8/20/53; Laertes, *Hamlet*
8/21/53; Benedick, *Much Ado About Nothing*
8/22–31/53; Dandy Cox 9x; Sir William Wellesey, *The Roebuck*
9/1/53; Junius Brutus Booth Jr.'s benefit; Sir William Wellesey; Dandy Cox
9/2–5/53; Dandy Cox 4x
9/6–7/53; Sir Giles Overreach, first known performance, *A New Way to Pay Old Debts*; Dandy Cox
9/8/53; Booth's benefit, Shylock, *Merchant of Venice*, first known performance; Petruchio, *Katherine and Petruchio*
9/9/53; Charles Oakley, *The Jealous Wife*
9/10/53; Harriet Mace Booth's benefit, Walker, *Leap Year*
9/12/53; Don Caesar de Bazan, *Don Caesar de Bazan*, first known performance
9/13/53; Citizen Sangfroid, *Delicate Ground*

1853–1854

9/19/53; San Francisco Theatre; Charles Surface, *The School for Scandal*
9/20/53; Don Manuel, *Where There's a Will There's a Way* a/k/a *The Queen's Husband*; Petruchio, *Katherine and Petruchio*
9/21/53; Duke de Chartres, *The Follies of a Night*
9/22/53; Duke de Chartres, *The Follies of a Night*
9/23/53; Lord Townley, *A Provoked Husband*
9/24/53; Lord Townley, *A Provoked Husband*; Petruchio, *Katherine and Petruchio*
9/25/53; Don Caesar de Bazan
9/26/53; Charles Surface, *The School for Scandal*
9/30–10/1/53; Don Caesar de Bazan 2x
10/3/53; Doricourt, *The Belle's Stratagem*
10/4/53; Laertes, *Hamlet*; Petruchio, *Katherine and Petruchio*
10/5/53; Duke de Chartres, *The Follies of a Night*; Charles Surface, *The School for Scandal*
10/6/53; Doricourt, *The Belle's Stratagem*
10/7/53; Don Manuel, *Where There's a Will There's a Way* a/k/a *The Queen's Husband*
10/8/53; Doricourt, *The Belle's Stratagem*
10/11/53; Douglas Trafford, *The People's Advocate*
10/12/53; Douglas Trafford, *The People's Advocate*; Duke de Chartres, *The Follies of a Night*
10/13/53; Douglas Trafford, *The People's Advocate*
10/14/53; Don Manuel, *Where There's a Will There's a Way* a/k/a *The Queen's Husband*
10/15/53; Don Philip, *Gil and Giraldi*; Petruchio, *Katherine and Petruchio*
10/16/53; Don Philip, *Gil and Giraldi*
10/17/53; Douglas Trafford, *The People's Advocate*; Don Philip, *Gil and Giraldi*
10/18/53; Cressford, *Ellen Wareham*; Don Philip, *Gil and Giraldi*
10/19/53; Cressford, *Ellen Wareham*; Duke de Chartres, *The Follies of a Night*
10/20/53; Cressford, *Ellen Wareham*; Don Philip, *Gil and Giraldi*
10/21/53; Cressford, *Ellen Wareham*; Don Manuel, *Where There's a Will There's a Way* a/k/a *The Queen's Husband*
10/22/53; Cressford, *Ellen Wareham*; Doricourt, *The Belle's Stratagem*
10/23/53; Don Philip, *Gil and Giraldi*
10/24/53; Sacramento Theatre; Benedick, *Much Ado About Nothing*
10/25/53; Paul Lafont, *Love's Sacrifice*
10/26/53; Cressford, *Ellen Wareham*; Petruchio, *Katherine and Petruchio*
10/27/53; Doricourt, *The Belle's Stratagem*; Duke de Chartres, *The Follies of a Night*
10/28/53; Petruchio, *Katherine and Petruchio*
10/29/53; Charles Surface, *The School for Scandal*
10/29/53; Cressford, *Ellen Wareham*
11/3–6/53; San Francisco Theatre; Don Caesar de Bazan 4x
11/7/53; Alfonso, *Lucretia Borgia*
11/14, 16, 19, 22, 27/53; Mr. Jones Brown Smith 5x, *Little Toddlekins*
12/5/53; Ernest Maltravers, *Alice, the Forsaken*

12/6/53; Ernest Maltravers, *Alice, the Forsaken*; Title role, *Charles II*
12/9/53; Charles, *My Sister Kate*
12/10/53; Silver Jack, *The Rent Day*
12/12/53; Maladine, *Moll Pitcher*; Petruchio, *Katherine and Petruchio*
12/13/53; Iago, *Othello*; Maladine, *Moll Pitcher*
12/14/53; Iago third act, *Othello*
12/16/53; Richard III
12/17/53; Junius Brutus Booth Jr.'s benefit; Pythias, *Damon and Pythias*
12/18/53; Charles
12/19/53; Booth's benefit, Title Role, *Bertram*; Don Caesar de Bazan
Booth's benefit at the San Francisco Theatre on Dec. 19, 1853, was not financially successful possibly because he performed Bertram, which was not as well known as some of his other roles or possibly because it was scheduled on a Monday.
12/20/53; Delaval, *Matrimony*; Petruchio, *Katherine and Petruchio*
12/21/53; Catherine N. Sinclair's benefit; Delaval, *Matrimony*
12/24/53; New San Francisco Theatre; Mr. Jones Brown Smith, *Little Toddlekins*
12/25/53; Richard III
12/28/53; Metropolitan Theatre, San Francisco; Col Mannering, *Guy Mannering*
12/30/53; Laertes, *Hamlet*
12/31/53; Iago, *Othello*
1/1/54; Pythias, *Damon and Pythias*; Delaval, *Matrimony*
1/5/54; Francis, *The Stranger*
1/6/54; DeMauprat, *Richelieu*
1/7/54; Macduff, *Macbeth*
1/11/54; Francis, *The Robbers*
1/12/54; Stuckley, *The Gamester*
1/13/54; Col. Mannering, *Guy Mannering*
1/14–15/54; Title role, *Pizzaro* 2x
1/17/54; Richard III
1/19/54; Mr. Jones Brown Smith, *Little Toddlekins*
1/24/54; Charles II
1/29/54; Mr. Jones Brown Smith, *Little Toddlekins*
2/13/54; Romeo
2/15/54; St. Pierre, *The Wife*
2/16/54; Count de Saxe, *Adrienne the Actress*
2/17/54; Sir Thomas Clifford, *The Hunchback*
2/18/54; Title role, *Fazio*
2/20/54; Macduff, *Macbeth*, originally announced for Paul Lafont [*Love's Sacrifice*] cancelled due to illness of Matilda Heron
3/10/54; Mr. Jones Brown Smith, *Little Toddlekins*
3/14/54; Ruy Gomez, *Faint Heart Never Won Fair Lady*
4/6/54; Wildrake, *The Love Chase*
4/7/54; Claude Melnotte, *The Lady of Lyons*
4/8/54; Duke Aranza, *The Honeymoon*; Howard Leslie, *Two Can Play at That Game*
On Apr. 15 1854, Modus, the San Francisco critic for *The Spirit of the Times*, wrote: "Young Edward [*sic*] Booth, the light comedian possesses extraordinary talent for the profession, and he bids fair with exertion, to rival his father in his palmiest days."
4/23/54; Sunday performance; Richard III
4/25/54; Macbeth first known performance
5/22/54; Don Manuel, *Where There's a Will There's a Way* a/k/a *The Queen's Husband*
5/24/54; Petruchio, *Katherine and Petruchio*
5/26/54; Lieut. Worthington, *The Poor Gentleman*
5/29/54; Fazio, *Fazio*
5/31/54; Macbeth
6/1/54; Huon, *Love, or the Countess and the Serf*
6/2/54; Count de Saxe, *Adrienne the Actress*; Captain Murphy Maguire, *A Serious Family*
6/3/54; Claude Melnotte, *The Lady of Lyons*
6/6/54; Booth's benefit, Hamlet
6/7/54; Catherine Sinclair's benefit; Sir Thomas Clifford, *The Hunchback*
6/9/54; Lafont, *Love's Sacrifice*
6/19/54; Duke de Chartres, *The Follies of a Night*
6/21/54; Frank Heartall, *The Soldier's Daughter*
6/24/54; Don Manuel, *Where There's a Will There's a Way* a/k/a *The Queen's Husband*
6/28–7/1/54; Gilmore 4x, *Mother's Trust, or California in 1849*
7/2/54; American Theatre, San Francisco Complimentary Benefit for Vinson and McClosky; Richard III Fifth Act
7/3–4/54; Gilmore 2x, *Mother's Trust, or California in 1849*
7/11–18/54; Luis 6x, *De Soto: Or The Hero of the Mississippi*
On July 23, 1854, Edwin and D. C. Anderson were making "active preparations" to go to Australia. On July 29, it was reported that the ship would sail "tomorrow." With Anderson and Booth were going "Mr. Milne, a very meritorious actor, Mr. Rowe, the well known Circus proprietor and Mr. Charles Devere the most accomplished rider that has appear in the 'ring' in California. Capt. Barnes, of the M. A. Jones was to be accompanied by his wife, an actress named Madame Dupres and two Australian actors Mr. and Mrs. Evans."
8/4/54; Iago, *Othello*
10/23/54; Royal Victoria Theatre, Sydney; Claude Melnotte, *The Lady of Lyons*
In Sydney Booth was billed as the son of the late "James Booth." *The Empire* critic wrote: "Mr. Booth is a young actor of great promise, His 'Claude Melnotte' was really a clever performance; it has rarely, in fact, been excelled in the colony. The love scenes were rendered with much pathos and tenderness, and in the farewell of Melnotte to Pauline and his mother on his proceeding to join the armies of the Republic, Mr. Booth was particularly effective, delineating faithfully the fiery zeal and independence of the proud and patriotic French-

man.... On Wednesday evening 'The Stranger' was produced, with marked success, the pourtrayal [sic] of the misanthrope's pride, agony and tenacity of honour [sic], stamping Mr. Booth as an actor of the highest order.... In the character of 'Hamlet' last evening, Mr. Booth fully sustained his reputation as a good tragedian, the various speeches and perorations being rendered by him in a most effective manner — particularly the magnificent soliloquy on Death, commencing, 'To be or not to be.'"

10/24/54; Shylock, *Merchant of Venice*
10/25/54; The Stranger, *The Stranger*, first known performance
10/26/54; Claude Melnotte, *The Lady of Lyons*
10/27/54; Hamlet
10/28/54; Benedick, *Much Ado About Nothing*
10/29/54; Hamlet; Howard Leslie, *Two Can Play at That Game*; Claude Melnotte, *The Lady of Lyons*
10/31/54; Philip Augustus, *Philip of France*
11/1/54; Benedick, *Much Ado About Nothing*
11/2/54; The Count Horace de Beauval, *Pauline*; Ruy Gomez, *Faint Heart Never Won Fair Lady*
11/3/54; Richard III
11/4/54; Connor, *The Rash Knight of Arva*; The Count Horace de Beauval, *Pauline*
11/20–21/54; The Queen's Theatre, Melbourne, Australia; Benedick 2x, *Much Ado About Nothing*
11/22/54; Claude Melnotte, *The Lady of Lyons*
11/23/54; Richard III
11/24/54; Role unknown, *Plot and Passion*; Role unknown, *Grist to the Mill*
3/3/55; Royal Hawaiian Theatre, Honolulu; Dick Dashall, *My Aunt*; Diggory, *All the World's a Stage*
3/8/55; Role unknown, *The Golden Farmer*; Role unknown, *The Review*
3/10/55; Sir Edward Mortimer, *The Iron Chest*, first known performance; Master Dobbs, *The Omnibus*
3/22/55; Booth's Farewell benefit; Richard III
3/24/55; Richard III; Claude Melnotte, *The Lady of Lyons*

Booth's company opened in Honolulu on Feb. 24 and appears to have performed approximately three times a week. They played a performance on Feb. 26 and on Mar. 3, 1855. Tickets were one dollar for a box and fifty cents in the pit. By Mar. 10, 1855, they were performing *The Iron Chest* and a comic afterpiece called *The Omnibus*. Booth performed in both the main pieces and the one-act farces that followed. In 1885 Booth told his daughter Edwina: "The story of my acting Hamlet & Toodles is not true; the latter I never played, the former I did not act in Honolulu.... But — I played Richard & Tommy Dobbs [in *The Omnibus*]."

4/30/55; Metropolitan Theatre, San Francisco; Richard III scheduled but did not take place.

5/2–3/55; Benedick 2x, *Much Ado About Nothing*
5/4/55; Richard III
5/27/55; Ruy Gomez, *Faint Heart Never Won Fair Lady*
5/28–30/55; Armand Duval, *Camille* 2x
5/31/55; Huon, *Love, or the Countess and the Serf*
5/31/55; Sir Thomas Clifford, *The Hunchback*
6/2, 4/55; Silius 2x, *Valeria*
6/5/55; Julian St. Pierre, *The Wife*
6/6/55; Armand Duval, *Camille*
6/7/55; Armand Duval, *Camille*. Performance did not take place although scheduled.
6/9/55; Charles Surface, *The School for Scandal*
6/15/55; Armand Duval, *Camille*; Doricourt, *The Belle's Stratagem*
7/10/55; Benefit for Mrs. Woodward; Role unknown, *Morning Call*
7/30/55; American Theatre, San Francisco; Corinthian Tom, *Tom and Jerry, or Life in London*

1855–1856

8/4/55; Sacramento Theater; Jack Spriggs, *Look Before You Leap*
8/6, 8/55; Jack Spriggs 2x, *Look Before You Leap*
8/9/55; Citizen Sangfroid, *Delicate Ground*
8/11/55; Richard III
8/13/55; Macbeth
8/14/55; Citizen Sangfroid, *Delicate Ground*
8/18/55; Hamlet
8/20–23/55; Demetrius 4x, *A Midsummer Night's Dream*
8/24/55; Malvolio, *Twelfth Night*
8/27/55; Demetrius, *A Midsummer Night's Dream*
8/28/55; Antipholis of Syracuse, *A Comedy of Errors*
8/29/55; Antipholis of Syracuse
8/30/55; Elizabeth Thoman's benefit; Lionel Lyn, *Married Life*
8/31/55; Mr. Bucket, *Bleak House*
9/1/55; Benefit of Mrs. Judah; Jack Spriggs, *Look Before You Leap*
9/6, 8/55; Master Wildrake, *The Love Chase*
9/10/55; Mr. Oakley, *The Jealous Wife*
9/11/55; Antony Latour, *Love's Fetters*
9/13/55; Benefit of Adelaide Gougenheim; Duke of Richmond, *Court and Stage*
9/14/55; Duke of Richmond, *Court and Stage*
9/15/55; Duke of Richmond, *Court and Stage*; Captain Charles, *Who Speaks First*
9/17/55; Duke Aranza, *The Honeymoon*
9/18/55; Mr. Oakley, *The Jealous Wife*; Sir Edward Ardent, *A Morning Call*
9/19/55; Antony Latour, *Love's Fetters*; Captain Charles, *Who Speaks First*
9/20/55; Benefit of Joey Gougenheim; Sidney Maynard, *The Housekeeper*; Captain Murphy Maguire, *A Serious Family*
9/21/55; Sir Edward Ardent, *A Morning Call*; Sidney Maynard, *The Housekeeper*

9/22/55; Master Wildrake, *The Love Chase*; Sidney Maynard, *The Housekeeper*

9/24–27/55; Marysville Theatre; Unknown roles Booth and the Gougenheim sisters opened in Marysville on Sept. 24, 1855, and the local critic said that Booth "is yet very young; but he bids fair to inherit and wear with honor the mantle of his almost matchless father." Tickets in Marysville were $1 and $2.

9/29, 10/1/55; Duke of Richmond 2x, *Court and Stage*

10/2/55; Wildrake, *The Love Chase*; Robert Shelly, *Momentous Question*

10/8/55; American Theatre, San Francisco; Wildrake, *The Love Chase*

10/9/55; Duke Aranza, *The Honeymoon*

10/10/55; Mr. Oakley, *The Jealous Wife*

10/11/55; Duke of Richmond, *Court and Stage*

10/12/55; Duke of Richmond, *Court and Stage*; Captain Charles, *Who Speaks First*

10/13/55; Duke of Richmond, *Court and Stage*

10/14/55; Antony Latour, *Love's Fetters*

10/15/55; Master Wildrake, *The Love Chase*

10/16/55; Mr. Oakley, *The Jealous Wife*; Captain Charles, *Who Speaks First*

10/17/55; Sidney Maynard, *The Housekeeper*; Anthony Latour, *Love's Fetters*

10/18–20/55; Murtogh 3x, *The Green Bushes* Frank Mayo, then a sixteen-year-old boy, remembered seeing Booth play Murtogh in *The Green Bushes*, "running about on the stage, dragging his coat after him — the Irish defiance — swinging his shillelalah over his head and challenging for somebody to tread on his coat."

10/21/55; Duke of Richmond, *Court and Stage*

10/22/55; Sir Edward Mortimer, *The Iron Chest*

10/23/55; Hamlet

10/26/55; Iago, *Othello*

10/28/55; Charles II; Richard III

11/6/55; Edwin Forrest Theater, Sacramento, California; Benedick, *Much Ado About Nothing*

11/7/55; Charles Surface, *The School for Scandal*

11/8/55; Young Marlowe, *She Stoops to Conquer*

11/27/55; Sacramento Theater, Sacramento, California; Capt. Murphy Maguire, *A Serious Family*

11/28/55; Claude Melnotte, *The Lady of Lyons*

11/29/55; Petruchio, *Katherine and Petruchio*

11/30/55; Doricourt, *The Belle's Stratagem*

12/1/55; Richard III

12/3/55; John Mildmay, *Still Waters Run Deep*; Petruchio, *Katherine and Petruchio*

12/4/55; Duke de Chartres, *The Follies of a Night*

12/5/55; John Mildmay, *Still Waters Run Deep*; Doricourt, *The Belle's Stratagem*

12/6/55; Claude Melnotte, *The Lady of Lyons*

12/7/55; The Stranger

12/8/55; Ruy Gomez, *Faint Heart Never Won Fair Lady*; Capt. Murphy Maguire, *A Serious Family*

12/10–25/55; Raphael DuChalet/Phidias 14x, *The Marble Heart*

12/26–27/55; Father Radcliffe 2x, *Two Loves and a Life*

12/28–29/55; Raphael/Phidias 2x, *The Marble Heart*

12/31/55–1/1/56; Fabien del Franchi 2x, *The Corsican Brothers*

1/3/56; Claude Melnotte, *The Lady of Lyons*; Petruchio, *Katherine and Petruchio*

1/4/56; Catherine Sinclair's benefit; Raphael DuChalet, *The Marble Heart*

1/5/56; Booth's benefit, Richard III

1/7/56; Raphael DuChalet, *The Marble Heart*

1/11/56; Complimentary Benefit for Booth; Raphael DuChalet, *The Marble Heart*

1/12/56; Marysville Theatre, Marysville, California; Raphael DuChalet, *The Marble Heart*

1/14–19/56; Metropolitan Theatre, San Francisco; Raphael DuChalet 7x, *The Marble Heart*

1/24–29/56; Marysville Theatre; Raphael DuChalet 4x, *The Marble Heart*

1/30/56; Booth's benefit, Claude Melnotte, *The Lady of Lyons*

1/31/56; Petruchio, *Katherine and Petruchio*

2/1–3/56; Theatre, Oroville, California; Raphael DuChalet 3x, *The Marble Heart*

2/6–9/56; Theatre, Nevada, California; Raphael DuChalet 4x, *The Marble Heart*

2/19–20/56; Edwin Forrest Theatre, Sacramento; Phidias/Raphael 2x, *The Marble Heart*

2/21/56; Claude Melnotte, *The Lady of Lyons*

2/22/56; Bertrand in *Madelaine, or the Foundling of Paris*

2/23/56; Joint benefit of Booth and Sedley; Bertrand, *Madelaine, or the Foundling of Paris*; Petruchio, *Katherine and Petruchio*

3/1/56; Complimentary Testimonial to Mrs. Catherine Sinclair; Duke de Chartres, *The Follies of a Night*

3/8/56; Sir Thomas Clifford, *The Hunchback*

3/11/56; Ludovico, *Evadne; or the Statue*

3/12/56; Armand, *Armand or, The Peer and the Peasant*

3/13/56; Ruy Gomez, *Faint Heart Never Won Fair Lady*

3/14–15/56; Genarro 2x, *Lucrezia Borgia, or, The Poisoner*

4/8–9/56; Citizen Sangfroid 2x, *Delicate Ground*

4/11/56; Charles II

4/12/56; Sir William, *Rough Diamond*

4/14/56; Ghost, *Hamlet*

4/15/56; Ghost, *Hamlet*

4/16/56; Sanguinbeck, *Cherry and Fair Star, or, The Children of Cyprus*

4/17/56; Sanguinbeck, *Cherry and Fair Star, or, The Children of Cyprus*

4/19/56; Booth's Complimentary benefit; Sir Edward Mortimer, *The Iron Chest*; Hamlet 3rd act; Mr. Jones Robinson Brown Smith, *Little Toddlekins*

4/21/56; Claude Melnotte, *The Lady of Lyons*; Mr. Jones Robinson Brown Smith, *Little Toddlekins*
4/22/56; Sir Edward Mortimer, *The Iron Chest*; Hamlet 3rd act, *The Iron Chest*; Mr. Jones Robinson Brown Smith, *Little Toddlekins*
4/26/56; Sacramento Theater; Richard III
4/28/56; Othello, first known performance, *Othello*
4/30/56; Bertram, *Bertram*
5/1/56; Lucius Junius Brutus, first known performance, *Brutus*
5/2/56; Othello
5/3/56; Booth's benefit, Sir Giles Overreach, *A New Way to Pay Old Debts*
5/5/56; Union Theatre San Francisco; Hamlet
5/6/56; Claude Melnotte, *The Lady of Lyons*
5/7/56; Brutus, *Julius Caesar*, first known performance
5/8/56; Othello
5/9/56; Richard III
5/10/56; Booth's benefit, Sir Edward Mortimer, *The Iron Chest*; Hamlet Act III
5/12/56; Macbeth
5/13/56; Junius Brutus Booth Jr.'s benefit; Mr. John Mildmay, *Still Waters Run Deep*; Ruy Gomez, *Faint Heart Never Won Fair Lady*
5/15/56; Shylock, *Merchant of Venice*
5/16/56; Lucius Junius Brutus, *Brutus*
5/17/56; Richard III
5/19/56; Pescara, *The Apostate*, first known performance
5/20–21/56; Sir Giles Overreach 2x, *A New Way to Pay Old Debts*
5/22/56; Romeo
5/23/56; Sir Edward Mortimer, *The Iron Chest*
5/24/56; Richelieu first known performance
5/27/56; Metropolitan Theatre, San Francisco. Benefit of C. Tibbitts, the prompter; Richelieu
5/29/56; Union Theatre, San Francisco; Harriet Booth's benefit; Mr. Jones Brown Smith, *Little Toddlekins*
5/31/56; Forrest Theater, Sacramento, California; Pescara [*The Apostate*] scheduled but Booth did not appear.
6/5/56; Pescara, *The Apostate*
6/6/56; Richelieu
6/7/56; Benjamin A. Baker's benefit; Julien St. Pierre, *The Wife*
6/9/56; Jackson Theatre, Jackson, California; Role unknown
6/12, 14, 16/56; Georgetown, California; Roles unknown
6/27/56; Placerville Theatre; Fazio, *Fazio*
7/4–5/56; Roles unknown
7/10–11/56; Auburn, California; Roles unknown
7/13/56; Frisbie's Theatre, Nevada, California; Sir Edward Mortimer, *The Iron Chest*
7/14/56; Petruchio, *Katherine and Petruchio*
7/15/56; Richelieu
7/16/56; Hamlet
7/17/56; Booth's benefit, Richelieu
7/19/56; Concert Hall, Nevada City, California; Scheduled but did not take place because of fire.
Unknown dates; Diamond Springs, California; Roles unknown
Unknown dates; National Theatre, Downieville, California; Roles unknown
8/9/56; Forrest Theater, Sacramento, California; Richard III
8/19/56; Hamlet
8/20/56; Lucius Junius Brutus, *Brutus*
8/21/56; Richard III
8/22/56; Macbeth
8/23/56; Grand Complimentary Farewell Testimonial; Richelieu
9/1/56; Grand Complimentary and Farewell Benefit; Iago, *Othello*
9/3/56; Metropolitan Theatre, San Francisco Benefit; King Lear, first known performance, *King Lear*

1856–1857

10/15/56; Front Street Theatre, Baltimore; Hamlet
10/16/56; Richelieu
10/17/56; Richard III
10/18/56; Sir Edward Mortimer, *The Iron Chest*
10/20/56; Richard III
10/21/56; Pescara, *The Apostate*; Petruchio, *Katherine and Petruchio*
10/22/56; Romeo
10/23/56; The Stranger
10/24/56; Pescara, *The Apostate*
10/25/56; Booth's benefit, Sir Giles Overreach, *A New Way to Pay Old Debts*; Mr. Jones Robinson Brownsmith, *Little Toddlekins*
11/17/56; Washington, D.C.; Richard III
11/18/56; Richelieu
11/19/56; Hamlet
11/20/56; Pescara, *The Apostate*
11/21/56; Booth's benefit, Shylock, *Merchant of Venice*; Petruchio, *Katherine and Petruchio*
11/22/56; Sir Edward Mortimer, *The Iron Chest*; Mr. Jones Brown Smith, billed as John Jobson Brownsworth, *Little Toddlekins*
11/24/56; Richmond Theatre; Richard III
Booth's Richmond review reads "Young Booth is of stature perhaps a little above his father's and he does not seem quite so stout. The features of his face ... resemble his father's as does his voice."
11/25/56; Romeo
This was the performance during which Booth first acted with Mary Devlin, who would become his first wife.
11/26/56; Sir Giles Overreach, *A New Way to Pay Old Debts*
11/27/56; Iago, *Othello*
11/28/56; Booth's benefit, Sir Edward Mortimer, *The Iron Chest*; Jay Robinson Brownsmith, *Little Toddlekins*

11/29/56; Lucius Junius Brutus, *Brutus*
12/1/56; Richelieu
12/2/56; Sir Edward Mortimer, *The Iron Chest*
12/3/56; Claude Melnotte, *The Lady of Lyons*
12/4/56; King Lear
12/5/56; Booth's benefit, Shylock, *Merchant of Venice*; Petruchio, *Katherine and Petruchio*

At Booth's final Richmond benefit, on Dec. 5, 1856, Mary Devlin played Katherine to his Petruchio; however, another actress played Portia to his Shylock, probably because Portia was a heavier dramatic role and not in Mary's "line of business."

12/6/56; Pescara, *The Apostate*
12/8/56; National Theatre, Washington D.C.; Sir Edward Mortimer, *The Iron Chest*
12/9/56; Iago, *Othello*
12/10/56; Sir Giles Overreach, *A New Way to Pay Old Debts*
12/11/56; Lucius Junius Brutus, *Brutus*
12/12/56; Complimentary Benefit; King Lear
12/13/56; Richard III

In Dec. 1856 Washington D.C.'s *National Intelligencer* told its readers that Booth's "enunciation is forcible, and not a word was lost from beginning to end of the piece, a pleasure often denied the audience with other performers. It is to be hoped that avoidance of overstraining so good a voice will be his care."

12/22/56; Pittsburgh Theatre; Lucius Junius Brutus, *Brutus*
12/23/56; Sir Giles Overreach, *A New Way to Pay Old Debts*
12/24/56; Richelieu
12/27/56; Sir Edward Mortimer, *The Iron Chest*
12/29/56; Pescara, *The Apostate*
12/30/56; Shylock, *Merchant of Venice*
1/3/57; Richard III
1/5/57; Athenaeum. Wheeling, West Virginia; Sir Edward Mortimer, *The Iron Chest*
1/6/57; Richelieu

On Jan. 9, 1857, the critic for the *Wheeling Daily Intelligencer* wrote of Booth's Richelieu: "His efforts to tremble were too palpable, and out of all keeping with his voice, which had a steady, stentorian ring.... Mr. Booth did not personate Richelieu in his weakness nor in his general bearing. His motions were entirely too rapid and energetic."

1/7/57; Pescara, *The Apostate*
1/8/57; Shylock, *Merchant of Venice*; Jones Robinson Brownsmith, *Little Toddlekins*
1/9/57; Booth's benefit, Richard III
1/10/57; Bertram, *Bertram or The Castle of Street Aldabrand*; Petruchio, *Katherine and Petruchio*

Benjamin Baker, Booth's first manager later remembered: "The theater in Wheeling was over a carriage maker's shop. It was a bare, bleak, whitewashed place, heated in winter by two stoves in the parquet [orchestra] and one in the gallery. That bitter night Ted played Richard. When he went on for the "Now is the winter of our discontent" speech, he looked over the house, and seeing nobody, came toward the prompt side and said to me, "Where's all the audience, Ben?" The few half-frozen people in front were huddled about the three stoves trying to keep warm.... The stage was so dirty there that I wouldn't let Ted wear the new fifty-dollar *Richelieu* robe that we had recently bought.... I made most of the costumes he wore on that tour myself. After the performance I would sit up for a couple of hours in the double-bedded room we always occupied and sew ... while Ted sat by smoking his pipe, waxing the thread and threading my needles. We had to do it, for ... neither of us could afford to buy wardrobe.... Ted had only one pair of shoes. I wore boots. He borrowed my boots to wear on the stage.... The widow of Old Booth gave Edwin her husband's wardrobe.... We managed to make that serve for everything. We used to sew the ermine cap of Richard onto Richelieu's robe and then rip it off again when the crookbacked monarch had to have it." Baker's reminiscences date from a point between 1879 and 1881. Baker contended: "Booth and I used to sleep in the same room, and it was his habit frequently to rehearse a whole play after a hard day's work. After playing Richard, for instance, he would go through Lear, I acting as prompter, until the night had far advanced. He has always been an indefatigable worker, but he slept after eating only a light supper and smoking a mild pipe-full. Booth always knows whether he has done well after the excitement of the play is over. And when is he is not equal to himself he display great chagrin. 'Kick me,' he said one day; 'I haven't done decently. I ought to be thrashed.'" Barton Hill echoed Baker's description: "Every afternoon it was our custom to sit in his room at the old Clarendon Hotel, on Main Street, smoking our clay-pipes, all three of us—Edwin, Ben Baker and myself—working like beavers if not like tailors, sewing 'concaves' on his shirt of mail to complete his armor for *Richard* or *Macbeth*." When Hill reminded Booth of the incident, he contended that Booth said: "And when the concaves were all sewed on and that armor was donned, I felt more real satisfaction than I ever got out of the 'sumptuous' trappings that I wore in later years. Ah me. But that was many years ago."

1/19/57; People's Theatre, St. Louis, Missouri; Role unknown
1/20/57; Hamlet
1/21/57; Iago, *Othello*
1/22/57; Sir Edward Mortimer, *The Iron Chest*
1/23/57; Booth's benefit; King Lear
1/24/57; Lucius Junius Brutus, *Brutus*
1/26/57; Bertram, *Bertram*
1/27/57; Richelieu
1/28/57; Sir Edward Mortimer, *The Iron Chest*; James R. Brownsmith, *Little Toddlekins*

1/29/57; Pescara, *The Apostate*
1/30/57; Booth's benefit, Sir Giles Overreach, *A New Way to Pay Old Debts*; Petruchio, *Katherine and Petruchio*
1/31/57; Richard III
2/2/57; Woods' Theater, Cincinnati, Ohio; Richard III
2/3/57; Hamlet
2/4/57; Richelieu
2/5/57; Sir Edward Mortimer, *The Iron Chest*; Petruchio, *Katherine and Petruchio*
2/6/57; Booth's benefit, King Lear
2/7/57; Richard III
2/9/57; Pescara, *The Apostate*
2/10/57; Lucius Junius Brutus, *Brutus*
2/11/57; Sir Giles Overreach, *A New Way to Pay Old Debts*
2/12/57; Richard III
2/13/57; Booth's benefit, Iago, *Othello*
2/14/57; Sir Giles Overreach, *A New Way to Pay Old Debts*
3/9/57; Mobile Theatre; Richard III
  At Booth's Mobile debut on March 9, 1857, "the excessive rain ... rendered the Theatre unapproachable" except through the "process of ... wading."
3/10/57; King Lear
3/13/57; Booth's benefit, Sir Edward Mortimer, *The Iron Chest*; Mr. Jones Robinson Brownsmith, *Little Toddlekins*
3/14/57; Richard III
3/16/57; St. Charles Theatre, New Orleans; Richard III
3/17/57; Hamlet
3/18/57; Richelieu
3/19/57; Sir Giles Overreach, *A New Way to Pay Old Debts*
3/20/57; Pescara, *The Apostate*
3/21/57; Booth's benefit, King Lear
3/22/57; Lucius Junius Brutus, *Brutus*
3/24/57; Claude Melnotte, *The Lady of Lyons*
  New Orleans' *Daily Picayune* noted that the large audience at the St. Charles Theatre in Mar. 1857, found the "same natural ability" they had observed in Junius Brutus Senior. On Mar. 24, 1857, thirty-five male citizens of New Orleans offered to sponsor a complimentary benefit for Booth. Two days later he accepted and published both letters in the local newspaper.
3/25/57; Richelieu
3/26/57; St. Pierre, *The Wife*
3/27/57; King Lear
3/28/57; Complimentary Benefit; Sir Giles Overreach, *A New Way to Pay Old Debts*
4/3/57; Mobile Theatre; Richelieu; Petruchio, *Katherine and Petruchio*
4/20/57; Boston Theatre; Sir Giles Overreach, *A New Way to Pay Old Debts*
  Booth opened in Boston on Apr. 20, 1857 as Sir Giles Overreach. Asia Booth Clarke described his opening as a "thin house," but the *Boston Advertiser* noted that the house was "well filled." The critic for the *Boston Evening Transcript* was lavish in his praise, faulting Booth only for "a slight drawling tendency." The box office took in $272.00 because of the weather.
4/21/57; Richelieu
  The Boston Theatre box office took in $185.75 due to bad weather
4/22/57; Richard III
  The Boston Theatre box office took in $713.75
4/23/57; Pescara, *The Apostate*
  The Boston Theatre box office took in $461.25
4/24/57; Booth's benefit, Bertram, *Bertram*; John Robinson Brownsmith, *Little Toddlekins*
  The Boston Theatre box office took in $981.75
4/25/57; Matinee—first known matinee performance; Bertram, *Bertram*
  The Boston Theatre box office took in $267.62
4/27/57; Hamlet
  The Boston Theatre box office took in $782.25
4/28/57; King Lear
  The Boston Theatre box office took in $426.25
4/29/57; Lucius Junius Brutus, *Brutus*
  The Boston Theatre box office took in $542.50. By Apr. 29, 1857, a group of Bostonians, including the Harvard Professors Benjamin Peirce Agassiz, and C. C. Felton, requested another performance of Hamlet.
4/30/57; Richard III
  The Boston Theatre box office took in $699.50
5/1/57; Booth's benefit, Sir Edward Mortimer, *The Iron Chest*; Petruchio, *Katherine and Petruchio*
  The Boston Theatre box office took in $1,241.75
5/2/57; Matinee, Petruchio, *Katherine and Petruchio*; Brownsmith, *Little Toddlekins*
  The Boston Theatre box office took in $280.25. At the closing performance in Boston, the audience demanded a speech. Booth stood there, "unassuming, timid and really embarrassed" and said: "*Ladies and Gentlemen*—I am a very poor speechmaker. Seldom do I undertake the task, but I feel it my duty this night to say that at least I appreciate your kindness. The tremendous greeting ... is sufficient to impress indelibly on my heart the grateful remembrance of Boston. I was told you were cold and critical, but I have found you warm and generous towards me. Perhaps, however, this is due to the love you bear the memory of my father, rather than to any merit of my own. [Enthusiastic and prolonged applause]. Let me assure you, I shall hail with delight my return to this city. Let me trespass a moment longer on your patience to return my thanks to Mr. [Thomas] Barry [the theatre's manager] and the ladies and gentlemen connected with the theatre, for the kind manner in which they have treated me. Once more, ladies and gentlemen, I thank you." The Boston correspondent for the *Spirit of the Times* wrote: "Young Booth greatly re-

sembles his distinguished parent in personal appearance; he has a good but somewhat slight figure, a handsome and expressive face, lit up by a marvelously brilliant and fiery eye, which he used with remarkable effect; his voice is strong, of good quality and compass, and with care in cultivating the proper intonations, is capable of becoming exceedingly musical.... There was all that nervous energy and impassioned manner which characterized the acting of his father in his palmiest days."

5/4/57; Burton's New Theatre, New York; Richard III

On Apr. 18, 1857, Burton and Booth signed a contract for twelve New York performances from May 4 until May 16. Booth, agreeing to a 50 percent share of the theatre profits after $350 per night had been deducted from the gross. In addition Booth received a clear third of the receipts of the profits on his first Friday benefit and a clear half of the profits on his second. According to legend, Booth intended to open with Sir Giles Overreach, but on the day of his debut, May 4, 1857, newspapers announced him in *Richard III*, and Booth supposedly had no choice but to appear as Richard. The story is only possibly true. He had used Sir Giles as his opening piece in Boston and given his triumph there, may well have wanted to use it on opening night in New York. On the other hand, he had opened with *Richard III* in Cincinnati, Mobile and New Orleans. *The New York Clipper* reviewer wrote: "EB's appearance as Richard III, at Burton's is said by good judges to have been a very creditable performance. Last Monday night was rather busy in the theatrical way, and we took the liberty of judging that we would see his Richard some other night. Hope no offense to Mr. Booth's intense and se-va-ge-rous [sic] admirers. From our omnipresent friends, we learn that Nedwin continues to improve rapidly. His fine person and early opportunities for observation are now beginning to harmonize into that dramatic power which will enable him to carry out his usually correct conceptions. In Shakespearean characters especially such an actor is much needed, and we are proud of Mr. Booth's accumulated success." *The New York Herald* found Booth hesitant in the opening acts of *Richard* but thought that the final acts "showed an accelerated force and a very even admirable execution, rising in point to great power and grandeur." *The New York Herald* review includes: "In the sinister aspects ... there was nothing beyond detail points which was not conceived in the most masterly style.... That in which he was perhaps at fault, was in the lack of a sufficiently free play of ... Richard['s] ... scoffing, sardonic humorous mockery. The passion and the malice were allowed too much scope.... In the hypocritical scenes, the wooing of Anne, and the interview with the Lord Mayor the artifice in them was rather transparent.... Mr. Booth's elocution and gesture suggest those of his father at every turn of a phrase. There could hardly be well conceived a more difficult ordeal for any actor, than the anticipations and associations of the audience.... Doubtless he strongly felt this himself, and the feeling was evident in the care and hesitation with which the earlier scenes of the play were acted. As he progressed his action naturally gained more freedom and boldness, the first act, and perhaps the second being more slow and less impressive in the artistic rendering than the others. The closing acts showed an accelerated force and a very even admirable execution, rising in point to great power and grandeur. His conception ... is not ... finished to that detail ... which he will doubtless attain.... his conceptions ... suggest ... the cartoon of a great master [rather] than his final work. This, however, is one of the most satisfactory and interesting aspects of his acting.... In person he is slight, handsome, nervous and active." The review from the *New-York Daily Times* reads in part: "...although an imperfect performance in some respects, it was superior to any we have seen on the stage of late years and sufficient to place him above the mediocrities ... of his profession. Mr. Booth has a fine intelligent bearing; a keen eye, susceptible of extreme dilation; a well-balanced elocution; and a walk not extremely theatrical.... The performance last night was more remarkable for well-sustained finish than for startling originality of conception.... He was cordially received and called out frequently." *The Tribune* reviewer, however, was divided in his estimation: "Mr. Booth is the most unequal actor we remember ever to have seen; and his fine careful acting in one scene is no guaranty that he will not walk feebly through the next and let it go by default. He omits many opportunities, for making technical points, and slurs over many sentences which, in other hands, have seldom failed to gain the audible approval of the house; but, on the other hand, when he takes up a favorite scene, he renders the passage with a vigorous truthfulness which startles his audience into wild enthusiasm, and brings down a perfect storm of applause." *The Albion* reviewer wrote: "The average Richard of the stage is either a rantipole ruffian, or a sheer lunatic.... Mr. Booth ... enjoys a real refinement of vision.... but he will not trust himself to refinement of execution. His tone is frequently too glaring.... Mr. Booth shows no quality more promising than his evident respect for the modesty of nature. If he will but cast out the very small theatrical demon which is in him, ... he will certainly make a very fine actor.... He has acquired a wonderful control over what may be called the mechanism of his person, and though his walk is sometimes a little awkward and constrained there is a pervading naturalness and ease to his carriage and bearing, from which he is not likely to lapse into any tricks." R. S. Chilton, a member of the diplomatic corps who admired Booth's performances, wrote, from Washington, D.C., to encourage him saying that "you have permitted your reception in New York which from bad weather or some other cause appears to have been ... less enthusiastic than you or your friends had a right to expect to rob you of that ... spirit which you were wont to have" and encouraging Booth "to keep 'due on' regardless of thin houses, newspaper critics & other annoyances."

5/5/57; Richelieu
5/6/57; Sir Giles Overreach, *A New Way to Pay Old Debts*
5/7/57; Shylock, *Merchant of Venice*
5/8/57; Booth's benefit, King Lear
5/9/57; Richard III
5/11/57; Romeo
5/12/57; Hamlet
5/13/57; Claude Melnotte, *The Lady of Lyons*
5/14/57; Iago, *Othello*
5/15/57; Booth's benefit, Sir Edward Mortimer, *The Iron Chest*

The review of Booth's performance as Sir Edward Mortimer in the *New-York Daily Times* of May 16, 1857 reads in part: "...although an imperfect performance in some respects, it was superior to any we have seen on the stage of late years, and sufficient to place him above the mediocrities ... of his profession. Mr. Booth has a fine intelligent bearing; a keen eye, susceptible of extreme dilation; a well-balanced elocution; and a walk not extremely theatrical.... The performance last night was more remarkable for well-sustained finish than for startling originality of conception.... He was cordially received and called out frequently."

5/16/57; Sir Giles Overreach, *A New Way to Pay Old Debts*
5/18/57; Julien St. Pierre, *The Wife*
5/19/57; The Stranger; Petruchio, *Katherine and Petruchio*
5/20/57; Pescara, *The Apostate*
5/21/57; Richelieu
5/22/57; Booth's benefit, Pescara, *The Apostate*; Brownsmith, *Little Toddlekins*
5/23/57; King Lear
5/26, 28/57; Lucius Junius Brutus, *Brutus*
5/30/57; Booth's benefit, Richard III

The critic William Winter added to the legend of Booth's modesty about his prospects at the time, contending that having made his reputation in the provinces, he hoped to become the leading actor in a New York stock company, like his friend Joseph Jefferson at Laura Keene's theatre. Booth supposedly told Winter: "The height of my expectation was to become a leading actor in a New York theatre, after my starring tour — which I supposed would last a season or two." In actuality there is no evidence that he ever pursued such a career move, although he certainly recommended it to others. Until 1860 he worked primarily as a touring star outside New York where critical success eluded him.

6/1/57; Walnut Street Theatre, Philadelphia; Sir Giles Overreach, *A New Way to Pay Old Debts*
6/2/57; Richelieu
6/3/57; Iago, *Othello*
6/4/57; Pescara, *The Apostate*
6/5/57; Booth's benefit, Sir Edward Mortimer, *The Iron Chest*; Petruchio, *Katherine and Petruchio*
6/6/57; Richard III
6/8/57; Hamlet
6/9/57; Sir Giles Overreach, *A New Way to Pay Old Debts*
6/10/57; Lucius Junius Brutus, *Brutus*
6/11/57; Richard III
6/12/57; Booth's benefit, King Lear
6/13/57; Lucius Junius Brutus, *Brutus*

1857–1858

8/31/57; Burton's New Theatre, Broadway, New York; Sir Giles Overreach, *A New Way to Pay Old Debts*

The company at Burton's in the fall of 1857 included Booth's future partner Lawrence Barrett. Unreserved admission to every part of the house was fifty cents, the cost of two railway rides from Manhattan to Flushing, Long Island or two boat rides from Manhattan to Port Monmouth, New Jersey or one bottle of Murray and Lanham's Florida water for removing "roughness of the skin or one bottle of J. R. Stafford's olive tar for weak lungs, coughs or colds"; reserved balcony chairs were seventy-five cents, the cost of half a dozen teaspoons; orchestra chairs were one dollar, the cost of a three pound box of tea, or four boxes of Durno's Catarrh snuff, a cure for coughs; proscenium boxes were six dollars, the cost of twenty-four piano lessons; family private boxes holding ten people were ten dollars, the cost of two tons of home-delivered coal and three dollars more than a maid who did the laundry and cooking made each week.

9/1/57; Lucius Junius Brutus, *Brutus*
9/2/57; Richelieu, originally advertised as Pescara, *The Apostate*
9/3/57; Pescara, *The Apostate*
9/4/57; Booth's benefit, Sir Edward Mortimer, *The Iron Chest*; Petruchio, *Katherine and Petruchio*
9/5/57; Richard III
9/14/57; Boston Theatre; Sir Giles Overreach, *A New Way to Pay Old Debts*

When Booth opened in Boston, the critic for the *Boston Courier* wrote: "His voice last night was a little rough, but that was owing to a severe bronchial complaint under which he has suffered for two or three days." The day he opened the *Boston Evening Transcript* reported that he had "recovered from his recent severe hoarseness."

9/15/57; Richelieu
9/16/57; Iago, *Othello*
9/17/57; Shylock, *Merchant of Venice*
9/18/57; Booth's benefit, Richard III
9/19/57; Matinee, Shylock, *Merchant of Venice*
9/21/57; Othello
9/22/57; Sir Edward Mortimer, *The Iron Chest*
9/23/57; Hamlet
9/24/57; Richard III
9/25/57; Booth's benefit, Lucius Junius Brutus, *Brutus*; Petruchio, *Katherine and Petruchio*
9/26/57; Matinee, Sir Edward Mortimer, *The Iron Chest*
10/5/57; Wood's Theater, Cincinnati, Ohio; Sir Giles Overreach [*A New Way to Pay Old Debts*] scheduled but Booth was detained elsewhere and did not appear
10/6/57; Richard III
10/7/57; Pescara, *The Apostate*
10/8/57; Sir Giles Overreach, *A New Way to Pay Old Debts*
10/9/57; Booth's benefit, Sir Edward Mortimer, *The Iron Chest*; Petruchio, *Katherine and Petruchio*
10/10/57; Richard III
10/12/57; Hamlet
10/13/57; King Lear
10/14/57; Richard III
10/15/57; Charles de Moor, *The Robbers*
10/16/57; Booth's benefit, Hamlet
10/17/57; Charles de Moor, *The Robbers*
10/19/57; Louis, Richard III
10/20/57; Pescara, *The Apostate*
10/21/57; Wellborn
10/22/57; Charles de Moor, *The Robbers*
10/23/57; Booth's benefit, Sir Edward Mortimer, *The Iron Chest*; Petruchio, *Katherine and Petruchio*
10/24/57; Charles de Moor, *The Robbers*
10/26/57; Lucius Junius Brutus, *Brutus*
10/27/57; Romeo
10/28/57; Shylock, *Merchant of Venice*
10/29/57; Charles de Moor, *The Robbers*
10/30/57; Booth's benefit, Richard III
10/31/57; Charles de Moor, *The Robbers*; Petruchio, *Katherine and Petruchio*
11/9/57; Plunkett's Metropolitan Theatre, Rochester, New York; Sir Giles Overreach, *A New Way to Pay Old Debts*
11/10/57; Richelieu
11/11/57; Iago, *Othello*
11/12/57; Pescara, *The Apostate*
11/13/57; Booth's benefit, Richard III
11/14/57; Charles de Moor, *The Robbers*; Petruchio, *Katherine and Petruchio*
Ben Baker remembered: "[In] Rochester ... [we] were hard up for funds. There was a large German population, and I conceived the idea of doing Schiller's *Robbers* [on Nov. 14, 1857]. Ted had no dress for the part of Franz, but I faked one up out of my frock coat, to the collar and skirts of which I sewed a lot of imitation fur."
11/16/57; Metropolitan Theatre, Buffalo, New York; Richard III
When Booth opened at Buffalo's Metropolitan Theatre in Nov. 1857, billed as "The Wonder of the Age." His Sir Giles Overreach was described as "one of the most brilliant specimens of acting we have ever witnessed." Booth's Richelieu did not draw well in Buffalo, and a storm resulted in low attendance at his benefit. The weather remained unfavorable during most of Booth's engagement. His benefit there, however, was packed.
11/17/57; Richelieu
11/18/57; Lucius Junius Brutus, *Brutus*
11/19/57; King Lear
11/20/57; Booth's benefit, Sir Edward Mortimer, *The Iron Chest*; Petruchio, *Katherine and Petruchio*
11/21/57; Charles de Moor, *The Robbers*
11/23/57; Hamlet
11/24/57; Richard III
11/25/57; Pescara, *The Apostate*
11/26/57; Sir Giles Overreach, *A New Way to Pay Old Debts*
11/27/57; Complimentary Benefit; Richelieu
11/28/57; Iago, *Othello*
12/21/57; Crisp's Gaiety Theatre, Memphis; Richard III
When Booth opened in Memphis in Dec. 1857, Miss [Adah Isaacs] Menken opened with him, although her name never appeared in the theatre's advertisements.
12/22/57; Richelieu
12/23/57; Sir Giles Overreach, *A New Way to Pay Old Debts*
12/24/57; Lucius Junius Brutus, *Brutus*
12/25/57; Charles de Moor, *The Robbers*
12/26/57; Booth's benefit, Sir Edward Mortimer, *The Iron Chest*; Petruchio, *Katherine and Petruchio*
12/28/57; Hamlet
12/29/57; Sir Giles Overreach, *A New Way to Pay Old Debts*
12/30/57; Iago, *Othello*
12/31/57; Hamlet
1/1/58; Pescara, *The Apostate*; Petruchio, *Katherine and Petruchio*
1/2/58; Booth's benefit, Richard III
1/10/58; Crisp's Gaiety Theatre, New Orleans; Sir Giles Overreach, *A New Way to Pay Old Debts*
1/11/58; Richelieu
1/12/58; Shylock, *Merchant of Venice*
On Jan. 15, the *Picayune* reported: "Until last evening we do not remember that we ever had occasion to witness the necessity of raising the curtain prematurely dropped, to enable the actors to present the catastrophe of the piece to the audience....

The audience were [sic] very naturally indignant, and amidst the most unmistakable expressions of that feeling, on their part, the curtain was again raised, and the last scene was partially repeated."
1/13/58; Iago, *Othello*
1/14/58; Lucius Junius Brutus, *Brutus*
1/15/58; Charles de Moor, *The Robbers*
1/16/58; Booth's benefit, Richard III
1/17/58; Charles de Moor, *The Robbers*; Petruchio, *Katherine and Petruchio*
1/18/58; Hamlet
1/19/58; King Lear
1/20/58; Benedick, *Much Ado About Nothing*
1/21/58; Richelieu
1/22/58; Pescara, *The Apostate*
1/23/58; Booth's benefit, Sir Edward Mortimer, *The Iron Chest*
1/24/58; Richard III
The Spirit of the Times, on Jan. 30, 1858, called Booth "a born genius," while warning that "it remains entirely with himself, if his life is spared a few years, whether he will or not be one of the greatest actors of the age."
2/1/58; Crisp's Gaiety, Nashville, Tennessee; Richard III scheduled but Booth did not appear
Mrs. Adah Isaacs Menken sometimes spelled Menkin was scheduled to play Queen Elizabeth to Booth's Richard III at Crisp's Gaiety in Nashville on Feb. 1, 1858.
2/10/58; Concert Hall/Theatre, Augusta, Georgia; Hamlet
2/11/58; Richelieu
2/12/58; Iago, *Othello*
2/13/58; Richard III
2/15/58; Sir Giles Overreach, *A New Way to Pay Old Debts*
2/16/58; Benefit of Mr. G. F. Marchant; Richelieu
2/17/58; Theatre, Charleston, South Carolina; Richelieu cancelled because of "the non-arrival of the Company, caused, according to the *Charleston Daily Courier*, by a detention of the cars on the road from Augusta.
2/18/58; Richelieu
2/19/58; Sir Giles Overreach, *A New Way to Pay Old Debts*; Petruchio, *Katherine and Petruchio*
2/20/58; Richard III
2/23/58; Richmond. Virginia; Richard III
2/27/58; Charles de Moor, *The Robbers*
3/2/58; King Lear
3/3/58; Booth's benefit, Richard III
3/8/58; Holliday Street Theatre, Baltimore; Richelieu
3/9/58; Sir Giles Overreach, *A New Way to Pay Old Debts*
3/10/58; Hamlet
3/11/58; Lucius Junius Brutus, *Brutus*
3/12/58; Booth's benefit, Richard III
3/13/58; Charles de Moor, *The Robbers*
3/15/58; King Lear
3/16/58; Romeo
3/17/58; Richelieu
3/18/58; Richard III
3/19/58; Complimentary benefit; Sir Edward Mortimer, *The Iron Chest*; Petruchio, *Katherine and Petruchio*
3/20/58; Matinee Benefit for Mount Vernon Association, Shylock, *Merchant of Venice*, Act IV; Richelieu, Act IV; Evening, Pescara, *The Apostate*
3/23/58; Boston Theatre; Richelieu
At the Boston Theatre in 1858, a private box was six dollars; seats in the parquette, balcony and first tier of boxes were fifty cents; in the family circle twenty-five cents and in the amphitheatre fifteen cents.
3/24/58; Hamlet
3/25/58; Iago, *Othello*
3/26/58; Booth's benefit, Richard III
3/27/58; Matinee, Sir Edward Mortimer, *The Iron Chest*
3/29/58; King Lear
3/30/58; Sir Giles Overreach, *A New Way to Pay Old Debts*
3/31/58; Othello
4/1/58; Pescara, *The Apostate*
4/2/58; Farewell Benefit, Charles de Moor, *The Robbers*; Petruchio, *Katherine and Petruchio*
4/3/58; Matinee, Charles de Moor, *The Robbers*
4/5/58; Burton's Theatre, New York; Pescara, *The Apostate*
4/6/58; Richelieu
4/7/58; Hamlet
4/8/58; Sir Giles Overreach, *A New Way to Pay Old Debts*
4/9/58; Booth's benefit, Richard III
4/10/58; Charles de Moor, *The Robbers*; Petruchio, *Katherine and Petruchio*
4/12/58; Wallack's Theatre, New York; Iago, *Othello*
When Booth appeared in New York on Apr. 12, 1858, the lobbies and staircases were "choked up with people.... The overture being over, ... the bell tinkled; our pulses quickened, for Iago, in the person our young favorite, Booth, was immediately to appear; up went the curtain; Roderigo entered, and shortly after him, one, whose graceful person, expressive face and dignified demeanor, are not ... surpassed by any living actor.... As I looked on Booth's handsome and naturally amiable attractive countenance was disfigured by the foul and dastardly vindictiveness of Iago. I involuntarily thought ... of that 'fallen Cherub,' who was ... the most beautiful of the sons of the morning, but whose black heart made that beauty ... become as terrible as it had formerly been attractive." Called before the curtain at the end of the Jarrett benefit, Booth appeared next to his co-star E. L. Davenport; Davenport was dressed in his Othello cos-

tume; Booth was already in his street clothes, "hastily put on;" he looked ready to go home. *The Spirit of the Times* described his clothing as "somewhat primitive undress."
4/27/58; Louisville Theater; Sir Giles Overreach, *A New Way to Pay Old Debts*
4/28/58; Richelieu
4/29/58; Richard III
4/30/58; Booth's benefit, Sir Edward Mortimer, *The Iron Chest*; Petruchio, *Katherine and Petruchio*
5/1/58; Charles de Moor, *The Robbers*
5/3/58; King Lear
5/4/58; Pescara, *The Apostate*
5/5/58; Sir Giles Overreach, *A New Way to Pay Old Debts*
5/6/58; Macbeth
5/7/58; Booth's benefit, Benedick, *Much Ado About Nothing*
5/8/58; Role unknown
5/10/58; St. Louis Theatre; Hamlet
5/11/58; Charles de Moor, *The Robbers*
5/12/58; Richelieu
5/13/58; Sir Giles Overreach, *A New Way to Pay Old Debts*
5/14/58; Booth's benefit, Richard III
5/15/58; Charles de Moor, *The Robbers*
5/17/58; Iago, *Othello*
5/18/58; Lucius Junius Brutus, *Brutus*
5/19/58; King Lear
5/20/58; Sir Edward Mortimer, *The Iron Chest*; Petruchio, *Katherine and Petruchio*
5/21/58; Richard III
5/24/58; Wood's Theater, Cincinnati, Ohio; Hamlet
At Wood's Theatre in St. Louis in 1858, prices were fifty cents for the dress circle and orchestra chairs; twenty-five cents for the parquette.
5/25/58; Richelieu
5/26/58; Julien St. Pierre, *The Wife*
5/27/58; Booth's benefit, Richard III
5/28/58; Iago, *Othello*
5/31/58; McVicker's Theatre Chicago; Sir Giles Overreach, *A New Way to Pay Old Debts*
6/1/58; *Othello*, role unknown
6/2/58; Richelieu
6/3/58; Lucius Junius Brutus, *Brutus*
6/4/58; Booth's benefit, Richard III
6/7/58; Hamlet
6/8/58; Pescara, *The Apostate*
6/9/58; Richelieu
6/10/58; Macbeth
6/12/58; Richard III
6/21/58; Metropolitan Theatre Buffalo; Richelieu
6/22/58; Iago, *Othello*
6/23/58; Lucius Junius Brutus, *Brutus*
6/24/58; King Lear
6/25/58; Booth's benefit, Richard III
6/26/58; Charles de Moor, *The Robbers*
6/28/58; Pescara, *The Apostate*
6/29/58; Macbeth
6/30/58; Richelieu
7/1/58; Sir Giles Overreach, *A New Way to Pay Old Debts*
7/2/58; Sir Edward Mortimer, *The Iron Chest*; Petruchio, *Katherine and Petruchio*
7/3/58; Richard III
7/5/58; Benedick, *Much Ado About Nothing*
8/2/58; Academy of Music, New York Dramatic Fund Benefit; Richelieu Selection

1858–1859

8/23/58; Holliday Street Theatre, Baltimore; Richelieu
8/24/58; Iago, *Othello*
8/25/58; King Lear
8/26/58; Sir Giles Overreach, *A New Way to Pay Old Debts*
8/27/58; Booth's benefit, Richard III
John Wilkes Booth, billed as Wilkes Booth, plays Richmond
8/28/58; Sir Edward Mortimer, *The Iron Chest*; Petruchio, *Katherine and Petruchio*
8/30/58; Hamlet
8/31/58; Lucius Junius Brutus, *Brutus*
9/1/58; Romeo
9/2/58; Shylock, *Merchant of Venice*; Richelieu Act IV
9/3/58; Booth's benefit, Macbeth
9/4/58; Richard III
9/6/58; New Washington Theatre; Richelieu
9/8/58; King Lear
9/9/58; Sir Edward Mortimer, *The Iron Chest*
9/10/58; Booth's benefit, Hamlet
9/11/58; Sir Giles Overreach, *A New Way to Pay Old Debts*
9/13/58; Richard III
9/14/58; Shylock, *Merchant of Venice*
9/15/58; Richard III
9/16/58; Macbeth
9/17/58; Pescara, *The Apostate*
9/18/58; Charles de Moor, *The Robbers*
9/27/58; Richmond Theatre a/k/a Marshall Theatre; Role unknown
9/28/58; Richelieu
9/30/58; Sir Edward Mortimer, *The Iron Chest*; Petruchio, *Katherine and Petruchio*
10/1/58; Booth's benefit, Richard III
10/6/58; Booth's benefit, Richard III
10/7/58; Iago, *Othello*
10/8/58; Shylock, *Merchant of Venice*; Petruchio, *Katherine and Petruchio*
10/12/58; Henry V, *Henry V*
10/13/58; King Lear
10/14/58; Lucius Junius Brutus, *Brutus*
10/15/58; Booth's benefit, Benedick, *Much Ado About Nothing*
10/16/58; Role unknown

10/25/58; Boston Theatre; Iago, *Othello*
10/26/58; Richelieu
10/27/58; Sir Giles Overreach, *A New Way to Pay Old Debts*
10/28/58; Shylock, *Merchant of Venice*
10/29/58; Booth's benefit, Richard III; Role unknown, *Only a Half Penny*
10/30/58; Matinee, Sir Giles Overreach, *A New Way to Pay Old Debts*; Evening, Iago, *Othello*

On Oct. 31, 1858, Edwin wrote to his brother Junius Brutus: "I remain here two weeks longer — old Burton played his first engagement here prior to mine, and drew immensely of course — they tried to buy me off, so as to give him a longer run — but I wouldn't budge though I should have made more money by so doing — I couldn't give up my little revenge — he swindled me in N.Y. last summer.... I have allowed myself plenty of time to rest between engagements this time — something that Baker never did.... The clock has struck three — so I will not prolong this but adjourn to get some sleep — which I have tasted little of lately.... I think this is going to be a good season for our business, for, though my houses here have been rather slim, my previous engagements in Balt<u>o</u> Washington & Richmond were better than ever before, and from all I hear the theatres are doing well all over the country."

11/1/58; Macbeth
11/2/58; Sir Edward Mortimer, *The Iron Chest*
11/3/58; Hamlet
11/4/58; Richard III
11/5/58; Booth's benefit, Pescara, *The Apostate*; Petruchio, *Katherine and Petruchio*
11/6/58; Matinee, Sir Edward Mortimer, *The Iron Chest*
11/8–9/58; King Lear 2x
11/10/58; Hamlet
11/11/58; Macbeth
11/12/58; Booth's benefit, Romeo; Petruchio, *Katherine and Petruchio*
11/13/58; Matinee, Richard III
11/22/58; New National Theatre, Cincinnati Ohio; Hamlet
11/23/58; Sir Giles Overreach, *A New Way to Pay Old Debts*
11/24/58; King Lear
11/25/58; Richelieu
11/26/58; Role unknown
11/27/58; Charles de Moor, *The Robbers*
11/29/58; Hamlet
11/30/58; Iago, *Othello*
12/1/58; Macbeth
12/2/58; Sir Edward Mortimer, *The Iron Chest*
12/3/58; Farewell Benefit; Sir Edward Mortimer, *The Iron Chest*; Petruchio, *Katherine and Petruchio*
12/4/58; Richard III
12/6/58; Louisville Theatre; Sir Giles Overreach, *A New Way to Pay Old Debts*

At the Louisville Theatre in Dec. 1858, seats in the dress circle and parquette were seventy-five cents; the second tier was thirty-five cents; the third tier was twenty-five cents; private boxes for whites were five dollars; colored boxes were fifty cents and the colored gallery was twenty-five cents.

12/7/58; Richelieu
12/8/58; Richelieu or Pescara, *The Apostate*
12/9/58; Lucius Junius Brutus, *Brutus*
12/10/58; Booth's benefit, Richard III
12/11/58; Sir Edward Mortimer, *The Iron Chest*; Petruchio, *Katherine and Petruchio*
12/13/58; Hamlet
12/14/58; King Lear
12/15/58; Lucius Junius Brutus, *Brutus*; Petruchio, *Katherine and Petruchio*
12/16/58; Macbeth
12/17/58; Booth's benefit, Richelieu
12/18/58; Richard III
12/21/58; Wood's Theatre, St. Louis; Sir Giles Overreach, *A New Way to Pay Old Debts*
12/22/58; Richelieu

On Dec. 23, a St. Louis critic described "the curse of Rome" speech from *Richelieu*: "The curse, at the conclusion of the fourth act, was, to our mind, the most imposing scene we ever witnessed; the audience sat perfectly transfixed until the end of the speech, when their enthusiasm knew no bounds, in fact it was so great that it was impossible to proceed with the performance for some minutes. At the end of the fourth act Mr. Booth was called before the curtain, and also at the conclusion of the play, when he was received amidst the hearty shouts of a well pleased audience."

12/23/58; Iago, *Othello*
12/24/58; Booth's benefit, Richard III
12/25/58; Charles de Moor, *The Robbers*
12/27/58; Hamlet
12/28/58; Richard III
12/29/58; King Lear
12/30/58; Charles de Moor, *The Robbers*
12/31/58; Booth's benefit, Macbeth
1/1/59; Benefit of J. H. Bagwell, treasurer of the theatre; Sir Edward Mortimer, *The Iron Chest*; Petruchio, *Katherine and Petruchio*
1/17/59; St. Charles Theatre, New Orleans; Hamlet

At the St. Charles Theatre in New Orleans in 1859, prices were seventy-five cents for the dress circle and parquette; fifty cents for the second circle; twenty-five cents for the gallery and six dollars for a private box. On Jan. 17, 1859, Booth opened as Hamlet in New Orleans where audiences proved "first rate." The local critic "noted ... some indefensible liberties taken with the text" and felt that Booth played "several characters much better than he plays Hamlet."

1/18/59; Macbeth

Of Booth's Macbeth on Jan. 18, the New Orleans critic wrote: "Long dead levels of monotonous

reading are ... relieved occasionally by bursts of fine and telling powers of speaking and acting."
1/19/59; Iago, *Othello*
1/20/59; Lucius Junius Brutus, *Brutus*
1/21/59; Booth's benefit, Richard III
Booth's Richard III Jan. 21 received a mixed review, the critic indicating that Booth merely recited rather than acted the soliloquies.
1/22/59; Richelieu
Booth played Richelieu on Jan. 22. Despite the fact that he was performing "with a bad cold," he was called before the curtain after the "Curse of Rome" speech. A local critic, however, thought that "at times his acting was "careless and indifferent. At others, he ... showed by the care he devoted to the delivery of his speeches that he had thought about them. But the performance, taken as a whole, was a strikingly uneven one."
1/23/59; Charles de Moor, *The Robbers*
1/24/59; Hamlet
1/25/59; Macbeth
1/26/59; Sir Giles Overreach, *A New Way to Pay Old Debts*
1/27/59; King Lear
1/28/59; Richelieu
1/29/59; Booth's benefit, Sir Edward Mortimer, *The Iron Chest*; Petruchio, *Katherine and Petruchio*
1/30/59; Charles Pope's benefit; Richard III
The critic for New Orleans' *Daily Picayune* wrote of his Richard III: "He lacks the hardiness which ... [an] improved physique will yet bring."
1/31/59; Romeo
2/1–12/59; Mobile Theatre; Role unknown
2/21/59; Crisp's Gaiety, Memphis, Tennesse; Richard III scheduled but the *Kate Frisbee*, the boat carrying Booth, did not arrive on time
2/22/59; Sir Giles Overreach, *A New Way to Pay Old Debts*
2/23/59; Richard III
2/24/59; Lucius Junius Brutus, *Brutus*
2/25/59; Booth's benefit, Richelieu
On Feb. 25, 1859, when Booth played Memphis for the second time, the theatre was "very well attended ... when we take into consideration the almost impassable condition of our streets and the threatening aspect of the weather."
2/26/59; Sir Edward Mortimer, *The Iron Chest*; Petruchio, *Katherine and Petruchio*
2/28/59; King Lear
3/1/59; Pescara, *The Apostate*
3/2/59; Iago, *Othello*
3/3/59; Sir Giles Overreach, *A New Way to Pay Old Debts*
3/4/59; Hamlet
3/5/59; Booth's benefit, Hamlet
3/7/59; Crisp's Gaiety, Nashville, Tennessee; Sir Edward Mortimer, *The Iron Chest*, scheduled but Booth did not arrive until 11 P.M. that evening due to an accident on the Memphis and Charleston Railroad. Booth got stranded at Murfreesboro. Mr. Crisp announced this at 9 P.M. When Booth appeared on Mar. 8, he apologized to the audience for the problem after the performance. In Nashville "at the conclusion of the play, Mr. Booth was called before the curtain, and elevated himself a niche higher in our [the critic's] estimation by bowing a declination of acceptance to a boisterous invitation from certain lovers of 'oratory' in the parquette, to make a 'speech.'"
3/8/59; Richard III
When Booth performed Richard III in Nashville on Mar. 8, 1859, the audience consisted "chiefly of ladies, and every available seat was taken, so that numbers of gentlemen were compelled to stand during the entire performance—blocking the lobbies and crowding the aisles in the dress circle."
3/9/59; Hamlet
3/10/59; Sir Giles Overreach, *A New Way to Pay Old Debts*
3/11/59; Booth's benefit, Richelieu
The critic for Nashville's *Republican Banner* wrote in Mar. 1859: "we feared that from the apparent tameness in the first three acts, the great tragedian would disappoint his audience, but this apprehension was dispelled in the fourth act when we discovered that according to his own original manner of impersonating the character of 'Cardinal Richelieu' or from physical inability, perhaps, he had 'saved himself' up to this point to invest it with a spirit and power that was electrifying."
3/12/59; Sir Edward Mortimer, *The Iron Chest*; Petruchio, *Katherine and Petruchio*
3/14/59; Pescara, *The Apostate*
3/15/59; Lucius Junius Brutus, *Brutus*
3/16/59; King Lear
3/17/59; Iago, *Othello*
3/18/59; Booth's benefit, Macbeth
3/19/59; Richard III
3/22/59; Theatre, Charleston, South Carolina; Sir Giles Overreach, *A New Way to Pay Old Debts*
3/23/59; Hamlet
3/24/59; Richelieu
3/25/59; Booth's benefit, Richard III
3/26/59; Sir Edward Mortimer, *The Iron Chest*; Petruchio, *Katherine and Petruchio*
3/28/59; Iago, *Othello*
3/29/59; Pescara, *The Apostate*
3/30/59; Richelieu
In Charleston, the local critic wrote on Mar. 30, 1859: "The performance was sometimes marred by loud conversation on the part of some of the audience.... Persons gain admittance to the pit, and even the boxes sometimes, under the garb of a genteel exterior, and then do not hesitate to rival the vulgarity of the "National" or "Bowery" by their conduct. If such gentry have not sufficient respect

for the presence of ladies, to behave with quietness and decorum, the police should be in readiness to convey them to the exterior of the building."
3/31/59; Hamlet
4/1/59; Booth's benefit, Macbeth
4/2/59; Richard III
4/4/59; Macbeth
4/5/59; King Lear
4/6/59; Pescara, *The Apostate*
4/7/59; Benefit in aid of the School Ship of the Port Society; Sir Edward Mortimer, *The Iron Chest*
4/8/59; Booth's benefit, Iago, *Othello*
4/9/59; Richelieu
4/11/59; Benefit of G. F. Marchant; Lucius Junius Brutus, *Brutus*
4/18/59; Richmond Theater; Pescara, *The Apostate*
4/19/59; Sir Edward Mortimer, *The Iron Chest*
4/20/59; King Lear
4/21/59; Macbeth
4/22/59; Booth's benefit, Richard III
4/23/59; Lucius Junius Brutus, *Brutus*
4/25/59; King Lear
4/26/59; Sir Giles Overreach, *A New Way to Pay Old Debts*
4/27/59; Hamlet
4/28/59; Phoenix Hall, Petersburg, Virginia; Hamlet
4/29/59; Sir Giles Overreach, *A New Way to Pay Old Debts*
4/30/59; Booth's benefit Matinee, Richard III
4/30/59; Richmond Theatre; Benefit of John Wilkes Booth; Iago, *Othello*
7/2, 4/59; Front Street Theatre, Baltimore; Sir Edward Mortimer 2x, *The Iron Chest*
7/30/59; Niblo's Garden, New York; Iago, *Othello* The critic for *The New York Daily Times* wrote: "The audience did not ... exhibit the dignified repose which might be supposed to indicate profound sympathy with the inspired language of Shakespeare. They stamped considerably, yelled outrageously, whistled fearfully, and "cat-called" profusely. Some, too, brought their little family matters into the parquet, and resuming at the point where they had left off at home, discussed them audibly throughout the greater part of the performance.... In the scene where Iago hypocritically expresses his surprise at the trouble he has occasioned in *Othello*'s family circle, one extremely rural person in the parquette was good enough to make to us the ... observation: 'Look at that now, and he is the very fellow that's been and done the whole of it.'" The results were, according to *The Albion*, disastrous. Booth's "*Iago* was slurred throughout."

1859–1860

8/27/59; Wheatley & Clarke's Arch Street Theatre, Philadelphia; Richelieu
8/29/59; Iago, *Othello*
8/30/59; Pescara, *The Apostate*
8/31/59; Hamlet
9/1/59; Lucius Junius Brutus, *Brutus*
9/2/59; Booth's benefit, Sir Edward Mortimer, *The Iron Chest* Petruchio, *Katherine and Petruchio*
9/5–9/59; Booth's benefit on 9/9/59; Richard III 5x
9/10/59; Charles de Moor, *The Robbers*
9/12/59; Sir Giles Overreach, *A New Way to Pay Old Debts*
9/13/59; Hamlet
9/14/59; Othello
9/15/59; King Lear
9/16/59; Booth's benefit, Sir Edward Mortimer, *The Iron Chest*; Petruchio, *Katherine and Petruchio*
9/17/59; Richard III
9/19/59; Macbeth
9/20/59; Shylock, *Merchant of Venice*
9/21/59; Macbeth
9/22/59; Pescara, *The Apostate*; Petruchio, *Katherine and Petruchio*
9/23/59; Booth's benefit, Benedick, *Much Ado About Nothing*; Shylock trial scene, *Merchant of Venice*
9/24/59; Romeo
10/3/59; Metropolitan Theatre, Buffalo, New York; Iago, *Othello*
10/4/59; Sir Giles Overreach, *A New Way to Pay Old Debts*
10/5/59; Richelieu
10/6/59; Hamlet
10/7/59; Booth's benefit, Richard III
10/8/59; King Lear
10/10/59; Richelieu
10/11/59; Sir Edward Mortimer, *The Iron Chest*; Petruchio, *Katherine and Petruchio*
10/12/59; Richard III
10/13/59; Pescara, *The Apostate*
10/14/59; Booth's benefit, Shylock, *Merchant of Venice*; Don Caesar de Bazan
10/17/59; Howard Athenaeum, Boston, Massachusetts; Hamlet
10/18/59; Sir Giles Overreach, *A New Way to Pay Old Debts*
10/19/59; Richelieu
10/20/59; Richard III
10/21/59; Booth's benefit, Shylock, *Merchant of Venice*; Petruchio, *Katherine and Petruchio*
10/22/59; King Lear
10/24/59; Macbeth
10/25/59; Hamlet
10/26/59; Richard III
10/27/59; Richelieu
10/28/59; Booth's benefit, The Stranger; Don Caesar de Bazan
10/29/59; Macbeth

10/31/59; Hamlet
11/1/59; Pescara, *The Apostate*
11/2/59; Claude Melnotte, *The Lady of Lyons*
11/3/59; Hamlet
11/4/59; Booth's benefit, Sir Giles Overreach, *A New Way to Pay Old Debts*; Don Caesar de Bazan
11/5/59; Richard III
11/7/59; Othello
11/8/59; Cassius, *Julius Caesar*, first known performance
11/9/59; Iago, *Othello*
11/10/59; Hamlet
11/11/59; Booth's benefit, Claude Melnotte, *The Lady of Lyons*; Ruy Gomez, *Faint Heart Never Won Fair Lady*

On Nov. 11, 1859, at Booth's benefit at the Howard Athenaeum, "the house was so crowded that the orchestra had to vacate their seats to give room to the public and play from the stage. A long time before the curtain was rung up, every part of the theatre was packed like herrings in a box! While hundreds went away, unable to get even standing room in the lobbies, all of which were crowded. A large number of high stools were procured and placed in the lobbies, to accommodate ladies who seem determined to ... remain ... throughout the entire performance, even if they stood up all evening."

11/12/59; Sir Edward Mortimer, *The Iron Chest*; Petruchio, *Katherine and Petruchio*
12/5/59; Athenaeum, Savannah, Georgia; Sir Giles Overreach, *A New Way to Pay Old Debts*
12/6/59; Hamlet
12/7/59; Richelieu
12/8/59; Iago, *Othello*
12/9/59; Booth's benefit, Sir Edward Mortimer, *The Iron Chest*
12/10/59; Richard III
12/12/59 Crisp & Canning's Gaiety Theatre, Columbus, Georgia aka Temperance Hall; Hamlet

During a six-day engagement in Columbus, Georgia in 1859, prices were seventy-five cents and twenty-five cents for "coloured persons."

12/13/59; Iago, *Othello*
12/14/59; Richelieu
12/15/59; Richard III
12/16/59; Booth's benefit, Sir Edward Mortimer, *The Iron Chest*; Petruchio, *Katherine and Petruchio*
12/17/59; Charles de Moor, *The Robbers*
12/19/59; Crisp & Canning's Gaiety Theatre, Montgomery, Alabama, Hamlet
12/20/59; Iago, *Othello*
12/21/59; Richard III
12/23/59; Booth's benefit, Sir Edward Mortimer, *The Iron Chest*; Petruchio, *Katherine and Petruchio*
12/24/59; Sir Giles Overreach, *A New Way to Pay Old Debts*
12/26/59; Richard III
12/27/59; Hamlet
12/28/59; Richelieu
1/2/60; St. Charles Theatre, New Orleans; Hamlet

When Booth appeared at the St. Charles Theatre in New Orleans in 1860, tickets were seventy-five cents in the dress circle and parquette; fifty cents in the second circle and twenty-five cents in the gallery. Private boxes were six dollars each. In the period white people could be treated for an eye infection for $3.50 to $5 a day; Negroes for $1.50; Burnett's Cocoaine, a compound of "Cocoa Nut Oil, &c." designed to prevent hair loss cost fifty cents a bottle.

1/3/60; Richelieu
1/4/60; Sir Giles Overreach, *A New Way to Pay Old Debts*
1/5/60; Iago, *Othello*
1/6/60; King Lear
1/7/60; Booth's benefit, Sir Edward Mortimer, *The Iron Chest*; Petruchio, *Katherine and Petruchio*
1/8/60; Richard III
1/9/60; Lucius Junius Brutus, *Brutus*
1/10/60; Macbeth
1/11/60; Richelieu
1/12/60; Richard III
1/13/60; Hamlet
1/14/60; Booth's benefit, Pescara, *The Apostate*; Don Caesar de Bazan
1/15/60; Sir Edward Mortimer, *The Iron Chest*
1/16/60; Title role *Henry II*

The title role of *Henry II* was Booth's only attempt at an original role written by an American. The authors were two lawyers, John Denison Champlin and his son-in-law Gideon Hiram Hollister. Working in Milwaukee during the summer of 1859, they turned out a five-act historical drama in a month, publishing it anonymously, to preserve their reputations, under the title *Thomas a Becket*, "a Tragedy by George Harvey." They sent it to Booth who called upon them in New York with Adam Badeau and offered them two hundred dollars for the play and an additional twenty dollars for each performance. In late Dec. 1859 *The New York Clipper* carried the news that Booth had a new tragedy by "a literary gentleman of New York." Mary Devlin had doubts about the commercial possibilities of a blank verse play, and Adam Badeau did not like the first act, but Booth, who was interested in playing Henry II, gained sole rights to its representation for his money. Badeau, Hollister and possibly Booth cut the play to four acts and renamed it. He began performing *Henry II or the Death of Thomas A Beckett*, with "new scenery" at the St. Charles Theatre in New Orleans on Jan. 16, 1860. According to *The Daily Picayune*, the best scene in the play was a confrontation between Henry and Becket with an obvious echo of *Richelieu*: "Becket, summoned to the royal presence, to answer to accusations of simony, and other crimes of which he was innocent, comes before the king and his court, armed with the holy symbol of his office, and defies his enemies both royal and noble.... The churchman, cross in hand, fixes his eye upon the monarch, in stern rebuke of his tyrannic conduct; the King, stung to madness, rises from the throne, throws off his royal robe, seizes an axe, springs upon the council table, and thence to the floor, and is in the very act of striking the bold prelate to the earth, when holding aloft the cross, the latter exclaims: 'Henry Plantagenet, I curse you in the name of Rome!' The monarch falls prostrate beneath the withering anathema, the courtiers, nobles, all shrink from him, and the power of the church is triumphant." Booth tried *Henry II* four times. The correspondent for *The New York Clipper* wrote: "the novelty possesses merit but is overdone with 'talk.'" From New Orleans Booth wrote to Champlin and to Hollister, sending each a royalty check for $20 per performance: "I did all I could to render *Henry* the part of the piece — but *Becket* has the sympathies of the audience...; therefore I deem it advisable to end the play with his death; ... I have so arranged it now ... in four acts; I have carried the females along till the last act. I think I had better reserve it now till I get an opening in New York for it.... I have had no opportunity to do it decently here.... The fourth act was terrific. I arranged some very effective 'business,' and a fine tableau at its conclusion, which was loudly applauded, and on each night, the curtain had to be raised on it. The two first nights were tolerably good, the third and fourth very poor. I thought it advisable to run it through for its reputation elsewhere." Booth was trying out a new play in what he considered to be an inferior theatre outside New York. It was not financially successful, but he performed Henry, hoping to build word of mouth at his next venue — Mobile. He apparently changed his mind and wrote to the young author/lawyer by Feb. 5, 1860: "I have been requested to 'do' Henry 2d; so shall let them have a taste of it but cannot possibly give it more than once.... I think the best thing we can do is to let the piece rest for awhile — that is — you drop it for a couple of months, and I'll keep up the thinking, and if any telling point should present themselves, ... I'll let you know.... The printed — original — copy I cut to pieces, and put them together again in a different shape — so as to do the play in 4 acts.... I got sick over it, and have not looked at it for a week.... The first three acts were complained of as being ... slow. Don't bother your brains about it for awhile — probably in a few months some new idea may strike you for the ending. I am going to try the play as I have fixed it, some day, in order to get square on the bargain — if nothing else. So soon as I get a clear copy of it as it stands in four acts, I'll send it to you, but I must first become calm and tranquil — I get so infernally excited when overhauling a knotty point; wouldn't do for a lawyer would I?" The next day Booth sent Hollister a sketch of his revision of the play, telling him: "I merely tried my hand at it with the idea of doing Becket; but as you say I must play the King. Of course another act must be given him. As I have imagined it — B. ends all the acts; the women are carried through the play till the end, and the King is disposed of pretty decently before the death of B.... 'Tis better to get rid of the boys—children are invidious on the stage as they are anywhere but in 'dream-land,' so leave them out if possible.... I shall, of course, bring 'Henry' out in N.Y. as soon as possible; but theatricals are in such a grim state there now that I am I doubt if I ever get a chance at the place again. They won't have tragedy — that is the managers won't I'm sure the public are ready for it, for it's nearly two years since they have had any. I can't conceive an ending for 'Henry' unless it be a sick bed with fever, cursing his sons etc."

1/17–19/60; Henry II 3x
1/20/60; Romeo
1/21/60; Richard III
1/22/60; Benefit of Charles Pope; Macbeth
1/24/60; Mobile Theatre; Hamlet
1/25/60; Romeo
1/26/60; Iago or Othello, *Othello*
1/27/60; Sir Giles Overreach, *A New Way to Pay Old Debts*
1/28/60; Booth's benefit, Richard III
1/30/60; Richelieu
1/31/60; Claude Melnotte, *The Lady of Lyons*
2/1/60; King Lear
2/2/60; Iago, *Othello*
2/3/60; Booth's benefit, Richelieu
2/4/60; Macbeth
2/6/60; Hamlet
2/7–9/60; Phydias and Raphael 3x, *The Marble Heart*
2/10/60; Booth's benefit, Sir Edward Mortimer, *The Iron Chest*; Don Caesar de Bazan
2/13/60; Pescara, *The Apostate*; Petruchio, *Katherine and Petruchio*
2/14/60; Richelieu

In Jan., 1860, the critic for *The Mobile Daily Register* wrote: "At times ... Mr. Booth delivers himself in too low a tone, this having the effect to destroy, to those farthest from the stage, the pleasure consequent to a full hearing of every word of the play."

2/20/60; New Memphis Theatre; Hamlet

In 1860 Booth wrote from Memphis: "My trade would be good here — were it not for the infernal rain, which ever falls in torrents when I come; it is my opinion that the Lord, for some evils in this place, is, by a slow process of hydropathy, washing this town, out of the map altogether, and if a new settlement should ever spring open upon its site — all their records will date from the Memphian flood." In Memphis in 1860, the dress circle, parquette and balcony were seventy-five cents; private boxes were five and ten dollars; and the third tier and coloured gallery were twenty-five cents.

2/21/60; Sir Giles Overreach, *A New Way to Pay Old Debts*
2/22/60; Richard III
2/23/60; Romeo
2/24/60; Booth's benefit, Sir Edward Mortimer, *The Iron Chest*; Don Caesar de Bazan
2/25/60; Pescara, *The Apostate*
2/27–28/60; Raphael 2x, *The Marble Heart*

On February 28, 1860, Booth wrote to his fellow actor Lawrence Barrett from Memphis: "Speaking of rain — it fell in more sense than one, the other night — in a scene between Raphael & Volage — just as I — the former — exclaimed — "Peace — peace"!, the rain-box gave way, and all the peas came spluttering over the stage — so I did not cry out in vain."

2/29/60; Richard III
3/1/60; Richelieu
3/2/60; Booth's benefit, Raphael, *The Marble Heart*; Petruchio, *Katherine and Petruchio*
3/3/60; Macbeth
3/5/60; Crisp's Gaiety, Nashville, Tennessee; Hamlet

In 1860, the critic for Nashville's *Republican Banner* found "Booth's colloquialism" as Hamlet: "a little too rapid and not sufficiently declamatory."

3/6/60; Sir Giles Overreach, *A New Way to Pay Old Debts*
3/7/60; Richard III
3/8/60; Richelieu
3/9/60; Booth's benefit, Sir Edward Mortimer, *The Iron Chest*; Petruchio, *Katherine and Petruchio*
3/10/60; Pescara, *The Apostate*
3/12/60; Macbeth
3/13/60; Iago, *Othello*
3/14/60; Richelieu
3/15/60; Charles de Moor, *The Robbers*
3/16/60; Booth's benefit, Richard III
3/17/60; Benefit of Mrs W. H. Crisp; Pescara, *The Apostate*; Petruchio, *Katherine and Petruchio*
3/20/60; Charleston Theatre; Sir Giles Overreach, *A New Way to Pay Old Debts*
3/21/60; Iago, *Othello*
3/22/60; Richelieu
3/23/60; Booth's benefit, Benedick, *Much Ado About Nothing*
3/24/60; Richard III
3/26/60; Phidias and Raphael, *The Marble Heart*
3/27/60; Hamlet
3/28/60; Richelieu
3/29/60; Richard III
3/30/60; Booth's benefit, Sir Edward Mortimer, *The Iron Chest*; Petruchio, *Katherine and Petruchio*
3/31/60; Macbeth
4/2/60; Romeo
4/3/60; Shylock, *Merchant of Venice*; Petruchio, *Katherine and Petruchio*
4/4/60; Booth's benefit, Lucius Junius Brutus, *Brutus*; Don Caesar de Bazan
4/9/60; Wood's Theatre, Cincinnati, Ohio; Richelieu

In Cincinnati in 1860 the gallery cost twenty-five cents, the price of a bottle of Mrs. Winslow's Soothing Sirup [sic] for Children Teething.

4/10/60; Hamlet
4/11/60; Sir Giles Overreach, *A New Way to Pay Old Debts*

The *Daily Cincinnati Gazette* criticized Booth's Sir Giles Overreach in Apr. 1860 saying: "Throughout the entire piece he seemed careless, and his stage business was at times bad. This may have partially been the result of physical inability."

4/12/60; Macbeth
4/13/60; Booth's Benefit; Richard III
4/14/60; Lucius Junius Brutus, *Brutus*

Of Booth's Lucius Junius Brutus, the Cincinnati critic wrote: "In the closing scene, where he parts with 'Titus,' passing the dreadful penalty of death upon his own son, there was a lack of feeling that a father is supposed to bear towards a child; there was passion, but not tenderness, and when he exclaimed, 'Brutus is childless, and Rome is free!' we doubt if one of the audience felt that Brutus had made any very great sacrifice."

4/16/60; King Lear
4/17/60; Richard III
4/18/60; Pescara, *The Apostate*
4/19/60; Sir Edward Mortimer, *The Iron Chest*; Petruchio, *Katherine and Petruchio*
4/20/60; Booth's Benefit; Shylock, *Merchant of Venice*; Don Caesar de Bazan
4/23/60; St. Louis Theatre; Hamlet

At the St. Louis Theatre, in 1860, seats in the dress circle and orchestra were fifty cents; seats in the pit twenty-five cents; gallery seats twenty-five cents; boxes five dollars and "coloured boxes" fifty cents.

4/24/60; Richelieu
4/25/60; Romeo
4/26/60; Sir Giles Overreach, *A New Way to Pay Old Debts*
4/27/60; Booth's benefit, Sir Edward Mortimer, *The Iron Chest*; Petruchio, *Katherine and Petruchio*
4/28/60; Richard III
4/30–5/1/60; Raphael 2x, *The Marble Heart*
5/2/60; Macbeth
5/3/60; Booth's benefit, Richard III
5/4/60; Pescara, *The Apostate*; Don Caesar de Bazan
5/9/60; Wheatley and Clarke's Arch Street Theatre, Philadelphia; Lucius Junius Brutus, *Brutus*

5/10/60; Iago, *Othello*
5/11/60; Richelieu
5/12/60; Macbeth
5/14/60; Hamlet
5/15/60; Pescara, *The Apostate*; Don Caesar de Bazan
5/16/60; Richard III
5/17/60; Othello
5/18/60; Macbeth
5/19/60; Charles de Moor, *The Robbers*
5/21/60; Richard III
5/22/60; Shylock, *Merchant of Venice*; Petruchio, *Katherine and Petruchio*
5/23/60; Sir Edward Mortimer, *The Iron Chest*

1860–1861

9/3/60; Howard Athenaeum, Boston, Massachusetts; Pescara, *The Apostate*
9/4/60; Richelieu
9/5/60; Macbeth
9/6/60; Richard III
9/7/60; Booth's benefit, Sir Edward Mortimer, *The Iron Chest*; Don Caesar de Bazan
9/8/60; Pescara, *The Apostate*
9/10–15/60; Booth's benefit on 9/15/60; Hamlet 6x
9/17/60; Claude Melnotte, *The Lady of Lyons*
9/18/60; Hamlet
9/19/60; Macbeth
9/20/60; Hamlet
9/21/60; Booth's benefit, Sir Giles Overreach, *A New Way to Pay Old Debts*; Petruchio, *Katherine and Petruchio*
9/22/60; Othello
9/24/60; Bertuccio, first known performance, *The Fool's Revenge*
9/25/60; Hamlet
9/26/60; Bertuccio, *The Fool's Revenge*
9/27/60; Richard III
9/28/60; Booth's benefit, Julien St. Pierre, *The Wife*; Petruchio, *Katherine and Petruchio*
9/29/60; Matinee, Claude Melnotte, *The Lady of Lyons*
10/8–10/60; Baltimore; Richard III 3x
10/11/60; Romeo
10/12/60; Booth's benefit, Lucius Junius Brutus, *Brutus*
10/15/60; Hamlet
10/17/60; Iago, *Othello*
10/18/60; Othello
10/19/60; Booth's benefit, Hamlet
10/21/60; Sir Edward Mortimer, *The Iron Chest*
10/22/60; Booth's benefit, Bertuccio, *The Fool's Revenge*
10/31/60 Wheatley & Clarke's Arch Street Theatre, Philadelphia; Richard III
11/1/60; Iago, *Othello*
11/2/60; Richelieu
11/3/60; Cassius, *Julius Caesar*
11/5–10/60; Booth's benefit on Nov. 5, 1860; Bertuccio 6x, *The Fool's Revenge*
11/12–15/60; Hamlet 4x
11/16/60; Booth's benefit, Cassius, *Julius Caesar*; Petruchio, *Katherine and Petruchio*
11/17/60; Bertuccio, *The Fool's Revenge*; Petruchio, *Katherine and Petruchio*
11/26–28/60; Winter Garden Theatre, New York Hamlet 3x

One of the odd practices of the Winter Garden management was that Booth's benefits were often staged on a Monday rather than at the traditional Friday performance. Mondays were traditionally the weakest box office night of the week. *Frank Leslie's Illustrated Newspaper* wrote of Booth's 1860 Hamlet: "From the first scene to the last, 'the fruitful wen of the eye and deject'd 'havior o the visage' denote his conception of the part truly. This gentleman ... repeats the words of the text — not always correctly — with an apparent indifference as to their meaning and accompanies them with gesture more or less suited to said words. During Mr. Booth's previous engagements in this city, we took occasion to witness all of his representations but failed to discover wherein lay the secret of his success in the provinces—for that he is successful in all other places but New York is abundantly verified. To us, he appears a young man of average ability, with a good figure, pleasant voice and quiet manner; his shortcomings as an artist are not glaring but ... he will never reach the goal that injudicious friends claim he has already attained." The critic for *The Evening Post* wrote: "In happy contrast to most Hamlets is Mr. Booth's in the demeanor of the Prince of Denmark towards his mother. The insolent brutality which most representatives of the part assume in their interviews with the Queen is replaced by an earnestness mingled with pity." The critic for the *New York Dispatch* praised Booth's decision to include the scene in which Hamlet finds the King praying and the conversation between Hamlet and Horatio before the entrance of Osric but criticized his elocution as: "too pedantic. Nay, at times, it actually verges upon a sing-songy and rhythmical style of declamation.... Moreover in the employment of his hands Mr. Booth is somewhat too profuse." The critic for *The New York Daily News* wrote that Booth "played with his former general carelessness and fugitive flashes of genius. He has neither improved nor deteriorated; And we should imagine is as far as ever beyond the influence of correction, and as remotely removed from anything like a first-class position as when he performed here, three years ago." The critic for *The New York Times* saw Booth and Edwin Forrest as representatives of "the intellectual and physical schools" and wrote of the opening night performance: "Mr. BOOTH is almost ... unknown to a New-York audience....

Last night, in the first act of *Hamlet*, he seemed timid in consequence, as if he had to become acquainted with his audience and his audience with him.... But in the second and especially in the third and fifth acts, Mr. BOOTH played admirably, still being a little faulty and immature at times, as if either the first timidity had crept back upon him, or that he had so much dread of the loud-voiced Forrest school, that he went to the other extreme of whispers. In portions of the closet scene, a few paces from the stage, he was nearly inaudible.... Of all tragedians of the present time, ... we prefer Mr. BOOTH. He has little muscular force, but with several faults, he has decided and discriminating intellectual talent." Booth restored the scene in which Hamlet almost kills the king while the latter prays. According to the critic for *The New York Times*, it had not been seen on the stage since the time of Garrick and with good reason. "It offends," the critic wrote, "the sense of propriety of many people and does not add anything to the grand features of the play."

11/29/60; Pescara, *The Apostate*

11/30/60; Richelieu

On Dec. 1, 1860, the critic for *The New York Times* wrote of *Richelieu*: "The house was well filled, but was not crowded. We predict, however, thronged houses, henceforth, every night that Mr. BOOTH repeats this personation.... Mr. BOOTH fully equals [William Charles Macready].... Gradually rising in grandeur, as the play proceeded, Mr. BOOTH, at the close of the fourth act, on being called before the curtain, not only received the applause of the electrified audience, but unable to restrain themselves, they broke into loud and long articulated 'Bravos.'" "In those passages, 'in the hands of men entirely great, the pen is mightier than the sword,' and 'take away the sword. States can be ruled without them,' the audience looked upon them as quite applicable to the present disturbed state of the country, and testified their appreciation of the sentiments in the most vociferous manner, many of the present rising to their feet, waving hats, handkerchiefs, and cheering like they had been hired to do the hurraing at a political mass meeting."

12/1/60; Pescara, *The Apostate*

12/3–4/60; Booth's benefit on 12/2/60; Richard III 2x

12/5–7/60; Richelieu 3x

12/8/60; Richard III

12/10–14/60; Booth's benefit on 12/14/60; Richelieu 5x

12/15/60; Iago, *Othello*

At the end of Booth's third week, the critic for *Frank Leslie's Illustrated Newspaper* wrote: "Despite the futile attempts made by certain papers to manufacture public opinion in his behalf, we fancy that the public proper will feel no ... grief at parting with this young man. He has been more persistently overpraised than any artist of late years."

12/17/60; Hamlet

12/18/60; Othello

12/19/60; Romeo

12/20/60; Richelieu

12/21/60; Booth's benefit, Hamlet

12/22/60; Lucius Junius Brutus, *Brutus*; Petruchio, *Katherine and Petruchio*

Mrs. Sam Cowell wrote in her diary: "On Saturday last Sidney and I went to the Winter Garden, to see Edwin Booth play Brutus and Petruchio—It was his last night and the theatre was very full. Sometimes a little tendency to rant distressed me but the earnestness of his acting made amends for that fault."

1/1/61; American Academy of Music, Philadelphia; Booth's benefit on 1/3/61 and Charlotte Cushman's benefit on 1/4/61; Macbeth 5x

1/7–8/61; Cardinal Wolsey 2x, *Henry VIII*; first known performance

1/9–10/61; Shylock 2x, *Merchant of Venice*, paired with Petruchio, *Katherine and Petruchio*, on 1/10/61

1/21, 23/61; Winter Garden, New York City; Lucius Junius Brutus 2x, *Brutus*

Booth reopened at the Winter Garden as Lucius Junius Brutus on Jan. 21, 1861, playing only four nights a week at first—Monday, Wednesday, Friday and Saturday, copying the pattern that Edwin Forrest had followed in his performances at Niblo's. After one week, however, he resumed playing every night. In New York, in Jan. 1861, critics were still divided in their opinions of Booth's acting. The *New York Dispatch* thought he had "degenerated into the unenergetic and so called intellectual school" and found him "partially imitative when forcible and weak when not imitative." The critic for *The New York Daily News*, hitherto hostile, praised Booth's Iago, Othello and Richard III, although he thought the supernumeraries "want drilling badly." *The New York Times* reported that Booth's performances had been initially "affected by the weather" but that he was doing "brilliantly" by the end of the week.

1/25–26/61; Richard III 2x

1/28–31/61; Richelieu 4x

In Feb. 1861, Mrs. Sam Cowell wrote: "We went to the Winter Garden ... to see 'Richelieu' by Edwin Booth—and down came *that* statue from its pedestal. He looked like an old woman, and played alternately as if in the last agonies of death from exhaustion, and the raging passion of a man in full health. I liked him so little that I shall say no more about him." On Jan. 28, 1861, Booth performed Richelieu to a large audience "composed of the *elite* of the city," while Edwin Forrest performed the same role at Niblo's.

2/1–2/61; Booth's benefit, Sir Giles Overreach 2x,

A New Way to Pay Old Debts; Petruchio 2x, *Katherine and Petruchio*
2/4–5/61; Macbeth 2x
2/6–7/61; Hamlet 2x
2/8–9/61; Sir Edward Mortimer 2x, *The Iron Chest*; Don Caesar de Bazan 2x
2/11–16/61; Shylock 6x, *Merchant of Venice*
Even the critic of the *New York Dispatch,* normally negative about Booth, was positive about his Shylock, noting, however, that the supporting roles were "terribly done." *The Spirit of the Times* wrote of Booth's Shylock: "It is true, that as with Edmund Kean ... to some degree, the Promethean fire blazes forth in lightning flashes, failing to illuminate steadily the whole of his conception. But it is there, ever and anon lighting up a fierce passion, as in the scene with Tubal ... and again, as once or twice in the trial scene.... Booth passed over the sorrow of "I had it from Leah when I was a bachelor."
2/18/61; Iago, *Othello*
2/19/61; Othello
Of Booth's 1861 Othello, the critic of *The Spirit of the Times* wrote: "If we were to criticize we should say that he paints his face too darkly for the Moor.... The slightest Negro tinge which seems to be too often reached in Othello is artistically offensive and historically false." The critic for *The New York Clipper* preferred Booth's Shylock to his Othello and thought that Booth "sees his faults, and seems determined to correct them."
2/20/61; Iago, *Othello*
2/21/61; Othello
2/22/61; Booth's benefit, Iago, *Othello*; Petruchio, *Katherine and Petruchio*
2/23/61; Iago, *Othello*; Petruchio, *Katherine and Petruchio*
3/21/61; Academy of Music, New York. New York Benefit performance with Charlotte Cushman for the Dramatic Fund Association; Macbeth
For the Booth/ Cushman benefit on Mar. 21, 1861, *The Spirit of the Times* reported that the Academy of Music in New York was "thronged from parquette to dome, though the weather was almost tempestuous and the streets in a state not to be trodden. The Academy is a wretched place for the exhibition of any other than a lyrical drama, for the scenery is very limited, and the voices of the speakers can scarcely be heard in its cavernous spaces. Not one half the audience, we presume, heard the play as they desired to hear it, and the melodious tones of Booth even failed to reach all parts of the house.... The army of Macduff was most shabbily represented.... composed of four chiefs and five ranked file."
4/8/61; Wheatley & Clarke's Arch Street Theatre, Philadelphia; Sir Giles Overreach, *A New Way to Pay Old Debts*
4/9/61; Role unknown
4/10–11/61; Bertuccio 2x, *The Fool's Revenge*
4/12/61; Booth's benefit, Shylock, *Merchant of Venice*; Petruchio, *Katherine and Petruchio*
4/13/61; Richelieu
4/15–16/61; Winter Garden, New York; Shylock 2x, *Merchant of Venice*
4/17–18/61; Othello 2x
4/19–20/61; Booth's benefit on 4/19/61; Hamlet 2x
4/22–23/61; Richelieu 2x
4/24/61; Sir Giles Overreach, *A New Way to Pay Old Debts*; originally scheduled as Macbeth
4/25/61; Iago, *Othello*; originally scheduled as Macbeth
4/26/61; Booth's benefit, Shylock, *Merchant of Venice*; Petruchio, *Katherine and Petruchio*
4/27/61; Shylock, *Merchant of Venice*; originally scheduled as Iago, *Othello*; Petruchio, *Katherine and Petruchio*
5/13/61; Howard Athenaeum, Boston, Massachusetts; Richelieu
5/14/61; Richard III
5/15/61; Iago, *Othello*
5/16/61; Richelieu
5/17/61; Booth's benefit, Shylock, *Merchant of Venice*; Petruchio, *Katherine and Petruchio*
5/18/61; Pescara, *The Apostate*
5/20/61; Hamlet
5/21/61; Macbeth
5/22/61; Hamlet
5/23/61; Claude Melnotte, *The Lady of Lyons*
5/24/61; Booth's benefit, Hamlet
5/25/61; Richard III
5/27/61; Richelieu
5/28/61; Sir Edward Mortimer, *The Iron Chest*; Petruchio, *Katherine and Petruchio*
5/29/61; Claude Melnotte, *The Lady of Lyons*
5/30/61; Romeo
5/31/61; Booth's benefit, Lucius Junius Brutus, *Brutus*; Don Caesar de Bazan
6/1/61; Sir Giles Overreach, *A New Way to Pay Old Debts*; Petruchio, *Katherine and Petruchio*
6/3/61; Cassius, *Julius Caesar*
6/4/61; Hamlet
6/5/61; Othello
6/6/61; Cassius, *Julius Caesar*
6/7/61; Booth's benefit, Fazio, *Fazio*; Sir Edward Mortimer, *The Iron Chest*
6/8/61; Cassius, *Julius Caesar*
6/10–11/61; Bertuccio 2x, *The Fool's Revenge*
6/12/61; Lucius Junius Brutus, *Brutus*
6/13/61; Shylock, *Merchant of Venice*; Don Caesar de Bazan
6/14/61; Booth's benefit, Macbeth
6/15/61; Matinee, Hamlet

1861–1862

9/30/-10/4/61; Theatre Royal, Haymarket, London; Shylock 3x, *Merchant of Venice*
The Haymarket was crowded on opening night, and when "Booth appeared upon the stage as Shy-

lock, ... he was very warmly greeted, and throughout the performance applause was bestowed.... Of course, too, at the close of the fourth act, where the serious incidents of the play terminate, he was summoned before the curtain, and when he retired it was amid unanimous indications of enthusiasm." The reviewer in *The Daily News* wrote: "Those who came expecting any startling outburst, any new readings, any marked points, must have been disappointed." London critics found his acting as Shylock "forced and spasmodic, particularly during the trial scene, in which he indulged in an unendurable excess of facial contortions, ... which were so unnatural as to border on the grotesque." He was judged "a judicious actor," "a careful artist, who eschews rant, discriminates his emphases, and controls his wildest declamation with judgment," one whose "acting, though at times restrained and wanting in vigour [sic], bespoke study and stage experience," "sometimes careful and judicious, occasionally even spirited and impressive, but almost invariably conventional." *The Literary Gazette* reported: "As regards the 'get-up' we just protest against the absence of beard. *Antonio* could scarcely have 'voided his rheum' upon the beard of Mr. Booth." *The Era*'s critic wrote: "Mr. Edwin Booth, is, we believe, only in his 27th year, and the youthful appearance which he presents when, by a rapid change of dress, he comes forward in the costume of private life to acknowledge the plaudits of the public, will strengthen the hopes of those who look forward to his future advancement." "Mine was," Booth wrote, "the first tragedy effort that had been made there [at the Haymarket Theatre] for several years. The company in comedy were highly celebrated, but when they appeared with me, it was one of the most unsatisfactory and awkward attempts that had ever been witnessed on the stage."

10/7–9/61; Sir Giles Overreach 2x, *A New Way to Pay Old Debts*

The London Illustrated News critic found his Sir Giles Overreach lacking in passion. "His Sir Giles is a decent, respectable man of the world, who behaves himself remarkably well. But when he begins to rage, it is with startling suddenness and obstinate persistency. Mr. Booth closed his fourth act effectively with a burst of exultation, which brought down the house. The part of Sir Giles is ... a bold bad man, who scorns conscience and follows his own interest exclusively, with a spice also of demoniac cruelty to his disposition.... The actor must ... throw himself into it with an unreasoning confidence.... Mr. Booth is evidently a very judicious actor, and is more intent on the proprieties of the scene than the passion." The critic for *John Bull* agreed: "The part itself is not a good one.... Mr. Booth's conception is not marked by a strong originality, although sensible and consistent. He made all the points of the play with considerable force and discrimination, and in the last and most important scene displayed powers of expression of no mean order. In the days when a strong and complete dramatic company existed, Mr. Booth would have proved a most valuable acquisition to the stage; but it is to be feared that he has not fire enough to re-create an interest in plays which modern audiences, whenever they are induced to go to see them, rather submit to than enjoy." The critic for *Bell's Life in London* wrote: "Mr. Booth is not our *beau ideal* of Sir Giles Overreach; his style is too colloquial and too real, but he is painstaking, and has evidently made a study of the part. His talent is conspicuously shown in some of the conversational passages of the play." *The Illustrated London News*' reviewer observed a "reservation of strength, and consequent long intervals of level and rapid, too rapid, speaking between the more energetic passages" as well as a "willful missing of opportunities, and the dropping of words and phrases that ought to be rendered emphatic; and the unexpected power at occasional spasmodic display."

10/11/61; Shylock, *Merchant of Venice*

10/14/61; Sir Giles Overreach, *A New Way to Pay Old Debts*

10/17, 19/61; Shylock 2x, *Merchant of Venice*

10/28–29/61; Richard III 2x

The critic for *The Daily Telegraph*, wrote of Booth's *Richard III*: "The manner in which he dashes from his couch in the tent-scene, waving his sword about in half-awakened agony and terror, is really both picturesque and fearful, but his death is too painfully elaborated to be impressive. His general performance, however, though lacking the brilliancy and vigor of genius, is careful and judicious; the only particular in which he can be said seriously to offend against good taste being in the too frequent display of his handkerchief." In 1871, the reviewer of *The Albion* remembered Booth's London performance as Richard III: "The ludicrous support given by the comedians on that occasion was more easily imagined than described. With the exception of the central figure, the whole affair was a mere travestie."

10/30/61; Shylock, *Merchant of Venice*

10/31–11/9/61; Booth's benefit on 11/9/61; Richelieu 9x

The critic for *The Illustrated London News* wrote of Booth's *Richelieu*: "He was better supported than on former occasions.... The scenery provided for the occasion was appropriate, and in one instance new and pleasing." The critic for *The Daily Telegraph* wrote that "in the pathetic passages, Mr. Booth is oftentimes touching and natural, his manner being more easy and unstudied than it was in his last representation. He might be a little more dignified at times, but then he never sinks into commonplace, even when he is more conversational in tone than the text seems to warrant." The critic for the *Sunday Times* wrote: "He kept subdued the exhibition of all those inconsistencies of trembling decrepitude and boisterous expression by which the part is best known.... He did not at one moment gasp for breath, and next declaim with a whirlwind vehemence, alternating between the extremest debility and the most robustious fire." *The Literary Gazette* wrote: "Where is there any of the mirth or even the satire, of the great minister? When the 'grand monarque,' defeated in his design upon the life of the husband of *Julie*, and even refused by the *Cardinal* permission to love his proposed victim, demands petulantly, "Whom, then, can I love?" who but Mr. Booth could have supposed that *Richelieu* was serious in his suggestions that if the *King* must love some one, let him love him, his faithful minister? Yet such is the case; no smile breaks over his face, nor is there any hint of the humor which *Richelieu* displays both here and in other portions of the play. Altogether we think this one of the worst conceptions that we have ever seen set before a London audience."

11/11–16/61; Theatre Royal, Manchester; Hamlet 6x
11/18–19/61; Othello 2x
11/20/61; Shylock, *Merchant of Venice*
11/21/61; Iago, *Othello*
11/22/61; Shylock, *Merchant of Venice*
11/23/61; Othello
11/25/61; Hamlet
11/26/61; Sir Giles Overreach, *A New Way to Pay Old Debts*
11/27/61; Richard III
11/28/61; Othello
11/29–30/61; Booth's benefit on 11/29; Romeo 2x; Petruchio 2x, *Katherine and Petruchio*
2/24/62; Royal Amphitheatre, Liverpool; Hamlet
2/25/62; Richelieu
2/26/62; Macbeth
2/27–3/1/62; Richelieu 3x
3/3/62; Richard III
3/4/62; Hamlet
3/5/62; Shylock, *Merchant of Venice*
3/6/62; Sir Giles Overreach, *A New Way to Pay Old Debts*
3/7/62; Sir Edward Mortimer, *The Iron Chest*; Petruchio, *Katherine and Petruchio*
3/8/62; Othello

1862–1863

9/29–10/2/62; Winter Garden, New York; Hamlet 4x
10/3–4/62; Othello 2x
10/6–7/62; Lucius Junius Brutus 2x, *Brutus*
10/8–9/62; Shylock 2x, *Merchant of Venice*
  The reviewer for *The New York Clipper* wrote of Booth's Shylock: "At times, in action and voice, he appears far too young, ... but, in his interview with Tubal, in the third act ... Edwin Booth is thought to be second to no living actor. Only four acts were played — the Cibber-Tate version — thereby detracting much from its being properly performed. At a house like the Winter Garden we had a right to expect the Launcelot unabridged, dog and all ... with only a two hours' performance and no afterpiece, the manager can hardly expect overflowing benches."
10/10–11/62; Booth's benefit on 10/11/61; Iago 2x, *Othello*
10/13–22/62; Richelieu 9x
10/23/62; Richard III
10/24–25/62; Booth's benefit on 10/24/62; Richelieu 2x
  Petruchio 2x, *Katherine and Petruchio*
10/27–28/62; Romeo 2x
  The critic for *The Albion* wrote: "In some parts of 'Richelieu' ... and in that banging blue-bottle tragedy of 'Richard III,'" Booth could "rant in a manner most violent and astonishing. But in *Hamlet, Romeo, Iago* and *Shylock*, he exaggerated with ... delicacy, consistency and finish."
10/29/62; Hamlet
10/30/62; Shylock, *Merchant of Venice*
10/31–11/1/62; Richard III 2x
11/3–6/62; Claude Melnotte 4x, *The Lady of Lyons*
  When Booth did Claude Melnotte during his third week in New York, the critic for *The New York Times* wrote: "*Claude*, in his hands, is a crafty deceiver, as full of shrugs as *Iago*, and as wide awake as *Mephistophiles*, a wily conspirator who knows the risk, and takes the chances—not a passionate swain blinded by the possible attainment of his heart's desire." *Frank Leslie's Illustrated Newspaper* was negative to the point of making snide remarks about the handsome young actor: "Mr. Edwin Booth is a very sorry kind of lover on the stage, ... whatever he may be in private life. His Claude Melnotte was a shade worse than his Romeo.... The want of ... individuality in those characters may have blinded Mr. Booth to ... their ... difficulty ... and the increased necessity for study.... If he deemed them beneath his study, he should not have included them in his repertoire. He, however, redeemed himself by his ... personation of ... Sir Giles Overreach."
11/7–13/62; Sir Edward Mortimer 6x, *The Iron Chest*; Don Caesar de Bazan 6x
11/14/62; Booth's benefit, Shylock 4th act only, *Merchant of Venice*; Pescara, *The Apostate*
11/15/62; Shylock, *Merchant of Venice*; Pescara, *The Apostate*
11/24–25/62; Boston Theatre; Hamlet 2x
11/26–27/62; Othello
11/28–29/62; Matinee on 11/29/62; Romeo 2x
12/1–2/62; Richelieu 2x
12/3/62; Claude Melnotte, *The Lady of Lyons*

The *Boston Post* critic wrote that Booth "no longer listlessly waits for special points at which great efforts may be made." The same critic thought Booth's Claude Melnotte looked repulsive.

12/4/62; Iago, *Othello*
12/5/62; Shylock, *Merchant of Venice*; Petruchio, *Katherine and Petruchio*
12/6/62; Matinee, Hamlet
12/8/62; Sir Giles Overreach, *A New Way to Pay Old Debts*
12/9/62; Shylock, *Merchant of Venice*; Petruchio, *Katherine and Petruchio*
12/10/62; Richelieu
12/11/62; Pescara, *The Apostate*
12/12/62; Sir Edward Mortimer, *The Iron Chest*; Petruchio, *Katherine and Petruchio*
12/13/62; Matinee, Richelieu
12/15/62; Richard III
12/16/62; Benedick, *Much Ado About Nothing*
12/17/62; Richard III
12/18/62; Hamlet
12/19–20/62; Booth's benefit on 12/19/62 and matinee on 12/20/62; Sir Edward Mortimer 2x, *The Iron Chest*; Don Caesar de Bazan 2x
12/22–23/62; Brooklyn Academy of Music; Richelieu 2x

The *Brooklyn Daily Eagle*'s critic, Walt Whitman, wrote that, as Richelieu, Booth lacked "the presence necessary to complete the illusion. He does not look the priest nor prime minister…. Mr. Booth's Richelieu is an uneven performance. His "Curse of Rome" speech, however, elicited "tumultuous applause," and although Whitman preferred Forest's version, he admitted: "there are times when Booth, as Richelieu, rises a head and shoulders above any man that we have seen in the part."

12/24/62; Sir Edward Mortimer, *The Iron Chest*; Don Caesar de Bazan

The Academy of Music published a request by sixteen Brooklyn citizens that Booth perform there and a letter from Booth agreeing to do so. That not all the actors in Brooklyn had performed in Boston is attested to by the fact that an 11 A.M. rehearsal was called on Dec. 24, 26 and 27, 1862.

12/25/62; Sir Edward Mortimer, *The Iron Chest*; Petruchio, *Katherine and Petruchio*
12/26/62; Shylock, *Merchant of Venice*; Petruchio, *Katherine and Petruchio*
12/27/62; Shylock, *Merchant of Venice*; Don Caesar de Bazan
2/9/63; Winter Garden, New York; Hamlet
2/10/63; Othello
2/11/63; Hamlet
2/12/63; Othello
2/13–14/63; Hamlet 2x
2/16–17/63; Shylock 2x, *Merchant of Venice*
2/18/63; Hamlet
2/19/63; Iago, *Othello*
2/20/63; Richard III
2/21/63; Richard III scheduled but did not occur.
2/23/63 Richelieu scheduled but did not occur because of the death of Mary Devlin Booth.

1863–1864

8/22, 24/63; American Academy of Music, Philadelphia; Richelieu 2x
8/25/63; Richard III
8/26/63; Iago, *Othello*
8/27/63; Cassius, *Julius Caesar*
8/28/63; Hamlet
8/29/63; Booth's benefit, Shylock, *Merchant of Venice*; Petruchio, *Katherine and Petruchio*
8/31/63; New Chestnut Street Theatre, Philadelphia; Sir Edward Mortimer, *The Iron Chest*; Don Caesar de Bazan
9/1/63; Hamlet
9/2–3/63; First known performance on 9/2/63; Ruy Blas 2x, *Ruy Blas*
9/4/63; Booth's benefit, Ruy Blas, *Ruy Blas*; Bertuccio, *The Fool's Revenge*
9/12/63 American Academy of Music, Philadelphia, Benefit for the U.S. Sanitary Commission; Macbeth
9/14/63; Tweedle Hall, Albany, New York; Hamlet
9/15/63; Richelieu
9/16/63; Othello
9/17/63; Richelieu
9/18/63; Booth's benefit, Sir Edward Mortimer, *The Iron Chest*; Petruchio, *Katherine and Petruchio*
9/19/63; Richelieu; Petruchio, *Katherine and Petruchio*
9/21–26/63; Winter Garden, New York; Hamlet 6x
9/28/63; Othello
9/29/63; Shylock, *Merchant of Venice*
9/30/63; Iago, *Othello*
10/1–3/63; Booth's benefit on 10/2/63; Richard III 3x
10/5–6/63; Richelieu 2x
10/7/63; Iago, *Othello*
10/8/63; Macbeth
10/9–10/63; Booth's benefit on 10/9/t63; Lucius Junius Brutus 2x, *Brutus*; Petruchio 2x, *Katherine and Petruchio*
10/12/63; Ruy Blas, *Ruy Blas*
10/13/63; Richard III
10/14–17/63 Ruy Blas 4x, *Ruy Blas*, including Booth's benefit on 10/15/63, unusual because it is a Thursday.
10/22/63; Academy of Music, New York; benefit for the U.S. Sanitary Commission; Macbeth
10/26/63; Boston Theatre; Hamlet
10/27/63; Hamlet
10/28–29/63; Richelieu 2x
10/30/63; Shylock, *Merchant of Venice*
10/31/63; Pescara, *The Apostate*
11/2–4/63; Richard III 3x

11/5/63; Sir Giles Overreach, *A New Way to Pay Old Debts*
11/6/63; Booth's benefit, Sir Edward Mortimer, *The Iron Chest*; Petruchio, *Katherine and Petruchio*
11/7/63; Richard III
11/9/63; Macbeth
11/10/63; Lucius Junius Brutus, *Brutus*
11/11/63; Othello
11/12/63; Richelieu
11/13/63; Iago, *Othello*
11/14/63; Shylock, *Merchant of Venice*; Petruchio, *Katherine and Petruchio*
11/16–18/63; Ruy Blas 3x, *Ruy Blas*
11/19/63; Macbeth
11/20/63; Booth's benefit, Lucius Junius Brutus, *Brutus*; Don Caesar de Bazan
11/21/63; Matinee, Hamlet; Evening, Pescara, *The Apostate*
11/23/63; Cassius, *Julius Caesar*
11/24/63; Othello
11/25/63; Cassius, *Julius Caesar*
11/26/63; National Thanksgiving Night; Richard III
11/27/63; Booth's benefit, Sir Edward Mortimer, *The Iron Chest*; Ruy Blas, *Ruy Blas*
11/28/63; Matinee, Ruy Blas, *Ruy Blas*; Don Caesar de Bazan
Evening, Iago, *Othello*
1/1/64; Academy of Music, Brooklyn, New York; Hamlet
1/1–2/64; Richelieu 2x
1/5–6/64; Shylock 2x, *Merchant of Venice*
1/8/64; Othello
1/9/64; Richard III
1/11/64; Hamlet
1/12/64; Romeo
1/13–15/64; Macbeth 3x
1/16/64; Winter Garden Theatre, New York; Hamlet
1/18/64 Academy of Music, Brooklyn; Cardinal Wolsey, *The Roebuck*; Booth did not appear due to bad weather.
1/19/64; Booth's benefit, Shylock, *Merchant of Venice*; Petruchio, *Katherine and Petruchio*
1/20/64; Cardinal Wolsey, *The Roebuck*
1/21/64; Richelieu
2/15/64; Grover's Theatre, Washington D.C.; Hamlet
2/16/64; Othello
2/17/64; Shylock, *Merchant of Venice*
2/18/64; Richelieu
2/19/64; Sir Edward Mortimer, *The Iron Chest*; Petruchio, *Katherine and Petruchio*
2/20/64; Richard III
2/22–24/64; Ruy Blas 3x, *Ruy Blas*
2/25/64; Lucius Junius Brutus, *Brutus*
President and Mrs. Lincoln attended the play.
2/26/64; Shylock, *Merchant of Venice*; Don Caesar de Bazan
President and Mrs. Lincoln attended the play.
2/27/64; Macbeth
2/29/64; Sir Giles Overreach, *A New Way to Pay Old Debts*
3/1/64; Ruy Blas, *Ruy Blas*
3/2/64; Hamlet
President and Mrs. Lincoln attended the play.
3/3/64; Booth's benefit, Iago, *Othello*
3/4/64; Richelieu
President and Mrs. Lincoln attended the play.
3/5/64; Richard III
3/7/64; Bertuccio, *The Fool's Revenge*
President and Mrs. Lincoln attended the play.
3/8/64; Bertuccio, *The Fool's Revenge*
3/9/64; Macbeth
3/10/64; Richelieu
President and Mrs. Lincoln attended the play.
3/11/64; Hamlet
3/12/64; Pescara, *The Apostate*; Don Caesar de Bazan
3/28–4/15/64; Niblo's Garden, New York; Bertuccio 17x, *The Fool's Revenge*
4/16/64; Benefit of the Sanitary Fair; Sir Edward Mortimer, *The Iron Chest*; Petruchio, *Katherine and Petruchio*
4/18–22/64; Raphael 5x, *The Marble Heart*, including Booth's benefit on 4/22/64
4/23/64; Winter Garden, New York
Benefit for statue of Shakespeare in Central Park. 300th anniversary of Shakespeare's birth; Romeo
5/3/64; Winter Garden, New York; Hamlet
5/4/64; Richelieu
5/5/64; Shylock, *Merchant of Venice*
5/6/64; Hamlet
5/7/64; Richard III
5/9/64; Richelieu
5/10/64; Hamlet
5/11/64; Othello
5/12/64; Hamlet
5/13/64; Booth's benefit, Iago, *Othello*
5/14/64; Hamlet

1864–1865

9/5–8/64; Walnut Street Theatre, Philadelphia; Hamlet 4x
9/9–10/64; Shylock 2x, *Merchant of Venice*; Petruchio 2x, *Katherine and Petruchio*
9/12/64; Richelieu
9/14/64; Hamlet
9/15/64; Richard III
9/16/64; Don Caesar de Bazan
9/17/64; Don Caesar de Bazan
9/19–22/64; Ruy Blas 4x, *Ruy Blas*
9/23/64; Don Caesar de Bazan
9/24/64; Lucius Junius Brutus, *Brutus*
9/26/64; Hamlet
9/27/64; Richard III
9/28–29/64; Hamlet 2x
9/30/64; Shylock, *Merchant of Venice*; Petruchio, *Katherine and Petruchio*

10/1/64; Richard III
11/25/64; Winter Garden, New York
  Benefit for the erection of a statue of Shakespeare in Central Park. Three Booth brothers perform; Brutus, *Julius Caesar*
11/26/64–3/22/65; Matinees on 2/18, 25/65; 3/4, 11, 18/65 Hamlet 100x
  On Jan. 10, 1865, Booth wrote to Emma F. Cary: "I've scarcely had breathing-time since I began operations at the Winter Garden.... This terrible success of *Hamlet* seems to swallow up everything else theatrical, and the desire I have to follow it up with something still better done, if it can be, in the way of costumes and scenery, keeps me far off in fairyland, day and night, in my dreams and in my days. I believe you understand how completely I 'ain't here' most of the time. It's an awful thing to be somebody else all the while."
3/23–24/65; Friday Matinee on 3/24/65; Iago, *Othello*
3/27/65; Boston Theatre; Hamlet
3/28/65; Iago, *Othello*
3/29/65; Macbeth
3/30/65; Richelieu
3/31/65; Booth's benefit, Lucius Junius Brutus, *Brutus*; Petruchio, *Katherine and Petruchio*
4/1/65; Matinee, Hamlet
4/3/65; Macbeth
4/4/65; Richelieu
4/5/65; Hamlet
4/6/65; Shylock, *Merchant of Venice*
4/7/65; Richard III
4/8/65; Matinee, Sir Edward Mortimer, *The Iron Chest*; Petruchio, *Katherine and Petruchio*
4/10/65; Hamlet
4/11/65; Othello
4/12/65; Hamlet
4/13/65; Richard III
4/14/65; Sir Edward Mortimer, *The Iron Chest*; Don Caesar de Bazan
4/15/65 Farewell Matinee, Hamlet
  Did not occur because of presidential assassination.

1865–1866

1/3–23/66; Winter Garden, New York; Hamlet 17x, including one matinee
1/24/66; Matinee, Ruy Blas, *Ruy Blas*
1/25–26/66; Hamlet 2x
1/27/66; Ruy Blas, *Ruy Blas*
1/29–30/66; Hamlet 2x
1/31/66; Matinee, Ruy Blas, *Ruy Blas*
2/1–23/66; Richelieu 24x
  Booth wrote to Emma Cary: "It would be difficult to explain the many little annoyances I have been subjected to in the production of 'Richelieu,' but when I tell you that it far surpasses 'Hamlet' and exceeds all my expectations, you may suppose that I have not been very idle all this while. I wish you could see it.... It really seems that the dreams of my past life — so far as my profession is concerned — are being realized. What Mary and I used to plan for my future, what Richard and I used laughingly to promised ourselves in *our model theatre*, seems to be realized — in these two plays, at least.... I have been offered from all parts of the country the means to a speedy and an ample fortune, but prefer the limit I have set, wherein I have the power to carry out my wishes, though 'on half pay' as it were.... I am in a state of 'crazy.' Acting such parts night after night is a dreadful drain upon the nervous system and affords no rest either to mind or body; so I am not myself at any time when under their influence."
2/24/66 Matinee Benefit for the House of Reception for Orphans; Ruy Blas, *Ruy Blas*
2/24–3/6/66; Richelieu 9x
3/7/66; Matinee, Hamlet
3/8–13/66; Richelieu 5x
3/14/66; Matinee, Ruy Blas, *Ruy Blas*; Petruchio, *Katherine and Petruchio*
3/21/66; Matinee, Hamlet
3/28/66; Petruchio, *Katherine and Petruchio*
3/24/66 Matinee. Benefit Union Home and School for the Children of Volunteers in the United States Service. Supported destitute children of soldiers and sailors killed in the Civil War. Role unknown
3/26/66; Ruy Blas, *Ruy Blas*; Petruchio, *Katherine and Petruchio*
3/27/66; Hamlet
3/28/66; Matinee, Don Caesar de Bazan; Petruchio, *Katherine and Petruchio*
3/29/66; Booth's benefit, Richelieu
4/23/66; Walnut Street Theatre, Philadelphia; Othello, originally scheduled as Hamlet
4/24/66; Romeo
4/25/66; Iago, *Othello*
4/26/66; Romeo
4/27/66; Booth's benefit, Shylock, *Merchant of Venice*; Petruchio, *Katherine and Petruchio*
4/28/66; Richard III
4/30–5/1/66; Ruy Blas 2x, *Ruy Blas*; Don Caesar de Bazan 2x
5/2/66; Richard III
5/3–17/66; Hamlet 13x, including two Booth benefits
5/18/66; Booth's benefit, Richelieu
5/19/66; Shylock, *Merchant of Venice*; Petruchio, *Katherine and Petruchio*
5/21/66; Hamlet
5/22/66; Richelieu
5/23/66; Hamlet
5/24/66; Iago, *Othello*
5/25/66; Booth's benefit, Richelieu
5/26/66; Richard III
5/28/66; Hamlet
5/29/66; Shylock, *Merchant of Venice*; Petruchio, *Katherine and Petruchio*

Although Booth did not like Philadelphia audiences, they still liked him. On May 29, 1866, he wrote: "So long as business [at the Winter Garden] continues good, Clarke thinks it folly to break off—and so do I; yet will I be glad when my eng^t terminates—for never was poor mortal so weary of making money.... Day after tomorrow is 'settling day' at the two theatres—here & at the Winter Garden; I am afraid at the latter place Barney Williams [Irish comic actor] has added little or nothing to the treasury, but here there will be 'much spoils'.... The play of Hamlet has been—comparatively as great a success here as in N.Y. The receipts—for the same number of nights—are larger here—I've acted it some 16 or 17 times to full houses, and although I have played a number of other parts Hamlet draws the best audiences—in every sense. I think it better mounted than at the Winter Garden." In all, Booth appeared in *Hamlet* twenty-one times in Philadelphia in the spring of 1866.

5/30/66; Richelieu
5/31/66; Hamlet
6/1/66; Booth's benefit, The Stranger
6/2/66; Bertuccio, *The Fool's Revenge*
6/4/66; Hamlet
6/5/66; Bertuccio, *The Fool's Revenge*
6/6/66; The Stranger; Don Caesar de Bazan
6/7/66; Bertuccio, *The Fool's Revenge*
6/8/66; Booth's benefit, Hamlet
6/9/66; Bertuccio, *The Fool's Revenge*
6/11/66; Sir Giles Overreach, *A New Way to Pay Old Debts*
6/12/66; Hamlet
6/13/66; Lucius Junius Brutus, *Brutus*
6/14/66; Richelieu
6/15/66; Booth' benefit; Othello
6/16/66; Pescara, *The Apostate*
6/18/66; Bertuccio, *The Fool's Revenge*
6/19/66; Hamlet
6/20/66; Ruy Blas, *Ruy Blas*; Petruchio, *Katherine and Petruchio*

1866–1867

9/3/66; Boston Theatre; Othello
9/4/66; Romeo
9/5/66; Othello
9/6/66; Shylock, *Merchant of Venice*
9/7/66; Richard III
9/8/66; Matinee, Romeo; Evening, Lucius Junius Brutus, *Brutus*
9/10–29/66; Hamlet 14x, including 3 matinees
10/1/66; Richard III
10/2/66; Othello
10/3/66; The Stranger; Petruchio, *Katherine and Petruchio*
10/4/66; Hamlet
10/5/66; Shylock, *Merchant of Venice*
10/6/66; Matinee, Ruy Blas, *Ruy Blas*
10/8–9/66; Richelieu 2x
10/10/66; Matinee, Don Caesar de Bazan; Evening, Bertuccio, *The Fool's Revenge*

On Oct. 10, 1866, the Boston critic Epes Sargent wrote to Booth: "The 'Richelieu' was grand last evening. I was sorry to see that his cough was not wholly simulated. Pray take care of it."

10/11–12/66; Booth's benefit on 10/11/66; Ruy Blas 2x, *Ruy Blas*; Petruchio 2x, *Katherine and Petruchio*
10/13/66; Matinee, The Stranger
10/15/66; Walnut Street Theatre, Philadelphia; Iago, *Othello*
10/16/66; Sir Giles Overreach, *A New Way to Pay Old Debts*
10/17/66; Othello
10/18/66; Lucius Junius Brutus, *Brutus*
10/19–20/66; Booth's benefit on 10/19/66; Romeo 2x; Petruchio 2x, *Katherine and Petruchio*
10/22/66; Shylock, *Merchant of Venice*
10/23/66; Othello
10/24/66; The Stranger
10/25/66; Ruy Blas, *Ruy Blas*
10/26/66; Booth's benefit, Shylock, *Merchant of Venice*; Don Caesar de Bazan
10/27/66; The Stranger; Don Caesar de Bazan
10/29/66; Romeo; Petruchio, *Katherine and Petruchio*
10/30/66; Ruy Blas, *Ruy Blas*; Don Caesar de Bazan
10/31/66; Richard III
11/1/66; Iago, *Othello*
11/2–3/66; Booth's benefit on 11/2/66; Richard III 2x
11/5–7/66; Richelieu 3x
11/8/66; Pescara, *The Apostate*
11/9/66; Booth's benefit, Sir Giles Overreach, *A New Way to Pay Old Debts*; Petruchio, *Katherine and Petruchio*
11/10/66; Matinee, Hamlet; Evening, The Stranger
11/12/66; Hamlet
11/13/66; Bertuccio, *The Fool's Revenge*
11/14/66; Hamlet
11/15/66; Bertuccio, *The Fool's Revenge*
11/16/66; Booth's benefit, Hamlet
11/17/66; Matinee, Richelieu; Evening, Richard III
11/19/66; Richelieu
11/20/66; The Stranger; Don Caesar de Bazan
11/21/66; Hamlet
11/22/66; Romeo; Petruchio, *Katherine and Petruchio*
11/23/66; Booth's benefit Matinee, Shylock, *Merchant of Venice*; Don Caesar de Bazan
11/24/66; Matinee, Hamlet; Evening, Pescara, *The Apostate*
11/27–29/66; Winter Garden Theatre, New York; Hamlet 3x
11/30/66; Brooklyn Academy of Music; Hamlet

On Nov. 30, Stuart presented Booth and the Winter Garden company including their "costumes, appliances and appointments" at the Brooklyn Academy of Music. Tickets were one dollar; reserved seats were fifty cents extra; family circle seats were fifty cents. For fifty cents women could visit a clairvoyant; gentlemen paid one dollar. $1.50 bought a ladies or children's ticket to the Chichester's Skating pond.

12/1/66; Winter Garden Theatre; Richard III
The Albion commented on Dec. 1, 1866: "It evidently needs no effort on the part of Mr. Booth to put himself *en rapport* with the ideal of the great Bard.... [Hamlet's characteristics and circumstances] are all 'felt' by the actor with an ease and naturalness which bespeak many points of resemblance between the 'melancholy Dane' and the artist who portrays him."

12/4/66; Richelieu
12/5/66; Matinee, The Stranger; Don Caesar de Bazan
12/6/66; Richelieu
12/7/66; Brooklyn Academy of Music; Richelieu
12/8/66; Winter Garden Theatre; The Stranger; Don Caesar de Bazan
12/11/66; Richelieu
12/12/66; Matinee, The Stranger; Petruchio, *Katherine and Petruchio*
12/13/66; Richelieu
12/14/66; Brooklyn Academy of Music; The Stranger; Don Caesar de Bazan
12/15/66; Winter Garden Theatre; Pescara, *The Apostate*

Pescara was a great success and the reviewer for *Frank Leslie's Illustrated Newspaper* likened Booth's performance to that of his father. A reporter for *The New York Clipper* wrote: "We reached the theatre just ten minutes before eight and found the lobby, from the box office to the door-keeper's gate, a mass or surging men and women. So great was the crowd that it took us eight minutes to get into the house.... The orchestra has been enlarged by placing therein over two hundred stuffed chairs, carrying the railing considerable of a distance up the parquet. The supports of the first circle have been touched up with gold leaf, and present a very neat and clean appearance. In the dress circle adjoining the proscenium, on box sides of the stage, six small private boxes like those of the French Theatre, have been built.... The curtain rose upon a brilliant assemblage, the house being crowded in every part, and hundreds were turned from the box office unable to get standing room. The sign announcing 'standing room only' was to be seen before eight o'clock. Mr. Booth's appearance was the signal for applause ... lasting several minutes. He was called before the curtain at the close of every act."

12/18/66; Hamlet
12/19/66; Matinee, Ruy Blas, *Ruy Blas*; Petruchio, *Katherine and Petruchio*
12/20/66; Hamlet
12/21/66; Brooklyn Academy of Music; Ruy Blas, *Ruy Blas*; Petruchio, *Katherine and Petruchio*
12/22/66; Winter Garden Theatre; Richard III
In Dec. 1866, the critic for *The Albion* wrote: "If there is an objection to Mr. Booth's *Richard [III]*, it is to be found in the fact that nature has not formed him for the part."

12/24/66; Benefit of the Masonic Hall Asylum Fund; The Stranger
12/26/66; Richelieu
12/27/66; Matinee, Benefit for Mr. Lingard, former proprietor of the Bowery Theatre; Role unknown
12/28/66 Brooklyn Academy of Music, Brooklyn, New York Booth's Benefit; Hamlet
Since he was one of the theatre's lessees, Booth had a great deal of freedom in the distribution of complimentary tickets. On Dec. 28, 1866, he wrote to John B. Murray: "If you do not desire the box of this evening, you can have the same for the next performance.... only let me know as soon as possible please, that the box may be disposed of — but if you can't decide just now, I'll hold it for you until the last moment."

12/29/66; Winter Garden Theatre; Iago, *Othello*
The critic for the *New-York Daily Tribune* wrote: "The theatre was not merely full — it was absolutely overwhelmed.... The play was produced with inadequate scenery.... Mrs. Methua-Scheller spoke in German in *Desdemona's* scenes with *Othello* but in all other scenes dropped ... into English.... Mr. Dawison's stage walk is at times curious and amusing. Moreover he makes the Moor a Negro in appearance. *Othello* is not a negro but a Moor, and should be represented neither as a black nor a mullatto [sic] but with a tawny or olive hue." During the run of the polyglot *Othello*, Booth played on alternate nights and gave matinees to benefit various charities. On Monday, Jan. 7, 1867, he gave a matinee benefit for the Masons and on Thursday, Jan. 10 for J W. Lingard, the manager of the burned New Bowery theatre.

12/31/67; Hamlet
1/1/67; Pescara, *The Apostate*; Petruchio, *Katherine and Petruchio*
1/2/67; Iago, *Othello*
1/3/67; Richard III
1/4/67; Iago, *Othello*
1/5/67; Pescara, *The Apostate*; Petruchio, *Katherine and Petruchio*
1/7/67; Lucius Junius Brutus, *Brutus*
1/8/67; Sir Giles Overreach, *A New Way to Pay Old Debts*
1/9/67; Lucius Junius Brutus, *Brutus*
1/10/67; Sir Giles Overreach, *A New Way to Pay Old Debts*
1/11/67; Romeo
1/12/67; Richard III

1/14–15/67; Bertuccio 2x, *The Fool's Revenge*
1/16/67; Romeo
1/17–19/67; Bertuccio 3x, *The Fool's Revenge*
1/21/67; Romeo
1/22/67; Hamlet
1/23/67; Richard III
1/24–25/67; Hamlet 2x
1/26/67; Othello
1/28–3/16/67; Shylock 41x including 2 matinees, *Merchant of Venice*

The New York Clipper's critic wrote about the acting in *The Merchant of Venice*: "Mr. Booth's Shylock was by no means a satisfactory performance.... With the exception of the first scene in the third act, when he learns of Antonio's losses, and the trial scene, he was very tame. In the trial scene, he was excellent. Few of those present will forget his manner of delivering his reason of revenge to the Duke:—'You'll ask me why I chose to have a weight of carrion flesh, &c' The cold blooded reply, so indicative of his unalienable hate: 'An oath, an oath, I have an oath in heaven;' and the bitterness of revenge in 'Ay, his *breast*, So says the *bond*. Doth it not, noble judge? Nearest his *heart*, those are the very words,' at the same time pointing with a malignant smile, with his knife, to the bond. Still more was the soul of the vindictive Jew exhibited when Portia asks him if he had a surgeon to stop the wounds of Antonio lest he do bleed to death, and he replied—'Is it so *nominated* in the *bond*?' His appearance when justice returns the ingredients of the chalice to his own lips, his dropping of the knife and scales, and the look he gave Antonio at leaving the Senate house were natural and judicious. But these few beauties do not make up for Mr. Booth's short-comings.... As Mr Booth is such a lover of Shakespeare, we are surprised to see him close the piece with the fourth act, cutting out altogether the fifth act. This was done, no doubt, because Shylock does not appear." *The Merchant of Venice* ran until Mar. 16, when Booth returned to Hamlet. Booth began doing Saturday matinees of *Merchant* on Mar. 9 but did not perform in the evenings of matinee days. As the season wore on, he limited his Saturday performances to matinees, allowing other members of the company to take their benefits on Saturday evening.

3/18/67; Hamlet
3/19/67; Ruy Blas, *Ruy Blas*
3/20/67; Richelieu
3/21/67; Romeo originally scheduled as Pescara, *The Apostate*
3/22/67; Lucius Junius Brutus, *Brutus*
3/23/67; Matinee, Romeo
3/25/67; Pescara, *The Apostate* [scheduled but not performed due to Winter Garden fire]
3/26/67; Hamlet [scheduled but not performed due to Winter Garden fire]

On Mar. 28, 1867, Launt Thompson wrote to Adam Badeau: "The fire at the Winter Garden destroyed every vestige of Booth's magnificent wardrobe, including souvenirs, presents, recent purchases—<u>everything</u>—dressing case & unworn laces—not a thing left belonging to his father—wig—toga—nor sword—Edwin is very sorry for the loss of the things that he cannot replace, nor money buy—like the jewels—that he had that were once worn by Mrs. Siddons, John Philip Kemble & Edmund Kean & the relics of his father's wardrobe.—Financially, it only set him back a while, and he takes it like a philosopher, it doesn't seem to ruffle his temper—except when he thinks that he moved his things to the theatre to save <u>Jim</u>, his donkey the trouble of daily carrying his dresses down there—his loss will be over sixty thousand dollars. Stuart just got out of theatre with his life—without taking watch or wallet—I saw him last Sunday at Edwin's going in the bedroom to put on one of Ned's shirts—When Booth told Edwina that 'Papa's theatre is burned down'—she said 'O! papa. I'm so sorry—but then you won't come home tired any more—will you?'—little darling. Booth is not 'crying over spilt milk' but is busy preparing for future action.—He was left without a pair of tights but has a score of tailors at work for him—It will not interfere with his moving into his thirty third street house—The scenery & properties for Othello were never seen by the public—Great pity! Isn't it—Shylock you saw—He improved in his part very much before the close."

4/4/67; Academy of Music, New York. Benefit for members of the Winter Garden Company; Hamlet

Stuart's testimonial benefit at Niblo's was given by three fellow managers—Jarrett, Palmer and Wheatley, at which time Stuart got the profits from an evening of the musical hit *The Black Crook*. All the members of the cast, the corps de ballet, the stage-hands and musicians gave up their salary on the night. But no benefit was given for Booth. Madame Methua Scheller, Mr. and Mrs. Leffingwell, Messrs. Gotthold, Barton Hill, Davidge and Burroughs all lost their wardrobes. Consequently Booth gave a benefit for members of the company, supported by those individuals, at the Academy of Music on Apr. 4, 1867. The receipts including outside donations reached about $3,200–$4,000 "which was divided according to the amount of salary among the company."

4/8–13/67; Boston Theatre; Hamlet 6x, including 1 matinee
4/15/67; Romeo
4/16/67; Sir Giles Overreach, *A New Way to Pay Old Debts*
4/17/67; Romeo
4/18/67; Othello
4/19/67; Lucius Junius Brutus, *Brutus*

On Apr. 19, [1867] Booth wrote to Epes Sargent from Boston: "Having now no wardrobe the few leisure moments I usually have between rehearsal and the play are employed in looking up the many little articles necessary to my costume."

4/20/67; Matinee, Romeo
4/22/67; Benedick, *Much Ado About Nothing*
4/23/67; Hamlet
4/24/67; Sir Giles Overreach, *A New Way to Pay Old Debts*
4/25/67; Booth's benefit, Shylock, *Merchant of Venice*; Petruchio, *Katherine and Petruchio*
4/26/67; Academy of Music, Providence, Rhode Island; Hamlet

The box office for one performance of *Hamlet* in Providence in Apr. 1867 was reported by *The New York Clipper* as $1,723 and by the *Boston Daily Evening Transcript* as $1,940. The ticket prices in Providence were "greatly increased from the ordinary rates."

4/27/67; Boston Theatre; Richard III
4/29–5/4/67; Richelieu 6x including 1 matinee
5/6/67; Sir Giles Overreach, *A New Way to Pay Old Debts*
5/7/67; Pescara, *The Apostate*
5/8/67; Lucius Junius Brutus, *Brutus*
5/9/67; Othello
5/10/67; Richard III
5/11/67; Matinee, Richard III
5/13/67; Richelieu
5/14/67; Hamlet
5/15/67; Richard III
5/16/67; Pescara, *The Apostate*
5/17/67; Booth's benefit, Macbeth
5/18/67; Matinee, Petruchio, *Katherine and Petruchio*; The Stranger; Evening, Iago, *Othello*
6/3–4/67 McVicker's Theatre, Chicago; Hamlet 2x

During Booth's Chicago engagement in June 1867 McVicker's Theatre charged eight, ten and thirteen dollars for private boxes. A thirteen dollar box was the equivalent of fifty-two gallery, seats which went for twenty-five cents each.

6/5–6/67; Shylock 2x, *Merchant of Venice*
6/7/67; Romeo
6/8/67; Matinee, Shylock, *Merchant of Venice*; Evening, Lucius Junius Brutus, *Brutus*

On June 9, 1867, Booth wrote to Launt Thompson from Chicago: "Money is coming in very rapidly, but I fear the hot weather will choke it off.... Will be back by July 4th."

6/10/67; Romeo

The Chicago correspondent for *The New York Clipper* wrote of Mary McVicker: "Her performance was a success, although the lady will require a deal of study before she can play leading roles to general satisfaction."

6/11/67; Richelieu

Of Mary McVicker's Julie de Mortimer on June 11, 1867, the critic for the *Chicago Tribune* wrote: "Miss McVicker's Julie was a much better performance than her Juliet. Her nervousness is ... wearing away. Except in long involved passages ... which she delivers unevenly, she did remarkably well for one so young and unused to the stage while in little, quiet, pathetic passages, she was even better than many actors of established reputation."

6/12/67; Richelieu
6/13/67; Hamlet

The critic for the *Chicago Tribune* wrote: "Miss McVicker's Ophelia was, like her Juliet and Julie, uneven in its development, the unevenness which will always be noticed in an unfinished player.... In her first scene, the farewell to Laertes and the confession to Polonius of Hamlet's tenders of love, she strove too hard and succeeded only in mincing the text and by too marked emphasis and too high a pitch of voice deprived her delivery of ... naturalness.... In the interview with Hamlet in the third act, she appeared to much better advantage and read the final soliloquy with ... pathos.... Her personation of the [mad] scene was very successful. If in the delivery of these pathetic passages, however, she would curb her tendency to prolong and sustain her phrasing, she would have appeared to still better advantage. Of her rendering of the little minor melodies and the lighter and more vivacious Valentine songs, ... we cannot speak in too high terms.... Study and proper training of the voice may yet enable her to accomplish a marked success."

6/14/67; Pescara, *The Apostate*
6/15/67; Matinee, Romeo; Evening, Pescara, *The Apostate*
6/17/67; Macbeth
6/18/67; Iago, *Othello*
6/19/67; Sir Giles Overreach, *A New Way to Pay Old Debts*
6/20/67; Richard III
6/21/67; Hamlet
6/22/67; Matinee, The Stranger; Evening, Richelieu
6/24/67; Benedick, *Much Ado About Nothing*

On June 24, 1867, McVicker played Beatrice opposite Booth's Benedick, and on June 27, Lady Macbeth to his Macbeth. Despite the fact that these are roles calling for a mature actress, she received a positive review from the critic of the *Chicago Tribune* whose only significant criticism was that her voice lacked power. During Booth's June engagement McVicker's took in $29,590 as opposed to $10,645.50 the preceding month.

6/25/67; Hamlet
6/26/67; Othello
6/27/67; Macbeth
6/28/67; Petruchio, *Katherine and Petruchio*; The Stranger
6/29/67; Matinee, Don Caesar de Bazan

6/29, 7/1/67; Evening performance on 6/29/67; Richard III 2x

7/2/67; Benedick, *Much Ado About Nothing*

7/3/67; Booth's benefit, Hamlet

7/4/67; Matinee, Romeo; Evening, Richard III

1867–1868

9/9/67; Holliday Street Theatre, Baltimore; Richard III; originally scheduled as Sir Giles Overreach, *A New Way to Pay Old Debts*

Booth and Mary McVicker opened a three-week engagement at Baltimore's Holliday Street Theatre on Sept. 9, 1867, with *Richard III*. *The Sun*'s critic wrote: "The Holliday Street Theatre was more densely crowded last night on the appearance of Mr. Booth's King Richard III than it has been on any other occasion this season. The house was really so full in all parts that even standing room could not be obtained. The audience ... [called] Mr. Booth before the curtain at the close of each act, amidst enthusiastic applause. Extra police were needed to deal with the traffic." When Booth gave a matinee at the end of his first week, "special tickets" were sold in Washington "including railroad fare." The management of the Holliday Street Theatre published the following: "This early announcement is made of the benefit of country patrons to enable them to see Mr. Booth and return home in daylight."

9/10/67; Romeo

9/11/67; Richard III

The Baltimore correspondent for *The New York Clipper* wrote: "The advent of Edwin Booth, after an absence of six [actually seven] years, has been a marked one. Each night throngs of persons are unable to gain admission to the theatre after the raising of the curtain. On the 11th, he appeared as 'Richard III,' when the excitement amounted to a *furore*; and it may be safely estimated that at least one thousand persons were denied the pleasure of witnessing the gifted young actor, so densely was the theatre packed. Booth was to have continued the present week, but having been wounded on the evening of the 12th accidentally by a pistol, his engagement closed that evening." *The Clipper*'s correspondent corrected himself the following week, stating that it was a wound made by a dagger but incorrectly identified the place as Booth's right hand.

9/12/67; Pescara, *The Apostate*

9/13/67; Benedick, *Much Ado About Nothing*

9/14/67; Richard III

9/16/67; Hamlet scheduled but cancelled

9/17/67; Hamlet scheduled but cancelled

9/18/67; Hamlet scheduled but cancelled

9/19/67; Lucius Junius Brutus scheduled but cancelled, *Brutus*

9/20/67; Shylock, *Merchant of Venice*, scheduled but cancelled

9/21/67; Matinee, The Stranger scheduled but cancelled; Petruchio [*Katherine and Petruchio*] scheduled but cancelled; Evening, *Othello* [play] scheduled but cancelled

9/23–24/67; Hamlet 2x

9/24/67; Hamlet

9/25/67; Role unknown

9/26/67; Brutus scheduled, *Julius Caesar*. Romeo substituted. On Sept. 26, 1867, during the Baltimore run, *Romeo and Juliet* was substituted for *Brutus*, "it being necessary for Mr. BOOTH to avoid the naked arms that the character of 'Brutus' requires. At the second performance of *Hamlet*, the house was exceedingly crowded though every available space was filled with temporary seats." Secured seats in the Dress circle were one dollar; secured orchestra chairs were $1.50; General Admission to the Parquette & Dress Circle was seventy-five cents; general admission to the family circle was fifty cents.

9/27/67; Booth's benefit, Shylock, *Merchant of Venice*

9/28/67; Matinee, The Stranger; Petruchio, *Katherine and Petruchio*; Evening, Othello

9/30/67; Richelieu

10/1/67; Richard III

10/2/67; Lucius Junius Brutus, *Brutus*

Booth and McVicker played Brutus and Tarquina on Oct. 2, 1867 "before a large house." As Tarquina in John Howard Payne's *Brutus* McVicker "played ... admirably. For one so young she is a most accomplished artiste. Her undoubted talent and capacity, full voice, and clear enunciation invest her acting with a rare degree of attractiveness."

10/3/67; Richelieu

10/4/67; Booth's benefit, Hamlet

10/7/67; Opera House, Pittsburgh, Pennsylvania; Hamlet

10/8/67; Shylock, *Merchant of Venice*

10/9/67; Romeo

10/10/67; Richelieu

10/11/67; Booth's benefit, Hamlet

10/12/67; Matinee, The Stranger; Evening, Richard III

In Pittsburg, "on Thursday, Friday and Saturday evenings, even standing room could not be had at any price. The gallery was filled by the most respectable and wealthy citizens who preferred to sit and stand there rather miss seeing Mr. Booth. Miss McVicker's Ophelia in 'Hamlet' was a very fine piece of acting." In Oct., 1867, the Pittsburg theatre took in $13, 273.00, the highest amount for any month in 1867.

10/14/67; National Theatre, Cincinnati, Ohio; Sir Giles Overreach, *A New Way to Pay Old Debts*

10/15/67; Romeo

When Booth and McVicker played Romeo and Juliet, in Cincinnati, he received a luke-warm review, but Mary was praised particularly for her ability to show Juliet's increasing isolation and personal growth from a "sympathy-seeking girl" to a "determined and desperate woman." The Cincinnati critic wrote: "The Juliet of Miss McVicker was a very creditable performance. The balcony scene bore the marks of the workshop, but all traces of mere acting disappeared in the subsequent scenes."

10/16/67; Othello
10/17/67; Pescara, *The Apostate*
10/18/67; Shylock, *Merchant of Venice*
When Booth and McVicker performed Shylock and Portia on Oct. 18, the Cincinnati critic wrote: "we had thought the fifth act of the play implied at least, if not nominated in the bond, but the management withhold it, and the audience, after patiently (for once) sitting till the curtain fell on what proved to be the final act, (the fourth) were obliged to be informed that the play was over."
10/19/67; Matinee, Benedick, *Much Ado About Nothing*
10/19/67; Evening, Richard III
10/21–23/67; Hamlet 3x
When Booth played Hamlet in Cincinnati on Oct. 21, the critic for the *Cincinnati Commercial* wrote: "For four hours and a half last evening, the brilliant audience assembled at the National followed the actor through the greatest of tragedies.... We were gratified that the vulgar persons who marred the close of the tragedy, by a miserable rush to get first to the doors were heartily hissed."
10/24–25/67; Richelieu 2x
10/26/67; Matinee, Iago, *Othello*; Evening, Macbeth
10/28/67; Bertuccio, *The Fool's Revenge*
10/29/67; Richelieu
10/30–31/67; Hamlet 2x
11/1/67; Booth's benefit, The Stranger; Petruchio, *Katherine and Petruchio*
11/2/67; Matinee, Romeo; Evening, Richard III
Despite the rise in prices to "double the normal rates" "all eligible seats" at the Louisville Theatre were "engaged" by the time Booth and McVicker opened, and *The Louisville Daily Journal* expected that the opening night house would be "packed." "Every portion of the house, dress-circle, parquette, and galleries was crowded, and the audience was ... the most distinguished for fashion, beauty, and culture that ever assembled in the new theatre," because Booth had not played there in nine years. In Louisville box seats went for five and eight dollars; seats in the dress circle for one dollar; reserved seats were raised to two dollars; unreserved seats in the dress circle, parquette and orchestra were raised to for $1.50 and second tier seats for fifty cents. Colored boxes were fifty cents and the gallery twenty-five cents
11/4/67; Louisville Theatre; Hamlet
An interviewer in Louisville, in 1867 wrote of Booth: "A few delicate lines about the mouth and chin mark distinctly great decision of character, but there is something about his countenance that denotes the deepest melancholy, which the eminent author, E. A. Steadman, and the poet Stoddard, have attributed to the close study of Hamlet, whose nature and character is said to have become his own. He said he looked on Hamlet as a rational being, and that if any of us were placed in Hamlet's situation, and surrounded by the same circumstances, that we would in all probability have acted in the very same way; and that he would not under any circumstances believe Hamlet insane." The critic for the *Louisville Daily Courier* wrote of McVicker's Ophelia: "We never saw the character better portrayed." When *Hamlet* was produced, the newspaper said that the support [the Louisville stock company] was "very bad.

11/5/67; Richelieu
When Booth and McVicker performed Richelieu and Julie de Mortimer, the critic for *The Louisville Daily Journal* wrote: "After his denunciation of the conspirator, Baradas, at the end of the third act, Mr. Booth was compelled to respond to the overwhelming call to the footlights.... Miss Mary McVicker showed herself a thorough artiste." The Louisville correspondent for *The New York Mirror* wrote: "Miss McVicker as Ophelia and Julie De-Mortimer obtained a success rarely accorded to so young a *debutante*.... She has that within which will, in time, astonish the country, and give another Ristori and [Jean Davenport] Lander to the stage.... [Booth's] support, with the exception of Miss McVicker, has been but meager, and had the strength of the company been adequate to their tasks, there had been nothing to complain of."
11/6/67; Richelieu originally scheduled as Iago, *Othello*
The Louisville correspondent for *The New York Clipper* wrote: "On the 6th 'Othello' was billed with Booth as Iago, but owing to Miss McVicker having been taken suddenly ill during the day, 'Richelieu' was substituted.
11/7/67; Hamlet
11/8/67; Booth's benefit, Shylock, *Merchant of Venice*; Petruchio, *Katherine and Petruchio*
11/9/67; Matinee, The Stranger originally scheduled as Romeo; Evening, Richard III
The Louisville correspondent for *The New York Clipper* wrote of Booth's *Richard III* in November 1867: "At the end of the 4th act, when the curtain should have fallen on a picture, it failed, notwithstanding Mr. Booth gave two distinct signals at the proper moment, and Richard rose from his knees and made his exit R. 1st E., venting his wrath on the prompter.... As the curtain fell on the death of Richard and amidst the cries of 'Long live Richmond, King of England,' I thought I heard the prostrate Gloster exclaim: 'For this relief much thanks,' alluding undoubtedly to the termination of his engagement."

11/11/67; DeBar's Opera House St. Louis, Missouri; Hamlet
11/12/67; Richelieu
11/13/67; Pescara, *The Apostate*
11/14/67; Hamlet
11/15/67; Booth's benefit, Benedick, *Much Ado About Nothing*
11/16/67; Richard III
11/18/67; Hamlet
11/19/67; Romeo
11/20/67; Richard III
11/21/67; Hamlet
11/22/67; Booth's benefit, Iago, *Othello*
11/23/67; Shylock, *Merchant of Venice*; Petruchio, *Katherine and Petruchio*
12/2/67; Mobile Theatre; Hamlet
12/3/67; Shylock, *Merchant of Venice*
12/4/67; Richelieu
12/5/67; Hamlet

On Dec. 2, 1867, after an absence of eight years, Booth opened as Hamlet in Mobile. The critic for the *Mobile Daily Advertiser and Register* wrote: "Booth exceeds [Edwin Forrest, Edwin Adams and Charles Kean] in his rendition of the poetic — the ideal — the spiritual beauty of the character.... The support given Mr. Booth by the company was much better than in 'Richelieu.' Miss McVicker's *Ophelia* was admirable — much superior to her *Julie de Mortimer*."

12/6/67; Romeo
12/7/67; Richard III
12/9/67; Sir Giles Overreach, *A New Way to Pay Old Debts*
12/10/67; Othello
12/11/67; Richelieu
12/12/67; Macbeth
12/13/67; Richelieu
12/14/67; Booth's benefit, Benedick, *Much Ado About Nothing*

In Dec. 1867 a Mobile critic thought Booth's Benedick, particularly in the first act, "one of the most nearly perfect pieces of acting that we have ever witnessed. Mr. Booth's Benedick was not a *merely* gay, witty, brilliant superficial ruffler. There was a degree of passion, sentiment ... infused into the character."

12/15/67; Matinee, Role unknown; Evening, The Stranger
12/16/67; Varieties Theatre, New Orleans; Romeo

When Booth and McVicker opened in New Orleans on Dec. 16, 1867, the critic for *The Daily Picayune* wrote: "Miss McVicker's *Juliet* was a charming piece of acting, if we may except some few of the situations where her voice seemed to be unequal for the portrayal of the deeper passions. This young lady is quite pretty, reads well, and possesses a certain naviete of manner which makes her very attractive." The New Orleans correspondent for *The New York Clipper* wrote: "A large, fashionable and discriminating audience greeted [Booth's] appearance with rapturous applause which continued throughout the entire performance."

12/17/67; Shylock, *Merchant of Venice*

The critic for *The Daily Picayune* wrote: "In that passage in the third act, where Shylock replies to Salarino's inquiry as to 'whether Antonio have had any loss at sea or no,' Mr. Booth's acting was thrillingly effective, and called forth loud bursts of applause from the large and brilliant audience, as also did his rendering of the next passage, commencing: 'To bait a fish withal.' The scene which follows between *Shylock* and *Tubal* was a perfect piece of acting, and when he rushed from the stage, the house, which had been as still as death, broke out in deafening applause, which brought Mr. Booth before the curtain to bow his thanks."

12/18/67; Othello
12/19/67; Sir Giles Overreach, *A New Way to Pay Old Debts*
12/20/67; Booth's benefit, Benedick, *Much Ado About Nothing*
12/21/67; Matinee, Romeo

On Dec. 21, Booth played Romeo for the matinee followed by The Stranger and Petruchio for the evening performance. The price of tickets for the matinee was one dollar. The critic for *The Daily Picayune* was amazed: "When the curtain fell upon the final act of 'Taming of the Shrew' last evening, it is natural to presume Mr. Booth must have been wearied. Playing *Romeo* at noon [actually 1 P.M.] at the matinee, and the *Stranger* and *Petruchio* at night was certainly enough to have exhausted almost any one; and yet the manner in which he dashed through the latter *role*, now courting his 'bonnie Kate,' and anon chasing the attendants about the stage, gave no evidence of weariness.... Miss McVicker's personation of the willful and perverse *Katherine* was most admirable. The more we see of this little lady, the more are we pleased with her. Her sweet girlish face and petite graceful figure win for her at once the hearts of the ladies, and the gentlemen, if they withhold their praise at first, find themselves applauding as loudly as their lady friends and laughing despite themselves." The critic for *The Daily Picayune* wrote: "On the 21st, there was a large array of ladies present at the *matinee* to witness the Romeo and Juliet of Mr. Booth and Miss McVicker. I take it that *matinees* will become a permanent feature at this favorite establishment during the season, and in view of the success of the experiment on Saturday."

12/21/67; Evening, The Stranger; Petruchio, *Katherine and Petruchio*
12/23–24/67; Hamlet 2x
12/25–26/67; Richelieu 2x
12/27/67; Iago, *Othello*
12/28/67; Matinee, Claude Melnotte, *The Lady of Lyons*; Evening, Richard III

12/30/67; Macbeth
12/31/67; Hamlet
1/1/68; Richard III
1/2/68; Richelieu
1/3/68; Booth's benefit, Macbeth
1/4/68; Matinee, Benedick, *Much Ado About Nothing*; Evening, Richard III

When Booth and McVicker opened at the New Memphis Theatre in Jan., 1868, general admission was one dollar; reserved seats were ten cents extra; third tier and colored gallery tickets were twenty-five cents and colored boxes were fifty cents. In Memphis, one dollar bought four pounds of coffee, a bushel of sweet vegetables or half a gallon of whiskey.

1/7/68; New Memphis Theater; Romeo
1/8/68; Shylock, *Merchant of Venice*
1/9/68; Richelieu

Of Booth's Richelieu, the Memphis critic wrote: "If in the first portions of the play he appeared cold and comparatively tame, he made up for it as act followed act, and reached the full grandeur of the character when he guards Julia with the awful power of the church, and bids Baradas to lose not a single trick. At the termination of the act, he was enthusiastically called before the curtain. The close of the play was very effective and was most attentively awaited by the large audience, the refinement of which was shown by none moving until the curtain was down."

1/10/68; Booth's benefit, Shylock, *Merchant of Venice*

When Booth performed Shylock for his benefit, the Memphis critic wrote: "Every seat in the dress circle and parquette was taken before the doors were opened, and the lobby was filled with standers compactly pressed against each other. The upper part of the house was likewise good.... As in witnessing his *Richelieu*, the audience was silent in its applause, so deep and thorough was its appreciation." "At his benefit ... the house was fuller and more fashionable than on any previous evening, although he repeated Shylock.... Our newspapers have not been pleased with Miss McVicker, and for a day or two, after speaking slightingly of her, have ignored her altogether. She is, in my opinion, a charming little actress, and for one so young, truly artistic. Her features are not regular, and her figure is *petite*, but she has an eloquent eye. Her voice is musical, full toned, and her emphasis true and marked. If I were to object it would be at her length of stride."

1/11/68; Matinee, Claude Melnotte, *The Lady of Lyons*; Evening, Richard III

Booth's matinee performance of *The Lady of Lyons* "did not draw a large but a very respectable audience, among which the ladies predominated; however the house was 'overflowing' for his Richard III at night." The Memphis correspondent for The *New York Clipper* wrote: [of Booth and McVicker's *Romeo and Juliet*]: "There was a fine house and some excellent acting ... [of their *Merchant of Venice*] the dress circle and the parquet were full.... *Richelieu* drew even a better house.

1/13/68; Hamlet
1/14/68; Richelieu

After Booth and McVicker appeared in *Hamlet*, on Jan. 14, 1868, a Memphis critic wrote: "Notwithstanding the sleet in the afternoon, and the two inches or more of slushy snow in the evening, the theater was crowded."

1/15/68; Macbeth
1/16/68; Hamlet
1/17/68; Booth's benefit, Claude Melnotte, *The Lady of Lyons*
1/18/68; Matinee, Role unknown; Evening, Richard III

In January 1868 Booth wrote to his friend the critic John E. Russell: "I was delighted to hear from you in melancholy Memphis—muddy, murderous Memphis! Let me hear again while here in chilly Chicago. Lost 24 hours of my life on the way from there to here—arrived safely, after many ups and downs, and colds and curses; rest until Monday—then at it again."[1]

1/27/68; McVicker's Theatre, Chicago; Shylock, *Merchant of Venice*
1/28/68; Richelieu

The Chicago correspondent for *The New York Clipper* wrote that Booth and McVicker opened in *The Merchant of Venice* "to a very large audience." The next day they played *Richelieu* "to a still larger audience, although the greatest conflagration ever known in Chicago was raging but a few blocks away." In Chicago there was no increase in prices at McVicker's Theatre except for the fact that matinees were priced the same as evening performances. Admission was seventy-five cents for unreserved seats and one dollar for "secured seats."

1/29/69; Claude Melnotte, *The Lady of Lyons*
1/30/68; Hamlet
1/31/68; Booth's benefit, Richelieu
2/1/68; Matinee, Claude Melnotte, *The Lady of Lyons*
2/1/68; Evening, Iago, *Othello*
2/3/68; Richard III

On Feb. 3, *The Chicago Tribune* reported: "The houses have been crowded every night, and on two or three occasions hundreds have been turned away, unable to obtain even standing room."

2/4/68; Hamlet

On Feb. 4, a member of the company (Mrs. Myers) played Ophelia "owing to the illness of Miss McVicker." Booth was also forced to substitute *The Stranger* and *Katherine and Petruchio* for *Romeo and Juliet* on Feb. 5.

2/5/68; The Stranger originally scheduled as Romeo; Petruchio, *Katherine and Petruchio*

2/6/68; Macbeth
2/7/68; Booth's benefit, Hamlet
2/8/68; Matinee, Romeo; Evening, Richard III
2/10/68; Music Hall, Milwaukee, Wisconsin; Hamlet

On Feb. 10, Booth and McVicker went to Milwaukee where they were supported by a portion of the Chicago company. The local critic, while grateful for Booth's presence, felt the company supported him "in some respects inadequately" and felt that the Saturday matinee of Hamlet was marked by carelessness.

2/11/68; Shylock, *Merchant of Venice*
2/12/68; Richelieu
2/14/68; Richard III
2/15/68; Booth's benefit, The Stranger; Petruchio, *Katherine and Petruchio*
2/16/68; Matinee, Hamlet; Evening, Iago, *Othello*

Booth and McVicker played a week's engagement at the Young Men's Hall in Detroit beginning Feb. 17, 1868, opening with *Hamlet*. Tickets were $1.50; one dollar in the center gallery and fifty cents in the side galleries. There was no extra charge for securing seats, and out-of-towners could do so by mail or telegraph. Theatre-goers could have *The Detroit Free Press* delivered for twenty cents per week. A bottle of Hoofland's German Bitters for ailments of the stomach and liver cost a dollar. Admission to the skating rink cost twenty-five cents. One dollar bought a center seat in the front of the gallery or a package of "French safes, a sure preventative to disease and pregnancy" while two dollars bought two center seats or a box of Dr. DeLos' Female Regulating Pills "by which those who, from any cause, deem it necessary to avoid an increase in family, can do so."

2/17/68; Young Men's Hall, Detroit, Michigan; Hamlet

In Detroit, Booth and McVicker were touring stars playing with the local stock company. "Last night the hall was densely crowded, every available seat, either in the galleries or in the body of the house being taken, as well as a huge portion of the standing-room."

2/18/68; Shylock, *Merchant of Venice*

The local critic thought that McVicker was more successful as Portia than as Ophelia.

2/19/68; Richelieu

The local critic thought that McVicker's Julie was not as "interesting as it might have been, but the fault was evidently in her natural endowments, rather than any lack of study of want of conception of the part."

2/20/68; Macbeth

As Lady Macbeth, "Miss McVicker was very successful in her closing scene at the end of the fourth act, and was called before the curtain."

2/21/68; Hamlet

When Booth performed Hamlet for a second time, "all three of the galleries were literally overflowing; every seat in the body of the hall was occupied; the space allotted to the orchestra between the front seats and the stage was crowded with chairs, all of which were taken before the curtain rose."

2/22/68; Matinee, Romeo; Evening, Richard III

When Booth and McVicker opened in Cleveland, "the buying of tickets" commenced several days in advance and on opening day, "there was a perfect rush for them so that the Academy was densely crowded."

2/24/68; Academy of Music, Cleveland, Ohio; Hamlet
2/25/68; Shylock, *Merchant of Venice*
2/26/68; Richelieu
2/27/68; Macbeth
2/28/68; Booth's benefit, Romeo
2/29/68; Matinee, Claude Melnotte, *The Lady of Lyons*; Evening, Richard III
3/9/68; Romeo
3/10/68; Shylock, *Merchant of Venice*
3/11/68; Iago, *Othello*
3/12/68; Richelieu
3/13/68; Hamlet
3/13/68; Matinee, Claude Melnotte, *The Lady of Lyons*; Evening, Richard III
3/30/68; Walnut Street Theatre, Philadelphia, Shylock, *Merchant of Venice*

Booth opened at the Walnut Street Theatre in Philadelphia on Mar. 30, 1868 and closed on May 2, 1868. His 34 performances took in $21,673, an average of only $637 each. This was, however, the second-highest monthly amount taken in by any Philadelphia theatre from May 1867 through Apr. 1868. The highest amount was $24,489 taken in Nov., 1867 when Edwin Forrest appeared.

3/n.d./68; Newark, New Jersey; Shylock, *Merchant of Venice*
3/31/68; Lucius Junius Brutus, *Brutus*
4/1/68; Sir Giles Overeach
4/2/68; Claude Melnotte, *The Lady of Lyons*
4/3/68; Booth's benefit, Shylock, *Merchant of Venice*; Petruchio, *Katherine and Petruchio*
4/4/68; Pescara, *The Apostate*
4/6/68; Richelieu
4/7/68; Macbeth
4/8/68; Othello
4/9/68; Richelieu
4/10/68; Booth's benefit, Claude Melnotte, *The Lady of Lyons*
4/11/68; Macbeth
4/13/68; Easter Monday matinee, Claude Melnotte, *The Lady of Lyons*; Evening, Iago, *Othello*
4/14/68; Iago, *Othello*, originally scheduled as Hamlet
4/15/68; Romeo
4/16/68; Hamlet
4/17/68; Booth's benefit, Benedick, *Much Ado About Nothing*

4/18/68; Bertuccio, *The Fool's Revenge*
4/20–22/68; Hamlet 3x
4/23/68; Richard III
4/24/68; Romeo
4/25/68; Matinee, Benedick, *Much Ado About Nothing*; Evening, Richard III
4/27/68; Edwin Forrest in the audience; Macbeth
4/28/68; Romeo
4/29/68; Bertuccio, *The Fool's Revenge*
4/30/68; Claude Melnotte, *The Lady of Lyons*
5/1/68; Booth's benefit, The Stranger; Petruchio, *Katherine and Petruchio*
5/2/68; Matinee, Claude Melnotte, *The Lady of Lyons*; Evening, General Grant in a box; Richard III

After Booth and McVicker played Philadelphia in Mar.-Apr. 1868, George Allen, an elderly wealthy man who had befriended Booth wrote: "If Miss McVicker would care anything for the opinions of an old non-playgoing student, please tell her with what profound sympathy and interest I followed her in her bold, but most successful, attempt to fill the part of Lady Macbeth. Mr. [Asa Israel] Fish [a wealthy admirer of Booth and Shakespeare] and myself shared entirely the feeling of the house. We could not have expected one so young and so inexperienced to have placed herself so suddenly by the side of the great artists of her profession.... As it is, mere girl as we now see her, she has already (but I forget she was a girl) 'won her spurs.' I have seen no lady under Ristori that has inspired me with so much satisfaction of the moment and so much hope for the future." The Philadelphia correspondent for *The New York Clipper* wrote: "The attendance has been equally large throughout the week. Mr. Booth is supported by Miss McVicker, who, as she becomes better acquainted with the good people of the Quaker City, may make a good impression."

5/11/68; Music Hall, Worcester, Massachusetts; Hamlet
5/12/68; Academy of Music, Providence, Rhode Island; Hamlet
5/13/68; Music Hall, Springfield, Massachusetts; Hamlet
5/14/68; Tweedle Hall, Albany, New York; Hamlet
In Albany, in 1868, one dollar bought a pair of ladies' kid gloves or a reserved seat.
5/15/68; The Stranger; Petruchio, *Katherine and Petruchio*
5/16/68; Richelieu
5/18/68; Allyn Hall, Hartford, Connecticut; Hamlet
5/19/68; Richelieu
5/20/68; Music Hall, New Haven, Connecticut; Hamlet
5/21/68; Richelieu
5/22/68; Academy of Music, Providence, Rhode Island Richelieu
5/23/68; The Stranger; Petruchio, *Katherine and Petruchio*
5/25/68; Shannahan's Opera House, Newport, Rhode Island; Hamlet

When Booth played Hamlet in Newport, Rhode Island on May 25, 1868, tickets were $1.50 for reserved chairs in the orchestra and parquette, one dollar for general admission and for reserved seats in the family circle and fifty cents for general admission to the family circle.

5/26/68; Liberty Hall, New Bedford, Massachusetts; Hamlet
5/27/68; Salem, Massachusetts; Role unknown
5/28–29/68; Portland, Maine; Roles unknown
5/30/68; Music Hall, Lowell, Massachusetts; Richelieu
6/1/68; Academy of Music, Providence, Rhode Island; Richard III
6/4/68; Griswold Opera House, Troy, New York; Hamlet
6/5–6/68; Roles unknown

1868–1869

In the fall of 1868 still in need of money, Booth went back to work as a traveling star, supported by stock companies in Pittsburgh, Cincinnati, Toledo, Detroit, Boston, Chicago and Buffalo. The stock company was far from dead in medium-sized and large American cities; however, the Toledo company accompanied him to Detroit, and when he played Milwaukee, he had to use a company put together from McVicker's Chicago Theatre the same way June had put one together the preceding year. When he played Toledo, and Detroit, he was playing under the management of Barney Macauley.

9/7/68; New Opera House, Pittsburgh, Pennsylvania; Role unknown
9/8/68; Lucius Junius Brutus, *Brutus*
9/9/68; Richelieu
9/10/68; Hamlet
9/11/68; Booth's benefit, Shylock, *Merchant of Venice*; Petruchio, *Katherine and Petruchio*
9/12/68; Matinee, Claude Melnotte, *The Lady of Lyons*; Evening, Richard III
9/14/68; National Theatre, Cincinnati, Ohio; Hamlet

In Cincinnati in Sept. 1868 the local critic complained: "The business of the play, always under the direction of the reigning star, was well performed under Mr. Booth's superintendence, but the support given last night hardly filled the measure of expectation. The bane of minor characters, rant, appeared in larger quantity than the audience have yet experienced."

9/15/68; Shylock, *Merchant of Venice*
9/16/68; Hamlet
9/17/68; Richelieu
9/18/68; Booth's benefit, Benedick, *Much Ado*

About Nothing; Petruchio, *Katherine and Petruchio*
9/19/68; Matinee, Claude Melnotte, *The Lady of Lyons*; Evening, Richard III
9/21/68; White's Hall, Toledo, Ohio; Hamlet
9/22/68; Shylock, *Merchant of Venice*
9/23/68; Richelieu
9/24/68; Iago, *Othello*
9/25/68; Booth's benefit, Hamlet
9/26/68; Matinee, Claude Melnotte, *The Lady of Lyons*; Evening, Richard III
9/28/68; Young Men's Hall, Detroit, Michigan; Hamlet
9/29/68; Richelieu
9/30/68; Lucius Junius Brutus, *Brutus*
10/1/68; Richard III
10/2/68; Matinee, Claude Melnotte, *The Lady of Lyons*; Evening, Booth's benefit, Benedick, *Much Ado About Nothing*
10/5–8/68; Boston Theatre; Hamlet 4x
10/9/68; Benedick, *Much Ado About Nothing*
10/10/68; Matinee, Claude Melnotte, *The Lady of Lyons*; Evening, Shylock, *Merchant of Venice*; Petruchio, *Katherine and Petruchio*
10/12–14/68; Richelieu 3x
10/15/68; Othello
10/16/68; Booth's benefit, Claude Melnotte, *The Lady of Lyons*; Petruchio, *Katherine and Petruchio*
10/17/68; Matinee, Romeo; Evening, Richard III
10/19/68; Hamlet
10/20/68; Richelieu
10/21/68; Claude Melnotte, *The Lady of Lyons*; Petruchio, *Katherine and Petruchio*
10/22/68; Richard III
10/23/68; Booth's benefit, Lucius Junius Brutus, *Brutus*; Don Caesar de Bazan
10/24/68; Matinee, Hamlet; Evening, Macbeth
10/26/68; Shylock, *Merchant of Venice*; Petruchio, *Katherine and Petruchio*
10/27/68; Richard III
10/28/68; Lucius Junius Brutus, *Brutus*; Don Caesar de Bazan
10/29/68; Eugene de Morny in *Love's Ordeal* by Edmund Falconer
10/30/68; Booth's benefit, Eugene de Morny, *Love's Ordeal*
10/31/68; Matinee, Eugene de Morny, *Love's Ordeal*; Evening, Richard III
11/2/68; Benefit of Mrs. Junius Brutus Booth Jr.; Othello
11/3/68; Macbeth
11/16/68; McVicker's Theatre Chicago; Lucius Junius Brutus, *Brutus*

Booth opened in Chicago on Nov. 16, 1868, as Lucius Junius Brutus. The local critic thought his "support was mediocre and in some instances very bad." The critic for the *Chicago Tribune* felt that "although ... still juvenile in her action," McVicker "made a very acceptable Julie, dressed ... with exquisite taste." The local reviewer for the *Chicago Tribune* thought "her physique" was "well adapted" to Ophelia. Financially the engagement was a great success, "attracting overflowing houses." In Oct., 1868, McVickers took in $17,974, in comparison to its nearest competitor, Wood's Museum, which took in $11,952.

11/17/68; Shylock, *Merchant of Venice*

When Booth performed Shylock, in 1868, the *Chicago Tribune* critic wrote: "The stereotyped notion of the meanly clad, cringing, servile Israelite who never, in the presence of his superiors, rises above his submission to a dominant race, but chews in silence the bitter cud of contumely, is totally set aside by Booth, who dresses *Shylock* ... in the rich, fanciful garb affected by the wealthy Jews of that period, with iron-gray hair and beard, brown and green gaberdine [sic], scarlet belt, leathern pouch, and the orange bonnet worn as a badge of sufferance. The gait is infirm and tottering the expression dark, scowling and cunning.... Mr. Booth's personification of Shylock intentionally deprived the character of any traits ... calculated to enlist sympathy ... the contemptuous shrug of the shoulder, the sardonic leer, the affected gaiety at the bare idea of the "merry bond" ... are perfection ... the cold sordid calculating Jew ... cares more for a jewelled [sic] ring than for 'a wilderness of'— daughters;... in the interview with Tubal ... Booth ... raves and groans over the reckless prodigality of his daughter, and now chuckles with fiendish exultation over the straits of his hated creditor."

11/18/68; Richelieu

In Nov. 1868 the *Chicago Tribune* critic wrote: "Mr. Booth ... has not fallen into the common error of making Richelieu some twenty years older than he really was. His make-up is not so old as that of Kean or Forrest, and in fact represents Richelieu very nearly at his real age.... Although weak, feeble and tottering and although racked with a cough that is painfully natural, he yet preserves a large degree of life ... and nervous energy.... In the second act the lifting of the falchion, and the prostration and coughing consequent upon the effort, was an effective piece of physical action, but like the sharpening of the knife upon in the shoe in The Merchant of Venice, we think it detracts from the dignity of the play."

11/19/68; Othello
11/20/68; Hamlet
11/21/68; Matinee, Shylock, *Merchant of Venice*; Evening, Pescara, *The Apostate*
11/23/68; Richard III
11/24/68; Romeo
11/25/68; Hamlet
11/26/68; Matinee, The Stranger; Petruchio, *Katherine and Petruchio*; Evening, Lucius Junius Brutus, *Brutus*

11/27/68; Richelieu
11/28/68; Matinee, Romeo; Evening, Richard III
11/30/68; Macbeth

In Nov., 1868, the receipts for Booth's first two weeks in Chicago, where he played to 24,198 people, totaled $24,484.00. The Chicago receipts were Monday, Brutus, $1,582; Tuesday, Shylock, $1,400; Wednesday, Richelieu, $1,747; Thursday, Othello, $1,488; Friday, Hamlet, $2,098; Saturday, Shylock (matinee), Pescara (evening) $2,897; Total first week $11,212.00; Monday, Richard III, $1,740; Tuesday, Romeo, $1,738; Wednesday, Hamlet, $1,983; Thursday, The Stranger, Petruchio, $1,494; Thursday, Brutus, $2,026; Friday, Richelieu, $1,611; Saturday, Romeo (matinee), Richard III (evening) $2,680.00; Weekly total $13,272.00. Saturdays were profitable, because he played two performances. The Thanksgiving Thursday matinee played to a fairly small house, but the performance that evening, was far more successful, presumably because audience members had already had their family dinner. Booth performed Hamlet and Richelieu on Friday night, because they were his big draws and remained so throughout his career. In this case, however, *Richelieu* drew poorly, because it was scheduled on the night after a holiday, traditionally a slow day in the nineteenth-century American theatre.

12/1/68; Claude Melnotte, *The Lady of Lyons*
12/2/68; Richelieu
12/3/68; Hamlet
12/4/68; Richard III
12/5/68; Matinee, Claude Melnotte, *The Lady of Lyons*; Evening, Hamlet
12/8/68; Music Hall, Milwaukee, Wisconsin; Hamlet
12/9/68; Richard III
12/10/68; Matinee, Claude Melnotte, *The Lady of Lyons*; Evening, Romeo
12/14/68; Academy of Music, Buffalo, New York; Hamlet
12/15/68; Richelieu
12/16/68; Richard III
12/17/68; Romeo
12/18/68; Booth's benefit, Hamlet
12/19/68; Matinee, Claude Melnotte, *The Lady of Lyons*; Evening, Othello

Five nights in Buffalo in Dec. 1868 grossed $7,189.00 of which Booth and his manager, James McVicker, got 50 percent. The Dec. 14–19, 1868, receipts in Buffalo were Monday, *Hamlet* $1072; Tuesday, *Richelieu*, $965; Wednesday, *Richard III*, $1,129; Thursday, *Romeo*, $970; Friday (Booth's benefit) *Hamlet* $1,329; Saturday matinee, *The Lady of Lyons*, $712.50, Saturday evening, *Othello*, $1,003.50. The Buffalo correspondent for *The New York Clipper* wrote that "had the house been capable of accommodating more people, the receipts would have been larger."

12/21/68; New Opera House, Pittsburgh, Pennsylvania; Richard III

On Dec. 21, 1868, Booth opened in Pittsburgh under McVicker's management. The local critic wrote of Mary: "We were not particularly pleased with Miss McVicker, though a charming and spirited actress. None will gainsay Miss McVicker's talent and ability in most of the roles she assumes, but she fails to put enough feeling or to render with a conspicuous brilliancy the faithful, loving and constant Julie." Tickets at the New Opera House in Pittsburgh were $10 for Private Boxes, two dollars for orchestra chairs, one dollar for reserved seats in the parquette and dress circle as well as general admission and fifty cents for the gallery.

12/22/68; Richelieu
12/23/68; Hamlet
12/24/68; Shylock, *Merchant of Venice*
12/25/68; Matinee, Benedick, *Much Ado About Nothing*; Evening, Iago, *Othello*
12/26/68; Matinee, Hamlet; Evening, Iago, *Othello*
2/3–4/10/69; Booth's Theatre, New York; Romeo 58x including 7 matinees

The critic for the *New York Herald* wrote that both Booth and McVicker had a tendency to "overact." The correspondent for Washington's *Daily National Intelligencer* thought her Juliet "marred by shy timidity." The critic for the *Leader* wrote: "We do not know why it is, but actresses of Western education and experience lack perfection of grace; their tones, in expressing sentiment, seem odd and harsh, and Miss McVicker is no exception to this judgement." Only the critic for *The New York Albion* thought Mary McVicker's Juliet work "noteworthy," because her stature was well suited to "a heroine of fourteen." The *Dispatch* said that "in the balcony scene, ... [Booth] was ineffective and boyish and by far too volatile and light of foot and gesture." The critic for *The New York Leader* wrote that Booth "never is the character. He always acts it. He plays not Romeo but the handsome vain and pensive Booth.... Throughout the play it seems as if Mr. Booth were continually advancing to the footlights and in his weirdest and most somber manner asking his audience whether they are not astonished at the perfection of his art and his ability to sustain the histrionic reputation of the Booths." William Winter's review criticizing Booth's Romeo for its lack of "a certain dashing manliness of personality," illustrates a vision of the part so constant in the nineteenth century that many actresses specialized in the role. In addition to Charlotte Cushman, Mrs. Malverna Jones played Romeo to her daughter Avonia's Juliet; Mrs. Alexina Fisher Baker played the role to Matilda Heron's Juliet at the American Theatre in San Francisco on Jan. 2, 1854; Susan Denin played Romeo to her sister Kate's Juliet at the same theatre on Apr. 15, 1854. Winter's review includes: "Juliet was a thoroughly intelligent performance. It was a good deal from the head, however, and not enough from the heart. The lady's beauty lacks softness, and, so too, apparently does her temperament. She seemed always to possess the character and scarcely ever to be possessed by it." On Feb. 12, 1869, Booth wrote to John E. Russell: "I opened on the 3rd — you can guess the particulars. Lester Wallack requested me to defer it till then to give him a chance to use the 1st & so I yielded for the sake of the cause I battle for." On Mar. 15, 1869, Booth wrote to John E. Russell: "Lent has hurt my trade a little, but the success is great — In spite of the blackguardians & the pot-house lawyers, and the silence w<u>h</u> now prevails—finding their abuse did no harm, they have concluded to say nothing. Winter has done all he could — having pledged to do as little as he possibly could. Giving all the praise to Wallack's tawdry, wretched burlesque of Shakespeare, with his shabby leaves & tinsely drapes. I'll have to live this thing down. Everybody is delighted with the acting of every member of my company — many private assurances by letter & otherwise convince me of this— in addition to the great applause & strict attention paid to everything from the beginning to the end of the play. Stuart has broken his leg — the wrong end — unfortunately, and until he dies, I will not look for fairness from the papers here. He has done his work well.... I'll fight through Lent, and then do Othello. Adams is unwell, but the audiences as yet don't know it — I hope they won't. If I discharge him the crickets [critics] w<u>d</u> deluge me with abuse —for they try to elevate him above me. I look for nothing but abuse now, and must be content to grin & bear it." Lester Wallack had opened a production of *Much Ado About Nothing* at this theatre on Feb. 1, two days before Booth opened *Romeo*. It received a positive review in *The New York Times*, but following the initial notices, the production faded into journalistic obscurity. On Mar. 27, 1869, *The New York Albion* reported that Booth's Theatre had taken in $43,751 in the first month of *Romeo and Juliet*. The burlesque show at Niblo's had taken in $54,486; Wallack's revival of *Much Ado About Nothing* took in $24,409 and Brougham's revival of *The Merchant of Venice* $11,295. By late Feb. the lower part of the house was still crowded, but the gallery "was not so liberally patronized." In Mar. 1869, Booth's Theatre took in $35,343, making it third to Wallack's ($35,602) and Niblo's Garden ($41,013).

4/12–24/69; Othello 12x including 2 matinees
4/26–5/6/69; Iago 10x including 1 matinee, *Othello*
5/7/69; Academy of Music, New York Matinee Rehearsal; Manfred, *Manfred*
5/7–8/69; Booth's Theatre, New York; Matinee on 5/8/69, Iago, *Othello*
5/8/69; Evening Academy of Music Philharmonic Society Concert Manfred — Booth read Byron's tragic poem to Schumann's incidental music. Booth ultimately agreed to do a reading of Manfred on the basis that the text would be put in large type so that the book could be placed on a music stand.
5/10–15/69; Booth's Theatre, New York; Othello 6x including one matinee

Othello was due to open on Apr. 5, 1869, but was postponed for a week. On opening night, the scenery did not work "smoothly," and the play finished at a quarter to twelve. The reviewer for *The New York Albion* wrote: "Throughout the earlier scenes the dignified mien of the officer is preserved, and the insidious approaches of jealousy ... are finely portrayed. The *Desdemona* of Miss McVicker is a very pleasing performance but by no means a great one. The bed scene of the last act is especially weak, the preparations for her murder being apparently regarded by her without the slightest terror.... Miss McVicker's *Juliet* was a much better performance. The critic for *The Sun* wrote of Booth's make-up: "The old doubt recurs as to what complexion Othello had. It does not seem to us that Mr. Booth has hit the mark. His glass may tell him that he looks dark enough to be like the Moor, but that is certainly not the effect from the auditorium. His color is decidedly not that of an oriental of any nation whatever. There is no swarthiness or sunburn in it." The critic for *The New York Leader* wrote of Booth's *Othello*: "There is not a speech, not a dialogue, not a scene in which Othello figures, where Booth seems even to forget his individual presence and reputation.... Mr. Booth makes Othello more of a scholar than a soldier.... Mr. Booth makes Othello an intellectual hero, familiar with the art of oratory.... When Othello appeals to the duke in the second act, Mr. Booth impresses us with the most skillful flourishes such as no rude soldier is supposed to be familiar with.... Instead of seeming incapable of discerning the contradictions in Iago's conduct and conversation, Booth apparently penetrates the arch intriguer's meaning at a glance and while the text of the play makes him extol the honesty of Iago, he seems to know that it is hollow and false.... He may be accused of "playing with his eyes" too much, but this could easily be forgotten if he would put aside other mannerisms peculiar only to Booth.... Miss McVicker makes an easy and fluent Desdemona, and what she lacks in force makes up in sweetness.... But she still maintains the questionable habit of dressing contrary to the requirements of her part. All her costumes are anachronisms. While all the dresses are rich, costly and elegant, they are not suited to the time and customs of the play.... Her voice in singing loses all the harshness and bad intonation which characterizes most of her elocutionary efforts. The reviewer for *The New York Leader* wrote of Booth's

Iago: "Having traveled the gamut of Shakespearean characters, Mr. Booth has settled down into the tamest and most commonplace Iago that ever trod the stage. He ambled as Romeo, glared as Othello but is eminently mild as Iago. He is the most gentle and civilized Iago we ever remember to have seen.... It is throughout a cold, apathetic spiritless Iago.... Mr. Booth is an effect of puffery.... He can play Edwin Booth off upon the public, but nothing else. So that whether he plays Richelieu or Hamlet, or Romeo, or Othello or Iago, the personation is identical in gesture, in monotone, in lackadaisical in gesture, in monotone, in lackadaisicality, in look, in stride, in claptrap, the only difference being that there are differences in textual variations. He never merges Edwin Booth in any personation.... Some critic has ... unjustly and ridiculously accused Mr. Booth of filling up his company with mediocre actors [in order to show how fine his own acting is].... Some of the members of his company would be more generally liked in the capacity of ushers in the lobby than as actors upon the stage." The reviewer for *The New York Herald* wrote: "It was a performance so toned down as to lose all point." The critic for *The New York Dispatch* wrote: "The *Iago* of Mr. Booth has been made the subject of severe condemnation by one or two of our leading local journals, and in this we think that we see more of individual spite — or, at least of ill-feeling — than a desire to do even-handed justice. Indeed, some of the strictures upon Mr. Booth's *Iago* have shown something that was very nearly akin to venom, though veiled at times under the specious professions of candour, and at other times illustrated by very high sounding phrases for which the dictionary must have been drawn upon.... That Mr. Booth's *Iago* is not the best that has been given in this metropolis during the present generation, we freely admit; but there are few actors of the present day who are his superior in the part." Despite the mediocre reviews, during the first week of *Othello*, every seat in the orchestra and the first two balconies was occupied.

5/17/69; Iago, *Othello*
5/18/69; *Othello*
5/19/69; Iago, *Othello*
5/20/69; *Othello*
5/21/69; Iago, *Othello*
5/22, 24/69; *Othello* 2x
5/25/69; Iago, *Othello*
5/26/69; Matinee, Manfred, "assisted by the members of the Philharmonic Society with Schumann's original music. Chorus under the direction of Mr. Agricolpauer, Conductor of the Liederkranz Society. The violinist Ole Bull took part in the performance"; Evening, Othello
5/27/69; Iago, *Othello*
5/28/69; Benefit of Mary McVicker; *Othello*
5/29/69; Matinee, Last performance by Mary McVicker; Iago, *Othello*

In June 1870 Booth's Theatre took in $19,375, lagging behind the New York Circus ($21,574), Wallack's ($24,496), the Olympic ($26,506) and Niblo's Garden ($29,869). In July, Booth's theatre ranked third in box office receipts, having taken in $23,542, behind the Olympic ($23,613) and Niblo's Gardens ($24,066). In Aug. 1869, Booth's took in $41,834 as opposed to its nearest competitor, Niblo's which only took in $23,833. In Sept., the theatre took in $49,144 as opposed to Niblo's $35,595. In all, Booth's took in $383,437 in 1869; it was the highest gross of any theatre in the city, followed only by Niblo's Garden at $381,997 and Wallack's Theatre at $345,573. The monthly box office receipts for Booth's were Feb., 1869, $45,754; Mar., 1869, $35,343; Apr., 1869, $41,495; May, 1869, $33,917; June, 1869, $19,375; July, 1869, $20,842; Aug., 1869, $41,804; Sept., 1869, $41,144; Oct., 1869, $34,339 (as opposed to $27,422 earned by Wallack's); Nov., 1869, $33,814 (with Wallacks running a close second at $34,488 and Niblo's third at $38,450); Dec., 1869, $23,580. On Thanksgiving Day, Booth's took in $2,388, coming in second only to Niblo's Garden (3,327.75). During the last week of his engagement, Booth played Othello and Iago, each on three nights. On May 24 and 25, Mrs. Winters played Desdemona due to Mary McVicker's "absence." On June 13, the *New York Dispatch* told its readers: "It is rumored that Miss McVicker has retired from the stage." In May, the theatre took in $33,917 to $28,818 for the Olympic and $23,096 for Niblo's.

1869–1870

9/10/69; Academy of Music, New York J. G. Hanley Benefit Fund; Iago, *Othello*
9/20–22/69; Walnut Street Theatre, Philadelphia; Hamlet 3x

Booth opened at the Walnut Street Theatre on Sept. 20 and closed on Oct. 30, 1869, taking in $22,370 during 44 performances for an average of only $508 per performance. Opening night at the Walnut (9/20/1869), the theatre "was literally crammed in every part, the sultry and oppressive atmosphere proved no drawback. On Sept. 25, 1869, Edwin Forrest wrote to his friend James Oakes from Philadelphia: "I went to the Walnut Street Theatre on Monday night last to see Edwin Booth's Hamlet and was sorely disappointed — It was the most purposeless performance of the part I ever saw — he did not even read it intelligently."

9/23/69; Shylock, *Merchant of Venice*
9/24–25/69; Booth's benefit on 9/24/69 and a matinee on 9/25/69; Claude Melnotte 2x, *The Lady of Lyons*
9/25/69; Evening, Pescara, *The Apostate*
9/27–29/69; Hamlet 3x

9/30/69; Claude Melnotte, *The Lady of Lyons*
10/1–2/69; Booth's benefit on 10/1/69 and a matinee on 10/2/69; Benedick 2x, *Much Ado About Nothing*
10/2/69; Evening, Shylock, *Merchant of Venice*
10/4/69; Richelieu
10/5/69; Lucius Junius Brutus, *Brutus*
10/6/69; Iago, *Othello*
10/7/69; Richelieu
10/8/69; Booth's benefit, Othello
10/9/69; Matinee, Claude Melnotte, *The Lady of Lyons*; Evening, Richard III
10/11/69; Macbeth
10/12/69; Claude Melnotte, *The Lady of Lyons*
10/13/69; Richard III
10/14/69; Bertuccio, *The Fool's Revenge*
10/15–16/69; Matinee on 10/16/69; The Stranger 2x
10/16/69; Evening, Macbeth
10/18/69; Richelieu
10/19/69; The Stranger; Don Caesar de Bazan
10/20/69; Othello
10/21/69; Hamlet
10/22/69; Booth's benefit, Shylock, *Merchant of Venice*; Don Caesar de Bazan
10/23/69; Matinee, Don Caesar de Bazan; Petruchio, *Katherine and Petruchio*; Evening, Richard III
10/25/69; The Stranger; Petruchio, *Katherine and Petruchio*
10/26/69; Hamlet
10/27/69; Shylock, *Merchant of Venice*; Don Caesar de Bazan
10/28/69; Claude Melnotte, *The Lady of Lyons*
10/29–30/69; Matinee on 10/30/69; Hamlet 2x
10/30/69; Evening, Role unknown
11/4/69; Boston Theatre; Hamlet

After Philadelphia, Booth toured for two weeks to the Boston Theatre then managed by his brother June. He opened in Boston on a Thursday "to an audience which occupied every seat and every inch of standing room, but, according to *The New York Clipper*, "his support in some cases was good, but it was by no means what a first-class theatre should provide." He planned to return for a four-week engagement in the spring of 1870, but this did not materialize.

11/5/69; Richelieu
11/6/69; Matinee, Claude Melnotte, *The Lady of Lyons*; Evening, Richard III
11/8/69; Hamlet
11/9/69; Richelieu
11/10/69; Richard III
11/11/69; Shylock, *Merchant of Venice*; Petruchio, *Katherine and Petruchio*
11/12/69; Booth's benefit, Hamlet
11/13/69; Matinee, The Stranger; Petruchio, *Katherine and Petruchio*; Don Caesar de Bazan; Evening, Macbeth
11/15/69; Music Hall, New Haven, Connecticut; Hamlet
11/16/69; Richelieu
11/17/69; Roberts' Opera House, Hartford, Connecticut; Hamlet
11/18/69; The Stranger; Petruchio, *Katherine and Petruchio*

In the fall of 1869 Booth played with stock companies in Boston and Philadelphia but worked with a touring company from the Boston Theatre in a tour of smaller New England cities. Hartford was a disaster artistically, although financially reasonable. The total receipts for the two nights were "$3,014, making a net profit to Edwin of $1,150 as he takes one-half of the gross income"; however, the local critic reported: "A miserable support was given in 'Hamlet' on Wednesday evening, owing to the fact that the company here was only a fragment of the Boston theatre company, the manager having a portion of his stock in Worcester and the rest in Providence on the same night; but on Thursday evening an entirely new support was furnished.... The comedy [*Katherine and Petruchio*] was horribly cut up — worse by considerable than the usual stage version. No orchestra was furnished on either evening, the management depending upon local musicians who were all previously engaged for Thanksgiving parties, but a Weber piano was substituted and was skillfully manipulated by Mr. Phelps organist at the Center Church."

11/19/69; Music Hall, Worcester, Massachusetts; Hamlet
11/20/69; Boston Theatre, Benefit of Junius Brutus Booth Jr.; Richard III
11/22/69; Music Hall, Portland, Maine; Hamlet
11/24/69; Academy of Music, Providence, Rhode Island; Hamlet

In Providence, the local critic wrote: "The sadness of the delineation would have become painfully oppressive, if it were not that the unequal support Mr. Booth received turned into a partial comedy what was intended to be a deep tragedy. Ophelia was lackadaisical and painfully uninteresting; the Queen had stentorian lungs; the King looked like a barber; and Laertes like a popinjay while the solemnity of the ghostly visitant degenerated into a farce."

1/5–2/12/70; Booth's Theatre, New York; Hamlet 34x including 6 matinees

The critic for *The New York Albion* wrote: "The revival of 'Hamlet,' now running at Booth's Theatre, has been signalized by lavish expenditure in scenic illustration." The *New York Dispatch*, thought Booth's work "a typification of genius" but his support "mediocre." *The New York Times* described the revival as "sumptuous" but flawed. "The costumes adopted are significant rather of originality than of demonstrable correctness…. Whether Danish or not, his <u>Hamlet</u> dresses are in general harmony with the North of Europe costume of the supposed period of the tragedy.... The dress of the Ghost ... might be better. It looks too modern, and has a white look that is not ... ghostly.... On the first night, Mr. Waller [as the ghost] was sometimes slightly at fault in the words.... In a general way the acting is rather too much subordinated to the principal figure for the best possible effect. It is undoubtedly true that most people go mainly to see Mr. BOOTH, and equally so that subordination of the same sort has been habitually carried further by most prominent actors than it is carried by him." The Player Queen was performed by the fifteen year old theatre call boy, Master Willie Seymour. Booth restored Claudius' third act soliloquy. Booth's original plan was to perform only on Monday, Wednesday and Friday evenings and Saturday matinees, leaving the rest of the time for Emma Waller to give her Meg Merrilies in *Guy Mannering*. As it turned out, Waller played Monday, Tuesday and Saturday evenings, and Booth performed Wednesday, Thursday Friday evenings and Saturday matinee. In Jan. 1870 the critic for *The New York Times* wrote: "The free use of seats from which to deliver the soliloquies and long speeches gives variety to the scene." On Jan. 18, 1870, Charles W. Clarke, then twenty-one, a bookkeeper and correspondent in New York, attended the first of eight *Hamlet* performances he would see. Although Booth saw Shakespeare in terms of romantic realism, Clarke understood that the plays were far more abstract: "Booth's Hamlet is not natural. Shakespeare's Hamlet is not natural.... Booth's Hamlet is full of art, full of mechanical rhetoric ... too ideal for life. Yet ... full of human nature." Clarke reported that when Hamlet says to Ophelia: "I could interpret between you and your love if I could see the puppets dallying," Booth spoke "the first half of the sentence as an aside ... inaudible to Ophelia and ... spoken with sort of melancholy" and then turned "if I could see the puppets dallying" into an expression of impatience connecting it with "Begin murderer; leave thy damnable faces and begin." Clarke described the end of the closet scene: When Hamlet says: "Once more, good night," Booth bowed his head. Gertrude looked at him and started away "with her hands at her face." She then turned impulsively and stepped "toward him, raising both hands over him as if to impart benediction." He raised "his head sadly" and saw them there. He started and drew in a "breath audibly," reach up and pushed "her hands away with the manner of one who is interrupting a sacrilege." She threw "her head a little back with look of misery" as she noted the import of his action. He rose slowly, "with some dignity and spoke ... "When you are desirous to be blessed I'll blessing beg of you." Tickets for the 1870 *Hamlet* at Booth's Theatre could be purchased two weeks in advance. The gross receipts at Booth's Theatre for the first ten nights of "Hamlet" were as follows: Wednesday, Jan. 5th, $3,303.50; Thursday, Jan. 6th, $3,145.50; Friday, Jan. 7th, $2,757.50; Saturday matinee, Jan. 8th, $2,380; Monday, Jan. 10th, $2,450; Tuesday, Jan. 11th; $2,675; Wednesday, Jan. 12th, $2,960; Thursday, Jan. 13th, $2,705.50; Friday, Jan. 14th, $2,808; Saturday matinee, Jan. 15th, $2,113.50. The total was $27,290. In Jan., 1870 Booth's Theatre took in $54,423, as opposed to its nearest competitor, Wallack's with $32,879. In Feb., the theatre took in $36,327, coming in second to the Grand Opera House's $38,819. *Hamlet* averaged consistently over $2,000 a night the first weeks, then went down to $1,700, closing at $2,513.70 with constant good sales. Booth restored the entire passage in Act I, scene v in which Hamlet mocks the Ghost. He later regretted the decision, telling William Winter: "So much depends on the subordinate actors that I really have regretted the restoration of such a simple bit as the "Truepenny" & c in Hamlet; Horatio and Marcellus cannot comprehend the little required of them there, and invariably mar all I try to do."

2/12/70; Steinway Hall, New York; Reading of Collins' The Passions

2/14–3/19/70; Booth's Theatre; Hamlet 30x including 5 matinees. By Mar. 12, "the upper gallery was not largely attended" during *Hamlet*, although it was "impossible to obtain a seat in the orchestra or the parquet circle for a week in advance, excepting from the speculators."

3/21–23/70; Sir Giles Overreach 3x, *A New Way to Pay Old Debts*

The critic for the *New York Dispatch* thought Booth "made the character of Sir Giles "horribly repulsive, full of wild rage and animal excitement." *The New York Times* critic thought his Sir Giles Overreach far superior to his Hamlet: "When Mr. Booth tries to depict vacillation, he gives us languid monotony.... But when he tries to depict intensity, he has merely to reproduce himself." On Mar. 26, 1870, *The New York Albion* critic wrote that Booth's Sir Giles Overreach was "too studied; nothing is left to the impulse."

3/24–26/70; Matinee on 3/26/70; Claude Melnotte 3x, *The Lady of Lyons*

The critic for *The Evening Post* was positive about *The Lady of Lyons*, noting that Booth had moved from the old age of Sir Giles to the youth of Claude Melnotte, "like a crab" going "backwards." The critic for *The New York Times* wrote: "The character of the enthusiastic young French peasant is one by no means well suited to Mr. Booth's histrionic powers.... The performance ... is mechanical."

3/28–4/13/70; Macbeth 15x

The reviewer for *The New York Times* wrote of Booth's Macbeth: "In spite of bad weather the house was crowded.... The scenery and dresses are in some respects worthy of praise for the attempt, at least, at archaeological accuracy.... The only thing in truth that seems to suggest incongruity is the figure of Mr. Booth himself. There is something in his person and bearing quite foreign to the military or heroic ideal." The interior scenery for *Macbeth* was borrowed from *Hamlet*.

4/14–15/70; Claude Melnotte 2x, *The Lady of Lyons*

4/16/70; Matinee, Macbeth; Evening, Claude Melnotte, *The Lady of Lyons*

4/20/70; Fort Wayne, Indiana; Role unknown

In 1870 Booth purchased:
One pair turret-topped, plum colored morocco boots for Sir Giles Overreach, $28.00
One pair scarlet silk high-tongue shoes for Cardinal Richelieu, $12.00
One pair silk velvet Venetian shoes with cut point front and back toe and instep, $12.00
One pair red morocco Roman sandals for Brutus, $10.00
One pair King Richard strapped shoes, long pointed toe, of plum-colored velvet (very elegant), $16.00
One pair, bucket-top boots, King Charles the First style, plum-colored morocco, made very high and to fold over lined with the same material, using three skins, $25.00
One pair black silk velvet shoes, with three straps for Hamlet, $12.00.

1870–1871

9/5/70; McVicker's Theatre, Chicago; Brutus, *Julius Caesar*

9/6/70; Shylock, *Merchant of Venice*

9/7/70; Iago, *Othello*

9/8/70; Sir Giles Overreach, *A New Way to Pay Old Debts*

9/9–10/70; Matinee on 9/10/70; Benedick 2x, *Much Ado About Nothing*

9/10/70; Evening, Brutus, *Julius Caesar*

9/12–13/70; Hamlet 2x

9/14–15/70; Richelieu 2x

9/16/70; Booth's benefit, The Stranger; Petruchio, *Katherine and Petruchio*

9/17/70; Matinee, Iago, *Othello*; Evening, Richard III

9/19–20/70; Hamlet 2x

9/21/70; Macbeth

9/22/70; Richard III

9/23/70; Richelieu

9/24/70; Matinee, The Stranger; Petruchio, *Katherine and Petruchio*; Evening, Macbeth

9/26–27/70; Bertuccio 2x, *The Fool's Revenge*

9/28/70; Claude Melnotte, *The Lady of Lyons*

9/29/70; King Lear

9/30/70; Farewell Benefit; Shylock, *Merchant of Venice*; Petruchio, *Katherine and Petruchio*

10/1/70; Matinee, Hamlet; Evening, Bertuccio, *The Fool's Revenge*

10/4/70; DeBar's Opera House, St. Louis, Missouri; Othello or Iago, *Othello*

Booth began performing at DeBar's Opera House in St. Louis on Oct. 4, 1870. It was Fair Week in St. Louis; tourists flooded the city, and Booth played "the most successful engagement thus far ever known in St. Louis. The theatre has been packed every night, the gallery, corridor and aisles full of those who thought themselves fortunate to secure even standing room."

10/5/70; Richelieu

10/6/70; Shylock, *Merchant of Venice*

10/7/70; Booth's benefit, Hamlet

10/8/70; Matinee, Claude Melnotte, *The Lady of Lyons*; Evening, Macbeth

10 10/70; Hamlet

10/11/70; Richelieu

10/12/70; Claude Melnotte, *The Lady of Lyons*

10/13/70; Macbeth

10/14/70; Booth's benefit, The Stranger; Petruchio, *Katherine and Petruchio*

10/15/70; Matinee, Othello or Iago, *Othello*; Evening, Richard III

10/17/70; Bertuccio, *The Fool's Revenge*

10/18/70; King Lear

10/19/70; Hamlet

10/20/70; Richelieu, originally scheduled as Bertuccio, *The Fool's Revenge*

10/21/70; Booth's benefit, King Lear

10/22/70; Matinee, The Stranger; Petruchio, *Katherine and Petruchio*; Evening, Richard III

10/25/70; National Theatre, Cincinnati, Ohio; Iago, *Othello*

10/26/70; Shylock, *Merchant of Venice*

10/27/70; Claude Melnotte, *The Lady of Lyons*

10/28/70; Macbeth

10/29/70; Matinee, Claude Melnotte, *The Lady of Lyons*; Evening, Macbeth

10/31–11/1/70; Hamlet 2x

11/2/70; Richelieu

11/3/70; Richard III

Booth began to appear in Cincinnati on Oct. 25, 1870. When the company did *Richard III*, the local critic wrote: "The soldiers moved with more than their usual sleepiness, and the same might also be said of the delivery of some of the principal actors, all doubtless due to the bad ventilation of the theater, the air in which was so exhausted of vitality that even an actor might be excused for dropping asleep."

11/4/70; Hamlet

11/5/70; Matinee, The Stranger; Petruchio, *Katherine and Petruchio*; Evening, Richard III

11/7/70; King Lear

11/8–9/70; Claude Melnotte 2x, *The Lady of Lyons*

11/10/70; Richelieu

11/11/70; Benedick, *Much Ado About Nothing*

11/12/70; Matinee, Hamlet; Evening, Shylock, *Merchant of Venice*; Petruchio, *Katherine and Petruchio*

11/15/70; Opera House, Pittsburgh, Pennsylvania; Iago, *Othello*

When he played Pittsburgh in Nov. 1870, Booth performed with the local stock company. Private Boxes were eight dollars; orchestra chairs, two dollars; parquette chairs $1.50; reserved dress circle chairs $1.00; dress circle general admission seventy-five cents and the gallery thirty-five cents.

11/16/70; Shylock, *Merchant of Venice*

11/17/70; Richard III

11/18/70; Richelieu

11/19/70; Matinee, Iago, *Othello*; Evening, Richard III

11/21–22/70; Hamlet 2x

11/23/70; Richelieu

11/24/70; Claude Melnotte, *The Lady of Lyons*

11/25/70; Booth's benefit, King Lear

"An evening of rain and slush, cold and cheerless as possible, did not prevent our people from crowding the Opera House on the occasion of Mr. Booth's benefit ... Lear." His second performance of Lear, however, was played to a "slim" audience.

11/26/70; Matinee, Hamlet; Evening, King Lear

12/5/70; Walnut Street Theatre, Philadelphia; Iago, *Othello*

12/6/70; Shylock, *Merchant of Venice*

12/7/70; Richelieu

12/8/70; Macbeth

12/9–10/70; Booth's benefit on 12/9/70 and matinee on 12/10/70; Claude Melnotte 2x, *The Lady of Lyons*

On Dec. 10, 1871, Booth wrote to John E. Russell: "The critics are all a funny lot—take them as you will—now they are all for me and Hamlet, a little while ago and they were lashing me, a little while hence and I'll catch it again—they are even now divided on the position as to whether my company is d—d bad or only tolerably so."

12/10/70; Evening, Richard III

On Dec. 11, 1870, Booth wrote to Richard Robertson: "As to a good company, Dick, I can't agree with you that we have not always had a good one—as they go. Hamlet never was cast or acted better in America, nor is there a company anywhere better than ours has always been. However, we'll try what a host of strong names will do.... Again we are to expect a terrible increase of our pay roll—for ... [Lawrence] Barrett, [Edwin] Adams & even [Lester] Wallack & [Edgar Loomis, "E. L."] Davenport (all excellent in the stock) require their $300 per week. And then again—say you get them (as I hope to & will try to)—where are the plays in wʰ we can use them all? You see—Wallack reserves the right to decline any part he does not like, and two men of equal popularity (Barrett & Adams &c) will object to act together except in equal parts.

It's a puzzling question what to do with your good material when you've got it, & the history of all theatrical management is alike disastrous where 'great actors' are in the stock.... I think of ... do[ing] away with the star system altogether. But you see the difficulties—first to get your actors at something like reasonable prices, and then to get the plays to use them in. We can but try & I have already instructed Harry to open negotiations with Wallack & [D.P.] Bowers—I will try Barrett & Adams & see what can be done. These chaps all require their names to be at the head of bill & in the largest letters and (as a secondary consideration) to receive as much as they get by 'starring'—to say nothing of declining to play seconds to each other. I still contend & will always do so that our company has been the best in the country—but that is not sufficient, we will hereafter try what names will do—if they draw, their salaries will not be grudged—I'm sure; but after a few weeks the same old cry of bad company will be heard again.... If we can make these d—d idiots pull together I don't care what we pay them or how many we have—it was my original plan to collect together a huge array of names, but our expenses frightened me & I have your interest to consider as well as my own. I might be satisfied with the fame of [the] thing & the profits of my engagements elsewhere—but that is not altogether what you built a theatre for. I've been scared—I confess, but more by my knowledge of the idiots' (actors) vanity & constant squabbles and the doubt of being able to use them, than by the expense—though that's enough to frighten the devil."

12/12–13/70; Hamlet 2x

12/14/70; Richard III

12/15/70; King Lear

Booth opened in Philadelphia on Dec. 5, 1870. He performed Lear there with a text that restored the Fool on Dec. 15. It was the first time he had ever done the play in Philadelphia.

12/16/70; Booth's benefit, Hamlet

On Dec. 16, 1870, Booth wrote to Launt Thompson from Philadelphia: "My business here is good, for Philadelphia, where the prices are always less than elsewhere. I long to get back to New York, but not to act, for I am heartily tired, and need rest—but I see at least three long months of hard work yet before me." In the same period, he wrote to William Bispham: "I shall be home at Xmas (God willing) and will follow Jefferson at Booth's in Jan. This is rather unexpected, tho' I'm rather glad of it, for I am sick of traveling, and it is not the thing for Mary, who has been confined to the house for a week past.... My business has been excellent, and I have accomplished a great deal toward the liquidation of my indebtedness on the theatre; a few years more and I will feel at ease, if I don't kill myself in the West I tell you it is not child's play rehearsing two and three hours a day, and acting the same at night. The strain upon the nervous system is terrific. I can't rest enough in one night to revive my energies."

12/17/70; Matinee, The Stranger; Petruchio, *Katherine and Petruchio*; Evening, Sir Giles Overreach, *A New Way to Pay Old Debts*

Reviewing Booth's *A New Way to Pay Old Debts*, the critic for *The New York Clipper* wrote that Booth "was not as ably supported as in other parts he has performed in his theatre. The drama was presented to full houses for three nights though a falling off was perceptible on the third night."

12/19/70; Sir Edward Mortimer, *The Iron Chest*; Benedick, *Much Ado About Nothing*

12/20/70; Shylock, *Merchant of Venice*; Don Caesar de Bazan

12/21/70; Macbeth

12/22/70; Sir Edward Mortimer, *The Iron Chest*; Petruchio, *Katherine and Petruchio*

12/23/70; Booth's benefit, The Stranger; Don Caesar de Bazan

12/24/70; Matinee, Hamlet; Evening, Pescara, *The Apostate*; Don Caesar de Bazan

1/9–18/71; Booth's Theatre, New York; Richelieu 10x including one matinee

1/19/71; Matinee, George Holland Testimonial; Petruchio, *Katherine and Petruchio*; Evening, Richelieu

1/20–3/4/71; Richelieu 38x including 7 matinees

The critic for *The World*, writing about Booth's Richelieu in 1871 noted: "He can call the blood to his temples yet, and laugh, weep and even perspire by the mere effort of a will that seems to hold all the involuntary functions of the body in subjection." *The New York Herald* review of *Richelieu* includes: "The audience was unenthusiastic during the first three acts, and the "telling scenes" of the fourth and fifth acts were greeted with "mild applause.... Until the excommunication scene, there was nothing like a genuine burst of applause." *The New York Leader* review includes: "In that familiar scene where the cardinal threatens to launch the anathema of the church upon Barabas, ... Booth becomes the representative of the church. He takes refuge in the power of the sanctuary to save Julie. It is a solemn duty, and there is something of solemnity in his use of the means as a last resort." Augustus R. Cazauran, writing under the pseudonym Johan S Moray, loathed the 1871 production of *Richelieu* and published a four-page diatribe ridiculing Booth's diction, gestures and height and referring to his reputation as an alcoholic. As a result, Harry Magonigle, Booth's business manager barred both Cazauran and his editor Paul F. Nicholson from the theatre. Booth was sued successfully by the two men and publicly humiliated in newspapers all over New York. He wrote to William Winter: "In consequence of Harry's lack of judgment in excluding Cazauran & Nicholson, I find myself posted in all the papers as an ass."

3/6–18/71; Benedick 13x including 2 matinees, *Much Ado About Nothing*

Reviewing *Much Ado About Nothing*, the critic for *The Star* wrote: "Ned Booth doubtless thinks he can play *Benedick* to the life. He can't do it.... Booth lacks humor and the appreciation of it.... His industry takes the shape of ... physical acting which ... wears monotonous. " The critic for *The New York Albion* wrote: "Mr. Booth's Benedick is a misconception from the commencement to the end." Another critic praised Booth's Benedick but wrote: "Mr. Booth['s] brilliant and admirable acting in the church scene was marred by an occasional gesture or bit of facial expression, which savored more of *Don Caesar* or *Petruchio*.

3/20/71; Othello

Reviewing Booth's 1871 Othello, the critic for the *New York Commercial Advertiser* wrote; "Mr. Booth has many physical advantages for this character; and if his Oriental face and costume leave anything to be desired ... we should mark an apparent lack of the sinewy strength that marks not only the children but the far off descendents of the desert.... There is a greatness in the Moor even when everything within him is unhinged, that we failed to see in Mr. Booth's frequent and convulsive weeping." Booth and Lawrence Barrett alternated roles for two weeks. By the first Thursday of the run, Booth was already "hoarse, either from cold or heavy exertion, and it was plain that acting was rather up-hill work with him. He made some slips in the text, not of course from want of knowledge, that were signs of this. For example, in the passage: 'Were she to give you so much of her lips/ As of her tongue she oft bestows on me/ You'd have enough.' Mr. Booth unluckily transposed 'lips' and 'tongue' and in the beginning of the great scene in the third act, he said: 'Did Michael Cassio when you knew my lady.' Although he went back and substituted the proper word 'woo'd' afterward.... Of the grinding, harsh monotony that impairs his delivery in *Othello*, in *Iago* he furnishes very little." Bianca was restored in Booth's 1871 production of *Othello*.

3/21/71; Iago, *Othello*
3/22/71; Othello
3/23/71; Iago, *Othello*
3/24/71; Othello
3/25/71; Matinee, Iago, *Othello*; Evening, Othello
3/27/71; Iago, *Othello*
3/28/71; Othello
3/29/71; Iago, *Othello*
3/30/71; Othello
3/31/71; Iago, *Othello*
4/1/71; Matinee, Othello; 4/1/71; Evening, Iago, *Othello*
4/3–15/71; Bertuccio 10x including 1 matinee, *The Fool's Revenge*

The critic for *The New York Herald* wrote: "Mr. Booth as the Court fool, was completely transmogrified, but it is a strong character charged with revenge and full of the caustic and pungent diabolisms of Iago and of the deep redeeming home affection of Shylock. Accordingly it is exactly in the line of Mr. Booth's especial dramatic qualifications." The critic for the *New-York Daily Tribune* thought that Booth acted Bertuccio "to absolute perfection except that, by reason of the care and toil of the year, he was physically feebler than he used to be, in two or three of the great situations." The critic for the *New York Evening Express* wrote that "women shuddered and strong men grew pale, and when the curtain descended, a perfect torrent of applause called the actor before an audience that recognized the most grand and perfect piece of art that he had ever given to them." The critic for *The Albion*, however, wrote: "In 'The Fool's Revenge,' Mr. Edwin Booth has achieved a great success, although we do not believe that the character is suited to his individuality.... in 'The Fool's Revenge,' there is all the gamut of human nature to play between 'Bottom the Weaver' and 'Lear' and to such a part Mr. Booth is unequal.... The tragedy was admirably placed upon the stage, and was received with so well-merited applause as to make us regret its withdrawal after so short a run.... Next week Mr. Booth plays Richelieu for the closing nights of his engagement. For a provincial tour we could better spare a better man, but unfortunately that better man is not to be found." Booth did not perform Bertuccio on Wednesday evenings or the Saturday evening performance during his first week and the Saturday matinee performance during his second week. These were devoted to Lawrence Barrett.

4/17–18/71; Richelieu 2x
4/20/71; Bertuccio, *The Fool's Revenge*
4/21/71; Richelieu
4/22/71; Matinee, Bertuccio, *The Fool's Revenge*; Evening, Richelieu
7/16/71; Richelieu

1871–1872

On Oct. 18, 1871, Booth wrote to Edwina: "Miss Cushman & I act tomorrow night—in Macbeth—for the benefit of the Chicago sufferers—and on Saturday we start for Boston.... A letter has come today from Mr. McVicker—they are all safe & well, but—of course—very unhappy over their great losses." On Oct. 19, 1871, Booth and Charlotte Cushman did a benefit for the sufferers of the Chicago fire. Tickets were twice the usual price. Every seat was occupied, and patrons were felt lucky if they got standing room.

10/19/71; Booth's Theatre, New York; Macbeth
10/23–24/71; Boston Theatre; Hamlet 2x
10/25–27/71; Richelieu 3x
10/28/71; Matinee, The Stranger; Petruchio, *Katherine and Petruchio*; Evening, Richard III
10/30/71; Macbeth
10/31/71; Hamlet
11/1/71; Sir Edward Mortimer, *The Iron Chest*; Don Caesar de Bazan
11/2/71; Sir Giles Overreach, *A New Way to Pay Old Debts*
11/3/71; Lucius Junius Brutus, *Brutus*
11/4/71; Matinee, Hamlet; Evening, Macbeth
11/6/71; Richard III
11/7/71; Sir Edward Mortimer, *The Iron Chest*; Petruchio, *Katherine and Petruchio*
11/8/71; Lucius Junius Brutus, *Brutus*
11/9/71; Richelieu
11/10/71; Booth's benefit, Shylock, *Merchant of Venice*; Petruchio, *Katherine and Petruchio*
11/11/71; Matinee, Claude Melnotte, *The Lady of Lyons*; Evening, Richard III
11/20/71; Mrs. F. B. Conway's Brooklyn Theatre; Hamlet
11/21/71; Richelieu
11/22/71; Shylock, *Merchant of Venice*
11/23/71; Hamlet
11/24/71; Richelieu
11/25/71; Matinee, Claude Melnotte, *The Lady of Lyons*; Evening, Richard III
12/4–8/71; Booth's Theatre, New York; Hamlet 5x
12/9/71; Matinee, Claude Melnotte, *The Lady of Lyons*
12/9–16/71; Hamlet 7x
12/16/71; Matinee, Claude Melnotte, *The Lady of Lyons*
12/18–23/71; Matinee on 12/23/71, Hamlet 6x
12/23/71; Evening, The Stranger; Petruchio, *Katherine and Petruchio*
12/25–1/16/71; Brutus 23x including 3 matinees, *Julius Caesar*
1/17/72 Niblo's Garden, New York; Matinee Benefit for Matilda Heron; Petruchio, *Katherine and Petruchio*
1/17–3/2/72; Booth's Theatre, New York; Brutus 48x including 8 matinees, *Julius Caesar*
3/4–9/72; Cassius 7x including 1 matinee, *Julius Caesar*
3/11–16/72; Marc Antony including 1 matinee, *Julius Caesar*
3/18–19/72; Sir Edward Mortimer 2x, *The Iron Chest*
3/20–22/72; Bertuccio 3x, *The Fool's Revenge*
3/23/72; Matinee, Sir Edward Mortimer, *The Iron Chest*; Evening, Bertuccio, *The Fool's Revenge*
3/25/72; Walnut Street Theatre, Philadelphia; Brutus, *Julius Caesar*
3/26/72; Cassius, *Julius Caesar*
3/27/72; Marc Antony, *Julius Caesar*
3/28/72; Richelieu
3/29/72; Hamlet
3/30/72; Matinee, Claude Melnotte, *The Lady of*

Lyons; Evening, Shylock, *Merchant of Venice*; Petruchio, *Katherine and Petruchio*
4/1/72; Cassius, *Julius Caesar*
4/2/72; Marc Antony, *Julius Caesar*
4/3/72; Macbeth
4/4/72; Hamlet
4/5/72; Shylock, *Merchant of Venice*; Petruchio, *Katherine and Petruchio*
4/6/72; Matinee, Brutus, *Julius Caesar*; Evening, Macbeth

In Apr. 1872, the critic for *The Philadelphia Inquirer* wrote: "His slender physique is not fitted to meet one's ideal of 'Macbeth.'"

4/8–9/72; Hamlet 2x
4/10/72; Richard III

Richard III was done in six acts and, on opening night, lasted until 11:30 P.M.

4/11/72; Richelieu
4/12/72; Iago, *Othello*
4/13/72; Matinee, Hamlet; Evening, Pescara, *The Apostate*
4/15/72; Richard III
4/16/72; Othello
4/17/72; Bertuccio, *The Fool's Revenge*
4/18/72; Macbeth
4/19/72; Booth's benefit, Hamlet
4/20/72; Matinee, The Stranger; Petruchio, *Katherine and Petruchio*; Evening, Bertuccio, *The Fool's Revenge*
4/22/72; Booth's Theatre, New York; Sir Edward Mortimer, *The Iron Chest*
4/25/72; Brutus, *Julius Caesar*
4/26/72; Bertuccio, *The Fool's Revenge*
4/27/72; Matinee, Sir Edward Mortimer, *The Iron Chest*; Evening, Bertuccio, *The Fool's Revenge*
5/1–3/72; Richard III 3x
5/4/72; Matinee, Claude Melnotte, *The Lady of Lyons*
5/4–18/72; Richard III 14x
5/11/72; Matinee, The Stranger
5/18/72; Matinee, Don Caesar de Bazan
5/22/72 Benefit for the sufferers from the fire at Niblo's Garden given with company from Wallack's Theatre; The Stranger
5/27/72; Griswold's Opera House, Troy, New York; Hamlet

After he finished work at his New York theatre, he traveled to Troy, New York where he spent a week starring with a stock company run by Emma Waller. It was the longest period of time he had ever performed in so small a city. When the season ended, Booth and the company, left on the Sunnyside, for Poughkeepsie, where, after three performances, the troupe disbanded.

5/28/72; Richelieu
5/29/72; Sir Edward Mortimer, *The Iron Chest*
5/30/72; The Stranger; Petruchio, *Katherine and Petruchio*
5/31/72; Booth's benefit, Hamlet
6/1/72; Matinee, Claude Melnotte, *The Lady of Lyons*; Evening, Richard III
6/3/72; Collingwood Opera House, Poughkeepsie, New York; Hamlet
6/4/72; Richelieu
6/5/72; Matinee, Claude Melnotte, *The Lady of Lyons*; Evening, Richard III

1872–1873

7/13/72; Norwich, Connecticut; Role unknown
9/14/72; Roberts' Opera House, Hartford, Connecticut; Hamlet
9/16/72; Richelieu
9/17/72; Haynes's Opera House, Springfield, Massachusetts; Hamlet
9/18/72; Richelieu

On Sept. 17 and 18, Booth played Hamlet and Richelieu at Haynes's Opera House in Springfield, Massachusetts. Tickets went on sale at the local drug store a week in advance. Receipts were slightly short of $1,800, which according to a local critic was "a larger sum than has been taken by any company which has visited Springfield for many months."

9/21/72; Music Hall, Lowell, Massachusetts; Hamlet
9/23/72; Richelieu
9/28/72; Saunders Hall, Lawrence, Massachusetts; Hamlet
9/30/72; Richelieu

Booth played Saunders Hall in Lawrence, Massachusetts on Sept. 28 and 30, 1872. The local critic lamented the fact "that the City Hall is not finished so that the stage and scenic effect could better keep pace with his powerful delineations."

10/3/72; The Temple, Portsmouth, New Hampshire; Hamlet

In October 1872 when Booth's company played *Richelieu* at the Temple Theatre in as small a town as Portsmouth, New Hampshire, the cast included seventeen speaking roles plus various supernumeraries.

10/4/72; Richelieu

On Oct. 3, Booth played The Temple in Portsmouth, New Hampshire. Reserved seats were one dollar; unreserved seats in the parquette were seventy-five cents and balcony seats were fifty cents. In Portsmouth a dollar bought a full sized quilt or six towels. The local newspaper reported: "The sale of reserved seats at Preston's drug store, yesterday, was quite large, and Edwin Booth is likely to be greeted by large audiences if the sales today and tomorrow are correspondingly good. We hear of one gentleman who invested about $10 in tickets, Wednesday, who declared that he did so for the sole purpose of encouraging the manager who dares bring such an array of talent to our city. Probably the Booth company is the most complete organization of the kind, which has visited us...."

The prices of admission are by no means too large, considering the great expense attendant. We are informed that the daily expenses of the company exceed $600."

10/5/72; Music Hall, Portland, Maine; Hamlet
10/7/72; Sir Edward Mortimer, *The Iron Chest*
10/8/72; Richelieu
10/9/72; Shylock, *Merchant of Venice*
10/10/72; Don Caesar de Bazan
10/11/72; Sir Edward Mortimer, *The Iron Chest*; Petruchio, *Katherine and Petruchio*

Tickets at Lewiston and Portland, Maine, were one dollar for reserved seats.

10/12//72; Lyceum Hall, Lewiston, Maine; Hamlet
10/14/72; Richelieu
10/15/72; Shylock, *Merchant of Venice*
10/16/72; Granite Hall, Augusta, Maine; Hamlet
10/17/72; Richelieu
10/18/72; Norombega Hall, Bangor, Maine; Hamlet
10/19/72; Richelieu
10/21/72; Sir Edward Mortimer, *The Iron Chest*

When Booth gave three performances in Bangor, a special train to outlying areas was scheduled after the performance, and passengers could buy a round trip ticket for the cost of a one-way fare on the afternoon train. During the performance, seats were placed in the aisles.

10/22/72; Granite Hall, Augusta, Maine; Sir Edward Mortimer, *The Iron Chest*; Petruchio, *Katherine and Petruchio*
10/23/72; Lyceum Hall, Lewiston, Maine; Sir Edward Mortimer, *The Iron Chest*; Petruchio, *Katherine and Petruchio*
10/24/72; Music Hall, Portland, Maine; Macbeth

When Booth gave his Portland performance on Oct. 24, seats were sold in the aisles, and even every inch of standing room was taken; tickets were being scalped for as high as five dollars. Of course, scalped tickets profited the scalper and not the box office.

10/25/72; City Hall, Biddeford, Maine; Hamlet
10/26/72; Richelieu
10/27/72; Saco, Maine; Role unknown
10/28/72; Music Hall, Portland, Maine; The Stranger
10/29/72; Richard III
11/1/72; Music Hall, Manchester, New Hampshire; Hamlet
11/2/72; Richelieu
11/4/72; Phoenix Hall, Concord, New Hampshire; Hamlet
11/5/72; Richelieu

When Booth gave two performances in Concord, New Hampshire on Nov. 4 and 5, 1872, the audience at the second performance was not as great as the audience at the first "owing to the distractions of election."

11/7/72; Place unknown; Sir Edward Mortimer, *The Iron Chest*; Petruchio, *Katherine and Petruchio*
11/8/72; City Hall, Gloucester, Massachusetts; Hamlet
11/9/72; Richelieu
11/12/72; Chelsea Academy of Music, Chelsea, Massachusetts; Hamlet
11/13/72; Richelieu
11/19/72; Liberty Hall, New Bedford, Massachusetts; Hamlet
11/20/72; Richelieu
11/21/72; Opera House, Newport, Rhode Island; Hamlet
11/22//72; Providence Opera House, Providence, Rhode Island; Hamlet
11/23/72; Richard III

When Booth played Richard III at the Providence Opera House on Nov. 23, 1872, the local critic wrote that "the support was unequal throughout, and the scenic effect [turned] the evening entertainment into a partial comedy."

11/25/72; Richelieu
11/26/72; Macbeth
11/27/72; Shylock, *Merchant of Venice*; Petruchio, *Katherine and Petruchio*
11/28/72; Fletcher's Music Hall, Woonsocket, Rhode Island; Hamlet
12/3/72; Carll's Music Hall, New Haven, Connecticut; Richelieu
12/4/72; Shylock, *Merchant of Venice*; Petruchio, *Katherine and Petruchio*
12/9/72; Taylor's Opera House, Trenton, New Jersey; Hamlet
12/10/72; Richelieu
12/12/72; Newark Opera House, Newark, New Jersey; Hamlet
12/13/72; Richelieu
12/14/72; Matinee, Shylock, *Merchant of Venice*; Petruchio, *Katherine and Petruchio*; Evening, Sir Edward Mortimer, *The Iron Chest*

Booth "and the rest of the company from Booth's Theatre, in New York" toured with their "costumes, properties and appointments" to Trenton, New Jersey for two performances on Dec. 9 and 10, 1872. Tickets were one dollar. A dollar purchased a large size of Holloway's Pills and Holloway's Ointment used for "purifying the turgid blood and expelling corrupt humors from the system." The box office in Trenton sold "Correct Books of the Play" and photographs of Booth.

Date unknown; after 12/19/72, Patterson, New Jersey; Role unknown
12/30/72; Booth's Theatre, New York; Richard III
1/4/73; Matinee, Don Caesar de Bazan
1/4, 6/73; Evening, Richard III 2x
1/11/73; Matinee, Don Caesar de Bazan
1/20–31/73; Lucius Junius Brutus 11x, *Brutus*
1/25/73; Matinee, Benedick, *Much Ado About Nothing*

2/1/73; Matinee, Claude Melnotte, *The Lady of Lyons*, originally scheduled as Brutus, *Julius Caesar*
2/1/73; Evening, Lucius Junius Brutus, *Brutus*
2/5/73; Detroit Opera House, Detroit, Michigan; Hamlet
2/6/73; Richelieu
2/7/73; Richard III
2/8/73; Matinee, Don Caesar de Bazan; Evening, Shylock, *Merchant of Venice*
2/11/73; Union Hall, Kalamazoo, Michigan; Hamlet
2/12/73; Luce's Hall, Grand Rapids, Michigan; Hamlet
2/13/73; Richard III
2/21–22/73; McVicker's Theatre, Chicago; Shylock 2x, *Merchant of Venice*
3/6/73; Benedick, *Much Ado About Nothing*
3/7–8/73; Macbeth 2x
3/10–15/73; Hamlet 6x
3/17–22/73; Brutus, *Julius Caesar*, 7x including 1 matinee
3/24–28/73; Richard III 3x

On Mar. 25, 1873, Booth wrote to Jervis McEntee: "I hope you obtain a glimpse of the silver lining to that dark cloud that seems to have settled over the artistic life in this prosaic country of ours. I have been very successful [in Chicago] up till the beginning of last week, when my business fell on Julius Caesar & the present fearful weather prevents Richard (a more popular play) from reviving the waning 'star.'"

3/29/73; Matinee, Hamlet; Evening, Shylock, *Merchant of Venice*
4/date unknown/73; Utica, New York; Role unknown
4/6/73; Quincy, Illinois; Role unknown
Date unknown; Jacksonville, Illinois; Role unknown
4/15/73; Academy of Music, Indianapolis, Indiana; Hamlet
4/16/73; Matinee, Don Caesar de Bazan; Evening, Richelieu
4/17/73; Richard III

On April 17, 1873, when Booth played Richard III in Indianapolis, "the poverty of his support" approached "burlesque." "No army ever led by Richmond ever created so much sensation as that docile host of four with tin pan halberds and broom stick spears.... Richmond [vanquished] Richard's grim hosts (five stalwart figures with rejected dusters as gaudy plumes and venerable sacques as coats of mail) ... the lamb like warriors of Richmond smashed their kettles over the beplumed sconces of the crook backed tyrant's hosts."

4/22/73; Turner's Opera House, Dayton, Ohio; Hamlet
4/30/73; Fort Wayne, Indiana; Role unknown
5/3/73; New Opera House, Lansing, Michigan; Hamlet
5/8/73; Opera House, Detroit, Michigan; Richelieu
5/9/73; Hamlet
5/10/73; Richard III

1873–1874

In the fall of 1873, Booth began his tour by working with a stock company at the Boston Theatre.

10/6/73; Boston Theatre; Iago, *Othello*
10/7/73; Shylock, *Merchant of Venice*
10/8/73; Sir Edward Mortimer, *The Iron Chest*
10/9–10/73; Richelieu 2x
10/11/73; Matinee, Iago, *Othello*; Evening, Richard III
10/13/73; Shylock, *Merchant of Venice*
10/14–16/73; Hamlet 3x
10/17/73; Sir Edward Mortimer, *The Iron Chest*; Petruchio, *Katherine and Petruchio*
10/18/73; Matinee, Claude Melnotte, *The Lady of Lyons*; Evening, Macbeth
10/20/73; Richard III
10/21/73; Richelieu
10/22/73; Hamlet
10/23/73; Richelieu

On Oct. 23, 1873, Booth wrote to Launt Thompson from Boston: "I have arranged all my travel this season with a view to comfort — breaking the long journeys by an occasional 'lay over' and taking a week here and there for a 'blow' after each engagement."

10/24/73; Booth's benefit, Othello
10/25/73; Matinee, Hamlet; Evening, Richard III
11/3–8/73; Booth's Theatre, New York; Hamlet 6x

For the week beginning Nov. 3, Booth's theatre took in $10,277.75, $6,444.25 more than the previous week. On Tuesday, Nov. 4, Joseph Booth commented: "This being election night, it was not anticipated that the house would be large; so often has this night been detrimental to theatres."

11/8/73; Matinee, Claude Melnotte, *The Lady of Lyons*
11/10–15/73; Richelieu 6x

The following week, beginning Nov. 10, Booth switched to Richelieu with a Saturday matinee performance as Benedick. No figures are available for the Monday night performance. The total of $5,699.25, however, means that even if figures were available for that performance, the theatre would have taken in less than the preceding week. Booth was now performing at Saturday matinees as well as Saturday evenings, and his brother Joseph attributed the decrease in box office revenue to opposition from the opera at the Lyceum and the Academy of Music, the performance of *Ours* at Wallacks and P. T. Barnum's last Saturday matinee and evening performance.

11/15/73; Matinee, Benedick, *Much Ado About Nothing*; Evening, Richelieu
11/17–22/73; Lucius Junius Brutus 6x, *Brutus*

The following week, beginning Nov. 17, Booth switched to Lucius Junius Brutus with a Saturday matinee performance as Don Caesar de Bazan. Total receipts for the week were $4,990.25, $709 less than the available box office receipts for the preceding week.

11/22/73; Matinee, Don Caesar de Bazan
11/24–25/73; Othello 2x
11/26/73; Iago, *Othello*
11/27–29/73; Shylock 3x, *Merchant of Venice*

On Thanksgiving week, Booth began three performances of *Othello*. Then on Thanksgiving night, Thursday, Nov. 27, he switched to Shylock for three performances. The Saturday matinee that week was a double bill of *The Stranger* and *Katherine and Petruchio*. The critic for *The Daily Graphic*, however, thought: "The exceptional badness of the company which now supports Mr. Booth, and which ... might have been recruited from an Oshkosh variety show, constituted a safety-valve upon which critical vigor to a great extent expended itself on Tuesday morning, to the manifest advantage of Mr. Booth."

11/29/73; Matinee, The Stranger; Petruchio, *Katherine and Petruchio*

Booth played New England with a company comprised of members of the Providence Opera House.

12/1/73; New Haven, Connecticut; Hamlet
12/2/73; Robert's Opera House, Hartford, Connecticut; Iago, *Othello*

In Hartford, on Dec. 2, 1873, there were nearly two thousand people in the opera house, and the box office receipts were between $1,600 and $1,700.

12/3/73; Springfield, Massachusetts; Iago, *Othello*; originally scheduled as The Stranger and Petruchio, *Katherine and Petruchio*
12/4/73; Worcester Theater; Iago, *Othello*; originally scheduled as The Stranger and Petruchio, *Katherine and Petruchio*

The *Worcester Daily Spy*'s critic noted that of most of the actors "not much [was] to be said, save that they followed the text."

12/8/73; Providence Opera House, Providence, Rhode Island; Othello
12/9/73; Shylock, *Merchant of Venice*
12/10–11/73; Richelieu 2x
12/12/73; Iago, *Othello*; originally scheduled as Shylock, *Merchant of Venice*
12/13/73; Matinee, The Stranger
12/29/73; Walnut Street Theatre, Philadelphia; Shylock, *Merchant of Venice*
12/30/73; Othello
12/31/73; Benedick, *Much Ado About Nothing*
1/1/74; Pescara, *The Apostate*
1/2/74; Booth's benefit, Lucius Junius Brutus, *Brutus*
1/3/74; Matinee, Benedick, *Much Ado About Nothing*; Evening, Pescara, *The Apostate*
1/5/74; Richelieu
1/6/74; Lucius Junius Brutus, *Brutus*; originally scheduled as Claude Melnotte, *The Lady of Lyons*
1/7/74; Bertuccio, *The Fool's Revenge*
1/8/74; Richelieu
1/9/74; Booth's benefit, Iago, *Othello*
1/10/74; Matinee, Claude Melnotte, *The Lady of Lyons*; Evening, Shylock, *Merchant of Venice*
1/12–15/74; Hamlet 4x
1/16/74; Booth's benefit, Bertuccio, *The Fool's Revenge*
1/17/74; Matinee, Don Caesar de Bazan; Evening, Macbeth
1/19/74; Richard III
1/20/74; Claude Melnotte, *The Lady of Lyons*
1/21/74; Richard III
1/22/74; Hamlet
1/23/74; Booth's benefit, Macbeth
1/24/74; Matinee, Hamlet; Evening, Shylock, *Merchant of Venice*; Petruchio, *Katherine and Petruchio*
1/26/74 Mrs. F. B. Conway's Brooklyn Theatre, Brooklyn, New York; Hamlet

When Booth opened at Mrs. F. B. Conway's Brooklyn Theatre on Jan. 26, 1874, the local critic, who referred to Booth's Hamlet as an "emasculated misrepresentation" wrote: "The dresses were chiefly either those used at the theatre Mr. Booth formerly occupied in New York or excellent copies thereof.... The scenery of course was not comparable."

1/27/74; Richelieu
1/28/74; Shylock, *Merchant of Venice*
1/29/74; Richard III

Booth's 1874 Brooklyn production of *Richard III* used twenty-four actors plus "Aldermen, Priests, Soldiers, Banner Men, Pages, Ladies of the Court and Attendants." In part, these numbers were generated by Booth's avoidance of double casting. Double casting, so prevalent in modern Shakespearean productions, was antithetical to the nineteenth-century's concern for physical realism on stage. Of the thousands of Booth performances examined for this book, only six examples of double casting have been found.

1/30/74; Hamlet
1/31/74; Lucius Junius Brutus, *Brutus*
2/9/74; Detroit Michigan; Shylock, *Merchant of Venice*
2/10/74; Hamlet
2/11/74; Benedick, *Much Ado About Nothing*
2/12/74; Richelieu
2/13/74; Hamlet
2/14/74; Matinee, Don Caesar de Bazan; Evening, Iago, *Othello*
2/16/74; Wheeler's Opera House, Toledo, Ohio; Shylock, *Merchant of Venice*
2/17/74; Hamlet

2/18/74; Matinee, Don Caesar de Bazan; Evening, Iago, *Othello*
2/19/74; Richelieu
2/23/74; McVicker's Theatre, Chicago; Shylock, *Merchant of Venice*
2/24/74; Othello or Iago, *Othello*
2/25/74; Benedick, *Much Ado About Nothing*
2/26/74; Pescara, *The Apostate*
2/27/74; Lucius Junius Brutus, *Brutus*
2/28/74; Matinee, Benedick, *Much Ado About Nothing*; Evening, Pescara, *The Apostate*
3/2/79; Richelieu
3/3/74; Claude Melnotte, *The Lady of Lyons*
3/4/74; Bertuccio, *The Fool's Revenge*
3/5/74; Richelieu
3/6/74; Iago, *Othello*
3/7/74; Matinee, Claude Melnotte, *The Lady of Lyons*; Evening, Bertuccio, *The Fool's Revenge*
3/9–11/74; Hamlet 3x
3/12/74; Shylock, *Merchant of Venice*
3/13/74; Macbeth
3/14/74; Matinee, Don Caesar de Bazan; Evening, Macbeth
3/16/74; Richard III
3/17/74; Othello or Iago, *Othello*
3/18/74; Richelieu
3/19/74; Lucius Junius Brutus, *Brutus*
3/20/74; Richard III
3/21/74; Matinee, Hamlet; Evening, Shylock, *Merchant of Venice*
3/24/74; DeBar's Grand Opera House, St. Louis, Missouri; Hamlet
3/25/74; Benedick, *Much Ado About Nothing*
3/26/74; Othello
3/27/74; Booth's benefit, Richelieu
3/28/74; Matinee, Don Caesar de Bazan; Evening, Shylock, *Merchant of Venice*
4/2/74; Richelieu
4/3/74; Booth's benefit, Hamlet
4/4/74; Matinee, Claude Melnotte, *The Lady of Lyons*; Evening, Richard III
4/7/74; Macauley's Theatre, Louisville, Kentucky; Hamlet
4/8/74; Richelieu
4/9/74; Richard III
4/10/74; Benedick, *Much Ado About Nothing*
4/11/74; Matinee, Claude Melnotte, *The Lady of Lyons*; Evening, Shylock, *Merchant of Venice*
4/13/74; Richelieu
4/14/74; Othello
4/15/74; Richard III
4/16/74; Iago, *Othello*
4/17/74; Hamlet
4/18/74; Matinee, The Stranger; Evening, Macbeth
In Apr., 1874 Booth performed in Cincinnati with a touring stock company from McCauley's Theatre in Louisville.
4/20/74; Wood's Theatre, Cincinnati, Ohio; Richelieu
4/21/74; Shylock, *Merchant of Venice*
4/22/74; Hamlet
4/23/74; Othello
4/24/74; Claude Melnotte, *The Lady of Lyons*
4/25/74; Matinee, Benedick, *Much Ado About Nothing*; Evening, Richard III

On Apr. 26, 1874, Booth wrote to Ford that he could not "act Richelieu at the Matinee & Richard at night — I have made a slight change in your programme, giving you a tragedy part (Iago) for the day with Brutus at night — this is the best I can do, & nothing could be better for both sides." He reminded Daly: "I am not loath to work 'my hardest,' but when I perform a 'heavy' part at the matinee I must have light one for the evening or vice versa." While Booth was concerned about his leading lady, he recognized that he would have to accept the actors in Ford's Baltimore company. Ford wanted him to open in Baltimore on Monday, May 11, 1874. Booth was closing in Pittsburgh on the 9th and as much as he needed money to pay off the debts incurred in his bankruptcy, he needed an extra day's break. Ford also suggested a schedule that had Booth playing two of his heavy roles back to back on a Saturday. Booth did not agree. He was also worried about the heat that he might encounter during the Wilmington run: "It is impossible for me to begin with you on Monday night; altho' my general health is good enough — the 'wear & tear' of brain & the nervous system is too apparent, & I must, in justice to myself & all concerned with me, relax a little now & then, or 'this machine will not be to him — Hamlet' &c, very long: I have not acted in B. for seven years, & the 2 weeks bus. will be great — it will make up to you any loss the Monday night may occasion. God knows I need the money now — every dollar I can get — as much as you, and yet I am too painfully aware that rest is of far more value. Nor can I act Richelieu at the Matinee & Richard at night — I have made a slight change in your programme, giving you a tragedy part (Iago) for the day with Brutus at night — this is the best I can do, & nothing could be better for both sides. In accepting the Wilmington eng.^t I was influenced by a desire to visit some friends there. That is why I was so anxious to know if the report ... was true. When I received your reply I wrote these friends ... that I w^d surely be there the last three nights of the week instead of the first, as originally intended; you then thought of giving Baltimore 3 nights of the third week. As it now stands (Baltimore Monday, Wilmington Tuesday & Wednesday) they will arrive 'just in time to be too late,' & find me gone! I'd rather give up the time after Baltimore altogether — for the weather will be killing hot, I've no doubt; but, if you so wish it & think it best for your interests I'll do as you suggest — play Richard on the Monday of the third week in Baltimore & 'do' Wilmington Tuesday & Wednesday.... I will take it as a great favor if you will secure me rooms at the best hotel. We (my wife & I) have had everywhere parlor bedroom with bath attached, late supper & breakfast in rooms for $16 per day in most of the places, in St. Louis they charged by $12 & gave us all our meals privately.... I remain 4 nights longer then Pittsburgh. Booth was writing from the Burnet House in Cincinnati. The 1874 negotiation between Booth and Ford was as follows:

Booth's proposal: Tue., Shylock; Wed., Othello; Thurs., Richelieu; Fri., Claude; Sat. mat., Don Caesar; Sat., Richelieu; Mon., Hamlet; Tue., Hamlet; Wed., Iago; Thurs., Richelieu; Fri., Hamlet; Sat. mat., Claude; Sat., Richard Ford's proposal: Tue., Hamlet; Wed., Hamlet; Thurs., Hamlet; Fri., Othello; Sat. mat., Claude; Sat., Shylock; Mon, Richelieu; Tue., Richelieu; Wed., Iago; Thurs., Richard; Fri., Hamlet; Sat. mat., Don Caesar; Sat., Richelieu What Booth actually performed: Tue., Richelieu; Wed., Richelieu; Thurs., Shylock; Fri., Othello; Sat. mat., Claude; Sat., Richard III; Mon., Hamlet; Tue., Hamlet; Wed., Hamlet; Thurs., Hamlet; Fri., Iago; Sat. mat., Don Caesar; Sat., Lucius Junius Brutus; Mon., Richard III

The result was an enormous success "grossing over $20,000 in two weeks. Tickets sold rapidly, especially for Hamlet.... [A Baltimore musician named Alonzo] May [paid] $3.00, his week's wages, to sit on a camp stool in the center aisle behind the orchestra leader to see the fourth performance of *Hamlet*.... The house was full on opening night, with many 'standees,' and included 'the best people of Baltimore, many who had not attended [the theatre] for a long time,' and three coach-loads of Washington patrons. Chief Justice White of the Supreme Court and the Italian tragedian Tomasso Salvini, who performed ... after Booth's engagement closed, stood in line for tickets."

4/27/74; Hamlet
4/28/74; Richard III
4/29/74; Richelieu
4/30/74; The Stranger; Petruchio, *Katherine and Petruchio*
5/4/74; Pittsburgh Opera House, Pittsburgh, Pennsylvania; Hamlet
5/5/74; Richelieu
5/6/74; Shylock, *Merchant of Venice*
5/7/74; Othello
5/8/74; Booth's benefit, Hamlet
5/9/74; Matinee, Claude Melnotte, *The Lady of Lyons*; Evening, Richard III

In May Booth played Pittsburgh and Baltimore, with resident stock companies, the latter managed by John T. Ford. In May 1874, the critic for *The Pittsburgh Commercial* wrote: "We ... think there should be more of the General in the character [of Othello]." Booth performed at the Pittsburgh Opera House in May, 1874, the local critic wrote: "His support was not at all good, there seeming to be something of embarrassment on the part of most. We have often seen them do the same parts better. A night or two with the famous star will wear off the rigidity of their manner and possibly quicken the memories of a few." The month before Edwin opened at Ford's Grand Opera House in Baltimore on May 12, 1874, Ford proposed extending the tour, using the Baltimore company to play Wilmington, Delaware and Harrisburg, Pennsylvania. The two men began an exchange of letters in which Booth negotiated for his lead actress and time to rest. While fairly fussy about costumes, he was casual about the scenery: "Would like very much to have M<u>rs</u> Pateman if you can get her. 3 nights in Wilmington; Harrisburg No— it will be on the back track & I want as little travel as possible. Heavy stone arches, with tapestry curtains to be drawn across them, are the safest for Hamlet scenery—this is all I can do for you at this distance, & it is quite sufficient to suggest the epoch, and be in harmony with the tone of the play. In the way of costumes, of course, no velvets, silks or satins should be used, and the furniture should be of the very earliest pattern; but (tho' all this would be useful for many other plays) it is not necessary to go to such expense & trouble for only a few nights. Booth was writing to Ford from Cincinnati.

5/12–13/74; Ford's Grand Opera House, Baltimore; Richelieu 2x
5/14/74; Shylock, *Merchant of Venice*
5/15/74; Othello
5/16/74; Matinee, Claude Melnotte, *The Lady of Lyons*; Evening, Richard III
5/18–21/74; Hamlet 4x
5/22/74; Iago, *Othello*
5/23/74; Matinee, Don Caesar de Bazan; Evening, Lucius Junius Brutus, *Brutus*
5/26/74; Wilmington, Delaware, Theatre unknown; Role unknown

On May 24, 1874, Booth wrote to Launt Thompson from Baltimore: "Although our trip this season has been very pleasant, at least not so unpleasant as usual, we are migtely [sic] glad it is at an end; on Tuesday night, in Wilmington I howl my last for some months to come I hope, and on Saturday next we expect to be at 'Cos Cob.'"

5/25/74; Richard III

1874–1875

On June 3, 1874, Booth wrote to John E. Russell: "I hope not to act this season—at all events very little & not 'till very late in the winter." He asked William Winter to spread the rumor that he was suffering from nervous dyspepsia which had caused his "temporary retirement." Booth's was not the only theatre in trouble. *Frank Leslie's Illustrated Newspaper* reported: "The last season has been disastrous in theatrical enterprises. Not half a dozen established theatres have made a cent, and most of them lost heavily. Among the latter may be mentioned Booth's, Daly's, and Niblo's, New York; McVicker's Aiken's and Hooley's Chicago; DeBar's in New Orleans; all the Philadelphia houses except the Walnut and all the Washington and Baltimore theatres.... Booth's losses are put down at $40,000; Jarrett & Palmer's at $60,000 and Daly's at $80,000."

12/14–15/74; McVicker's Theatre, Chicago; Shylock 2x, *Merchant of Venice*
12/16–18/74; Othello or Iago 3x, *Othello*
12/19/74; Matinee, Shylock, *Merchant of Venice*; Evening, Othello or Iago, *Othello*
12/21–23/74; Hamlet 3x
12/28–29/74; Richard III 2x
1/2/75; Matinee, Hamlet; Evening, Shylock, *Merchant of Venice*
1/25/75; Walnut Street Theatre, Philadelphia; Shylock, *Merchant of Venice*
1/26/75; Richelieu
1/27/75; Hamlet
1/28/75; Lucius Junius Brutus, *Brutus*
1/29/75; Richelieu
1/30/75; Matinee, The Stranger; Petruchio, *Katherine and Petruchio*; Evening, Lucius Junius Brutus, *Brutus*
2/1/75; Hamlet
2/2/75; Richard III
2/3/75; Iago, *Othello*
2/4/75; Richard III
2/5–6/75; Booth's benefit on 2/5/75 and matinee on 2/6/75, Hamlet 2x
2/6/75; Evening, Pescara, *The Apostate*
2/15/75; Ford's Grand Opera House, Baltimore; Hamlet
2/16/75; Richelieu
2/17/75; Othello
2/18/75; Hamlet
2/19/75; Shylock, *Merchant of Venice*
2/20/75; Matinee, The Stranger; Petruchio, *Katherine and Petruchio*; Evening, Richard III
3/15/75; Boston Theatre; Shylock, *Merchant of Venice*
3/16/75; Othello
3/17/75; Richelieu
3/18/75; Othello
3/19/75; Richelieu
3/20/75; Matinee, Claude Melnotte, *The Lady of Lyons*; Evening, Pescara, *The Apostate*
3/22–23/75; Hamlet 2x
3/24/75; Richard III
3/25/75; Lucius Junius Brutus, *Brutus*
3/26/75; Shylock, *Merchant of Venice*
3/27/75; Matinee, The Stranger; Petruchio, *Katherine and Petruchio*; Evening, Richard III
3/29/75; Richelieu
3/30/75; Hamlet
3/31/75; Richelieu
4/1/75; Richard III
4/2/75; Pescara, *The Apostate*; Petruchio, *Katherine and Petruchio*
4/3/75; Matinee, Iago, *Othello*; Evening, Richard III

1875–1876

Booth was scheduled to appear at Augustin Daly's Fifth Avenue Theatre in the fall of 1875. Daly began negotiations by offering financial terms to Booth, through James McVicker, who was acting as Edwin's business manager. Booth replied: "Mr. McVicker submitted to me your two propositions for an engagement of six weeks (beginning Octr. 4th) at your theatre, viz: Six thousand dollars per week (seven performances) or: Half the gross receipts up to fifteen hundred dollars and two thirds of all over that amount. Either will satisfy me, and I leave it to you the preference." Daly decided on the latter method rather than the certainty. Booth, in turn, asked for "a list of the characters you wish me to perform," reminding Daly: "I think it advisable to change the bill frequently — I am not loath to work 'my hardest,' but when I perform a 'heavy' part at the matinee I must have light one for the evening or vice versa." He also requested "the names of the principal ladies & gentlemen" Daly intended to "furnish" and promised to provide "all necessary information regarding costumes & scenery for the plays you select." When Augustin Daly sent a list of plays, Booth advised him that several "would give us trouble on your stage on account of 'armies' & 'fiddlers'— perhaps it would be better to omit Richd 3rd & Macbeth. Richard in the original would be a novelty, however; so I intend to do it — unless you prefer Colley Cibber." Booth was originally scheduled to begin performing at the Fifth Avenue Theatre on Oct. 4, 1875. His opening was delayed because of his carriage accident. On Oct. 8, 1875, he wrote to John E. Russell: "Don't know when I can act — am in a <u>slough</u> from w^h I but <u>slowly</u> emerge; 'tis very <u>costive</u> to me at present." On Oct. 10, Booth wrote to Edwina: "Your Papa Booth is still in a sling but can raise the arm high enough to scratch his nose." When he played the Fifth Avenue Theatre in New York in 1875, Booth had his choice of receiving a certainty of "six thousand dollars per week (seven performances @ $857 a performance) or half the gross receipts up to fifteen hundred dollars and two thirds of all over that."

10/25–27/75; Daly's Fifth Avenue Theatre, New York City; Hamlet 3x

The New York season was delayed for 3 weeks and cut from 6 weeks to 4. On Oct. 25, 1875, Booth opened at the Fifth Avenue Theatre under the

management of Augustin Daly. "The applause began before he had fairly entered upon the stage.... The actor bowed repeatedly.... Mr. Booth bears sad traces of his recent accident. His face is somewhat paler and thinner than it was formerly, and his left arm hangs powerless by his side." During the first week, Booth acceded to Daly's suggestions:
   First Week
   Daly's suggestion: Mon., Hamlet; Tues., Hamlet; Wed., Hamlet; Thurs., Hamlet; Fri., Hamlet; Sat. mat., Hamlet; Sat. eve.; Shylock
   What was actually performed: Mon., Hamlet; Tues., Hamlet; Wed., Hamlet; Thurs., Pescara; Fri., Hamlet; Sat. mat., Hamlet; Sat. eve., Pescara

The critic for the *New York Dramatic News* wrote of Booth: "His 'Hamlet' is not the 'Hamlet' of ten years ago— not even of five He has changed some of his readings of well-known passages.... The disposition to rant is altogether gone; ... the elocution is improved; the affectation of his delivery is almost gone.... The enunciation of the words to Horatio, 'I'll put [on] an antic disposition" is too distinct to leave a doubt as to Hamlet's sanity.... The advice to the players (only one player coming on) was rendered with rare skill and beauty or gesture, despite the loss of the use of the left arm (which still hangs in the sling).... For the cast there is much excuse to be made. They are colloquial actors, accustomed to light comedy and they are weak and tame in Shakespearean tragedy.... Regarding the scenery — it is fine, though incorrect in many particulars. Even in the first act, a few moments after the sentry complains of the bitter cold and we have the idea of the northern winter in our mind, we are introduced to a forest bedecked in lavish green.... Again the costumes do not accord with the scenery. *Francisco* and *Bernardo* wear casques of the winged barbarian type in the first scene, while *Hamlet* gives his advice to the players in a chamber decorated with armors of the twelfth and thirteenth centuries.... It is hardly necessary to say anything of the company which supports Mr. Booth. They seem to have become hardened to the lash, and they have never played so badly. It is well known that Mr. Booth has ceased not only to be a stage director, but to instruct a stage director as to his methods or the work he wishes done. In such a case, even so good a stage manager as Mr. Daly is powerless, and the actors play carelessly, unsympathetically and very often perfunctorily. The setting of the stage was more creditable; it was as good as was to be expected of a star theatre setting a play for a night." O. B. Bunce wrote: "One of the innovations by Mr. Booth in his recent appearance in this part is to enter upon the stage in his first scene at a somewhat later moment than has been usual. Ordinarily either *Hamlet* and the court are discovered as the scene opens, or the king and queen, followed by their courtiers, enter upon the stage —*Hamlet* lingering ... upon the outskirts of the party. But Mr. Booth now chooses to stalk rapidly and in a pronounced manner upon the stage, just as the cue for his first speech is to be given. A characteristic of Mr. Booth is that he never seems to be satisfied with his conceptions. His performances are marked by ceaseless change. Of course, this disposition gives opportunity for improvement and development, but unfortunately it is with this actor more frequently manifested in mere details of "business" than in expression of idea. He restlessly changes his entrances, his exits, his poses, his situations, his effects, but these transpositions rarely bring him any nearer a just knowledge of the essential spirit of the part. We fear that he does not change his ideal, because he has no adequate ideal to change. The character is mainly what he can make it by stage situations."

10/28/75; Pescara, *The Apostate*
10/29–30/75; Matinee on 10/30/75; Hamlet 2x
10/30/75; Evening, Pescara, *The Apostate*
11/1/75; Richelieu

Booth expected perfect memorization from the actors around him. John Drew who performed with Booth as a young actor in Daly's company in 1875 remembered: "At the rehearsals of *Richelieu*, in which I was to play *Francois*, I was extremely nervous. *Francois* is the character that *Richelieu* sends to get the papers containing the names of the plots, *Gaston, Orleans*, and the others. *Francois* is also the character to whom the famous lines are spoken: 'In the lexicon of youth, which fate reserves/ For a bright manhood, there is no such word/ As fail.' When *Francois* returns with the important paper which will confound all those who have plotted against the king, he kneels and says: 'My lord, I have not failed.' For some reason or other I said: 'My liege.' Booth said: 'Don't say that: it isn't 'my liege.'"

11/3/75; Iago, *Othello*

During the second week at Daly's Booth became ill and gave only two performances:
   2nd week
   Daly's suggestion: Mon., Richelieu; Wed., Richelieu
   What was actually performed: Mon., Richelieu; Wed., Iago, *Othello*

11/7–9/75; Richard II 3x
11/10/75; Matinee, Claude Melnotte, *The Lady of Lyons*; Evening, Richard II; first known performance
11/11/75; Hamlet
11/12/75; Richard II
11/13/75; Matinee, Richelieu; Evening, Shylock, *Merchant of Venice*

Frederick Warde, a member of the company, later described playing *The Merchant of Venice* against "a background of a modern American street with advertisements painted on it" and Hamlet interviewed the Ghost in "a dense wood" and Booth wrote to William Winter that he had had to "struggle against" Daly's "'duffers' & cheap, tawdry costumes & scenery." In order to make up for five lost performances the previous week, Booth appeared nine times during the third week, including two matinees and a Sunday performance, his heaviest performance schedule since his days in California.

3rd week

Daly's suggestion: Sun, Nothing scheduled; Mon., Othello; Tues., Othello; Wed. mat., Nothing scheduled; Wed. eve., Othello; Thurs., Othello; Fri., Othello; Sat. mat., Othello; Sat. eve., Iago, *Othello*

What was actually performed: Sun, Richard II, Mon., Richard II; Tue., Richard II; Wed. mat., Claude Melnotte, *The Lady of Lyons*; Wed. eve., Richard II; Thurs., Hamlet; Fri., Richard II; Sat. mat., Richelieu; Sat. eve., Shylock

11/15/75; Hamlet

11/16/75; King Lear

11/17/75; Matinee, The Stranger; Petruchio, *Katherine and Petruchio*; Evening, King Lear

11/18/75; Hamlet

11/19/75; Richelieu

11/20/75; Matinee, Hamlet; Evening, Iago, *Othello*

4th week

Daly's suggestion: Mon., Lear; Tues., Lear; Wed. mat., Nothing scheduled; Wed. eve., Lear; Thurs., Lear; Fri., Lear; Sat. mat., Lear; Sat. eve., Pescara

What was actually performed: Mon., Hamlet; Tues., Lear; Wed. mat., Richelieu; Wed. eve., Shylock; Thurs., Hamlet; Fri., Lear; Sat. mat., The Stranger/Petruchio; Sat. eve., Lear

5th week

Daly's original suggestions: *Richard II* 5 nights & matinee. Claude Melnotte, *The Lady of Lyons*, Saturday night. No actual performances.

6th week

Daly's original suggestions: *Macbeth* 4 times; Brutus 2 times, *Julius Caesar*. No actual performances.

11/22–23/75; Walnut Street Theatre, Philadelphia; Richelieu 2x

In November 1875 Booth wrote from Philadelphia: "With [the evangelist Dwight Lyman]Moody and [the evangelist Ira D.] Sankey & the Kellogg [opera] troupe against me I can form no notion of my prospects here.... I may gain a hearing on some of their off-nights—if it don't rain."

11/24/75; Pescara, *The Apostate*

11/25/75; Matinee, The Stranger; Evening, Othello or Iago, *Othello*

11/26/75; *Othello*, later changed to Richelieu

11/27/75; Matinee, Iago, *Othello*; Evening, Pescara, *The Apostate*

11/29–30/75; Hamlet 2x

12/1/75; Sir Giles Overreach, *A New Way to Pay Old Debts*

12/2/75; Claude Melnotte, *The Lady of Lyons*

12/3/75; Shylock, *Merchant of Venice*

12/4/75; Matinee, Hamlet; Evening, The Stranger; Petruchio, *Katherine and Petruchio*

12/6–8/75; Richard II 4x

12/9–10/75; King Lear 2x

12/11/75; Matinee, Richard II; Evening, Claude Melnotte, *The Lady of Lyons*

12/13–14/75; Cardinal Wolsey 2x, *The Roebuck*

12/15/75; Richard II

12/16–17/75; Hamlet 2x

12/18/75; Matinee, Claude Melnotte, *The Lady of Lyons*; Evening, Cardinal Wolsey, *The Roebuck*; Petruchio, *Katherine and Petruchio*

In Dec., 1875, "the supporting company at the Walnut Street Theatre in Philadelphia was "not as good as the necessities require." The local critic thought that five of the resident actors were "artists of recognized ability, but these few ladies and gentlemen unfortunately do not comprise the entire company."

In the spring of 1876, Booth toured the South under the management of John Ford. Ford had suggested the tour, two years before, but Booth was initially reluctant. He did not like touring; he was enmeshed in the financial complications of his bankruptcy. He had promised to perform for his brother June who was still running Booth's Theatre in New York; consequently he put off Ford's offer. By the spring of 1875, however, he needed the money enough to accept Ford's offer. When he accepted John Ford's offer for a Southern tour in the spring of 1876, he began researching the route—unusual for a touring star. Routing, railroad timetables etc. were the work of the tour's manager, but Booth was concerned that Ford would overtax him, and he was not above reminding Ford that other managers were interested in his southern tour and that he needed to have his requirements met: "The enclosed (following your route) is the result of careful investigation of R.R. time-tables &c. The inconvenient hours at which many of the trains start—and to avoid night travel—renders it impossible to do better. By this arrangement we have 2 more performances (52) than you have stated (50), & to make them 'worth the money' I must avoid as much fatigue as possible in going from place to place—early rising & late arrivals; as it is, I can't avoid several 'ungodly' hours.... Might it not be arranged to engage special trains—where none run on Sunday, or in cases where they start at day-break, or so late in the evening? ... it might save the loss of several nights. [C. W.] Tayleure has just written to know if I'd take the trip with him, & Charley Jefferson desired to 'boss' it also—likewise McVicker—but I told them I had promised—if I went at all I'd go with you; but 'mark me, Master Ford,' as you jerk me from 'hither to yon' o'er rough roads, from sunrise 'till he set again, and look for me to play that night—ye will not find me; I cannot, must not, will not do it! ... As to the terms: your offer of thirty thousand for the trip (of 50, or 52 performances—as I make it) and travel paid—3 in number [meaning three people in Booth's party—himself, Mary McVicker and Edwina]—I will accept (if I understand it rightly); but any programme additional to the above I must be paid for 'pro rata' or ½ of the house." The tour began on Jan. 3, 1876, at Ford's Opera House in Baltimore and ended on Mar. 3 in Bowling Green, Kentucky. Edwin had agreed to tour for a flat fee of $30,000, and wrote to William Winter that Ford "has surely cleared $50,000 by me, while, after deducting my expenses, about $3,000, I rec$\underline{d}$ 27,000. Booth believed that Ford had provided a "very mild" company bought together a "trifling expense" and that he had publicly stated that Booth's salary was so large "that he was compelled to raise his prices on that acct., expecting to realize [only] 3 or 4,000" through the tour.

1/3/76; Ford's Opera House, Baltimore; Hamlet
1/4/76; Richelieu
1/5/76; Iago, *Othello*
1/6/76; Richard II
1/7/76; Booth's benefit, Hamlet
1/8/76; Matinee, Claude Menotte; Evening, Cardinal Wolsey, *The Roebuck*; Petruchio, *Katherine and Petruchio*
1/10/76; Othello
1/11–12/76; King Lear 2x
1/13–14/76; Richard II 2x
1/15/76; Booth's benefit, Hamlet
1/17/76; Theatre, Richmond, Virginia; Hamlet
1/18/76; Richelieu
1/19/76; Iago, *Othello*
1/20/76; Richard II
1/21/76; King Lear
1/22/76; Matinee, Shylock, *Merchant of Venice*; Evening, Booth's Benefit, Cardinal Wolsey, *The Roebuck*; Petruchio, *Katherine and Petruchio*
1/24–25/76; Charlotte, North Carolina; Roles unknown
1/26/76; Hamlet

In Charleston, South Carolina, The sale of reserved seats for Booth's engagement for the week ending Feb. 5 began on Jan. 26th. There was "a general rush to secure places, and consequently almost every seat for the entire week" was taken. "There have been several attempts made by different parties to buy an entire house for speculative purposes, but in each case Mr. Arthur, the agent for the Academy, refused to sell the parties more than a given number of tickets, for which refusal, it is reported, he will be sued."

1/28–29/76; Girardey's Opera House, Augusta, Georgia; Hamlet 2x

Booth's performance of Hamlet at Augusta, Georgia, in Feb., 1876 brought in $1,800. On Sunday, Jan. 30, 1876, Booth wrote to Edwina: "We left Augusta this A.M. at 10 o'clk & reached here [Charleston, South Carolina] at 5."

1/31/76; Owens' Academy of Music, Charleston, South Carolina; Hamlet
2/1/76; Richelieu
2/2/76; Iago, *Othello*
2/3/76; Richard II
2/4/76; King Lear
2/5/76; Matinee Booth's benefit, Cardinal Wolsey, *The Roebuck*; Petruchio, *Katherine and Petruchio*

At Booth's farewell matinee benefit, at Charleston South Carolina's Owen's Academy of Music, Ford gave a "'Booth Souvenir' (worthy of being treasured) ... to each" of the thousand ladies present. It was a photo-lithograph of Booth. He did the same thing for the matinee in Savannah and for performances in Atlanta and Nashville.

2/7/76; Savannah Theatre, Georgia; Hamlet
2/8/76; Richelieu
2/9/76; Iago, *Othello*
2/10/76; Richard II
2/11/76; King Lear
2/12/76; Matinee, Booth's benefit, Cardinal Wolsey, *The Roebuck*; Petruchio, *Katherine and Petruchio*

In Savannah, Georgia "the ladies at the Booth matinee turned out in full force ... crowning him with a laurel wreath, entwined with flowers and ribbons." On Feb. 12, 1876, Booth wrote to Edwina from Savannah: "We start for Macon at 9 A.M. tomorrow [Sunday, Feb. 13]."

2/14/76; Ralston Hall, Macon, Georgia; Hamlet
2/15/76; Opera House, Columbus, Georgia; Hamlet
2/17/76; Montgomery Theatre, Alabama; Hamlet
2/18/76; Richelieu
2/19/76; Iago, *Othello*
2/21/76; DeGive's Opera House, Atlanta, Georgia; Hamlet

Seats for Booth's 1876 Atlanta performances went on sale on February 16. Even before the opening of the piano and organ store, where they were sold, "a crowd had collected on the sidewalk in front, and when they were admitted in, they went with a rush. From that time until late in the afternoon, when the sale was suspended, the jam was tremendous.... When [a newspaper reporter] called in about 11 o'clock, [he was] informed that there were parties there who had been waiting in vain for two hours to get reserved seats.... Some of the more violent of the crowd accidentally broke a few of the glasses of some picture frames by being pressed against them.... Gentlemen, hopelessly in the rear, who looked from the rate at which they were advancing, that they might reasonably expect to reach the ticket box by ... the next day, would put their hands over the heads of the fortunate ones in front and ask friends to do their purchasing for them.... Many gentlemen bought as many as $40 and $50 worth of seats at a time." Booth's first night in Atlanta grossed $2,700; Booth's four performances in Atlanta grossed $9,000, and the entire tour probably took in $90,000. As Booth wrote to William Winter: "It certainly was the most profitable engagement for the manager that was ever made. I was fool enough to give him 2 nights free, because I was led to believe the theatres were very small & the people very poor all of wh. was not so.... My tour has been delightful & all the stages easy; with the exception of murderous cooking at several hotels—all has been digestable."

2/22/76; Richelieu

2/23/76; Iago, *Othello*

2/24/76; Cardinal Wolsey, *The Roebuck*; Petruchio, *Katherine and Petruchio*

Tickets for Booth's performance of *Hamlet* in Chattanooga on Feb. 26, 1876, were advertised as early as Feb. 17 at which date, John Ford's advance agent was in the city, calling upon local newspapers. The advance man had told the newspaper that in Atlanta "the rush was so great for reserved seats that considerable damage was done in Messrs. Phillips and Crews Book Store." A decision was made to sell the tickets at the James Hall box office. They went on sale Feb. 19. Secured seats were $2.50 and two dollars. The local newspaper predicted that Messrs. Gledhill and Cady, at whose store the tickets were to be sold, would "call upon Mayor Fort for a posse of policemen to regulate the crowd who will rush for secured places at 9 o'clock." "At six o'clock some persons began to arrive and assume positions near the office window by nine o'clock the crowd had become a perfect jam in the narrow hall."

2/26/76; James Hall, Chattanooga, Tennessee; Hamlet

On Feb. 27, 1876, Booth wrote: "The night I arrived in Chattanooga, I was surrounded by a 'scheechy' band. I tell you, I was frightened. I should have made a speech and asked them to take a glass of wine, but I didn't; I got hold of the hotel proprietor (whose brother led the band) & he thanked them for me."

2/28/76; Masonic Opera House, Nashville, Tennessee; Hamlet

2/29/76; Richelieu

On Feb. 29, 1876, *The Daily American* of Nashville, Tennessee reported that "Mr. Booth's support [in *Hamlet*] was such as would not invite enthusiasm from a critical audience." The touring company, organized by John Ford, in the spring of 1876, was described as being "of the so-so order."

3/1/76; Iago, *Othello*

3/2/76; Booth's benefit, Cardinal Wolsey, *The Roebuck*; Petruchio, *Katherine and Petruchio*

3/3/76; Bowling Green, Kentucky; Hamlet

On Mar. 5, 1876, John T. Ford wrote to William Winter: "I parted with Edwin at the Mammoth Cave or rather Cave City near the M.C. He was in good health, fine spirits and evidently fully satisfied with his trip.... We began in Baltimore Jan. 3rd and ended in Bowling Green Ky ... on Mar. 3rd just two months, both dates inclusive. E. B. traveled like a prince special trains special apartments, special fare, He was a Sensation Every Where, but all in respect to the people, I Never heard a rude remark, He was ... very affable; the company voted him a trump of a gentleman, charming in his familiarity; he made all feel at home in his presence. Nashville gave us the best business, Baltimore 2nd and Atlanta 3rd. We commenced every night precisely on time, never had a delay between the acts of over 5 minutes, and in the entire route never a moment behind in our rail movement.... It was a remarkable trip in every feature and a success beyond precedent of its kind. The number of performances given 52. and the prompter's voice never heard, or needed."

3/13/76; Macauley's Theatre, Louisville, Kentucky; Hamlet

3/14/76; Richelieu

3/15/76; Iago, *Othello*

3/16–17/76; King Lear 2x

3/18/76; Matinee, Claude Melnotte, *The Lady of Lyons*; Evening, Shylock, *Merchant of Venice*

3/20/76; Richelieu

3/21/76; Sir Giles Overreach, *A New Way to Pay Old Debts*

3/22/76; Hamlet

3/23–24/76; Richard II 2x

3/25/76; Matinee, Hamlet; Evening, Cardinal Wolsey, *The Roebuck*; Petruchio, *Katherine and Petruchio*

3/27/76; Wood's Theater, Cincinnati, Ohio; Hamlet

3/28/76; Richelieu or Richard II

3/29/76; King Lear

3/30/76; Iago, *Othello*

3/31/76; Richelieu

4/1/76; Matinee, Claude Melnotte, *The Lady of Lyons*; Evening, Shylock, *Merchant of Venice*

4/3/76; Richelieu

4/4/76; Hamlet

4/5/76; Cardinal Wolsey, *The Roebuck*; Petruchio, *Katherine and Petruchio*

4/10–12/76; McVicker's Theatre, Chicago; Richard II 3x

4/13/76; Shylock, *Merchant of Venice*

4/14/76; Othello

4/15/76; Matinee, The Stranger; Petruchio, *Katherine and Petruchio*; Evening, Pescara, *The Apostate*

4/17–19/76; King Lear 3x

On Apr. 19, 1876, Booth wrote to John Ford who wanted him to do a double bill of Cardinal Wolsey and Petruchio at a benefit in June: "Both Wolsey & Petruchio are hot parts—for hot weather—the one all padding & the other all go—but I think it would be, perhaps, a stronger card than any one play."

4/20/76; Claude Melnotte, *The Lady of Lyons*
4/21/76; Richelieu
4/22/76; Matinee, Benefit for the Shakespeare Memorial; Benedick, *Much Ado About Nothing*; Evening, Richard II
4/24–26/76; Hamlet 3x
4/27/76; Richelieu
4/28/76; Iago, *Othello*
4/29/76; Matinee, Claude Melnotte, *The Lady of Lyons*; Evening, Sir Giles Overreach, *A New Way to Pay Old Debts*
5/1/76; Shylock, *Merchant of Venice*
5/2/76; Cardinal Wolsey, *The Roebuck*; Petruchio, *Katherine and Petruchio*
5/3/76; Richelieu
5/4/76; Hamlet
5/5/76; Benedick, *Much Ado About Nothing*
5/6/76; Matinee, Iago, *Othello*; Evening, Cardinal Wolsey, *The Roebuck*; Petruchio, *Katherine and Petruchio*
5/8/76; Good's Opera House, South Bend Indiana; Hamlet
5/9/76; Opera House, Adrian, Michigan; Shylock, *Merchant of Venice*
5/10/76; Wheeler Opera House, Toledo, Ohio; Hamlet
5/11/76; Shylock, *Merchant of Venice*
5/12/76; Richelieu
5/13/76; Matinee, Claude Melnotte, *The Lady of Lyons*; Evening, Iago, *Othello*
5/15/76; Whitney's Opera House, Detroit, Michigan; Hamlet

When Booth appeared in Detroit in May 1876, an advance man for James McVicker arranged that "all lines of street cars and either the steamer Fortune or Victoria will be waiting at the close of performance."

5/16/76; Richelieu
5/17/76; Benedick, *Much Ado About Nothing*
5/18/76; Shylock, *Merchant of Venice*
5/19/76; Richard II
5/20/76; Matinee, Claude Melnotte, *The Lady of Lyons*; Evening, Iago, *Othello*
5/22/76; Mechanics' Hall, Hamilton, Ontario; Hamlet
5/23/76; Mrs. Morrison's Grand Opera House, Toronto, Canada; Hamlet
5/24/76; Queen's Birthday; Matinee, Claude Melnotte, *The Lady of Lyons*; Evening, Richelieu
5/25/76; Richard II
5/26/76; Shylock, *Merchant of Venice*
5/27/76; Matinee, Benedick, *Much Ado About Nothing*; Evening, Iago, *Othello*
5/28/76; Theatre Unknown, St. Catherine's, Ontario; Role Unknown
5/29/76; Academy of Music, Buffalo, New York; Hamlet

On May 29, 1876, Booth opened in Buffalo with a company he had picked up at McVicker's Theatre in Chicago, and the local reviewer wrote: "Generally the company that supports the great tragedian is very poor; but such is not the case now; on the contrary, it has elements of decided strength and talent."

5/30/76; Richelieu
5/31/76; Benedick, *Much Ado About Nothing*
6/1/76; Shylock, *Merchant of Venice*
6/2/76; Richard II
6/3/76; Matinee, Claude Melnotte, *The Lady of Lyons*; Evening, Iago, *Othello*

1876–1877

6/19/76; Ford's Opera House, Baltimore Fundraiser, Ladies' Centennial Commission; Cardinal Wolse, *The Roebucky*; Petruchio, *Katherine and Petruchio*

In terms of negotiating with managers financially, Booth referred to himself as a "slider," meaning someone who worked on a percentage of the house. On July 16, 1876, he wrote to John Ford: "If I am able to visit Balt.º at all next season it cannot be before Mar.—it is just now impossible for fix any definite date. My terms hereafter will be on the basis of a 'sliding scale' as it is called. 'Twas thus I played with Daly & he derived therefrom so satisfactory a profit that he wished a continuance of it & is now anxious for me to arrange time with him for the Winter. The method I propose gives me a fairer share of the proceeds of my labor than I was silly enough to accept for my Southern tour—in which, of course, you were not to blame (except in the matter of 'support') but which was far less than a continuance of my N. Y., eng.ᵗ would have yeilded [sic]. I shall require managers to give me an exact statement of the capacity of their houses, their nightly expenses & then share with them in such a way as will yeild [sic] them a reasonable profit & pay me well on the large houses. So let me have a diagram, with prices, of your theatre, your nightly expenses &c, and when I can positively say when (if) I can act with you next season I will let you have my terms." There is no evidence that Booth actually undertook this kind of laborious business detail. In the fall of 1876 he played with a San Francisco stock company run by the actor John H. McCullough and used James McVicker as his personal assistant. He then toured with McCullough's company to Sacramento, left for New York City and opened there seventeen days later, using a new company now managed by

McVicker. Subsequently he took that company touring through the East from November 1876 until May 1877. McVicker paid Booth $600 a night or $4200 a week, although in Brooklyn he worked for $500 a show and in Philadelphia for 75 percent of the gross receipts. Booth augmented his salary or share by selling play texts, and photographs and/or engravings of himself at the box office.

9/4–8/76; California Theatre, San Francisco; Hamlet 5x

Booth's first week in San Francisco brought in $16,147, averaging over $2,300 per performance with boxes going at auction for between $20 and $100. The 56 San Francisco performances grossed $96,000, averaging out to $1,700 per appearance. The San Francisco correspondent for *The New York Dramatic News* wrote: "Instead of Edwin Booth playing Gloster, Gloster was playing Edwin Booth.... Of Edwin Booth we cannot say that he is unconscious of self; on the contrary he is always Edwin Booth.... In Hamlet he slaps his forehead every night at the very same word (why does he slap his forehead?) and after a representation or two, we know exactly what he will do next with as much accuracy as he were naught but a machine."

9/9/76; Matinee, Benedick, *Much Ado About Nothing*; Evening, Hamlet
9/11/76; Richelieu
9/12/76; Iago, *Othello*
9/13/76; Richelieu
9/14/76; Othello
9/15/76; Richelieu
9/16/76; Matinee, Iago, *Othello*; Evening, Richelieu
9/18–19/76; Richard II 2x
9/20/76; Hamlet, originally scheduled as Richard II
9/21–22/76; King Lear 2x
9/23/76; Matinee, Don Caesar de Bazan; Evening, King Lear
9/25–27/76; Bertuccio 3x, *The Fool's Revenge*
9/28–29/76; Shylock 2x, *Merchant of Venice*
9/30/76; Matinee, Hamlet; Evening, Pescara, *The Apostate*
10/2–4/76 Matinee and Benefit of St. Luke's Hospital, San Francisco Female Hospital 10/4/76; Marc Antony 3x, *Julius Caesar*
10/4–5/76; Evening, Cassius 2x, *Julius Caesar*
10/6–7/76; Matinee and Evening of 10/7/76; Brutus 3x, *Julius Caesar*
10/9–13/76; Richard III 5x
10/14/76; Matinee, The Stranger; Evening, Richard III
10/16/76; Hamlet
10/17–18/76; Lucius Junius Brutus 2x, *Brutus*
10/19/76; Claude Melnotte, *The Lady of Lyons*
10/20/76; Macbeth
10/21/76; Matinee, Claude Melnotte, *The Lady of Lyons*; Evening, Macbeth
10/23/76; Hamlet
10/24/76; Iago, *Othello*
10/25/76; Richelieu
10/26/76; Hamlet
10/27/76; Farewell benefit of Booth, Shylock, *Merchant of Venice*; Petruchio, *Katherine and Petruchio*
10/28/76; Matinee, Ruy Blas, *Ruy Blas*; Evening, Hamlet

In 1876–1877 Booth's performances in San Francisco, after thirteen years' absence, netted $32,000 in six weeks. The San Francisco correspondent for *The New York Dramatic News* wrote of Booth's performance of Richard III: 'Mr. Booth does not dress the part — a common fault with this great artist, who, as Richelieu, resembles, in his costume, a Monsignor, as Othello a Greek and as Richard III *Je ne sais quoi*.... [The critic wanted costumes copied from portraits of Richard in the Society of Antiquaries in Somerset House, London]."

10/31/76; Metropolitan Theatre, Sacramento, California; Hamlet
11/1/76; Richelieu
11/2/76; Iago, *Othello*
11/3/76; Richard III
11/20–24/76; Lyceum Theatre, New York; Hamlet 5x
11/25/76; Matinee, Claude Melnotte, *The Lady of Lyons*; Evening, Hamlet
11/27–12/1/76; Thanksgiving Matinee on 11/30/76; Bertuccio 6x, *The Fool's Revenge*

In Dec.1876, the critic for *The New York Dramatic News* wrote: "This moping, mooning, monotonous figure in black, stalking across the stage as if sad from indigestion and seeking pepsine more than revenge ... is the Hamlet of Mr. Booth." *The New York Dramatic News*, in Dec. 1876, criticized Booth's speech: "While his elocution is mainly good, it suffers from a drawl which strikes the reader with a monotonous and ever recurring cadence." A critic for *The New York Dramatic News* wrote "Mr. Booth's method of study ... is that of the automaton, inasmuch as it always lacks inspiration. What Mr. Booth does at the stroke of nine on one night, he does precisely at the stroke of nine on the next, with the same intonation, the same gesture, the same expression.... He never forgets himself."

12/2/76; Matinee, The Stranger
12/4–8/76; Richard II 5x
12/9/76; Matinee, Don Caesar de Bazan
12/11/76; Othello
12/12/76; Othello or Iago, *Othello*
12/13–14/76; Shylock 2x, *Merchant of Venice*
12/15/76; Othello or Iago, *Othello*
12/16/76; Matinee, Iago, *Othello*
12/18–22/76; Richelieu 5x
12/23/76; Matinee, Benedick, *Much Ado About Nothing*

12/25–29/76; Richard III 5x

12/30/76; Matinee, Ruy Blas, *Ruy Blas*

12/31/76–1/7/77; Lucius Junius Brutus 7x, *Brutus*

When Booth played Brutus in New York in 1876, under McVicker's management "the Lyceum Romans looked like the last run of shad. There was not a decent air of antiquity in the lot, except so far as their costumes were concerned. Barnum's never held a more curious conglomeration of old clothes fitted to proportionless trunks than were here exhibited.... The ladies in the cast struggled vainly with blank verse.... It was a star performance where one rocket was attached to a great many sticks."

1/6/77; Matinee, Benedick, *Much Ado About Nothing*

1/8–10/77; King Lear 3x

1/11/77; Ruy Blas, *Ruy Blas*; Petruchio, *Katherine and Petruchio*

1/12/77; Role unknown

1/13/77; Matinee, King Lear

1/14/77; Role Unknown

1/15–16/77; Hamlet 2x

1/17/77; Bertuccio, *The Fool's Revenge*

1/18/77; Othello

1/19–20/77; Matinee on 1/20/77; Richelieu 2x

1/20/77; Evening, The Stranger; Petruchio, *Katherine and Petruchio*

1/22/77; Shylock, *Merchant of Venice*

1/23/77; Lucius Junius Brutus, *Brutus*

1/26/77; Don Caesar de Bazan

1/27/77; Ruy Blas, *Ruy Blas*

1/29/77; Academy of Music, Brooklyn, New York; Hamlet

1/30/77; Iago, *Othello*

1/31/77; Richelieu

In Brooklyn in January, 1877, the local critic wrote: "The chief and most conspicuous failure of Mr. Booth was his utter inability to keep up a continuous representation of old age. [Mr. Booth's] lower limbs hobbled as if they were in the early stages of paralysis, and [his] hands and fingers kept up a jerky twitching that looked for all the world like a bad case of St. Vitus Dance. ...He represented a very nervous and volatile elderly gentleman whose spine had been jarred up by a railroad accident or a steamboat explosion.... The voice was the voice of Edwin Booth, slightly bronchial, loud, resonant, and characteristically given to rolling "r's" and hissing "s's." ...When *Richelieu* calls for his sword, the old man inspired by the sight of the rusty weapon, shakes off his senile languor.... Mr. Booth ... called for the sword as any respectable middle-aged gentleman.... And when he got the sword he made an immense show of trying to lift it. ...Then after toying with the weapon, which last night intensified the situation by being about eight feet long, Mr. Booth in a muffled voice ... described his encounter with the Englishman at Rochelle, smacking his lips as he pictured him 'cloven to the waist'—very much as an enthusiastic butcher might anticipate the possible sausage meat to which he had just reduced his plumpest pig. All of a sudden, as if recollecting with a burst that it was part of the 'business' of the situation to faint, Mr. Booth hastily dropped the sword, coughed with amazing vigor for about a minute, gasped and gargled convulsively and then fell with a thump into the easy chair arranged to receive him."

2/1/77; Shylock, *Merchant of Venice*

2/2/77; Bertuccio, *The Fool's Revenge*

2/3/77; Matinee, Ruy Blas, *Ruy Blas*; Evening, Lucius Junius Brutus, *Brutus*

2/5/77; Richard III

2/6/77; Claude Melnotte, *The Lady of Lyons*

In Brooklyn in Feb. 1877, the local critic wrote: "'Young Edwin' must have played *Claude* better than he does now, seeing that neither he nor any other actor could possibly play it worse. ...His elocution is even worse in 'The Lady of Lyons' than in 'Richard.' ... Despite his fine eyes ... he makes love very indifferently.... He has no ... sense of comedy.... There is a dreadful cannibalistic, determined air about him as he clutches her by the wrist, and pours his love into her ear, much as he would his into it the announcement of his unalterable intention to cut her throat.... He seems to be not simply a bad lover but a bad man.... He presents ... a middle aged roué."

2/7–8/77; Hamlet 2x

In Feb. 1877 the critic for the *Brooklyn Daily Eagle* wrote: "The fencing scene was not very well done. At its conclusion Mr. Booth rolled himself up into a little ball and dived head forward on the stage, which set the audience to laughing, and the tragedy ended with a peal of merriment."

2/9/77; Ruy Blas, *Ruy Blas*; Petruchio, *Katherine and Petruchio*

2/10/77; Matinee, Don Caesar de Bazan; Evening, King Lear

2/19–22/77 Mrs. John Drew's Arch Street Theatre, Philadelphia; Hamlet 4x

2/23/77; Bertuccio, *The Fool's Revenge*

2/24/77; Matinee, Claude Melnotte, *The Lady of Lyons*; Evening, Bertuccio, *The Fool's Revenge*

2/26, 28/77; Richelieu 2x

When Booth played Richelieu, under James McVicker's management, at the Arch Street Theatre in Philadelphia, in Feb., 1877, the local critic wrote: "It must be very difficult for Mr. Booth to do himself justice when acting with such a company as that which is now supporting him."

3/1/77; Shylock, *Merchant of Venice*

3/2/77; Hamlet

3/3/77; Matinee, Don Caesar de Bazan; Evening, Shylock, *Merchant of Venice*

3/5/77; Richard III

3/6/77; Claude Melnotte, *The Lady of Lyons*

3/7/77; Othello
3/8/77; Richard III
3/9/77; Booth's Benefit, Ruy Blas, *Ruy Blas*; Petruchio, *Katherine and Petruchio*
3/10/77; Matinee, Hamlet; Evening, Benedick, *Much Ado About Nothing*
3/12/77; Ford's Opera House, Baltimore; Iago, *Othello*
3/13/77; Richelieu
3/14/77; Hamlet
3/15/77; Bertuccio, *The Fool's Revenge*
3/16/77; Shylock, *Merchant of Venice*
3/17/77; Matinee, Ruy Blas, *Ruy Blas*; Evening, King Lear

On Mar. 18, 1877, Booth wrote to Jervis McEntee: "I have eight weeks yet before my season closes & verily I yearn for that blessed time, for I am mightily fatigued."

3/19/77; Richard III
3/20/77; Hamlet
3/21/77; Bertuccio, *The Fool's Revenge*
3/22/77; Richelieu
3/23/77; Booth's Benefit, Ruy Blas, *Ruy Blas*; Petruchio, *Katherine and Petruchio*
3/24/77; Matinee, Benedick, *Much Ado About Nothing*; Evening, Richard III

In Apr. 1877 The *New York Dramatic News and Society Journal* informed its readers: "Edwin Booth's agent engaged Howe's new Opera House, in Bridgeport, for Easter Monday evening. The building not being ready, the engagement was broken off. Mr. Booth and his company will play Hamlet on the evening in question at Stamford, Conn. Mr. Booth is adverse to playing during holy week. In fact he is a truly good actor, particularly as no manager will give him his terms this week. Religion and bankruptcy fit so well together in this choicest of Heaven's creatures."

4/2/77; Town Hall, Stamford, Connecticut; Hamlet

When he played the town hall in Stamford Connecticut on Apr. 2, 1877, the house "was two-thirds full — and a great majority paid from $1.00 to $1.50 each for their tickets," although "the roads were bad" and "the weather throughout the afternoon and evening was rainy and disagreeable."

4/3/77; Music Hall, New Haven, Connecticut; Hamlet

When Booth played New Haven in Apr. 1877, he was accompanied by thirty-five actors.

4/4/77; Shylock, *Merchant of Venice*; Petruchio, *Katherine and Petruchio*

In Apr. 1877 "quite a crowd gathered in the corridor of the City Hall building ... before 8 o'clock to secure seats for" Booth's first performance in Waterbury, Connecticut. "The first man put in an appearance at 6:30 and had to wait over an hour, before he could have his choice of the best seats in the house."

4/5/77; City Hall, Waterbury, Connecticut; Hamlet
4/6/77; Roberts' Opera House, Hartford, Connecticut; Hamlet
4/7/77; Shylock, *Merchant of Venice*; Petruchio, *Katherine and Petruchio*
4/9/77; Springfield, Massachusetts; Hamlet
4/10/77; Shylock, *Merchant of Venice*; Petruchio, *Katherine and Petruchio*
4/11/77; Worcester Theatre, Worcester, Massachusetts; Hamlet
4/12/77; Shylock, *Merchant of Venice*; Petruchio, *Katherine and Petruchio*
4/13/77; Academy of Music, Fall River, Massachusetts; Hamlet
4/14/77; Shylock, *Merchant of Venice*; Petruchio, *Katherine and Petruchio*
4/16/77; Providence Opera House, Providence, Rhode Island; Hamlet
4/17/77; Iago, *Othello*
4/18/77; Bertuccio, *The Fool's Revenge*
4/19/77; Hamlet
4/20/77; Richard II
4/21/77; Matinee, Ruy Blas, *Ruy Blas*; Evening, King Lear
4/23/77; Richelieu
4/24/77; Richard III
4/25/77; Shylock, *Merchant of Venice*
4/26/77; Bertuccio, *The Fool's Revenge*
4/27/77; Ruy Blas, *Ruy Blas*; Petruchio, *Katherine and Petruchio*
4/28/77; Matinee, Claude Melnotte, *The Lady of Lyons*; Evening, Richelieu
4/30/77; Globe Theatre, Boston; Richard II
5/1/77; Iago, *Othello*
5/2/77; Shylock, *Merchant of Venice*
5/3/77; Richard II
5/4/77; Benedick, *Much Ado About Nothing*
5/5/77; Matinee, Ruy Blas, *Ruy Blas*; Evening, King Lear
5/7/77; Hamlet
5/12/77; Richard III

On May 13, 1877, Booth wrote to Jervis McEntee from Boston: "This week will end my labors for the season, unless the manager insists upon paying me a large certainty for another week of doubtful business. Doubtless because the large audiences are chiefly composed of numerous stockholders & private friends of Cheney (the proprietor) who seems to delight in squandering his money & managing a theatre for the mere fun of it. This does not affect me, however, for he pays me a certain amount per week; but I have a curious antipathy to a wholesale gobble of all the profits."

5/14/77; Richelieu
5/15/77; King Lear
5/16/77; Lucius Junius Brutus, *Brutus*
5/17/77; Richard III
5/18/77; The Stranger; Petruchio, *Katherine and Petruchio*

5/19/77; Matinee, Hamlet; Evening, Lucius Junius Brutus, *Brutus*

The 1876–1877 season netted Booth $121,353.

1877–1878

In 1877 Booth told Ferdinand Ewer that he was undertaking a revised version of *Richard III* to "educate the ignorant who suppose Cibber's book to be Shakespere's [sic] tragedy." That same year he wrote to the inveterate autograph seeker L. J. Cist: "I am very glad that you were so well pleased with the new (old) Richard; it will be I hope, the accepted acting version, I shall strive my utmost to establish it as such in lieu of Colly Cibber's claptrap melodrama. Shakespeare's Lear has at last ousted Nahum Tate's trash and I have faith in the Master's Richard over Cibber's crook-back'd bastard." On July 1, 1877, Booth wrote to Augustin Daly: "Negotiations which have been pending for some time, and are still in abeyance, prevent my replying definitely to several offers (your own among them) relative to my next appearance in New York. During the next thirty days Mr Horace McVicker [Booth's brother-in-law and manager] will advise you whether or not I shall be free to close with you." When Booth performed in Chicago in the fall of 1877, he used a stock company; when he moved on to Louisville and Cincinnati, he worked with a touring company organized by Barney McCauley; when he went to Cleveland, he worked with a stock company again.

9/10–11/77; McVicker's Theatre, Chicago; Hamlet 2x

9/12–13/77; King Lear 2x

9/14/77; Lucius Junius Brutus, *Brutus*

9/15/77; Matinee, Claude Melnotte, *The Lady of Lyons*; Evening, Lucius Junius Brutus, *Brutus*

9/17–19/77; Richelieu 3x

9/20–21/77; Bertuccio 2x, *The Fool's Revenge*

9/22/77; Matinee, The Stranger; Evening, Bertuccio, *The Fool's Revenge*

9/24–26/77; Shylock 3x, *Merchant of Venice*

9/27–28/77; Hamlet 2x

9/29/77; Matinee, Don Caesar de Bazan; Evening, Hamlet

William Winter was urging Booth to undertake an English tour, citing his own positive experiences as a tourist, and on Sept. 29, 1877, Booth responded: "Your experience, so different from mine in England, made me yearn to try a bout with the Island mastiffs: once again, and it may be I shall do so, when I am old enough — before my teeth fall out."

10/1/77; Othello, originally scheduled as Richard III

10/2–3/77; Richard III 2x

10/4/77; Richelieu

10/5/77; Bertuccio, *The Fool's Revenge*

10/6/77; Matinee, Hamlet; Evening, Iago, *Othello*

10/9/77; DeBar's Grand Opera House, St. Louis, Missouri; Richelieu

When Booth appeared with the local stock company at DeBar's Grand Opera House in St. Louis, seventy-five cents was the cost of a reserved balcony seat or a French felt hat or a bottle of London hair restorer or of having a coat cleaned at the Steam Dye Works.

10/10/77; Hamlet

10/11/77; Iago, *Othello*

10/12/77; Booth's benefit, Bertuccio, *The Fool's Revenge*

10/13/77; Matinee, Hamlet; Evening, Shylock, *Merchant of Venice*

Booth wrote to Ferdinand Ewer on Oct. 14, 1877: "'May a time and oft' hath my busy little B. (Mrs B. of course) asked: 'When will you write to Dr Ewer?' ... My wife has — ever since our first year together — kept a record of events — domestic & dramatic, and commenced last year to put the latter into form for future use. The first criticism of my acting was written by yourself (tho' many puffs had previously appeared), and what you then wrote would be an interesting addition to the many selections she has collected concerning my theatrical career."

10/15/77; Richard III

10/16/77; Hamlet

10/17/77; King Lear

10/18/77; Richelieu

10/19/77; Booth's benefit, Richard II

10/20/77; Matinee, Ruy Blas, *Ruy Blas*; Evening, Richard III

10/23/77; Robinson's Opera House, Cincinnati, Ohio; Hamlet

10/24/77; Othello

10/25/77; Richelieu

10/26/77; Cardinal Wolsey, *The Roebuck*; Petruchio, *Katherine and Petruchio*

10/27/77; Matinee, Claude Melnotte, *The Lady of Lyons*; Evening, Richard III

10/29/77; Hamlet

10/30/77; King Lear

10/31/77; Richelieu

11/1/77; Academy of Music, Philadelphia; Benefit for the Roman Catholic Orphan Asylum; Shylock, *Merchant of Venice*, Act III

11/2/77; Mrs. John Drew's Arch Street Theatre, Philadelphia; Richard III

11/3/77; Matinee, Ruy Blas, *Ruy Blas*; Evening, Lucius Junius Brutus, *Brutus*

11/5/77; Richard III

From Philadelphia in Nov. 1877 he wrote: "The early village cock will soon remind me that I have a rehearsal at 10½ in the morning, and that, you know, is an unusual hour for my appearance."

11/6/77; Claude Melnotte, *The Lady of Lyons*

11/7/77; Othello

11/8/77; Richard III

11/9/77; Booth's benefit, Ruy Blas, *Ruy Blas*; Petruchio, *Katherine and Petruchio*
11/10/77; Matinee, Hamlet
11/19/77; Euclid Avenue Opera House, Cleveland, Ohio; Hamlet
11/20/77; Richelieu
11/21/77; Richard III
11/22/77; Cardinal Wolsey, *The Roebuck*; Petruchio, *Katherine and Petruchio*
11/23/77; Booth's benefit, Richelieu
11/24/77; Matinee, Ruy Blas, *Ruy Blas*; Evening, Lucius Junius Brutus, *Brutus*
11/26/77; Richard III
11/27/77; Hamlet
11/28/77; King Lear
11/29/77; Iago, *Othello*
11/30/77; Richard II
12/1/77; Matinee, Hamlet; Evening, Shylock, *Merchant of Venice*
12/3/77; Academy of Music, Buffalo, New York; Hamlet
12/4/77; Shylock, *Merchant of Venice*
12/5/77; Hamlet
12/6/77; Richelieu

In Dec.1877 a Buffalo reviewer wrote of Booth's Richelieu: "The ... palpable haste and slurring over of good passages ... was very noticeable during the first three acts, throughout.... He seemed to be reserved himself for ... the fourth."

12/7/77; Richard III
12/8/77; Matinee, Cardinal Wolsey, *The Roebuck*; Evening, Richard III

After Booth played Buffalo in the fall of 1877, the company under the management of the Meech brothers supported him in Lockport, Rochester, Syracuse and Utica.

12/10/77; Hodge Opera House, Lockport, New York; Hamlet

In Lockport, New York in Dec. 1877 "a passenger train" traveled "east at 11:00 P.M. to accommodate those attending from Middleport, Medina, [and] Albion. Parties from Niagara Falls could also return on the same night."

12/11/77; Opera House, Rochester, New York; Hamlet
12/12/77; Matinee and Evening, Richelieu 2x
12/13/77; Wieting Opera House, Syracuse, New York; Hamlet

In Syracuse in 1877 three dollars bought two reserved tickets to see Booth or a day's room and board at the Delavan House.

12/14/77; Opera House, Utica, New York; Hamlet

In 1877 the Utica newspaper wrote: "Trains are to be run on the Black River, Midland and Central Roads to suit the accommodation of outside friends."

12/17/77; Leland Opera House, Albany, New York; Hamlet
12/18/77; Shylock, *Merchant of Venice*
12/19/77; Richelieu
12/20/77; Richard III
12/21/77; Othello or Iago, *Othello*
12/22/77; Matinee, Cardinal Wolsey, *The Roebuck*; Evening, Richelieu
12/23/77; Richard III
12/24/77; Othello or Iago, *Othello*
12/25/77; Matinee, Cardinal Wolsey, *The Roebuck*; Evening, Richard III

During the summer of 1877 Booth decided to manage his own company for a six-week engagement at the New York theatre that bore his name, using his wife's step-brother Horace McVicker as his business manager. He was essentially producing a short-term stock company, resurrecting the enterprise that had failed four years before. He leased the theatre from Jan. 7, 1878, until Feb. 16, 1878, from Oliver Ames II and Oakes A. Ames for eight hundred dollars a month and a promise to provide the Ameses with four good seats in the parquette for all performances. Booth was immediately involved in hiring a company and turned primarily to actors employed by Ford in Baltimore. As a possible leading lady he thought first of Rose Eytinge who was managed by Max Strakosch and then as a backup Eleanor Carey who was under contract to Ford. Eytinge had played Fiordelisa to Booth's Bertuccio at the premiere of *The King's Jester* at Niblo's Garden in 1864, but by 1878 she was a touring star. Booth made what she later described as "a very liberal" offer to "support him ... at the evening performances" while playing her own specialties at matinees and on Saturday night, thus limiting Edwin to five performances a week. Either Etynge or her manager kept Booth waiting, and he wrote to Ford: "The negotiation [sic] with Miss Eytinge is still in abeyance, and if she agrees to proposals I have offered, I shall not require Miss Cary. If, on the contrary, the former lady declines, the position will be open, & I shall be pleased to have Miss Cary. I cannot, however, determine for some time yet. I may want some of your other people, but cannot take M^{rs} [Octavia] Allen—at least so it looks at present. I shall do all I can to make the leading members of my company very prominent. From all I can learn M^{r} [Louis] James will suit me better than M^{r} [Charles] Coghlan, about whom there has been some correspondence between his manager & Horace McVicker—who attends to my business affairs. Please let me know soon what the terms would be. Let all who may come to me understand that if Miss Eytinge is with me there will be some specialty of hers given on Saturday nights and also on Wednesday Matinees." A month later, on Oct. 14 Booth wrote to Ford: "I have waited to hear further from Strakosch, regarding terms I offered him for Eytinge, before writing you—but as no reply has come, and I have waited long enough, I shall take the changes with Miss Cary. I saw the lady but once — as Becky Sharpe, in which I could not fairly judge of her tragic element, but I thought she evinced qualities that would well suit the female roles of my repertory — such as Julie, Ophelia, Desdemona, Queen Elizabeth &c, but if I do Macbeth I would prefer Etyinge (if I can get her), and for Queen Margaret as well. Let me know what people you have that I may select therefrom; I may be able to relieve you of many. I will have an opportunity — by using your people — to make mention of your name in connection with the engagement." On Nov. 11, 1877, Booth wrote to John T. Ford advising him that Etyinge's "agents advise her not to risk what w^d indeed be a sure profit to her artistically as well as financially." In her memoirs, published 28 years later, Eytinge "regretted" her decision. This left Booth with Eleanor Carey. He wrote to Ford on Nov. 11, 1877: "I shall want Miss Cary of course to do Ophelia & Queen Elizabeth — unless she has great power & would assume the wrinkles &c of Q. Margaret. I doubt if I shall do more than four plays during the six weeks, but, of course, that depends. I want James for Laertes & Richmond, Mauprat & Edgar &c. I consider the ghost of far less importance to the piece as well as to myself to waste the leading man upon it. For others of your co— would it not be unwise to increase my expenses by paying 'little people' extra wages— when the same can be had in N.Y., without the additional fee?" Louis James jumped at the chance. Within four days, Ford, who was sub-contracting James to Booth replied: "Mr. James advised all the parts agreeable to him. Carey will suit you admirably in all parts of the grade of Desdemona She is not strong but exceedingly well trained and versed in parts like Ophelia, Julie De Mortimer, etc. Mrs. Octavia Allen with me, is the best heavy woman that I have ever had under engagement, a very fine actress I think, and I feel sure you will agree with me if you know her." Unfortunately, by mid–Dec., with only three weeks before opening, Louis James was having second thoughts about accepting the engagement, and Booth wrote to Ford. James wanted to play the Ghost in *Hamlet*, often considered the leading man's part when a star played the title role. Booth did not agree and wrote to Ford on Dec. 18, 1877: "I expressly stated that I wanted James for the part of Laertes— not for the ghost, a cheaper actor can do the latter part as well as he, but not so with Laertes. The gentleman will have an excellent opening part — Richmond & when Hamlet is played he need have no dread of losing his close of Act 4th. He will have Othello, Dell Aquila (in Fool's Rge) Mauprat, Henry 8th, and other first-rate opportunities for the exercise of his talents, and I think he will be foolish if he lets this chance slip. Several actors (poor [Edwin] Adams among them) have expressed to me their deep regret for having declined what I offered them, & if Mr James will make good use of the advantage now proposed he will some day thank me for it." James passed on the opportunity and by Dec. 26 Booth had substituted Joseph F. Wheelock for as his leading man and was rationalizing the change to Ford: "Wheelock has played all the parts while — I understand upon good authority — Mr James is seldom perfect in the text, owing to his poor study; he will have more time now to perfect himself for the Balt^o engagement. The part of Queen Elizabeth will be sent at once to Miss Carey to your theatre — see that she gets it quick.... Has she ever acted in New York? Of course, Booth was responsible not only for cast but also for the costumes, scenery, props etc. and decided to "trust entirely to a hired set of dresses, properties, &c., furnished by the costumer, Eaves, who doubtless, will follow Planche's suggestions as he promises to supply correct dress, &c." Since he was planning on only six weeks at Booth's followed by a week at the Brooklyn Academy of Music, he felt: "I cannot afford to do much in the way of new scenery &c., for so short a time; but I am told that most of my Shakespearean scenery is still intact and but little worn." Just doing the planning while simultaneously acting on tour exhausted him and he wrote to William Winter: "This [letter] has been a desperate effort for me, this morning, a raging headache has more than once tempted me to throw the scrawl into the fire."

1/7–11/78; Booth's Theatre, New York; Richard III 5x

The company opened in New York on Jan. 7, 1878, using Booth's restored version of *Richard III*. The play, in Booth's words, was "a go." Most of the supporting cast was not. *The New York Times*' critic described Eleanor Carey as "a lady whose face is comely and inexpressive and whose delivery is intelligent and feeble." Three days after opening, Booth wrote to Ford: "Miss Carey is very weak [and] has not impressed the people here, I am sorry to say. Her salary is about $60 too much." He wanted to return the actress he had borrowed and asked Ford: "Don't you want Carey? I can get as good (maybe a stronger woman) for my plays for less pay. Perhaps she will please better in Ophelia. My wife & I were exceedingly well pleased with her in California but she seems to be unequal to the tragedy business."

1/12/78; Matinee, Cardinal Wolsey, *The Roebuck*; Evening, Richard III

1/14–17/78; Richard III 4x

1/17/78; Matinee Benefit for John Brougham; Role unknown

1/18/78; Role unknown

1/19/78; Cardinal Wolsey, *The Roebuck*; Petruchio, *Katherine and Petruchio*

1/21–26/78; Matinee on 1/26/78; Hamlet 6x

1/26/78; Evening, Othello or Iago, *Othello*

1/28/78; Othello
In Jan.1878 a reporter from the *New York Tribune* wrote: "He makes the murder of Desdemona a solemn and terrible sacrifice — and not an insane butchery."

1/29/78; Shylock, *Merchant of Venice*

1/30/78; Bertuccio, *The Fool's Revenge*

1/31/78; Matinee, Claude Melnotte, *The Lady of Lyons*; Evening, Brutus, *Julius Caesar*

By the end of the month, Eleanor Carey was presenting personal as well as professional problems. On Jan. 31, 1878, Booth wrote to E. C. Benedict: "The illness & death today, of Miss Carey's mother have kept Mary & myself 'on the go' all this week. The girl is so helpless that Mary could not leave her to the really cruel treatment of those she was surrounded by in the Union Plaza Hotel [Booth was at the Everett House], & consequently has devoted all her time to the dying woman & her daughter. We sat with them all one night & most of the next, and tonight we were with her [the daughter] after the play ... it is now 10 o'clk.... I have been dreadfully upset & bothered by this misfortune; for it leaves me without a leading actress & I have been obliged to borrow [his sister-in-law] M⁻ Agnes Booth next week. How I will get over the next 3 weeks, I am at a loss to say at present; am telegraphing all over the country for help. So much for management!"

2/2/78; Matinee, Othello or Iago, *Othello*; Evening, Bertuccio, *The Fool's Revenge*

2/5, 7, 8, 14 /78; Richelieu 3x

2/11/78; Hamlet

2/12/78; Richard III

2/13/78; Shylock, *Merchant of Venice*

2/14/78; Richelieu

2/15/78; Richard II

2/16/78; Matinee, Ruy Blas, *Ruy Blas*; Evening, King Lear

2/18/78; Brooklyn Academy of Music, Brooklyn, New York Richard III

In Brooklyn in Feb. 1878 the local critic pointed out that in Booth's Richard III, "there is intense feeling in some of the passages, but others are hurried as though he feared they might become tedious to the audience." In the last scene Booth's Richard III entered running and fighting. Stabbed, he fell upstage but continued to fight, "lying on his side," working his way "along the ground until he had almost reached the footlights. Hurt to the heart, at last," he gave "one mad leap into the air." "His sword gone, with clenched hand," he defied "his rival in a look concentrating all the hate and bitterness of his evil heart," and then "fell upon his head and shoulders, turning completely over dead at the feet of Richmond." The company that played with Booth in New York also followed him to Brooklyn. *The Brooklyn Daily Eagle* referred to the actors as "his own company."

2/19/78; King Lear

2/20/78; Hamlet

2/21/78; Richelieu

2/22/78; Matinee, Hamlet; Evening, Iago, *Othello*

2/23/78; Matinee, Shylock, *Merchant of Venice*; Evening, Bertuccio, *The Fool's Revenge*

On Feb. 24, 1878 Booth wrote to William Winter: "Brooklyn did well but less than any former engagement there.... I have made a special point to mount ... [Hamlet] in nearly all the leading cities, both with scenery & costume as correctly as Planche & other authorities have enlightened us.... Since my production of Richd 2d at Daly's I have made alterations.... I shall start about Saturday next for Boston; after 3 weeks there I shall rest a few days & start for Pittsburgh, thence to Baltimore — where I close my season on May 4th."

3/4/78; Boston Theatre, Boston, Massachusetts; Hamlet

3/5/78; Othello

The *Boston Post* critic wrote in Mar. 1878: "Nature did not fashion Mr. Booth for an Othello.... Othello was a splendid animal, a magnificent brute.... Mr. Booth's portrayal of the jealousy, rage, madness and despair of the Moor cost efforts that are too painfully apparent. In his appearance upon the scene of the drunken fray ... his coming is unimpressive; his assumption of authority [is] marred by ... exaggerated staginess."

3/6/78; King Lear

3/7/78; Hamlet

3/8/78; King Lear

3/9/78; Matinee, Iago, *Othello*; Evening, Macbeth

On March 10, 1878, Booth wrote to E. C. Benedict from Boston: "My first week's agony is ended.... I ache all over ... business good and audiences enthusiastic There's life in the old dog yet, opposition has been great too — Modjeska & various literary entertainments, balls & every night."

3/11/78; Richelieu

3/12/78; Hamlet

3/13/78; Richelieu

3/14/78; Shylock, *Merchant of Venice*; Petruchio, *Katherine and Petruchio*

3/15/78; Hamlet

3/16/78; Matinee, Richelieu; Evening, Lucius Junius Brutus, *Brutus*

3/18/78; Richard III

3/19/78; Shylock, *Merchant of Venice*; Petruchio, *Katherine and Petruchio*

3/20/78; Richard III

3/21/78; Hamlet

3/22/78; Booth's benefit, Ruy Blas, *Ruy Blas*; Don Caesar de Bazan

3/23/78; Matinee, Hamlet

4/1/78; Pittsburgh Opera House; Hamlet

4/2/78; Othello

4/4/78; Shylock, *Merchant of Venice*

4/5/78; Hamlet

4/6/78; Matinee, Ruy Blas, *Ruy Blas*; Evening, Richelieu

On Apr. 7, 1878, Booth wrote to Jervis McEntee: "I think I can afford to rest six months of the year now, & it is better than to wear my life out as I have been doing these many years past."

4/12/78; Richard II

4/13/78; Richard III

On Apr. 14, 1878, he wrote again to Winter: "I must needs devote more time to rest than action; my vacation this year will be until Oct., and when I begin I shall sandwich my engagements with long intervals of rest." On Apr. 19 he wrote to David C. Anderson: "I've been 'loafing' for a week — but dyspepsia has marred my enjoyment of it. Have worked hard the past two years, but have made [sic] and I invested them in bonds. Have taken furnished rooms in New York for two years, and hope to act seldom and travel little." Booth continued to negotiate with mangers about scheduling, scenery, venues, casting, hotels, meals and salary. Prior to his opening at Ford's Grand Opera House on Apr. 22, 1878, he wrote to Ford, skeptical about scheduling *Hamlet* on Shakespeare's birthday, concerned about the lack of scenery at the theatre as well as its geographic location and worried about the money to be made, probably because he was acting for a percentage of the house: "Let Hamlet be for the birth day as you wish — but no sentiment will add a cent to our account therefor [sic].... I am told that the 'Broad' is devoid of scenes, grooves &c, &c and that the least rain prevents people going there because of no street cars. How is it? Am I to perform the 'drop' game? [perform in front of painted drops rather than three-dimensional scenery] ... I have no desire to act at the reduced Matinee prices — which is customary at some theatres, and I want this borne in mind as to the Broad. By-the-by I'd rather not have it known too early that I am going to act there; I have declined to treat with managers yet — deferring them 'till later in the Spring; if they see me announced elsewhere they'll be boring me to death, & I want to feel free for awhile before talking or even thinking of next season's business." Booth opened at Ford's Theatre on Apr. 22, 1878. He was playing with Ford's company and was concerned about Ford's casting, particularly his use of Marion Booth, June's daughter, now billed as Marie. On Apr. 14, 1878, when Edwin was deciding what roles his niece Marie should play in Baltimore, it was Mary who corresponded with Marie. Booth wrote to Ford: "I think [Rosa] Rand had better do Elizabeth; Marie, Lady Anne; [Octavia] Allen Margaret [in *Richard III*]. Marie had better do Marion de Lorme & Rand Julie, in Richelieu; it would be as yet too heavy (Julie, I mean) for Marie. Rand for Portia, Marie Nerissa; Marie Desdemona, Allen or Rand Emelia. Ophelia is too much for Marie as yet — the mad scene requires more experience than she has had; Rand had better play it, Marie the "player queen" (my new version makes it a better part than the ordinary one) and Allen the Queen. Marie can do Cordelia & the Queen in Richard 2nd — also Fiordelisa, in the Fools' [sic] Revenge, also Hero in Much Ado." Ford wanted to publicize the fact that Booth would be playing with his niece, but Edwin had great doubts about his niece's abilities: "I thought she c^d be gaining experience by playing certain small parts — say the 'player queen' — 'Marion de Lorme' — 'Cordelia' 'Nerissa' or 'Jessica' &c — but for a novice to do more would be ruinous. Remember such slight parts as she has had thus far are very different from Shakespearian verse & the heroic characters. Now, a word to the wise: I don't want any feature to be made of this Booth business; no 'uncle & niece' bosh, you know. Marie is already endeavoring to work on the Edwina Booth plan of advertising ... it annoys me considerably; for I dislike such 'dodges' for popularity — I am anxious for her welfare & will do all I can to aid her in her profession, but both she & her managers must be content with her unbolstered abilities. It will be doing the girl a serious injury, if she is bepuffed & pushed beyond her powers at the very outset of her career — before she has learnt the alphabet of her profession.... Many thanks for your kindness about the rooms. I shall take them, but I do not understand if the food is included in the price named.... I cannot accept less than the terms I receive from you & have received elsewhere this season. I have not the Broad faith you & John [Sleeper Clarke] possess." When Booth performed at Ford's Grand Opera House in Baltimore in Apr. 1878, admission was one dollar for the first floor, fifty cents for the second floor and twenty-five cents for the third floor.

4/22–23/78; Ford's Grand Opera House, Baltimore; Hamlet 2x

"This evening will be marked by the presence of visitors of the greatest distinction from Washington, representing the Senate and House of Representatives — both parties and all sections, the Supreme Court, the President's Household, the Foreign Embassies, the Army and Navy &c. — who come especially to pay homage to the great Poet and to witness the grandest work of his genius, interpreted by the Greatest of Actors.... It is understood that special cars will be run from Washington to accommodate visitors from that city."

4/24/78; Richelieu

4/25/78; Macbeth

4/26/78; King Lear

4/27/78; Matinee, Benedick, *Much Ado About Nothing*

4/27/78; Shylock, *Merchant of Venice*; Petruchio, *Katherine and Petruchio*

4/29–30/78; Richard III 2x

5/1/78; Richelieu
5/2/78; Bertuccio, *The Fool's Revenge*
5/3/78; Booth's benefit, Richard II
5/4/78; Matinee, Hamlet; Evening, Iago, *Othello*
When William Winter suggested that Booth restore the scene in Act IV of *Othello*, in which Othello overhears Cassio and Iago speaking, Booth contended in a letter dated June 2, 1878: "My long and varied experience has taught me that the closer and the quicker tragedy can be acted, the better is the audience pleased. [The German actor Bogumil] Dawison and I did the scene in question and it seemed to drag.... The play is long enough with all its cuts, and I think any additional matter would detract from the enjoyment of its representation." On June 18, 1878, Booth wrote to Jervis McEntee about some portraits he was painting of Edwin in costume: "The wigs shall be properly dressed & Mary will arrange them for me, as she does in preparing me for the stage."

1878–1879

On Oct. 2, 1878, Booth wrote: "Am already groaning at the prospect of work. I'm not lazy — but I don't like play-acting any more."
10/14–15/78; Broad Street Theatre, Philadelphia; Hamlet 2x
10/16–17/78; Macbeth 2x
On Oct. 16, 1878, Booth wrote to Winter who was editing an edition of Booth's plays: "I really know nothing of Ruy Blas; hardly the silly stuff I *have to recite* in that character.... It is usually styled a drama — I don't know indeed what it is."
10/18/78; Richelieu
10/19/78; Matinee, Hamlet
10/21/78; Richelieu
10/22–23/78; Richard III 2x
10/24/78; King Lear
10/25/78; Hamlet
10/26/78; Matinee, Ruy Blas, *Ruy Blas*; Petruchio, *Katherine and Petruchio*
10/28/78; Bertuccio, *The Fool's Revenge*
10/29/78; Bertuccio, *The Fool's Revenge*, or Hamlet
10/30/78; Iago, *Othello*
10/31/78; Hamlet
11/1/78; Bertuccio, *The Fool's Revenge*
11/2/78; Matinee, Benedick, *Much Ado About Nothing*; Shylock, *Merchant of Venice*
On Nov. 8, 1878, Booth, writing from 68 Madison Avenue, told Jervis McEntee: "I dread my coming five weeks engagement here, besides, the financial outlook is not promising."
11/11–13/78; Fifth Avenue Theatre, New York; Hamlet 3x
11/14/78; Iago, *Othello*
11/15/78; Othello
11/16/78; Matinee, Hamlet; Evening, Iago, *Othello*
11/18–23/78; Richelieu 7x
11/25/78; King Lear
11/26, 28/78; Roles unknown
11/27/78; Shylock, *Merchant of Venice*
11/29/78; Richard II
11/30/78; Matinee, Hamlet; Evening, Shylock, *Merchant of Venice*
12/2/78; Hamlet
12/3/78; Richelieu
12/4–5/78; Richard III 2x
12/6/78; Bertuccio, *The Fool's Revenge*
12/7/78; Matinee, Iago, *Othello*; Evening, Richard III
12/9/78; Bertuccio, *The Fool's Revenge*
12/10/78; Richelieu
12/11/78; Bertuccio, *The Fool's Revenge*
12/12/78; Hamlet
12/13/78; Shylock, *Merchant of Venice*
12/14/78; Matinee, Claude Melnotte, *The Lady of Lyons*; Evening, Hamlet
4/7/79; Detroit Opera House; Hamlet
When Booth played Detroit Apr. 7–11, 1879, the sale of seats began on Apr. 4. By the time the box office opened, so "many applications for seats were received ... by telegraph from Adrian, Ann Arbor, Ypsilanti, Pontiac, Flint and other interior towns," that the manager of the opera house arranged for excursion rates on the railroad for those from out of town. A picture of the Detroit Opera House can be found in *Frank Leslie's Illustrated Newspaper*, July 27, 1878: 362; an article on "The District Telephone System" in the same newspaper, May 3, 1879: 137 shows a standing sandwich board outside a telegraph office advertising a Booth performance of *Hamlet*.
4/8/79; Shylock, *Merchant of Venice*
4/9/79; Richelieu
4/10/79; Iago, *Othello*
4/11/79; Richard III
4/14/79; McVicker's Theatre, Chicago; Hamlet
When Edwin played Chicago in April–May 1879, "business" was "very poor" for his first two weeks. The critic for *The Chicago Tribune* attributed this "to the draft of the Carnival, among the class who have generally substantially patronized Mr. Booth." In Apr. 1879 the critic for *The Chicago Tribune* wrote: "Mr. Booth's personal attractions are well know and recognized as particularly fitting him for the character of *Hamlet*, — his light and graceful figure, his pale face bordered with dark and clinging hair, his features well chiseled and mobile, and his large expressive eyes."
4/15/79; Matinee, Hamlet
4/15, 17/79; Richard III 2x
4/18/79; Hamlet
4/19/79; Richard III
4/21–22/79; Richelieu 2x
4/23–24/79; Richard II 2x
4/25–26/79; Bertuccio 2x, *The Fool's Revenge*
4/28–29/79; Lucius Junius Brutus 2x, *Brutus*
4/30/79; Hamlet

5/1/79; Richelieu
5/2–3/79; King Lear
5/5/79; Othello
5/6/79; Iago, *Othello*
5/7/79; Shylock, *Merchant of Venice*; Petruchio, *Katherine and Petruchio*
5/8/79; Shylock, *Merchant of Venice*; Petruchio, *Katherine and Petruchio*
5/9/79; Macbeth
5/10/79; Matinee, Hamlet

1879–1880

On July 27, 1879, Booth wrote to Winter: "I find rest & a relief from travel are of more value to me than dollars—while I can earn sufficient for family requirements by less wear and tear." In the fall of 1879 Booth performed with a combination company organized by John T. Ford in Baltimore and Philadelphia.

10/6–10/79; Ford's Opera House, Baltimore; Hamlet 5x

In Oct. 1879 a critic for the *Baltimore Gazette* wrote: "That Mr. Booth does learn is evinced by the fact that two years ago he would have walked from the entrance to the footlights to deliver his "Soliloquy" but now he throws himself dejectedly into a chair *à la* Fechter, and only rises and dreams and moves to the front when his thoughts of the dream that may come after death shock him into activity."

10/11/79; Bertuccio, *The Fool's Revenge*
10/13–14/79; Richelieu 2x
10/15/79; Iago, *Othello*
10/16/79; Bertuccio, *The Fool's Revenge*
10/17/79; Shylock, *Merchant of Venice*; Petruchio, *Katherine and Petruchio*
10/18/79; Matinee, Hamlet
10/20–24/79; Ford's South Broad Street Theatre Philadelphia; Hamlet 4x
10/25/79; Hamlet or Bertuccio, *The Fool's Revenge*
10/27–28/79; Richelieu 2x
10/29/79; Iago, *Othello*
10/30/79; Bertuccio, *The Fool's Revenge*
10/31/79; Shylock, *Merchant of Venice*; Petruchio, *Katherine and Petruchio*
11/1/79; Matinee, Hamlet; Evening, Iago, *Othello*
11/10–14/79; Grand Opera House, New York; Roles unknown
11/15/79; Matinee, Hamlet; Evening, Ruy Blas, *Ruy Blas*; Petruchio, *Katherine and Petruchio*
11/17–22/79; Hamlet 7x
11/24–30/79; Roles unknown
12/1–2/79; Richelieu 2x

On Dec. 2, 1879, Booth wrote: "I have many originators who appeal to my friendship &c, for the trifling favor to let them act with me. The favor is about as trifling as it would be to a painter or a sculptor to grant the request of an amateur to practice a little on his picture or bust. It is a very serious interruption to the regular stage work of the theatre when 'star' engagements are on; managers of 'stock' theatres can more easily offer openings for the trials of beginners."

12/3/79; Shylock, *Merchant of Venice*; Petruchio, *Katherine and Petruchio*
12/4/79; Shylock, *Merchant of Venice*
12/5–6/79; Bertuccio 2x, *The Fool's Revenge*
12/6/79; Matinee, Shylock, *Merchant of Venice*
3/4/80; Academy of Music, New York; Benefit for Irish sufferers; Hamlet, third act; Othello, one act; Petruchio, *Katherine and Petruchio*

In the spring of 1880, Booth played with a stock company in Boston that stayed with him during his four-week New York run at Booth's Theatre under the management of Henry E. Abbey.

3/8–11/80; Park Theatre, Boston, Massachusetts; Hamlet 4x
3/12/80; Macbeth
3/13/80; Matinee, Hamlet; Evening, Iago, *Othello*
3/15–17/80; Richelieu 3x
3/18–19/80; Bertuccio 2x, *The Fool's Revenge*
3/20/80; Matinee, Don Caesar de Bazan; Evening, Richard III
3/22/80; Macbeth
3/23/80; Hamlet
3/24/80; Richard III
3/25/80; Richelieu
3/26/80; Booth's benefit, Benedick, *Much Ado About Nothing*
3/27/80; Matinee, Iago, *Othello*; Evening, Shylock, *Merchant of Venice*; Petruchio, *Katherine and Petruchio*
3/29–31/80; Booth's Theatre, New York; Macbeth 3x
4/1–2/80; Richelieu 2x

On Apr. 2, 1880, he wrote to William Winter: "Things are in such a bad way (among scenery, props &c at Booth's to say nothing of the 'dogans') that I have to attend rehearsals nearly every day—although the same people were with me in Boston & I have an experienced man at the helm."

4/3/80; Matinee, Benedick, *Much Ado About Nothing*

William Winter wrote of Booth's Benedick in Apr. 1880: "Mr. Booth's temperament ... does not lend itself easily to the comedy mood; and therefore his personation of Benedick is unreal, forced and fantastic.... The performance leaves the impression of a bit of a masquerade. The declaration of love to Beatrice is so little really felt that the actor has to reinforce it with grimaces that are actually farcical." *The New York Mirror* told its readers: "The company was not above the ordinary Boothian average. Mr. Booth had many old friends behind as well as in front of him—we refer to the venerable Shakespearean scenery that has done duty since the time of the opening of the theatre.... There were long and tedious delays too, and ragged and slow work on the part of scene shifters." Nine years later, a reviewer for *The New York Mirror* wrote: "I remember seeing Booth and Mrs. Bowers in Much Ado at Booth's Theatre a long time ago [Apr. 3, 1880]. It was put on for a matinee bill, and ye gods! What a vile performance it was. Booth didn't know his lines, and the tragic Mrs. Bowers scarcely the character of the girl who was born under a star that danced. The support was not much better than the principals. Mrs. Bowers and I were laughing over the recollections of that lamentable exhibition only the other day."

4/3/80; Evening, Richelieu

The New York Mirror of Apr. 3, 1880 reported: "Thursday night Booth's Theatre was crowded from orchestra to gallery with an immense assemblage of people who had come together to witness the first night performance of Edwin Booth's farewell engagement prior to his departure for Europe.... One could not help contrast the interior as it stood under Booth's management and as it appears now. The garish gold and crimson decorations, the contraction of the proscenium arch, and the projection into the audience of the stage—all seem to unfit the theatre for the purposes of grand tragedy.... Booth's first entrance Monday night was the signal for [applause] and it was some minutes before the actor was permitted to proceed with his lines."

4/5/80; Matinee Academy of Music, New York, Herald Irish Relief Fund Benefit; Hamlet, one act; Iago, one act, *Othello*; Petruchio, *Katherine and Petruchio*

4/5–6/80; Booth's Theatre; Richard III 2x

When Booth performed at Booth's Theatre in the spring of 1880, his support was savaged by the critic of *The New York Mirror*: "It is to be deplored ... that it is next to impossible to gather together a company at all fitted to meet the requirements of the legitimate drama. Booth's company is a very inferior one, that is in no way capable of giving the tragedian the proper and necessary support; and it is a matter of surprise that a cultured audience will sit through a performance ... and watch a raft of bandy-legged people struggle with the language, the simple words of which they are unable to comprehend.

4/7/80; Richard III

4/8/80; Othello

Booth's Othello was not well attended, because according to *The New York Mirror*'s critic it "is not popular with the theatre going public." Again the supporting cast was heavily criticized. "Of the support there is little good to be said. It hung like a millstone around the star's neck, and its effect upon him was almost as detrimental as it was upon the people in front. In Apr. 1880 when Booth was forty-seven, the critic for *The New York Mirror* wrote: "To begin with one cannot recognize in the slight, youthful figure of Booth, the stalwart Moor that Shakespeare drew.... Booth seems puny in the part." On Apr. 8, 1880, Jervis McEntee wrote in his diary: "I went to see Booth in Othello this evening. He was fine but in the more passionate parts I feel a lack of physique. I like him better in his emotional parts." The critic for *The New York Mirror* wrote, in 1880, of the faults in Booth's vocal technique: "They ... consist ... of a nasal pronunciation, a sing-song monotony, and tediousness of reading."

4/9/80; Bertuccio, *The Fool's Revenge*

4/10/80; Matinee, Iago, *Othello*; Evening, Bertuccio, *The Fool's Revenge*

4/12–15/80; Hamlet 4x

On Apr. 13, 1880, Booth wrote to William Winter: "When you are in the theatre why don't you find your way into my room? Merely send word by an usher & the door is opened for you."

4/16/80; Macbeth

4/17/80; Matinee, Hamlet; Evening, Shylock, *Merchant of Venice*; Petruchio, *Katherine and Petruchio*

4/19/80; Richelieu

4/20/80; Iago, *Othello*

4/21/80; Macbeth

4/22/80; Bertuccio, *The Fool's Revenge*

4/23/80; Macbeth

4/24/80; Matinee, Ruy Blas, *Ruy Blas*; Evening, Bertuccio, *The Fool's Revenge*

4/30/80; Academy of Music, Brooklyn, New York; Macbeth

5/1/80; Matinee, Iago, *Othello*; Evening, Richard III

5/3/80; Hamlet

5/4/80; Richelieu

5/5/80; Bertuccio, *The Fool's Revenge*

5/6/80; Othello

5/8/80; Matinee, Hamlet; Evening, Shylock, *Merchant of Venice*; Petruchio, *Katherine and Petruchio*

5/31/80; Wallack's Theatre, New York; Complimentary testimonial for W. R. Floyd; Iago, *Othello*

6/2/80; Booth's Theatre, New York; Iago, *Othello*

On June 2, 1880, Booth wrote to Jervis McEntee: "I have just finished the performance of Iago—the house was jammed with doctors from all parts of the country—a house-full of 'dead heads.' 'Skull & cross-bones' would have been a fit emblem for the occasion."

6/28/80; Madison Square Theatre, New York. Benefit for Poe Statue Fund; Iago, *Othello*; Petruchio, *Katherine and Petruchio*

Charles W. Clarke wrote: "Booth is a light weight compared with many of the brawny tragedians upon the stage. He is more intellectual; he commands good bodily resources, and the very intelligence of his passions make them superior to the soulless flingings of most of the heavier men."

Booth himself agreed with this assessment. In 1880, for instance, he declined a play manuscript based on the life of Oliver Cromwell, because he felt "deficient" in that "sturdy quality," so necessary to the "perfect personation of the 'Protector.'"

1880–1881

Tickets at the Princess's Theatre were one to eight guineas for a private box; ten shillings for the stalls, five shillings for the dress circle, three shillings for the upper boxes, two shillings for the pit, and one shilling for the gallery. Two people could sit in the dress circle for the cost of a dozen perfumed Christmas cards or in the pit for the price of a dozen Christmas crackers. The receipts for the Princess's Theatre, figured on a Saturday to Friday basis, using only pounds were:

Week	Gross	Expenses	Net Profit	Booth's Share
Nov. 6–12, 1880	£630	£457	£172	£86
Nov. 13–19, 1880	£686	£460	£225	£112
Nov. 20–26, 1880	£694	£460	£233	£116
Nov. 27–Dec. 3, 1880	£845	£468	£377	£188
Dec. 4–10, 1880	£687	£468	£222	£111
Dec. 11–17, 1880	£587	£463	£123	£61
Dec. 18–24, 1880	£700	£462	£237	£118
Dec. 25–31, 1880	£738	£382	£356	£178
Jan. 1–7, 1880	£776	£612	£164	£82
Jan. 8–14, 1880	£778	£615	£163	£81

At this point, there is a divergence between the box office memorandum and the bank account credits that Booth recorded.

Date	Gross	Expenses	Net	Bank Account
Jan. 15–21, 1880	£522	£8	£513	1/25/80 £185
Jan. 22–28, 1880	£430	£5	£424	
Jan. 29–Feb. 1, 1880	£511	£7	£504	
Feb. 5–11, 1880	£523	£9	£514	
Feb. 12–18, 1880	£623	£608	£15	
Feb. 19–25, 1880	£735	£611	124	
Feb. 26–Mar. 4, 1880	£572	£510	£62	3/2/80 £62
Mar. 5–11, 1880	£506	£8	£497	3/9/80 £31
Mar. 12–18, 1880	£608	£497	£111	
Mar. 19–25, 1880	£540		£405	
Mar. 26, 1880	£147	£103	£43	4/1/80 £38

11/6–19/80; Royal Princess's Theatre London; Hamlet 12x

In 1880 the critic for London's *Morning Advertiser* wrote that "when telling the players to follow Polonius, Mr. Booth, instead of saying, 'And look you, mock him not,' makes a pause on the word 'look' and throws a stress upon the succeeding word 'you.' In London in Nov. 1880 Booth performed 'To be or not to be,' having thrown himself on a couch. D. A., the critic for *Bell's Life in London* wrote that Booth belonged to: "the old and stilted school. He mouths his words and rolls his eyes and waves his arms.... His conception of the part [Hamlet] is too whimpering ... funereal and dispiriting." Joseph Knight, the *Sunday Times* critic wrote that Booth looked and sounded well and had "a method long-studied and carefully trained" but lacked "vigor." The *Daily Chronicle* (Nov. 8) "found him to be too colloquial, too natural especially in the advice to the players and the 'To be or Not to be' soliloquy." Mr. May Morris, the critic for *The Daily News* wrote: "Though there were some slight tokens of opposition from some parts of the house, yet ... the welcome was ... enthusiastic.... His performance is not any new conception.... Nearly all the depth of pathos, while he is dying in the arms of Horatio is sacrificed in his restless movements. Altogether, Mr. Booth's impersonation does not leave the impression of a great performance, though it is essentially refined." The critic for *The Observer* wrote: "Momentary satisfaction alternates with disappointment throughout the whole of Booth's performance. A soliloquy which begins with a promise of natural effect, ends in a mere rhetorical display. A clever piece of new or unusual business dies away in measured obedience to the artificial mannerisms of conventional tragedy. Booth is at his best in the highly difficult interview with Ophelia; at his worst where anything like ease of humor is required.... His rendering of several of the most important passages is that of a thoughtful scholar cramped by tradition." Mr. Howe, the critic of the *Morning Advertiser* (Nov. 8) ... wrote that Booth's Hamlet was "picturesque and impassioned" and that Booth was "'a fine actor' whose style had 'power' and 'careful finish.'" Alfred Watson of *The Standard* wrote: "Mr. Booth's performance was a disappointment.... He is never emphatic in speech and gesture. He does not soliloquize but recites a set speech. In the scene with Ophelia, his tenderness is touching." Palgrave Simpson in *The Theatre* wrote: "The house was crowded in every part; and it may be said at once, that the performance of Hamlet by the new-comer was hailed throughout by the general public with the most enthusiastic acclamation. Nevertheless the recognized great artist ... does not seem to have wholly satisfied the more critical judges among the audience. He said by some to be the mere traditional follower of the 'old school' of acting.... By others we are told he is 'stagey.' ... Instead of being the slave of 'tradition' I found him constantly neglecting old traditional points—of which his manner after the 'Play Scene,' when his exultation would not give time to wait until the crowd had wholly disperse, was, perhaps, the most notable example.... Another instance may be given in his delivery of the words, 'I'll rant as well as thou,' which were not howled and ranted, as is commonly the case, but uttered with a profound feeling of contempt of the ranting of Laertes.... To my mind ... Edwin Booth was eminently natural, and to be looked on as an admirable exponent of the more approved 'new school.'" Charles Dunphie, the critic for *The Post*, wrote: "The vehemence and celerity of his performance rob it of its pensive philosophy and meditative grace. The earlier scenes of the play were good, but after those Mr. Booth no longer acted with continuous skills and spirit. The play was languid, but Booth rallied rightly in the last scene, and his fine fencing was universally admired. On Dec. 19, 1880, Booth wrote from London: "I'd rather be at home, somewhere in America, quiet and secure from the publicity my profession brings, than be here feted and applauded, and tired with what's called fame. Bosh! It's my liver, I dare say; the doctors tell me so. I suppose I'd be dissatisfied with my other lot. I'm a chronic growler, I fear."

11/20–12/24/80; Richelieu 30x

The English novelist, journalist and manager Joseph Hatton wrote: "I saw both Booth's impersonation of [Richelieu] and the new Princess's Theatre together for the first time I can now understand how heavily the American tragedian was handicapped by circumstances and how much greater his success is than it appears to be. During Mr. Gooch's management of the Princess's, the old house was the home of melodrama — not classic melodrama, but strong, realistic, ... 'blood and thunder' melodrama; it was practically an East-End theatre at the West. A Bowery theatre in Madison Square is the parallel idea for New York. *Guinea Gold, Jane Shore, It Is Never Too Late to Mend, Drink, The Streets of London*, were its most successful plays. In the height of its money-making history in this line, Mr. Gooch pulled the theatre down. It was old, dusty, inconvenient; it smelled of sawdust, orange-peel and gas; it was draughty, afflicted with rats, and the stage was positively dangerous; but the cheap parts were crowded every night.... Now and then the better class of playgoers came; but the money was in pit, gallery and upper circle, not in the boxes or stalls.... Today the old house is no more. On the historic site has arisen a clean, comfortable, and handsome theatre, with a beautiful entrance-hall, artistically-decorated corridors, pleasant waiting rooms, a cheerful salon.... The gallery boys ... were not even represented.... The stalls and dress circle of the theatre were occupied by persons of a higher grade than one usually sees at the Princess's.... Under the circumstances Mr. Booth was as much handicapped as if he had to make the reputation of a new theatre. He gained nothing by the early traditions of the old house; and in producing classic plays he had to contend against the modern fashions of gorgeous scenery and costly furniture; for Mr. Gooch had not stock of scenery and properties in his new theatre that would enable him to carry out the Booth policy of a frequent change of progamme from one historical work to another.... It is impossible ... to be secure of a good all-round company to the claims of *Hamlet, Richelieu, Macbeth and Othello*." Unfortunately Booth was stuck with the casts Gooch had hired. England was proving to be just like America in that respect. On Nov. 25, 1880, he wrote to W. C. Day an actor who was seeking employment as Othello. Day had apparently pointed out how poor the supporting company was, and Booth agreed, but was legally committed. "Mr. Gooch has already an actor engaged for the part who, though he may not satisfactorily sustain it, is under salary, and the expenses are already so great that I cannot in fairness, demand a change. My support is indeed very poor; I hoped to find better material here than we have in America — but such as I have at the Princess's is really weaker than any I've had for years." In Nov. 1880, the critic for *Lloyd's* wrote: "Mr. Booth several times changes his dress. In the first act, he wears a handsome amber-satin robe, deeply edged with fur, and tied with a light blue cord." In Dec. 1880, the London magazine *Punch* asked "what authority he has for *Richelieu* in a yellow dressing-gown trimmed with fur?— a robe far more appropriate to an old *beau* ... in his bedroom, than a Cardinal in his reception-room."

12/27/80–1/15/81; Boxing Night (12/27); Bertuccio 18x, *The Fool's Revenge*

The supporting company fared better in *The Fool's Revenge*, than they had in *Hamlet* or *Richelieu*, although some of them were still savaged. The critic for the *Saturday Review* wrote: "They would do well to learn ... that Manfredi does not rhyme to Macready, and one of them, at least, should remember that Malatesta does not assume a final *r* before a vowel. They pronounced Bolgona "baloney." According to a cable sent to the *New York Herald*, the stage management was scarcely satisfactory, the costumes certainly not being of the period assigned to the play ... while the dummy, which was carefully handed down a ladder, was a very palpable dummy, with very stiff black feet." The journalistic abuse that Booth anticipated for his work in Bertuccio was, in *The Illustrated London News*, leveled not at him but at the play: "The Bertuccio of Mr. Edwin Booth was, throughout, magnificent.... So nearly did the extremes of the grotesque and the terrible touch each other, that, for a moment, one scarcely knew whether to smile at it or to be appalled at the ravings of the brokenhearted father. This was especially the case in the whimpered 'Take me in, Take me in!' entreaty of the jester to the courtier, when Bertuccio is repulsed from the door of the banqueting-chamber. He fondles, he fawns upon, he pats the knees of the man who he thinks has influence enough to take him into the presence of Fiordilisa and her abductor. His yell of immeasurable despair when his suit is denied, and he is rudely thrust from the door with a rough reminder that his 'ape's tricks' are not wanted within, is something agonising [sic] to hear.... It is not Mr. Booth's fault if throughout the part of Bertuccio ... there runs a strong vein of 'stagey' unreality.... The final catastrophe and scene of reconciliation, ... have been altered by Mr. Edwin Booth himself from the text of Mr. Taylor." On Jan. 5, 1881, Booth wrote to William Winter: "Everything connected with the management is distasteful to me. Gooch, a cheap-John Jew, has taken a vile advantage of me & coerced me into a filthy bargain on his own terms—closing my engagement at a time when it should be in its bloom (next Mar.), and hampering me every way—with a wretched low company.... He is about the vilest cur I ever dealt with—not excepting Robertson, Clarke Bell, Barnett or John E. Russell.... What have I gained by acting here? ... It seems to me a loss of time & labor. I shall leave no impression—there seem to be few minds here worth impressing. The actor's art is judged by his costumes and the scenery. If they are not 'esthetic" (God save the mark!), he makes no stir.... I was at the same ill work at home—but was fortunately checked, by fire first and afterwards by bankruptcy. I do not regret my losses now—since I've seen the evil results of 'grand revivals.' ... My head aches & I've had a severe cough. The business is what is called good in London—for this season, at home I'd think queer; all London is one huge dead-head, particularly the wealthy & 'Nobby' part of it.... Gooch is anxious to get rid of stars & likes the cheap & nasty drama better than Shakespeare." On Jan. 10, 1881, Booth wrote to Laurence Hutton: "All that people here seem to require of the theatre is fine scenes & dresses, if these are lacking they don't like the acting a bit at all."

1/17/81; Othello

About Booth's Othello, Clement Scott wrote in *The Daily Telegraph*: "Every actor living has some trick or mannerism, something that can be imitated in a greater or less degree. Hitherto the very marked style of Mr. Booth, his rolling eyes, his long pauses, his staccato words and laboured process of accentuation, were observed to be strongest in his Hamlet. In 'Othello' ... we feel ourselves occasionally distracted from the scene by this excess of preparation and these constant pauses between each particular syllable.... There was fine elocution of the purely elocutionary school in the speech to the Senate; no fire, no rapture; all cold, correct and formal. Dignity there was but little tenderness; method but very slight inspiration.... Sentences such as 'Never more be officer of mine' and 'Wife What wife? I have no wife,' became a succession of marked pauses."

1/18/81; Othello

1/19/81; Iago, *Othello*

In London, in Jan. 1881, the critic for the *Sunday Times* wrote: "While the ... duel is being conducted, Iago issues noiselessly from his house, goes between the combatants and knocking up the sword of Roderigo ... lays his victim open to the assault of Cassio. Before Cassio can recover from his lunge, Iago cuts at him with his sword. Returning noiselessly into his house, he comes out again with a loud outcry, speaks to Cassio, and runs his sword through the heart of Roderigo. This action accomplished, he turns again to Cassio, whom he sees kneeling, for the purpose of binding up with his handkerchief the wound in his leg. The moment is so favourable, he is about to attack him again, and complete the partially-accomplished murder, when he spies the approach of Ludovico and Gratiano, and abandons his purpose."

1/20/81; Iago, *Othello*

1/21/81; Othello

The most negative criticism of Booth's production of *Othello* came from the critic of *Society* who faulted Booth's cutting of "the scene in which *Othello* hides and hears *Cassio's* praise of *Bianca* ... and the scene in which *Othello* strikes his wife in the presence of the envoy from Venice." He did not like the fact that Booth played the scenes with Iago in "an exposed spot in the seaport of Cyprus" rather than "the private room they are usually played." He pointed out that the "stage management provoked continual laughter. Mysterious hands came and drew the curtain when *Desdemona* was dead, and the voice of Mr. Booth was heard behind the scenes commanding silence." But the critic heaped the greatest scorn on Booth's Othello: "It is a part for which he is physically unsuited. He is small in stature, and cannot look dignified. In every scene he is dwarfed and stunted. Rolling eyes and scowls and groans, premonitory howls, don't add one cubit to an actor's stature.... He was the actor *Hamlet*, not the man. He was the actor of trick as *Richelieu,* not the Cardinal. He was the contortionist *Bertuccio*, not the jester with a pierced heart.... He forced his voice, and the effect was lamentable. His style was marred by all the affectations and mannerisms of the 'bow-wow' drama. Each sentence was accentuated 'til it became ridiculous. '*Cas-si-o*-I-love-thee-but-nev-er-more be-off-i-cer-of mine.' ... He threw his dagger away and his turban off, he stalked about and stamped and groaned.... It was all theatrical and false, hollow and tinselly."

1/22/81; Iago, *Othello*

1/24/81; Othello
1/25/81; Iago, *Othello*
> On Jan. 25, 1881, Booth wrote to E. C. Benedict about his predicament at the Princess's Theatre: "The manager is a cheap-John Jew & is grasping, of course, he don't believe in 'high-art' and expensive stars, but wants his ballet — legs & *Drink* again, so after I quit, the theatre will go back to the beastly business & I shall cool my heels 'till next season." Gooch wants the "blood & thunder" drama without a star to share his profits with.... He's a low-priced pig, of the 'Far-away-Moses' tribe. His name is Gouge, mollified to Gooch."

1/26/81; Othello
1/27/81; Iago, *Othello*
1/28/81; Othello
1/29/8; Iago, *Othello*
1/31/1; Othello
2/1/81; Iago, *Othello*
2/2/81; Othello
2/3/81; Iago, *Othello*
2/4/81; Othello
2/5/81; Iago, *Othello*
2/7/81; Othello
2/8/81; Iago, *Othello*
2/9/81; Othello
2/10/81; Iago, *Othello*
2/11/81; Othello
2/12/81; Iago, *Othello*
2/14–16/81; King Lear 3x
> Charles Dunphie in the *Morning Post* wrote that Booth's *Lear* had "touches of beauty and grandeur as pure and as lofty as any within the reach of any actor." Joseph Knight of the *Sunday Times*, wrote that it was a "remarkable performance," "a brilliant illustration of method and capacity" which had "seldom, if ever, been seen on our stage." Only Clement Scott, the critic for *The Daily Telegraph* was negative. He wrote: "Down to a certain point in the play, the success of the actor was purely theatrical. It was an actor's triumph, adorned with intelligence, but unenlightened with inspiration. We shall be told that after the curse of Goneril, and the lament over the infidelity of Regan, Mr. Booth was called again and again before the curtain; that he roused the audience to enthusiasm, and stirred them to excitement. There is literally nothing to be desired in the Lear of Edwin Booth.... After a sudden spasm of convulsion, the ruined king stands erect and grand only to fall dead, a monument of fallen greatness. There are unfortunately, but few exceptions ... to be made to the general condemnation that the cast must receive, when it is pronounced uneducated and unworthy of the dramatic times win which we live.... The tragedy of 'Lear' is seldom acted, no doubt; but actors and actresses by profession scarcely need tradition or example to guard them against the crudities and imperfections here exhibited.

2/17/81; Lyceum Theatre, F. B. Chatterton's benefit; Morning performance, Richelieu, 4th act
2/17–3/19/81; Princess's Theatre; King Lear 16x
2/28/81; Drury Lane, Royal Theatrical Fund benefit; Matinee, Petruchio, *Katherine and Petruchio*
3/21–26/81; Shylock 3x, *Merchant of Venice*; Petruchio 3x, *Katherine and Petruchio*
> A critic for *The New York Dramatic News and Society Journal* of Apr. 16, 1881, wrote: "Edwin Booth is no fool. No man knows better than himself how little of a good actor he really is, and how much of a mere mime aping and parroting the business and speech his good memory stores up from his experiences of the past.... The fact that his father was a great actor gave Edwin Booth a dramatic 'boost' at the start, and the glamour of his name, and the advertisement of his rash brother's crime afforded him, served him in good stead till their newness wore away. People went to see him first because he was Booth's son, then because he was John Wilkes Booth's brother. He acted well enough to please rude tastes which we almost satisfied by merely seeing a man whose name was in everyone's mouth, and so gained a certain spurious smoothness by practice.... Booth knows himself to be a counterfeit great man and does not intend to test his business by a genuine standard. This is the reason he always plays with people who are such hod-carriers of art that his mechanical facility looms into almost dazzling eminence among them. He has never but once shared in anything like a equal performance with a really strong man since he has been parading his false title to fame. Then the other was a German, and his ignorance of our language destroyed all fear of rival comparison." Negotiating with Booth about their joint appearance, Irving suggested *Venice Preserved*, but Booth had "no fancy for it"; they discussed reviving *Julius Caesar*, but Booth felt that "it would cost a fortune to mount" the piece "in the Lyceum style." On Mar. 4, 1881, Irving wrote to Booth: "I would like, if possible, to play Iago first.... I should be most uncomfortable with the part hanging over my head."

5/2–6/81; Royal Lyceum Theatre, London; Othello 3x
5/9–13/81; Iago 3x, *Othello*
5/16–20/81; Othello 3x
> As Othello in 1881, at age 47, "he stabbed himself standing then turned convulsively, tried unsuccessfully to mount the steps leading to Desdemona's bed, clutched at the curtain, reeled and fell."

5/23–27/81; Iago 3x, *Othello*
5/28–6/4/81; Morning Performance (5/28); Othello 4X
6/7/81; Iago, *Othello*
6/8/81; Morning Performance, Othello
6/9, 11/81; Iago 2x, *Othello*

6/15/81; Othello
6/19/81 End of Performances with Irving; Benefit for Ellen Terry; Role unknown
Irving and Booth had dressing rooms on the side of the stage opposite the rest of the company. The box office took in £1,135 the first week, £1,140 the second, £1,224 the third, £1,155 the fourth and £1975. The amounts Booth received were:

Date	Amount
May 7, 1880	£227
May 14, 1880	£228
May 21, 1880	£244
May 28, 1880	£304
June 7, 1880	£231
June 13, 1880	£395

1881–1882

10/3–4/81; Booth's Theatre, New York; Richelieu 2x
10/5–6/81; Macbeth 2x
10/7/81; Othello
10/8/81; Matinee, Iago, *Othello*; Evening, Richelieu
The grosses in New York for the week beginning Oct. 3, 1881, were: Oct. 3, 1881, $1,784.25; Oct. 4, 1881, $1,839.00; Oct. 5, 1881, $1,631.00; Oct. 6, $1,502.50; Oct. 7, 1881, $1,732.50; Oct. 8, 1881 (mat), $1,086.50; Oct. 8, 1881 (eve), $1,977.50.
10/10/81; Bertuccio, *The Fool's Revenge*
10/11/81; Bertuccio, *The Fool's Revenge*
10/12–13/81; Hamlet 2x
10/14/81 Matinee, Fifth Avenue Theatre, Booth-Barrett Matinee Benefit for Michigan Fire Sufferers; Iago, *Othello*; Booth's Theatre, Evening, Iago, *Othello*
10/15/81; Matinee, Hamlet; Evening, Bertuccio, *The Fool's Revenge*
The grosses in New York for the week of Oct. 10–15, 1881, were: Oct. 10, 1881, $1,106.50; Oct. 11, 1881, $1,487.00; Oct. 12, 1881, $1,667.25; Oct. 13, 1881, $1,771.50; Oct. 14, 1881 (eve), $1,518.00; Oct. 15, 1881 (mat), $1,703.75; Oct. 15, 1881 (eve), $1,873.50.
10/17–18/81; King Lear 2x
10/19/81; Shylock, *Merchant of Venice*; Petruchio, *Katherine and Petruchio*
10/20–21/81; Richard III 2x
10/22/81; Matinee, Richelieu; Evening, Richard III
The grosses in New York for the week of Oct. 17–22, 1881, were: Oct. 17, 1881, $955.00; Oct. 18, 1881, $1,192.75; Oct. 19, 1881, $1,604.25; Oct. 20, 1881, $1,539.75; Oct. 21, 1881, $1,614.50; Oct. 22, 1881 (mat), $1,809.50; Oct. 22, 1881 (eve), $1,782.25
10/24/81; Role Unknown
10/25/81; Richelieu
10/26/81; Shylock, *Merchant of Venice*
10/27/81; Richard III
10/28/81; Richelieu
10/29/81; Either matinee or evening. One role unknown; Hamlet
The grosses in New York for the week of Oct. 24–29, 1881, were: Oct. 24, 1881, $1,419.75; Oct. 25, 1881, $1,629.75; Oct. 26, 1881, $1,346.75; Oct. 27, 1881, $1,651.75; Oct. 28, 1881, $1,761.75; Oct. 29, 1881 (mat), $1,679.75; Oct. 29, 1881 (eve), $1,772.25.
10/31/81; Haverly's Theatre, Brooklyn, New York; Richelieu
11/1/81; Macbeth
11/2/81; Othello
11/3/81; Bertuccio, *The Fool's Revenge*
11/4/81; Hamlet
11/5/81; Matinee, Iago, *Othello*; Evening, Shylock, *Merchant of Venice*; Petruchio, *Katherine and Petruchio*
Business was poor in Brooklyn. The grosses for Oct. 31-Nov. 5, 1881 were: Oct. 31, 1881, $872.25 company's share, $647.80 (74 percent share); Nov. 1, 1881, $835.75; Nov. 2, 1881, $1,026.00; Nov. 3, 1881, $363.00; Nov. 4, 1881, $548.75; Nov. 5, 1881 (mat), $905.00; Nov. 5, 1881 (eve), $401.00.
11/7–8/81; Lyceum Theatre, Philadelphia; Richelieu 2x
11/9–10/81; Macbeth 2x
11/11/81; Othello
11/12/81; Matinee, Iago, *Othello*; Evening, Shylock, *Merchant of Venice*; Petruchio, *Katherine and Petruchio*
11/14/81; Hamlet; cancelled due to Mary McVicker's death
11/15/81; Bertuccio, *The Fool's Revenge*; cancelled due to Mary McVicker's death
11/16/81; Shylock, *Merchant of Venice*; cancelled due to Mary McVicker's death; Petruchio, *Katherine and Petruchio*; cancelled due to Mary McVicker's death
11/17/81; Richelieu; cancelled due to Mary McVicker's death
11/18/81; Iago, *Othello*; cancelled due to Mary McVicker's death
11/19/81; Matinee, Hamlet; cancelled due to Mary McVicker's death; Evening, Bertuccio, *The Fool's Revenge*; cancelled due to Mary McVicker's death
Business in Philadelphia was mediocre with a high gross of $1,257.00 on Saturday evening, in part due to a top ticket price of $1.50. The company played to a 75 percent share. The grosses for the week of Nov. 7–12, 1881, were: Nov. 7, 1881, $722.00; Nov. 8, 1881, $1,097.75; Nov. 9, 1881, $879.00; Nov. 10, 1881, $1,027.75; Nov. 11, 1881, $1,138.50; Nov. 12, 1881 (mat), $650.00; Nov. 12, 1881 (eve), $1,257.00.
11/21/81; Academy of Music, Baltimore; Richelieu
11/22/81; Hamlet
11/23/81; Othello
11/24/81; Matinee, Iago, *Othello*; Evening, Shylock, *Merchant of Venice*; Petruchio, *Katherine and Petruchio*
11/25/81; Macbeth

11/26/81; Matinee, Hamlet; Evening, Bertuccio, *The Fool's Revenge*

The grosses in Baltimore for the week of Nov. 21–26 were: Nov. 21, 1881, $1,180.50; the Company received $944.40 or 80 percemt; Nov. 22, 1881, $1,548.50; Nov. 23, 1881, $880.50; Nov. 24, 1881 (mat), $774.25; Nov. 24, 1881 (eve), $ 253.25; Nov. 25, 1881, $1,385.75; Nov. 26, 1881 (mat), $1,279.50; Nov. 26, 1881 (eve), $1356.75. In Baltimore, "over three hundred people awaited on the pavement the opening of the doors.... As the curtain fell after each act, the applause came, and Mr. Booth was called to the front." Booth wrote to Laurence Hutton: "My business is very fine, weather bad and my acting not much to boast of; I am *absent* & very weary."

11/28/81 City Hall, Waterbury, Connecticut; Hamlet; originally scheduled as Richelieu; originally advertised as Shylock, *Merchant of Venice*; Petruchio later cut, *Katherine and Petruchio*

11/29/81; Carll's Opera House, New Haven, Connecticut; Hamlet

One performance of *Hamlet* in New Haven, Connecticut, on Nov. 29, 1881, brought in $1,355, but the local manger made only $100.

11/30/81; Opera House, Meriden, Connecticut; Hamlet

12/1/81; Robert's Opera House, Hartford, Connecticut; Hamlet

In Hartford, on Dec. 1, 1881, "long before the opening of the doors for the entertainment, every seat in the parquet, parquet circle, and dress circle had been sold, and at the commencement of the play, even the seats in the upper gallery were occupied and in the body of the house advantageous standing room was difficult to obtain.... The receipts ... amounted to $1,745. According to the local newspaper, "by his contract with Mr. Abbey, Mr. Booth received thirty-five percent of the net profits"— $610.75.

12/2/81; New Opera House, Springfield, Massachusetts Hamlet

When Booth played Springfield, Massachusetts, "people began to form in line at 7 o'clock the night before, though the sale did not begin until 2 o'clock" the next afternoon. "The theatre rotunda was filled by a motley crowd, but the sale was conducted so smoothly that at 3 o'clock all the dress-circle seats were gone, and soon after four nothing remained down stairs but the three back rows, the sale footing up $900. A large number of tickets went into the hands of speculators, and most of them disposed of their seats in a short time at advanced rates.... The rest of the seats [were] put on sale [the following] morning at Whiting's music store; but admission to the gallery and standing room [was] not ... sold until the night of the performance."

12/3/81; Worcester Theatre, Worcester, Massachusetts; Hamlet

12/4/81; Low's Opera House, Providence, Rhode Island; Hamlet

12/5–6/81; Park Theatre, Boston, Massachusetts; Richelieu 2x

12/7–8/81; Macbeth 2x

12/9/81; Othello

12/10/81; Matinee, Iago, *Othello*; Evening, Richelieu

The grosses for the week of Dec. 5–10, 1881, at the Park Theatre in Boston were: Dec. 5, 1881, $858.75; Dec. 6, 1881, $1,087.40; Dec. 7, 1881, $1,105.65; Dec. 8, 1881, $1,190.95; Dec. 9, 1881, $1,154.35; Dec. 10, 1881 (mat). $ 975.15; Dec. 10, 1881 (eve). $1285.25.

12/12–13/81; Bertuccio 2x, *The Fool's Revenge*

12/14–15/81; Hamlet 2x

12/16/81; Iago, *Othello*

12/17/81; Matinee, Hamlet; Evening, Bertuccio, *The Fool's Revenge*

12/19/81; Hamlet

12/20/81; Shylock, *Merchant of Venice*

12/21/81; King Lear

12/22–23/81; Richard III 2x

12/24/81; Matinee, Richelieu; Evening, Richard III

The grosses in Boston for the week of Dec. 19–24, 1881, were: Dec. 19, 1881, $1,147.50; Dec. 20, 1881, $860.30; Dec. 21, 1881, $1,096.75; Dec. 22, 1881, $1,074.95; Dec. 23, 1881, $1,049.35; Dec. 24, 1881 (mat), $1,064.10; Dec. 24, 1881 (eve), $ 812.55.

12/26/81; Macbeth

12/27/81; Hamlet

On Dec. 27, 1881, Booth wrote to Jervis McEntee: "Go often to some funny shop, if not to the <u>niggers</u> [minstrel shows], see Patience [Gilbert and Sullivan] & other bouffes—come see <u>me</u> when I act in N.Y. and I'll make you laugh—or <u>sleep</u>, I'll warrant you. The weather is dismal & I feel malarial."

12/28/81; Richelieu

12/29/81; Iago, *Othello*

12/30/81; Bertuccio, *The Fool's Revenge*

12/31/81; Matinee, Hamlet; Evening, Richard III

The grosses in Boston for Dec. 26–31, 1881 were: Dec. 26, 1881, $1,308.70; Dec. 27, 1881, $1,147.65; Dec. 28, 1881, $1,170.70; Dec. 29, 1881, $1,103.90; Dec. 30, 1881, $1,176.20; Dec. 31, 1881 (mat), $1,265.70; Dec. 31, 1881 (eve), $1,246.60

1/2/82; Academy of Music, Fall River, Massachusetts; Iago, *Othello*

The one performance of *Othello* at the Academy of Music in Fall River, Massachusetts, on Jan. 2, 1882, grossed $1,417.25.

1/3/82; Low's Opera House, Providence, Rhode Island; Richelieu

1/3/82; Iago, *Othello*

The performance of *Richelieu* at Low's Opera House in Providence, Rhode Island, on Jan. 3, 1882, grossed $1,654.25; the performance of *Othello* on Jan. 4, 1882, grossed $1,529.50. The company played at an 80 percent share.

1/6/82; Able Opera House, Easton, Pennsylvania; Hamlet, originally scheduled as Iago [*Othello*], probably because S. W. Piercy became too ill and could not do Othello. The performance of *Hamlet* at the Able Opera House in Easton, Pennsylvania, on Jan. 6, 1882, grossed $959.00.

1/7/82; Academy of Music, Scranton, Pennsylvania; Richelieu

One performance of *Richelieu* at the Academy of Music in Scranton, Pennsylvania, on Jan. 7, 1882, grossed $1,511.75.

1/9/82; Music Hall, Wilkes-Barre, Pennsylvania; Hamlet

On Jan. 9, 1882, Booth's leading actor, Samuel W. Piercy, died of smallpox in Boston. He was replaced by Barton Hill. There were 150 people on line when the Wilkes-Barre sale began on the Wednesday before performance. A thousand dollars worth of tickets was sold between nine and eleven A.M. at $1.50 per ticket. No one was permitted to buy more than six seats. "Booth concluded not to stay over Sunday in Scranton and ... proceeded to New York on the midnight line. He returned to Pennsylvania on Monday "in the handsome palace car named ... Jerome Miller" and "made his headquarters at the Valley house. Holders of tickets to the performance came early, and long before ... [the] orchestra tuned up their instruments, every seat in Music Hall was occupied.... The gentlemen on this occasion overlooked the ladies' towering hats.... Sooner than disturb a lady on account of the wideness of her brim or the tallness of her crown, the gentlemen put their overcoats on their seats, which raised them a peg higher." The performance on Jan. 9 at Wilkes Barre lasted until 11:45 P.M. and grossed $1,611.50.

1/10/82; Grand Opera House, Harrisburg, Pennsylvania; Iago

One performance of *Othello* at the Grand Opera House, Harrisburg, Pennsylvania, on Jan. 10, 1882, grossed $1,237.50, despite the fact that it was snowing. The local critic thought most of Booth's support scarcely "fair to middling."

1/11/82; Library Hall, Pittsburgh, Pennsylvania; Richelieu

1/12/82; Hamlet

On Jan. 12, 1882, Booth wrote to William Winter from Pittsburgh: "Business is good. We two [Booth and Edwina] are good, too, but mighty dull in smoky Pittsburgh. Where we stop longer than one night we abandon the car for hotels—as here."

1/13/82; Bertuccio, *The Fool's Revenge*

1/14/82; Matinee, Hamlet; Evening, Othello or Iago

The grosses for five performances at Pittsburg were: Jan. 11, 1882, $1,184.25; the Company share was $1,006.61 (85 percent); Jan. 12, 1882, $1,782.50; Jan. 13, 1882, $1,590.50; Jan. 14, 1882 (mat), $1,222.00; Jan. 14, 1882 (eve), $935.75. All tickets at the matinee were one dollar. When Booth played Hamlet, the local critic wrote that he "was well received by his audience ... which ... was probably the largest that ever witnessed a theatrical representation in Library Hall.... Mr. Booth's company is not a strong one.... People become very much disgusted when prices are advanced for an organization of this kind."

1/16/82; Macauley's Theatre, Louisville, Kentucky; Richelieu

1/17/82; Hamlet

1/18/82; Iago, *Othello*

The grosses for the three nights in Louisville were Jan. 16, 1882—$1,186.00 with the company's share being $948.80; Jan. 17, 1882—$1,630.50 with the company's share being $1304.40; Jan. 18, 1882—$1,382.00 with the company's share being $1,104.00. The company's share was 80 percent.

1/19/82; Leubrie's Theatre, Memphis, Tennessee; Richelieu

1/20/82; Bertuccio, *The Fool's Revenge*

1/21/82; Matinee, Hamlet; Evening, Iago, *Othello*

Four performances at Leubrie's Theatre in Memphis, Tennessee, on Jan. 19, 20 and 21 grossed $6,458.50. The performance of *Richelieu* ("bad weather and streets") on Jan. 19, 1882, grossed $1454.50; *The Fool's Revenge* ("rain and wind") on Jan. 20 grossed $1705.00; the matinee of *Hamlet* on Jan. 21 ("weather fine") grossed $1889.50; the evening performance of *Othello* grossed $1409.50. The company received an 80 percent share. When Booth appeared in *Hamlet*, "every seat was filled up stairs and down and a double row of people stood up along the walls of the dress circle. Many ladies were seen sitting on the steps in the aisles of house.... When the curtain fell on the third act, Mr. Barton Hill of the company, came before the curtain and made a most welcome announcement. He said that in consequence of the desire expressed by many citizens to see Mr. Booth the fourth time during the present engagement, he would appear at night, in Othello, taking the role of Iago. The Mozart Society who had engaged the theater ... resigned it to Mr. Booth, and in the name of the management, Mr. Hill returned thanks to the society.... The announcement was received with great cheering, and when it was over, Mr. Hill announced that the sale of seats for the night performance would begin immediately after the final fall of the curtain. As soon as the audience had dispersed, the ticket office ... became thronged with eager applicants for reserved seats, and in less than half an hour a full house was assured.... The house downstairs was sold in an hour and fifty minutes after the ticket office was opened—and this in a town that does not, as a rule, support the theater on Saturday night. When the curtain rose the theater was filled downstairs and in the balcony. The gallery was also fairly tenanted."

1/24/82; Tremont Opera House, Galveston Texas; Richelieu

By Galveston, Booth's weariness was showing in his performances. The local critic wrote: "Throughout the first act" of *Richelieu*. "there was something of coldness. In the succeeding act there seemed to be but little more warmth but later when the death scene was enacted a specimen of the power of the great actor was given. The climax was not reached until [the curse of Rome scene]."

1/25/82; Macbeth

When Booth performed Macbeth, "an entire act was disclosed before there was any great degree of enthusiasm."

1/26/82; Hamlet

1/27/82; Bertuccio, *The Fool's Revenge*

1/28/82; Matinee, Iago, *Othello*

When Othello was presented "there was not that freshness nor finish that marked other of his works during the week, nor did his support tend to strengthen the merit of the play." Nevertheless, six performances brought in $8,641.00.

Evening, Shylock, *Merchant of Venice*, originally scheduled as *Othello*

The New York Mirror of Jan. 28, 1882, reported: "Booth's vaccination still troubles him, but he is recovering from the scald he received some days ago. Neither interfered with his acting." "Mr. Maze Edwards manager of the company and Mr. W[illiam] E. Miller, business manager for Mr. Booth" were with the company in Galveston. The grosses for five performances were: Jan. 24, 1882, $1,323.50; Jan. 25, 1882, $1113.00; Jan. 26, 1882, $1,583.00; Jan. 27, 1882 (mat), $1,018.00; Jan. 27, 1882 (eve), $1,481.00. The company received an 80 percent share. Booth left Galveston on Jan. 29, 1882 for New Orleans and then continued eastward through the South to Montgomery, Atlanta, and Chattanooga, where, after the show he wrote to William Winter: "Being in a car, bounced from end to end all day & acting at night unfits one for such pastime [writing letters].... I have just finished Hamlet & am in my car—to start at 5 A.M. tomorrow.... The horrid weather has kept me confined all day—but the house was well-filled, in spite of mud & rain. The leader of Orchestra was drunk so we did à la Francaise—without music. I have pic-nic'd my company several times—for Edwina's sake—and had jolly times, once at Galveston, by the Mexican Gulf, & again 'neath the pines of Alabama—where we had a set of darkies to sing, dance & 'cut up' for us.... Thank God! I am on the return voyage—if He spares us in our travels over these infernal roads, I shall never cease my thanks and will never take such a trip again."

1/30/82; Sales Grand Opera House, New Orleans; Richelieu

In New Orleans, "the desire here to see this eminent tragedian, ... notwithstanding the price of reserve seats" produced "very large houses.... His supporting company, with the exception of Bella Pateman, who is admirable, is not worthy of the star." The local critic wrote of *Richelieu* "The theatre was crowded.... The support given Mr. Booth by the company, all parts considered, was unworthy of the theatre and the great star."

1/31/82; Othello

When Booth played Othello, the critic thought the support was "fairly good." When he played Hamlet, the local critic wrote that "Mr. Booth's towering excellence in so great a part in so great a play only makes the inferior company about him seem more weak than it is."

2/1/82; Hamlet

2/2/82; Macbeth

2/3/82; Bertuccio, *The Fool's Revenge*

2/4/82; Matinee, Iago, *Othello*; Evening, Richelieu

The grosses for the six performances in Sales Grand Opera House were: Jan. 30, 1882, $1,211.50; Jan. 31, 1882, $1,071.00; Feb. 1, 1882, $1,820.50; Feb. 2, 1882, $1,304.00; Feb. 3, 1882, $1,613.50; Feb. 4, 1882 (mat), $1,572.00, Company share $1,179.00 (75 percent share); Feb. 4, 1882 (eve), $1,598.00.

2/6/82; Montgomery Theatre, Alabama; Iago, *Othello*

2/7/82; Hamlet

Two nights in the Montgomery Theatre in Montgomery, Alabama, grossed a total of $2,645.00. The performance of *Othello* on Feb. 6, 1882, grossed $1,155.00; the performance of *Hamlet* on Feb. 7 grossed $1490.00. The company received an 80 percent share. In Montgomery the first seats to be sold were for a combination of both nights. The next day, seats for individual performances were sold. "Excursion rates were allowed on nearly all the roads in the state to parties desiring to see Booth." "The S. & N. R. R. from Birmingham and intermediate stations; the Selma division of the W. R. R; the M. & M. from Evergreen and intermediate stations, the Western R. R. from West Point, Opelika, Auburn and Chehaw" sold "round trip tickets for one fare. The Western R. R. ... only [sold] excursion tickets for the 7th, the other roads for both nights. Tickets for the theatre [could also] be ordered by telegraph." Booth remained in his railroad car on a siding while in Montgomery. In Feb. 1882, Booth wrote to Laurence Hutton: "Here & there I give the party a pic-nic—for Edwina's enjoyment,& it does 'em all good here particularly At Galveston by the Gulf, & 'neath the pine trees of Alabama, out of Montgomery, we had jolly times. At the latter place we had the genuine plantation darkies, with bones & tambourine (but no banjo), a jewsharp & lots of dancing, juba, and tumbling & songs, etc. I have so much writing to do that I fear I shall not be able to treat them during this week." On Feb. 7, 1882, the day before Booth performed Hamlet at DeGive's Opera House, there were still "485 reserved seats to sell in the dress circle and balcony and the whole second gallery, also two boxes."

2/8/82; De Give's Opera House, Atlanta, Georgia; Hamlet

The sale of tickets for Booth's Feb. 8 performance of *Hamlet* in Atlanta began on the morning of Jan. 30. Some 800 tickets were sold before one P.M. Speculators sold tickets for three to five dollars each. The performance of *Hamlet* in Atlanta grossed $2,238.00. The company received an 80 percent share.

2/9/82; St. James Hall, Chattanooga, Tennessee; Hamlet

Tickets for Booth's performance at St. James' Hall in Chattanooga on Feb. 9, 1882, went on sale six days prior to his opening, and "there was a great rush for them." By opening "every seat in the parquet and dress circle except forty of fifty was reserved." Booth sequestered himself in his private car, although he and Edwina "took a short walk down Market street ... and attracted ... attention." People came from Dalton, Georgia; Huntsville, Alabama; Knoxville, Tennessee; Scottsboro and other towns in Kentucky, Tennessee and Georgia. "There was a rush" for unreserved seats, "as soon as the doors opened," and the total receipts was $1,109.00. "The hall was not jammed, yet comfortably full, containing probably more people than was ever before assembled there.... The orchestra which Mr. Stoop engaged failed to materialize, for the reason, he states, that some of the members became intoxicated."

2/10/82; Masonic Theatre and Grand Opera House, Nashville, Tennessee; Richelieu

On Feb. 5, 1882, when tickets for Booth's Nashville performances went on sale, "an immense assemblage filled the street and sidewalk.... The jam was such ... that the large doors gave way with a crash, and the crowd rushed in pell-mell, yelling at the top of their voices. Men were run over and trampled upon, faces bruised, arms broken and pockets picked. Seats were upturned and the stage was packed with the crowd, forcing the postponement of the sale of tickets" until the next day. When Booth performed Richelieu on Feb. 10, 1882, "not a decent seat remained and much of the standing room was occupied. Many ladies contented themselves with the view from the gallery," and the local critic thought that "the company is the best Mr. Booth has ever had South." The performance grossed $1,400.00.

2/11/82; Matinee, Iago, *Othello*

The performance of *Othello* at the matinee on Feb. 11 grossed $1,232.00.

2/11/82; Evening, Hamlet

The performance of *Hamlet* that evening grossed $1,872.00. The company received an 80 percent share.

2/13/82; Grand Opera House, St. Louis, Missouri; Richelieu

When Booth opened in St. Louis on Feb. 13, 1882, as Richelieu "the audience filled every seat ... and much of the standing space was claimed.... Fashionable ladies [sat] ... everywhere, in the boxes and in the lower and second circles." The local critic, however, found "the supporting company" only "fair" and felt that Booth had: "shorn the role of *Richelieu* of much of the force with which he played it several years ago, passing through the earlier scenes without infusing into them the fiery elocution which he formerly put into many of the strong passages and almost entirely reserving his strength until he reached the great scenes of the fourth act ... when *Richelieu*, with the light of the coming triumph in his eyes, and the boldest defiance on his lips, cries out to the quivering *Baradas* 'Avaunt! My name is Richelieu! I defy Thee!" ... That the actor's voice has lost a little of its pristine strength was noticeable. He was called out at the end of every act, and was obliged to come forward three times after the curse scene, the house greeting him with shouts and waving handkerchiefs."

2/14/82; Macbeth

2/15/82; Hamlet

2/16/82; Bertuccio, *The Fool's Revenge*

When Booth did Bertuccio on Feb. 16, 1882, the audience "at the close of the play held their seats and applauded and stamped until the curtain was rolled up again, the lights turned on and Mr. Booth with Miss Pateman, came forward to bow his acknowledgements amid a wild outburst of bravos from every part of the house."

2/17/82; Iago, *Othello*

2/18/82; Matinee, Hamlet; Evening, Shylock, *Merchant of Venice*

The grosses in St. Louis from Feb. 13–18, 1882, were: Feb. 13, 1882, $1,549.50; Feb. 14, 1882, $1,326.50; Feb. 15, 1882, $2,162.00; Feb. 16, 1882, $1,747.50; Feb. 17, 1882, $1,919.00; Feb. 18, 1882 (mat), $2,120.50; Feb. 18, 1882 (eve), $1,550.00. On Feb. 19, 1882, Booth was interviewed. He "lay stretched upon the sofa in his parlor at the Southern Hotel ... with, as he expressed it 'a raging headache.' ... Wrapped in a beautiful dressing gown, he reclined at full length, the right hand resting under his head and the feet encased in slippers.... The company say he is beginning to evince an interest in the details of their own work, and now and then kindly furnishes advice and suggestions in matters that were formerly left entirely to the stage manager. [Booth discussed his plans for England and Germany. The reporter met Maze Edwards in the lobby and Edwards said:] 'You would be astonished at the amount of interest he shows in the welfare of the company. Mr. Booth has a special car in which he travels, and often he inquires 'Are your ladies comfortably fixed?' and 'Are your gentlemen entirely satisfied?' And when we were nearing Galveston I suggested that it would be pleasant for our party to visit the beach. Instantly he replied, with a smile, 'By all means. Get some hacks and a band of music, and we'll have a picnic. I'll ride in the band wagon myself.' ... He was naturally of a thoughtful and retiring disposition and was always glad to be relieved of business, while his wife and mother-in-law were deeply interested in managing him and his affairs.' 'Does he manage his own affairs?' 'Not in detail. He is very nervous and excitable over small matters and such things as dismissals and company engagements annoy him greatly. So they are all left to the management.'"

2/20/82; Grand Opera House, Evansville, Indiana; Richelieu

2/21/82; Opera House, Terre Haute, Indiana; Hamlet

Booth's performance in Terre Haute on Feb. 21, 1882, was announced on Feb. 12. On Feb. 15, 1882, tickets went on sale at nine A.M., and people could register for them from seven to nine that morning. No more than six tickets were sold to any one person unless they were not residing in the city. The first day's sales reached $1,100. A representative from Kansas, Illinois reserved twenty-nine seats, and various speculators bought six tickets at a time. Rumors circulated in Terre Haute that Booth would cancel his engagement there because of exaggerated reports of a small-pox outbreak, the company having lost an actor named Sam Piercy to that disease in Boston. According to the local paper, "he has canceled here every season for many past." One performance in Terre Haute Indiana, on Feb. 21, 1882, grossed $1,638.50 from which the company, playing at an 80 percent share received $1,310.80.

2/22/82; Grand Opera House, Lafayette, Indiana; Hamlet

The New York Mirror reported a $1,300 house in Lafayette, Indiana. The actual house was $1,101.25 with the company getting an 85 percent share.

2/23/82; Academy of Music, Fort Wayne, Indiana; Hamlet

Booth's appearance in Fort Wayne on Feb. 23, 1882, was first announced on Feb. 13. His advance man E. F. Gillett had arrived and arranged for Booth and Edwina to have a parlor suite of rooms at the Robinson Hotel and for their meals to be served in their rooms so they did not have to use the dining room. Members of the local press were admitted free, but dramatic correspondents for out-of-town newspapers were not entitled to complimentary tickets. Gillett also limited the number of tickets given to the press which infuriated the local critic so that he rained abuse on Booth even after the actor had left the city. Tickets went on sale at the box office on Feb. 17, 1882. The public was informed that the police would be on hand to preserve order. One hour after the box office opened in Fort Wayne, every seat in the house was taken, and the theatre had taken in either $1,200 or $1,700, according to variant accounts. The local newspaper noted that "at least four of the local clergy will sanction the performance by attending." By Feb. 21 speculators were getting three or four dollars a ticket for the Booth performance. The company arrived in the "Jerome Marble" from Lafayette over the Wabash Railroad on the morning of the performance. Apparently Booth decided not to use the hotel and walked from his car to the theatre. The gross in Fort Wayne on Feb. 23, 1882, was $1,473.00 from which the company received $1,178.40 or 80 percent.

2/24/82; Dickson's Grand Opera House, Indianapolis, Indiana; Bertuccio, *The Fool's Revenge*, originally announced as Richelieu

When Booth appeared for the first time in nine years in three performances at Dicksons' Grand Opera House in Indianapolis on Feb. 24 and 25, 1882, the theatre's free list (complimentary tickets to shareholders) was suspended. Excursions of fifty to one hundred people were arranged from "cities contiguous" to Indianapolis. His performance was advertised as early as Feb. 10, and tickets went on sale on Feb. 17, first at the Grand Opera House and later at a local music store. When tickets went on sale, checks for the best seats were given to people who arrived between 5 A.M. and 10 A.M. at the Opera House, and no one was allowed to buy more than six tickets for each performance to prevent speculation. Sixteen men spent the night at the opera house in order to get the best seats. The day tickets went on sale, the theatre took in $3,714. By the end of the day, every seat on the main floor and in the first balcony for *Hamlet* was gone. Tickets for *Hamlet* sold first, but by the end of the second day, there were few seats left on the ground floor for any performance. The audience that attended included "the culture, beauty and fashion of the city." During *The Fool's Revenge*, the audience demanded that Booth appear before the curtain prior to the second act. Hundreds were turned away who could not even get standing room. It was the most successful engagement in the history of the Indianapolis theatre. As reported in the statements given to Booth, *The Fool's Revenge* took in $2,048.75; *Othello* grossed $2,118, and *Hamlet* brought in $2,463.75 for a grand total of $6,630.95.

2/25/82; Matinee, Othello, originally announced as Shylock, *Merchant of Venice*; Evening, Hamlet

2/27/82; Robinson's Opera House, Cincinnati, Ohio; Richelieu

2/28/82; Macbeth

3/1/82; Hamlet

3/2/82; Bertuccio, *The Fool's Revenge*

3/3/82; Iago, *Othello*
3/4/82; Matinee, Hamlet; Evening, Shylock, *Merchant of Venice*

The advance sale in Cincinnati was $6,000. The local critic thought that in Richelieu, Booth's support ranged "from good to perfect." Overall, at the end of the week, the critic thought the company was "good to tolerable." The grosses for the week of Feb. 27–Mar. 4, 1882, were: Feb. 27, 1882, $1,319.50; Feb. 28, 1882, $1,340.00; Mar. 1, 1882, $1,804.50; Mar. 2, 1882, $1,308.50; Mar. 3, 1882, $1,499.50; Mar. 4, 1882 (mat), $1,242.00; Mar. 4, 1882 (eve), $1,877.00.

3/6/82; Grand Opera House, Springfield, Ohio; Hamlet

One performance of *Hamlet* in Springfield, Ohio, grossed $1,439.00.

3/7/82; Music Hall, Dayton, Ohio; Hamlet

At the end of the day after tickets went on sale in Dayton, for one performance of *Hamlet* on Mar. 7, the whole lower half of the house was sold. The performance grossed $1,641.00 from which the company, playing at an 85 percent share, received $1,394.85. According to the record given to Booth, one performance of *Hamlet* grossed $2,011.50. Seventy-seven extra chairs were needed.

3/8/82; Comstock Opera House, Columbus, Ohio; Hamlet
3/9/82; Academy of Music, Akron, Ohio; Hamlet
3/10/82; Academy of Music, Youngstown, Ohio; Hamlet

One performance of *Hamlet* at the Youngstown Opera House grossed $1,506.00. An article in the *Akron Daily News* of Mar. 10, 1882, read: "The elegant palace car "Jerome Marble," belonging to the Worcester Palace Excursion Car Company was found yesterday standing on the side-track of the Cleveland, Akron and Columbus RailRoad in this city, and a *News* man was sent out to visit it and its occupants. On applying for entrance, it was denied on the grounds that Mr. Booth was just then taking his breakfast; but upon being urged to seek Mr. Booth and see if he would not extend the courtesy to *The News* man, the maid entered and asked the gentleman, and upon learning that he was from so enterprising a paper as *The News*, very courteously granted the request.... Miss Edwina Booth is a very fine pianist and during the interview the dulcet strains that were proceeding from the piano in the salon, were the product of her artistic skill."

3/11/82; Biemiller's Opera House, Sandusky, Ohio; Hamlet

One performance in Sandusky, Ohio, grossed $1111.50 with Booth playing to an 85 percent share.

3/13/82; Wheeler's Opera House, Toledo, Ohio; Hamlet

When Booth appeared in Toledo on Mar. 13, 1882, there was no extra charge for reserved seats. No person was allowed to buy more than six seats.

"Every seat in the Opera House was filled ... and standing room in the lower floor was at a premium. The placard 'standing room only,' which" seldom appeared "at Wheeler's was displayed early in the evening." The local critic wrote: "His support, although good, appeared to poor advantage, as their defects were more clearly noticed when brought in comparison with the polished acting of the great star. That the audience was thoroughly pleased may be judged from the frequent applause bestowed upon the company, Mr. Booth being called before the curtain several times." The gross was $1,662.75 of which the company received $1,330.20 or 80 percent.

3/14/82; Detroit Opera House, Detroit, Michigan; Richelieu
3/15/82; Hamlet

The performance of *Richelieu* in Detroit on Mar. 14, 1882, grossed $1,685.25; the performance of *Hamlet* on Mar. 15 grossed $2,219.75. The company received an 80 percent share. When Booth played Hamlet the next night, he "packed the opera house to suffocation. Hundreds of people stood up all over the house.... Ladies eagerly paid $1.50 each for the privilege of sitting in the orchestra pit with the musicians. Patrolman Thomas Thompson ... routed out scores of young men who tried to sit on the steps of the aisles free the entire evening." The local newspaper reported: "the great tragedian was in poor health, having been confined to his room all day with a cold, but after the first act he warmed to his work, and barring some degree of hoarseness, gave 'Richelieu' in a manner calculated to excite a high pitch of enthusiasm."

3/16/82; Powers' Opera House, Grand Rapids, Michigan; Hamlet

At the end of the first day of ticket sales for one performance in Grand Rapids, Michigan, on Mar. 16, the box office had taken in $1,400, and the gross receipts were $1,820. Playing at an 80 percent share, the company received $1,456.00. By the time he opened almost every seat had been taken. In Detroit, "no person" was allowed to buy more than six seats. Seats [could] be secured by telegraph or telephone. "Mr. Marcus R. Mayer, who has been managing Edwin Booth's business in the south and west, says Mr. Booth's tour has been a continued series of ovations. The seats are all sold for his performance here on Thursday [Mar. 16, 1882 in Grand Rapids Michigan] and while there will not be quite so much money in the house as Bernhardt had, it will be the largest audience ever known here." In Grand Rapids, Michigan, where Booth performed on Mar. 16, 1882, the reserve ticket sale at the end of the first day of sale was $1,400.

3/17/82; Grand Opera House, Milwaukee, Wisconsin; Richelieu

When Booth played two evenings and a matinee at the Grand Opera House in Milwaukee on

Mar. 17 and 18, the opera house "was filled from parquet to balcony with an appreciative and discriminating audience." Booth still suffered from hoarseness—the result of "a sudden but brief illness suffered a few days ago in Detroit. By Saturday morning, the only seats left for Saturday night were in the balcony." The performance of *Richelieu* on Mar. 17 grossed $1,217.50; the performance of *Othello* at the matinee on Mar. 18 grossed $1,269.00 and the evening performance that night grossed $1,920.00 The company received an 80 percent share.

3/18/82; Matinee, Iago, *Othello*; Evening, Hamlet

3/20/82; Hooley's Opera House, Madison, Wisconsin; Hamlet

3/21/82; Opera House, Rockford, Illinois; Hamlet

The performance of *Hamlet* at the Opera House in Rockford, Illinois, on Mar. 21, 1882, grossed $1,281.50, with the company receiving $1,089.28.

3/22/82; Harper's Opera House, Rock Island, Illinois; Richelieu

The performance of *Richelieu* at Harper's Opera House in Rock Island, Illinois, on Mar. 22, 1882, grossed $1,406.50.

3/23/82; Burtis's Opera House, Davenport, Iowa; Role unknown

The performance at Burtis's Opera House in Davenport Iowa on Mar. 23, 1882, grossed $1,202.75.

3/24/82; New Opera House, Burlington, Iowa; Hamlet

The performance of *Hamlet* at the New Opera House in Burlington, Iowa, on Mar. 24, 1882, grossed $1,631.00. When Booth played Burlington, excursions were "arranged from several of the neighboring cities for the occasion, at the price of best seats placed at three dollars. Standing room tickets were sold at $1.50 each."

3/25/82; Touser's Opera House, Rock Island Illinois; Hamlet

The performance of Hamlet at Touser's Opera House in Rock Island, Illinois on Mar. 25 grossed $1,115.00.

3/27–28/82; Haverly's Theatre, Chicago; Richelieu 2x

3/29–30/82; Hamlet 2x

3/31/82; Bertuccio, *The Fool's Revenge*

4/1/82; Matinee, Hamlet; Evening, Iago, *Othello*

4/3/82; Macbeth

The mediocrity that had plagued the entire tour continued in Chicago. On Apr. 3, 1882, when Booth performed Macbeth, "the scenic management was all at odds and it seemed to be impossible to get a pair of flats to fit or a door to shut. Much amusement was created ... when half a palace and half a forest were slid into opposite grooves , and there were too many scene-shifters and assistants in plain view on several occasions during the play."

4/4/82; Richelieu

4/5/82; Othello

In 1882 the critic for the *Chicago Tribune* wrote: "In the course of the play, *Othello* is called upon for the exercise of considerable muscular power, and in one scene is supposed to slam *Iago* around with considerable violence and dust the furniture with him.... Last night Mr. Barton Hill, who is about a foot taller than Mr. Booth, took the part of *Iago*, and when Mr. *Othello* Booth began to wrestle with Mr. Hill and finally threw him, it looked as though, like other wrestling matches, it was a put-up job.... Mr. Booth ... possesses neither the physique, nor the temperament necessary to a complete realization of this hot-blooded, semi-civilized character. To imagine that such a cold, calculating, refined figure as Mr. Booth ... would ever allow himself ... to murder his wife is a great stretch of the imagination."

4/6/82; Shylock, *Merchant of Venice*

4/7/82; Hamlet

A Chicago critic wrote: "The company supporting Mr. Booth on his present tour is without doubt the best with which he has ever been surrounded while traveling.... The stage setting and costuming of the play were all that could be desired." Booth's Hamlet on Apr. 7, 1882, in Chicago took in nearly $2,000.

4/8/82; Matinee, Richelieu; Evening, Bertuccio, *The Fool's Revenge*

4/10/82; Academy of Music, Buffalo, New York; Richelieu

4/11/82; Hamlet

Two performances at the Academy of Music in Buffalo, New York, on Apr. 10–11, 1882, grossed $2,360.00. The performance of *Richelieu* at the Academy of Music in Buffalo, New York, on Apr. 10, 1882, grossed $989.50. The company's share was $791.60. The performance of *Hamlet* on Apr. 11 grossed $1,370.50.

4/12/82; Grand Opera House, Rochester, New York; Hamlet

One performance of *Hamlet* at the Grand Opera House, Rochester, New York, on Apr. 12, 1882, grossed $1,607.00. The company received an 80 percent share.

4/13/82; Utica Opera House, Utica, New York; Hamlet

When Booth played Hamlet at the Utica Opera House on Apr. 13, 1882, 1,500–1,600 people attended. He was called before the curtain three times. "The curtain rose nearly on time, and the waits between the acts were very short; yet it was after 11 o'clock when the final scenes were enacted." The performance grossed $1,793.00.

4/14/82; Leland Opera House, Albany, New York.; Richelieu

Booth gave three performances in Albany, from Apr. 14–15 1882. The performance of *Richelieu* on Apr. 14, 1882 grossed $1,111.50. The company received a share of $950.35; the performance of *Oth-*

ello at the matinee on Apr. 15 grossed $871.75; the performance of *Hamlet* that evening grossed $1,236.50.

4/15/82; Matinee, Iago, *Othello*; Evening, Hamlet
4/17/82; Booth's Theatre, New York; Richelieu
4/18/82; Othello
4/19/82; Macbeth
4/20/82; Bertuccio, *The Fool's Revenge*
4/21/82; Iago, *Othello*
4/22/82; Matinee, Richelieu; Evening, Bertuccio, *The Fool's Revenge*
4/24/82; Hamlet
4/25/82; King Lear
4/26/82; Richelieu
4/27/82; Hamlet
4/28/82; Bertuccio, *The Fool's Revenge*
4/29/82; Matinee, Hamlet; Evening, Richard III

The receipts for the two weeks in Apr. in New York were: Apr. 17, $1,371.25; Apr. 18, $1,121.75; Apr. 19, $1,265.50; Apr. 20, $1.634.00; Apr. 21, $1,174.00; Apr. 22 (mat), $1,768.75; Apr. 22 (eve), $1,814.25; Apr. 24, $1,323.00; Apr. 25, $1,257.75; Apr. 26, $1,879.25; Apr. 27, $2,000.75; Apr. 28, $1,860.75; Apr. 29 (mat), $1,947.25; Apr. 29 (eve), $2,065.00.

1882–1883

By Aug. 26, 1880, word of a possible German engagement had reached the editor of the *Kleine Journal* in Berlin who wrote, asking for permission to arrange the tour. Booth had a secretary write, saying that he did "not at present contemplate a professional visit to your country." The editor wrote again on Nov. 18, 1881, when word reached Germany that Booth was coming. One of the actors hired for the provincial English tour was Booth's nephew, Creston Clarke, On Sept. 24, Booth wrote to William Winter from Harrowgate: "I have one of Clarke's boys with me — but I fear he is dull." Booth wrote to the Aldrichs on June 1, 1882: "I am to open there (Adelphi) on the 26th & I can't reach London before 24th! A close shave! ... Lillie Taylor has translated *Richelieu* & *The Fool* for me — both of which plays are unknown on the German stage." The Adelphi Theatre, where Booth performed in the summer of 1882, was located at 411 Strand and is extant. At the Adelphi Robert Pateman was Booth's stage manger, and Edwin performed under the business management of Wynn Miller. Only one member of the cast returned from the 1880–1881 company. In the audience opening night was Sir Theodore and Lady Martin (Helen Faucit) who had played the original Julie to Macready's Richelieu in 1839. At some point during his stay in London, Booth went to a "drawing-room reading" of *Much Ado About Nothing* with Helen Faucit (Lady Martin) and Sir Henry Irving in the leading roles.

6/26–7/22/82; Adelphi Theatre, London; Richelieu 14x

Booth opened in London on June 26, 1882, in *Richelieu*. "Besides figuring in the ordinal cardinal's garb, ... [he] appeared in the first scene in a handsome robe of old gold brocade trimmed with costly fur. The programmes were printed on white satin and enclosed in a gilt-edged covers with flowers painted on the back." The production values got mixed reviews. The critic for *Society* wrote: *Richelieu* is sumptuously mounted, the furniture and upholstery having been specially manufactured by the eminent firm of White, Winter and Co., of Percy Street, Tottenham Court Road.... I may especially mention the real Venetian chandelier and the Louis XIII furniture.... The painting of the Throne room is too garish and dauby and is not in keeping with the furniture, and we certainly look for something better nowadays in the matter of skies and ceilings than Mr. Charles Brookes and assistants have provided. The critic for the *Weekly Dispatch* wrote, however, that "the drama is placed upon the stage with as much care as if it were intended to run for a lengthy period. The whole of the scenes are rich and tasteful, except in the last act, where a blue moon [is] surrounded by a green sky." The last act was copied from a print in the British Museum. In June 1882 the critic for *The Globe* thought that when Booth played Richelieu, his "delivery [was] slow and deliberate, and the shake of the fingers [was] too frequently employed." The critic for *The Echo* wrote: "Too much is made of the cough."

7/24–8/2/82; Bertuccio 9x, *The Fool's Revenge*

When Booth began to perform Bertuccio in London, on July 24, the Adelphi ... was crowded, and ... Booth was literally pelted with largest of bouquets." Making "his appearance on the stage ... clothed in singularly picturesque rags and tatters, he was greeted with rounds and rounds of applause that threatened to be continuous and to quite stop the play." The *mise-en-scène* of the production was somewhat problematic. The critic for *The Globe* thought the "properties ... lacking in realism." The critic for the *Referee* noted that "in the first act of "Fool's Revenge," there is a moon. The moon has a man in it as usual. It is a gasman. You can't see him, but you can see the gas." He also complained that "the audience was not able to get away until about twenty minutes before midnight" but added that "they have altered all that since then." The *Reynolds'* critic wrote that "the music of 'Rigoletto' was ... made to do good service ... in some scenes." Booth was called before the curtain twice.... Bouquets were thrown at him, and a large laurel wreath was handed up." In changing the ending of *The Fool's Revenge*, Booth weakened the tragic predicament of his character, at least in the eyes of the critic for the *London Times* who wrote on July 27, 1882: "It is impossible to feel very keenly for a personage whose daughter suffers no more than an abortive abduction." As Bertuccio in 1882, at age 49, Booth contrived "during three long acts, to simulate the gait of a man with incurably crooked legs," giving "to each of [his] legs the temporary aspect of the letter 'C.'"

8/3/82; Matinee, Don Caesar de Bazan

On Aug. 3, Booth gave a special matinee of *Don Caesar de Bazan*. It was a benefit for Wynn Miller, although not announced as such. "As too often happens at morning representations, the piece had been but inadequately rehearsed, and the prompter had a busy time of it." "There were delays, misreadings, wrong entrances and exits, and other signs of hasty and immature preparation." "It was stated that the performance would commence at one o'clock, but few habitual theatre-goers imagined that the chief feature of the entertainment would head the bill. As it was, a large number of persons missed the first act." The Scarborough contract was made out on Sept. 5, 1881. The contract to play Birmingham was made on Feb. 14, 1882. The contract to play Manchester was made out on Mar. 21, 1882. The contracts for Dundee and Aberdeen were not signed until after Booth had begun his English tour. None of these contracts were signed by anyone representing Booth. The contract for Liverpool was signed on Aug. 3, 1881, by W. E. Miller. The contract for Dublin was signed by William H. Griffiths, acting as a agent on behalf of Edwin Booth on Mar. 14, 1882. All other contracts for the English tour had been originally made out in Sept. 1881 but the original month was crossed out and the Nov. dates inserted. These contracts were signed by Miller. At Scarborough, Booth received 65 percent of the gross receipts. At Newcastle-upon-Tyne, Glasgow, Edinburgh, Leeds, Dublin, Manchester and Birmingham he received 60 percent of the gross receipts. At Hull he received 65 percent of the receipts, "providing that such receipts for the week amount to the sum of six hundred pounds but should the receipts not amount to the sum of six hundred pounds then it is agreed that the said Edwin Booth shall receive only sixty per cent of the gross receipts." In Dundee and Aberdeen, Booth received two-thirds of the gross receipts. In Liverpool, he received 55 percent of the gross.

8/3–5/82; Bertuccio 3x, *The Fool's Revenge*

9/11/82; New Theatre Royal, Sheffield, England; Richelieu

Booth opened in Sheffield on Sept. 11, 1882. "The house was only a small one." "There was a very large attendance in the pit, but the higher-priced parts of the house were certainly not so well-filled as one would have expected on the visit of so great a actor." Sheffield people had "a way of not coming out in numbers the first evening," and Booth's first "night was no exception." It was also "Doncaster week and the minds of thousands" were "filed with 'the Leger' [St. Leger horserace in Doncaster] to the exclusion of almost every other subject." and the dress circle was "far too deserted." The critic for *The Sheffield Daily Telegraph* wrote: "Mr. Booth, on his first appearance last evening, in the scene with De Mauprat, was most cordially received, and at the end of the act had a hearty recall. At the outset he seemed to be somewhat frigid in his manners.... [As] warmly as the actor had been welcomed on his first entrance, the curtain fell in comparative silence upon the two opening acts; the audience was chilled by his lack of fire, and the general feeling was one of distinct disappointment." The "audience could scarcely wait the close of his words [curse of Rome speech[] before they burst into enthusiastic applause, again and again renewed.... At the close of the third act, ... the occupants of the pit seemed to rise en masse from their seats to demand the appearance of the ... actor before the curtain, and when he came [they expressed their] enthusiasm ... in every way, including the waving of hats and handkerchiefs." In Sheffield, England in 1882 "occasionally the words seemed to come somewhat rapidly, and the voice dropped towards the end of certain sentences."

9/12/82; Hamlet

9/13/82; Richelieu

"The address to the Senate—the apology as it is usually called—was much too hurried, though every word fell clear from the lips of the skilled elocutionist."

9/14/82; Othello

9/15/82; Bertuccio, *The Fool's Revenge*

9/16/82; Shylock, *Merchant of Venice*; Petruchio, *Katherine and Petruchio*

9/18/82; Theatre Royal, York; Richelieu

9/19/82; Londesboro Theatre, Scarborough; Richelieu

9/20/82; Hamlet

On Sept. 20, [1882], Booth wrote to David C. Anderson from Scarborough: "After a smoky visit at Sheffield & a delightful day at York we arrived here yesterday—a charming place! Just on the beach of the German Ocean stands the Grand hotel at which I am now—a splendid house, but rather too fashionable. I opened to full and fashionable house last night, but the theatre is so small that very little money is received. The weather is gloomy & that is better for business than if it was fair."

9/21/82; Bertuccio, *The Fool's Revenge*

9/22/82; Shylock, *Merchant of Venice*; Petruchio, *Katherine and Petruchio*

9/23/82; Spa Rooms, Harrowgate; Role unknown

9/25/82; Theatre Royal, Newcastle-Upon Tyne; Richelieu

9/26/82; Hamlet

A Newcastle critic wrote: "On Tuesday Mr. Booth appeared as *Hamlet*, to a large audience. It has been said that he is an actor of the 'old school,' and that in his performance of the Prince of Denmark he is merely the follower of tradition. This, in our judgment, is not so, for not only is he free from the rant which some have charged him with being possessed of, but he has not hesitated to introduce new readings in several passages, all of which, we are bound to say are thoroughly consistent with intelligence.... Mr. Booth does not go in for what is known as point-making.... Unfortunately his efforts were to an extent marred by the great noise behind. The hurrying of feet, the moving of scenery, and bustle that were going on, must have disturbed the actor much more than it did the audience. Mr. Pateman, the stage-manger, would do well to instruct his minions to combine silence with energy."

9/27/82; Othello

On Sept. 27, 1882, Booth wrote to Laurence Hutton from Newcastle: "The papers are enthusiastic — so is the audience but sixpenny admissions make an 'allow [hollow] show!'" One Newcastle critic thought "the pronunciation of a word here and there betrays his nationality.... Not an instant unoccupied does he pass on the stage; when not speaking he is listening, all the time doing something, which, though trifling in itself, is natural." A Newcastle critic wrote: "On Wednesday Mr. Booth appeared as *Othello*. We liked him less in this part than any other we have seen him in. We cannot exactly define our reason for this, unless it was the quiet, subdued manner in which Mr. Brooke played Iago that formed so strong a contrast as to make us think Mr. Booth rather noisy in his scenes with him."

9/28/82; Bertuccio, *The Fool's Revenge*

The critic of the *Dundee Courier and Argus* wrote about *The Fool's Revenge*: "Mr. Booth ... with remarkably good taste, has ... amended upon Tom Taylor, having altered the final catastrophe and scene of reconciliation.... We can imagine nothing finer than the piteous whine of the poor jester, 'Let me in, let me in!' when he is driven away from the door of the banqueting chamber. His yell of unutterable despair when repulsed with the rude intimation that his 'ape tricks' are not wanted within was agonizing to hear."

9/29/82; Richelieu

9/30/82; Shylock, *Merchant of Venice*; Petruchio, *Katherine and Petruchio*

10/2/82; Theatre Royal, Dundee; Richelieu

In Dundee, "an immense house congregated to welcome" Booth in *Richelieu*, the auditorium being "literally crammed from floor to ceiling." Hundreds were turned away each night in the "most successful engagement ever known" there. The critic for *The Dundee Courier and Argus* wrote: "We ... regard his Hamlet as a far less satisfactory performance than his Richelieu.... More dependence was placed upon the enunciation of the words for the conveyance of the dramatist's meaning, and less upon action and facial expression, than was the case in the role of the great Cardinal ... a little more passion would be an improvement."

10/3/82; Hamlet

The critic for the *Dundee Advertiser* wrote: "The Hamlet of Booth is quietly pensive.... You can see that he utterly loathes the marriage of his mother with her deceased husband's brother; but the dislike is not active to hostility, it is rather a well-bred loathing ... and accordingly the uncle-father and the aunt-mother are treated with the utmost deference.... Even to the spies who are set to watch him ... he is always courteous, and this is in striking contrast to the conventional Hamlets, who are always fiercely cynical to the younger men and offensively rude to the old Chamberlain."

10/4/82; Bertuccio, *The Fool's Revenge*

10/5/82; Her Majesty's Theatre, Aberdeen; Richelieu

In Aberdeen the critic for the *Aberdeen Evening Express* wrote of Richelieu: "Mr. Booth gave us an interpretation of the part to which we have hitherto been strangers. The leading feature of his conception is quietness and dignity. Indeed Booth made a distinctly marked impression.... Another fine touch is the lifting of the rosary to his lips ere he swoons." The critic for Aberdeen's *Daily Free Press* wrote: "No 'star' in his northern wanderings ever had the surrounding of dramatic talent to aid him in his work such as the American tragedian can happily command.... Mr. Booth ... was called and recalled at the close of each act."

10/6/82; Hamlet

Of his Hamlet the critic for Aberdeen's *Daily Free Press* wrote: "he never forces the action in order to 'make points,' and never for an instant courts or waits for applause." When Booth played Hamlet in Aberdeen: "the house was crowded from floor to ceiling; the 'circle seats' were booked before the opening of the doors; and the other parts of the building were filled so soon and so completely as to show that here at all events, Shakespeare ... does not spell ruin. Mr. Booth is not superlatively gifted by nature of the part of Hamlet, and accordingly his first coming on the stage, despite the plaudits with which it was hailed was not such as to prejudice the audience in his favour. Mr. Booth commenced his performance quietly and therein struck the key note of his entire conception.... He does not indulge in the wild and seemingly uncontrollable outbursts that mark the rendering of Mr. Irving and his school. Mr. Booth does not countenance the newer readings— many of which by the way, display more ingenuity than literary discrimination or acuteness. He sticks to the "handsaw," the "sea" of troubles, the "backed like a weasel" We think he is right. The substitution of "hemshaw," "Heron-pshaw!" the "siege" of troubles, or the "ouzel" ... have appeared to us to show more imaginativeness than taste."

10/7/82; Bertuccio, *The Fool's Revenge*
In Aberdeen the performance of *Richelieu* on Oct. 5, 1882 grossed ninety-nine pounds and sixteen shillings. The performance of *Hamlet* on Oct. 6, 1882 grossed 113 pounds and twelve shillings. The performance of *The Fool's Revenge* on Oct. 7, 1882 grossed 114 pounds, six shillings and six pence.

10/9/82; Gaiety Theatre, Glasgow, Scotland; Richelieu
Booth opened in Glasgow for a week on Oct. 9, 1882, to "an audience filling, if not exactly crowding, the Gaiety Theatre. During *Richelieu*, he was called before the curtain after every act." His Hamlet, however, and his Othello, were not as well received. In the opinion of the critic from the *Glasgow Evening News*, Booth was too restrained, "the setting of the scenes ... not only meagre but inappropriate" and the orchestra in serious need of "overhauling." The critic for the *Glasgow Herald* wrote that Booth's "style was easy, graceful, dignified; his elocution as near perfection as can well be reached." Despite critical reservations, Booth played to "splendid business" and was serenaded by the theatre orchestra on his final performance with "The Star-Spangled Banner." Booth described his make-up for the role as "wrinkling his face." He used this in both *The Iron Chest* and *Richelieu*. Not everyone agreed with his depiction of Richelieu's age. The *Glasgow News*' critic wrote: "It may have been noticed that in the opening scenes, and especially in Richelieu's first, that the cardinal wanted the infirmity that his age implies.... It is not reasonable to imagine a disgraced Minister lying full length on a couch toying with a maid-of-honor's tresses, even though she be his ward, in the presence of a sovereign dealing with affairs of state."

10/10/82; Hamlet
A Glasgow review of Booth's Hamlet reads: "Mr. Booth was weakest in the closet scene, especially in the first part of it.... [He] spoke with good elocution ... but absolutely without the appearance of understanding a word he said. But his acting upon, and after the entrance of the ghost obliterated ... the remembrance of this unfortunate lapse. Perhaps Mr. Booth's finest qualities were displayed ... in the wandering utterances to *Ophelia*."

10/11/82; Othello
A Glasgow review of Booth's Othello reads: "His *Othello* is much fainter than his *Hamlet*.... His grasp of the character is fitful. Now he is violent and overbearing; how he reflects too much, like a very Hamlet.... His sobs and tears are feminine; his cries of next to no quality; and one humming nasal sound, which he often uses, is rather mawkish. The spontaneity, which in spite of much mannerisms, distinguishes this actor; his chastity of gesture ... and his admirable power of facial expression, appeared strikingly here.... The restraint which he puts on himself enables Mr. Booth, when he finds or makes an opportunity for passion, to produce powerful effects. This part of his method stood him in good stead at the end of the first and second acts and in the play scene.... The absence of any great resource of passion emasculates Mr. Booth's *Othello*." The critic for *The Evening Citizen* wrote of Booth's Othello: "Now and then to be sure, a scene or a speech seemed to be slurred over, to be delivered without due emphasis ... and again there was at times something of hurry in the style and method of the actor. But this was only at times, and it was occasioned, as was very evident by the desire to husband his resources to preserve himself for the great and more arduous passages of the tragedy. And in these Mr. Booth was all energy and passion. So intense was he so high was the note he struck, even in the earlier scenes of the third act, that it seemed as if something like an anti-climax must take place before the close. All such fear happily however, proved groundless."

10/12/82; Bertuccio, *The Fool's Revenge*

10/13/82; Richelieu

10/14/82; Shylock, *Merchant of Venice*

10/16/82; Theatre Royal, Edinburgh; Richelieu
On Oct. 16, 1882, Booth, dressed in a "fur trimmed yellow robe" opened *Richelieu* to "a large audience" and mixed reviews at the Theatre Royal in Edinburgh. The critic for *The Daily Review* wrote: "Last night a large Edinburgh audience endorsed in an unusually expressive manner the general appreciation of the *Richelieu* of Mr. Edwin Booth.... Even in acknowledging the double recall and enthusiastic cheers of the audience, he did not disillusionize the onlookers as is so often the case; he is too much identified with the character he portrays to obtrude his individual personality.... In the scene, for instance, with the king, in which the latter turns his back upon the great statesman, he portrayed a dejection of spirit with a pathetic intensity it would be difficult to surpass." The critic for *The Edinburgh Evening News* wrote: "No one in the audience last night could fail to recognize in him a powerful and accomplished actor, but those sufficiently familiar with the higher melodrama to maintain a critical attitude could not but feel that the cheers bestowed on the actor were largely referable to the situations in which he appeared.... In no scene could a substantially different rendering be wished for, the only fault to be found with the performance — apart from notice of the actor's rather marked mannerism of elocution — being that the ring of the merely theatrical which is so strongly association with all Lytton's work is never long absent from Mr. Booth's acting."

10/17/82; Hamlet
When he played Hamlet, the next night, a local critic felt that the character showed "certain pecu-

liarities of intonation betraying the actor's nationality." His arm was still bothering him, and he was fencing with his left hand. The critic for *The Edinburgh Evening News* wrote: "It is difficult to decide how far the unfortunate disablement of the right arm from which he is at present suffering, and which compelled him to fence with his left hand, may have affected his delivery of his lines.... A desire to think as highly of the performance as possible would induce the supposition that as a whole it suffered somewhat from nervous disturbance consequent on the surgical treatment Mr. Booth is announced to be undergoing.... The faults of the performance will be found to consist chiefly in a hurried and ill-emphasized delivery of many speeches and a frequent want of feeling, as distinguished from violence of utterance.... The address to the ghost, the adjuration to Ophelia, and several of the soliloquies, as given last night, were certainly unsatisfactory.... Not the least serious weakness was the omission of a number of lines, notably the passage, "Well said, old mole!" the elision of which amounts to throwing away a fine opportunity."

10/18/82; Bertuccio, *The Fool's Revenge*

The critic for *The Edinburgh Evening News* wrote of Booth's Bertuccio: "His best points last night lay in good and his weak ones in bad melodramatic acting. Among the latter was his delivery of the various speeches in which the hunchback declares his hatred for men in general and one in particular; the actor's declamation here being mere hoarse sound and fury ... while in almost all of his jesting scenes he played with striking masculine power, indicating excellent capacity for the higher comedy."

10/19/82; Hamlet

10/20/82; Richelieu

10/21/82; Othello

The critic for *The Edinburgh Evening News* wrote of Booth's Othello: "He made a good impression on his first entrance, well suggesting the force of Othello's character by his firm dignity of speech and manner; and in this and several other situations he delivered level sentences in that natural and unaffected fashion which he sometimes adopts, with such excellent effect. As in his Hamlet, however, he failed to give the requisite weight to the more elevated speeches in the part. His address to the senators was given with a fluency which belied Othello's concession that he was rude in speech, the effect being merely that of a well-delivered recitation, conveying no impression of character.... The stage setting was satisfactory, save for the circumstance that one or two scenes were made to do duty both in Venice and Cyprus."

10/23/82; Theatre Royal, Hull; Richelieu

In Hull, "again and again 'twas the actor summoned to the front." The critic for Hull's *Eastern Morning News* noted that "the innumerable excellencies of Mr. Booth's acting ... would fill a volume, and we must content ourselves with particularizing the strikingly impressive delivery of the prophetic warning to Baradas, 'Walk blindfold on, the headsman stalks behind thee.'"

10/24/82; Hamlet

Of Booth's Hamlet, the Hull critic wrote: "Despite that apparent annoyance occasioned by a slight affection [*sic*] of the chest, the very acme of elocutionary power was shown.... The performance, in which new readings of the text were observable, was full of beauty.... The scenic arrangements which were presumably carried out according to Mr. Booth's idea, were in one or two instances novel in Hull"

10/25/82; Bertuccio, *The Fool's Revenge*

10/26/82; Othello

On Oct. 26, 1882, Booth wrote to David C. Anderson from Hull: "My tour continues, successful— so far as puffery & enthusiasm goes. I about pay expenses. It is pleasant enough, when the sun shines—which isn't *every* day.... The audiences are quiet & appreciative — applauding warmly "in the proper places," but the men all keep their hats on. It looks jolly queer! Next week I shall spend in Leeds—where I'm told the theatre surpasses any that we have in America. I go to Dublin from there, but I do not like the idea of even a short sea-trip at this season, as the channel is generally rough & the winds violent. Two weeks there and the worst part of my tour will be ended. I thought of spending the few weeks' vacation before going to Germany in Rome — but the journey there & thence to Berlin would be too fatiguing, so I shall go to a few nearby places in England & fetch up at Paris for a rest."

10/27/82; Richelieu

10/28/82; Shylock, *Merchant of Venice*; Petruchio, *Katherine and Petruchio*

10/30/82; Grand Theatre, Leeds; Richelieu

Booth opened in Leeds on Oct. 30 to a disappointingly small audience. The critic for *The Leeds Express* wrote: "We had expected to see a larger gathering in the Grand last evening, but Leeds playgoers have a habit of trusting to report to ascertain the first-night qualities of an entertainment, and if it is good, coming up strongly for the rest of the week."

10/31/82; Hamlet

11/1/82; Bertuccio, *The Fool's Revenge*

On Nov. 1, 1882, Booth wrote to William Bispham from Leeds: "This is the eighth week of my country tour, and with the exception of two of three old-time towns, such as York and Dundee and Edinboro, of course it has been dull enough. To be sure I've had applause sufficient to satisfy the most ambitious, but as I shall never revisit these places. I consider it a waste of time and labor. In Germany, as in London, I look for nothing but approval, and shall be satisfied even if I fall short of my expenses a little.... The theatre in this place is the most complete ... I have seen in either country.... All it lacks to make it perfect is full seats, which, they tell me, it sometimes has for some fashionable 'catch.'"

11/2/82; Othello

On Nov. 2, 1882, Booth wrote to Winter from Leeds which he described as: "this miserable place — where we've had not a ray of sunshine, but rain & fog every day, has made us all wretched enough — but I hope for better news tonight & better weather too when we leave Leeds. In many respects the theatre here is the best I've ever seen; too large or anything but Opera & Pantomime, the 'shows' on which they chiefly depend, but in all the arrangements 'fore & aft' it is perfect — thousands of pounds have been spent in needless decoration, of course, & on useless conveniences — such as baths & marble tileing, Roman pavements — even at the back door, &c, but it is superb.... The Opera last week took all the money & I am acting to vacancy, of course."

11/3/82; Richelieu

11/4/82; Shylock, *Merchant of Venice*; Petruchio, *Katherine and Petruchio*

On Nov. 4, 1882, Booth wrote to David C. Anderson from Leeds: "We start for Dublin toward 7 A.M. & cross the channel in a storm, I fear, for it has rained and hailed & howled here all the week. [Speaking of Leeds] A most dismal place — with the grandest theatre I ever saw anywhere — except the Paris Opera House. It is superb & *empty* all the time; had what they call here a good house last night, but —!... Feel *measley* today & expect to be dreadfully sea-sick tomorrow, for I am bilious."

11/6/82; Gaiety Theatre, Dublin; Richelieu

Booth opened in Dublin on Nov. 6 "for an engagement of two weeks at the Gaiety Theatre, presenting his entire repertoire with the exception of Iago. It was undoubtedly the most successful engagement of his tour.... The gross receipts for the first week amounted to 834.18 pounds and for the second week 829.12.6, the largest of his tour. *The Dublin Journal* that served as "the leading organ of the English or landlord party" was critical, but students crowded the pit, the pit stalls and the galleries. The critic for *The Evening Irish Times* wrote of his Richelieu: "His voice, although just now a little hoarse, possibly from the effect of cold, has great sweetness at times, and is full and sonorous in the lower register.... The house was crowded in every part.... Mr. Booth's 'business' in this part of the play [the two-handed sword] was rather different to that to which we have been accustomed. Instead of the chair in the centre of the stage, he occupied a sofa on the side, and with more propriety but less dramatic effect than might be had,

he refrained from stamping on the document, which is supposed to symbolize the enemies of France. As compared with other distinguished actors ... Mr. Booth is more subdued, more quiet and restrained.... We thought that Mr. Booth did not get all he might out of the scene with Francois when he warns that luckless lad that in the lexion of youth the word "fail" has no place.... If we say that occasionally Mr. Booth's declamation is somewhat precise — pedantic is too strong a word — we have said all that can with justice be urged in comparative dispraise ... the defect, though noticeable enough to ask for comment, is not sufficiently remarkable to damage a performance."

11/7/82; Hamlet

11/8/82; Bertuccio, *The Fool's Revenge*

A Dublin critic wrote, of Booth's Bertuccio: "We have had occasion to find fault with him for lack of passion and intensity for a certain methodical and measured elaboration of effect.... What we missed on the two former occasions we found last night.... He is more human, more genuine, more powerful by many degrees.... There was a tangible interval between his entrance and the prolonged applause with which he was welcomed.... Mr. Booth is at present suffering from a cold, the consequences of which must be very embarrassing to an actor.... Mr. Booth is particularly fortunate in his support."

11/9/82; Othello

Of Booth's Othello, the critic for *The Evening Irish Times* wrote: "His enunciation was always clear, and no syllable was missed even in the passages which strained his utterance most. In accent and gesture Mr. Booth manifested no exaggeration, and it was very plain that he was not prepared to deduce the passion of Othello from his Southern sensuality. It may be noted that the play suffered somewhat from the injudicious compilation in the acting edition.... Upon the termination of the great scenes in which he appeared, he was called before the curtain, and repeatedly cheered with a heartiness which testified the satisfaction of the audience.... Some few improvements might with advantage be introduced by the stage management, which usually has proved efficient. Between some of the acts last night there were tedious waits, for which there was no apparent reason." On Nov. 12, 1882, Edwin wrote to William Winter: "I have been very successful here, but strange to say Othello, not Richelieu (as expected), nor Hamlet, has been the hit, & it has been so much talked of & asked for at the box office that I shall repeat it this week. This is my first experience of the kind — for either Richelieu or Hamlet has, everywhere, for years, been the preferred play — never before has Othello been called for, though Iago has been frequently as strong a card as the other two. The press has been kind, the audiences fashionable. I have received many kind offers here but declined them all. I keep very close — being hard worked & very tired."

11/10/82; Richelieu

11/11/82; Shylock, *Merchant of Venice*; Petruchio, *Katherine and Petruchio*

When Booth presented a double bill of *The Merchant of Venice* and *Katherine and Petruchio*, the critic for *The Evening Irish Times* wrote: "We do not think that Mr. Booth was wise in arranging a mixed programme.... In the 'Merchant of Venice' there were transpositions of scenes.... Of the taste exhibited in these alterations, the critical listener could not approve. The play ended with the trial scene. This of itself was a mistake. We should have preferred to have seen the last act, with its exquisite fancy, poetical situations, and elegance of thought and diction, than the few scenes of the 'Taming of the Shrew,' which had something of the effect of a pantomime in their isolated fashion, while as parts of a complete and symmetrical play, they would undoubtedly have won credit and applause.... The quiet and subdued character of Mr. Booth's acting is of itself attractive because of its novelty.... He appeals very little to the sensibility which is not fine or the judgment which is not educated.... We do not think that Mr. Booth was seen to better advantage anywhere in the play — not even in the trial scene — than in the scene with Tubal, which, by the way, is made to come just before the trial scene."

11/13/82; Hamlet

11/14/82; Richard III

Of Booth's Richard III, the critic for *The Evening Irish Times* wrote: "That his rendering of the part lacks force must be acknowledged from the outset. We thought, at the commencement, that the observable weakness was due to the indisposition from which he has recently suffered.... Thus at the conclusion of the play yesterday evening, some of the denizens of the 'top' exhibited dissatisfaction because the sword-play was not fast and furious enough to stimulate their fancy. The somewhat ridiculous exhibition of the 'super'-soldiers they allowed to pass without condemnation. In the quieter scenes, those with the Lady Anne, with the Mayor and Corporation — a very 'seedy' deputation, by the way — with Buckingham, &c., Mr. Booth showed much art and subtlety.... The phantom scene was less powerful than we should have expected, but the whole impersonation, like everything he has shown us, bore a seal and impress of undoubted talent very near akin to genius.... We are grateful to Mr. Booth for having chosen the text proper as the basis of the play."

11/15/82; Othello

On Nov. 15, 1882, Booth wrote to Launt Thompson from Dublin: "I remain six nights longer here, where I have been most successful, so far as praise & full houses go, but the profit is by no means enormous. Have been offered many kindnesses here but have declined all — for I am very much fatigued & must keep very close to husband what strength I have."

11/16/82; Macbeth

11/17/82; King Lear

Of his Lear, the critic for *The Evening Irish Times* wrote: "The house last night was crowded from floor to ceiling, and during an exceptionally lengthy performance, every incident of the action was closely watched. Of course, the play was much shortened, and there was considerable modification in the disposition of the scenes.... In the day when scenery was wholly imaginary, frequent changes, duly placarded, offered a slight practical difficulty, but now nearly every shift entails complicated operations.... Scenes and speeches were transposed and inverted, and the thread of the story was in some parts imperfect. Mr. Booth ... likes best the romanticism of the play.... Mr. Booth was tempted, in several instances, to attach truculent features to Lear's character."

11/18/82; Bertuccio, *The Fool's Revenge*

11/20/82; Prince's Theater, Manchester, England; Richelieu

On Nov. 20, Booth opened in Manchester, a "booming textile town whose wealthy citizens had founded a university, an art museum, libraries and an orchestra." It did not, however, support theatre. Booth opened as Richelieu in "inclement weather" to a house "not crowded from floor to ceiling," and it was not until he closed that he was playing to houses "in which every seat was occupied, and in which even standing room was not easily to be had." About opening night, the critic for *The Manchester Courier and Lancashire General Advertiser* wrote: "Mr. Booth's eminence is due apparently rather to his art as an actor than to his skill as an elocutionist. The delivery is not always even, and, though it is always clear and impressive, it is occasionally marred by a peculiar hardness of intonation and abruptness of utterance, which detracts somewhat at time from the effect.... One of the most striking features of the performance was the wonderful way in which gradual physical decay was counterfeited. Every succeeding act showed the ambitious prelate more aged and more feeble, and when in the last act he lay, almost, as it seemed on the brink of the grave, there was nothing startling in the outburst of vitality when the stolen dispatch was suddenly restored to him. Notwithstanding the exceedingly inclement state of the weather there was a numerous audience.... The Richelieu presented by Mr. Booth is not wholly conventional. There are new readings of important passages, and it is open to question whether they are entitled in all cases to complete approval, to say nothing of preference.... The recalls at the close of each act were phenomenal. In some cases he was called more than once, and the loud clapping of hands was accompanied by those shouts of satisfaction which seem to make the cheers so honest and impressive."

11/21/82; Hamlet
11/22/82; Bertuccio, *The Fool's Revenge*
11/23/82; Shylock, *Merchant of Venice*; Petruchio, Katherine and Petruchio
11/24/82; Richelieu
11/25/82; Richard III

When Booth performed Richard III, the critic for the *Manchester Guardian* felt that in the tent scene as well as the final battle scene, Booth showed that he was "a little wearied and overdone by the labours of the week. Bella Pateman's dress for Ophelia "was badly managed and the high-heeled boots intolerable." On Nov. 26, 1882, he wrote to David C. Anderson from The Queens Hotel in Manchester: "Business, like the weather, very bad until last night when *Richard* drew more money than I've taken any night on the tour. A good *one night* stand in Manchester. I did — what they call — *splendidly* in Dublin, two weeks, and left to increasing business. The boys in front were quiet enough during the play — spoke to me once or twice, I believe, but I did not experience any of the old time fire I've heard or read about. In this hotel we have the best cooking & a greater variety of food yet found in England. A fine busy city — beautiful theatre & excellent hotel & I shall be glad to get away from 'em all: the weather has been beastly! It always is here, they say; 'tis called the 'watering-pot' of England."

11/27/82; Royal Alexandra Theatre, Liverpool, England; Richelieu
11/28/82; Hamlet
11/29/82; Bertuccio, *The Fool's Revenge*
11/30/82; Othello
12/1/82; King Lear
12/2/82; Richard III
12/4/82; Shylock, *Merchant of Venice*; Petruchio, Katherine and Petruchio
12/5/82; Bertuccio, *The Fool's Revenge*
12/6/82; Othello
12/7/82; Hamlet
12/8/82; Richelieu
12/9/82; Macbeth
12/11/82; Theatre Royal, Birmingham, England; Richelieu

Booth opened in Birmingham on Dec. 11, "suffering from a severe indisposition" which had plagued him for two weeks. He began with Richelieu and "after every act he was ... called before the curtain, and after the fourth act, the recall was a double one." Booth wrote to Winter from Birmingham: "I close here Saturday night & hurry on to Berlin — expecting to arrive there day before Xmas; I shall stop but a day or perhaps two in London.... Such beastly god-forsaken places as these provincial towns can only be equaled by miserable London — which, after the Summer sets, is the embodiment of wretchedness & the horrors! ... I was so prostrated by nervous exhaustion & consequent loss of sleep that I had a doctor see me in Liverpool, who lifted me up in the course of a few days and I now get my rest o'nights & 'nap' but the gloom & dampness & the reaction from my night's labors depress me very much.... Business averages about the same pit & gallery full, sparse elsewhere." In Birmingham, the supporting cast performed in a "very indifferent way," but the *Birmingham Daily Post* praised Booth's *Richelieu*, noting: "Although American characteristics are often so marked not only in natives, but in Englishmen who have played long to American audiences, Mr. Booth showed no trace of his nationality, or any peculiarities of voice and style, but appeared as a gentleman of high culture, finished taste, great refinement, and extraordinary dramatic power. Mr. Booth has ... one of the most remarkable ... voices ever heard on the stage.... At the end of each of the acts he had a warm reception and a call before the curtain."

12/12/82; Hamlet

The following day Booth did Hamlet, and the critic for the *Birmingham Daily Post* wrote: "The contrast of his *Hamlet* with his *Richelieu* was ... remarkable.... He fairly lost himself in each, so much so that except for the sustained richness and music of the voice, the personality of the player seemed lost. The critic for *The Dart* wrote: "Mr. Booth is supported by a very indifferent company, and his efforts are assisted by the ordinary stage fixtures."

12/13/82; Bertuccio, *The Fool's Revenge*
12/14/82; Othello
12/15/82; Richelieu
12/16/82; Richard III

The gross receipts for the English provincial tour were:

Date	City	Amount
Sept. 11–16, 1882	Sheffield	343 pounds
Sept. 18–23, 1882	York Scarboro, Harrowgate	425 pounds
Sept. 25–30, 1882	Newcastle	480 pounds
Oct. 2–7, 1882	Dundee, Aberdeen	562 pounds
Oct. 9–14, 1882	Glasgow	634 pounds
Oct. 16–21, 1882	Edinboro	794 pounds
Oct. 23–28, 1882	Hull	460 pounds
Oct. 30–Nov. 4, 1882	Leeds	523 pounds
Nov. 6–11, 1882	Dublin	834 pounds
Nov. 13–18, 1882	Dublin	829 pounds
Nov. 20–25, 1882	Manchester	688 pounds
Nov. 27–Dec. 2, 1882	Liverpool	493 pounds
Dec. 3–8, 1882	Liverpool	378 pounds
Dec. 10–16, 1882	Birmingham	572 pounds

By Jan. 3, 1883, Booth was staying at the Hotel de Rome in Berlin. He described his rehearsals as follows: "When a word of sentence sounds very English, as if frequently the case, it rather confuses me for tho' I have not acquired a word of the language, I seem to think it & comprehend it while I am acting with the Germans; ... at rehearsal I've had to ask my interpreter to give me the last few sentences of a speech in German when he has endeavored to assist me in English. I shall be glad when I get through with this tour — it's terrible work, as I have to mentally recite in English what the Germans are saying in order to make the speeches fit." On Jan. 7, 1883, Booth wrote to Laurence Hutton from Berlin: "I arrived here Sunday last & expected to begin rehearsals for *Richelieu*, at the *Victoria Theatre*, Tuesday. But, to my surprise, on Monday my agent told me that under pretence that my prompt books for the German Co. were not sufficiently clear to suit the manager my engagement would have to be postponed for at least a month. It seems that he had been losing money until Xmas when a new play made a "hit" for him; & he used this petty excuse to put me off to get rid of me altogether rather than take off his running piece. Of course by law I could have got the better of him, but law means delay & expense, & the result w^د have been the loss my Berlin advent, which I most desired. So, I agreed to defer the date of opening: — still he 'hung fire' & I saw he was inclined to trick me in any event. At the last moment a lady *star*, who was to commence this week at the *Residenz* (a Court) Theatre, was taken ill & the offer was made to my agent (who had been inquiring among the managers) that, if I could get free from my *Victoria* bond, I sh^د go there & fill even a longer time than my original contract gave me at the last named house. Well, it was amiably settled. I open there on Thursday next if scenery &c. are ready; rehearsals will begin Monday, day after tomorrow.... I begin with Hamlet will follow with Othello if time & the players *study* permit will end my brief engagement with Lear. I may do Richelieu in other towns. I shall act next in Hamburgh; from Feb. 15 to 23rd — in Bremen; 25th till Mar 1st — in Cologne; & Bonn Mar. 2nd–7th; 8th–14th at Hannover; 18th–21st at Leipsic & expect to wind up at Vienna the last few days of Mar.: all the engts. except the last are settled." On Jan. 7, 1883, Booth wrote to William Bispham from Berlin: "I arrived a week ago and found the manger had a successful play running which he hopes to keep on for many weeks. He resorted to a paltry quibble to defer my engagement a month. I consented, as all other places were shut to me, being occupied by other attractions. Finding the fellow inclined to trick me again, I set my German agent to work who came to me the next day in rapture; a lady star was ill, and could not fulfill her contract with the Residenz Theatre — a very small but more fashionable house than the Victoria, which is a large and cheerless place. The chance came like a miracle, and matters were amicably arranged for me to shift my quarters, and on Thursday next I open with 'Hamlet.' To-morrow my rehearsals begin, and as several of the actors speak a *little* English, and have already acted the parts they will play with me, I may not have such trouble as I expected.... After ten or fifteen performances here I go to Hamburg, thence to Bremen, Cologne, Bonn, Hanover, Leipsic, and perhaps Vienna —'t is not yet settled: a few nights only in each place. If all goes well by that time, the close of Mar., I shall *tour* a little in Italy for recreation, and go home for 'good and all.'" At the Victoria Booth was to receive half of the gross receipts minus five hundred marks. At the Residenz Theater he shared 50 percent after three hundred marks. The performances in Berlin grossed 16,740.75 marks.

1/11–20/83; Residenz Theater, Berlin; Hamlet 9x
Accompanying Prince Frederick to the opening of *Hamlet* in Berlin was his preceptor, Professor Karl Werder, a prominent Shakespearian student. They returned for Booth's fifth performance as Hamlet. On Jan. 20, 1883, *The New York Mirror* told its readers: "Edwin Booth was once asked in our hearing if there was one ambition he yet longed to satisfy. 'Yes,' was the tragedian's reply. 'It is to act in Berlin.' His wish has just been fulfilled and under circumstances of the most gratifying character. The cable flashes the story of his debut in the German capital.... Booth is the first native actor to carry the banner of dramatic art into Germany.... The Crown Prince has witnessed the performance on three different nights, and expresses his intention of going again to see it. The American and British legations were present on the opening night.... The *National Zeitung* eulogizes the actor's careful study and effects, and considers that he does not obtrude on his American nationality. The *Tageblatt* says: "The strange effect of the polyglot performance was soon removed by the interest in the chief impersonation." ... The *Vossische Zeotung* says the impersonation was full of life and spirit. The *Liosen Courier* ... says the impersonation is a perfect living whole.... The *Barsen Leotung* says in eloquence and gesture Booth stands on the same line with Rossi and Salvini, and perhaps surpasses them in minute power of suggestion."

On Jan. 29, 1883, Booth wrote to William Winter from the Hotel de Rome in Berlin: "I have been suffering ... with a racking cough & headache, and have had wearisome rehearsals every day.... Lear seems to have taken even a deeper hold on Shakespearian Germans than Hamlet .... I shall play Iago next week for a few nights, then Othello after which a repeat of Lear & Hamlet to close the engagement.... It may be that I shall return in Apr.

or May, but my movements will be controlled by Edwina's health and wishes.... I was too ill to rehearse this evening (I have one night off) after a tiresome tug this morning.... The death of the Emperor's brother [Prince Karl, the brother of Kaiser Wilhelm I, died on Jan. 21, 1883] has put a stop to my 'Royal patronage,' as the Court will be mourning til after my engagement ends. I learned, at the only dinner I have accepted, that it was intended by some of the 'Nobs' here to have a grand fete of some kind to which I wd. Be invited & presented to the Imperial folks, but that's upset."

2/1–2/83; Hamlet 2x

2/3–4/83; Iago 2x, *Othello*

The critic of the *Borsen Zeitung* (Feb. 4) characterized Booth's Iago as a "fine elegant Venetian with all the mobility, cunning and perfidy of an Italian Tartuffe" and reminded his readers that "Iago, after all, is not a '*Lieutenant*' but a "*Feldwebel* [Sergeant]." "The well-known 'Put money in thy purse' ... is spoken by him in an ordinary tone.... We are well aware, that a representation of 'Iago' more boisterous, more pointed, and painted in stronger colours than Mr. Booth's impersonation would perhaps have still better pleased the German part of the audience." On Feb. 4, 1883, Edwina wrote to Mrs. Ole Bull from the Hotel de Rome in Berlin: "Papa is feeling quite unwell, the result of overwork.... We find the audiences more appreciative and sympathetic than the English, and although 'Lear' and 'Iago' have pleased them — they cry for more 'Hamlet.' This Papa will reproduce next week — his last in Berlin. He was requested to appear before the court, but circumstances unfortunately prevented. The death of Prince Charles keeps away many of the high aristocracy.... We start soon for Hamburgh [*sic*] where Papa next appears. Our winter will be passed in Germany, and we hope to spend Apr. in Italy.

2/6/83; Othello

Otto Brahm, who would assume the directorship of the Deutsches Theater in 1894, saw Booth play both Iago and Othello in Berlin: "He deplored his playing of Iago as an elegant gentleman with none of the 'rough and hard' qualities of the original. When Booth played Othello at a subsequent performance, he could "produce none of those eruptive outbursts that make the role so compelling." "The Othello whose powerfully exploding passion devastates all around him and the dearest to him, and then drives him to commit murder on himself — him I saw less clearly and believed in less willingly."

2/7/83; Hamlet

In 1886 a Boston critic, present at the time in Berlin wrote: "He had a cordial greeting from the newspaper critics at first. The military caste, however, was not among his first audiences, and the substantial burgher of Berlin did not, in the beginning of the engagement, analyze the presentation ... to his family at dinner.... Mr. Booth was forced to appear in the little and remote Residenz Theatre.... His support was poor. In 'Hamlet,' they carried themselves in a dull heavy manner.... In 'Othello,' the general mediocrity was improved. The language used in every play was German.

2/8–13/83; Benefit for the Berlin Newspaper Press Fund on 2/13/83; Othello 6x

2/15/83; Thalia Theater, Hamburg; Hamlet

On Feb. 15, 1882, Booth opened at the Thalia Theater in Hamburg. He played with a one third share after three hundred marks had been deducted. In Hamburg his houses averaged 3,800 marks.

2/17/83; King Lear

2/19/83; Hamlet

On Feb. 19 an English traveler wrote from Hamburg: "Edwin Booth began his engagement here, last Friday, the 16th as *Hamlet*, to a crowded house. Indeed all the seats for the three performances announced were sold nearly a fortnight ago, and the prices might have been trebled.... Last Saturday night, when Booth was playing *King Lear*, it was truly a most pathetic sight to see the people, at the wings, weeping. When the curtain fell, he was repeatedly recalled and vociferously cheered, and after that he was embraced by all the dramatic company — except the poor little extra girls who acted as pages. These are not "supers" here, in our acceptation of the word, but young ladies who are at the foot of the ladder, and studying to become actresses. As he left the theater, these girls were waiting for him in the hall, and, in a perfectly artless and modest manner, one of them and, in broken English, said through her tears: 'Mr. Booth, you make us cry — we do want so much to kiss you.' After the osculations of a number of enthusiastic German gentlemen, this surely was no bad change; and I observed that the tragedian was enabled to endure, with quite a becoming resignation, the caresses of these charming little devotees.... He had to take home a number of floral contributions, and as he passed to his carriage several hundred persons were in waiting to catch a glimpse of him and to say good night. This evening, he repeated *Hamlet*. Not a vacant seat in the house. Speculators got as much as twenty marks apiece for the four mark seats. He received seven beautiful wreaths, two or three bouquets, and a great basket of flowers from the girls of the ballet.... From Hamburg he goes to Bremen." On Feb. 20, 1883, Edwina Booth wrote to William Winter from the Hotel de l'Europe in Hamburg: "The Germans are vile stage-dressers, their costumes being all out of character, as to time and place. It was amusing to see 'Horatio' in military boots, and armed with a sword, and Ophelia in satins and gold lace.... I am sure we should find more care more knowledge in these matters, even amongst our poorest companies in America.... Most of the actors know ... no English whatever, and thus jump their cue, interrupting Papa's lines. Yet he follows them with great accuracy, never saying the wrong thing, even when more than the usual text is spoken. It is curious how, even the oldest actors, depend, almost entirely upon the aid of the prompter, who sits in his little box facing the stage, giving them every word in an audible whisper — this too, whilst Papa is reciting his lines, which is most annoying as well as confusing."

2/21–22/83; King Lear 2x

2/24/83; Bremen Stadt-Theater; Hamlet

Booth played at the Bremen Stadt Theater from Nov. 24 through 28, 1882. He received 50 percent of the net receipts after three hundred marks had been deducted from the gross. The gross receipts were 4,814 marks.

2/25/83; King Lear

2/27/83; Othello

2/28/83; Hamlet

"At the end of his engagement, after a performance of Hamlet that drew four curtain calls, Booth was leaving the stage; he was met at the wings by the entire company and chorus of the theatre, who commenced to sing ... a beautiful 'Farewell.' ... Mr. Booth, ... as the company advanced, retreated to the middle of the stage, where he was motioned to be seated. As the song finished the prompter's bell rang, and the curtain rose again. The audience, hearing the singing, had not left their seats. A young lady of the company then came on to the stage, bearing a velvet cushion upon which reposed a silver wreath, upon each leaf of which was inscribed the names of those who had played with him, including that of the director. The 'King' then made a ... speech in English, and Mr. B. responded with his 'usual' few words. Then Horatio called for three cheers for Mr. B., in which the audience heartily joined. The floral wreaths and bouquets so filled the carriage that there was scarcely room for the actor and his business manager to ride home to the hotel. In the morning the chorus of the theatre serenaded him at the hotel and the station was thronged [with people there] to see him depart."

3/2/83; Cologne; Hamlet

3/4/83; Stadt-Theater in Bonn; Othello

3/6/83; Cologne; Othello

3/8/83; Residenz Theater, Hanover; Othello

On Mar. 8, 1883, he wrote to David C. Anderson from Hanover: "I am tired and full of aches tonight. Success continues, but no more silver wreaths since Bremen, though flowers, laurels and ribbons galore. I stop here a week; then after several days' rest, go to Leipsic [sic]; another two weeks' rest, and then for Vienna, where I close what I regard as the most important engagement of my life. I wish I had a full year to revisit the places I have been to, and to play other parts, but I must rest satisfied with what I've got, though the managers are all asking me to return."

3/9/83; Iago, Othello

3/10/83; Hamlet

3/12/83; King Lear

3/13/83; Hamlet

Booth played in Cologne on the second and the sixth of Mar. and in Bonn on the 4th. He got half the gross receipts minus three hundred marks for expenses. Booth played at the Residenz Theater in Hanover from Mar. 8 through Mar. 14. He received half of the box office receipts after two hundred marks had been deducted for daily expenses. One performance in Hanover brought in 4,315 marks or over $1,000. The theatre grossed 5,637.50 marks. In Leipzig Booth received a third of the net profits. "For the three evenings on which he played there, every seat in the Stadttheater not occupied by the regular subscription audience could have been sold twice over." The theatre grossed $1,758.94 marks. On Mar. 17, Booth wrote to Laurence Hutton: "We have had deep snow & real old fashioned winter the past ten days—after the most glorious weather, from our arrival in Berlin 'till we reached Hanover." "On the night of Booth's first appearance in Leipzig, Baron von Leon, Intendant of the Grand Ducal Theatre in Weimar, called, after the third act, [with] ... an invitation to appear before the Court in Weimar." Edwin would have gladly gone, but he was already expected in Vienna, and there was no possibility of postponing his engagement." He told von Leon: "I never had a will of my own; I always found myself, as now, under the yoke of obligations which others assumed for me."

3/19/83; Neues Leipziger Stadt-Theater; Hamlet

3/20/83; Othello

3/21/83; King Lear

3/31, 4/2/83; Wiener Stadt-Theater, Vienna, Austria; Hamlet 2x

4/4–5/83; Othello 2x

In Vienna Booth received half the receipts minus six hundred guilder. The theater grossed 5,398.10 guilders. "The Viennese critics generally commended him but were much more reserved in their assessments of his Hamlet and Othello than had been the Berlin critics. Most of them complained of Booth's lack of passion, of force ... as Hamlet, especially in the scene at Ophelia's grave.... Othello also was criticized for its lack of force and passion, especially in the first two acts.... The third act impressed most critics. Booth's King Lear was perhaps his most successful impersonation in Vienna.... Booth was called before the curtain after every act, often every scene and at the end of the performance was presented with garlands of flowers and wreaths of laurel." He appeared as Othello on Apr. 4 and King Lear on Apr. 7. The house was "crammed to the roof," and his engagement was extended for another five performances during which he repeated Lear and Hamlet.

4/7, 9, 11/83; King Lear

On Apr. 9, 1883, Booth wrote to David C. Anderson from the Hotel Imperial in Vienna: "You see I have not lost Vienna after all. My two first roles did not seem to take the critics *fully*, although the people were enthused & I had many private commendations sent me, but as *Lear*, Saturday, the crowded house went wild & all the papers yesterday & today are full of my triumph & even begin to hint at a repetition of Hamlet & Othello; it seems the impression left by those parts was stronger than they at first realized. The result is a renewal of my engagement & all the tickets gone for tonight. I shall not stay longer than a week, however, for I want rest & have little time to visit the places I've promised Edwina that she shall see — old Nuremburg particularly.... The climate of this beautiful city is worse than ours: snow & heat of summer, rain & cold winds during a single day on several occasions."

4/12/83; Hamlet

4/14, 16/83; King Lear

4/17/83; Benefit of the Concordia Club; Iago, *Othello*

On Apr. 18, "a number of critics, such as the critic of the *Neue Freie Presse* complained that Booth's Iago was more of a devil than a soldier. After the second act of Lear, the members of the Stadt-Theater company and its manager gathered backstage and presented Booth with a laurel wreath. In Vienna the average box office income was 1,740 florins or about $728. Booth regularly received twenty-five per-cent of the total receipts, making between $175 and $200 a performance, far less than he would have received in America. On May 5, 1883, Booth wrote to William E. Miller: "Secure rooms at Morely's for evening of May 16th — Wednesday; we will leave here on the morning of that day & remain in London 'till June 8th. If too late for Morley's try some of the small hotels in the neighborhood — there are several in the vicinity in Cockspur S^t ... The Paris journalists have tried to interview me & want my photo. I might have worked up a few nights here." On May 8, Booth wrote to Miller from the Hotel Meurice, saying that he could not leave until the 20th. "I want to see Irving in the Bells & if possible get me two seats in the balcony — directly in front where I can see the entire stage. — I want to see all the 'parts of him' that I have not seen — Ch^{as} 1st, & Hamlet, as well as Mathias.... Can you conveniently meet me at the station when I arrive?" On May 9, Booth wrote to William E Miller from the Hotel Meurice, 228 Rue de Rivoli: "Yes, I do want the rooms & the one berth.... I shall leave here Sunday 20th at 9.40 & reach London about 7 or 7.30, I forget the exact hour of arrival, nor do I know the station: — by way of Dover.... Some Americans are trying to get up one night for me to act Othello at the Odeon, so I hear — it come [*sic*] third-hand to me.... Weather here is lovely & the city full." On May 10, 1883, Booth wrote to William E. Miller from the Hotel Meurice in Paris: "I have consented to act Othello at the Odeon Sat^r 19th for benefit of some Asylum, under the patronage of the first folks of Paris & the Am^{rn} Colony, provided I can arrange the play for the French actors as we do it in English and if my costume arrives in time. If no hitch occurs I will telegraph you — in the meantime wire me if the things are in London. Let Stevens bring the dresses, wig &c. &c. in a basket or a trunk which he can hire for the occasion. If the trunks are at Gillig's let Stevens get the prompt book of Othello and send it to me at once & have the costumes ready to bring — for I shall require a dresser. I hardly think he need bring the swords — I can hire them here; In fact I can get costumes, but the "fat" is all important & that I could not hire or have made in time. If he forgets to bring that with the other et ceteras necessary for my make up I will evaporate him. Othello is selected because it has lately been acted here & the actors are 'up' in it, & the scenery & costumes are ready for immediate use. It will not be known definitely until tomorrow whether the theatre can be obtained for that particular date. Stevens had better have ballet-skirts washing at once — if not fit for use." That same day Booth wrote to Launt Thompson: "I have been here three weeks today, having abandoned the Italian trip, & very glad am I that we did not go, for several Americans just returned from Rome are down with the fever & had I once got into Italy I would have surely gone to the Infernal city. Must defer that visit till you & I can be there together. In spite of the gayety & excitement of Paris I am having a rest here — doing things moderately & we are both in better condition than usual. It may be that I shall act here, once only, for some charitable purpose, just to give the French "a taste of my quality," but 'tis not yet decided.... I shall go to London Sunday 20th, to remain 'till I sail — June 9th." On May 16, Booth wrote: "The idea of my acting here is abandoned. The prime mover in the affair has been flying about to Brussells [*sic*], to Antwerp & to London the past few day in hopes of getting either a French or an English C^o, but in vain. Bernhardt regrets she cannot assist me but offers her theatre, &c. At the Odeon they are rehearsing new plays & the actors are afraid of the experiment though would much like to have me act &c. The time is too breif [*sic*] to do anything & so we give up the scheme. I hope you have got all my boxes together without trouble. It would be well to send word to Adele forbidding the sale of my photos; he has made money by my inconvenience — to which I submitted after his repeated requests for my portrait. My nerves are all of a shake this morning—yet I've drunk nothing stronger than coffee for more than a week—the weather is intensively hot & makes me 'fidget.'"

1883-1884

11/5-6/83; Globe Theatre, Boston; Richelieu 2x
Booth opened his two-week engagement at the Globe in Boston in *Richelieu*. "The piece was finely mounted, care and attention having been paid to the smallest detail in the stage-setting. The support, however, was inferior." On opening night in Boston, Booth "was recalled after each act, including the last, and after the fourth was brought before the curtain ... six times." When Booth played Richelieu at the Globe Theatre in Boston in Nov. 1883 a local critic wrote: "There was ... in the first three acts ... a lack of inspired enthusiasm.... Many of the salient points of the action were lost in the tameness of the feeling.... In the fourth act the spirit and vigor of the drama were fully realized ... and it was received with tumultuous applause, and at its close, Mr. Booth was four times called before the curtain."

11/7/83; Macbeth
When Booth performed *Macbeth*, "every seat was taken and "every place that permitted a view of the stage was occupied."

11/8-9/83; King Lear 2x
11/10/83; Matinee, Richelieu
11/12/83; Othello
11/13/83; Iago, *Othello*
11/14-15/83; Bertuccio 2x, *The Fool's Revenge*
11/16/83; Shylock, *Merchant of Venice*; Petruchio, *Katherine and Petruchio*
11/17/83; Matinee, Iago, *Othello*
11/19-20/83; Hamlet 2x
11/21/83; King Lear
11/22/83; Shylock, *Merchant of Venice*; Petruchio, *Katherine and Petruchio*
11/23/83; Richelieu

On Nov. 23, 1883, Booth wrote to Laurence Hutton: "Business is very fine but the house is small you know; the company compares favorably with the one I had last season: only this, & nothing more; the critics don't consistently abuse it though—so all's well that goes well, I suppose."

11/24/83; Matinee, Hamlet
On Dec. 1, 1883, *The New York Mirror* told its readers: "At the Globe, with the exception of Hamlet, Edwin Booth appeared in characters sustained by him during the two previous weeks.... Edwin Booth can well feel proud of the crowd which assembled nightly and the ovations tendered him by those present, appearing as he did before audiences which filled the theatre to such an extent that even standing room was difficult to obtain. The only drawback in making this engagement favorable in every manner was caused by the acting of the support! I need say no more on this subject, as sufficient has been written and said, and it is to be hoped that when Booth again appears in this city he will bring with him a co that will make the other characters stand forth with greater prominence."

12/10-11/83; Star Theatre, New York; Richelieu 2x
"The company had arrived from Boston only a few hours before the play began and were strange to the stage"; nevertheless, "cheers rang through the house at the rising of the curtain, and they were repeated at the end of the fourth act, and at the close of the play. "[Booth] is apparently in excellent health, and the somewhat listless manner noted a year or so ago has entirely disappeared."

12/12-14/83; King Lear 3x
12/15/83; Matinee, Richelieu
On Dec. 15, 1883, William Winter wrote to Booth: "The Star people have not given you such scenery as they ought to have given you, for the plays thus far seen. As to the Company—I received a letter from one of your oldest admirers in Boston, bewailing that it was so incompetent.... What I see [is]—the best tragic actor in the English language acting most nobly in the greatest of plays & surrounded with old 'fakements' for scenery & with persons who ... are out of their depth, and ... are painful sticks." Booth agreed. On Dec. 20, 1883, he wrote to Winter: "Regarding the little matters of stage business you refer to—at rehearsals I have had such matters noted & my instructions followed satisfactorily, yet so d-nably dull are the wretched idiots that compose the rank & file of my profession that none of the details are remembered or comprehended.... God grant there be no actors in the other life! Apropos of [Affie] Weaver (& of Davey [David C. Anderson] too) there's where my foolish weakness interferes with my business. I promised Horace [McVicker] to let her have a chance without really knowing ought of her; & I somehow couldn't decline Uncle Dave, who thinks he can act Shakespearian characters, wh. he can't.... The same weakness has hampered me always. 'Save me from my friends!' Affie Weaver was the wife of Booth's manager Horace McVicker's, and Horace had clearly used his influence with Booth to get her a position in the company, playing Ophelia, Fiordelisa and Julie de Mortimer. It is not true, however, that Booth did not know her acting. She had performed major roles opposite him in Apr. and May 1879. When Booth performed Shylock in New York a local critic wrote on Dec. 16, 1883: "The setting of the piece was only fair and the stage management decidedly bad, several inexcusable stage waits breaking the continuity of the acting."

12/17-18/83; Hamlet 2x
12/19-21/83; Bertuccio 3x, *The Fool's Revenge*
12/22/83; Matinee, Hamlet
12/24/83; Othello

In Dec. 1883, *The New York Mirror* told its readers:

"Although [Othello] is one of our tragedian's most thoughtful impersonations, like Lear, it fails to draw the public. One reason is that people have formed the opinion that the Moor cannot be satisfactorily acted save by a human bullock. They want a muscular vociferous actor for the part. While there is no foundation for this view, except that Salvini has popularized the idea, its existence cannot be denied." In Dec. 1883 *The New York Mirror* told its readers: "Edwin Booth is in private life a somewhat phlegmatic gentleman; but his unhappiest hours are spent on the stage of a theatre when a rehearsal of one of his plays is proceeding. The artistic detail so dear to Mr. Irving is utterly distasteful to the American actor.... The player, experienced or otherwise, who comes to Booth for direction or instruction, is usually told to "come on in the usual way," and "go off L.C.," or is given some other order, which teaches the intelligent actor, at least the lesson that his best plan is to take Mr. Booth as he finds him." Booth did not perform on Christmas day

12/26/83; Iago, *Othello*

12/27–28/83; Shylock 2x, *Merchant of Venice*; Petruchio 2x, *Katherine and Petruchio*

12/29/83; Matinee, Iago, *Othello*

12/31/83–1/1/84; Macbeth 2x

In Jan. 1884 *The New York* Mirror told its readers: "The Star was only moderately filled Monday night (Dec. 31, 1883) when Mr. Booth appeared as Macbeth. His acting in this part ... lacks that robostiousness and great physique which tradition has association with the successful personation of the role, but in other respects it is smooth and thoughtful."

1/2–4/84; Hamlet 3x

1/5/84; Matinee, Macbeth

1/7–8/84; Richelieu 2x

1/9–10/84; Bertuccio 2x, *The Fool's Revenge*

1/11–12/84; Matinee on 1/12/84; King Lear 2x

1/14/84; Hamlet

1/15/84; King Lear

1/16/84; Shylock, *Merchant of Venice*; Petruchio, *Katherine and Petruchio*

1/17/84; Macbeth

1/18/84; Richelieu

1/19/84; Matinee, Hamlet; Evening, Richard III

On Jan. 21 the company left New York at 11:10 A.M. by train and arrived in Philadelphia at 1 P.M. That night they opened in Richelieu.

1/21/84; Walnut Street Theatre, Philadelphia; Richelieu

1/22/84; King Lear

1/23/84; Evening, Iago, *Othello*

The theatre has a matinee but Booth does not appear.

1/24/84; Shylock, *Merchant of Venice*; Petruchio, *Katherine and Petruchio*

1/25/84; Bertuccio, *The Fool's Revenge*

1/26/84; Matinee, Richelieu; Evening, Richard III

1/28/84; Hamlet

1/29/84; Macbeth

1/30/84; Bertuccio, *The Fool's Revenge*

The theatre has a matinee, but Booth does not perform.

1/31/84; Iago, *Othello*

2/1–2/84; Matinee on 2/2/84, Hamlet 2x; Evening, Richard III

"At the farewell matinee [in Philadelphia] ... Walnut Street was completely blocked with people for half a square on either side of the theatre entrances. Admission tickets only were sold, and finally the windows had to be closed. At least a thousand persons were unable to obtain even a view of the lobby. The total receipts for Friday night and the Saturday matinee reached to within a fraction of $4,500. The company left Philadelphia at 9 A.M. on Sunday Feb. 3 and arrived in Baltimore at 12:30, opening the next day, again in Richelieu. The advance sale in Baltimore was reported as nearly $9,000. The aggregate receipts were reported as upward of $20,000. At a later date the *Tribune* reported over $26,000. In Baltimore, the orchestra was "pushed from its place," and "at every performance, crowds of people" were "turned from the doors."

2/4/84; Holliday Street Theatre, Baltimore; Richelieu

2/5/84; King Lear

2/6/84; Iago, *Othello*

The company has a matinee, but Booth does not perform.

2/7/84; Shylock, *Merchant of Venice*; Petruchio, *Katherine and Petruchio*

On Feb. 7, 1884, Booth wrote to Laurence Hutton from Baltimore: "I must go [to Boston] from here, it seems, in consequence of some failure on the part of my managers to fix the Brooklyn date. After next week I jump to Boston for twelve performances, thence to Brooklyn &, as ill luck will have it, then to the 14th Street shop in New York — time at all other places being filled by other 'shows'; it will bring me in opposition to Irving, too, which I have tried to avoid; but New York is big enough for both & doubtless he will cut a broader swath than I. There is a sort of possibility that he & I may act together a few nights— Abbey comes here to talk over such a plan, but he wants me to go to Cincinnati for the 'hurrah' festival which I won't!— To my surprise the business in Phila was very great & here it holds out quite as well — New York alone deserted me, in a measure. Wretched weather & counter-attractions in the shape of balls, &c., do not affect the excellent business that I am doing. In my boyhood it was very difficult to muster a corporals' guard to attend the strongest theatrical attraction in Balto; now it works as one of the best 'show towns' in the country." Booth was writing from the Mt. Vernon Hotel in Baltimore.

The change in schedule meant that his second run in both Boston and New York was opposite Irving and, in the case of New York at an inferior house—the Fourteenth Street Theatre, because everything else was booked.

2/8/84; Bertuccio, *The Fool's Revenge*
2/9/84; Matinee, Richelieu; Evening, Richard III
2/11/84; Hamlet
2/12/84; Macbeth
2/13/84; Matinee, Richard III; Evening, Bertuccio, *The Fool's Revenge*
2/14/84; Iago, *Othello*
2/15–16/84; Matinee on 2/16/84; Hamlet 2x

Booth did not play the Saturday evening performance. During Booth's second week, even standing room was sold out, and "the receipts amounted to about $26,000. The Saturday matinee, when Booth appeared as Hamlet, was the biggest ever known" in Baltimore, and Booth's "personal share" o/f the profits was $1,200. "People were turned away from the doors by the hundreds. Ladies ... with campchairs ... sat wherever they could, and the sidewalks were blocked with people.... And all this ... in the face of the most disagreeable spell of weather known" in Baltimore "in years." Booth was to go on to Brooklyn, but the schedule got fouled up, and he returned to Boston for two weeks. On Sunday Feb. 17, 1884, the company left Baltimore at 8 A.M. They had lunch in New York left New York at 4:30 P.M. and arrived in Boston at 11 P.M., where the advance sale was over $11,000.

2/18/84; Globe Theatre, Boston; Hamlet
2/19/84; King Lear
2/20/84; Iago, *Othello*
2/21/84; Bertuccio, *The Fool's Revenge*

In Feb. 1884 Horace Howard Furness sent Booth a cane that he subsequently used for both Shylock and Bertuccio.

2/23/84; Matinee, Hamlet; Evening, Macbeth
2/25/84; King Lear
2/26/84; Hamlet
2/27/84; Shylock, *Merchant of Venice*; Petruchio, *Katherine and Petruchio*
2/28–29/84; Hamlet 2x
3/1/84; Matinee, Richelieu
3/1/84; Evening Benefit for Associate Charities, Richelieu

On Mar. 1, 1884, *The New York Mirror* told its readers: "The co. in support of the great American tragedian it is hardly necessary to say, is not a great one but it really is not so bad as many would make it out to be. In these days of combinations, when every fair member of a stock company thinks he is a star, it is difficult to get a good co. at figures that will justify a manager in engaging them." *The New York Tribune* admitted that "good actors in Shakespeare are not plentiful anywhere." When he returned to Boston in Mar. 1884, "the constant rain injured" Booth's "first three nights" there "but when it ceased Thursday the houses were packed," and a Hamlet matinee on the first Saturday was "crowded," despite bad weather. The aggregate gross for the Boston run was $14,000. Although he was appearing at the same time as Henry Irving, Booth wrote to Winter from Boston: "The indications are that my business will not suffer..., but I am sorry that circumstances have placed us in opposition & will do so again in New York."

On Mar. 1, Booth gave his last Boston performance for that season and went to Newport with Edwina for a week's rest. On Mar. 8, 1884, *The New York Mirror* told its readers: "It has been a good thing for Boston and indeed for Edwin Booth in the long run, that he and Henry Irving played against each other last week. It has shown, to thinking persons, the American's superiority to the Englishman in all but superb stage presentation and management; and that, after all, is not the actor's immediate business. He should see that it is done, but not necessarily do it. Mr. Booth may not be a closer student of Shakespeare or of human nature generally than Mr. Irving; but, undeniably, he can make that study manifest to greater advantage, while he has not strong mannerisms to mar his work. His left leg may not be a poet, but his whole organization is refined tragedy personified. With such a co. as Mr. Irving's in support, Mr. Booth's great superiority would be manifest to anyone not prejudiced."

3/10/84; Haverly's Theatre, Brooklyn, New York; Hamlet

Booth opened in Brooklyn on Mar. 10, 1884. The house was "completely filled with a cultured and refined audience." "[In Brooklyn] Lent has not had the slightest effect at any of the theatres.—Over a hundred tickets were refused to speculators by Treasurer Wilson, last Tuesday." It was the first day of the advance sale of seats for Booth.

3/11/84; King Lear

When Booth played Hamlet in Brooklyn on Mar. 11, 1884, there was about $1,200 in the house. When Booth played Lear the next day, his lead comic actor Owen Fawcett noted "Although Lear is one of the best things that Mr Booth plays—it attracts the worst houses—yet he will play it."

3/12/84; Iago, *Othello*
3/13/84; Bertuccio, *The Fool's Revenge*
3/14/84; Macbeth
3/15/84; Matinee, Hamlet; Evening, Richard III
3/17/84; Richelieu
3/18/84; Hamlet
3/19/84; Shylock, *Merchant of Venice*; Petruchio, *Katherine and Petruchio*
3/20–21/84; Hamlet 2x
3/22/84; Matinee, Richelieu
3/24/84; Fourteenth Street Theatre, New York; Hamlet
3/25/84; Bertuccio, *The Fool's Revenge*

"Tuesday night the Fourteenth Street was crowded by a notably fashionable audience, collected to witness Edwin Booth's splendid performance of Bertuccio in The Fool's Revenge. It was followed with intense interest from beginning to end, and applauded most liberally.... Whether lashing Manfredi's courtiers with his bitter wit, bestowing fierce paternal love upon his close-kept child, or gloating over the supposed abduction of his enemy's wife, the actor rivets the attention of the audience and plays upon the whole gamut of their emotions. The scene with Fiordelisa was magnificently done, the bitterness of the jester and tenderness of the father alternately outcropping, In the last act, where revenge, grief, remorse and terror follow quick upon one another, the star fairly outdid himself. The audience were strangely affected by his acting, and when, concealing his anguish beneath the antics of the fool the wretched man pleads for admittance to the banquet-hall where his child is captive in the hands of her would-be undoers, a tremor and a sob ran over the spectators.... After each act he was called out, and when the play had finished the people rose to their feet to a man and cheered enthusiastically."

3/26/84; Iago, *Othello*

3/27/84; Hamlet

3/28/84; Shylock, *Merchant of Venice*; Petruchio, *Katherine and Petruchio*

3/29/84; Matinee, Hamlet

No evening performance. *The New York Mirror* of Mar. 29, 1884 reported: "Manager Colville gave Hamlet an admirable setting. Several of the scenes were new and they materially contributed to the enjoyment of the production." Even when new scenery was used, as in the case of Booth's second New York run, at the 14th Street Theatre, the management still provided "modern furniture" for interior scenes.

3/31/84; Richelieu

4/1–2/84; Hamlet 2x

On Apr. 1, 1884, Booth wrote to E. C. Benedict: "I've an offer $5,000 for one week in Combination at Metropolitan, but don't like the jobby look of the thing & will decline it."

4/3/84; Bertuccio, *The Fool's Revenge*

4/4/84; Richelieu

4/5/84; Evening, Hamlet; No matinee performance.

1884–1885

On Nov. 13, 1884, *The New York Mirror* told its readers: "Preparations have been going on for four months at the Boston Museum for Edwin Booth's revivals this season, but the preparations were scenic, and "four rehearsals were hardly enough for the smooth functioning of Hamlet."

11/17–21/84; Boston Museum; matinee on 11/22/84, Hamlet 7x

11/24/84; Othello

When Booth played Othello on Nov. 24, a local reviewer wrote: "the support given by the Museum company was, on the whole, quite good."

11/25/84; Iago, *Othello*

11/26, 28/84; Richelieu 2x

11/29/84; Matinee, Iago, *Othello*; Evening, Macbeth

On Nov. 29 *The New York Mirror* told its readers: "Boston Museum ... crowded on Monday evening, and crowded houses have ruled during the entire week.... Possibly in elocution, [Booth's Hamlet] was more mellow than of yore.... Manager Stetson is making great preparation for the Booth season at the Fifth Avenue The production of *The Apostate*, which Mr. Booth has not done in many years, will necessitate costly mounting."

12/1–2/84; King Lear 2x

12/3/84; Hamlet

12/4/84; Shylock, *Merchant of Venice*; Petruchio, *Katherine and Petruchio*

12/5–6/84; Matinee on 12/6/84; Richelieu

12/6/84; Evening, King Lear

12/8–9/84; Bertuccio 2x, *The Fool's Revenge*

12/10/84; Richelieu

12/11/84; Hamlet

12/12/84; Macbeth

12/13/84; Matinee, Macbeth; Evening, King Lear

On Jan. 1, 1885, Booth wrote to William Winter. He complained of "malaria, contracted some years ago when 'on the road' with Ford. I am well enough & take good care of myself, but now & then my nerves collapse & I can do nothing but glare — unable to think or read; & smoke mechanically — a stolid idiot.... I am sorry that [Barrett] and I must play against each other in New York, but I guess he is safe: I have not so much confidence in my own engt. At the 5th Ave: — my first one there yielded me within a fraction of $1,000 per night, the 2d didn't pay at all — & the theatre closed, you may remember, after I finished."

1/19/85; Fifth Avenue Theatre, New York; Iago, *Othello*

On Jan. 24, 1885, the critic for *The New York Mirror* wrote: "The ordinary Iago is such an out-and-out scoundrel that one wonders why his villainies are not apparent to all the persons of the play. Mr. Booth, however, is so nearly genuine in his counterfeit frankness and integrity that even the spectator would be deceived were it not for the moments when Iago, alone and undisturbed, unmasks and shows his hand."

1/20/85; Othello

1/21–22/85; Sir Edward Mortimer 2x, *The Iron Chest*

1/23/85; Macbeth

1/24/85; Matinee, Ruy Blas, *Ruy Blas*; Evening, Macbeth

On Jan. 24, 1885, *The New York Mirror* reported: "We may say at once that of late years Mr. Booth has not been surrounded by such a competent company.... When the nervousness natural to a first appearance in the Metropolis has worn off, we shall be able to take correct measure of their worth." During his engagement at the Fifth Avenue, Booth revived two roles — Sir Edward Mortimer and Pescara — in which he had not appeared for over ten years." He had last performed Sir Edward Mortimer on Oct. 17, 1873, and Pescara on Sept. 30, 1876. On Jan. 25, 1885, *The Boston Gazette* published a piece about Booth's work in New York: "There is not much that is new, to say of Mr. Booth, except that he has grown stouter and grayer, and that there are signs of thinness in his hair."

1/26–29/85; Hamlet 4x

1/30/85; Pescara, *The Apostate*

1/31/85; Matinee, Don Caesar de Bazan; Evening, Pescara, *The Apostate*

On Jan. 31, 1885, *The New York Mirror* told its readers: "Mr. Booth's engagement at the Fifth Avenue Theatre has proved gratifyingly successful in a pecuniary sense thus far. The houses have been only limited by the capacity of the auditorium.... Every night he has been called before the curtain again and again and cheered to the echo."

2/2–4/85; Richelieu 3x

2/5–7/85; Matinee on 2/7/85; Bertuccio 2x, *The Fool's Revenge*

2/7/85; Evening, Shylock, *Merchant of Venice*; Petruchio, *Katherine and Petruchio*

The New York Mirror of Feb. 7, 1885, told its readers: "The Apostate was very well staged. The scenery and costumes were new and for the most part correct. At the matinee Saturday Mr. Booth played Don Caesar de Bazan to a house crowded with ladies.... On Monday when Mr. Booth played Richelieu, there was a slight falling in the attendance at the Fifth Avenue. Still there were not many vacant seats in the house."

2/9–12/85; Ruy Blas 4x, *Ruy Blas*; Don Caesar de Bazan 4x

2/13/85; Richard III

2/14/85; Matinee, Sir Edward Mortimer, *The Iron Chest*; Evening, Bertuccio, *The Fool's Revenge*

The New York Mirror of Feb. 14, 1885, noted "Edwin Booth probably never acted Bertuccio ... to a more thoroughly responsive and delighted assemblage than that which greeted him last Thursday night at the Fifth Avenue Theatre.... After the first and second acts of the play Mr. Booth was called before the curtain. At the close of the performance he was summoned four distinct times and then, as if more applause were an insufficient mode of expressing their pleasure and appreciation the gallery in response to a demand for three cheers from one enthusiast among them gave them with a will. Previously the tragedian had preserved his habitual dignified mien but this unlooked-for demonstration up aloft caused his features to relax into a smile of grateful recognition." "For the past four weeks the Fifth Avenue Theatre has been the scene of great enthusiasm nightly, and matinees have been gala days. At every performance for the last two weeks the orchestra has been sent beneath the stage. At the matinee last Saturday over two hundred ladies were obliged to stand in the aisles and many were standing in the boxes. It was stated at the box-office that up to Tuesday night over $45,000 had been received and that on the conclusion of the engagement on Saturday night, very little short of $50,000 will have been paid to see the leading American tragedian."

2/16/85; Carll's Opera House, New Haven, Connecticut; Ruy Blas, *Ruy Blas*; Don Caesar de Bazan

In New Haven, "the terrible storm of the day subsided at almost eight o'clock last evening , and though it yet continued threatening, Carll's was crowded.... The plays were excellently well produced, and after every act but one, Booth was called before the curtain. The audience was very enthusiastic and applauded repeatedly during the acts." On Feb. 17, 1885, Booth wrote to Edwina about his performances in New Haven: "The plays went finely & the house was full in spite of the terrific storm. I get a certainty, so do not know the amount of money taken."

2/17/85; Robert's Opera House, Hartford, Connecticut; Ruy Blas, *Ruy Blas*; Don Caesar de Bazan

2/18/85; Opera House, Holyoke, Massachusetts; Iago, *Othello*

When he appeared as Iago in Holyoke, Massachusetts, on Feb. 18, 1885, "Mr. Booth was recalled after the third, fourth and fifth acts."

2/19/85; Academy of Music, Haverhill, Massachusetts; Iago, *Othello*

The Daily Evening Bulletin of Haverhill, Massachusetts told its readers on Feb. 16, 1885: "Long before the office hour for the sale of tickets for the play of 'Othello' at the Academy of Music, this morning, a large crowd of purchasers were in waiting. The line, which extended from the office around the hallway balustrade to the office again, contained some 125 persons. At 9 o'clock the sale commenced and was continued until about 11 o'clock, when the last reserved ticket was disposed of, and the office was closed.... Among the purchasers were many of our business men, but all classes were represented. Quite a number of tickets were ordered from Merrimac, Georgetown, Exeter and other towns. In Haverhill Mr. Barron and Mr. Booth were both called "before the curtain several times."

2/20/85; Providence Opera House, Providence, Rhode Island; Hamlet

On Feb. 20, 1885, Booth wrote to Edwina: "I ...

went to Haverhill at five o'clk. Acted there in a very large, very fine & very comfortable theatre. I start for Providence at 3.30 & will leave there Sunday morning about 8 — getting here [Boston] to breakfast about ten o'clk."

2/21/85; Matinee, Iago, *Othello*; Evening, Sir Edward Mortimer, *The Iron Chest*; Petruchio, *Katherine and Petruchio*

In Providence Booth and the Boston Museum company played to packed houses for three performances on Feb. 20–21. "It is said the receipts for Friday evening amounted to $2,300, the largest by over $500 ever before received at this house." On Mar. 22, 1885, he wrote to Winter: "There is little doubt (tho' 'tis not definitely settled) that Ristori & I will give Macbeth in N.Y., Phila. & Boston — one night each — sometime in May, the 1st week — probably.... Tomorrow I begin my last week here, I wish it was the last of my season, for I am very tired. I shall be a few days, nearly a week, in N.Y. at the Albemarle, after this week. "New Way" seems to have hit 'em here but not Apostate."

2/23/85; Theatre, Worcester, Massachusetts; Hamlet

In Worcester Massachusetts in Feb. 1885 the local critic wrote: "The support company was a whole was only fair." Booth performed "to the largest house eve gathered in the theatre. Receipts $1,800."

2/24/85; Grand Opera House, New Bedford, Massachusetts; Hamlet

2/26/85; Huntington Hall, Lowell, Massachusetts; Hamlet

In Lowell, Booth played to standing room only. "Mr. Booth is no longer 'young Hamlet,' and his face wears the traces of age a well as the assumed gravity of the moody Dane, but there is no lack of vigor in his portrayal.... The audience manifested a disposition to applaud in the wrong place occasionally, and was quite willing to laugh at any of 'Hamlet's' sarcastic or witty words. The support given by the Boston Museum company was fair, and by no means excellent.... The play was mounted as well as the resources of the stage would admit, but some annoyance was caused by the scene shifting during some of the most interesting scenes.... The horse cars ran to all parts of the city at the close and found numerous patrons."

2/27/85; Opera House, Lawrence, Massachusetts; Hamlet

In Lawrence, where he had not played in thirteen years, Booth was "called several times before the curtain." He was supported by the Boston Museum Company. An advertisement in the local newspaper read: "Wanted Twenty Supernumeraries for above performance. Apply to Stage Manager at Stage Entrance of Opera House, Friday at 3 P.M.... Admission tickets to a limited number will be sold for Booth tonight at 7:45. The prices will be fifty cents for balcony and seventy-five cents orchestra admission."

2/28/85; City Theatre, Brockton, Massachusetts; Iago, *Othello*

3/2–3/85; Boston Museum; Sir Edward Mortimer 2x, *The Iron Chest*

3/4–5/85; Sir Giles Overreach 2x, *A New Way to Pay Old Debts*

In Boston on Mar. 4, 1885, he revived Sir Giles Overreach, a role he had not performed "for over ten years." The Boston correspondent for *The New York Mirror* thought *The Iron Chest* "a stupid sort of an affair, though it is played superbly not only by Mr. Booth himself but by the co. in support as well."

3/6–7/85; Pescara 2x, *The Apostate*

3/7/85; Matinee, Don Caesar de Bazan

The company performed without Booth on Saturday night.

3/9–14/85; Richard III 6x

3/14/85; Matinee, Claude Melnotte, *The Lady of Lyons*

3/16–18/85; Ruy Blas 3x, *Ruy Blas*; Don Caesar de Bazan 3x

3/19/85; Sir Giles Overreach, *A New Way to Pay Old Debts*

3/20–21/85; Matinee on 3/21/85, Claude Melnotte 2x, *The Lady of Lyons*

3/21/85; Pescara, *The Apostate*; Petruchio, *Katherine and Petruchio*

3/23/85; Richelieu

3/24/85; Othello

3/25–26/85; Ruy Blas 2x, *Ruy Blas*; Don Caesar de Bazan 2x

3/27–28/85; Matinee on 3/28/85, Shylock 2x, *Merchant of Venice*; Petruchio 2x, *Katherine and Petruchio*

3/28/85; Evening, Iago, *Othello*

On Apr. 4, 1885, the Boston correspondent for *The New York Mirror* wrote: "the co. in support has met with particular favor improving constantly, as lines were learned more thoroughly and ease was gained.... All the co. needs is good stage management and a chance to work together. It will have both next season."

4/6–8/85; Chestnut Street Opera House, Philadelphia Hamlet 3x

On Apr. 8 Booth wrote to Edwina: "Last night the house was again crowded & the audience very demonstrative & I think I acted even better than the first night. The people seem to be far more demonstrative than any that I've acted to elsewhere; it may be there is a little bit of national feeling in the case — since the gush over Irving." In Apr. 1885 Booth wrote to Edwina: "My health is good, acting ditto & the business great. This being a continuation of my crazy arrangement with Fields, he, of course, gets the hog's share of the 'swag'; my last dealings with him — out of Boston, at all events — there the terms were equitable."

4/9/85; Bertuccio, *The Fool's Revenge*
4/10/85; Shylock, *Merchant of Venice*; Petruchio, *Katherine and Petruchio*
4/11/85; Matinee, Don Caesar de Bazan; Evening, Macbeth

During the Philadelphia run, Booth wrote to Edwina: "Business continues great & Fields is happy, but I shall soon file a complaint w<u>h</u> will make him <u>shudder</u>! ... This afternoon I play <u>Don Caesar</u> & <u>Macbeth</u> tonight. Have just heard that Miss Clark is ill, & it is barely possible a change to <u>Fool's Revenge</u> may be necessary — she gets ill about 8 times a week, it seem & I wish she w<u>d</u> retire permanently." During the Philadelphia run, Booth wrote to Edwina: "After the play last night I went into the clover-room across the hall from mine and was received with great enthusiasm, cheered and be-speeched & made an honorary member along with Mark Twain. Business continues great — the greatest I've ever had (in money) in this city & as my luck w<u>d</u> have it, Fields gets the cream of it — I made my terms easy, because formerly my engagements here were not very great."

4/13–14/85; Richelieu 2x
4/15/85; Ruy Blas, *Ruy Blas*; Don Caesar de Bazan
4/16/85; Iago, *Othello*

During the Philadelphia engagement, Booth wrote to Edwina on Apr. 16, 1885: "Last night a laurel wreath with white ribbon was passed to me from front, no name on the card.... The papers seem to be full of me & my acting — have heard so, seen by The Times. Houses are jammed every night & I am told that <u>all</u> the papers have been unusually kind."

4/17/85; Bertuccio, *The Fool's Revenge*
4/18/85; Matinee, Claude Melnotte, *The Lady of Lyons*; Evening, Pescara, *The Apostate*; Petruchio, *Katherine and Petruchio*

On Apr. 18 the Philadelphia correspondent for the *New York Mirror* wrote: "Edwin Booth's engagement at the Opera house has thus far been a phenomenal success.... At the last representation of Hamlet people were turned away. The Boston Museum co., as a whole is inadequate to the work cut out for it.... The Penn Club will tender a reception to Edwin Booth on Friday evening."

4/20–21/85; Richelieu 2x
4/22/85; Ruy Blas, *Ruy Blas*; Don Caesar de Bazan
4/23/85; Iago, *Othello*
4/24/85; Bertuccio, *The Fool's Revenge*
4/25/85; Matinee, Claude Melnotte, *The Lady of Lyons*; Evening, Pescara, *The Apostate*; Petruchio, *Katherine and Petruchio*

On Apr. 25 the Philadelphia correspondent for *The New York Mirror* wrote: "Edwin Booth closed the most successful season he has ever played in this city with the performance of *The Apostate*. The Opera House has been filled to overflowing every night of the engagement, the total receipts being $20,000."

5/4/85; New York Academy of Music; Macbeth
c.5/5/85; New York; Poe tribute
5/7/85; Academy of Music, New York or Philadelphia; Macbeth
5/9/85; Macbeth

1885–1886

On June 28, 1885, Booth wrote to Edwina: "I shall be at home most of the season — I act only 14 weeks, 8 or 9 of which will be spent in Boston, but the following season I shall act longer."

11/9/85; Academy of Music, Baltimore; Richelieu
11/10/85; Iago, *Othello*
11/11/85; Hamlet
11/12/85; Bertuccio, *The Fool's Revenge*
11/13/85; Macbeth
11/14/85; Matinee, Don Caesar de Bazan; Evening, Sir Edward Mortimer, *The Iron Chest*

According to *The New York Mirror*, "the first week of ... Booth's engagement at the Academy of Music was a crush at every performance. Every available inch of room was utilized; the aisles were filled from the stage to the door, and the orchestra was crowded from its place," and by its end, "the seats were nearly all sold" for the second week. "This is probably the most brilliant engagement Mr. Booth ever played here. Usually Baltimore audiences are noisy and pronounced in their enthusiasm, but last week, they were quiet in their appreciation, though it was nonetheless sincere and hearty. The support of the Boston Museum co. was excellent"

11/16/85; King Lear
11/17/85; Hamlet
11/18/85; Pescara, *The Apostate*
11/19/85; Richelieu
11/20/85; Sir Giles Overreach, *A New Way to Pay Old Debts*
11/21/85; Matinee, Hamlet; Evening, Ruy Blas, *Ruy Blas*; Petruchio, *Katherine and Petruchio*

According to *The New York Mirror*, "during the second week, ... the house was packed at every performance and people were turned from the door every night." The total receipts of Booth's fortnight in Baltimore were a little over $20,000.

11/23/85; Academy of Music Brooklyn New York; Richelieu

"Edwin Booth began a week's engagement at the Academy, [Brooklyn] with a powerful portrayal of Richelieu.... He has been so badly treated in this city that he intended making n.d. here until too late for the regular theatres."

11/24/85; Iago, *Othello*
11/25/85; Ruy Blas, *Ruy Blas*

On Nov. 25 Booth wrote to Edwina: "The rain has injured my business [in Brooklyn], but it is the best of all the theatres."

11/26/85; Bertuccio, *The Fool's Revenge*

11/27/85; Hamlet

11/28/85; Ruy Blas, *Ruy Blas*; Petruchio, *Katherine and Petruchio*

The Brooklyn correspondent for *The New York Mirror*, however, told its audiences, on Nov. 28, 1885 that "the town has turned to him.... He will not play to less than $7,000 for the week, at popular prices. The support has something to do with it." After Brooklyn, Booth rested for a month, opening in Boston on Dec. 28 for a five-week season.

12/28/5–1/2/86; Boston Museum Matinee on 1/2/86, Lucius Junius Brutus 7x, *Brutus*

1/4–9/86; Matinee on 1/9/86; Hamlet 6x

1/9/86; Evening, Iago, *Othello*

1/11–13/86; Richelieu 3x

1/14/86; Shylock, *Merchant of Venice*; Petruchio, *Katherine and Petruchio*

1/15/86; Bertuccio, *The Fool's Revenge*

1/16/86; Matinee, Richelieu; Evening, Sir Giles Overreach, *A New Way to Pay Old Debts*

1/18/86; Hamlet

1/19/86; Macbeth

1/20/86; Bertuccio, *The Fool's Revenge*

1/21/86; King Lear

1/22/86; Richard III

When Booth performed *Richard III* on Jan. 22, 1886, a Boston critic wrote: "The want of historic exactness in the ladies' dresses was more than usually noticeable; Mrs. Ryan's (Duchess of York), save for the train, would hardly have excited comment on Temple place any shopping afternoon you please."

1/23/86; Matinee, Iago, *Othello*; Evening, Richard III

1/25–30/86; Matinee on 1/30/86; Brutus 7x, *Julius Caesar*

2/1–5/86; Fifth Avenue Theatre New York; Hamlet 5x

2/6/86; Iago, *Othello*

2/8–10/86; King Lear 3x

2/11–14/86; Matinee on 2/13/86; Lucius Junius Brutus 4x, *Brutus*

On Feb. 13, 1886, *The New York Mirror* told its readers: "Edwin Booth's house on Monday night was not as large as he has had since the beginning of his present engagement. This falling off was accounted for by the fact that *King Lear* was the bill. Of all Shakespeare's acting plays, *King Lear* is least attractive to the public. Mr. Booth acted the part superbly. and the audience were aroused several times to enthusiastic admiration of his impersonation. After each act he was called before the curtain. The company failed to give satisfactory support. This evening John Howard Payne's *Brutus* will be presented, and for the rest of the week. On Feb. 14, 1886, Booth wrote to Edwina: "The past week's business was greatly injured by the storms. 'Brutus' made a tremendous hit & had the weather been decent the theatre w$^{\underline{d}}$ not have held the crowds that would have come. I never knew more enthusiasm for any play, nor so much — ever — for Brutus I played it twice yesterday — to fine audiences that stood & waved & cheered; it amazed me! And I'm not easily amazed by applause." "It is stated that the business of the first week of the engagement of Edwin Booth at the Fifth Avenue Theatre was larger than that of the corresponding week of last season, when the tragedian played to an average business of over $10,000 per week for four weeks. At the matinee on Saturday the receipts were the largest ever taken at this theatre for any performance at regular prices. It was $40 better than Mr. Booth's best house last season, and it was $200 better than any *Mikado* performance except the Sullivan night, when the prices were advanced. Many persons who wanted to see *Hamlet* neglected to apply for tickets until late in the week, and hundreds of people were turned away on Friday night and on Saturday afternoon unable to get even standing room."

2/15/86; Macbeth

2/16–17/86; Sir Giles Overreach 2x, *A New Way to Pay Old Debts*

On Feb. 17, 1886, Booth wrote to Edwina from New York City: "The operas, weather, & new plays at other houses have injured my business seriously." In Feb. 1886 Booth wrote to Edwina: "Business is still good — but the weather kills the nights sales."

2/18–20/86; Matinee on 2/20/86; Richelieu 4x

On Feb. 20, 1886, *The New York Mirror* told its readers: "Edwin Booth's engagement at the Fifth Avenue is attended by a succession of large and enthusiastic audiences. On Tuesday last [actually Thursday] he acted Brutus superbly in John Howard Payne's tragedy, but his support was something so deplorable as to defy an adequate description. On Monday *Macbeth* was acted, the star's well-known impersonation evoking the usual measure of admiration. On Tuesday *A New Way to Pay Old Debts* was given, Mr. Booth appearing as Sir Giles Overreach for the first time in a number of years. The piece is tiresome and the leading character has little opportunity for effective acting except in the last act. Here Mr. Booth thrilled the house by his marvelous exhibition of impotent rage, and his awful dying speech was delivered with tremendous power.... The scenery was a series of antique, shabby daubs, that cause a succession of involuntary titters. The mounting of some of the pieces during the Booth season has been disgraceful." On Feb. 21, 1886, Booth wrote to Edwina: "I acted Richelieu twice yesterday & have not yet recovered from my fatigue.... I am to take a tour as far as California, next season.... Sir Giles & Brutus seem to have stirred the town."

2/22–23/86; Bertuccio 2x, *The Fool's Revenge*

2/24–25/86; Richard III 2x

2/26–27/86; Matinee on 2/27/86; Brutus 3x, *Julius Caesar*

On Feb. 28, 1886, Booth wrote to William Winter from New York: "Tomorrow at 11 A.M. I shall go to Phila — to be absent two weeks.... My sojourn here has not been a pleasant one & I shall be glad when the next fortnight ends and my connection with Fields (outside of Boston, at least) shall terminate. I have worked hard & am weary. With the exception of one misstep (Iago) I have done my duty well — until Friday when, to my utter dismay I found that Brutus has slipped from my memory! I recently acted the part, 7 times, to my own & the public's satisfaction & felt so sure of myself that I did not rehearse or read the part — but when I entered the scene my wits flew off & I made a bungle of the part. At the Matinee, next day, I was but a trifle better — although I read & re-read the lines; at night — last night — I felt my way cautiously & consequently my acting was indifferent, yes — bad! I never had anything of the sort happen to me 'till now.... I have but two more weeks of work & then comes a good long respite." In New York Hamlet was given six times; Richelieu and Lucius Junius Brutus four; King Lear and Shakespeare's Brutus three; Sir Giles Overreach, Richard III and Bertuccio two; and Macbeth once. *The New York Mirror* reported that "although prices were not raised for his engagement, his first matinee took in more money than any matinee at regular prices in the theatre's history." Yet Booth wrote to Edwina: "All day yesterday & last night a heavy snow storm prevailed & it is intensely cold. This & two successful operas have hurt my business seriously. Have not yet had a really good house — while the operas are doing finely."

3/1/86; Chestnut Street Opera House, Philadelphia; Hamlet
3/3/86; Richard III
3/4/86; Lucius Junius Brutus, *Brutus*
3/5/86; Iago, *Othello*
3/6/86; Matinee, Hamlet; Evening, Sir Giles Overreach, *A New Way to Pay Old Debts*
3/8/86; Macbeth
3/9/86; King Lear
3/10/86; Brutus, *Julius Caesar*
3/11/86; Bertuccio, *The Fool's Revenge*
3/12–13/86; Matinee on 3/13/86; Richelieu 2x
3/13/86; Evening, Iago, *Othello*
4/26–29/86; New York Academy of Music; Iago with Salvini 4x, *Othello*

Booth's letter to Edwina written circa Apr. 29, 1886, reads: "After the violent scene with Salvini where he throws me to the ground & picks me up — my heel caught in the ragged carpet & I fell flat — The audience was for a moment startled, but all went well after that.... I am charmed with Salvini — personally as well as professionally — he is a great actor.... Saturday night I shall take Salvini to my club."

4/30/86; Hamlet with Salvini
5/1/86; Matinee, Iago with Salvini, *Othello*
5/3, 5/86; Academy of Music, Philadelphia; Iago with Salvini 2x, *Othello*
5/7/86; Hamlet with Salvini
5/8/86; Matinee, Iago with Salvini, *Othello*
5/10, 12/86; Boston Theatre; Iago with Salvini 2x, *Othello*
5/14/86; Hamlet with Salvini
5/15/86; Matinee, Iago with Salvini, *Othello*

A. C. Wheeler, under the pseudonym Nym Crinkle wrote in *The New York Mirror* of Sept. 4, 1886: "I need not remind you when Cushman opened her 'ponderous and marble jaws' the house was awestruck. And Ned Booth, when he played with her, always reminded me of a lion tamer about to perform the perilous feat of thrusting his head into the leonine mouth. I am bound to say, however, that he never lost his head with her. That catastrophe was reserved until he played with Salvini."

1886–1887

Booth was concerned about the venues he was scheduled to play during the 1886–1887 season. He did not want to wear out his attractiveness through over-exposure. "I don't want to 'play myself out' in Boston which is apt to be the case if I act long engagements there every season — last season I played two engagements at the Museum, and this time I am there for five weeks — with the same old plays, with nothing for a run." He also objected to specific theatres — for instance, Ford's Opera House in Baltimore, and had Barrett arrange for the Baltimore Theatre instead. Barrett selected Arthur Branscomb Chase for the position of road manger. Booth, who had never met Chase, had already offered the job to Charles H. Thayer who had managed his 1884–1885 and 1885–1886 tours. Chase's name was published before Booth broke the bad news to Thayer, and Thayer resented being shunted aside. Booth wrote to Winter: "It is awkward for me to face the man to whom I had partly committed myself — for the article mentions Mr. Chase I think it is, as my agent. He is Barrett's man of business whom I have never seen — to my knowledge, nor even held any kind of communication with; I must now tell my man the entire facts rather than let him think that I have thrown him over for another agent" In terms of hiring actors for the 1886–1887 season, the question was not only one of quality but also of price. Booth, for instance, liked H. C. Albaugh, who was touring with him in 1885–1886, but, as he told Barrett: "'tis merely a question of ducats — for you to determine.... Charley Wolcott is a good fellow &c, in modern comedy, a good actor — but, altho' he has acted often in all my pieces, I never regarded him as a 'tragedy cuss,' and — with the kindest feelings for the man — I would prefer another, ... but what other I cannot say—for I cannot keep the run of actors in mind & lose their very names." Neither man was hired. On July 3, 1886, *The New York Mirror* told its readers: The leading men for Edwin Booth and Lawrence Barrett next season are Charles Barron and Newton Gotthold." Barron made $125 a week. Booth's complained that Osric was always played by young women; his complaints, however, were exaggerated. The overwhelming number of his Osrics were male; however he did, occasionally, performed with female Osrics including: Lillie Graham at the Louisville Theatre on Apr. 27, 1858; Fanny Denham at Wood's Theatre in Cincinnati on Apr. 10, 1860; Maria Boniface at Grover's Theatre in Washington, D.C. on Feb. 15, 1864; Mary Young at Taylor's Opera House in Trenton, New Jersey on Dec. 9, 1872; Emma Stockman who toured with Booth under John T. Ford's management Jan., Feb. and Mar., 1876, throughout the south and Lydia Denier [sometimes spelled Dennen] at Macauley's Theatre in Louisville, Kentucky on Nov. 5, 1877. Kitty Molony played Osric at the Detroit Opera House at the matinee on Sept. 18, 1886. Cast changes continued through the 1886–1887 tour. Miss Rock got to try Marion de Lorme and the Player Queen (the latter two at Kitty Molony's expense). Walter Thomas was replaced by John T. Sullivan as Francois in *Richelieu*. The child playing the Duke of York in *Richard III* and his accompanying mother were dropped in Baltimore. Booth was able to hire a child in San Francisco for five dollars a week. Ida Rock who usually played Gentlewomen and pages got to try Regan, because, in Booth's view, Mrs. Sarah A. Baker, originally hired for the role looked "antique enough to spank old Lear. The Fool's line about making 'thy daughters thy mothers,' is not, in her case, at all inappropriate."

9/13/86; Academy Theatre Buffalo, New York; Richelieu
9/14/86; Macbeth
9/15/86; Hamlet
These dates were originally scheduled for Buffalo and then changed to Detroit and then back to Buffalo.
9/16/86; Opera House, Detroit, Michigan; Richelieu
9/17/86; Macbeth
9/18/86; Matinee, Hamlet
9/18/86; Evening, Iago, *Othello*
9/20/86; New Opera House, Bay City, Michigan; Hamlet
This date was originally scheduled for Grand Rapids, Michigan
9/21/86; Academy of Music, East Saginaw, Michigan; Hamlet
9/22/86; Academy of Music, Kalamazoo Michigan; Hamlet
9/23/86; Powers' Opera House, Grand Rapids, Michigan; Hamlet
9/24/86; Grand Opera House Milwaukee, Wisconsin; Richelieu
9/25/86; Matinee, Hamlet; Evening, Iago, *Othello*
The New York Mirror told its readers that "Edwin Booth is having a triumphal march in Michigan. The houses on the circuit are sold out for two to three days in advance of his coming and at increased prices." Arthur Chase was doing his job—filling the nation's premiere theatrical newspaper with the Booth legend. In actuality, the increased prices resulted in reduced ticket sales. Chase found that two dollars was generally the most he could charge, although some seats could go up to $2.50. He made money, however, by saving on expenses, negotiating with the Michigan Central Railroad for a special coach and baggage car and for free transport of 6000 pounds of excess baggage.
9/27/86; Grand Opera House, Minneapolis, Minnesota; Richelieu
On Sept. 27, 1886, Chase wrote to Barrett from Minneapolis: "I think if St. Paul holds up as well as this city the gross will amount to about $13,000—for present week—Mr Conklin estimates it will run $15,000.
9/28/86; Iago, *Othello*
9/29/86; Hamlet
After *Hamlet* on Sept. 29 the company moved to St. Paul, put in a long rehearsal of *King Lear* on Friday and, after two Saturday performances, left for Chicago at 7 P.M. on Oct. 3.
9/30/86; Grand Opera House St. Paul, Minnesota; Richelieu
Booth, "clad in a heavy ulster, his long grey hair protruding from under a black derby hat, set well back on his head" was "drawing on his gloves for a morning walk" when approached by a reporter in the lobby of the Ryan Hotel in St. Paul. His response was: "Oh I must beg you to excuse me. I don't like to be interviewed. Mr. Chase, my manager, can tell you anything you wish to know but I—I am never interviewed." When asked about newspaper reports of his retirement, Booth said: "I see many of the newspapers have so announced, but it did not come from me. I hope not—I hope to continue a good many years yet."
10/1/86; Bertuccio, *The Fool's Revenge*
10/2/86; Matinee, Hamlet; Evening, Iago, *Othello*
10/4/86; Chicago Opera House, Chicago Illinois; Richelieu
10/5/86; Iago, *Othello*
10/6/86; Macbeth
On Nov. 6 Arthur Branscomb Chase wrote to Lawrence Barrett: "I had a platform built in Orchestra & placed 40 camp chairs there at 1.^{50} each, more as an advertisement than anything else as the Balcony was not sold out. The seating capacity of the Star is not as large as I supposed. It is 646 Orchestra;

379 Balcony; 464 Gallery; Total 1,489. With every seat Or[chestra] & Bal[cony] Sold at 1^{50} & entire gallery at 50 cents the house would amt to only $1,764.58, without the boxes which do not sell well. None sold this P.M. & this is without deducting Press & other comps.—Since writing above, Mr. Burnham has told me that the present engagement is way ahead of Mr. Booth's last season's engagement at Fifth Avenue. He was the Treasurer there—says Mr. Booth's houses ran from $800 to $1,600—the latter sum on only one occasion."
10/7/86; Richelieu
On Nov. 7, 1886, Booth wrote to Edwina: "I've had an unpleasant griping trouble for several days—if not a cold, it must be the effect of <u>canned</u> corn.... I got a medicine that relieved me."
10/8–9/86; Matinee on 10/9/86; Hamlet 2x
10/9/86; Evening, Iago, *Othello*
10/11/86; Hamlet
10/12/86; Bertuccio, *The Fool's Revenge*
10/13/86; Richard III
10/14/86; Hamlet
10/15/86; Bertuccio, *The Fool's Revenge*
10/16/86; Matinee, Richelieu; Evening, Shylock, *Merchant of Venice*; Petruchio, *Katherine and Petruchio*
A Chicago critic in 1886 wrote: "Mr. Booth paints the Jew, not the Hebrew.... Mr. Booth does not allow us a moment of sympathy with Shylock. He makes the character odious even in its piety."
10/18/86; Olympic Theatre, St, Louis, Missouri; Richelieu
10/19/86; Hamlet
10/20/86; Bertuccio, *The Fool's Revenge*
10/21/86; Richard III
10/22/86; Macbeth
10/23/86; Matinee, Hamlet; Evening, Iago, *Othello*
10/25/86; Opera House, Cleveland, Ohio; Richelieu
10/26/86; Hamlet
10/27/86; Bertuccio, *The Fool's Revenge*
10/28/86; Richard III
10/29/86; Shylock, *Merchant of Venice*
10/30/86; Matinee, Hamlet; Evening, Iago, *Othello*
11/1–6/86; Star Theatre, New York Matinee on 11/6/86; Hamlet 6x
11/6, 8/86; Evening, Bertuccio 2x, *The Fool's Revenge*
11/9/86; Bertuccio, *The Fool's Revenge*—cancelled
11/10/86; Bertuccio, *The Fool's Revenge*—cancelled
11/11/86; Richelieu—cancelled
11/12/86; Richelieu—cancelled
11/13/86; Matinee, Richelieu—cancelled; Evening, Macbeth—cancelled
11/15–17/86; Iago 3x, *Othello*
11/18–20/86; Richelieu 3x
11/20/86; Matinee, Iago, *Othello*
11/22/86; Hamlet
11/23/86; Bertuccio, *The Fool's Revenge*
11/24/86; Shylock, *Merchant of Venice*; Petruchio, *Katherine and Petruchio*
11/25/86; Matinee, Iago, *Othello*; Evening, Hamlet
11/26/86; Bertuccio, *The Fool's Revenge*
11/27/86; Matinee, Hamlet; Evening, Shylock, *Merchant of Venice*; Petruchio, *Katherine and Petruchio*
11/29/86; Park Theatre, Brooklyn, New York; Richelieu
Performing in Brooklyn in late Nov., early Dec. 1869, Booth complained of "a distressful weariness (malaria, I think)." "My head cold (no longer my belly, <u>thank God</u>!) and the low temperature keep me indoors.... Headaches have been the rule with me for several weeks past & it is at the splitting point now while I write."
11/30/86; Hamlet
12/1/86; Iago, *Othello*
12/2/86; Richelieu
12/3/86; Shylock, *Merchant of Venice*; Petruchio, *Katherine and Petruchio*
12/4/86; Matinee, Hamlet; Evening, Bertuccio, *The Fool's Revenge*
12/5/86; Boston Theatre; Richelieu
12/7/86; Hamlet
12/8/86; Bertuccio, *The Fool's Revenge*
12/9/86; Richelieu
12/10/86; Shylock, *Merchant of Venice*; Petruchio, *Katherine and Petruchio*
12/11/86; Matinee, Hamlet; Evening, Iago, *Othello*
12/13/86; Richard III
12/14/86; Macbeth
12/15/86; King Lear
On Dec. 15, 1886, Arthur Branscomb Chase wrote to Lawrence Barrett: "Mr. Levy [Booth's advance man] is here. He has Hamlet laid out for Springfield. As Mr Booth gives Hamlet at Holyoke just ahead and there having been a large sale to Springfield people, don't you think it advisable to give them something different to draw from both towns."
12/16/86; Hamlet
12/17/86; Bertuccio, *The Fool's Revenge*
12/18/86; Matinee, Richelieu; Evening, Richard III
12/20/86; Worcester Theatre, Worcester, Massachusetts; Iago, *Othello*
12/21/86; Opera House, Holyoke, Massachusetts; Hamlet
12/22/86; Leland Opera House, Albany, New York; Richelieu
In Dec. 1886 when Booth was fifty-three, the critic for the *Albany Journal*, wrote: "Of the robust roles which call for a physique that's bespeaks strong animality and the art which can picture massive heroes like *Spartacus* and *Othello* ... one looks to a Salvini for interpretation." [*Richelieu*] gives opportunity for the full display of the strong elocutionary method which characterizes this great actor [Booth], and which, perhaps, unfits him, in a

measure, for parts which call for less of convention and calculation and more of informality."

12/23/86; Opera House, Utica, New York; Iago, *Othello*

12/24/86; Academy of Music, Oswego, New York; Iago, *Othello*

12/25/86; Wieting Opera House, Syracuse, New York; Matinee, Hamlet; Evening, Iago, *Othello*

12/27/86; Opera House, Rochester, New York; Hamlet

12/28/86; Wagner Opera House, Bradford, Pennsylvania; Hamlet

12/29/86; Elmira Opera House, Elmira, New York; Hamlet

12/30/86; Academy Theatre, Scranton, Pennsylvania; Hamlet

12/31/86; Fulton Opera House, Lancaster, Pennsylvania; Hamlet

1/1/87; Grand Opera House, Newark, New Jersey, Matinee, Iago, *Othello*; Evening, Hamlet

1/3/87; Chestnut Street Opera House, Philadelphia; Richelieu

1/4/87; Hamlet

On Jan. 4, 1887, Arthur Branscomb Chase wrote to Lawrence Barrett who was contemplating renting The Academy of Music in New York: "I spoke to Mr. Booth regarding it & he replied his ambition had been gratified as to a N.Y. theatre."

1/5/87; Bertuccio, *The Fool's Revenge*

1/6/87; Richelieu

1/7/87; Shylock, *Merchant of Venice*; Petruchio, *Katherine and Petruchio*

1/8/87; Matinee, Hamlet; Evening, Iago, *Othello*

1/10/87; Richard III

1/11/87; Macbeth

1/12/87; Hamlet

1/13/87; King Lear

1/14/87; Hamlet

1/15/87; Matinee, Richelieu; Evening, Richard III

1/17/87; Baltimore Theatre; Richelieu

1/18/87; Hamlet

1/19/87; Bertuccio, *The Fool's Revenge*

1/20/87; King Lear

1/21/87; Shylock, *Merchant of Venice*; Petruchio, *Katherine and Petruchio*

1/22/87; Matinee, Hamlet; Evening, Iago, *Othello*

1/24/87; Ellsler's Opera House, Pittsburgh, Pennsylvania; Richelieu

1/25/87; Hamlet

1/26/87; Bertuccio, *The Fool's Revenge*

1/27/87; King Lear

1/28/87; Shylock, *Merchant of Venice*; Petruchio, *Katherine and Petruchio*

1/29/87; Matinee, Hamlet; Evening, Iago, *Othello*

1/31/87; Grand Opera House, Cincinnati, Ohio; Richelieu

2/1/87; Hamlet

2/2/87; King Lear

On Feb. 2, 1887, Chase wrote to Barrett from Cincinnati about plans for Booth's San Francisco engagement due to start Mar. 7: "Will you suggest the repertoire for Frisco? How would it do for second or third week to put up *Hamlet* as long as it runs profitably?"

2/3/87; Richelieu

2/4/87; Shylock, *Merchant of Venice*; Petruchio, *Katherine and Petruchio*

2/5/87; Matinee, Hamlet; Evening, Iago, *Othello*

2/7/87; Macauley's Theatre, Louisville, Kentucky; Richelieu

On Feb. 7, 1887, Booth wrote to Furness: "My notion of Shylock is of the traditional type, which I firmly believe to be "the jew that Shakespeare drew." Not the buffoon that Daggett gave according to Lord Lonsdale's version of the play, but the strongly marked & somewhat grotesque character which Macklin restored to the stage, in which he was followed by Cooke, by Edmund Kean and by my father. 'Tis nonsense to suppose that Shylock was represented in other but a serious vein by Burbage, merely because he 'made up' doubtless after some representation of Judas — with red hair, to emphasize the vicious expression of his features. Is there any authority for the assertion that some make that he also wore a long nose? What if he did? A clever actor once played the part of Tubal with one & wore red hair & a hook'd nose. He did not make the audience laugh; 'twas not his purpose, but he looked the very creature that could sympathize with Shylock. His 'make up' was admirable. He is the son of the once famous John Drew & is himself an excellent actor — at present a leading member of Mr Daly's company. Let Burbage have the long nose, if you will, but I am sure that he never, under Shakespeare's nose, made the character ridiculous. No not 'till Londsdale's bastard came, did the jew make the unskillful laugh and the judicious grieve. From that time, perhaps, until Macklin restored the original method of representing the character, it was treated as a 'low comedy' part. I doubt if Macklin or Cooke wore red wig for Shylock — but no matter, Burbage did and neither he nor they were funny. If Edmund Kean was the first to wear black hair when red was the usual color worn by actors of the part at the time, 'tis easily accounted for when you reflect that he was very poor and probably had a very limited stock of stage 'props' — he doubtless had no other old man's wig (except a white one for Lear) and the 'black bald' did service for Sir Giles Overreach & several other elderly gentlemen besides Shylock. I know that such was my father's case and also mine in my strolling days. I believe that Burbage, Macklin, Cooke & Kean (as did my father) made Shylock what was technically termed a "character-part"— grotesque not so pronounced, perhaps as my personation has been sometimes censored for.- I think Macready was the first to lift the uncanny jew out of the darkness of his native element of revengeful selfishness into the light of the venerable Hebrew, the martyr, the Avenger. He has had several followers, and I once tried to view him in that light, but there he does not cast a shadow sufficiently strong to contrast with the sunshine of the comedy — to do which he must be to a certain extent repulsive, a sort of party that one doesn't care to see about the dainty revellers [sic] of Venice in her prime, &c. Antonio's liver-trouble is gloom enough for them, but to heighten their brilliancy for us a heavier cloud is necessary and it takes the form of Shylock — "an inhuman wretch uncapable of pity, void and empty from any dram of mercy." — It has been said that he is an affectionate father and a faithful friend. When, where and how does he manifest the least claim to such commendation? Tell me that and unyoke! 'Twas the money value of Leah's ring that so grieved him, not its association with her else he would have shown some affection for her daughter, which he did not — or she would not have called her home a hell, robbed and left him. Shakespeare makes her do these un-Hebrew things to intensify the baseness of Shylock's nature. If we side with him in his self-defense 'tis because we have charity, which he has not; if we pity him under the burthen [sic] of his merited punishment 'tis because we are human, which he is not — except in form and even that, I think, should indicate the crookedness of his nature. His refusal to accept thrice the amount he loaned seems to have given some critics the idea that as a great avenger of his wronged people he rises above all selfish considerations, but had he accepted what a lame & impotent conclusion it would have been. No, this other un-jew-like action was necessary for stage-effect. Do not forget, my histrionic boy, when you read the Poet's plays, that he was a player and mark you! A theatrical manager with a keen eye to stage-effects; witness the 'gag' of Shylock's sharpening his knife — a most dangerous 'bit of business' and apt to cover a laugh, be careful of that 'point.' — would the heroic Hebrew have stooped to such a paltry, Jew-like action? NO, not in its very white-heat of his pursuit of Vengeance. But Vengeance is foreign to Shylock's thought, 'tis Revenge he seeks, and he gets just what all who seek it get — sooner or later, as the saying is. Had his motive been the higher one Shakespeare would have, somehow, contrived his success without doubt; but Shylock has grown too strong for him. 'Tis said ... he had to kill Mercutio else the merry fellow would have killed his tragedy so Shylock would have killed the Comedy had he been intended to personify Vengeance. — The storm-cloud of his evil passions having burst he is forgotten in the moonlight of fair Portia's garden."

2/8/87; Hamlet
2/9/87; Iago, *Othello*
2/10//87; New Memphis Theatre, Tennessee; Richelieu
2/11/87; Hamlet

On Feb. 11, 1887, Booth wrote to Lawrence Barrett: "The 'critics' have gone for my thin grey pate & wrinkled face with a vengeance — even the friendly ones have been aroused to these disappointments. Well, I presume I must begin to shelve my inkey cloak [Hamlet costume] & rely on Lear & Richelieu."

2/12/87; Matinee, Hamlet; Evening, Iago, *Othello*
2/14/87; Grand Opera House, New Orleans; Richelieu
2/15/87; Hamlet
2/16/87; Bertuccio, *The Fool's Revenge*
2/17/87; King Lear
2/18/87; Shylock, *Merchant of Venice*; Petruchio, *Katherine and Petruchio*
2/19/87; Noon Matinee, Hamlet; Evening, Iago, *Othello*
2/21/87; Tremont Opera House, Galveston, Texas; Richelieu
2/22/87; Hamlet
2/23/87; Pillot's Opera House, Houston, Texas; Hamlet
2/24/87; Opera House, Dallas, Texas; Hamlet
2/25/87; Opera House, Austin, Texas; Hamlet
2/26/87; Opera House, San Antonio, Texas; Matinee, Richelieu; Evening, Hamlet
3/2/87; Grand Opera House, Los Angeles, California; Richelieu

Booth wrote to Barrett the day after he arrived in Los Angeles: "Monster! Through the land of the Cactus & Cowboy I ached my alkaline way &, to my surprise, 'am not ded yit' — But for our worthy Arch & patron-saint, D. Garick Eq^{re}, [Booth's private railway car] I might not now be writing here. But with all the comforts he afforded, the trip is extremely well 'played out' last night."

3/3/87; Hamlet
3/4/87; Shylock, *Merchant of Venice*; Petruchio, *Katherine and Petruchio*
3/5/87; Matinee, Hamlet; Evening, Iago, *Othello*
3/7–12/87; Baldwin's Theatre, San Francisco; Matinee on 3/12/87, Hamlet 6x
3/12/87; Evening, Iago, *Othello*

The nightly box office receipts for five evenings and a matinee of *Hamlet* and Saturday evening performance in *Othello* in San Francisco in 1877 were $3,425; $2,012; $2,085; $2,147; $2,295; $1,870 and $2,313.

3/14/87; Macbeth
3/15/87; King Lear
3/16/87; Bertuccio, *The Fool's Revenge*
3/17/87; Othello
3/18/87; Shylock, *Merchant of Venice*; Petruchio, *Katherine and Petruchio*
3/19/87; Matinee, Iago, *Othello*; Evening, Bertuccio, *The Fool's Revenge*

On Mar. 20, 1887, Booth wrote to Thomas Bailey Aldrich: "In my private car, the David Garrick, I table with me the best of the company — all very agreeable folk and live at ease — with every joint jostled out of plumb and all my nerves shattered, I feel like a heavy drunk after an all-night trip; but not a drunk of the lightest sort has yet been indulged in by any member of my corps, nor by my own corpse, neither; ginger-ale has been my only tonic & I've somehow lost my liking for my blessed beer; Tobacco, alas, still hold me in its thrall — that I cannot escape from I am & must be ever its abject slave! — The strange mirage of the desert & the snow-mountains, seemingly close at hand, made the hot & arid sand — through which I journeyed three days — very interesting despite the inconveniences of that home of the Cactus & Cowboy — of wh I saw galore."

3/21/87; Richelieu
3/22/87; Hamlet
3/23/87; Sir Giles Overreach, *A New Way to Pay Old Debts*
3/24/87; Bertuccio, *The Fool's Revenge*
3/25/87; Richelieu
3/26/87; Matinee, Bertuccio, *The Fool's Revenge*; Evening, Richard III
3/28/87; Hamlet
3/29/87; Shylock, *Merchant of Venice*; Petruchio, *Katherine and Petruchio*
3/30/87; Othello
3/31/87; Hamlet
4/1–2/87; Matinee on 4/2/87; Richelieu 2x
4/2/87; Evening, Hamlet
4/6/87; California Theatre, San Jose, California; Hamlet
4/7/87; Avon Theatre, Stockton, California; Hamlet
4/8/87; New Metropolitan Theatre, Sacramento, California; Hamlet
4/9/87; Matinee, Richelieu; Evening, Iago, *Othello*
4/12/87; Salt Lake Theatre; Richelieu
4/13/87; Hamlet
4/14/87; Bertuccio, *The Fool's Revenge*
4/15/87; Shylock, *Merchant of Venice*; Petruchio, *Katherine and Petruchio*
4/16/87; Matinee, Hamlet; Evening, Iago, *Othello*

The critic of *The Salt Lake City Daily Tribune* wrote in 1887: "He is one of the most uneven of actors, and moody in his work. He might play 'Hamlet' with delightful fervor one night, as he did on Wednesday, and a few nights thereafter he might repeat the same lines with absolutely no feeling or power."

4/18/87; Opera House, Cheyenne, Wyoming, then Western Territory; Hamlet
4/19/87; Tabor Grand Opera House, Denver, Colorado; Richelieu
4/20/87; Hamlet
4/21/87; Bertuccio, *The Fool's Revenge*
4/22/87; Shylock, *Merchant of Venice*; Petruchio, *Katherine and Petruchio*
4/23/87; Matinee, Hamlet; Evening, Iago, *Othello*
4/25/87; Opera House, Omaha, Nebraska; Richelieu

In Omaha on Apr. 25, 1887, Booth wrote to Barrett: "All continues well — except my pregnant cold, which have marred my voice considerably the past three weeks. The house was packed tonight; as we get a certainty I know not the exact receipts.... Dim eyes and a constant weariness prevent reading much & as for writing — you may judge from my letters to you."

4/26/87; Hamlet
4/27/87; Iago, *Othello*
4/28/87; Coates Opera House, Kansas City, Missouri; Richelieu
4/29–30/87; Matinee on 4/30/87; Hamlet
4/30/87; Evening, Iago, *Othello*

By early May 1887 Arthur Branscomb Chase was reporting that Booth's net share of the profits had reached $300,000, but this was an exaggeration of Booth's box-office supremacy.

5/2/87; Morris' Opera House, Des Moines, Iowa; Hamlet

Booth left Kansas City on May 1, writing to Edwina: "I leave today for ... I forgot the name.... The excitement here over my 4 performances was tremendous! The largest money I ever played to in my life.... The hotel is a miserable affair.... My general health is good, I suppose, but I suffer from excessive weakness during the day & have a persistent cold in the head." The town he could not remember was Des Moines where he played Hamlet on May 2 "to the largest house of the season at advanced prices."

5/3/87; Grand Opera House, Peoria, Illinois; Hamlet

Next day, the same production in Peoria also brought out "one of the largest houses of the season." From there, Booth wrote to Edwina: "I have not felt so entirely well for months as I did all day yesterday & last night, but today I have all the aches that flesh is heir to & am utterly weary. A hard ride with no wink of sleep caused it — I presume. This is another wonderful city: the hotel & theatre superb & the other public buildings & fine streets are wonderful.... There are a number of similar places in these far western states & territories where I am solicited to act that would fill up weeks of my time and yeild [*sic*] large sums in payment — all places unknown to me; I wish I could have realized this some five years ago ... the oddest part of it is — the refinement & total absence of roughness that marks the masses that are up in arms to see me & all express themselves satisfied. One w^d suppose that my performances, especially Hamlet, would bore and disappoint them, but if any distinction can be noted it is in favor of the cheaper part of the audience.... Tomorrow I go elsewhere—I forget the name of the town, but 'tis a short trip.

5/4/87; Chatterton Opera House, Springfield, Illinois Hamlet

The "short trip" was to Springfield, Illinois, where "the best people" attended Booth's performance of Hamlet on May 4; yet the house "was much smaller than either Mr. Booth's manager or the manager of the Opera House expected" and the Springfield correspondent for *The New York Mirror* thought that "Booth's voice and face plainly show the mark of age" and that his "wrinkles and furrows" were "poorly hidden" by his make-up.

5/5/87; English's Opera House, Indianapolis, Indiana; Hamlet

56/87; Grand Opera House, Dayton, Ohio; Richelieu

5/7/87; Metropolitan Opera House, Columbus, Ohio; Shylock, *Merchant of Venice*; Petruchio, *Katherine and Petruchio*

5/9/87; Opera House, Harrisburg, Pennsylvania; Hamlet

5/10/87; Star Theatre, New York; Complimentary Testimonial C. W. Couldock, Hamlet, Third act; Brutus Quarrel scene, *Julius Caesar*

5/11/87; Hyperion Theatre a/k/a Carll's Opera House, New Haven, Connecticut; Richelieu

5/12/87; Opera House, Hartford, Connecticut; Richelieu

The company played New Haven and Hartford and then got stuck in Providence, where there was no engine to pull Booth's car to Fall River, necessitating a change of trains.

5/13/87; Academy of Music, Fall River, Massachusetts; Richelieu

5/14/87; Grand Opera House, New Bedford, Massachusetts; Richelieu

1887–1888

To design the company's limited scenery, Barrett and Booth turned to John Doud, a theatrical jack-of-all-trades. As early as December 1867 Doud had played opposite Booth as Laertes and Iago in Mobile, Alabama. During 1886–1887, he was a member of Edwin's company, playing utility roles (Marcellus, the First Murderer in Macbeth) and also functioning as a call boy and 'stage director.' In April 1867 Doud presented Booth with a series of sketches for drops to be used in the upcoming season. The sketches were turned into scenery in New York. In smaller towns the company used Doud's arches and drops which could be rolled up and carried easily on the train.

9/10/87; Academy of Music, Buffalo; Macbeth scheduled but did not occur

9/12/87; Brutus, *Julius Caesar*

9/13/87; Hamlet

9/14/87; Iago, *Othello*

9/15/87; Opera House, Detroit, Michigan; Iago, *Othello*

9/16/87; Shylock, *Merchant of Venice*

9/17/87; Matinee, Hamlet; Evening, Brutus, *Julius Caesar*

The Detroit engagement was originally scheduled 9/22–24/87.

9/19/87; Hennepin Avenue Theatre, Minneapolis, Minnesota; Brutus, *Julius Caesar*

9/20/87; Hamlet

9/21/87; Iago, *Othello*

9/22/87; Macbeth

9/23/87; Shylock, *Merchant of Venice*

9/24/87; Matinee, Hamlet; Evening, Brutus, *Julius Caesar*

9/26/87; Grand Opera House, Duluth, Minnesota; Brutus, *Julius Caesar*

Booth and Barrett were originally scheduled to open in Milwaukee on 9/26/87

9/27/87; Opera House, Eau Claire, Wisconsin; Brutus, *Julius Caesar*

9/28/87; Opera House, Oshkosh, Wisconsin; Brutus, *Julius Caesar*

9/29/87; Opera House, Milwaukee, Wisconsin; Brutus, *Julius Caesar*

9/30/87; Macbeth

10/1/87; Matinee, Hamlet; Evening, Iago, *Othello*

10/3–8/87; Chicago Opera House, Illinois; Brutus 7x, *Julius Caesar*

10/10/87; Iago, *Othello*

10/11/87; Hamlet

10/12/87; Macbeth

10/13/87; Othello

10/14/87; King Lear

10/15/87; Matinee, Hamlet; Evening, Iago, *Othello*

10/17/87; Shylock, *Merchant of Venice*

10/18/87; Brutus, *Julius Caesar*

10/19/87; Shylock, *Merchant of Venice*

10/20/87; Brutus, *Julius Caesar*

10/21/87; Hamlet

10/22/87; Matinee, Shylock, *Merchant of Venice*; Evening, Brutus, *Julius Caesar*

10/24/87; Warder Opera House, Kansas City, Missouri; Iago scheduled but cancelled, *Othello*

10/25/87; Iago, *Othello*

10/26/87; Matinee, Brutus, *Julius Caesar*; Evening, Hamlet

10/27/87; Macbeth

10/28/87; Othello

10/29/87; Matinee, Hamlet; Evening, Brutus, *Julius Caesar*

The "roofless" theatre that the company found "unfit for use" was "a little better Tuesday night." Booth wrote to Edwina: "At nine o'clock at night, there were fifty workmen removing lumber, driving nails & doing all sorts of work, amid a perfect whirlwind of noise & freezing blasts of wind. At ten o'clk a half-scene and a red sheet were drawn aside & the play—Othello—began, to about 75 people in hats, over-coats & heavy fur wraps—most of whom left as the play progressed, unable to endure the cold. Not a door was in its place & the sky was in full view above the auditorium and part of the stage. We cd use but one scene — an interior, and that we used throughout the entire play, out doors & in. It was a freezing performance. Next day (yesterday) we tried Caesar for a Matinee — this was given to make up for the loss of Monday night. One scene (a street) served for the Capitol, Brutus' tent, the Forum, and the fields of Philippi — about 16 cold boys and girls in front. Last night we had some stoves, a tarpaulin cover for a roof, several scenes & played Hamlet to about 200 people. The house shd not have been opened for three months — but the wealthy fool had vowed it shd open this week with Booth and Barrett & having paid us a large certainty & sold a great many tickets at five dollars per head, the promise was kept with only the delay of one night. The hotel we are at is not much better, but a warm wave is on & I keep well…. I send a satin bones program of the first night that was to be, and didn't."

10/31/87; Olympic Theatre, St. Louis, Missouri; Brutus, *Julius Caesar*

11/1/87; Hamlet

11/2/87; Iago, *Othello*

11/3/87; King Lear

When Booth did Lear, the *St. Louis Post-Dispatch* praised "the scene with Edgar in the storm, the kindly sheltering of the poor fool under his robe, the purposeless handling of straws as the poor king chattered aimlessly of life … the plucking at the fringe of his robe as Lear's mind sought in the mists of confusion for recognition of Cordelia."

11/4/87; Shylock, *Merchant of Venice*

11/5/87; Matinee, Hamlet; Evening, Brutus, *Julius Caesar*

A St. Louis reviewer wrote "A few big-jointed, cotton-tighted tinsel-made soldiers can hardly represent the legions of Rome and a fiddle and a brass horn do not adequately stand for a decisive battle; nor do a couple of poles fastened together covered with a piece of fur and borne by four supers fill the measure of glory in the way of funeral honors to the body of dead Caesar. In this way it was no better and no worse than the average of combination tragedy."

11/7/87; Grand Opera House, Cincinnati, Ohio; Brutus, *Julius Caesar*

11/8/87; Hamlet

11/9/87; Iago, *Othello*

11/10/87; King Lear

11/11/87; Shylock, *Merchant of Venice*

11/12/87; Matinee, Hamlet; Evening, Brutus, *Julius Caesar*

11/14/87; Euclid Avenue Opera House, Cleveland, Ohio; Brutus, *Julius Caesar*

11/15/87; Hamlet

11/16/87; Matinee, Shylock, *Merchant of Venice*; Evening, Iago, *Othello*

11/17/87; Wheeler's Opera House, Toledo, Ohio; Brutus, *Julius Caesar*

11/18/87; Park Opera House, Erie, Pennsylvania; Brutus, *Julius Caesar*

11/19/87; Opera House, Youngstown, Ohio; Brutus, *Julius Caesar*

11/21/87; Grand Opera House, Pittsburgh, Pennsylvania; Brutus, *Julius Caesar*

11/22/87; Iago, *Othello*

11/23/87; Hamlet

11/24/87; Matinee, Brutus, *Julius Caesar*; Evening, Macbeth

11/25/87; Shylock, *Merchant of Venice*

11/26/87; Matinee, Hamlet; Evening, Othello

11/28–12/3/87; Chestnut Street Opera House, Philadelphia; matinee on 12/3/87, Brutus 7x, *Julius Caesar*

12/5/87; Iago, *Othello*

The *Philadelphia Ledger and Transcript* informed its readers: "The Senate scene was a finely painted interior, with splendid groupings, and the fortress at Famagusta, in Act III, a remarkably good piece of stage perspective, giving a long view of the fortress walls retiring from the spectator, with the sea beyond. A rich Byzantine interior showed the island home of Othello and Desdemona, and even the street scene, where Roderigo is killed, was made much of in its architectural arrangement…. The last act passes in the bed chamber of Desdemona, a rich effect of draperies with the bed … in the moonlight…. The management of the stage itself left nothing to be desired, but the waits between some of the acts, made necessary by the elaborate stage setting, were tiresome and interfered, to some extent, with the action of the piece."

12/6/87; Shylock, *Merchant of Venice*

12/7/87; Hamlet

12/8/8; King Lear

12/9/87; Shylock, *Merchant of Venice*

12/10/87; Matinee, Hamlet; Evening, Iago, *Othello*

12/12–17/87; Boston Theatre; Matinee on 12/17/87, Brutus 7x, *Julius Caesar*

12/19/87; Iago, *Othello*

12/20/87; Hamlet

12/21/87; King Lear

12/22/87; Iago, *Othello*

12/23/87; Shylock, *Merchant of Venice*

12/24/87; Matinee, Iago, *Othello*; Evening, Macbeth

12/26/87–1/7/88 Academy of Music New York; Mon. 12/31/87 and 1/7/88; Brutus 7x, *Julius Caesar*

1/9/88; Holliday Street Theatre, Baltimore; Iago, *Othello*

1/10/88; Brutus, *Julius Caesar*

1/11/88; Hamlet

1/12/88; King Lear

1/13/8; Shylock, *Merchant of Venice*
1/14/88; Matinee, Iago, *Othello*; Evening, Macbeth
By the time they were touring through the South, it was estimated that the Booth-Barrett combination would make no less than $600,000 during the season, 60 percent going to Booth, 30 percent to Barrett and 10 percent to their tour manager Arthur Branscomb Chase.
1/16/88; Richmond Theatre; Iago, *Othello*
1/17/88; Owens' Academy of Music, Charleston, South Carolina; Iago, *Othello*
1/18/88; Savannah Theatre; Iago, *Othello*
1/19/88; Academy, Macon, Georgia; Iago, *Othello*
1/20/88; De Give's Opera House, Atlanta, Georgia; Iago, *Othello*
1/21/88; Matinee, Hamlet; Evening, Brutus, *Julius Caesar*
1/23/88; Theatre Vendome, Nashville, Tennessee; Iago, *Othello*
1/24/88; Hamlet
1/25/88; Matinee, Shylock, *Merchant of Venice*; Evening, Brutus, *Julius Caesar*
1/26/88; New Memphis Theatre, Tennessee; Iago, *Othello*
1/27/88; Shylock, *Merchant of Venice*
1/28/88; Matinee, Hamlet; Evening, Brutus, *Julius Caesar*
1/30/88; New Opera House, Chattanooga, Tennessee; Iago, *Othello*
1/31/88; Brutus, *Julius Caesar*
2/1/88; New Opera House, Birmingham, Alabama; Brutus, *Julius Caesar*
2/2/88; Iago, *Othello*
2/3/88; Montgomery Theatre, Montgomery, Alabama; Iago, *Othello*
2/4/88; Old Theatre, Mobile, Alabama; Iago, *Othello*
2/6/88; Grand Opera House, New Orleans; Iago, *Othello*
2/7/88; Hamlet
2/8/88; King Lear
2/9/88; Matinee, Brutus, *Julius Caesar*; Evening, Macbeth
2/10/88; Shylock, *Merchant of Venice*
2/11/88; Matinee, Hamlet; Evening, Brutus, *Julius Caesar*
2/13/88; Tremont Opera House, Galveston, Texas; Iago, *Othello*
2/14/88; Brutus, *Julius Caesar*
2/15/88; Pillot's Opera House, Houston, Texas; Matinee, Brutus, *Julius Caesar*; Evening, Iago, *Othello*
2/16/88; Opera House, Dallas, Texas; Iago, *Othello*
2/17/88; Matinee, Hamlet; Evening, Brutus, *Julius Caesar*
2/18/88; Opera House, Fort Worth, Texas; Matinee, Hamlet; Evening, Brutus, *Julius Caesar*
2/20/88; Garland Opera House, Waco, Texas; Brutus, *Julius Caesar*
2/21/88; Opera House, Austin, Texas; Matinee, Brutus, *Julius Caesar*; Evening, Iago, *Othello*
2/22/88; Grand Opera House, San Antonio, Texas; Iago
2/23/88; Brutus, *Julius Caesar*
2/24/88; Mayer's Opera House, El Paso, Texas; Brutus, *Julius Caesar*
2/27/88; Grand Opera House, Los Angeles, California; Iago, *Othello*
On February 27, 1888, Booth wrote from Los Angeles: "The trip here over the desert was very hot & fatiguing. I arrived this morning and ache in every joint — half choked with alkali dust, too.... I feel greatly in need of some kind of tonic — which medicine does not supply to my system. I am become bald very rapidly — my sight is dimmer than ever & glasses are painful, my teeth, too, are troublesome while roomertix [rheumatism] is plentiful; altogether I'm pretty well, I thankee."
2/28/88; Hamlet
2/29/88; Matinee, Brutus, *Julius Caesar*; Evening, King Lear
3/1/88; Macbeth
3/2/88; Shylock, *Merchant of Venice*
3/3/88; Matinee, Iago, *Othello*; Evening, Brutus, *Julius Caesar*
3/5–10/88 Baldwin Theatre, San Francisco; Brutus 7x, *Julius Caesar*
3/12/88; Iago, *Othello*
3/13/88; Shylock, *Merchant of Venice*
3/14/88; Othello
3/15/88; Shylock, *Merchant of Venice*
3/16/88; Iago, *Othello*
3/17/88; Matinee, Shylock, *Merchant of Venice*; Evening, Macbeth
3/19/88; Hamlet
3/20/88; Brutus, *Julius Caesar*
3/21/88; Hamlet
3/22/88; Iago, *Othello*
3/23/88; King Lear
3/24/88; Matinee, Hamlet; Evening, Shylock, *Merchant of Venice*
3/26/88; Avon Theatre, Stockton, California; Brutus, *Julius Caesar*, scheduled but did not occur
3/27/88; New Metropolitan Theatre, Sacramento, California; Brutus, *Julius Caesar*
3/28/88; Matinee, Iago, *Othello*
3/30/88; Salt Lake Theatre, Utah; Iago, *Othello*
3/31/88; Matinee, Hamlet
3/31/88; Brutus, *Julius Caesar*
4/2/88; Tabor Grand Opera House, Denver, Colorado; Iago, *Othello*
The manager in Denver offered 87 percent for a whole week and 85 percent for half a week.
4/3/88; Brutus, *Julius Caesar*
4/4/88; Hamlet
4/5/88; Macbeth
4/6/88; Shylock, *Merchant of Venice*

4/7/88; Matinee, Iago, *Othello*; Evening, Brutus, *Julius Caesar*
4/9/88; Boyd's Opera House, Omaha, Nebraska; Brutus, *Julius Caesar*
4/10/88; Shylock, *Merchant of Venice*
4/11/88; Matinee, Hamlet
4/11/88; Evening, Originally the end of the tour; Macbeth
4/12/88; Kunkes Opera House, Lincoln, Nebraska; Brutus, *Julius Caesar*
4/13/88; Crawford's Opera House, Topeka, Kansas; Iago, *Othello*
4/14/88; Crawford's Opera House, Wichita, Kansas; Matinee, Brutus, *Julius Caesar*; Evening, Iago, *Othello*
4/16/88; Crawford's Opera House, Leavenworth, Kansas; Iago, *Othello*
4/17/88; Tootle's Opera House, St. Joseph, Missouri; Iago, *Othello*
4/18/88; Grand Opera House, Des Moines, Iowa; Iago, *Othello*
4/19/88; Greene's Opera House, Cedar Rapids, Iowa; Brutus, *Julius Caesar*
4/20/88; Opera House, Dubuque, Iowa; Brutus, *Julius Caesar*
4/21/88; Burtis' Opera House, Davenport, Iowa; Brutus, *Julius Caesar*
4/23/88; Opera House, Peoria, Illinois; Brutus, *Julius Caesar*

On Apr. 23, 1888, Booth wrote to Edwina from Peoria: "We arrived here yesterday (Sunday) morning. Altho' we are to be but one night here, Barrett & I decided to quit the car & come to the hotel for a bath or two. I took one last night and this morning I thought it would be necessary to have a gang of workmen with shovels to dig the mud from the tub, before I could take another dip. I am led to hope, however, that 'twas the sediment of the river water and not me that muddied the bath. One has to rough it — even in a palace-car — when travelling [sic] night & day over the "per-rairies."

4/24/88; Chatterton Opera House, Springfield, Illinois; Brutus, *Julius Caesar*
4/25/88; Opera House, Bloomington, Illinois; Brutus, *Julius Caesar*
4/26/88; Naylor's Opera House, Terre Haute, Indiana; Iago, *Othello*
4/27/88; English Opera House, Indianapolis, Indiana; Iago, *Othello*
4/28/88; Matinee, King Lear; Evening, Brutus, *Julius Caesar*
4/30/88; Grand Opera House, Lafayette, Indiana; Iago, *Othello*
5/1/88; Masonic Temple, Fort Wayne, Indiana; Iago, *Othello*
5/2/88; Academy of Music, Kalamazoo, Michigan; Brutus, *Julius Caesar*
5/3/88; Powers' Grand Opera House, Grand Rapids, Michigan; Iago, *Othello*
5/4/88; New Opera House, Bay City, Michigan; Brutus, *Julius Caesar*
5/5/88; Academy of Music, East Saginaw, Michigan; Matinee, Iago, *Othello*; Evening, Brutus, *Julius Caesar*
5/7/88; Opera House, Ann Arbor, Michigan; Brutus, *Julius Caesar*
5/8/88; Opera House, Springfield, Ohio; Iago, *Othello*
5/9/88; The Grand Opera House, Dayton, Ohio; Brutus, *Julius Caesar*
5/10/88; Southern Exposition Music Hall, Louisville, Kentucky; Hamlet
5/11/88; King Lear
5/12/88; Matinee, Iago, *Othello*; Evening, Brutus, *Julius Caesar*
5/14/88; Amphion Academy, Williamsburgh, Brooklyn, New York; Brutus, *Julius Caesar*
5/15/88; Macbeth
5/16/88; Hamlet
5/17/88; King Lear
5/18/88; Shylock, *Merchant of Venice*
5/19/88; Matinee, Iago, *Othello*; Evening, Brutus, *Julius Caesar*
5/21/88; Metropolitan Opera House, New York Benefit for Lester Wallack Hamlet
5/24/88; Boston Theatre, Boston, Massachusetts; Matinee for the Actor's Fund, Iago scene, *Othello*

1888–1889

Booth and Barrett started from New York on September 8 in a special car, and the company opened *Julius Caesar* at the now completed Warder Grand Opera House in Kansas City, Missouri, on September 10, 1888. Despite hot weather and "political excitement in the streets," receipts were excellent. The 3,000-seat Warder was "crowded every evening, and *Hamlet*, on September 13, with five hundred people in standing room and hundreds turned away, took in over four thousand dollars. The receipts for the week were $25,113.00. It turned out to be the largest weekly gross of the season.

9/10/88; Warder Opera House, Kansas City, Missouri; Brutus, *Julius Caesar*
9/11/88; Shylock, *Merchant of Venice*
9/12/88; Othello
9/13/88; Hamlet
9/14/88; Shylock, *Merchant of Venice*
9/15/88; Matinee, Brutus, *Julius Caesar*; Evening, Iago, *Othello*
9/17/88; Grand Opera House, Minneapolis, Minnesota; Brutus, *Julius Caesar*
9/18/88; Shylock, *Merchant of Venice*
9/19/88; Matinee, Hamlet; Evening, Iago, *Othello*
9/20/88; Opera House, St. Paul, Minnesota; Brutus, *Julius Caesar*
9/21/88; Hamlet
9/22/88; Matinee, Shylock, *Merchant of Venice*; Evening, Iago, *Othello*

9/24–29/88; Chicago Opera House, Chicago; Matinee on 9/29/88, Brutus 7x, *Julius Caesar*

In their first three stops—Kansas City, Minneapolis and St. Paul—Booth and Barrett still employed the stock scenery provided by local theatres; however, in Chicago, they picked up the sets designed for them by Ernest Albert, the scenic artist of the Chicago Opera company and used them for the rest of the tour. The Forum scene in the first and fourth acts of *Julius Caesar* was a collection of Roman temples and "colossal statues of mighty conquerors." The second act used two sets—a garden terrace with "distant foliage," for Brutus' house and the interior of Caesar's palace. The Capitol, in act three, based on Jean-Leon Gerome's painting "The Death of Caesar," was constructed in a semicircle, with "the Senators … elevated upon circular platforms," giving "the effect of an amphitheatre." The fifth act showed the exterior and interior of Brutus' tent at Sardis and the sixth "the battlefield on the Plains of Philipi, with a "rocky foreground, … gentle slopes [and] billowy fields, stretching far away in the distance to … precipitous mountains, all bathed in the purple light of a southern sun." "When the last word of 'Julius Caesar' [was] spoken, a drop display[ing] a funeral urn fell. When it [was] raised," a papier-mâché likeness of Booth as Brutus laid in profile "on a funeral pyre" was discovered, around which were grouped soldiers singing "a threnody … composed by the leader of [the production's] choir." Despite this elaborateness, the critic for *The Chicago Daily Tribune* questioned "the use of black for Roman mourning, the wearing of mustaches by the citizens or the custom, which seems to be traditional, of confining Antony to the tunic when his age and station should entitled him to the toga.… Of the funeral pyre and the change here superadded, it is enough to say that the ceremony is superfluous."

10/1–6/88; Matinee on 10/6/88; Shylock 7x, *Merchant of Venice*

On Sunday September 30, the company had a night rehearsal "of the scenery" provided by the Chicago Opera House for *The Merchant of Venice*." The opening scene represented "the Grand Piazza at Venice with the façade of the Doge's Palace on the right" and a "quay, with its shipping and gondolas" on the left. The second act opened with Portia "looking out upon the terrace of Belmont." This, in turn, disclosed "the great scene of the second and third acts, the home of Shylock." "The hall at Belmont where Bassanio makes his choice," in Booth's fourth act, was a semi-circular or octagonal columned apartment with a domed paneled ceiling painted to resemble gray and gold "colored marble," with figures in the panels of the dome, rising "twenty-eight feet above the stage, … four feet higher than any piece of scenery ever put on the Opera House stage." For the fourth act courtroom, Albert produced "an exact reproduction of one of the Council Chambers in the [Venetian] Ducal Palace." The trial scene was also the sumptuous chamber of the ducal palace used in "Othello." The last act again in Belmont showed "a dreamy Italian garden by moonlight with rose-colored lamps and far twinkling stars."

10/8/88; Iago, *Othello*

Booth and Barrett added a scenically lavish production of *Othello* to the repertoire during their third week in Chicago. The play opened with the scene of Brabantio's house as seen by moonlight. The acting area was closed in with an arched-drop through which Iago and Othello entered. The set for the island of Cyprus showed "the walls of Famagosta," ending in the entrance of the round Torro del Moro, the headquarters of Christofore Moro, painted from photographs showing the walls and tower as they stood at the end of the nineteenth century, as authenticated from materials in the collection" of General Luigi Palma di Cesnola, the first director of the Metropolitan Museum of Art. When a reporter commented that the "authenticity" of the general's collection had "been disputed," Bromley replied: "It is authentic enough for the stage. We shall have an old sundial in the background.… And the tower of Cristoforo del Moro is a bit of scenery which archaeologists will approve." Othello's room had a "Byzantine interior," "with a magnificent decoration of mosaic glass upon a ground of gold." Desdemona's bedchamber had "painted gilt partitions; the walls were "hung with tapestries" and moonlight streamed in "through panes of real glass." Most importantly the bed, "surrounded by blue curtains" was built so as "to show its entire interior." The production was praised for "the introduction of many details such as the music from the gondolas at the rise of the curtain and the sound of the trumpets as the dawn breaks upon Iago's scene of 'pleasure and action.'"

10/9/88; Hamlet
10/10/88; Iago, *Othello*
10/11/88; Hamlet
10/12/88; Iago, *Othello*
10/13/88; Matinee, Hamlet; Evening, Iago, *Othello*
10/15/88; Grand Opera House, Cincinnati, Ohio; Brutus, *Julius Caesar*
10/16–17/88; Iago 2x, *Othello*
10/18–20/88; Matinee on 10/20/88; Shylock 3x, *Merchant of Venice*
10/20/88; Evening, Hamlet
10/22/88; Olympic Theatre, St. Louis; Brutus, *Julius Caesar*
10/23–24/88; Iago 2x, *Othello*
10/25–27/88; Matinee on 10/27/88; Shylock 3x, *Merchant of Venice*
10/27/88; Evening, Hamlet
11/12–13/88; Fifth Avenue Theatre New York; Iago 2x, *Othello*

11/14/88; Shylock, *Merchant of Venice*
11/15/88 Benefit Performance for the Actor's Fund. Grand Opera House, New York; Matinee, Role unknown
11/15/88; Shylock, *Merchant of Venice*
11/16/88; Iago, *Othello*
11/17/88; Matinee, Shylock, *Merchant of Venice*; Evening, Iago
11/19/88; Shylock, *Merchant of Venice*
11/20/88; Iago, *Othello*
11/21/88; Shylock, *Merchant of Venice*
11/22/88; Iago, *Othello*
11/23/88; Shylock, *Merchant of Venice*
11/24/88; Matinee, Iago, *Othello*; Evening, Shylock, *Merchant of Venice*
11/26/88; Iago, *Othello*
11/27/88; Shylock, *Merchant of Venice*
11/28/88; Iago, *Othello*
11/29/88; Matinee and Evening, Shylock 2x, *Merchant of Venice*
11/30/88; Iago, *Othello*

In Dec. 1888, A. C. Wheeler, under the pseudonym Nym Crinkle, wrote: "When you tell me an American actor cannot wear a dress coat, you must mean Edwin Booth.... Do you know why the American actor can't? It is because great acting doesn't depend on a dress coat, and the dress coat drama has risen just in proportion as ladies and gentlemen took the place of women and men on the stage."

12/1/88; Matinee, Shylock, *Merchant of Venice*; Evening, Iago, *Othello*
12/3/88; Shylock, *Merchant of Venice*
12/4/88; Iago, *Othello*
12/5/88; Shylock, *Merchant of Venice*
12/6/88; Iago, *Othello*
12/7/88; Shylock, *Merchant of Venice*
12/8/88; Matinee, Iago, *Othello*; Evening, Shylock, *Merchant of Venice*
12/10–22/88; Matinees on 12/15/88 and 12/22/88; Brutus 14x, *Julius Caesar*
12/24/88; Bertuccio, *The Fool's Revenge*
12/25/88; Matinee, Brutus, *Julius Caesar*; Evening, Bertuccio, *The Fool's Revenge*
12/26–29/88; Matinee on 12/29/88; Bertuccio 5x, *The Fool's Revenge*; Bertuccio, *The Fool's Revenge*
12/31/88; Shylock, *Merchant of Venice*
1/1/89; Iago, *Othello*
1/2/89; Brutus, *Julius Caesar*
1/3–5/89; Matinee on 1/5/89; Bertuccio 4x, *The Fool's Revenge*
1/7/89; Grand Opera House, Pittsburgh, Pennsylvania; Brutus, *Julius Caesar*
1/8/89; Shylock, *Merchant of Venice*
1/9/89; Iago, *Othello*
1/10/89; Hamlet
1/11/89; Iago, *Othello*
1/12/89; Matinee, Shylock, *Merchant of Venice*; Evening, Bertuccio, *The Fool's Revenge*
1/14/89; Albaugh's Holliday Street Theatre, Baltimore; Brutus, *Julius Caesar*
1/15/89; Shylock, *Merchant of Venice*
1/16/89; Iago, *Othello*
1/17/89; Matinee, Brutus, *Julius Caesar*; Evening, Hamlet
1/18/89; Iago, *Othello*
1/19/89; Matinee, Shylock, *Merchant of Venice*; Evening, Bertuccio, *The Fool's Revenge*
1/21/89; Boston Theatre, Massachusetts; Iago, *Othello*
1/22/89; Othello
1/23/89; Iago, *Othello*
1/24/89; Othello
1/25/89; Iago, *Othello*
1/26/89; Matinee, Othello; Evening, Iago, *Othello*
1/28–2/2/89; Matinee on 2/2/89; Shylock 7x, *Merchant of Venice*
2/4/89; Brutus, *Julius Caesar*
2/5/89; Hamlet
2/6/89; Brutus, *Julius Caesar*
2/7/89; Hamlet
2/8/89; Brutus, *Julius Caesar*
2/9/89; Matinee, Hamlet; Evening, Brutus, *Julius Caesar*
2/11/899; Shylock, *Merchant of Venice*
2/12/89; Hamlet
2/13/89; Iago, *Othello*
2/14–16/89; Matinee on 2/16/89; Bertuccio 3x, *The Fool's Revenge*
2/16/89; Evening, Macbeth
2/18–20/89; Chestnut Street Opera House, Philadelphia; Iago 3x, *Othello*
2/21/89; Shylock, *Merchant of Venice*
2/22–23/89; Matinee on 2/23/89; Shylock 3x, *Merchant of Venice*
2/25–27/89; Hamlet 3x
2/28–3/1/89; Brutus 2x, *Julius Caesar*
3/2/89; Matinee, Hamlet; Evening, Brutus, *Julius Caesar*
3/4/89; Shylock, *Merchant of Venice*
3/5/89; Iago, *Othello*
3/6/89; Brutus, *Julius Caesar*
3/7/89; Hamlet
3/8–9/89; Matinee on 3/9/89; Bertuccio 3x, *The Fool's Revenge*
3/11/89; Taylor's Opera House, Trenton, New Jersey; Iago, *Othello*
3/12/89; Hawe's Opera House, Bridgeport, Connecticut; Iago, *Othello*
3/13/89; Hyperion Theatre, New Haven, Connecticut; Iago, *Othello*
3/14/89; Roberts Opera House, Hartford, Connecticut; Iago, *Othello*
3/15/89; Holyoke Opera House, Holyoke, Massachusetts; Shylock, *Merchant of Venice*
3/16/89; Gilmore's Opera House, Springfield, Massachusetts; Iago, *Othello*

3/18–19/89; Providence Opera House, Providence, Rhode Island; Shylock 2x, *Merchant of Venice*
3/20/89; Brutus, *Julius Caesar*
3/21–22/89; Iago 2x, *Othello*
3/23/89; Matinee, Hamlet; Evening, Bertuccio, *The Fool's Revenge*
3/25–26/89; Amphion Academy, Williamsburgh [Brooklyn], New York; Shylock 2x, *Merchant of Venice*
3/27/89; Brutus, *Julius Caesar*
3/28–29/89; Iago 2x, *Othello*
3/30/89; Matinee, Hamlet; Evening, Bertuccio, *The Fool's Revenge*
4/1/89; Academy of Music, Scranton, Pennsylvania; Iago, *Othello*
4/2/89; Elmira Opera House, Elmira, New York; Brutus, *Julius Caesar*
4/3/89; Lyceum Theatre, Rochester, New York; Iago, *Othello*
4/15/89; Euclid Avenue Opera House, Cleveland, Ohio; Iago, *Othello*
4/16/89; Shylock, *Merchant of Venice*
4/17/89; Matinee, Hamlet; Evening, Brutus, *Julius Caesar*
4/18/89; Metropolitan Opera House, Columbus, Ohio; Iago, *Othello*
4/19/89; English's Opera House, Indianapolis, Indiana; Shylock, *Merchant of Venice*
4/20/89; Matinee, Hamlet; Evening, Bertuccio, *The Fool's Revenge*
4/22/89; New Opera House, Burlington, Iowa; Iago, *Othello*
4/23/89; Moore's Opera House, Des Moines, Iowa; Brutus, *Julius Caesar*
4/24/89; Peavey Grand Opera House, Sioux City, Iowa; Hamlet
4/25/89; Iago, *Othello*
4/26/89; Boyd's Opera House, Omaha, Nebraska; Shylock, *Merchant of Venice*
4/27/89; Matinee, Iago; Evening, Bertuccio, *The Fool's Revenge*
4/29/89; Tabor Grand Opera House, Denver, Colorado; Shylock, *Merchant of Venice*
4/30/89; Iago, *Othello*
5/1/89; Brutus, *Julius Caesar*
5/2/89; Shylock, *Merchant of Venice*
5/3/89; Iago, *Othello*
5/4/89; Matinee, Hamlet
5/6/89; Salt Lake Theatre; Shylock, *Merchant of Venice*
5/7/89; Brutus, *Julius Caesar*
5/8/89; Bertuccio, *The Fool's Revenge*
5/13/89; New California Theatre, San Francisco; Iago, *Othello*
5/14/89; Othello
5/15/89; Iago, *Othello*
5/16/89; Othello
5/17/89; Iago, *Othello*
5/18/89; Matinee, Othello; Evening, Iago, *Othello*
5/20–25/89; Matinee on 5/25/89; Shylock 7x, *Merchant of Venice*
5/27–28/89; Brutus 2x, *Julius Caesar*
5/30/89; Hamlet
5/31/89; Bertuccio, *The Fool's Revenge*
6/1/89; Matinee, Hamlet; Evening, Bertuccio, *The Fool's Revenge*
6/13/89; Metropolitan Opera House, New York; Benefit for sufferers of the Johnstown Flood; Iago, *Othello*

1889–1890

9/23/89; MacAuley's Theatre, Louisville, Kentucky; Shylock, *Merchant of Venice*
9/24/89; Richelieu
9/25/89; Matinee, Bertuccio, *The Fool's Revenge*; Evening, Iago, *Othello*
9/26/89; Macbeth
9/27/89; Hamlet
9/28/89; Matinee, Benedick, *Much Ado About Nothing*; Evening, Brutus, *Julius Caesar*
9/30/89; Grand Opera House, Pittsburgh, Pennsylvania; Shylock, *Merchant of Venice*
10/1/89; Hamlet
10/2/89; Richelieu
10/3/89; Hamlet
10/4/89; Richelieu
10/5/89; Matinee, Benedick, *Much Ado About Nothing*; Evening, Bertuccio, *The Fool's Revenge*
10/7/89; Euclid Avenue Opera House, Cleveland, Ohio; Shylock, *Merchant of Venice*
10/8/89; Hamlet
10/9/89; Richelieu
10/10/89; Hamlet
10/11/89; Richelieu
10/12/89; Matinee, Benedick, *Much Ado About Nothing*; Evening, Bertuccio, *The Fool's Revenge*
10/14–18/89; Broadway Theatre, New York; Richelieu 5x
10/19/89; Matinee, Benedick, *Much Ado About Nothing*; Evening, Richelieu
10/21–25/89; Richelieu 5x
10/26/89; Matinee, Benedick, *Much Ado About Nothing*; Evening, Richelieu

The critic for *The New York Mirror* wrote of the matinee: "The performance was disgracefully ragged, uneven and unsatisfactory. Insufficiency of rehearsal was constantly evinced; the players did not know their positions or business, some of them did not know their lines, and the prompter played a prominent and lively part throughout. Mr. Booth's Benedick was just such a careless performance as that gifted actor can give when he does not choose to waste his energies. He is really an admirable comedian, but nobody would have supposed it who had only his spiritless and perfunctory acting on Saturday to judge by. Madame Modjeska was a charming Beatrice in so far as personal grace and lovely gowns were concerned. But her lines were spoken almost unintelligibly, and the blunders of her associates were a source of constant trial. If Modjeska could only pronounce English as well as she understands its meaning, what a delightful Shakespearean actress she would be."

10/28–11/2/89; Matinee on 11/2/89; Shylock 7x, *Merchant of Venice*
11/4–8/89; Hamlet 5x
11/9/89; Matinee, Don Caesar de Bazan; Evening, Hamlet
11/11–16/89; Matinee on 11/16/89; Hamlet 6x
11/16/89; Evening, Don Caesar de Bazan
11/18–22/89; Macbeth 5x
11/23/89; Matinee, Richelieu; Evening, Macbeth
11/25–27/89; Bertuccio 3x, *The Fool's Revenge*
11/28/89; Matinee, Shylock, *Merchant of Venice*; Evening, Richelieu
11/29/89; Shylock, *Merchant of Venice*
11/30/89; Matinee, Hamlet; Evening, Bertuccio, *The Fool's Revenge*
12/2/89; Shylock, *Merchant of Venice*
12/3/89; Richelieu
12/4/89; Hamlet
12/5/89; Richelieu
12/6/89; Benedick, *Much Ado About Nothing*
12/7/89; Matinee, Hamlet; Evening, Bertuccio, *The Fool's Revenge*
12/9/89; Burtis Opera House, Auburn, New York; Hamlet
12/10/89; Jacob and Proctor's Opera House, Utica, New York; Hamlet
12/11/89; Wieting Opera House, Syracuse, New York; Shylock, *Merchant of Venice*
12/12/89; Macbeth
12/13/89; Lyceum Theatre, Rochester, New York; Shylock, *Merchant of Venice*
12/14/89; Matinee, Richelieu; Evening, Hamlet
12/16/89; Hammerstein's Opera House, Harlem, New York; Shylock, *Merchant of Venice*
12/17/89; Hamlet
12/18/89; Richelieu
12/19/89; Bertuccio, *The Fool's Revenge*
12/20/89; Hamlet
12/21/89; Matinee, Benedick, *Much Ado About Nothing*; Evening, Macbeth
1/6/90; Providence Opera House, Providence, Rhode Island; Shylock, *Merchant of Venice*
1/7/90; Hamlet
1/8/90; Macbeth
1/9/90; Richelieu
1/10/90; Hamlet
1/11/90; Matinee, Benedick, *Much Ado About Nothing*; Evening, Bertuccio, *The Fool's Revenge*
1/13/90; Academy of Music, Fall River, Massachusetts; Shylock, *Merchant of Venice*
1/14/90; Opera House, Holyoke, Massachusetts; Macbeth
1/15/90; Gilmore's Opera House, Springfield, Massachusetts; Shylock, *Merchant of Venice*

In 1890 the critic for the *Springfield Republican* wrote: "Mr. Booth's creation lays bare the malignant, hardened side of the Jew's soul, pulsating with its thirst for revenge, at the expense of the sympathy that from a modern audience is due a character representing as Shylock does a race that has suffered unjustly, long continued and cruel persecution."

1/16/90; Hyperion Theatre, New Haven, Connecticut; Shylock, *Merchant of Venice*
1/17/90; Roberts Opera House, Hartford, Connecticut; Hamlet
1/18/90; Matinee, Shylock, *Merchant of Venice*; Evening, Macbeth
1/20/90; Boston Theatre, Boston, Massachusetts; Shylock, *Merchant of Venice*
1/21/90; Benedick, *Much Ado About Nothing*
1/22/90; Richelieu
1/23/90; Bertuccio, *The Fool's Revenge*
1/24/90; Richelieu
1/25/90; Matinee, Benedick, *Much Ado About Nothing*; Evening, Macbeth
1/27/90; Hamlet
1/28/90; Shylock, *Merchant of Venice*
1/29/90; Hamlet
1/30/90; Macbeth
1/31/90; Shylock, *Merchant of Venice*
2/1/90; Matinee, Hamlet; Evening, Richelieu
2/3/90; Opera House, Bridgeport, Connecticut; Shylock, *Merchant of Venice*
2/4/90; Academy of Music, Brooklyn, New York; Shylock, *Merchant of Venice*
2/5/90; Hamlet
2/6/90; Richelieu
2/7/90; Bertuccio, *The Fool's Revenge*
2/8/90; Matinee, Benedick, *Much Ado About Nothing*; Evening, Macbeth
2/10/90; Chestnut Street Opera House, Philadelphia; Shylock, *Merchant of Venice*
2/11/90; Macbeth
2/12/90; Richelieu
2/13/90; Bertuccio, *The Fool's Revenge*
2/14/90; Richelieu
2/15/90; Matinee, Benedick, *Much Ado About Nothing*; Evening, Macbeth
2/17/90; Hamlet
2/18/90; Shylock, *Merchant of Venice*
2/19/90; Hamlet
2/20/9; Macbeth
2/21/90; Shylock, *Merchant of Venice*
2/22/90; Matinee, Hamlet; Evening, Richelieu
2/24/90; Albaugh's Holliday Street Theatre, Baltimore; Shylock, *Merchant of Venice*
2/25/90; Benedick, *Much Ado About Nothing*
2/26/90; Richelieu
2/27/90; Bertuccio, *The Fool's Revenge*
2/28/90; Hamlet
3/1/90; Matinee, Benedick, *Much Ado About Nothing*; Evening, Macbeth
3/3/90; Hamlet

3/4/90; Bertuccio, *The Fool's Revenge*
3/5/90; Richelieu
3/6/90; Macbeth
3/7/90; Shylock, *Merchant of Venice*
3/8/90; Matinee, Hamlet; Evening, Richelieu
3/10–11/90; Chicago Opera House, Chicago; Shylock 2x, *Merchant of Venice*
3/12–13/90; Hamlet 2x
3/14/90; Richelieu
3/15/90; Matinee, Shylock, *Merchant of Venice*; Evening, Richelieu
3/17–18/90; Macbeth 2x
3/19/90; Benedick, *Much Ado About Nothing*
3/20/90; Bertuccio, *The Fool's Revenge*
3/21/90; Hamlet
3/22/90; Matinee, Benedick, *Much Ado About Nothing*; Evening, Macbeth
3/24/90; Richelieu
3/25/90; Shylock, *Merchant of Venice*
3/26/90; Hamlet
3/27/90; Don Caesar de Bazan
3/28/9; Shylock, *Merchant of Venice*
3/29/90; Matinee, Hamlet; Evening, Richelieu
3/31/90; Olympic Theatre, St. Louis, Missouri; Richelieu
4/1/90; Hamlet
4/2/90; Shylock, *Merchant of Venice*
4/3/90; Richelieu
4/4/90; Hamlet
4/5/90; Matinee, Benedick, *Much Ado About Nothing*; Evening, Macbeth
4/8/90; Hamlet
4/9/90; Richelieu
In 1890 Booth wrote to Edwina from St. Louis: "H. W." & "H. W."—(Holy Week & Hellish Weather) have hurt the business considerably.
4/7–10/90; Grand Opera House, Cincinnati, Ohio; Shylock 4x, *Merchant of Venice*
4/11/90; Hamlet
4/12/90; Matinee, Benedick, *Much Ado About Nothing*
4/12/90; Evening, Macbeth
4/14/90; Detroit Opera House, Detroit, Michigan; Richelieu
4/15/90; Hamlet
4/16/90; Shylock, *Merchant of Venice*
4/17/90; Wheeler's Opera House, Toledo, Ohio; Shylock, *Merchant of Venice*
4/18/90; Academy of Music, East Saginaw, Michigan; Shylock, *Merchant of Venice*
4/19/90; Powers' Grand Opera House, Grand Rapids, Michigan; Hamlet
4/21/90; Grand Opera House, Milwaukee, Wisconsin; Hamlet
4/22/90; Richelieu
4/23/90; Opera House, Cedar Rapids, Iowa; Shylock, *Merchant of Venice*
4/24/90; Burtis' [Grand] Opera House, Davenport, Iowa; Shylock, *Merchant of Venice*
4/25/90; Opera House, Peoria, Illinois; Shylock, *Merchant of Venice*
4/26/90; Powers' New Opera House, Decatur, Illinois; Hamlet
4/28/90; Bloomington, Illinois; Macbeth
4/29/90; English's Opera House, Indianapolis, Indiana; Macbeth
4/30/90; Opera House, Vincennes, Indiana; Hamlet
5/1/90; Auditorium, Louisville, Kentucky; Richelieu
5/2/90; Macbeth
5/3/90; Matinee, Hamlet; Evening, Shylock, *Merchant of Venice*
5/5/90; Grand Opera House, Dayton, Ohio; Shylock, *Merchant of Venice*
5/6/90; Schultz's Opera House, Zanesville, Ohio; Richelieu
5/7/90; Opera House, Wheeling, West Virginia; Shylock, *Merchant of Venice*
5/8/90; Opera House, Youngstown, Ohio; Richelieu
5/9/90; Star Theatre, Buffalo, New York; Richelieu
5/10/90; Matinee, Hamlet; Evening, Shylock, *Merchant of Venice*

1890–1891

11/3/90; Albaugh's Lyceum Theatre, Baltimore; Shylock, *Merchant of Venice*
11/4/90; Hamlet
11/5/90; Iago, *Othello*
11/6/90; Shylock, *Merchant of Venice*
11/7/90; Macbeth
11/8/90; Hamlet
11/10/90; Brutus, *Julius Caesar*
11/11/90; Shylock, *Merchant of Venice*
11/12/90; Macbeth
11/13/90; Brutus, *Julius Caesar*
11/14/90; Iago, *Othello*
11/15/90; Matinee, Hamlet
11/17/90; Chestnut Street Opera House, Philadelphia; Brutus, *Julius Caesar*
11/18/90; Shylock, *Merchant of Venice*
11/19/90; Iago, *Othello*
11/20/90; Richelieu
11/21/90; Shylock, *Merchant of Venice*
11/22/90; Brutus, *Julius Caesar*
11/24/90; Hamlet
11/25/90; Richelieu
11/26/90; Othello
11/27/90; Thanksgiving Matinee, Hamlet
11/28/90; Shylock, *Merchant of Venice*
11/29/90; Macbeth
12/1/90; Park Theatre, Boston, Massachusetts; Brutus, *Julius Caesar*
12/2/90; Shylock, *Merchant of Venice*
12/3/90; Iago, *Othello*
12/4/90; Richelieu
12/5/90; Shylock, *Merchant of Venice*

12/6/90; Brutus, *Julius Caesar*
12/8/90; Hamlet
12/9/90; Richelieu
12/10/90; Othello
12/11/90; Macbeth
12/12/90; Shylock, *Merchant of Venice*
12/13/90; Matinee, Hamlet
12/15/90; Providence, Rhode Island, Providence Opera House; Brutus, *Julius Caesar*
12/16/90; Hamlet
12/17/90; Iago, *Othello*
12/18/90; Richelieu
12/19/90; Shylock, *Merchant of Venice*
12/20/90; Matinee, Hamlet

In Dec. 1890 when Booth was four months away from retirement, the critic for *The Providence Daily Journal* wrote: "A master of technique, Mr. Booth's fondness for change, for experimenting with new details of movement and gesture or facial expression is well known."

3/2–4/91; Broadway Theatre, New York; Shylock 3x, *Merchant of Venice*
3/5–6/91; Brutus 2x, *Julius Caesar*
3/7/91; Matinee, Shylock, *Merchant of Venice*
3/9–11/91; Hamlet 3x
3/12/91; Othello
3/13/91; Iago, *Othello*
3/14/91; Matinee, Hamlet
3/16–18/91; Richelieu 3x

On March 8, 1891, the critic for *The World* wrote: "His [Booth's] performance indicates mental indolence and artistic indifference rather than physical weakness. It certainly does not require any great expenditure of physical strength to make himself up as carefully and properly in Shylock as he once did. And he need not exhaust himself by a little attention to the subordinate scenes. It was apparent to his friends who saw him in Shylock that the greater part of his work was perfunctorily done; that he took no pains to hide his weariness in doing it and that he got through the heavier scenes with an automatic simulation of his former earnestness and spirit.... Mr. Booth's frame is not paralyzed. His interest is. He is not careworn; he is careless.... In 'Julius Caesar' he shut his eyes at times and waited as if he were bored to death. At other times, he started and recalled the duties of the moment suddenly."

3/19–20/91; Macbeth 2x
3/21/91; Matinee, Richelieu

After Barrett's death Albert Bruning took Barrett's role as the ghost and Ben G. Rogers did both Polonius and the First Gravedigger (a role normally played by Booth's nephew Wilfred Clarke who was ill). The company finished out its season at the Broadway theatre with Lawrence Hanley and John Lane playing Barrett's roles.

3/23/91; Shylock, *Merchant of Venice*, cancelled due to Lawrence Barrett's death
3/24/91; Hamlet
3/25/91; Iago, *Othello*
3/26/91; Richelieu
3/27/91; Brutus, *Julius Caesar*
3/28/91; Matinee, Hamlet
3/30/91; Brooklyn Academy of Music; Hamlet
3/31/91; Shylock, *Merchant of Venice*
4/1/91; Othello
4/2/91; Richelieu
4/3/91; Macbeth
4/4/91; Matinee, Hamlet

Notes

Abbreviations

ABC	Arthur Branscomb Chase
Barstow Scrapbook	Booth Bills & Reviews, 1883–1890, collected by Mary C. Barstow, Hampden Booth Theatre Library of The Players Foundation for Educational Research
Columbia	Dramatic Museum Collection, Rare Book and Manuscript Library, Columbia University
EB	Edwin Booth
ECS	Edmund Clarence Stedman
EwB	Edwina Booth
EBG	Edwina Booth Grossman
Folger	Folger Shakespeare Library
Hampden-Booth	Hampden-Booth Theatre Library of The Players Foundation for Educational Research
Harvard	Harvard Theatre Collection
McE	Jervis McEntee
LB	Lawrence Barrett
LC	Library of Congress
LH	Laurence Hutton
Maryland	Maryland Historical Society
NYPLPA	New York Public Library for the Performing Arts
Pennsylvania	H. H. Furness Memorial Library Manuscript Collection, Van Pelt Library, University of Pennsylvania
Princeton	Department of Rare Books and Special Collections, Princeton University Libraries
Rochester	University of Rochester Library
TBA	Thomas Bailey Aldrich
Texas	Harry Ransom Humanities Research Center. University of Texas at Austin
Tulsa	McFarlin Library, University of Tulsa
WW	William Winter

Introduction

1. Richard Lockridge, *Darling of Misfortune* (New York: The Century Company, 1932), 3.
2. William Winter, *Life and Art of Edwin Booth* (1893; reprint, New York: Greenwood Press, 1968), vii.
3. Asia Booth Clarke, *The Elder and the Younger Booth* (Boston: James R. Osgood and Company, 1882), 178, 179; LB, "Edwin Booth," *The Life and Art of Edwin Booth and his Contemporaries* (Boston: L. C. Page & Company, 1886), 66; EBG, *Edwin Booth*, 1894 (reprint, Freeport, New York: Books of Libraries Press, 1970), 24.
4. Eleanor Ruggles, *Prince of Players* (New York: W. W. Norton & Company, Inc., 1953), xii; L. Terry Oggel, *Edwin Booth: A Bio-Bibliography* (New York: Greenwood Press, 1992), 7.
5. EB to EBG, May 11, no year [1888 penciled in], NYPLPA; LB, "EB," *Edwin Booth and his Contemporaries* (Boston: L. C Page & Company, 1886), 59.
6. Daniel Watermeier, *Between Actor and Critic* (Princeton, New Jersey: Princeton University Press, 1971), 303.
7. EB to LH, Feb. 22, 1882, Princeton; Otis Skinner, *The Last Tragedian: Booth Tells his own Story* (New York: Dodd, Mead & Company, 1939), 7; Oggel, *Bio-Bibliography*, 8.

8. For information about Booth's attempts to write an autobiography, see EB to WW, Mar. 15, 1870, Mar. 12, 1878 (penciled copy prepared by Jefferson Winter), May 9, July 12, 1878, Dec. 7, 1885, Folger; EB to EBG, Oct. 3, 1886, EBG, note to EB, typed fragment, Jan. 9, 1888, NYPLPA; EB to McE, no month, n.d. [Mar. 15], 1880, to LB, Apr. 25, 1887, to EBG, July 14, no year [1888 penciled in], Hampden-Booth; to LH, Nov. 27, no year, Princeton; Watermeier, *Between Actor and Critic*, 273, 273, n. 45; Hamlin Hill, ed., *Mark Twain's Letters to his Publishers 1867–1894* (Berkeley: University of California Press, 1967), 262, 263; Nicola Humble, ed., *Mrs. Beeton's Book of Household Management* (Oxford: Oxford University Press, 2000), 30; Clipping, "A Blow to Mr. Booth," newspaper clipping, n.d. Hampden–Booth.

PART I

Chapter One

1. LH, "EB," EB Scrapbook, p. 19, Harvard; Asia Booth Clarke, *The Elder and the Younger Booth*, 121; EB to Mr. Cist," Apr. 29, 1874, Simon Gratz Collection, The Historical Society of Pennsylvania.

2. A caul is a portion of the amnion, the "thin, tough, membranous sac that encloses the embryo." EB, to EwB, Nov. 14, 1869, Oct. 18, 1871, Nov. 15, 1874, Nov. 15, 1871, NYPLPA; to LB, n.d. [summer 1886], Harvard; John T. Ford to WW, Mar. 9, 1894 in WW, *Life and Art of EB*, Folger; Stephen M. Archer, *Junius Brutus Booth: Theatrical Prometheus* (Carbondale, Illinois: Southern Illinois University Press, 1922), 127, 308, n. 47; Clarke, *The Elder and the Younger Booth*, 119; Katherine Goodale, *Behind the Scenes with Edwin Booth* (Boston: Houghton Mifflin Company, 1931), 109; Edwina Booth Grossman, *Edwin Booth: Recollections by his Daughter* (New York: The Century Co., 1894), 32, 39, 40; *The Evening Post* (New York), Nov. 13, 1833: 3.

3. Junius Brutus Booth wrote to his mother-in-law on May 30, 1815, saying that he had married Adelaide on the 8th of that month: "Vous avez par ce terme sans doute recue ma letter avec une copie scrite du certificat de notre Mariage du 8 courant." In 1847 Adelaide and Junius Brutus Booth swore that they had entered into a separate maintenance agreement in 1826. Junius Brutus Booth, to Madame Delannoy, May 30, 1815, Taper Collection; EB to EwB, June 2, 1875, NYPLPA; to McE, June 2, 1880, Tulsa; Mary Ann Holmes Booth to EwB, Oct. 14, 1881, Hampden-Booth; Asia Booth to Jean Anderson, May 22, 1855, Maryland; Clarke, 52; Archer, *Junius Brutus Booth*, 7, 17, 22, 23, 46, 66, 67, 68, 181, 296, n. 31, 318, 319.

4. Archer 178–181, 185, 197; *The Sun* (Baltimore), Mar. 11, 1858: 2; Clipping, Junius Brutus Booth Scrapbook, Folger; *New York Clipper*, Mar. 20, 1858: 383.

5. EB to EBG, Jan. 19, 1888, NYPLPA; Asia Booth Clarke, *Passages, Incidents, and Anecdotes in the Life of Junius Brutus Booth*, New York: G. W. Carleton, 1866, in Copeland, n.p., extra-illustrated edition, Harvard; *The New York Clipper*, Apr. 22, 1865: 11; *The Philadelphia Inquirer*, Apr. 24, 1865: 2; Clippings: "Tombs of the Booths," no source, n.d. Folger; "Another Booth Skeleton," no source, n.d. Barstow scrapbook, Hampden-Booth; "Death of EB's Mother," Junius Brutus Booth & Family Miscellaneous Manuscript Collection, LC.

6. In late Oct. Junius Brutus Booth was managing the Tremont Street Theatre in Boston; by early Nov. he had moved to New York to perform at the Bowery Theatre, leaving his wife and at least one child in Boston. In a letter to Junius Brutus Booth, the proprietor of the inn where the Booths had been staying wrote to Junius Brutus Booth that Mary Ann "was afraid to come home to you and that she was not sorry for the death of the child for that she thought it was happy and that the only thing she was afraid of was to meet you. She best knows the reason." The Booths skipped town owing fifty-five dollars. A. R. Charnock to Junius Brutus Booth, Dec. 4, 1828, University of Pennsylvania; Archer, *Junius Brutus Booth*, 259.

7. Shortly after Asia's birth, Junius Brutus Booth wrote to his wife: "Call the little one Asia, in remembrance of the country where God first walked with man, and Frigga because she came to us on Friday, which day is consecrated to the Northern Venus"; however, Asia used Asia Sydney in early letters, and Junius Brutus Booth referred to her as Asia Sydney when she was four months old. EB to Richard Booth, Jan. 8, 1836, Princeton; to WW, Xmas 1871, Junius Brutus Booth Scrapbook, Folger; to EwB, Jan. 30, 1876, n.d. [Apr. 1885 penciled in], to EBG, Oct. 3, 1886, Apr. 13, no year [1887 penciled in], NYPLPA; Asia Booth to Jean Anderson, Nov. 19, 1856, Maryland; EB to J. E. Fries, Feb. 10, 1886, Harvard; Terry Alford, ed., *John Wilkes Booth: A Sister's Memoir* (Jackson, Mississippi: University Press of Mississippi, 1996), 5, 55; Archer, 74, 123, 124, 133, 137, 141, 146, 147, 156, 159, 226, 227, 228, 306 n. 12; Goodale, 152; Oggel, *Bio-Bibliography*, 57; Winter, *Life and Art*, 3, 10, 266, 267; *The New York Clipper*, Apr. 29, 1865: 19; Clipping, "Mrs. J. S. Clarke Buried," William Cushing Bamburgh, *Tributes, Sketches, Souvenirs, Portraits, Memorials and Programmes Edwin Thomas Booth*, Theatre Collection, Harvard; Clipping, "A Famous Stage Family," *Baltimore Sun*, June 10, 1900, NYPLPA.

8. John Sleeper Clarke to EB, Nov. 28, 1890, Hampden-Booth; Edward Alford, 11, 15, 21; Archer, *Junius Brutus Booth*, 171, 229; Hamilton Bell, "Mr. J. S. Clarke," *EB and his Contemporaries*, ed. Brander Matthews and Laurence Hutton (Boston: Page, 1900), 99, 100, 101; *Sketch of the Life of Mr. John S. Clarke Comedian* (London: J. W. Last & Co., 1872), n.p; William Stuart, "John S. Clarke, Comedian," *Lippincott's Magazine of Popular Literature and Science*, II (Nov., 1881): 498, 499; Clipping, "EB's Boyhood," *Tribune*, Oct. 8, 1892, Folger.

9. Booth always remembered "Miss Susan," as well as her niece Augusta Hyde, whom he later described as "my first sweetheart." Asia, writing her 1882 biography under her brother's tutelage, took pains to accord him academic credentials, claiming that Edwin was a pupil of an old French naval officer named Louis Dugas, that he "went to a university," and studied under a Mr. Kearney, who encouraged class dramatics. Terry Alford identified Asia's "Mr. Kearney" as Martin J. Kerney, who operated a school on Exeter Street near the Booth's home. Education was part of the legend she created to elevate a family whose public image was riddled with scandal. Mrs. L.M. Baltzele to EB, May 4, 1868, Susan Hyde to EB, Nov. 23, 1881, Hampden-Booth; EB to McE, Oct. 12, 1879, Taper Collection; to EBG, Mar. 13, no year [1887 penciled in], NYPLPA; to LB, Bunker-day, 1888, Harvard; to "Dear Furness" [Horace Howard Furness], June 17, 1888, Pennsylvania; EB, "Some Words about my Father," E-8, Princeton; Alford, 7; LB, "EB," *The Life and Art of EB and his Contemporaries* (Boston: L.C. Page & Company, 1886), 58; Clarke, *The Elder and the Younger Booth*, 121; LH, "EB," EB Scrapbook, 19, Harvard.

10. EB to "My dear Madame," June 18, 1859, Harvard; to EwB, n.d. Feb. 5, 1872, Clippings: "Portrait of EB," 154, EB Clipping Collection; "The Heart of Hamlet," *New York Herald*, Nov. 1, 1903, EB Scrapbook, NYPLPA; Asia Booth Clarke, *The Older and the Younger Booth*, 114; Grossman, 34, 49; Watermeier, *Between Actor and Critic*, 8.

11. EB to EwB, Sept. 27, Nov. 15, Dec. 27, 1874, Apr. 23, 1876, NYPLPA; to McE, Oct. 4, 1877, Hampden-Booth; to Richard Henry Stoddard, n.d. to Laurence Hutton, n.d. Princeton; to McE, May 12, n.d. [1882], Tulsa; to TBA, Jan. 21, no year, to Lillian Woodman Aldrich, Wednesday, n.d. Harvard; to John E. Russell, Oct. 8, 1875, Rochester; to Ferdinand Ewer, Oct. 14, 1877, Folger; Watermeier, *Between*

Actor and Critic, 8, 118; Clipping, "Portrait of EB," 154, EB Clipping Collection, NYPLPA.

12. EB to LH, Oct. 8, 1885, Princeton.

13. John L. Booth, "Extract from letter," n.d. Asia Booth Clarke to EB, Nov. 1, 1867, Julia Chapman to EB," Mar. 22, no year [1881], Hampden-Booth; Mrs. Elijah B. Rogers to Stump Forwood, n.d. LC; Clarke, *Elder and Younger Booth*, 122, 123; William H. Crane, *Footprints and Echoes* (New York: E. P. Dutton & Company, 1925), 93; Goodale, 229; Grossman, 11; Watermeier, *Between Actor and Critic*, 174; Clippings: EB's Boyhood," "An Actor King," *The Illustrated American* (June 24, 1893): 727, NYPLPA; "Booth off the stage," Baltimore newspaper, 1890, Scrapbook, Tours of EB, Season 1886–87, Hampden-Booth; " Booth Gone," LC.

14. Two of Booth's fellow performers recalled that John Wilkes had told Junius Brutus Booth that Edwin had stolen his costume for one of these performances. This is likely to be part of the demonization of John after Lincoln's assassination. Clarke, *Elder and Younger Booth*, 122; Percy MacKaye, *Epoch: The Life of Steele MacKaye*, II (New York: Boni & Liveright, 1927), 219; Titone, 100, 101; "An Actor King": 727; *The New York Clipper*, Apr. 20, 1861: 8, Sept. 30, 1865: 196; *New York Dramatic News and Society Journal*, Apr. 2, 1881: 3; Clippings: "Ned is Getting Gray," St. Louis newspaper, no source, n.d. Scrapbook, 1886–1887 season, 27, "Flowers and Good Wishes for Mr. Booth," no source [Baltimore newspaper], n.d. [Nov. 14, 1890], Barstow Scrapbook, Hampden-Booth; "Booth's Debut," Harvard; "The First Appearance of Two Famous Actors," Columbia.

15. Francis Wilson, *EB*, unpublished manuscript, 1933, 7, 23, Hampden-Booth; Archer, *Junius Brutus Booth*, 120; Clarke, *Elder and Younger Booth*: 112, 113, 121; Oggel, *Bio-Bibliography*, 9; Winter, *Life and Art*, 3; Stephen M. Archer, "Edwin Booth's Bel Air Appearance[s]," *Theatre History Studies*, 9 (1989): 133–137; Adam Badeau, "EB on and off the Stage," *McClure's Magazine*, 1 (Aug., 1893): 257; LB "EB": EB Scrapbook, 20, 58, Harvard.

16. Asia quotes her brother John, whom she called Wilkes, as saying: "We know that two-thirds of the funny anecdotes about our own father are disgraceful falsehoods." Wilson, 5; Alford, 51; *National Gazette and Literary Register* (Philadelphia), Dec. 15, 1829: 2; *Utica Daily Observer*, Dec. 15, 1877: 1.

17. Booth purchased an embarrassing letter written by his father from R. C. Davis, because "I would not have it fall into cruel hands." EB to R. C. Davis Esq., May 31, 1870, Harvard; to Wm. G. Hale, Esq., Feb. 22, 1872, Folger; Archer, *Junius Brutus Booth*, 260, 276; Clarke, *Elder and Younger Booth*, 101, 110; *Public Ledger* (Philadelphia, Pennsylvania), Jan. 1 (3), Mar. 4 (3) 1851.

18. Shortly after Edwin's death, his friend Adam Badeau wrote that Mary Ann had acted as Junius' dresser and taken Edwin with her. On Oct. 23 and 26, 1847, Mary Ann Booth performed Queen Elizabeth to her husband's Richard III at Baltimore's Front Street Theatre. It was generally considered the leading tragic female role in the play. On Oct. 25 she performed Goneril to his Lear. She also acted and sang in the one-act farces that followed the main piece. After Booth's engagement Mrs. Booth stayed on as a company member, performing a britches role in *Richelieu*. Her husband appeared for her benefit on Nov. 5, 1847. She was a member of the company at the Holliday Street Theatre in Baltimore by July 4, 1850, playing singing leads in the theatre's one-act farces. When she performed with the company on July 4, she was billed as making "her first appearance for years." Mary Ann's interest in the theatre, particularly box office receipts, is shown in letters to Edwin dated Jan. 13 and Jan. 29, 1863. A letter from Junius Brutus Booth to Mary Ann dated June 23, 1840, makes it clear that she made his costumes. In a letter to Laurence Hutton from New Haven, Connecticut, Booth says that a photograph of his father was taken in Albany in 1848 and that "I sat beside him in the original, but I looked so pale & sheepish that my brother Joe—when having it copied—very properly had me left out, for which I thanked him!" In 1882 Edwin contended that his eldest brother "never traveled with father, at least when my mother did." Traveling with his father became important after Lincoln's assassination when Booth distanced himself from his brother John and when his sister Asia avoided linking the two in her biopography. If Edwin was with his father, he could not have been at home with John, and not having known John was a legend that Edwin created to protect himself. Junius Brutus Booth to Richard Booth, Oct. 26, 1834, Mary Ann Holmes Booth to EB, Jan. 13, 29, 1863, EB to E. H. Hazard Esq., Feb. 14, 1882, Hampden-Booth; EB to LH, Tuesday, n.d. Princeton; Program, Boston Theatre, Oct. 1, 1847, extra-illustrated edition of Charles Copeland, Harvard, 18f; Booth, "Some Words about my Father," E-4; Archer 132, 150, 162, 168, 271; Badeau, "EB on and off the Stage": 256; *American and Commercial Daily Advertiser* (Baltimore), Oct. 22 (3), 23 (3), 25 (3), 26 (4), 28 (3), Nov. 1 (3), 5 (3) 1847; July 4 (3), 1850; *The Sun* (Baltimore), July 4, 1850: 3; *Boston Courier*, June 8, 1842: 3; The *Providence Daily Journal*, Jan. 5, 1882: 6; Item 1418235165, ebay.com.

19. Henry Sedley, "The Booths—Father and Son," *Harper's Weekly* 37 (Nov. 11, 1893): 1083.

20. EB to WW, May 17, 1880, typewritten copy prepared by Robert Young, Folger; to EBG, Oct. 22, 1888, NYPLPA; Archer, *Junius Brutus Booth*, 274, 275; Andrew Barr, *Drink: A Social History of America* (New York, Carroll & Graf Publishers, Inc., 1999), 44; Edward Kohn, "Creator of Compromise: William Henry Sedley and the Boston Museum's *Uncle Tom's Cabin*," *Theatre Survey*, 41:2 (Nov. 2000): 77.

21. EBG's annotation to EB to EBG, Apr. 15, no year [1889 penciled in], NYPLPA.

22. June's expertise in fencing is attested to by the fact that for his farewell benefit at Maguire's Opera House in San Francisco on Apr. 11, 1864, he "appeared in the foil and broadsword exercise with Colonel Monstery and afterwards in a set-to with Bill Clarke." Wilson, 4; Oggel *Bio-Bibliography*, 9; Sedley: 1083; *The New York Clipper*, May 21, 1864: 46.

23. EB to Oakley Colos, Esq., Dec. 14, [1880], Folger.

24. *Utica Daily Observer*, Dec. 15, 1877: 1; George J. Manson, "These Our Actors," *Spirit of the Times* (New York), Feb. 9, 1884, in EB Clipping Collection, NYPLPA.

Chapter Two

1. Clarke, 125; *Boston Evening Transcript*, Apr. 20, 1857: 2.

2. Thoman was a Philadelphia-born actor and the husband of Elizabeth Anderson, Joseph Jefferson's first cousin. Program, Boston Museum, Aug. 20, no year [1849], extra-illustrated edition of Charles Copeland, *The Life of EB*, Harvard; Helene Wickham Koon, *How Shakespeare Won the West: Players and Performances in America's Gold Rush, 1849–1865* (Jefferson, North Carolina: McFarland, 1989), 137, 155; WW, *Life and Art*, 4; *The Boston Semi-Weekly Atlas*, Aug. 15, 1849: 3; Clipping, EB scrapbook, Robinson Locke Collection, 78, NYPLPA.

3. Clipping, Barton Hill, "Personal Recollections of EB," no title, n.d. EB Scrapbook, NYPLPA.

4. EB, "Some Words about my Father," E-11; Oggel, *Bio-Bibliography*, 57; ECS, "EB," *The Atlantic Monthly*, XVII, 99 (1866): 587.

5. EB to "Dear Sir," Oct. 28, no year [1866 penciled in, perhaps in Booth's handwriting], Oct. 21, no year [1866], Folger; Otis Skinner, 8.

6. Archer, 275; *The Providence Daily Journal*, Sept. 27 (3) 1849; *Public Ledger* (Philadelphia), May 22, 1850: 3; Mar. 5, 1851: 3; *Cummings' Evening Telegraphic Bulletin* (Philadelphia), May 22, 1850: 3; *The Charleston Courier,* Feb. 16, 1860: 3; *The Daily Picayune* (New Orleans), Jan. 28, 1859: 1.

7. The text reads: "Baltimore Apr. 8th, 1850 Mr. Sefton Dear Sir Will you be kind enough to inform me if my Father is in Richmond, and whether he is ill, for we've not heard a word from him since he left here. I see by the Richmond paper Friday that he was not announced to play that night. We feel anxious to know something [abo]ut him. Answer this by return of mail and oblige Yours truly Edwin Booth In Haste." This is the earliest extant EB letter. The Booths may have known Sefton, who was a member of the Baltimore Museum Company in 1849. Archer, 275; EB to John Sefton, Apr. 8, 1850, NYPLPA; *The Sun* (Baltimore), Feb. 17, 1849: 3, Apr. 3, 1850: 2; Clipping, Hill, "Personal Recollections of EB," NYPLPA.

8. The story circulated by John Sleeper Clarke, Asia Booth Clarke and Mrs. Elijah B. Rogers that a "Negro billsticker" pasted the advertisements upside down all over town was probably a racist piece of comic relief designed to illustrate Booth's humble beginnings. Asia Booth to Jean Anderson, Apr. 4, 1854, Maryland; Mrs. Elijah B. Rogers to W. Stump Forwood, Aug. 10, 1886, LC; Clarke, 126, 128; *The Sun* (Baltimore), Supplement, Nov. 10, 1890: 4; *The Pittsburg Dispatch*, Jan. 13. 1882: 5S; Clipping, "The First Appearance of Two Famous Actors," Columbia.

9. EB, "Some Words about my Father," E-18, 19.

10. Arthur W. Bloom, *Joseph Jefferson: Dean of the American Theatre* (Savannah: Frederic C. Beil, 2000), 38; Winter, *Life and Art*, 6; Oggel, *Bio-Bibliography*, 9; *The New York Post*, Sept. 27, 1850: 3; *The New York Herald*, Sept. 27 (5), Oct. 4 (5), 1850.

11. *Spirit of the Times* (New York), Sept. 28, 1850: 384; Apr. 5 (84), Sept. 20 (372), 1851.

12. St. Louis Theatre Petition, "Mr. EB," Jan. 28, 1851, Hampden-Booth; *The Sun* (Baltimore), Nov. 2(3), Nov. 12 (1) 1850; *Daily National Intelligencer* (Washington, D. C.), Nov. 11, 1850: 3; *The Brooklyn Daily Eagle*, Dec. 11, 1850: 3; Clipping, Joseph Jefferson, "In Memory of EB," no source, n.d. Hampden-Booth.

13. EB, "Some Words about My Father," E-11; Archer, 275, 276; Clarke, 129; "An Actor King": 727, 728; *The Evening Post* (New York), Apr. 5, 1851: 1; *The New York Herald*, Apr. 5, 1851: 1, 7.

14. Clarke, 129, 130; Winter, *Life and Art*, 6, 7; *The New York Dramatic Mirror*, Aug. 27, 1901: 3; Clipping, no source, n.d., Robinson Locke Collection, 78, LH, "EB," EB Collection, NYPLPA.

15. Booth, "Some Words about My Father," E-11.

16. Clipping, *Burton's Daily Bulletin*, May 14, 1857, Mr. and Mrs. Frank Rea Collection, NYPLPA.

17. *Daily National Intelligencer* (Washington), May 8, 1851: 1; *American Telegraph* (Washington), May 17, 1851: 2.

18. *American Telegraph* (Washington), May 19, 1851: 2.

19. Archer, 277; *The Sun* (Baltimore), May 28, 1851: 3; Feb. 11 (3), 12 (3), Mar. 6 (3) 1852; *Daily Chronicle and Sentinel* (Augusta, Georgia), Apr. 1 (3), 2 (3), 1852; *The Charleston Mercury*, Mar. 22 (3), 26 (3), 1852; *The American and Commercial Daily Advertiser* (Baltimore), Nov. 2, 1852: 3.

20. *The Sun* (Baltimore), Sept. 9 (2), Nov. 9 (3), 1850; Feb. 24, 1852: 3.

Chapter Three

1. Helene Wickham Koon believes that June and Harriet Mace were not married when they arrived in California and that he went East in Sept. 1854 to "settle a discreet divorce arrangement with Clementine DeBar and make Harriet an honest woman." Mary DeBar was still billed as "Mrs. J. B. Booth Jr." in Dec. 1855. Edwin later performed with his ex-sister-in-law at the St. Charles Theatre in New Orleans. Blanche visited Asia Booth Clarke in June 1859, and Asia wrote to Jean Anderson: "I found her restless, coquettish, altogether *fast* and yet I was pleased with her too (She is no relative or mine or connection of ours, but the step daughter of my brother). I call that nothing." On Mar. 18, 1865, Clementina's brother, the New Orleans manager Ben DeBar, sent John Wilkes Booth a letter with a review of Blanche's work telling him: "I have sent June a bill to prove to him I have no wish that the girl should have any other than my name." At the time of Lincoln's assassination, however, Blanche referred to herself as Blanche Booth and contended that June was her father. Ben DeBar also claimed that June was her father. A report of the arrests of Ben DeBar and Blanche DeBar includes the following information: "Although Ben DeBar was instrumental in procuring a divorce for his sister from her husband, there has been a bad feeling existing between them for some time, and he will not allow Blanche to have any intercourse with her mother whose character it is alleged is decidedly questionable." The report states that in 1865 Blanche was 24, which would place her birth in 1841, about the time that June married her mother. Asia Booth to Jean Anderson, n.d. [1852], "My Dear Jean," [Jean Anderson], June 19, 1859, Maryland; Statement of J. H. Baker, M599 Roll # 1 (35), Ben DeBar to John Wilkes Booth, Mar. 18, 1865, Roll # 2 (0335), J. H. Baker to Hon. C. A. Dana, Roll 2 (0408–0413), "Statement of Ben DeBar," Apr. 22, 1865, Roll 2 (0420), "Statement of Blanche Booth," Apr. 22, 1865, Roll 2 (0422), *Investigation and Trial Papers Relating to the Assassination of President Lincoln*, National Archives; Archer, 165, 225, 227; Michael W. Kauffman, *American Brutus* (Random House: New York, 2004), 417, n. 21; Koon, 61, 71; George C. D. Odell, *Annals of the New York Stage* V (New York: Columbia University Press, 1931), 42; Oggel, *Bio-Bibliography*, 9; Winter, *Life and Art*, 7–8; *The Sun* (Baltimore), Feb. 10, 1851: 1; *Boston Daily Evening Transcript*, Apr. 18, 1851: 3; *Daily Morning News* (Boston), Apr. 25, 1852: 2; *Sacramento Daily Union*, Dec. 19, 1855: 3; *New York Clipper*, Apr. 24 (7), June 11 (62), Oct. 1 (191), 1859; Feb. 29, 1862: 365, Mar. 19, 1864: 387; Aug. 12, 1865: 142; *The Spirit of the Times* (New York), Oct. 18, 1859: 411; *The Daily Picayune* (New Orleans), Mar. 19, 1867: 2; Clippings: "The Eccentric Booths," *The Sun* (Baltimore), Mar. 27, 1891, Folger; *New York Sun*, Mar. 28, 1897, EB scrapbook, NYPLPA; "Another Booth Gone," no source, LC.

2. During the week of May 31, 1852, Junius Brutus Booth Senior had a "farewell" engagement at the Holliday Street Theatre in Baltimore, during which time Edwin played Edgar to his father's Lear. According to Winter, Junius Brutus Senior started off to California alone but was full of foreboding at the ordeal before him and stopped to send for Edwin. According to Asia Booth Clarke, the elder Booth went to New York, became ill, returned to Baltimore and then set out a second time, taking Edwin with him. Asia Booth to Jean Anderson, Jan. 8, 1854, Maryland; Clarke, 130; George R. MacMinn, *The Theater of the Golden Era in California* (Caldwell, Idaho: The Caxton Printers, Ltd., 1941), 44; Malcolm J. Rohrbough, *Days of Gold* (Berkeley: University of California Press, 1997), 80; Winter, *Life and Art*, 8; *Spirit of the Times* (New York), Mar. 15 (43), May 3(122), Dec. 6 (504) 1851; Mar. 27 (63), Apr. 3 (84), May 29 (170) 1852; *The San Francisco Daily Herald*, Jan. 10 (2), Feb. 23 (2), Mar. 4 (2) 1852; *The San Francisco Daily Herald*, Mar. 19, 1852: 2, 3; *The Sun* (Baltimore), May 31 (3), June 1 (3), 2 (3), 3 (3), 4 (3), 5 (3), 1852.

3. Douglas Fetherling, *The Gold Crusades: A Social History of Gold Rushes, 1849–1929* (Toronto: University of Toronto Press, 1997), 31; John Haskell Kemble, *The Panama Route 1848–1869* (Berkeley: University of California Press, 1943), 58, 64; *New-York Daily Times*, Mar. 2 (3), Mar. 20 (4), Apr. 17 (1, 3), 27 (4), July 29 (8), Nov. 4 (7), 20 (7) 1852; Dec. 31, 1853: 7; Feb. 20 (8), 21 (8), 1854.

4. Kemble, *Panama Route*, 22, 120, 150, 231; Kemble, "The Gold Rush to Panama, 1848–1851," *Rushing for Gold*, ed. John Walton Caughey (Berkley, California: University

of California Press, 1949), 46; Joseph L. Schott, *Rails Across Panama* (Indianapolis, Indiana: The Bobbs-Merrill Company, Inc., 1967), 121; *Boston Daily Evening Transcript*, Apr. 22, 1851: 4; *New-York Daily Times*, June 22, 1852: 3; *New-York Daily News*, June 29, 1857: 1.

5. George Forby to Elizabeth Dowd Forby, Apr. 4, 1852, The Huntington Library; H. W. Brands, *The Age of Gold* (New York: Doubleday, 2002), 79; Clarke, *The Elder and The Younger Booth*, 102; J. S. Holliday, *The World Rushed In* (New York: Simon & Schuster, 1981), 435, 436; Donald Dale Jackson, *Gold Dust* (New York: Alfred A. Knopf, 1980), 77, 78; Polly Welts Kaufman, ed., *Apron Full of Gold: The Letters of Mary Jane Megquier from San Francisco 1849–1856* (Albuquerque: University of New Mexico Press, 1994), 14; Kemble, *Panama Route*, 59, 167, 169, 186; Schott, 28, 47, 53, 69, 104, 105, 106, 108, 110, 111, 113; John Easter Minter, *The Chagres: River of Westward Passage* (New York: Rinehart & Company, Inc., 1948), 213, 221; Alex Perez-Venero, *Before the Five Frontiers: Panama from 1821–1903* (New York: AMS Press, 1978), 84, 88; *The Daily Journal* (Wilmington, North Carolina), Apr. 14, 1852: 2; *The Nevada Journal* (Nevada, California), Aug. 7, 1852: 2.

6. John H. Eagle to Margaret H. Eagle, Feb. 7, 1852, Forby, Apr. 4, 1852, The Huntington Library; Brands, 80, 81; Clarke, 130–131; Fetherling, 31; J. S. Holliday, *The World Rushed In*, 433–444; Joseph Henry Jackson, *Gold Rush Album* (New York: Charles Scribner's Sons: 1949), 113, 116; Joseph Henry Jackson, *Anybody's Gold: The Story of California's Mining Towns* (San Francisco: Chronicle Books, 1970), 30; Kemble, *Panama Route*, 173; Kemble, "The Gold Rush to Panama, 1848–1851," 53; Perez-Venero, *Before the Five Frontiers*, 88; *The San Francisco Daily Herald*, Nov. 23, 1852: 4.

7. Eagle, Feb. 7, 1852; Forby, Apr. 4, 1852; Brands, 81, 84; Kemble, *Panama Route*, 177.

8. Victor M. Berthold, *The Pioneer Steamer California, 1848–1849* (Boston: Houghton Mifflin Company, 1932), 1; Holliday, 416, 417, 428, 429, 430; Kemble, *Panama Route*, 159; John E. Pomfret, ed., *California Gold Rush Voyages, 1848–1849* (San Marino, California: The Huntington Library, 1954), 177; Schott, 13, 14, 58; *Boston Daily Evening Transcript*, May 1, 1851: 3.

9. J. J. McCloskey, "How I Met EB," *New York Dramatic Mirror*, Dec. 25, 1904: xvi; J. J. McCloskey, "EB in Old California," *Green Book*, June, 1911, in EB Scrapbook, NYPLPA.

10. McCloskey, "EB in Old California," NYPLPA; *Daily Alta California* (San Francisco), July 30, 1852: 3.

11. *Placer Times and Transcript* (San Francisco), July 30 (2), 31 (2), 1852; *The San Francisco Daily Herald*, July 31 (2), Aug. 1 (2), 1852; *Daily Alta California* (San Francisco), July 31, 1852: 2.

12. Charles H. Shattuck, "Edwin Booth's First Critic," *Theatre Survey*, VII, 1 (May 1966): 6; *Daily Placer and Transcript* (San Francisco), July 31 (2), Aug. 2 (2), 1852; Clipping, "The High Church Apostle," no source, July 27, no year, Ferdinand C. Ewer file, Hampden-Booth.

13. Winter, *Life and Art*, 8; *Daily Alta California* (San Francisco), July 18 (3), 25 (3), 29 (3), 30 (2), 1852; *Spirit of the Times* (New York), Nov. 6, 1852: 451.

14. Clarke, 131; Holliday, 302; Charles H. Shattuck, *The Hamlet of Edwin Booth* (Urbana: University of Illinois Press, 1969), 3; Winter, *Life and Art*, 8; *The Daily Union* (Sacramento), July 15 (1), Aug. 18 (2), 19 (2, 3), 23 (3), Nov. 4 (1), 1852; *Daily Alta California* (San Francisco), Nov. 5 (2), 22 (1), 1852.

15. EB to TBA, Apr. 10, no year [1887], Harvard; Clarke, 132; *McCabe's Journal* quoted in *San Francisco Theatre Research*, 46; *The Daily Union* (Sacramento), Aug. 25 (2), 28 (2), Sept. 4 (2) 1852; Clipping, "Another Booth Gone," LC.

16. Edwin Booth, "Some Words about My Father," E-14; *The San Francisco Herald*, Sept. 26, 1852:3; *Daily Placer and Transcript* (San Francisco), Sept. 27 (3), Oct. 1 (3), 1852: 3; *The Daily Union* (Sacramento), Sept. 29, 1852: 2; *The San Francisco Herald*, Oct. 1, 1852: 4; *The Weekly Placer Herald* (Auburn, California), Oct. 2, 1852: 2; *Spirit of the Times* (New York), Nov. 6, 1852: 451.

17. James H. Simpson recorded what transpired on board: "I had taken passage on the steamer, J. W. Chenowith, from New Orleans to Cincinnati at the same time [as] Booth.... One day out from New Orleans, ... I noticed a man walking back and forth in the saloon, with his hands behind him, his head bowed in ... thought.... A gentleman ... remarked: 'That is the tragedian, Booth.' I then remembered having seen him in his last play at the Saint Charles Theatre, New Orleans. The second day out, he was absent from the saloon, and, on inquiry, I found that he was confined to his stateroom very sick. Well knowing the careless regard strangers have on boats for one who is sick, I at once visited his room, apologizing for my intrusion and offered my services to him.... After scanning me with a look of penetration and surprise, ... he accepted the offer. On examining his room, I found that he had been neglected. I immediately called the porter, had the room cleaned out, clean linen put on him and on the bed, [and] ordered some gruel made for him, as he was too weak for stronger nourishment, but there was no medical attention at hand, and he wasted away very fast. The third day after he was taken, he could not turn over without help. I saw that he was getting in an helpless condition, and thinking to stimulate his energies, gave him some brandy and water, having to saturate a rag and place it between his teeth, his jaws having become rigid, but on tasting it, he made an effort to remove it from his lips and spoke with difficulty: 'No more in this world.' I saw that he had no hopes of living and felt anxious in regard to his hope for the future, but being a young man and an entire stranger, I felt it to be a very delicate situation for one of my experience, but with a mental prayer that I might be sustained, I commenced by asking him if he had a wife. He answered with a look of astonishment and an emphatic 'Certainly I have.' I then asked him if he had any message to send her, but I could not understand him; but he seemed to say in his look and features, 'O, that I could talk.' But, poor man, his power of utterance was so impaired that he could scarcely utter a word distinctly. He attempted to tell me of his travels in California, but I could understand nothing but that he had suffered a great deal and been exposed very much. On the fourth day after he was taken, I asked him if I should read to him from my testament. He seemed anxious that I should, when I selected an encouraging chapter, and read, while he gave deep attention. I then asked him if I might pray for him. His eyes became dim with moisture, and he signified his consent, while I knelt beside his bunk and besought the Great Father of us all, before whom he was so shortly to appear, to receive him, though at this late hour, for the sake of him who died, that sinners might trust in his mercy. He seemed very grateful, attempted to put his arms around my neck, as I bent over him to smooth his pillow. On the fifth day about 1 o'clock, he died. Winter, *Life and Art*, 10, 11; *New-York Daily Times*, Nov. 30, 1852: 2; *The Spirit of the Times* (New York), Dec. 11 (516), 18 (520), 1852; *New-York Daily Times*, Dec. 10, 1852: 1; Clipping, "Freaks of the Elder Booth," Robinson Locke Collection 78, NYPLPA.

18. *Daily Alta California* (San Francisco), Jan. 6, 1853: 2; *The Daily Union* (Sacramento), Jan. 12, 1853: 1; *The San Francisco Daily Herald*, Jan. 6, 1853: 2.

19. For information on the mining camps and towns that Booth played in California, see David Allan Comstock, *Gold Diggers and Camp Followers* (Grass Valley, California: Comstock Bonanza Press, 1982), 264, 265, 322; Holliday, *The World Rushed In*, 298, 379; Holliday, *Rush for Riches*, 141, 185, 203; Jackson, *Anybody's Gold*, 71, 103, 133; W. P. Morrell, *The Gold Rushes* (Chester Springs, Pennsylvania: Dufour,

1968), 83 n. 1, 90; James J. Sinnott, *Downieville: Gold Town on the Yuba* (Fresno: Mid-Cal Publishers, 1983), 5; Jack R. Wagner, *Gold Mines of California* (Berkeley: Howell North Books, 1970), 5; *The Sun* (Baltimore), Aug. 24, 1850: 1; *The Nevada Journal* (Nevada, California), Oct. 14, 1853: 2.

20. EB to LB, Dec. 28, 1886, Harvard.

21. Clippings: EB, "Notes to Macready's Reminiscences," Bamburgh, Harvard; "EB's Injuries," *The Daily Graphic*, Aug. 17, 1875, Folger.

22. In an account written in Downieville in 1881 the Waller company was described as sinking to the level of the Vincent Crummles' company in Dickens's *Nicholas Nickleby*. The finale of Mrs. Waller's benefit at Downieville "was a tableau, representing the arms and shield of California. Mrs. Waller enthroned [as] the Goddess of Liberty, with miners picking and panning in red shirts and big boots, and a good-sized young grizzly bear chained to the centre of the group, comprised the scene. The curtain slowly rose, the orchestra played, the grouped actors sang the Star Spangled Banner, and the bear reared on its hind legs and howled in [what] critics would call the 'upper register' and nearly drowned the voices of all the rest; and not being used to facing such an audience, in his excitement, he did what a bear ought to do only in his native wilds, and he made a burlesque of the beautiful Tableau, and the curtain fell amidst the wildest shouts of both audience and actors." Sinnott, 129; *Nevada Journal* (Nevada City, California), Dec. 31, 1852: 3; *Daily Chicago Tribune*, July 17, 1881: 18.

23. The snowstorm hemmed the company in at Grass Valley or Red Dog or Nevada City, depending on whose account is read. J. J. McCloskey contented that Booth and the Wallers were stranded in Red Dog. Asia Booth Clarke places the event in Nevada. Newspapers have the company in Grass Valley. Clarke, 133, 134; H. P. Davis, *Gold Rush Days in Nevada City* (Nevada City, California: Berliner & McGinnis, 1948), 57; Holliday, *Rush for Riches*, 187, 203; M. A. DeWolfe Howe, *Memories of a Hostess: A Chronicle of Eminent Friendships drawn chiefly from the Diaries of Mrs. James T. Fields* (Boston: The Atlantic Monthly Press, 1922), 203; MacMinn, 183; Rohrbough, 150, 162; *San Francisco Theatre Research*, 47; Shattuck, 4; Sinnott, 15; McCloskey, "How I Met Edwin Booth": xvi; *The Daily Union* (Sacramento), Nov. 16 (3), 17 (3), 25 (1), 26 (2), 1852; *Placer Times and Transcript* (San Francisco), Nov. 25, 1852: 2; *The San Francisco Daily Herald*, Nov. 29, 1852: 2, Jan. 9, 1853: 2; *The Weekly Placer Herald* (Auburn, California), Dec. 18, 1852: 3; *The Mountain Echo* (Downieville, California), Dec. 18, 1852: 3; *Daily Alta California* (San Francisco), Dec. 25, 1852: 2, Jan. 15, 1853: 2, 3; *Placer Times and Transcript* (San Francisco), Dec. 30, 1852: 2.

24. Clarke, 135; Goodale, 149; *Daily Alta California* (San Francisco), Feb. 2, 1853: 3; *Placer Times and Transcript* (San Francisco), Feb. 3, 1853: 3; *The Golden Era* (San Francisco), Feb. 6, 1853: 2.

25. EB to EwB, Mar. 2, 1873, NYPLPA; Grossman, 36; Winter, *Life and Art*, 15; *Daily Alta California* (San Francisco), Aug. 7, 1853: 2; *San Francisco Examiner*, June 7, 1893, quoted in *San Francisco Theatrical Research*, 86.

26. Shattuck, 9; Ferdinand Ewer, "Editor's Table," *The Pioneer, or California Monthly Magazine* III (Jan.–June, 1855): 374; *Daily Alta California* (San Francisco), Mar. 24 (2), Apr. 17 (2), 1853; *Placer Times and Transcript* (San Francisco), Apr. 20, 1853: 2.

27. *Daily Alta California* (San Francisco), Apr. 21 (3), 22 (2), 1853; *The San Francisco Daily Herald*, Apr. 22, 1853: 2.

28. *Daily Placer Times and Transcript* (San Francisco), Apr. 22 (2), 27 (3), May 3 (2), 1853.

29. *Daily Placer Times and Transcript* (San Francisco), Apr. 26, 1853: 2; *Daily Alta California* (San Francisco), Apr. 27(2), June 14 (3), 1853.

30. EB to David C. Anderson, July 22, 1876, Hampden-Booth; Comstock, 96; Grossman, 204; *San Francisco Theatre Research*, 52, 92; *The San Francisco Daily Herald*, Feb. 12 (3), June 3 (2), 1852; *The Nevada Journal* (Nevada, California), June 10, 1853: 3; *Daily Placer Times and Transcript* (San Francisco), July 2, 1853: 3; *Daily Alta California* (San Francisco), July 4, 1852: 3; Mar. 16 (3), Oct. 2 (3), 1853; *New-York Daily Times* Aug. 25, 1853: 3; *Spirit of the Times* (New York), Jan. 6 (2), Feb. 18 (7), June 3 (189), 1854; Nov. 17, 1855: 457; Clippings: McCloskey, "The Earlier Life of Edwin Booth," NYPLPA; "Short Bits," San Francisco newspaper, no source, n.d. [circa Mar. 7, 1887], Scrapbook, Tour of EB — Season 1886–87, 35, Hampden-Booth.

31. In 1877 Booth could still write to his California friend Mateo Game in Spanish that Game described as "faultless." Game married a cousin of Booth's second wife Mary McVicker named Clara Belle. Mateo Game to EB, Sept. 18, 1877, Hampden-Booth; Clipping, Henry Sedley, "The Booths-Father and Son," NYPLPA.

32. *Spirit of the Times* (New York), Apr. 26 (120), July 12 (252), Sept. 20 (361), 1851; Jan. 10, 1852: 564; *Daily Placer Times and Transcript* (San Francisco), Dec. 27, 1854: 2; Clippings: J. J. McCloskey, "How I Met EB": xvi, Henry Sedley, "The Booths—Father and Son," NYPLPA.

33. Clipping, *The Christian Union*, post–1882, Edwin Booth Scrapbook, NYPLPA.

34. Oggel, *Bio-Bibliography*, 11; Shattuck, 9; Clipping, "The Heart of Hamlet," *New York Herald*, Nov. 1, 1903, in EB Scrapbook, NYPLPA.

35. EB to David C. Anderson, May 3, 1874, Hampden-Booth; Grossman, 42.

36. Oggel, *Bio-Bibliography*, 10; McCloskey, "How I Met Edwin Booth," xvi; *The San Francisco Daily Herald*, Jan. 12, 1852: 2; *The Spirit of the Times* (New York), Apr. 16 (108), 23 (114), Nov. 20 (470), 1852; Nov. 5, 1853: 446; *The Daily Union* (Sacramento), May 7 (1), 30 (2), June 8 (2), 15 (1), 30 (1), July 11 (3), 15 (1), 27 (3), Aug. 9 (2), 12 (2), Sept. 11 (2), Dec. 28 (2), 1853; *Daily Alta California* (San Francisco), May 7 (3), 9 (3), 11 (2), 19 (3), June 20 (3, 4), July 18 (3), Aug. 22 (3), Dec. 23 (2), 1853; Feb. 14, 1854: 2; *Daily Placer Times and Transcript* (San Francisco), May 13 (2), 18 (2), 1853; *New-York Daily Times*, Aug. 10 (3), Sept. 26 (2), June 22 (2), 1853; July 10 (1), 20 (6), Sept. 21 (6), 1854.

37. *Daily Placer Times and Transcript* (San Francisco), June 1 (3), 3 (3), July 4 (2), 5 (2), Aug. 23 (3), 1853; *Daily Alta California* (San Francisco), June 11 (3), 24 (3), 27 (3), July 4 (2), Aug. 2 (3), 3 (2), 20 (3), Sept. 6 (3), 8 (3), 1853; Feb. 14, 1854: 2; *The Spirit of the Times* (New York), Aug. 13 (307), Sept. 17 (362), 1853.

38. J. J. McCloskey, "How I Met Edwin Booth": xvi; *Daily Alta California* (San Francisco), Sept. 10 (3), 11 (2), 18 (3), Oct. 15 (2), 19 (2), 21 (2), 1853; *Daily Placer Times and Transcript* (San Francisco), Sept. 12 (2), 14 (2), 24 (2), 1853.

39. Winter, *Life and Art* 15, 16; *Daily Alta California* (San Francisco), Aug. 14 (2), Sept. 12 (2), Nov. 3 (3), 4 (2), Dec. 21 (3), 24 (3), 25 (2, 3), 26 (2), 28 (3), 1853, Jan. 15, 1854: 2; *The Daily Union* (Sacramento), Sept. 26 (2), Oct. 24 (2), 25 (2), 26 (2), 31 (2), Nov. 1 (2), Dec. 29 (2), 1853; *Daily Democratic State Journal* (Sacramento, California), Oct. 25, 1853: 2; *Daily Placer Times and Transcript* (San Francisco), Dec. 20, 1853: 2; *The Golden Era* (San Francisco), Jan. 22, 1854: 2; *San Francisco Daily Evening News*, Feb. 15, 1854: 2; *The New York Clipper*, Feb. 19, 1870: 366; Clipping, Hill, "Personal Recollections of EB," NYPLPA.

40. Denounced by his co-star, Booth supposedly told friends he felt it "keenly." Ferdinand Ewer, "Editor's Table," *The Pioneer, or California Monthly Magazine* I (Jan.-June 1854): 249; *New-York Daily Times*, Sept. 2, 1853: 5; *The Spirit of the Times* (New York), Dec. 3, 1853: 504; *Daily Alta California* (San Francisco), Mar. 25 (2), Apr. 3 (2), 6 (2), 8 (2), 9 (2), 1854; *The Nevada Journal* (Nevada, California), Apr. 7, 1854: 2; *The Golden Era* (San Francisco), Apr. 7, 1854: 2; *Marysville Daily Herald* (Marysville, California), Apr. 8,

1854: 2; *California Chronicle* (San Francisco), Apr. 8, 1854: 2; *The Wide West* (San Francisco, California), Apr. 9, 1854: 2.

41. Stewart Edward White, *The Forty-Niners* (New Haven, 1920), 173, quoted in MacMinn, 145, n. 16; *The Wide West* (San Francisco), June 11, 1854: 2; *The Golden Era* (San Francisco), July 9 (2), 23 (2), 1854; *The Marysville Herald* (Marysville, California), July 11, 1854: 2; *Daily Placer Times and Transcript* (San Francisco), July 25 (2), 29 (2), Aug. 1 (2), 1854.

42. Nora Titone contends that Booth and Laura Keene were in love. Their relationship in San Francisco and later in Hawaii points in the opposite direction. Titone, 150; *Daily Alta California* (San Francisco), Apr. 10 (2), May 1 (3), June 26 (3), Aug. 2 (2, 3), 16 (1, 2), Dec. 9 (2), 1854; *Spirit of the Times* (New York) July 29, 1854: 288; *Daily Placer Times and Transcript* (San Francisco), July 31 (3), Aug. 2 (2, 3), 1854; *California Chronicle* (San Francisco), Aug. 1 (2, 3), 3 (3), 1854; *The Golden Era* (San Francisco), Aug. 6, 1854: 2; *New-York Daily Times*, Sept. 9, 1854: 2; *Weekly Alta California* (San Francisco), Oct. 28, 1854: 3.

43. Broadsides, Royal Victoria Theatre, Sydney, Australia, Oct. 25, 31, no year [1854], Hampden-Booth; Eric Irvin, "Laura Keene and Edwin Booth in Australia," *Theatre Notebook*, XXIII, 3 (Spring, 1969): 95, 98; *Sacramento Daily Union*, Sept. 13, 1856: 2; *The Empire* (Sydney), Oct. 30, 1854: 5; *Spirit of the Times* (New York), Mar. 17, 1855: 49.

44. Irvin: 99, 100; Richard Waterhouse, "High Culture and Low Culture: The Changing Role of Shakespeare, 1833–2000," John Golder and Richard Madelaine, eds., *O Brave New World: Two Centuries of Shakespeare on the Australian Stage* (Sydney: Currency Press, 2001), 25; *New-York Daily Times*, Aug. 12, 1854: 2, Dec. 15, 1883: 6, Dec. 25, 1904; *The Argus* (Melbourne), Nov. 21 (4), 22 (4), 29 (4), Dec. 2 (4) 1854; *Daily Placer Times and Transcript* (San Francisco), Dec. 13. 1854: 2; *Spirit of the Times* (New York), May 5, 1855: 135.

45. The Argus (Melbourne), Nov. 22 (7), 25 (4), Dec. 2 (4), 1854.

46. Index to Passenger Manifests, Box 1002811, Passenger List, *City of Norfolk*, Ship Manifests, Box 1009965, Index to Passenger Manifests, Box 1002814, Archives Division, Department of Accounting and General Services, State of Hawaii, Honolulu; Pauline King, ed., *The Diaries of David Lawrence Gregg: An American Diplomat in Hawaii* (Honolulu: Hawaiian Historical Society, 1982), 566, n. 10; *The Friend* (Honolulu), Mar. (24), Apr. (32), 1855; *Daily Alta California* (San Francisco), Mar. 16, 1855: 2; *New-York Daily Times*, Apr. 16 (1), 25 (1), May 25 (1), 1855; *Oroville Daily Butte Record* (Oroville, California), July 24, 1856: 2; Clipping, *Fact* (London), Mar. 19, 1881, Scrapbook, 1880–1881, Hampden-Booth.

47. "Reminiscences of the Stage in Honolulu," *Hawaiian Almanac and Annual for 1906* (Thomas G. Throm: Honolulu, 1905): 94, 95; *Daily Placer Transcript and Times* (San Francisco), Mar. 20 (3), 23 (2), Apr. 2 (3), 7 (2), 9 (3), 10 (2), 1855.

48. "Booth in Honolulu," *The Evening Telegraph* (Philadelphia), Oct. 14, 1889, extra-illustrated edition, Matthews and Hutton, V, pt. 2, Harvard.

49. Alexander Liholiho, *Journal of the voyages made to the United States, England and France*, typed manuscript, Hawaiian collection, Hamilton Library, University of Hawaii, n.p.; Jacob Adler, ed., *The Journal of Prince Alexander Liholiho* (Honolulu: University of Hawaii Press, 1967), xv, xix, 16, 99, 100, 101, 102, 127; Archer, 275, 376; Clarke, 141; Jacob Adler, "King Kamehameha IV's Attitude towards the United States," *The Journal of Pacific History*, III (1968): 107–113; *Alta California* (San Francisco), Oct. 18, 1849: 2, Aug. 23, 1850: 5; *Alta California for the Steamer California* (San Francisco), Nov. 1, 1849: 7.

50. King, 217, 218, 219, 226; Caroline Bengston, "Hawaii in 1855," *The Hawaiian Journal of History*, IX (1975): 58. n.4; *The Polynesian* (Honolulu), Jan. 13, 1855: 2; *The Nevada Journal* (Nevada City, California), Jan. 19, 1855: 2; *The New Era and Argus* (Honolulu), Mar. 29, 1855: 2.

51. Booth may have been referring to Apia, the capital of Upolu, in Western Samoa. It is possible that the City of Norfolk stopped there on the way to Tahiti. EB to WW, June 13, 1878, to ECS, May 8, 1881, Folger.

52. Index to Passenger Manifests, Box 1002811, Hawaii; EB to DCA, Apr. 19, 1878, Hampden-Booth; Asia Booth to Jean Anderson, Aug. 1, 1855, Maryland; Winter, *Life and Art*, 16, 17; Oggel, *Bio-Bibliography*, 58; *The Golden Era* (San Francisco): Apr. 29, 1855: 2; *Daily Placer Transcript and Times* (San Francisco), May 3, 1855: 2.

53. Shattuck, 8; Koon, 117; *San Francisco Daily Evening News*, May 28 (3), June 2 (2), 6 (2) 1855; *The New York Clipper*, July 20, 1861: 108; *The New York Dramatic Mirror*, June 24, 1893: 14; *Daily Alta California* (San Francisco), May 30 (2), 31 (2), June 6 (2), 1855; Clipping, Margaret Spencer, "EB's Prentice Days," EB Scrapbook, Harvard.

54. *The Wide West* (San Francisco), June 17, 1855: 2.

55. Koon, 100; *San Francisco Daily Evening News*, June 9 (2), 15 (3), July 10 (3), 1855; *Daily Alta California* (San Francisco), July 30, 1855: 3; *Mountain Democrat* (Placerville, California), June 9 (2), 16 (2), 1855; *Georgetown Weekly News* (Georgetown, California), June 14 (2), 21 (2), 1855; Clipping, "Talk about Booth," *Buffalo Commercial*, June 7, 1893, Scrapbook. Tributes of the Press to EB Memorial Notices collected by The Players, 1893, collected by William Cushing Bamburgh, Dec. 9, 1902, Hampden-Booth.

56. Koon, 116; *Daily Placer Times and Transcript* (San Francisco), Sept. 8 (2), Nov. 29 (2), 1854, July 29 (2), Nov. 8 (2), 24 (2), 26 (2), Dec. 8(2), 13 (2), 1855; *The Nevada Journal*, Nov. 10 (2), 17 (1) 1854; *Sacramento Daily Union*, Aug. 4 (2), 7 (2), 8 (3), 1855; *Daily Alta California* (San Francisco), Aug. 18 (1), Oct. 5 (1, 2, 3), 6 (3), 24 (3), 1855; *The Marysville Herald*, Sept. 11 (2), 25 (2), 27 (2) 1855; *New-York Daily Times*, Apr. 23 (5), Oct. 15(2), 31 (1), 1855; Clipping, Sacramento Theatre, Aug. 28, 1855, Tennessee.

57. McCloskey, "The Earlier Life of EB": xviii; *Sacramento Daily Record-Union*, Oct. 31, 1876: 3; *Sacramento Daily Record-Union*, Apr. 8, 1887: 3.

58. *Sacramento Daily Union*, Nov. 6 (2), Dec. 10 (2), 13 (2), 17 (3), 21 (2), 29 (3) 1855; Clippings: McCloskey, "How I Met EB," and "The Earlier Life of EB," EB Scrapbook, NYPLPA.

59. MacMinn, 162; *Daily Placer Times and Transcript* (San Francisco), July 2 (3), Aug. 21 (2), Dec. 13 (3), 1855; *Daily Alta California* (San Francisco), July 4, 1855: 3, Feb. 12 1856: 2; *California Chronicle* (San Francisco), Jan. 1 (1), Mar. 1 (3) 1856; *San Francisco Daily Evening News*, Jan. 14 (3), 15 (2, 3), 19 (3), 1856; *The Chicago Tribune*, Apr. 27, 1879: 7; *The New York Dramatic Mirror*, Sept. 13, 1890: 5.

60. *San Francisco Daily Evening News*, Jan. 19 (2), 26 (2), 1856; *Marysville Daily Herald*, Jan. 24 (2), 30 (2), 1856; *Daily Alta California* (San Francisco), June 1, 1856: 1; Clipping, Sedley, "The Booths—Father and Son," NYPLPA.

61. *The North Californian* (Oroville, California), Feb. 9, 1856: 2.

62. *Evening Bulletin* (San Francisco), Feb. 18 (2), May 5 (2), 6 (2, 3), 8 (2), May 10 (2)1856; *Sacramento Daily Union*, Apr. 18 (3), 26 (3), 28 (3), May 1 (3), 1856; *San Francisco Daily Evening News*, Aug. 16, 1855: 3; McCloskey, "How I Met Edwin Booth," NYPLPA.

63. H. P. Davis, *Gold Rush Days in Nevada City* (Nevada City, California: Berliner & McGinnis, 1948), 58; Winter, *Life and Art*, 18; *New-York Daily Times*, Mar. 31, 1852: 1; May 17 (1), Aug. 14 (8), 1856; *California Chronicle* (San Francisco), Feb. 2, 1854: 2; *The Placer Press* (Auburn, California), June 9, 1855: 2; *Mountain Democrat* (Placerville), June 30, 1855: 2; *Sacramento Daily Union*, May 31 (2), June 1 (2), 2 (3), 5 (2), 6 (2), July 2 (2), 1856 *Nevada Democrat* (Nevada, California), July 9, 1856: 2; *Evening Bulletin* (San Francisco), July

10 (3), 11 (1), 21 (2), 1856; *The Placer Herald* (Auburn, California), July 12, 1856: 2; *The Nevada Journal* (Nevada, California), July 18, 1856: 2, 3; *Placer Press* (Auburn, California), July 26, 1856: 3; *Frank Leslie's Illustrated Newspaper* (New York), Sept. 20, 1858: 227.

64. *Sacramento Daily Union*, Apr. 18 (3), May 31 (3), Aug. 19 (3), 1856.

65. Watermeier, *Between Actor and Critic*, 135; J. Alan Hammack, "An American Actor's Diary—1858," *Educational Theatre Journal*, VII (Dec., 1955): 324, 325; *Sacramento Daily Union*, May 29, 1856: 2; Clippings: Charles Pope, "The Eccentric Booths," *New York Sun*, Mar. 28, 1897, Sedley, "The Booths—Father and Son," NYPLPA.

66. Rumors persisted throughout Booth's life that the family had "a strain of Jewish blood." Titone, 23; *Sacramento Daily Union*, Sept. 1 (3), 2 (3), 1856; *The New York Dramatic Mirror*, Oct. 26, 1889: 2.

67. EB to McE, Jan. 9, 1876, Hampden-Booth; Alexander Liholiho, *Journal of the voyages made to the United States, England and France*, typed manuscript, Hawaiian collection, Hamilton Library, University of Hawaii, n.p.; Clarke, 145; Holliday, *The World Rushed In*, 418; Kemble, *Panama Route*, 195, 227; John Haskell Kemble, ed, *Gold Rush Steamers* (The Book Club of California, 1958), 9; Minter, 283; Perez-Venero, *Before the Five Frontiers: Panama from 1821–1903*: 61, 68, 98, 278–281; Schott, 11; *Marysville Daily Herald* (Marysville, California), Feb. 20, 1854: 2; *Daily California Chronicle* (San Francisco), Feb. 21, 1854: 1; *New-York Daily Times*, Feb. 9 (1), Mar. 2 (1), 7 (2), Apr. 21 (4), 1855; May 1 (1), 17 (1) 1856; *Daily Alta California* (San Francisco), Aug. 17 (1), 20 (2), Sept. 3 (2), 5 (2), 6 (2), 1856; *Star and Herald* (Panama): Sept. 18 (1), 20 (2), 1856; *The Chicago Tribune*, Apr. 27, 1879: 7.

68. Shirt Tail Canyon and Lone Gulch Shirt-Tail Hill both existed, but Cock-Tail Canyon appears to be imaginary and a reference to Booth's drinking. EB to McE, Dec. 24, 1875, to David C. Anderson, Sept. 16 1879, Dec. 17, 1880, Hampden-Booth; Edwin G. Gudde, *California Gold Camps* (Berkeley, California: University of California Press, 1975), 198, 318; Grossman, 196, 215–218; Oggel, *Bio-Bibliography*, 58; *San Francisco Theatrical Research*, 117; Watermeier, *Between Actor and Critic*, 35–36; Winter, *Life and Art*, 17; Clipping, WW, "Booth in California," *Tribune*, Aug. 24, 1902, Folger.

Chapter Four

1. Shattuck, 10; *Frank Leslie's Illustrated Newspaper* (New York), Aug. 2, 1856: 119; Clippings: "Booth's First Manager," Columbia; "Stories of Booth," EB collection, NYPLPA.

2. Clarke, 145; Winter, *Life and Art*, 20; *Frank Leslie's Illustrated Newspaper* (New York), Aug. 9 (131), Sept. 6 (199), Nov. 1 (323), 1856; *Daily Alta California* (San Francisco), Sept. 3, 1856: 2; *Boston Evening Transcript*, Sept. 8 (3), 16 (3), 19 (3), 29 (3), Oct. 6 (3), 21 (3), Dec. 15 (3), 20 (3), 1856; Feb. 2 (3), Mar. 9 (3), 30 (3), Apr. 25 (3), 1857; *New-York Daily Times*, Sept. 29, 1856: 8; *The Sun* (Baltimore), Oct. 15 (3), 23 (3) 1856; *The Daily Baltimore Republican*, Oct. 15, 1856: 3; Clipping, "Stories of Booth," EB collection, NYPLPA.

3. George Kunkel to J.T. Ford, Feb. 27, 1858, John Ford Sollers, *The Theatrical Career of John T. Ford* (Diss. Stanford University, 1962): 70.

4. Shattuck, 10; *New York Clipper*, Oct. 15, 1856: 215; *Evening Star* (Washington), Nov. 18, 1856: 3; *Richmond Daily Dispatch* as quoted in *Spirit of the Times* (New York), Dec. 20, 1856: 537; *The Daily Picayune* Afternoon Edition (New Orleans), Mar. 17, 1857: 2; *Spirit of the Times* (New York), Mar. 21 (62), May 2 (133), 9 (145, 156), 1857.

5. *The Cincinnati Daily Commercial*, Feb. 4, 1857: 2; *The Daily Picayune* (New Orleans), Mar. 21, 1857: 3; *Boston Evening Transcript*, Mar. 24, 1858: 2.

6. *The Daily Picayune* (New Orleans), Jan. 18, 1859: 4; *The Albion* (New York), Mar. 23, 1867: 139.

7. Shattuck, 11; *Boston Evening Transcript*, Apr. 23, 1857: 2; *Rochester Union and Advertiser*, Nov. 9, 1857:3; Clipping, no place, n.d. [circa 1858], Melvin Scrapbook, Hampden-Booth.

8. EB to Robert C. Davis Esq., June 7, 1870, Simon Gratz Collection, The Historical Society of Pennsylvania; to H. B. Bult, July 29, 1881, Folger; to LB, Oct. 11, 1882, Princeton; Stephen Van Dulken, *Inventing the 19th Century* (New York: New York University Press, 2001), 20–21; Grossman, 281; ECS, "EB," *The Atlantic Monthly*, Vol. 17, 99 (1866): 590; *The New-York Daily Times*, Dec. 27, 1852: 6; *Spirit of the Times* (New York), Oct. 16, 1858: 432; *The Daily Picayune* (New Orleans), Jan. 19, 1859: 4; *The New York Clipper*, Sept. 10, 1859: 166; Clipping, Charles Pike Sawyer, "The Mirror of the Stage," EB Collection, NYPLPA.

9. Adam Badeau to EB, Nov. 12, 1859, Launt Thompson to EB, Feb. 23, 1864, Hampden-Booth; Oggel, *Letters and Notebooks of Mary Devlin* (New York: Greenwood Press, 1987), 26, 30; *The New York Clipper*, Sept. 17, 1859: 174; Clipping, "Celebrities at Home," n.d. Scrapbook, 1880–1881, Hampden-Booth.

10. *Buffalo Morning Express and Daily Democracy*, Nov. 16 (2), 28 (2), 1857; *Buffalo Daily Courier*, Nov. 19 (3), 21 (3), 27 (3). 28 (3), 1857; *Chicago Daily Tribune*, June 2, 1858: 1.

11. *New York Clipper*, Dec. 27, 1856: 287, Apr. 25 (3), May 2 (15), 9 (23), 1857; *The Mobile Daily Register*, Mar. 14, 1857: 3; Clippings: Hill, "Personal Recollections of EB," EB Scrapbook, NYPLPA, *Porter's Spirit of the Times*, Dec. 19, no year [1856], Scrapbook, *Journal Book No. 2*, Hampden-Booth.

12. Hammack: 324, 325.

13. EB to Joseph Jefferson, Apr. 26, 1858, Hampden-Booth. The letter is transcribed in Asia Booth Clarke, *The Unlocked Door* (New York: Faber and Faber, 1938), 17, 194, 195, 196.

14. EB to Junius Brutus Booth Jr., n.d. [late Mar. 1858], Texas; *Spirit of the Times* (New York), Apr. 18, 1857: 109; *The Chicago Tribune*, Apr. 27, 1879: 7; *The New York Dramatic Mirror*, Sept. 20, 1890: 3; Clippings: "Some Stories of Booth," EB Collection, Hill, "Personal Recollections of EB," EB Scrapbook, NYPLPA; "Booth's First Manager," Columbia.

15. EB to Junius Brutus Booth Jr., [circa July 4, 1858], Harvard.

16. EB to Wright," July 23, 1858, Special Collections, Washington University Libraries, Washington University in St. Louis; "Dear Write," July 29, 1858, Folger; Watermeier, *Between Actor and Critic*, 18.

17. *Boston Evening Transcript*, Apr. 28, 1857: 2; *Republican Banner* (Nashville), Mar. 19, 1859: 3.

18. John C. Burnham, *Bad Habits* (New York: New York University Press, 1993), 51; Watermeier, *Between Actor and Critic*, 31; *Daily Evening Transcript* (Boston), Sept. 25, 1857: 2; *Spirit of the Times* (New York), Feb. 6, 1858: 614.

19. EB to Walter Brackett, Feb. 6, 1859, Texas; *Daily Cincinnati Gazette*, Nov. 23, 1858: 2; Apr. 12 (2), 13 (2), 16 (2), 1860.

20. EB to Junius Brutus Booth, Jr., Oct. 31, 1858, Harvard; Richmond Croom Beatty, *Bayard Taylor: Laureate of the Gilded Age* (Norman, Oklahoma: University of Oklahoma Press, 1936), 105; Clarke, 148; Winter, *Life and Art*: 21; Watermeier, *Between Actor and Critic*: 30; *Boston Evening Transcript*, Apr. 21 (2), 22 (2) 1857; *The Spirit of the Times* (New York), Apr. 25 (1), May 2 (133) 1857; *Boston Advertiser*, in *Rochester Union and Advertiser*, Nov. 9, 1857: 3.

21. Agreement between EB and William Burton, Apr. 18, 1857, Hampden-Booth; EB to Harry [Magonigle], Nov. 14, 1874, in Robert Cohen, "Booth Notes," n.p, University of California, Irvine; *New York Daily-Times*, May 1 (3), 16 (5) 1857; *The New York Herald*, May 5 (3), 11(4), 1857; *Frank Leslie's Illustrated Newspaper* (New York), May 13, 1876: 157.

22. Shattuck, 17; *New York Clipper*, June 6 (54), 27 (7) 1857.
23. The sketch for *Richelieu* appears on the back of a collection of poetry written by C. M. Keteltas and can be found in the file of Kelteltas letters to Booth in the Hampden-Booth library. Playbill, May 8, 1857, Rea Scrapbook, NYPLPA; John E. Owens to EB, Oct. 24, 1859, Hampden-Booth; Ireland, 2, 670; LB, "EB," 62; *Spirit of the Times* (New York), July 11 (264), Aug. 29 (318), Sept. 5 (360), 1857; *New York Clipper*, Aug. 29 (150), Sept. 5 (158), 1857; *The New-York Daily Times*, Aug. 31 (6), Sept. 1 (4), 7 (7), 8 (3, 6), 9 (5, 7), 10 (7), 11 (7), 12 (6), 17 (7), 19 (8), 21 (5), 26 (8), 30 (7), 1857.
24. Clipping, "Theatrical Matters," Rea Collection, NYPLPA.
25. *New-York Daily Tribune*, Sept. 2, 1857: 6.
26. E. Douglas Branch, *The Sentimental Years* (New York: Hill and Wang: [1934] 1966), 31; *Rochester Union and Advertiser*, Nov. 9, 1857:3; *Buffalo Daily Courier*, Nov. 17, 1857: 3; *Spirit of the Times* (New York), Jan. 30 (612), Apr. 10 (108), 1858; *Republican Banner* (Nashville, Tennessee), Feb. 2, 1868: 3; *The Charleston Daily Courier*, Feb. 22, 1858: 2; *The New York Herald*, Apr. 6, 1858: 7; *The Albion* (New York), Apr. 10 (176), 17 (188), 1858; *New York Clipper*, Apr. 10 (407), Nov. 13 (239), 1858.
27. *New-York Daily Times*, Apr. 30, 1855: 4; *New York Herald*, Aug. 30, 1857: 7; *New York Dramatic News*, July 15, 1876: 6; Clipping, *Spirit of the Times* (New York), Oct. 7, 1858, EB Collection, NYPLPA.
28. EB to Walter Brackett, June 22, 23, 1858, Texas; *Spirit of the Times* (New York), Jan. 2, 1858: 564; *New York Clipper*, May 1 (14), July 31 (119), 1858.
29. EB to Walter Brackett, June 11, n.d. [late 1850s], Texas; John Rhodehamel and Louise Taper, "*Right or Wrong, God Judge Me*," *The Writings of John Wilkes Booth* (Urbana: U of Illinois Press, 1997), 42.
30. EB to Junius Brutus Booth, Jr., Oct. 31, 1858, Harvard.
31. EB to "Dear Walter," [Brackett], Jan. 30, 1859, Texas.
32. On July 2, 1859, Joseph, under the stage name Joseph Adrian, appeared in a minor role in *The Iron Chest* along with Edwin at the Front Street Theatre in Baltimore. By Nov. 1861 he was studying medicine, an attempt he abandoned only to pick it up again in later life. Asia Booth to Jean Anderson, no month, no day, 1854, Nov. 16, 1861, Maryland; EB to Junius Brutus Booth Jr., n.d. [late Mar. 1858], Texas; to Junius Brutus Booth Jr., Dec. 12, 1858, Harvard; *The Sun* (Baltimore), June 1, 1859: 2.
33. EB to Junius Brutus Booth, Jr., Dec. 12, 1858, Harvard.
34. EB to "My dear Walter," [Brackett], Feb. 6, 1859, Texas.
35. *Boston Evening Transcript*, Nov. 1, 1859: 2; *The New York Clipper*, Nov. 19 (247), Dec. 3 (263), 1859; *The Spirit of the Times*, Nov. 5, 1859: 463; *Public Ledger* (Philadelphia), Aug. 29, 1859: 1.

Chapter Five

1. Bispham: 243, Bamburgh, Harvard; Badeau: 261.
2. EB to David C. Anderson, n.d. [circa Dec., 1857], Hampden-Booth; to WW, Apr. 27, 1879, Folger; Paul Lewis, *Queen of the Plaza: A Biography of Adah Isaacs Menken* (New York: Funk & Wagnalls, 1964), 109; Watermeier, *Between Actor and Critic*, 129; *The Memphis Daily Appeal*, Dec. 22, 1857: 3; *Nashville Daily Gazette*, Jan. 31 (2), Feb. 2 (3), 1858; *The Louisville Daily Journal*, Dec. 6 (3), 7 (3), 8 (3), 9 (3), 10 (3), 11 (3), 13 (3), 14 (3), 15 (3), 18 (3), 1858; *Louisville Daily Courier*, Dec. 6 (2) 1858; *The Chicago Tribune*, Apr. 27, 1879: 7; Clipping, "Some Stories of Booth," EB Collection, NYPLPA.
3. Jonathan Ned Katz has suggested that "Oriental" also had connotations of homosexual practices. While there is no indication that the people who describe Booth's appearance as "Oriental" intended this inference, Booth's "Oriental" good looks gave him a soft romantic appearance that was particularly appealing to women. Jonathan Ned Katz, *Love Stories: Sex between Men before Homosexuality* (Chicago: The University of Chicago Press, 2001), 207; Joel Myerson and Daniel Shealy, *The Selected Letters of Louisa May Alcott* (Boston: Little, Brown and Company, 1987), xlv, 39, 47.
4. Edith [last name unknown] to EB, Feb. 4, 1866, Hampden-Booth.
5. M.E.P. to EB, Jan. 13, 1865, Adele [last name unknown] to EB, Mar. 22, 1865, Hampden-Booth; Oggel, *Bio-Bibliography*, 18; Clippings: "Booth Relics Sold," *Herald*, Dec. 17, 1901, "Relics of EB Sold," *Sun*, Dec. 17, 1901, Folger.
6. *New Orleans Daily Crescent*, quoted in *Rochester Union and Advertiser*, Nov. 9, 1857: 3.
7. Program, Boston Theatre, May 4, 1857, Rare Books Department, Boston Public Library; *Boston Evening Transcript*, May 1, 1857: 2; *Spirit of the Times* (New York), May 9, 1857: 145.
8. Shattuck, 30; Peter Gay, *Schnitzler's Century* (New York: W. W. Norton & Company, 2002), 76.
9. EB to Junius Brutus Booth, Jr., Oct. 31, Dec. 12, 1858, Harvard; Shattuck, 30, 31; *The New York Herald*, Aug. 2, 1858: 7.
10. For information about Josephine Orton see Barry B. Witham, ed. *Theatre in the United States: A Documentary History*, I, *1750–1915: Theatre in the Colonies and United States* (Cambridge: Cambridge UP, 1996), 177; *New-York Daily Times*, Oct. 16, 1856: 5, Aug. 17, 1857: 6; *Boston Evening Transcript*, Sept. 7, 1860: 3, Apr. 10, 1865: 3; *The New York Clipper*, Sept. 10, 1864: 174, Aug. 4, 1866: 134, July 13, 1867: 110, Oct. 24, 1868: 230, May 15 (46), June 29 (86), 1869, Feb. 26, 1870: 374; *The Philadelphia Inquirer*, Oct. 3, 1864: 8; *Public Ledger* (Philadelphia), May 10 (1), Sept. 28 (1), 1866; Apr. 16, 1867: 1; *New York Dramatic News*, July 29, 1876: 5; Josephine Orton Clipping Collection, Harvard.
11. Adam Badeau to EB, Oct. 7, 1858, Hampden-Booth.
12. Jervis McEntee, Diary, Feb. 7, 1879, Smithsonian.
13. EB to Walter Brackett, June 22, 1858, Texas.
14. Joseph Jefferson, "In Memory of EB," *Modern Eloquence*, 692.
15. John Sleeper Clarke to EB, Mar. 7, 1863, EB to EBG, n.d. [Feb. 2, 1886], n.d. [Jan. 15, 1891 penciled in], NYPLPA; Program, Howard Athenaeum, May 17, 1855, extra-illustrated edition of Copeland, 50f, Harvard; Oggel, *Letters*; *Wilkes' Spirit of the Times* (New York), July 21, 1860: 320; *The New York Dramatic Mirror*, Feb. 23 (14), Mar. 26 (14), Apr. 20 (14), 1901.
16. *Richmond Enquirer*, Sept. 5 (3), 9 (2), 26 (2), Oct. 7 (2), 24 (2), 31 (3), Nov. 7 (3), 18 (2), 21 (3), 1856; *Daily Dispatch* (Richmond), Sept. 11 (1), Nov. 3 (2), 4 (2), 6 (1) 17 (2), 24 (2), 25 (2), 1856; Jefferson, 691.
17. Joseph Jefferson to John T. Ford, n.d. [Fall 1857], Ford papers, LC; Oggel, *Bio-Bibliography*, 13; *Richmond Enquirer*, Dec. 5, 1856: 2, 3; *Daily Dispatch* (Richmond), Dec. 30, 1856: 2; *Spirit of the Times* (New York), Mar. 14, 1857: 50.
18. Adam Badeau to The Adjt. Genl. Of the Army, Oct. 30, 1865, Badeau papers, National Archives; Henry Adams, *The Education of Henry Adams* (New York: The Modern Library, 1996), 263; politicalgraveyard.com/bio/baczkowski-baile.
19. Adam Badeau to EB, May 17, no year [1857], Hampden-Booth.
20. Adam Badeau to EB, June 15, 1857, Hampden-Booth.
21. EB to Adam Badeau, n.d. extra-illustrated edition, Copeland: 78f, Harvard; to Walter Brackett, Feb. 6, 1859, Texas; Adam Badeau to EB, Apr. 14, no year [1860], Hampden-Booth.
22. Shattuck, 19; *New-York Daily Times*, Dec. 1, 1856: 4.
23. Ann Douglas, *The Feminization of American Culture*

(New York: Alfred A. Knopf, 1977), 17; Katz, 165; *The Sun* (Baltimore), Jan. 11 (1), Feb. 5 (1), 1850; *The Spirit of the Times* (New York) Apr. 12, 1859: 90, Apr. 13, 1861: 150; *The New-York Times*, Aug. 22, 1860: 1.

24. For further references of the expression of love between same-sex friends see Mary Devlin Booth to Emma Cushman, n.d. [mid–Nov., 1862], Taper Collection; B. C. to Mr. EB, May 17, 1859, John B. Murray to EB, May 23, 1863, Dec. 2, 1867, EB to Richard Stoddard, Nov. 19, 1863, to Charles Carryl, Oct. 15, 1890, Ferdinand Ewer to EB, Dec. 17, 1878, Lucius Hart to EB, May 28, 1881, Hampden-Booth; to Mary Anderson, Feb. 26, 1883, Rochester; to Horace Howard Furness], June 17, 1888, Pennsylvania; Grossman, 139; Carroll Smith-Rosenberg, *Disorderly Conduct*, 27, 56; Katz, 144, 242, 39; Davis S. Reynolds, *Walt Whitman's America: A Cultural Biography* (New York: Vintage Books, 1996), 396, 397; Douglas, 20; Gay, 54, 66, 67; Susan Lee Johnson, *Roaring Camp The Social World of the California Gold Rush* (New York: W. W. Norton & Company, 2000), 159.

25. Nora Titone contends that "Badeau had ... an openness about his homosexuality that was rare in nineteenth-century New York." There is no evidence for "openness." For further possible nineteenth-century homosexual references, see Adam Badeau to EB, n.d. [after May 17, 1859], Apr. 5, 14, 18, no year [1860], Hampden-Booth; Douglas, *The Feminization of American Culture*, 18; Johnson, 171, Titone, 172.

26. For information on Mary Devlin's career see Oggel, *Letters*, x; *New York Clipper*, Aug. 1, 1857: 118; Feb. 2, 1858: 359; *The Sun* (Baltimore), Nov. 17 (2), Dec. 7 (2), 11 (2) 16 (2), 21 (2), 23 (2), 24 (2), 28 (2), 1857, Jan. 9, 1858: 2; *American and Commercial Advertiser* (Baltimore), Jan. 1 (3), Mar. 12 (2), 15 (2), 16 (2), 17 (2), 19 (2), 20 (2), 1858; *Spirit of the Times* (New York), Feb. 20, 1858:24.

27. EB to Junius Brutus Booth, n.d. [late Mar. 1858], Texas.

28. For further information on EB and Mary Devlin in 1858 see EB to Junius Brutus Booth, n.d. [late Mar. 1858], to Walter Brackett, May 13, no year [1858], Texas; Asia Booth to Jean Anderson, Oct. 11, 1853, Maryland; Boston Theatre Programs, May 31-June 11, 1858, Rare Books Department, Boston Public Library; Oggel, *Letters*, x; Winter, *Life and Art*, 23; Hammack: 328; *The Sun* (Baltimore), Apr. 6 (2), 9 (2), 14 (2), 17 (2), 19 (2), 23 (2), 24 (3), 26 (2), 28 (2), 29 (2), 30 (2), May 1 (2), 5 (2), 6 (2), 11 (2), 14 (2), 15 (2), 1858; *The New-York Times*, June 22 (3), 24 (3), 28 (3), 30 (6), 1858; *Spirit of the Times* (New York), June 26, 1858: 240; Clipping, "Letter from 'Acorn,'" *Spirit of the Times*, c. June 7, 1858, Jean Davenport, Frederick Lander papers, LC.

29. Emma C. Cushman, "Charlotte Cushman: A Memory": 1, 2, Biographical Data, XV, Clipping, "Mr. E. C. Cushman Jr. Married," Family Members, Cushman Papers, Manuscript Division, LC.

30. John T. Ford to My dear Sir, [no name], July 16, no year [1858], Ford papers, Manuscripts, LC.

31. EB to Walter Brackett, June 2, 1858, Texas.

32. EB to Walter Brackett, June 22, 1858, Texas; Oggel, *Letters*, xii.

33. *Spirit of the Times* (New York), July 10, 1864: 264.

34. For information on the performances of Mary Devlin, Josephine Orton and EB at the Boston Theatre company see Boston Theatre Programs, Sept. 15-June 7, 1859, Boston Public Library; Program, Boston Theatre, Oct. 29, 1858, extra-illustrated edition of Copeland, 50f, Program, Boston Theatre, Oct. 26, 1858, Broadside, "EB will appear at the National Theatre!" n.d. [1856], extra-illustrated edition, Matthews and Hutton, V, pt. 2, Harvard; *Boston Evening Transcript*, Sept. 11 (3), 17 (3), Oct. 4 (3) 13 (3), 18 (3), 25 (3), 26 (3) 27 (3), 29 (2), Nov. 2 (3), 4 (3), 8 (3), 16 (3), 23 (3), 26 (3), 1858; *Spirit of the Times* (New York), Feb. 12 (12), Mar. 5 (38), 1859; Mar. 17, 1860: 63.

35. Playbill, Boston Theatre, Nov. 2, 1858, Folger; EB to Walter Brackett, Jan. 30, 1859, Texas; to EBG, n.d. [June 24, 1888 penciled in], NYPLPA; *The New York Times*, Dec. 23, 1919: 9.

36. EB to Walter Brackett, Feb. 6, 1859, Texas; Adam Badeau to EB, n.d. [after May 17, 1859], n.d. [Spring 1859], Apr. 14, no year [1860], Hampden-Booth; Cohen, Booth-notes, 44; Shattuck, 21, 22; Badeau: 255–67; *The Albion* (New York), May 23, 1857: 248; *The New-York Times*, Jan. 5 (5), July 30 (3), 1858; *The Charleston Mercury*, Mar. 30, 1859: 1.

37. Adam Badeau to EB, Apr. 14, no year [1859], Hampden-Booth.

38. Oggel, *Letters*, 4, 5.

39. Adam Badeau to EB, Apr. 21, 1859, Hampden-Booth.

40. Asia Booth Clarke to Jean Anderson, Thursday, Aug. 1859, Hampden-Booth; Oggel, *Letters*, 5; *The New York Clipper*, July 9, 1859: 94.

41. C. Dallett Hemphill, *Bowing to Necessities: A History of Manners in America, 1620–1860* (New York: Oxford University Press, 1999), 191.

42. Asia Booth Clarke to Jean Anderson, Thursday, Aug., 1859, Hampden-Booth; Oggel, *Letters*, 5, 6, 10, 12, 38; *The Albion* (New York), Feb. 28, 1863: 103.

43. EB to Dr. and Mrs. Beale, July 26, 1859, Folger; Oggel, *Letters*, xiii; Shattuck, 31.

44. EB to My dear Walter [Brackett], Sept. 12, 1859, Harvard.

45. G. J. Baker-Benfield, *The Horrors of the Half-Known Life* (New York: Harper & Row, 1976), 198.

46. Asia Booth to Jean Anderson, Sept. 10, 1856, Thursday 1860 [incorrectly labeled, actually four months after she was married on Apr. 28, 1859], n.d. [Fall 1859], Mar. 7, 1860, Feb. 9, 1862, Maryland; Oggel, *Letters*, xii, 7, 9, 10; *The New York Herald*, Feb. 22, 1863: 8.

47. Oggel, *Letters*, 11, 16.

48. Oggel, *Letters*, 20, 45; "The Break between Player & Poet," *The New York Herald*, Nov. 1, 1903: 2.

49. Lystra, 39; Oggel, *Letters*, 15, 16. 21.

50. Adam Badeau, *The Vagabond*, 1859.

51. Adam Badeau to EB, Jan. 28, no year [1860], Hampden-Booth; Oggel, *Letters*, 18, 27, 28, 36, 46; Shattuck, 35.

52. Carl Bode, *The Anatomy of American Popular Culture 1840–1861* (Berkeley: University of California Press, 1959), 82; Grossman, 73; Oggel, *Letters*, 7, 8, 31, 47; Shattuck, 32; *New-York Daily Times*, June 6, 1855: 5.

53. Grossman, 25.

54. Oggel, *Bio-Bibliography*, 13; Carroll Smith-Rosenberg, *Disorderly Conduct* (New York: Alfred A. Knopf, 1985), 13, 25; Marilyn Yalom, *A History of the Wife* (New York: HarperCollins Publishers, 2002), 189, 202; Elizabeth Reitz Mullenix, "So Unfemininely Masculine": Discourse, True/False Womanhood and the American Career of Fanny Kemble," *Theatre Survey*, 40, 2 (Nov. 1999): 27.

55. Shattuck, 28.

56. Adam Badeau to EB, Apr. 5, no year [1860], Hampden-Booth.

57. Adam Badeau to EB, Apr. 22, 1860, n.d. [May 8, 1860], May 12, no year, May 17, no year, Hampden-Booth.

58. Nora Titone writes that "John Wilkes was the only member of the Booth family who agreed to be a witness." I have found no evidence that anyone else in the Booth family was invited. EB to Walter Brackett, Feb. 10, no year [1860], Texas; R. S. Chilton to EB, Dec. 17, 1860, Hampden-Booth; Mabel Osgood Foreght to WW, July 7, 1893, in Winter, *Life and Art*, Folger; Shattuck, 29; Titone, 13; Yalom, 198; Adam Badeau: 263.

59. Asia Booth Clarke to Jean Anderson, Aug. 21, 1860, Maryland; Oggel, *Letters*, 14; Winter, *Life and Art*, 22; Adam Badeau: 263; *The New York Clipper*, July 14, 1860: 102.

60. Mrs. Thomas Bailey Aldrich, *Crowding Memories* (Boston: Houghton Mifflin Company, 1920), 8.

61. Asia Booth Clarke to Jean Anderson, Oct. 28, 1860, Maryland.

Chapter Six

1. Adam Badeau to EB, n.d. [May 1860], Hampden-Booth; Henry Adams, *The Education of Henry Adams* (New York: The Modern Library, 1996), 264; Aldrich, *Crowding Memories*, 25, 28; Humble, ed., 7; Oggel, *Letters*, 99; Ellen M. Plante, *Women at Home in Victorian America* (New York: Facts on File, Inc: 1997), 32; Shattuck, 28.
2. Oggel, *Letters*, 11, 30.
3. Grossman, 132–133.
4. EB to Junius Brutus Booth Jr., Dec. 12, 1858, Harvard; Adam Badeau to EB, Apr. 14, no year [1860], Apr. 18, no year [1860], Apr. 22, 1860, Hampden-Booth; Oggel, *Letters*, 46; *The New York Clipper*, Nov. 30, 1861: 263.
5. EB to My dear Sir, Dec. 9, 1860, Folger.
6. EB to John T. Ford, Nov. 14, 1860, Ford Papers, LC; Edwin Duerr, *The Length and Depth of Acting* (New York: Holt, Rinehart and Winston, 1963), 363 as quoted in John Perry, *James A. Herne: The American Ibsen* (Chicago: Nelson-Hall, 1978), 8; *New York Clipper*, Nov. 3, 1860: 231.
7. EB, to John T. Ford, Nov. 8, 14, 1860, Ford Papers, LC, to LB, n.d. [1860], Hampden-Booth.
8. *The New-York Times*, Apr. 12, 1858: 4.
9. EB to Harry Magonigle, Nov. 14, 1874, in Robert Cohen, "Booth Notes," n.p.
10. EB to LB, n.d. [1860], Nov. 21, 1860, Jan. 9, 1861, Hampden-Booth; *The Spirit of the Times* (New York), Jan. 28 (612), June 16 (228), Sept. 8 (360), Oct. 27 (464), 1860; *The New York Clipper*, Sept. 3 (4), 10 (7), 1860; Mar. 31, 1866: 406; *New York Dramatic News*, Sept. 16, 1876: 7; *The New-York Times*, Mar. 21, 1895: 5.
11. EB to LB," Nov. 21, 1860, Jan. 9, 1861, n.d. [1860], Hampden-Booth.
12. *New York Evening Express*, Nov. 26, 1860: 1; *The New-York Times*, Nov. 27, 1860: 1; *New York Morning Express*, Nov. 27, 1860: 2; *Frank Leslie's Illustrated Newspaper* (New York), Dec. 8, 1860: 35.
13. *The New-York Times*. Nov. 26 (5), 27 (1), 1860: 5; *New-York Daily Tribune*, Nov. 27, 1860: 5.
14. *The Evening Post* (New York), Dec. 6, 1860: 2; *The New-York Times*, Dec. 1, 1860: 4. Oct. 18, 1862: 7.
15. *New-York Tribune*, Dec. 7, 1860: 1, 7; *The New-York Times*, Dec. 7, 1860: 4, Apr. 18, 1861: 5; *The Evening Post* (New York), Dec. 6, 1860: 2.
16. Grossman, 133, 134.
17. *The Evening Post* (New York), Dec. 4, 1860: 2; *The New-York Times*, Dec. 10 (5), 17 (5), 20 (4, 5), 1860: 5; Jan. 21, 1861: 7; *New York Clipper*, Dec. 22, 1860: 286; *New York Morning Express*, Dec. 20, 1860: 2; *The New-York Daily Tribune*, Dec. 20, 1860: 5.
18. *Frank Leslie's Illustrated Newspaper* (New York), Dec. 13 (51), 29 (83), 1860.
19. M. Wilson Disher, *The Cowells in America* (London: Oxford University Press, 1934), 226, 227.
20. EB to LB, Dec. 23, 1860, Hampden-Booth.
21. EB to LB, Dec. 23, 1860, Hampden-Booth; Grossman, 133, 134; *The New-York Times*, Dec. 10, 1860: 5; *Public Ledger* (Philadelphia), Jan. 1 (3), 2 (2), 8 (3), 10 (3), 11 (3), 1861; *The New York Clipper*, Nov. 21, 1863: 252; Drawing of Forrest as Macbeth, *Edwin Forrest Memorials*, Temple University.
22. *New York Dispatch*, Feb. 9 (5), 16 (5), 1861; *The New-York Times*, Feb. 12 (4), 18 (5), 1861; *New York Clipper*, Feb. 16 (350), 23 (358), 1861.
23. *The Spirit of the Times*, Feb. 23, 1861: 218.
24. *The New-York Daily Tribune*, Dec. 17, 1860: 8; *New York Clipper*, Apr. 27 (14), May 4 (22), 1861: 14.
25. *The New York Clipper*, May 18 (36), June 8 (62), 1861.
26. EB to LB, July 1, 1861, Hampden-Booth.
27. Emma Cary to Mary Devlin Booth, July 15, 1861, Hampden-Booth; EB to John T. Ford, July 19, 1861, Ford Papers, LC, to Walter Brackett, Nov. 3, 1861, Texas; Grossman, 135, 137; Oggel, *Letters*, 51; *New York Daily-Times*, Apr. 30, 1857: 2; *The New York Clipper*, Aug. 31, 1861: 156.
28. Oggel, *Letters*, 51; *Post Office London Directory* (London: Frederic Kelly, 1861), 145.
29. *Post Office London Directory*, 1776; Winter, *Life and Art*, 25; *The Daily Telegraph* (London), Oct. 1, 1861: 2; *The Times* (London), Oct. 1, 1861: 6; *The Daily News* (London), Oct. 1, 1861: 2; *The Detroit Free Press*, Feb. 16, 1868: 3.
30. For information about the critical reaction to Booth's Shylock see *Morning Star and Dial* (London), Oct. 1, 1861: 3; *The Evening Star and Dial* (London), Oct. 1, 1861: 1; *The Times* (London), Oct. 1, 1861: 6; *The Morning Post*, Oct. 2, 1861: 5; *The Literary Gazette* (London), Oct. 5, 1861: 333, 334; *The Illustrated London News*, Oct. 5, 1861: 344; *Bell's Life in London and Sporting Chronicle*, Oct. 6, 1861: 3.
31. Jim Davis and Victor Emeljanow, *Reflecting the Audience: London Theatregoing, 1840–1880* (Iowa City: University of Iowa Press, 2001), 189, 194.
32. *The Daily Telegraph* (London), Oct. 1, 1861: 2; *Sunday Times* (London), Oct. 6, 1861: 3.
33. Oggel, *Letters*, 54.
34. EB to Lorimer Grahman, Oct. 6, 1861, Taper Collection; to Thomas Hicks, Oct. 13, 1861, Hampden-Booth; *The New York Clipper*, Oct. 26, 1861: 223.
35. Mary Devlin Booth to Emma Crow Cushman, Oct. 4, no year [1861], Taper Collection; Oggel, *Bio-Bibligrahy*, 15; Oggel, *Letters*, 56, 79; Clipping, "EB," Sept. 28, 1875, Folger.
36. Cyril Maude *The Haymarket Theatre* (New York: E.P. Dutton & Co., 1903), 143, 144; *Frank Leslie's Illustrated Newspaper* (New York), Sept. 14, 1861: 283; *The Standard* (London), Oct. 8, 1861: 3; *The Illustrated London News*, Oct. 12 (368), Nov. 2 (448), 1861; *John Bull* (London), Oct. 12 (652), Nov. 2 (701) 1861; *Bell's Life in London and Sporting Chronicle*, Oct. 13 (3), Nov. 3 (3), 1861; *Sunday Times*, Oct. 13 (3), 20 (3)1861; *Sunday News* (London), Nov. 3, 1861: 3.
37. *The Illustrated London News*, Nov. 9, 1861: 469; *Bell's Life in London*, Nov. 10, 1861: 3.
38. *The Literary Gazette* (London), Nov. 9, 1861: 455.
39. EB to Thomas Hicks, Oct. 13, 1861, Hampden-Booth.
40. Adam Badeau to Major Charles Graham Halpine, June 30, 1861, Huntington; EB to Walter Brackett, Nov. 3, 1861, Texas.
41. Shattuck, 35.
42. Adam Badeau to EB, Dec. 4, 1862, Hampden-Booth.
43. EB to Adam Badeau, Apr. 12, 1862, Pennsylvania.
44. EB to Walter Brackett, Nov. 3, 1861, Texas; to Lorimer Graham, Jan. 29, 1863, Special Collections Library, The Pennsylvania State University.
45. EB to Lorimer Graham, Dec. 3, no year [1861], to Thomas Hicks], Dec. 9, 1861, Taper Collection.
46. EB to Thomas Hicks, Dec. 9, 1861, Taper Collection; Gay, 47; Stephen M. Frank, *Life with Father* (Baltimore: The Johns Hopkins University Press, 1998), 7.
47. Adam Badeau to EB, Apr. 18, 1861, to Mrs. C. C. Felton, Dec. 12, 1861, to EBG, Feb. 22, 1886, Hampden-Booth; to EwB, June 19, 1873, NYPLPA; to Lorimer Graham, Dec. 9, 1861, Mary Devlin Booth to My darling friend, [Emma Crow Cushman], Jan. 1862, Feb. 26, 1862, Taper Collection; Asia Booth Clarke to Jean Anderson, Feb. 26, 1862, Maryland; Gay, 46; Goodale, 96; Oggel, *Letters*, 56, 62, 75; Winter, *Life and Art*, 23.
48. Asia Booth Clarke to Jean Anderson, Feb. 26, 1862, Maryland; Oggel, *Letters*, 61, 65, 66, 69; Plante, 33.
49. Mary Devlin Booth to Emma Crow Cushman, Jan. 1862, Feb. 26, 1862, Taper Collection; Grossman, 137, 138; Oggel, *Letters*, 66.
50. EB to Lorimer Graham, Mar. 14, 1862, Mary Devlin

Booth to Emma Cushman, Apr. 12, 1862, Taper Collection; Watermeier, *Between Actor and Critic*, 303.
51. EB to Adam Badeau, Apr. 8, 1862, Folger; to Lorimer Graham, May 21, n.d. [1863], Penn State; Bill Hotel des Arts, May 3–9, 1862, NYPLPA; Oggel, *Letters*, 73, 74, 79; Clipping, "EB Dead," *Boston Journal*, June 7, 1893, EB Scrapbook, 2, Harvard.
52. EB to Lorimer Graham, Sept. 5, 1862, Penn State; to G. M. Clayton, "EB Esq.," Apr. 15, 1879, Hampden-Booth; William H. Miller, Jr., *Pictorial Encyclopedia of Ocean Liners 1860–1994* (New York: Dover Publications Inc., 1995), 55; Arnold Kludas, *Record Breakers of the North Atlantic: Blue Ribboned Liners 1838–1952* (Washington D. C.: Brassey's Inc., 1999), 26, 71.
53. EB to Lorimer Graham, Sept. 5, 1862, Penn State; EB to William Henry Huntington, Nov. 18, n.d. [1862], Texas; W. R. Sutton to EB, Jan. 28, 1863, EB to David C. Anderson, Dec. 17, 1880, Hampden-Booth; EB to WW, Sept. 9, 1877, Folger; Grossman, 140; Oggel, *Bio-Bibliography*, 15.

Chapter Seven

1. Richmond Croom Beatty, *Bayard Taylor: Laureate of the Gilded Age* (Norman, Oklahoma: University of Oklahoma Press, 1936), 252, 256, 257; Dumas Malone, ed., *Dictionary of American Biography*, XVIII (New York: Charles Scribner's Sons, 1936), 53, 54, 57–59; *Frank Leslie's Illustrated Newspaper* (New York), June 16, 1877: 255.
2. The Carys were a well-connected Boston family. Cary's sister Elizabeth married the Harvard professor Louis Agassiz, and his sister Mary Louisa married Cornelius Conway Felton, a professor of Greek at Harvard who later became the institution's president (1860–1862). Felton mixed with James Russell Lowell, Henry Wadsworth Longfellow and was one of a party who entertained William Makepeace Thackeray in Boston in Oct. 1852 and in New York in Dec. 1855. Richard Cary to EB, May 20, 1862, Emma Cary to Mary Devlin Booth, Sept. 19, 1862, Hampden-Booth; EB to James Lorimer Graham, Jr., Sept. 5, 1862, Pennsylvania; Mary L. Felton to Mary Devlin Booth, Sept. 7, no year [1862], EBG, footnote to typed manuscript of EB to Emma F. Cary, Mar. 5, 1863, NYPLPA; Richard Carey file, National Archives, LC; Beatty, 182, 256; Branch, 276; Frederick H. Dyer, *A Compendium of the War of the Rebellion* (Wilmington, North Carolina: Broadfoot Publishing Company, 1994), 157, 657, 897, 900, 906, 1248; Gale, 119, 120; Grossman, 134; James B. Hewett, *The Roster of Union Soldiers 1861–1865* (Wilmington, North Carolina: Broadfoot Publishing Company, 1997), 252; Oggel, *Letters*, 47, 80, 83; Pattee, 86; *Boston Evening Transcript*, August 11 (3), 12 (2), 15 (4), 18 (2), 1862.
3. EB to Geo. Karnes, Nov. 8, 1862, Taper Collection; EB to William Henry Huntington, Nov. 18, n.d. [1862], Texas; *New-York Daily Tribune*, Nov. 24, 1862: 3.
4. EB to William Henry Huntington, Nov. 30, 1862, Taper Collection; Oggel, *Letters*, 86.
5. Mary Devlin Booth to Emma Crow Cushman, Dec. 13, 1862, Taper Collection; EB to Elizabeth Stoddard, Dec. 14, 1862, Hampden-Booth; Oggel, *Letters*, 87, 88.
6. EB to Richard Henry Stoddard, n.d. to Richard Henry and Elizabeth Stoddard, January 13, 1863, Hampden-Booth; Oggel, *Letters*, 96–99; www.word-detective.com/081203.html.
7. EB to Richard Henry Stoddard, January 22, 1863, to Elizabeth Stoddard, Feb. 1, no year, Mary Ann Holmes Booth to EB, January 29, 1863, Hampden-Booth; Mary Devlin Booth to Emma Crow Cushman, January 22, no year [1863], Taper Collection; EB to James Lorimer Graham Jr., January 29, 1863, Pennsylvania; Oggel, *Letters*, 101, 103; *Boston Evening Transcript*, January 21, 1863: 3.
8. Grossman, 14, 142–145, 169.
9. Aldrich, *Crowding Memories*, 35; *The New York Herald*, Feb. 10, 1863: 5; *The New-York Times*, Feb. 8 (7), 11 (5), 19 (7), 1863; *The New-York Daily Tribune*, Feb. 16, 1863: 8; *The New York Leader*, Feb. 21, 1863: 5; *The Albion* (New York), Feb. 21, 1863: 91.
10. Aldrich, *Crowding Memories*, 34; Oggel, *Letters*, 105; Florence Marion Howe Hall, "The Friendship of EB and Julia Ward Howe," *New England Magazine* (Nov. 1893): 318, 319; *Boston Evening Transcript*, Feb. 11, 1863: 2.
11. Transcription of Diary of Francis Ware, provided by her great-great grandson Allen MacNeill, Feb. 18, 1863, Hampden-Booth. I am indebted to Michael Morrison for this information.
12. Orlando Tompkins to EB, Feb. 18, 1863, NYPLPA.
13. Erasmus D. Miller to EB, Feb. 19, no year [1863], NYPLPA.
14. Orlando Tompkins to EB, Feb. 19, 1863, NYPLPA; Frances Ware, transcribed Diary, Feb. 20, 1863, Lucy J. Pry to Elizabeth Stoddard, Feb. 21, no year [1863], Hampden-Booth.
15. Frances Ware, transcribed Diary, Feb. 21, 1863, Hampden-Booth.
16. EB to Elizabeth Stoddard, Mar. 11, 1863, Hampden-Booth; to WW, Mar. 15, 1870, Folger.
17. EBG to EBG, n.d. NYPLPA.
18. Frances Ware, transcribed diary, Feb. 22, 23, 1863, Hampden-Booth.
19. EB to Mrs. Charles E. Russell, n.d. Rochester; Junius Brutus Booth, Jr., *Diary*, June 1, 1864, Frances Ware, Diary, transcribed Feb. 27, 1863, Hampden-Booth; Aldrich, *Crowding Memories*, 39, 40; Winter, *Life and Art*, 23, 24, notes on page 24; Ireland, II, 579; *Philadelphia North American and United States Gazette*, Feb. 23 (3), 24 (3), Mar. 2 (2, 3), 1863; *Utica Daily Observer*, Dec. 15, 1877: 1; Clippings: "The Funeral of Mrs. EB," Charlotte Cushman papers, LC; "Booth's Memory Fitly Honored," *New York Herald*, June 10, 1893, Folger.
20. EB to Adam Badeau, July 3, [1863], Folger.
21. Asia Booth Clarke to Jean Anderson, Mar. 3, 1863, Maryland.
22. The Rev. Samuel Osgood to EB, Mar. 3, 1863, Hampden-Booth; EB to the "Rev. Samuel Osgood," Nov. 7, 1863, Folger; Grossman, 1.
23. EB to LB, n.d. [1863], Hampden-Booth.
24. EB to Adam Badeau, n.d. Harvard; John T. Ford to J. B. Wright, June 27, 1863, Ford papers, LC; Grossman, 146; Winter, *Life and Art*, 30.
25. Deed, June 11, 1863, Liber 884: 165, Register's Office, New York, New York; Grossman, 151, 152; "The Break between Player & Poet," *The New York Herald*, Nov. 1, 1903: 2.
26. Adam Badeau to EB, Mar. 8, 1863, Apr. 9, 1863, Hampden-Booth.
27. Ulysses S. Grant to Brig Genl. L. Thomas, May 19, 1863, "Supreme Court of the United States, Nos. 659 and 749," Adam Badeau to Sir, July 29, 1863, Adam Badeau papers, National Archives; *The New York Herald*, June 6, 1863: 3; *The Sunday Mercury* (New York), June 7, 1863; ebay.com, item 530841131.
28. EB to Adam Badeau, June 6, 1863, Hampden-Booth; Adam Badeau to the Adjt Gen. of the Army, Oct. 7, 1863, Dec. 22, 1863, "Surgeon's Certificate for Leave," Oct. 8, 27, 1863, National Archives; *The New-York Times*, June 7, 1963: 1.
29. EB to Adam Badeau, Tuesday, n.d. to Col T. A. Brown, July 28, 1888, Folger; Kenneth T. Jackson and Davis S. Dunbar, eds., *Empire City: New York through the Centuries* (New York: Columbia University Press, 2002), 202; *Philadelphia North American and United States Gazette*, Sept. 10, 1863: 3; *The New York Clipper*, Nov. 28, 1863: 259; Clipping, "Sketch of Charlotte Cushman," General Reviews, Cushman papers, LC.

30. Adam Badeau, "EB on and off the Stage": 264.
31. EB to Adam Badeau, n.d. [after Feb. 1863], Harvard.
32. "The Break between Player & Poet": 2.
33. EB to Capt. A. Badeau, May 18, 1863, Hampden-Booth; to Lorimer Graham, May 21, n.d. [1863], Pennsylvania; Grossman, 147, 148; Leach, *Bright Particular Star*, 323. Clipping, "Life Tragedy of EB," *Sunday Herald*, Nov. 1, 1903, Harvard.
34. Grossman, 141–145.
35. EB to Adam Badeau, n.d. [after Feb. 1863], Harvard; "The Break between Player & Poet": 2.
36. Laura Edmonds to EB, n.d. Hampden-Booth; *The New-York Times*, Dec. 30, 1857: 3; Dec. 22, 1858: 4; Nov. 29, 1859: 4.
37. Laura Edmonds to EB, no month, 25, no year, Hampden-Booth.
38. EB, Adam Badeau, Sept. 13, no year, Folger, Launt Thompson to EB, Sept. 15, 1864, Hampden-Booth.

Chapter Eight

1. EB to Harry Magonigle, Nov. 14, 1874, in Cohen, "Booth Notes," n.p.
2. Agreements between William Stuart, EB and John S. Clarke, Sept. 26, 1863, Jan. 2, 1866, Hampden-Booth.
3. EB to Adam Badeau, Tuesday, n.d. to Col T. A. Brown, July 28, 1888, Folger; Oggel, *Bio-Bibliography*, 14; *The New York Clipper*, June 13 (67), Sept. 26 (195), 1863; *The New York Herald*, Sept. 20 (8), 22 (7), 1863; *Frank Leslie's Illustrated Newspaper* (New York), Oct. 3 (27), 17 (55), 24 (67), 1863; Clipping, "Sketch of Charlotte Cushman," General Reviews, Cushman papers, LC.
4. Nora Titone cites the fact that John Wilkes Booth was not brought into the partnership as evidence of the animosity between John and Edwin and John Sleeper Clarke. There is no evidence of any such intention on the part of the two partners. It is likely that both John and June were excluded from the partnership because they had no money to contribute. EB to Harry Magonigle, Nov. 14, 1874 in Cohen, *Booth Notes*, n.p; Titone, 303; Edward Hamilton Bell, "Mr. J. S. Clarke," *EB and his Contemporaries*, 101; *The New York Clipper*, Dec. 12, 1863: 275, Mar. 19, 1864: 390.
5. EB to Adam Badeau, Nov. 18, 1863, Texas; Winter, *Life and Art*, 31; Clippings: "The Playhouse," *The Illustrated London News*, The Theatre Museum, London; Laurence Hutton, "EB," EB Scrapbook, 24, Harvard.
6. Rose Eytinge, *The Memories of Rose Eytinge* (New York: Frederick A. Stokes Company, 1905), 28, 29, 30.
7. Winter, *Life and Art*, 32; *The Evening Post* (New York), Mar. 29, 1864: 2; *The New York Clipper*, Apr. 9 (411), 30 (22), 1864.
8. *The New York Leader*, Mar. 26 (4), Apr. 9 (5), 1864; *New-York Daily Tribune*, July 28, 1864: 5.
9. EB to LB, May 25, no year [1864], Hampden-Booth.
10. EB to Emma F. Carry, Aug. 26, 1864, Hampden-Booth; Grossman, 153, 154; *New-York Daily Times*, July 31, 1864: 3.
11. EB to Launt Thompson, n.d. [Aug. 1864 penciled in], copy by Edwina Booth Grossman, NYPLPA.
12. EB to Thomas Bailey Adrich, Aug. 23, no year [1864], Harvard; to Adam Badeau, Sept. 26, no year, Folger.
13. EB to Emma F. Cary, Aug. 26, 1864, Hampden-Booth; *New-York Daily Times*, July 31, 1854: 3.
14. Laurence Hutton, "EB," EB Scrapbook, 24, Harvard; *New York Herald*, Aug. 15, 1864: 7.
15. Junius Brutus Booth Jr., *Diary*, various dates, Folger; EB, "My dear Launt," [Launt Thompson], Sept. 16, no year [1864], NYPLPA; *The New York Clipper*, Sept. 24, 1864: 198.
16. EB to "J. E. Tilton & Co.," Apr. 11, 1865, to Adam Badeau, Sept. 26, no year, Folger; to Thomas Bailey Aldrich, Oct. 3, 1864, Harvard; *The New York Clipper*, Oct. 8, 1864: 206.
17. Grossman, 154, 155.
18. EB to Richard Henry Stoddard, Friday eve, n.d. Hampden-Booth; Advertisement, Winter Garden Theatre, Nov. 25, 1864, Folger; Winter, *Life and Art*, 33, 34, 35.
19. *New York Herald*, Nov. 23, 1864: 7; *The New York Leader*, Dec. 3, 1864: 5; *The New York Clipper*, Dec. 10, 1864: 278.
20. *The New York Clipper*, Dec. 3, 1864: 270.
21. *New-York Daily Tribune*, Nov. 25 (3), 28 (5), 1864.
22. Lucia Gilbert Calhoun, "EB," *The Galaxy*, Jan. 1869: 79–82.
23. EB to "J. E. Tilton & Co.," Apr. 11, 1865, Folger; *The New York Clipper*, Dec. 10, 1864: 278, Feb. 3, 1865: 342; *New-York Daily Tribune*, Dec. 10, 1864: 3, Jan. 11 (5), Feb. 20 (5), 27 (5), 1865; *Frank Leslie's Illustrated News* (New York), Dec. 24, 1864: 211, Mar. 25, 1865: 3; *The New York Herald*, Nov. 30 (7) Dec. 24 (7), 1864; *The New York Leader*, Dec. 31, 1864: 5; Clipping, "Winter Garden," no source, [1864–1865], scrapbook collected by Helen Weston, 1863, Hampden-Booth.
24. EB to Emma F. Cary, Jan. 10, 1865, Hampden-Booth; Grossman: 167, 168; Oggel, *Bio-Bibliography*, 19; *Frank Leslie's Illustrated News* (New York), Dec. 24, 1864: 219; *The New York Leader*, Jan. 14, 1865: 4, 5; *The Albion* (New York), Mar. 25, 1865: 139.
25. Winter, *Life and Art*: 43, 44, n.l.
26. Aldrich, *Crowding Memories*, 60; Grossman: 170, 171, 172; *Boston Evening Transcript*, Mar. 28, 1865: 2.
27. Aldrich, *Crowding Memories*: 61, 66.

Chapter Nine

1. Grossman, 227, 228.
2. In 1886 when asked how many children there were in his family, he named nine, as if John had never existed. He clearly did not know about the child who died in Boston in 1858. Goodale, 95.
3. While John Wilkes Booth has come down in history bearing three names, EB usually called him "John" or "Wilkes." In Richmond in 1858 John was using the stage names J.B. Wilkes and Wilkes Booth, but Edward Valentine, a Richmond historian and art collector, writing in his diary notes: "In the evening took a walk — Met John Booth." It is possible that John, as a member of the Richmond company, played subordinate roles during his brother's Richmond engagement of Sept. 10 through Oct. 16. On Oct. 2, 1858, Mary Anne Holmes Booth wrote to her eldest son June, still in California, from 7 High Street in Baltimore: "Edwin is playing now in Richmond. I found a letter awaiting my return —& he says his first night — last Monday — was very glad — and he thinks he will do a fine business— John is in Richmond too & Edwin thinks he will get along first rate — he plays some very good parts— he played Richmond in Baltimore to Edwin's Richard —& he acted very well —& looked well & his Voice is so like Edwin's you could scarcely tell them apart…. Joseph has a situation as assistant Treasurer in Baltimore at the Holliday St. He receives 4 dollars a week. It just about keeps him in liqors [sic]. John got 11." The following Oct. and Nov., John may have supported his brother for three performances during an engagement at the Howard Athenaeum. Programs for performances on Oct. 19, Oct. 26, Oct. 29 and Nov. 5, 1859, show a Mr. Wilkes (Oct. 19, Oct. 26, Nov. 5) or Wilks (Oct. 29) in the company of the Howard Athenaeum. If this is John Wilkes Booth, he was suddenly relegated to the most minor of roles (Blount in *Richard III*, the second officer in *Macbeth* and the third secretary in *Richelieu*) after having performed major roles elsewhere. Moreover the commercial nature of the nineteenth-century theatre makes it unlikely that if two Booth brothers appeared

together, one would hardly be unnoticed in the cast lists. Having the two of them together would be good box office. Programs, Howard Athenaeum, Oct. 19, 26, 29, Nov. 5, 1859, Michael A. Morrison collection, New York, New York; Mary Ann Holmes Booth to Junius Brutus Booth, Jr., Oct. 2, 1858, Taper Collection; Gordon Samples, *Lust for Fame: The Stage Career of John Wilkes Booth* (Jefferson, North Carolina: McFarland & Company Inc., 1982), 205, 206; *The Daily Dispatch* (Richmond), May 2, 1859: 2.

4. Mary Ann Holmes Booth to EB, Jan. 29, 1863, Hampden-Booth; Rhodehamel and Taper, 45.

5. John also played roles Edwin never tried — e.g. Alfred Evelyn in Bulwer Lytton's *Money*. EB to My dear Brother [Junius Brutus Booth Jr.], Dec. 12, 1858, Harvard; to My dear Larry [Lawrence Barrett], Dec. 23, 1860, Hampden-Booth; Oggel, *Letters*, 106; Rhodelhamel and Taper, 7; Arthur G. Sullivan, "Theatre Notes on English's Opera House and J. Wilkes Booth": 46, Indiana State Library, Indianapolis; *The New York Clipper*, Mar. 16 (383), 23 (391), Apr. 27 (14) 1861; *Chicago Tribune*, Nov. 30 (4), Dec. 1 (4), 7 (4), 9 (4), 10 (4), 11 (4) 12 (4), 13 (4), 17 (2), 19 (2), 1862; May 17 (2), 18 (2), 19 (2), 22 (2), 23 (2), 24 (2), 26 (2), 27 (2), 28 (2), 29 (4), 30 (2), 31 (2), June 1 (2), 5 (2), 6 (2), 1863.

6. *The Spirit of the Times* reported that John, billed as Mr. J. B. Wilks," was "spoken well of by the Richmond ... critics." Rhodelhamel and Taper, 45; *Spirit of the Times* (New York), Dec. 10, 1859: 224.

7. Mary Devlin Booth was less enthusiastic about John's Pescara and wrote to Emma C. Cushman on the same day: "We were very much pleased with him — but he has a great deal to learn and unlearn." The Richmond, Virginia, correspondent for *The New York Clipper* wrote in May 1862, that as Pescara, John was "greatly superior to his brother." "Bully boy with a glass eye" means "a good fellow" or "a fair-haired boy." By using the phrase, Edwin was implying that John would be very successful. On May 20, 1862, Richard Cary wrote to Booth after Cary had been to Washington and seen John act: "I ... went down to see J. Wilkes Booth play Macbeth.... The performance reminded me of something, but for a long time, I could not think what it was; at last it struck me. At the old Federal St theatre in Boston, I once saw a blood & thunder melodrama full of sheet iron and burnt rosin & ghosts & other horrors which made a great impression upon my juvenile imagination. I had not thought of it for years, but it all was vividly recalled by the acting that night.... I came from the theatre with the impression strong upon me that whatever he may be able to do by & by, he cannot act Shakespeare yet in a way to please "the judicious few." Some of his business is good, though that in the dagger scene, I thought very bad, & he has a melodramatic power which is at times effective but which approached altogether too much ranting to please me. Many of the tones of his voice are wonderfully like your own, but he lacks expression of face & consequently supplies its place by a "make up" which however good must be carried through the scene then in action. I see by the newspapers that Richard is considered his best part, & I should think it probable that it was, there being more scope for his particular energy than in most of the characters he undertakes." Blood and thunder were John's specialties. Speaking of his performance as Charles de Moor in Schiller's *The Robbers*, the critic of *The Albion* wrote: "He made a good deal of noise and was tempestuous after his kind, but ... noise is not elocution." He had, in this critic's eye, "the prestige of a great name and the fire of uncultured genius ... a man of genius but to the last degree rough and raw." Nora Titone contends that "the one thing Edwin was determined to prevent was his brother's acting in New York." Her statement is based on Asa Booth Clarke's comment that John "felt it rather premature that Edwin should mark off for himself the North and East, and leave the South ... to Wilkes." Titone places this decision in 1860.

At that point Edwin is a salaried actor in the Winter Garden theatre. At no time did he ever have enough power to prevent any other actor from performing in New York. Richard Cary to EB, May 20, 1862, EB to Richard Henry Stoddard, Jan. 22, 1863, Hampden-Booth; Mary Devlin Booth to Emma Crow Cushman, Jan. 22, no year [1863], Taper Collection; Alford, 80; Oggel, *Letters*, 101; Titone, 182, 220; *The Albion* (New York), Mar. 22 (139), 29 (151)1862; http://www.word-detective.com/currentpage2.html.

8. On Nov. 11, 1860, Booth wrote to Emma F. Cary: "I voted (for Lincoln) t'other day — the first vote I ever cast; and I suppose I am now an American citizen all over, as I have ever been in heart." Lincoln reportedly said after seeing EB perform *The Merchant of Venice*: "I had a thousand times rather read it at home if it were not for Booth's playing." Abraham and Mary Todd Lincoln saw Booth perform Hamlet on Mar. 2 1864, at Grover's Theatre in Washington D. C. Leonard Grover, the manager of Grover's Theatre in Washington, remembered a dinner at the home of Secretary Seward in honor of EB to which Grover was invited. "Mr. Lincoln," wrote Grover, "attended EB's performances several times. He particularly admired his *Ruy Blas*, a part expressing sentiment, while Seward's admiration was for the crafty *Richelieu*. Lincoln, Mrs. Lincoln, Secretary Seward and Senator Harris saw Booth perform Richelieu on Mar. 3, 1864. During the war Booth wrote to Adam Badeau: "'Tis said the rebels are retreating, God grant it may be so and that the traitors may be 'squelched' by 'little Mac' before they get back to their nest of damnation.... Grant looks the man he is — solid, true and honest — God grant that the next blow he strikes may drive the nail clean up to the head." In the letter in which Booth comments on Badeau's suggestion to enlist, he went on to write: "It wouldn't be so much like suicide, though, did I take his advice. Despair (I think?) would choose the rank and file." EB to James Lorimer Graham Jr., Sept. 5, 1862, Penn State; to Adam Badeau, Sept. 14 [no year], Apr. 2, [no year] Sept. 26 [no year], Folger; Edward F. Kuntz to EB, Apr. 19, 1865, Hampden-Booth; Aldrich, *Crowding Memories*, 60; Grossman, 155, 171; Dorothy Meserve Kunhardt and Philip B. Kunhardt Jr., *Twenty Days* (N.P.: Castle Books, 1965), 22; "The Break between Player & Poet": 2; Leonard Grover, "Lincoln's Interest in the Theater," *The Century Magazine* (1909): 946; *Daily National Intelligencer* (Washington, D. C.) Mar. 1 (1), 2 (1), 4 (1) 1864.

9. In the late 1870s Booth wrote to Edwina that "in Jan. neither Betty nor Joseph could write their names — now they can, and Betty has written Mamma quite a long letter." When Betty had difficulties about property she had bought, Booth hired "a lawyer to look into it." John D. Seville to EB, Nov. 23, 1866, Hampden-Booth; EB to EBG, May 29, no year [1885], NYPLPA.

10. Laurence Hutton later remembered Booth providing a pass for "Black Betty" and her husband to go to the theatre after she had left his service. Calvert, 206, 207; Laurence Hutton, "A Group of Players,"*Harper's New Monthly Magazine*, XCVI, 572: 200.

11. Hagar accompanied the Junius Brutus Booth senior family to England in 1836. EB to Elizabeth Campbell Winter], July 17, 1886, Folger; Archer, *Junius Brutus Booth*, 143; Watermeier, *Between Actor and Critic*, 274.

12. EB to Junius Brutus Booth, Jr., Dec. 12, 1858, Harvard; to WW, Dec. 7, 1879, Folger; to EwB, Feb. 17, 1885, to EBG, July 7, 1886, NYPLPA; Alford, 81, 82; C. Dallett Hemphill, *Bowing to Necessities: A History of Manners in America, 1620–1860* (New York: Oxford University Press, 1999), 139, 141; *The Great Conspiracy* (Philadelphia: Barclay & Co., 1866), 27.

13. EB to EBG, July 2, no year [1885], NYPLPA.

14. EB to LB, Nov. 7, no year [1886], Feb. 1, 1887, Harvard.

15. EB to EwB, Jan. 16, Feb. 12, 1876, NYPLPA; EB, to Jervis McEntee, Jan. 18, 1876, Hampden-Booth; Howe, 200.

16. Booth's sister Asia shared his attitudes toward people

of color, writing, in 1854, to her friend Jean Anderson: "I've got my *darkey* girl — she's only 6 years old. She kneels at my knee and says her prayers every night…. This *nigger* of mine has an endless tongue and a memory surpassing everything. She's chattering now out on the grass to the puppies and keeping up a deaf'ning clatter." Asia played Lady Bountiful to the black people of the region. "I paid my weekly visit to my darkey neighbors on Monday. It is a joy to me, to be welcomed into poor houses— Children and all flock round me — and I really think I am *beloved* among the poor and black around us." Asia Booth to Jean Anderson, Jan. 30, Apr. 4, May 1854, Maryland; EB to EwB, Mar. 12, 1876, NYPLPA.

17. "Statement of Junius Brutus Booth," M599, Roll # 2 *Investigation and Trial Papers Relating to the Assassination of President Lincoln*, National Archives, 0258–0259.

18. At the time he joined the army, John was one of the sixteen men and thirteen women who formed the Richmond Theatre company. The tone of Mary's letter implies that its writer is a mature woman looking at the misdeeds of a young boy. In actuality she was two years younger than John. The actor Edwin Adams claimed at the time of the Lincoln assassination that "I remember that at Richmond, Va. he [John Wilkes Booth] forced himself upon the cars, having been repeatedly pushed off by the soldiers. And armed with pistols and knife [he] secreted himself in the baggage car until the train had got far upon his journey when he shewed himself and was made either an assistant commissary or quartermaster." Asia Booth Clarke to Jean Anderson, n.d. [Fall 1859], Maryland; Edwin Adams to Reikert, Apr. 17, 1865, National Archives, 0061; Oggel, *Letters*, 22, 27; *The Spirit of the Times* (New York), Sept. 3, 1859: 360; *Daily Dispatch* (Richmond), Nov. 23, 1859: 1.

19. Although June was writing in Oct. 1862, John sent the money to Edwin and Mary in England some time previously. Junius Brutus Booth Jr. to EB, Oct. 20, 1862, Hampden-Booth; "Junius Brutus Booth states," May 4, 1865, Roll # 3, 0742, *Investigation*, National Archives; Oggel, *Letters*, 69.

20. Rhodehamel and Taper, 86.

21. "The Break between Player & Poet": 2.

22. John Wilkes Booth wrote a letter to John Ford from Edwin's 17th Street home on Sept. 17, 1863, and to Isabel Sumner from the 19th Street address on June 7, 1864. John Wilkes Booth to John T. Ford Esq.," Sept. 17, no year [1863 penciled in], Ford papers, LC; EB to Adam Badeau, Oct. 14, no year, Tuesday, n.d. to Col T. A. Brown, July 28, 1888, Folger; Rhodehamel and Taper, 90, 110; "The Break between Player & Poet": 2; "Sketch of Charlotte Cushman," General Reviews, Cushman papers, LC; *Frank Leslie's Illustrated Newspaper* (New York), Sept. 7, 1872: 411.

23. Badeau was always looking for heroes and always anxious to connect himself with celebrities — the Booth brothers, "Left Arm" Wilson and finally Ulysses S. Grant. If he stayed at the Booth home, he did not stay long. His foot was wounded on May 27, 1863. Assuming that it would have taken him at least two weeks to get home, he probably missed John, who was in St. Louis from June 15 to June 26 and in Cleveland from June 30 to July 3. If John nursed Adam, it was probably in early July 1863, because by July 29 Badeau was at the Busteeds' house in Jamaica, Long Island, and by Oct. 7 at their Manhattan address at 102 Madison Avenue, where he remained until at least Jan. 22, 1864. On Oct. 8 a surgeon reported that the wound was "yet open and requiring frequent dressing." EB to Adam Badeau, June 6, 1863, Hampden-Booth; Adam Badeau to the Adjt Gen. of the Army, Oct. 7, Dec. 22, 1863, "Surgeon's Certificate for Leave," Oct. 8, 27, 1863, Jan. 22, 1864, Adam Badeau papers, National Archives; Adam Badeau, "EB on and off the Stage": 264; *The New-York Times*, June 7, 1963: 1.

24. EB to Adam Badeau, n.d. Harvard; Clipping, "Booth Relics Sold," *Herald*, Dec. 17, 1901, Folger.

25. Mary Ann Holmes Booth felt the need to "take care" of Joe. By May 10, 1862, the family had learned that Joe had sailed for Europe, and Mary Ann wrote to Edwin in Paris: "Ere this I hope you have seen Joseph — I have no doubt he will be delighted with Paris, I wish you were all worth Millions— so that you could travel and see everybody. I sometimes think he is not contented, as he has not written one line to me since he left New York — I was in hopes to have had a long letter from him telling me all his adventures for in the confusion & hurry of his departure I heard nothing. I only knew that he was alive and well…. Joe says I treat him as if he was still a baby; he don't [*sic*] think that I love him just the same — as if he were — I pray to God to protect him." Whether Joe ever made it to Paris is unclear. Rose A. Booth to EB, Mar. 12, 1860, NYPLPA; EB to Adam Badeau, Apr. 8, 1862, Folger; Mary Ann Holmes Booth to EB, May 10, 1862, Hampden-Booth; Rhodehamel and Taper, 78, 79.

26. In an interrogation after the assassination, Joseph Booth stated that he had suffered from "melancholy insanity." Junius Brutus Booth, Jr. to EB, Oct. 20, 1862, Hampden-Booth; Alford, 137, 138.

27. Nora Titone has Edwin "no doubt seizing John and forcing him out the front door and into the street." This seems unlikely, given how strong John was. There is no evidence that Edwin was ever prone to physical confrontation. Rhodehamel and Taper, 110, 114, 115, Titone, 340.

28. "Statement of J. B. Booth," National Archives: 0261–0268.

29. Samuel B. Arnold later testified that he and Michael O'Laughlin met John in Baltimore in late Aug. or early Sept. 1864, when they discussed a plan to kidnap Lincoln. He contended that he later received a letter saying that John was "laid up with erysipelas in his arm." Erysipelas is a form of *cellulitis*, a bacterial infection affecting the most superficial layers of the skin…. Symptoms and signs of erysipelas are usually abrupt in onset and often accompanied by general illness in the form of fevers, chills and shivering…. The affected skin is red, swollen and may be finely dimpled (like an orange skin). It may be blistered. Bleeding into the skin may cause *purpura* (purple patches)." By July 7 June, Edwin and John were living together at Edwin's 19th Street house in New York. John returned to Boston later that month, but on July 27 John Sleeper Clarke, Asia, their children and June's daughter Mary arrived from Philadelphia at noon and at 5 P.M. that afternoon, "all left" for New London, Connecticut, on the City of New York. They slept on board and arrived the next morning at William Stuart's country house for breakfast. On July 30 John came down to New London from Boston and stayed until Aug. 2, when he and Edwin left for New York. They remained in New York on until Aug. 7 when, accompanied by John Sleeper Clarke, they left for Philadelphia. Edwin brought Edwina down to Philadelphia on Aug. 2, 1864. Junius Brutus Booth, Jr., *Diary*, Apr. 16, 1864, Folger; Asia Booth Clarke to Jean Anderson, Aug. 25, 1864, Maryland; Grossman, 164; *The New York Clipper*, July 4, 1863: 9, May 7 (31), 28 (54), 1864; *The New-York Times*, Dec. 29, 1886: 1, Jan. 19, 1869: 8; www.dermnetnz.org/bacterial/erysipelas.html.

30. In his diary, June recorded: "[June] 6th … John cut his nose against a clothes line…. June-9 John & Joe Simonds left for Oil City. On June 21 [June] and Edwin left on the General Stockton at 2 P.M. from New York and after stopping in Perth Amboy and Camden, arrived in Philadelphia at 7 P.M. They stayed "at 1025 Callowshill St." Asia was "at home" but John Sleeper Clarke "was at Washington playing." Clarke returned from Washington sometime between June 23 and 25. On the 29th at noon June left with Edwin, [John Sleeper] Clarke & [William] Stuart for New London and arrived at Stewart's [Stuart's] farm by 7. M. On July 4 "Ed & Stewart [Stuart] & rest left at 10 P.M. for N.Y." On Nov. 18, 1864, Asia and John Sleeper Clarke moved from Callowhill Street to

229 North 18th Street to what June called "their new house. It was "just opposite the Square on the corner of Summer Street." Asia Booth Clarke wrote to Jean Anderson Sherwood: "My great charge Mollie Booth [Junius' daughter] is the wildest hoyden that ever skipped. She is full of gay spirits and keeps me constantly correcting her. Her father is in Boston, Wilkes is in Washington and my John [Sleeper Clarke] is fulfilling his engagement at the Arch [in Philadelphia]." Junius Brutus Booth, Jr. opened at the Walnut Street Theatre on Jan. 16, 1865, and played until Jan. 28. Junius Brutus Booth, *Diary*, Nov. 18–30, 1864, Folger; Asia Booth Clarke to Jean Anderson, Dec. 1, 1864, Maryland; *The New York Clipper*, Oct. 8 (206), 22 (222), Dec. 10 (278), 1864.

31. June was playing an unsuccessful engagement at the New-Chestnut Street Theatre in Philadelphia. Audiences were so poor for June's engagement that the management had to couple his show with a fairy burlesque. *The New York Clipper*, Jan. 28 (334), Feb. 4 (842), 1865.

32. John Wilkes Booth to Junius Brutus Booth, Jr., Jan. 17, no year [1865], Princeton.

33. Michael W. Kauffman writes that John Booth and John Surratt were in New York in Feb. and that John introduced Surratt to Edwin, Mary Ann and Rosalie at Edwin's home and that John went to New York on Mar. 21 to see Edwin's last night as Hamlet on Mar. 22 and visited Edwin during a rehearsal of Hamlet, probably on Apr. 5, 1865, in Boston. John planned to be at Edwin's New York address on Feb. 11, 1865. "Statement of J. B. Booth," National Archives: 0261–0268; Kauffman, 89, 171, 204; Rhodehamel and Taper, 134.

34. Aldrich, *Crowding Memories*, 71; Winter, *Life and Art*, 36.

35. *The New York Dramatic News*, Jan. 13, 1877: 5.

36. The theatre reopened on Apr. 20, 1865, featuring the Irish comedians Mr. and Mrs. Barney Williams. The detective was identified only as G. H. H. John T. Ford begged Booth to do a performance in Washington for the Custer Memorial that President Hayes, "all the prominent generals north and south and many of the senators and congressmen from both sections" would attend, but Booth refused. Playbills, Boston Theatre, Apr. 14, 20, 1865, Boston Public Library; John T. Ford to EB, Nov. 24, no year [1877?], Hampden-Booth; Oggel, *Bio-Bibliography*, 19; "An Actor King": 730; *Boston Evening Transcript*, Apr. 17, 1865: 3; *Frank Leslie's Illustrated Newspaper* (New York), July 8, 1865: 245; Clippings: "By an Ex-Editor," Glase Scrapbook, Free Library of Philadelphia; "EB's Baggage Searched," *Boston Gazette*, Folger.

37. Barnum's Museum reopened on the 20th and the Varieties on the 21st. Boston Theatres reopened on Apr. 20. During the week of Apr. 24, most theatres reopened. In comparison, when James Garfield died on Sept. 19, 1881, theatres remained closed until after Oct. 1, when he was buried. David Beasley, *McKee Rankin and the Heyday of the American Theater* (Waterloo, Ontario: Wilfred Laurier University Press, 2002), 176; *Boston Daily Advertiser*, Apr. 20, 1865: 1; *The New York Clipper*, Apr. 22 (14), 29 (19), May 6 (30), 1865.

38. Launt Thompson and Thomas Bailey Aldrich also urged Booth to remain in Boston. John B. Murray to EB, Apr. 16, 1865, Launt Thompson to EB, Apr. 16, 1865, TBA to EB, Apr. 16, 1865, Hampden-Booth; Clippings: "Circumstances of the Arrest of Junius Brutus Booth," *Philadelphia Ledger*, Apr. 29, 1865, "Arrest of John S. Clarke, the Actor, a Brother-in-Law of the Assassin," *Philadelphia Ledger*, Apr. 29, 1865, "Affidavit of Mr. J. S. Clarke, the Comedian," Folger; http://www.hawkins.com/firm_history.asp.

39. The full poem reads:
All feeling hearts must feel for him
Who felt this picture. Presage dim —
Dim inklings from the shadowy sphere
Fixed him and fascinated here.
A demon-cloud like the mountain one
Burst on a spirit as mild
As this urned lake, the home of shades.
But Shakespeare's pensive child
Never the lines had lightly scanned,
Steeped in fable, steeped in fate;
The Hamlet in his heart was 'ware
Such hearts can antedate.
No utter surprise can come to him
Who reaches Shakespeare's core;
That which we seek and shun is there—
Man's final lore.

Melville subtitled his poem "A Picture by S. R. Gifford, and owned by Edwin Booth. Included in the N. A. Exhibition, Apr. 1865." *American Poetry: The Nineteenth Century*, II (New York: The Library of America, 1993), 13, 962, n 13.2, 13.3; Launt Thompson to EB, n.d. [Apr. 1865], W. B. to EB, Apr. 15, 1865, George Allen to EB, Apr. 17, 1865, EB to Emma F. Cary, May 6, 1865, One of your party to EB, May 10, 1865, "Outraged Humanity" to EB, May 6, 1865, "Justicer" to EB, n.d. Elizabeth C. Agassiz to EBG, Apr. 6, 1901, Hampden-Booth; E. Douglas Branch, 275; Gale, 3, 4; Grossman, 178; Andrew Wilton and Tim Barringer, *American Sublime Landscape Painting in the United States 1820–1860* (London: Tate Publishing, 2002), 162; *Boston Daily Advertiser — Supplement*, Apr. 17, 1865: 1; *Boston Daily Advertiser*, Apr. 20, 1865: 2; *Boston Evening Transcript*, Apr. 20, 1865: 2; *The Playbill* (New York), Apr. 21, 1865: 1 in Bamburgh, Harvard; *Frank Leslie's Illustrated Newspaper* (New York), Jan. 19, 1867: 277; Clippings: "Letter to EB and his Reply," no source, Apr. 18, 1845, no source, n.d. [Apr., 1865], Weston scrapbook, Hampden-Booth; "The Loyalty of Mr. EB," c. Apr. 18, 1865, Folger; http://www.capenet.com/capemay/allen/history.html

40. The incident, in all likelihood, occurred on Feb. 14, 1864, since Booth opened in Washington the next day. *The New York Clipper*, Apr. 28, 1865: 19.

41. David C. Anderson to EB, June 13, 1865, Hampden-Booth.

42. EB to Adam Badeau, Apr. 16, n.d. [1865], The Beinecke Rare Book and Manuscript Library, Yale University.

43. Ben Baker also wrote a condolence letter to Booth on Apr. 19, 1865. Adam Badeau to EB, Apr. 19, 1865, Benjamin A. Baker to EB, Apr. 19, 1865, Hampden-Booth.

44. For information on the subsequent career and life of Adam Badeau as well as his relationship to Booth see Adam Badeau to EB, Dec. 23, 1866, to John Davis, Oct. 2, 1883, Nov. 29, n.d. [1883], to Robert Besley," July 26, 1870, Letter Book, U. S. Consul General, London, Robert R. Hill to Adam Badeau, Aug. 30, 1881, Copies of Dispatches from the Department of State to Adam Badeau, Adam Badeau, Dispatches to the State Department, Aug. 12, 1883-Apr. 14, 1884 from the United States Consulate, Havana. Special Collections & University Archives, Rutgers University Libraries; EB to EwB, Apr. 25, 1875, Hampden-Booth; to John E. Russell, Apr. 25, 1875, Rochester; to Adam Badeau, Apr. 25, 1875, Nov. 30, [1885], Folger; to EwB, May 9, 1875, to EBG, n.d. [Feb. 21, 1886, Sept. 25, 1887, May 15, 1888], Adam Badeau, "In consideration of the sum," Nov. 19, 1888, NYPLPA; EB to Adam Badeau," Nov. 15, 188-[5], Rare Book and Manuscript Library, Columbia University; Longacre, 233; Jean Edward Smith, *Grant*, 459, 475; Badeau, "EB on and off the Stage": 265; *The New-York Times*, Mar. 21, 1895: 5, 9; May 18, 1915: 131; Feb. 24, 1925: 19; ebay item 418289242.

45. Evidence # 104, Apr. 28, 1865, Record of statement of J. H. Baker, Apr. 24, 1865, M599 Roll # 1 (22, 35), John A Foster, to H. L. Burnett, Apr. 27, 1865, Roll # 2 (0401–0402), Captain G. B. Russell, to Col H. H. Wells, May 9, 1865, Roll 2 (0904–0913), *Investigation*, National Archives; Eleanor Ruggles quoted in Don Rhodes, "Booth Family was Favored for Tragedies," *The Augusta Chronicle*, web posted July 2, 1999; Clipping, "Junius Brutus Booth," Apr. 15, 1865, Folger.

46. June later repudiated the published letter stating: "It [the letter] urged him to have nothing to do with the rebellion.... We have always been fearful of J. Wilkes knowing his sympathy for the South, and have again and again advised him to have nothing to do with it. We have tried to get him away from Washington, knowing that here he would see so much of military life and besides being so close to Southern soil." "Statement of Junius Brutus Booth," National Archives: 0258–0259.

47. *The New York Clipper* reported that "Mr. [Junius Brutus] Booth, who had been up late the previous night, left his room and went direct to Pike's Opera House on Saturday morning to attend rehearsal totally unaware of what had transpired. An excited crowd had already clamored at the door for him, torn down the bill in which he was announced, and had only left on assurance that he would not play and that no performance would be had that evening. When he appeared on the stage, Mr. Simmonds, acting manager, drew him to one side, and cautioned him against too much publicity. He inquired why, and on being told the news, exclaimed: —'My God can it be possible!' swooned away and was conveyed from the stage in an insensible condition." The *Philadelphia Inquirer* of Apr. 23, 1865 told its readers: "An order for the arrest of Junius Brutus Booth Jr. was received by telegraph, from the authorities at Washington, and its execution was entrusted to Isaac M. Krupp, Special Agent of the Fourth District of Philadelphia. About 3 o'clock on Tuesday afternoon Mr. Krupp proceeded to the residence of a relative of Booth's [Asia Booth Clarke] in the western part of the city, where he (Booth) was stopping, and after obtaining an interview with him, informed him that he had a warrant for his arrest in irons, and instructions to convey him to Washington. [Junius] Booth seemed for a moment dumbfounded at the announcement, but soon after said: 'Do you know if it is in regard to that letter?' The officer, not being there to answer questions, gave him no satisfaction, but informed him that although he had authority to take him in irons, he would dispense with the use of them. Booth thanked him, and in a state of considerable agitation prepared to leave the house at once. The twain proceeded on foot to the Station House, 13th and Brandywine streets, where Booth remained for several hours. While there he employed part of his time in copying extracts from the Bible, some of which were from the Forty-ninth Psalm.... During the evening he was conveyed in a carriage to the Baltimore depot, and left in company with Officer Krupp in the 11 o'clock train.... Arriving at Washington at 6 1/2 A.M. on Wednesday he was furnished with a good breakfast and at 9 o'clock was taken to the War Department.... After the interview at the War Department he was taken to the Old Capitol prison where he was safely quartered at five minutes of 4 o'clock, having been kept at the War department for several hours. Officer Krupp returned to this city yesterday and sent by Adams Express a quantity of clothing, &c., to Booth, at his particular request. Mr. Booth arrived in Philadelphia on Wednesday last, from Cincinnati, and kept his apartment closely until the time of his arrest." On Apr. 27 A. H. Burnett ordered that "the letter written by Junius Brutus Booth to his brother, signed 'Jun,' in which he advises his brother, now that Richmond is taken, to abandon the oil business" be forwarded to him. On Apr. 27 Burnett ordered that June "not be ironed." On May 22 Asia Booth Clarke wrote to Jean Anderson: "Junius and John Clarke have been today confined in the Old Capital, Washington. Junius wrote an innocent letter from Cincinnati which by as wicked misconstruction has been the cause of his arrest. John Clarke was arrested for having in his house a package of papers upon which he never laid his hands or eyes, but after this occurrence when I produced them, thinking it was a will put here for safekeeping, John took them to the U. S. Marshal who reported to headquarters. Hence this long imprisonment for two entirely innocent men." Burnett ordered Cary Clay Ford released on June 2, 1865. John Ford was released by May 29, 1865. He attempted to reopen his theatre on July 10, 1865, but was prevented from doing so by federal troops. The War Department contended that arson had been threatened, if the building were reopened as a theatre. It was eventually purchased by the government. John T. Ford to Thomas A. Hall Apr. 19, 1865, typescript, George Ford to John T. Ford, no month [May penciled in] 1, no year [1865 penciled in]; J. H. Rosewald *et al* to John T. Ford, May 29, 1865, Ford papers, LC; Asia Booth Clarke to Jean Anderson, May 22, 1865, Hampden-Booth; H. L. Burnett to Major General C. C. Auger, Apr. 25, 1865, to A. B. Crec, Apr. 26, 1865, to Col. J. A. Foster, Apr. 27, 1865, to Major General C. C. Auger, Apr. 27, 28, 29, 1865, to Hon. E. M. Stanton, June 2, 1865, M599 Roll # 1 (4, 6, 9, 10, 11, 13, 14, 52), Louis H. Pelonze, to Colonel L C. Baker, Apr. 17, 1865, Roll # 2 (51), National Archives; *Boston Evening Transcript*, Apr. 27, 1865: 2; *The Philadelphia Inquirer*, Apr. 28, 1865: 4; *The New York Clipper*, Apr. 29 (19), July 22 (118), 1865.

48. Edward Spangler, the theatre's stage carpenter was arrested for "making the braces with which Booth fastened the door between the dress circle and the box." Col. H. S. Olcott recommended Ford's release to Col. H. L. Burnett on Apr. 28, 1865. Col. H. S. Olcott to Col. H. L. Burnett, Apr. 28, 1865, Roll 5: 0497–0498, National Archives; J. T. Ford, "Rough Memoranda of Events in Old Capital," n.d. in J. T. Ford III papers, Sollers: 203; *Boston Daily Advertiser*, Apr. 19, 1865: 1.

49. When the theatre community of Philadelphia met on Apr. 21 to draft resolutions of sympathy, Clarke sent a note reading: "The affliction under which I am suffering, worse than death, prevents my attendance; Proclaim my entire concurrence with any measures expressive of sympathy for the loss of our lamented President [and] loyalty to our Government." The letter discovered in the Clarke home is the "Right or wrong, God judge me" letter until recently at The Players. The oil stocks referred to were John's investments in the western Pennsylvania oil field strike centered in Titusville. Clarke complained to Asia who, in turn, wrote to her brother: "I believe that he was really angry that you had had an exciting affair that would bring fresh sympathy and increase of popularity, and not even a scratch for it.... If he [Clarke] had never rushed into print with — the letter — he would never have gone to prison — that is the truth as I will always declare — but I never say it to him now — having said it once, and wrought him up to fury pitch — he thinks June brought that ignominy on him." Asia Booth Clarke to EB, Jan. 3, 1879, Hampden-Booth; H. L. Burnett to Major Junius Hayden, Apr. 26, 1865, National Archives: 14; Gale, xvii; *Boston Evening Transcript*, Apr. 20, 1865: 2; Clipping, "Important Letter from J. Wilkes Booth," *The Philadelphia Press*, Apr. 19, 1865, Folger.

50. According to Lillian Aldrich, Thomas Bailey Aldrich gave Mary Ann Booth a copy of a daily newspaper when he left her as the train was pulling out. According to Mrs. James T. Fields, Aldrich told her that the person with Mary Ann was Launt Thompson. "The old woman would have the paper. He was her 'Johnnny' after all," said T. B. Aldrich, *Crowding Memories*, 76; Howe, 198; *Mobile Daily Advertiser and General Register*, Oct. 11, 1867: 1.

51. Two days after John's death, on Apr. 28, 1865, Richard Stoddard wrote to Booth: "When I heard of the dreadful calamity which has fallen upon us, my sorrow was twofold — for the Nation and for you. My impulse was to write you at once and say so, but I did not for several reasons. First, I could say nothing which could ... mitigate your grief or which you would not be likely to hear ... from others. Second, it seemed to me that you should be left to yourself, alone with your woe and God. Third I knew that if you ever understood me, and I think you did once, you would un-

derstand my silence as well as my speech. Fourth I have always made it the rule of my life when I have lost a friend or a friend has lost me, to take no steps, and to permit none to be taken ... towards renewing the old relationship. There is no cement in this world ... strong enough to bind a broken friendship.... *Now*, however, I write you, as you see, and why? Because it seems to me that the 'shadow of death' has passed or will pass from you soon, now that the black curtain has fallen. Because John is dead, not by the rope, which he could not have escaped and by which *I* would not have had him die, for your sake, and your mother's and the memory of your great dead father, but by a bullet, fighting for his life. Because all is over with him, I write you, rejoicing, although with tears, for your sake and his own. For my own part, I remember him well and kindly. I saw no ill in him when I met him at your house, and shall think of him, or try to, as he seemed to me then, than as we are told he was later and as he must have been at last. That God may sustain you, and help you, and pardon *him*, is the prayer of your once-friend and never enemy. Farewell." Richard Henry Stoddard to EB," Apr. 28, 1865, Hampden-Booth; EB to Mrs. John Murray, Thursday, n.d. [Apr. 27, 1865], Manuscript Department, The New-York Historical Society; Jervis McEntee, Diary, Mar. 10, 1876.

52. On May 7, 1865, Mrs. James T. Fields records remarks by a minister named Bellows who had just been to see EB and reportedly said: "Ah! if it had been a fellow like myself who had done this dreadful dead, the world would not have wondered — but Johnny!!" Junius Brutus Booth, Jr., Diary, Special Collections, Boston University; Howe, 199; *The New York Clipper*, May 20, 1865: 46.

53. John Adams Dix was an American politician from New York. He served as Secretary of the Treasury, U.S. Senator, and Governor. He was also a distinguished Civil War General. On May 20, 1865, J. H. Brown of the Treasury department wrote to Edward Stanton, Secretary of War: "I have just received information from California that Joseph A. Booth left San Francisco for New York on one of the last steamers and that he was aware of the plot and conspiracy against the Executive officers of the Government. J." H. Brown to Edward M. Stanton, May, 17, 1865; Roll 3: 0702, National Archives, EB to John B. Murray, May 11, 1865, Hampden-Booth; Alford, 132–140; http://en.wikipedia.org/wiki/John_Adams_Dix.

54. On May 27 June wrote: "John [Sleeper Clarke] released. I detained till further investigations to see if anything might transpire to implicate me. Judge Hal said he had not seen my letter of the 12. or my statement to Stanton. Promised to do so and release me immediately 31. Spent my time reading Spenser's works & such books as I could lay hands on. Many of the Prisoners have left & those remaining have more liberty.... Edwin came on to the trial & dined with me. June from the 1st to the 10th the same. Daily hopes of release.... 10. Joined the mess of Room 25.... 22 informed of my release. Hemper of Pha had presented a petition & letters to the Sec of War from David Paul Brown, I H. Brewster & other leading Philadelphians which doubtless expedited it — together with Stuart's letters to Ast Sec. Danna 22. After eight long weeks imprisonment left for Pha at 7.pm. 23. 3 A.M. in Pha & found all up waiting for me." Junius Brutus Booth, Jr., Diary, Special Collections, Boston University; H. L. Burnett to Edward M. Stanton, June 2, 1865, National Archives, 57; *The New York Clipper*, June 10, 1865: 70.

55. Booth was writing to John B. Murray from 229 North 18th Street in Philadelphia. Lillian Aldrich claims that she and her then fiancée Thomas Bailey Adrich met Booth on the spiral staircase outside the court. EB to John B. Murray, June 1, n.d. [1865], Hampden-Booth; Aldrich, *Crowding Memories*, 82.

56. Clipping, "Asia Booth Clarke," in Extra Illustrated Version of Asia Booth Clarke, *Junius Brutus Booth and EB*, n.p., Harvard.

57. Lillian Woodman Aldrich's sister, Martha S. Woodman, was a friend of both Edwin and Mary Devlin Booth. Elizabeth Barstow Stoddard to Wilson Barstow, 16th Monday [Mar., 1865], Martha S. Woodman to EwB, Oct. 25, 1881, Hampden-Booth.

58. EB to Emma F. Cary, May 6, 1865, Hampden-Booth; Howe, 198.

59. On May 21, Jervis McEntee wrote to Booth, inviting him to McEntee's home in Rondout, New York: "I see no reason why you should not go out and indeed I think it would be advisable for you to begin to go out." John B. Murray to EB, May 21, 1865, Jervis McEntee to EB, May 21, 1865, EB to John B. Murray, May 23, 1865, Hampden-Booth; Asia Booth Clarke to Jean Anderson, May 22, 1865, Maryland; Howe, 198.

60. On Feb. 27, 1880, McEntee wrote in his diary: "Booth came and we talked for an hour or so. He told me that when he was engaged to Miss Hanel [sic] he was sitting near her and talking about their approaching marriage and some remark was made as whether any thing could happen to interfere with it, when suddenly there was a small puff of smoke close to them, like an explosion with no noise but a strong smell of gun powder." Jervis McEntee, Diary, Feb. 27, 1880.

61. EB to Emma F. Cary, Nov. 24, 1865, Hampden-Booth; Grossman, 174.

62. Asia Booth Clarke to Jean Anderson Sherwood, Feb. 15, 1866, Maryland.

63. EB to EBG, Oct. 9, no year [1887 penciled in], NY-PLPA.

64. Mrs. Elijah B. Rogers wrote: "Well John Wilks had deposit 2000 in gold in Canada, for the purpose of escaping there after the deed was done of shooting President, and after John was dead some time, there was advertisement of this gold for the friends, of John Booth to come on and get the money, but would not go. I proposed for Roslie and I would go with her for Company but Edwin said no let the money go to the government, after A space of time it was Advertize again, saying if they did not come by such A date it would go the government British government. So it was never sent for and was lost to there family John had one daughter Ogretia and one Son Alonso, Olgretia was beautyfull Alonso was very much like the old Mr. Richard Booth. Johns wife is still living. Her name was Izalia. I do not know her maiden name. John told Roslie he would give her two oil wells, and he wished her to take care of those two children, which she did although they ware with there Mother. Rosie calls them her children. John was not married to there Mother. After Johns Death Izalia she went with the Children A way to Ilinoise they the children are both married now poor children.... None of the family takes any account of John Wilks' Children but Rosalie; she is very kind to them; does not visit them, but sends them money every spring and fall. Calls them her children." Booth wrote to Edwina [date penciled in is Dec. 5, 1885] "Today's Tribune contains a wretched lie about John Wilkes' family, not one word of truth in it from end to end; I suspect it is the beginning of a 'black-mail scheme' of which I had some intimation months ago thro' a Boston lawyer.... The *widow* of this Tribune article is only one of twenty that wrote to me just after John's death & is the one, I suspect, who got all poor Rose's money — some *$10,000* from her. Rose says all that is ended now & that she will save her money — I hope she is not deceiving me." Junius Brutus Booth Jr., to EB, Apr., n.d. 1865, EB to Emma F. Cary, Apr. 22, 1866, to EBG, n.d. Dec 5/85 penciled in, Hampden-Booth; to LH, Saturday, n.d. [May 1885?], Princeton; Mrs. Elijah B. Rogers to W. Stump Forwood, n.d. Junius Brutus Booth & Family Miscellaneous Manuscript Collection, LC; *The New York Mirror*, Mar. 17, 1888: 6.

65. Rankin claimed that shortly before the assassination,

he had met John in Boston. "He said he had just come from Montreal from which place he had shipped his wardrobe to Havana upon a little blockade runner." The blockade-runner, a schooner called the Marie Victoria, bound for Richmond, via Nassau, was "wrecked in the Gulf of St. Lawrence" in the fall of 1864. According to Rankin, the wreck took place on the very night of Lincoln's assassination. Unclaimed, Booth's trunk was taken over by the Canadian Vice Admiralty Court and sold for salvage on July 18. At auction, Booth's dressing case went for fifteen dollars; his costumes for twenty and twenty-five dollars and his stage swords for $4.75. Rankin's brother George, then in the Civil Service in Quebec City, bought the things for Rankin, thinking they would be of use to him in his theater work, and shipped them to their home in Windsor. Rankin picked them up when he returned briefly to Windsor after his Boston engagement. When, in 1865–1866, he was playing at the Arch Street Theatre in Philadelphia, he told the theatre's manager, Mrs. John Drew, that he had the costumes with him, "although he had left Booth's swords and other properties with his brother in Windsor. She became greatly excited and begged him to tell no one. If word leaked out, the public fury against actors because of the assassination would turn on Rankin and ruin not only his career but endanger the season at her theater. Since the costumes were sea-stained and useless, Rankin boxed up the trunk to conceal the name 'J. Wilkes Booth' on the cover and put it away." When EB played Philadelphia, Rankin "took the opportunity to write Booth a note explaining how his brother's trunk had come into Rankin's possession. Expecting that Booth would be eager to possess his brother's belongings, he offered him possession of the trunk and was surprised that Booth did not reply. When Booth left the city, John Clarke wrote in carefully worded terms that Booth had not responded, because he feared any connection with his brother's "heinous deed." In Mar. 1867 Rankin met Barton Hill at the Metropolitan House Café on the corner of Prince and Broad Streets in New York. Hill, then a member of Booth's company at the Winter Garden, told Rankin that "he [Hill] wanted to buy John Wilkes Booth's trunk, containing his wardrobe. Astounded that Barton Hill knew that he was in possession of Booth's wardrobe.... Rankin told him that the costumes were sea-stained and of no use. Hill was persistent, offering him $75, and Rankin relinquished the trunk the next morning. Later that evening the actor Claude Burroughs, another member of Booth's company, greeted Rankin with the words: 'Hello Mac! I hear you sold Wilkes Booth's wardrobe to Ned!' He then revealed that Hill had bought the trunk for EB." Rankin assumed that the trunk had burned with Booth's other belongings at the Winter Garden. "According to a story told by the actor Otis Skinner in later years it was [John] McCullough to whom [John Wilkes Booth] entrusted his trunk of costumes while McCullough was touring in Canada, and it was to Rankin that EB turned several years later to retrieve it when the general suspicion of actors had abated. The story was incorrect, and Rankin tried to correct it, but his reminiscence recorded by Henry Kirk was not published." On Sept. 14, 1867, while Booth was playing Baltimore, *The Washington Express* told its readers: "At the time of the assassination John Wilkes Booth ... was stopping at the National Hotel in this city. The morning following ... the crime the War Department seized what baggage he had in the hotel and examined it, but allowed it to remain, though ordering that it should not be delivered to any claimants. The proprietors of the hotel to-day received a letter from C. B. Bishop, the well-known comedian, who writes on behalf of EB, who is now playing in Baltimore, in which he requests that his brother's trunk be forwarded to him, as the family are anxious to obtain possession of all the Wilkes Booth effects. The letter states that EB is prepared to pay whatever may be the amount of his brother's indebtedness to the hotel on presentation of the bill. The proprietors of the hotel took this letter to the War Department this morning and requested permission to forward the trunk, but this request, we are informed was positively refused." The next day *The Sun* (New York newspaper) published what it termed a correction indicating that Booth "hearing for the first time in Baltimore of the whereabouts of the trunk, accepted an offer of a friend to procure it, that friend having previously learned that it has been for two years and five months at the National Hotel, Washington ready to be delivered on demand. The government never took possession of it; the refusal to permit its delivery now is, by the orders from the office of Military Justice." The incident in which Edwin burned his brother's possessions supposedly took place in Booth's Theatre, when *Richard III* was having a short successful run. According to Skinner, Booth went down, with the Booth Theatre's "basket boy," Garrison or "Garrie" Davidson, to the furnace room of the theatre, removed the costumes, wigs and props and a packet of personal letters, one by one from the trunk, and with tears pouring down his cheeks, burnt them. It took three hours to destroy them all. The 1896 article on which Skinner based his story has none of the background information about the weather or year that Skinner provides. In the original Booth throws the articles himself into the furnace. In Skinner's version he hands them to Davidson. Davidson interviewed in 1896, said he asked Booth for a coat with a fur collar and that Booth replied: "No Garry, it must not be. There is no man living I would more willingly give that coat to than you. But I cannot endure the thought that any man, not even you, Garry, is wearing a coat that my poor misguided brother had worn. It must disappear in the flames forever." Garrie Davidson, who assisted Booth in the costumes' destruction, remembered that *Richard* III was playing at Booth's Theatre. He remembered that one of the costumes was an Indian dress "with a photograph of John Wilkes in the same costume, dated Richmond, Virginia 1859–1860. In 1927, Francis Wilson wrote to EwB: "Willie Seymour says your father told him in 1869 (at Booth's Theatre) that J. W. B.'s wardrobe was burnt with many precious relics in the Winter Garden fire in 1867!!! Seymour queried Skinner who smiled & said that his version 'was good reading.'" Francis Wilson to EBG, May 11, 1927, Hampden-Booth; Oggel, *Bio-Bibliography*, 20; Rhodehamel and Taper, 47–48; Otis Skinner, "The Last of John Wilkes Booth," *The American Magazine*," 73–77, McKee Rankin "The Story of John Wilkes Booth's Wardrobe. An account of what became of Booth's clothes," 1909, Lincoln Collection Misc., 1909, in Beasley: 45, 46, 59, 448, 448, n. 87; *The New York Clipper*, July 29, 1865: 126; *The Sun* (Baltimore), Sept. 17, 1867: 3; Clipping, "The Property Man," *Tribune*, Jan. 26, 1896, Folger.

66. *The New-York Tribune* of Apr. 29, 1865, told its readers that Booth was in Washington and had requested his brother's body. In July 1867 John Ford offered to help and Booth wrote to him: "Many thanks for yr. kindness in this matter. Do what you can—whatever you think can be done—I shall not forget it. Any reference to this fearful subject serves to open all my wounds afresh—and God knows the shame & sorrow heaped upon my family is enough already.... Anything that can be done to lighten the agony should—for humanity' sake—be done & I am grateful to you for yr. kind feelings." Booth's letter to Grant dated Sept. 1867 reads: "Having once received a promise from Mr Stanton that the family of John Wilkes Booth should be permitted to obtain the body when sufficient time had elapsed, I yielded to the entreaties of my Mother and applied for it to the 'Secretary of War'—I fear too soon, for the letter was unheeded—if, indeed, it ever reached him. I now appeal to you—on behalf of my heart-broken Mother—that she may receive the remains of her son.—You, sir, can understand what a consolation it would be to an aged parent to have the

privilege of visiting the grave of her child, and I feel assured that you will, even in the midst of your most pressing duties, feel a touch of sympathy for her — one of the greatest sufferers living. May I not hope too that you will listen to our entreaties and send me some encouragement — how and when the remains may be obtained? By so doing you will receive the gratitude of a most unhappy family, and will — I am sure — be justified by all right-thinking minds should the matter ever become known to others than ourselves. I shall remain in Baltimore two weeks from the date of this letter — during which time I could send a trust-worthy person to bring hither and privately bury the remains in the family grounds, thus relieving my poor mother of much misery. Apologizing for my intrusion, and anxiously awaiting a reply to this — I am, sir, with great respect Y^r ob^t ser^t." Booth was writing from Barnum's Hotel in Baltimore. EB to J. T. Ford, July 15, 1867, to General Ulysses S. Grant," Sept. 11, 1867, Hampden-Booth; Sollers: 236; *Boston Evening Transcript*, Apr. 29, 1865: 2; *New-York Daily Tribune*, Apr. 29, 1865: 5; *Frank Leslie's Illustrated Newspaper* (New York), May 20, 1865: 1; *The Sun* (Baltimore), Oct. 4, 1867: 4; *Mobile Daily Advertiser and General Register*, Oct. 11, 1867: 1; *The New York Clipper*, Feb. 27, 1869: 314.

67. Booth wrote to Andrew Johnson "There is also (I am told) a trunk of his at the National Hotel which I once applied for but was refused — it being under seal of the War Dept., it may contain relics of the poor misguided boy — which would be dear to his sorrowing Mother, and of no use of any one." EB to Andrew Johnson, Feb. 10, 1869, Hampden-Booth.

68. Telegram, J. T. Ford to EB, Feb. 15, 1869, Anonymous to Major General G. D. Ramsay, Feb. 15, 1869, Andrew Johnson to The Honorable The Secretary of War, Feb. 15, 1869, D. Ramsey to Maj. Gen. E. O. Townsend, Feb. 16, 1869, Hampden-Booth; Sollers: 237; Hans L. Trefousse, *Andrew Johnson: A Biography* (New York: W. W. Norton & Company, 1989), 351; *The Sun* (Baltimore), Feb. 18, 1869: 1.

69. *The New-York Times*, Feb. 17, 1869: 1; *The Sun* (Baltimore), Feb. 15(1), 16 (1), 17 (1), 18 (1), 19 (1), 1869; *The New York Clipper*, Feb. 27, 1869: 314.

70. Mrs. Elijah B. Rogers to W. Stump Forwood, n.d. Junius Brutus Booth & Family Miscellaneous Manuscript Collection, LC.

71. *The New York Clipper*, June 26 (94), July 3 (102) 1869; *The Sun* (Baltimore), June 28, 1869: 1.

72. For further information on the later life of Asia Booth Clarke see William Bispham to EB, Jan. 23, 1868, Launt Thompson to EB, Feb. 17, 1868, Luke A. Lockwood to Mrs. Asia Clarke Morgan, Nov. 25, 1891, Hampden-Booth; Asia Booth Clarke to Jean Anderson Sherwood, Feb. 4, 23, 1868, Feb. 12, 1871, Dec. 6, 1874, Maryland; Clipping, "Mr. and Mrs. Wilfred Clarke," Miscellaneous Documents file, Hampden-Booth.

73. EB to LH, Dec. 27, 1881, Princeton; *Frank Leslie's Illustrated Newspaper* (New York), Jan. 22, 1870: 319.

74. On Apr. 19, 1876, Booth wrote to John T. Ford: "I have seen, in several Southern letters to Eastern papers, some very brutal references to my tour & the excitement it caused — attributing it solely to their curiosity — to see the brother of J. W. B.— I feared this sort of thing & regret I ever went among them." On Feb. 15, 1876, WW wrote to John T. Ford: "I am rejoiced over Edwin's success in the South, so tell him, with my love. It is a pity some of these Southern editors have neither sensibility, discretion, tact or principle, which would shut their mouths as to John Wilkes Booth. He was a maniac, and that is the only extenuation for one of the most cruel, cowardly, and horrid murders ever committed on this earth. To revive this subject, in any form, must be exquisite torture to Edwin." EB to Nat Levin, Mar. 1, 1876, Hampden-Booth; to John T. Ford, Apr. 19, 1876, WW to John T. Ford, Feb. 15, 1876, Ford papers, LC.

75. Several years later, Booth sent Garrett a collection of books. In an 1878 interview, John Ford said, that he "had no doubt that Wilkes Booth formed his design of killing Mr. Lincoln from the example in the two pieces of 'Brutus' and 'Julius Caesar,' in both of which his father and himself were conspicuous" and that he had "no doubt that Wilkes Booth was insane." "EB read this statement and wrote in protest, charging that Ford had 'revived a scandal ... for ... selfish motives,'" namely to draw in audiences to a performance from which he stood to gain financially (the interview occurred a few days before a performance of *Julius* Caesar, on June 17, 1878, given as Ford's benefit). Correspondence must have continued over the summer, because, in Oct., Booth wrote that, while differing with Ford "as to the result, which amounts to nothing — beyond the revival of painful memories," he was "willing to believe" that Ford's "motive was sincere, but it was ill-timed — in view of your approaching benefit.... I am willing to bury the subject, but protest against any repetition of such *friendly* acts." R. B. Garrett to EB, Mar. 11, 1877, to EB, Feb. 13, 1880, Miss M. L. Burroughs to EB, Nov. 5, 1887, Hampden-Booth; John T. Ford to EB, Summer 1878, EB to John T. Ford, Oct. 6, 1878, Oct. 6, 1878, Ford papers, LC; Sollers: 438, 439; Clipping, "The Experience of a Veteran, *The Daily Graphic* (New York), Apr. 7, no year (1879 penciled in), Ford Papers, LC.

76. EB to LB, Sept. 14, 1885, Harvard.

77. EB to Jervis McEntee, Sept. 24, 1865, Tulsa; Goodale, 95; *Daily National Intelligencer* (Washington), Aug. 18, 1867: 1.

Chapter Ten

1. Junius Brutus Booth, Jr., Diary, Boston University; *The New York Clipper*, Sept. 16, 1865: 182.

2. EB to McE, June 11, n.d. [1865 penciled in], Sept. 24, 1865, Tulsa; John D. Seville to EB, June 12, 1865, EB to Emma F. Cary," July 31, 1865, Hampden-Booth; Grossman, 173; *The New York Clipper*, January 7(310), August 26 (58) 1865, January 6, 1866: 310; January 19, 1867: 326.

3. EB to Emma F. Cary," July 31, 1865, H. H. Coolidge to EB," Dec. 30, 1865, Hampden-Booth; Grossman, 173; Oggel, *Bio-Bibliography*, 21–22; Eugene Tompkins, *The History of the Boston Theatre 1854–1901* (Boston and New York: Houghton Mifflin Company, 1908), 111, 127; Bell, "J. S. Clarke," 102; *Chicago Tribune*, June 6, 1867: 2; *The New York Clipper*, Aug. 5 (134), Sept 30 (199), 1865; Clipping, no source, n.d. [1865], Weston Scrapbook. Hampden-Booth.

4. Winter, *Life and Art*, 37; *The New York Clipper*, Nov. 25, 1865: 262; January 6, 1866: 310.

5. *The New York Herald*, Dec. 24, 1865 in Cohen, Boothnotes, 76.

6. *The New York World*, January 4, 1866 in Cohen, Boothnotes, 76.

7. *The New York Clipper*, January 6, 1866: 310; *The Albion* (New York), January 6, 1866: 7.

8. *Frank Leslie Illustrated Newspaper* (New York), Apr. 7, 1856: 35.

9. EB to Emma F. Cary," Apr. 22 1866, to John B. Murray, August 12, 1866, Hampden-Booth; to Charles Barron, August 9, 1866, Harvard; Oggel, *Bio-Bibliography*, 21; Clipping, "EB Dead," *Boston Journal*, June 7, 1893, EB Scrapbook, p. 3, Harvard; *New York Dispatch*, Feb. 11 (4), Mar. 25 (5), 1866; *The New York Clipper*, Apr. 7 (416), August 11 (142), 1866, January 12, 1867: 31.

10. EB to John B. Murray, Oct. 11, 1866, Junius Brutus Booth, Note of indebtedness to EB and John Sleeper Clarke, Nov. 7, 1866, Hampden-Booth; *The New York Clipper*, Oct. 20 (222), Dec. 8 (278), 1866.

11. EB to Launt Thompson, n.d. [Nov. 1866], transcription by EBG, NYPLPA.

12. *The New York Clipper*, Oct. 15, 1864: 214, January 12 (310), May 18 (46) 1867; *New-York Daily Tribune*, Dec. 31,

1856: 8; *Frank Leslie's Illustrated Newspaper* (New York), Dec. 1 (163), 8 (179), 15 (195), 29 (227), 1866; January 5 (243), 12 (259), 19 (275), 26 (291), Feb. 2 (309), 1867; *The New York Leader*, Dec. 29, 1866: 4; *The Albion* (New York), January 5, 1867: 7; *Boston Daily Evening Transcript*, May 17, 1867: 2; *Boston Daily Advertiser*, Nov. 2, 1868: 1.

13. Winter, *Life and Art*, 41; *The New York Clipper*, Feb. 9, 1867: 350; *The Sun* (New York), January 30, 1867: 4; *Frank Leslie's Illustrated Newspaper*, Feb. 10 (338), Mar. 30 (19), Apr. 6 (35), 1867; *The New York Clipper*, Mar. 9, 1867: 382.

14. *New-York Daily Tribune*, Mar. 25, 1867: 8; *The Sun* (New York), Mar. 25, 1857: 4; *New York Dispatch*, Mar. 24, 1867: 1.

15. Count Johannes to EB, Apr. 9, 1867, Hampden-Booth; EB to Epes Sargent, Apr. 19, no year [1868?], Taper Collection; Winter, *Life and Art*, 44, 45, 46; *The New York Herald*, Mar. 24, 1867: 5; *Daily National Intelligencer* (Washington), Mar. 25, 1867: 2; *Chicago Tribune*, Mar. 27, 1867: 4; *Frank Leslie's Illustrated Newspaper*, Apr. 6 (37), 13 (51), 20 (67) 1867; *The New York Clipper*, Apr. 7, 1867: 6, January 11, 1868: 315; *Boston Daily Evening Transcript*, May 16, 1867: 2; Clipping, "Great Fire on Broadway," Bamburgh, Harvard.

16. EB to John E. Russell, Apr. 21, 1867, Rochester; William Stuart, Receipt, Sept. 6, 1867, NYPLPA.

17. EB to John B. Murray, June 13, 1867, Asia Booth Clarke to EB, Nov. 1, 1867, EB to McE, Nov. 21, 1867, McE to EB, Dec. 10, 1867, Hampden-Booth.

18. J. G. Boyd to EB, August 18, 1869, NYPLPA; EB to John E. Russell, June 22, 1874, Rochester; to Mrs. E. L. Davenport, Dec. 12, 1879, Department of Special Collections, University of California, Davis; to Mr. Asa Israel Fish, n.d. Folger; Watermeier, *Between Actor and Critic*, 48, 283; *The New York Clipper*, Apr. 20, 1867: 14; *The New-York Times*, Dec. 29, 1886: 1; *The New York Mirror*, January 1, 1887: 7.

19. Witham, I: 175–176; *The New York Clipper*, May 11, 1867: 38, Apr. 4 (414), August 8 (142) 1868.

Chapter Eleven

1. *The New York Dramatic Mirror*, June 24, 1893: 14.
2. EwB to EB, Sept. 19, 1875, Hampden-Booth; EB to EwB, Sept. 18, 1873, Sept. 27, 1874, to EBG, Aug. 24, 1885, Oct. 22, 1887, NYPLPA; Manhattan Death Certificate 40402, Nov. 13, 1881, Birth Death and Marriage Certificate Office, New York, New York; *New-York Daily Times*, Feb. 4 (4), Mar. 11 (4), July 22 (3), 1856; *Daily Missouri Republican* (St. Louis), Jan. 19 (3), 20 (3), 21 (3), 22 (3), 23 (3), 24 (3), 26 (3), 27 (3), 28 (3), 29 (3), 30 (3), 31 (3), 1857; *Spirit of the Times* (New York), Oct. 24, 1857: 444; *Boston Evening Transcript*, Sept. 10 (3), 23 (3) 1859; *The Chicago Tribune*, Dec. 3 (4), 19 (4), 1862, Nov. 14, 1881: 5; *The New York Clipper*, June 22, 1867: 86; *The Albion* (New York), June 12, 1869: 338; *The New York Mirror*, Nov. 19, 1881: 6; Find a Grave, Rose Hill Cemetery, wysiwyg://131http:// www. Findagrave.com/pictures/8231.html.
3. Clipping, "Some Stories of Booth," NYPLPA; Clarke, 150.
4. On Sept. 12, 1859, Mary McVicker joined the Boston Museum company as a touring star and appeared as Blanche in *Angel Child* and then went on to the Green Street Theatre in Albany. She appeared at the St. Louis Theatre on Nov. 25 1859, supported by her father. There she also made her debut as a concert singer. The *New York Clipper* announced that she had made a great hit singing the *Marseilles Hymn* [sic] and noted her success imitating Charlotte Cushman, as Lady Macbeth, although telling its readers: "We should rather not see such a sight." In 1859 she toured to Burlington, Iowa, singing her hit "Meet me by moonlight," and *The New York Clipper* advised her to go to England and sing before Queen Victoria. On Dec. 10 she performed the first act of *Hamlet* and *The Little Treasure* at the beginning of a week-long engagement at the St. Louis Theatre, but she was not successful; houses were as low as $60 per night. When she performed at the Odd Fellows' Hall in Mobile, Alabama, for six nights and a matinee in Feb. 1860, Mary McVicker was billed as "Little Mary McVicker, who has been honored by the great operatic artists of the day with the cognomen of 'THE GENIUS OF MUSIC.' Her sweet vocalization and capital rendition of the works of the great masters of music, create an enthusiasm on the part of her hearers, who look upon her as the CHILD WONDER." The local critic in Mobile thought that Mary McVicker was ten years old. M. E. Gilman, a Memphis reviewer, later remembered that "as a girl she wore high heels and cork soles to give her height." Anon. to Mary McVicker, Aug. 29, Sept. 12, 1865, Cashinne [?] to Mary McVicker, Nov. 3, 1864, James B. Runnion to Mary McVicker, Apr. 14, 1864, Henry W. Cleveland to EB, May 15, 1870, Hampden-Booth; Katherine K. Preston, *Opera on the Road* (Urbana: University of Illinois Press, 1993), 143, 147, 246, 459, 472, 476; *The New York Clipper*, Sept. 18, 1858: 174; Feb. 5 (334), Aug. 20 (142), 27 (150), Sept. 17(174), 24 (183), Oct. 1 (190), Dec. 10 (271), 17 (279) 1859; Oct. 21 (215), 27 (223), Dec. 29 (295), 1860; Jan. 5, 1861:303; Feb. 29, 1864: 371; *The Spirit of the Times*, Mar. 26, 1859: 84; *Boston Evening Transcript*, Sept. 10 (3), 23 (3), 1859; *The Mobile Daily Register*, Feb. 23 (3), 25 (3), 29 (3) 1860; *Wilkes' Spirit of the Times* (New York), Sept. 22, 1860: 48; *The New York Clipper*, Jan. 24, 1868: 334; *Chicago Tribune*, Nov. 14, 1881: 5.

5. EB to Launt Thompson, June 9, no year [1867], transcription by EBG, NYPLPA; *Chicago Tribune*, June 2 (2), 4 (5), 5 (4), 7 (4), 8 (4), 12 (4), 22 (1), 23 (4), 28 (4), 1867; *The New York Clipper*, June 22 (86), 29 (94), Aug. 3 (184) 1867.

6. Theatre Programs, Walnut Street Theatre, Mar. 26-May 2, 1868, Theatre Collection, The Free Library of Philadelphia; *Mobile Daily Advertiser*, July 18, 1867: 2; *The New York Clipper*, July 27, 1867: 126; *The Sun* (Baltimore), Sept. 12 (2), 14 (2), 1867.

7. EB to Launt Thompson, Dec. 21, no year [1867], transcription by EBG, NYPLPA; EB to WW, n.d. [July 13 written in Winter's handwriting], Folger; *The Cincinnati Commercial*, Oct. 15 (8), 16 (8), 19 (8), 20 (8) 22 (8)1867; *The New York Clipper*, Oct. 19 (222), 26 (230), Nov. 23 (262) 1867; Jan 18 (326), 24 (334), Feb. 1 (342), 1868; *The Louisville Daily Journal*, Nov. 7 (3), 11 (1) 1867; *Memphis Daily Appeal*, Jan. 14, 1868: 3.

8. Asia Booth Clarke to Jean Anderson Sherwood, Mar. 12, 1868, Maryland; Laura Edmonds to EB, June 29, 1868, Hampden-Booth; *Springfield Republican* (Springfield, Massachusetts), May 13, 1868: 1.

9. Grossman, 156, 157, 158.
10. Launt Thompson to EB, Feb. 28, 1864, Hampden-Booth; EB to EwB, Sept. 29, 1872, NYPLPA.
11. Asia Booth to Jean Anderson, n.d. [1852], May 22, 1855, to Jean Anderson Sherwood, Aug. 25, 1864, Feb. 4, 1868, Maryland.
12. EB to EwB, Sept. 5, 1868, NYPLPA.
13. EB to EwB, Sept. 15, 1868, NYPLPA.
14. *The New-York Times*, May 6, 1869: 7; Clipping, Dr. G. [sic] Ogden Doremus, "EB and Ole Bull": 235, Robert Young Jr. Research Materials, LC.
15. A. O. Kellogg to EB, June 11, 1869, Hampden-Booth; J. H. Schenck, *Album of Long Branch* (New York: John F. Trow, 1868), 105; Watermeier, *Between Actor and Critic*, 113; *The Albion* (New York), June 12, 1869: 338; *The New-York Times*, June 13, 1869: 5.
16. EB to John E. Russell, June 22, no year [1869], Rochester.
17. EB to TBA and Lillian Woodman Aldrich, Aug. 22, 1869, Harvard.
18. Laura Edmonds to EB, Feb. 17, 1882, Hampden-Booth.

Chapter Twelve

1. Grossman, 134, 139.
2. I. Abbott to EB, Nov. 11, 1868, Hampden-Booth.
3. EB to John B. Murray, May 29, 1866, Jan. 15, 1867, to Mrs. John B. Murray, July 27, 1866, to Emma F. Cary, n.d. Hampden-Booth; to Launt Thompson, May 8, [1867, 1868 incorrectly written in], transcription by EBG, NYPLPA; to John E. Russell, Apr. 21, 1867, Rochester.
4. EB to Anon., June 30, 1867, Pennsylvania; to John B. Murray, Oct. 5, 1867, Hampden-Booth; Winter, *Life and Art*, 75; *Chicago Tribune*, June 2, 1867: 2.
5. Launt Thompson to EB, Oct. 3, 1867, Hampden-Booth; Oct. 17, 1867. transcription by EBG, NYPLPA.
6. Richard A. Robertson to EB, Apr. 4, 1863, Hampden-Booth; Robert Cohen, *EB in Performance*, 15, University of California, Irvine.
7. EB to John E. Russell, Mar. 21, no year [1868], Rochester; James H. Hackett to EB, Mar. 31, 1868, Hampden-Booth; EB to Launt Thompson, Apr. 8, no year [1868 written in], transcription by EBG, to EwB, Dec. 9, 1868, NYPLPA; Program, Walnut Street Theatre, Apr. 11, 1868, Free Library of Philadelphia; "Booth's Theatre," *Harper's Weekly*, 13 (Jan. 12, 1869): 22; *The New York Clipper*, Aug 24 (154), Nov. 30 (270), 1867, Apr. 18, 1868: 14; *The New York Times*, Mar. 11 (8), Apr. 9 (1), 1868; *The Tribune* (New York) Nov. 18, 1868: 5 in Boothnotes, 90; Clippings: "EB," Sept. 28, 1875, Folger; *Home Journal* (New York), Dec. 25, 1872, Scrapbook, 1871–1872, Hampden-Booth.
8. EB to John E. Russell, Jan. 24, n.d. [1868], Rochester; to Launt Thompson, Jan. 30, 1868, to EwB, Feb. 25 [1868 penciled in], transcription by EBG, NYPLPA; Grossman, 177; *Public Ledger* (Philadelphia), June 30, 1866: 1; *The New York Dramatic Mirror*, June 5, 1889: 8; *The New York Clipper*, June 6, 1868: 70; *The Chicago Tribune*, Sept. 27, 1868: 2.
9. EB to Launt Thompson, Oct. 25, no year [1866], Jan. 30, 1868, transcription by EBG, to Launt Thompson and McE, Apr. 27, 1869, NYPLPA; Launt Thompson to EB, Feb. 17, 1868, EB, to McE, Nov. 21, 1867, Hampden-Booth; to TBA, Oct. 3, 1872, Harvard; *Harper's Weekly* (New York), May 22, 1869:.
10. Edwin Adams to EB, Dec. 1, 1868, Hampden-Booth; *The New York Clipper*, Nov. 2, 1867: 236, June 6 (70), July 11 (110) 1868.
11. Program, English's Opera House, Indianapolis, Indiana, Dec. 23–24, 1881, Will E. English Theatre Program Collection, William Henry Smith Memorial Library, Indiana Historical Society; Grossman, 177; *The New-York Times*, Jan. 25 (5), Feb. 2 (7), 16 (5), 1869; *Frank Leslie's Illustrated Newspaper* (New York), July 25, 1868: 291; *Pittsburg Gazette*, Sept. 11, 1868: 2; *The New York Albion* (New York), Jan. 30, 1869: 57; *Frank Leslie's Illustrated Newspaper* (New York), Apr. 23, 1870: 83.
12. Cohen, *EB in Performance*, 25.
13. EB to Richard Robertson, Sunday, n.d. Folger.
14. Richard A. Robertson to EB, Jan. 13, 1869, Hampden-Booth.
15. Charles W. Clarke, *Diary*, Column 4, Folger; EB to Richard A. Robertson, Apr. 3 no year [1869], Michael A. Morrison Collection; *New York Dispatch*, Jan. 31, 1869: 4; *New York World*, probably Feb. 4, 1869 in Boothnotes, 100; *The New-York Times*, Feb. 4, 1869: 5.
16. Cohen, *EB in Performance*, 14, 21, 24; O. B. Bunce, *Booth's Theatre, Behind the Scenes* (New York, 1870), 9; Watermeier, *Between Actor and Critic*, 146, 147, n. 29; *The New-York Times*, Jan. 25, 1869: 5; *The New York Albion* (New York), Feb. 6, 1869: 66, 68; *New York Dispatch*, Feb. 7, 1869: 5.
17. *The New-York Times*, Feb. 4, 1869: 5; *The New York Albion* (New York), Feb. 6, 1869: 68; *Frank Leslie's Illustrated Newspaper* (New York), Feb. 20, 1869: 355; *The New York Leader*, Feb. 6 (4), 13 (1), 1869; Watermeier, *Between Actor and Critic*, 21; Clippings: *The World* (New York), Feb. 3, 1869, no source, Mar. 29, 1869, Scrapbook, 1869–1870, Booth's Theatre, Hampden-Booth.
18. EB to John E. Russell, St. Paddy's day, 1869, Rochester; to Mrs. Gray, Mar. 16, 1869, Beinecke Rare Book and Manuscript Library, Yale University Library; *The New-York Times*, Feb. 1 (7), 2 (5), 1869.
19. Watermeier, *Between Actor and Critic*, 20–23.
20. EB to WW, Feb. 7, 1869, Folger.
21. Epes Sargent to EB, Sept. 17, 1866, Hampden-Booth; EB to John E. Russell], St. Paddy's day, 1869, Rochester.
22. *The New York Clipper*, Sept. 19, 1868: 186.
23. *The New York Clipper*, Apr. 17, 1869: 14.
24. *The New-York Times*, Apr. 4 (5), 13 (4), 1869; *The Sun* (New York), Apr. 13, 1869: 1; *The New York Clipper*, Apr. 17 (14), 24 (22), May 1 (30), May 8 (38), 1869; *The New York Albion* (New York), Apr. 17 (210), 24 (228), 1869; Clippings: no source, n.d. [Apr. 13, 1869], *Daily Star*, Apr. 13, 1869, *Citizen* (New York), Apr. 17, 1869, Scrapbook, 1869–1870, Booth's Theatre, Hampden-Booth.

Chapter Thirteen

1. *The New York Albion* (New York), June 5 (312), 12 (338), 1869; *The New York Clipper*, June 5, 1869: 70.
2. *The New York Leader*, June 5, 1869: 5.
3. EB to Launt Thompson and McE, Apr. 27, 1869, NYPLPA; to John E. Russell, June 22, no year [1869], Aug 22, 1869, Rochester; to Charlotte Cushman, July 23, 1871, Letters to Charlotte Cushman, IX, Charlotte Cushman Papers, LC; Edward L. Partridge, "EB to John E. Russell," *The Outlook*, 127 (Apr. 20,. 1921): 638; *The New York Albion* (New York), Aug 14, 1869: 481; *The New York Clipper*, Oct. 2 (206), 30 (238) 1869; Clipping, "City Summary," Folger.
4. EB to Launt Thompson, Nov. 9, 1869, transcription by EBG, NYPLPA; Boston Theatre Programs, Nov. 4–13, 1869, Boston Public Library; *The Philadelphia Inquirer*, Sept. 21, 1869: 3; *The New York Clipper*, Nov. 13 (254), Dec. 4 (279), 1869; *Hartford Daily Courant*, Nov. 20, 1869: 2; *Providence Daily Journal*, Nov. 25, 1869: 1.
5. EB to Launt Thompson, Dec. 5, 1869, transcription by EBG, NYPLPA; *The New-York Times*, June 27, 1869: 5; *The New York Albion*, Sept. 4 (530), 18 (562), Nov. 25 (722) 1869; *The New York Clipper*, July 31 (134), Nov. 27 (270), Dec. 11 (286), 1869, Jan. 1 (310), 29 (342), Feb. 12 (358), 1870.
6. For reviews of Booth's 1870 *Hamlet*. see *The New York Clipper*, Dec. 11, 1869: 286, Jan. 8 (319), Feb. 5 (350), 26 (374), Mar. 12 (390), 1870; *New-York Daily Tribune*, Jan. 6, 1870: 4; *New York Herald*, Jan. 6, 1870: 7; *The Evening Post* (New York), Jan. 6, 1870: 2; *The Sun* (New York), Jan. 6, 1870: 2; *The Evening Post* (New York), Jan. 6, 1870: 2; *New York Dispatch*, Jan. 8, 1870: 5; *The New York Times*, Jan. 9, 1870: 5; *The New York Albion* (New York), Jan. 15, 1870: 40–41; Clipping, "Booth's Theatre — Hamlet," no name, n.d. [circa Jan. 5, 1870], Melvin Scrapbook, Hampden-Booth.
7. For a detailed description of the 1870 *Hamlet* see Charles H. Shattuck's *The Hamlet of Edwin Booth*; Cohen, *EB in Performance*, 33, Boothnotes, 103; Watermeier, *Between Actor and Critic*, 109; *Frank Leslie's Illustrated Newspaper* (New York), Jan. 8 (275), Mar. 26 (19), 1870; *New-York Daily Tribune*, Jan. 19, 1870: 3; *The New York Clipper*, Jan. 22 (334), 29 (342), Feb. 26 (374), Mar. 26 (406), 1870; *The New York Times*, Jan. 23, 1870: 5; *New York Herald*, Feb. 11(2), 13 (2), 14 (5), 15 (7), 1870; *The Evening Post*, Feb. 28, 1870: 4; Clippings: no source, Mar., 1869, Scrapbook, 1869–1870, Booth's Theatre, New York newspaper, n.d. [Jan. 1870], Melvin Scrapbook, Hampden-Booth.
8. *The New York Albion* (New York), Mar. 19 (186), 26 (202), Apr. 2 (218), 1870; *The Evening Post* (New York), Mar. 22 (2), 24 (2), 25 (2), 1870; *The Sun* (New York), Mar. 22,

1870: 2; *The New York Times*, Mar. 26, 1870: 5; *New York Dispatch*, Mar. 27, 1870: 5; *The New York Albion*, Apr. 2, 1870: 218; Clipping, *The New York Times*, n.d. [circa Mar. 21, 1870], Scrapbook, 1869–1870, Booth's Theatre, Hampden-Booth.
   9. *The New York Clipper*, Apr. 2, 1870: 414.
   10. EB to John E. Russell, Apr. 2, 1870, Rochester; Cohen, Boothnotes, 58, 62, 101; *The Sun* (New York), Mar. 25, 1870: 2; *The Evening Post* (New York), Mar. 29, 1870: 2; *The New York Times*, Mar. 29 (4), 30 (4), 1870; *The New York Albion* (New York), Apr. 2, 1870: 218; *New York Dispatch*, Apr. 3, 1870: 5.
   11. EB to McE, June 13, 1870, to John S Clarke, Lease, June 23, 1870, Hampden-Booth; Watermeier, *Between Actor and Critic*, 42; *The New York Clipper*, July 21, 1869: 126; *Frank Leslie's Illustrated Newspaper* (New York), Mar. 12 (427), 19 (3), Apr. 2 (35), 1870; *The New York Albion*, Mar. 26 (202), Apr. 2 (218), May 28 (346), June 4 (362), 1870.
   12. Watermeier, *Between Actor and Critic*, 25, 26; *Frank Leslie's Illustrated Newspaper* (New York), May 21 (147), July 16 (275), 23 (291) 1870; *The New York Albion*, July 2 1870: 424.
   13. http://en.wikipedia.org/wiki/Oakes_Ames.
   14. Richard A. Robertson to EB, Oct. 11, 1870, Hampden-Booth; EB to Launt Thompson, Dec. 16, 1870, transcription by EBG, NYPLPA; Bispham, "Memories and Letters of EB": 135; *The New York Albion*, Dec. 3 1870: 777.
   15. Program, Booth's Theatre, Feb. 4, 1871, Matthews and Hutton, V, pt. 2, Harvard; EB to John E. Russell, Feb. 12, 1871, Rochester; *The New-York Times*, Feb. 3, 1869: 7, Jan. 1, 1871: 4; *Frank Leslie's Illustrated Newspaper* (New York), Jan. 7 (275), 28 (327), 1871; *The World* (New York), Jan. 10, 1871: 1; *The Evening Post*, Jan. 10, 1871: 2; *New York Evening Express*, Jan. 10, 1871: 2; *The New York Albion*, Jan. 14, 1871: 25, 26.
   16. Cohen, Boothnotes, 91, 101, 102; Watermeier, *Between Actor and Critic*, 71; *The New York Times*, Apr. 1 (4), 20 (4, 5), 1869; *The Tribune* (New York), Apr. 13, 1869: 5; *New-York Daily Tribune*, Apr. 26, 1871: 5; *The New York Albion* (New York), Apr. 29, 1871: 268; *Frank Leslie's Illustrated Newspaper* (New York), May 13 (129), 21 (173, 179), 22 (311), 1871.
   17. Entries, Mar. 21 1871, Mary Francis Booth from Grantor Jeremiah T. Smith, liber 229, 516, June 3, 1871 Mary Francis Booth from Grantor Jeremiah T. Smith, Liber 232, 127, June 3 1871, Edwin T. Booth from Grantor Jeremiah T. Smith, Liber 234A, 44–45, June 6, 1871 Mary Francis Booth from Grantor John Corlies White, Liber 234A, 64, Long Branch, Monmouth County, New Jersey Land Records, County Clerk's Office, Freehold, New Jersey; Cohen, *EB in Performance*, I, 34, Boothnotes, 103; Bispham: 135; *The New York Albion* (New York), May 6 (284), 27 (332), June 3 (348, 364), 1871; *Frank Leslie's Illustrated Newspaper* (New York), June 17, 1871: 219.
   18. *Frank Leslie's Illustrated Newspaper* (New York), Aug 19 (387), 26 (395) 1871.
   19. EB to LB, Sept. 9, 1871, Hampden-Booth; Charles W. Clarke, *Diary*, Column 4, Folger; Watermeier, *Between Actor and Critic*, 31, 32, 39; *The Albion* (New York), Aug 19, 1871: 324.

Chapter Fourteen

   1. Charlotte Cushman to EB, June 21, 1871, Hampden-Booth; Emma Stebbins, *Charlotte Cushman: Her Letters and Memories of her Life* (Boston: Houghton, Osgood and Company, 1878), 256; Clipping, "Charlotte Cushman," Obituaries, Part II, Charlotte Cushman Papers, LC.
   2. Charlotte Cushman to EB, July 1, 1871, Hampden-Booth.
   3. EB to Charlotte Cushman, July 23, 1871, Letters to Charlotte Cushman, IX, LC; Clipping, T. F. & Fam., n.d. Scrapbook, Booth Newspaper Clippings: 1871–1873, Hampden-Booth.
   4. Charlotte Cushman, to EB, July 27, July 30, 1871, EB to LB, Sept. 9, 1871, Hampden-Booth; EB to Charlotte Cushman, August 4, 1871, Letters to Charlotte Cushman, IX, LC; *The New-York Times*, Oct. 25 (7), Nov. 26 (3) 1860; *The Albion* (New York), Nov. 11, 1871: 717.
   5. EB to John E. Russell, July 19, no year [1871], Rochester; to LB, Oct. 6, 1871, Hampden-Booth; Mary F. Booth Grantor to Richard A. Robertson, Nov. 16, 1871, Liber 236, 95, Monmouth County Clerk's Office, Freehold, New Jersey.
   6. EB to EwB, Oct. 18, 1871, NYPLPA, to LB, Nov. 3, 1871, Hampden-Booth; Cohen, *EB in Performance*, 14; Watermeier, *Between Actor and Critic*, 33; Clippings: "The Drama," "Booth's Theatre," no source, n.d. [1871] General Review File, Cushman Papers, LC.
   7. *The New York Herald*, Dec. 5 (2), 23 (2), 1871.
   8. Cohen, *EB in Performance*, 35; *New-York Tribune*, Mar. 4 (7), 11 (7), 1872; *The Evening Post* (New York), Mar. 5 (2), 12 (2), 1872; *The New-York Times*, Mar. 5, 1872: 5; *New York Evening Express*, Mar. 6, 1872: 2; *New-York Daily Tribune*, Mar. 18, 1872: 5; Clippings: *Watson's Art Journal*, Mar. 9, 1872, *The Express* (New York), Mar. 15, 1872, *Weekly Review* (New York), Mar. 16, 1872, Woodhull & C[?], Mar. 20, 1872, Scrapbook, Booth Newspaper Clippings: 1871–1873, Hampden-Booth.
   9. EB to Charlotte Cushman, July 14, 1872, Letters to Charlotte Cushman, IX, LC
   10. *Hartford Daily Courant*, Sept. 16, 1872: 2; *Springfield Republican* (Springfield, Massachusetts), Sept. 12(2), 18 (2) 1872; *Daily Kennebec Journal* (Augusta, Maine), Oct. 12, 1872: 3; *Concord Daily Monitor* (Concord, New Hampshire), Oct. 30, 1872: 2; *The Providence Daily Journal*, Nov. 23, 1872: 1.
   11. EB to TBA, Oct. 3, 1872, Harvard.
   12. D. W. Waller to EB, Feb. 5, 1873, McE to EB, Mar. 28, 1873, Hampden-Booth; EB to McE, Mar. 25, 1873, Tulsa; Watermeier, *Between Actor and Critic*, 42; *New York Dramatic News and Society Journal*, Mar. 10, 1877: 5; Clipping, "Booth's Theatre," June 16, 1873, Folger; Item 356741060, ebay.com.
   13. Joseph Adrian Booth, Box Office Report, Booth's Theatre, Sept. 1-Oct. 4, 1873, Washington State University Libraries; *Frank Leslie's Illustrated Newspaper*, Sept. 20 (67), Nov. 22 (183), 29 (203) 1873.
   14. EB to EwB, Oct. 5, 1873, NYPLPA; Joseph Booth, Box Office Report, Booth's Theatre, Oct. 6–18, 1873, Washington State; EB to TBA, Oct. 15, 1873, Harvard; Clipping, "Booth's Bankruptcy," no name, n.d. Melvin Scrapbook, Hampden-Booth.
   15. James H. McVicker to EB, Oct. 11, 1873, Hampden-Booth; Joseph Booth, Box Office Report, Booth's Theatre, Oct. 20-Nov. 1, 1873, Nov. 3–29, Washington State; EB to John E. Russell, Oct. 22, 1873, Rochester; to Launt Thompson], Oct. 23, 1873, transcription by EBG, NYPLPA; EB to John E. Russell, Nov. 9, 1873, Rochester; Oggel, *Bio-Bibliography*, 23; Clippings: "Amusement Feuilleton," no source, Nov. 4, 1873, Melvin Scrapbook, Hampden-Booth; Clipping, "Booth's Bankruptcy," Sept. 20, 1874, Folger.
   16. Clark Bell to Samuel L. M. Barlow, June 4, 1873, R. A. Robertson to Oliver Ames, May 5, 1876, The Huntington Library; James H. McVicker, to EB, Nov. 27, 1873, Hampden-Booth; Watermeier, *Between Actor and Critic*, 43; Clippings: "EB's Rights," no source, Nov. 23, 1876, Folger; "Booth's Bankruptcy," no source, n.d. Melvin Scrapbook, Hampden-Booth.
   17. Bispham: 135, Harvard.
   18. Junius Brutus Booth, Jr. to EB, Mar. 4, 1874, Hampden-Booth; Receipt signed by Mary G. Booth, DeBar's Opera House, Apr. 4, 1874, Harvard; EB to John E. Russell, Apr. 29, 1874, Rochester; Watermeier, *Between Actor and Critic*, 44, 46, 47; *Frank Leslie's Illustrated Newspaper* (New York), Mar. 7, 1874: 427.

19. Watermeier, *Between Actor and Critic*, 47, 49; *Frank Leslie's Illustrated Newspaper* (New York), July 25, 1874: 311; Clipping, "Booth's Bankruptcy," Sept. 29, 1874, Folder.
20. Watermeier, *Between Actor and Critic*, 47.
21. EB to John E. Russell, Feb. 19, 1874, Rochester.
22. James H. McVicker to EB, May 2, 1875, Jan. 4, 1876, EB to David C. Anderson, July 22, 1876, Hampden-Booth; to WW, Apr. 30, 1876, typewritten copy, Folder; McE, Diary, Jan. 13, 17, 1876; EB to John E. Russell, Jan. 23, 1874, Mar. 2, 1875, Rochester; *The News and Courier* (Charleston, South Carolina), Feb. 1, 1876: 1; *The New York Dramatic News*, Feb. 5 (7), July 29 (3)1876; Clippings: "The Drama, EB's Bankruptcy," no source, 1874, Folder; "EB's Estate," *Tribune* (New York), Jan. 30, 1896.
23. EB to EwB, Nov. 29, 1874, to McE, June 29, 1875, Hampden-Booth; to EwB, Nov. 29, 1874, June 2, 1875, NYPLPA; Hampden-Booth; Mary Ann Holmes Booth to EwB, Nov. 9, 1875, Taper Collection.
24. *Detroit Daily Free Press*, Feb. 7 (3), Mar. 7 (3), 1857.
25. Booth's first experience with a limited range combination company came in Apr. 1867, when he gave one performance of *Hamlet* at the Providence Opera House supported by the Boston Theatre company with which he had been performing. For the day Booth and the company "were conveyed to and from Providence by a special train." They returned to Boston in time to play a matinee the following day. *Boston Daily Evening Transcript*, Apr. 27, 1867: 2.
26. Beasley, 118.
27. *The New York Dramatic Mirror*, Aug. 22 (7, 8, 9), Sept. 12 (8) 1891.
28. EB to E.C. Benedict, Oct. 28, 1877, to David C. Anderson, Apr. 19, 1878, ABC to LB, Jan. 4, 1886, Hampden-Booth; EB to WW, Dec. 9, 1877, typewritten copy probably prepared by Jefferson Winter, Folder.
29. EB to LB, Jan. 20, 1881, Harvard.
30. EB to WW, 1880–1881, typewritten copy prepared by Robert Young, Folder; to E.H. House, Mar. 29, 1881, John Crouse Autograph Collection, Bentley Historical Library, University of Michigan; E. H. House, "EB in London," *The Century Magazine*, Dec. 1897: 272.
31. EB to McE, Oct. 14, 1877, Hampden-Booth; Program, Booth's Theatre, Apr. 30 1883, Folder; *The Indianapolis Times*, Feb. 27, 1882: 4; *The New York Mirror*, Apr. 7 1883: 7; *The New York Mirror*, May 5 (6), June 9 (11), Oct. 13 (2), 1883; Clippings: *Advertiser* (Boston), Dec. 23, 1882, Scrapbook, EB, 1881–1882 Season, *New York Tribune*, Apr. 29, 1888, Scrapbook, Booth Memorial, I, Hampden-Booth.

Chapter Fifteen

1. Ellen M. Plante, *Women at Home in Victorian America* (New York: Facts on File, Inc: 1997), 39.
2. EB to TBA, July 4, 1870, Harvard; to John E. Russell, July 4, 1870, Rochester; to McE, July 25, 1870, Hampden-Booth; to EwB, Nov. 24, 1872, to EBG, Apr. 13, no year [1887 penciled in], NYPLPA.
3. EB to Jean Davenport Lander, Oct. 20, 1878, Folger; to John E. Russell, Sept. 29, 1870, Rochester.
4. James McVicker, "My dear Edwin," [EB], Feb. 8, 1871, Hampden-Booth; EB, "My dear daughter," [EwB], Nov. 10, 1872, NYPLPA; Receipt signed by Mary G. Booth, DeBar's Opera House, Apr. 4, 1874, Harvard; EB to John T. Ford, Apr. 14, 1878, n.d. [mid–Apr. 1878], Ford Papers, LC; EB to Asa Israel Fish, Jan. 20, no year, Folger; Grossman, 179; Watermeier, *Between Actor and Critic*, 106; Clipping, *The Globe* (New York), Mar. 11, 1870, Hampden-Booth.
5. EB to EwB, Jan. 1, 1876, NYPLPA; to WW, Dec. 10, 1876, Folger.
6. EB to Launt Thompson, Dec. 16, 1870, transcription by EBG, to EwB, Oct. 1, 1871, NYPLPA; James H. McVicker to EB, Feb. 19, 1871, Hampden-Booth; Deed Books, 229 (516), 232 (127), 234 (44, 64), County Clerk's Office, Freehold, New Jersey; EB to John E. Russell, June 19, 1871, Rochester; to LB, July 3, Sept. 9, 1871, LB to EB, July 9, 1871, Hampden-Booth;.
7. EB to EwB, Oct. 1, 1871, NYPLPA; to LB, Oct. 6, 1871, Hampden-Booth; Deed Book, 236, 95, County Clerk's Office, Freehold, New Jersey.
8. EB to TBA, Oct. 3, 1872, Harvard; to John E. Russell, Oct. 17, 1873, Rochester; to EwB, June 2, Sept. 12, 1875, NYPLPA; Clippings: "EB's Injuries," *The Daily Graphic*, Aug. 17, 1875, "EB Assurances of his Speedy Recovery," Aug. 17, 1875, Folder.
9. T. J. Barrett to EB, Aug. 5, 1872, Hampden-Booth
10. EB to LB, n.d. [1887–1888], Harvard.
11. EB to EwB, Jan. 29, 1873, NYPLPA.
12. EB to EwB, Feb. 2, 15, 1873, NYPLPA.
13. EB to EwB, Mar. 2, 1873, NYPLPA.
14. EB to EwB, June 13, 1873, NYPLPA.
15. A. O. Kellogg to EB, n.d. [After Aug. 16, 1875], Aug. 27, 1875, Hampden-Booth; EB to EwB, Sept. 12, 1875, NYPLPA.
16. EB to WW, n.d. [received July 13, 1878, penciled in by WW], Folger; Mary Ann Holmes Booth to EB, Aug., 1875, EwB to McE, Aug. 18, n.d. [1875], Hampden-Booth; McE, Diary, Aug. 17–19 1875; EB to EwB, Sept. 12, 1875, NYPLPA; Clippings: "EB's Injuries," *The Daily Graphic*, Aug. 17, 1875, "Actor Perhaps Fatally Injured," no source, Folder.
17. McE, Diary, Aug. 23, 1875; EB to McE, Aug. 29, 1875, Hampden-Booth; to Augustin Daly, Sept. 2, 1875, Clipping, "EB's Injuries," *The Daily Graphic*, Aug. 17, 1875, Folder.
18. EB to WW, Sept. 5, 1875, Folger; to EwB, Sept. 5, 1875, NYPLPA.
19. EB EwB, Sept. 12, 1875, NYPLPA.
20. EB to Augustin Daly, Sept. 6, 1875, Folger; EB to John E. Russell, Oct. 5, 8, 1875, Rochester; to Augustin Daly, Oct. 5, 1875, Folger; to EwB, Oct. 10, 1875, NYPLPA.
21. EB to EwB, Oct. 24, 1875, NYPLPA, WW to John T. Ford, Mar. 13, 1876, John T. Ford to WW, Aug. 15, 1876, Letter fragment, no addressee, n.d. [Fall 1876], Ford Papers, LC; *New York Dramatic News*, Oct. 16 (6), 30 (2), Nov. 18 (4), 1875; Clipping, "EB as Hamlet," *The New York Herald*, Oct. 26, 1875, Melvin Scrapbook, Hampden-Booth.
22. *The New York Dramatic News*, Mar. 11, 1876: 5.
23. Miscellaneous, Book 45, 48, 49, 50, Greenwich Town Hall, Greenwich, Connecticut; J. H. McVicker to EB, Dec. 31, 1878, EB to EwB, Jan. 1, 1876, NYPLPA; to EwB, Jan. 1, 1876, to McE, May 14, 1876, to David C. Anderson, July 22, 1876, Hampden-Booth; McE, Diary, May 28, June 2, 9, 1876; John T. Ford to WW, n.d. [late June 1886 penciled in], Ford Papers, LC; Watermeier, *Between Actor and Critic*, 89; *New York Dramatic News*, July 15, 1876: 5, 3.
24. John McCullough to EB, Apr. 3, 1876, to McE, July 15, 1876, Hampden-Booth; EB to McE, Oct. 1, 1876, Tulsa; Watermeier, *Between Actor and Critic*, 58; *The Chicago Daily Tribune*, Aug. 6, 1876: 16; *Deseret Evening News* (Salt Lake City, Utah), Aug. 18, 1876: 2; *Daily Alta California* (San Francisco), Aug. 19, 1876: 2; *The Salt Lake City Daily Tribune*, Aug. 23, 1876: 3; *New York Dramatic News*, Aug. 26 (6), Sept. 16 (6), 1876.
25. EB to John McCullough, Nov. 19, 1876, Harvard; to McE, June 10, 1877, July 22, no year [1877], Aug. 29, 1877, Hampden-Booth; Postcard to WW, June 27 [1877 written in Winter's handwriting], to WW, Aug. 25, 1877, Folger; *New York Dramatic News and Society Journal*, June 16 (3), 23 (5), July 7 (2, 5), Sept. 8 (4), 1877.
26. EB to WW, no salutation or date, [Spring 1878], Mar. 22, 1878, Folger; to E. C. Benedict, Mar. 20, 1878, Hampden-Booth; Watermeier, *Between Actor and Critic*, 97; *The New York Mirror*, Feb. 26, 1882: 6.
27. EB to McE, n.d. [Summer, 1878], Hampden-Booth.
28. *The Chicago Tribune*, Apr. 24, 1879: 1–2.

29. EB to Ferdinand C. Ewer, Apr. 27, 1879, to E. C. Benedict, Apr. 27, 1879, to David C. Anderson, May 1, 1879, June 20, 1879, Hampden-Booth; to McE, Apr. 27, 1879, Taper Collection; to ECS, Apr. 27, 1879, The New-York Historical Society; to WW, Mar. 20, 1882, Folger; Grossman, 197–198; Watermeier, *Between Actor and Critic*, 135; *The Chicago Tribune*, Apr. 26 (6), 28 (5), 1879; *The Chicago Daily Tribune*, May 11, 1879: 10.
30. *St. Louis Globe-Democrat*, June 11, 1893: 1.
31. LH, "A Group of Players": 198.
32. EB to ECS, Nov. 8, 1879, to WW, Dec. 3, 1879, Folger; McE, Diary, Jan. 21, 1880.
33. For information on the symptoms of pulmonary tuberculosis see Thomas Dormandy, *The White Death. A History of Tuberculosis* (New York: New York University Press, 2000), 22, 23s, 114, 117, 124.
34. Dormandy, 134; Rothman, 248.
35. EwB to EB, n.d. Spring, 1880, NYPLPA.
36. Carroll Smith-Rosenberg, *Disorderly Conduct*: 208; "The Female World of Love and Ritual: Relations Between Women in Nineteenth-Century America," *Signs* I (1975): 1–29 cited in Frank, *Life with Father*, 160.
37. EB to LH, Mar. 5, no year, [1880], Princeton; EB to WW, Mar. 5, 1880, Folger.
38. EB to WW, Mar. 17, 1880, Apr. 20, 23, 1880, Folger; to McE, Apr. 16, 1880, Hampden-Booth; to LH, Apr. 16, 1880, Princeton; McE, Diary, Apr. 20, 21, 1880.
39. EB to WW, n.d. [June 29, 1880 written in hand of Jefferson Winter], Folger.
40. McE, Diary, May 11, 1880, EB to EwB, May 30, 1880, Hampden-Booth; to LH, May 30, 1880, Harvard, McE, June 2, 1880, Tulsa.
41. McE, *Diary*, May 14, 1880.
42. EB to LH, June 17, June 22, 1880, June 22, 1880, Harvard.
43. EB to LH, June 17, to TBA, June 22, 1880, Harvard; Hemphill, 191; Watermeier, *Between Actor and Critic*, 154; *The New York Times*, June 5 (4), 14 (5) 1880.
44. EB to Frederick Paulding, June 20, 1880, Hampden-Booth; to TBA, June 22, 1880, Harvard; McE, Diary, June 21, 1880; Bispham: 137, Harvard.
45. EB to LH, July 6, 1880, Princeton.

Chapter Sixteen

1. EB to Richard Robertson, Dec. 11, 1870, Clipping, *The New York Mirror*, Dec. 4, 1880, Scrapbook, 1880–1881, Hampden-Booth.
2. McE, Diary, Mar. 17, 1879.
3. EB to ECS, Apr. 27, 1879, The New-York Historical Society; to LH, Aug. 15, 1879, Princeton; to David C. Anderson, Sept. 16, 1879, Hampden-Booth; to McE, Sept. 20, 1879, Tulsa; *St. Louis Daily Globe-Democrat* May 18 (10), June 1 (9), 1879; *The New York Times*, Aug. 24, 1879: 7.
4. From Dublin the Booths went to Belfast, stopping several times to see "ruins, battlefields, etc." There they spent "a day or two" and went on to Kingston, now called Dún Laoghaire or Dunleary, then to a seaport on Dublin Bay, south of the city of Dublin (July 14), Portrush (July 18), back to Belfast and then across the channel to Scotland. There they visited Glasgow, Abbotsford, Melrose, Stirling, Loch Lomond, the Trossachs (a small woodland glen made famous by Sir Walter Scott), and Edinburgh. They went south to Derwentwater and the Lake District, Chester, Knutsford, Wales, Lichfield, Charlecote, Leamington (Aug. 14–16), Stratford-upon-Avon (Aug. 17), Clopton (Aug. 18), Oxford (Aug. 19–21), Salisbury (Aug. 22), Sarum and Tunbridge Wells. EB to David C. Anderson, July 15, 1880, to LH, July 13, 1880, Princeton; to TBA, Nov. 21, 1880, Harvard; to McE, July 20, 1880, Taper collection; to ECS, Sept. 4, 1880, Folger; McE to EB, Aug. 8, 1880, Ferdinand C. Ewer to EB, Sept. 15, 1880, Hampden-Booth; Grossman, 210–213; Watermeier, *Between Actor and Critic*, 155, 156, 160; Bispham: 138, Harvard; Hutton, "A Group of Players": 197; *The New York Mirror*, Aug. 7, 1880: 6; Clipping, *Lloyd's* (London), Nov. 7, 1880, Scrapbook, 1880–1881, Hampden-Booth.
5. McE to EB, Aug. 8, 1880, Walter Gooch, Abstract of Engagement between Mr. EB and Mr. Walter Gooch, Aug. 9, 1880, EB to John Sleeper Clarke, Aug. 9, 1880, Hampden-Booth.
6. EB to LH, Aug. 29, 1880, Princeton; McE, *Diary*, Aug. 30, 1880; EB to McE, Sept. 19, 1880, Taper Collection; to Ferdinand C. Ewer, Dec. 19, 1888, Hampden-Booth; Grossman, 218, 219; Watermeier, *Between Actor and Critic*, 163, 164, 165; Bispham: 138, *The New York Mirror*, Sept. 25, 1880: 2.
7. EB to McE, Nov. 10, 1880, Taper Collection; to David C. Anderson, Nov. 14, 1880, Hampden-Booth; *The New York Mirror*, July 21, 1881: 21.
8. Watermeier, *Between Actor and Critic*, 170–173; *The New York Mirror*, July 21, 188: 21.
9. EB, "My dear Sir," Oct. 7, 1880, Thomas Swinbourne et al to EB, Oct. 16, 1880, R. Eves to EB, Oct. 29, 1880, EB to Ferdinand C. Ewer, Dec. 19, 1880, to E. C. Benedict, Jan. 25, 1881, Hampden-Booth; to LB, Jan. 20, 1881, Harvard; Grossman, 218, 219.
10. EB to TBA, Nov. 21, 1880, Harvard; to E. C. Benedict, Dec. 19, 1880, Hampden-Booth; http://mypage.uniserve.ca/~canyon/qv_ladies.htm#Ladies.
11. Box office memorandum, Nov. 6, 1880-Mar. 26, 1881, File, EB, Tour of England, Scotland and Ireland, 1882, EB to Ferdinand C. Ewer, Dec. 19, 1880, to David C. Anderson, June 6, 1881, Henry Irving, Telegram to EB, n.d. [circa Apr. 27, 1883], Hampden-Booth; EB to LH, Dec. 19, 1880, Princeton; to ECS Dec. 24, 1880, Folger; to LH, Jan. 10, 1881, Princeton; to EBG, n.d. [Nov. 17, incorrectly labeled Nov. 18, 1886], NYPLPA; Grossman, 218, 219, 221.
12. EB to ECS, Nov. 13, 1880, Folger; EB to LH, Jan. 10, 1881, Princeton; to E. C. Benedict, Jan. 25, 1881, Henry Irving to EB, Nov. 15, 1880, Hampden-Booth; Bispham: 241, Harvard; Grossman, 213, 214; Watermeier, *Between Actor and Critic*, 170–173.
13. EB, Financial memorandum, Nov. 12–31, no year [1880], Walter Gooch, "The engagement between EB and Walter Gooch," Jan. 1, 1881, Hampden-Booth; EB to LH, Jan. 10, 1881, Princeton; to LB, Sept. 14, 1885, Harvard.
14. EB to ECS, Dec. 24, 1880, Folger; Programme, *Othello*, Princess's Theatre, n.d. [Jan. 17, 1881 penciled in], The Theatre Museum, London; Grossman, 221; *The Daily Telegraph* (London), Jan. 18, 1881: 2.
15. EB to LB, Jan. 20, 1881, Harvard; to E. C. Benedict, Jan. 25, 1881, Hampden-Booth; Clippings: *Life* (London), Jan. 22, 1881, *New York Tribune*, n.d. Scrapbook, 1880–1881, Hampden-Booth.
16. EB to LH, Nov. 9, 1880, Princeton; to LB, Jan. 20, 1881, Harvard; Madge Kendal, *Dame Madge Kendal by Herself* (London: John Murray, 1933), 227, 228.
17. Franklin Taylor to Mary McVicker Booth, Jan. 8, 1881, Hampden-Booth; Barr, *Drink*, 12; Rene and Jean Dubos, *The White Plague: Tuberculosis, Man, and Society* (New Brunswick, New Jersey: Rutgers University Press, 1996), 64; 205, 206; Kendal, 229.
18. EB to E. C. Benedict, Jan. 25, 1881, Hampden-Booth.
19. Asia Booth Clarke to EB, n.d. [1881], Hampden-Booth.
20. EB to Harry Magonigle, Mar. 1881, Yale; Henry Irving to EB, Mar. 4, 1881, to Mr. Collier, Mar. 6, no year [1881], Hampden-Booth; Watermeier, *Between Actor and Critic*, 183; House: 275, 276; *Bell's Life in London and Sporting Chronicle*, Mar. 5, 1881: 11.
21. EB to McE, Mar. 1, 1881, Taper Collection; Dormandy, 155.
22. On Apr. 5, 1881, Mary Ann Holmes wrote to Edwina

suggesting that Mary McVicker be put in a "quiet careful spot ... where she could do no harm." EB to Harry Magonigle, Mar. 1881, Yale; to McE, Mar. 20, 1881, to E. H. House," Mar. 29, 1881, John Crouse Autograph Collection, Bentley Historical Library, University of Michigan; to TBA, Mar. 29, 1881, to E. H. House," Apr. 6, no year [1881], Harvard; to McE, Apr. 24, 1881, Mary Ann Holmes Booth to EwB, Apr. 5, 1881, Taper Collection; to ECS, May 8, 1881, Folger; Record of Expenses and Deposits, 1880–1881, Hampden-Booth; Grossman, 225, 226; House: 271, 272, 277; Laurence Hutton, "A Group of Players": 197; *New York Dramatic News and Society Journal*, Mar. 26 (8), Apr. 30 (7), 1881; *The New York Mirror*, Apr. 2 (7), 9 (6), July 21 (14), 1881.

23. Watermeier, *Between Actor and Critic*, 187.

24. Laurence Irving, *Henry Irving: The Actor and His World* (New York: The Macmillan Company, 1952), 372.

25. Laurence Irving, 375; *The New York Mirror*, Apr. 9, 1881: 6; *The New York Dramatic News and Society Journal*, May 7, 1881: 2; *The Chicago Daily Tribune*, May 7 (5), 22 (19) 1881; Clippings: *The Illustrated London News*, May 7, 1881, The Theatre Museum, London *Truth* (London), May 12, 1881, Scrapbook, Winter-Spring, 1883, Hampden-Booth.

26. EB to E.C. Benedict, May 10, 1881, Taper Collection; to Mr. Meller, May 24, 1881, to Adam Badeau, June 3, 1881, Folger; Record of Expenses and Deposits, 1880–1881, Hampden-Booth; Watermeier, *Between Actor and Critic*, 188, 189; Bispham:242, Harvard.

27. EB to David C. Anderson, June 6, 1881, Hampden-Booth.

Chapter Seventeen

1. McE, Diary, May 31, June 7, 1881; EB to Miss Henrietta Bube, June 14, 1881, to William E. Miller, Aug. 16, no year [1881], Record of Expenses and Deposits, 1880–1881, Hampden-Booth; EB to McE, July 25, 1881, Taper Collection; EB to WW, n.d. [Received by Winter Aug. 10, 1881], Folger; EB to Major Walters, July 29, 1884, Harvard; EB to LB, n.d. Princeton; *New York Dramatic News and Society Journal*, Apr. 30 (7), May 7 (7), 1881; *The Daily Chicago Tribune*, July 12, 1881: 7; *The New York Mirror*, July 30, 1881: 10.

2. EB to McE, Thanksgiving, no year [1881], Taper Collection; William G. Rothstein, *American Physicians in the Nineteenth Century* (Baltimore: The Johns Hopkins University Press, 1972), 195.

3. EB to McE, July 1, 1881, Tulsa; to Mrs. Gray, July 7, 1881, Yale; to EwB July 8 [1881 penciled in], McE to EB, July 10, 1881, Hampden-Booth; EB to ECS, July 8, 1881, to WW, July 9, 1881, Saturday, n.d. [note that the letter was received on July 23, 1881 in Winter's handwriting], Folger; *The New York Mirror*, July 9, 1881: 6.

4. EB to WW, n.d. [Answered by Winter Feb. 12, 1879], Saturday, n.d. [note that the letter was received on July 23, 1881 in Winter's handwriting], Folger; to McE, July 25, 1881, Taper Collection; *The New York Mirror*, July 30, 1881: 10.

5. William Alex, *Calvert Vaux: Architect & Planner* (New York, Ink, Inc., 1994), 1.

6. EB to McE, Nov. 21, 1867, Downing Vaux to EB, Jan. 7, 1882, Hampden-Booth; McE, Diary, July 11, 1872, 14, no year [1872], Oct. 4, 1876, Feb. 8, 18, 1878, July 27, 1880; *Dictionary of America Biography*, XIX (New York: Charles Scribner's Sons, 1936), 238.

7. McE, Diary, Dec. 3, 1879; Sr. Agnes Mary to EwB, July 29, 1880, Julia D. Vaux to EwB, Oct. 3, 1880, McE to EB, May 8, 1881, Hampden-Booth; EB to McE, July 1, 1881, Tulsa; Watermeier, *Between Actor and Critic*, 192, n. 3; Clipping, "Was EB's Manager," *Chicago Post*, n.d. [June, 1893], Scrapbook. Tributes of the Press to EB, Memorial Notices, Hampden-Booth.

8. EB to McE, July 25, 1881, Taper Collection; Downing Vaux to EwB, Aug. 8, 22, 1881, Hampden-Booth; *The New York Mirror*, July 30, 1881:10.

9. McE, Diary, Sept. 26, 27, 30, 1881; McE to EwB, Sept. 30, 1881, Hampden-Booth.

10. Marilyn Yalom, *A History of the Wife* (New York: HarperCollins Publishers, 2001), 178; *The New York Mirror*, Oct. 22, 1881: 6.

11. Booth received eighty percent of the net profits and Abbey twenty percent. According to his stage manager Maze Edwards, Booth netted $120,000 during the 1881–1882 tour. Agreement between Henry E. Abbey and EB, Aug. 17, 1881, Hampden-Booth; *The Daily Chicago Tribune*, June 19, 1881:18; *The New York Mirror*, July 30, 1881:10; Clipping "Was EB's Manager," *Chicago Post*, n.d. [June, 1893], Scrapbook, Tributes of the Press to EB, Hampden-Booth.

12. Manhattan Death Certificate 40402, Nov. 13, 1881, Birth Death and Marriage Certificate Office, New York, New York; Clinton Wagner to EB, Nov. 13, 1881, Lyceum Theatre, Philadelphia, Pennsylvania, Box Office Record, Nov. 15–17, 19, 1882, Sr. Agnes Mary to EwB, Nov. 29, 1881, Hampden-Booth.

13. McE to EB, Nov. 17, 1881, Hampden-Booth; *The Chicago Tribune*, Nov. 14, 1881: 5; *The Cincinnati Commercial*, Nov. 17, 1881:1; Clipping, "Death of EB's Wife, *New-York Daily Tribune*, Nov. 14, 1881, "Mrs. Booth's Funeral in Chicago," *New York Mirror*, Nov. 26, 1881, Folger.

14. *The Chicago Daily Tribune*, Nov. 19 (11), 20 (22), 1881; *The New York Mirror*, Nov. 19, 1881:6; Watermeier, *Between Actor and Critic*, 195; www.Findagrave.com/pictures/8231.

15. Mary L. Booth to EB, Nov. 19, 1881, Hampden-Booth; Goodale, 106, 107; Watermeier, *Between Actor and Critic*, 197; *The New-York Times*, Mar. 6, 1886: 5.

16. William Bispham to EB, Nov. 22, 1881, Hampden-Booth; to LH, Nov. 23, 1881, Princeton.

17. Calvert, 208, 209, 210; Watermeier, *Between Actor and Critic*, 195, 196; *Waterbury Daily American*, Nov. 29, 1881: 4; Clipping, no source, n.d. Scrapbook, 1881–1882 Season, Hampden-Booth.

18. EB to LH, Dec. 27, 1881, Princeton; to McE, Dec. 27, 1881, Hampden-Booth;, *Between Actor and Critic*, 199, 200; *Easton Express* (Easton, Pennsylvania), Jan. 2, 1882: 2; *The Providence Daily Journal*, Jan. 5, 1882: 8.

19. EB to LH, Feb. 14, 22, 1882, Princeton, to E. H. Hazard, Feb. 14, 1882, Folger; *The New York Mirror*, Jan. 21, 1882: 3; *The Terre Haute Express*, Feb. 12, 1882: 3.

20. EB, letter fragment, no addressee [Laurence Hutton], n.d. Princeton; Watermeier, *Between Actor and Critic*, 201; *Fort Wayne Daily Sentinel*, Feb. 23, 1882: 1.

21. EB to WW, Apr. 13, 1882, Folger; to LH, Apr. 15, 1882, Princeton.

22. EB to WW, Jan. 10, [1882, penciled in], Apr. 24, 1885, Folger; McE, Diary, Apr. 18, 1882; EB to LH, Apr. 27, 1883, Princeton; to EBG, Sept. 19, 1886, Oct. 3, 1887, NYPLPA; Grossman, 74; Watermeier, *Between Actor and Critic*, 265.

Chapter Eighteen

1. EB to WW, May 6, 1882, Folger; to LH, May 6, 1882, Princeton; Wynn E. Miller to EB, Aug. 16, 1881, EB to Wynn E. Miller, May 15, 1882, Hampden-Booth; *The New York Mirror*, Nov. 26, 1881: 6.

2. EB to Mary Booth, May 25, 1882, Harvard; to Wynn E. Miller, May 27, 1882, Hampden-Booth; Grossman, 229; Watermeier, *Between Actor and Critic*, 223, 224, 225; *Frank Leslie's Illustrated Newspaper*, Jan. 4, 1879: 294, 295.

3. Wynn E. Miller to EB, Aug. 16, 1881, EB to McE, Feb. 23, 1882, McE to EB, Dec. 10, 1867, Julia Vaux to EwB, Dec. 27, 1881, EB to Launt Thompson, n.d. [May 1882], Hampden-Booth; to LH, Feb. 24, 1881, Mar. 3, 1882, Princeton; to TBA, May 14, 1882, Harvard; McE, Diary, May 12, 1882; Watermeier, *Between Actor and Critic*, 216, 217.

4. EB to Mrs. Ole Bull, Jan. 10, no year [1882], to William E. Miller, May 27, 1882, Hampden-Booth; to WW, May 17, 19, 1882, n.d. [annotation by WW that it was written on May 24, 1882], Folger; McE, *Diary*, May 17, 1882.
5. EB to William E. Miller, May 27, 1882, to Launt Thompson, May 29, 1882, Hampden-Booth.
6. EwB to EB, Jan. 8, 1882, to Launt Thompson, June 4, 1882, Hampden-Booth; to WW, n.d. [June 4, 1882 penciled in], Folger; to Lester Wallack, June 5, 1882, Harvard; *The New York Mirror*, June 6, 1882: 9.
7. Program, Adelphi Theatre, June 26, 1882, Hampden-Booth; Watermeier, *Between Actor and Critic*, 208; *The Times* (London), June 26, 1882: 8; *The New York Mirror*, July 1 (6), 15 (7), 1882; Clippings: *Evening News* (London), June 24, 1882, *Daily Telegraph* (London), June 24, 1882, *The Echo* (London), June 27, 1882, *Life* (London), June 29, 1882, *Whitehall, Review* (London), June 29, 1882, Scrapbook, 1882, Hampden-Booth.
8. Watermeier, *Between Actor and Critic*, 210–215.
9. EB to LH, n.d. [July 1882], July 7, 1882, Princeton; to David C. Anderson, July 23, [1882], Hampden-Booth; Watermeier, *Between Actor and Critic*, 208, 209.
10. EB to "Dear Doctor," July 27, no year [1882], Folger; Watermeier, *Between Actor and Critic*, 209.
11. EB to David C. Anderson, Aug. 12, 1882, Hampden-Booth.
12. EB to LH, Aug. 25, 1882, Princeton; Watermeier, *Between Actor and Critic*, 210, 211, 212, 223, 224, 225.
13. Agreement between W. A. Waddington and EB, Sept. 5, 1881, Agreements between Charles Bernard and EB, Nov. 21, 24, 28, 1881, Agreements between Wilson Barrett and EB, Nov. 23, 1881, Agreement between J. B. Howard and EB, Nov. 24, 1881, Agreement between Mercer H. Simpson and EB, Feb. 14, 1882, Theatre Royal, Dundee, Terms, Sept. 14, 1882, Memorandum of Agreement, Royal Alexandria Theatre, Liverpool, Aug. 30, 1881, Terms, Her Majesty's Theatre, Aberdeen, Sept. 14, 1882, Memorandum of Agreement, Gaiety Theatre, Dublin, Mar. 14, 1882, File, Tour of England, Scotland and Ireland, 1882, Hampden-Booth; Watermeier, *Between Actor and Critic*, 210, 211, 212.
14. *The Sheffield Daily Telegraph*, Sept. 12 (6), Sept. 14 (3), 1882; Clippings: "Prince's Theatre, Mr. EB in 'Richelieu,'" "Mr. EB in 'Richard III,'" *Manchester Guardian*, n.d. [Nov. 21–25, 1882], The Theatre Museum, London; *Glasgow Evening News*, Oct. 12, 1882, Scrapbook, 1882, Hampden-Booth.
15. EB to David C. Anderson, Oct. 26, 1882, Hampden-Booth; Grossman, 238, 239; Watermeier, *Between Actor and Critic*, 213, 214, 215.
16. EB to David C. Anderson, Sept. 20, [1882], Hampden-Booth; to LH, Sept. 27, no year [1882], Princeton; Grossman, 237, 238.
17. McE, *Diary*, Oct. 13, 16, 1882.
18. McE, *Diary*, Nov. 1, 1882.
19. EB to David C. Anderson, Dec. 21, 1882, Box office receipts, File, EB, German and Austrian Tour, 1883, Hampden-Booth; EB to WW, Dec. 26, 1882, Folger; McE, *Diary*, Jan. 1, 1883; Grossman, 241; Watermeier, *Between Actor and Critic*, 222–225.
20. EB to Paul R. Schweitzer, Jan. 3, 1883, Folger; EB, to David C. Anderson, Jan. 29, 1883, Hampden-Booth; Grossman, 242; Watermeier, *Between Actor and Critic*, 229, 230, 231.
21. EB to LH, Jan. 7, 1883, Princeton; Watermeier, *Between Actor and Critic*, 227, 228.
22. Lorraine Commeret, "Edwin Booth's Tour of Germany and Austria in 1883: A Perspective on the Critical Responses," *Theatre History Studies*, IX (1989): 43; Clippings: "EB in Berlin," no source, Jan. 17, no year [1883], The Theatre Museum, London; Emanuel Lederer, trans., "EB in Germany," n.d. 5–7, NYPLPA; *The New York Tribune*, Jan. 12, 1883, *The New York Tribune*, Jan.13, 14, 17, 1883, Scrapbook, Booth Memorial Vol. 1, Hampden-Booth.
23. EB to David C. Anderson, Jan. 29, 1883, Hampden-Booth; to LH, n.d. [c. Jan. 1883], Princeton; Grossman, 242; Clipping, Lederer: 5, 6, 7, NYPLPA.
24. EB to LH, n.d. [c. Jan. 1883], Princeton.
25. EB to David C. Anderson, Jan. 29, 1883, Hampden-Booth; to LH, Feb. 4, 1883, Princeton; McE, *Diary*, Mar. 3, 1883; Grossman, 242; Watermeier, *Between Actor and Critic*, 229, 230, 231.
26. Clipping, *New York Herald*, Apr. 24, 1883, Scrapbook, Winter-Spring, 1883, Hampden-Booth.
27. EB to David C. Anderson, Feb. 18, 1883, Hampden-Booth; Grossman, 2472, 243, 244.
28. "The farewell performance of Mr. Booth Thalia Theater Hamburg," translation of newspaper article, NYPLPA; Watermeier, *Between Actor and Critic*, 234, 325, 236.
29. EB to LH, Mar. 7, 1883, Princeton; Commeret: 49; Clipping, "EB at Bremen," no source, n.d. [late Feb.-early Mar. 1883], The Theatre Museum, London.
30. Watermeier, *Between Actor and Critic*, 236–239.
31. Clipping, "EB in Vienna, no source, n.d. The Theatre Museum, London.
32. Clipping, no source, n.d. [after Apr. 17, 1883], Scrapbook, Winter-Spring, 1883, Hampden-Booth.
33. Watermeier, *Between Actor and Critic*, 239, 240, 241, 243, 246, 247, 248; Commeret: 49; Clippings: "EB in Vienna, no source, Mar. 18, 1883, "Mr. EB in Vienna," no source, n.d. The Theatre Museum, London; no source, n.d. [after Apr. 17, 1883], Scrapbook, Winter-Spring, 1883, Hampden-Booth.
34. EB to David C. Anderson, Apr. 27, 1883, Hampden-Booth; to LH, Apr. 27, 1883, Princeton; to McE, May 4, 1883, Taper Collection; Grossman, 246, 247; Watermeier, *Between Actor and Critic*, 243–248.
35. EB to David C. Anderson, Apr. 27, 1883, Hampden-Booth; to McE, May 4, 1883, Taper Collection; to LH, Apr. 27, 1883, Princeton; Grossman, 246, 247.
36. McE, *Diary*, May 7, 8, 1883.
37. McE, *Diary*, May 9, 10, 12, 13, 14, 20, 21, 1883; EB to McE, May 21, no year, [1883], Taper Collection; *The New-York Times*, May 9 (5), 10 (8) 1883: 8.
38. EB to David C. Anderson, May 21, 1883, to E. de Wartegg, Jan. 10, no year, Hampden-Booth; to Major Walters, July 29, 1884, Harvard; to LH, Oct. 1, 1884, May 4, 1887, Princeton; to Mr. Lederer, Oct. 30, 1884, Texas; to EBG, Aug. 16, Sept. 9, 1885, NYPLPA; Mary Anderson, *A Few Memories* (New York, n.p., 1896), 209; Watermeier, *Between Actor and Critic*, 248.

Chapter Nineteen

1. EB to LH, Apr. 27, 1883, Princeton.
2. EB to McE, July 16, 1883, Taper Collection; Clipping *The New York Tribune*, July 24, 1883, Scrapbook, Booth Memorial Vol. 1, Hampden-Booth.
3. EB to WW, July 25, no year [1883], Folger; McE, *Diary*, July 26, 27, Sept. 4, Oct. 13, 1883.
4. EB to WW, n.d. [Answered by Winter Feb. 12, 1879], Folger; William Bispham to EB, Mar. 23, 1882, Hampden-Booth; *Middletown Rhode Island Houses: History, Heritage* (Middletown, Rhode Island: The Middletown Historical Society, 1990), 66; James L. Yarnell, "Edwin Booth's Life in Paradise," *Newport History*, 68, part 3 Number 236, 1997: 113–116, 119, 123, 131; *The New York Clipper*, August 4, 1866: 134; *The New York Mirror*, Feb. 15 (4), June 21 (4) 1879; Bispham: 137, Bamburgh, Harvard.
5. EB to LH, August 24, 1883, Princeton; Letter Fragment beginning "The bill," n.d. [Feb. 1879], 8; to EwB, June 11, Sept. 15, 1872, NYPLPA, to David C. Anderson, Sept. 16,

Dec. 10, 1879, Hampden-Booth; Mary Anderson, 208; Grossman, 202, 203; *The New York Clipper*, May 19, 1866: 42; Clipping, "Another Booth Gone," Junius Brutus Booth & Family Miscellaneous Manuscript Collection, LC.

6. EB to David C. Anderson, January 29, 1883, Hampden-Booth; to LH, Sept. 25, 1883, Princeton; to McE, Sept. 27, 1883, Tulsa; to EBG, Oct. 9, no year [1887 penciled in], NYPLPA; *The New-York Times* Sept. 16 (6), 18 (4), 1883; *Newport Daily News*, Sept. 17 (1), 18 (1), 1883; *The New York Mirror*, Sept. 22, 1883: 6; *New York Amusement Gazette*, Dec. 16, 1889: 195; Clippings: "Death of Junius Brutus Booth," *New-York Daily Tribune*, Sept. 18, 1883, "Junius Brutus Booth's Estate," no source or date listed, "Breaking a Will," *The New-York Herald*, Dec. 16, 1883, Folger; *The New York Tribune*, Sept. 19, 1883, Scrapbook, Booth Memorial Vol. 1, Hampden-Booth, "Mrs. Agnes Booth as Mrs. Ralston in 'Jim the Penman,'" "Agnes Booth," Glase Scrapbook, Theatre Collection, Free Library of Philadelphia.

7. EB to LH, Sept. 25, 1883, Princeton; Clipping, *The New York Times*, Sept. 19, 1883, Scrapbook, Booth Memorial Vol. 1, Hampden-Booth.

8. EB to WW, n.d. [Oct. 8, 1883 penciled in], Folger.

9. EB to R. M. Field, Apr. 12, 1883, to LH, July 7, 1883, Princeton, to TBA, Oct. 10, 19, 1883, Harvard; Watermeier, *Between Actor and Critic*, 211; *Newport Daily News*, Oct. 13, 1883: 2; Clipping, "Recollections of Mr. Booth," *Boston Herald*, June 8, 1893, Scrapbook, Tributes of the Press to EB, Memorial Notices collected by The Players, 1893, Hampden-Booth.

10. Watermeier, *Between Actor and Critic*, 257.

11. Watermeier, *Between Actor and Critic*, 251, 253.

12. Downing Vaux went on to become a landscape architect, laying out Kingston Point Park and Downing Park in Newburgh, New York, as well as his most famous project, Riverside Drive in New York. He never married, and the last years of his life were spent at the Y.M. C. A. in Kingston, New York. There on the morning of May 15, 1926, he got up early to watch the sunrise. He fell from the roof and was found dead on the sidewalk, wearing only his night clothes. McE, Diary, Dec. 26, 27, 1883, Jan. 2, Apr. 8, 1884, Feb. 11, July 11, 1885; EB to McE, Dec. 30, 1883, July 27, 1884, Taper Collection; to Bowyer Vaux, May 5, 1884, Tulsa; to David C. Anderson, July 27, 1884, to McE, Dec. 14, 1884, Hampden-Booth; *The New York Mirror*, June 7, 1884: 6; *The New York Times*, May 16, 1926: 28.

13. EB to David C. Anderson, July 27, 1884, Hampden-Booth; to McE, July 27, 1884, Taper Collection; to WW, n.d. [Summer 1884 penciled in], Folger; Grossman, 252, 253.

14. EB to Major Walters, July 29, 1884, Harvard; to LH, Aug. 17, Nov. 13, 1884, Princeton; to James R. Osgood & Co., Sept. 18, 1884, Folger; to Mr. Lederer, Oct. 30, 1884, Texas.

15. Grossman, 254; *The New York Mirror*, Dec. 13, 1884: 10.

16. EB to Launt Thompson, Christmas 1884, Hampden-Booth.

17. EwB to Ignatius R. Grossman, Nov. 24, 29, no year [1884], Dec. 11, 1884, NYPLPA.

18. EB to EwB, Feb. 17, 1885, NYPLPA; Grossman genealogical material, Miscellaneous file, Hampden-Booth; Grossman Tombstone, Mount Auburn Cemetery, Boston, Massachusetts.

19. EB to LH, Nov. 30, 1884, Princeton; to Adam Badeau, n.d. [Jan.-Feb. 1885], Texas; Watermeier, *Between Actor and Critic*, 264; *The Philadelphia Inquirer*, Apr. 7 1885: 7; *Evening Bulletin* (Philadelphia), Apr. 10, 1885: 5; Clipping, *Boston Gazette*, Jan. 25, 1885; Matthews and Hutton, V, pt. 2, Harvard.

20. Daniel Frohman, *Encore* (New York: Lee Furman, Inc., 1937), 90.

21. EB to EwB, Apr. 7, 1885, n.d. [Apr., 1885 penciled in], NYPLPA; Mary Mann to Ignatius Grossman, Apr. 12, 1885, Hampden-Booth; Grossman, 54.

22. EB to WW, Apr. 24, 1885, Folger; Watermeier, *Between Actor and Critic*, 265.

23. Wedding invitation, "Mr. EB requests the pleasure of your company," Harvard; Marriage Certificate, May 16, 1885, NYPLPA; McE, Diary, May 19, 1885; Frank, 17; Clipping, "EB in Boston," Harvard.

24. EB to EBG, May 24, no year [1885], NYPLPA.

25. EB to WW, Aug. 14 1885, Folger; to TBA, Aug. 16, no year [1885], to LB, Sept. 14, 1885, Harvard.

26. EB to WW, Sept. 28, no year [1885], Folger.

27. Mary Ann Holmes Booth to EwB, Mar. 3, 1881, Taper Collection.

28. EB to WW, Jan. 27, Feb. 24, Mar. 10, 1884, Folger; to David C. Anderson, July 27, 1884, to E. C. Benedict, Feb. 19, 1884, Hampden-Booth; to LH, Feb. 7, Aug. 17, 1884, Princeton; to McE, Feb. 14, 1884, Taper Collection; to McE, Mar. 1, 1885, Tulsa; *The New York Mirror*, Jan. 26, 1884: 6.

29. EB to Mrs. David C. Anderson, Dec. 21, no year, Hampden-Booth; *The New York Times*, Oct. 17 (5), 18 (5) 1884; Clipping, *The New York Tribune*, Oct. 20, 1884, Scrapbook, Booth Memorial Vol. 1, Hampden-Booth.

30. Clipping, "Death of Mrs. Booth," Junius Brutus Booth & Family Miscellaneous Manuscript Collection, LC.

31. EB to WW, Oct. 22, 1885, Folger; Grossman, 65, 66; "Death of EB's Mother," Clipping, Junius Brutus Booth & Family Miscellaneous Manuscript Collection, LC.

32. Death Certificate 544068, Oct. 22, 1885, Birth, Marriage and Death Certificates, New York, New York; EB to LB, Oct. 27, no year [1885], Harvard; *The Sun* (Baltimore), Oct. 26, 1885: 1.

33. EB to EBG, July 14, 1885, Hampden-Booth; to LH, Aug. 15, 1885, Princeton; *The Sun* (Baltimore), Nov. 3, 1885: 1.

34. McE, Diary, Dec. 4, 1885.

35. EB to EBG, n.d. [Nov. 1885 penciled in but the actual date was Jan. 31, 1886], NYPLPA; *The New York Mirror*, Feb. 6, 1886: 2.

36. EB to EBG, n.d. [New York 1886 penciled in, actually Feb. 27, 1886], NYPLPA; Watermeier, *Between Actor and Critic*, 271, 272.

37. EB to LB, Mar. 23, no year [1886], Harvard; to WW, Mar. 25, 1866, Folger.

38. EB to LH, n.d. [Spring 1886], Princeton; *The New York Mirror*, May 8, 1886: 6.

39. EB to EBG, n.d. [Apr. 24, 1886], NYPLPA.

40. McE, Diary, Apr. 28, 29, 1886; Clipping, "Howard's Gossip," Harvard.

41. EB to LB, May 4, no year [1886], Harvard; *The Philadelphia Inquirer*, Apr. 30 (1), May 1 (7) 1886; Clippings: *The Tribune*, Apr. 30, 1886: 31, Scrapbook, 1886–1887 Season: 27, Hampden-Booth; Clipping, "Mr. Booth's Condition," Harvard.

42. EB to LB, n.d. [July 1886], Harvard.

43. Watermeier, *Between Actor and Critic*, 275, 276, 277.

44. 442. EB to EBG, Sept. 16, 1886, NYPLPA; to E. C. Benedict, n.d. Hampden-Booth; Watermeier, *Between Actor and Critic*, 277, 280.

Chapter Twenty

1. The 1886–1887 tour, announced publicly on Oct. 17, 1885, is one of most documented in Booth's career. In addition to his regular correspondents (Aldrich, Bispham, McEntee, Winter), Booth wrote regularly to both Edwina and to Barrett; the troupe's comedian, Owen Fawcett, kept a log book of travel times and performances with occasional notes. Forty five years, later one of the company's ingenues, Kitty Molony, later Katherine Goodale, published an account of the tour. Like many of the actors hired, she came out of LB's troupe to play roles such as Jessica, the Player Queen in *Hamlet,* Lucretia in John Howard Payne's *Brutus*, Lazarillo in *Ruy Blas* and the Prince of Wales in *Richard III*. While

her perception of the tour is not completely reliable, her memoir still provides insight into the day-to-day workings of the troupe. Moreover, Booth's road manager Arthur B. Chase sent letters to Barrett that document both the personal and the financial aspects of the company's work. Together these documents provide one of the most comprehensive views of a late nineteenth-century tour available. E. C. Benedict, Account Statement, Jan. 1, 1885, Hampden-Booth; EB to McE, June 9, 1885, Tulsa; EB to LB, June 10, no year, [1885], Oct. 27, no year [1885], Harvard; to WW, Sept. 28, no year [1885], Folger; Watermeier, *Between Actor and Critic*, 259, 260, 261.

2. *The New York Mirror*, July 17, 1886: 6.

3. Goodale, 13, 14, 15, 21; *The Detroit Free Press*, Sept. 17, 1886: 2.

4. Fawcett, Diary, Sept. 6, 1886, Tennessee; Program, Star Theatre, New York City, Nov 24, 1886, Hampden-Booth; EB to EBG, Sept. 8, no year [1886], NYPLPA; Bispham: 245, Harvard; *The Daily Era* (Bradford, Pennsylvania), Dec. 24, 1886: 4.

5. ABC to LB, Sept. 11, Oct. 6, 1886, Hampden-Booth; Fawcett, Diary, Sept. 11, 12, 1886, Tennessee; EB to EBG, Sept. 13, 1886, NYPLPA.

6. Goodale, 19, 20, 22, 23, 169, 170, 173; Clipping, *Buffalo Courier*, Sept. 14, 1886, Scrapbook, Tours of EB.—Season 1886–1887, 1, Hampden-Booth.

7. ABC to LB, Sept. 16, 1886, Hampden-Booth; Goodale, 17, 19.

8. ABC to LB, Nov 2, 1886, Hampden-Booth.

9. EB to EBG, Sept. 19, 1886, NYPLPA; Grossman, 74.

10. ABC to LB, Sept. 27, 1886, Hampden-Booth.

11. ABC to LB, Sept. 27, 1886, Hampden-Booth.

12. EB to EBG, Oct. 3, 1886, NYPLPA.

13. ABC to LB, Sept. 27, 1886, Hampden-Booth; EB to EBG, Oct. 3, 1886, NYPLPA.

14. ABC to LB, Nov 1, 2, 1886, Hampden-Booth.

15. EB to LB, Nov 7, no year [1886], Harvard.

16. ABC to LB, Nov 13, 23, 1886, Recapitulation of Booth Tour Season 1886–1887, Receipt Book, Booth Tours, 1886–1891, Hampden-Booth; EB to EBG, n.d. [Dec. 1886], NYPLPA; Goodale, 71; *New York Amusement Gazette*, Nov 1 (3), 15 (6) 1886.

17. ABC to LB, Nov 10, 1886, Hampden-Booth; EB to EBG, n.d. [Nov 10, 11, 1886], NYPLPA; to TBA, Nov 18, 1886, Harvard; Watermeier, *Between Actor and Critic*, 282.

18. Clipping, *The New-York Times*, Nov 16, 1886, Scrapbook, 1886–1887 season, 31, Hampden-Booth.

19. ABC to LB, Dec. 4, 1886, Hampden-Booth; EB to LB, Dec. 7, no year [1886], n.d. Winter 1885–1886, Harvard.

20. Statements for Weeks of Dec. 20, 27, 1886, Receipt Scrapbook for Tours of EB, 1886–1891, Hampden-Booth.

21. Watermeier, *Between Actor and Critic*, 284.

22. EB to LB, Jan. 4, 1887, Harvard.

23. EB to LB, Jan. 27, 1887, Harvard; Goodale, 95; Clippings: *Baltimore American and Commercial Advertiser, The Morning Herald* (Baltimore, Maryland), Jan. 19, 1887, Scrapbook, Tour of EB—Season 1886–1887: 53, Hampden-Booth.

24. ABC to LB, Feb. 8, 1887, Hampden-Booth.

25. ABC to LB, Feb. 8, 15, 1887, Hampden-Booth.

26. ABC to LB, Jan. 30, Feb.15, 1887, Hampden-Booth; EB to LH, Feb. 19, no year [1887], Princeton, to EBG, Feb. 21, no year [1887 penciled in], Feb. 23, 1887, NYPLPA; to LB, n.d. [May 1887], Harvard; Goodale, 113, 115, 144.

27. *The New York Mirror*, Mar. 5, 1887: 8.

28. Fawcett, Diary, Feb. 27, Mar. 1, 1887, Tennessee; EB to EBG, Feb. 26, 1887, Mar. 1, no year [1887 penciled in], NYPLPA; Bispham: 245, Harvard; *The Los Angeles Times*, Mar. 3, 1887: 1.

29. EB to EBG, Mar. 1, no year [1887 penciled in], Mar. 3, no year [1887 penciled in], NYPLPA; to LB, Mar. 2, no year [1887], Harvard; Bispham: 245, Harvard.

30. ABC to LB, Mar. 4, 1887, Hampden-Booth; EB to TBA, Mar. 5, no year [1887], Harvard; Fawcett, *Diary*, Mar. 6, 1887, Tennessee; Goodale, 162, 163, 164; Grossman, 79.

31. Saunders was Elizabeth Thoman when Booth first performed with her. When Booth left California he gave Saunders a book; in the leaves was a check for $1,000. Joseph Jefferson, Saunders's first cousin, mentioned the gift in a eulogy a year after Booth died without mentioning the actress's name. Goodale, 173–176 178–182; *Daily Alta California*, Mar. 8, 1887: 3; *The New York Mirror*, May 28, 1887: 7.

32. EB to TBA, Apr. 10, no year [1887], to LB, Apr. 16, no year [1887], Harvard.

33. EB to TBA. Mar. 20, no year [1887], Apr. 10, no year [1887], Harvard; Fawcett, Diary, Apr. 4, 1887, Tennessee; Goodale, 222, 223.

34. EB to LB, Apr. 16, no year [1887], Harvard.

35. EB to LB, Apr. 25, 1887, Hampden-Booth; to EBG, Apr. 25, 28, no year [1887 penciled in], NYPLPA; *The New York Mirror*, May 7, 1887: 4.

36. ABC to LB, Nov 14, 1886, Feb. 3, 1887, Hampden-Booth.

37. ABC to LB, Mar. 7, 1887, Hampden-Booth; Goodale, 273.

38. Malcolm Dale Owen to Dear Mother-Father Father-Mother, May 7, 1887, The Lilly Library, University of Indiana; *The New-York Times*, Jan. 1, 1887: 2

39. EB to LH, Apr. 21, 1887, Princeton; *New York Amusement Gazette*, Apr. 25, 1887: 4; *The New York Mirror*, May 14, 1887: 6.

40. Goodale, 273, 283, 284, 285, 289, 292, 296; *The New York Mirror*, May 28, 1887: 7.

Chapter Twenty-One

1. Clara Morris, *Life on the Stage* (New York: McClure, Phillips & Co., 1892): 221.

2. EB to LB, Sept. 26, n.d. [1886], Harvard.

3. ABC to LB, Oct. 4, 9, 10, 1886, Aug. 24, 1887, Hampden-Booth.

4. ABC to LB, Sept. 27, 1886, Hampden-Booth.

5. Agreement between EB and LB, Oct. 1, 1886, ABC to LB, Oct. 15, 1886, Hampden-Booth.

6. EB to LB, Oct. 10, 16, Nov. 17, 1886, n.d. [Jan. 1887], n.d. [Winter 1885–1886], Jan. 4, 27, Feb. 1, 11, 15, Mar. 25, Apr. 25, 26, 1887, Harvard; ABC to LB, Oct. 12, 14, 16, 20, Nov. 4, Dec. 4, 7, no year [1886], 23, 30, 1886, n.d. Jan. 7, 19, 23, 26, 27, Feb. 6, 8, Mar. 2, 7, 13, 20, June 29, July 8, 21, 1887, Hampden-Booth; Fawcett, Diary, Jan. 10, July 8, 1887, Tennessee; EB to EBG, May 5, no year [1888 penciled in], NYPLPA; Watermeier, *Between Actor and Critic*, 286; *The New York Mirror*, May 7 (5), July 16 (7), 1887; *The Daily American* (Nashville, Tennessee), Jan. 23, 1888:5; *The Terre Haute Express*, Apr. 19, 1888:1.

7. ABC to LB, Dec. 15, 1886, Jan. 23, 27, 30, Feb. 6, 18, Mar. 4, 27, Apr. 28, June 20, 22, 25, 27, 30, July 5, 10, 22, 24, Aug. 6, 7, 13, 18, 21, 1887, Hampden-Booth; *The New York Mirror*, Mar. 10, 1887: 4.

8. ABC to LB, Mar. 18, 1887, Hampden-Booth; EB to LB, Apr. 3, no year [1887], Harvard.

9. *The New York Mirror*, June 2 (3), 9 (9), 1888.

10. ABC to LB, June 20, 22, 1887, Hampden-Booth.

11. ABC to LB, Aug. 24, Sept. 1, 5, 1887, Hampden-Booth; *The New York Mirror*, July 16, 1887: 7.

12. EB to EBG, n.d. [Nov. 1887 penciled in], Nov. 5, no year [1887 penciled in], NYPLPA.

13. ABC to LB, Aug. 17, 20, 24. 1887, Hampden-Booth.

14. *The Courier Journal* (Louisville, Kentucky), May 11, 1888: 3; *The Daily Picayune* (New Orleans), Jan. 30, 1888: 3; *The Omaha Republican*, Apr. 10, 1888: 3; Clippings: *The North American*, Nov. 29, 1887, Mathews and Hutton, extra-illustrated, Harvard; *The Daily Nebraska State Journal*, Apr. 13, 1887, Scrapbook, 1888–1893, Hampden-Booth.

15. ABC to LB, " Aug. 13, 17, 20, 27, 31, Sept. 1, 5, 1887, Hampden-Booth; *The New York Mirror*, July 16, 1887: 7; *The Chattanooga Daily Times*, Jan. 23, 1888: 5; *The Daily American* (Nashville, Tennessee), Jan. 23, 1888:5; *Memphis Avalanche*, Jan. 27, 1888: 1.

16. EB to EBG, Sept. 15, no year [1888 penciled in; actually 1887], 25, Oct. 9, no year [1887 penciled in], NYPLPA; Program, Detroit Opera House, Sept. 16, 1887, Hennepin Avenue Theatre, Sept. 19, 1887, Chicago Opera House, Oct. 19, 1887, Scrapbook, Booth-Barrett Season, 1887–1888, Hampden-Booth; Grossman, 81, 82.

17. EB to EBG, Oct. 9, no year [1887 penciled in], NYPLPA; to WW, Oct. 12, 1887, handwritten copy, Folger; to TBA, Oct. 21, n.d. [1887], Harvard.

18. ABC to LB, Sept. 5, 1887, Hampden-Booth; EB to TBA, Oct. 21, n.d. [1887], to EBG, Oct. 24, no year [1887 penciled in], NYPLPA; Bispham: 246, Harvard.

19. Edwin Milton Royle, "EB as I Knew Him": 842- 843.

20. LB to EB, July 7, no year [1887], ABC to LB, Aug. 13, 1887, Hampden-Booth; EB to LH, n.d. [late summer 1887], Harvard; to EBG, Nov. 5, no year [1887 penciled in], Nov. 20, no year [1887 penciled in], Feb. 27, 1888, Mar. 31, no year [1888 penciled in], NYPLPA; Grossman, 80.

21. EB to LB, n.d. Winter 1885–1886, Harvard; Augustin Daly to LB, Dec. 28, 1886, Hampden-Booth; EB to EBG, May 3, 11, 20, no year [1888 penciled in], NYPLPA.

22. Augustin Daly to LB, Dec. 28, 1886, Hampden-Booth; EB to EBG, May 11, no year [1888 penciled in], May 20, no year [1888 penciled in], NYPLPA; *The Courier Journal* (Louisville, Kentucky), May 11, 1888: 3; *The New York Mirror*, May 12 (4), 26 (2), 1888; *New York Dramatic News*, Feb. 28, 1891: 12, 14; Clipping, "Hail Wallack," no source, n.d. [May 22, 1888], Melvin Scrapbook, 1874, no source, May 29, 1888, Scrapbook, Tours of EB 1888–1893, Hampden-Booth.

23. EB to EBG, June 7, 1888, NYPLPA; *The Evening Leader* (Grand Rapids, Michigan), May 4, 1888: 1; *The New York Mirror*, May 26, 1888: 3.

24. Watermeier, *Between Actor and Critic*, 289, 290; *Youngstown Weekly Telegram*, Nov. 18, 1887: 2.

Chapter Twenty-Two

1. *The New York Mirror*, June 11, 1887: 2.

2. EB to LB, no month [May], 29–30, 1887, n.d. [late June 1887], Harvard; to E. C. Benedict, n.d. Hampden-Booth; Otis Skinner, 7.

3. EB to David C. Anderson, Apr. 19, 1878, to WW, May 18, June 19, 1879, to F. J. Walton, Sept. 26, 1879, Folger; to McE, June 18, 1878, Hampden-Booth; to TBA, Oct. 19, 1883, Harvard; to McE, Oct. 29, 1882, Taper Collection; Batterberry, 143; *The New York Dramatic News*, Feb. 3, 1877: 5.

4. Photograph, LH Papers, Princeton; EB to LB, n.d. [mid–June 1887], Harvard; to LH, June 23, 1886 [1887], Hampden-Booth; to EBG, June 28, no year [1887 penciled in], July 3, no year [1887 penciled in], n.d. [July 11, 1887 penciled in; more likely July 18, 1887], n.d. [July 18, 1887 penciled in], n.d. [July 20, 1887 penciled in], July 27, no year [1887 penciled in], n.d. [July 30, 1887 penciled in], Aug. 3, no year [1887 penciled in], Aug. 6, no year [1887 penciled in], n.d. [Aug. 12, 1887 penciled in], NYPLPA; to LH, July 6, no year [1887], July 16 or 17 , no year [1887], Princeton; to McE, July 16, n.d. [1887], Tulsa.

5. ABC to LB, Aug. 6, 1887, Hampden-Booth; EB to LB, July 12, no year [1888], Harvard; TBA to WW, Nov. 1, 1893 in WW, *Life and Art of EB*, facing page 308, Folger; Clipping, New York newspaper, n.d. [circa Jan. 1, 1899], Scrapbook, 1888–1891, Hampden-Booth.

6. Clipping, New York newspaper, Dec. 30, 1888, Scrapbook, 1888–1891, Hampden-Booth.

7. By Dec. 26, 1888, Bispham was the treasurer of The Players. William Bispham to Stanford White, Jan. 18, 27, 1888, Hampden-Booth; to Samuel L. M. Barlow, Dec. 26, 1888, The Huntington Library; Grossman, 85; *The New York Mirror*, Jan. 14 1888: 6.

8. EB to EBG, Apr. 19, no year [1888 penciled in], NYPLPA; EB to LH, Apr. 24, 1888, Hampden-Booth.

9. EB to EBG, May 3, 1888, NYPLPA; Deeds, Jan. 26, 1863, Liber 870: 145, May 28, 1888, Liber 2148: 87, City Register's Office, New York, New York; Charles Lockwood, *Bricks and Brownstone: The New York Row House, 1783–1929* (New York, New York: Abbeville Press, 1972); 38; Jerry E. Patterson, *The First Four Hundred: Mrs. Astor's New York in the Gilded Age* (New York: Rizzoli, 2000), 93; *The Chicago Daily Tribune*, Sept. 24, 1888:2; Clipping, New York newspaper, n.d. [circa, Jan. 1, 1899], Scrapbook, 1888–1891, Hampden-Booth.

10. EB to EBG, n.d. Friday [Sept. 7, 1888, penciled in], NYPLPA; David Garrard Lowe, *Stanford White's New York* (New York: Watson-Guptill Publications, 1999), 151–153; Paul R. Bake, *Stanny: The Gilded Life of Stanford White* (New York: The Free Press, 1989), 137; Clipping, New York newspaper, n.d. [Dec. 30, 1888], Scrapbook, 1888—1891, Hampden-Booth.

11. EB to LH, June 5, 7, 1888, Harvard; William Bispham to Stanford White, n.d. Sept. 29, 1888, to McKim, Mead & White, Nov. 7, 1888, Hampden-Booth; Watermeier, *Between Actor and Critic*, 296.

12. EB to EBG, n.d. [June 3, 1888 penciled in], NYPLPA; to Augustin Daly, Nov. 26, 1891, Folger; to LH, Sept. 9th, no year, Princeton; Grossman, 103; *Los Angeles Daily Herald*, Feb. 26, 1888: 6; *The New York Dramatic Mirror*, Apr. 11, 1891: 4.

13. Watermeier, *Between Actor and Critic*, 289, 290.

14. EB to McE, May 28, no year [1888], Hampden-Booth; to Horace Howard Furness, June 4, 1888, University of Pennsylvania; to LH, June 5, no year [1888], Princeton; *The New York Mirror*, June 23, 1888: 7; Clipping, New York newspaper, n.d. [Dec. 30, 1888], Scrapbook, 1888–1891, Hampden-Booth.

15. Jefferson had an illegitimate son in Australia. It is not clear that Booth would have known that. The son did not contact Jefferson until 1889, but Jefferson was aware of his birth. It is also possible that one of the "vices" (note the plural) would have been drinking. Sex and drink were the only "vices" within the range of Booth's experience. EB to LB, July 12, no year [1888], Harvard; Benjamin McArthur, *The Man Who Was Rip Van Winkle* (New Haven, Yale University Press, 2007), 204, 312, 313.

16. Clippings: *The New York World*, Jan. 1889, *The New York World*, Jan. 1, 1889, New York newspaper, n.d. [circa Jan. 1, 1889], Scrapbook, 1888–1891, Hampden-Booth.

17. EB to LB, n.d. [May 1888], Harvard.

18. EB to LB, June 7, 1888, Harvard; William Bispham to Stanford White, n.d. [1888], Hampden-Booth; EB to EBG], June 2, [1890 penciled in], NYPLPA.

19. Clipping, New York newspaper, n.d. Scrapbook, 1888–1891, Hampden-Booth.

20. EB to EBG, Jan. 6, 9, 1889, NYPLPA; *The New York Dramatic Mirror*, Feb. 16 (3), May 4 (8), Nov. 15 (8), 1889; Clippings: Philadelphia newspaper, n.d. [circa Feb., 1889], Scrapbook, 1888–1891, Hampden-Booth; "Booth's Princely Gift," Fawcett Collection, Tennessee.

Chapter Twenty-Three

1. Agreement between EB and LB, Oct. 20, 1887, Hampden-Booth; EB to EBG, July 14, no year [1888 penciled in], NYPLPA; to LB, July 12, no year [1888], Harvard; Grossman, 87; *The New York Mirror*, July 14 (8), 21 (3), August 25 (11), 1888.

2. ABC to LB, August 13, 1887, Hampden-Booth; *The*

New York Mirror, June 2 (2), July 28 (2), 1888; Clipping, no source, May 29, 1888, Scrapbook, Tours of EB, 1886–1893, Hampden Booth.

3. Fawcett, Diary, Sept. 6–10, 1888, Mar. 7, 10, 1889, Tennessee; *The New York Mirror*, Sept. 8, 1888: 7; Statements for weeks beginning Sept. 10, 1888, Feb. 18, 1889, Booth Tours, 1886–1891, Hampden-Booth.

4. EB to EBG, Oct. 12, 1888, Clipping, Boston newspaper, n.d. Scrapbook, 1888–1891, Hampden-Booth; *The Chicago Daily Tribune*, Sept. 24, 1888:2; *The Denver Republican*, Apr. 22, 1889: 4; *Rocky Mountain News* (Denver, Colorado), Apr. 30 (7), May 3 (4), 1889.

5. *The Daily Chicago Tribune*, Oct. 14, 1888: 32.

6. EB to EBG, Oct. 22, 1888, NYPLPA; *St. Louis Post-Dispatch*, Oct. 28, 1888: 10; *The St. Louis Republic*, Oct. 28, 1888: 22.

7. EB to EBG, Nov. 8, 1888, Hampden-Booth.

8. *The New York Dramatic Mirror*, Nov. 17, 1888: 2.

9. Clipping, *Commercial Advertiser* (New York, New York), Nov. 13, 1888, Hampden Booth.

10. Rosalie died at 668 Lexington Avenue at 10 P.M. of "Bulber Paralysis and Progressive Spinal Sclerosis." She was buried in Baltimore on Jan. 17, 1889. Death Certificate 1793, Jan. 15, 1889, Birth, Marriage and Death Certificates, New York, New York; Fawcett, Diary, Dec. 17, 1888, Tennessee; EB to EBG, Wednesday, n.d. [Dec. 19, 1888 penciled in], Dec. 27, no year [1888 penciled in], NYPLPA; *The Sun* (Baltimore), Jan. 18, 1889: 4.

11. Watermeier, *Between Actor and Critic*, 295, 296; Clippings: no source [Boston newspapers], Jan. 29, 1889, n.d. [circa Feb. 5, 1889], Scrapbook, 1888–1891, Hampden-Booth.

12. Clippings: "EB Ill," Rochester, New York newspaper, Apr. 3, 1889, Fawcett Collection, Tennessee, "Mr. Booth Too Ill to Play," *New York Tribune*, Apr. 4, 1889, Scrapbook, 1888–1891, Hampden-Booth.

13. Clipping, "His First Paralytic Stroke," 1893, Tennessee.

14. *The New York Dramatic Mirror*, Apr. 13, 1889: 11; *The Union and Advertiser* (Rochester, New York), Apr. 4, 1889: 3.

15. *The Union and Advertiser* (Rochester, New York), Apr. 4, 1889: 2; Clippings: "EB Ill," Rochester newspaper, Apr. 3, 1889, Tennessee; Rochester newspaper, Apr. 4, 1889, Scrapbook, 1888–1891, Hampden-Booth.

16. EB to EBG, n.d. [Apr. 6, 1889 penciled in], NYPLPA; *The Union and Advertiser* (Rochester, New York), Apr. 4, 1889: 2; Clippings: Rochester newspaper, Apr. 4, 5, 1889, Scrapbook, 1888–1891, Hampden-Booth; Clipping, "His First Paralytic Stroke," 1893, Tennessee.

17. EB to EBG, Apr. 15, no year [1889 penciled in], May 3, no year [1889 penciled in], May 11, no year [1889 penciled in], NYPLPA; EB to Sadie & Lulu Benedict, Apr. 16, no year [1889], The Historical Society of the Town of Greenwich, Greenwich, Connecticut; *The New York Dramatic Mirror*, Apr. 20, 1889: 3.

18. EB to EBG, Apr. 22, no year [1889 penciled in], May 7, 1889, NYPLPA.

19. EB to EBG, Apr. 15, no year [1889 penciled in], Apr. 17, 1889, Apr. 22, no year [1889 penciled in], May 3, no year [1889 penciled in], NYPLPA; Grossman, 96, 97.

20. EB to Thomas Bailey and Lillian Woodman Aldrich, May 7, 1889, Harvard.

21. *Daily Alta California* (San Francisco), May 11, 1889: 8.

22. EB to EBG, May 11, no year [1889 penciled in], May 13, no year [1889 penciled in], May 21, 1889, NYPLPA; Grossman, 99; *Daily Alta California* (San Francisco), May 11, 1889: 8; *The New York Dramatic Mirror*, June 1, 1889: 2.

23. Fawcett, Diary, June 2, 10, 1889, Tennessee; EB to EBG, May 27, no year [1889 penciled in], NYPLPA; *The New York Dramatic Mirror*, June 1 (2), 29 (12), 1889.

Chapter Twenty-Four

1. Jeanette Leonard Gilder, "Madame Modjeska," *The Life and Art of EB and his Contemporaries*, 195, 197, 198, 199, 200, 202, 203; Item 330 ... 15PDT, ebay.com; http://en.wikipedia.org/wiki/Helena_Modjeska.

2. EB to E. C. Benedict, Mar. 10, 1878, Helena Modjeska to EB, June 13, 1881, Hampden-Booth; EB to WW, Sept. 9, no year [1878?], Folger; to EBG, n.d. [Nov. 14, 1886 penciled in], NYPLPA; Sir Johnston Forbes-Robertson, *A Player Under Three Reigns* (Boston: Little Brown, and Company, 1925), 106; Watermeier, *Between Actor and Critic*, 96.

3. EB to EBG, Dec. 9, 1888, NYPLPA; Watermeier, *Between Actor and Critic*, 295, 296; Clippings: *The Boston Record*, n.d. [circa Feb. 1889], New York newspaper, n.d. Scrapbook, 1888–1891, Hampden-Booth.

4. EB to ABC, Aug. 28, 1889, Texas; Clippings: Philadelphia newspaper, Mar. 23, 1889, no place, n.d. "Tour of EB, Mme Modjeska 1889–1890," Scrapbook, 1888–1891, Hampden-Booth; *The New York Dramatic Mirror*, Feb. 9 (8), Mar. 30 (2) 1889.

5. EB to EBG, Mar. 24, 1889, n.d. [Aug. 17, 1889 penciled in], NYPLPA; *The New York Dramatic Mirror*, Aug. 3 (3), Sept. 21 (5, 6) 1889; *New York Amusement Gazette*, Aug. 26, 1889: 14; Clipping, Pittsburgh newspaper, Oct. 8, 1889, Scrapbook, 1888–1891, Hampden-Booth.

6. EB to EBG, July 3, no year [1889 penciled in], NYPLPA; to ABC, Aug. 28, 1889, Texas; to LH, Aug. 21, 1889, Princeton; *The New York Dramatic Mirror*, July 27 (4), Aug. 17 (2, 6) 1889; *New York Amusement Gazette*, Aug. 26, 1889: 14; Clipping, New York newspaper, circa Oct. 28, 1889, Scrapbook, 1888–1893, Hampden-Booth.

7. EB to LH, July 11, 1889, Princeton; to EBG, n.d. [Summer 1889], NYPLPA; Grossman, 100.

8. Fawcett, Diary, Sept. 4, 9, 1889, Tennessee; Playbill, Broadway Theatre, 1889, Pennsylvania; Watermeier, *Between Actor and Critic*, 296; Items 319197483, 319 ...47PDT, ebay.com.

9. EB to EBG, n.d. [Sept. 20, 1889 penciled in], n.d. [Sept. 21, 1889 penciled in], NYPLPA; Fawcett, Diary, Sept. 27, 28, 29, 1889, Tennessee; Statement for week of Sept. 23–28, 1889, Booth Tours 1886–1891, Hampden-Booth; *The New York Dramatic Mirror*, Aug. 31, 1889: 3; Clipping, Louisville newspaper, n.d. Scrapbook, 1888–1893, Hampden-Booth.

10. EB to EBG, Oct. 1, no year [1889 penciled in], NYPLPA; Clipping, Pittsburgh newspaper, Oct. 8, 1889, Scrapbook, 1888–1891, Hampden-Booth.

11. EB to EBG, Oct. 8, no year [1889 penciled in], Oct. 11, 1889, typed and abridged copy of letter, NYPLPA.

12. *Toledo Daily Blade*, Apr. 17, 1890: 5.

13. *New York Amusement Gazette*, Oct. 14 (83), 21 (95), 28 (106), Nov. 18 (144), 25 (156), Dec. 2 (168), 1889.

14. EB to ABC, n.d., Texas.

15. *The New York Dramatic Mirror*, Nov. 16, 1889: 3.

16. EB to EBG, n.d. [Nov. 11, 1889 penciled in], NYPLPA.

17. EB to EBG, n.d. [Feb. 12, 1890], NYPLPA.

18. Fawcett, Diary, Feb. 8, 1890, Tennessee.

19. EB to LH, Sunday, Feb. 3, 1890, Princeton; to EBG, n.d. [Feb. 12, 1890], Feb. 18, no year [1890 penciled in], Hampden-Booth; to LH, Wednesday n.d. [c. Feb. 1890], Princeton; to EBG, Feb. 23, 1890, NYPLPA; Bispham: 248, Harvard.

20. Fawcett, Diary, Feb. 3, 1890, Tennessee; EB to LH, Mar. 5, 1890, Princeton; to EBG, Mar. 6, no year [1890 penciled in], Hampden-Booth; *The New York Dramatic Mirror*, Mar. 8, 1890: 6; Clipping, "Booth Off the Stage," Tennessee.

21. EB to EBG, Mar. 23, no year [1890 penciled in], Hampden-Booth; Apr. 3, [1890 penciled in], NYPLPA.

22. EB to EBG, Apr. 7, [1890 penciled in], NYPLPA; Fawcett, Diary, May 6, 1890, Tennessee.

23. Fawcett, Diary, Apr. 30, 1890, Tennessee; Otis Skinner, 6.

24. EB to EBG, May 5, no year [1890 penciled in], NYPLPA; Fawcett, Diary, May 9, 1890, Tennessee; Otis Skinner, Introduction, Francis Wilson, *EB*, unpublished manuscript, 1933, 1, Hampden-Booth; *The New York Dramatic Mirror*, May 3 (3), 17 (3), 1890.

Chapter Twenty-Five

1. EB to LH, Sept. 9, no year [1890], Princeton; Watermeier, *Between Actor and Critic*, 300.
2. EB to Edward V. Valentine, July 10, 1891, The Valentine Museum, Richmond, Virginia; to EBG, n.d. to LB, Sept. 2, no year, Hampden-Booth; to LH, Sept. 2, no year, Princeton.
3. EB to EBG, n.d. [Nov. 24, 1889 penciled in], NYPLPA; to "You dear old Party" [Nov. 1889], Hampden-Booth.
4. EB to TBA, Nov. 30, 1887, Harvard; Watermeier, *Between Actor and Critic*, 301, 302, n. 59; Clipping, "The Baltimore Theatres," *The Sun* (Baltimore, Maryland), Nov. 4, 1890, Barstow Scrapbook, Hampden-Booth.
5. Watermeier, *Between Actor and Critic*, 302.
6. Clippings: "Providence Opera House, Julius Caesar," *Providence Journal*, n.d. [Dec. 16, 1890], Barstow Scrapbook, New York newspaper, Mar. 3, 1891, Scrapbook, EB 1888–1893, Hampden-Booth.
7. EB to LH, May 1, 1891, Princeton; to EBG, Mar. 7, no year [1891 penciled in], Mar. 11, 1891, NYPLPA; Clipping, "Mr. Booth Looks Pale and Ill," no source, n.d. [circa Feb. 1891], Barstow Scrapbook, Hampden-Booth; *New York Amusement Gazette*, Mar. 2 (254), 9 (262) 1891.
8. Clipping, no source, n.d., Bamburgh, Harvard.
9. Grossman, 117, 118, 119; Clippings: "EB as Macbeth," no source, n.d., Bamburgh, Harvard; "EB as Macbeth," no source, n.d. [Mar. 20, 1891], Barstow Scrapbook, Hampden-Booth.
10. EB to EBG, Mar. 22, 1891, NYPLPA; Grossman, 121; Item 1414065363, ebay.com.
11. EB to EBG, Mar. 22, 1891, NYPLPA; Grossman, 121; Clippings: "Notes," Clipping Scrapbook, EB 1888–1893, "EB as Macbeth," no source, n.d. [Mar. 21, 1891], "EB in 'Hamlet,'" no source, n.d. [Mar. 25, 1891], Barstow Scrapbook, Hampden-Booth.
12. Clipping, New York newspaper, Apr. 5, 1891, Scrapbook, EB 1888–1893, Hampden-Booth.
13. Clipping, "EB at Brooklyn," Apr. 5, no year [1891], The Henry E. Huntington Library; "EB Dead," *Boston Journal*, June 7, 1893: 5, Harvard.
14. EB to EBG, Apr. 1, 7, 1891, NYPLPA; Card, Miscellaneous Booth File, Folger.
15. EB to TBA, Oct. 9, 1891, Bispham: 248, Harvard; *New York Dramatic News*, July 18, 1891: 16.
16. EB to WW, Sat, 23, no month, no year [1892 penciled in], The Lilly Library, Indiana University; Bispham: 250, Harvard.
17. Clippings: "EB's Condition," *The World*, Oct. 1892, Folger; "EB's History," no source, n.d. [circa Apr., 1893], Melvin Scrapbook, Hampden-Booth.
18. Clipping, "Mr. Booth's Birthday Not Forgotten," *New York Herald*, Nov. 13, 1892, Folger.
19. Badeau: 266.
20. EB to EBG, n.d. [Dec. 21, 1892 penciled in], NYPLPA.
21. *The Sunday Advertiser* (Honolulu), July 5, 1908: 13.
22. EB to EBG, Feb. 19, no year [1893 penciled in], Feb. 26, no year [1893 penciled in], NYPLPA; Grossman, 123, 124, 125; Watermeier, *Between Actor and Critic*, 303; Clippings: *The World*, Feb. 19, 1893, Tennessee; "Death of EB," *The New York Dramatic News*, n.d., 14, Glase Scrapbook, Free Library of Philadelphia.
23. EB to EBG, n.d. [Apr. 17, 1893 penciled in], NYPLPA; Grossman, 128.
24. Clipping, "Mr. Edwin Booth Ill," no source, Apr. 20, 1892, Folger.
25. Clippings: "EB's Illness" *New York Herald*, Apr. 21, 1892, "Dr. Smith's Statement," no source, n.d., Folger.
26. St. Clair Smith, Reports on Booth's condition, May 16, June 5, 1893, *Chicago Journal*, June 5, 1893, Scrapbook, Tributes of the Press to EB Memorial Notices collected by The Players, 1893, Clippings: "EB Dead," *New York Tribune*, June 7, 1893 [mislabeled 1894], Scrapbook, compiled by A. Sandor Grossman, 1895, Hampden-Booth; Clippings: *The New-York Times*, June 7, 1893, "EB Died Early this Morning," no source, n.d., *The Press*, June 7, 1893, Folger; "Death of EB," *The New York Dramatic News*, n.d.: 14; Glase Scrapbook, Free Library of Philadelphia.
27. WW, *Life and Art of EB*, notes, 156, Clippings: "Honors Paid to Booth's Memory," *New York Herald*, June 9, 1893, "Booth Laid in the Earth," *Daily Tribune*, June 10, 1893, "Death of EB, *The New York Dramatic News*, n.d.: 14, Glase Scrapbook, Free Library of Philadelphia.
28. Clippings: "EB's Funeral," no source, n.d., "Booth's Memory Fitly Honored," *New York Herald*, June 10, 1893, "Booth Laid in the Earth," *Daily Tribune*, June 10, 1893, Folger; *Dramatic Mirror*, June 17, 1893 in EB scrapbook, pp. 14, 15, "EB in Boston," Harvard; "Death of EB," *The New York Dramatic News*, n.d., 14, Glase Scrapbook, Free Library of Philadelphia.
29. Winter, *Life of Belasco*, I, 96; Clippings: "Relics of Booth Sold for $3,230," "Boothiana at a Penny Sale," Folger.
30. EB to Mr. de Zayas, July 27, 1884, Folger.
31. Booth left an estate of $600,000, the bulk of which was bequeathed to Edwina. He left $10,000 to Joseph; $10,000 to Marie; $5,000 each to Asia Clarke Morgan, Adrienne Clarke, Junius B. Booth, Sidney Booth, Creston Clarke and Wilfred Clarke; $2500 each to his cousins Charlotte Mitchell and Robert Mitchell, $5000 to Maria Anderson, the widow of David C. Anderson; $10,000 each to John H. Magonigle and his wife; $5,000 to Margaret Devlin; $5,000 each to the Actors' Fund, the Actor' Order of Friendship of Philadelphia, the Trustees of the Masonic Hall and Asylum Fund of New York, and the Home for Incurables at West Farms, New York. The rest was left to Edwina. A clipping in Harvard notes that "the appraiser of the estate ... has fixed the value of personal property at ... $602,675" and that the "residuary" after "debts, legacies and expenses" was $462,335. Edwina described her inheritance as "a handsome fortune in Trust for me & my children." EB, "Some Words about My Father," E-9, Princeton; to EBG, Apr. 14, [1890 penciled in], NYPLPA; EBG to Edward V. Valentine, May 20, 1925, The Valentine Museum, Richmond, Virginia; Tombstone, EB, Mount Auburn Cemetery, Boston, Massachusetts; Grossman 110; Watermeier, *Between Actor and Critic*, 303; Clippings: "EB's Will," *The Dramatic Times*, Folger; "EB's Estate," EB scrapbook, Harvard.

PART II

In a career that spanned more than 6,122 known performances, Booth gave 1,230 performances of Hamlet; 687 of Richelieu; 439 of Iago; 429 of Shylock; 392 of Richard III; 303 of Petruchio; 280 of Bertuccio; 263 of Brutus; 233 of Macbeth; 198 of Othello; 180 of King Lear; 130 of Romeo; 128 of Claude Melnotte; 118 of Sir Edward Mortimer; 115 of Lucius Junius Brutus; 109 of Don Caesar de Bazan; 107 of Sir Giles Overreach; 93 of Pescara; 88 of Benedick; 75 of Ruy Blas; and 66 of The Stranger.

For information on EB's performances prior to the summer of 1852, see St. Louis Missouri Petition to Mr. EB, Jan.

28, 1851, Wilson, 58, Hampden-Booth; Junius Brutus Booth Senior to John Rogers, Oct. 21, 1851, Taper Collection; to Mr. Furnell Esq.," Apr. 20, 1852, Program, Holliday Street Theatre, Mar. 13, 1852, extra-illustrated edition of Charles Townsend Copeland, *The Life of EB*, Harvard; Archer, 275; Winter, *Life and Art*, 4–7; Ireland, 2:579; Oggel, *Bio-Bibliography*, 9, 10, 57; LB, "EB": 97.98; *The Daily Evening Transcript* (Boston), Sept. 10, 1849: 3; *The Boston Atlas*, Sept. 10, 1849: 3; *Boston Courier* Sept. 10, 1849: 3; *The Providence Daily Journal*, Sept. 27 1849: 3; *The Pittsburgh Daily Dispatch*, Dec. 10, 1849: 2; *The Charleston Courier* Feb. 16, 1850: 3; *The New York Herald*, Sept. 27 (5), Oct. 4 (5), 1850; *Daily National Intelligencer* (Washington, D.C.), Nov. 7 (3), Nov. 8 (3) 1850, May 5 (3), 6 (3), May 7 (3), May 8 (1), 14 (3), 15 (3), 16 (3), 1851; *American and Commercial Daily Advertiser* (Baltimore), Nov. 2, 1850: 3; *Lowell Daily Journal and Courier*, Jan. 8, 1851: 3; *The Lowell Advertiser*, Jan. 14 (3), 16 (3) 1851; Feb. 11 (3), 12 (3), 1852; *Brooklyn Daily Eagle*, Dec. 10, 1850: 3; *The Daily Union* (Washington), Feb. 23 (4), 26(4), May 16 (3), 1851; *The Sun* (Baltimore), Mar. 6 (3), 8 (3), May 29 (3), 30 (2) 1851; Feb. 11 (3), Feb. (3), June 3 (3), 1852; *The American Telegraph* (Washington, D.C.), May 14–19, 1852; Clippings, Barton Hill, "Personal Recollections of EB," *Dramatic Mirror* (New York), Dec. 26, 1896 in EB Scrapbooks, NYPLPA.

For information on EB's performances in the West from the summer of 1852 until he returned from Australia and Hawaii (1852–1853; 1853–1854; 1854–1855) see Program, National Theatre, Aug. 23, 1850, Glase Scrapbook, Theatre Collection, The Free Library of Philadelphia; Programs, Metropolitan Theatre, San Francisco, Dec. 28, 1853, Apr. 25, 1854, extra-illustrated edition, Charles Copeland 38f, 40f; San Francisco Theatre, Aug. 15, 1853, Royal Victoria Theatre, Oct. 26, 1854, extra-illustrated edition, Matthews and Hutton, V, pt. 2, Harvard; Broadsides, Royal Victoria Theatre, Sydney Australia, Oct. 23, 25, 31, no year [1854], Royal Hawaiian Theatre, Mar. 10, 1855, Hampden-Booth; Broadside, Hawaiian Theatre, Dec. 23, 1861, Archives Division, Department of Accounting and General Services, State of Hawaii, Honolulu; EB, "Some Words about My Father," E-14; Asia Booth to Jean Anderson, Jan. 8, 1854, Maryland; EB to EBG, n.d. [Jan. 11, 1889 penciled in], NYPLPA; Archer, 278; Brands: 80, 81; Clarke, 130, 131, 140, 141; Pauline King, ed., *The Diaries of David Lawrence Gregg: An American Diplomat in Hawaii* (Honolulu: Hawaiian Historical Society, 1982), 566, n. 10; Koon, 141; Oggel, *Bio-Bibliography*, 9, 10, 11, 58; *San Francisco Theatre Research*, 55, 77, 81; Winter, *Life and Art*, 8–19; Anon, "Reminiscences of the Stage in Honolulu," *Hawaiian Almanac and Annual for 1906* (Thomas G. Throm: Honolulu, 1905): 94–95; Barrett, "EB," 61; Caroline Bengston, "Hawaii in 1855," *The Hawaiian Journal of History*, IX (1975): 39, 40; Richard A. Greer, "Honolulu in 1847," *The Hawaiian Journal of History*, IV (1970): 75; Eric Irvin, "Laura Keene and EB in Australia," *Theatre Notebook*, XXIII, 3 (Spring, 1969): 95, 98, 99, 100; Robert C. Schmitt, "Some Firsts in Island Leisure," *The Hawaiian Journal of History*," XII (1978): 102; Richard Waterhouse, "High Culture and Low Culture: The Changing Role of Shakespeare, 1833–2000," John Golder and Richard Madelaine, eds., *O Brave New World: Two Centuries of Shakespeare on the Australian Stage* (Sydney: Currency Press, 2001): 25; *The Sun* (Baltimore), May 31 (3), June 1 (3), 2 (3), 3 (3), 4 (3), 5 (3), 1852; *Daily Alta California* (San Francisco), July 29 (2), 30 (3), 31 (3), Aug. 2 (3) 3 (3), 8 (3), 11 (3), 21 (2) 1852; Feb. 2 (3), 19 (3), 21 (3), 25 (3), 27 (3), Mar. 1 (3), 11 (3), 28 (3), 29 (3), 30 (3), 31 (3), Apr. 3 (3), 9 (3), 13 (3), 14 (3), 15 (3), 16 (3), 17 (3), 18 (3), 20 (3), 21 (3), 22 (3), 23 (3) 24 (3), 25 (3) 26 (3), 27 (3), 28 (3), 29 (3), 30 (3), May 1 (3), 2 (3), 5 (3). 6 (3), 7 (3), 8 (3), 10 (3), 12 (3), 14 (3), 15 (3) 16 (3), 17 (3), 20 (3), 20 (3), 22 (3), 25 (3), June 11 (3), 13 (3), 14 (3), 15 (3, 17 (3), 18 (3), 20 (3), 21 (3), 22 (3), 23 (3), 24 (3), 25 (3), 26 (3), 27 (3), 28 (3) 29 (3), July 1 (3), 2 (3), 6 (3), 7 (3), 8 (3), 10 (3), 11 (3), 13 (3), 14 (3), 15 (3), 17 (3) 22 (3), 25 (3) 26 (3), 29 (3), 30 (3), 31 (3), Aug. 1 (3), 2 (3), 5 (3), 8 (3), 10 (3), 11 (3) 12 (3), 13 (3), 14 (2, 3), 15 (3), 16 (3), 17 (3), 19 (3), 20 (3), 22 (3), 23 (3), 24 (3), 25 (3), 26 (3), 27 (3), 28 (3), 29 (3), 30 (3), 31 (3), Sept. 1 (3), 2 (3), 3 (3), 4 (3), 5 (3), 6 (3), 7 (3), 8 (3), 9 (3), 18 (3), 20 (3), 21 (3), 22 (3), 23 (3), 24 (3), 25 (3), 26 (3), 30 (3), Oct. 3 (3), 4 (3), 5 (3), 6 (3), 7 (3), 11 (3), 12 (3), 13 (3), 14 (3), 15 (3), 16 (3), 17 (3), 18 (3), 19 (3) 21 (2, 3), 22 (3), 23 (3), Nov. 3 (3), 4 (2, 3), 5 (3), 6 (3), 7 (3), 14 (3), 16 (3), 19 (3), 22 (3), 27 (3), Dec. 5 (3), 6 (3), 10 (3), 12 (3), 13 (3), 16 (3), 17 (3), 18 (3) 19 (3), 20, 24 (3), 25 (3), 30 (3) 31 (3), 1853; Jan. 1 (3), 6 (3), 11 (3), 12 (3), 4 (3) 15 (3), 19 (3), 24 (3), 29 (3), Feb. 13 (3), Feb. 15 (3), Feb. 16 (3), 17 (3), Mar. 10 (3), 15 (3), 21 (3), 22 (3), 23 (3), 24 (2, 3), 25 (3), 26 (3), 27 (3), 28 (3), 29 (3), Apr. 6 (3), 7 (3), 8 (3), 10 (2), 23 (3), 24 (3), May 1 (3), 21 (3), 24 (3), 29 (3), 31 (3), June 1 (3), 2 (3), 3 (3), 6 (3), 8 (3), 10 (3), 26 (3), 29 (3), Aug. 2 (2, 3), 16 (1, 2), Dec. 9 (2), 1854, Mar. 16, 1855: 2; *The Daily Union* (Sacramento), July 30, 1852: 2, Aug. 20 (3), 21 (3), 23 (3), 24 (3), 25 (3), 26 (3), 27 (3), 28 (3), 30 (2), 31 (3), Sept. 2 (3), 3 (3), 6 (3), 1852; Oct. 23 (2), 24 (2), 25 (2), 26 (2), 27 (2), 28 (2), 29 (2), 1853; *Sacramento Daily Union*, Apr. 13 (2), 17 (2), 18 (2) 1854, Sept. 13, 1856: 2; *The San Francisco Herald*, Sept. 26 (2, 3), Oct. 1 (4), 24 (2), 25 (2), 26 (2), 31 (2), Nov. 1 (2), 1853; 1852; *Nevada Journal* (Nevada, California), Oct. 15 (2), 22 (2), 29 (2), Nov. 12 (2), Nov.19 (2), Nov. 26 (2), Dec. 10 (2), 24 (3), 31 (3), 1852; *Daily Placer Times and Transcript* (San Francisco), July 29, 1852: 3; Aug. 12 (3), Sept. 27 (3), Oct. 1 (3), Nov. 15 (3), 1852; Feb. 5 (3), 12 (3), 18 (3), 22 (3), 23 (3), 28 (2), Mar. 16 (3), 24 (2), 25(2) Apr. 1 (2, 3), 4 (3), 6 (3), 13 (3), May 4 (3), 5 (3), 6 (3), 11 (3), 30 (2), June 2 (3), 9 (2), 19 (3), 21 (3), 24 (3), 28 (4), July 4 (3, 4), July 18 (3), 19 (3), 20 (3), 23 (3), 25 (3), Aug. 2 (2, 3), 10 (3), 11 (3), 12 (3), 13 (3), 16 (3), 22 (3), 31 (3), Sept. 1 (3), 8 (3), 10 (3), 12 (3), Oct. 8 (3), 20 (3), Nov. 8 (3), Dec. 9 (3), 12 (3), 13 (3), 15 (3), 21 (3), 24 (3) 1853; Feb. 20 (3), 21 (2), Mar. 20 (3), 23 (2), Apr. 2 (3), 7 (2), 9 (3), 10 (2), July 25 (2), 29 (2), 31 (2), Aug. 1 (2) Dec. 13 (3), 1854; July 28, 1855: 3; *Spirit of the Times* (New York), May 29 (170), Nov. 6 (451) 1852, May 20 (159), June 3 (189), July 29 (288), 1854, Mar. 17 1855: 49, July 5, 1856: 241; *The San Francisco Daily Herald*, Feb. 14 (2), Mar. 24 (2), 19 (2, 3), July 29 (2), Aug. 27 (2), Nov. 23 (4) 1852, Feb. 10 (2), Apr. 4 (3), May 3 (3), 11 (3), 13 (2), 23 (3), June 4 (2); 16 (3), July 18 (3), 19 (3), 28 (2, 3), 29 (3), 30 (3), 1853; *The Golden Era* (San Francisco), Dec. 26, 1852: 2; *The Golden Era* (San Francisco), July 9 (2), 23 (2), 1854; *The Marysville Herald* (Marysville, California), July 11, 1853: 2; *The Weekly Argus* (Honolulu), Sept. 7, 1853: 3; *The Polynesian* (Honolulu), Oct. 15, 1853:90; *Daily Democratic State Journal* (Sacramento, California), Oct. 25, 1853: 2; *Daily California Chronicle* (San Francisco), Dec. 14 (2), 21 (2), 1853; *California Chronicle* (San Francisco), Dec. 19 (3), 21 (2) 1853, Jan. 5 (3), 7 (3), 1854; *San Francisco Daily Evening News*, Jan. 11 (3), 12 (3), 13 (3), 14 (3), 17 (3), 19 (3), 21 (3), 24 (3), Feb. 13 (3), 15 (3), 16 (3), 17 (3), 18 (3), 20 (3), 21 (2), Mar. 10 (3), 14 (3), Apr. 6 (3), 7 (3) 25 (3), May 24 (3), 29 (3), July 1 (3), 3 (3), 11 (3), 12 (3), 13 (3), 14 (3), 15 (3), 18 (3), Aug. 1 (3), 1854; *Daily California Chronicle* (San Francisco), Feb. 16, 1854: 3; *California Chronicle* (San Francisco), Aug. 1 (2, 3), 3 (3), 1854; *New-York Daily Times*, Aug. 12 (2), Sept. 9 (2) 1854, Apr. 16 (1), 25 (1), May 25 (1), 1855; *The Empire* (Sydney), Oct. 23 (4), 24 (4), 28 (4), 30 (4, 5), 31 (4), Nov. 1 (4), 2 (4), Nov. 3 (4), Nov. 4 (4), 1854; *Weekly Alta California* (San Francisco), Oct. 28 1854: 3; *The Golden Era* (San Francisco): July 2 (2), Aug. 6 (2) 1854; Apr. 29, 1855: 2; *The Argus* (Melbourne), Nov. 21 (4), 22 (4), 29 (4), Dec. 2 (4), 1854; *The Polynesian* (Honolulu), Feb. 24, 1855: 166; *The Friend* (Honolulu), Mar. (24), Apr. (32), 1855; *The New Era and Weekly Argus* (Honolulu), Mar. 8 (2), 29 (2) 1855, Apr. 12, 1858: 2; *Oroville Daily Butte Record* (Oroville, California), July 24, 1856: 2; *The New*

York Clipper, Feb. 19, 1870: 366; *Saturday Press* (Honolulu), July 30, 1881: 1; *The Pacific Commercial Advertiser* (Honolulu), June 7, 1892: 3; *The Sunday Advertiser* (Honolulu), June 11, 1911: Feature Section, 4; *The Honolulu Advertiser*, June 21, 1925: Society Section, 12; Clippings, *Fact* (London), Mar. 19, 1881, Scrapbook, 1880–1881; "Short Bits," San Francisco newspaper, no source, n.d. [circa Mar. 7, 1887], Scrapbook, Tour of EB — Season 1886–87: 35, Hampden-Booth; Barton Hill, "Personal Recollections of EB," *Dramatic Mirror* (New York), Dec. 26, 1896, J. J. McCloskey, "How I Met EB," *New York Dramatic Mirror* Dec. 25, 1904, xvi in EB Scrapbooks, NYPLPA.

For information about Booth's performances in California after his return from Australia in 1855 see EB to Gentlemen, Apr. 16, 1856, Taper Collection; Program, Forrest Theater, Feb. 19, 1856, Bamburgh, Harvard; Koon, 73; *San Francisco Daily Evening News*, Apr. 30 (3), May 2 (3), 4 (2, 3), 28 (3), 29 (3), 30 (3), 31 (3), June 1 (3), 2 (3), 5 (3), 6 (3), 7 (3), 9 (3), 15 (3), July 10 (3), 1855; Jan. 14 (3), 15 (3), 16 (3), 17 (3), 18 (3), 19 (3), 26 (2), 28 (2), Feb. 18 (2), 1856; *Evening Bulletin* (San Francisco), May 8 (2), 9 (2), 10 (2), 12 (2), 13 (2), 29 (2), 1856; *Daily Alta California* (San Francisco), June 1 (2), July 30 (3), Oct. 8 (3), 9 (3), 10 (2, 3), 11 (3), 12 (3), 13 (3), 14 (3), 15 (3), 16 (3), 17 (3), 18 (3), 19 (3), 20 (3), 21 (3), 22 (3), 23 (3), 26 (3), 28 (3), Nov. 26 (2), 1855; Feb. 8(2), Feb. 11 (2), May 27 (2), 1856; *The Marysville Herald*, Sept. 25 (2), Oct. 2 (2), 1855; Jan. 10 (2), 24 (2), 25 (2), 26 (2), 29 (2), 30 (2), 31 (2), 1856; *Sacramento Daily Union*, Aug. 4 (2), 6 (2), 7 (2), 8 (2), 11 (2), 14 (2), 18 (2), 20 (2), 23 (2), 24 (2), 27 (2), 28 (2), 30 (2), 31 (2), Sept. 1 (2), 6 (2), 8 (2), 10 (2). 11 (2), 13 (2), 14 (2), 15 (2), 17 (2), 19 (2), 20 (2), 21 (2), 22 (2), Nov. 6 (2), 7 (2), 8 (2), 27 (2), 28 (2), 29 (2), 30 (2), Dec. 1 (2), 3 (2), 4 (2), 5 (2), 6 (2), 7 (2), 8 (2), 10 (2), 11 (2), 12 (3), 13 (3), 14 (3), 15 (3), 17 (3), 18 (3), 19 (3), 20 (3), 21 (3), 22 (3), 24 (5), 25 (3), 26 (3), 27 (3), 28 (3), 29 (3) 1855; Jan. 1 (3), 3 (3), 5 (3), Feb. 21 (3), 22 (3), 23 (3), Mar. 8 (3), 11 (3), 12 (3), 13 (3), Apr. 8 (3), 14 (3), 16 (3), 18 (3), 19 (3), 22 (3), May 1 (3), 15 (3), 16 (3), 17 (3), 19 (3), 20 (3), 21 (3), 22 (3), 23 (3), 24 (3), 31 (3), June 5 (3), 6 (2), 7 (3), 10 (3), Aug. 9 (3), 15 (3), 16 (2,3), 20 (3), 21 (3), 22 (3), 23 (3), 1856; *Daily Placer Times and Transcript* (San Francisco), July 10 (2), Aug. 21 (2), Sept. 24 (2), Oct. 12 (2), 23 (2), Nov. 12 (2), 1855; *The Nevada Journal* (Nevada, California), Feb. 8(2), 15 (2), July 18 (2, 3), 1856; *New-York Daily Times*, Dec. 31, 1855: 2; *The North Californian* (Oroville, California), Feb. 2, 1856: 3; *The Placer Herald* (Auburn, California), July 12, 1856: 2; Clippings, Sacramento Theatre, Aug. 28, 1855, Tennessee; "Talk about Booth," *Buffalo Commercial*, June 7, 1893, Scrapbook. Tributes of the Press to EB Memorial Notices collected by The Players, 1893, collected by Bamburgh, Dec. 9, 1902, Hampden-Booth.

For information on the 1856–1857 season see Joseph Jefferson to John T. Ford, n.d. [Fall 1857], Ford Papers, LC; EB to Junius Brutus Booth Jr., n.d. [late Mar. 1858], Texas; Benjamin Peirce to EB, Program, Boston Theatre, Apr. 27, 1857 and "Notes," *Boston Transcript*, June 27, 1925, Fred G. Ross EB Scrapbook, Programs, May 8, 13, 1857, Rea Collection, NYPLPA; Agreement between EB and William Burton, Apr. 18, 1857, R. S. Chilton to EB, May 8, 1857, "Proceeds from Booth's 1857 appearance in Boston,"s Hampden-Booth; EB to Harry Magonigle, Nov. 14, 1874, in Robert Cohen, "Booth Notes," n.p.; EB to J. H. Furlong Esq.," Mar. 15 1870, Program, Burton's Theatre, May 4, 1857 in Extra Illustrated Edition of Clarke, *Junius Brutus Booth and EB*, 69, Folger; Celebrity Index, Philadelphia Theatre Index, Program, Boston Theatre, Apr. 24, 1857, Glase Scrapbook, The Free Library of Philadelphia; Program, Boston Theatre, May 1, 1857, extra-illustrated edition, Copeland 48f, Harvard; Clarke, *Junius Brutus Booth and EB*, I (Boston, no publisher: 1882), 69; 148; Ireland, II, 663; Oggel, *Bio-Bibliography*: 13; Shattuck, 10, 11, 16, 17; Winter, *Life and Art*, 20, 21; Water-

meier, *Between Actor and Critic*, 30; *Frank Leslie's Illustrated Newspaper* (New York), Aug. 2, 1856: 119, May 13, 1876: 157; *The New York Clipper*, Aug. 16 (134), Oct. 4 (190), 15 (215), Dec. 27 (287), 1856, Apr. 10 (407), 25 (3), May 2 (15), 9 (23), 1857; Aug. 19, 1865: 147; *Boston Evening Transcript*, Sept. 8 (3), 16 (3), 19 (3), 29 (3), Oct. 6 (3), 21 (3), Dec. 15 (3), 20 (3), 1856; Feb. 2 (3), Mar. 9 (3), 30 (3), Apr. 21 (2), 22 (2), 23 (2), 25 (3), 1857; *The Sun* (Baltimore), Oct. 15 (3), 16 (3), 17 (3), 18 (3), 20 (3), 21 (3), 22 (3), 23 (3), 24 (3), 25 (3), 1856; Jan. 31, 1857: 607; *Richmond Enquirer*, Oct. 31 (3), Nov. 7 (3), Dec. 5 (2, 3), 1856; *Spirit of the Times* (New York), Nov. 8, 1856: 469; Mar. 14 (50), 21 (62), Apr. 4 (85), 11 (108), 18 (109), 25 (121), May 2 (133), 9 (145, 156), June 13 (206), July 11 (264), 1857; *Evening Star* (Washington), Nov. 17 (2), 18 (2), 19 (2, 3), 21 (2), 22 (2, 3), Dec. 8 (2), 11 (2), 1856; *New York Clipper*, Nov. 22 (247) Dec. 6 (262) 1856; May 16 (30), 23 (38), 30 (46), 1857; *Daily Dispatch* (Richmond), Nov. 24 (2), 25 (2), 1856; *Daily Dispatch* (Richmond), Nov. 24 (2), 26 (2), 27 (2), 28 (2), 29 (2), Dec. 1 (2), 3 (2), 4 (2), 1856; *Richmond Enquirer*, Nov. 25 (3), 28 (2), Dec. 2 (2), 5 (3), 1856; *National Intelligencer* (Washington, D.C.), reprinted in *Natchez Daily Courier*, Dec. 4, 1856: 2; *Daily National Intelligencer* (Washington, D.C.), Dec. 12, 1856: 1; *Richmond Daily Dispatch* as quoted in *Spirit of the Times* (New York), Dec. 20, 1856: 537; *The Daily Pittsburgh Gazette*, Dec. 22 (3), 23 (3), 24 (3), 29 (3), 30(3), 1856; Jan. 3, 1857: 3; *Daily Dispatch* (Richmond), Dec. 30, 1856: 2; *Wheeling Daily Intelligencer*, Jan. 5 (2), 6 (2), 7 (2), 8 (2), 9 (2), 10 (2), 1857; *Daily Missouri Republican* (St; Louis), Jan. 19 (3), 20 (3), 21 (3), 22 (3), 23 (3), 24 (3), 26 (3), 27 (3), 28 (3), 29 (3), 30 (3), 31 (3), 1857; *The Cincinnati Daily Commercial*, Feb. 2 (3), 3 (3), 4 (3), 5 (3), 7 (3), 9 (3), 10 (3), 11 (3), 12 (3), 13 (3), 14 (3), 1857; *Frank Leslie's Illustrated Newspaper* (New York), Feb. 14, 1857: 163; *The Mobile Daily Register*, Mar. 10 (3), 13 (3), 14 (3), Apr. 3 (3), 1857; *The Daily Picayune* (New Orleans), Mar. 15 (5), 17 (2, 4), 18 (5), 19 (5), 20 (5), 21 (5), 22 (5), 24 (4, 5), 25 (5), 26 (4,5), 27 (5), 1857; *The New York Herald*, Apr. 25 (1), May 2 (133), 3 (7), 5 (3), 11(4), 1857; *Boston Evening Transcript*, Apr. 25 (2), 27 (3), 28 (3), 29 (2), 30 (2), May 1 (3), 1857; *New-York Daily Times*, May 2 (3), 4 (6), 6 (3), 7 (6), 8 (6), 11 (6), 12 (3), 13 (6), 14 (6), 15 (6), 16 (5, 6), 18 (4), 21 (6), 23 (6), 26 (3), 30 (3), Aug. 31 (4, 6), Sept. 1 (4), 2 (6), 3 (3), 4 (6), 1857; Mar. 2, 1858: 2; *New York Herald*, May 3 (7), 7 (9), 9 (9), 10 (7), 12 (7), 14 (7), 15 (8), 16 (7), 17 (7), 19 (7), 20 (8), 21 (7), 22 (7), 23 (7), 1857; *The Albion* (New York), May 9 (224), 23 (248), 1857; *New-York Daily Times*, May 1 (3), 16 (5), 1857; *Public Ledger* (Philadelphia), June 1 (3), 2 (3), 3 (4), 4 (3), 5 (3), 6 (3), 8 (3), 9 (3), 10 (3), 11 (3), 12 (3), 13 (1), 1857; *The Chicago Tribune*, Apr. 27, 1879: 7; *The New York Dramatic Mirror*, Sept. 20, 1890: 3; Clippings, no place, n.d. [circa 1858], Melvin Scrapbook Hampden-Booth, "Some Stories of Booth," EB collection, Hill, "Personal Recollections of EB," EB Scrapbook, "Stories of Booth," EB collection, NYPLPA; "Booth's First Manager," Columbia University.

For information on the 1857–1858 season see George Kunkel to John T. Ford, Feb. 27, 1858, Ford papers, LC; Programs, Boston Theatre, Apr. 1, 1858, Boston Theatre, Apr. 2, 1858, extra-illustrated edition of Copeland 48f, Burton's Theatre, Apr. 9, 1858, extra illustrated edition of Clarke, Asia Booth, *Junius Brutus Booth and Edwin Booth*, I (Boston, no publisher: 1882), 69, Harvard; Boston Theatre, Mar. 23-Apr. 3, 1858, Rare Books Department, Boston Public Library; EB to Walter Brackett, July 23, 1858, Texas; EB to Write, July 29, 1858, Folger; Edward V. Valentine to Edwina Booth Grossman, Nov. 27, 1922, Nov. 26, 1928, Edward V. Valentine, Biographical Index, The Valentine Museum, Richmond, Virginia; Playbill, May 8, 1857, Rea Scrapbook, NYPLPA; Coder: 72; Ireland, 2, 663, 670; Shattuck, 16, 17; Winter, *Life and Art*, 22; *Spirit of the Times* (New York), Dec. 13, 1856: 528; July 11 (264), Aug. 29 (318), Sept. 5 (360), 12

(372) Nov. 28 (504), 1857, Jan. 2 (564), 30 (612), Feb. 6 (614), 20 (2), 27 (36), Mar. 13 (60), 27 (84), Apr. 3 (84), 10 (108), 17 (120), 24 (125), May 15 (168), July 3 (252), 1858; *New York Clipper*, Aug. 29 (150), Sept. 5 (158), 12 (166), 19 (174), 1857; *The New-York Daily Times*, Aug. 31 (6), Sept. 1 (4), 7 (7), 8 (3, 6), 9 (5, 7), 10 (7), 11 (7), 12 (6), 17 (7), 19 (8), 21 (5), 26 (8), 30 (7), 1857; *The New York Herald*, Sept. 1 (7), Sept. 2 (7), 1857; *Boston Evening Transcript*, Sept. 14 (2), 15 (3), 16 (3), 17 (3), 18 (3), 1857; Mar. 23 (3), 24 (3), 25 (30), 26 (3), 27 (3), 29 (3), 30 (3), 31 (3), Apr. 1 (3), 2 (3), 1858; *New York Clipper* Oct. 3, 1857: 191; Jan. 23 (319), Feb. 20 (351), May 22 (39), 29 (46), 1858; *Cincinnati Daily Commercial*, Oct. 5 (3), 6 (3), 7 (3), 8 (3), 9 (3), 10 (3), 12 (3), 13 (3), 14 (3), 15 (3), 16 (3), 17 (3), 1857; *Daily Missouri Republican* (St. Louis), Oct. 19 (3), 20 (3), 21 (3), 22 (3), 23 (3), 24 (3), 26 (3), 27 (3), 28 (3), 29 (3), 30 (3), 31 (3) 1857; May 10 (3), 11 (3), 12 (3), 13 (3), 14 (3), 15 (3), 17 (3), 18 (3), 19 (3), 20 (3), 21 (3), 1858; *The Mobile Daily Register*, Oct. 30, 1857: 3; *Boston Advertiser* and *Boston Courier* in *Rochester Union and Advertiser*, Nov. 9, 1857: 3; *Rochester Union and Advertiser*, Nov. 9 (2), 10 (2), 11 (2), 12 (2), 14 (2), 1857; *Buffalo Morning Express and Daily Democracy*, Nov. 16 (2), 17 (2), 18 (2), 19 (2), 20 (2), 21 (2), 23 (2) 24 (2), 25 (2), 26 (2), 27 (2), 28 (2), 1857; *Buffalo Daily Courier*, Nov. 16 1857:3; June 21 (3), 22 (3), 23 (3), 24 (3), 25 (3), 26 (3), 28 (3), 29 (3), 30 (3) July 1 (3), 2 (3) 3 (3), 5 (3), 1858; *The Memphis Daily Appeal*, Dec. 22 (2,3), 23 (2), 24 (2), 25 (2), 27 (2), 29 (2), 30 (2), 31 (2), 1857; Jan. 1, 1858: 2; *The Daily Picayune* (New Orleans), Jan. 10 (5), 11 (1), 12 (1, 3), 13 (4), 14 (5), 15 (1, 4), 16 (4), 17 (2), 18 (1), 19 (7), 20 (5), 21 (5), 22 (5), 23 (4), 24 (5), 1858; *Nashville Daily Gazette*, Jan. 31 (2), Feb. 2 (3), 1858; *Buffalo Morning Express and Daily Democracy*, Nov. 16 (2), 28 (2), 1857; *Buffalo Daily Courier*, Nov. 19 (3), 21 (3), 27 (3). 28 (3), 1857; *The Daily Picayune* (New Orleans), Afternoon Edition, Jan. 12, 1858: 1; *The Daily Constitutionalist* (Augusta, Georgia), Feb. 10 (2), 11 (2), 12(2), 13 (2), 15 (2), 16 (2), 1858; *The Charleston Daily Courier*, Feb. 16 (2), 17 (2), 18 (2), 19 (3), 20 (3), 1858; *The Charleston Mercury*, Feb. 17, 1858: 2; *American and Commercial Advertiser* (Baltimore), Mar. 11 (2), 12 (2), 13 (2), 15 (2), 16 (2), 17 (2), 18 (2), 19 (2), 20 (2), 1858; *New York Clipper*, Mar. 13, 1858: 375; *The Sun* (Baltimore), Mar. 20, 1858: 2; *The New York Herald*, Apr. 6, 1858: 7; *The Albion* (New York), Apr. 10 (176), 17 (188), 1858; *Daily Louisville Democrat*, Apr. 25 (3), 27 (3), 28 (3), 29 (3), 30 (3), May 1 (3), 2 (3), 4 (3), 5(3), 6 (3), 7 (3), 1858; *Daily Missouri Republican* (St. Louis), May 9, 1858: 3; *Cincinnati Daily Gazette*, May 24 (1), 25 (1), 26 (1), 27 (1), 28 (1), 1858; *Chicago Daily Tribune*, May 31 (1), June 2 (1), 3 (1), 4 (1), 8 (1), 1858; *Chicago Daily Tribune*, June 2, 1858: 1; Clippings, Hill, "Personal Recollections of Edwin Booth," EB Scrapbook, "Theatrical Matters," Rea Collection, NYPLPA; *Porter's Spirit of the Times*, Dec. 19, no year [1856], Scrapbook, *Journal Book No. 2*, Hampden-Booth; "Edwin Booth's First Appearance in Boston as Othello," Folger.

For information on the 1858–1859 season, see EB to Junius Brutus Booth, Jr., Oct. 31, 1858, Dec. 12, 1858, Harvard; to Walter Brackett, Jan. 30, Feb. 6, 1859, Texas; to Natt Levin, Mar. 26, 1859, Adam Badeau to EB, Apr. 21, 1859, Hampden-Booth; Program, Boston Theatre, Nov. 2, 1858, Folger; Edward V. Valentine, Biographical Index, Valentine Museum, Richmond; Odell, 6, 527; Oggel, *Letters and Notebooks of Mary Devlin Booth*, x; Gordon Samples, *Lust for Fame: The Stage Career of John Wilkes Booth* (Jefferson North Carolina: McFarland & Company Inc. 1982), 202; Watermeier, *Between Actor and Critic*, 18; J. Alan Hammack, "An American Actor's Diary—1858," *Educational Theatre Journal*, VII (Dec., 1955): 324; *The New York Herald*, Aug. 1, 1858: 7; *The Sun* (Baltimore), Aug. 23 (3), 24 (2), 25 (2), 26 (2), 27 (2), 28 (2), 30 (2), 31 (2), Sept. 1 (2), 2 (2), 3 (2), 4 (2) 1858, July 1 (2), 4 (2), 1859; *New York Clipper*, Aug. 28 (150), Sept. 18 (174), Oct. 16 (206), Nov. 13 (239), 27 (254), Dec. 18 (278),

1858; Jan. 1 (295), 29 (326), Feb. 12 (342), Mar. 19 (382), 26 (390), July 2 (86), 1859; *Spirit of Times* (New York), Sept. 25 (396), Oct. 16 (432), 30 (445), Nov. 13 (480), 20 (492), Dec. 25 (552), 1858; *Richmond Enquirer*, Sept. 28 (3), Oct. 1 (3), 8 (3), 15 (3), 1858; *Boston Evening Transcript*, Oct. 25 (3), 26 (3), 27 (3), 28 (3), 29 (3), 30 (3), Nov. 1 (3), 3(3), 3 (2,3), 4 (3), 5 (2,3), 8 (3), 9 (3), 10 (3), 11 (3), Nov. 12 (3), 1858; *Cincinnati Daily Gazette*, Nov. 22 (1), 23 (1, 2), 24 (1), 25 (1), 27 (1), 29 (1), 30 (1), Dec. 1 (1, 2), 2 (1), 3 (1), 4 (1), 1858; *The Louisville Daily Journal*, Dec. 6 (3), 7 (3), 8 (3), 9 (3), 10 (3), 11 (3), 13 (3), 14 (3), 15 (3), Dec. 16 (3), Dec. 17 (3), Dec. 18 (3), 1858; *Louisville Daily Courier*, Dec. 6, 1858: 2; *Daily Missouri Republican* (St. Louis), Dec. 21 (3), 22 (3), 23(2, 3), 24 (3), 25 (3), 28 (3), 29 (3), 30 (3), 31 (3) 1858, Jan. 1 (2), 1859; *The Daily Picayune* (New Orleans), Jan. 17 (1), 18 (1), 19 (1, 4), afternoon edition (1), 20 (1), 21 (1, 3), 22 (1), afternoon edition (4), 23 (1), 24, afternoon edition (1), 25 (1, 3), 26 (1), 27 (1), 28 (1), 29 (1), 30 (1), 31, afternoon edition (1), 1859; *The Memphis Daily Appeal*, Feb. 20 (2), 22 (2, 3), 23 (2), 24 (2), 25 (2), 26 (2), 27 (2), Mar. 1 (2), 2 (2), 3 (2), 4 (2), 5 (2), 1859; *The Memphis Daily Avalanche*, Feb. 25(3), 26(3), 1859; *Nashville Daily Gazette*, Mar. 6 (2), 8 (3), 9 (3), 1859; *Republican Banner* (Nashville, Tennessee), Mar. 8 (3), 10 (2), 11 (3), 12 (3,3), 15 (2), 16 (2), 17 (2), 18 (2), 19 (2, 3), 1859; *The Charleston Daily Courier*, Mar. 22 (2), 23 (2), 24 (2), 25 (2), 26 (2), 28 (2), 29 (2), 30 (1, 2), 31 (2), Apr. 1 (2), 2 (2), 4 (2), 5 (2), 6 (2), 7 (2), 8 (2), 9 (2), 11 (2), 1859; *The Charleston Mercury*, Apr. 5, 1859: 2; *The Daily Dispatch* (Richmond), Apr. 18 (2), 19 (2), 20 (2), 21 (2), 23 (2), 25 (2), 26 (2), 27 (2), 1859; *The Daily Express* (Petersburg, Virginia): Apr. 28 (1), 30 (2), 1859; *The New York Daily Times*, July 29 (7), Aug. 1 (4), 1859; *The Albion* (New York), Aug. 6, 1859: 379.

For information on the 1859–1860 season see EB to Walter Brackett, Sept. 12, 1859, Harvard; to LB, Jan. 13, 1860, Feb. 25, no year [1860], Adam Badeau to EB, Nov. 12, 1859, Hampden-Booth; Program Nov. 11, 1859, Fred G. Gross Scrapbook, NYPLPA; EB to Gideon Hollister, Feb. 5, 1860, Folger; Feb. 6, 1860, Special Collections and Archives, Wesleyan University; EB to Walter Brackett, Feb. 10, no year [1859], Texas; Celebrity Index, Philadelphia Theatre Index, Free Library of Philadelphia; Coder: 77; Oggel, *Letters and Notebooks of Mary Devlin*, 27, 28, 45, 123; Shattuck, 27; *The New York Daily Times*, Aug. 1 (4), Dec. 12 (2), 1859; *Public Ledger* (Philadelphia), Aug. 27 (3), 29 (3), 30 (3), 31 (1, 3), Sept. 1 (3), 2(3), 12 (3), 13 (2), 16 (3), 17 (4), 19 (3), 20 (3), 21 (3), 22 (3), 23 (3), 24 (4), 1859; May 9 (3), 10 (3), 11 (3), 12 (3), 14 (3), 15 (3), 16 (3), 17 (3), 18 (3), 19 (3), 21 (3), 22 (3), 23 (3), 1860; *The New York Clipper*, Sept. 10 (166), 24 (183), Oct. 1 (191) Nov. 19 (247), Dec. 24 (287), 31 (235) 1859; Feb. 4 (335), 20 (367), Mar. 17 (383), Apr. 14 (415), 1860; *Buffalo Daily Courier*, Oct. 3 (2), 4 (2), 5 (2), 6 (2), 7 (2), 8 (2), 10 (2), 11 (2), 12 (2), 13 (2), 14 (2), 1859; *Boston Evening Transcript*, Oct. 17 (3), 22 (3), Nov. 1 (2), 12 (3), 1859; *The Spirit of the Times*, Nov. 5 (463), 26 (192), Dec. 3 (208), 1859; *Wilkes' Spirit of the Times* (New York), Jan. 28 (336), May 12 (160), Sept. 27 (396), 1860; *The New York Clipper*, Nov. 19 (247), Dec. 3 (263), 1859, Feb. 4, 1860: 335; *The Savannah Republican*, Dec. 5 (2), 6 (2), 7 (2), 8 (2), 10 (2), 1859; *The Daily Sun* (Columbus, Georgia), Dec. 12 (2, 3), 13 (2), 14 (2), 15 (2), 16 (2), 17 (2), 19 (2), 1859; *The Daily Confederation* (Montgomery, Alabama), Dec. 18 (2), 20 (2), 21 (2), 23 (2), 24 (2), 25 (2). 28 (2, 3), 1859; *The Daily Picayune*, Jan. 3 (1), 4 (1,2), 5 (1), 6 (1), 7 (1, 6), 8 (1), 10 (1, 2), 11 (1), 12 (1), 13 (1), 14 (1), 15 (1), 17 (1, 8), 18 (1, 7), 19 (1, 3), 20 (1), 21 (1, 12), 27 (1), 28 (6, 7), 1860; *The Mobile Daily Register*, Jan. 24 (3), 25 (3), 27 (3), 28 (3), 30 (3), Feb. 1 (3), 2 (3, 3), 4 (3), 6 (3), 7 (3), 8 (3), 9 (3), 10 (3), 11 (3), 13 (3), 14 (3), 1860; *The Memphis Daily Appeal*. Feb. 19 (3), 21 (2), 22 (2), 24 (3), 25 (2), 26 (2), 28 (2), 29 (2), Mar. 1 (2), 2 (2), 1860; *Nashville Union and American*, Mar. 4 (4), 6 (3), 7 (2), 9 (2, 3),

10 (2), 11 (2), 13 (2), 15 (2), 16 (2), 17 (2), 1860; *The Charleston Daily Courier*, Mar. 20 (3), 21 (3), 22 (3), 23 (3), 24 (3), 26 (3), 27 (3), 28 (3), 29 (3), 30 (3), 31 (3), Apr. 2 (3), 3 (3), 4 (3), 1860; *Cincinnati Daily Gazette*, Apr. 9 (1), 10 (1), 11 (1), 12 (1,2), 13 (1, 2), 14 (1), 16 (1,2), 17 (1), 18 (1), 19 (1, 3), 20 (1, 2), 1860; *Daily Missouri Republican* (St. Louis), Apr. 24 (3), 25 (4), 26 (4), 27 (4), 28 (4), 29 (4), May 1 (4), 2 (4), 3 (4), 4 (4), 1860; Clippings, Robinson Locke Collection, 78, John Denison Champlin, "EB's 'Becket," *The Looker-On* (Mar. 1897), EB Scrapbook, NYPLPA.

For information on the 1860–1861 season see Programs, Howard Athenaeum, Sept. 17, 29, 1860, Holliday Street Theater, Oct. 2, 1860, Winter Garden Theatre, Jan. 28, 1861, Howard Athenaeum, June 1, 1861, extra-illustrated edition, Matthews and Hutton, V, pt. 2, Harvard; EB to LB, n.d. [1860], Nov. 21, Dec. 23, 1860, Jan. 9, July 1, 1861, Hampden-Booth; Programs, American Academy of Music, Jan. 10, 1861, Winter Garden Theatre, New York, Jan. 21, Feb. 1, 8 13,, 1861, Howard Athenaeum, Boston, May 17, 27, June 15, 1861, Glase Scrapbook, ; Celebrity Index, Philadelphia Theatre Index, The Free Library of Philadelphia; Asia Booth Clarke to Jean Anderson, Mar. 3, 1861, Maryland; EB to Harry Magonigle, Nov. 14, 1874 in Cohen, "Booth Notes, n.p.; Disher, *The Cowells in America*, 226, 227, 322, 247; Grossman, 133; Leach, *Bright Particular Star*, 308; *Boston Evening Transcript*, Sept. 3 (3), Sept. 4 (3), Sept. 5 (3), Sept. 6 (3), Sept. 7 (3), Sept. 8 (3) Sept. 10 (3), 11 (3), 12 (3), 14 (3), 15 (3), 19 (3), 20 (3), 21 (3), 22 (3), 26 (3), 27 (3), 1860, May 13 (3), 14 (3), 15 (3), 16 (3), 17 (3), 20 (3), 21 (3), 22 (3), 23 (3), 24 (3), 25 (3), 29 (3), 30 (3), June 3 (3), 4 (3), 5 (3), 6 (3), 8 (3), 10 (3), 12 (3), 13 (3), 14 (3), 1861; *The New York Clipper*, Sept. 8 (167), 15 (175), 22(183), 29 (191), Oct. 21 (215), Dec. 1 (262), 8 (270), 15 (278), 22 (286), 29 (294), 1860; Jan. 26 (327), Feb. 23 (358), Apr. 20 (7), 20 (5, 7), 27 (14), May 4 (14, 22), June 8 (63), 15 (70), 22 (79), 1861; *Wilkes' Spirit of the Times*(New York), Oct. 20 (112), 27 (128), Nov. 3 (144) 1860, Feb. 23 (218), Mar. 21 (64), 30 (128), 1861; *Public Ledger* (Philadelphia), Oct. 31 (4), Nov. 1 (3), 2 (3), 3 (3), 5 (3), 6 (3), 7 (3), 8 (3), 9 (3), 10 (3), 12 (3), 13 (3), 14 (3), 15 (3), 16 (3), 17 (3), 1860; Jan. 1 (3), 2 (2), 3 (3), 4 (3), 5 (3), 8 (3), 8 (3), 9 (3), 10 (3), Apr. 8 (3), 9 (3), 10 (3), 11 (3), 12 (3), 1861; *The New-York Times*, Nov. 26 (5), 27 (1), Dec. 1 (4), 3 (7), 7 (4), 10 (5), 17 (5), 20 (4, 5), 22 (7) 1860, Jan. 21 (7), Apr. 18 (5), 1861; *New-York Daily Tribune*, Nov. 27 (5), Dec. 7 (1, 7), 20 (5), 1860, Mar. 22, 1861: 8; *The Evening Post* (New York), Nov. 27 (2), Dec. 4 (2), 6 (2), 1860; *The New York Daily News*, Nov. 27, 1860: 5, Jan. 28 (4), Feb. 19 (4), 1861; *New York Dispatch*, Dec. 1, 1860: 5, Jan. 26 (8), Feb. 16 (5), 1861; *Frank Leslie's Illustrated Newspaper* (New York), Dec. 8 (35), 13 (51), 29 (83), 1860, Apr. 30, 1861: 371; *New York Morning Express*, Dec. 11 (2), 20 (2), 1860; *The New York Herald*, Jan. 21 (6), 23 (6), 25 (6), 26 (6), 29 (4), 30 (4), 31 (4), Feb. 1 (4), 2 (6), 5 (4), 6 (4), 7 (4), 9 (6), 17 (7), 20 (4), 21 (7), 22 (7), Apr. 15 (4), 17 (4), 18 (7), 21 (7), 25 (7), 26 (4), 27 (4), 1861; *The Philadelphia Inquirer*, Apr. 12 (5), 13 (4), 1861; Clippings, "Mr. Edwin Booth as Iago," *New York Tribune*, Dec. 17, 1860, *New York Evening Express*, Feb. 5 1861, Rare Book Department, Boston Public Library.

For information about the 1861–1862 season see Emma Cary to Mary Devlin Booth, July 15, 1861, EB to Thomas Hicks, Oct. 13, 1861, Hampden-Booth; to John T. Ford, July 19, 1861, Ford papers, LC, to Walter Brackett, Nov. 3, 1861, Texas; Mary Devlin Booth to Emma Crow Cushman, Oct. 4, no year [1861], May 11, 1862, EB "My to Lorimer Graham, Dec. 3, no year [1861], to Thomas Hicks, Dec. 9, 1861, Taper Collection; Grossman, 135, 137; Oggel, *Bio-Bibliography*, 5; Oggel, *Letters*, 51, 54, 55, 56, 78, 79; *Post Office London Directory*, 1776; Winter, *Life and Art*: 25; *New York Daily-Times*, Apr. 30, 1857: 2; *The New York Clipper*, Aug. 31 (156), Oct. 26 (223), Nov. 23 (255), 1861; *Frank Leslie's Illustrated Newspaper* (New York), Sept. 14, 1861: 283; *The Times* (London), Sept. 30 (6), Oct. 1 (6), 2 (6), 4 (6), 7 (6), 9 (6), 11 (6), 1861; *The Daily Telegraph* (London), Oct. 1, 1861: 2; *The Daily News* (London), Oct. 1, 1861: 2; *Morning Star and Dial* (London), Oct. 1, 1861: 3; *The Evening Star and Dial* (London), Oct. 1 (3), 2 (1), 5 (1), 14 (1), 17 (1), 30 (1), 31 (1), Nov. 4 (1), 5 (1), 6 (1), 7 (1), 8 (1), 9 (1), 1861; *The Morning Post*, Oct. 2 (5), 31 (5), 1861; *The Literary Gazette* (London), Oct. 5, 1861: 333, 334; *The Illustrated London News*, Oct. 5 (344, 348), 12 (368, 372), 19 (396), 26 (420), Nov. 2 (444, 448), 9 (469), 1861; *Bell's Life in London and Sporting Chronicle*, Oct. 6 (3), 13 (3), Nov. 3 (3), 1861; *The Standard* (London), Oct. 8, 1861: 3; *Sunday Times*, Oct. 13 (3), 20 (3), Nov. 3 (3), 10 (3), 1861; *The Daily Telegraph* (London), Oct. 29 (3), Nov. 1 (3), 1861; *John Bull* (London), Nov. 2, 1861: 701; *Sunday News* (London), Nov. 3, 1861: 3; *The Literary Gazette* (London), Nov. 9, 1861: 455; *Manchester Weekly Times— Supplement*, Nov. 9, 1861: 46; *Manchester Daily Examiner & Times* (England), Nov. 11 (1), 12 (1), 13 (1), 18 (1), 19 (1), 20 (1), 21 (1), 21 (1), 23 (1), 25 (1), 27 (1), 30 (1), 1861; *The Liverpool Mail*, Feb. 22 (4), Mar. 1 (4) 1862; *The Detroit Free Press*, Feb. 16, 1868: 3; *The Albion* (New York), Apr. 8, 1871: 220; Clipping, "Edwin Booth," Sept. 28, 1875, Folger.

For information on Booth's performances during the 1862–1863 season see EB to Geo. Karnes, Nov. 8, 1862, Mary Devlin Booth to Emma Crow Cushman, n.d. [mid-Nov., 1862], Taper Collection; EB to William Henry Huntington, Nov. 18, n.d. [1862], Texas; EB to Adam Badeau, Nov. 30, no year, [1862], Programs, Boston Theatre, Nov. 29, Dec. 2, n.d. [1862], Dec. 6, 9, 1862, Brooklyn Academy of Music, Dec. 23–26, 1862, Mathews and Hutton, extra-illustrated, V, pt. 2, Harvard; Mary Ann Holmes to EB, Jan. 29, 1863, Hampden-Booth; Oggel, *Letters*, 83, 86, 91, 93; *Chicago Daily Tribune*, Aug. 9, 1862: 4; *The New York Herald*, Sept. 24 (4), 29 (7), 30 (7), Oct. 1 (7), 2 (7), 4 (7), 5 (4), 7 (4), 8 (4), 9 (4), 11 (7) 12 (4), 14 (4), 15 (4), 16 (4), 17 (4, 7), 18 (4), 20 (4), 21 (4), 22 (4, 7), 26 (4), 28 (4), 29 (4, 7), 31 (4), Nov. 1 (4), 2 (4), 4 (4), 5 (4), 6 (4), 7 (4, 7), 8 (4), 11 (4), 12 (4), 13 (4), 14 (4, 7), 15 (4) 17 (7), 21 (4), 1863; *The Albion* (New York), Oct. 4 (475), 18 (499) Nov. 1 (523) 1862; Feb. 21, 1863: 91; *The New-York Daily Tribune*, Oct. 6 (3), Nov. 24 (3) 1862, Feb. 16, 1863: 8; *The New York Clipper*, Oct. 11 (207), 18 (215), Nov. 1 (230), 8 (238), 1862; *The New-York Times*, Oct. 27 (5), Nov. 4 (5), Dec. 24 (2, 7), 25 (7), 26 (7), 27 (3, 7), 29 (2), 1862, Feb. 19, 1863: 7; *Frank Leslie's Illustrated Newspaper* (New York), Nov. 8 (107), 15 (119), 22 (133), 1862; *Boston Post*, Nov. 24 (3) 25 (3), 26 (3), 29 (4), Dec. 1 (3).4 (3), 5 (3), 6 (4), 10 (3), 11 (3), 15 (3), 16 (3), 17 (3), 19 (3), 20 (3), 1862; *The Brooklyn Daily Eagle*, Dec. 22 (1), 24 (2), 1862; he Albion (New York), Feb. 21, 1863: 91; Clippings, Review by Athens for the *United States Gazette*, Macbeth reviews, Cushman papers, LC, "EB Dead," *Boston Journal*, June 7, 1893, EB Scrapbook, 3, Harvard.

For information on Booth's performances during the 1863–1864 season see EB to Adam Badeau, Tuesday, n.d., Sept. 26, no year, to "Col T. A. Brown," July 28, 1888, Junius Brutus Booth Jr., *Diary*, various dates, Folger; Programs, Boston Theatre, Oct. 26-Nov. 28, 1863, Rare Books Department, Boston Public Library; Programs, Boston Theatre, Oct. 31, Nov. 21, 1863, Glase Scrapbook, Celebrity Index, The Free Library of Philadelphia; Program, Boston Theatre, Nov. 25, 1863, extra-illustrated edition, Copeland, 56f, Programs, Niblo's Garden, Mar. 29, Apr. 5, 1864, Winter Garden Theatre, May 9, 1864, Bamburgh, Harvard; Broadsides, Winter Garden, Apr. 23, 1864 May 14, 1864, T. J. Hind Scrapbook, Folger; Rose Eytinge, *The Memories of Rose Eytinge* (New York: Frederick A. Stokes Company, 1905), 28, 29, 30; Grossman, 153, 154, 161, 162; Oggel, *Bio-Bibliography*, 14; Titone, 433; Winter, *Life and Art*, 32; Edward Hamilton Bell, "Mr. J. S. Clarke," *Edwin Booth and his Contemporaries*: 101; *North American and United States Gazette* (Philadelphia), Aug. 24

(2), Aug. 25 (3), Aug. 27 (3), Aug. 28 (3), Aug. 29 (3), Aug. 31 (3), Sept. 2 (3), Sept. 3 (3), Sept. 4 (3), 1863; *Albany Evening Journal*, Sept. 14 (3), Sept. 15 (3), Sept. 16 (3), Sept. 17 (3), Sept. 18 (3), Sept. 19 (3), 1863; *The New York Herald*, Sept. 20 (8), Sept. 22 (4), Sept. 23 (4), Sept. 24 (6), Sept. 26 (6), Sept. 28 (6), Oct. 2 (1), Oct. 3 (1), Oct. 4 (4), Oct. 6 (6), Oct. 7 (1) Oct. 8 (1, 4) Oct. 9 (4), Oct. 10 (4, 7), Oct. 13 (6), Oct. 14 (2), Oct. 15 (1), Oct. 16 (4), Oct. 17 (1) 1863; Mar. 29 (7), Mar. 31 (4, 10), Apr. 2 (6), Apr. 3 (4), Apr. 6 (4), Apr. 7 (4), Apr. 8 (4), Apr. 9 (4), Apr. 10 (4), Apr. 12 (4), Apr. 13 (10), Apr. 14 (4), Apr. 15 (4, 7), Apr. 19 (4), Apr. 20 (4), Apr. 21 (10) Apr. 22 (10), May 3 (10), May 4 (4), May 5 (7), May 6 (4), May 7 (4, 7), May 11 (10), May 12 (4, 10), 1864; *Frank Leslie's Illustrated Newspaper* (New York), Oct. 3 (27), Oct. 17 (55), Oct. 24 (67) 1863; May 11 (116), 21 (131), 1864; *The New York Clipper*, Oct. 10 (203), Dec. 12 (275) 1863, Apr. 9 (111), 30 (22), Sept. 24 (198), Oct. 8 (206), 1864;Apr. 30, 1864: 22, Jan. 9 (307), Jan. 16 (315), Jan. 23 (323), Jan. 30 (331), Feb. 20 (355), May 7 (30), 1864; *The Albion* (New York), Oct. 17 (439), Oct. 24 (511) 1863: 439; Apr. 16, 1864: 187; *The Brooklyn Daily Eagle*, Jan. 2 (3), Jan. 5 (1, 3), Jan. 8 (1), Jan. 9 (1), Jan. 11 (1), Jan. 12 (1), Jan. 13 (1), Jan. 14 (1), Jan. 21 (1), 1864; *Daily National Intelligencer* (Washington, D.C.), Feb. 15 (3), Feb. 16 (3), Feb. 17 (3), Feb. 18 (3), Feb. 20 (1), Feb. 23 (1), Feb. 24 (1), Feb. 26 (1), Feb. 27 (1), Feb. 29 (1), Mar. 2 (1), Mar. 7 (1), Mar. 8 (1) Mar. 9 (1), Mar. 10 (1), Mar. 12 (1), 1864; *The Evening Post* (New York), Mar. 29, 1864: 2; *The New York Leader*, Apr. 9 (4) 23 (5), 1864; *The New York Herald*, May 3 (10), 17 (10), June 17 (7), 1864; *New-York Daily Times*, July 31, 1864: 3; *Utica Daily Observer*, Dec. 15, 1877: 1; Clippings, Mar. 5, 1864, T. J. Hind Scrapbook, Folger; Advertisement for benefit of Sept. 12, 1864, General Reviews file, Emma C. Cushman, "Charlotte Cushman A Memory," 15, Biographical Data, XV, "Sketch of Charlotte Cushman," Cushman papers, LC; Edward R. Byram, "EB in Boston," Harvard.

For information on the 1864–1865 season see EB to Adam Badeau, Aug. 18, 1864, to J. E. Tilton & Co., Apr. 11, 1865, Folger; to McE, Aug. 18, 1864, Oct. 25, [n.d., 1864 penciled in], Tulsa; to TBA, Aug. 18, 1864, Aug. 23, no year [1864], Oct. 3, 1864, Harvard; to Emma F. Cary," Aug. 26, 1864, Jan. 10, 1865, to Richard Henry Stoddard], Friday eve, n.d., Hampden-Booth; to Launt Thompson, Sept. 16, no year [1864], NYPLPA; to Harry Magonigle, Nov. 14, 1874 in Robert Cohen, Boothnotes, n.p., 38; Robert Cohen, *Edwin Booth in Performance* Ms., University of California, Irvine, I, 11; Programs, n.d. [Jan. 9, 1865 penciled in], Winter Garden, Mar. 20, 1865, Bamburgh, Harvard; Program, Winter Garden Theatre, New York, Mar. 17, 1865, Glase Scrapbook, Celebrity Index, Philadelphia Theatre Index, Free Library of Philadelphia; Playbills, Boston Theatre, Mar. 20-Apr. 14, 1865, Rare Books Department, Boston Public Library; Aldrich, *Crowding Memories*, 66; Grossman, 154, 155, 165–170; Oggel, *Bio-Bibliography*, 19; Lucia Gilbert Calhoun, "Edwin Booth," *The Galaxy*, Jan. 1869: 79–82; *The New York Clipper*, Nov. 28, 1864: 262; Feb. 18 (358), Mar. 25 (398), 1865; *Frank Leslie's Illustrated News* (New York), Dec. 24, 1864: 219; *The New York Leader*, Jan. 14, 1865: 4, 5; *The Albion* (New York), Mar. 25, 1865: 139; *Boston Evening Transcript*, Apr. 3 (3) 1865; Clippings, "The One Hundredth Night of 'Hamlet'" Advertisement, Winter Garden Theatre, Nov. 25, 1864, Folger; Edward R. Byram, "Edwin Booth in Boston," Extra-illustrated edition, Copeland, 78f, Harvard; item 332040695, ebay.com.

For information on the 1865–1866 season see EB to McE, June 11, n.d. [1865 penciled in], Tulsa; John D. Seville to EB, June 12, 1865, EB to Emma F. Cary, July 31, 1865, H. H. Coolidge to EB, Dec. 30, 1865, EB to John B. Murray, Jan. 21, Apr. 27, May 29, Aug. 12, 1866, Hampden-Booth; Broadside, Winter Garden Theatre, Jan. 24.1866, Programs, Winter Garden Theatre, Jan. 10, 1866 , Feb. 21, 1866, EB to Henry Hinton, Folger; to William Henry Huntington, July 28, no year [correct date Saturday, July 28, 1856 or Sunday July 29, 1856], Texas; Programs, Walnut Street Theatre, May 10, 1866, Extra-illustrated edition, Copeland, 82f, Program, Winter Garden Theatre, Jan. 19, 1866, Bamburgh, Harvard; Coder: 38; Program, Walnut Street Theatre, June 18, 1866, Celebrity Index, Philadelphia Theatre Index, Free Library of Philadelphia; Owen Fawcett, Diary, 1866, Tennessee; Cohen, *Edwin Booth in Performance* Ms., University of California, Irvine, I, 12, Boothnotes, 50; Grossman, 156, 157, 158, 173, 174. 175; Oggel, *Bio-Bibliography*, 21, 22; Eugene Tompkins, *The History of the Boston Theatre 1854–1901* (Boston and New York: Houghton Mifflin Company, 1908), 111, 127; "An Actor King": 730; Bell, "J. S. Clarke": 102; *Public Ledger* (Philadelphia), Apr. 23 (1), Apr. 25 (1), Apr. 27 (1), Apr. 28 (1), Apr. 30 (1), May 1 (1), May 2 (1), May 3 (1), May 7 (1), May 14 (1), May 15 (1), May 16 (1), May 17 (1), May 18 (1), May 21 (1), May 22 (1), May 28 (1), May 29 (1), May 30 (1), May 31 (1), June 1 (1), June 2 (1), June 4 (1), June 5 (1), June 6 (1), June 9 (1), June 11 (1), June 12 (1), June 13 (1), June 15 (1), June 16 (1), June 20 (1), 1866; *New-York Tribune*, Jan. 5 (3), Jan. 6 (3), Jan. 8 (3), Jan. 9 (3), Jan. 11 (3), Jan. 12 (3), Jan. 13 (3), Jan. 16 (3), Jan. 18 (3), Jan. 20 (3), Jan. 24 (3), Jan. 27 (3), Feb. 5 (3), Feb. 6 (3), Feb. 8 (3), Feb. 9 (3), Feb. 10 (3), Feb. 12 (3), Feb. 15 (3), Feb. 16 (3), Feb. 19 (3), Feb. 26 (3), Mar. 2 (3), Mar. 3 (3), Mar. 12 (3), Mar. 13 (3), 1866; *The New York Clipper*, Jan. 6 (310), Aug. 26 (58) Sept. 30 (199) 1865, Jan. 6 (310), Jan. 19 (326, 327), Jan. 27 (335), Feb. 3 (350), Feb. 17 (358, 359), Mar. 24 (398, 399), Mar. 31 (406, 407), 1866; *The Albion* (New York), Jan. 6 (7), Feb. 3 (55), Mar. 10 (115) 1866; *Frank Leslie Illustrated Newspaper* (New York), Apr. 7, 1865: 35; *Chicago Tribune*, June 6, 1867: 2; Clippings, no source, n.d. [1865], Weston Scrapbook , Hampden-Booth; Robinson Locke Collection, 78, NYPLPA; Ebay items 15247226147, 1530263000.

For information about the 1866–1867 season see Anon to EB, Oct. 10, no year, [1866], EB to John B. Murray], Dec. 28, 1866, June 13, 1867, Count Johannes to EB, Apr. 9, 1867, Program Winter Garden Theatre, Dec. 20, 1866, Weston Scrapbook, Hampden-Booth; Launt Thompson to Adam Badeau, Mar. 28, 1867, Badeau General Correspondence, Manuscript Division, LC; EB to Epes Sargent, Apr. 19, no year [1867], Taper Collection; E to John E. Russell, Apr. 21, 1867, June 22, 1874, Rochester; William Stuart, Receipt, Sept. 6, 1867, J. G. Boyd to EB, Aug. 18, 1869, EB to Launt Thompson, June 9, no year [1867], transcription by Edwina Booth Grossman, NYPLPA; EB to Mrs. E. L. Davenport, Dec. 12, 1879, Department of Special Collections, The University Library, University of California, Davis; EB to Asa Israel Fish, n.d., Folger; Boston Theatre Playbills, Sept. 3-Oct.13, 1866, Boston Public Library; Fawcett, Diary, Tennessee; Programs, Winter Garden Theatre, Jan. 1, Mar. 15, 21, 1867, Bamburgh, Harvard; Cohen, Boothnotes, 39, 50; Oggel, *Bio-Bibliography*, 21; Watermeier, *Between Actor and Critic*, 48; Winter, *Life and Art*, 41, 45, 46; *The New York Clipper*, Sept. 8 (175), Oct. 15 (214), Nov. 10 (246), Dec. 1 (270), 15 (286), 22 (295) 1866; Jan. 5 (311), 19 (327), 26 (335), Feb. 2 (343), 9 (350), Mar. 9 (382), 16 (391), 23 (380), Apr. 2 (403), 6 (414), 7 (416), May 4 (31), June 29 (94), Aug. 3 (184), 11 (142), Nov. 10 (246), Dec. 1 (270), 8 (278), 15 (286) 1866, Jan. 12 (310, 311), Feb. 9 (350), Apr. 7 (6), May 18 (46), June 22 (86), 1867; *Public Ledger* (Philadelphia), Sept. 1 (1), Oct. 13 (1), 16 (1), 17 (1), 18 (1), 20 (1), 22 (1), 27 (1), 30 (1), 31 (1), Nov. 1 (1), 2 (1), 3 (1), 5 (1), 6 (1), 8 (1), 9 (1), 10 (1), 12 (1), 13 (1), 14 (1), 15 (1), 16 (1), 21 (1), 24 (1), 1866; *The New-York Times*, Nov. 21(7), 27 (7) 1866; Dec. 1 (7), 4 (7), 5 (4), 6 (7), 1866; *Daily National Intelligencer* (Washington), Sept. 8, 1866: 1; *The Brooklyn Daily Eagle*, Nov. 30 (1), Dec. 1 (1, 4), 7 (3), 8 (1, 3), 10 (1), 17 (1), 24 (1), 1866; *Frank Leslie's Illustrated Newspaper* (New York), Dec. 1 (163), 8 (179), 15 (195), 29 (227), 1866; Jan. 5 (243), 12 (259), 19 (275), 26 (291), Feb. 2 (309),

10 (338), Mar. 30 (19), Apr. 6 (35, 37) 13 (51), 20 (67), 1867; *York Leader*, Dec. 22 (4), 29 (4), 1866; *New-York Daily Tribune*, Dec. 31, 1856:8, Jan. 5 (9), 9 (7), 25 (7), 30 (8), 31 (7), Feb. 1 (4, 7), 2 (7), 4 (7), 5 (7), 6 (7), 7 (7), 8 (7), 9 (7), 11 (7), 12 (7), 13 (7), 14 (7), 15 (7), 16 (7), 18 (7), 19 (7), 20 (2), 21 (7), 22 (7), 23 (7), 25 (7), 26 (7), 27 (7), 28 (7), Mar. 1 (7), 2 (7), 3 (7), 4 (7), 6 (7), 8 (7), 12 (7), 13 (7), 19 (7), 20 (7), 1867; *The Albion* (New York): Dec. 1 (571), 8 (583) 1866, Feb. 2 (55), Mar. 16 (127), 1867; *The Evening Post* (New York), Dec. 24, 1866: 2; *Boston Daily Evening Transcript*, Mar. 6 (2), Apr. 3 (2), May 5 (2), 1867; *The New York Herald*, Mar. 24, 1867: 5; *Daily National Intelligencer* (Washington), Mar. 25, 1867: 2; *Chicago Tribune* Mar. 27 (4), June 2 (2), 4 (5), 5 (4), 7 (4), 8 (4), 12 (4), 22 (1), 23 (4), 28 (4), 1867; *Boston Daily Evening Transcript*, Apr. 26 (2), 27 (2), 29 (2), May 16 (2), 17 (2), 1867; *Chicago Daily Tribune*, June 3 (4), 4 (5), 12 (4), 16 (4), 19 (4), 22 (1), 23 (4), 30 (4), 1867; *Boston Daily Advertiser*, Nov. 2, 1868: 1; Clippings, "EB," *Boston Journal*, June 7, 1893, EB Scrapbook, 3, "Great Fire on Broadway," Bamburgh, Harvard.

For information on the 1867–1868 season see EB to General Ulysses S. Grant, Sept. 11, 1867, to John B. Murray, Oct. 5, 1867, Asia Booth Clarke to EB, Nov. 1, 1867, Anon. to EB, Nov. 7, 1867, EB to McE, Nov. 21, 1867, McE to EB, Dec. 10, 1867, A. O. Kellogg to Jan. 15, 1868, George Allen to EB, n.d., Hampden-Booth; EB to John E. Russell, Jan. 24, n.d. [1868], University of Rochester Library; Robinson Locke Collection, 78, EB to Launt Thompson, Oct. 17, 1867, transcription by Edwina Booth Grossman to EwB, Feb. 13, 1868, 25 [1868 penciled in], Programs, Academy of Music, Cleveland, Ohio, Feb. 27, 1868, Walnut Street Theatre, Philadelphia, Pennsylvania, Apr. 8, 1868, EB to EwB, n.d. [Jan. 7, 1887 penciled in], NYPLPA; Programs, Ford's Holliday Street Theatre, Baltimore, Sept. 1867, Walnut Street Theatre, Mar. 26-May 2, 1868, Glase Scrapbook, Celebrity Index, Philadelphia Theatre Index, Free Library of Philadelphia; Fawcett, Diary, Apr. 27, May 2, 1868, Tennessee; Sollers: 249; Taylor, 233; *Mobile Daily Advertiser and Register*, July 18 (2), 28 (2), Dec. 1 (3), 3 (3), 7 (3), 8 (2), 11 (3), 15 (3), 1867; *The New York Clipper*, July 27 (126), Sept. 21 (190), 28 (198), Oct. 19 (222), 26 (230), Nov. 16 (254), 23 (262), 30 (270) 1867, Jan. 4 (311), 18 (327), 24 (334), Feb. 1 (342), 8 (350), Mar. 7 (382), 14 (390), Apr. 11 (6), May 16 (46), 23 (54), 30 (62), June 6 (70), 13 (78), 1868; *Daily National Intelligencer* (Washington), Aug. 18 (1), Sept. 6 (1), 1867; *The Sun* (Baltimore), Sept. 9 (2), 10 (2), 11 (2), 12 (2), 13 (2), 14 (2), 16 (2), 23 (2), 24 (2), 25 (2), 26 (2), 27 (2), 28 (2), 30 (2), Oct. 1 (2), Oct. 2 (2), 1867; *The Sun* (Baltimore), Sept. 9 (2), 10 (2), 12 (2), 14 (2), 16 (2), 24 (1, 2), 25 (2), 28 (2), Oct. 3 (2), 1867; *The Cincinnati Commercial*, Oct. 13 (8), 15 (8), 16 (8), 18 (4), 19 (8), 20 (8), 22 (8), 26 (8), 1867; *The Louisville Daily Journal*, Nov. 2 (3), 4 (2, 3, 4), 5 (3), 6 (3), 7 (3), 8 (3), 9 (3), 11 (2), 1867; *Louisville Daily Courier*, Nov. 4 (3), 5 (4), 11 (1), 1867; *The Missouri Republican* (St. Louis), Nov. 11 (2), 12 (2), 14 (2), 15 (2), 17 (2), 23 (2), 1867; *Boston Daily Evening Transcript*, Nov. 15, 1867: 2; *Mobile Daily Advertiser and Register*, Dec. 3 (3), 6(3), 7 (3), 15 (2), 1867; *The Daily Picayune* (New Orleans), Dec. 15 (5), 17 (5), 17, afternoon edition (2), 18 (5, 8), 19 (5, 8), 20, afternoon edition (2, 5), 21 (5), 22 (7), 24 (5), 25 (5), 27 (5), 28 (5), 29 (5), 30 (5), 1867; Jan. 1 (4), 2 (4), 3 (4), 4 (4, 8), 1868; *The Memphis Daily Appeal*, Jan. 7 (2), 8 (2), 9 (3), 10 (3), 11 (3), 12 (3), 14 (2, 3), 16 (2), 18 (3), 1868; *The Daily Memphis Avalanche*, Jan. 16 (2), 17 (2), 18 (2), 1868; *The Chicago Tribune*, Jan. 24 (4), 26 (4), 28 (4), 31 (4) 1867; Feb. 3 (4), 5 (4), 7 (4), 1868; *The Detroit Free Press*, Feb. 9 (1), 11 (2, 3), 12 (2), 14 (3), 18 (1), 19 (1), 20 (1), 21 (1), 22 (1), 1868; *Milwaukee Sentinel*, Feb. 10 (1), 14 (1), 17 (1), 1868; *The Detroit Free Press*, Feb. 11, 1868: 2; *Cleveland Daily Plain Dealer*, Feb. 24 (2), 25 (4), 26 (4), 27 (4), 28 (4), 29 (4), 1868; *Newark Daily Advertiser* (Newark, New Jersey), Mar. 2 (3), 11 (2), 1868; *Daily Evening Bulletin* (Philadelphia), Mar. 30 (6), 31 (6), Apr. 2 (6), 4 (6), 7 (6), 8 (6), 11 (6), 1868; *Public Ledger* (Philadelphia), Apr. 15 (1), 17 (1), 20 (1), 21 (1), 22 (1), 24 (1), 25 (1), 27 (1), 1868; *Springfield Republican* (Springfield, Massachusetts), May 7, 1868: 4; Jan. 12, 1890: 3; *Hartford Courant*, May 12, 1868: 1; *Albany Evening Journal*, May 12 (3), 13 (1) 1868; *Morning Journal and Courier* (New Haven, Connecticut), May 20, 1868: 2; *Newport Mercury* (Newport, R. I), May 23, 1868: 3; *The Daily Mercury* (New Bedford, Massachusetts), May 25, 1868: 3; *Lowell Daily Courier*, May 26, 1868: 3; *Providence Daily Journal*, May 30, 1868: 3;

For information on the 1868–1869 season (including the building of Booth's Theatre) see EB to John B. Murray, May 29, 1866, Jan. 15, June 13, 1867, Oct. 5, 1867, to LB, June 13, 1867, to Mrs. John B. Murray, July 27, 1866, to Emma F. Cary, n.d. [Jan. 1868], to to Launt Thompson, Oct. 3, 1867, Joseph Booth to EB, Dec. 2, 1867, John B. Murray to EB, Dec. 2, 1867, McEntee to EB, Dec. 10, 1867, Program, Boston Theatre, Nov. 3, 1868, Edwin Adams to EB, Dec. 1, 1868, May 12, no year [1869?], Mortgage, EB to John S Clarke, Apr. 5, 1869, Mrs. Henry P, Gray to Edwin Booth, Mar. 2, 1869, Marie Potter to EB, May 9, 1869, EB to John E. Russell, May 28, 1869, Jerome Buck to Ignatius R. Grossman, Dec. 6, 1908, Hampden-Booth; EB to Launt Thompson, May 8, [1867/1868 incorrectly written in], transcription by EBG, Oct. 17, 1867. transcription by EBG, Jan. 30, 1868, to EwB, Feb. 25 [1868 penciled in], transcription by EBG, Sept. 5, 15, Dec. 9, 1868, Sept. 28, no year [1869 penciled in], May 28, n.d. [1869 penciled in], Feb. 27, 1872, to Launt Thompson, Sept. 22, 1868, transcription by EBG, to Launt Thompson and McE, Apr. 27, 1869, NYPLPA; EB to John E. Russell, Apr. 21, 1867, Jan. 24, n.d. [1868], Feb. 12, 1869, St. Paddy's day, 1869, June 22, no year [1869], Rochester; Deeds, May, 1, 1867, Liber 1024: 83; June 10, 1867, Liber 1019: 441; Sept. 11, 1867, Liber 1022: 387, 389; Sept. 18, 1867, Liber 1013: 674, 675; Register's Office, New York, New York; EB to Anon., June 30, 1867, Program, Booth's Theatre, Feb. 3, 1869, University of Pennsylvania; Playbills, Boston Theatre, Oct. 5-Oct. 31, 1868, Boston Public Library; EB to Mrs. Gray, Mar. 16, 1869, Beinecke Rare Book and Manuscript Library, Yale University Library; EB to TBA, Sept. 27, no year [1868 penciled in], Program, Boston Theatre, Oct. 30, 1868, Matthews and Hutton, V, pt. 2, EB to Bouncer Cox, Feb. 8, 1871, Harvard; Program English's Opera House, Indianapolis, Indiana, Dec. 23–24, 1881, Will E. English Theatre Program Collection, William Henry Smith Memorial Library, Indiana Historical Society; EB to Asa Israel Fish, n.d., Program Booth's Theatre, Mar. 22, 1869, Mortgage John S Clarke and Edwin T. Booth to Richard A. Robertson for $54,000 in 3 years with int. half yearly Assigned to The Fidelity Insurance Trust & Safe Deposit Company Assigned to Joseph B. Myers, May 3, 1869, Folger; Cohen, *Edwin Booth in Performance* Ms., Irvine, I, 13, 31–32, Boothnotes: 74, 90, *The Tribune* (New York) Mar. 5, 1869: in Boothnotes: 91; Newspaper Index, Buffalo and Erie County Historical Society; Coder: 140; Paul R. Bake, *Stanny: The Gilded Life of Stanford White* (New York: The Free Press, 1989), 150; Charles C. Baldwin, *Stanford White* (New York: Da Capo Press, 1976), 145; Grossman, 177; Taylor, 235, 236; Watermeier, *Between Actor and Critic*, 24, 27, 52; Winter, *Life and Art*, 75; *Daily Placer Times and Transcript* (San Francisco), Jan. 2 (3), Apr. 15 (3), 1854; *New-York Daily Times*, Sept. 6, 1856: 3; *Public Ledger* (Philadelphia), June 30, 1866: 1; *The New York Albion* (New York), Jan. 19, 1867: 31, Jan. 30 (57), Feb. 6 (68) Mar. 27 (164), Apr. 17 (210), 24 (228), May 15 (274), 1869; *The Cincinnati Commercial*, Sept. 15 (8), 17 (8), 1868; *The Detroit Free Press*, *The Detroit Free Press*, Sept. 20 (1), 24 (2), Oct. 1 (1), 2 (1) 1868; *Toledo Blade*, Sept. 21, 1868: 1; *The New York Clipper*, Nov. 2, 1867: 236, June 6 (70), July 11 (110), 21 (126) Sept. 26 (198), Oct. 10 (214), Nov. 7 (246), 21 (262, 270), Dec. 5 (278), 1868, Jan. 2 (310), 23 (334) 30 (342), Feb. 27 (374), Apr. 17 (14), 24

(22), May 1 (30), 8 (38), 22 (54), June 26 (94), 1869; *Chicago Tribune,* June 2, 1867: 2, Nov. 17 (1), 18 (1), 19 (4), 21 (4), 29 (2,4), Dec. 1 (4), 1868; *Newport Mercury.* May 23, 1868: 3; *Frank Leslie's Illustrated Newspaper* (New York), July 25, 1868: 291; *Pittsburg Gazette,* Sept. 7 (8), 8 (7), 9 (7), 10 (7), 12 (7), Dec. 21 (7), 22 (7), 23 (7), 24 (7), 25 (7), 1868;*The Cincinnati Commercial,* Sept. 12 (8), 13 (8), 1868; *The Chicago Daily Tribune,* Sept. 27 (2), Nov. 17 (1), 20 (4), 22 (2), 25 (4), 28 (4), Dec. 5 (4), 1868; *Boston Daily Evening Transcript,* Oct. 5 (2), Dec. 1 (2), 1868; *Milwaukee Sentinel,* Dec. 7, 1868: 1; *Pittsburg Gazette,* Sept. 11 (2), Dec. 21 (7), 23 (8), 1868, Apr. 23, 1870: 83; *Buffalo Daily Courier,* Dec. 11 (2), 12 (2), 15 (2), 16 (2), 17 (1), 18 (2), 19 (2), 1868; *The New-York Times,* Jan. 25 (5), Feb. 1 (7), 2 (7), 4 (4, 5), 5 (4), 6 (4), 7 (5), 8 (4), 9 (4), 10 (4), 11 (4), 12 (6), 13 (4), 15 (4), 16 (4, 5), 17 (4, 7), 18 (4,7), 19 (4), 22 (4, 5,7), 23 (4, 5, 7), 24 (4), 25 (4), 26 (4), Mar. 1 (5), 2(7), 4 (5), 14 (7), 22 (4), 23 (4), 24 (6), 25 (6), 26 (4), 27 (6), 28 (4), Apr. 4 (5), 11 (7), 13 (4), 25 (7), May 2 (7), 6 (7), 7 (7), 16 (7), 24 (7), 25 (4), 1869; *New York Herald,* Feb. 4 (7), Apr. 27 (9), 1869; *Daily National Intelligencer* (Washington), Feb. 6, 1869: 1; *The New York Leader,* Feb. 6 (4), 13 (1), Apr. 17 (1), 24 (5), May 1 (5), 20 (4), 1869; *The Albion* (New York), Apr. 3 (179), 10 (195), 17 (210), May 1 (242), 8 (258), 15 (274), 29 (306), 1869;*The Sun* (New York), Apr. 13, 1869: 1; *New York Dispatch,* May 2 (4), 9 (3), 30 (4), June 13 (5), 1869; *New York Dramatic News,* Sept. 16, 1876: 6; *The New York Dramatic Mirror,* June 5, 1889: 8; Clippings, LH, "EB," EB Scrapbook, 24, Harvard; Dr. G. [*sic*] Ogden Doremus, "Edwin Booth and Ole Bull": 235, Robert Young Jr. Research Materials, LC; *The Dispatch* (New York), Feb. 7, 1869, *Rochester Chronicle,* Apr. 5, 1869, no source, n.d. [Apr. 13, 1869], *Daily Star,* Apr. 13, 1869, *Citizen* (New York), Apr. 17, 1869, *The Sun* New York, May 16, 1869, Scrapbook, Booth's Theatre, 1869–1870, Hampden-Booth; http://www.journals.uchicago.edu/doi/abs/10.1086/507500

For information about Booth's performances during the 1869–1870 season see EB to John E. Russell, June 22, no year [1869], Aug. 22, 1869, Rochester; Celebrity Index, Philadelphia Theatre Index, Program, Walnut Street Theatre, Sept. 22, 1869, Free Library of Philadelphia; Programs, Walnut Street Theatre, Oct. 27, 1869, Booth's Theatre, New York, Jan. 27, 1870, extra-illustrated edition, Matthews and Hutton, V, pt. 2, EB to TBA, Nov. 13, 1869, Program, Booth's Theatre, Jan. 5, 1870, Bamburgh, Harvard; to Launt Thompson and McE, Apr. 2, 1869, to Launt Thompson, Nov. 9, 1869, transcription by EBG, Dec. 5, 1869, transcription by EBG, to EwB, Nov. 14, 1869; Apr. 20, 1870, NYPLPA; Programs, Booth's Theatre, Jan. 4, Mar. 21, 1870, to WW, Mar. 15, 1870, Charles W. Clarke, *Diary,* Column 1, 102, 107, 142, 148, 149, Folger; EB to John E. Russell, Apr. 2, 1870, Rochester, to Mrs. Allen, June 1, 1870, to H. T. Tuckerman, Oct. 26, 1869, to McE, June 13, 1870, to John S Clarke, Lease, June 23, 1870, Hampden-Booth; Playbills and Broadsides, Boston Theatre, Nov. 4–13, 1869, Boston Public Library; EB to Charlotte Cushman, July 23, 1871, Letters to Charlotte Cushman, IX, LC; Edwin Forrest to James Oakes, Sept. 25, 1869, Princeton University Library; Cohen, *Edwin Booth in Performance,* 33, Boothnotes, 58, 62, 101, 103; Watermeier, *Between Actor and Critic* 23, 25, 42, 109; Edward L. Partridge, "Edwin Booth to John E. Russell," *The Outlook,* 127 (Apr. 20,. 1921): 638; *The New York Albion* (New York), June 5 (312); 12 (338), Aug. 14 (481), Sept. 4 (530), 18 (562), Nov. 25 (722) 1869, Jan. 15 (40–41), Feb. 12 (106), 19 (122), 26 (138), Mar. 19 (398), 26 (202), Apr. 2 (218), 9 (234), 16 (250), May 28 (346), June 4 (362), July 21 (226), 1870; *The New York Clipper,* June 5 (70), July 31 (134), Oct. 2 (206), 30 (238), Nov. 13 (254), 20 (262), 27 (270–271), Dec. 4 (278, 279), 11 (286) 1869, Jan. 1 (310), 8 (319), 22 (334), 29 (342), Feb. 5 (350), 12 (358), 26 (374), Mar. 5 (382), 12 (390), 26 (406), 1870; *The New-York Times,* June 27, 1869: 5, Jan. 9 (5), 23 (5), Mar. 26 (5), 29 (4), 30 (4), 1870; *The New York Times,* Jan. 7, 1870: as quoted in Witham, 201, 202, 203; *The Philadelphia Inquirer,* Sept. 20 (8), 21 (3), 27 (2, 8), 28 (8), 29 (8), 30 (8), Oct. 1 (8), 4 (8), 5 (8), 6 (8), 7 (8), 8 (8), 9 (8), 11 (3, 8), 15 (8), 16 (8), 18 (8), 19 (8), 23 (8), 25 (8), 27 (8), 1869; *Worcester Daily Spy,* Nov. 13, 1869: 3; *Morning Journal and Courier* (New Haven), Nov. 13, 1869: 3; *Hartford Daily Courant,* Nov. 15 (3), 20 (2) 1869; *Providence Daily Journal,* Nov. 20 (5), 25 (5), 1869; *The New-York Daily Tribune,* Jan. 6 (4), 10 (3), 17 (3), 19 (3), 24 (3), 31 (3), Feb. 5 (7), 7 (7) 14 (4), 15 (3) 1870; *New York Herald,* Jan. 6 (7), Feb. 11(2), 13 (2), 14 (5), 15 (7), 1870; *The Evening Post* (New York). Jan. 6 (2), Feb. 28 (4), Mar. 12 (4), 22 (2), 24 (2), 25 (2), 29 (2), 30 (4), Apr. 1 (4). 2 (2), 4 (4), 12 (4), 1870; *The Sun* (New York), Jan. 6 (2), Mar. 22 (2), Mar. 25 (2) 1870; *New York Dispatch,* Jan. 8 (5), Mar. 22 (5), Apr. 3 (5), 1870; *Frank Leslie's Illustrated Newspaper* (New York), Jan. 8 (275), Mar. 12 (427), 19 (3), 26 (19), Apr. 2 (35), 16 (67), 1870; Clippings, *The Tribune* (New York), Sept. 10, 1869, Scrapbook, 1869–1870, no source, Mar. 1869, *The New York Times,* n.d. [circa Mar. 21, 1870], *The Globe,* Mar., 1870, *Evening Gazette* (New York), Mar. 26, 1870, Scrapbook, 1869–1870, Booth's Theatre, New York newspaper, n.d. [Jan. 1870], "Booth's Theatre—Hamlet," no source, n.d. [circa Jan. 5, 1870], Scrapbook Booth's Theatre, Melvin Scrapbook, Hampden-Booth; "City Summary," no source, n.d. (1869) Folger; ebay.com 459567394.

For information on the 1870–1871 season see Richard A. Robertson to EB, Sept. 15, Oct. 11, 1870, Dan W. Waller to EB, Sept. 22, 1870, EB to Richard A. Program, Booth's Theatre, Feb. 3, 1871, Scrapbook, Booth's Theatre, 1870–1871, Hackett to EB, Mar. 4, 1871, George W. Ryerson to EB Feb. 7, 1871, Programs, Booth's Theatre, Apr. 14, Dec. 26, 1871, Scrapbook, Booth Theatre, 1884, J. W. Shackleford to EB, July 17, 1871, Hampden-Booth; Receipt signed by EB, DeBar's Opera House, Oct. 19, 1870, to Mrs. Lander," Oct. 20, 1870, to WW, n.d. [circa Apr. 17, 1871], Folger' EB to Launt Thompson, Dec. 16, 1870, transcription by EBG, NYPLPA, Receipt signed by EB, DeBar's Opera House, Oct. 10, 1870, Programs, Walnut Street Theatre, Dec. 5, 6, 8, 9, 10, 12, 23, 1870, Program, Booth's Theatre, Jan. 11, 1871, Programs, Booth's Theatre, Feb. 4, Mar. 18, 27, Apr. 22, 1871, Matthew & Hutton, V, pt. 2, Harvard; EB to "Friend Hicks," Feb. 8, 1871, Texas; EB to John E. Russell, Feb. 12, 1871, Rochester; Cohen, *Edwin Booth in Performance,* Ms., I, 33, 77, 88, 139, Boothnotes, 40, 91, 101–103; Celebrity Index, Philadelphia Theatre Index, Free Library of Philadelphia; Grossman, 33; Taylor, 237, 238; Watermeier, *Between Actor and Critic,* 28, 29, 71; Bispham: 135; Partridge: 638; *The Chicago Daily Tribune,* Sept. 4 (2), 6 (4), 7 (4), 8 (4), 11 (2), 15 (4), 16 (4) 18 (2), 19 (4), 20 (4), 25 (2), 30 (4), 1870; *The Missouri Republican* (St. Louis), Oct. 4 (2), 10 (2), 17 (2), 20 (2), 1870; *The Cincinnati Commercial,* Oct. 24 (8), 27 (8), 31 (8), Nov. 6 (8), 1870; *The Pittsburgh Commercial,* Nov. 15 (4), 28(4). 1870; *The New York Albion,* Dec. 3 1870: 777, Jan. 14 (25–26), Mar. 4 (140), 11 (157), Apr. 1 (204), 8 (220), 29 (268), 1871; *The Philadelphia Inquirer,* Dec. 12 (3), 13 (8), 17 (8), 19 (8), 20 (8), 21 (8), 1870; *The New-York Times,* Feb. 3, 1869: 7, Jan. 1 (4), Apr. 1 (4), 20 (4, 5), 1871; *Frank Leslie's Illustrated Newspaper* (New York), Oct. 15, 1870: 67; Jan. 7 (275), 28 (327), Mar. 18 (3), May 13 (129), 21 (173, 179), 22 (311), Apr. 15 (67), 1871; *The New York Times,* Jan. 1 (4), Apr. 13 (7) 1871; *New-York Daily Tribune,* Jan. 9 (7), 16 (7), 23 (7), 30 (7), Feb. 6 (7), 13 (7), 20 (7), 27 (7), Mar. 6 (7), 13 (7), 20 (7), M21 (5), 27 (7), Apr. 3 (7), 5 (4), 10 (7), 13 (5), 17 (7), 1871; *The World* (New York), Jan. 10 (1), Mar. 21 (2), 1871; *The Evening Post,* Jan. 10 (2), Mar. 7 (4), 1871: 2; *New York Evening Express,* Jan. 10 (2), Mar. 21 (2), Apr. 4 (2). 1871;*The New York Herald,* Jan. 10 (3), Mar. 21 (3), Apr. 4 (3), 1871; *The New York Leader,* Jan. 14 (4), Feb. 18 (5), 1871; *The New York Dramatic Mirror,* Feb. 1, 1889: 5; *The Star* (New York), Mar. 7, 1871: 2; *The New York Clipper,* Apr. 2, 1870:

414; *New York Commercial Advertiser,* Apr. 4, 1871: 1; Clippings, *The World,* Feb. 26, 1871, "Much Ado about Nothing" at Booth's Theatre, review, n.d. [Mar. 18, 1871 penciled in], Matthews and Hutton, V, pt. 2, Harvard; no source, n.d. [Mar. 21, 1871], Scrapbook, 1869–1870, Booth's Theatre, Hampden-Booth.

For information on the 1871–1872 season see Charlotte Cushman to EB, July 12, 27, 30, 1871, William Creswick to EB, July 3, 22, 1871, EB to LB, Sept. 9, Oct. 6, Nov. 3, 1871, Program, Booth's Theatre, Oct. 19, 1871, to EwB, Nov. 6, 1871, Mar. 19, 1872, T. J. Barnett to EB, Dec. 19, 1871, Jan. 27, Feb. 17, 21, 23, Apr. 23, 26, Aug. 5, 1872, EB to John E. Russell, Feb. 5, 1872, James H. McVicker to EB, July 9, 1872, Hampden-Booth; EB to John E. Russell, July 19, no year [1871], Nov. 1, 3, 1871, Rochester; EB to Charlotte Cushman, Aug. 4, 1871, Mar. 6, 1872, Letters to Charlotte Cushman, IX, LC; EB to EwB, Oct. 18, 1871, Mar. 6, May 13, 1872, NYPLPA; Programs, Boston Theatre, Oct. 23-Nov. 11, 1871, Rare Books Department, Boston Public Library; Program, Boston Theatre, Nov. 10, 1871, Extra-illustrated edition, Copeland, 134f, Booth's Theatre, Apr. 26, 27, May 7, 1872, Matthews and Hutton, V, pt. 2, Harvard; Program, Booth's Theatre, Jan. 19, 1872, The Valentine Museum, Richmond, Virginia; Mary F. Booth Grantor to Richard A. Robertson, Liber 236 p. 95, Monmouth County Clerk's Office, Freehold, New Jersey; Program, Walnut Street Theatre Apr. 5, 1872, EB to WW, Apr. 10 1872, Program, Booth's Theatre, May 10, 1872, Folger; Cohen, *Edwin Booth in Performance,* 14, 26, 34, 35, Boothnotes, 40, 52; Celebrity Index, Philadelphia Theatre Index, Program, Boston Theatre, Nov. 4, 1871, Program, Booth's Theatre, New York, Dec. 14, 1871, Program, Walnut Street Theatre, Apr. 20, 1872, Glase Scrapbook, Free Library of Philadelphia; Watermeier, *Between Actor and Critic,* 33; *The Brooklyn Daily Eagle,* Nov. 20 (1), 21 (1), 1871; *The New York Herald,* Dec. 5 (2), 23 (2), 24 (2), 31 (2), 1871; *The Evening Post* (New York), Dec. 26, 1871: 2, 5, Mar. 5 (2), 12 (2), 1872; *The New-York Times,* Dec. 26, 1871: 5, Mar. 5, 1872: 5; *New York Evening Express,* Dec. 26 (2), Mar. 6 (2), 1872; *The New York Leader,* Dec. 30, 1871: 5; *The Albion* (New York), Dec. 30, 1871: 826; Jan. 6, 1872: 10; *New-York Daily Tribune,* Jan. 8 (7), 15 (7), 22 (7), 29 (7), Feb. 5 (7). 12 (7), 19 (7), 26 (7), Mar. 4 (3, 7), 11 (7), 18 (3,5), May 2 (7), 6 (11), 13 (7), 1872; *The Philadelphia Inquirer,* Mar. 23 (8), 25 (8), Apr. 4 (3), 8 (3, 8), 11 (5), 15 (8), 16 (8), 17 (5), 18 (5), 1872; *Frank Leslie's Illustrated Newspaper* (New York), May 12 (131), June 8 (203), 1872; *The Troy Daily Press,* May 24 (1), 28 (2), 29 (2),30 (2), June 1 (2), 1872; *Troy Daily Whig,* May 27 (3), 31 (3), 1872; *Troy Daily Times,* May 30 (3), June 3 (3), 1872; *Poughkeepsie Daily Eagle,* June 1, 1872: 3; *Stamford Advocate,* Mar. 30, 1877: 2, 3; Clippings, "The Drama," "Booth's Theatre," no source, n.d. [1871] General Review File, Cushman Papers, LC; *Era* (New York), n.d. [1872], *Watson's Art Journal,* Mar. 9, 1872, *The Express* (New York), Mar. 15, 1872, *Weekly Review* (New York), Mar. 16, 1872, Scrapbook, Booth Newspaper Clippings, 1871–1873, *Our Society* (New York), May 18, 1872, *Express* (New York), May 17, 1872, *Watson's Art Journal* (New York), Apr. 20, May 8, 1872, Scrapbook, Booth Newspaper Clippings, 1871–1872, Hampden-Booth.

For information about Booth's performances during the 1872–1873 season see EB to TBA, Oct. 3, 1872, Folger; Program, Booth's Theatre, Jan. 4, 1873, Bamburgh, Program, Booth's Theatre, Feb. 1, Mar. 18, 1873, Matthews and Hutton, V, pt. 2, Harvard; Program, Chelsea Academy of Music Nov. 12, 1872, Program, Music Hall, Dec. 3, 1872, D. W. Waller to EB, Feb. 5, 1873, EB to David C. Anderson, Feb. 14, 1873, McEntee to EB, Mar. 28, 1873, Hampden-Booth; Program, Taylor's Opera House, Dec. 9, 1872, Program, Booth's Theatre, Week ending Feb. 1, 1873, Folger; EB to EwB, Sept. 15, 29, Oct. 13, 27, Nov. 10, 24, 1872, Jan. 29, Feb. 2, Apr. 6, Apr. 30, May 4, 1873, NYPLPA; Program, Booth's Theatre, New York, Week ending Jan. 25, 1873, Glase Scrapbook, Theatre Collection, The Free Library of Philadelphia; EB to McE, Mar. 25, 1873, Tulsa; Edwin Booth against Henry C. Jarrett and Henry D. Palmer, 1; Bruce and Virginia Ronald, *Now Playing An Informal History of the Victoria Theatre* (Dayton, Ohio: Landfall Press, Inc., 1989): 16; Taylor, 241, 242, Watermeier, *Between Actor and Critic,* 35, 42; *Frank Leslie's Illustrated News* (New York), July 13 (275), 27 (307), Aug. 17 (355), Nov. 30 (183), 1872; Jan. 23 (315), Feb. 1 (331), 1873; *Springfield Republican* (Springfield, Massachusetts), Sept. 12 (2), 18 (2), 1872, Jan. 12, 1890: 3; *Hartford Daily Courant,* Sept. 13 (3), 16 (2), 17 (2). 1872; *Lowell Daily Courier,* Sept. 16, 1872: 4; *Lawrence Daily Eagle,* Sept. 23 (2), 30 (2) 1872; *Daily Eastern Argus* (Portland, Maine), Sept. 28 (3), Oct. 18 (3), 5 (3), 1872; *Portsmouth Daily Chronicle* (Portsmouth, New Hampshire), Sept. 30 (2), Oct. 3 (2, 3), 4 (3), 1872; *The Daily Evening Times* (Portsmouth, New Hampshire), Oct. 2, 1872: 3; *Lewiston Evening Journal,* Oct. 5 (3), 8 (3), 10 (3), 12 (3), 14 (3), 15 (3), 21 (3), 23 (3), 24 (3), 1872; *Daily Eastern Argus* (Portland, Maine), Oct. 5 (3), Oct. 24 (3), 25 (3), 1872; *Daily Kennebec Journal* (Augusta, Maine), Oct. 12 (3), 21 (3), 1872; *Bangor Daily Whig and Courier,* Oct. 15 (3), 21 (3), 1872; *The Maine Democrat* (Biddeford), Oct. 23, 1872: 2; *Concord Daily Monitor* (Concord, New Hampshire), Oct. 30 (2), Nov. 7 (3), 1872; *Manchester Daily Union* (Manchester, New Hampshire), Oct. 31, 1872: 2; *The Gloucester Telegraph* (Gloucester, Massachusetts), Nov. 6, 1872: 3; *Newport Mercury* (Newport, Rhode Island), Nov. 16, 1872: 2, 3; *The Providence Daily Journal,* Nov. 22 (3), 23 (1, 3), 26 (1), 27 (3), 1872; *Woonsocket Patriot and Rhode Island State Register,* Nov. 28, 1872: 5; *Daily State Gazette* (Trenton, New Jersey), Dec. 7 (2), 10 (4), 1872; *The Detroit Free Press,* Feb. 8, 1873: 1, *Kalamazoo Daily Telegraph,* Feb. 10, 1873: 1; *Daily Morning Democrat* (Grand Rapids Michigan), Feb. 12, 1873: 4; *The Detroit Free Press,* Apr. 4 (6), May 3 (3), 1879; *New York Dramatic News and Society Journal,* Mar. 10, 1877:5; *The Indianapolis Daily Sentinel,* Apr. 12, 1873: 5; *The Lansing State Republican,* May 1, 1873: 3; ebay item 4915939; Clippings, *Newark Daily Journal,* Dec. 13, 1872, *Sunday Call* (Newark, New Jersey), Dec. 15, 1872, *Patterson Press* (Patterson, New Jersey), Dec. 19, 1872, *Sunday* (New York), Dec. 29, 1873, Scrapbook, 1871–1872, Hampden-Booth; Clipping, "Booth's Theatre," June 16, 1873, Folger; ebay items 356741060, 7571225428.

For information about Booth's performances during the 1873–1874 season see Clark Bell to Samuel L. M. Barlow, June 4, 1873, R. A. Robertson to Oliver Ames, May 5, 1876, The Huntington Library; Joseph Booth, Box Office Report, Booth's Theatre, Sepember 1-Nov. 29, 1873, Washington State University Libraries; EB to Jean Davenport Lander," Sept. 15, 1873 [incorrectly dated 1883], Program, Walnut Street Theatre, Jan. 9, 1874, EB to WW, Apr. 26, 1874, to Maurice Grau, May 11, 1874, Folger; Boston Theatre Playbills, Oct. 6-Oct. 25, 1873, Boston Public Library; EB to TBA, Oct. 15, Dec. 4, 1873, Program, Booth's Theatre, Nov. 15, 1873, Bamburgh, Receipt signed by Mary G. Booth, DeBar's Opera House, Apr. 4, 1874, Harvard; James H. McVicker to EB, Oct. 11, Nov. 27, 1873, EB to EwB, Nov. 4, 1873, Feb. 8, Apr. 9, 1874, EB to McE, Feb. 15, 1874, J. H. McVicker, Box Office and Expense Sheet, McVicker's Theatre, Mar. 2–21, 1874, EB to David C. Anderson, May 3, 1874, McE to EB, Nov. 17, 1874, Hampden-Booth; EB to John E. Russell, Oct. 22, Nov. 9, 28, 1873, Jan. 23, Apr. 29, May 24, 1874, Rochester; EB to Launt Thompson, Oct. 23, 1873, transcription by EBG, EB to EwB, Nov. 30, Dec. 5, 1873, Feb. 1, 1874, Apr. 13, 29, 1874, to Launt Thompson, Jan. 24, 1874, transcription by EBG, May 24, 1874, transcription by EBG, NYPLPA; EB to Horace Howard Furness, Jan. 21, 1874, University of Pennsylvania; Programs, DeBar's Grand Opera House, Mar. 24, Apr. 2, 1874, Glase Scrapbook. Theatre Collection, Celebrity Index, Philadelphia Theatre Index, The Free Library of Philadelphia; EB to John T. Ford, Apr. 21,

1874, Ford Papers, LC; EB to Prof. Corson, May 3, 1874, Rare and Manuscript Collections, Carl A. Kroch Library, Cornell University; Edwin Booth against Henry C. Jarrett and Henry D. Palmer, 1; Daly, 198. 199; Grossman, 38, 178, 179, 182; Oggel, *Bio-Bibliography*, 23; Watermeier, *Between Actor and Critic*, 43–48; Taylor, 244, 245; *Frank Leslie's Illustrated Newspaper*, Sept. 13 (7), 20 (67), Nov. 22 (183), 29 (203), 1873, July 18, 1874: 295; *Springfield Republican* (Springfield, Massachusetts), Nov. 27 (1), Dec. 3 (1, 3), 1873; *Worcester Daily Spy*, Dec. 1 (3), 5 (1), 1873; *Hartford Daily* Courant, Dec. 2, 1873: 2; The *Providence Daily Journal*. Dec. 8 (3), Dec. 9 (3), 11 (1), 1873; *The Philadelphia Inquirer*, Dec. 29, 1873: 8; Jan. 1 (8), 2 (4), 7 (8), 12 (8), 13 (4), 16 (8), 19 (3), 1874; *The Brooklyn Daily Eagle*, Jan. 26 (1) 27 (3), 28 (2), 29 (2), 30 (2), 31 (1, 2), 1874; *Toledo Daily Blade*, Feb. 14, 1874: 5; Mar. 9, 1882: 3; *The Courier-Journal* (Louisville, Kentucky), Apr. 5 (4), 10 (5), 12 (4), 1874;*The Cincinnati Commercial*, Apr. 18 (10), 25 (10), 1874; *The Pittsburgh Commercial*, May 4 (4), 5 (4), 7 (4), 8 (4) 9 (4), 1874; *The Sun* (Baltimore, Maryland), May 11 (1), 18 (1), 19 (1), 20 (1), 1874; Clippings "Booth's Bankruptcy," no source, Sept. 20, 1874, "Edwin Booth's Rights," no source, Nov. 23, 1876, Folger; "Amusement Feuilleton," no source, Nov. 4, 1873, Melvin Scrapbook, Hampden-Booth;

For information on the 1874–1875 season see EB to John E. Rusell, June 3, 22, 1874, Mar. 2, 1875, Rochester; Celebrity Index, Philadelphia Theatre Index, Programs, Boston Theatre, Mar. 24, Apr. 2, 1875, Glase Scrapbook, Theatre Collection, Free Library of Philadelphia; Broadsides and Playbills Boston Theatre, Boston Public Library; Taylor, 246; Watermeier, *Between Actor and Critic*, 47; *Frank Leslie's Illustrated Newspaper* (New York), July 25, 1874: 311; *The Philadelphia Inquirer*, Jan. 25 (3) 26 (5), 27 (5), 29 (5), 30 (3), Feb. 1 (8), 2 (8), 4 (5), 1875; *The Sun* (Baltimore, Maryland), Feb. 15 (1), 16 (1), 1875; Clipping, "Booth's Bankruptcy," Sept. 29, 1874, Folger; Item 14900249539, e-bay.com.

For information on the 1875–1876 season, see EB to John T. Ford, Jan. 14, 1874, Maryland Historical Society; Jervis McEntee, Diary, Jan. 19, 1875; EB to John T. Ford, Apr. 21, 1874, Apr. 20, 1875, WW to John T. Ford, Feb. 15, 1876, John T. Ford to WW, Mar. 5, 1876, Ford Papers, LC; EB to McE, June 29, Dec. 24, 1875, Jan. 9, 18, Mar. 11, Apr. 2, May 7, 14, 1876, to Clark Bill, Jan. 14, 1876, G. Herbert Sass to EB, Feb. 7, 1876, James H. McVicker to EB, Feb. 23, 1876, EB to Nat Levin, Mar. 1, 1876, TBA to EB, May 23, 1876, Hampden-Booth; EB to John E. Russell, Oct. 5, 8, 1875, Rochester; EB to EwB, Oct. 10, Nov. 14, 1875, Jan. 16, 30, Feb. 12, 27, May 7, 21, June 4, 1876, NYPLPA; Program, Daly's Fifth Avenue Theatre, Nov. 8, 1875, extra-illustrated edition Copeland, 108f, EB, "Dear Madam" Nov. 12, 1875, Harvard; Program, Walnut Street Theatre, Dec. 6, 1875, EB to Seniors, Holyoke Academy, Louisville, Mar. 10, 1876, to WW, June 21, 1876, Folger; Program, Walnut Street Theatre, Dec. 11, 1875, Program, Wood's Theatre, Apr. 5, no year [1876], Program, McVicker's Theatre, Chicago, May 1, 1876, Glase Scrapbook, Celebrity Index, Philadelphia Theatre Index, Free Library of Philadelphia; EB to Edward V. Valentine, Jan. 21, Feb. 4, 1876, The Valentine Museum, Richmond, Virginia; EB to G. Herbert Sass, Feb. 10, 1876, South Caroliniana Library, The University of South Carolina; Daly; 198, 199, 200; *Memories of Daly's Theatres* (New York: Aug.in Daly, 1896); 118; John Drew, *My Years on the Stage* (New York: E. P. Dutton & Company, 1921), 57; Grossman, 46, 182; Joel Myerson and Daniel Shealy, *The Selected Letters of Louisa May Alcott* (Boston: Little, Brown and Company, 1987), 217, n2; Taylor, 249, 250; Watermeier, *Between Actor and Critic*, 55, 57, 58, 59, 62; O. B. Bunce, "Mr. Booth's Hamlet," *Appleton's Journal*, 14 (Nov. 27, 1875), 657, 658, 59, 689, 690, 691; Don Rhodes, "Booth family was favored for tragedies," *The Augusta Chronicle*, web posted July 2, 1999; *The Detroit Free Press*, May 3, 1875: 3, May 14 (3), 16 (1), 1876; *Frank Leslie's Illustrated Newspaper* New York, Sept. 18 (23), Oct. 9 (71), 1875; *New York Dramatic News*, Oct. 30 (2), Nov. 6 (8), Dec. 25 (23) 1875, Jan. 29 (3), Feb. 5 (3), 12 (3), 19 (3), Mar. 4 (3), 11 (5), Apr. 8 (3), 15 (5), 22 (6), May 13 (3), 20 (6), 27 (6), June 10 (2), 1876; *The Philadelphia Inquirer*, Nov. 20 (8), 29 (8), 1875; *The Sun* (Baltimore, Maryland), Jan. 3 (1), 4 (2), 5 (1), 6 (1), 8 (1), 11 (1), 1876; *Daily Dispatch* (Richmond, Virginia), Jan. 15 (2), 17 (2), 24 (1), 1876; *The News and Courier* (Charleston, South Carolina), Jan. 31 (2), Feb. 3 (2), 4 (2), Feb. 5 (4), 1876; *Savannah Morning News*, Feb. 7 (2), 8 (2), 10 (2) 11 (2), 1876; *Montgomery Daily Advertiser*, Feb. 10, 1876: 3; *Chattanooga Daily Times*, Feb. 11, 17 (1, 4), 19 (4), 21 (4), 1876; *The Macon Telegraph and Messenger*, Feb. 11, 1876: 4; *Columbus Daily Enquirer* (Columbus, Georgia), Feb. 16, 1876: 4; *The Constitution* (Atlanta, Georgia), Feb. 18 (3, 4), 24 (3), 1876; *The Daily American* (Nashville), Feb. 27 (2), 29 (2, 4), Mar. 1 (4), 1876; *The Courier-Journal* (Louisville, Kentucky, Mar. 7 (4), 16 (4), 24 (4), 1876; *The Daily Times* (Grand Rapids, Michigan), Mar. 12, 1882: 4; *The Cincinnati Commercial*, Mar. 26 (8), 30 (8), Apr. 1 (8), 1876; *The Chicago Daily Tribune*, Apr. 10 (7), 16 (12), 23 (8), 30 (6), 1876; *South-Bend Daily Tribune*, May 3, 1876: 4; *The Adrian Daily Times*, May 5, 1876: 4; *Toledo Daily Blade*, May 9, 1876: 2; *The Detroit Free Press*, May 14, 1876: 1; *The Globe* (Toronto, Canada), May 20 (4) 1876; *Hamilton Daily Spectator* (Hamilton, Ontario), May 23, 1876: 3; *Buffalo Commercial Advertiser*, May 27 (2), 30 (3), 1876; Clippings, "The Fifth Avenue Theatre," Oct., 1875, Mathews and Hutton, Harvard, no source, n.d. [Oct. 26, 1875], Scrapbook, Hampden-Booth; Robinson Locke Collection, 78, Edwin Booth Clipping Collection, NYPLPA; "The Drama, Fifth Avenue Theater—Edwin Booth as Hamlet, clipping, Oct. 26, 1875, "Fifth Avenue Theatre Special Card," 1875, "Fifth Avenue Theatre, Special," 1875, "Edwin Booth in Baltimore," Jan. 10, 1876; Fifth Avenue Theatre Advertisements, Week of Nov. 15, 1875, Folger.

For information on the 1876–1877 season see penciled notations to John T. Ford to WW, n.d. [late June 1876 penciled in], EB to John T. Ford, July 16, 1876, Ford Papers, LC; to David C. Anderson, July 22, Aug. 9, Nov. 3, 1876, Mar. 11, 1877, to McE, Mar. 18, Apr. 22, May 13, 1877, to Wm Brewston, Aug. 31 1876, Hampden-Booth; to McE, Oct. 1, 1876, McFarlin Library, Tulsa; Programs, California Theatre, Oct. 10, 1876, Lyceum Theatre, Nov. 29, 1876, Bamburgh, Academy of Music, Brooklyn, New York Feb. 2–10, 1877, The Globe, Apr. 30, 1877, extra-illustrated edition, Matthews and Hutton, V, pt. 2, Boston Theatre, May 4, 1877, Extra-illustrated edition, Copeland, 110f, EB to TBA, May 22, 1877, Harvard; Programs California Theatre, Oct. 10, 14, 1876, Programs Lyceum Theatre, Nov. 20, 27, 28, 30, 31, 1876, Glase Scrapbook, Celebrity Index, Philadelphia Theatre Index, The Free Library of Philadelphia; Programs, Metropolitan Theatre, Sacramento, California, Oct. 31, Nov. 2, 1876, California State Library, Sacramento; Robinson Locke Collection, 78, NYPLPA; McE, Diary, Nov. 25, Dec. 6, 26, 1876; Jan. 21, 27, 1877; EB to WW, Jan. 25, 1877, 29, Mar. 23, 1877, Program, Mrs. John Drew's Arch Street Theatre, Feb. 26, 1877, Folger; to Asa Israel Fish, Mar. 13, 1877, Pennsylvania; Sollers, 369; Grossman, 184; Watermeier, *Between Actor and Critic*,70, 71, 72, 78, 81; Winter, Life of David Belasco, I, 94; *Daily Alta California* (San Francisco), Sept. 4 (1), 8 (4), 9 (1, 4), 14 (1, 4), 20 (1, 4), 29 (1), Oct. 5 (4), 9 (4), 10 (4), 11 (1), 12 (4), 19 (1), 1876; *The New York Dramatic News*, Oct. 14 (4), 16 (8), 23 (8), Nov. 4 (4), Dec. 1 (1, 5), 4 (3), 9 (2), 11 (3), 28 (6), 1876, Feb. 10, 1877: 5; *Springfield Republican* (Springfield, Massachusetts), Jan. 12, 1890: 3; *The Brooklyn Daily Eagle*, Feb. 6, 1877: 3; *The Philadelphia Inquirer*, Feb. 19 (5), 20 (5), 21 (5), 22 (5), 26 (8), 28 (3), Mar. 1 (5), 2 (5), 5 (5), 6 (5), 1877; *The Sun* (Baltimore), Mar. 12 (1), 16 (1), 20 (1), 23 (1), 1877; *New York Dramatic News and*

Society Journal, Apr. 1, 1877: 5; *Morning Journal and Courier* (New Haven, Connecticut), Apr. 2 (3), 3 (2), 1877; *Waterbury Daily American,* Apr. 4 (1, 3), 5 (2), 1877; *Hartford Courant,* Apr. 5, 1877: 1; *Stamford Advocate* (Stamford, Connecticut), Apr. 6, 1877: 2; *Worcester Daily Spy,* Apr. 7, 1877: 1; *Fall River Evening News* (Fall River, Massachusetts), Apr. 9, 1877: 3; *The Providence Daily Journal,* Apr. 16 (3), 17 (3), 20 (3), 23 (3), 25 (3), 1877; Clippings, "Gold behind the Footlights," Sept. 1876, "Lyceum Theatre," *The New York Times* Nov. 21, 1876, "Mr. Booth at the Lyceum," Jan. 1877 (incorrectly labeled 1876), "Our Dramatic Stars," Feb. 25, 1877, Folger; E-bay item 3306703629.

For information on the 1877–1878 season see EB to WW, Aug. 25, 1877, Apr. 30, 1878, to John T. Ford, Sept. 17, Oct. 14, Nov. 11, Dec. 18, 26, 1877, Jan. 10, Apr. 14, 18, n.d. [mid–Apr. 1878], 1878, Ford Papers, LC; John T. Ford to EB, Nov. 15, no year, [1877 penciled in], Lease, Oliver Ames II and Oakes A. Ames to EB, Aug. 22, 1877, EB to E. C. Benedict, Nov. 1, 1877, Jan. 31, no year [1878], to McE, Apr. 7, June 18, 1878, to David C. Anderson, Apr. 19th 1878, Hampden-Booth; EB to Aug.in Daly, July 1, 1877, to Ferdinand Ewer, Oct. 14, Nov., 11, 1877, to Mr. Cist, Nov. 11, 1877, to WW, Dec. 4, 1877, typewritten copy probably prepared by Jefferson Winter, n.d.; Spring 1878, to John T. Ford, Apr. 14, 1878, Folger; McE, Diary, Feb. 18, 1878; Eytinge, *The Memories of Rose Eytinge,* 28, 32; Grossman, 188, 189; Watermeier, *Between Actor and Critic,* 86, 91, 92, 93, 103, 104, 105, 108. 109; Badeau, "Edwin Booth on and off the Stage": 261; Bispham, "Memories and Letters of Edwin Booth": 135; Lucia Gilbert Calhoun, "Edwin Booth": 78; *New York Dramatic News and Society Journal,* Sept. 15, 1877: 3; *St. Louis Dispatch,* Oct. 1 (1), 8 (1, 3), 9 (2), 10 (3), 11 (3), 1877; *The Cincinnati Commercial,* Oct. 28, 1877: 8; *The Philadelphia Inquirer,* Feb. 27, 1877: 4, Oct. 20 (5), 21 (2), 1877; *Cleveland Daily Plain Dealer,* Nov. 16 (4), 19 (1), 1877; *Buffalo Commercial Advertiser,* Dec. 7 (3), 8 (2), 1877; *Buffalo Daily Courier,* Dec. 10, 1877: 2; *Lockport Daily Journal* (Lockport, New York), Dec. 10, 1877: 4; *Utica Daily Observer,* Dec. 12 1877: 2; *Rochester Daily Union and Advertiser,* Dec. 13, 1877: 3; *The Syracuse Daily Journal,* Dec. 15, 1877: 1; *The Brooklyn Daily Eagle,* Feb. 17 (3), 21 (2), 1878; *Boston Post,* Mar. 6, 1878:3; *The Sun* (Baltimore), Apr. 22, 1878: 1, 2; Clipping,"Music and the Drama," *New York Tribune,* Jan. 30, 1878, Mathews and Hutton, Harvard.

For information on the 1878–1879 season see EB to WW, Oct. 2, Dec. 3, 1878, Programs, Broad Street Theatre, Oct. 14, 30. 1878, Folger; to David C. Anderson, Oct. 17, Dec. 15, 1878, Samuel Osgood to EB, Nov. 14, 30, 1878, Ferdinand C. Ewer, to EB, Dec. 5, 7, 1878, Hampden-Booth; Program, Fifth Avenue Theatre, Nov. 11, 1878, to Mr. Davidge," Dec. 5, 1878, Harvard; Celebrity Index, Philadelphia Theatre Index, Advertisement, Globe Theatre, Nov. 5, 1883, Program, Fifth Avenue Theatre, Nov. 15, 1878, Glase Scrapbook. Theatre Collection, The Free Library of Philadelphia; to McE, Nov. 8, 1878, Tulsa; McE, Diary, Dec. 15, 1878; Grossman, 188, 189; Watermeier, *Between Actor and Critic,* 122, 123, 125, 131; *The Philadelphia Inquirer,* Oct. 21 (8), 26 (8) 1878; *The Detroit Free Press,* Apr. 4 (6), 5 (1), 10 (2), 13 (6), 1879; *The New York Mirror,* Apr. 5 (6), 12 (7), 1879; *The Chicago Daily Tribune* Apr. 13 (5), 15 (4), 19 (7), 23 (5), 27 (10), May 2 (7), 1879; Clippings, "Dramatic," n.d. [*The New York Times,* Nov. 30, 1878 penciled in], n.d., *The New York Times,* [Dec. 15, 1878, penciled in], extra-illustrated edition, Matthews and Hutton, V, pt. 2, Harvard.

For information on the 1879–1880 season see EB to LH, Mar. 9, 1879, Princeton; EB to David C. Anderson, Apr. 13, May 1, Sept. 16, Dec. 10, 1879, Feb. 14, Mar. 20, Apr. 25, 1880, Hampden-Booth; EB to WW, Oct. 16, 1879, [Jan.-Feb., 1880], Mar. 5, 1880, to Geo. H. Howard," Jan. 28, 1880, Charles W. Clarke, *Diary,* Column 9, EB to WW, Apr. 13, 1880, n.d. [1878 penciled in], Folger; Programs, Grand Opera House, n.d. [Nov. 15, 1879, penciled in], Park Theatre, Mar. 12, 18, 19 no year [1880], Booth's Theatre, Apr. 9, 1880, Brooklyn Academy of Music, May 5, 1880 extra-illustrated edition, Matthews and Hutton, V, pt. 2, to TBA, May 7, 1880, Harvard; EB to McE, no month, n.d., [Mar. 15], 1880, Program, Madison Square Theatre, June 28, 1880, Hampden-Booth; EB to McE, Oct. 12, Nov. 16, 1879, Taper Collection; Programs, Grand Opera House, New York Dec. 1, 6, 1879, Pennsylvania; EB to D. Allatengne, Dec. 2, 1879, Texas; to Mrs. E. L. Davenport, Jan. 4, 1880, Department of Special Collections, The University Library, University of California, Davis; McE, Diary, Dec. 3, 1879, Mar. 5, Apr. 8, 19, 20, June 10, 1880; EB to LH, June 1, 1880, Princeton; to McE, June 2, 1880, Tulsa; Robinson Locke Collection, 78, NYPLPA; Celebrity Index, Philadelphia Theatre Index, Free Library of Philadelphia; Grossman, 206, 208; Watermeier, *Between Actor and Critic,* 135, 136, 145, 147, n. 30, 31, 47, 151, 153; *The New York Mirror,* July 5 (6), Aug. 2 (3), 9 (4), Oct. 18 (3), 25 (4), Nov. 1 (4) 29 (6), Dec. 13 (2) 1879, Jan. 10 (4), 31 (4), Feb. 7 (7), 28 (10), Mar. 20 (3), Apr. 3 (7), 10 (7), 17 (7), 24 (6, 7), 1880; *The New York Dramatic Mirror,* Oct. 19, 1889: 3; *The Philadelphia Inquirer,* Oct. 20 (5), 21 (5), 22 (5), 28 (5), 1879; *Boston Evening Transcript,* Mar. 6 (5), 15 (5), 22 (1), 24 (5), 1880; *The Brooklyn Daily Eagle,* Apr. 29 (1), May 1 (1), 3 (1), 1880; Clippings, "Amusements," *The Gazette* (Baltimore), Oct. 7, 10, 1879, Ford Papers, LC; "Edwin Booth as Benedick," *Tribune,* Apr. 5, 1880: 10, Robert Young's research notes, Folger; ebay item 458887390.

For information on the 1880–1881 season, see Account of expenses and deposits, 1880–1881, Box office memorandum, Princess's Theatre, Nov. 6, 1880-Mar. 26, 1881, File, Edwin Booth, Tour of England, Scotland and Ireland, 1882, EB to David C. Anderson, Nov. 14, 1880, June 6, 188, to E. C. Bendict, Jan. 25, 1881, Henry Irving to EB, Mar. 4, Apr. 16, 1881, EB to Mr. Collier, Mar. 6, no year [1881], Bram Stoker to EB, May 7, 13, 20, June 3, 11, 1881, EB to Ferdinand C. Ewer, Dec. 19, 1888, Hampden-Booth; EB to W. C. Day, Nov. 25, no year [1880], to ECS, Dec. 24, 1880, Folger; to LH, Jan. 10, 1881, Princeton; *The Illustrated Sporting and Dramatic News* (London), Nov. 13 (201), Dec. 30 (no page) 1880, Programs, Royal Princess's Theatre, n.d. [Nov. 20, 1880 penciled in], *Othello,* Princess's Theatre, n.d. [Jan. 17, 1881 penciled in], Royal Lyceum Theatre, May 2, May 9, 1881, The Theatre Museum, London; EB to LH, Feb. 24, 1881, Princeton; to McE, Mar. 1, 1881, Taper Collection; Program, Lyceum Theatre, May 25, 1881, Bamburgh, Harvard; Copeland 122, 123; Percy Fitzgerald, 128, 129, n. 1; Grossman, 219, 221; Laurence Irving, 375; Watermeier, *Between Actor and Critic,* 178–181, 183, 202, 203; Bispham: 241, 242, Bamburgh, Harvard; E. H. House, "Edwin Booth in London," *The Century Magazine,* Dec. 1897: 275, 276; *The Times* (London), Nov. 6 (8), 8 (8), 10 (8) 11 (8), 12 (8), 13 (8), 15 (8), 16 (8), 17 (8), 18 (8), 19 (8), 20 (8), 22 (8), 23 (8), 24 (8), 25 (8), 26 (8), 27 (8), 29 (8), 30 (8), Dec. 1 (8), 2 (8), 3 (8), 4 (8), 6 (8), 7 (8), 8 (8), 9 (8), 10 (8), 11 (8), 13 (8), 14 (8), 15 (8), 16 (8), 17 (6), 18 (8), 20 (8), 21 (8), 22 (8), 23 (6), 24 (8), 25 (8), 27 (8), 28 (6), 29 (6), 30 (8), 31 (6), 1880; *Sunday Times* (London), Nov. 14, 1880: 3; *The Daily Telegraph* (London), Dec. 24 (4) 25 (4), 1880; Jan. 1 (4), 3 (4), 4 (4), 5 (4), 6 (4), 7 (4), 8 (4), 10 (4), 11 (4), 12 (4), 13 (5), 14 (4), 15 (4), 17 (4), 18 (2, 4), 19 (4), 20 (4), 21 (4), 22 (4), 24 (4), 25 (4), 26 (4), 27 (4), 28 (4), 29 (4), 31 (4), Feb. 1 (4), 2 (4), 3 (4), 4 (4), 5 (4), 7 (4), 8 (4), 9 (4), 10 (4), 11 (4), 12 (4), 14 (4), 15 (4) 16 (4), 17 (4), 18 (4), 19 (4), 21 (4), 22 (4), 23 (4), 24 (6), 25 (4), 26 (4), 28 (4), Mar. 1 (3), 2 (4), 3 (6), 4 (4), 5 (4), 7 (4), 8 (4), 9 (4), 10 (6), 11 (4), 12 (4), 14 (4), 15 (4), 16 (4), 17 (4), 18 (4), 19 (4), 21 (4), 22 (4), June 15 (4), 1881; *The New York Mirror,* Mar. 12 (9), Apr. 9 (6), July 21 (21), 1881; *New York Dramatic News and Society Journal,* Apr. 16, 1881: 10; *The New York Dramatic News and Society Journal,* May 7, 1881: 2; *The Chicago Daily Tribune,* May 7 (5), May 22 (11, 19) 1881; Clippings, *Morning*

Notes — Part II

Advertiser (London), Nov. 8, 1880, no source, Nov. 11, 1880; *Bell's Life in London and Sporting Chronicle*, Nov. 13, 1880: 11; *The New York Mirror*, Nov. 13, 1880: 2; *Saturday Review*, Nov. 13, 1880, *The South African*, Nov. 18, 1880, *Lloyd's*, Nov. 21, 1880, *The New York Times*, Nov. 25, 1880, *Punch*, Dec. 4, 1880: 256; *New York Herald*, Dec. 23, 1880, *Echo*, Jan. 1, 1881, *Pan*, Jan. 1, 1881, *Sunday Times* (London), Jan. 29, 1881, Clipping, *Truth* (London), May 12, 1881, Scrapbook, 1880–1881, Hampden-Booth, "The Playhouses," *The Illustrated London News*, n.d., "Society," Jan. 22, May 7, 1881, The Theatre Museum, London.

For information on the 1881–1882 season see EB to David C. Anderson, July 6, 1881, Wynn E. Miller to EB," Aug. 16, 1881, McE to EB, Nov. 13, 1881, William Bispham to EB, Nov. 22, 1881, EB to McE, Dec. 17, 27, 1881, Feb. 23, 1882, Henry G. Parker to EB, Dec. 27, 1881, EwB to EB, Jan. 6, 1882, Charles T. Nash to EB, Feb. 28, 1882, Ernest Victor Chamberlain to EB, Mar. 4, no year [1882], Route Card "Edwin Booth and Company under the Management of Henry E. Abbey, Spring 1882, Booth's Theatre, Box Office Returns, Oct. 3–8, Oct. 10–15, Oct. 17–22, Oct. 24–29, 1881, Haverly's Theatre, Brooklyn, New York, Box Office Records, Oct. 31-Nov. 5, 1881, Lyceum Theatre, Philadelphia, Pennsylvania, Box Office Returns, Nov. 7–12, 1881, Academy of Music, Baltimore, Maryland, box office reports, Nov. 21–26, 1881, Park Theatre, Boston, Massachusetts, Box Office Returns, Dec. 5–10, Dec. 19–24, Dec. 26–31, 1881, Low's Opera House, Providence, Rhode Island, Box Office Statement, Jan. 4, 5, 1882, Able Opera House, Easton, Pennsylvania, Box Office Report, Jan. 6, 1882, Academy of Music, Scranton, Pennsylvania, Ticket Agent's Report, Jan. 7, 1882, Music Hall, Wilkes-Barre, Pennsylvania, Box Office Record, Jan. 9, 1882, Grand Opera House, Harrisburg, Pennsylvania, Box Office Report, Jan. 10, 1882, Library Hall, Pittsburg, Pennsylvania, Box Office Statements, Jan. 11–14, 1882, Macauley's Theatre — Box Office Returns, Jan. 16, 17, 18, 1882, Leubrie's Theatre, Memphis, Tennessee, Box-Office Statement, Jan. 19, 20, 21, 1882, Tremont Opera House, Galveston, Texas, Box Office Report, Jan. 24–27, 1882, Sales Grand Opera House, New Orleans, Louisiana, Box Office Report, Jan. 30-Feb. 4, 1882, Grand Opera House, LaFayette, Indiana, Box Office Statement, Feb. 2, 1882, Montgomery Theatre, Montgomery, Alabama, Statements, Feb. 6. 7, 1882, DeGive's Opera House, Atlanta, Georgia, Account of Sales, Feb. 8, 1882, Masonic Theatre and Grand Opera House, Nashville, Tennessee, Ticket Sale Statement, Feb. 10, 11, 1882, Grand Opera House, St. Louis, Missouri, Returns, Feb. 13–18, 1882, No place [Grand Opera House, Evansville, Indiana], Report, Feb. 20, 1882, Academy of Music, Fort Wayne, Indiana, Statement, Feb. 23, 1882, Grand Opera House, Springfield, Ohio, Box Office Report, Mar. 6, 1882, Youngstown Opera House, Statement, Mar. 10, 1882, Biemiller's Opera House, Sandusky, Ohio, Box Office Record, Mar. 11, 1882, Wheeler's Opera House, Toledo, Ohio, Box Statement, Mar. 13, 1882, Opera House, Terre Haute, Indiana, Box Office Statement, Feb. 21, 1882, Dickson's Grand Opera House, Indianapolis, Indiana, Statements, Feb. 24, 25, 1882, Robinson's Opera House, Cincinnati, Ohio, Box Office Records, Feb. 27-Mar. 4, 1882, Music Hall, Dayton, Ohio, Record, Mar. 7, 1882, Comstock's Opera House, Columbus, Ohio, Mar. 8, 1882; Detroit Opera House, Box Office Statements, Mar. 14, 15, 1882, Powers Opera House, Grand Rapids, Michigan, Box Office Return, Mar. 16, 1882, Grand Opera House, Milwaukee, Wisconsin, box office report, Mar. 17, 18, 1882, Hooley's Opera House, Madison, Wisconsin, Box office record, Mar. 20, 1882, Opera House, Rockford, Illinois, Statement of Receipts, Mar. 21, 1882, Burtis' Opera House, Davenport, Iowa, Box Office Record, Mar. 22 1882, Box Office Record, Mar. 23, 1882, Harper's Opera House, [Rock Island, Illinois], New Opera House, Burlington, Iowa, Box Office Record, n.d. [Mar. 24, 1882], Touser's Opera House, No place [Rock Island, Illlinois], Box Office Statement, Mar. 25, 1882, Academy of Music, Buffalo, New York, Box Office Report, Apr. 10, 11, 1882, Grand Opera House, Rochester, New York, Box-Office Statement, Apr. 12, 1882, Utica Opera House, Utica, New York, Box Office Report, Apr. 13, 1882, Leland Opera House, Albany, New York, Box Office Report, Apr. 14, 15, 1882, Booth's Theatre, Box Office Returns, Apr. 17–29, 1882, Programs, Springfield Ohio, Mar. 6, 1882; Dayton, Ohio, Mar. 7, 1882; Columbus, Ohio, Mar. 8, 1882; Akron, Ohio, Mar. 9, 1882; Youngstown, Ohio Mar. 10, 1882, Sandusky, Ohio, Mar. 11, 1882, Madison, Wisconsin, Mar. 20, 1882; Rockford, Illinois, Mar. 21, 1882, Albany, New York, Apr., 15, 1882, New York, New York, Apr. 17–22, 1882, Scrapbook, Edwin Booth, 1881–1882 Season, Hampden-Booth; McE, *Diary*, Oct. 3, 1881, Apr. 17, 20, 28, 1882; Program, Booth's Theatre, Oct. 7, 1881, EB to WW, Dec. 6 [1881 penciled in], Dec. 11, 1881, Jan. 10, 1882, Mar. 20, 1882; Apr. 2, 13, 1882, Folger; Program, Booth's Theatre, Oct. 17, 1881, Pennsylvania; EB to John E. Russell, Dec. 4, 1881, Rochester; EB to John E. Russell, Dec. 14, 1881, Washington University Libraries, Washington University in St. Louis; Programs, Park Theatre, Boston, Dec. 20, 22, 23, 24, 1881, Mar. 31, Apr. 1, 1882, Haverly's Opera House, Chicago, Mar. 29, 1882, Booth's Theatre, New York, Apr. 27, 1882, Glase Scrapbook. Theatre Collection, The Free Library of Philadelphia; Program, Park Theatre, Boston, Dec. 31, 1881, program, Adelphi Theatre, June 26, 1882, extra-illustrated edition, Matthews and Hutton, V, pt. 2, Harvard; EB to LH, Dec. 20, 27, 1881, Jan. 12, Feb. 14, 22, Mar. 15, 22, 28, Apr. 15, 1882, Princeton; EB to McE, n.d. [Apr. 5, 1882 on envelope], Tulsa; EB to A.M. Palmer, Apr. 6, 1882, Texas; Program, Park Theatre, Boston, Apr. 14, 1882, John Herbert Corning Scrapbook, LC; EB to TBA, no day or month, 1882, Harvard;Mrs. Charles Calvert, *Sixty-Eight Years on the Stage*, 206, 208; Copeland, 127; *In Memoriam, Samuel W. Piercy*, n.d. [1882], NYPLPA; Watermeier, *Between Actor and Critic*, 191, 192, 193, 201, 202, 205; Bispham: 242, 243, Bamburgh, Harvard; *New York Dramatic News and Society Journal*, June 16, 1877: 3; *The New York Mirror*, June 12, 1880: 6, Aug. 27(6), Oct. 8 (2), 22 (2), 29 (4), Nov. 5 (4, 5), 12 (4), 19 (5), 26 (4), Dec. 10 (4, 8), 1881; Jan. 28 (6), Feb. 4 (4), 11 (5,8), 18 (4, 5, 8), 25 (4, 5, 10), Mar. 4 (4, 8, 10), 11 (5, 8), 18 (5), 25 (5), Apr. 1 (4, 5), 8 (4), 15 (11), 22 (2), 29 (2), 1882; *The Chicago Daily Tribune*, Oct. 16 (19), Nov. 8 (5), 1881, Mar. 28, 1882; *Daily Brooklyn Eagle*, Oct. 30 (3), Nov. 2 (3), 1881; *The Philadelphia Inquirer*, Nov. 7 (5), 12 (5), 1881; *The Sun* (Baltimore), Nov. 21 (1), 23 (3), 1881; *Meriden Daily Republican* (Meriden, Connecticut), Nov. 22: 1881: 2; *Waterbury Daily American* (Waterbury, Connecticut), Nov. 23 (1), 28 (1), 29 (4), 1881; *Springfield Daily Republican* (Springfield, Massachusetts), Nov. 25 (6), 29 (1), 1881; *Worcester Daily Spy*, Nov. 28, 1881: 3; *The Wilkes-Barre Record*, Jan. 3 (4), 5 (4), 10 (4), 1882; *Boston Evening Transcript*, Dec. 5 (5), 19 (4), 1881; *The Providence Daily Journal*, Jan. 3 (4, 5) 1882; *The Scranton Republican*, Jan. 2 (2), 5 (4), 9 (3), 1882; *Easton Express* (Easton, Pennsylvania), Dec. 27 (2), Dec. 30 (2) 1881; Jan. 2 (2), 7 (3) 1882; *The Harrisburg Daily Patriot*, Jan. 9 (4), 11 (1) 1882; *The Pittsburg Dispatch*, Jan. 11 (4), 12 (3), 13 (4), 14 (8) 1882; *The Galveston Daily News*, Jan. 17 (1), 22 (1), 25 (4), 26 (4), 27 (4) 1882: 1; *The Courier-Journal* (Louisville, Kentucky), Jan. 15 (10), 18 (3, 8), 19 (8), 1882; *The Memphis Daily Appeal*, Jan. 20 (4), 21 (1), 22 (4), 1882; *The Galveston Daily News*, Jan. 22 (1), 25 (1), 29 (4), 1882; *The Daily Picayune* (New Orleans), Jan. 27 (5), 31(2), Feb. 2 (2), 1882; *The Atlanta Constitution*, Jan. 31(8), Feb. 7 (4), 9 (5), 1882; *Montgomery Daily Advertiser*, Feb. 1(4), Feb. 3 (4), 7 (4), 8 (4) 1882; *The Atlanta Constitution*, Feb. 5, 1882: 5; *Daily Journal* (Evansville, Indiana), Feb. 9 (4), 10(4), 11 (4), 12 (4), 14 (4), 15 (4), 18 (4), 19 (4), 1882; *The Indianapolis Times*, Feb. 9 (4), 11 (3, 7), 14 (2), 16 (1, 4), 17 (2), 18 (6), 21 (3, 4), 22 (4), 24 (3), 25 (8), 27 (2, 4), Mar. 1 (2), 1882; *The Daily News* (Chattanooga, Tennessee), Feb. 10,

1882: 4; *The Daily American* (Nashville), Feb. 11, 1882: 4; *The Morning World* (Nashville, Tennessee), Feb. 11, 1882: 4; *Fort Wayne Daily Sentinel*, Feb. 11 (3), 12 (1,3), 15 (3), 18 (3), 20 (3), 21 (3), 23 (1), 25 (3), 1882; *St. Louis Globe-Democrat*, Feb. 11 (5), 12 (6), 17 (6), 18 (6), 1882; *The Terre Haute Express*, Feb. 12 (3), 16 (4), 1882; *Daily Journal* (Evansville, Indiana), Feb. 12, 1882: 5; *Fort Wayne Daily Sentinel*, Feb. 13 1882: 3; *The Cincinnati Commercial*, Feb. 26 (8), 28 (8), Mar. 5, Extra Sheet (1), 1882; *Sandusky Daily Register*, Mar. 7, 1882: 3; *Toledo Daily Blade*, Mar. 9 (3), 14 (3), 1882; *The Evening News* (Detroit), Mar. 11 (3), 15 (4), 16 (4), 1882; *The Daily Times* (Grand Rapids, Michigan), Mar. 12, 1882: 2; *Milwaukee Daily Sentinel*, Mar. 17 (4, 5), 18 (5, 8), 1882; *The Chicago Daily Tribune*, Mar. 26 (16), Apr. 1 (7), 1882; *Utica Daily Observer*, Apr. 10 (3), 14 (2), 1882; *Albany Journal*, Apr. 13 (3), 15 (1), 17 (1), 1882; Clippings, *New York Tribune*, Oct. 6, 1881, *New Haven Union*, n.d. [Nov. 30, 1881], *Hartford Express*, Dec. 2, 1881, *Memphis Daily Avalanche*, Jan. 22, 1881, *Lafayette Journal* (Lafayette, Indiana), Feb. 2, 3, 23, Mar. 11 (10), 1882; no newspaper cited, Feb. 6, 1882, *Ohio State Journal* (Columbus), Mar. 9, 1882, *Akron Daily News*, Mar. 10, 1882, *Detroit Free Press*, Mar. 16, 1882, *Chicago Tribune*, Apr. 4, 1882, Scrapbook, Edwin Booth, 1881–1882 Season, Hampden-Booth; Clippings, "Music and the Drama," *New York Tribune*, Apr. 23, 1882, Matthews and Hutton, Edward R. Byram, "Edwin Booth in Boston," Harvard; ebay.com items 321823375, 439270066.

For information on the 1882–1883 tour see C. Carlotta to EB, Aug. 26, 1880, Nov. 18, 1881, Program, Adelphi Theatre, June 26, 1882, Gastpiel Contract, Stadt Theater, Bremen, Germany, Aug. 22, 1882, Gastspiel-Contract, Aug. 23, 1882, Memorandum of Agreement, Royal Alexandria Theatre, Liverpool, Aug. 30, 1881, Memorandum of Agreement between W. A. Waddington and EB, Sept. 5, 1881, Memorandum, Box Office Receipts, Sept. 11-Dec. 16, 1882, EB to David C. Anderson, Sept. 20, [1882], Oct. 26, Nov. 4, 26, 1882, Jan. 29, Apr. 9, May 21, 1883, Xerox of Broadside, Theatre Royal, Edinburgh, Oct. 16 [1882], EB to Launt Thompson, Nov. 13, 1882, May 10, 1883, Memorandum of Box Office Receipts, Gastpiel Contract, Stadt Theater, Leipzig, Germany, Nov. 14, 1882, EB to Launt Thompson, Nov. 15 1882, Agreements between Wilson Barrett and EB, Nov. 23, 1881, Agreements between Charles Bernard and EB, Nov. 24, 28, 1881, Mar. 21, 1882, Agreement between J. B. Howard and EB, Nov. 24, 1881, Agreement between Mercer H. Simpson and EB, Feb. 14, 1882, Memorandum of Agreement, Gaiety Theatre, Dublin, Mar. 14, 1882, Agreement between Charles Bernard and EB, Mar. 21, 1882, Gastpiel Contract, Victoria Theatre, Berlin, Germany, July 14, 1882, T Gastpiel Contract, Thalia Theater, Hamburg, Germany, Aug. 15, 1882, Theatre Royal, Dundee, Terms, Sept. 14, 1882, Terms, Her Majesty's Theatre, Aberdeen, Sept. 14, 1882, Her Majesty's Theatre, Aberdeen, Summary of House Returns, Program, Residenz-Theater, Jan. 19, 23, Feb. 3, 1883, EwB to Mrs. Ole Bull, Feb. 4, 1883, Program, Bremer Stadt-Theater, Feb. 28, 1883, Gastspiel Contract, Mar. 6 1883, Memorandum of box office receipts, File, EB, Tour of England, Scotland and Ireland, 1882, Program Stadt-Theater in Bonn, Mar. 4, 1883, Dr. Carl Michael to EB, Mar. 5, 1883, Program, Neues Leipziger Stadt — Theater, Mar. 21, 1883, Wiener Stadt-Theater, Mar. 31, Apr. 4, 7, 1883, EB to William E. Miller, May 8, 9, 10, no year [1883], to E. de Wartegg, Jan. 10, no year, Hampden-Booth; EB to TBA, June 1, 1882, to Major Walters, July 29, 1884, Harvard; to LH, Sept. 27, no year, [1882], Jan. 7, 1883, Oct. 1, 1884, May 4, 1887, Princeton; to Paul R. Schweitzer, Jan. 3, 1883, to Mrs. Lippincott, Feb. 18, 1883, to WW, Feb. 26, 1883, Folger; McE, *Diary*, May 9, 10, 12, 13, 14, 20, 21, 22, 23, 26, 27, 28, June 1, 2, 3, 5, 7, 12, 1883; EB to William E. Miller," May 16, no year [1883], Huntington Library; to McE, Oct. 29, 1882, Taper Collection; to Mr. Lederer, Oct. 30, 1884, Texas; EB to EBG, Aug. 16, Sept. 9, 1885, NYPLPA; Anderson, 209; Carol Jones Carlisle, *Helen Faucit: Fire and Ice on the Victorian Stage* (London: The Society for Theatrical Research, 2000), 239, 240; Grossman, 237–240, 242; *Post Office London Directory 1861* (London, Frederic Kelly, 1861), 1776; Watermeier, *Between Actor and Critic*, 210, 211, 212, 218, 219, 221–225, 228–234, 239–243, 248; Simon Williams, *Shakespeare on the German Stage*, I (Cambridge: Cambridge University Press, 1990), 200, 201; Bispham: 243, Bamburgh, Harvard; *The Times* (London), June 27 (12), June 28 (10), June 29 (8), June 30 (8), 1880; *The New York Mirror*, Nov. 26, 1881: 6 July 15, 1882: 9; *John Bull* (London), July 1 (415), 8 (418), 15 (434), 22 (451), 29 (466), Aug. 5 (483), 1882; *The Daily Post* (London), July 17 (4), 18 (4), 19 (4), 20 (4), 21 (4), 22 (4), 31 (4), Aug. 1 (4), 2 (4), 3 (4), 4 (4), 5 (4), 1882; *The Sheffield Daily Telegraph*, Sept. 11 (1), 12 (1), 13 (1), 14 (1), 15 (1), 1882; *The Sheffield Daily Telegraph*, Sept. 12 (6), 14 (3, 5), 15 (2), 1882; *The Sheffield and Rotherham Independent*, Sept. 12, 1882: 2; *The Sheffield Daily Telegraph*, Sept. 12, 1882: 6; *The York Herald* (York, England), Sept. 18 (1), 19 (1), 1882; *The Newcastle Daily Journal*, Sept. 25, 1882: 1; *Tyneside Daily Echo and North Durham Advertiser* (Newcastle-upon-Tyne), Sept. 26, 1882: 3, *The Northumbrian* (Newcastle-upon-Tyne), Sept. 30, 1882: 268, *The Dundee Courier & Argus*, Oct. 2, 1882: 1; *The Dundee Courier and Argus*, Oct. 3 (5), 4 (2), 5 (3) 1882; *Aberdeen Evening Express*, Oct. 4, 1882: 1; *Aberdeen Evening Express*, Oct. 6 (4), 7 (4), 9 (4), 1882; *The Daily Free Press* (Aberdeen), Oct. 6 (5), 7(5), 1882; *The Evening Citizen* (Glasgow), Oct. 9 (3), 11 (4), 14 (1), 1882; *The Daily Review* (Edinburgh), Oct. 16 (1), 17 (1), 18 (1), 19 (1), 20 (1), 21 (2). 1882; *The Edinburgh Evening News*, Oct. 17 (2), 18 (2), 19 (2), 20 (2), 1882; *The Eastern Morning News Lincolnshire Express and Hull Advertiser*, Oct. 24 (2), 26 (3), 1882; *The Leeds Express*, Oct. 31 (3), Nov. 2 (3), 1882; *The Leeds Mercury*, Oct. 31, 1882: 5; *The Hull Packet and East Riding Times* (Hull, England), Oct. 20 (1), 27(1), 1882; *The Eastern Morning News Lincolnshire Express and Hull Advertiser*, Oct. 26, 1882:1; *The Leeds Times*, Oct. 28 (5) Nov. 4 (5), 1882; *The Yorkshire Post and Leeds Intelligencer*, Oct. 30, 1882: 1; *Leeds Daily News*, Nov. 3, 1882: 3; *The Daily Express* (Dublin), Nov. 6 (1), 7 (1), 9 (1), 11 (1), 13 (1) 1882; *The Manchester Courier and Lancashire General Advertiser*, Nov. 21, 1882: 1; *Evening Express* (Liverpool), Nov. 27 (1), Dec. 1 (1), 6 (1) 1882; *The Daily Express* (Dublin), Nov. 6 (1), 7 (1), 9 (1), 11 (1), 13 (1), 1882; *The Evening Irish Times* (Dublin), Nov. 7 (4), 9 (7), 10 (4), 13 (7), 15 (4), 18 (4), 1882; *The New-York Times*, May 10, 1883: 8; Clippings, *The Echo* (London), June 27, 1882, *The Globe* (London), June 28, July 25, 1882, *Whitehall Review*, June 29, 1882, *Society* (London), July 1, Aug. 5, 1882, *Weekly Dispatch*, July 2, 1882, *Lloyd's* (London), July 2, 1882, *Reynolds' Newspaper* (London), July 2, 30, 1882, *The Times* (London), July 27, 1882, *Illustrated London News*, July 29, 1882, *Referee* (London), July 30, Aug. 6, 1882, *Morning Post* (London), Aug. 4, 1882, *Weekly Times* (London), Aug. 6, 1882, *Daily Chronicle* (London), n.d., "Mr. EB as Hamlet," *Dundee Advertiser*, n.d. [Oct. 1882], "Sheffield, Theatre Royal," no source, n.d., "Sheffield — Royal," no source, n.d., "York, Theatre Royal," no source, n.d., "York-Royal," no source, n.d., "Newcastle-Upon-Tyne, Theatre Royal," no source, n.d., "Newcastle — Royal," no source, n.d.,"Scarborough — Londesboro," no source, n.d., "Scarborough, Londesborough Theatre," no source, n.d., "Dundee. Theatre Royal," "Mr. EB in The 'Fool's Revenge," Dundee, Scotland, no source, n.d. [Oct. 1882], "Mr. Booth's Acting," no newspaper [Glasgow], Oct. 16, 1882, *Glasgow News*, Oct. 10, 1882, "Mr. Booth at the Gaiety," *Glasgow Herald*, n.d. [mid–Oct. 1882], no place [Glasgow], n.d. [mid–Oct. 1882], Oct. 16, 1882, *Glasgow Evening News*, Oct. 12, 1882, *The Evening Citizen* (Glasgow), Oct. 12, 1882: 3, "Provincial Theatricals, no source, Oct. 14, 1882, *The Daily Review* (Edinburgh), Oct. 17, 1882: 4, Clippings, "Hull, Theatre Royal," "Hull — Royal," no source, n.d., *Leeds Express*,

Oct. 31, 1882, "Leeds—The Grand Theatre," no source, n.d., *Manchester Courier*, Nov. 21, 1882, "Liverpool, Royal Alexandra Theatre," no source, n.d. [Nov. 1882], Nov. 22, 1882, "Mr. EB at the Alexandra Theatre," no source, n.d. [Dec. 1882], *Manchester Guardian*, n.d. [Nov. 21–25, 1882], "Prince's Theatre, Mr. EB in "Richelieu," "Mr. EB in "Richard III," "Mr. EB at the Alexandria Theatre," *Liverpool Daily Post*, Nov. 25, 1882, "Music and the Drama," *Liverpool Courier*, Nov. 31, 1882, "Last Five Nights," no source, n.d., *Birmingham Daily Post*, Dec. 12, 1882, *Birmingham Daily Post*, Dec. 12, 13, 1882, *The Dart* (Birmingham, England), Dec. 15, 1882, "Mr. EB at Berlin," *The Times* (London), Jan. 13, 1883, "Booth in Berlin," no source, Jan. 16, 1883, EB in Berlin," no source, Jan. 17, 1883, "EB at Bremen," *Era* (London), Mar. 12, 1883, "Mr. EB in Berlin," no source, Feb. 5, 8, 1883, "On Saturday evening last," no source, n.d. [early Feb. 1883], "Mr. EB, the American actor," *The Times* (London), Feb. 13, 1883, "EB in Vienna," no source, n.d., "EB at Vienna," no source, Mar. 18, 1883, "Mr. EB," clipping, no source, Feb. 16, 1883, Program, Thalia Theater, Feb. 17, 1883, "Mr. EB," no source, n.d. [Feb. 22, 1883], "Mr. EB in Vienna," no source, n.d., Theatre Museum, London; "Memories of EB," Boston newspaper, no name, n.d., Scrapbook, 1886–1887 season: 35, *Weekly Times* (London), Aug. 6, 1882, *The Northumbrian* (Newcastle-upon-Tyne), Sept. 30, 1882; Program, Adelphi Theatre, Aug. 3, no year [1882], *The New York Tribune*, Jan. 12, 13, 14, 17, 1883, Dr. C. Carlotta, "Mr. EB as 'Iago,'" *Fremdenblatt*, Feb. 6, 1883, *New York Tribune*, Mar. 26, 1883, *Evening Post* (New York), Apr. 28, 1883, Scrapbook, 1882, Scrapbook, Winter-Spring, 1883, File, German and Austrian Tour, Scrapbook, Booth Memorial Vol. 1, Hampden-Booth; "EB in Dublin," "EB How He was Received in Austria and Germany," no source, n.d., Harvard; Emanuel Lederer, trans., "EB in Germany," n.d., 5–7, Leo Newmark, "EB," Jan. 29, 1883, NYPLPA; ebay.com item 370800839.

For information on the 1883–1884 season see EB to WW, n.d. [Answered by Winter Feb. 12, 1879], Sept. 11, 1883, to WW, Oct. 25, no year [1883 penciled in], Jan. 27, Feb. 24, 1884 May 2, no year [1884 penciled in], in WW, *Life and Art of EB*, to Mrs. House, Feb. 15, 1884, Folger; to McE, n.d. [Apr. 5, 1882 on envelope], Aug. 16, 1883, to Bowyer Vaux, May 5, 1884, Tulsa; William Bispham, to EB, Mar. 23, 1882, to TBA and Lillian Aldrich Sept. 11, Dec. 13, 1883, to LH, Aug. 24, 1883, Nov.t 23rd, [1883], Feb. 7, 1884, Princeton; Program, Jan. 2, 1884, EB to Horace Howard Furness, Feb. 27, 1884, Pennsylvania; Program, Star Theatre, Dec. 27–28, n.d. [1883], extra-illustrated edition, Matthews and Hutton, V, pt. 2, to E. C. Benedict, [Apr. 1], 1884, Harvard; to E.C. Benedict, Feb. 19, 1884, to Mrs. Ole Bull, June 10, 1884, to LB, July 14, no year [1885 penciled in], Hampden-Booth; Fawcett, Diary, Jan. 1, 12, 21, 24, 30, Feb. 3, 15, 16, 23, 25, Mar. 10, 11, 22, 29, 1884, Tennessee; EB to EBG, n.d. [incorrectly labeled Philadelphia 1886; circa Apr. 29, 1884], Robinson Locke Collection, 78, NYPLPA; Celebrity Index, Philadelphia Theatre Index, Programs, Globe Theatre, Nov. 7, 10, 15, 1884, Walnut Street Theatre, Philadelphia, Jan. 21, Feb. 1, 1884, Glase Scrapbook. Theatre Collection, Free Library of Philadelphia; Grossman, 250; Watermeier, *Between Actor and Critic*, 250, 251, 253–256, 258; Bispham: 137, Bamburgh, Harvard; *The New York Clipper*, Aug. 4, 1866: 134; *The New York Mirror*, Feb. 9 (4), 15 (4), June 21 (4) 1879; Sept. 29 (8), Nov. 17 (4), 19 (6), Dec. 1 (4, 8), 8 (6), 15 (2), 22 (9), 29 (2) 1883; Jan. 5 (2), 24 (6), 26 (4, 8) Feb. 9 (6), Feb. 16 (4), 23 (3, 4, 10), Mar. 1 (4, 8, 10), 8 (4), 29 (2), Apr. 5 (2, 6, 7), 1884; *The Daily Transcript* (Holyoke, Massachusetts), Feb. 17, 1885: 2; Clippings, "EB at the Globe," n.d. [Nov. 6, 1883, penciled in], "Mr. EB is Richelieu," *Journal*, [Boston], Nov. 6, 1883, Matthews and Hutton, Harvard; *The New York Tribune*, Nov. 6, 8, 1883, Scrapbook, Booth Memorial Vol. 1, "Mr. Booth as Hamlet," no source [Boston newspaper], Nov. 20, 1883, Barstow Scrapbook, Booth Bills & Reviews, 1883–1890, *The New York Tribune*, Dec. 11, 1883, Feb. 5, 17, "Booth Again in Baltimore," "Amusements," Feb. 8, 1884, Miscellaneous file, *The New York Tribune*, Feb. 19, 23, "EB's Season," *The New York Tribune*, Feb. 26, 1884, "A Reception to EB," *The New York Tribune*, Mar. 2, 1884, Scrapbook, compiled by Alfred Sandor Grossman, 1895, Hampden-Booth.

For information on the 1884–1885 season see Programs, Boston Theatre, Nov. 17–Dec. 6, 1884, Rare Books Department, Boston Public Library; Programs, Boston Museum, Nov. 29, Dec. 1, 1884, Academy of Music, May 9, 1885, Glase Scrapbook, Celebrity Index, Philadelphia Theatre Index, Free Library of Philadelphia; EB to LH, Nov. 30, Dec. 7, 1884, Princeton; Programs, Boston Museum, Nov. 25, 1884, Fifth Avenue Theatre, n.d. [Feb. 2, 1885 penciled in], Matthews and Hutton, Boston Museum, Dec. 8,9, 12, 13, 1884, Mar. 2, 7, 20, 21, 27, 28, 1885, EB Scrapbook, EB to LB, n.d., [spring 1885], Harvard; EB to EwB, Feb. 17, 18, Apr. 8, 1885, [Apr. 15, 1885 penciled in, actually Feb. 20, 1885], Apr. 16, 1885, n.d. [Apr. 1885, penciled in], NYPLPA; Program, Fifth Avenue Theatre, Week ending Jan. 24, 1885, EB to T. H. Morrell Esq.," Feb. 15, 1885, to Charles Dudley Warner, Feb. 18, 1885, to Augustin Daly, Mar. 15, 1885, to WW, Mar. 22, 1885, n.d. [May 8, 1884 penciled in], to Horace Howard Furness, May 5, 1885, Folger; McE, *Diary*, Feb. 18, 1885; EB to EwB, Apr. 15, 1885, to Mrs. Ole Bull, June 2, 1885, Hampden-Booth; Grossman, 57, 254, 256, 258; Watermeier, *Between Actor and Critic*, 260, 251, 262, 262, n. 21; *The New York Mirror*, Sept. 13 (2), 1884: 2, Nov. 22 (10), 29 (4, 7), Dec. 20 (4), 27 (11), 1884; Jan. 10 (9), 17 (3), 24 (2), 31 (2), Feb. 7 (2), 14 (2, 6, 8), 21 (9), 28 (8, 10), Mar. 7 (5, 9), 14 (4), 28 (4), Apr. 4 (4), 18 (4), 25 (4), 28 (4), 1885; *Morning Courier and Journal* (New Haven, Connecticut), Feb. 7 (3), 17 (2) 1885: 3; *Hartford Courant*, Feb. 9, 1885: 1; *The Daily Transcript* (Holyoke, Massachusetts), Feb. 13 (4), 19 (2) 1885; *Daily Evening Bulletin* (Haverhill, Massachusetts), Feb. 16 (3), 18 (2), 20 (3), 1885; *The Daily Transcript* (Holyoke, Massachusetts), Feb. 19, 1885: 2; *The Providence Daily Journal*, Feb. 19, 1885: 5; *Worcester Daily Spy*, Feb. 18 (1), 24 (4), 1885; *Lowell Daily Courier*, Feb. 26 (1), 27(8), 1885; *The Lawrence American*, Feb. 27, 1885: 3; *The Philadelphia Inquirer*, Apr. 7 (7), 10 (7), 11 (3), 13 (7), 17 (7), 1885; *Evening Bulletin* (Philadelphia), Apr. 13, 1885: 5; Clippings, "Mr. Booth as Othello," no source [Boston newspaper], n.d., [Nov. 25, 1884], Barstow Scrapbook, Hampden-Booth; *Evening Transcript* (Boston), Nov. 18, 1884, Mar. 3, 1885, *Boston Gazette*, Jan. 25, 1885, Mathews and Hutton, Edward R. Byram, "EB in Boston," extra-illustrated edition, Matthews and Hutton, V, pt. 2, Bispham, "Memories and Letters of EB": 244, Program, Academy of Music, May 7, 1885, Bamburgh, Harvard; Items 3371780, 359505433 ebay.com.

For information on the 1885–1886 season see EB to EBG, June 28, no year [1885], Nov. 13, n.d. [Nov. 25, 1885 penciled in], Dec. 3, 1885, Jan. 4, no year [1886 penciled in], Feb. 17, no year [1886], n.d. [Feb. 21, 1886], n.d. [circa Feb., 1886], n.d. [Winter, 1885 penciled in, actually Feb. 1886], n.d. [New York 1886 penciled in, actually Feb. 27, 1886], NYPLPA; EB to WW, Sept. 28, no year [1885], Program, Fifth Avenue Theatre, Feb. 16, 17, 1886, Folger; EB to McE, Nov. 15, no year [1885], ABC to LB, Jan. 4, 1886, EB to EBG, Feb. 14, no year [1886], Hampden-Booth; Programs, Boston Museum, Dec. 28, 1885, Jan. 9, 23, Chestnut Street Opera House, Mar. 13, 1886, Glase Scrapbook, Theatre Collection, Celebrity Index, Philadelphia Theatre Index, Free Library of Philadelphia; McE, *Diary*, Apr. 27, 28, 29, 1886; EB to Mrs. Martha H. Brooks, May 23, 1886, Texas; Grossman, 66, 67, 69, 264, 265; Watermeier, *Between Actor and Critic*, 268, n. 34, 271, 272, 274; *The New York Mirror*, Oct. 17 (4), Nov. 14 (4, 6), Nov. 21 (4), 28 (4, 6), 1885, Jan. 16 (4,6), Jan. 23 (7), 30 (4), Feb. 6 (6), 13 (2, 7, 10) 20 (2), 1886; *The Sun* (Baltimore), Nov. 9 (1), 12 (1) 1885; *The Philadelphia Inquirer*, May 1, 1886: 5; *Boston Evening Transcript*, Jan. 1(5), 2 (5), 4 (1), 25

(1) 1886; *New York Amusement Gazette*, Feb. 6 (1), 18 (1), 20 (1) 1886; Clippings, "Howard"s Gossip," Harvard, "'Richard III' at the Museum," no source, n.d. [Jan. 23, 1886], Barstow Scrapbook, Hampden-Booth.

For information on the 1886–1887 season see EB to LB, July 14, no year [1885 penciled in], Aug. 2, 1885, to EBG, June 23 no year [1886 penciled in], Sept. 16, 21, 25, Oct. 15, no year [1886], 19, 21, 25, n.d. [Nov. 14], n.d. [Nov. 17], n.d. [Nov. 19, labeled Nov. 18], n.d. [Nov. 23], n.d. [Nov. 29], n.d. [Dec. 21], Dec. 26, 1886, Feb. 3, 9, 11, 19, 26, Mar. 5, May 7, 1887, n.d. [Nov. 17, 1886], n.d. [Nov. 29, 1886 penciled in], n.d. [Dec. 1886], May 1, 3, 1887, NYPLPA; EB to LB, Sept. 14, Oct. 19, 27, 30, Nov. 17, Dec. 8, no year [1886], Feb. 1, 11, 19, Mar. 2, 14, 23, Apr. 16, no year [1887], n.d. [May 1887], to TBA Oct. 3, no year [1886], Mar. 20, no year [1887], Apr. 10, no year [1887], no year [1887], Program, Star Theatre, Nov. 6, 1886, extra-illustrated edition, Matthews Hutton, V, pt. 2, to Wm. J. Anthony, Feb. 23, no year [1887], May 1, 1887, Harvard; to WW, n.d. [Nov. 18, 1886, penciled in], Dec. 3, no year [1886 according to notation on envelope in Winter's hand], to Augustin Daly, Dec. 10, 1886, EB to Aug.in Daly, Apr. 27, 1887, in Memorial edition of *The Taming of the Shrew* (New York: no publisher, 1887), 127, Folger; McEntee, *Diary*, Dec. 5, 1886; ABC to LB, Jan. 4, Sept. 16, 23, 27, 28, Oct. 26, 28, Nov. 4, 23, Dec. 15, 30, 1886, Feb. 2, 1887, EB to Mildred Grossman, Oct. 17, 1886, to George P. Goodale, Dec. 12, 1886, to EBG, Jan. 7, no year [1887], Mar. 18, 1887, May 17, no year [1887 penciled in], June 17, 1887, Statement for week of Mar. 28, 1887, Receipt Scrapbook for Tours of EB, 1886–91, Recapitulation of Booth Tour Season of 1886–87, penciled notation on the back of statement for May 9, 1887, Receipt Book, Booth Tours, 1886–91, Program, Chestnut Street Opera House, Philadelphia, Pennsylvania, Jan. 8, 1887, Scrapbook, EB Season 1886–87 Under the Management of LB, 114, EB to LB, Apr. 25, 1887, Hampden-Booth; to LH, attached to Mrs. Hutton, Oct. 12, 1886, May 4, 1887, Princeton; to Mary M. Ahlfield, Dec. 6, 1885, Sothebys.com item 1580847170, to Horace Howard Furness, Feb. 7, 1887, Pennsylvania; "Tour of EB 1886–87. Statement for Week Apr. 25, 1887," Texas; Malcolm Dale Owen, to Mother-Father Father-Mother, May 7, 1887, Complimentary Testimonial C. W. Couldock, Star Theatre, May 10, 1887, The Lilly Library, University of Indiana; Boston Theatre programs, May 10, 12, 14, 15, 1886, EB Clipping Collection, Programs, Chicago Opera House, Oct. 8, 16, 1886, Programs, Boston Theatre, Dec. 9, 13, 13, 17, 1886, Glase Scrapbook, Theatre Collection, The Free Library of Philadelphia; Goodale, 7, 9–13, 85, 86; Grossman, 73, 74, 76, 78, 267, 268; Watermeier, *Between Actor and Critic*, 266, 267, 268, 279, n. 1, 280; Winter, *Life and Art*, 287; Bispham: 245, Bamburgh, Harvard; *The New York Mirror*, May 16, 1885: 6, May 22 (2), July 3 (3), Aug. 14 (8), 28 (8), Sept. 4 (6) 25 (5, 8), 1886, Feb. 17 (8), Mar. 5 (8), Apr. 2 (5), 23 (4, 5), 30 (5, 6), May 7 (5, 7, 8), 14 (5), 21 (5), 1887; *New York Amusement Gazette*, Sept. 6 (4), Nov. 1 (3), 15 (3, 6), 22 (3, 4, 6), 29 (5), 1886; *Kalamazoo Daily Telegraph*, Sept. 16, 1886: 2; *The Evening Press* (Bay City, Michigan), Sept. 18, 1886: 2; *Rochester Daily Union and Advertiser*, Dec. 11, 1877: 1; Apr. 11, 1882: 1; *The Daily Transcript* (Holyoke, Massachusetts), Dec. 13, 1886: 2; *Worcester Daily Spy*, Dec. 15, 1886: 1; *Albany Journal* (Albany, New York), Dec. 22 (4), 23 (4) 1886; *The Oswego Palladium* (Oswego, New York), Dec. 22, 1886: 4; *The Daily Era* (Bradford, Pennsylvania), Dec. 24, 1886: 4; *The Lancaster Intelligencer* (Lancaster, Pennsylvania), Dec. 27, 1886: 4; *Newark Evening News*, Dec. 30, 1886: 3; *The Los Angeles Times*, Feb. 24, 1887:1; *Los Angeles Daily Herald*, Mar. 2, 1887:5; *The Denver Republican*, Apr. 10, 1887: 8; *The Salt Lake City Daily Tribune*, Apr. 15, 1887:4; Clippings, "Booth Will Not Retire," St. Paul newspaper, no source, n.d., "Booth's Farewell," Chicago newspaper, no source, n.d., "The Mimic Stage," San Francisco newspaper, no source, n.d. [Circa Mar. 7, 1887], Denver newspaper, no source, n.d., [Apr. 19–24, 1886], Omaha newspaper, no source, n.d. [Apr. 25–27, 1886], Clipping Scrapbook, Tour of EB — Season 1886–1887, Hampden-Booth; item 1151266917, 1527285173, 1541099088, ebay.com.

For information on the 1887–1888 season see EB to WW, Sept. 2, 1887, n.d. [letter received Sept. 9, 1887], Program, The Academy of Music, Buffalo, Sept. 12, 1887, Programs, Chicago Opera House, Oct. 12, 14, 15, 17, 18, 20, 22, EB to Creston Clarke, Dec. 6, 1887, Folger; Tour of Booth-Barrett 1887–1888, Statement for Week of Oct. 3, 1887, "Tour of Booth-Barrett 1887–88. Statement for Week Oct. 10, 1887," "Statement for Week Oct. 24, 1887," "Statement for the Week of Dec. 12, 1887," "Statement for Week of Dec. 19, 1887," "Statement for Week of Mar. 5, 1888," "Statement for the Week of Mar. 12, 1888," "Statement for the week of Mar. 19, 1888." "Statement for the week of Apr. 9, 1888," "Statement for the Week of May 7, 1888," Texas; EB to EBG, Sept. 22, Oct. 27, no year [1887 penciled in], Nov. 12, 26, 1887, Feb. 5, 9, Apr. 14, 16, 23, 1888, NYPLPA; EB to TBA, Nov. 2, 1887, Feb. 7, 1888, Program, Chestnut Street Opera House, Nov. 28, n.d. [1887], extra-illustrated edition, Matthews and Hutton, V, pt. 2, EB to Mr. Palmer, Jan. 14, 1888, to LB, n.d. [May 1888], Harvard; Programs, Opera House Pittsburgh, Pennsylvania, Nov. 21, 1887, Tabor Grand Opera House, Denver, Colorado, Apr. 3, 1888, Fawcett collection, Tennessee; EB to EBG, Mar. 11, 1888, Apr. 29, no year [1888], ABC to LB, Mar. 27, 1887, Statement, Booth Tours, 1886–91, "The Edwin Booth-Lawrence Barrett 1887–1888" tour schedule, Miscellaneous file, Hampden-Booth; to Revd. H. W. Cleveland, June 8, 1888, Edward Carrigan, SJ Theatre Collection, Loyola University Chicago Archives; to Horace Howard Furness, June 17, 1888, Pennsylvania; EB to Ada Rehan, Nov. 26, 1891, Pennsylvania; Celebrity Index, Philadelphia Theatre Index, Free Library of Philadelphia; Newspaper Index, Buffalo and Erie County Historical Society; Grossman, 80–85; James L. Haley, *Sam Houston* (Norman, Oklahoma: University of Oklahoma Press, 2000), 436, n. 8; Winter, *Life and Art*, 288, 289, 290; Bispham: 243, 247, Harvard; *The New York Mirror*, Oct. 1 (5), 8 (8) 1887, Jan. 21 (8), Feb. 11 (9), 25 (8), Mar. 17 (4), 31 (4), Apr. 21 (8), 23 (4), 28 (4, 5), May 5 (5), 12 (5), 19 (8), 26 (4), 1888; *St Louis Post-Dispatch*, Nov. 1 (5), 4 (4), 1887; *New York Amusement Gazette*, Dec. 26, 1887: 1; Jan. 2, 1888: 1; *The Chattannoga Daily Times*, Jan. 30, 1888: 4; *The Los Angeles Times*, Feb. 27(1), 29 (4). 1888; *Los Angeles Tribune*, Mar. 3, 1888: 1; *Daily Alta California* (San Francisco), Mar. 11, 1888: 2; *The Indianapolis News*, Apr. 16, 1888: 2; *The Terre Haute Express*, Apr. 17 (4), 25 (2) 1888; *The Fort Wayne Sentinel*, May 1, 1888: 2; *The Evening Leader* (Grand Rapids, Michigan), May 1, 1888: 2; *Bay City Tribune* (Bay City, Michigan), May 1, 1888: 2; Clippings, *The Daily Picayune* (New Orleans), Feb. 12, 1888, *San Francisco News Letter*, Mar. 10, 1888, Owen Fawcett Diary, 1888, Owen Fawcett Collection, Tennessee; "Edwin Booth Dead," *Boston Journal*, June 7, 1893, Harvard; item 339111031, ebay.com.

For information on the 1888–1889 season see EB to Horace Howard Furness, June 17, 1888, Pennsylvania, to EBG, n.d., Friday [Sept. 7, 1888, penciled in; Sept. 14, 1888 is the correct date], Sept. 11, 1888, Sept. 15, no year [1888 penciled in], Sept. 19, no year [1888 penciled in], Sept. 24, no year, [1888 penciled in], Jan. 6, Mar. 21, Apr. 25, no year, [1889 penciled in], Apr. 29, no year [1889 penciled in] 1889 NYPLPA; Owen Fawcett, Diary, Sept. 6–10, 30, 1888, Mar. 7, 10, 1889, Programs, Warder Grand Opera House, Sept. 10–15, 1888; Grand Opera House, Minneapolis, Minnesota, Sept. 17–19, 1888; Opera House, St. Paul, Minnesota, Sept. 20–22, 1888; Chicago Opera House, Sept. 24-Oct. 13, 1888, Grand Opera House, Cincinnati Ohio, Oct. 15–20, 1888, Olympic Theatre, St. Louis, Missouri, Oct. 22–27, 1888, Fifth Avenue Theatre, Nov. 12, 1888-Jan. 5, 1889, Grand Opera

House Pittsburgh, Pennsylvania, Jan. 7–12, 1889, Albaugh's Holliday Street Theatre Baltimore, Maryland, Jan. 14–19, 1889, Boston Theatre, Boston, Massachusetts Jan. 21-Feb. 16, 1889, Chestnut Street Opera House Philadelphia, Pennsylvania, Feb. 18-Mar. 9, 1889; Taylor's Opera House Trenton, New Jersey, Mar. 11, 1889; New Opera House Bridgeport, Connecticut, Mar. 12, 1889, Hyperion Theatre New Haven, Connecticut, Mar. 13, 1889; Roberts Opera House, Hartford, Connecticut, Mar. 14, 1889, Holyoke Opera House Holyoke, Massachusetts, Mar. 15, 1889, Gilmore's Opera House Springfield, Massachusetts, Mar. 16, 1889, Providence Opera House Providence, Rhode Island, Mar. 18–23, 1889, Amphion Academy Williamsburgh [Brooklyn], New York, Mar. 25–30, 1889, Euclid Avenue Opera House Cleveland, Ohio, Apr. 15–17, 1889, Metropolitan Opera House Columbus, Ohio Apr. 18, 1889, English's Opera House Indianapolis, Indiana, Apr. 19–20, 1889, Grand Opera House Burlington, Iowa, Apr. 22, 1889, Moore's Opera House Des Moines, Iowa, Apr. 23, 1889, Peavey Grand Opera House, Sioux City, Iowa, Apr. 23–24, 1889, Boyd's Opera House Omaha, Nebraska, Apr. 26–27, 1889, Tabor Grand Opera House, Denver, Colorado, Apr. 29-May 4, 1889, Salt Lake Theatre Salt Lake City, Utah, May 6–8, 1889, California Theatre, San Francisco, May 13-June 3, 1889, Owen Fawcett Collection, Owen Fawcett Diary 1888, Tennessee; EB to LH, Sept. 14, 1888, Princeton; Program, [Daly's Fifth Avenue Theatre, Nov. 12, 1888, penciled in], Programs, Chestnut Street Opera House, Feb. 18, [Feb. 25, 1889] Matthews and Hutton, V, pt. 2, Program, Metropolitan Opera House, June 13, 1889, Bamburgh, Harvard; McE, *Diary*, Dec. 11, 1888; EB to Augustin Daly, Jan. 10, Feb. 4, 1889, Mar. 8, no year [1889 penciled in], Folger Celebrity Index, Philadelphia Theatre Index, Programs, Boston Theatre, Jan. 21, Feb. 2, 9, 16, 1889, Chestnut Street Opera House, Feb. 26, 1889, Glase Scrapbook, Theatre Collection, The Free Library of Philadelphia; Henry E. Abbey to EB, Mar. 6, 1889, Hampden-Booth; Bake, 137; Grossman, 88–92, 94, 95, 97; 275; Bispham: 247–248, Harvard; "An Actor King," *The Illustrated American*, 13 (June 24, 1893): 730; *The Daily Chicago Tribune*, Sept. 24 (2), 25 (4), Oct. 2, 1888: 4; *The Chicago Daily Tribune*, Oct. 11, 1888: 3; *The New York Mirror*, Oct. 27 (3), Dec. 29 (1) 1888, Mar. 26 (11, 13), Apr. 20 (2), 1889; *New York Amusement Gazette*, Nov. 12 (95), 19 (107), 26 (117), 3 (127), 10 (137), 17 (148), 24 (157), 31 (167), 1888; *Springfield Republican* (Springfield, Massachusetts), Mar. 5, 1889: 1; *The Denver Republican*, May 5, 1889: 1; *Daily Alta California* (San Francisco), May 19, 1889: 2; Clipping, Boston newspaper, Jan. 29, 1889, Scrapbook, 1888–1891, Hampden-Booth; item 3306737400, ebay.com.

For information on the 1889–1890 season see "Tour of Booth-Barrett, 1889–1890, Statement for Week of Sept. 23 to 28 1889, Texas; EB to EBG, Oct. 8, no year [1889 penciled in], May 5, no year [1890 penciled in], NYPLPA; Souvenir program, Louisville, Kentucky, Sept. 25, 1889, Scrapbook, compiled by Frank Lodge, 1889–1890, Playbills, Broadway Theatre, Nov. 2, 25, 1889, Harlem Opera House, Dec. 21, 1889, Pennsylvania; EB to Constance Carryl, Dec. 27, 1889, "Tour of Edwin Booth, Mme Modjeska 1889–1890," EB to EBG, Mar. 23, no year [1890 penciled in] 28, no year [1890 penciled in], n.d. [Apr. 20, 1890 penciled in], Box Office Receipts, Boston Theatre, Feb. 1, 1890 (matinee and evening), Hampden-Booth; EB to L. Clarke Davis, no month, 20, 1889, Beinecke Rare Book and Manuscript Library, Yale University; EB to LH, n.d. [circa Feb. 1890], Princeton; Programs, Chestnut Street Opera House, Feb. 13, 15 [1890], extra-illustrated edition, Matthews and Hutton, V, pt. 2, Harvard; Celebrity Index, Philadelphia Theatre Index, Program, Chestnut Street Opera House, Feb. 22, 1890, Glase Scrapbook, Theatre Collection, Free Library of Philadelphia; 1889–1890 Booth-Modjeska Tour Statement for the Week of Apr 7 to 12, 1890, Folger; Program, *Hamlet* and *Richelieu*, n.d., Junius Brutus Booth & Family Miscellaneous Manuscript Collection, LC; Grossman, 99, 102, 103, 107; Kotsilibas-Davis, *Good Times, Great Times*, 301; *New York Amusement Gazette*, Oct. 14 (83), 21 (95), 28 (107), Nov. 4 (119), 11 (132), 18 (144), Dec. 2 (168), 16 (192), 1889, Feb. 3, 1890: 276; *The Utica Observer*, Dec. 11, 1889; 5; *The New York Dramatic Mirror*, Dec. 14, 1899: 13; Apr. 19 (12, 13), May 3 (11), 17 (12), 1890; *Springfield Republican* (Springfield, Massachusetts), Jan. 7 (1,6), 16 (5), 1890; *The Evening Leader* (Grand Rapids, Michigan), Apr. 16, 1890: 2; Clippings, Clipping, *Daily Advertiser* (Auburn, New York), Dec. 9, 1889, Owen Fawcett Diary, 1889, Tennessee; *The Press*, Feb. 18, 1890, Harvard; items 319197483, 319 ... 47PDT, 321789510, ebay.com.

For information on Booth's performances during the 1890–1891 season, see EB to EBG, Nov. 4, Dec. 6, 1890, Dec. 19, no year [1890 penciled in], NYPLPA; Program, Chestnut Street Opera House, Nov. 17, 1890, extra-illustrated edition, Matthews and Hutton, V, pt. 2, Harvard; EB to Mr. Woolett," Dec. 8, 1890, Hampden-Booth; EB to Augustin Daly, Dec. 19, 1890, Folger; Programs, Broadway Theatre, Mar. 28, 1891, Brooklyn Academy of Music, Mar. 30, 1891, Pennsylvania; Celebrity Index, Philadelphia Theatre Index, Free Library of Philadelphia; Grossman, 113, 114, 115, 117, 118, 119, 121; *The Sun* (Baltimore), Nov. 3 (1), 10 (1) 1890; *New York Amusement Gazette*, Nov. 29 (64), Dec. 1 (150) 1890, Mar. 2 (254), 9 (262), 16 (270), 23 (278), 1891; *Boston Evening Transcript*, Dec. 2, 1890: 4; *The New York Dramatic Mirror*, Dec. 6 (11), 20 (11), 27 (11), 1890; *The Providence Sunday Journal*, Dec. 14 1890: 8; *The Providence Daily Journal*, Dec. 20, 1890: 8; *New York Dramatic News*, Mar. 14, 1891: 3; Clippings, "On Mr. Booth's Birthday," Nov. 14, 1890, Manuscript Room, Milton S. Eisenhower Library, The Johns Hopkins University; "Edwin Booth Dead," *Boston Journal*, June 7, 1893: 4,

Bibliography

Manuscripts

Major collections of Booth letters and manuscripts can be found at:

The Hampden-Booth Theatre Library at The Players Educational Foundation.
Department of Special Collections, Charles E. Young Research Library, University of California at Los Angeles.
The Library of Congress.
The Folger Shakespeare Library, Washington D.C.
Harvard University.
Department of Rare Books and Special Collections, Princeton University Libraries.
The New York Public Library for the Performing Arts, Taper Collection.
The Harry Ransom Humanities Research Center, The University of Texas at Austin.

Books

Alford, Terry, ed. *John Wilkes Booth: A Sister's Memoir by Asia Booth Clarke.* Jackson: University of Mississippi Press, 1996.
Archer, Stephen M. *Junius Brutus Booth: Theatrical Prometheus.* Carbondale: Southern Illinois University Press, 1992.
Bloom, Arthur. *Joseph Jefferson: Dean of the American Theatre.* Savannah, GA: Frederic Beil, 2000.
Bulwer-Lytton, Edward George. *The Lady of Lyons.* New York: Harper & Brothers, 1838.
_____. *Richelieu.* New York: Harper & Brothers, 1839.
Calvert, Mrs. Charles [Adelaide Helen]. *Sixty-Eight Years on the Stage.* London: Mills & Boon, 1911.
Clarke, Asia Booth. *The Elder and the Younger Booth.* Boston: James R. Osgood, 1882.
Coleman, Mario Moore. *Fair Rosalind: The American Career of Helena Modjeska.* Cheshire, CT: Cherry Hill Books, 1969.
Copeland, Charles Townsend. *The Life of Edwin Booth.* Boston: Small, Maynard, 1901.
Court of Common Pleas in and for the City and County of New York. *Edwin Booth against Henry C. Jarrett and Henry D. Palmer.* New York: Douglas Taylor, 1877.
Daly, Joseph Francis. *The Life of Augustin Daly.* New York: Macmillan, 1917.
Goodale Katherine. *Behind the Scenes with Edwin Booth.* Boston: Houghton Mifflin, 1931.
Grossman, Edwina Booth. *Edwin Booth: Recollections by His Daughter.* New York: Century, 1894.
Henneke, Ben Graf. *Laura Keene: A Biography.* Tulsa: Council Oak Books, 1990.
Hinton, Henry, adapter. *Shakespeare's Tragedy of Macbeth as produced by Edwin Booth.* New York: Henry L. Hinton, 1868.
_____. *Shakespeare's Tragedy of Othello The Moor of Venice as produced by Edwin Booth.* New York: Henry L. Hinton, n.d.
Ireland, Joseph N. *Records of the New York Stage.* Vol. 2. 1866–1867. Reprint, New York: Burt Franklin, 1968.
Irving, Laurence. *Henry Irving: The Actor and His World.* New York: Macmillan, 1952.
Koon, Helene Wickham. *How Shakespeare Won the West: Players and Performances in America's Gold Rush, 1849–1865.* Jefferson, NC: McFarland, 1989.
_____. *Gold Rush Performers: A Biographical Dictionary of Actors, Singers, Dancers, Musicians, Circus Performers and Minstrel Players in America's Far West, 1848–1869.* Jefferson, NC: McFarland, 1994.
Kotsilibas-Davis, James. *Great Times Good Times.* Garden City, New York: Doubleday, 1977.
Leach, Joseph. *Bright Particular Star: The Life & Times of Charlotte Cushman.* New Haven: Yale University Press, 1970.
Matthews, Brander and Hutton, Laurence. *The Life and Art of Edwin Booth and His Contemporaries.* Boston: L.C. Page, 1886.
The New York Times Theatre Reviews, I, II. New York: The New York Times & Arno Press, 1978.
Odell, George C.D. *Annals of the New York Stage*, V, VI. New York: Columbia University Press, 1931.

Oggel, L. Terry, ed. *The Letters and Notebooks of Mary Devlin*. New York: Greenwood, 1987.

_____. *Edwin Booth. A Bio-Bibliography*. New York: Greenwood, 1992.

Rhodehamel, John and Taper, Louise. "*Right or Wrong, God Judge Me*": *The Writings of John Wilkes Booth*. Urbana: University of Illinois Press, 1997.

Samples, Gordon. *Lust for Fame: The Stage Career of John Wilkes Booth*. Jefferson, NC: McFarland, 1982.

San Francisco Theatre Research, I. San Francisco: WPA Project 8386, 1938.

Shakespeare, William, altered by Garrick, David and Kemble, John Philip. *Taming of the Shrew; or, Katharine and Petruchio*. London: John Cumberland, n.d.

Shattuck, Charles H. *The Hamlet of Edwin Booth*. Urbana: University of Illinois Press, 1969.

Shiel [sic], Richard Lalor. *The Apostate*. New York: Samuel French, n.d.

Sketch of the Life of Mr. John Sleeper Clarke, Comedian. London: J.W. Last, 1872.

Skinner, Otis. *The Last Tragedian: Booth Tells His Own Story*. New York: Dodd, Mead, 1939.

Selby, Charles. *The Marble Heart*. Boston: William V. Spencer, n.d.

Stebbins, Emma. *Charlotte Cushman: Her Letters and Memories of her Life*. Boston: Houghton, Osgood, 1878.

Stoker, Bram, *Personal Reminiscences of Henry Irving*. New York: Macmillan, 1906.

Von Kotzebue, Augustus Frederic Ferdinand. *The Stranger*. New York: William Taylor, 1846.

Watermeier, Daniel, ed. *Between Actor and Critic*. Princeton, NJ: Princeton University Press, 1971.

Williams, Simon. *Shakespeare on the German Stage*, I. Cambridge: Cambridge University Press, 1990.

Winter, William. *The Comedy of Don Caesar de Bazan as presented by Edwin Booth*. New York: Francis Hart, 1878.

_____. *Payne's* Tragedy of Brutus; *or the Fall of Tarquin as presented by Edwin Booth*. Boston: Charles H. Thayer, 1878.

_____. *Prompt-Book of Shakespeare's Comedy of* The Merchant of Venice *as performed by Mr. Edwin Booth and Mr. Lawrence Barrett*. Philadelphia: Penn, 1895.

_____. *The Shakespearean Plays of Edwin Booth*, I. Philadelphia: Penn, 1899.

_____. *Shakespeare's Comedy of* Much Ado About Nothing *as presented by Edwin Booth*. New York: J.H. Magonigle, 1890.

_____. *Edwin Booth's Prompt-Book of* Henry the Eighth. Philadelphia: Penn, 1913.

_____. *Shakespeare's Tragedy of* King Richard II *as presented by Edwin Booth*. Philadelphia: Penn, 1894.

_____. *Shakespeare's Tragedy of* King Richard III, *as presented by Edwin Booth*. New York: Francis Hart, 1878.

_____. *Tom Taylor's Tragedy of* The Fool's Revenge *as presented by Edwin Booth*. Boston: Charles H. Thayer, 1878.

_____. *Victor Hugo's Drama of* Ruy Blas *as Presented by Edwin Booth*. New York: Francis Hart, 1878.

_____. *Life and Art of Edwin Booth*. 1893. Reprint, New York: Greenwood, 1968.

_____. *The Life of David Belasco*. 2 volumes. New York: Moffat, Yard, 1918.

Witham, Barry B., ed. *Theatre in the United States: A Documentary History*, I, *1750–1915: Theatre in the Colonies and United States*. Cambridge, England: Cambridge University Press, 1996.

Articles

"An Actor King." *The Illustrated American*, 13 (June 24, 1893): 727–730.

Bacon, Dolores Marbourg. "The Break Between Player & Poet." *The New York Herald*, Nov. 1, 1903: 2.

Badeau, Adam. "Edwin Booth On and Off the Stage." *McClure's Magazine* I (August, 1893): 256–267.

Bispham, William. "Memories and Letters of Edwin Booth." *The Century* William Cushing Bamburgh, *Tributes, Sketches, Souvenirs, Portraits Memorials and Programmes Edwin Thomas Booth*, Harvard Theatre Collection.

"Booth's Theatre." *Harper's Weekly*, 13 (January 12, 1869): 21–22.

Bowers, Mrs. D.P. "Memories of Edwin Booth." *The Californian* V, 1 (Dec., 1893): 471–477.

Bunce, O.B. "Mr. Booth's Hamlet." *Appleton's Journal* 14 (Nov. 20, 1875): 657–659.

_____. "Mr. Booth's Hamlet" *Appleton's Journal* 14 (Nov. 27, 1875): 689–691.

Byram, Edward R. "Edwin Booth in Boston." Clippings: Harvard Theatre Collection.

Calhoun, Lucia Gilbert. "Edwin Booth." *The Galaxy* (January 1869): 77–87.

Carson, William G.B. "Under the Calcium Lights." *Missouri Historical Society Bulletin* (July 1956): 333–357.

Clapp, Henry A. "Reminiscences of a Dramatic Critic." *The Atlantic Monthly* 88, 528: 433–576.

_____. "Edwin Booth." *Atlantic Monthly* 72 (1893): 308–317.

Cohen, Robert. "Hamlet as Edwin Booth." *Theatre Survey* 10, 1 (May 1969): 53–74.

Commeret, Lorraine. "Edwin Booth's Tour of Germany and Austria in 1883: A Perspective on the Critical Responses." *Theatre History Studies* 9 (1989): 41–53.

Davis, Peter A. "From Stock to Combination: The Panic of 1873 and Its Effects on the American Theatre Industry." *Theatre History Studies*, 8 (1988): 1–9.

"Edwin Booth and Lincoln." *The Century* (1909): 919–920.

Ewer, Ferdinand. "Editor's Table." *The Pioneer, or California Monthly Magazine* I (January–June 1854): 246–256.

Grover, Leonard. "Lincoln's Interest in the Theater." *The Century* (1909): 943–950.

Hall, Florence Marion Howe. "The Friendship of

Edwin Booth and Julia Ward Howe." *New England Magazine* (Nov. 1893): 315–320.

Hammack, J. Alan. "An American Actor's Diary—1858." *Educational Theatre Journal* VII (Dec., 1955), 324–337.

House, E.H. "Edwin Booth in London." *The Century Magazine* (Dec. 1897): 269–279.

Hutton, Laurence. "A Group of Players." *Harper's New Monthly Magazine* XCVI, 572: 196–210.

Irvin, Eric. "Laura Keene and Edwin Booth in Australia." *Theatre Notebook* XXIII, 3, Spring, 1969: 95–102.

McArthur, Benjamin. "Theatrical Clubs of the Nineteenth Century: Tradition versus Assimilation in the Acting Community." *Theatre Survey* XXIII, 2 (Nov. 1982): 197–212.

McCloskey, J.J. "How I Met Edwin Booth." *The New York Dramatic Mirror* (Dec. 24, 1904): xvi.

_____. "The Earlier Life of Edwin Booth" *The New York Dramatic Mirror* (Dec. 22, 1906): xviii.

Partridge, Edward L. "Edwin Booth to John E. Russell." *The Outlook* 127 (Apr. 20,. 1921): 637–639.

Phillips, Levi Damon. "Arthur McKee Rankin's *The Danites* 1877–1881: Prime Example of the American Touring Process." *Theatre Survey* XXV, 2 (Nov., 1984): 225–247.

"Reminiscences of the Stage in Honolulu." *Hawaiian Almanac and Annual for 1906* (Thomas G. Throm: Honolulu, 1905), 93–96.

Royle, Edwin Milton. "Edwin Booth as I Knew Him." *Harper's Magazine* 132 (May 1916), 840–849.

S.H.L. "Reminiscences of Theatricals in Honolulu." *Hawaiian Almanac and Annual for 1881* (Thos. G. Throm: Honolulu, 1881): 34–39.

Sedley, Henry. "The Booths—Father and Son." *Harper's Weekly* 37 (Nov. 11, 1893): 1082–1084.

Shattuck, Charles H. "Edwin Booth's First Critic." *Theatre Survey* VII, 1 (May 1966): 1–14.

Shettel, James W. "J. Wilkes Booth at School." *The New York Dramatic Mirror* (Feb. 26, 1916): 3–5.

Skinner, Otis. "The Last of John Wilkes Booth." *The American Magazine* (Nov. 1908): 73–77.

Stedman, E.C. "Edwin Booth." *The Atlantic Monthly* XVII, 99 (1866): 585–593.

Stuart, William. "John Clarke, Comedian." *Lippincott's Magazine of Popular Literature and Science* II (Nov., 1881), 497–502.

Watermeier, Daniel J. "Edwin Booth's Iago." *Theatre History Studies* VI (1986): 32–55.

Williams, Hugh Blake. Clipping, "Booth's Fondness for Tobacco." *Chicago Post*, Folger Shakespeare Library.

Yarnell, James L. Edwin Booth's Life in Paradise." *Newport History* 68, part 3 Number 236 1997.

Newspapers

Albany Evening Journal
The Albion
American and Commercial Daily Advertiser
Bell's Life in London, and Sporting Chronicle
Boston Evening Transcript
The Brooklyn Daily Eagle
Buffalo Daily Courier
The Charleston Daily Courier
The Charleston Mercury
The Chicago Daily Tribune
The Cincinnati Daily Commercial
The Courier-Journal
Daily Alta California
The Daily American
Daily California Chronicle
Daily Dispatch
Daily Evening Transcript
Daily Missouri Republican
Daily National Intelligencer
The Daily Picayune
Deseret Evening News
Detroit Daily Free Press
The Evening Post
Fall River Evening News
The Golden Era
Hartford Daily Courant
The Memphis Daily Appeal
The Memphis Daily Avalanche
Mobile Daily Advertiser and Register
The Mobile Daily Register
Morning Journal and Courier
New York Amusement Gazette
The New York Clipper
New York Commercial Advertiser
The New York Daily News
New-York Daily Times
The New York Times
New-York Daily Tribune
New-York Dispatch
New York Dramatic News
New York Evening Express
New York Herald
The New York Leader
The New York Mirror
The Philadelphia Inquirer
The Pittsburgh Daily Gazette
The Providence Daily Journal
Public Ledger
Richmond Enquirer
Rochester Union and Advertiser
Sacramento Daily Union
The Salt Lake City Daily Tribune
Spirit of the Times
Springfield Republican
The Sun
Toledo Blade
The Weekly Placer Herald
Worcester Daily Spy

Index

Abbey, Henry E. 125, 126, 174
Abbotsford, Scotland 321
Aberdeen, Scotland 129, 262, 263, 264
Able Opera House (Easton, Pennsylvania) 255
Academy (Macon, Georgia) 289
Academy of Music (Baltimore, Maryland) 253, 279
Academy of Music (Brooklyn, New York) 203, 204, 206, 207, 239, 244, 248, 279, 294, 296
Academy of Music (Buffalo, New York) 217, 237, 242, 260, 287
Academy of Music (Cleveland, Ohio) 214
Academy of Music (East Saginaw, Michigan) 282, 290, 295
Academy of Music (Fall River, Massachusetts) 240, 254, 287, 294
Academy of Music (Fort Wayne, Indiana) 258
Academy of Music (Haverhill, Massachusetts) 277
Academy of Music (Indianapolis, Indiana) 228
Academy of Music (Kalamazoo, Michigan) 282, 290
Academy of Music (New York) 91, 137, 139, 143, 191, 200, 203, 208, 218, 219, 247, 248, 279, 281, 284, 288
Academy of Music (Oswego, New York) 284
Academy of Music (Philadelphia, Pennsylvania) 203, 241, 281
Academy of Music (Providence, Rhode Island) 209, 215, 220
Academy of Music (Scranton, Pennsylvania) 255, 293
Actors' Fund 156
Adams, Edwin 99, 100, 102, 212, 223, 243, 311n18
Adams, Henry 41
Adelphi Theatre (London, England) 128, 129, 261
Adelphi Theatre (San Francisco, California) 19

Adelphi Theatre (Washington, D.C.) 14, 177
Adrienne the Actress 181
Agassiz, Louis John Rudolphe 81, 308n2
Ahrendt, Carl 147
Albany, New York 49, 65, 299n18, 317n4
Albaugh, H.C. 281
Albaugh's Holliday Street Theatre (Baltimore, Maryland) 170, 292, 294, 295
Albert, Ernest 161, 291
Alcott, Louisa May 36, 37, 66
Aldrich, Lillian Woodman 49, 50, 62, 80, 84, 97, 126, 165, 314n55
Aldrich, Thomas Bailey 19, 49, 61, 62, 82, 84, 107, 108, 118, 153, 156, 157, 165, 312n38, 313n55
Alfonso (*Lucretia Borgia*) 180
Alice, the Forsaken 180, 181
All for Love or The Lost Pleiad 179
All the World's a Stage 182
Allen, George 215
Allen, Mrs. Octavia 242, 243, 245
Allworth (*A New Way to Pay Old Debts*) 178
Allyn Hall (Hartford, Connecticut) 215
American Academy of Music (Philadelphia, Pennsylvania) 199, 203
American Dramatic Fund 38
The American Fireman 21, 178
American Theatre (Sacramento, California) 19, 178
American Theatre (San Francisco, California) 26, 181, 182, 183, 217
Ames, Oakes A. 104 108, 242
Ames, Oliver 104, 108, 109, 242
Amphion Academy (Brooklyn, New York) 290, 293
Anderson, David C. 22, 24, 26, 27, 31, 82, 110, 123, 129–131, 133, 134, 245, 262, 265, 266, 268, 271, 273
Anderson, Jean (Sherwood) 60, 85, 94, 300n1, 311n16, 312n30, 313n47
Anderson, Marie 138
Anderson, Mary 135
Antietam, Maryland 51, 57

Antipholis of Syracuse (*Comedy of Errors*) 26, 182
Antoine Bellard (*The Carpenter of Rouen*) 15, 178
Antonio (*The Merchant of Venice*) 56, 208, 212, 285
Antony Latour (*Love's Fetters*) 182, 183
Antwerp, Belgium 129, 272
The Apostate 7, 13, 27, 62, 177, 184, 185, 186, 188, 189, 190, 191, 192, 193, 194, 195, 196, 197, 198, 199, 200, 202, 203, 204, 206, 207, 208, 209, 210, 211, 212, 214, 216, 217, 219, 224, 226, 229, 230, 232, 233, 234, 236, 238, 277, 278, 279, 284, 285, 286
Arch Street Theatre (Philadelphia, Pennsylvania) 51, 177, 194, 197, 198, 200, 239, 241, 315n65
Armand (*Peer and Peasant*) 182
Armand Duval (*Camille*) 26, 51, 182, 183
Aspinwall, Panama 17
Astley's Theatre (London, England) 56
Athenaeum (Savannah, Georgia) 195
Athenaeum (Wheeling, West Virginia) 185
Athenaeum, Howard (Boston, Massachusetts) 27, 40, 80, 194, 195, 198, 200, 309n3
Auburn, California 27, 185
Auditorium (Louisville, Kentucky) 295
Austin, Texas 146, 285, 289
Avon Theatre (Norfolk, Virginia) 177
Avon Theatre (Stockton, California) 286, 289

Badeau, Adam 1, 31, 36–38, 40–42, 44, 47–51, 57–59, 62, 64–67, 173, 175, 195, 208, 299n18, 306n25, 310n8, 311n23, 312n44
Bagwell, J.H. 192
Baker, Alexina Fisher 215
Baker, Benjamin A. 14, 27, 28, 29,

31, 32, 35, 36, 39, 90, 184, 185, 189, 192, 312*n*43
Baker, Sarah A. 282
Baldwin's Theatre (San Francisco, California) 285
Baltimore, Maryland 5, 6, 7, 13, 15, 16, 19, 25, 29, 31, 34, 35, 40, 42, 43, 49, 51, 69, 74, 75, 81, 87, 88, 94, 126, 136, 139, 145, 152, 155, 163, 177, 178, 184, 190, 191, 194, 198, 210, 230, 231, 232, 235, 236, 237, 240, 242, 244, 245, 247, 253, 254, 274, 275, 279, 281, 282, 284, 288, 292, 294, 295, 299*n*18, 300*n*2, 300*n*7, 305*n*32, 309*n*3, 313*n*47, 316*n*66
Baltimore Museum 40
Bancroft, Squire 120
Bangs, Francis C. 107
Banks, Nathaniel P. 65
Baradas (*Richelieu*) 26, 209, 211, 213, 257, 265
Barbacoas, Panama 18
Barnett, T.J. 108, 109, 11
Barnum's American Museum (New York) 39, 228, 239, 312*n*37
The Barrack Room 180
Barras, Charles M. 113
Barrett, Lawrence 1, 20, 33, 51, 52–54, 64, 69, 76, 88, 98, 105, 110, 118, 138, 139, 142–150, 152–154, 161–171, 188, 197, 223, 224, 225, 253, 276, 281, 282, 283, 284, 285, 286, 287, 288, 289, 290, 291, 296
Barron, Charles 277, 282
Bassanio (*The Merchant of Venice*) 152, 291
Beatrice (*Much Ado About Nothing*) 167, 209, 247, 293
Bel Air, Maryland 5, 7, 13, 33, 34, 47, 75, 138, 175
Belfast, Ireland 321*n*4
Bell, Clarke 108, 109, 251
The Belle's Stratagem 180, 182, 183
Benedick (*Much Ado About Nothing*) 26, 105, 167, 179, 180, 182, 183, 190, 191, 194, 197, 203, 209, 210, 211, 212, 213, 214, 215, 216, 217, 220, 222, 224, 228, 229, 230, 237, 238, 239, 240, 245, 246, 247, 293, 294, 295
Benedict, E.C. 124, 157, 244, 252, 276
Bennett, James Gordon 89, 90
Berlin, Germany 129–132, 261, 265, 269, 270, 271
Bertram (*Bertram*) 27, 181, 184, 185, 186
Bertrand (*Madelaine, or the Foundling of Paris*) 183
Bertuccio (*The Fool's Revenge*) 69, 167, 198, 200, 203, 204, 206, 208, 211, 215, 220, 222, 224, 225, 226, 229, 230, 238, 239, 240, 241, 242, 244, 246, 247, 248, 250, 251, 253, 254, 255, 256, 257, 258, 260, 261, 262, 263, 264, 265, 266, 267, 268, 273, 274, 275, 276, 277, 279, 280, 281, 282, 283, 284, 285, 286, 292, 293, 294, 295
Bethel, Maine 54

Bingen, Germany 129
Birmingham, England 129, 256, 262, 268, 289
Bispham, William 104, 108, 115, 140, 156, 157, 168, 172, 174, 223, 265, 269
The Black Crook 91, 107, 113, 184, 208
Bleak House 182
Boniface, Maria 282
Bonn, Germany 269, 271
Booth, Amelia 5
Booth, Clemintina Mary deBar (Mrs. Junius Brutus Booth, Jr.) 17, 216, 300
Booth, Edgar 112
Booth, Elizabeth 6, 87
Booth, Frederick 6, 87
Booth, Harriet Mace 17, 34
Booth, Henry Byron 6
Booth, John Wilkes 6, 7, 10, 34, 47, 49, 62, 64, 65, 69, 74–80, 82–84, 87–89, 92, 116, 252, 306*n*58, 309*nn*3,4, 310*n*7, 311*n*18, 312*n*30, 313*n*46
Booth, Joseph Adrian 6, 7, 10, 34, 35, 36, 45, 47, 49, 52, 60, 65, 74, 75, 78–80, 82, 84, 87, 88, 94, 99, 100, 103, 108, 109, 114, 136, 138
Booth, Junius Brutus, Jr. 5, 7, 9, 10, 12, 17, 19, 21, 23, 31, 33–36, 39, 52, 69, 74, 75, 78–80, 82–84, 87–89, 102, 103, 108, 109, 114, 135, 136
Booth, Junius Brutus, Sr. 5, 6, 7, 8, 9, 10, 11, 12, 13, 14, 15, 17, 18, 19, 25, 34, 36, 47, 55, 74, 75, 77, 79, 87, 132, 144, 175
Booth, Marian Agnes Lane Rookes Perry 135, 244
Booth, Mary (Marie, Mollie. Marion) 34, 79, 94
Booth, Mary Ann (child) 6, 87
Booth, Mary Ann Holmes 5, 6, 7, 9, 34, 35, 49, 52, 64, 65, 74, 75, 77–82, 84–88, 94, 103, 109, 114, 124, 135, 138
Booth, Mary Christine Adelaide Delannoy 5, 6, 9
Booth, Mary Devlin 1, 22, 31, 36, 40, 42–52, 54, 56, 57, 59–66, 68, 75, 76, 78, 84, 85, 93, 97, 112, 117, 136, 139, 144, 156, 157, 185, 195, 203, 310*n*7, 314*n*57
Booth, Mary McVicker 93, 94, 96, 99–105, 108, 109, 112–126, 128, 135, 139, 206, 207, 209, 210, 211, 217, 219, 235, 253, 322*n*22
Booth, Richard 5, 9
Booth, Rosalie Ann (Rose) 6, 10, 34, 35, 45, 52, 64, 74, 77, 80, 81, 86–88, 103, 135, 138, 163
Booth's Theatre (New York) 68, 98–111, 113, 125, 126, 156, 217, 218, 219, 220, 221, 224, 225, 226, 227, 228, 234, 243, 247, 248, 253, 261, 315*n*65
Boston, Massachusetts 6, 12, 25, 30, 32, 33, 34, 37, 39, 40, 51, 62, 63, 68, 69, 73, 75, 76, 79, 80, 81, 91, 103, 117, 135–137, 139–141, 145, 148, 152, 161–163, 171, 175
Boston Academy 61, 62

Boston Museum 74, 109, 136, 139, 177, 276, 278, 279, 280, 317*n*4
Boston Theatre 39, 43, 44, 63, 73, 81, 89, 91, 92, 98, 170, 186, 188, 190, 192, 202, 203, 205, 206, 208, 209, 216, 220, 225, 228, 232, 244, 281, 283, 288, 290, 292, 294, 306*n*28, 312*n*37, 320*n*25
Boucicault, Dion 51, 162
Bowers, D.P. 223
Bowery Theatre (New York) 5, 156, 207, 250, 298*n*6
Bowling Green, Kentucky 235, 236
Boyd's Opera House (Omaha, Nebraska) 290, 293
Brackett, Walter 35, 43, 44, 46, 54, 59, 63
Brahm, Otto 270
Breach of Promise 179, 180
Bremen, Germany 131, 132, 269, 270, 271
Bremen Stadt-Theater 271
Bridgeport, Connecticut 126, 292, 294
Broad Street Theatre (Philadelphia, Pennsylvania) 246, 247
Broadway Theatre (New York) 29, 166, 167, 171, 293, 296
Bromley, Theodore 171
Brookline, Massachusetts 17
Brooklyn, New York 62, 136, 139, 152, 154, 156, 168, 171
Brooks & Dixon 136
Brougham, John 218, 243
Brutus (*Julius Caesar*) 8, 13, 69, 107, 139, 148, 152, 153, 163, 171, 178, 184, 195, 198, 200, 203, 204, 205, 210, 222, 225, 226, 228, 238, 244, 280, 281, 287, 288, 289, 290, 316*n*75
Brutus 15, 27, 184, 185, 186, 188, 189, 190, 191, 192, 193, 194, 195, 197, 198, 199, 200, 202, 203, 204, 205, 206, 207, 208, 209, 210, 214, 215, 216, 220, 225, 227, 228, 229, 230, 231, 232, 238, 239, 240, 241, 242, 244, 246, 280, 281
Bryant, William Cullen 41
Buckstone, J.B. 54, 56
Buffalo, New York 126, 143, 152, 164, 189, 191, 194, 215, 217, 237, 242, 260, 282, 287, 295
Bull, Ole 219
Bull, Mrs. Ole 270
Bunce, O.B. 233
Burlington, Iowa 260, 293
Burnett, Col. H.S. 82
Burtis' Opera House (Davenport, Iowa) 260, 290, 295
Burton, William Evans 33
Burton's New Theatre, Broadway (New York) 33, 34, 41, 43, 187, 188, 190
Busteed, Richard 41, 306*n*23
Buzzard's Bay, Massachusetts 170, 172

Calhoun, Lucia Gilbert 73
California Theatre (San Francisco, California) 166, 238, 293

Calvert, Mrs. Charles 77
Calverton Hall (*The State Secrets*) 178
Camille 26, 182
Capen, Nahum 74
Capt. Absolute (*The Rivals*) 179, 180
Capt. Charles (*Who Speaks First*) 182, 183
Capt. Murphy Maguire (*A Serious Family*) 181, 182, 183
Cardinal Wolsey (*Henry VIII*) 199
Cardinal Wolsey (*The Roebuck*) 204, 234, 235, 236, 237, 241, 242, 243
Carey, Eleanor 242–244
Carll's Music Hall (New Haven, Connecticut) 227, 254, 277
Carrollton, Louisiana 57
Carryl, Charles P. 174
Cary, Emma F. 54, 56, 69, 70, 81, 85, 90, 205, 310n8
Cary, Richard F. 42, 51, 52, 57, 60, 61, 66, 68, 69, 81, 98, 310n7
Cassio (*Othello*) 12, 59, 163, 177, 178, 246, 251
Cassius (*Julius Caesar*) 8, 13, 69, 107, 148, 152, 195, 198, 200, 203, 204, 225, 226, 228
Cazauran, Augustus R. 224
Cedar Cliff 113, 114
Cedar Mountain, Virginia 61
The Century Club 101, 118
Chagres River, Panama 18
Champlin, John Denison 195, 196
Chanfrau, Frank 27
Charlecote, England 321n4
Charles (*My Sister Kate*) 179, 181
Charles de Moor (*The Robbers*) 75, 189, 190, 191, 192, 193, 194, 195, 197, 198
Charles Franklin (*Sweethearts and Wives*) 178
Charles Oakley (*Jealous Wife*) 179, 180
Charles II/*Charles II* 178, 181, 183
Charles Surface (*The School for Scandal*) 23, 179, 180, 182, 183
Charleston, South Carolina 13, 15, 78, 88, 152, 177, 178, 190, 193, 235, 289
Charleston Theatre 177, 178, 197
Charlotte, North Carolina 235
Chase, Arthur Branscomb 142–147, 149, 150, 164, 175, 281, 282, 283, 284, 286, 289
Chatterton Opera House (Springfield, Illinois) 287, 290
Chelsea Academy of Music (Chelsea, Massachusetts) 277
Cherry and Fair Star, or The Children of Cyprus 183
Chestnut Street Opera House (Philadelphia, Pennsylvania) 203, 278, 281, 284, 288, 292, 294, 295, 312n31
Cheyenne, Wyoming 147, 286
Chicago, Illinois 19, 74, 93, 109, 112, 114, 115, 125–127, 142, 144, 150, 152, 153, 161, 162, 165, 168, 209, 213, 214, 215, 216, 217, 222, 225, 228, 230, 232, 236, 237, 241,
246, 250, 260, 282, 283, 287, 291, 295
Chicago Opera House 282, 287, 291, 295
The Child of the Regiment or The Trumpeter's Daughter 178
Chilton, R.S. 188
Church, Frederick 41
Cibber, Colley 11, 202, 232, 241
Cincinnati, Ohio 145, 162, 186, 189, 191, 192, 197, 210, 211, 215, 222, 230, 231, 236, 241, 258, 259, 274, 282, 284, 288, 291, 295, 301n17, 313n47
Cist, L.J. 241
Citizen Sangfroid (*Delicate Ground*) 180, 182, 183
City Hall (Biddeford, Maine) 227
City Hall (Gloucester, Massachusetts) 227
City Hall (Waterbury, Connecticut) 126, 240, 254
City Theatre (Brockton, Massachusetts) 278
Clarke, Asia Booth (Asia Sydney, Asia Frigga) 1, 5, 6, 7, 9, 10, 11, 17, 25, 45, 47, 49, 60, 64, 67, 73, 75, 78, 79, 81, 83, 85, 87, 89, 121, 135, 155, 186, 298nn7,9, 299n16, 300nn1,2, 302n23, 310n16, 311nn16,29,30, 312n30, 313n47,49, 316n72
Clarke, Creston, 89, 261, 328n31
Clarke, John Sleeper 7, 8, 10, 13, 61, 64, 68–70, 79, 80, 83, 84, 87–92, 110, 119, 121, 245, 300n8, 309n4, 311nn29,30, 312n30, 314n54
Clarke, Lillian 89
Clarke, Wilfred 290, 328n31
Claude Melnotte (*The Lady of Lyons*) 23, 24, 27, 75, 104, 179, 181, 182, 183, 184, 185, 186, 188, 195, 196, 198, 200, 202, 212, 213, 214, 215, 216, 217, 219, 220, 221, 222, 223, 225, 226, 228, 229, 230, 231, 232, 233, 234, 236, 237, 238, 239, 240, 241, 244, 246, 278, 279
Claudius (*Hamlet*) 126, 130, 148, 221
Clemens, Samuel (Mark Twain) 157
Cleveland, Grover 173
Cleveland, Ohio 110, 144, 164, 167, 214, 241, 242, 259, 283, 288, 293, 311n23
Clopton, England 321n4
Coates' Opera House (Kansas City, Missouri) 286
Cohasset, Massachusetts 158, 161
Collingwood Opera House (Poughkeepsie, New York) 226
Cologne, Germany 269, 271
Col. Mannering (*Guy Mannering*) 179, 181
Col. Terrier (*The Barrack Room*) 180
Columbus, Ohio 147, 259, 287, 293
Columbus Theatre 150
A Comedy of Errors 26, 182
Concert Hall (Nevada City, California) 184
Concert Hall/Theatre (Augusta, Georgia) 190
Connaught, Duke of (Arthur) 120
Connor (*The Rash Knight of Arva*) 182
Connor, Mr. and Mrs. Edmon S. 47, 159
Connor's Arch Street Theatre (Philadelphia, Pennsylvania) 177
Consumption 115, 117, 120–122, 125
Conway, Mrs. F.B. 225, 229
Cook, Dutton 123
Cordelia (*King Lear*) 43, 245, 288
Cork, Ireland 119
The Corsican Brothers 62, 76, 183
Cos Cob, Connecticut 113–115, 124, 135
Couldock, C.W. 148, 287
Count Horace de Beauval (*Pauline*) 182
Count de Saxe (*Adrienne the Actress*) 180
Court and Stage 183
Cowell, Mrs. Sam 53, 199
Crabtree, Lotta 105
Crane, William H. 116
Crawford's Opera House (Leavenworth, Kansas) 290
Crawford's Opera House (Topeka, Kansas) 290
Crawford's Opera House (Wichita, Kansas) 290
Cressford (*Ellen Wareham*) 180
Crisp, Mrs. W.H. 197
Crisp & Canning's Gaiety Theatre a/k/a/ Temperance Hall (Columbus, Georgia) 195
Crisp & Canning's Gaiety Theatre (Montgomery, Alabama) 195
Crisp's Gaiety Theatre (Memphis, Tennessee) 189, 193
Crisp's Gaiety Theatre (Nashville, Tennessee) 190, 193, 197
Crisp's Gaiety Theatre (New Orleans, Louisiana) 189
Cruces, Panama 18
Cushman, Charlotte 42, 43, 46, 51, 53, 55, 56, 106, 119, 199, 200, 217, 225, 317n4
Cushman, Emma Crow 43, 56, 60, 62, 66
Cushman, Susan 42

Dallas, Texas 146, 285, 290
Daly, Augustin 114, 230, 232, 233, 234
Daly, Judge Joseph F. 157
Daly's Fifth Avenue Theatre (New York) 110, 232
Damon and Pythias 181
Dandy Cox (play unknown) 180
Davenport, Edgar Loomis 190, 223
Davenport, Jean (Lander) 15, 26, 118, 178, 211
Davidge, William 208
Davidson, Garrison (Garrie) 315n65
Dawison, Bogusmil 90, 91, 207, 246
Day, W.C. 250
The Day After the Wedding 15, 178

Dayton, Ohio 169, 228, 259, 287, 290, 295
Dazzle (*London Assurance*) 179, 180
DeBar, Ben 45, 83, 300*n*1
DeBar, Blanche 17, 83, 103
DeBar's Opera House (St. Louis, Missouri) 212, 222, 230, 232, 241
Dedham, Massachusetts 17
DeGive's Opera House (Atlanta, Georgia) 235, 256
Delafield, Louis L. 81
Delaval (*Matrimony*) 181
Delicate Ground 180, 182, 183
Delmonico's 118, 146, 157
DeMauprat (*Richelieu*) 171, 178, 181
Demetrius (*A Midsummer Night's Dream*) 26, 182
Denham, Fanny 288
Denier, Lydia 282
Denin, Kate 217
Denin, Susan 217
Denver, Colorado 147, 152, 286, 289, 293
Derrickville, Pennsylvania 20
Derwentwater, England 321*n*4
Desdemona (*Othello*) 102, 122, 133, 139, 207, 218, 219, 243, 244, 245, 251, 288, 291
De Soto: Or the Hero of the Mississippi 181
Detroit, Michigan 110, 114, 143, 153, 214, 215, 216, 228, 229, 237, 246, 259, 260, 282, 287, 295
Detroit Opera House 228, 246, 259, 282, 295
Detroit Theatre 110
Diamond Springs, California 184
Dick Dashall (*My Aunt*) 182
Dick Dowlas (*The Heir at Law*) 178, 179
Dickson's Grand Opera House (Indianapolis, Indiana) 258
Diggory (*All the World's a Stage*) 182
Dinsmore, Amy Elliot 53
Dix, John Adams 84
Dombey (*Dombey and Son*) 179
Don Caesar de Bazan (*Don Caesar de Bazan*) 60, 73, 167, 174, 179, 180, 181, 194, 195, 196, 197, 198, 200, 202, 203, 204, 205, 206, 207, 209, 216, 220, 224, 225, 226, 227, 228, 229, 230, 231, 238, 239, 241, 244, 247, 262, 277, 278, 279, 294, 295
Don Manuel (*Where There's a Will There's a Way* a/k/a *The Queen's Husband*) 180, 181
Don Philip (*Gil and Giraldi*) 180
Dona Diana 167
Donalbain (*Macbeth*) 143
Doncaster, England 130, 262
Dorchester, Massachusetts 62, 63, 75
Doremus, R. Ogden 94
Doricourt (*The Belle's Stratagem*) 180, 182, 183
Douglas 15, 177
Douglas Trafford (*The People's Advocate*) 180

Downieville, California 20, 26, 184, 302*n*22
Dramatic Hall (Nevada, California) 178
Dresden, Germany 132
Drew, John 47, 233, 284
Drew, Mrs. John 47, 74, 239, 241, 315*n*65
Dublin, Ireland 262, 265, 266, 267, 268, 321*n*4
Dugas, Louis 298*n*9
Duke Aranza (*The Honeymoon*) 179, 181, 182, 183
Duke de Chartres (*Follies of a Night*) 180, 181, 183
Duke of Richmond (*Court and Stage*) 182, 183
Dundee, Scotland 262, 263, 265, 268
Dunphie, Charles 250, 252
Durant, Dr. Ghislahi 116
Dusseldorf Gallery (New York) 48
Duster, William E. 84

Eddy, Jerome H. 164
Edgar (*King Lear*) 15, 152, 177, 178, 288, 300*n*2
Edinburgh, Scotland 129, 262, 264, 265, 321*n*4
Edmonds, Judge J.W. 81
Edmonds, Laura 66, 67, 81, 85, 97
Edward, Prince of Wales 120, 133
Edwards, Maze 256, 257, 322*n*11
Edwin Forrest Theatre (Sacramento, California) 183
The Elder and the Younger Booth 1
Elko, Nevada 147
Ellen Wareham 180
Ellsler, John 110
Ellsler's Opera House (Pittsburgh, Pennsylvania) 284
Elmira Opera House 284, 293
Ely, Lady Jane, Dowager Marchioness 120
English's Opera House (Indianapolis, Indiana) 287, 293, 295
Ernest Maltravers (*Alice, the Forsaken*) 180, 181
Erysipelis 80, 130
Euclid Avenue Opera House (Cleveland, Ohio) 242, 289, 293
Eugene de Morny (*Love's Ordeal*) 216
Evadne, or the Statue 183, 251
Ewer, Ferdinand 19, 21, 22, 23, 24, 26, 42, 241
Eytinge, Rose 69, 242, 243

Fabien del Franchi (*The Corsican Brothers*) 183
Faint Heart Never Won Fair Lady 181, 182, 183, 184, 195
The Fair One with the Golden Locks 179
Father Radcliffe (*Two Loves and a Life*) 183
Fawcett, Owen 169, 275, 324*n*1
Fazio/*Fazio* 181, 184, 200
Fechter, Charles Albert 104, 247
Felton, C.C. 186, 308*n*2

Field/s, Mrs. James T. 85, 313*n*50, 314*n*52
Fields/Field, Robert Montgomery 136, 139, 166, 278, 279
Fifth Avenue Hotel (New York) 49
Fifth Avenue Theatre (New York) 110, 137, 232, 246, 253, 276, 277, 280, 291
Fiordelisa (*The Fool's Revenge*) 167, 242, 245, 273, 276
Fletcher's Music Hall (Woonsocket, Rhode Island) 227
Flohr, Henry 31, 116
Florence, William Jermyn 47, 154, 158
Floyd, W.R. 248
Flynn, Thomas 6, 9
The Follies of a Night 180, 181, 183
The Fool's Revenge 51, 120, 121, 129, 167, 198, 200, 203, 204, 206, 208, 211, 215, 220, 222, 224, 225, 226, 229, 230, 238, 239, 240, 241, 242, 244, 246, 247, 248, 250, 251, 253, 254, 255, 256, 257, 258, 260, 261, 262, 263, 264, 265, 266, 267, 268, 273, 274, 275, 276, 277, 279, 280, 281, 282, 283, 284, 285, 286, 292, 293, 294, 295
Ford, Cary Clay 83
Ford, John T. 29, 40, 51, 83, 87, 114, 231, 234, 235, 236, 237, 310*n*66
Ford's Grand Opera House (Baltimore, Maryland) 231, 232, 245
Ford's South Broad Street Theatre (Philadelphia, Pennsylvania) 247
Ford's Theatre (Washington, D.C.) 80, 81, 83, 245
Forrest, Edwin 6, 21, 23, 41, 51–53, 61, 66, 106, 119, 198, 209, 212, 214, 215, 219
Fort Wayne, Indiana 222, 228, 258, 290
Fourteenth Street Theatre (New York) 275, 276
Francis (*The Stranger*) 178, 179
Frank Heartall (*The Soldier's Daughter*) 178, 179, 180, 181
Fred Jerome (*The American Fireman*) 21, 178
Frisbie's Theatre (Nevada, California) 184
Frohman, Daniel 137
Front Street Theatre (Baltimore, Maryland) 15, 29, 184, 194, 299*n*18, 3015*n*32
Fulham, England 59
Furlbond (*The Yellow Dwarf*) 179
Fulton Opera House (Lancaster, Pennsylvania) 284
Furness, Horace Howard 1, 42, 275, 284

Gaiety Theatre (Dublin, Ireland) 266, 323*n*13
Gaiety Theatre (Glasgow, Scotland) 129, 264
Gale, Minna 150, 168
Galveston, Texas 126, 146, 256, 258, 285, 289
The Gamester 178, 181

Garland Opera House (Waco, Texas) 289
Garrett, R.B. 88
Garrick, David 94
Garrick Club, London, England 120
Gaspar (*The Lady of Lyons*) 178
Genarro (*Lucrezia Borgia, or the Poisoner*) 183
George (*The Green Bushes*) 179, 183
Georgetown, California 27, 184
Gertrude (*Hamlet*) 126, 221
Ghost (*Hamlet*) 152, 183, 221, 243, 264, 265
Gifford, Sanford Robinson 61, 109, 312*n*39
Gil and Giraldi 180
Gillett, E.F. 258
Gillmore, Gen. Quincy A. 57
Gilmore (*A Mother's Trust, or California in 1849*) 181
Gilmore's Opera House (Springfield, Massachusetts) 292, 294
Girardey's Opera House (Augusta, Georgia) 235
Gisippus 178
Givemesum (play title unknown) 180
A Glance at New York 27
Glasgow, Scotland 262, 264, 268, 321*n*4
Globe Theatre (Boston, Massachusetts) 240, 273, 275
The Golden Farmer 182
Goneril (*King Lear*) 252, 299*n*18
Gooch, Walter 90, 119, 120, 121, 250, 251, 252
Good's Opera House (South Bend, Indiana) 237
Gorgona, Panama 18
Gotthold, Newton 208, 282
Gougenheim, Joey and Adelaide 26, 182
Graham, James Lorimer 56, 59–61, 63, 66
Graham, Lillie 282
Grand Opera House (Cincinnati, Ohio) 284, 288, 291, 295
Grand Opera House (Dayton, Ohio) 287, 290, 295
Grand Opera House (Des Moines, Iowa) 290
Grand Opera House (Duluth, Minnesota) 287
Grand Opera House (Evansville, Illinois) 258
Grand Opera House (Harrisburg, Pennsylvania) 255
Grand Opera House (Lafayette, Indiana) 258, 290
Grand Opera House (Los Angeles, California) 146, 285, 289
Grand Opera House (Milwaukee, Wisconsin) 259, 282, 295
Grand Opera House (Minneapolis, Minnesota) 282, 290
Grand Opera House (New Bedford, Massachusetts) 278, 287
Grand Opera House (New Orleans, Louisiana) 256, 285, 289
Grand Opera House (New York) 247, 292

Grand Opera House (Newark, New Jersey) 284
Grand Opera House (Peoria, Illinois) 286
Grand Opera House (Pittsburgh, Pennsylvania) 289, 292, 293
Grand Opera House (St. Louis, Missouri) 257
Grand Opera House (San Antonio, Texas) 289
Grand Theatre (Leeds, England) 265
Granite Hall (Augusta, Maine) 227
Grant, Ulysses S. 65, 82, 86, 87, 311*n*23
Grass Valley, California 20, 178, 302*n*23
Gratiano (*The Merchant of Venice*) 15, 20, 177, 178, 180, 183
Gray, Mark 36
The Green Bushes 179, 183
Green Mount Cemetery (Baltimore, Maryland) 19, 87
Green Street Theatre (Albany, New York) 317*n*4
Greene's Opera House (Cedar Rapids, Iowa) 290
Greenwich, Connecticut 124
Griffiths, William H. 262
Grist to the Mill 182
Griswold Opera House (Troy, New York) 215, 226
Grossman, Edwin Booth (Ted) 63, 147
Grossman, Edwina Booth 2, 6, 59, 60, 63–65, 73, 77, 78, 80, 94–97, 99, 109, 113–115, 117, 124–133, 135–141, 145, 147, 154, 156, 159, 165, 170–175, 182, 208, 225, 235, 245, 255, 256, 257, 258, 259, 270, 272, 275, 277, 278, 279, 280, 281, 283, 286, 287, 290, 295, 297, 310*n*9, 311*n*29, 314*n*64, 321*n*22, 324*n*1, 328*n*31
Grossman, Ignatius R. 137–140, 145, 147, 167
Grossman, Mildred 139
Grover's Theatre (Washington, D.C.) 204, 282, 310*n*8
Guy Mannering 178, 179, 181, 221

Hackett, James 61, 99
Hamburg, Germany 129, 131, 132, 269, 270
Hamlet/*Hamlet* 2, 7, 9, 13, 19, 21, 24, 26, 29, 32, 37, 52, 53, 59, 63, 64, 66, 68, 70–73, 75, 79, 89, 91, 98, 103, 105, 109, 114, 116, 120, 126, 129–133, 139, 143, 146, 147, 167, 171, 178, 179, 181, 182, 183, 184, 185, 186, 188, 189, 190, 191, 192, 193, 194, 195, 196, 197, 198, 199, 200, 202, 203, 204, 205, 206, 207, 208, 209, 210, 211, 212, 213, 214, 215, 216, 217, 219, 220, 221, 222, 223, 224, 225, 226, 227, 228, 229, 230, 231, 232, 233, 234, 235, 236, 237, 238, 239, 240, 241, 242, 243, 244, 245, 246, 247, 248, 249, 250, 251, 253, 254, 255, 256, 257, 258, 259, 260, 261, 262, 263, 264, 265, 266, 267, 268, 269, 270, 271, 272, 273, 274, 275, 276, 277, 278, 279, 280, 281, 282, 283, 284, 285, 286, 287, 288, 289, 290, 291, 292, 293, 294, 295, 296, 310*n*8, 312*n*33, 317*n*4, 318*n*6, 320*n*25, 324*n*1
Hammerstein's Opera House (Harlem, New York) 294
Hanel, Blanche 67, 85, 86
Hanley, J.G. 219
Hanley, Lawrence 171, 296
Hanlon Brothers 70
Hare, Sir John 121
Harrisburg, Pennsylvania 83, 148, 231, 255, 287
Harrowgate, England 261, 262, 268
Harry Stanly (*Paul Pry*) 178, 179
Hatton, Joseph 120, 250
Haverly's Theatre (Brooklyn, New York) 253, 275
Haverly's Theatre (Chicago, Illinois) 260
Hawaii 26, 29, 182
Hawe's Opera House (Bridgeport, Connecticut) 292
Haymarket Theatre (London, England) 54–56, 200, 201
Haynes's Opera House (Springfield, Massachusetts) 226
The Heir at Law 178, 179
Hemeya (*The Apostate*) 13, 14, 177, 178
Hemphill, C. Dallett 45
Hennepin Avenue Theatre (Minneapolis, Minnesota) 287
Henry II/*Henry II* 195, 196
Henry V/*Henry V* 191
Henry VIII/*Henry VIII* 199
Henry Hamilton (*Maidens Beware*) 178, 179, 180
Henry Meadows (*Rosina Meadows*) 178
Hepworth, Rev. George H. 81
Her Majesty's Theatre (Aberdeen, Scotland) 263
Herald, David E. 84
Herman (*The Robbers*) 15, 178
Heron, Matilda 23, 37, 41, 51, 181, 217, 225
Hicks, Thomas 57, 59
Hill, Barton 86, 185, 208, 255, 260, 315*n*65
Hinton, Henry 89
Hoboken, New Jersey 45, 47
Hodge Opera House (Lockport, New York) 242
Holland, George 224
Holliday Street Theatre (Baltimore, Maryland) 6, 15, 35, 43, 168, 177, 178, 190, 191, 210, 274, 288, 292, 294, 299*n*18, 300*n*2, 309*n*3
Hollister, Gideon Hiram 195, 196
Home, John 15
The Honeymoon 179, 181, 182, 183
Honolulu, Hawaii 24, 182
Horatio (*Hamlet*) 75, 198, 221, 233, 249
Hosmer, Harriet 42
The Housekeeper 182, 183
Houston, Texas 146, 285, 289

Howard Leslie (*Two Can Play at That Game*) 181, 182
Howe, Julia Ward 41, 64
Howe's Opera House (Bridgeport, Connecticut) 240
Hull, England 129
Humboldt, California 147
The Hunchback 23, 181, 182, 183
Huntington Hall (Lowell, Massachusetts) 278
Huon (*Love, or the Countess and the Serf*) 181, 182
Hutton, Laurence 8, 116, 118, 125, 126, 130, 131, 136, 139, 156–158, 167, 251, 254, 256, 263, 269, 271, 273, 274, 297, 299n18, 310n10
Hyde, Augusta 299n9
Hyde, Susan 7, 299n9
Hyperion Theatre a/k/a Carll's Opera House (New Haven, Connecticut) 287, 292, 294

Iago (*Othello*) 7, 23, 28, 54, 55, 75, 90, 102, 107, 121, 122, 139, 152, 153, 171, 178, 180, 181, 183, 184, 185, 186, 188, 189, 190, 191, 192, 193, 194, 195, 196, 197, 198, 199, 200, 202, 203, 204, 205, 206, 207, 209, 211, 212, 213 214, 216, 217, 218, 219, 220, 222, 223, 224, 226, 228, 229, 230, 231, 232, 233, 234, 235, 236, 237, 238, 239 240, 241, 242, 243, 244, 246, 247, 248, 251, 252, 253, 254, 255, 256, 257, 259, 260, 261, 263, 266, 269, 270, 271, 272, 273, 274, 275, 276, 277, 278, 279, 280, 281, 282, 283, 284, 285, 286, 287, 288, 289, 290, 291, 292, 293, 295, 296
Icilius (*Virginius or The Roman Father*) 178
Indianapolis, Indiana 147, 165, 228, 258, 287, 290, 293, 295
Ingomar 15, 28, 177
Interlocken, Switzerland 129
Inter-state law 150
Invisible Prince 178
The Iron Chest 7, 13, 177, 182, 183, 184, 185, 186, 188, 189, 190, 191, 192, 193, 194, 195, 196, 197, 198, 200, 202, 203, 204, 205, 224, 225, 226, 227, 228, 276, 277, 278, 279, 305n32
Irving, Henry 59, 119–123, 128, 129, 133, 152, 261, 275

Jabber (*Breach of Promise*) 179, 180
Jack Cade/*Jack Cade* 178
Jack Spriggs (*Look Before You Leap*) 182
Jackson, Hart James (A.W. Jackson, Black Jackson) 52, 54, 61, 63, 64, 68, 69
Jackson Theatre (Jackson, California) 27, 184
Jacksonville, Illinois 228
Jacob and Proctor's Opera House (Utica, New York) 294
Jaffier (*Venice Preserved*) 19, 178
James, Louis 150, 178, 242, 243
James Hall (Chattanooga, Tennessee) 236, 257
Janauschek, Fanny 91
Jarrett, Henry C. 34, 40, 81, 91, 109, 190, 208, 232
Jealous Wife 179, 180, 182, 183
Jeems Pipes *see* Massett, Stephen
Jefferson, Charles Burke 174, 234
Jefferson, Joseph 13, 31, 40, 46, 48, 74, 92, 93, 103, 104, 108, 119, 154, 157–159, 170, 172, 174, 188, 223, 299n2, 325n31, 326n15
Jefferson, Margaret Lockyear 13
Jenner, Dr. William 121
Jenny Lind Theatre (San Francisco, California) 17, 18, 178
John Drew's National Theatre (Philadelphia, Pennsylvania) 40
John Mildmay (*Still Waters Run Deep*) 183, 184
Johnson, Pres. Andrew 86, 87
Johnson, Eastman 61
Jones, Alvonia 217
Jones, Mrs. Malverna 217
Julie de Mortimer/Mortimar (*Richelieu*) 167
Juliet (*Romeo and Juliet*) 40, 53, 90, 93, 94, 100, 209, 210, 211, 212, 217, 218
Julius Caesar 13, 80, 106, 107, 139, 148, 152, 159, 161, 170, 178, 184, 195, 198, 200, 203, 204, 205, 210, 222, 225, 226, 228, 238, 244, 280, 281, 287, 288, 289, 290, 316n75

Kalamazoo, Michigan 144, 228, 282, 290
Kamehameha IV (Alexander Liholiho) 25
Kansas City, Missouri 147, 150, 152, 153, 161, 286, 287, 290, 291
Katherine (*Katherine and Petruchio*) 43, 94, 185, 212
Katherine and Petruchio 94, 129, 143, 153, 179, 180, 181, 183, 184, 185, 186, 188, 189, 190, 191, 192, 193, 194, 195, 196, 197, 198, 199, 200, 202, 203, 204, 205, 206, 207, 209, 210, 211, 212, 213, 214, 215, 216, 217, 220, 222, 223, 224, 225, 226, 227, 228, 229, 231, 232, 234, 235, 236, 237, 238, 239, 240, 241, 242, 243, 244, 245, 246, 247, 248, 252, 253, 254, 262, 263, 265, 266, 267, 268, 273, 274, 275, 276, 277, 278, 279, 280, 283, 284, 285, 286, 287
Katz, Jonathan Ned 43, 305n3
Kean, Charles 70, 72, 99, 102, 110, 119, 212
Kean, Edmund 43, 55, 200, 208, 284
Keene, Laura 23, 24, 25, 29, 31, 61, 83, 188, 302n40, 303n42
Kellogg, A.O. 97, 114
Kendal, Madge Robertson 121
Kendal, W.H. Grimston 121
Kerney, Martin J. (Kearney) 298n9
Killarney, Ireland 119
King Lear/*King Lear* 7, 15, 28, 29, 30, 43, 114, 131, 132, 145, 177, 178, 184, 185, 186, 188, 189, 190, 191, 192, 193, 194, 195, 196, 197, 222, 223, 234, 235, 236, 237, 238, 239, 240, 241, 242, 244, 245, 246, 247, 252, 253, 254, 261, 267, 268, 269, 270, 271, 272, 273, 274, 275, 276, 279, 280, 281, 282, 283, 284, 285, 287, 288, 289, 290, 299n18, 300n2, 328
The King's Pleasure 152, 153
Kingston, Ireland (Dunlaoghaire, Dunleary) 321n4
Kirby, Mrs. Hudson 43
Knight, Joseph 249, 252
Kotzebue, August von 13
Kunkel, George 29, 40
Kunkes Opera House (Lincoln, Nebraska) 290

LaCoste, Anna 100
Lady Anne (*Richard III*) 94, 245, 267
Lady Macbeth (*Macbeth*) 53, 91, 166, 167, 209, 214, 215, 317n4
The Lady of Lyons 94, 104, 179, 181, 182, 183, 184, 185, 186, 188, 195, 196, 198, 200, 202, 212, 213, 214, 215, 216, 217, 219, 220, 221, 222, 223, 225, 226, 228, 229, 230, 231, 232, 233, 234, 236, 237, 238, 239, 240, 241, 244, 246, 278, 279
Lady Teazle (*The School for Scandal*) 23
Laertes (*Hamlet*) 13, 59, 107, 153, 177, 178, 180, 181, 209, 220, 243, 287
Lancaster, Pennsylvania 143, 284
Lane, John 296
The Last Days of Pompeii 179
Leamington, England 321n4
Leap Year 179, 180
Leeds, England 129, 130, 262, 265, 266, 268
Leland Opera House (Albany, New York) 242, 260, 283
Leonid meteor shower 5
A Lesson for Ladies 179
Leubrie's Theatre (Memphis, Tennessee) 255
Levin, Natt 88
Liberty Hall (New Bedford, Massachusetts) 215, 227
Library Hall (Pittsburgh, Pennsylvania) 255
Lichfield, England 321n4
Lt. Worthington (*The Poor Gentleman*) 181
Life and Art of Edwin Booth 1, 73
Lincoln, Pres. Abraham 66, 75, 76, 81, 82, 89, 202, 204, 299nn14,18, 300n1, 310n8, 311nn18,29, 315n65, 316n75
Lincoln, Robert 82
Lionel Lyn (*Married Life*) 182
Little Eva (*Uncle Tom's Cabin*) 93
Little Toddlekins 180, 181, 184
Liverpool, England 54, 124, 129, 202, 262, 268
Lockridge, Richard 1
Lodge, Frank 142, 164
Londesboro Theatre (Scarborough, England) 129, 130, 262
London, England 54, 56, 59, 60, 78,

116, 117, 119, 200, 201, 202, 238, 241, 249, 250, 251, 252, 261, 266
London Assurance 179, 180
Lone Gulch, California 28, 304*n*68
Long Branch, New Jersey 77, 94, 97, 105, 107, 112, 113, 124, 135
Look Before You Leap 182
Lord Rivers (*The Day After the Wedding*) 15, 178
Lord Sparkles (*Love in Livery*) 178, 179
Lord Townley (*A Provoked Husband*) 180
Los Angeles, California 142, 146, 150, 165, 285, 289
Louisville, Kentucky 31, 35, 126, 145, 191, 230, 236, 241, 255, 284, 290, 293, 295
Louisville Theatre 192, 211, 282
The Love Chase 181, 182, 183
Love in Livery 178, 179
Love, or the Countess and the Serf 181, 182
Love's Fetters 182, 183
Love's Ordeal 216
Love's Sacrifice 179, 180, 181
Low's Opera House (Providence, Rhode Island) 254
Luce's Hall (Grand Rapids, Michigan) 228
Lucille 179
Lucius Junius Brutus (*Brutus*) 13, 15, 27, 94, 184, 185, 186, 188, 189, 190, 191, 192, 193, 194, 195, 197, 198, 199, 200, 202, 203, 204, 205, 206, 207, 208, 209, 210, 214, 215, 216, 220, 225, 227, 228, 229, 230, 231, 232, 238, 239, 240, 241, 242, 244, 246, 280, 281
Lucrezia Borgia, or the Poisoner 180, 183
Ludovico (*Evadne, or the Statue*) 183, 251
Luis (*De Soto: Or The Hero of the Mississippi*) 181
Lyceum Hall (Lewiston, Maine) 227
Lyceum Theatre (London, England) 119, 123, 128, 129, 252
Lyceum Theatre (New York) 110, 238
Lyceum Theatre (Philadelphia, Pennsylvania) 253
Lyceum Theatre (Rochester, New York) 293, 294
Lydon (*The Last Days of Pompeii*) 179
Lykon (*Ingomar*) 15, 178

Macauley's Theatre (Louisville, Kentucky) 230, 236, 255, 282, 284, 293
Macbeth/*Macbeth* 13, 15, 26, 27, 53, 75, 91, 104, 137, 143, 167, 168, 177, 178, 181, 184, 185, 191, 192, 193, 194, 195, 196, 197, 198, 199, 200, 202, 203, 204, 205, 209, 211, 212, 213, 214, 215, 216, 217, 220, 221, 222, 223, 224, 225, 226, 227, 228, 229, 230, 234, 238, 243, 244, 245, 246, 247, 248, 250, 253, 254, 256, 257,
258, 260, 261, 267, 268, 273, 274, 275, 276, 279, 280, 281, 282, 283, 284, 285, 287, 288, 289, 290, 292, 293, 294, 295, 296, 307*n*21, 310*n*7, 317*n*4
Macduff (*Macbeth*) 15, 152, 177, 178, 181, 200
Macready, William Charles 59, 199, 250, 261, 284
Magonigle, John Henry (Harry) 44, 49, 94, 98, 100, 114, 122, 142, 156, 173, 174, 328*n*31
Magonigle, Kate Devlin 44, 49
Maguire's Opera House (San Francisco, California) 299*n*22
Maidens Beware 178, 179, 180
Maladine (*Moll Pitcher*) 181
Malcolm (*Macbeth*) 178
Malone, John T. 148
Malvolio (*Twelfth Night*) 26, 182
Manchester, England 129, 130, 262, 267, 268
Manchester, New Hampshire 227
Manchester-by-the-Sea, Massachusetts 135, 136
Manfred/*Manfred* 97, 218, 219
The Marble Heart 26, 27, 183, 197
Marc Antony (*Julius Caesar*) 107, 225, 226, 238
Marchant, G.F. 190, 194
Marco (*The Marble Heart*) 26, 27
Margaret Overreach (*A New Way to Pay Old Debts*) 44, 94
Marlowe/Young Marlowe (*She Stoops to Conquer*) 178, 179, 180, 183
Married Life 182
Marshall, Caleb E.A. 29
Marysville, California 20, 21, 26, 183
Masonic Opera House (Nashville, Tennessee) 236
Masonic Theatre and Grand Opera House (Nashville, Tennessee) 257
Massett, Stephen (Jeems Pipes) 22
Master Dobbs (*The Omnibus*) 182
Matrimony 181
Mayer's Opera House (El Paso, Texas) 289
Mayo, Frank 26, 183
McCloskey, J.J. 18, 26, 175, 302*n*23
McCullough, John 115, 315*n*65
McEntee, Gertrude Vaux 124, 135
McEntee, Jervis 39, 61, 82, 85, 88, 109, 115, 117, 118, 120, 122, 124, 125, 130, 133, 135, 136, 139, 142, 228, 240, 245, 246, 248, 254, 297, 314*nn*59,60
McFarland, A. 110
McVicker, Harriet G. Meyers Weaver Runnion 93, 94, 114, 115, 117, 118, 122, 123–125, 127
McVicker, Horace 116, 241, 242, 273
McVicker, James 93, 97, 108, 109, 114, 115, 118, 122, 123–125, 127, 217, 225, 232, 234, 237, 238, 239, 241
McVicker's Theatre (Chicago, Illinois) 93, 115, 116, 191, 209, 213,
216, 222, 228, 230, 232, 236, 237, 241, 246
Mechanics' Hall, Hamilton, Ontario, Canada 237
Meg Merriles (*Guy Mannering*) 5, 221
Melbourne, Australia 24, 182
Melrose, Scotland 321*n*4
Melville, Herman 82, 312*n*39
Memphis, Tennessee 126, 145, 162, 188, 189, 193, 196, 197, 213, 255, 285, 289, 317*n*4
Menken, Adah Isaacs 189
The Merchant of Venice 13, 15, 20, 56, 90, 91, 129, 142, 161, 167, 180, 182, 184, 185, 188, 189, 190, 191, 192, 194, 197, 198, 199, 200, 201, 202, 203, 204, 205, 206, 208, 209, 210, 211, 212, 213, 214, 215, 216, 217, 219, 220, 222, 223, 224, 225, 226, 227, 228, 229, 230, 231, 232, 233, 234, 235, 236, 237, 238, 239, 240, 241, 242, 244, 245, 246, 247, 248, 252, 253, 254, 256, 257, 258, 259, 260, 262, 263, 264, 265, 266, 267, 268, 273, 274, 275, 276, 277, 278, 279, 280, 283, 284, 285, 286, 287, 288, 289, 290, 291, 292, 293, 294, 295, 296, 307*n*30, 310*n*8, 328
Methua-Scheller, Marie Mme. 91, 207
Metropolitan Opera House (Columbus, Ohio) 287, 293
Metropolitan Opera House (New York) 154, 290, 293
Metropolitan Theatre (Buffalo, New York) 189, 191, 194
Metropolitan Theatre (Sacramento, California) 238, 286, 289
Metropolitan Theatre (San Francisco, California) 23, 24, 26, 27, 28, 181, 182, 183, 184
A Midsummer Night's Dream 26, 182
Millais, John Everett Sir 121
Miller, Erasmus, Dr. 62, 63
Miller, Wynn 128, 132, 133, 261, 262
Miller's Maid 178
Milwaukee, Wisconsin 144, 195, 214, 215, 217, 259, 282, 287, 295
Minneapolis, Minnesota 161, 282, 287, 290
Minnehaha Falls, Minnesota 144
Mr. Bromley/Bromly (*A Lesson to Merchants* a/k/a *Simpson & Co.*) 178, 179, 180, 291
Mr. Bucket (*Bleak House*) 182
Mr. F.B. Conway's Brooklyn Theatre 22, 225, 229
Mr. Jones Brown Smith/John Robinson Brownsmith (*Little Toddlekins*) 180, 181, 184
Mr. Oakley (*The Jealous Wife*) 182, 183
Mitchell, Jane Booth 7
Mitchell's Olympic Theatre (New York) 27
Mobile, Alabama 29, 187, 196, 287, 289, 317*n*4
Mobile Theatre 186, 193, 196, 212

Modjeska, Helena (Helen Opid, Helene Opido) 110, 154, 165–168
Moll Pitcher 181
Molony, Kitty (Goodale, Katherine, Kate) 143, 146, 282, 324n1
Monterey, California 147, 165
Montgomery Theatre 195, 235, 256, 289
Moore's Opera House (Des Moines, Iowa) 293
Morant, Fanny 100, 102
A Morning Call 182
Morris, Clara 142
Morris, Mr. May 249
Morris' Opera House (Des Moines, Iowa) 286
A Mother's Trust, or California in 1849 181
Moulton, Ben F. 26
Mount Auburn Cemetery (Cambridge, Massachusetts) 64, 112, 175
Mount Vernon Association 190
The Mountaineers 178
Mrs. John Drew's Arch Street Theatre (Philadelphia, Pennsylvania) 74, 239, 241, 337
Mrs. Morrison's Grand Opera House (Toronto, Canada) 237
Much Ado About Nothing 105, 179, 180, 182, 183, 190, 191, 194, 197, 203, 209, 210, 211, 212, 213, 214, 215, 216, 217, 220, 222, 224, 228, 229, 230, 237, 238, 239, 240, 245, 246, 247, 293, 294, 295
Munich, Germany 119
Murdoch, James 23
Murray, John B. 81, 85, 90, 92
Murray, Master 14
Murtogh (*The Green Bushes*) 183
Music Hall (Lowell, Massachusetts) 215, 226
Music Hall (Manchester, New Hampshire) 227
Music Hall (Milwaukee, Wisconsin) 214, 217
Music Hall (New Haven, Connecticut) 215, 220, 240
Music Hall (Portland, Maine) 220, 227
Music Hall (Springfield, Massachusetts) 215
Music Hall (Wilkes-Barre, Pennsylvania) 255
Music Hall (Worcester, Massachusetts) 215, 220
My Aunt 182
My Sister Kate 179, 181

Narragansett Pier, Rhode Island 140, 165, 167, 170, 172, 173
Nashville, Tennessee 162, 190, 193, 197, 235, 236, 257, 289
National Hall (Washington, D.C.) 15, 177
National Theatre (Cincinnati, Ohio) 210, 215, 222
National Theatre (Downieville, California) 184
National Theatre (New York) 13, 14, 177

National Theatre (Washington, D.C.) 27
Naylor's Opera House (Terre Haute, Indiana) 290
Neues Leipziger Stadt-Theater (Germany) 133, 271
Nevada City, California 20, 27, 28, 178, 184, 302n23
New Chestnut Street Theatre (Philadelphia, Pennsylvania) 203, 312n31
New Haven, Connecticut 215, 220, 227, 229, 240, 254, 277, 287, 292, 294, 299n18
New London, Connecticut 79, 311nn29,30
New Memphis Theatre 196, 213, 285, 289
New Metropolitan Theatre (Sacramento, California) 286, 289
New National Theatre (Cincinnati, Ohio) 192
New Opera House (Bay City, Michigan) 282, 290
New Opera House (Birmingham, Alabama) 289
New Opera House (Burlington, Iowa) 260, 293
New Opera House (Chattanooga, Tennessee) 289
New Opera House (Lansing, Michigan) 228
New Opera House (Pittsburgh, Pennsylvania) 215, 217
New Opera House (Springfield, Massachusetts) 254
New Orleans, Louisiana 19, 29, 30, 33, 35, 37, 44, 65, 126, 145, 150, 152, 186, 187, 189, 192, 193, 195, 196, 212, 232, 256, 285, 289, 300n1, 301n17
New San Francisco Theatre 23, 181
New Theatre Royal (Sheffield, England) 129, 130, 262
A New Way to Pay Old Debts 94, 178, 180, 184, 185, 186, 187, 188, 189, 190, 191, 192, 193, 194, 195, 196, 197, 198, 199, 200, 201, 202, 203, 204, 206, 207, 208, 209, 210, 212, 221, 222, 224, 225, 234, 236, 237, 278, 279, 280, 281, 286
New York 17, 31, 33, 34, 40, 43, 60, 65, 68, 69, 79–81, 89, 90, 97, 98, 103, 105, 109, 114–117, 123–125, 135–137, 139, 141, 144, 152, 162, 163, 177, 187, 188, 189, 190, 191, 194, 195, 196, 198, 199, 200, 202, 203, 204, 205, 206, 207, 208, 209, 210, 211, 213, 215, 217, 218, 219, 220, 221, 223, 224, 225, 226, 227, 228, 229, 232, 233, 234, 237, 238, 239, 240, 241, 242, 243, 244, 245, 246, 247, 248, 250, 253, 255, 260, 261, 273, 374, 275, 276, 277, 279, 280, 281, 282, 283, 284, 287, 288, 290, 292, 293, 294, 295, 296
Newark, New Jersey 214, 227, 284
Newark Opera House 227
Newcastle-Upon-Tyne, England 262

Newport, Rhode Island 130, 135, 136, 140, 145, 215, 227, 275
Niagara Falls 49, 121
Niblo's Garden (New York) 45, 52, 69, 73, 194, 204, 218, 219, 225, 226, 242
Nobles, Milton 150
Norfolk, Virginia 13, 152, 177
Norombega Hall (Bangor, Maine) 227
Norval (*Douglas*) 15, 177
Norwich, Connecticut 226

Oakes, James 219
The Octaroon 52
Ogden, Utah 147
Oggel, L. Terry 2
Old Theatre (Mobile, Alabama) 289
Olympic Theatre (St. Louis, Missouri) 283, 288, 291, 295
Omaha, Nebraska 147, 152, 286, 290, 293
The Omnibus 182
Only a Half Penny 44, 192
Opera House (Adrian, Michigan) 237
Opera House (Ann Arbor, Michigan) 290
Opera House (Austin, Texas) 285, 289
Opera House (Bloomington, Illinois) 290
Opera House (Cedar Rapids, Iowa) 295
Opera House (Cheyenne, Wyoming) 286
Opera House (Cleveland, Ohio) 283
Opera House (Columbus, Georgia) 235
Opera House (Columbus, Ohio) 235
Opera House (Dallas, Texas) 285, 289
Opera House (Detroit, Michigan) 228, 282, 287
Opera House (Dubuque, Iowa) 290
Opera House (Eau Claire, Wisconsin) 287
Opera House (Fort Worth, Texas) 289
Opera House (Harrisburg, Pennsylvania) 287
Opera House (Holyoke, Massachusetts) 277, 283, 294
Opera House (Lawrence, Massachusetts) 278
Opera House (Meriden, Connecticut) 254
Opera House (Milwaukee, Wisconsin) 287
Opera House (Newport, Rhode Island) 227
Opera House (Omaha, Nebraska) 286
Opera House (Oshkosh, Wisconsin) 287
Opera House (Peoria, Illinois) 290, 295

Opera House (Pittsburgh, Pennsylvania) 210, 215, 217, 223, 231, 244
Opera House (Rochester, New York) 242, 284
Opera House (San Antonio, Texas) 285
Opera House (Springfield, Ohio) 290
Opera House (Terre Haute, Indiana) 258
Opera House (Utica, New York) 242, 284
Opera House (Vincennes, Indiana) 168, 295
Opera House (Wheeling, West Virginia) 295
Opera House (Youngstown, Pennsylvania) 288, 295
Ophelia (*Hamlet*) 69, 73, 94, 98, 100, 103, 107, 154, 167, 209, 210, 211, 212, 213, 214, 216, 220, 221, 243, 245, 249, 264, 265, 268, 270, 271, 273
Oroville, California 27, 31, 183
Orton, Josephine (Josie) 38, 39, 44, 109
Osgood, The Rev. Samuel 49, 64
Othello/*Othello* 7, 28, 54, 55, 59, 75, 90, 91, 102, 121, 122, 129, 132, 133, 139, 143, 152, 153, 161–163, 177, 184, 189, 190, 194, 195, 196, 198, 199, 200, 202, 203, 204, 205, 206, 208, 209, 210, 211, 212, 214, 216, 217, 218, 219, 220, 222, 224, 226, 228, 229, 230, 231, 232, 234, 235, 236, 238, 239, 240, 241, 242, 243, 244, 246, 247, 248, 251, 252, 253, 254, 255, 256, 260, 261, 262, 263, 264, 265, 266, 267, 268, 270, 271, 273, 274, 276, 278, 285, 286, 287, 289, 290, 292, 293, 295, 296
Otway, Thomas 19
Our American Cousin 80
Owen, Malcolm Dale 147, 148
Owens' Academy of Music (Charleston, South Carolina) 235, 289
Oxford, England 129

Palmer, A.M. 157, 173
Panama City, Panama 18, 28
Paradise Valley, Pennsylvania 43
Paris, France 60, 119, 129, 133
Park Opera House (Erie, Pennsylvania) 288
Park Theatre (Boston, Massachusetts) 170, 247, 254, 295
Park Theatre (Brooklyn, New York) 283
Parsons, Anna 64
Parsons, Thomas 64
Pateman, Bella 231, 256, 257, 268
Pateman, Robert 128, 261, 263
Paul Lafont (*Love's Sacrifice*) 179, 180, 181
Paul Pry 178, 179
Pauline (*The Lady of Lyons*) 94, 182
Payne, John Howard 210, 280, 324n1
Peavey Grand Opera House (Sioux City, Iowa) 293

Peer and Peasant 183
The People's Advocate 180
People's Theatre (St. Louis, Missouri) 185
Pescara (*The Apostate*) 7, 13, 14, 27, 53, 62, 75, 184, 185, 186, 188, 189, 190, 191, 192, 193, 194, 195, 196, 197, 198, 199, 200, 202, 203, 204, 206, 207, 208, 209, 210, 211, 212, 214, 216, 217, 219, 224, 226, 229, 230, 232, 233, 234, 236, 238, 277, 278, 279, 284, 285, 286, 310n7, 328
Petruchio (*Katherine and Petruchio*) 23, 43, 53, 75, 179, 180, 181, 183, 184, 185, 186, 188, 189, 190, 191, 192, 193, 194, 195, 196, 197, 198, 199, 200, 202, 203, 204, 205, 206, 207, 209, 210, 211, 212, 213, 214, 215, 216, 217, 220, 222, 223, 224, 225, 226, 227, 228, 229, 231, 232, 234, 235, 236, 237, 238, 239, 240, 241, 242, 243, 244, 245, 246, 247, 248, 252, 253, 254, 262, 263, 265, 266, 267, 268, 273, 274, 275, 276, 277, 278, 279, 280, 283, 284, 285, 286, 287
Philadelphia, Pennsylvania 13, 33, 45, 51, 53, 64, 68, 69, 73, 80, 81, 83–85, 89, 92, 99, 103, 114, 125, 136, 137, 139, 140, 145, 152, 161, 163, 168, 177, 188, 194, 197, 198, 199, 200, 203, 204, 205, 206, 214, 215, 219, 220, 223, 225, 229, 232, 234, 238, 239, 241, 246, 247, 253, 274, 278, 279, 281, 284, 288, 292, 294, 295, 299n2, 311nn29,30, 312nn30,31, 313nn47,49, 314nn54,55, 328n31
Philip Augustus (*Philip of France*) 182
Phillippe (*The Child of the Regiment, or The Trumpeter's Daughter*) 178
Phoenix Hall (Concord, New Hampshire) 227
Phoenix Hall (Petersburg, Virginia) 194
Pike's Opera House (Cincinnati, Ohio) 83, 313n47
Pillot's Opera House (Houston, Texas) 285, 289
Pittsburgh, Pennsylvania 13, 145, 154, 163, 185, 210, 215, 217, 223, 230, 231, 244, 255, 284, 288, 292, 293
Pittsburgh Theatre 185
Pizzaro 23
Placerville, California 20, 27, 28, 184
Placerville Theatre 184
The Players 156–159, 164, 170, 172–174, 313n49
Plot and Passion 182
Plunkett's Metropolitan Theatre (Rochester, New York) 189
Points 30
The Poor Gentleman 181
Pope, Charles 28, 193, 196
Portia (*The Merchant of Venice*) 91, 167, 185, 208, 211, 214, 245, 285, 291

Portland, Maine 215, 220, 227
Portrush, Ireland 321n4
Potter, Virginia Mitchell 157, 159
Poverty Flat, California 20
Powell, Lewis Thornton (Payne) 84
Powers' Grand Opera House (Grand Rapids, Michigan) 290, 295
Powers' New Opera House (Decatur, Illinois) 295
Prince of Players 2
Princess's Theatre, London, England 119–121, 249, 250, 252
Privilege ("opening with the privilege") 106
Providence, Rhode Island 170, 177, 209, 215, 220, 227, 229, 240, 254, 277, 293, 294, 296, 320n25
Providence Museum 12, 177
Providence Opera House 227, 229, 240, 277, 293, 294, 296, 320n25
A Provoked Husband 180
Pythias (*Damon and Pythias*) 181

Queen Elizabeth (*Richard III*) 190, 243, 299n18
The Queen's Theatre (Melbourne, Australia) 182
Queenstown, Ireland 119, 128
Quincy, Illinois 228

Ralston Hall (Macon, Georgia) 235
Ramsey, Maj. Gen. G.D. 87
Rand, Rosa 245
Rankin, McKee 86, 314n65, 316n65
Raphael Du Chalet/Phidias (*The Marble Heart*) 26, 27, 75, 183, 197
The Rash Knight of Arva 182
Red Dog, California 20, 302n23
Reno, Nevada 147
The Rent Day 181
Renwick, James 98, 99
Residenz Theater (Berlin, Germany) 130, 131, 269, 270
Residenz Theater (Hanover, Germany) 129, 269
The Review 182
Rice, John Blake 74
Richard II/*Richard II* 115, 116, 233, 234, 235, 236, 237, 238, 244, 245, 246
Richard III/*Richard III* 5, 7, 11, 14, 15, 19, 21, 23, 25, 26, 27, 30, 40, 43, 53, 56, 58, 70, 75, 94, 107, 144, 177, 178, 179, 181, 182, 183, 184, 185, 186, 187, 188, 189, 190, 191, 192, 193, 194, 195, 196, 197, 198, 199, 200, 201, 202, 203, 204, 205, 206, 207, 208, 209, 210, 211, 212, 213, 214, 215, 216, 217, 220, 222, 223, 225, 226, 227, 228, 229, 230, 231, 232, 238, 239, 240, 241, 242, 243, 244, 245, 246, 247, 248, 253, 254, 261, 267, 268, 274, 275, 277, 278, 280, 281, 282, 283, 284, 286, 299n18, 309n3, 315n65, 328
Richelieu/*Richelieu* 13, 26, 27, 28, 30, 33, 43, 52, 56–60, 73, 91, 104, 105, 107, 128, 129, 143, 147, 167,

171, 177, 178, 181, 184, 185, 186, 188, 189, 190, 191, 192, 193, 194, 195, 196, 197, 198, 199, 200, 201, 202, 203, 204, 205, 206, 207, 208, 209, 210, 211, 212, 213, 214, 215, 216, 217, 219, 220, 222, 223, 224, 225, 226, 227, 228, 229, 230, 231, 232, 233, 234, 235, 236, 237, 238, 239, 240, 241, 242, 244, 245, 246, 247, 248, 250, 251, 252, 253, 254, 255, 256, 257, 258, 259, 260, 261, 262, 263, 264, 265, 266, 267, 268, 269, 273, 274, 275, 276, 277, 278, 279, 280, 281, 282, 283, 284, 285, 286, 287, 293, 294, 295, 296, 299n18, 305n23, 309n3, 310n8, 328
Richmond (*Richard III*) 14, 15, 75, 177, 178, 182
Richmond, Virginia 13, 15, 29, 40, 42, 43, 75, 76, 152, 177, 235, 310n7, 315n65
Richmond Greys 78
Richmond Theatre/Marshall Theatre (Richmond, Virginia) 13, 40, 184, 191, 194, 289, 311n18
Rip Van Winkle 103, 108, 124, 129
Ristori, Adelaide 137
The Rivals 179, 180
The Robbers 15, 75, 178, 181, 189, 190, 191, 192, 193, 194, 195, 197, 198
Robert Shelly (*Momentous Question*) 183
Roberts' Opera House (Hartford, Connecticut) 220, 226, 229, 240, 254, 277, 292, 294
Robertson, Agnes 51
Robertson, Richard 99, 100, 104, 107–109, 113, 223
Robinson's Opera House (Cincinnati, Ohio) 241, 258
Rochester, New York 163, 189, 242, 260, 284, 293, 294, 297
Rock, Ida 282
The Roebuck 179, 180, 204, 234, 235, 236, 237, 241, 242, 243
Rogers, Ben G. 296
Rogers, Mrs. Elijah B. 87
Roland (*All for Love or The Lost Pleiad*) 179
A Roland for an Oliver 179
Romeo 23, 27, 40, 75, 80, 90, 93, 100, 179, 181, 184, 188, 189, 190, 191, 192, 193, 194, 196, 197, 198, 199, 200, 202, 204, 205, 206, 207, 208, 209, 210, 211, 212, 213, 214, 215, 216, 217, 219
Romeo and Juliet 90, 99, 100, 102, 104, 111, 178, 179, 210, 213, 214, 218
Rondout, New York 124–126, 129, 135
Rose Hill Cemetery (Chicago, Illinois) 126
Rosina Meadows 178
Rough and Ready, California 20
Royal Alexandra Theatre (Liverpool, England) 268
Royal Amphitheatre (Liverpool, England) 202

Royal Hawaiian Theatre (Honolulu, Hawaii) 24, 182
Royal Victoria Theatre (Sydney, Australia) 24, 181
Royle, Edwin Milton 153
Ruggles, Eleanor 2
Russell, John E. 97, 101, 104, 105, 108, 114, 213, 218, 223, 231, 232, 251
Ruy Blas/*Ruy Blas* 203, 204, 205, 206, 207, 208, 238, 239, 240, 241, 242, 244, 245, 246, 247, 248, 276, 277, 278, 279, 280, 310n8, 324n1, 328
Ruy Gomez (*Faint Heart Never Won Fair Lady*) 181, 182, 183, 184, 195

Saco, Maine 227
Sacramento, California 19, 21, 23, 26, 28, 147, 178, 179, 180, 183, 184, 237, 238, 286, 289
Sacramento Theatre 27, 182, 184
St. Catherine's, Ontario, Canada 237
St. Charles Theatre (New Orleans, Louisiana) 19, 186, 192, 195, 300n1
St. Cupid, or Dorothy's Fortune 179
St. Cyr (*Lucille*) 179
St. James Hall (Chattanooga, Tennessee) 257
St. Louis, Missouri 14, 43, 144, 150, 154, 162, 185, 191, 192, 197, 212, 222, 230, 231, 241, 257, 288, 291, 295, 311n23, 317n4
St. Paul, Minnesota 161, 282, 290, 291
St. Pierre/Julien St. Pierre (*The Wife*) 181, 182, 184, 186, 188, 191, 198
St. Val (*A Lesson for Ladies*) 179
Salem, Massachusetts 215
Sales Grand Opera House (New Orleans, Louisiana) 256
Salisbury, England 321n4
Salt Lake City, Utah 147, 289
Salt Lake Theatre 289
Salvini, Alexander 174, 175
Salvini, Tomasso 133, 139, 140, 231, 269, 274, 281, 283
San Antonio, Texas 146, 285, 289
Sand Lake, New York 40
San Francisco, California 17, 18, 19, 21, 24, 26, 27, 82, 115, 142, 146, 150, 178, 180, 181, 182, 183, 184, 217, 237, 238, 282, 284, 285, 289, 293, 299n22, 314n53
San Francisco Theatre 21, 178, 180, 181
Sanguinbeck (*Cherry and Fair Star, or The Children of Cyprus*) 183
Sanitary Fair 204
San Jose, California 147, 286
San Juan del Sud, Panama 19
Saratoga, New York 116
Sargeant, Epes 206, 209
Sarum, England 321n4
Saunders Hall (Lawrence, Massachusetts) 226
Savannah, Georgia 77, 150, 195, 235, 289

Savannah Theatre 235, 289
Saxe-Meiningen, Georg II, Duke of 162, 163
Scarborough, England 262
The School for Scandal 23, 179
Schultz's Opera House (Zanesville, Ohio) 295
Scott, Clement 251, 252
Scott, John R. 14
seconds 15
Sedley, Charles 10, 12, 22, 26, 27
Sedley, Henry 10
Sefton, John 13
A Serious Family 181, 182, 183
Seymour, Willie 221, 315n65
Shakespeare statue, Central Park, (New York) 70
Shannahan's Opera House (Newport, Rhode Island) 215
She Stoops to Conquer 178, 179, 180, 183
Sheffield, England 262, 268
Sheil, Richard 13
Sherman, William Tecumseh, General 157
Shirt-Tail Bend, California 20, 28, 304n68
Shirt-Tail Canyon, California 20
Shylock (*Merchant of Venice*) 7, 9, 23, 27, 53, 55, 56, 59, 75, 91, 167, 171, 179, 180, 182, 184, 185, 186, 189, 190, 191, 192, 194, 197, 198, 199, 200, 201, 202, 203, 204, 205, 206, 208, 209, 210, 211, 212, 213, 214, 215, 216, 217, 219, 220, 222, 223, 224, 225, 226, 227, 228, 229, 230, 231, 232, 233, 234, 235, 236, 237, 238, 239, 240, 241, 242, 244, 245, 246, 247, 248, 252, 253, 254, 256, 257, 258, 259, 260, 262, 263, 264, 265, 266, 267, 268, 273, 274, 275, 276, 277, 278, 279, 280, 283, 284, 285, 286, 287, 288, 289, 290, 291, 292, 293, 294, 295, 296, 307n30, 328
Sidney Maynard (*The Housekeeper*) 182, 183
Silius (*Valeria*) 182
Silver Jack (*The Rent Day*) 181
Simonds, Joseph H. 78
Simpson, Palgrave 249
Sinclair, Catherine N. 23, 26, 27, 181, 183
Sir Alfred Highflyer (*A Roland for an Oliver*) 179
Sir Charles Rivers (*The Trumpeter's Wedding*) 178, 179
Sir Edward Ardent (*A Morning Call*) 182
Sir Edward Mortimer (*The Iron Chest*) 7, 13, 15, 18, 20, 27, 73, 82, 182, 183, 184, 185, 186, 188, 189, 190, 191, 192, 193, 194, 195, 196, 197, 198, 200, 202, 203, 204, 205, 224, 225, 226, 227, 228, 276, 277, 278, 279, 328
Sir Giles Overreach (*A New Way to Pay Old Debts*) 7, 23, 27, 30, 31, 44, 56, 104, 180, 184, 185, 186, 187, 188, 189, 190, 191, 192, 193, 194, 195, 196, 197, 198, 199, 200, 201,

Index

202, 203, 204, 206, 207, 208, 209, 210, 212, 221, 222, 224, 225, 234, 236, 237, 278, 279, 280, 281, 286
Sir Thomas Clifford (*The Hunchback*) 23, 181, 182, 183
Sir Valentine May (*St. Cupid, or Dorothy's Fortune*) 179
Sir William Wisby (*The Roebuck*) 179
Skinner, Otis 12, 86, 166, 168, 169, 315n65
Slasher and Crasher 11
Smith, Betty (Black Betty, Brown Betty, Yeller gal) 77, 119, 128, 129, 140
Smith, Elizabeth Oakes 112
Smith, Dr. St. Clair 144, 164, 174, 175
Smoking 10, 31, 41, 50, 129, 153, 156, 164, 173, 174, 185
The Soldier's Daughter 178, 179, 180, 181
Southern Exposition Music Hall (Louisville, Kentucky) 290
Spa Rooms (Harrowgate, England) 129, 130, 262
Spangler, Edward 313n48
Spofford, Richard Smith, Jr. 45
Springfield, Massachusetts 107, 215, 226, 229, 240, 254, 259, 287, 290, 292, 294
Stadt-Theater in Bonn, Germany 271
Stamford, Connecticut 114, 240
Stanton, Edwin M. 80, 84, 86
Star Theatre (Buffalo, New York) 295
Star Theatre (New York) 136, 144, 148, 273, 283, 287
The State Secrets 178
Stebbins, Emma 42
Stedman, Edmund Clarence 12, 26, 61, 175
Steinway Hall (New York) 221
Still Waters Run Deep 183, 184
Stirling, Scotland 311n4
Stock Company 13, 15
Stockbridge, Massachusetts 172
Stockman, Emma 282
Stockton, California 147, 281, 284
Stoddard, Elizabeth Drew Barston 47, 50, 61–63, 85, 124, 140
Stoddard, Richard Henry 61, 62, 124, 211, 313n51
Strakosch, Max 242
The Stranger/*The Stranger* 13, 20, 24, 75, 178, 179, 181, 182, 183, 184, 188, 194, 206, 207, 209, 210, 211, 212, 213, 214, 215, 216, 217, 220, 222, 224, 225, 226, 227, 229, 230, 231, 232, 234, 236, 238, 239, 240, 241
Stratford-upon-Avon, England 311n4
Stuart, William 33, 51, 52, 61–64, 68–70, 73, 79, 89–92, 206, 208, 218, 311nn29,30, 314n54
Stuckley (*The Gamester*) 178, 181
Sullivan, John T. 282
Supernumeraries 110, 161, 162

Sweethearts and Wives 178
Sydney, Australia 24, 181

Tabor Grand Opera House (Denver, Colorado) 286, 289, 293
Tahiti 24
Tarquina (*Lucius Junius Brutus*) 94, 210
Taylor, Bayard 61
Taylor, Lillie 261
Taylor, Tom 69, 263
Taylor's Opera House (Trenton, New Jersey) 227, 282, 292
The Temple (Portsmouth, New Hampshire) 107, 226
Terry, Ellen 122, 253
Thalia Theater, Hamburg, Germany 270
Thaxter, Celia 137
Thayer, Charles H. 281
Theatre Royal (Birmingham, England) 268
Theatre Royal (Dundee, England) 129, 130, 263
Theatre Royal (Edinburgh, Scotland) 264
Theatre Royal (Hull, England) 265
Theatre Royal (Manchester, England) 59, 202
Theatre Royal (Newcastle-upon-Tyne, England) 129, 130, 262
Theatre Royal (York, England) 129, 130, 262
Theatre Vendome (Nashville, Tennessee) 289
Thoman, Elizabeth (Saunders, Elizabeth, Anderson, Elizabeth) 27, 146, 182, 325n31
Thoman, Jacob Wonderly 11, 27, 299n2
Thomas, Walter 143, 282
Thompson, John 81
Thompson, Launt 69, 88, 137, 208, 209, 223, 228, 231, 259, 267, 272, 312n38, 313n50
Timon of Athens 39
Titus (*Brutus*) 13, 15, 177, 178, 197
Titusville, Pennsylvania 313n49
Tom and Jerry, or Life in London 182
Tompkins, Orlando 63
Tootle's Opera House (St. Joseph, Missouri) 290
Town Hall (Stamford, Connecticut) 240
Tremont Opera House (Galveston, Texas) 256, 285, 289
Tremont Street Theatre (Boston, Massachusetts) 298n6
Trenton, New Jersey 82, 227, 282, 292
Tressel (*Richard III*, Colley Cibber version) 11, 12, 27, 177, 179
The Trossochs, Scotland 321n4
Troy, New York 40, 215, 226
Troy Museum 40
Tubal (*The Merchant of Venice*) 56, 200, 202, 212, 216, 267, 284
Turner's Opera House (Dayton, Ohio) 228

Tweedle Hall (Albany, New York) 203, 215
Twelfth Night 26, 182
Two Can Play at That Game 181, 182
Two Loves and a Life 183

Uncle Tom's Cabin 93
Union Hall (Kalamazoo, Michigan) 228
Union Theatre (San Francisco, California) 24, 184
U.S. Sanitary Commission 203, 204
Ursuline Convent Academy 94
Utica, New York 97, 228, 242, 260, 284, 294

Valentine, Edward 309n3
Valeria 182
Van Schanck, Comilins 109
Varieties Theatre (New Orleans, Louisiana) 212, 312n37
Vaux, Calvert 61, 82, 124, 125, 130, 133, 135
Vaux, Downing 124–126, 128, 130, 131, 133, 135, 136, 138, 324n12
Vaux, Julia 124, 125, 128, 129, 131, 133, 135
venereal disease 39, 44, 45, 47, 48
Venice Preserved 13, 19, 178, 252
Vernon, Ida 127
Victoria, Queen of England 120, 317n4
Victoria Theatre (Berlin, Germany) 130, 269
Victoria Theatre (Sydney, Australia) 24, 181
Vienna, Austria 132, 133, 269, 271, 272
Vincennes, Indiana 295
Vincent, Felix A. 110
Virginius or the Roman Father 178
Virolet (*The Mountaineers*) 178
Volage (*The Marble Heart*) 26

Wagner Opera House (Bradford, Pennsylvania) 284
Wales 321n4
Walker (*Leap Year*) 179, 180
Wallack, James William 41
Wallack, James William, Jr. 54
Wallack, Lester 154, 218, 219, 223, 290
Wallack's Theatre (New York) 34, 51, 189, 190, 226, 228, 248
Waller, Dan Wilmarth 20, 100, 178, 221, 302nn22,23
Waller, Emma 20, 100, 221, 226, 302nn22,23
Walnut Street Theatre (Philadelphia, Pennsylvania) 33, 69, 70, 89, 90, 98, 188, 204, 205, 206, 214, 219, 223, 225, 229, 232, 234, 274, 312n30
Warde, Frederick 150, 233
Warder Opera House (Kansas City, Missouri) 153, 287, 290
Ware, Francis 62–64
Ware, Dr. John 62, 63
Warren, William 64, 74, 137, 159
Washington, D.C. 14, 15, 25, 43,

80–83, 86–88, 177, 184, 185, 188, 192, 204, 210, 217, 231, 232, 245, 282, 310nn7,8, 311nn30,36,40, 313nn46,47, 315nn65,66
Waterbury, Connecticut 126, 240, 254
Weaver, Affie 273
Weaver, John C. 86, 87
Wheatley & Clarke's Arch Street Theatre (Philadelphia, Pennsylvania) 194, 197, 198, 200
Wheeler, A.C. (Nym Crinkle) 281, 292
Wheeler's Opera House (Toledo, Ohio) 229, 237, 259, 288, 295
Where There's a Will There's a Way a/k/a *The Queen's Huband* 180, 181
White, Stanford 157–159, 175
White's Hall (Toledo, Ohio) 216
Whitman, Walt 203
Who Speaks First 182, 183
Wiener Stadt-Theater (Vienna, Austria) 132, 271
Wieting Opera House (Syracuse, New York) 242, 284, 294

The Wife 181, 182, 184, 186, 188, 191, 198
Wildrake (*The Love Chase*) 181, 182, 183
Wilford (*The Iron Chest*) 13, 18, 177, 178
William I, Emperor of Germany 131
Williams, Mr. and Mrs. Barney 73, 206, 312n36
Wilmington, Delaware 230, 231
Wilson, Francis 177, 315n65
Wilson, James Harrison 65
Windsor, England 120
Winter, William 1, 2, 8, 14, 17, 21, 26, 27, 33, 55, 56, 60, 62, 73, 101, 104, 108, 110, 117, 118, 123, 125, 127, 129, 132, 136, 137, 141, 145, 173, 174, 188, 217, 218, 221, 224, 231, 234, 235, 236, 237, 241, 243, 244, 245, 246, 247, 248, 251, 255, 256, 261, 266, 268, 269, 270, 273, 275, 276, 278, 281, 297
Winter Garden Theatre (New York) 2, 30, 51–54, 68–70, 72, 73, 79, 89–93, 98, 100, 110, 198, 199, 200, 202, 203, 204, 205, 206, 207, 208, 310n7, 315n65
The Winter's Tale 99, 104, 105
Witham, Charles W. 99, 103
Wolcott, Charles 281
Woodman, Mattie (Maty) 85, 126
Wood's Theatre (Cincinnati, Ohio) 197, 230, 282
Wood's Theatre/People's Theatre (St. Louis, Missouri) 191, 192
Worcester, Massachusetts 126, 215, 220, 229, 240, 254, 278, 283
Worcester Excursion Car (David Garrick, Junius Brutus Booth) 145–148, 152, 156
Worcester Theatre 240, 254, 283

The Yellow Dwarf 179
Young, Mary 282
Young Men's Hall (Toledo, Ohio) 214, 216
Youngstown, Ohio 259, 288, 295
Yuba River, California 21

www.ingramcontent.com/pod-product-compliance
Ingram Content Group UK Ltd.
Pitfield, Milton Keynes, MK11 3LW, UK
UKHW050543150426
5217IPUK00026B/2060